BY ARTHUR HERMAN

Douglas MacArthur: American Warrior

*The Cave and the Light: Plato Versus Aristotle,
and the Struggle for the Soul of Western Civilization*

*Freedom's Forge: How American Business
Produced Victory in World War II*

*Gandhi & Churchill: The Epic Rivalry That
Destroyed an Empire and Forged Our Age*

*To Rule the Waves: How the British Navy
Shaped the Modern World*

*How the Scots Invented the Modern World:
The True Story of How Western Europe's Poorest
Nation Created Our World & Everything in It*

*Joseph McCarthy: Reexamining the Life
and Legacy of America's Most Hated Senator*

The Idea of Decline in Western History

DOUGLAS
MacARTHUR

DOUGLAS MacARTHUR

★★★★★AMERICAN WARRIOR

Arthur Herman

RANDOM HOUSE

NEW YORK

Published in the United States by Random House, an imprint and division of Penguin Random House LLC, New York.

RANDOM HOUSE and the HOUSE colophon are registered trademarks of Penguin Random House LLC.

Grateful acknowledgment is made to the General Douglas MacArthur Foundation for permission to reprint excerpts from *Reminiscences* by General Douglas MacArthur (New York: McGraw-Hill, 1964), copyright © 1964 by the General Douglas MacArthur Foundation, and various archival materials housed at the General Douglas MacArthur Foundation including letters, poetry, and speeches. Used with the permission of the General Douglas MacArthur Foundation, MacArthur Square, Norfolk, Virginia 23510.

LIBRARY OF CONGRESS CATALOGING-IN-PUBLICATION DATA
Names: Herman, Arthur, author.
Title: Douglas MacArthur : American warrior / Arthur Herman.
Description: New York : Random House, 2016. | Includes bibliographical references and index.
Identifiers: LCCN 2015039817 | ISBN 9780812994889 | ISBN 9780812994896 (ebook)
Subjects: LCSH: MacArthur, Douglas, 1880–1964. | Generals—United States—Biography. | United States—History, Military—20th century. | United States. Army—Biography.
Classification: LCC E745.M3 H47 2016 | DDC 355.0092—dc23 LC record available at http://lccn.loc.gov/2015039817

Printed in the United States of America on acid-free paper

randomhousebooks.com

9 8 7 6 5 4 3 2 1

First Edition

Book design by Christopher M. Zucker

To Beth,
for everything

CONTENTS

PREFACE   *xi*

PROLOGUE   *3*

CHAPTER 1: **SON OF THE FATHER**   *7*

CHAPTER 2: **TURNING POINTS**   *23*

CHAPTER 3: **GLORY DAYS**   *39*

CHAPTER 4: **YOUNG MAN GOING EAST**   *54*

CHAPTER 5: **COUNTDOWN TO WAR**   *75*

CHAPTER 6: **INTO THE FIRE**   *103*

CHAPTER 7: **FIGHT TO THE FINISH**   *123*

CHAPTER 8: **BACK TO WEST POINT**   *151*

CHAPTER 9: **THE TUMULTUOUS YEARS**   *176*

CHAPTER 10: **SAVING THE ARMY**   *196*

CHAPTER 11: **SAVING FDR**   *226*

CHAPTER 12: **MISSION TO MANILA**   *253*

CHAPTER 13: **WAITING FOR THE ENEMY**   *288*

CHAPTER 14: **RAT IN THE HOUSE**   *314*

CHAPTER 15: **WHEN MEN MUST DIE**   *338*

CHAPTER 16: **BACK TO THE WALL**   *366*

CHAPTER 17: **I SHALL RETURN**   *395*

CHAPTER 18: **TAKING SUPREME COMMAND**   *416*

CHAPTER 19: **GREEN HELL**   *446*

CHAPTER 20: **DOING CARTWHEEL**   *473*

CHAPTER 21: **STEPPING-STONES TO VICTORY**   *498*

CHAPTER 22: **LIBERATION**   522

CHAPTER 23: **ON TO MANILA**   550

CHAPTER 24: **BATTLEGROUND**   578

CHAPTER 25: **DOWNFALL**   602

CHAPTER 26: **BRIEF ENCOUNTERS**   627

CHAPTER 27: **BEING SIR BOSS**   654

CHAPTER 28: **HEADWINDS**   682

CHAPTER 29: **WAR AGAIN**   705

CHAPTER 30: **INCHON AND BEYOND**   732

CHAPTER 31: **REVERSAL OF FORTUNE**   763

CHAPTER 32: **ENDGAME**   787

CHAPTER 33: **FADING AWAY**   818

CONCLUSION   843

ACKNOWLEDGMENTS   851

NOTES   853

INDEX   893

PREFACE

You can see him in your mind's eye. The khaki uniform and pressed pants, the gold-braided cap, the sunglasses, the corncob pipe firmly in his teeth and the ramrod-straight back.

In the mind's eye we see him wading ashore in the Philippines, sitting in a jeep in Korea, or accepting the surrender of the empire of Japan on board the USS *Missouri*. As the years passed, Americans grew to see him as a pillar of strength—or a tower of vanity. A man ready to be the savior of his country— or a man the country needed to be saved from.

He was Douglas MacArthur, arguably the last American public figure to be worshiped unreservedly as a national hero—and arguably the last to bring the romantic stirrings of a Custer or a Robert E. Lee to the American military tradition. Yet he also foresaw the greatest geopolitical shift for his nation's future since its founding, away from Europe and toward Asia and the Pacific Rim.

It's not difficult to find polarizing figures in American history, but none is more intriguing, or more significant, than Douglas MacArthur. Was he prophet or anachronism? Romantic hero or vain mountebank? It's what biographers and historians have debated back and forth in the half century since his death.

There are more than twenty-five separate biographies of Douglas MacArthur and many more books on his military campaigns, from World War One and the Philippines to Korea. Most, however, fall into two categories. There are the unrelenting critics like Richard Rovere and Arthur Schlesinger, Jr., *The General and the President* (New York, 1951), Gavin Long, *MacArthur as Military Commander* (London, 1969), Carol Petillo, *Douglas MacArthur: The Philippine Years* (Bloomington, IN, 1981), Michael Schaller, *Douglas MacArthur: The Far Eastern General* (Oxford, 1989), and, most recently, Russell Buhite, *Douglas MacArthur: Statecraft and Stagecraft in America's East Asian Policy* (Lanham, MD, 2008). Then there's the category of unashamed adulation, as in Frazier Hunt, *The Untold Story of Douglas MacArthur* (New York, 1964), Charles Willoughby and John Chamberlain, *MacArthur: 1941–1951* (New York, 1954), Courtney Whitney, *MacArthur: His Rendezvous with History* (New York, 1955), and MacArthur's own *Reminiscences* (New York, 1964).

As for the rest, the most scholarly biography, D. Clayton James's *The Years of MacArthur*, 3 volumes (New York, 1970–1985), is balanced but exhausting to read, and has become increasingly out of date. The only single-volume biographies for general readers, William Manchester's *American Caesar: Douglas MacArthur 1880–1964* (Boston, 1978) and Geoffrey Perret, *Old Soldiers Never Die: The Life of Douglas MacArthur* (New York, 1996), both suffer from unevenly critical perspectives on their subject, and never fulfill the promise of their themes or their authors.

In short, it is time for a biography of MacArthur that gives this larger-than-life figure his full due by peeling back the layers of myth, both pro and con, and revealing the marrow of the man, and his career. By using available archive sources, including the huge collection of materials from the MacArthur Library in Norfolk, Virginia, as well as newly declassified materials from the National Archives and U.S. Center of Military History; and the scholarship of leading Japanese as well as Australian and Korean scholars, it is now possible to set one of the legends of American history—in many ways, an American Churchill—firmly in his time and place and profession. This volume will show how much of the man remained hidden from the public image, and how and why the emergence of Douglas MacArthur as an American hero was actually a process of conscious self-creation.

This is also the first biography to make use of new Soviet and Chinese archive sources, which shed considerable new light on the events leading up to the outbreak of the war in Korea, particularly the real facts behind China's intervention in the conflict. In addition, it is the first to make full use of the complete 1998 oral interview with Jean MacArthur—the interview she swore she would never give—which is now safely ensconced in the archives of the MacArthur Memorial.

What readers will discover in these pages is that far from being a remote figure from the historical past, MacArthur was an individual whose life and career is very much one for our time. For example, more than any other American in the twentieth century, MacArthur understood the importance of Asia for his country's future destiny. As readers will learn, he was a far-sighted prophet who predicted the rise of the Pacific Rim after World War Two, and who remains a figure as significant in the history of Asia as in American history—possibly even more so.

"It was crystal clear to me," MacArthur once wrote, "that the future and, indeed, the very existence of America, were irrevocably intertwined with Asia."

He lived that conviction all his life. It motivated many of his key decisions, including in World War Two and Korea, and his impatience with American politicians who still saw Europe as the necessary focus of strategy and foreign policy was legendary.

By any measure, the man who warned John F. Kennedy not to get involved in Vietnam and who said "Anyone who starts a land war in Asia ought to have his head examined" deserves a fresh new look.

Indeed, from Vietnam and Nixon's 1972 opening to China, to the current crisis in Europe—not to mention the emergence of postwar Japan and the "little dragons" including Taiwan, Singapore, and South Korea, and the rise of mainland China as the next great superpower—MacArthur's life and career may be more relevant than ever for understanding our world today.

*   *   *

Certainly no one can deny the epic breadth of that life and career.

When MacArthur was born in the Little Rock army barracks, American soldiers were still reeling from the massacre at Little Bighorn four years before. When he died, American soldiers were deploying in Vietnam—the war he specifically warned President Kennedy to steer clear of.

When he entered West Point, generals who had commanded his father in the Civil War were still alive and Orville and Wilbur Wright's first flight was four years away. When he spoke at West Point for the last time in 1962, Americans were headed into space, and jet bombers carrying nuclear weapons circled the North Pole.

Over that span of eighty-four years Douglas MacArthur spent his entire career in uniform; indeed, he knew no other life. He was born and died in military hospitals. His first memory, as he recounted in his autobiography, was "the sound of bugles" at his father's tiny military post where he was born in 1880.

MacArthur's death in 1964 was treated as a national event, with his funeral broadcast on network TV with the scale and solemnity befitting the passing of a great national hero—a hero comparable to another titanic figure who died the following year, namely Winston Churchill. Yet even during his lifetime, armies of critics (some of whom had served with him in the field) dismissed him as a second-rate soldier and a vain, pompous, arrogant publicity hound. Then, and later, they could point to his failed defense of the Philippines at the outset of America's entry into the Second World War, which led to the biggest mass surrender in U.S. military history.

They pointed to the suppression of the Bonus Marchers during the Depression by troops under his command; his costly campaign in lives and treasure to retake the Philippines; and his disastrous march toward the Yalu after Inchon during the Korean War, which precipitated what MacArthur had assured everyone would never happen—China's entry into the conflict. Then, as Korea grew into the biggest and most dangerous conflict of the Cold War, MacArthur stunned many by threatening to use nuclear weapons to win it, until a frustrated President Truman dismissed him from command. No wonder biographer William Manchester and others have compared

MacArthur to a Greek tragic hero, brought down from the heights of power by his own pride and hubris—or even, some have argued, his incompetence.

His supporters and apologists, on the other hand, could point to his great success with the amphibious landings at Inchon in September 1950, which turned the tide of war and saved the U.S. Army and its NATO allies from being driven into the sea—and saved South Korea forever from the tyranny of its northern neighbor.

They could point to his campaign to retake New Guinea from the Japanese, with its brilliant use of land, sea, and air power. They were able to celebrate his bravery during World War One, which should have won him the Medal of Honor and which did make him the youngest brigadier general in American army history; his reorganization and modernization of West Point while superintendent in the twenties, and his tireless work in the thirties as army chief of staff trying to prevent the army's total collapse under the weight of shrinking budgets, congressional neglect, and the Great Depression.

Above all, they proudly pointed to his role after Japan's surrender in World War Two, when he used a combination of firmness and diplomatic skill to bring modern democracy and the traditions of an open society to that defeated country. Those years in Japan earned him the respect and admiration of an entire nation, which still reveres Douglas MacArthur as the equivalent of a modern Founding Father—the man whose actions and policies, as one Japanese historian has put it, "set the course of Japanese history in the second half of the twentieth century."

So which version is true?

My hope is that by the end of this book, readers will know the answer.

DOUGLAS MacARTHUR

PROLOGUE

Three men in uniform arrived at the airport looking tense and somber. They were America's Joint Chiefs of Staff, the men in charge of the nation's armed services, and they were there on a mission from the president. They were going to tell the supreme commander in the Far East, General Douglas MacArthur, to halt his plans to win the war in Korea.

At dawn on June 25, 90,000 North Korean soldiers backed by 150 Soviet-built tanks had poured across the border into a defenseless South Korea. Not even five years after the end of World War Two, the Cold War with the Soviet Union had suddenly turned hot.

The only troops available to repel the North Korean attack had been four undermanned, underequipped divisions in Japan under General Walton Walker. They faced a foe more than twice their number. Day by day, elements of the Twenty-fourth and Twenty-fifth Infantry Divisions and the First Cavalry went into battle, almost from the moment they arrived at Seoul airport. Tanks were in such short supply that M4 Shermans on display at Fort Knox were taken down from their concrete pedestals, had their engines reinstalled, and then were shipped overseas to join the fight.

By the end of July, 94,000 American and South Korean troops were clinging to a narrow perimeter around Pusan at the southern tip of Korea. The fighting was intense, sometimes hand to hand. General Walker told his men there was no retreat, because there was nowhere to go. "We must fight to the end."

If they had to die, he said, "at least we die fighting together."

From the moment General MacArthur had been named supreme commander in the Korean theater, he had been spending days and weeks trying to find a way not only to save his men at Pusan but also to reverse the tide of war and drive the Communists back. A bold amphibious landing far behind enemy lines, MacArthur believed, could allow him to liberate Seoul, relieve the pressure on Walker, and cut off the North Koreans' line of retreat before they recovered. The place he had chosen was Inchon, a port city 150 miles northwest of Pusan and 30 miles east of Seoul, the Korean capital now in Communist hands.

Instead of the American and South Korean armies being cut off and isolated, it would be the Communists. A landing at Inchon, MacArthur predicted, would turn imminent defeat into decisive victory.

The moment the Joint Chiefs in Washington got wind of MacArthur's plan, they were aghast. The army's General Lawton Collins, who had commanded troops in landings in New Georgia during the Second World War, the navy's Admiral Forrest Sherman, and the marines' Lemuel Shepherd all remembered the uncertainties and perils of large amphibious operations during the last war—and the high casualties. Collins's predecessor, General Omar Bradley, had told Congress that the army would never be part of a large amphibious landing again. President Truman and Secretary of Defense George Marshall were equally dubious.

Meanwhile, the more military experts studied the situation, the dicier it looked. "We drew up a list of nearly every natural and geographic handicap" an amphibious assault might face, one naval staff officer later remembered, "and Inchon had 'em all."

And if MacArthur's plan failed, everyone in Washington realized, it would mean catastrophe for the American cause in Asia.

So Truman had dispatched the Joint Chiefs to convince MacArthur to change his mind: no landing at Inchon. By mid-afternoon of July 23, they and their aides were jammed into a tiny conference room off MacArthur's office in the Dai-ichi Insurance building in Tokyo, where he had been presiding as de facto ruler of Japan since its surrender five years before.

At the head of the table was MacArthur. Tall, handsome, ramrod straight in spite of his seventy years, he was the veteran of American wars in Mexico and the Philippines, decorated commander in two world conflicts, and son of a Civil War hero. In 1950 he was the most instantly recognizable American soldier in the world. Many thought it likely he would be the next president of the United States.

But not if he lost Korea.

He sat silent and expressionless, his pipe gripped tightly in his teeth, as the Joint Chiefs laid out their objections.

They pointed out that Inchon's tides were among the largest and most unpredictable in Asia, and that a landing force might well find itself stranded on a series of mudbanks, becoming sitting ducks for Communist gunners.

They explained that the channel entering Inchon harbor was narrow and winding, and a ship sunk there by an enemy mine could block the entire channel, making the operation impossible.

They also protested that MacArthur's plan meant stripping the Pusan perimeter of the First Marine Brigade, leaving General Walker's men unnecessarily exposed to a sudden North Korean attack.

Finally, General Collins stated that even supposing the Inchon landing succeeded and MacArthur did drive on to Seoul, it was his personal belief that MacArthur would be too far away to link up with Walker at Pusan, and that if the Communists counterattacked he could easily find himself trapped with no hope of relief. The best plan, the Joint Chiefs had concluded, was for MacArthur to evacuate Pusan and resign himself, and America, to the fall of South Korea.

The conference room fell silent. MacArthur's chief of staff, General Edward Almond, shifted uneasily in his chair. The tension and the temperature in the tiny space steadily rose.

Then MacArthur pulled his pipe from his mouth and spoke.

He said he understood the objections and the obstacles to an amphibious landing, and that although they were substantial, they were not "insupera-ble."

He said, "My confidence in the Navy is complete, and in fact," he added with a sly smile as he glanced over at Admiral Sherman, "I seem to have more confidence in the Navy than the Navy itself."

MacArthur went on to explain that taking Inchon and Seoul would cut the enemy's supply line and seal off the entire peninsula. "This in turn will paralyze the fighting power of the troops that now face Walker," MacArthur predicted. "Without munitions and food they will soon be helpless, and can easily be overpowered by our smaller forces."

Then with a sweep of his arm, MacArthur got to his final point.

"The prestige of the Western world hangs in the balance," he said. "It is plainly apparent that here in Asia is where the Communist conspirators have elected to make their play for global conquest. . . . Make the wrong decision here—the fatal decision of inertia—and we will be done."

His eyes grew wide and more determined. "I can almost hear the ticking of the second hand of destiny. We must act now or die."

MacArthur rose to his feet and glanced around the stunned and silent room. "Inchon will not fail," he concluded. "Inchon will succeed. And it will save 100,000 lives."

Then his voice dropped to almost a whisper.

"We shall land at Inchon, and I shall crush them!"

Three abashed Joint Chiefs went back to the Tokyo airport and returned to Washington. Six days later their telegram arrived on MacArthur's desk, giving the go-ahead for his amphibious landing.

America's most distinguished military leader had just made his boldest move ever. And with the landings at Inchon in September 1950 he would witness his greatest triumph in half a century in the U.S. Army.

And yet in less than three months it would only appear as prelude to his most spectacular failure, and set the stage for the greatest clash between America's military and civilian leadership since the Civil War.

CHAPTER 1

SON OF THE FATHER

Nothing has stood longer than MacArthur, the hills, and the devil.

—SCOTTISH PROVERB

Anyone who wants to understand the life and career of Douglas MacArthur needs to start by understanding the father.

There is a photograph of Arthur MacArthur standing by a chair in his Civil War uniform. It's a shock to realize we are looking at a lieutenant in the U.S. Army. He looks more like a boy in costume dress-up, until you look at the face. Under the whiskerless cheeks still running to baby fat you can detect the hardness of granite in the mouth as well as in the eyes: a granite he would pass on to his son.

Arthur MacArthur was born in Springfield, Massachusetts, on June 2, 1845. His father, also named Arthur, was a popular lawyer, as well as judge advocate for the militia in the state's Western Military District. Judge Arthur MacArthur Senior had migrated to Massachusetts from Scotland in 1828. In America his considerable intelligence and even more considerable charm had won him a series of increasingly lucrative jobs. In little time he rose from teacher in a one-room school to law clerk in New York City. There he eventually opened his own law firm (in those days no one needed a formal law degree to pass the New York Bar) and found a wealthy wife, Aurelia Belcher, daughter of a Massachusetts iron manufacturer.[1]

Judge MacArthur, an accomplished storyteller and a delightful after-dinner speaker, was a hard man to dislike. People were irresistibly drawn to the man with dark, hooded eyes, tousled black hair, and quaint Scottish burr. But all the charm and smoothness that made the judge's career a success stuck with him. What was left for his son, Arthur, was the same perceptive intelligence yoked to a ferocity—even a rigidity—of will and an emotional opaqueness that would characterize Arthur MacArthur's entire career.

That ferocity certainly got him through America's bloodiest war. He showed an unflinching heroism from his first battle at Perryville to Stones River in December 1862, and then to Missionary Ridge in November 1863, where he single-handedly led the Twenty-fourth Wisconsin up the steep slopes under heavy fire, carrying the regimental flag and shouting, "On Wisconsin!," which would later become the state's motto.

From there MacArthur and the Twenty-fourth would march south and fight on, along the long, bloody road to Atlanta, the hub of Confederate resistance in the west. He was still only eighteen when the regiment's commanding officer was wounded and he took over command of the regiment. It was on the eve of fierce fighting at Resaca on the East Tennessee and Georgia Railroad line that passed through Atlanta—the first major hurdle in the North's bid to capture the transportation hub of the Confederacy, Atlanta itself.

Everyone realized this was no ordinary eighteen-year-old. MacArthur, a fellow officer in the Twenty-fourth Wisconsin named Ed Parsons, and a divisional staff officer were out examining the earthworks that the Wisconsin men had built to MacArthur's specifications. They looked sturdy enough, but the staff officer wondered if the Twenty-fourth had enough personnel to man them if the Confederates launched a full-scale attack. "Major," he asked MacArthur, "suppose the Rebs should make a charge and attempt to capture this position? What would you do?"

MacArthur told him fiercely, "Fight like hell."[2]

At the battle for Kennesaw Mountain, Major MacArthur took a bullet in the wrist and another in the chest, but miraculously continued to lead his troops in the fight, on to Peachtree Creek, and finally he and his men and the rest of the Army of the Cumberland marched into a smashed and deserted Atlanta. In 112 days the Army of the Cumberland had advanced 200 miles and fought thirteen major battles. It had cost the Twenty-fourth Wisconsin eight officers and ninety-two enlisted men killed and wounded—with the teenaged Arthur MacArthur in command almost all the way. [3]

Three months later, while the rest of Sherman's army was marching south into Georgia, the Twenty-fourth saw even tougher fighting at the Battle of Franklin near Nashville on November 30. There the nineteen-year-old's luck finally ran out. Two bullets, one in the knee and the other in the shoulder, finally laid him low in the battle that every survivor of the Twenty-fourth agreed was the worst they had ever fought, worse even than Missionary Ridge. When the last Confederate attack petered out around 9:00 P.M., MacArthur's men loaded their critically wounded commander into an ambulance wagon while fires from the burning houses of Franklin lit up the night sky. His friend Ed Parsons was left in charge of the regiment while doctors struggled to save MacArthur's leg (they did), and found to their relief that the bullet in the shoulder had passed clean through.[4]

So it was a relatively light price to pay for the slaughter at Franklin. When Parsons went to visit MacArthur in the hospital that evening, he remembered finding four blood-soaked generals lying side by side on the porch, all dead.

It wasn't until mid-February 1865 that Arthur finally returned to his regiment after recuperating at home in Milwaukee, where his mother had died shortly before he arrived. By now, most veterans of the Civil War were sick of the war, including his former commanding officer and the man who had coined the phrase "war is hell," General William Tecumseh Sherman himself.

"I confess without shame that I am tired of war," Sherman wrote to a friend. "Its glory is all moonshine. . . . Only those who have not heard a shot, nor heard the shrills and groans of the wounded and lacerated (friend or foe) . . . cry aloud for more blood and more vengeance [and] more desolation."[5] Another survivor of the same campaign, Lieutenant Oliver Wendell Holmes, had found the ordeal so shattering that he was never the same man again, even as Supreme Court justice.

Arthur MacArthur had the opposite experience. Far from being repelled by the violence, noise, and danger of war, he loved it, and he learned to close his mind and heart to the suffering it imposed. The supreme thrill of personally leading men through mortal peril to victory and glory would never leave him. In later years he came to wrap the experience of war and carnage around himself like an old friend—and he would pass that same thrill on to his son.

In April 1865 a beaten and battered Confederacy surrendered, and the Twenty-fourth Wisconsin was able to return home on June 5. Arthur MacArthur, now a lieutenant colonel by order of the Wisconsin state legislature, led his men in a triumphal dress parade down the streets of Milwaukee, while his father, along with the mayor and other dignitaries, proudly watched from their grandstand seats. Five days later the Twenty-fourth Wisconsin was officially disbanded, and Arthur was promoted to full colonel.

He was still not old enough to vote, but little more than a week after his twentieth birthday he was a war hero and a Wisconsin state legend. There was even talk of recommending him for the Medal of Honor for his bravery on Missionary Ridge. But the curtain of peacetime reality had now come down. Arthur MacArthur's dream was to remain in the army, but as the army had shrunk from a million men to fewer than 55,000, and from 15,000 officers to only 3,400—with thousands of other veterans clamoring for the handful of remaining vacancies—commands were few and very far between, even for a war hero.

So Judge MacArthur, the most popular man in Milwaukee and a growing power in Wisconsin state politics, got into the act. He wrote to his friend Alexander Randall, former Wisconsin governor and now postmaster general, to see if Randall could help get a promotion for young Arthur (the best the army could come up with for the former lieutenant colonel of the Twenty-fourth Wisconsin was second lieutenant in the Seventeenth Infantry, which was being reorganized in New York City). Randall obligingly spoke to President Andrew Johnson, as did a Wisconsin senator and the congressman for Milwaukee's district. On October 13, just as MacArthur's regiment had completed training and was setting out for Texas, Arthur MacArthur found himself promoted to captain.[6]

It was not the first time a MacArthur furthered his military career with the help of political patronage, and it would definitely not be the last. Both father and son firmly believed that in the making of a successful military career, there was no substitute for courage and competence and experience. In their long careers, both would display plenty of all three—plus the other attribute Napoleon said was indispensable for a great general, namely, luck.

MacArthur father and son also believed they had a kind of genius, a destiny, that would inevitably bring them the rewards they deserved. But why wait and do nothing when a brief but well-placed letter, a friendly meeting over lunch or after dinner, or a kind word from one powerful friend to another could help to speed up the inevitable?

"This fortunate promotion," Arthur MacArthur wrote to Postmaster Randall, "[may] decide my life. The undeveloped events of the future may place it in my power to reciprocate." Already he could see himself being in a position to one day return the favor.[7]

Arthur's unexpected promotion did ruffle some feathers in the Seventeenth Infantry. It turned out there were no vacancies for captains, certainly none for MacArthur; so Captain MacArthur was reassigned to the Thirty-sixth Infantry instead, which was stationed in the Nebraska Territory, helping to protect Union Pacific Railroad crews building the Transcontinental Railroad from Indian attacks. It was not until November, however, that he reached the headquarters of the Thirty-sixth Infantry and his first post–Civil War army post, Fort Kearny. He would have to wait twenty-three long years before he would see his next promotion.

What followed for Arthur MacArthur were two decades in what would come to be called the Old Army, as he traveled from one far-flung army post to another in a series of scenes that could have been from a John Ford movie: the wooden stockade guarding a small collection of whitewashed buildings clustered around a flagpole and a dusty parade ground; the tedious patrols and monotonous fatigue duties played out in front of endless stretches of prairie and sagebrush desert with sandstone cliffs or dark snowcapped mountains framing the horizon; occasional shots traded with disgruntled bands of Indians while a steady procession of Cheyenne, Sioux, Comanche, and Kiowa as well as buffalo, antelope, elk, and characters from future westerns—"the unshaven buckskin-clad frontiersman, the trapper, trader, trooper, and pioneer homeseeker"—paraded past each post and each patrol, from Nebraska and Arkansas to Texas, New Mexico, Utah, and Wyoming.[8]

Above all, there was boredom. Everywhere there was the same routine, from 5:45 first bugle call and reveille followed by raising of the flag at 6:10, through breakfast and assembly, to setting out for work on building bridges and stringing telegraph wires, to roll call in the evening and lights-out at 11:00 P.M. For Arthur, this routine was broken only occasionally, by some memorable event. He would be present, for example, on May 10, 1869, when Leland Stanford drove in the golden spike joining the Union Pacific and Central Pacific railroads at Promontory Summit, Utah, as America's Transcontinental Railroad was finally complete. In January 1871 he was given leave to attend the wedding of his father and his new wife, who was seven years the judge's junior, in Washington, D.C., where his father now made his home (this wife, Judge MacArthur's third, was the daughter of a highly successful congressman). But otherwise, those first eight years of army service were ones of brain-crushing tedium for an army officer with no vices except perhaps the occasional glass of whiskey during a game of whist for minor stakes.

To relieve the boredom, Arthur MacArthur mostly read. He would have the judge send books on to him at his various posts, in addition to stacks of journals like *Harper's Weekly, North American Review,* and *Blackwood's Magazine.* We know MacArthur had a fascination for economics and authors like Adam Smith, David Ricardo, John Stuart Mill, and Walter Bagehot, as well as works on ancient and modern history. There was also a growing shelf on China and Japan—not to mention everything and anything he could get his hands on regarding military strategy.[9]

But as he sat and read and pondered, or sat in the pew at his father's wedding among the delighted guests and the orange blossoms, he must have wondered when, if ever, *he* would be married. He was nearing thirty when his new regiment, the Eighteenth Infantry, was transferred to Jackson Barracks outside New Orleans. There he would meet the woman who would transform his life, and serve as a pillar of strength both for Arthur and for his even more famous son.

Mary Pinckney Hardy was a true Southern belle. If Arthur MacArthur was John Wayne from a John Ford western, "Pinky" Hardy was Scarlett O'Hara from *Gone with the Wind.*

Headstrong, vivacious, and darkly beautiful, she was the daughter of a wealthy merchant from Norfolk. Her son Douglas, for whom she would become the single most important person in his life, described her heritage this way:

> Mary Pinckney Hardy came from an old Virginia family dating back to Jamestown days. Her ancestors had fought under George Washington and Andrew Jackson, and her brothers, products of the Virginia Military Institute, had followed Robert E. Lee's flag on Virginia's bloody fields. A Hardy was at Stonewall Jackson's elbow that dark night when he fell on the sodden Plank Road near Chancellorsville.[10]

Despite the associations with the South's "lost cause," her father, Thomas, was no slave-owning plantation owner and Riveredge, the family home outside Norfolk, was no Tara. As a businessman specializing in fertilizer rather than cotton, he had emerged from the Civil War with his fortune more or less intact. Mary, born in 1852, was the eleventh of fourteen children, and had grown up in North Carolina and then Baltimore while the family home was occupied by Union general Benjamin Butler and then rebuilt after being used as an army hospital. Summers during and after the war were spent at a house in Massachusetts.

Three of her older sisters had already married Northerners when she, on a visit to New Orleans, caught the eye of a handsome but imperious-looking young Union officer at a ball. Although the Eighteenth was in town as part of the Reconstruction occupation of the South by federal troops, animosity toward the victors by the vanquished was less fierce in New Orleans than any other Southern city. Captain Arthur MacArthur had found himself accepted as part of the normal social scene. When the vibrant young Miss Hardy crossed his path, he impetuously proposed. She impetuously accepted, and the Catholic wedding ceremony took place at Saint Mary's church in Norfolk on May 19, 1875.[11]

Marrying Northerners was one thing in the Hardy family, but marrying a Yankee war hero was another. Two of Mary's brothers refused to attend; Mary's mother, already badly shaken by the war, fell deeper into a depression that hastened her death in 1881. But Mary refused to be daunted. She had chosen a man who represented the new American future, not the Southern past. She had chosen a man of no fortune except his talents and his brains, one whose career would inevitably take her to the remotest places in America. Yet her course was set—as was Arthur's. They would be devoted to each other for the next thirty-seven years in a marriage, as their son Douglas noted, "of perfect union"—though he would live to know just the opposite.

For a year and a half the married couple lived in suspended bliss. With the help of Judge MacArthur, the army adjutant general arranged for Captain MacArthur to enjoy sixteen months of detached duty in Washington, D.C., where Pinky was able to attend parties, delight in the judge's charming conversation at table with his influential friends, and on June 1, 1876, give birth to their first son, Arthur III. Even her husband's recall to duty in New Orleans in December didn't entirely disrupt the honeymoon, although life in Jackson Barracks was a rude introduction to the rigorous routine of army life. Pinky MacArthur took every opportunity to return to New England during the three years while her husband served as commander of K Company, Eighteenth Infantry, until October 1878, when a second son, Malcolm, was born in New Britain, Connecticut, while she was traveling with her mother.

The hammer fell in the spring of 1879 when, after rejoining her husband in New Orleans, an outbreak of yellow fever sent the Eighteenth Infantry fleeing north, first to Chattanooga (which must have been a grim reunion for the thirty-year-old Arthur) and then to Atlanta (ditto), until finally taking up quarters in Little Rock, Arkansas. Pinky was again pregnant. The plan was to have her bear her third child at Riveredge, but the baby came prematurely on January 26, 1880, while they were still settling in at the Little Rock barracks.

They named him Douglas. He was scrawny, small, and weak, like most premature babies. Some in her family wondered if he would be strong enough to survive. But Judge MacArthur was delighted. The boy had been born on his sixty-third birthday; Douglas would grow up to be his grandfather's favorite, although his mother and father were devoted to his brothers, Arthur and Malcolm.

The way the Norfolk papers covered the birth, as MacArthur later recalled, was "Douglas MacArthur was born on January 26, while his parents were away."[12] He was in some ways a provisional baby, the male backup in case his two elder brothers didn't survive (of the fourteen Hardy children, only ten had made it to adulthood). In fact, it was Douglas who would outlast and outshine them both, and become an army legend even exceeding his father's fame—a source of pride, but also ambivalence, for the rest of his life.

That July, Captain MacArthur was ordered to join Company K at Fort Wingate in New Mexico to help guard workers building the Atchison, Topeka, and Santa Fe Railway. Six-month-old Douglas was deemed strong enough to make the journey, so with the baby, four-year-old Arthur III, and nineteen-month-old Malcolm in tow, Pinky and her husband set out in the full heat of summer on a trek across Arkansas, Louisiana, and Texas, until they reached their destination, one hundred miles northwest from Albuquerque and a lifetime away from anywhere else.

The post was even worse than Pinky could have imagined. Set high in the Zuni Mountains along the Continental Divide, Wingate baked in summer and froze in winter. Rattlesnakes and Gila monsters haunted the nearby mesas and dry river basins. Their quarters were a small one-story adobe building with a flat dirt roof, with the inside ceiling lined with canvas to keep out the scorpions. The family of five shared two rooms and a kitchen, with a rough wooden floor. Quarters for the enlisted ranks did not even have that. No wonder that in 1881–82, 248 of the 440 enlisted men in the Thirteenth Infantry chose to desert.[13]

The same thought must have crossed Pinky's mind, but she had her delicate hands full nursing two babies and caring for toddler Arthur while her husband focused on camp duties. There were few women at Fort Wingate and even fewer opportunities for socializing, and so it was in the evening at dinner that Pinky must have poured out her frustrations to her husband and urged him over and over to resign his commission and go into business like her father.

Arthur refused. He loved the army, and performed his duties with a competence and rectitude that impressed every officer who had contact with him.[14] He was still convinced that he was destined for higher things. All he needed was the right opportunity, a lucky break, to show what he was meant to do—and take him and the family far away from the mesas, mountains, and the scorpions.

That break came in the autumn of 1881 following the death of Mary's mother. Arthur applied for leave to take the family east, and they arrived in Norfolk in early May 1882. Days were spent dividing up the Hardy estate (Arthur and Pinky came away with $40,000, a minor fortune in those days), and then Arthur set off for Washington to visit his father and his new wife at their house on N Street. His father's range of political contacts had grown to the highest levels of the government and included important figures in both political parties (there was even talk that the judge might be in the running for a seat on the U.S. Supreme Court).

One of those contacts was Ulysses S. Grant, Arthur's former commander in chief at Missionary Ridge and now a former president. He was delighted to learn that in addition to military history, Captain MacArthur had an interest in Asia and China. As it happened, Grant had just returned from Asia, and he had been deeply impressed by what he had seen.

The trip had been part of a world tour that Grant and his wife and sons had conducted in 1877, starting in England, where they had met Queen Victoria, and moving on to France, Germany, Russia, and Egypt. Back in the United States, the former president found himself stalked by scandal and accusations of incompetence during his administration. But abroad he was treated as a hero and a celebrity by adoring crowds and awestruck politicians, and so after visiting the Pyramids, Grant had decided to extend their tour for another year and press on to the Far East.

Ever since Commodore Perry had first sailed into Yokohama Harbor in 1854, Americans had been fascinated and drawn to Asia and the Pacific. "There is the east; there is India," proclaimed Thomas Hart Benton to an audience in St. Louis, as he pointed due west past the Rockies to California, which Americans of every political stripe saw as the gateway for American commerce and trade in Asia.[15]

The dream was that the networks of commerce flowing from the United States would free the East (what Walt Whitman called "venerable priestly Asia") from the shackles of superstition, tyranny, and poverty—while completing America's redemptive role as a beacon of freedom in the world.

In 1844 Secretary of State Caleb Cushing negotiated a most-favored-nation trading treaty with imperial China. In 1867 the United States purchased Alaska from Russia, in part to serve as a bridge to Asia; a year later America acquired a tiny atoll in the mid-Pacific that it dubbed Midway Island, since it sat midway between California and Japan. And in 1875 Grant himself had negotiated a reciprocity treaty with the independent kingdom of Hawaii, for shipping pineapples grown by American farmers in the islands to the United States.[16]

But Grant was also interested in something else. He spelled it out on his visit to China after spending several weeks in India, including touring the Taj Mahal. He told a large audience in Canton, "I am not prepared to justify the treatment the Chinese have received at the hands of the foreigner," meaning European powers like Britain and Russia. He foresaw a possible future role for the United States in Asia besides trade: that of protecting the nations of the region from outside aggressors as Asia emerged into the modern world.[17]

It was a point he returned to when he and his wife sailed into Nagasaki Harbor on June 21, 1879, on the USS *Richmond*. Japanese naval vessels fired ceremonial twenty-one-gun salutes while other ships circled the harbor waving American flags, as crowds waved from the quays and cliffs and set up bonfires to light their way at night.

Japan had embarked on its crash program of modernization, the Meiji reforms, eleven years earlier, and Grant was impressed by everything he saw. "The country is beautifully cultivated," he wrote to a friend. "[T]he scenery is grand, the people, from the highest to the lowest, the most kindly . . . in the world."[18]

He was particularly impressed by Japan's new railways and trains, as modern and up-to-date as anything on the Union Pacific line, and at the immense state dinner in his honor on June 23, he spoke to his rapt audience of his vision for the future of both Japan and America.

"America has great interests in the East. She is your next-door neighbor. She is more affected by the Eastern populations than any other Power," he told the Japanese, a clear reference to the growing Chinese and Japanese immigrant populations in California and on the American West Coast.

"We have rejoiced over your progress," he said. "We have watched you step by step. We have followed the unfolding of your old civilization and its absorbing the new. You have our profound sympathy in that work, and sympathy in the troubles which come with it, and our friendship. I hope it may continue—I hope it may long continue."[19]

The highlight of the visit was Grant's meeting with Japan's emperor, the Tenno, on August 10. It was not an entirely ceremonial meeting. While in China, the Chinese emperor's viceroy, General Li Hung-chang, had asked the former president if he would help negotiate a peace with Japan over some islands that both countries were claiming, the Ryukyus—the principal island of which was a twenty-square-mile rocky promontory called Okinawa. Grant had agreed, and during his meeting he managed to arrange the deal and secure a peace treaty, thus foreshadowing the role that Teddy Roosevelt would play in brokering an end to the Russo-Japanese War in 1905.

By the time he arrived back in San Francisco, Ulysses S. Grant had inaugurated a new era in U.S.-Asian relations. He would be eager to talk about it with the intelligent young army captain who seemed as enthusiastic about Asia as Grant was.

They spoke together over several days, with Grant describing his impressions of his visits with Chinese and Japanese politicians, and Captain MacArthur intently absorbing every detail. Grant was convinced that something extraordinary was happening, in both China and Japan. A new era in Asia's relations with the world was under way, and that the United States needed to be part of it.

"America has much to gain in the East," Grant was telling listeners. "No nation has greater interests—except America has nothing to gain except what insures them as much benefit as it does us. I'd be ashamed of my country," Grant emphasized, "if its relations with other nations, especially with these ancient and most interesting empires in the East, were based on any other ideas," and MacArthur no doubt would have enthusiastically agreed.[20]

Then Grant had an idea. Why didn't MacArthur apply to the War Department to be sent to China as a military attaché? Grant promised he would use what influence he had with the department and with President Chester Arthur to try to get him the post.

MacArthur was thrilled at the offer. He immediately filled out the paperwork for an application, while also seeking a six-month extension of his leave. By then, he hoped, the War Department would have weighed his case, read Grant's letters of recommendation (the ex-president wrote several), and he and Pinky and the boys would be bound for the exotic East.

It did not quite work out that way. First, his request for leave was denied and he was forced to make the 2,000-mile trip in just six days by himself—his wife absolutely refused to go and urged him to quit his commission rather than submit to the humiliation. It was not until October 1882 that he finally was granted leave to return to Norfolk and his family.

It was there that he put the final touches on what he considered his ace in the hole for securing the post in China. It was a forty-four-page manuscript that Arthur MacArthur had written and typed out himself, titled "Chinese Memorandum." It was in fact a scholarly tour d'horizon of American foreign policy in Asia, which he had put together with his usual ferocious concentration of energy and focus, the same technique that would mark his son Douglas's approach to any new or important task. He then sent it on to Grant, who forwarded it to President Arthur.

By any standard, it is an extraordinary document, especially considering it was written by someone who had never visited Asia. It did, however, reflect an intense reading of Oriental as well as European history, including the history of Russia; and although it antedates Alfred Thayer Mahan's *Influence of Sea Power Upon History,* and future pronouncements by Senator Henry Cabot Lodge, Albert Beveridge, and Theodore Roosevelt by almost a decade, their basic theme that the future of America lies westward in the Pacific is all there.

Indeed, ten years before Professor Frederick Jackson Turner published a famous essay prophesying the end of the U.S. frontier, MacArthur (who was actually serving on that frontier) did the same. America's overland expansion and settlement westward was all but over, MacArthur predicted. The nation would need a new challenge to mobilize its energies and peoples. That challenge, MacArthur announced, was Asia.[21]

Two nations in particular, he noted, "are making their way back into the old continent" where the Aryan race began. One was Great Britain, the other Russia.

MacArthur then described how in the past forty years Russia had annexed one swath of central Asia after another, until it now stood on the doorstep of imperial China. From the other end of the continent, Britain had advanced across the Indian subcontinent northward to Afghanistan and Nepal. Conventional wisdom had it that either Great Britain or Russia would dominate the future of Asia and particularly China which, despite long years of decadence and decline, was still "the richest Empire existing on the face of the Earth."

Arthur MacArthur, however, had a third candidate: America. Indeed, "the United States cannot exist as a commanding and progressive nationality unless we secure and maintain the sovereignty of the Pacific."[22]

It was a bold and daring proposition, one that—from the perspective of America's relative place in the world and the technologies of 1882—must have seemed beyond ordinary comprehension. But MacArthur saw this American dominance arising not through conquest but through trade. He proposed creation of a vast trans-Pacific commercial network that would open China to American influence and extend that influence beyond the borders of China, including to Japan and the rest of eastern Asia.

Indeed, MacArthur saw the competition for dominance in not material but ideological terms. There are two, and only two kinds of polities in the world today, he announced—the Empire and the Republic. One was embodied by Russia: ruthless and autocratic, the embodiment of the drive for military power and acquisition of wealth and territory at any cost. The other was reflected by the United States, the modern embodiment of the virtues of self-government and the rule of law, whose expansionist urges sprang from the bottom up rather than imperial diktat. America as the fulfillment of mankind's democratic impulses rather than its imperial ones, and the embodiment of a future built around commerce more than military might.

"It seems inevitable that the Empire and the Republic are destined to meet in Asia," MacArthur wrote. The fate of the world, indeed of freedom, hung in the balance of which principle prevailed.[23]

It was as if he could see in a crystal ball his son and his army's agonies on the Korean peninsula almost seventy years later.

America certainly had a material stake in expanding its markets into Asia. "The American Republic can never acquire its full complement of riches and power if it permits itself to be excluded from the field of Asiatic commerce," he wrote. But in Arthur MacArthur's mind, the issue went beyond commerce and moneymaking. American trade would serve as an opening for "the propagation of American ideas," including the concepts of republican liberty and human freedom.[24]

In the later pages of his "Chinese Memorandum" MacArthur even foresaw a day when California and America's West Coast would serve as a vast emporium of trade and influence spreading across the Pacific. In the process American trade would serve as a social and economic crucible in which the nations of Asia, including China, that seemed doomed to a state of decline and decadence might suddenly revive.

"Once let these torpid communities be set in motion," he predicted, "once mix them again by travel and commerce, and the aspect of things might quickly change. Asia," he wrote in a sentence that seems to leap gleaming off the page, "may yet be destined to exhibit the greatest of political wonders."

Yet if the Russian imperial ideal prevailed, the opposite would happen. The hegemony of Russia would have disastrous consequences both for America's future in geopolitical and ideological terms and also for the future enlightenment of China and the rest of Asia.

In short, "self-interest, sound economy, and pure morals, agree in their judgments," Captain MacArthur opined, "and corroborate each other, and point us to the Orient as the field of our future labors. There we must contend for commercial power, and perhaps combat for political supremacy."[25] That momentous fight, he believed, would begin with China, where "the possibility of a rapid development of an effectual military spirit in the Chinese Empire is, perhaps, as interesting and important as any . . . that may hereafter affect the civilization of the world." And he wanted to be part of that interesting and important mission, as military attaché.

In the end, it did not happen. Despite former president Grant's best efforts, MacArthur never got an appointment. In fact, it would be six years before the United States appointed military attachés to any foreign country, and then largely in Europe and Latin America.[26]

Yet as a document, MacArthur's "Chinese Memorandum" is also a personal landmark. From that date the future of the MacArthur family shifted decisively away from America or Europe and toward Asia. For both Arthur MacArthur and his son Douglas, Asia would be the arena in which their careers would take root and where they would earn their greatest laurels as military commanders. And for both father and son, the principles set forth in the 1882 memorandum would continue to influence their vision of America's role in Asia and what Asia's bright future could be with America's help.

For the present, however, the disappointment of not getting the post was overshadowed by a shattering event that would change the MacArthur family dynamic, and Douglas MacArthur, forever.

CHAPTER 2
TURNING POINTS

Captain MacArthur signed the finished copy of his "Chinese Memorandum" on January 15, 1883. Less than three months later a devastating bout of measles swept through the MacArthur family as they were staying at the Hardy estate at Riveredge, and on April 12 four-and-a-half-year-old Malcolm died.

The grief-stricken captain, Pinky, and their two surviving boys watched as Malcolm's little coffin was laid to rest in the Hardy family plot at Cedar Grove Cemetery. For Arthur MacArthur, the boy's death confirmed him in his steady retreat into the routine of work and duty. He avoided attending social events, stopped playing cards, and maintained a stony silence in the face of his wife's entreaties that he give up the army and start life over again in the civilian world.[1]

For three-year-old Douglas, the loss of the brother who had been his constant playmate must have been equally devastating, as well as frightening. As historian Carol Petillo, who has delved deeply into the MacArthur childhood, concluded, he suddenly found himself abandoned by his best friend, without understanding why.[2]

It was Pinky MacArthur for whom the death caused the greatest change, coming so soon after her mother's death, and in the same house. "His loss was a terrible blow to my mother," Douglas later admitted in his memoirs.[3] Her grief became at times overwhelming, as well as life-transforming. "Sometimes I nearly go crazy over my loss," she wrote to her sister Elizabeth, who had recently lost her husband. But she could take comfort that little Malcolm and Elizabeth's husband were now "before Jesus . . . pleading for us." It was a sad party that returned to Fort Wingate for that summer, fall, and winter. Only the news that Captain MacArthur had been reassigned to Fort Selden in far southern New Mexico, close to the Rio Grande—his first independent command—broke the routine of grief, silence, and collective misery.[4]

The three-hundred-mile trip to Selden involved considerable danger— Geronimo's band of Apaches was preparing one last breakout from their reservation near the MacArthurs' route—and hardship. But for three-year-old Douglas, it was filled with excitement, as well. In his memoirs, he records it as his first conscious memory. To him, the world of Fort Selden seemed like a Wild West story come to life. "It was here I learned to ride and shoot even before I could read or write," he remembered later, "indeed, almost before I could walk and talk." While his mother used to dress him in skirts and full blouses, and to curl his hair, which hung down to his shoulders, life at Fort Selden now introduced him to the world of masculine skills and duties and the romance of the West. It was "a land bright with promise scarred only by wind and weather—a land with unknown mountains to be climbed, alluring trails to be ridden, streams to be navigated by the strong and vigorous" and all of it guarded by strong men in blue, who marched out every day with their rifles on their shoulders into the blazing sun of summer or the freezing cold of winter and returned every night while "we would stand at attention as the bugle sounded the lowering of the flag."

There was even one comic moment when they were out riding and their horses and mules panicked at a strange smell. Then something suddenly loomed on the horizon, "a shaggy ghost out of the page of wonderful." It was an Egyptian camel, the pitiful survivor of the herd that Secretary of War Jeff Davis had bought for the army in 1855 as pack animals in the American desert—a clever experiment in cross-cultural exchange that never caught on.[5]

The memories of Fort Selden would become increasingly precious to

Douglas MacArthur. They would contain the last distant echoes of an American frontier way of life that was vanishing even then, as his father had predicted. "Life was vivid and exciting for me," he later wrote of those days, and his missing playmate, Malcolm, was soon all but forgotten.

But one person did not forget Malcolm. That was Pinky, who continued to nurse her grief and now directed all her love and attention on the one person who mattered most to her, her youngest son. After her husband left for work and her oldest son for school, she and Douglas would be alone for the entire day. Just as Arthur, the eldest, was increasingly a part of her husband's orbit and his clear favorite, so Douglas now became the center of her life.

She also did something extraordinary for her time and place. As she wrote to her sister from Fort Selden, "Arthur is in command and I can do just as I want." On one of her frequent trips east she had herself fitted with an early birth-control device called a pessary. The message to her husband was clear: there will be no more children. The four of them were now the only family they would have, and the emotional bond that her own mother had had to share with fourteen children, Pinky would focus on one in particular, her youngest son, Douglas.[6]

Until her death in 1935, she would be the single most important woman—indeed the most important person—in his life. When he was a boy she would be there to extricate him from dangers and build his self-confidence. When he was a man, she would reassure him at times of challenge and crisis, advise him at critical turning points in his military career, comfort him during times of loss, and share in moments of triumph. Nearly every day for the next fifty-two years, his mother would be his daily guide, support, and protector—and propel him forward to heights of accomplishment and fame that her husband, serving in the same profession, could only imagine.

The death of his brother Malcolm in 1883 was the first major turning point in Douglas MacArthur's life. The second came six years later when his father finally won the promotion to major that he had sought for so long, and moved the family to Washington, D.C.—and Douglas finally got to know his grandfather.

The tousled black hair had turned white, and there was now a decided paunch around the judge's middle. But the sparkling wit and beguiling charm that had won the hearts of three wives, won him a seat on the Supreme Court of the District of Columbia for seventeen years, and turned him from a down-at-the-heels Scottish immigrant into one of the most influential men in the nation's capital was still there. For the boys, used to their stern, subdued father, their grandfather was like a deep draught of a life-giving elixir.

"I could listen to his anecdotes for hours," Douglas later recalled. In their grandfather's study amid the books and leather-bound chairs, Arthur and Douglas would sit spellbound for hours as the judge wove stories about famous law cases together with tales about Scotland and the MacArthur clan, a branch of Clan Campbell that claimed to trace its roots back to King Arthur and the knights of the Round Table.

Through their grandfather's words they could visualize the MacArthur clan marching off to battle in the mists of the Highlands, wearing their tartans of green, black, and gold, and he could hear the clan motto, which the judge would repeat in his thickest Scottish burr:

> Tis Green for the sheen o' the pines
> And Black for the gloom o' of th' glen
> Tis Gold for the gleam of th' gorse
> The MacArtair tartan, ye ken.

Above all, Judge MacArthur told the boys about the battlefield exploits of their father. He recited for them by the hour the record of Arthur MacArthur's heroism on Missionary Ridge and at the Battle of Franklin and on Kennesaw Mountain. Douglas had rarely heard his father say anything about the Civil War, except in a self-deprecating way. It was his grandfather who turned a rather stuffy and unapproachable father into a figure of heroic, even epic proportions. Certainly the description in MacArthur's own autobiography of his father's charge up Missionary Ridge—"Gasping breath from tortured lungs! . . . The charge is losing momentum! They falter! . . . And then suddenly, on the crest the flag!"—conveys some flavor of what those exciting afternoons in his grandfather's study must have been like.[7]

Meanwhile, from his desk at the adjutant general's office at the War Department, Major MacArthur was busy in securing the Medal of Honor that he believed was rightfully his, for his actions on Missionary Ridge almost thirty years earlier. For years he, like other officers, had been told that the newly created Congressional Medal of Honor was reserved for enlisted men, not officers. But in April 1890, he discovered that Congress had amended the law in 1863 to allow commissioned officers to receive the medal. The War Department had ignored the change, but three commissioned officers *had* received medals after the war, and one of them—Captain John C. Burke— had won it for conspicuous bravery at the Battle of Murfreesboro: the very same battle in which MacArthur had distinguished himself for the first time.

So Major MacArthur submitted an application for his own Medal of Honor, complete with testimonials from the generals who had commanded him at Murfreesboro, Missionary Ridge, Kennesaw Mountain, and the Battle of Franklin, and even from fellow officers who had been eyewitnesses to the fighting.[8] The board was impressed, and on June 30, 1890, awarded him the Medal of Honor for conspicuous bravery at Missionary Ridge. They figured he deserved it equally well for his actions at Murfreesboro and Franklin, but Missionary Ridge was such a prominent example that it became the basis of the citation.

Persistence pays. Don't let the bureaucrats keep you down. Keep asking the same question until you get the answer you want. These were the lessons Douglas MacArthur would learn from his father's experience with the Medal of Honor. Indeed, winning the nation's highest military award for himself would become his own obsession as a soldier—one that would cause him considerable turmoil and generate controversy more than once.

The next turning point in Douglas's life was the move to San Antonio, Texas, when his father was assigned as assistant adjutant general to the military district there.

It was actually a happy time for the MacArthur family. His mother en- joyed the social life of San Antonio and the fort, where her husband was able to hire her a maid. She and other army wives were able to spend leisurely afternoons visiting the town's shops and restaurants—a far cry from life at Fort Selden. The major himself settled into the Fort Houston routine, know- ing that he was the master of his chosen work—"every duty assigned to you,

you have performed thoroughly and conscientiously," his commanding officer, General Kelton, wrote. "I regard your assignment to duty . . . a most fortunate circumstance for [this] office and the army"—and that he could count
on new promotions as time went on.[9]

Douglas's brother, meanwhile, had accepted a commission at the U.S.
Naval Academy and with Arthur III now out of the picture and safely ensconced at Annapolis, Pinky could concentrate all her attention on her
youngest son's scholastic attainments.

Up until now they had been pitiful. Later Douglas confessed, "I was only
an average student" at the various schools he had attended, including in
Washington. Both his father and his mother shook their heads over his mediocre grades and wondered aloud why he couldn't be more like his brother
Arthur, who was not only an excellent scholar but also a brilliant athlete who
broke the Annapolis record for the half-mile run.[10]

The place they chose for turning Douglas around was San Antonio's West
Texas Military Academy. It had been founded in 1893 by the Right Reverend
James Steptoe Johnson, a veteran of the Eleventh Mississippi during the Civil
War who fought in twelve engagements with the Army of Northern Virginia
and believed that "in a military school a boy most readily acquires the habits
of neatness, attention and obedience [and] which tend to make one upright
in principles and morals, as well as in bearing." His other goal was to develop
"the Christian character amongst the rising generation," and to teach them
that "character is the only true wealth."[11]

In any case, it was an environment that had an almost miraculous impact
on their youngest son's mind and spirit. "A transformation began to take
place in my development," he recorded seventy years later. "There came a
desire to know, a seeking for the reason why, a search for truth." His first year
at West Texas he maintained a 96.3 average out of 100 possible points, which
dipped to 95.15 the following year. His third year brought a 97.65 average
and a citation for "superior excellence" in scholarship; the boy whose main
interest had been sports was given a medal for the highest average in mathematics.[12]

What had happened? The impact of a strong, disciplined atmosphere with
a healthy competition from other students, many of whom came from the
San Antonio area and were, in the words of one graduate, "some of the mean-

est boys this side of hell," may have had something to do with it. The presence of strong-minded teachers and administrators like Reverend Johnson and Allen Burleson, the school's rector, probably helped. So did the hormonal boost of reaching the age when, as Dr. Johnson once said, the mind was most active and most retentive, and intellectual discovery becomes a thrill equal to scoring on the football field or—no doubt for some cadets—discovering girls.

Another part of it may simply have been the absence of an older brother who was accustomed to excelling and earning the approval of both parents while his younger sibling was forced to sit and listen. Now in the vacuum created by Arthur III's departure for Annapolis, Douglas finally had the chance to shine. Whatever the cause, he took full advantage of it.

"Abstruse mathematics began to appear as a challenge," he remembered later, "dull Latin and Greek seemed a gateway to the moving words of the leaders of the past, laborious historical data led to the nerve-tingling battlefields of the great captains, Biblical lessons began to open the spiritual portals of a growing faith, literature to lay bare the souls of men." As one of his awed classmates remembered, MacArthur "was doing Conic Sections when the rest of us were struggling with Elementary Algebra," and another said, "His ability to analyze a problem and arrive at a sound conclusion [is] just out of this world."[13]

At the same time, he was quarterback of the football team, played shortstop for the baseball team, which won seven out of eight games, and won the school's tennis championship.

Douglas's transformation was a matter of family as well as personal pride. His grandfather the judge had authored seven books; his father had built a library of nearly four thousand volumes in everything from Chinese history to political economy. The MacArthur men admired intellectual attainment as much as winning on the battlefield or winning the presidency; and now Arthur MacArthur's youngest son—Pinky's darling baby—had earned his place in the same exalted company. At West Texas he learned a lifelong love of books and ideas, and the mind that analyzed conic sections would later devote itself to organizing military operations from assaults on German positions on the Hindenburg Line to the liberation of the Philippines—and contemplating the logistics of nuclear war with Communist China.

Looking back six decades later, he wrote, "My four years there were the happiest of my life. Texas will always be a second home to me." Speaking of West Texas Military Academy to other graduates, he would always say, "This is where I started."[14]

On June 8, 1897, his proud parents sat in the pew in the school chapel as Douglas MacArthur, class valedictorian, recited James Jeffrey Roche's stirring poem "The Fight of the *General Armstrong*." Their son had won the school's highest honor, the Academy Gold Medal, as well as medals in Latin, mathematics, and public speaking. Reverend Burleson told them Douglas was "the most promising student that I have ever had in an experience of over ten years in schools both North and South."[15]

Their lives had changed too. For the second time in his life Arthur MacArthur was made lieutenant colonel. The first promotion had come at the end of the Civil War, when he was about to turn twenty. The second came on June 8, 1896, six days after his fifty-first birthday. That same month Arthur III graduated from Annapolis and set off for San Francisco as a cadet on the USS *Philadelphia*.

Then in August, Judge MacArthur died at a health clinic in Atlantic City. The *Atlantic City Daily Press, the Atlantic City Daily Union,* and the *Milwaukee Sentinel* all carried the news on their front pages, and his widow had conveyed the judge's body to be buried at Rock Creek Cemetery in Washington.[16] Two months later, in October 1896, Lieutenant Colonel Arthur MacArthur (with his father's death he had dropped the "Jr." from his signature) was assigned as the new adjutant general of the Department of the Dakotas, with headquarters in St. Paul, Minnesota.

The young graduate from West Texas Military Academy would be headed back north with him, but not to St. Paul. He would be living in Milwaukee, where his father and mother had hatched a plan to get Douglas past the next set of hurdles so he could enter the United States Military Academy at West Point. What none of them could know was that in less than a year events would disrupt all their plans, and a sudden explosion in Havana Harbor would change the destiny of the United States, and that of the MacArthur family.

*   *   *

"I never worked harder in all my life."

That was MacArthur's recollection many years later of the time he spent in the winter and spring of 1897–98 preparing for the next great hurdle he faced in his pursuit of a military career. "Always before me was the goal of West Point," MacArthur wrote, "the greatest military academy in the world."[17]

It had been his father's dream to attend, but he never did. Douglas tried to get an at-large appointment right after graduating from West Texas, but despite a sheaf of supporting letters from the commanding general of the Department of Texas, Wisconsin Senator John L. Mitchell (whose father had been one of the late Judge MacArthur's closest friends), four governors, two congressmen, and two bishops, President Grover Cleveland turned him down. He tried again later with the newly inaugurated President McKinley, but again the result was disappointment.

Now his parents sprang into action. Arthur MacArthur once told one of his aides, the future secretary of war Peyton March, that he had started planning to get Douglas into West Point the day the boy was born.[18] So he and Pinky devised what they considered a foolproof plan to get Douglas accepted, even though it had several moving parts.

The goal was to secure his nomination to West Point by Wisconsin Representative Theabald Otjen, yet another old friend of the late judge, by establishing residence in the congressman's district. They would do this by setting Douglas and his mother up in the swank Plankinton House hotel in Milwaukee, where she could supervise his studies for the West Point entrance exam while Arthur MacArthur would commute from St. Paul on weekends to see how things were progressing. In addition, Milwaukee was the home of a leading back specialist, Dr. Franz Pfister, who would treat the slight curvature of the spine that Douglas had developed at West Texas so that there could be no physical obstacles to his entering West Point.

Douglas and his mother moved into Plankinton House in October 1897. They had seven months before the competitive exam in May the following year. The schedule of study was unrelenting. In addition to his own course of reading under his mother's care, Douglas attended classes at Milwaukee's West Side High School to brush up on history, mathematics, English, and other topics covered in the exam, while the school's principal and its most popular history teacher, Miss Gertrude Hull, agreed to tutor the eighteen-year-old on whatever subjects posed the most difficult challenges.[19]

Monday through Friday Douglas went through the same grinding routine of walking the two miles to West Side to get there ahead of other students so he was already in class by the time they arrived, then returning home for more reading and study. On the weekends, however, there was time for church (he had been confirmed into the Episcopal Church while he was at West Texas) and for relaxation with his new Milwaukee friends. One was Frank McCutcheon, the assistant desk clerk at the Plankinton, with whom Douglas would sit and talk for hours, mostly about his dreams of a military career and joining the cavalry.[20]

Another was far more momentous for the future. The Mitchells, including Senator John L. Mitchell, had been MacArthur friends for decades. The senator had even served with Arthur MacArthur in the Twenty-fourth Wisconsin. Douglas soon struck up an acquaintance with John Mitchell's son William, as well as his sister. In fact, the sister was the object of Douglas's first teenage crush, and of the first lines of MacArthur poetry that survive. They are everything one would expect:

> Fair Western girl with life awhirl
> of love and fancy free,
> Tis thee I love
> All things above
> Why wilt thou not love me?

Even after she read these lines, it seems she never did.[21]

Douglas and William Mitchell never became close. Indeed, Douglas must have looked up to the twentysomething William, who was something of a local hero and who in 1898 had already embarked on the military career that Douglas coveted for himself. But after service in the Spanish-American War, William "Billy" Mitchell would choose military aviation as his field. He was destined to become the country's outspoken, if controversial, prophet of a new strategy for winning wars decisively: airpower. Then in 1928 he would be the subject of the most famous and significant court-martial in American history—one that would nearly doom America's ability to prepare for World War Two.

And on the opposite side of the court-martial table would be his old friend from Milwaukee, General Douglas MacArthur.

As February 1898 dawned and Milwaukee braced itself for one last bout of winter before the spring thaw, Douglas MacArthur and his mother were in the final stages of preparing him for the May competitive exam that would determine which prospective cadet got Congressman Otjen's nomination for West Point. Then one day the headlines of the Milwaukee papers were filled with news from the Spanish colony of Cuba that would turn the MacArthurs' lives, and the country, upside down.

On the night of February 15, a massive explosion ripped through the bowels of the battleship USS *Maine* as it was moored in Havana Harbor. It had been sent there to reassure American citizens in Cuba, who were caught in the bloody war between the Spanish colonial government and Cuban nationalist guerrillas. Instead, the ship became the watery grave of 260 Americans. To this day no one knows exactly what caused the *Maine*'s five tons of powder charges to explode, blowing away the entire front third of the battleship.[22] A hastily assembled American court of inquiry, however, decided it was a Spanish naval mine, perhaps deliberately set to deter the United States from intervening in the ongoing guerrilla war on the island. Spain's increasingly brutal counterinsurgent tactics, including confining thousands of Cubans in barbed-wire-lined detention camps, had offended Americans' sense of fairness and decency. Many reading the sensational articles about Cuba in Joseph Pulitzer's *New York World* and William Hearst's *New York Journal* had wondered aloud what the Monroe Doctrine was for, except to prevent a European imperial power from committing atrocities on a New World nation yearning to be free.

In March, as the death toll from the *Maine* disaster grew, the cry went up across America: "Remember the *Maine*! To Hell with Spain!" There was a pro-war march through Milwaukee, which Douglas no doubt watched and may even have joined. The calls for retaliation echoed not only in the streets of Milwaukee but in the halls of government and Congress as well. There,

America's leading exponents of the expansionist foreign policy that Arthur MacArthur had prophesied sixteen years earlier had been waiting for an opportunity like this one. They were led by Assistant Secretary of the Navy Theodore Roosevelt as well as Secretary of State John Hay, and two senators from Massachusetts, Albert Beveridge and Henry Cabot Lodge.

In their minds, it was time for the United States, the world's fastest-growing industrial power, to seize its rightful place on the world stage. They were more than willing to ride the outcry over the *Maine* to force a reluctant President McKinley to summon the nation to war—a war they were confident they could win. To this day, many historians, including most of MacArthur's biographers, have treated the rush to war in 1898 as a form of war hysteria "whipped up by a jingoistic press and fanned into flame by irresponsible politicians."[23]

In fact, motives for going to war were more complicated. They were a buoyant mixture of moral crusade and a belief in Manifest Destiny, weighed down by an additional calculation of Realpolitik. If the United States didn't use this chance to grab off portions of a moribund Spanish empire in the New World as well as the Pacific, went the reasoning, some other European power, such as Germany, likely would.

Besides, "have we no mission to perform, no duty to discharge to our fellow-man," Albert Beveridge proclaimed, unconsciously echoing Arthur MacArthur's words of a decade and a half earlier. "Shall America continue its march toward commercial supremacy over the world? Shall free institutions broaden their reign as the children of liberty wax in strength, until the empire of our principles shall be established over the hearts of all mankind?"[24]

Despite the wave of moral fervor in the media and in influential circles, it took almost two months for war to be declared. When it came, on April 20, Arthur MacArthur immediately got in touch with his friend Major General Henry Clark Corbin, the army's adjutant general, to ask for a combat command—his first since the Civil War twenty-seven years before. He knew that an army that had barely numbered 30,000 troops when the *Maine* was sunk would now have 125,000 volunteers to train and equip, a number that would swell to a quarter million the next year. The army was going to need every experienced field commander it could muster, and MacArthur was determined to be at the head of the line.

Corbin gave him what he wanted. Colonel Arthur MacArthur was ordered to report to Camp Thomas at Chickamauga, Georgia—ironically, the scene of the old Twenty-fourth Wisconsin's bloodiest fight—to assemble and train a brigade of volunteers as part of III Corps' invasion of Cuba while taking the rank of brigadier general.[25]

But then events on the other side of the world intervened. The first shots in the war with Spain were fired not in Cuba but across the Pacific, in the old Spanish colony of the Philippines. Theodore Roosevelt's plan for mobilizing the navy for war had included dispatching the U.S. Asiatic Fleet under Admiral George Dewey to Manila to attack the Spanish fleet there. On May 1, Dewey's fleet struck with devastating and decisive force, sinking all but one of Spain's older, undergunned warships. Total U.S. casualties came to nine wounded and one dead, from heatstroke.[26]

In the course of a single day, the way had opened for an American incursion into another Spanish colony, the Philippines. As it happened, like Cuba, the islands were home to another anti-Spanish insurgency. This one was led by a twenty-seven-year-old former provincial mayor named Emilio Aguinaldo, who had been in exile in Hong Kong when he learned the news of Dewey's stunning victory. Aguinaldo immediately set out to return home, where he soon upset all of America's plans for the Philippines.

Meanwhile, III Corps had set sail for Cuba in June. MacArthur, however, was not with them. Instead, he had been assigned to San Francisco to take command of the First Brigade, First Division, under the overall command of General Wesley Merritt, as they embarked for the Philippines on August 4. He was not the only MacArthur caught up in the war. The newly minted brigadier general had learned that his son Arthur was on his way to Cuba as part of the naval expedition that would eventually sink another Spanish fleet at Santiago, on July 3.[27]

But that was not all. General MacArthur had also received a letter from his wife informing him, to his pride and delight, that their other son, Douglas, was on his way to West Point.

Douglas was making final preparations for the all-important West Point exam when war broke out in April. Still, he and his friend Frank McCutcheon thought seriously of volunteering to join the fight. But in the end he did not dare. He and his mother and father had invested too much in passing the exam in May, and so he was forced to follow the course of the war in the newspapers until he finished the final round of study, closed the last book, and waited for the exam the next day at Milwaukee's city hall.

Sleep was impossible that night. The expectations of the entire MacArthur family—father, mother, older brother, the memory of his grandfather—seemed to weigh him down as he tossed and turned in bed. The next day, on the way to the city hall, he felt tired, haggard, and half defeated. He was also deeply nauseous, he writes in his memoirs, a nervous reaction that would haunt him in later moments of stress and indecision as well.

It was his mother, he remembered, who turned him around. "Doug," she said, tugging on his sleeve, "you'll win if you don't lose your nerve. You must believe in yourself, my son, or no one else will believe in you."

Her final words of advice before he entered the exam room were, "Be self-confident, self-reliant, and even if you don't make it"—Douglas must have drawn a sharp breath as she said it—"you will know you have done your best. Now, go to it."[28]

He did. When he left the examination room, he had scored 93.3 out of a possible 100—16 points ahead of the next applicant. When the results were announced in June, Douglas had won the congressional appointment.

"It was a lesson I never forgot," he wrote. "Preparedness is the key to success and victory." It also taught him that whatever his doubts and insecurities, and however distant his father seemed in both emotional and physical terms, his mother would be his pillar and rock, the one who would stand by him no matter what—and would believe in him when others did not.

It's no wonder then that when he finally stepped off the coach of the West Shore Railroad at the stop for West Point, New York, in early June 1899, and saw the cold gray granite buildings of the U.S. Military Academy for the first time, his mother was with him—and that she would be with him every single day for the next two years at the academy.[29]

*   *   *

She did not, of course, live on the grounds of the academy or in the dorm where Cadet Douglas MacArthur was housed. She took a room at the West Point Hotel, a broken-down boardinghouse on the northern edge of the West Point Plain. Pinky did not mind the shoddy rooms or the dirty facilities. She would be only a couple of hundred yards away from her son as he embarked on what was so far the greatest adventure of his life.

Physically he was more than prepared for what was coming. He was now nineteen years and four months old. His slight spinal curvature had been cured. He stood five feet ten inches tall and weighed 133 pounds. His physical report the day he registered pronounced him "*Normal.*"[30] A member of his class, Cadet Hugh Johnson (later head of the National Recovery Administration under Franklin Roosevelt), called him "the handsomest young man I have ever seen."[31]

Mentally and spiritually, though, there were serious challenges ahead.

One was that West Point was a closed world in more ways than one. A member of the cadet corps was allowed off the post exactly twice a year— once for the Army-Navy game and once for summer furlough at the end of the term year. Christmas never interrupted the regular routine of the Corps, let alone Thanksgiving.[32] A cadet who left sight of the Academy buildings was not allowed to dismount until he returned. He was not even allowed to handle money. Winston Churchill, who served with the Fourth Hussars cavalry regiment (no slouch in discipline), noted that West Point cadets were "cloistered almost to a monastic degree." Hence the academy's nickname— "Monastery on the Hudson."

A new cadet was also plunged into a world with its own language—a demerit was a "quill," because long ago a goose feather quill had been used to record them; a reprimand that required walking post was a "slug"; milk in the mess hall was "cow" and cream was "calf"; a plebe assigned to carve meat for upperclassmen was a "gunner." First-year cadets like MacArthur were "plebes," sophomores were "yearlings," and juniors were "second classmen." A senior was a "first classmen," and his female date a "drag," and roommates at the academy were "wives."

The physical conditions in which plebes lived were grim. Not much had changed since the institution had opened almost one hundred years before.[33]

The plumbing and standard of sanitation was ancient; the food was meant to sustain, not satisfy; and lights-out at night was at ten o'clock. But the real test, starting in July and August in what was known as "Beast Barracks," was the hazing.

It was an ancient ritual, harking back to militaristic societies like the Spartans and revered by every cadet who experienced it and survived to mete it out to others. Those living outside "the Monastery on the Hudson" saw it as brutal bullying, pure and simple. Cadets, alumni, and even professors understood it to be a necessary ritual for shaping a common esprit de corps—and weeding out the unsuitable.

By the time Douglas arrived, however, the hazing rituals had reached new levels of absurdity, even lethality—and he would become a principal target.

By West Point standards, it was easy to see why. Having his mother on hand did not help. The grandson of another army legend, U. S. Grant, was a member of the same West Point class and his mother, too, kept rooms at the West Point Hotel. Word quickly spread that both were "mama's boys," which brought the same malignant attention to Ulysses III from other cadets that Douglas had to endure.

But Douglas's problems also stemmed from his father. That summer Arthur MacArthur was fast becoming an army legend, not just for his Civil War exploits—Southern upperclassmen enjoyed making plebe MacArthur recite every detail of his father's campaigns—but for his growing success in the fighting in the Philippines.

CHAPTER 3

GLORY DAYS

The planting of liberty—not money—is what we seek. The human race has propagated its highest ideals in a succession of waves, and now its waves are passing beyond the Pacific.

—ARTHUR MACARTHUR, 1899

A s Arthur MacArthur and the five transports carrying the men of his First Brigade steamed into Manila Harbor on the morning of July 31, 1898, a strange sight greeted them. It was a long and dismal row of smokestacks sticking up from the water outside Cavite, the old Spanish naval base. It was all that remained of the Spanish fleet Admiral Dewey had sent to the bottom of the harbor on May 1, in the stunning victory that had left the Philippines open to the Americans—along with everyone else.

As the transports approached Manila, MacArthur and his men realized the Americans were far from alone. Fifty warships of four other nations—Britain, France, Germany, and Russia—filled the harbor, a veritable forest of masts and smokestacks, while Admiral Dewey's flagship *Olympia* and the other vessels of the American fleet watched them warily.[1]

For MacArthur the message was clear. If the Americans failed to fill the vacuum left by the defeat of Spanish colonial rule in the Philippines, others would fill it for them. Admiral George Dewey, meanwhile, had other problems on his mind. Following his smashing victory at Manila Bay, he had arranged for the young leader of the Filipino rebels, Aguinaldo, to leave his exile in Hong Kong and come to Manila. They had met on May 19, and to this day no one can agree on what they said to each other. Aguinaldo would later insist that Dewey supported his nation's claim for independence. Dewey would insist just as strongly he had said nothing of the sort.[2] In his mind his task was still to defeat the Spanish; what happened to the country afterward was none of his business, including its possible independence.

There was a huge problem, however. Although Dewey had told MacArthur and General Merritt, the overall commander, to "take no notice of the insurgents" as the Americans prepared to take Manila, the insurgents now controlled virtually all of the Philippines *except* Manila. In fact, on June 12—the very day MacArthur had left for San Francisco to join his command—Aguinaldo stole a march on Dewey and everyone else by formally declaring his country's independence.

Indeed, forces were unfolding in the Philippines that first MacArthur and then, more than thirty years later, his son would try to cajole, nudge, and bring into the American camp. It would be the same problem that would bedevil American policymakers in Vietnam, Iraq, and Afghanistan: how to unlock a people's desire to be free by force without having them turn back on their liberators.

The Filipino rebels were at first welcoming of their American liberators. The 15,000 men in the Spanish garrison in Manila were far more willing to surrender to the Americans than to the Filipinos, who could be expected to seek revenge for Spanish atrocities during the years of insurgency. After some light resistance, American troops entered Manila to accept the Spanish commander's surrender on August 13, 1898. MacArthur and his men breathed a sigh of relief. The streets of the old city, known as the Intramuros, wound themselves into a labyrinth of alleys and passages, many of which were so narrow that a man had to hug the stone walls to let another person pass. If the Spaniards had decided to fight house to house there, it could have taken days, even weeks, to winkle them out. The result would have been massive American casualties—as his son Douglas would discover almost half a century later.[3]

A few weeks passed before MacArthur and Merritt learned that the war in Cuba was over, following Theodore Roosevelt's stunning victory at San Juan Hill, that more American troops would be coming to the Philippines under

General Elwell E. Otis—and that Arthur MacArthur and General Thomas Anderson would assume command of Otis's two divisions, some 20,000 men.

That fall, under American occupation, Manila enjoyed the coming of peace. Martial law was lifted, and MacArthur was now commanding a division of more than 9,000 men, with more reinforcements on the way.

He was going to need them. On December 11 news came over the restored telegraph that President McKinley had decided, after considerable hesitation and second-guessing as well as prayer, that the United States would annex the Philippines rather than grant the islands outright independence. Independence without the means to safeguard it, some argued, would only leave the islands exposed to colonization by Germany, Britain, or France. Annexation by America was really the best solution.[4]

That feeling did not extend to the Philippine insurgents. Overnight McKinley's fateful decision turned Aguinaldo and the Filipino National Army from allies into enemies—and on the night of February 4, 1899, fighting broke out between a sentry of the First Nebraska Volunteers and Filipino troops. America's first land war in Asia had begun.[5]

Arthur MacArthur would distinguish himself in the fighting to clear the rebels from Manila and to drive them north, finally capturing Aguinaldo's capital at Malalos, twenty miles north of Manila. By May he was a national hero. Newspapers proclaimed, "Tis Dewey on the Sea, and MacArthur on the Land." But as the spring of 1899 dissolved into summer, an American army already weakened thanks to the exit of thousands of volunteers as their term of enlistment came due and they boarded ships for home, was weakened further by the outbreak of diseases like typhus, dysentery, and yellow fever.

Aguinaldo, in the meantime, refused to surrender. "We are no nearer a conclusion of hostilities here than we were three months ago," one officer wrote home to his wife on June 15. As the summer dragged on, Arthur MacArthur would have had to agree. They were going to need a lot more troops, and a much more aggressive commander than General Otis if they were going to win this war.

Meanwhile, Douglas's personal battle with hazing at West Point was reaching a climax.

Ordinarily, a cadet could escape the torture of hazing only by agreeing to a knockdown bare-knuckle fight with a skilled upperclassman, which usually left the plebe unconscious and bleeding. MacArthur was a skilled boxer, but he resigned himself to the hazing regime.

"We always prepared a warm reception for the sons of well-known men," said Robert Wood (later a close friend of Douglas MacArthur and CEO of Sears, Roebuck), and he was not kidding. Being forced to recite his father's military records and "making funny speeches," or hanging by his toes and fingers from a cot until he dropped from exhaustion, were just the start. Douglas MacArthur took all the hazing "with fortitude and dignity," Wood remembered, even after upperclassmen gave him a "sweat bath," by putting him in full dress uniform, wrapping him in a blanket and a raincoat, and making him sit up all night in the middle of summer.[6]

The turning point came one night when a gang of cadets led him blindfolded into a darkened tent, stripped him stark naked, and ordered him to do 250 "spread eagles" (meaning standing on his toes with arms extended, dropping to a stoop, flapping his arms and rising to a sitting position, then doing it again) over a bed of broken glass—followed by "wooden willys" that involved holding the regulation rifle at a fire position, dropping down to reload at the order of "ready," and then repeating the exercise until the upperclassmen decided to call it quits.

Douglas passed out before they called it quits. When they revived him, he went into severe convulsions, with arms and legs jerking uncontrollably.

He was still in convulsions when they carried him back to his room, where he asked his roommate to throw a blanket under his feet so that their involuntary thudding wouldn't alert the company officers to what had happened—and to jam a blanket in his mouth in case he cried out in pain.[7]

The next morning Douglas refused to go on sick report, as some urged him to do, or to speak about the incident. He turned out for drill and other duties like the other cadets, but when he was returning to his tent he was stopped by an upperclassman—the same one who had led the hazing the night before.

The man was ashamed about what had happened, but he also had a message.

"By your plucky work last night," he told MacArthur, "you have a bootlick from the entire Corps."

A bootlick meant he had earned the respect of every cadet at West Point for his endurance—and for keeping his mouth shut. It meant an end to hazing for Douglas MacArthur, and a new prestige among his fellow cadets.[8]

In short, "he emerged from camp with flying colors. He showed himself a true soldier," a colleague remembered. Others, however, took a very different view of things. When a cadet named Oscar L. Booz died as a result of hazing by members of MacArthur's class, the McKinley administration launched a formal inquiry, while a special committee of the House of Representatives decided to hold an investigative hearing. One of the former victims of hazing they particularly wanted to hear from was Cadet Douglas MacArthur.

MacArthur was in a quandary. On the one hand, he couldn't snitch on former classmates. "Come what may," he wrote later, "I would be no tattletale." On the other, he couldn't lie to the court of inquiry. He had already been summoned to the superintendent's office to name his original tormentors, and he had refused.[9] If McKinley's special court of inquiry demanded the offenders' names, and if MacArthur refused again, "It would in all likelihood mean my dismissal and the end of all my hopes and dreams. [Instead] it would be so easy and expedient to yield, to tell, and who would blame me?"

The answer, of course, was himself.[10]

The date was December 1900. Far away in the Philippines his father's war with insurgents, after a year and a half, had taken a strange but decisive turn.

Step by step, battle by battle, the Americans had finally cleared out resistance from the island of Luzon and broken the back of the Philippine National Army. With the rebel forces destroyed, General Otis and other officers assumed the war was over; Arthur MacArthur, however, did not. He grimly predicted that the insurgency was about to make a comeback. He also knew that the Americans had made themselves deeply unpopular in the Philippines and that unless they wrapped up the war quickly, this could turn into a protracted, costly stalemate—what a later generation would call a "quagmire."

Starting in January, the quagmire revealed itself. American control of Luzon steadily deteriorated; the number of engagements—always with small bands of hit-and-run partisans—rose, as did the number of American casualties. As in all guerrilla wars, the conduct of the war grew progressively more vicious, with each side taking the opportunity of atrocities by the other side to commit atrocities of its own.[11]

Finally, Washington had had enough and in March 1900 replaced Otis with Arthur MacArthur. At the same time, it appointed MacArthur military governor of the Philippines. The news left Aguinaldo and his guerrillas deeply worried. They knew who they would be dealing with. One of their leaders admitted, "MacArthur was the most able American General." They sensed the war was going to take a much tougher turn.[12]

They were right. MacArthur now had some 70,000 troops under his command, two-thirds of the entire U.S. Army, plus auxiliary units of Philippine ethnic minorities like the Macabebes and Illocanos, who hated the majority Tagalogs leading the insurgency.[13] MacArthur was ready to take the fight directly to the enemy. From December 1899 to September 1900, the U.S. Army fought more skirmishes with Filipino guerrillas and suffered more casualties—well over a thousand—than it had in every Indian war since 1865.[14]

Officials in Washington, and the public, were horrified. But as America's first great counterinsurgency strategist, the predecessor of future theorists such as David Petraeus and David Galula, MacArthur understood that the mounting casualties were the price of future success.[15] The goal was to push the insurgents off to the margins, deeper and deeper into the mountains and the jungle, while isolating them from the larger population. That population, he believed, was now united in its support of the revolutionaries. "That such unity exists is an undeniable fact," he wrote, whatever journalists and propagandists in Washington might think, along with Washington's sanguine emissary William Howard Taft, who arrived in June 1900 convinced that the fighting was all but over.[16]

MacArthur knew better. Victory would come, he believed, only after the majority of Filipinos finally decided that resistance to American occupation was futile—and that supporting the occupation could even be beneficial.

That was what he set out to do as military governor, a job combining economist, political theorist, civil engineer, business executive, and secondary school teacher all in one. Fortunately, Arthur MacArthur was prepared for all of them. From his headquarters in Manila he and his staff worked long days that dragged on through dinner, discussing problems in sanitation, education, economic development, and civil administration as well as the war. He also appointed boards of officers to study key issues like land reform, while he put soldiers to building schools, vaccinating civilians, setting up courts run by Filipino judges in pacified areas, and making sure municipal elections were safe and fair—much as his son would do in occupied Japan, and American soldiers would do in Iraq and Afghanistan more than a century later.

In the meantime, however, there was still a war to win. In December 1900—even as his son Douglas was about to be called as witness for the president's hazing investigation—Arthur MacArthur declared martial law throughout the Philippines. He applied a general order that President Lincoln had issued during the Civil War and General Sherman had used during his march through Georgia, declaring that combatants who were not in uniform, and civilians who helped them, would be subject to the death penalty.[17] He also ordered thirty-nine prominent insurrection leaders to be interned in Guam and had their property seized—including Aguinaldo's.

Either you're for us or you're against us, MacArthur was saying to the Philippine elites. Despite Taft's misgivings, the strategy worked. Insurgents began to surrender to their American pursuers; public support for the insurrection weakened. The final stroke came in March 1901, when by a simple ruse MacArthur was able to arrange for the capture of the Filipino leader Aguinaldo himself. That, combined with MacArthur's internment of key figures of the Filipino establishment, finally snapped the spine of the Filipino insurgency.

On April 19, after three weeks of intense negotiation, Aguinaldo— pressured by family and friends—threw in the towel. He agreed to swear allegiance to the United States and call on his followers to surrender in exchange for the immediate release of 1,000 prisoners, another 1,000 in May, and a further 1,000 a month later. Except for a few hot spots like Batangas province, south of Manila, and the island of Samar, the insurgency collapsed.[18]

As Arthur MacArthur sailed back to San Francisco on July 2, 1901, he could be satisfied with the outcome. He was now a major general; he had decisively won the most extensive guerrilla war that any Western nation, let alone the United States, had ever faced. He also had won the respect, even adoration, of a generation of American soldiers for whom he was, by general consent, the finest officer with whom they had ever served.

He had missed shaping his son Douglas's years at West Point, but he would leave him a far more valuable gift. This was that a number of the officers under whom Douglas would serve—Peyton March, Frederick Funston, John J. Pershing, Charles Summerall—would have earned their spurs in the Philippines under his father's command. The trust and respect they felt for the father would transfer when they took over command of the son, as all of them did. Some would be protective; most, like Funston and Summerall, would be tough but fair; John J. "Black Jack" Pershing would be brutal.

But all of them would remember the general who stood tall under enemy fire in the Philippines and found a way to win a war that most had thought unwinnable. Whatever Douglas's occasional flaws, they would give him the benefit of the doubt because they remembered the MacArthur who had risked everything to save his country from the humiliation of defeat, and gave his soldiers the prize they most craved: final victory.

The day the anti-hazing court met, Douglas MacArthur felt desperately ill— again, the paralyzing nausea that almost overwhelmed him the day of his qualifying exam in Milwaukee. And again it was his mother who came to his rescue. From the West Point Hotel, she sent him a letter. He opened it during a recess in the court, he tells us, and inside he found a poem:

> *Do you know that your soul is my soul such a part*
> *That you seem to be fiber and core of my heart?*
> *None other can pain me as you, son, can do;*
> *None other can please me or praise me as you.*
> *Remember the world will be quick with its blame*
> *If shadow or shame ever darken your name.*
> *Like mother, like son, is saying so true*
> *The world will judge largely of mother by you.*

MacArthur read the last four lines with tears in his eyes:

Be this your task, if task it shall be
To force this proud world to do homage to me,
Be sure it will say, when its verdict you've won
She reaps as she sowed: "This man is her son!"

With the poem folded in his pocket, MacArthur strode into the court-room. "I can still feel the beads of sweat on my brow," he wrote sixty years later. "I still feel my knees giving way under me and that dreadful nausea."[19] "I did my best to fend off the questions, to dodge the issues," but the judges, all retired military men, refused to be put off. They ordered him to divulge the names of his hazers.

"I pleaded for mercy; that my whole life's hope lay in being an officer; that always I had been with the colors; that my father, then on the battleline 10,000 miles away, was their comrade in arms of the Civil War and Indian wars; that I would do anything in the way of punishment, but not to strip me of my uniform."

There was a pause, and then the head of the court said, "Court is recessed. Take him to his quarters."[20]

Back in his room, Douglas MacArthur waited all day to be put under arrest. But the order never came. They were not about to arrest or expel the son of Arthur MacArthur, the hero of the Philippines; they found other ways of getting the names they wanted. When Douglas had to appear before the congressional committee, the questioning was more grueling—"you do not look very robust now," one congressman remarked sarcastically when MacArthur said having to endure the hours of "spread eagles" hadn't done him any lasting physical harm—but in a sense it was anticlimactic. The congressmen now had the names; what they really wanted was Cadet MacArthur to condemn hazing as a ritual institution. This he adamantly refused to do.

Q: Did you consider it cruel at the time?
A: I would like to have you define cruel.
Q: All right sir. Disposed to inflict suffering; indifference in the presence of suffering; hard-hearted; inflicting pain mentally or physically . . .
A: I should say perhaps it was cruel, then.

Q: You have qualified your answer. Was it or was it not cruel?

A: Yes sir.

Q: And you did not expect it was part of the essential education of an officer to be subjected to such cruelty?

A: I do not think it is essential; no sir.[21]

But was it cruelty? Decades later MacArthur still refused to see the hazing itself as anything but a natural part of how West Point shaped the character of its cadets to deal with adversity, how to uphold the solidarity of the Corps, how to endure—and get rid of those who couldn't take it. "Hazing was practiced with a worthy goal," he would write later, but sometimes "with methods that were violent and uncontrolled." The answer was regulation, not abolition.

He was not alone. John J. Pershing, who had been a vigorous, even hated TAC (tactical officer) at West Point two years before MacArthur arrived—cadets called him Lord God Almighty—had been an enthusiastic hazer as an upperclassman and did nothing to stop it during his time as TAC. He once told a friend, "I hope the day will never come when hazing is abolished."[22] MacArthur would have had to agree.

The investigations had come as Douglas MacArthur was in his third year as a cadet. He had already proved himself to be one of the best in West Point's history. As someone who served three years with him at the academy put it, "There was never another cadet quite like him."[23]

Photographs in his cadet uniform show him poised and confident, with strikingly handsome—almost beautiful—good looks (another reason he may have been a target for hazing early on). There's also a slightly faraway, visionary cast to his eyes that's familiar from myriad photographs of him during World War Two and Korea. That's no coincidence. The years at West Point created the essential core of the Douglas MacArthur the world would know for the rest of his life, the framework of values, habits, and attitudes that would sustain him for the next half century.

"Think of the sort of man he is today," his former West Point roommate said in 1953, "and you have exactly the picture of what he was when he graduated in 1903."[24]

One of those values was his love of the army, which bordered on religious idolatry. The barracks and facilities at West Point were broken down, unsanitary, and squalid. Two cadets shared a room with barely enough space for one of them to stand. There was no electricity, no running water. Instead, cadets had to fetch any water they needed with a five-gallon metal bucket from an outside spigot. From reveille at 6:00 A.M. until mandatory lights-out for underclassmen at 10:00 P.M., every day was a regimented routine of drill, classes, inspections, and parades.

Yet MacArthur was enchanted by it. To be in the same rooms, walk down the same halls, and attend the same classes—sometimes the same lectures— as Robert E. Lee (class of 1829), Ulysses S. Grant (class of 1843), Phil Sheridan (class of 1853), Jeb Stuart (class of 1854), George Armstrong Custer (class of 1861), and nearly every successful general currently serving in the army except his father was sometimes overwhelming. "As an Army brat, it was the fulfillment of all my boyish dreams," he wrote in 1947. "[T]he pride and thrill of being a West Pointer has never dimmed."[25]

To be part of West Point was to be part of history, but it was also a responsibility. "You are the leaven which binds together the entire fabric of our national defense," he once told a class of graduating cadets. "[F]rom your ranks come the great captains who hold the nation's destiny in their hands the moment the war tocsin sounds. The Long Gray Line has never failed us"—and he would never fail the Corps and what it stood for.

He had arrived at West Point determined not just to succeed but to surpass every one of his classmates in everything—and he nearly did. He "was one of the hardest working men I have ever known," his first roommate remembered. "His every energy was directed toward the attainment of . . . number one in his class." He was helped in this by the fact that his first roommate was also an upperclassman who had been impressed by MacArthur's drive and dedication the first time he set eyes on him during Beast Barracks, and invited him to be his roommate. That was a lucky break for Douglas, because first classmen had the privilege of keeping their lights on until 11:00 P.M., which for Douglas meant a precious extra hour of study. He was also regularly up an hour before reveille, hitting the books in everything from chemistry, physics, and mathematics (the mainstays of the curriculum at the Point) to geology, history, French, and Spanish (introduced after the start of the Spanish-American War).[26]

The teaching was perfunctory; none of the instructors in French, for example, could speak the language. Instead, cadets learned to prepare their lessons themselves, then come to class and recite the answers to questions instructors had assigned them during the previous class.[27] It wasn't an educational system designed to bring out much original thinking or creativity. But it gave a student like MacArthur, who possessed a virtual photographic memory and intense self-discipline, a guaranteed head start over students who were less responsive to rote memorization and didn't take books all that seriously.

But Douglas did, and by June 1900, of the 134 cadets still in his class he was first in math, first in English, first in drill regulations, and first on the Order of General Merit. Nor were his accomplishments limited to the classroom. He also worked hard at sports at the Point, starting with playing left field for the baseball team. "I was far from a brilliant ball player," he admitted years later. "I was no Ty Cobb but in those days I could run"—and as a classmate noted, he always managed to find a way to get on base either by drawing a walk or bunting his way to first. He managed to score the winning run in the very first Army-Navy baseball game at Annapolis, on May 18, 1901, earning him a dark blue letter "A," which he wore first on a sweater and then on a succession of gray dressing gowns for the rest of his life.[28]

What stood out in his mind sixty years later was not so much the score of the game but the raucous song the Navy cadets sang to him as he and the rest of the Army players walked onto the field:

> *Are you the Governor General*
> *Or a hobo?*
> *Who is the boss of this show?*
> *Is it you or Emilio Aquinaldo?*[29]

Yet it was from his father's years in the Philippines that Douglas MacArthur would draw valuable lessons for his own future, fighting in foreign lands.

The first lesson was that politicians in Washington, and their emissaries like William Howard Taft, never understand the real situation on the ground in making policy and so most of their recommendations are grounded in ignorance or bias, or both.

The second was that when an American army finds itself occupying a foreign country against its will, the best initial policy is a fierce severity. "You can't put down a rebellion," wrote Major General Lord Wheaton in 1900, "by throwing confetti and sprinkling perfumery." The severity, however, must be followed by mercy and a generosity that throws opponents off balance, and points the way to a lasting peace.[30]

Finally, Arthur MacArthur taught his son that America's role in Asia was different from those of other Western nations who were busy seizing trade concessions and colonies. It was to lend the light of liberty to people who had never experienced its warm, comforting glow, and to make America the symbol of freedom in a world that at times seemed to put a premium on its opposite.

Upon his return to the United States, Arthur MacArthur was ordered to appear before Congress. Representatives, especially on the Democratic side, were outraged by reported atrocities by American troops.

Arthur MacArthur deftly parried the attacks and criticism. He admitted that some individuals may have committed outrages, but said, "I doubt that any war—either international or civil, any war on earth—[has] been conducted with as much humanity, with as much careful consideration, with as much self-restraint . . . as have the American operations in the Philippine archipelago."

He also spoke highly of the Filipinos. "They like our institutions," he told the senators. "They have some mistrust of us individually, because our deportment is so entirely different." But "I have a good deal of faith, in them, they are smart, generous and intelligent people . . . I do not think there is a question about the power of the Filipino to reach any standard of excellence in almost any direction."

Then he finished by lecturing the senators on the importance of a continuing American presence in the Philippines, saying: "The archipelago's strategical position is unexcelled by that of any other position on the globe. [It is] relatively better placed than Japan . . . likewise, India . . . It affords a means of protecting American interest which, with the least output of physical power, has the effect of a commanding position . . . It is the stepping stone to commanding influence—political, commercial, and military supremacy in the East."[31]

It was a view his son would inherit, and uphold for the rest of his life.

The son, meanwhile, had created at West Point a record that was nothing less than astonishing.

Douglas MacArthur would rank first in his class for three of his four years, dropping to fourth in his third year—but still in the top five "distinguished cadets." When he graduated in 1903, the gap between MacArthur's merits total (2,424 out of a possible 2,470 or 98 percent) and that of the runner-up, Cadet Charles T. Leeds, was bigger than the gap separating Leeds from the man in fifth place. In addition to being the class First Captain, he led his class in mathematics, English, drill regulations, history, ordnance and gunnery, law, and military efficiency. His scores in English, history, and law were perfect—100 percent of all possible merits.[32]

Some said it was the most outstanding graduating record since Robert E. Lee's in the class of 1829. Most agreed it was the best in a quarter century.

But for Douglas, the highest reward was having both his parents present for the graduation ceremony on June 11, 1903. There was his father, Arthur, fresh from his triumphs in the Philippines, and his mother, Mary, with whom he spent a half hour every afternoon during the two years she had been with him at West Point, discussing his studies, his hopes, his problems—the person who had been his emotional rock in the most trying times of his life.

At West Point he had learned the power of self-discipline, and of self-assertion. It was customary in a cadet's last year that he could be exempted from taking the final exam in mathematics if he had maintained a certain grade point average.

When Douglas saw his name on the list of cadets who were *not* exempt—because the teacher insisted that he had missed a single quiz—he exploded. He told his instructor point-blank that he wouldn't take the exam, no matter what. "If my name is not off that list before 9 A.M. in the morning," he told his roommate at the time, George Cocheu, "I'll resign!"

Cocheu winced. "But what will your father say?"

"He will be terribly disappointed, but I believe he will see my attitude in the matter and approve my action."

At 8:50 MacArthur got the news. The instructor had relented.[33]

He also got his first experience in leadership. Even during summer camp of his first year, older cadets recognized that this was a person born to be in charge.

In his second year the tactical officer of A Company, an artillery officer, watched MacArthur drill a squad of inexperienced plebes. The officer turned to the cadet next to him and said with astonishment, "There's the finest drill master I have ever seen."[34]

At this point his identification with his father was total. His roommate Arthur Hyde remembered Douglas being obsessed with measuring up to his father's standard. "He often wondered if he would be as great a man as his father—and thought if hard work would make him so, he had a chance."[35] His years at West Point seemed to prove him right. But it was his mother, Mary, who had enabled him first to take on, and then endure, the most difficult of all the crises that he underwent at the Point. In the end, it was her trust and approval, even more than his father's, that would serve as the emotional foundation for his career and future.

His longtime aide and friend, Brigadier General Tommy Davis, who worked with him in the twenties and thirties, grasped this essential truth about the commanding officer whom he deeply admired but also understood. "The goal instilled in him was to be Superman," was how Davis explained it to a colleague. "MacArthur's tie to his mother . . . represented possessiveness and dominance, with the son never free of an imposed destiny or from fear of failing it."[36] Although the career he had chosen was his father's, and his goals the same as his, it was his mother who shaped the ways in which he would achieve those goals, starting at West Point.

For all these reasons, it was no wonder he could tell his roommate, "Next to my family, I love West Point," and tell the assembled cadets on the Plain fifty-five years later in his last public speech, "When I cross the river my last conscious thoughts will be of the Corps—and the Corps—and the Corps."[37]

It was a sincere declaration of what the academy had meant to him, but also what it had enabled him to become.

CHAPTER 4

YOUNG MAN GOING EAST

Asia is now the land of commerce, where the heated
imagination can indulge the boldest assumptions,
since it is essentially an unknown country.

—ARTHUR MACARTHUR,
"CHINESE MEMORANDUM," 1882

To a person just graduating from college, the world can seem a place of almost unlimited possibilities—or a place from which to seek permanent refuge. The first was true of Douglas MacArthur, and with good reason. After graduation from West Point, he enjoyed a two-month furlough with his parents in San Francisco before starting on his first assignment as a second lieutenant of engineers. Douglas had learned he would be heading to the country that his father had just left, the Philippines, in order to join the Third Engineer Battalion.

Now he would have a chance to see firsthand what his father had wrought in his four years as military governor there. The son would also start to forge his own links with the people and nation with whom he would be identified more than with any other country, including his own.

But before he left, the young West Point graduate spent many hours listening to his father explain his view that the Filipinos were America's future friends in Asia. Douglas would often spend the day in General MacArthur's San Francisco office now that his father was commander of the Division of the Pacific. Later the son would remember hearing Arthur MacArthur explain both to the state's governor and to railroad baron E. H. Harriman his

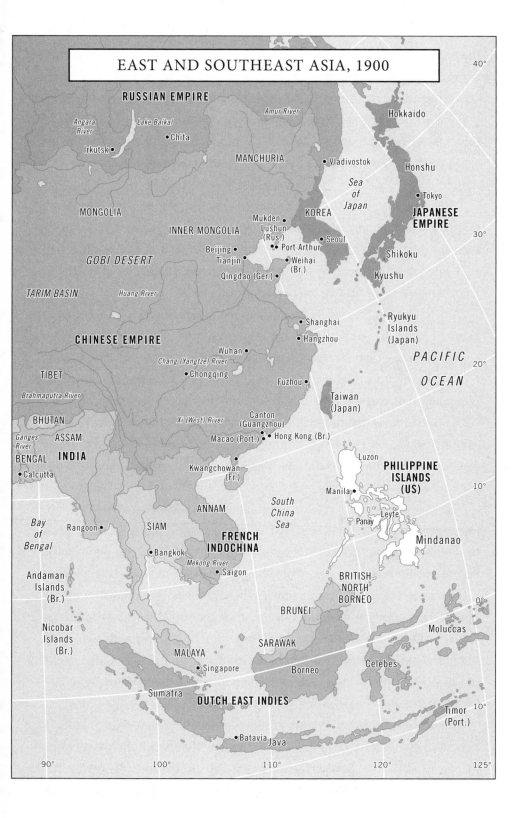

EAST AND SOUTHEAST ASIA, 1900

RUSSIAN EMPIRE

Angara River

Lake Baikal

• Chita

Irkutsk •

Amur River

MANCHURIA

• Vladivostok

Hokkaido

Sea of Japan

Honshu

• Tokyo

JAPANESE EMPIRE

MONGOLIA

INNER MONGOLIA

Mukden •

Lushun (Rus.)

KOREA

• Seoul

Shikoku

GOBI DESERT

Beijing •
Tianjin •

•• Port Arthur

• Weihai (Br.)

Kyushu

Qingdao (Ger.) •

TARIM BASIN

Huang River

CHINESE EMPIRE

• Shanghai

• Hangzhou

Ryukyu Islands (Japan)

PACIFIC

OCEAN

TIBET

Wuhan •

Chang (Yangtze) River

• Chongqing

Fuzhou •

Brahmaputra River

Taiwan (Japan)

BHUTAN

Ganges River

ASSAM

Xi (West) River

Canton (Guangzhou)

BENGAL

INDIA

Macao (Port.) •• Hong Kong (Br.)

• Calcutta

Kwangchowan (Fr.)

Luzon

PHILIPPINE ISLANDS (US)

Manila •

ANNAM

South China Sea

Leyte

Bay of Bengal

Rangoon •

SIAM

FRENCH INDOCHINA

Panay

Mindanao

• Bangkok

Mekong River

• Saigon

Andaman Islands (Br.)

BRITISH NORTH BORNEO

Nicobar Islands (Br.)

BRUNEI

Moluccas

SARAWAK

MALAYA

• Singapore

Borneo

Celebes

Sumatra

DUTCH EAST INDIES

Timor (Port.)

• Batavia Java

40°

30°

20°

10°

0°

10°

90°   100°   110°   120°   125°

idea of creating an artificial harbor in Los Angeles. "It was his belief that within fifty years such a port would become one of the leading handlers of commerce in the country," the son wrote, including trade with Asia. Creating a major western hub for American-Asian trade was yet another dream Arthur MacArthur had outlined in his "Chinese Memorandum" twenty years earlier, a dream that would be realized with the creation of the port of Los Angeles.[1]

It's a very fortunate second lieutenant who has the opportunity to be briefed on the country where he is about to do a duty tour by the country's former military governor. Certainly it was a well-informed Douglas MacArthur who set sail on the army transport *Sherman* from San Francisco with his fellow engineers for his first encounter with Asia and the Far East.

On October 28, 1903, MacArthur and the *Sherman* sailed into the blue-green expanse of Manila Bay. What impressed Douglas about Manila Bay, compared to San Francisco Bay, was its immense size. It measured thirty-five miles at its mouth, and the *Sherman* had to steam northeast for another five hours before it reached Manila. On the way they passed a sinister-looking rock-bound island that the Spanish had dubbed Corregidor, which was used as a fortress to guard the bay. Looming behind the island were the forbidding headlands of the Bataan Peninsula, sticking out like a swollen thumb to the west of Manila.

The *Sherman* was too large to unload at the Manila dock, so the big transport anchored offshore to discharge her passengers and cargo. From the deck the young lieutenant could see the red-tiled roofs of the old city, set in a low, flat plain, with row upon row of nipa huts stretching out from the city's suburbs into the interior of Luzon. Small skiffs or *bancas* rowed up with Filipinos offering goods and services to the disembarking Americans, and in a couple of hours Douglas MacArthur found himself wandering the streets of Manila, especially those of the sixteenth-century city nestled inside the old city walls, Intramuros, with access through drawbridges over the surrounding moat like a fairy-tale castle.

This was not his father's Manila of two years earlier, where tense patrols of American troops passed through streets lined with burned-out houses from the siege, as Dewey's cruisers grimly guarded the harbor with their guns pointed toward shore. The city had almost returned to its normal peacetime routines (although there was still guerrilla fighting up in the Sierra Madre and on the remoter islands). Shops, restaurants, and cafés catered to Americans and Filipinos alike, while after a leisurely lunch everything came to a halt for the two-hour siesta, until 4:00 P.M.

"The Philippines charmed me" at first sight, MacArthur admitted years later. But there wasn't a lot of time to enjoy the delights of the city. Almost the moment he docked, he was ordered to leave immediately for Iloilo on the island of Panay, where he would join the Third Engineer Battalion's I Company. The engineers were there to construct a new wharf and harbor for what was known as Camp Jossman, as part of the growing postwar American buildup in the islands.

He found life on the island amazingly primitive and amazingly hot, even for November. But Panay was also amazingly beautiful, with the rich tropical foliage and sparkling emerald-green vistas set against the cobalt-blue of the sea. There was also danger on Panay, MacArthur discovered, from poisonous snakes and the ever-present threat of malaria and yellow fever, but also from roaming gangs of brigands left over from Aguinaldo's army.

Every outing from Camp Jossman into the jungle therefore required an armed guard, and MacArthur learned to routinely carry his pistol when he set out on work duty. One day he and his men went to another island, Guimaris, to look for lumber for the piers and docks they were building. As he wandered down the jungle trail, and kept looking up ahead for trees tall and sturdy enough to cut down, he realized he had become separated from his work party.

At a turn in the trail he also came upon an armed man with a rifle blocking his path. MacArthur quickly glanced over his shoulder and found another blocking the path behind him.

There was no time to think. The first brigand raised his rifle and fired at MacArthur's head. The bullet whizzed through his sweat-stained campaign hat but somehow missed his skull, smacking into a sapling behind him instead—the first of Douglas MacArthur's many miraculous brushes with death.

By now he had his pistol out. He quickly fired one shot at the first brigand, dropping him in the path. Then he swiveled, aimed, and drilled the second through the head before the man had time to raise his rifle.

The sound of shots had drawn the attention of his sergeant foreman, who came running up to find his lieutenant standing over two dead bodies, his gun drawn and his hat still smoking from the first brigand's shot. The sergeant bent down to make sure the two guerrillas were dead. Then rolling his quid of tobacco into the hollow of his cheek (this was how MacArthur later remembered it), he slowly drew himself up to his full six feet, his heels clicking together, saluted, and drawled in his rich Irish brogue, "Beggin thu Loo'tenant's pardon, but all the rest of the Loo'tenant's life is pure velvet."[2]

In describing the incident in a letter to his mother, he wrote of the almost pleasant sound of a bullet whistle by his head. It was the kind of remark Winston Churchill might make, who had his baptism of fire on almost the same date in the Boer War, and famously said that nothing was more exhilarating than being shot at without result.[3]

Still, if a brigand's bullet couldn't cut him down, malaria did. To recuperate, he was given leave to return to Manila, where in the spring of 1904 he took and passed his examination for promotion to first lieutenant. One part of the exam was an oral question: What would Lieutenant MacArthur do, he was sternly asked, if he had to defend a harbor like Manila's from a combined naval and amphibious assault, but lacked any troops?

MacArthur thought for a moment, then said, "First, I'd round up all the sign painters in the community and put them to work making signs reading BEWARE—THIS HARBOR IS MINED. I'd float these signs out to the harbor mouth. After that I'd get down on my knees. Then I'd go out and fight like hell."

It was pure MacArthur, father and son. Douglas became a first lieutenant.[4]

Life became easier as a result. His superiors weren't as inclined to waste the son of the great Arthur MacArthur on tedious and dangerous duties out in the jungle as a first lieutenant. He settled down to a series of desk jobs as assistant to the chief engineer in Manila—although he was also sent out to survey the harbor at Mariveles, at the tip of the Bataan Peninsula, where he concluded that Aguinaldo had been right to plan to make his last stand in that rough, rugged terrain.

It never crossed his mind that three and a half decades later, forces under his command would be making their own last stand there, against a foe far deadlier than Aguinaldo.

In the evenings Douglas had time to come back to Manila, where he had been made a member of the Army and Navy Club, and where one evening he had dinner with two young Filipino lawyers who would play a major part in his later career. One was Sergio Osmeña, who would join MacArthur in the first landing in the Philippines in 1944 and would become the country's first president after the defeat of Japan.

The other was Manuel Quezon, a striking twenty-eight-year-old who had been Aguinaldo's chief aide but who had abandoned the insurrection after his master's capture. Quezon was part of a growing generation of young Eastern intellectuals who had learned to resent the dominance of white co-lonial powers over their peoples and were looking for ways to break free from dependence on the West while still retaining its respect. Quezon's greatest dream before and after the Spanish-American War was the indepen-dence of his country; if he couldn't do it by driving the Americans out, he concluded, then he would have to do it with their help. He had been im-pressed by the generosity of the postwar administration toward Filipinos, and by the work of reconstruction that Arthur MacArthur had begun.[5] Like his contemporary Sun Yat-sen, Quezon believed that Western-style politics, and a Western-style constitution, would make his people free and happy. He was on the lookout for American allies who could make it happen, and in his encounter with Douglas MacArthur he found one that he relied on until his death.

As for Douglas, the days when he wasn't on Bataan he was able to wander Manila's ancient winding streets. He walked past the stone-and-stucco houses, explored Intramuros's shops and lively market stalls, and rode the rickshaws (a mode of transport imported from Japan) that took a foreign visitor anywhere he wanted to go in the blazing heat of midday. Later he would remember with enthusiasm those palmy days, "the delightful hospi-tality, the respect and affection expressed for my father . . . and the languor-ous laze that seemed to glamorize even the most routine chores of life, the fun-loving men, the moonbeam delicacy of its lovely women, fastened me with a grip that has never relaxed."[6]

Unfortunately, the grip of malaria did not relax either, and in October he was ordered home to recover. He would spend a year in San Francisco recu-perating, with light duties supervising the Golden Gate harbor defenses. The rest of his time was devoted to chatting with his mother, traveling on horse-

back in the high country of the Sierra Nevada as part of a commission assigned to clean up the debris left by placer mining for gold—and dreaming
of the lush languor and moonbeam-delicate ladies of the Philippines. They
were days when it must have seemed as if he were drowning in honey—and
perhaps boredom.

Then on October 5, 1905, a telegram arrived that would transform his life.
It was from the army's acting chief of staff and was headed "Special Order
222."

It ordered MacArthur to be relieved of all duties and to proceed forthwith
to Tokyo, Japan. There he would be aide-de-camp to the acting American
military attaché, who had arrived there seven months earlier. That attaché
was none other than his father, Major General Arthur MacArthur.[7]

It was a dream come true for Lieutenant Douglas MacArthur: serving
full-time in an official capacity with the father he worshiped. For Arthur
MacArthur, it was a dream come true for other reasons. The job he had applied for in vain more than twenty years earlier was now his, except it was in
Japan rather than China—a change that represented a rapid shift in the balance of power in Asia.

Back in February, Japan had launched a surprise naval attack on Port Arthur, a Russian-held outpost in what had been Chinese Manchuria. The Russo-
Japanese War was on, and from his desk in San Francisco Arthur MacArthur
watched its progress with growing fascination. The Japanese had used a new
military technology, the torpedo, to cripple the Russian fleet at Port Arthur;
at the end of March their new modern navy wiped out the Russian fleet at
Vladivostok, while Russian and Japanese armies battled back and forth using
the new technologies of modern land war like the land mine, the field mortar, and the machine gun.

Arthur MacArthur grasped that point at once, and put in a request for
assignment to the Far East as a military observer. His hope was to witness at
least one major battle and study the field organization of the Japanese army.[8]
MacArthur's appointment that December lent seniority to a delegation of
American officers already headed for Tokyo, including three of MacArthur's
own protégés: Colonel Enoch Crowder, his former adjutant; Major Peyton
March, who had risen from the field artillery to become another MacArthur

aide; and Captain John J. Pershing, who had also served with MacArthur in the Philippines and was destined to be a rising star in the modern army.

On February 14, 1905, just as their son was settling into his desk duties in Manila, Arthur and Pinky set sail from San Francisco aboard the SS *Korea*. Also on board were Captain Pershing and his wife, and a friendship blossomed between the Pershings and the MacArthurs that would later bear strange fruit for their son Douglas.

They reached Yokohama on March 5, and when they arrived in Tokyo General MacArthur found to his surprise that he was the center of enormous attention. Japan's generals had studied his campaigns in the Philippines with intense interest, especially his war of rapid maneuver against the Philippine National Army. They had even adopted some of his tactics for their own campaign against the Russians in Manchuria, which reached a climax on March 8 at the Battle of Mukden—the same day the government held an enormous banquet in MacArthur's honor.

The banquet was regularly interrupted by hourly bulletins reporting the fighting at Mukden, prompting loud cheers from the Japanese attendees as the battle steadily tipped in Japan's favor. By the time the MacArthurs and Pershings returned to the Imperial Hotel, crowds filled the streets chanting "Banzai!" as the full extent of the victory became clear. Japan's rank as a great power was complete.[9]

Arthur MacArthur did not see any battles firsthand or modern weapons like machine guns used in action, but he did arrive in time to watch the Japanese mop up isolated pockets of Russian resistance, while the trip from Dairen, the main Japanese supply base in Manchuria, to Mukden revealed the dismal detritus of war: smashed villages, abandoned artillery and supply wagons, and thousands of unburied dead Russian soldiers.[10]

The Japanese let him talk to Russian prisoners of war who, at the time, were treated far better than the prisoners they would take from his son's army.[11] He also met the Japanese victors, including the commander of all Japanese forces in Manchuria, Field Marshal Oyama Iwao, and General Kuroki Tametomo, commander of the Japanese First Army, with whom Arthur MacArthur remained friends for the rest of his life. At every level, MacArthur found the Japanese to be superior soldiers than their Russian rivals. If anything, he was on the verge of becoming a true Nipponophile—and the Japanese Army on the verge of finding a new idol in the person of General Arthur MacArthur.

When MacArthur returned to Tokyo in August, however, he discovered that the general mood regarding Americans had abruptly changed.

Japan's victory on land at Mukden had been followed in May by victory at sea in the Tsushima Strait separating Korea and Japan, when Japanese admiral Togo sank or captured thirty-two of the thirty-five ships in the Russian Baltic Sea Fleet, which had traveled 18,000 miles to encounter complete and humiliating annihilation (total Japanese losses were 110 sailors). But then President Theodore Roosevelt decided it was time to bring Russia's string of defeats to an end and intervene—not with ships or soldiers, but with a pen.

He summoned the Russian and Japanese ambassadors from Washington to his vacation home in Portsmouth, New Hampshire, where under the president's watchful eye, they agreed to a peace treaty with Russia surrendering Manchuria and North Korea to Japan. Roosevelt saw the treaty as a way to maintain the complex and shifting balance of power between Japan and Russia—as well as a way to exert American influence in Asia for the first time. The Japanese, however, were furious at Roosevelt's compromise because it cheated them of the full fruits of victory. It also left Japan with an enormous war debt, which the government in Tokyo had told the Japanese public would be paid off by the Russians as part of a war indemnity.

Huge anti-American demonstrations broke out across the country, and hundreds of Japanese committed suicide over what they saw as a national humiliation.[12] Gazing from his hotel room at the angry crowds and anti-American signs, Arthur MacArthur realized his welcome in Japan was over (his own physical resemblance to Roosevelt, down to the barrel chest, bristling mustache, and pince-nez, certainly didn't help matters). Time to go, but to where?

There could be only one answer in his mind: the Philippines. He had already sent that wish on to the administration, which was why Taft was in Tokyo at the same time. He hoped to block MacArthur's return to the Philippines. During their time together the two men had clashed bitterly over American policy in the islands, especially on the issue of Philippine independence: Arthur MacArthur was a keen believer in granting it at once, while Taft and the rest of the Roosevelt administration preferred to wait. So rather than allow his rival to return to the Philippines and restore his influence there, Taft proposed an alternative. Why didn't MacArthur take an officially sanctioned tour of Asia, with his able young son Douglas as his military aide?

Surprised and delighted, MacArthur accepted on the spot. He forgot about returning to the Philippines (as Taft had hoped he would). This tour would not only reunite Pinky and him with their youngest son, but it would also allow his son to get his first look at the future face of modern war—not in Europe, where no one anticipated any military conflict, but in Asia, the crucible of empire building and America's future influence.

So the telegram had gone out to San Francisco, and on Sunday, October 29, 1905, Douglas MacArthur arrived in Japan for the first time. It was more than forty years before he would return.

At the time, "I was deeply impressed by and filled with admiration for the thrift, courage, and friendliness" of the ordinary Japanese, Douglas remembered, while the city of Tokyo itself would have galvanized his imagination with its strange contrasts between old and new. Trains and smokestacked factories surrounded the outskirts of Tokyo, while businessmen and officials dressed in suits and top hats bustled through the streets of the Ginza and Marunouchi districts just as they did in New York's Wall Street. Yet around the corner barefoot peddlers and rickshaws crammed ancient alleyways, along with men and women in kimonos, like scenes from a Japanese scroll painting. He also met many Japanese army officers—"grim, taciturn, aloof men of iron character and unshakeable purpose"—as well as the victor of Tsushima, Admiral Togo.[13]

The young lieutenant was also impressed by the ferocious discipline imposed on the Japanese soldier, especially the ordinary private. As one recruit later remembered, "Personality ceased to exist, there was only rank. You became lowest of the low, condemned to cook, clean, drill, and run from dawn to dusk. You could be beaten for anything—being too short or too tall, even because somebody didn't like the way you drank coffee. . . . Each man was schooled to accept unquestioningly the order of his group leader"—and above all the will of the emperor.[14]

One story in particular stuck in MacArthur's mind many years later. To combat an outbreak of beriberi, the government distributed a pill with the label: "to prevent beriberi take one pill three times a day." Like soldiers everywhere, MacArthur remembered, "they took the pill once, spat it out, then dumped the can into the mud." The surgeon in charge was stumped until a bright young officer suggested a new label: "The Emperor desires you to take one pill three times a day." The problem was solved: every pill was taken exactly as ordered. In fact, "[n]othing but death itself could stop the soldiers from taking the medicine."[15]

But the tour of military Japan was just the curtain-raiser for what Douglas MacArthur admitted later was "without doubt the most important factor of preparation in my entire life," in some respects even more important than West Point: an eight-month tour of Asia, from November 1905 to June 1906, that started in Singapore and ended back in Japan.

What Douglas MacArthur saw was the Asia that the European colonial powers had made, at the very end of the Victorian era. But he also saw the abundant opportunities for America to exert its commercial, military, and cultural muscle, once it had committed itself to a decisive turn to the Far East. In the words of Albert Beveridge, "the power that rules the Pacific . . . is the power that rules the world." To the MacArthurs, both father and son, that power was destined to be the United States.

The first stop on the tour was Singapore on November 23.[16] Founded in 1819, it was the main trading post for Great Britain in Asia, even greater than Hong Kong—and the military bastion of Britain's possessions east of India. Arthur and Douglas MacArthur met the British governor and reviewed the British troops on the island city. Then they toured other military bases on the Malay Peninsula, before settling sail for Djakarta in the Dutch East Indies on November 28.

The future capital of Indonesia, Djakarta (or Batavia, as the Dutch named it) bore the physical traces of a long colonial history, with European-style whitewashed buildings and houses, some dating back to the seventeenth century. The Dutch also maintained an impressive garrison of Dutch and native troops. But as with Singapore and other stops, MacArthur saw first-hand "the strengths and weakness of the colonial system," he wrote, "how it brought law and order, but failed to develop the masses along the essential lines of education and political economy."

As he walked the streets with his mother striding sturdily beside him, he "rubbed elbows with millions of underprivileged who knew nothing about economics or democracy" or anything else, but who were "interested only in getting a little more food in their stomachs, a little better coat on their backs, a little stronger roof over their heads."[17] A system of government that prom-ised more of all three, he realized, would mean more to ordinary Asians than any promises of constitutions or self-governance—or even civil liberties. It was a lesson that enabled him to understand the appeal of Communism in Asia after 1945, as well as the need for America and the West to forge the material and cultural, as well as military, tools to combat it.

The MacArthurs' time in the Dutch East Indies passed slowly. This was due in part because of "tropical heat and irregular connections," General MacArthur noted, but also because with his usual thoroughness he insisted on visiting no fewer than twelve military bases, covering 1,200 miles by train and carriage in a little over three weeks.[18] The trio then returned briefly to Singapore for Christmas before setting out for Burma. They traveled first to Mandalay in Upper Burma, which Winston Churchill's father, Randolph, had added to the British Empire in 1892, before traveling by steamer to what would be the heart of their Asian tour, India.

Starting on January 14 in Calcutta, the MacArthurs would spend nearly eight weeks in India, seeing everything from Calcutta and the Himalayas to Ceylon, Bangalore, the Northwest Frontier, and the Khyber Pass bordering on Afghanistan, while stopping at virtually every military installation along the way. "In order to expedite my observations," General MacArthur in-formed Washington, "all the Generals concerned practically put their com-mands under emergency orders." What he and Douglas witnessed was the deployment of the largest all-volunteer army in the world, nearly a quarter million strong and made up of every race and religion in India, with a small but sturdy cluster of British regiments to round out the force. The Indian army was the military juggernaut of Asia, and a reminder to both MacArthurs of what an alliance of Western and Eastern soldiers could accomplish, given enough resources and motivation.[19]

At the time, however, what Douglas particularly relished was the conversations between his father and the Indian army's commander in chief, Lord Kitchener. The greatest living British soldier and the greatest living American soldier (certainly in Douglas's mind) shared memories of past and present battles, including those with their own governments. Kitchener himself was in the midst of an imbroglio with the viceroy Lord Curzon about which he discoursed at bitter length. No doubt it also reminded Arthur MacArthur of his own problems dealing with William Howard Taft in the Philippines. Douglas's memoirs state that both men gave him a foretaste "of the age-old struggle between the civil and the military to fix the exact line of demarcation between executive control and the professional duty of the soldiers" while leaving him little doubt who should prevail, and who had no business prevailing, in that struggle.[20]

By the time the MacArthurs left India, they had logged no fewer than 19,000 miles of travel. But there was still more to come, including a stop in the one remaining independent power in Southeast Asia, Siam (today Thailand). They arrived in Bangkok on March 27, 1906, where their reception by King Chulalongkorn* and a formal dinner in their honor led American ambassador Hamilton King to report that "no man has been accorded such a royal and generous welcome as was the General since I have been in this country."[21]

According to a recently discovered diary kept by King's wife, the MacArthurs spent virtually every day touring military barracks, schools, and prisons in the Siamese interior, traveling by private railcar to Ratchapuri, the province west of Bangkok bordering Burma, with a Siamese aide-de-camp, before joining the entire party on a "picnic boat" to see the largest sitting Buddha in the world at Ayutthaya.

On returning to Bangkok they became virtual pet visitors of the king, especially Pinky, who with her usual combination of charm and audacity could be heard saying to the all-powerful monarch, "Oh! Your Majesty, you're a

---

* His father had been King Mongkut, made famous by the book *Anna and the King of Siam* and the musical *The King and I.*

darling!" and "Oh! I should like to see you on your throne!"—which he agreed to do, while she stood before him doing a series of mock bows, all to the horror of his courtiers. At one point she even took the king's arm as they walked through the palace, an unheard-of liberty, but to Pinky as natural as anything in the world.[22]

For Douglas, the highlight of the Bangkok visit was a ceremonial banquet during which the electric lights suddenly went out, plunging the entire court in darkness. "I had noticed a fuse box near where I was seated," he later recalled, "and promptly replaced the burned-out fuse." A grateful king offered to present the young lieutenant with a medal there and then. "Happily, I had the common sense to decline"—the first and last time Douglas MacArthur ever refused a decoration.[23]

From Bangkok the MacArthurs set out for Saigon, capital of French Indochina and cockpit of a future American land war; and then to Canton, which was their introduction to the tragic reality of China.

Humiliated by a series of treaties imposed on the imperial government by Europeans, crushed and broken by the defeat of the recent Boxer Rebellion, what was once the most sophisticated civilization in the world was now a shambling, moribund empire in the process of being pulled apart by stronger, more ruthless hands, including Japan, and teetering on national disaster. The Emperor's Mandate of Heaven that had ruled China for three thousand years had only five years left of life before it collapsed. Revolution and chaos would soon sweep the entire country. Eventually it would engulf the rest of Asia. Yet walking the streets of Shanghai with its large modern European buildings and Western-style shops and conveniences, and then gazing on the imperial capital of Peking with its elaborate fortifications and magnificent Forbidden Palace, not even a prescient observer like Arthur MacArthur could guess that the coming Chinese revolution would shake every nation involved in the continent, including the United States, and ultimately trigger a war that would propel his own son into the front lines.

But earthshaking news of a different kind was waiting for them when they returned to Japan. A great earthquake had hit San Francisco on April 18, making the MacArthurs anxious for news about Douglas's sister-in-law Mary and her son Arthur IV (Commander Arthur MacArthur had been at sea when the quake happened).[24] The mother and son were safe, but when the general and his wife returned to San Francisco on August 2, they came back to a shattered city. He would soon set aside his report on the Asian tour and plunge headlong into coordinating the army's effort to help rebuild.

But he had reasons to be satisfied. His Asian tour had been a huge personal and professional success. He was barely back a month before he received news that he had been promoted to lieutenant general, the army's highest rank, with a raise in salary from $7,500 to $11,000 a year (roughly $250,000 today). He had two and a half years to go before retirement, and he had every reason to assume that those years would be rounded out by appointment to the army's highest post, that of chief of staff.

Still, there were aspects to his Asian trip that had disquieted him. As he sat in his office in San Francisco, working on the report for the War Department that he would never finish, he saw looming before him and before America what he termed "the problem of the Pacific." He had witnessed firsthand the rise of Japan to great-power status, an advance that the Roosevelt administration had welcomed as a counterweight to Russia. But MacArthur realized that Japan's rise posed a potential threat not only to the stability of the region but to the survival of Western colonial empires, which, it seemed, were inclined to underestimate the challenge that Japan represented.[25]

The other country threatened by Japan's rise, he believed, was the Philippines. Those islands were still very much on his mind. After his tour of India, the Dutch East Indies, and Malaya, as well as Burma and the Chinese ports under European treaty, he had to concede "the general good administration apparent in certain colonial territories" but he went on to say that "self-supporting, germinal ideas, have not been introduced into any sphere of influence in the East, excepting in the Philippines," especially the idea of self-governing independence.

Then he pulled out his own crystal ball and predicted that this failure to expand Western-style opportunities for the Asian masses would fatally weaken "these ostentatious colonial governments . . . in the final struggle with the Orient," including possibly Japan. This would leave the United States as the one remaining Western power of significance, with the Philippines as its vital outpost and its closest Asian ally.

His one wish now was that the Philippines would continue as the living embodiment of the idea that "the imperishable ideas upon which free institutions are based," life, liberty, the rule of law, and the pursuit of happiness, can succeed with nonwhite populations in Asia. His own dream was that America would be both inspiration and protector of that precious ideal.

Both were audacious hopes. Certainly as a forecast of the rise of Japan signaling the twilight of Europe's colonial empires, General MacArthur was breathtakingly prescient. So was his prediction that America would be the great benefactor, but also beneficiary, of the new Asia that took their place. This in fact would be the great MacArthur family compact, embracing both father and son. Together they would support the proposition that the Philippines would light the lamp of America's Pacific destiny: not as a seaborne empire, like Great Britain's, or even a commercial power as Albert Beveridge and others hoped, but as the carrier of the ideal of human liberty to Asia.

This was why Arthur MacArthur was able to assert that the American occupation of the Philippines was the most important "event recorded in the annals of mankind since the discovery of this continent," meaning America itself, and why he believed that the essential mission for America was to strengthen the defenses of the Philippines before the coming storm, "in order to prevent its strategic position from becoming a liability rather than an asset to the United States."[26]

It would be left to his son to carry out the mission that the father outlined to his superiors in Washington three decades earlier.

As for Lieutenant Douglas MacArthur, the tour had certainly been an eye-opening experience. "The true historic significance and the sense of destiny that these lands of the western Pacific and Indian Ocean now assumed became part of me," he would write.

"Here lived almost half the population of the world, and probably more than half of the raw products to sustain future generations. Here was western civilization's last earth frontier. It was crystal clear to me that the future and, indeed, the very existence of America, were irrevocably entwined with Asia and its island outposts"—most particularly the Philippines. His father would be the first to wholeheartedly agree—and the first to reproach him if he ever let the mission down.[27]

*   *   *

When he returned to the United States that August, Douglas MacArthur was twenty-six years old and a rising star. He was West Point's most stellar graduate and the son of the army's most prominent general. He had seen things, and met people, that most officers in the U.S. Army barely dreamed of. A vigorous life and a promising career stretched out before him. His assignment that autumn to the elite engineering school at the Washington Barracks (now Fort McNair) clearly confirmed that. So did appointment in December as aide-de-camp to President Theodore Roosevelt himself.

Still, the mundane duties of an engineering classroom and standing at attention at social functions and shuffling papers, even if they were for the president of the United States, must have been a letdown after what he had seen and done in Asia. For the first and only time in his life, Douglas MacArthur became a slouch—and his efficiency reports showed it.

"I am sorry to report that during this time Lieutenant MacArthur seemed to take but little interest in his course at the school," read one evaluation written by the engineering school's commandant. "Throughout the time Lieutenant MacArthur was under my observation, he displayed, on the whole, but little professional zeal and his work was far inferior to that which his West Point record showed him capable of."[28]

Teddy Roosevelt certainly enjoyed his conversations with the young lieutenant and "was greatly interested in my views on the Far East and talked with me long and often," MacArthur later recalled.[29] But it was the efficiency reports that mattered, and they got worse when he was dispatched on "special duty" to Milwaukee in August 1907 to work on plans to refurbish several harbors on Lake Michigan. On the one hand, returning to Milwaukee also meant being reunited with his family (his father was serving out his last two years there on detached duty and had rented a large house at 575 Marshall Street).

On the other, his dissatisfaction with what seemed to him tedious duties that wasted his talents led to a direct conflict with his commanding officer, Major William V. Judson, and to reports like this:

"[Lieutenant MacArthur] exhibited less interest in and put in less time upon the drafting room, the plans and specifications for work and the works themselves than seemed consistent with my instructions . . . he was absent from the office during office hours more than I thought proper." When Judson tried to give him a different assignment he thought the lieutenant might profit from, MacArthur "remonstrated and argued verbally at length against assignment to this duty, which would take him away from Milwaukee for a considerable portion of the time," which meant away from his mother.[30]

Judson's efficiency report concluded, "Lieutenant MacArthur, while on duty under my immediate orders, did not conduct himself in a way to meet commendation. . . . his duties were not performed in a satisfactory manner." When MacArthur learned of the damning document, the result was an unholy row. He was already furious that he had been turned down for a teaching appointment at West Point; he also knew the Judson report would be a permanent part of his record. He fired off an angry letter to the brigadier chief of engineers, protesting "the ineradicable blemish Major Judson has seen fit to place on my military record" and trying to justify his frequent absences on the grounds that there didn't seem to be a lot to do and he wouldn't be missed.

What he got back was a stern rebuke from the brigadier, who reminded him that an officer's job was to obey orders and that MacArthur's special pleading was "itself justification of Major Judson's statement, in view of Mr. MacArthur's evident inclination to avoid work."[31] This led to a stormy family scene, with Pinky urging her son to think about resigning. She even sent a letter to his father's railroad baron friend E. H. Harriman, wondering if he might have some suitable position for her twenty-nine-year-old son.

When Douglas learned of her scheme, he was even more furious. He told Harriman's talent scout he had absolutely no plans to get out of the army; if he did, it certainly wouldn't be in the railroad. But the fact was he was bored. He couldn't help it if he came across like a spoiled brat; he was waiting for his next big career break, and it wasn't coming.

So like lots of bored young men, he fell in love.

Her name was Fanniebelle Stuart. She was from Milwaukee, and for the first time Douglas MacArthur thought seriously about getting married.[32]

What Miss Stuart thought we do not know; none of her letters survive. But what does survive is a series of romantic poems that Douglas composed for her, the earliest a twenty-six-page epic in rhyming couplets that tells us much more about Douglas's view on war, his profession, and his relationship with his father than it does about young love.

Although it starts conventionally enough with references to "songs of the birds and the hum of the bees," it soon shifts to a tragic narrative of a young soldier leaving his wife, Fan, to go to war. He goes "for home, and for children, for freedom, for bread

> *For the house of our God—for the graves of our dead"*
> *And she responds dutifully like a true Spartan wife:*
> *"I grudge you not, Douglas—die rather than yield,*
> *And, like the old heroes, come home on your shield."*

And so he goes—but soon returns gravely wounded after a battle that clearly takes place in the Civil War, and so after a long convalescence at home, he returns to the fight to find the hero's ultimate reward as Douglas merges into his father's image on Missionary Ridge:

> *Our cavalry bore themselves splendidly—far*
> *In front of his line galloped Colonel MacAr;*
> *Erect in his stirrups, his sword flashing high,*
> *and the look of a patriot kindling his eye . . .*
> *"Remember Wisconsin! Remember your wives!*
> *And on to your duty, boys!—on—with your lives!"*
> *He turned, and he paused, as he uttered the call*
> *Then reeled in his seat, and fell—pierced by a ball.*

The stanza ends with the hero Douglas having but one final wish: "to look on his wife."[33]

But his true wish was clearly for a chance to lead troops gallantly in battle like his father had, and to be the great hero.

That opportunity wasn't forthcoming, however, and so after a few more months of passionate love letters and poems, when Fanniebelle moved to New York City—"Fair Gotham girl with life awhirl of dance and fancy free; Tis thee I love All things above. Why canst thou not love me?"—the romance died of its own accord.

Love is at best a tragic joke
Begun in flames it ends in smoke.

But even as he was writing his last letter to her, wishing her "good luck and good luck," a friend of his father's had come to his rescue.

Major General J. Franklin Bell, the chief of staff, arranged for the wayward lieutenant to get a posting to Fort Leavenworth, Kansas, to train a company of new volunteers. Kansas looked bleak after Milwaukee, let alone Peking and Tokyo. The company, K Company, was the last on the list of twenty-six companies getting training at the post.

But this was what Lieutenant Douglas MacArthur had been waiting for: leading men, if not exactly into battle, at least into the rigors of a soldier's life, marching twenty-five miles a day, building pontoon bridges at record speed, learning marksmanship, horsemanship, and demolition. He fell in love with command at once. "I couldn't have been happier," he wrote, "if they had made me a general." He wrote a field manual on demolition, took over as the post's quartermaster, commissary officer, engineer officer, and disbursing officer, and managed the baseball team.[34] He turned his efficiency reports around. "A most excellent and efficient officer," the next one read. One day on the parade ground, he heard a veteran sergeant major tell his men, "Boys, there goes a soldier." It was a tribute that, MacArthur remembered almost sixty years later, "I prize more than any other."[35]

Others remembered him too. One was a Lieutenant Robert Eichelberger, who recalled seeing him in front of a drugstore one evening, "standing a bit aloof from the rest of us and looking off in the distance" with an expression that Eichelberger could only describe as Napoleonic. Another lieutenant at Leavenworth who regarded him with awe was Walter Krueger—thirty years later, the commander of MacArthur's Sixth Army. One lieutenant who didn't was a hard-faced, gravelly graduate from Virginia Military Institute named George Catlett Marshall. Their lack of love for each other would reach new heights during the Second World War, while both Krueger and Eichelberger would command armies for MacArthur in New Guinea and the Philippines.[36]

These were good days for MacArthur for another reason. In February 1911 his promotion came through to captain. He was finally going places in his career after eight years of struggle; he had the respect of the men serving under him and the officers serving with him.

Most who served with MacArthur at Leavenworth remembered him as a gregarious companion who drank little but loved long sessions at the poker table wreathed in cigar smoke. They remembered stag parties with MacArthur, Eichelberger, and the other officers draped around the piano while someone banged on the jangling keys and all sang one of the popular songs of the day, "Old Soldiers Never Die."

CHAPTER 5

COUNTDOWN TO WAR

Every head swiveled as Arthur MacArthur entered the room.

It was September 5, 1912, a warm Thursday. Across the Atlantic in Vienna, Archduke Franz Ferdinand of Austria was meeting with his father, Emperor Franz Josef, to decide what to do about troublesome Serbian nationalists in the Austrian province of Bosnia. Across the Pacific in Tokyo, courtiers and officials were preparing the ceremonial funeral for Emperor Mutsuhito, who had died in July. In a few days the proclamation would come of his successor, Emperor Taisho, and the next Crown Prince, Taisho's eleven-year-old son, Hirohito.

But here in Milwaukee the sixty-four remaining veterans of the Twenty-fourth Wisconsin were holding their fiftieth reunion. All day the Milwaukee Chamber of Commerce had held celebrations, a parade, and now there was a banquet at Wolcott Hall in their honor—and to honor their famous commander, who was to be the guest speaker.

The Arthur MacArthur who climbed the rostrum with difficulty was a changed man from the tough, confident Teddy Roosevelt look-alike who had triumphantly completed his tour of Asia, let alone the curly-haired eighteen-year-old who had charged up Missionary Ridge almost sixty years before.

That summer his kidneys had begun to give out and high blood pressure to set in. His stomach gave him constant problems with hyperacidity (a problem that would also plague his son in later years), and walking had become a growing challenge. But even worse, since he had returned from Asia his professional life had been one of constant disappointment.[1]

He had hoped to be appointed chief of staff, but in January 1907 the post went instead to J. Franklin Bell, the youngest major general in the army. MacArthur, the most senior lieutenant general in the army, bitterly protested being passed over for its youngest *major* general. President Roosevelt explained that they needed a man who would serve out the full four-year term as chief of staff, not one slated to retire in two years.

MacArthur was furious. He refused to accept the other commands they offered, including the Department of the East, headquartered in New York City, as unbefitting an officer of his rank. In the end, he angrily proposed that they send him home to Milwaukee on "detached duty" until retirement finally came in June 1909.[2]

"I'm glad to be back home," he told a newspaper reporter.[3] He had continued to read voraciously, had led long discussions on military history, economics, and geopolitics with Douglas, and had started work on his memoirs as he relived the campaigns that had made him a state and national hero, the greatest soldier Wisconsin had ever produced.

But the bitterness of personal defeat was written on his face, and it began to rack his body. That August his doctors had even put him to bed and advised him not to go to the fiftieth celebration on one of the hottest days of the year. But Arthur MacArthur was determined to meet his old comrades and speak to them one last time.

It was approaching ten o'clock before MacArthur was finally introduced by an old friend who had been with him in the famous charge up Missionary Ridge, former captain Ed Parsons. His fellow soldiers were now white-haired and bent with age, but they stood and cheered for six to seven minutes before he could begin to speak.

"Comrades," he began, "little did we imagine fifty years ago, that [we would ever] gather in this way. Little did we think that on that march to Atlanta so many of us would be spared to see Wisconsin again."[4]

He spoke of the joys and misery of those days, one participant recalled, and the valor they had all shown in the midst of the country's bloodiest conflict.

"Your indomitable regiment . . ."

Then Arthur MacArthur froze. He staggered slightly and grew pale.

"Comrades," he gasped, "I cannot go on. I am too weak. I must sit down."

There was a hushed gasp as he suddenly clutched at his heart, slumped in his chair, and closed his eyes. Then his head fell forward and every man in the room rushed to the podium.

Already his face "had assumed the pallor of death," one eyewitness said, "and he lay back in his chair breathing easily." They moved him to a couch, where two veterans who were also doctors tended to their old commanding officer.

Suddenly one of them grasped the general's wrist, laid his head on the man's breast, and then straightened up.

"Comrades," he said in a soft voice, "our commander has gone to his last rest." It had been a sudden aneurysm at the base of the brain. Death was almost instantaneous.

Heartbroken and with heads bowed, the surviving veterans of the Twenty-fourth began reciting the Lord's Prayer, led by one old soldier who could barely speak through his sobs. Another took up the flag they had brought with them from the state capitol, the same torn and begrimed flag that MacArthur had carried up Missionary Ridge, and draped it over his body.

Others gathered around Ed Parsons, who was devastated by the death of his old friend.

"We've been so long together," he kept saying in between bursts of tears. Then suddenly he grasped at his head and slumped to the floor. Dr. Cronyn sprang to the side of his second patient in as many minutes. Ed Parsons had suffered a massive stroke (he later recovered). Some carried him out of the room, while others gathered around the body of their fallen commander and continued to pray.[5]

So it was not Parsons but another old friend, Charlie King, who had to break the news to Pinky. Dr. Cronyn had called her at the Marshall Street house but could not bring himself to tell her that her husband was dead. He told her only that he had taken seriously ill. So King and two others who had attended the reunion walked to Marshall Street, where they found Pinky waiting on the steps.

"Is the general dead?" It was the first thing she said.

They sadly answered, "Yes." She went back into the house and was barely able to speak for the next four days.[6]

But she did have the strength to send the news to Douglas by telegram out at Leavenworth.

"My whole world changed that night," Douglas remembered. "Never have I been able to heal the wound in my heart."[7]

The man he revered as a hero and role model was gone. Indeed, for two weeks after his father's death Douglas suffered a prolonged bout of insomnia serious enough to alarm the doctors at Leavenworth. But even worse, the man whom his mother had relied on for emotional and financial support was gone, leaving her without the most important person in her life. For some sons, the loss of a larger-than-life, overbearing father might be liberating. Instead, it thrust Douglas deeper into emotional dependence on his mother, whose health began to deteriorate almost the same day her husband died. After the funeral (flags across Milwaukee flew at half-mast for four days, while tributes from soldiers, politicians, and foreign dignitaries poured in with every post), Douglas had to make arrangements for his mother's future. Despite the fact that her older son's wife and young family would have been happy to take her in, Pinky chose to rely on Douglas.[8]

Taking her to Leavenworth was out of the question. Instead, he began seeking a post in the nation's capital, since "Washington, on account of its proximity to Johns Hopkins Hospital, would offer more of advantage to Mrs. MacArthur than any other possible station," he told his commanding officer.[9] Of course, a posting to Washington wouldn't hurt his own career chances either.

It was another old friend of his father, General Leonard Wood, who came through this time. He caught a glimpse of Douglas's application for a transfer and passed it along to the new secretary of war, Henry L. Stimson, who, "in view of the distinguished service of General Arthur MacArthur," agreed to the transfer in the office of General Wood on the Engineering Board.[10]

He left Leavenworth in December 1912. He was embarking on what would be the next dramatic phase of his life, but without his father as teacher and mentor. He did have his mother's advice and unshakable support, as well as help from his father's protégés, like Bell and Wood. In normal times that would have been more than enough for an ambitious and gifted young officer.

But these were not normal times. Their world, and his, was about to explode in the greatest conflagration in history.

The Douglas MacArthur who appeared in Washington in 1913 was a slim and handsome bachelor of thirty-two years of age, the sort of elegant young man one would expect to meet in an ad for Arrow shirts of the day.

His was certainly an existence anyone could have envied, in or out of the army. He lived in a fashionable apartment building in Northwest Washington, the Hadleigh, with his ever-present mother. A black chauffeur drove him daily from Sixteenth Street to his equally enviable office job, first as aide to the popular and powerful General Wood, then starting in April 1913 as superintendent of the State, War, and Navy Building, which still stands on the corner of Seventeenth Street and Pennsylvania Avenue and is known as the Old Executive Office Building.

Besides his mother, his brother Arthur and his family had moved to Washington as well. In addition, Douglas was surrounded by senior officers who were his father's friends, including Wood, an army hero like his father who had helped capture Geronimo and who as commander in chief in Cuba supervised Captain Walter Reed's work to find a vaccine for yellow fever— and who, it seems, singled out Captain MacArthur as his favorite aide.

Even more important, the relationship with Wood brought him permanently onto the General Staff—the brains of the army—that September. He was the junior member of a staff of thirty-eight engaged in key strategic and operational planning; he was able to learn how important decisions were made in the army without yet assuming that responsibility himself. Douglas felt so comfortably ensconced that he turned down an offer from the new Democratic president, Woodrow Wilson, to become a presidential aide.

"The work was long and confining" at the General Staff, he wrote many years later, "and left me little time for relaxation, but it was rewarding." It was also preparing his way for a brilliant staff career.[11]

But there were still two things missing. One was the experience he had had at Leavenworth for too short a time: that of true leadership and command, even if it was only one company at a time. The other was something his father had known and lived for, but he still did not: the experience of battle.

Then out of nowhere the following spring, he got it, in Mexico.

On April 9, 1914, a detachment of sailors from the gunboat USS *Dolphin* went ashore at the Mexican port of Tampico to pick up a delivery of oil for their engines. It was no ordinary visit.

Mexico was in the throes of a civil war pitting followers of a monocled Mexican general named Huerta against the followers of Mexico's previous president, Madero, who were besieging Huerta's troops in Tampico. The soldiers on guard in Tampico were justifiably jumpy. When the American sailors arrived, wearing unfamiliar uniforms and unable to speak a word of Spanish, they were immediately arrested and taken down to division headquarters.

The next morning the Mexican soldiers turned them loose with an apology from General Huerta himself, but the commander of American naval forces in the region, Admiral Henry Mayo, was outraged. He demanded nothing less than a twenty-one-gun salute to the American flag to compensate for the arrests, and he let President Wilson know what he was doing.[12]

Wilson, as it happened, detested General Huerta. Huerta was a shameless freebooter who had assassinated his way into the Mexican presidency and shattered the country's fragile democracy. When Huerta, who detested Wilson with equal venom, refused Mayo's terms, Wilson decided it was time to act.

On April 20 he held a meeting with his top advisors and ordered Arthur MacArthur's former protégé Frederick Funston, now Major General Funston, down to Galveston, Texas. His orders were nothing less than to prepare an invasion of Mexico. The next day news reached Wilson that Huerta was receiving a massive shipment of arms from imperial Germany at the port of Veracruz—a blatant violation of the arms embargo against Mexico that Wilson had imposed two years earlier.

That was the last straw. Without waiting for Congress, Wilson ordered an immediate dispatch of navy ships and marines to take Veracruz. After a fierce battle that cost 500 casualties on both sides, the marines took the city as ordered. On April 30 Funston and his brigade of 7,000 soldiers arrived to occupy and hold Veracruz against Huerta's men.[13]

The next day a tall, spare figure in a battered campaign hat with two gold bars on his collar and a corncob pipe clenched between his teeth could be seen walking through the debris-strewn streets of Veracruz, dodging the stray dogs and vultures feasting on the dead animals and offal.

He was Captain Douglas MacArthur, in Mexico on personal orders from General Wood himself.

Just a week earlier he had been flat on his back recovering from acute tonsillitis when a message arrived at the Hadleigh from General Wood, to get down to the office at once. With his mother's help he had gotten dressed and headed to the War Department building, where he found Wood surrounded by stacks of paper and fresh from a meeting with Secretary of War Lindley Garrison.

Wood told him the president had ordered him to prepare and lead an expeditionary force into Mexico. He had intended to put MacArthur on his staff, but had decided instead to send his young aide out to Veracruz first under Wood's personal orders, to make an assessment of the situation.

"How soon can you leave?" Wood wanted to know.

"I can be off in an hour," MacArthur replied.[14]

Less than twelve hours later he was on board the battleship *Nebraska* sailing from New York, with a letter from Wood in his pocket ordering him "to obtain through reconnaissance and other means consistent with the existing situation, all possible information which would be of value in connection with possible operations."[15]

He was in effect Wood's personal secret agent, operating independently of General Funston or any other American authority in Veracruz—just the kind of daring assignment Captain MacArthur had dreamed of. It was the chance at last not just to use his own judgment free of interference from his superiors—an opportunity that not many junior staff officers receive—but also to use it to affect the outcome of a future military campaign, perhaps even shape the difference between victory and defeat.

The truth was, the American situation in Veracruz was desperate. Funston's troops were hemmed in on all sides by a Mexican force that outnumbered them almost three to two—shades of the senior MacArthur's predicament during the siege of Manila. If the Mexicans got any wind of Wilson's plans for a full-scale invasion of Mexico, they could make things very hot for Funston and his men, and for Captain MacArthur.

What Funston needed, he explained to Wood's young emissary, were two things. The first was transport, but there was none to be had in Veracruz. In the event of war, his orders would be to move forward and seize the town of Jalapa as a forward base for Wood's impending invasion, but without horses or mules or wagons his brigade was stuck fast. There were, however, plenty of railway wagons in Veracruz, Mac's friend Captain Constant Cordier of the Fourth Infantry Regiment, told MacArthur. But they had no railroad engines to move them.[16]

The other requirement was intelligence on what the Mexicans were up to, but Funston was leery of sending out anyone to do reconnoitering. One American had already been killed in a firefight near the town of Tejar south of the city, and Funston had no desire to trigger any more shooting incidents.

"Trouble is," Funston explained to his diary on May 3, "we, not being permitted to scout beyond outposts, cannot discover a concentration [of Mexican troops] close thereto." But one man might be able to, the man under secret orders, namely, Captain Douglas MacArthur.[17]

And here Cordier had an idea. He had met a Mexican rail engineer, he told MacArthur, who had informed him that there were locomotives down Alvarado way, forty miles southeast of Veracruz.

The man was a bit of drunkard, Cordier warned MacArthur, and since Cordier was under Funston's orders he couldn't go with him. But if MacArthur could somehow convince the man to show him where the locomotives were, and do some freelance reconnaissance at the same time, he just might be able to pull the Fifth Brigade out of its predicament.[18]

MacArthur eagerly agreed. He found the engineer at a sleazy Veracruz bar, got him sobered up, and told him in the Spanish he had learned in the Philippines that he would pay $150 in gold if he could take him to Alvarado and show him the locomotives. The engineer readily agreed, and made arrangements for the American captain to meet him at a railroad siding, where he would have a handcar waiting. He would also have two other Mexicans waiting farther down the line with another handcar, to take them all the way to Alvarado.

MacArthur agreed but was adamant that only when he and the engineer returned to Veracruz would the Mexicans get their $150—and not before. The engineer eagerly ducked his head in agreement. The deal was done.

MacArthur departed and went back to his rooms. He decided to take nothing except his .45 pistol, his dog tags, and a small Bible. He wasn't even traveling in uniform, though that meant that if he was caught he could be shot as a spy.[19]

Then as dusk settled and thunder rumbled in the distance (it was the beginning of the rainy season), Douglas MacArthur set off alone for the edge of the American lines near the Veracruz wireless station. There he disappeared into the darkness, not knowing whether he would ever come back alive.

He followed the railway line in the gloom until he found his engineer companion, waiting by the handcar.

The young American captain pointed his pistol and had the Mexican raise his hands while he frisked him and the man complained volubly. MacArthur took away the man's revolver and a small dirk and then had the Mexican search him, "so that he might better realize that there being nothing of value on me my death would afford him no monetary return," as MacArthur wrote later in his report to General Wood.[20]

They set off on the handcar and got as far as Boca del Rio, where MacArthur discovered that the railroad bridge across the Jamapa River was down. They abandoned the car, crossed the river with a small boat they found on the bank, then wandered along until they discovered two ponies tied up next to a shack. No one inside noticed as they surreptitiously slipped the tethers, mounted up, and after several detours found themselves back on the line to

Alvarado, which soon led them to their two companions with the second handcar. After a quick search of those two stalwarts, MacArthur and the engineer mounted up and they were off.

"Mile after mile we covered with no sign of the engines," MacArthur wrote. Once he had to threaten the men at gunpoint to get them to cross one of the rail bridges—no one knew when they might be fired upon by sentries or even if the bridge itself might collapse—but after that, he reported laconically, they took orders in stride and "after getting into the spirit of the thing their conduct was most admirable." MacArthur's having the only two guns in the party probably helped, as well.[21]

It was after one o'clock in the morning when they finally reached Alvarado, thirty-five miles from Funston's outposts. There the engineer led MacArthur to the siding where the locomotives were parked, five of them. Two, he saw, were only switch engines, useless for moving cars over a distance. But "the other three were just what we needed," MacArthur decided, "fine big road pullers in excellent condition" except for some spare parts that could be easily replaced.

He glanced at his watch. Time to go back. He and his companion had crept along as far as Salinas undetected, when suddenly five armed men loomed out of the darkness. They weren't wearing uniforms; MacArthur decided they were probably bandits, of which there were hundreds infesting the countryside. MacArthur and the engineer made a run for it, as the armed men opened fire and began chasing them. The pair managed to outdistance all except two, when "in order to save our lives" the young American turned and fired back, dropping one and then the other.

MacArthur was worried that the sound of gunfire might have scared his other two companions away, but they and the handcar were waiting, and soon they were whizzing away at top speed in a driving mist.

The trip home soon got eventful. At Pietra they ran into a party of fifteen mounted gunmen, who blazed away at the handcar as it sped by. MacArthur blazed back, hitting four of them while one of his Mexicans took a bullet in the shoulder. Still they sped on, pumping and pumping away as the miles clicked by. Then outside Laguna three more mounted men sprang up out of the predawn darkness, yelling and shooting and chasing the car on horseback. One of them, "unusually well mounted," managed to pass the car and straddle the track, then raised his gun and fired directly at the American.

MacArthur felt the first bullet tear at his shirt, but it passed through without touching him. Two more whizzed past his head as the cart screeched to a halt, then MacArthur aimed and fired again, killing both the man and his horse. It took some time to get the horse's carcass off the tracks, but the harried quartet finally managed it and they were soon under way again, not stopping until they reached Paso del Toro.

MacArthur and his engineer waved goodbye to their companions and the handcar, and managed to find the ponies they had left behind. They rode back to Boca del Rio, where—according to MacArthur—they left the animals at the shack where they had found them and set off on foot for the river.

They also found the boat they had used to cross the Jamapa, but this time it struck a snag and sank in midstream. Fortunately the river at that point was barely five feet deep, "for in our exhausted physical condition I do not believe we would have been capable of swimming."[22]

The first light of day was breaking as they reached the bank. They found the first handcar where they had left it and set off for the final stretch of the journey to the American lines, where MacArthur arrived exhausted but exultant just as the sun came up.

Mission accomplished—and his penchant for heroism under fire proved once and for all.

Still, it had been a harrowing twelve hours and when Cordier found him, "he still showed signs of the tremendous nervous strain he had been under." His shirt showed no less than four separate bullet holes, although MacArthur was unhurt. As it was, Cordier wrote, "knowing the outlying conditions as well as I do it is a mystery to me that any of the party escaped."[23] But knowing MacArthur "is the type that will never open his mouth with regard to himself"—not something many people would later say of Douglas MacArthur—Cordier composed a letter to General Wood urging that MacArthur be nominated for the Congressional Medal of Honor "for heroism displayed, for dangers braved, and for difficulties overcome."

The Medal of Honor.

In Douglas's mind it was still his father's medal, although he did not learn about Cordier's recommendation until later that summer. In the meantime, it turned out the locomotives were not needed after all. The crisis of war receded; Wilson canceled plans for invasion; Funston's brigade in Veracruz settled down to a routine of garrison duty; and MacArthur was reassigned as assistant engineer officer to Funston's staff. After a few weeks, his duties shifted from getting the Fifth Brigade ready for action to preparing for withdrawal.

Working in Veracruz in the summer heat, with temperatures soaring above 100 degrees and surrounded by flies, stray dogs, and vultures was a dismal contrast with staff life in Washington. It must have been with considerable relief that MacArthur learned he would be returning to the United States to rejoin Wood's staff. And so on August 29, 1914, in the sweltering humidity of Mexico's Gulf coast, he set out for home.[24]

It was a momentous time to be alive, let alone in uniform. On the other side of the Atlantic full-scale war had broken out among the European powers. Yet no Americans in late August 1914 could foresee that the fighting raging in Europe would ever involve their own country. On the contrary, the focus was on issues closer to home, from votes for women and the first telephone line between New York and San Francisco to the ongoing fighting in Mexico, where President Wilson would order the withdrawal of American forces on September 15 and Pancho Villa would declare war on Huerta's successor, General Carranza.

In Mexico, MacArthur had shown coolness under fire, an instinct for instant decision under desperate stress, and a willingness to take the initiative and risk his own life to accomplish a dangerous mission—all key ingredients of leadership. All the same, as he smoked a cigarette and draped himself over the rail on the voyage home, young Captain MacArthur could not have imagined that soon he and two million other Americans would march off to battle in France—or that in the process he would become an army legend rivaling his father.

Instead, he quietly came back to a Washington paralyzed by late-summer heat, wrote up his final report for General Wood on the last day of September, and waited.

The wheels of military bureaucracy moved slowly. It was not until the last week of November that General Leonard Wood, after rereading Cordier's letter and MacArthur's understated but still sensational report, recommended to the War Department that his young aide be awarded the Medal of Honor. The adjutant general duly forwarded all three pieces of paper to General Funston for comment, who finally pulled himself away from his duties in Veracruz to pen a reply.

Funston had been devoted to Douglas's father. Nonetheless, the reports came to him as an unwelcome surprise. "Captain MacArthur was not a member of my command at the time," he wrote in reply, "and as I had no knowledge of it until many months later, I am at a loss to know how I can properly make official recommendation on the subject." The truth was, Funston hadn't known about MacArthur's mission to Alvarado—indeed hadn't wanted to know, in case it went awry and he needed to preserve his own deniability.

It was also true that Funston was troubled by MacArthur's impulsive decision to take action without informing him beforehand. "I do not consider this the occasion to enter into a discussion of the advisability of this enterprise," he wrote archly, especially when MacArthur knew "that without specific instructions nothing was to be done that might lead to a resumption of hostilities," like venturing alone into enemy territory. The truth was, Funston was sore about what had happened, all without his authorization, regardless of any special orders from General Wood (which didn't include stealing locomotives and shooting up the countryside). Although Funston didn't think his old friend's son should lose the award due to any "error of judgment," his wasn't a ringing endorsement, either.[25]

So there it was. No good deed, and certainly no unauthorized one, goes unpunished, especially in the army. That lack of official authorization troubled members of the board meeting to consider the Medal of Honor award as well. They were also bothered by the fact that every recommendation for the Medal of Honor required two signed statements by eyewitnesses. That wasn't possible in these circumstances, they realized. They had only the letter from Cordier confirming certain important details, and a letter from Captain Ball, MacArthur's official contact in Veracruz, stating that "this officer clearly earned a Medal of Honor. I believe a grave injustice will be done if such action is not taken." Strong stuff—but not exactly the tone that was bound to move a wavering committee to embrace MacArthur's case.

In the end, the board decided against awarding the Medal of Honor. They ruled on the extraordinary grounds that "to bestow the award recommended might encourage any other staff officer, under similar conditions, to ignore the local commander, possibly interfering with reference to the enemy"— a clear disincentive for any officer to take the initiative no matter how important the cause.[26]

When he heard the news, MacArthur exploded. He drew up the kind of fiery letter of protest that his father would have sent, and with the same degree of ill consideration. He raged that he was "incensed" by the "rigid narrowmindedness and lack of information" on the part of the board (its chairman had been commandant of cadets during MacArthur's last two years at the Point), and shot copies off to Chief of Staff Scott and the secretary of war.[27]

There is no doubt that the letter did him no good in important circles. Certainly it made older and wiser heads shake in disbelief at his temerity and ill temper. Definitely his father's son, they might have said; the same hurt sense of pride, the same wounded pleading, with the same ineffectual results.

Others raised more serious questions, such as whether MacArthur's daring little adventure constituted military "action" in the proper sense required by the Medal of Honor rules. That doubt in turn led some MacArthur detractors to wonder later if the whole story was true at all or if he made the whole thing up.

In fact, there is no reason to suppose that he did, despite the lack of any physical evidence supporting his story. Captain Cordier himself confirmed what details he could by talking to the engineer and the Mexican firemen. Whether MacArthur could actually see how many bandits he had shot in the dark is really anyone's guess. Yet no one at the time ever doubted the veracity of MacArthur's story. His efficiency reports from Chief of Staff Scott, General Wood, and everyone else heaped high praise on him, almost in spite of his adventure with the locomotives, and that December 1914 he was promoted to major.[28]

Yet the entire enterprise, not excluding the incendiary letters to his superiors, far from helping his reputation, probably hurt him. It made him look like a potentially reckless gambler who, when the wheel runs against him, turns into a special pleader. But if he imagined that his one chance to win a Medal of Honor had passed him by forever, he was wrong. Events were on the move that would offer him many more opportunities to prove his valor on the battlefield—more, in fact, than any one American officer could expect to see and live.

On June 3, 1916, Woodrow Wilson stood before Congress and signed the National Defense Act. It was a momentous event, signaling a growing and dismal sense that America could no longer stay out of the war that was raging in Europe. It also reflected a major change of heart on the part of President Wilson—and about America's emerging role in the world.

A titanic clash was unfolding in Europe. German and Austrian armies battled imperial Russia for control of vast regions on the eastern front, while along a three-hundred-mile line of trenches from the Swiss border to the English Channel, German, French, and British forces were locked in a deadly embrace. Hundreds of thousands were dead already; mammoth clashes at Verdun and the Somme that year would claim many more. New and terrifying weapons of war—heavy artillery, massed machine guns, airplanes, flamethrowers, and poison gas—were turning armed conflict between nations into a charnel house that even Arthur MacArthur, with his tours of the battlefields of Manchuria, could only dimly imagine.

At the same time, fleets of warships and submarines roamed the world's oceans at will, hunting and killing one another as well as sinking neutral shipping with the goal of starving the enemy into submission and surrender. By 1915 German submarines were attacking American vessels without warning, and without mercy.

Wilson wanted to stay out of war. He had distractions enough, starting with the disintegrating situation in Mexico. When he learned that his General Staff was drawing up plans for a possible war with Germany, his first reaction was to have the entire staff fired.[29] But the possibility that America might be drawn into conflict in Europe through Germany's increasingly reckless submarine warfare could not be discounted. MacArthur's mentor Leonard Wood had led the way, declaring that the nation had to be prepared for the possibility of war. Backed by luminaries like Teddy Roosevelt, the voices for national preparedness gathered momentum, becoming especially urgent after the events of a May evening in 1915.

The British ocean liner *Lusitania* was loaded with American passengers, even though the German embassy had issued a warning to Americans not to sail in her because she was subject to being attacked once at sea. On the night of May 7, the *Lusitania* was torpedoed by a German submarine off the southern coast of Ireland. One hundred and twenty-eight Americans were among the dead.

The nation was as much shocked as outraged (few knew that despite a *New York Times* headline saying the *Lusitania* had been unarmed, she had actually been carrying 4.2 million rounds of ammunition plus thousands of empty shell cases and nonexplosive fuses destined for the British army). After manifestly trying to stay out of the war, Americans found themselves the inadvertent victims of it.[30]

In the face of American uproar, the Germans called off their unrestricted submarine warfare—for the time being. But it signaled a tide of events that no single president could control. America might soon find itself at war with a European great power for the first time since 1812.

That conflict had been a disaster. It was to prevent another that Wilson began to move in the direction of those, like General Wood, who were calling for a massive national effort at preparedness and rearmament. A sign of the change was that Wilson named a new secretary of war, Newton Baker, and then signed the National Defense Act. Prepared by the General Staff, it created America's first large standing army since the Civil War, consisting of 175,000 regular troops and 450,000 National Guard troops. The act also set up the nation's first Reserve Officers' Training Corps, or ROTC, to train a generation of young college students and graduates in the art of military command.

MacArthur had been in the thick of staff meetings drawing up the National Defense Act. He had been assigned to work with industry groups like the American Automobile Association to discuss building trucks for motor transport, as well as coordinating mobilization plans with the navy. In fact, the navy staff liked him so much they asked Wood to send MacArthur to them more often. One of those who took a particular liking to the young major was Assistant Secretary of the Navy Franklin D. Roosevelt. In those meetings they struck up an acquaintance that seemed to promise a lifelong friendship, although neither man could possibly guess what momentous events their relations would eventually trigger.

Roosevelt was not the only MacArthur fan. An Admiral Scott admired MacArthur's combination of impeccable manners and outgoing charm with an insatiable appetite for hard work. He's peculiarly "well fitted for positions requiring diplomacy and high grade intelligence," Scott remarked. Wood inwardly beamed. Clearly MacArthur seemed destined for a career as God's gift to staff work.[31]

Yet there was also trouble in General Staff paradise. Newton Baker's arrival at the Army and Navy Building had set off shock waves around the War Department. The former mayor of Cleveland, the prim, bespectacled Baker had the reputation of being not only a die-hard progressive but, incredibly for a secretary of war, a pacifist. "I'm so much a pacifist," he liked to quip, "I'm willing to fight for it." Many in and out of uniform shook their heads. This was the man who was supposed to get the nation ready for fighting a modern war?

They needn't have worried. Baker threw himself into his new job, and in looking to build the most dynamic and professional staff he could, he took an immediate shine to young Major MacArthur.

As for MacArthur's view of Baker, "I found him diminutive in size, but large in heart, with a clear, brilliant mind, and a fine ability to make instant and positive decisions"—especially when he listened to the advice of Major MacArthur. Later MacArthur branded Baker one of our greatest war secretaries, and "as an organizer of America's war resources he had no superior—perhaps no equal."[32]

With the National Defense Act already passed, preparing for war now had the support of the president and Congress. As a former mayor, Baker had the sense to realize that the challenge now was to get the rest of the nation on board as well. By May 1916 the bond of trust he had developed with MacArthur was such that he had asked MacArthur to head the department's Bureau of Information—in effect, its propaganda wing—and then act as official press censor. So that summer Mac exchanged his uniform and Sam Browne belt for a suit and straw boater, and became in effect the army's first public relations officer. His year at the Bureau of Information would leave a permanent stamp on the U.S. Army, and would be an enduring part of his own education.

For example, he learned how to deal with journalists, and how to be informal and relaxed with them without letting himself be caught off guard. He learned how to plant stories without making reporters feel manipulated by finding items that would catch their interest but also justified a policy—as when Woodrow Wilson surprised everyone by ordering General Pershing to set off after Pancho Villa in Mexico—or to shape a general narrative, as when the War Department decided that its public theme for the summer and autumn of 1916 would be the Necessity of Preparedness.[33]

MacArthur learned how to facilitate interviews with generals and officials, and he learned how to use his natural charm to head off the embarrassing stories and focus attention on the ones that put the army, and preparation for war, in a positive light.

His biggest test, however, and the most successful, was the draft.

Selective Service came into existence on May 18, 1917. Nothing like it had been seen since the Civil War, when the draft caused massive riots and became associated in people's minds with iniquitous practices like rich men's sons paying for substitutes. But by working closely with the two men who drew up the plan, Judge Advocate General Enoch Crowder (who had served under MacArthur's father in the Philippines) and fellow West Point classmate Lieutenant Colonel Hugh Johnson, MacArthur helped to craft a system that would be as fair as it was efficient—or at least it would seem so to the public.

They set aside the original plan for army-controlled conscription and replaced it with civilian draft boards for virtually every community in the country. This gave the appearance of local input into deciding who would qualify for the draft board and who would not; it even conveyed the impression of local control. The response from the media and Congress was overwhelmingly positive. Young men about to be drafted felt more comfortable sitting across the table from the president of the local bank or the local doctor or dentist rather than a row of expressionless men in khaki uniforms and Sam Browne belts. MacArthur had turned what could have been a public relations disaster into a national ritual accepted by all, and praised by many.

"Make no mistake," wrote public relations expert Ernest Dupuy many years later, "it was then Major Douglas MacArthur, Class of 1903, who sold to the American people the Selective Service Act"—and made it possible to create an American army that would swell in less than two years from barely over 100,000 to more than two million.[34]

MacArthur liked the job of public relations, and didn't mind the long hours. It turned out he had a gift for selecting what would attract media attention, and avoiding what would be a bore—a gift that would pay off in his own career from trench raids in France to the landings at Inchon.

"I am working very hard with my newspaper men," he wrote to his hero of the moment, General Wood. In the end, his overall assessment of journalists echoed that of a character in a novel a few years later: "if you tried to bamboozle them they were out for your blood, but . . . if you trusted them they would see you through."[35]

He learned that the press, if handled correctly, could be the kind of sympathetic prop and support that his mother had been, listening to and upholding his side of the story against attacks by the disapproving patriarchs of the army and the Washington establishment. MacArthur had resolved that he would never again make the mistake he made in Alvarado. Never again would he perform great deeds of bravery and skill, and allow the world not to hear about them.

As for the press's assessment of MacArthur, that was made plain in a letter sent to Secretary Baker and signed by twenty-nine Washington correspondents, including the representatives of the Associated Press, *The New York Times* and the *New York World,* the United Press, and the *Chicago Tribune, Washington Star,* and *Philadelphia Record.*

"We feel no doubt of what the future holds for Major MacArthur," it read. "Rank and honors will come to him if merit can come to any man; but we wish to say our thanks to him for his unfailing kindness, patience and wise counsel we have received from him in the difficult days that are past . . .

"He has put his personality in the task . . . and if wise decisions are reached eventually as to the military policy of our country, we cannot but feel that the major has helped, through us, to shape the public mind."[36]

The letter was dated April 4, 1917. Two days later America declared war on Germany.

It was news from Mexico, ironically enough, that finally forced Wilson to act. British naval intelligence had intercepted a telegram from German ambassador Arthur Zimmermann, promising large chunks of the western United States if Mexico followed an American declaration of war against Germany—a growing possibility now that Germany had resumed unrestricted submarine warfare—with a declaration of its own of war against the United States and allied itself with Germany. Wilson was so shocked by the news, and the fact that the German ambassador had arrogantly sent the secret message using the American commercial cable that Wilson had lent him at no charge, that he could only exclaim over and over again, "Good Lord! Good Lord!"[37]

Still, he dithered for almost another month until repeated torpedo attacks on American merchant ships finally convinced him to summon Congress on April 2. Four days later, on April 6, 1917, Congress formally declared war, joining Britain and France in what Wilson called "the war to end all wars" against Germany.

The next step was to send an army to Europe. The man to command it would not be the one originally slated for the job, General Frederick Funston. Arthur MacArthur's old friend and comrade from the Philippines, and Douglas MacArthur's commander from Veracruz, had suddenly died of a heart attack in San Antonio back in February. Ironically, it was MacArthur who brought the news to President Wilson personally, at Secretary Baker's house.

"What now, Newton, who will take the Army over?" Wilson had asked Baker. The secretary had paused and, as MacArthur later remembered, turned to the young public relations officer standing beside him.

"Whom do you think the Army would choose, Major?"

"For myself the choice would unquestionably be General Pershing," MacArthur promptly answered.

Wilson looked at him, MacArthur remembered, then said in a quiet voice: "It would be a good choice."[38]

It's a good story, and it's probably true. All the same, Wilson and Baker didn't need a thirty-seven-year-old major's advice to know that John Pershing was the right man for the job. Born in 1860 in Missouri, Pershing had attended West Point, where he had been a brutal hazer. But he had also taught at an African American school after he finished high school, and his fervent belief that black soldiers were as good as their white counterparts—a conviction confirmed by his command of the famous Buffalo Soldiers during the 1890s—earned him the nickname "Black Jack" (cadets he taught as an instructor at West Point used a more offensive word than "Black").

His expedition in Mexico against bandit leader Pancho Villa in 1916 (the same expedition where another young army officer, Lieutenant George Patton, first saw action) had made him a national hero and the inevitable choice for America's first overseas expeditionary force. So in April, Pershing was recalled from Mexico and dispatched to Paris to form a headquarters unit in advance of the impending arrival of his troops.

The big question was whether he would have any troops to lead.

The Selective Service Act passed by Congress created an army that would eventually number in the millions. But they would not be ready to go overseas for another year or two. There were some Regular Army divisions that could be ready, especially the well-equipped First Division. Its 7,000 officers and men, however, were not even close to the numbers America's new European allies wanted and expected. How was the War Department going to make up the difference?

It was Douglas MacArthur who championed the most obvious answer: mobilize the National Guard. It was active in all forty-eight states; its members at least had military training, and if they weren't up to the standards of the armies now fighting in Europe, they could be gotten ready for overseas service in a fraction of the time it would take to train new recruits. He also pointed out that some Guard divisions, like New York's, were nearly as well trained and equipped as some Regular units. In sum, "National Guard divisions should be able to fight proudly" alongside the Regular Army, MacArthur believed, even in the increasingly harsh conditions in Europe.

The rest of the General Staff, though, were to a man against the idea. A new staff study had come out, asserting that the optimal size for an American Expeditionary Force to France would be 500,000 men, all of whom should be recruited and trained by the Regular Army. No National Guard units were necessary, or even desirable, to augment that overseas force.

When the study reached MacArthur's desk, with the signatures of all the other members of the General Staff, all of whom endorsed it, filling up the last page, he dolefully added his. But he also added a tart note, saying, "I completely disagree with this conclusion, but I will not attempt to detail my reasons as I feel no one will give them the slightest attention."

Years later, he admitted, "It was a discourteous remark," and a potentially career-ending one—as he realized a few days later when he learned that Secretary Baker wanted to see him at once.

"What's it about, Sam?" MacArthur asked the elderly black messenger who brought the summons to his office at the War Department.

Sam had worked for MacArthur's father during his adjutant general days, and had known Douglas almost his entire life. Sam's answer was not reassuring.

"Don't know," he said, "but that little feller didn't smile at me."

With a dry throat and a sinking heart, MacArthur made his way to Baker's office, where he found the secretary of war puffing on his pipe and reading the report—especially MacArthur's note at the end.

The secretary, according to MacArthur, sat for a full minute in silence. Then he said, "Major, I have just read your endorsement."

MacArthur waited.

Baker went on, "I agree with you in this matter. Get your cap. We are going over to the White House to place the whole question before the President for his attention."[39]

They soon found themselves ensconced with President Wilson, and for a full hour they went over the arguments in favor of mobilizing the National Guard—the primary one being that it would increase manpower far beyond the half-million number recommended by the army's General Staff.

MacArthur recalled that Wilson listened intently, and finally said, "I am in general accord with your idea, Baker, to put this into effect. And thank you, Major," he added, turning to MacArthur, "for your frankness." From that moment, staff study or no staff study, the dispatch of National Guard units to France to serve in Pershing's American Expeditionary Force was official policy.

For MacArthur, certainly, it was a personal triumph. All the same, crossing one's superiors—including Chief of Staff Major General Hugh Scott, who had personally endorsed the report—wasn't a good precedent for the future.

Senior officers don't appreciate having their judgment questioned or their shortcomings pointed out by a young upstart, even if it's Arthur MacArthur's son. Nor would later senior politicians, including occupants of the White House, appreciate it, even when that upstart grew older and more distinguished. Yet it was a habit that MacArthur was never able to kick, especially as his confidence that he, and only he, had the right answer grew stronger with every run-in—and the results, more often than not, proved him right.

As one of his aides during the Korean War put it, "I knew he was positive that there wasn't anything anyone could do as well as he could do it. But at the same time," Edward Wright, MacArthur's former G3 (head of operations), added, "while I was learning this, I was learning he was right."[40]

MacArthur believed it too. And that confidence began to catch fire when he won his single-handed combat with the General Staff over sending the National Guard to France.

He and Baker still had one hurdle remaining. It was General Mann of the Militia Bureau, the officer who would be in charge of mobilizing the National Guard units, who pointed it out. Which National Guard divisions do we send? he asked Baker. New York and Pennsylvania are in the best shape, but if they go first, what will the other states say?

Baker, being a politician, saw the problem at once. "If we sent the New York National Guard first," he recalled, some in New York would ask why their boys got sent first. At the same time, other states would start "charging that we were preferring New York and giving it first chance."

They couldn't wait until all the National Guard units were ready. Time would run out. So how could they select one state without offending the rest? The problem seemed insoluble. So Baker turned to his public relations officer, the original champion of the National Guard plan, for advice.

"I disclosed my puzzle to Major MacArthur," Baker later recalled, "who suggested the possibility of our being able to form a division out of the surplus units from many states, the major part of whose National Guard organizations were [already] in multi-state divisions." Baker enthusiastically agreed, and at once set MacArthur and Mann to drawing up a list of individual regiments that would be ready to join.[41]

When they came back to Baker's office with their list ready, he was delighted to see the wide diversity of state units this new division would in-clude, from New England and New York all the way to Texas, Colorado, and California.

"It'll stretch like a rainbow clear across the United States," MacArthur said in a fit of enthusiastic eloquence. The name stuck.[42] Although officially num-bered as Forty-second, from that day forward the National Guard division that was to be the first to go to France was known as the Rainbow Division, with its divisional patch a rainbow semicircle of red, blue, yellow, purple, and green.

They had a division and a unit roster; next they needed a commander. MacArthur pushed for General Mann himself, although because Mann was approaching retirement age MacArthur in private urged Baker to pick the best colonel on the General Staff to serve as Mann's chief of staff, someone who was vigorous enough and competent enough to shoulder most of the general's burden.

Baker nodded. "I've already made my selection for the post."

MacArthur asked who it was.

Baker put his hand on MacArthur's shoulder. "It's you."

MacArthur was stunned. He managed to stammer his thanks, but pointed out he was only a major and not eligible.

"You're wrong," Baker said with a smile. "You are now a colonel. I will sign your commission immediately." He added, "I take it you will want to be in the Engineer Corps."

Suddenly MacArthur had a vision of his father, a young officer in blue waving a flag from the top of Missionary Ridge in 1863. "No, the Infantry," he promptly answered.

When Mann heard the news, Baker recalled, he was delighted. As for MacArthur, "I could only think of the old 24th Wisconsin Infantry," he con-fessed later—and of his father. Now it would be his turn to find glory on the battlefield in the ultimate test of honor and manhood.[43]

But first there was a division to organize. MacArthur found it the hardest task of his life.

*   *   *

They started showing up on Long Island in late August, on a 500-acre stretch of ground between Mineola and Garden City that MacArthur dubbed Camp Mills, after General Alfred Mills, who had commanded West Point when he had been there.

The first to arrive were men from New York's Sixty-ninth National Guard regiment, "the Fighting Irish," a regiment with deep Civil War roots, now dubbed the 165th. When they learned they were to be the New York representatives in the Rainbow Division, they were "full of excitement," according to a battalion chaplain, Father Francis X. Duffy.[44]

After the New Yorkers came men from MacArthur's home state, Wisconsin, and another Civil War–era regiment, the Fourth Ohio. The Ohioans and Wisconsinites were redesignated the 167th Infantry Regiment and formed with the New Yorkers one of the Rainbow's two combat brigades, the Eighty-third. By September, Camp Mills was also hosting the Fourth Alabama. MacArthur the Civil War student would have known that the Fourth Alabamans and the New York Sixty-ninths had actually fought each other at First Bull Run, and then again at Fredericksburg.

So together with a regiment drawn from three Iowa National Guard units, designated the 168th Infantry, the Alabamans (now renamed the 167th Infantry) became the Rainbow's other combat brigade, the Eighty-fourth Infantry Brigade. They would be led by a hard-nosed brigadier general named Robert A. Brown, whom MacArthur had gotten to know when they had served together on the General Staff—and from whom MacArthur would eventually take over as the brigade's commander.

Ohio, Wisconsin, New York, Alabama, and Iowa. These states now formed the fighting core of the Rainbow Division, the Eighty-third and Eighty-fourth Infantry Brigades. The rest—Californians, Coloradans, South Carolinians, Georgians, Kansans, forty-two states in all—were scattered through the division's other units, including supply, medical, and Signal Corps, as well as its machine-gun battalion (which was to be equipped with 260 of the latest .30-caliber Browning models) and its Field Artillery Brigade.[45] In an almost literal sense, America was marching off to war.

What the Rainbow lacked in equipment—very few of the machine guns it needed ever reached Camp Mills and tents were in such short supply that twelve men were sleeping in tents made for six—and experience, the division made up in enthusiasm and the quality of its officers, a large number of whom were Regular Army professionals. Out of their number would come two chiefs of staff of the army (including MacArthur himself), six major and lieutenant generals in World War Two, a secretary of the army as well as the air force, two big-city mayors and two governors—not to mention the man who would become America's top spymaster in World War Two.[46]

All the same, they were still far from France—and far from being ready to go there. One young Rainbow officer, John B. Coulter, remembered the chaotic atmosphere as "one of feverish preparation, from the Divisional Commander to the rawest recruit."[47]

And supervising it all was MacArthur. He developed at Camp Mills a routine that disposed of paperwork based on his father's policy in the Philippines: "never postpone until tomorrow what can be done today."

The routine was simple. Before MacArthur arrived at the office in the morning, he had usually worked out the salient issues of the day and their solutions in his mind while getting up and having breakfast. Thanks to his wide and varied reading, including his reading of the same reports his staff used to come to their decisions, and his nearly stenographic memory even of casual conversations, he never had to rely on a staff meeting to figure out or debate what to do next—not at Camp Mills and not thirty years later in Korea. Instead, he would attend a meeting to assign tasks that the chief of staff had left vacant and to absorb new information that might change or modify earlier decisions. Then he would quit the room, leaving the working out of details to subordinates.

Eventually, he learned to do away with staff meetings altogether. When a problem cropped up he would simply summon the relevant person for a one-on-one meeting, and they would work it out on the spot.[48]

It was a strange, even idiosyncratic, system. But MacArthur was an instinctive delegator, a habit that he found not only saved time but won trust and loyalty. He always delegated with a specific goal in mind—not to raise anyone's self-esteem or to groom successors (few on his staffs ever qualified for either category) but to free himself to think about the bigger picture. Once to a subordinate who felt it necessary to point out something he thought the boss had overlooked, MacArthur wrote a note that simply read

"I know everything." He meant it, and subordinates, including those at Camp Mills, would gradually come to realize it was probably true.

Certainly the task he had taken on at Camp Mills was all but overwhelming.

"During August and September," he wrote later, "the division worked day and night to whip into shape the 27,000 men who had arrived in different stages of training . . . There were no leaves, passes were limited, officers and men fared alike." He admired the men's spirit, their comradeship, and their willing cooperation with officers, many of whom they had never met before, including himself. But even the confirmed workaholic Lieutenant Colonel Douglas MacArthur couldn't work miracles.[49]

Secretary Baker and Major General Tasker Bliss, the army's new chief of staff, ventured out for an inspection of the Forty-second on September 30, when most of the division had been there barely six weeks. They were impressed by the intensive drills in close and extended order, sighting and aiming exercises, and training in "semaphore and wig wag." Things broke down, though, during parade review, when one regiment almost collided with another and when the command "eyes right" brought a flurry of hand salutes instead.

MacArthur shot a stern note around to all commanding officers afterward, but a second Baker-Bliss visit on October 7 did not go much better. An entire regiment, the 168th, got lost on the way to the parade ground and finally showed up when the rest of the review was nearly done. There were more stern notes; what Baker and Bliss thought is not recorded. Yet the Forty-second was leaving for France in just eleven days.[50]

Nothing could change that timetable. On the afternoon of October 18, MacArthur and his staff, along with the Eighty-third and Eighty-fourth Infantry Brigades as well as the Sixty-seventh Artillery Brigade, began boarding trains for Brooklyn. There they would transfer by ferry to Hoboken to meet the ships that would carry them to France.

October 1917 marked a new low point for the Allies in the war with Germany. Imperial Russia was collapsing into chaos; Italy was only days away from its worst disaster of the war, the Battle of Caporetto. The western front to which the Americans were headed had been reduced to an empty, devastated landscape, scarred by constant trench warfare. After three years of more or less constant fighting, the front lines had barely moved. The French and British hoped the newly arriving American divisions would change that situation and transform the war. MacArthur hoped they would not guess how inexperienced and unprepared his men really were.

He himself was now thirty-seven years old and still unmarried. In many ways—his dependence on his mother for emotional support, his reliance on his father's old comrades for promotion and favors, his self-absorbed touchiness that could not bear the least hint of contradiction or criticism from others, even his superior officers—he was still the young man who had graduated with top honors at West Point but was at bottom an immature boy. But now, even with America on the brink of its greatest overseas conflict, his life was about to change in ways that would have seemed unimaginable, both to himself and to those who knew him, a year or two earlier.

MacArthur, however, never hesitated. When the General Staff's chief of engineers reproached him for transferring to the Infantry, warning him he'd soon be back among the engineers, where he had spent his entire career until then, MacArthur had promptly replied, "You are wrong, Colonel. I shall never come back to you."[51]

It was true. Arthur MacArthur's son was finally going to war.

CHAPTER 6

INTO THE FIRE

*Sometimes it is the order
one disobeys that makes one famous.*

—DOUGLAS MACARTHUR

The *Covington* glided out from New York Harbor on October 18, 1917, and by nightfall was far out in the Atlantic. Because of the U-boat menace, there were no lights, and smoking on deck at night was forbidden since the faint red glow might catch the attention of a German periscope.

The men of the Forty-second, crammed belowdecks, had to wear life jackets even when they slept in case of submarine attack. Constant zigzagging to throw off any pursuing submarine meant that a trip that should have taken five days took almost two weeks.

But for Douglas MacArthur, standing in the darkness on deck, listening to the captain's voice intoning "Rudder right, rudder left," it was the beginning of his greatest adventure yet. Staring out into the blackness, he imagined he could see the cruiser *Chattanooga* on which his brother Arthur was serving, among the liner's armed escorts.

But in his mind's eye was also the image of his dead father, and of his still-living mother. He would arrive in France set on one thing: to make himself famous, as his father had, by a combination of bravery and leadership that would make him stand far above his colleagues. He intended to be constantly in the front lines, serving under fire along with his men. This meant that he and the Forty-second could not be sidelined by being placed in reserve. Yet as they finally disembarked at St Nazaire's harbor on November 1, that was exactly what General Pershing was planning to do.

Pershing and his staff sensed the desperation in the British and French armies, who wanted the Americans going into action at once, and so he made plans very different from the ones they had drawn up back in the States. They decided that their most experienced divisions of Regular Army troops—the First, Second, and Twenty-sixth—would go up into the line as soon as possible. The rest already in France, including the National Guardsmen of the Forty-second, would be used as replacements for those divisions, and would be fed in, battalion by battalion, as they were needed.

The news reached MacArthur while he was at the division's new French headquarters at Vaucouleurs, supervising the arrival of helmets, gas masks, artillery, and ammunition, as well as procuring 50,000 pairs of marching shoes. He was appalled and furious. Headquarters had already snatched away thirty-three of the Rainbow's best officers to serve in other divisions. Now MacArthur saw that Pershing was not only contemplating the breakup of the entire division, *his* division, but the plan might mean that he would never see action at all. The image of Douglas MacArthur sitting out the world's greatest war at a desk handling supply reports and personnel transfers was more than he could stand.[1]

He immediately launched a furious lobbying effort, starting with a cable to Secretary Baker and virtually anyone else who had a Washington, D.C., address. "The 42nd had been a uniting force as the nation mobilized for war," MacArthur argued. Breaking up the army's one truly national division "would be a shock to the nation."[2] Then he headed up to Chaumont, where Pershing had his headquarters, and burst in on his old friend James Harbord, who had introduced him to Manuel Quezon when they were serving in the Philippines and who now was a brigadier general and Pershing's chief of staff.

"Come and see the division," MacArthur urged him. "Judge for yourself whether such a splendid unit should be relegated to a replacement status."

So Harbord did, and he was impressed by what he saw, as MacArthur had known he would be. Conditions at Vaucouleurs were less than ideal, to say the least. The Rainbow artillerymen were housed in barracks previously used by German POWs. The rooms were so infested with lice the men had to strip down to their underwear to be deloused every morning before going to work.[3] Yet morale in the division was high and "its training has been on saner lines than any other division like to come," Harbord wrote afterward in a memo to Pershing, with "no trench or bomb nonsense, [just] straight soldier-making." Harbord also pointed out that breaking up the Forty-second, "the first division to arrive [in France] complete," might be politically difficult as well as militarily a mistake. The Rainbow Division "has figured more in the press and has more friends to resent the matter"—both of which were largely the result of MacArthur's influence.

Also, if Pershing tried to use it as a replacement division without letting Baker and the War Department know, his decision would almost certainly be reversed. "On the other hand if you ask the War Department . . . you will not be permitted to do it."[4]

Maybe they should rethink the plan, Harbord concluded. Pershing did. In the end, the Forty-second would remain intact, even as Chaumont ordered it to move out of Vaucouleurs for more intensive training. MacArthur's lobbying had saved the Rainbow from being broken up, even though he knew "my action was probably not in accord with normal procedure." As a result "it created resentment against me" inside Pershing's staff that would come back to bite MacArthur more than once.[5] But he had made sure that the Forty-second Division would end up in the front line, where there was fighting to be done and glory to be won—both for the living and for the dead.

MacArthur and the Rainbow celebrated a cold, comfortless Christmas at the new training area, located just north of Pershing's headquarters of Chaumont. The next day, December 26, they set out in a three-day snowstorm for their final training in the Marne Valley as part of I Corps. The men still had no overcoats and no winter underwear; many were still wearing the shoes they had first donned back in the States, which soon fell apart in the thirty-four-mile hike through the snow. MacArthur marched along with everyone else—something he would do for the rest of the war—and his staff aide,

Major Walter Wolf, couldn't help spotting bloody footprints in the snow. A private that Wolf passed, his feet wrapped in burlap and his pack heaped with ice, muttered bitterly, "Valley Forge—hell! There ain't no such animal."

Yet, Wolf later wrote, "from this march the spirit of the division was born."[6] It would be MacArthur's fate to constantly command soldiers who had to face extremes of climate as well as the enemy, whether it was the steamy jungles of Bataan and New Guinea or the ice-covered ridges of Korea. It all began with the Rainbow that winter in France.

Now that the Forty-second was assigned as the active reserve division for I Corps, a new commander had come in to replace Mann, General Charles Menoher. MacArthur proved to be the best chief of staff Menoher could have asked for: "One of the most efficient, energetic, and talented officers I have ever known," he would write after the war.[7]

MacArthur was a whiz at the paperwork, managing reports and personnel with a skill that earned him not only Menoher's admiration but that of his staff, and even a devotion that would prove a MacArthur trademark, then and later.

Albert Ettinger, a private from the 165th, found this out as a dispatch rider for MacArthur's HQ. One night in a driving rain he was carrying a bundle of dispatches for MacArthur when he was nearly run down by a truck, and wound up every few kilometers in the ditch trying to avoid columns of French troops tramping through the mud. When the exhausted and thoroughly saturated private got to battalion HQ, he was met by an astonished officer. "My God, Ettinger, what happened to you?"

On learning that Ettinger had been sent out in miserable weather for a bundle of very unimportant dispatches, MacArthur got up and went over to shake Ettinger's hand. "Ettinger," he said simply and solemnly, "you are a good soldier."

"I damn near died," Ettinger remembered. "Tears came to my eyes. No one, but no one, had ever called me a good soldier. . . . My heart went out to him there and then."

Then MacArthur had a sergeant major fetch Ettinger and get him a shower and not only a hot meal—"I mean a *good* meal," he ordered—and dry clothes, but sheets and a cot for the night. "I just worshiped the man," Ettinger wrote later—and that was true for many other men in the Rainbow as well.[8]

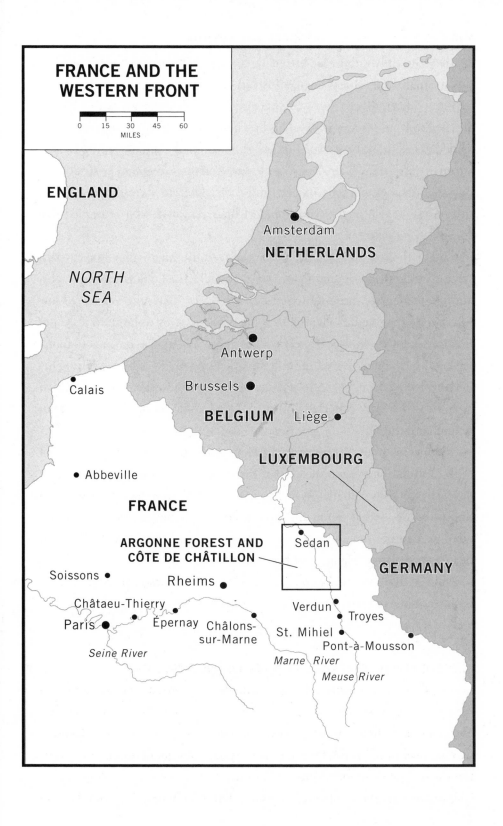

FRANCE AND THE
WESTERN FRONT

0   15   30   45   60
            MILES

ENGLAND

NORTH
SEA

NETHERLANDS

Amsterdam

Antwerp

Calais

Brussels

BELGIUM   Liège

LUXEMBOURG

Abbeville

FRANCE

ARGONNE FOREST AND
CÔTE DE CHÂTILLON   Sedan

GERMANY

Soissons   Rheims

Châtaeu-Thierry   Verdun
Paris   Épernay   Troyes
                            Châlons-   St. Mihiel
Seine River   sur-Marne   Pont-à-Mousson

                         Marne River
                                Meuse River

They certainly knew MacArthur by his appearance, which was unorthodox to an almost insolent degree. Instead of the standard olive-drab tunic of an army officer, MacArthur wore his gray West Point sweater with a blue A stitched in front—a memento of his baseball days at the Point. Instead of the standard gas mask or a sword or pistol, he carried a simple riding crop—"from my life on the plains," he liked to say. And instead of the classic doughboy steel helmet worn by officers and men alike, he wore a barracks cap tipped at a rakish angle, with the steel liner removed so it crumpled like someone had sat on it.

And as the war went on, he never changed the MacArthur Look—even when leading troops under fire or in a gas attack. The Look got some laughs, and the feelings of more-buttoned-down officers, including Pershing himself, can be imagined. But it also drew the news cameras, as he knew it would: the time spent working as Secretary Baker's press agent was paying off. Interviews with Colonel MacArthur accompanied by a photo of him featuring his hat and riding crop, began to dot newspapers around the country—which his mother lovingly collected and pasted into a scrapbook that soon began bulging out the sides.[9]

There were others in the army who found The Look refreshing, and even took to imitating parts of it. One of them was his friend from Milwaukee days, airman Billy Mitchell. When he met MacArthur at the front, he was so impressed by the hat minus the steel liner, that he pulled his own out and wore his cap the same way for the rest of the war. From Mitchell it would become the classic headgear of bomber pilots during World War Two, immortalized in photographs and films like *Twelve O'Clock High*: MacArthur's legacy not just to the Air Force but to Hollywood.[10]

The Look also got its first taste of battle, on February 26, 1918.

The last week of February MacArthur learned that French troops were planning a surprise raid on German positions along the Meurthe River. He and General Menoher approached the French commander, General Georges de Bazelaire, and asked if they and the brigade commanders could watch, as their first sight of action on the western front.

Bazelaire said yes and when Menoher left, MacArthur lingered. He had something else to ask the esteemed general. Would he be allowed to go along with the French raiding party doing reconnaissance before the attack? Baze-laire hesitated and would have said no, but MacArthur said, "I cannot fight them if I can't see them." So MacArthur got permission to go—but evidently never told Menoher about his plan.[11]

That night Menoher, MacArthur, and the others gathered on a low prom-ontory to watch the attack. MacArthur and another staff officer, Captain Thomas Handy, then quietly wandered down the line and met a party of French soldiers who were daubing black cork on their faces. They greeted the Americans like old friends, and a French lieutenant offered them wire clip-pers and trench knives, which MacArthur and Handy gratefully took. Then after blacking their own faces, they set off for the lip of the forward trench and waited to venture out into No Man's Land for the first time.

Trench raids were nightmarish affairs, whether it was a small raid of a few dozen soldiers or a big one with several hundred. There was no supporting artillery, no accompanying mortars or machine guns to help out, sometimes no weapons at all except a pistol and a brace of hand grenades. Yet crossing over to enemy trenches could be as dangerous as the raid itself, especially when the enemy kept the scene lit as bright as day. "The German loves his fireworks party every night," as another officer in the Forty-second, Major William Donovan, later wrote. German illumination shells and flares, fired at regular intervals throughout the night, gave the blasted black landscape a strange spectral quality—but also made discreet movement difficult, though not impossible.[12]

After a couple of nerve-racking hours crawling up to the edge of the Ger-man trenches, MacArthur and the raiding party paused. The signal to attack was supposed to be a grenade tossed into the German trenches, but accord-ing to MacArthur, at the last minute a German sentry spotted the soldiers huddled in the dark. "His gun flashed in the night," he wrote. "The alarm spread through the trench, across the front." As German shells and flares rained overhead, the party charged into the German trenches.

"The fight was savage and merciless"—just how savage is easy to guess from accounts of other, similar raids.[13] The tossed hand grenade, the en-trenching tool used as a bludgeon, the men stomped to death in the dark, the sudden pistol shot—except that MacArthur would not even carry a pistol.

Then and later, he maintained a strange fetish about carrying a sidearm that might mar the MacArthur Look. The truth was, the Look was more than an outlandish costume. It was visible proof of invulnerability, and a bold challenge to enemies as well as authority. Here I am, it said. See if you can get me.

A last grenade hurled into a German bunker finally ended the fight as the raiding party headed back to their own lines with an accompanying crowd of prisoners, including a German colonel MacArthur had subdued with his riding stick.

MacArthur's hosts congratulated him for having volunteered to come along on their risky mission. "Those veteran Frenchmen crowded around me, shaking my hand, slapping me on the back, and offering me cognac and absinthe." Eventually MacArthur and Handy got back to their post, where Menoher had been waiting for them. He had not been completely ignorant of what had gone on. "I saw them as they were taking a sneak around the point of a hill," he wrote in his report, "but said nothing, and we did not see them again until next morning."[14]

The division advocate general, Major Hugh Ogden, wrote in his diary, "We were scared to death" about MacArthur, "fearing something had happened to him." Instead he came in the HQ for breakfast, set a German spiked helmet he had taken in the raid on the table, and described the raid calmly and casually the way he might describe watching a football game. "He ought to stay back here and not do such crazy stunts," Ogden thought, but he and the others couldn't help feeling a sense of admiration—not to mention envy.[15]

MacArthur had ignored orders, but it hadn't done him any harm. General Bazelaire pinned him with a Croix de Guerre, and Menhoer himself recommended him for a Silver Star, which he won.[16] Asked about whether his heading off on the raid might have technically violated orders, he answered with a quip: "Sometimes it is the order one disobeys that makes one famous."

They were words he would make into a career.

On March 1, the Forty-second made its first move into the trenches, and on March 9 the Rainbows made their first over-the-top advance, with the Iowans of the 168th leading the way.

Zero hour was five o'clock plus five minutes. French artillery zeroed in on their targets along the front, prepared to pound five minutes before the men of the Rainbow were due to attack. The Germans, sensing what was coming, struck first, with a counterbarrage of their own that swept over the Rainbow trenches like a tornado of flame.

The Iowans hunkered down as the shells screamed and burst overhead and chunks of steel flew in all directions. Then some of them noticed a strange figure in their midst, dressed in a turtleneck sweater and muffler and carrying a riding crop. When someone offered him a pistol and a helmet, he refused.

"I couldn't figure out what a fellow dressed like that was doing out there," a private remembered. "When I found out who he was, you could have knocked me over with a feather."[17]

It was MacArthur.

"There was a cold drizzle," MacArthur remembered, "the air was sharp with coming storm, the mud ankle deep. . . . I began to feel uneasy. You never really know about men at such a time. They were not professionals. Few of them had ever been under fire." He started to walk the line, steadying the men amid the chill and the wet and the explosions in the darkness.

Then MacArthur's watch hand hit five of five. "The night trembled with the thunderous belch of sixty batteries," as the French gunners answered the German barrage.[18]

Around him were officers and sergeants with whistles in their teeth, waiting for the signal.

The barrage went on until two minutes past five. Then three minutes, five minutes. The French gunners started lowering their gun sights as zero hour approached, and the next round of steel landed just in front of the Americans' line. It was the start of the "creeping barrage" that would accompany the Americans all the way to the German trenches, to blast away anything in their path.

"All ready, Casey?" MacArthur shouted to F Company's battalion commander, Captain Charles Casey.

"Okay, Colonel," Casey bellowed back. A chorus of whistles sprang up and down the line.

"Up you go," Casey urged his men. "Keep alignment. Guide is right. Don't rush or you'll get your own barrage on your neck!"

Four thousand Americans hurled themselves out of their trenches. "I went over the top as fast as I could," MacArthur remembered, "and scrambled forward." The blast from the creeping barrage ahead "was like a fiery furnace." Then his uneasiness returned.

"For a dozen terrible seconds I felt they were not following me. But then, without turning around, I knew how wrong I was. . . . In a moment they were around me, ahead of me, a roaring avalanche of glittering steel and cursing men."[19]

The cursing, swarming men were his Iowans, moving relentlessly toward the German trenches. Many fell, but many more bounded through the broken, tangled German wire. "We carried the enemy position," MacArthur wrote later—the brief words barely disguising the sense of triumph and exultation. It was his first full-scale action and a tiny victory by western front standards, but it was a foretaste of what the Forty-second could do when it was ably led.

He was immensely impressed by the Iowans' performance. The 168th had served under his father in the Philippines, and Douglas told some fellow officers now, "Is it any wonder my father was so proud of this regiment?"[20] A French staff officer who had watched the Americans under fire, told MacArthur in awed tones, "They conduct themselves like veterans. I have never seen better morale."[21]

"From then on," MacArthur would write, with a touch of exaggeration enhanced by pride, "the Rainbow was rated by both friend and foe a fighting ace." So was its chief of staff, who won a Distinguished Service Cross for the action and a new nickname: "the Fighting Dude."

The Fighting Dude, the Beau Brummell of the AEF, the d'Artagnan of the Army. The nicknames expressed a certain amusement but also a growing respect, as it became clear that MacArthur's outlandish costume was backed by the real goods. Menoher's recommendation for the Distinguished Service Cross said as much. "In the face of the determined and violent resistance of the enemy," it read, "he lent actual advice on the spot to the unit commanders, and by his supervision of the operation not only guaranteed its success" but let everyone in the Forty-second know that their chief of staff was with them not just in spirit but in the flesh—even when the shells were falling and the machine-gun bullets were flying.[22]

On March 20 the Forty-second sustained its first massive gas attack. The shells loaded with German mustard gas rained down on their positions just as they were preparing for another trench raid. The men of the 165th got the worst of it, especially those in K Company. More than four hundred found themselves blinded and choking: mustard gas, Private Ettinger remembered later, wasn't fatal, but it burned any part of the body that secreted moisture, like the eyes, the mouth, the lungs, hair under the helmet's sweatband, and even the genitals. Men who hadn't gotten their gas masks on in time lay helpless on the road for hours, blind and in severe pain, as medics passed from one huddled group to the next.[23]

Mustard gas wasn't fatal, but phosgene gas was, and MacArthur had gotten a faceful of it in a German attack three days earlier. His refusal to carry a gas mask had finally caught up with him, and while he rated it a "slight gassing" and recovered in less than a week, the reports that got back to his mother made her frantic.

She had left Washington and was now living with his brother Arthur's family in Santa Barbara, and garbled newspaper reports that MacArthur had been "severely wounded" led her to send a cablegram to General Pershing himself. Pershing took the time to straighten the story out and replied to her that all was well.

"Only God alone knows how great the comfort your reassuring message was to me," she wrote back to Pershing, "and I thank you right from the core of my heart. . . . We know your courage and ability—and realize you are the right man—in the right place."[24]

In fact, MacArthur had recovered well enough to accompany Newton Baker on a tour of the front on March 19, just the day before the main German gas attack. The secretary of war had secretly hoped he might see some real action, and on his tour of the lines held by his fellow Ohioans of the 166th, he did. A German 105 mm shell slammed down out of the sky about seventy-five feet from his touring car.

"That was a shell, wasn't it?" Baker said eagerly.

"Yes!" bellowed MacArthur, as he frantically tried to push Baker back into his car to get him out of the area.

"Then I may say I've been under fire, mayn't I?" the pacifist from Cleveland chortled delightedly. The incident made his French tour.

Baker was equally delighted with his former protégé. MacArthur regaled him with stories of his daring trench raids, and even presented him with the brass helmet of a Bavarian officer he had taken in one of them, which Baker sent along to Douglas's mother.[25] MacArthur, the secretary of war later told a group of correspondents, was "the most brilliant young officer in the army."

But the Fighting Dude was just getting started.

On March 21, the day after the mustard gas attack on the Rainbow, the entire western front came alive.

The predawn sky lit up over a fifty-mile front, as massed German artillery belched forth a bombardment of shrapnel, high explosives, and chemical weapons, and the morning mist grew green with phosgene, chlorine, and mustard gas.

Seventy-six German divisions, many of them fresh from victory over Russia on the eastern front, erupted from their trenches and poured out toward the Allied lines between La Bassée in the south and Dixmude in the north, where the British Fifth Army had only twenty-eight divisions. Only an hour after the attack began, the Germans had opened a chasm in the British lines almost twelve miles wide; by noon they had reached the Fifth Army's main battle line, where resistance was fierce but increasingly desperate. That afternoon, resistance all but collapsed; as the sun finally set, the war in the west had taken a dangerous new turn.[26]

Over the next four days the forty-mile-wide and forty-mile-deep advance was propelling the British to the brink of collapse, and with it the entire Allied cause. An emergency meeting was held at Doullens near Amiens—once the anchor of the Allied rear but now only twenty miles from the German advance. It was attended by France's president and prime minister as well as leading British and French generals. When the conversation paused, the participants could hear the German guns in the distance. Everything now had to be thrown into steadying the line, they decided, including the Americans—whether they were ready or not.

General Pershing immediately put his four divisions at their disposal. The

First Division moved up into the line near Cantigny on the British front. The Second and Third, which included two regiments of marines, swung into the French sector, where eventually the marines would launch a bloody counterattack on German lines at Belleau Wood in June.

Meanwhile, Pershing's evaluation of the Forty-second was that they were still not ready for full front-line service. But he did note that the division's chief of staff was "a bright young chap—full of life and go who will soon settle down and make a name for himself"—MacArthur, of course—and had to admit that the division "performed its work with excellent spirit and aggressiveness" and had won the respect and admiration of the French. So as the crisis mounted, Pershing ordered the Forty-second to the fortified line around the town of Baccarat to relieve three French divisions heading north to protect Paris from the onrushing German tide.[27]

The men of the Forty-second held the Baccarat line from March 31 until June 21. There were no major offensives or battles, but it was no rest stop. As Menoher told his officers, "When we get into sector we will take over No Man's Land. We will take it over and keep it." And with MacArthur at its head, that was exactly what the Rainbow did.

"For eighty-two days," MacArthur wrote later, "the division was in almost constant combat." Most of it took the form of trench raids of between a couple of dozen and a couple of hundred soldiers rushing across No Man's Land into the enemy trenches, to shoot up Germans and take prisoners, and then scramble back to their own lines as artillery shells exploded around them. In the first two weeks of June alone there were more than ninety such raids, along with "extended patrols" that carried the Americans right to the edge of the German barbed wire.[28]

MacArthur participated in as many as he could. He did so without orders, and some thought he was being more reckless than daring. But his recklessness had collaborators in men like Colonel Frank McCoy, commander of the 165th New Yorkers and his First Battalion commander Major William Donovan, who enjoyed his own unauthorized trench raids. Menoher and the Eighty-third's Brigadier Charles Lenihan also secretly encouraged the Fighting Dude. Donovan once even declared it would be "a blamed good thing" if MacArthur managed to get himself shot while up in the line. It'll be a huge boost to American morale, Donovan declared, provoking gales of laughter in the dugout that night. But as Father Duffy noted, "All five of them are wild Celts, whose opinion no sane man like myself would uphold."[29]

Over those three months the Forty-second slowly mastered the routine of trench warfare: the dawn stand-to, the patrols and cleaning and reinforcing trenches and dugouts, responding quickly to sudden gas attacks or artillery bombardments, and the inevitable patrols and raids after dark, when the Americans would return disappointed if they didn't find any Germans to shoot or capture. MacArthur saw that as a sign of high morale and unit pride. It proved once again that as far as modern warfare went, Americans were more than up for the challenge. "American citizen soldiers could take their place beside the best troops the war had produced," wrote his friend Major Henry Reilly, later the division's official historian, "and equal their best performance."[30]

But it came at a price: the division suffered almost 2,000 casualties during the three months in Baccarat. No other officer risked life and limb more than MacArthur, and his commanding officer noticed it. In his official report Menoher pronounced MacArthur "a most brilliant officer" and noted how his "excellent staff work" had made the division into "a complete, compact, cohesive, single unit which ran like a well-oiled machine."

General Pershing himself, however, took a different view.

On June 16 he sent orders to Menoher and MacArthur to prepare the division to entrain for the Champagne front, where they would be assigned to the French Fourth Army under General Henri Gouraud. He showed up on a surprise inspection on June 21 at the loading ramp in the train station at Charmes, just as the loading of artillery caissons, medical supplies, tents, and personal gear was reaching a pandemonious climax.

He strode straight up to MacArthur, who was supervising the sweaty work, and who threw out a surprised salute. Pershing glared, his famous white mustache bristling with rage.

"This division is a disgrace," he barked. "The men are poorly disciplined and they are not properly trained. The whole outfit is just about the worst I've seen."

MacArthur stood in stunned amazement. Soldiers and junior officers were clustered around the loading ramp, listening to every word as the commander in chief reamed out the Fighting Dude inch by inch.

"MacArthur," Pershing rasped loudly, "I'm going to hold you personally responsible for getting discipline and order in this division. I'm going to hold you personally responsible . . . I won't stand for this. It's a disgrace!"

Reddening with shame and rage, MacArthur barked back, "Yes sir!" and flung out his hand in salute. Pershing turned and stomped away.

MacArthur's aide Major Wolf had witnessed the entire incident. He turned to MacArthur, and saw that his face, which had been beet red, was now drained of blood to a deathly white.

Without a word MacArthur walked down the loading ramp, with Wolf following. He walked into the town past the lines of wagons and caissons and clusters of men who had just marched sixty kilometers in the mud to the railroad station. He automatically returned salutes but said nothing until he found a bench and sat down.

Wolf tried to explain that this was only Pershing's way, the kind of brutal discipline he like to mete out even to officers who were his favorites or on his staff. MacArthur would have none of it. There had to be a reason, MacArthur insisted, that Pershing had singled him out and humiliated him in this way in front of his own men.

The only thing he could come up with was his father, he told Wolf. It must have to do with some ancient resentment toward his father, who had commanded Pershing during their military mission to Japan—some never-forgotten injury by the father that Black Jack was now visiting on the son.[31]

Yet just five days after Pershing's visit an envelope arrived from Chaumont. It was MacArthur's promotion to brigadier general, signed by Pershing himself.

The news came to Pinky like a burst of sunshine. She read the news about her son's promotion, along with forty-three other officers, in the newspapers. On June 29 she wrote a short note of effusive thanks to Pershing. "I am sending in return, a heart full, pressed down, and overflowing with grateful thanks and appreciation. . . . You will not find our Boy wanting!"[32]

That was June 29. More than two weeks earlier, on June 12, she had written a much longer letter to Pershing, urging him to consider her son for promotion to brigadier general—precisely the step he had just taken. "My hope and ambition in life is to live long enough to see this son made a General Officer," she had written in closing, "and I feel I am placing my entire life, in your hands."[33] What with passing through the hands of wartime censors and transatlantic mail delivery, it's highly unlikely that Pershing saw the letter in time for it to influence his decision. In fact, it was not Pershing at all, but Peyton March, the chief of staff, who had attached MacArthur's name to the recommendation list (possibly at Newton Baker's urging—we'll never know) after crossing out five names Pershing had put forward. Pershing had acquiesced, but was still seething over March's interference. Indeed, later he tried to have the chief of staff fired.[34]

All the same, Pershing telegraphed a nice note back to the wife of his former commanding officer, congratulating her on her son's promotion. It must have been doubly gratifying for Pinky, thinking that she had somehow had a hand in securing MacArthur's position as the youngest brigadier general in the United States Army.

As for MacArthur, it took almost a week for him to finally acknowledge the promotion to Pershing.

> The warm admiration and affection that both my Father and Mother have always expressed, and their confidence in the greatness of your future, have only served to make my own service in your command during the fruition of their prediction the more agreeable. May you go on and up to the mighty destiny a grateful country owes you.

It would, however, take a long time for the scars from the blows at Charmes to heal—and the bond of trust between the two men would never be fully restored.

On July 2 the Forty-second moved into Champagne, to take up its final position beside the French Fourth Army. Given the name, the Rainbows had half expected to find a verdant land of grape leaves and tangled vines where "the bottles grew on trees," as Father Duffy put it, "and the thirsty traveler had but to detach the wire that held them."

Instead they found a landscape that reminded them more of Nebraska, or even Texas: "A broad expanse of flat brookless country with patches of scrimpy trees that surely must be mesquite."[35] The Fourth Army's commander was a battle-scarred French army legend named Henri Gouraud who was convinced that the Germans were coming, and coming soon—even while Pershing's staff at Chaumont confidently believed the Germans didn't have the strength for another major offensive.

In fact, while Douglas MacArthur was getting news of his promotion to brigadier general, the German high command had been doing the numbers, and making some decisions.

After an initial success and high casualties, their great March 21 offensive was officially a failure. The German army chief Ludendorff had ordered the offensive halted on June 3. He was facing the reality that while he couldn't replace the 200,000 men he had lost in battle, or the other half million that had been struck down by influenza, the French were replacing their losses with Americans. Twenty divisions of the AEF were already in or behind the front lines, with another fifty-five on the way—altogether some four million men.[36]

Time, as well as men, was running out on Ludendorff. On July 15 he would make one last throw of the dice in a fifty-division attack against the British in Flanders, preceded by a diversionary assault with no less than forty-seven divisions along the Champagne front, in a two-pronged push. One prong would head down toward Épernay to the south of Rheims, and the other would thrust toward Chalôns-sur-Marne in the east—where the Forty-second was standing exactly in Ludendorff's way.

Gouraud hosted a late-afternoon luncheon for the officers of the Forty-second on July 14, Bastille Day. When it was done, he rose to his feet and gave a speech that brought tears to everyone's eyes, MacArthur's included. "You all know that a defensive battle was never fought under more favorable conditions," he told them. "You will fight on terrain that you have trans-formed into a redoutable fortress. . . . None shall look to the rear; none shall yield a step. . . . Each shall have but one thought, to kill, to kill until [the Boche] have had their fill."

Gouraud had cunningly hosted the meal early, thinking the Germans might try to attack the day after Bastille Day, to catch the French after a long night of celebrations. Sure enough, as MacArthur and the other Americans returned to their posts in the early twilight they were met by news. A French patrol had caught some German prisoners, who had divulged the entire plan: the main barrage to begin at midnight, with infantry on the attack to follow four hours later.[37] The Americans alerted their men, headed for their dugouts, and waited long, tense hours for the onslaught.

At 11:30 the silence of the night was shattered by the roar of artillery—not German this time, but French. Gouraud had taken advantage of his advance warning to use his own batteries to pound the attackers as they grouped for the attack. The effect, according to German sources, was devastating. Some units were so depleted they had to be replaced before even leaving their trenches. Nonetheless, the Germans answered back, as some 3,500 guns on both sides blasted away simultaneously. "The whole sky seemed to be torn apart with sound," Father Duffy wrote, "while the whole southern [horizon] was punctuated by quick bursts of light."[38]

MacArthur was in the same dugout as General Gouraud. As the German barrage opened up, the electric power went out. In the darkness the French general turned his face toward heaven.

"Thank God," he muttered. He knew his plan was going to work.[39]

Some 2,000 German batteries—one gun every twenty yards—were firing in answer to the French. It was the most intense artillery concentration of the entire war. German shells landed in Châlons, twenty miles away. Someone later told MacArthur that one hundred miles away the roar of the guns had awakened Parisian families from their beds.[40]

Then the gray-clad Germans clambered out of their lines and rushed forward into the Fifth and Forty-second's advance line, killing any survivors. Then they surged ahead again, over the withered and beaten ground, toward the intermediate line where MacArthur and the rest of the Forty-second were waiting for them.

At 4:17 French and American sentinels fired off red rockets, warning the main body that the Germans were coming. Artillerymen and infantry scrambled from the dugouts to take their positions along the firing line.[41] MacArthur was standing on the trench firing step when suddenly the French and American artillery opened up again, as a fresh wall of fire "descended like an avalanche" on the advancing Germans. Another eyewitness said it was like a "boiling bank of smoke" had blanketed the Germans. This had been Gouraud's plan all along: to let the Germans get out beyond the range of their own artillery and pound them as they wandered defenseless and stranded in between the advance and middle line.

For the next several hours the Germans charged, broke against the Allied line, and fell back, only to charge again. As the morning light came up over the horrible scene, the Germans still pressed on. MacArthur could see them coming on wave after wave, but "when they met the dykes of our real line they were exhausted, uncoordinated, and scattered, incapable of going further." Yet every time they rushed toward the American line, the artillery, machine-gun, and infantry fire drove them back, leaving mounds of writhing bodies on the barbed wire.[42]

It was the Americans' first full-scale battle. Yet "there was no flinching on the part of our men," one officer said. "Wounded artillerymen in their gas masks continued serving their guns; infantrymen knocked down and bruised by shells, picked up their rifles again and continued firing."[43]

Instead, it was the Germans who were at the end of their strength. "Their legs are broken," MacArthur heard a French corps commander say, watching their increasingly feeble attacks. MacArthur passed the grim but triumphant message on to a cluster of American artillerymen whose guns were now so hot they had to be swabbed out after every shot.[44]

At around 11:00 A.M. there came a pause, and the smoke-filled, shattered air carried the shrill sound of whistles from the American trenches. It was time to drive the exhausted Germans back. With a bound over the parapet, still unarmed and still without a steel helmet, MacArthur led the first wave of counterattacks. Each grew more relentless than the last, until by afternoon the men of the Forty-second were back in their original advance line, rounding up prisoners and counting their dead.

The Americans had lost some 750 men—losses Douglas's father had never experienced in a single battle for all his campaigns. To the west a few German units managed to shove back elements of the Fifth Army and had to be driven back over three days of intense fighting. But the battle had been fought, and won and lost. "The Germans' last great attack of the war had failed," MacArthur would write years later, "and Paris could breathe again."

General Gouraud was ecstatic. His next bulletin to his army sounded a loud note of triumph. "The German has clearly broken his sword on our lines. . . . We have in our midst in the most perfect fraternity of arms the

Forty-second American division. We esteem it and are honored to rival them in courage and nerve."

And MacArthur had earned his second Silver Star.[45]

A few nights later MacArthur and some fellow officers wandered down to Chalôns to celebrate. They picked out the AEF's favorite tune, "Mademoiselle of Armentières," on the piano. They poured down glass after glass of champagne, followed by brandy and Armagnac. But Douglas MacArthur was disquieted. He would go on to see many more battles, and more of the grotesque horrors the battlefield could offer. But the memory of those German body parts hanging on the wire and the smell of decayed human flesh that permeated the trenches would haunt him that night and for the rest of his life.

"Perhaps I was just getting old; somehow I had forgotten how to play."[46] The soldier who forty years later would speak of abolishing war forever was born that day.

Meanwhile, there was a lot more fighting to be done.

CHAPTER 7

FIGHT TO THE FINISH

The art of war is simple. Find where the enemy is, and get at him as quickly as you can. Then hit him as hard as you can, and keep moving on.

—ULYSSES S. GRANT

The men of the Rainbow had little time for rest or reflection. Just three days after their mammoth battle at Souain, the battalion and company commanders found this note waiting for them from Chief of Staff Douglas MacArthur:

"Pursuant to orders from the 4th French Army, the 42nd Division . . . will, beginning on the morning of July 21st, proceed westward, by rail. . . . The definite destination of the division is unknown."[1]

With the Germans now on the defensive, Marshal Ferdinand Foch had decided to move quickly to crush the so-called Marne salient, a forty-five-mile bulge of territory the Germans had taken in their massive attacks since March. The salient extended south to Château-Thierry, and stretched west of Soissons and just east of Rheims. The move meant bringing up the Americans under his command into the Château-Thierry sector, for the thrust north.

The Forty-second arrived shortly after the Germans had evacuated Château-Thierry and while their artillery and supply wagons were still pulling back across the Marne. MacArthur and Menoher assumed that their men, still recovering from the battle the week before, would be held in reserve, but on July 25 General Hunter Liggett, commander of I Corps, had grown unhappy with the performance of his Twenty-sixth Division and stuck the Rainbow in its place in the advance.

The two divisions traded places under a steady dismal rain, and the National Guardsmen didn't get very far before they ran into German resistance. There was a savage hand-to-hand fight for control of a local landmark called Croix Rouge Farm that cost heavy casualties and won a corporal from the 167th a posthumous Medal of Honor. It wasn't until the early evening of July 27 that advance elements of the Eighty-third Brigade passed through the last line of trees and looked out over the banks of a narrow, low-lying river.[2]

It was the river Ourcq, not much more than a trout stream, but with long sloping open fields on each bank that would make an easy crossing if there were no Germans—and absolute hell if there were.

That evening the order came down from Sixth Army headquarters to MacArthur's command post: the Forty-second was to conduct a full-scale advance across the Ourcq the next morning. MacArthur had his doubts; still edgy after the brutal fight at Souain, he knew that no one was sure how many Germans, if any, were still lurking on the far side of the river. Bill Donovan at the head of his battalion of New York Irishmen thought the sector looked "too quiet," and decided to make a quick reconnaissance.

As his men approached the tiny village on the near bank, they came under heavy German artillery that drove them back in the darkness to the far side of the hill overlooking the river. Even so, the fire was intense enough that while "kneeling down and talking to two or three officers a shell burst within ten feet of us, killing 7 next to me and smothering us with dirt."[3]

While Donovan and his men were hunkering down under the shell fire, MacArthur was pointing out to Sixth Army HQ that the Forty-second still didn't have any artillery to cover their advance. All the same, he barked into the field telephone, they would obey orders. The attack would begin at 4:30 on the morning of the 28th.

But if the artillery wouldn't be there to help, at least MacArthur would be.

As the Americans moved forward in the predawn darkness, Donovan's and MacArthur's worst fears were realized. Far from pulling back, the Germans had put no fewer than three divisions in the line overlooking the

Ourcq, along with what MacArthur that evening described as "one of the 'aces' of the German Army," the Fourth Guards. Their machine guns were pointed straight down on the men of the 165th's Third Battalion as they waded across the Ourcq.[4]

The moment they reached the water, the Germans opened up. The Third's lead company, K Company under Captain John Patrick Hurley, took the brunt of the firestorm. Within minutes three of Hurley's five lieutenants were dead, and another wounded. The Third Battalion's commander, Major MacKenna, was killed, then Hurley himself took a bullet when he scrambled back to talk to his commander, McCoy. But McCoy had no choice. He had to order his other battalions forward, including Donovan's.

MacArthur was close enough to the front to feel stray bullets whiz by as he watched the Irishmen stubbornly advance, then halt and wither under the hail of gunfire. The Second and Third Battalions finally dropped back, leaving Donovan and his men stranded at the crest of Meurcy Farm, with German guns firing at them from three sides and German airplanes strafing them mercilessly overhead. His battalion managed to hold its ground, but the rest of the assault that day stalled out. Alabamans and Iowans of the Eighty-fourth Brigade did manage to fight their way into the village of Sergy overlooking the crest three times, but each time they were driven out by a furious German counterattack.[5]

"A day of very fierce infantry fighting," MacArthur wrote at midnight in his terse intelligence report. "Along our whole front the battle rolled back and forth all day." The battle resumed before dawn and continued through the 29th, with groups of two or three soldiers crawling toward German machine-gun positions to toss a couple of hand grenades and then leap forward with bayonets. "It was savage," MacArthur remembered years later, "and there was no quarter asked or given."[6] When the sun finally set, Donovan's battalion was still holding on, although no one had any food or water— and every officer in his headquarters command except one was either dead or wounded.[7]

MacArthur meanwhile, passing from position to position to rally the men and coordinate attacks, received an unusual message. The ever-cautious General Brown of the Eighty-fourth Brigade had twice countermanded orders for artillery support, for fear it might land too close to his troops. Meno-her had finally had enough. He had relieved Brown and told his chief of staff that he, Douglas MacArthur, was now in charge of the Eighty-fourth.[8]

MacArthur was too busy dodging shell and machine-gun fire to reflect on this signal honor, his first combat command. But that night he led his men on a bayonet charge into Sergy much as his father might have done, and that night the Eighty-fourth took the village and kept it.

Still the fighting went on, day and night, for the next forty-eight hours. "The enemy made strong efforts to force us back beyond the Ourcq but failed at all points," MacArthur wrote in his intelligence brief. "Shell fire during the morning was heavier than the day before and [a] large proportion of gas was used."[9]

Meanwhile, at the crest of Meurcy Farm, Donovan still fought on. On the night of July 30–31, "I had no more than one and a half hours sleep all night," Donovan wrote to his wife later. In most of his companies the only surviving officers were second lieutenants.[10] It was not until the early-morning hours of the 31st that headquarters was able to get Donovan's men out of their positions at Meurcy Farm and down to Sergy, which MacArthur had captured two nights before. They had taken 600 casualties out of 1,000 men. The hearts of the other two battalions had also been cut out. More than half of the 165th Regiment, the old Fighting Sixty-ninth, were either dead or wounded. But the division was now firmly established across the Ourcq, and for his leadership and endurance in the battle Donovan would earn a Medal of Honor.

MacArthur, though, was worried what might happen next.

He knew the terrible price the 165th, and his own battalions, had paid. "The dead were so thick in spots we tumbled over them," he wrote later, remembering the path that led out from Sergy. "The stench was suffocating. . . . There must have been 2000 of those sprawled bodies. I identified the insignia of six of the best German divisions."[11] But the Germans were still out there, still ready for a fight or even a counterattack. Securing what had been won now depended on a steady advance forward along the entire heavily wooded four-kilometer front. MacArthur raced from "regiment to regiment, urging, pleading . . . for one last push" to consolidate the line.

All refused. They were exhausted and licking their wounds; they had no official orders to advance. Instead, rumor had it they were about to be relieved by the regulars of the Fourth Division, anyway. It wasn't until MacArthur reached Frank McCoy just before dawn and explained the situation—that if McCoy could get his men moving, the rest of the division might follow—that he got the answer he wanted.

McCoy summoned Meaney, commander of the 165th's Third Battalion now that MacKenna was dead, who listened stoically to MacArthur's plea. They had just buried Joyce Kilmer, the famous poet, who had been Donovan's acting sergeant major before he caught a German bullet in the brain.

Then Meaney said, "My men are few and they are tired, but they are willing to go anywhere they are ordered and," he added with a half smile, "they will consider an order to advance as a compliment." In a few minutes the weary survivors of the 165th rose to their feet and started cautiously forward. As MacArthur predicted, the other units saw them moving in the dim early light and began moving as well.

"By God," he swore to McCoy, "it takes the Irish when you want a hard thing done!"[12]

Back at headquarters the weary MacArthur met Menoher and Liggett, the corps commander. He explained what he had done, with difficulty. "I had not slept for four days and nights, and was so drowsy everything was beginning to black out." As Liggett spoke to Menoher about how to get his artillery across the river, MacArthur sank into a chair and fell fast asleep.

Liggett gazed down at the commander of the Eighty-fourth.

"Well, I'll be damned," he said. "Menoher, you better cite him."[13]

Menoher did. "In advance of orders," he wrote later, "and without delay he galvanized the entire division into a prompt pursuit. . . . General MacArthur personally instructed each of the infantry regiments of the division, moving along the entire divisional front of four kilometers and swung the artillery and supporting arms into immediate accompaniment despite a terrain which hardly offered a road."[14]

Mac had won not only his third Silver Star for his bravery in the fighting on July 28, but his fourth for his actions on the night of August 1, which had given the Allies control of the entire sector. It also brought them to the edge of the Vesle River, the Marne salient's last redoubt.

* * *

MacArthur's fifth Silver Star came a little over a month later.

In the days after Ourcq the Forty-second found itself in a furious chase north to the Nesle Forest and beyond. "Have personally assumed command of the line," ran MacArthur's breathless communiqué to Menoher marked 12:10 P.M. on August 2. "Have broken the enemy's resistance on the right. Immediately threw forward my left and broke his front. . . . I am using small patrols acting with great speed and continually flanking him . . . I am handling the columns myself, and my losses are extraordinarily light."[15]

Then suddenly in the early-morning hours of August 3, the Forty-second was relieved and dropped back as corps reserve, to the same battlefield they had fought across the week before. "In 8 days of battle," Donovan wrote, "our Division had forced the passage of the Ourcq, taken prisoners from 6 enemy divisions, met, routed, and decimated a crack division of the Prussian Guards . . . and driven back the enemy's line for 16 kilometers." But it had come at a high price. The Rainbow had suffered some 6,500 casualties, both officers and men. MacArthur's own brigade, the Eighty-fourth, had lost more than half of its effectives.[16]

Still, their success was due in no small measure to the Forty-second's former chief of staff and new brigadier, with his soft cap and sweaters and riding crop, and foppish exterior that disguised the heart of a warrior. When HQ in Chaumont tried to pull him away to train and command a brigade of a new division, the Eleventh, in the States, Menoher put up a furious fight to keep MacArthur at his side. He called him "the source of the greatest possible inspiration" and told Chaumont his men "are devoted to him."[17]

Pershing's HQ relented and MacArthur was allowed to stay. They would need him at the fighting front, and the Forty-second, for the punishing campaign ahead.

For two weeks in the rear the division found rest and replacements; "cannon fodder," as one cynical lieutenant in the 168th put it.[18] Then on August 28 they were on the move back to the front, and prepared themselves for the main offensive on the St. Mihiel salient.

This was a cluster of German fortified positions 200 miles in area and 16 miles deep, centered around the town of St. Mihiel and located just south of the major rail hub of Metz. Capture of St. Mihiel and Metz would not only put a serious crimp in the German front, it would also provide a major junction for pushing the Germans out of France, possibly even ending the war.[19] So Pershing was bringing almost a quarter million American and 110,000 French troops against St. Mihiel's defenders, with his blooded veteran divisions—the First, Second, Twenty-sixth, and the Rainbow Forty-second—leading the charge.[20]

The Forty-second had arrived at its forward position on the night of September 10–11 after tramping for days through incessant rain, with sodden patches of forest and roads turned to squelching mud at every step, while taking more than a thousand German prisoners, who were hustled off to the rear. Pleased with their rapid progress though he was, physically MacArthur felt worse and worse. He was coming down with a severe fever, and when he arrived at their position he was almost prostrate.

For now, however, he returned to his troops as all the next day the Americans jammed themselves into the lines of trenches—"a hopeless labyrinth, full of mud and water," future historian Walter Langer later remembered—facing the southern edge of the salient, with the Eighty-fourth Brigade tapped to lead the first wave of attack. The Rainbow learned that the scuttlebutt at Chaumont was that there could be as many as 75,000 casualties, and that the advance bombardment had been scaled back to catch the Germans by surprise.

MacArthur was as horrified as he was outraged. He consulted with his brigade artillery officers, who agreed they would pour on extra shells and not tell HQ. It was now that MacArthur quipped to Major Reilly the line that would become his trademark: "Sometimes it is the order one disobeys that makes one famous." At the time, however, it expressed less cockiness than it did desperation and anger—not to mention a high fever.[21]

MacArthur was in the full grip of his illness and sicker than he had ever been in his life. Yet he absolutely refused to be left behind. He told his headquarters staff he was going forward with his troops, even if they had to carry him on a stretcher. MacArthur and his men then spent the remaining hours of September 11, 1918, waiting for the bombardment to begin.

It came at 1:00 A.M. on the dot. "A man-made aurora borealis shot out of the wall of darkness," as Major Fred Palmer described it. "All the world, inclosed under canopy of night, was aflame." The bombardment went on for four hours, until at 5:00 A.M. the men of the Eighty-fourth Brigade rose out of their trenches into the lifting mists with bayonets fixed, and advanced.[22]

And advanced. And advanced. To their amazement, the resistance the Forty-Second met was weak and sporadic; the tanks they were supposed to have in support were all hopelessly stuck in the mud, but they weren't needed. The fact was, the Germans had gotten advance warning of the attack and were pulling out. Even better, the German artillery that was supposed to pound the Americans and French as they moved forward had been caught on the road by the American bombardment and virtually destroyed.

All the same, enough artillery shells passed overhead that at one point the brigade took shelter in a row of shell holes—all except MacArthur. That's where history stepped in. The colonel of the tanks supposed to support the Eighty-fourth came up on foot and found MacArthur alone, standing on a little hill and gazing ahead at the German lines. "I joined him and creeping barrage came along toward us," the colonel wrote to his wife that night. "I think each one of us wanted to leave but each hated to say so, so we let it come over us."

One shell did explode nearby, showering them with dirt but leaving them unhurt. The tank colonel told his wife he had flinched, but not ducked. MacArthur hadn't moved a muscle. "Don't worry, Colonel," he told him, "you never hear the one that gets you." They both laughed and shook hands. They never met again. But years later that colonel would command an army in the next world war.

His name was George S. Patton. He would set his own standard of courage under fire. But as he wrote to his family, in his opinion MacArthur was "the bravest man I ever met."[23]

Meanwhile, mile after mile MacArthur's men enveloped the Germans in their front from both flanks, as the prisoners headed back in droves, "with a doughboy in the rear prodding the laggards with a bayonet whenever necessary." Early that afternoon they passed their day's objective; before nightfall they had reached the objective for the second day.

On the second day the advance continued almost unhindered, and by afternoon MacArthur climbed a low hill and looked north. From the top of a small knoll on the third day, he could even see across the entire Woevre Plain to the hazy spires of Metz, barely a dozen miles away. "There it lay," he later wrote, "our prize wide open for the taking."[24] But their orders were to halt and dig in. On all fronts, the advance had been an amazing success. Instead of the 50,000 casualties Pershing had anticipated, there had been not more than 8,000, barely 2.5 percent of the troops engaged. Even as roads for miles jammed with Allied vehicles headed for Metz, Pershing and his officers relaxed to digest their relatively bloodless triumph.

But not MacArthur. As night fell he tapped his adjutant Major Wolf on the shoulder and the two of them managed to sneak their way several miles to the outskirts of Metz. There was no sign of the Germans; they had all pulled back to other sectors. "Here was an unparalleled opportunity to break the Hindenburg Line at its pivotal point," MacArthur believed, and he intended to convince his superiors of the same thinking.

But when he reached Pershing's HQ in the morning he met only stony faces. They could be in Metz, he heatedly argued, in forty-eight hours—and from there Pershing could drive straight into central Germany. "The President will make you a field marshal," he pleaded to Pershing himself. MacArthur was exhausted, still feverish, but above all exasperated at what he saw as the blind pigheadedness of the man.

Pershing, however, refused to change his plans. He had his Allies to think about; American unilateral action would trigger a fierce French and British reaction. Besides, what if MacArthur was wrong? He mentioned none of these things to MacArthur, but at last exasperated at being berated in his own office, Pershing barked, "Get out! And stay out!"

Outside, MacArthur shook his head ruefully. "I made a mistake," he told Wolf. "I should have taken Metz and then asked his permission."[25]

He may have been right, although the German commander in charge, General Max von Gallwitz, said after the war he believed Metz's defenses were strong enough to withstand any sudden American assault. On the other hand, Pershing's own assistant operations officer at GHQ, Colonel George C. Marshall, agreed that Metz was ripe for the taking. "There is no doubt in my mind," he later wrote, "but that we could have reached the outskirts of Metz by the late afternoon of the 13th, and quite probably have captured the city on the 14th"—which might have shortened the war by weeks, perhaps even a month. Marshall also dismissed the fear that the Germans might have had sufficient forces to mount a counterattack.[26]

Right or wrong in retrospect, for MacArthur it was a glaring example "of the inflexibility in the pursuit of previously conceived ideas," which, he added, was "too frequent in modern warfare. All too often, final decisions are made not at the front by those who are there but many miles away by those who can but guess at the possibilities and potentialities." His own frequent clashes with the Joint Chiefs during World War Two over strategy in the Pacific, and the final titanic clash with President Truman during the Korean War, all took first shape under the mist-covered spires of Metz.

And indeed, within a week the Germans had brought up reinforcements and the opportunity to take Metz was lost. In his memoirs Pershing had to agree.[27] But what he did not tell the brash young brigadier general was that Metz, tempting target though it was, no longer played a part in his plans. Pershing's mind was already fixed on his next objective, one that had been his final goal for weeks—and one in which Mac himself would play a major, even decisive, part.

This was the Argonne Forest.

On August 30 Supreme Commander Marshal Foch visited Pershing's HQ. The Germans were disorganized and on the retreat, he said, after the collapse of their last offensive. "We must not allow them an opportunity to reorganize," Foch urged. What he now proposed was that while the British continued to push toward Cambrai and Saint Quentin, and the French toward Mesnil, the Americans would bring their troops into the Aisne sector, far to the west of Verdun, for a decisive battle there.

Pershing thought for a moment and then said, "Why not have the Americans take the entire sector from the Meuse to the Argonne?" It was an unexpected, if not exactly strange, idea. It would prevent American troops from being split apart in the push forward, and allow the First Army to concentrate its forces on a single objective. Foch agreed, and on September 2 the plan was confirmed. This meant that when MacArthur confronted Pershing with his idea of sweeping on to Metz, the AEF commander had already made

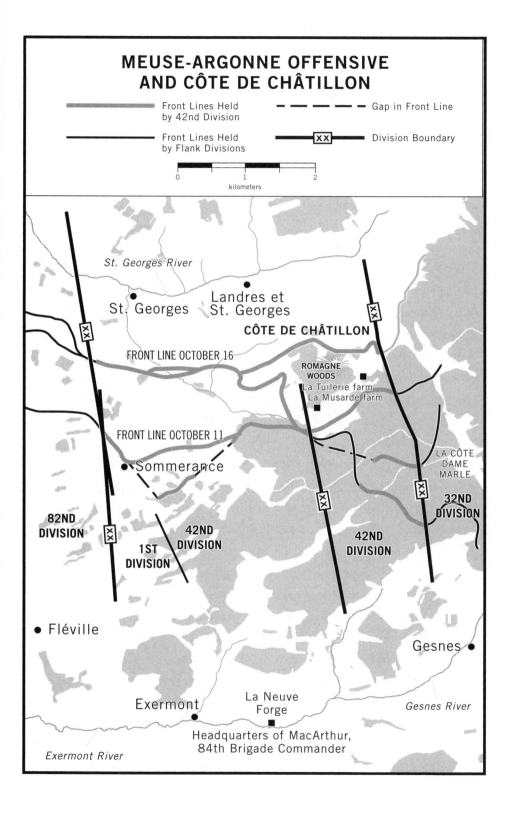

MEUSE-ARGONNE OFFENSIVE AND CÔTE DE CHÂTILLON

Front Lines Held by 42nd Division

Gap in Front Line

Front Lines Held by Flank Divisions

Division Boundary

0   1   2
kilometers

St. Georges River

St. Georges

Landres et St. Georges

CÔTE DE CHÂTILLON

FRONT LINE OCTOBER 16

ROMAGNE WOODS
La Tuilerie farm
La Musarde farm

FRONT LINE OCTOBER 11

Sommerance

LA CÔTE DAME MARLE

82ND DIVISION

1ST DIVISION

42ND DIVISION

42ND DIVISION

32ND DIVISION

Fléville

Gesnes

Exermont

La Neuve Forge

Gesnes River

Headquarters of MacArthur, 84th Brigade Commander

Exermont River

up his mind. The Americans' decisive push would not be toward Metz, but into the Argonne Forest.[28]

Unfortunately for Pershing's men, the forest formed a natural fortress bounded by two rivers and covered with thick woods and steep ridges, some rising as high as 750 feet above the valley. An American who fought over it described it as "a bleak, cruel country of white clay and rock and blasted skeletons of trees, gashed into innumerable trenches and scarred with rusted acres of wire, rising steeply into claw-like ridges and descending into haunted ravines, white as leprosy in the midst of that green forest, a country that had died years ago in pain." It was against this natural stronghold that Pershing would now commit his million-man force, a stronghold that Germany had fortified for four years with bunkers and hundreds of machine-gun nests and mortar outposts, not to mention miles of staked barbed wire.[29]

The decision was ratified on September 2, yet Pershing had gone ahead with his headlong assault on the St. Mihiel salient, which meant his most battle-toughened divisions, including the Forty-second, wouldn't be there to open the assault on the Argonne. Instead, he would have to rely on troops freshly arrived from New York State, like the Seventy-seventh, to crack open the German line.

Meanwhile, the Forty-second regrouped around St. Benoit for three weeks, where the magnificent château served as Brigadier General Douglas MacArthur's headquarters. German artillery was intermittent but menacingly accurate—one shell burst almost hit the room in which he was sleeping. But it wasn't until he learned from some German prisoners that a "big gun" was being brought up to bombard the château that he decided prudence demanded he shift headquarters. The next day, September 24, a massive 280 mm shell slammed squarely into the château, "leaving a smoldering heap of stone and a jagged mass of wall," one awed eyewitness, an Alabaman from the 167th Infantry, recounted, "its pink and blue draperies . . . its music room; its old tapestries hanging in its stone hallway—all gone."[30]

MacArthur's luck, or destiny, had held again. The story that he told officers of his staff, "All of Germany cannot fabricate a shell that will kill MacArthur," is almost certainly apocryphal—or a bad joke. But his stoic belief that when his time to die had come, it would come and not before, also prompted him to join in a particularly dangerous night raid on September 25—and earned him his sixth Silver Star.

When MacArthur and his men returned from the raid, far to the west they could hear what sounded like the distant rumble of thunder. It was in fact the rumble of the guns of war. Pershing's Argonne offensive was about to start.

Pershing's push into the Argonne opened on September 26 with 2,700 guns, 189 small tanks, and 821 airplanes flying in support, and quickly ground to a halt. The Americans soon discovered that they had, in historian Geoffrey Perret's words, "walked into a buzzsaw."

The plan was for a double thrust through the forest on either side of the main redoubt, the Romagne Heights. But too many of Pershing's divisions were still green, and the inexperienced troops simply dropped and hugged the ground in the face of withering German fire. Thousands of others fled to the rear. Only a few tried to press forward, and when they did they became disoriented and cut off. One of those units was the legendary Lost Battalion, six companies of the 308th Infantry and one company from the 307th from the Seventy-seventh Division, along with a machine-gun detachment, who held out surrounded for five days without food or water while the Germans pounded their position with machine-gun and mortar fire, and even flame-throwers. When relief came, half of those still alive had to be carried out by stretcher. It was heroic, but not the way to win a war.[31]

Finally, on October 1 Pershing decided he needed to refocus the attack around his veteran divisions, and take the Romagne Heights by frontal assault. He had run out of ideas, and options. "There is no course but to fight it out," he wrote in his diary. That meant the Forty-second was going into action again, and so MacArthur and the Eighty-fourth Battalion set out for the Romagne Heights and the Kriemhilde Redoubt.

The Germans called it the Kriemhilde Redoubt, or Kriemhilde Stellung, after one of Brunnhilde's sisters. Like the Valkyries of legend, it was broad, strong, and impregnable. It consisted of miles of barbed wire and concrete pillboxes, with hundreds of enfilading machine-gun nests and fortified bunkers. And at the heart of the complex was a cluster of fortified hills, one of which was known simply as Hill 288, while to its northeast sat the biggest, known locally as the Côte de Châtillon.

The Forty-second arrived at the foot of the Romagne Heights in a dismal rain on October 11. MacArthur could make out Hill 288 through the misting rain, and to its right the Côte, rising abruptly from the valley for several hundred feet. The Rainbows were taking over from the First Division. The men of the Big Red One had given their everything in attacking the twin hills and gotten nowhere. Decomposed bodies in olive drab lay on every side, and the Germans greeted the new arrivals with a withering gas attack.

MacArthur, who was up front with his troops as usual, caught a full whiff of the gas and for a while his adjutant, Major Wolfe, thought MacArthur's luck had finally run out and his part in the war was over. But MacArthur had seen that the position the 168th Regiment was supposed to start from would come directly under the next day's artillery fire.[32] There was no time to worry about himself. Instead he spent the evening going from point to point, moving the 168th to a safer position before he finally collapsed on his cot, ill and vomiting.

"I carry no gas mask because it hampers my movements," MacArthur later explained when an army board of inquiry asked about his unorthodox methods, adding, "I don't wear an iron helmet because it hurts my head. I go unarmed because it is not my purpose to engage in personal combat, but to direct others."[33] Maybe so, but MacArthur paid the price again the next day, with yet another dose of gas even as the Forty-second prepared for the main assault, as they relieved elements of the Thirty-second Division on their right and their main artillery came up. The plan was brutal and simple. The Eighty-third on the left would advance a mile across open ground to take the villages of St. George, where three separate lines of staked barbed wire with machine-gun nests in between awaited them. The Eighty-fourth's line of advance was slightly easier, but in order to take Hill 288 and the Côte from their jumping-off point they would be moving straight uphill.

MacArthur knew the hardship that was coming. On the march up he had watched the Thirty-second trying unsuccessfully to take the heights of Mont-faucon, and had seen the terrible price it paid. The mistake, he was beginning to realize, was trying to break the enemy by attacking his center, instead of finding a vulnerable flank. He began to have a growing sinking feeling as he looked around along the "heavily wooded valleys of death between . . . end-less folds of ridges," all of them under incessant heavy fire. Many men would die if he tried to get them around the German flank; but many more would die if he didn't.[34]

By evening the men of his brigade were as ready as they could be. Yet MacArthur told Menoher he had "many misgivings" about what would hap-pen the next day. Menoher asked him point-blank if his brigade could take the Côte. MacArthur answered, "As long as we are speaking in the strictest confidence, I am not certain."

Then that night MacArthur had an unexpected visitor. It was Major Gen-eral Charles Summerall, the new V Corps commander. Summerall had the reputation of being a tough man, headstrong and hard-driving, but that night when he dropped by MacArthur's command post he looked "tired and worn, and I made him a cup of steaming black coffee, strong enough to blis-ter the throat."

Summerall glared across his cup at the younger man. A career officer, Summerall had known MacArthur's father, and he had seen the Côte bleed his First Division in their desperate attacks already. He had no time for the Fighting Dude's fine attitudes or (it seemed to him) insouciant confidence.

"You will give me Côte de Châtillon tomorrow," he snapped, "or turn in a report of 5000 casualties."

MacArthur's smile faded and he stiffened to attention. "This brigade will capture Côte de Châtillon tomorrow, sir," he said in a matter-of-fact tone, "or you can report every man in it as a casualty. And at the top of the list will be the name of the brigade commander."

Summerall was taken aback, and tears seemed to well up in his eyes. The general said nothing else, then opened the door and stepped out into the blackness.[35]

The Forty-second's advance began just before dawn on October 14. The scene soon became a nightmare.

The Eighty-third Brigade had it worst. It ran straight into a curtain of fire that American artillery could do nothing to abate, and when men crawled forward to cut the wire, they were shot down one by one, their bodies left hanging on the wire like pigeons on a game line.

This part of the assault was supposed to be supported by tanks, but they quickly ran into difficulties. Twenty-five started out, of which sixteen actually made it to the front, but only ten managed to move forward over the rough, broken ground—and when the German shells zeroed in on their track they quickly turned around and went back. So the men of the Eighty-third, led by the redoubtable 165th, went ahead alone as the full weight of the German fire fell on them. A German counterattack followed, which the Irishmen of the 165th beat back, but they weren't advancing any farther that day.[36]

On the right, the Eighty-fourth Brigade's luck was just as bad. MacArthur, as usual, was in the first wave, and he remarked to one of his men as they climbed out of their trenches, "If this is good, I'm in it. And if it's bad, I'm in it, too." It *was* bad. The men of the Third Battalion, 167th got entangled in the enemy wire after advancing just 200 meters. They tried for three hours to get up the face of the Côte and failed, until their Lieutenant Colonel Bare called off any more attempts to get past that first line of wire. On the other side, the Iowans of the 168th managed, under very heavy machine-gun fire, to get almost to the crest of Hill 288 by 1:00 P.M. But when they tried to take the enemy trenches on the opposite slope with the help of men from the Thirty-second Division, they were bloodily repulsed. As darkness set in at 5:00 they were clinging to the southern slope near the crest, but barely clinging.[37]

Côte de Châtillon remained as defiant and impregnable as ever.

By that time an exhausted and frustrated MacArthur was back down at the command post on the telephone with Menoher.

"I will continue the attack during the night," he barked over the phone. "I will give orders to do no firing but to clean up with the bayonet." MacArthur had seen this done once before by the Alabamans of the 167th in the fight for Croix-Rouge, and figured it might clear the resistance off the Côte.

"Is it all right?" he asked.

"It is," squeaked Menoher's voice over the phone.

"All right, I will give those orders. Good night."[38]

MacArthur's plan was unorthodox and dangerous. The Alabamans, after all, had suffered 50 percent casualties. But that had been in broad daylight;

this would be at night and might catch the Germans napping. Besides, if General Summerall would be satisfied only with a defeat that meant lots of corpses, this was one grim and sure way to do it.

The other officers in the Eighty-fourth, however, were appalled and said so. Lieutenant Royal Little of 167th's Third Battalion thought "the order was so ridiculous that I immediately rushed to battalion headquarters to find out who had perpetrated this abortion." Major Revee Norris of the same regiment told his commander, Colonel Bare, "No firing! It's nothing short of murder to send men in on such an assault."[39] Ross of the 168th told MacArthur the order was physically impossible. To bypass the masses of machine-gun nests and wire by moving left toward Côte de Châtillon would leave them bumping into the 167th in the dark. Men might end up bayoneting one another instead of the enemy; and the overall commotion would mean the end of any surprise.

In any case, MacArthur's plan had to wait because Menoher decided to try an extensive artillery barrage that evening instead, to see if that would dislodge the Germans. It did not, although Lieutenant Little's company saw two men killed and several wounded in the darkness from the friendly fire.

The next day the Eighty-fourth tried five times to take Hill 288, but each time the heavy machine-gun fire from Châtillon drove them back. Each time MacArthur rallied his troops and led them up the hill again—only to see the assault break down as men prostrated themselves on the hillside to avoid the incessant fire.

As the sunlight faded to twilight the men returned to their trenches, waiting for darkness and the dreaded bayonet charge. MacArthur summoned Bare, Matthew Tinley of the 168th Iowa, and Major Cooper Winn, commander of his machine-gun battalion, to his dugout to discuss the plan. They had barely gotten started when the phone rattled. It was Summerall, checking in on the progress in taking Châtillon. He had already fired the commander of the Eighty-third for poor performance; now he wanted to know if the Eighty-fourth planned to do any better.

His voice was so loud that Bare could make out every angry syllable. Châtillon was the key to the entire show, Summerall kept saying; he wanted it taken by six o'clock on the 16th.

"We will take the Côte de Châtillon by tomorrow," MacArthur barked back, "or report a casualty list of 6000 dead. That will include me," he added and slammed the phone down.[40]

Then Mac turned to the sober little group. *Any ideas?* his grim face said. Now Bare spoke up.

"I have been up there forty-eight hours," he said. "I am to make the attack. Am I to have nothing to say about it?"

"Well, what have you got to say about it?" MacArthur wanted to know.

Bare explained that his Lieutenant Little, in storming the slopes of the hill, had noted that the wire along the northwestern side of the Côte was brand-new and barely completed. In fact, an aerial photograph (one of the few they had from Colonel Billy Mitchell's wing, which was focused more on bombing than reconnaissance) showed a gap in the German wire to the northeast, close to the hillside hamlet known as Musarde Farm.

MacArthur pondered. Maybe this was the opportunity he had been looking for: a double envelopment with his two regiments, the 167th and the 168th, swarming through the weakest parts of the German lines and then converging at the crest. He decided to call off the bayonet charge; a deeply relieved Bare told him there was an open ravine between Hill 263 and Tinley's 168th. If Bare could put a battalion in there, he said, with machine-gun fire from Winn's battalion keeping the Germans pinned down, his men could scramble up the northeast face of Châtillon and into the gap in the wire.[41]

Tinley enthusiastically agreed. "I will be delighted not only to cooperate in any way I can but will take orders if necessary from Colonel Bare." Then Winn spoke up. A massed machine-gun fusillade could pin down and distract the Germans; this was exactly the opportunity he was looking for, to prove his machine gunners' mettle. MacArthur agreed to the plan; the mood went at once from somber to enthusiastic, even ecstatic. The officers headed back to their units, and Bare picked Major George Glenn's Third Battalion to lead the way into the dark ravine.

That night MacArthur organized his own reconnaissance, leading a patrol along in the dark until they confirmed what Little had reported: the German wire, almost twenty feet thick and impenetrable at the center, dribbled out at the ends. A strike "with my Alabama cotton-growers on the left, my Iowa farmers on the right" with "every machine gun and every artillery piece as covering fire" just might work.[42]

Suddenly out of the darkness came a surprise German artillery barrage. The shells exploded around as men slithered into every available shell hole. The flashes of explosions lit up the battleground, the tangles of wire, the men lying silent in their shell holes. Then when it lifted, MacArthur went from hole to hole to rally the rest of the patrol. "Follow me," he whispered to each shaking the man's shoulder; "we're going to go back to the Rainbow lines."

No one moved. MacArthur shook one of his men harder. The figure slumped over in the darkness. Then MacArthur realized the truth: each and every man in his patrol was dead. All except him. Somehow he had been spared.

It was, MacArthur told a friend afterward, like a revelation. "It was God, He led me by the hand, the way he led Joshua." God had spared him as a matter of destiny—and that destiny was to lead the final charge the next morning.[43]

At dawn, MacArthur moved out for a last word with Ross, Bare, and the other commanders. Then at 5:30 he watched Ross's First Battalion of the 168th Iowa make their move out from Tuilerie Farm. A battalion from the 167th Alabama drawn from eight different companies was not far behind, moving right toward the opening in the wire.[44]

Then a deafening machine-gun barrage of sixty guns opened up on the German lines, sweeping their positions with more than a million rounds as the Germans hunkered down in their bunkers. Meanwhile, Ross's men had found the gap, and were pouring around the German flank; the Alabamans were doing the same on the left side of Châtillon, as men rose up and dashed forward across open ground, then dropped down as German bullets whizzed overhead.

"Officers fell and sergeants leaped to the command," MacArthur wrote, describing the scene. "Companies dwindled to platoons and corporals took over." Lieutenant Little and his fellow Alabamans found themselves pinned down on the slope from heavy machine-gun fire, but after conferring with one another, Little and the other officers agreed to give a whistle blow in unison and then "rush all forward together. It worked." The Germans panicked and pulled back, while Little's captain chased them up the hill. Little himself led one hundred men around to the southwest, where they found a passage through the wire into the German flank. In moments the trenches were theirs, as men scrambled to the crest.[45]

Meanwhile, Ross's men had found a similar breach on their side, slithered through, and reached the top of the Côte de Châtillon, only to see the Alabamans coming up in a frenzy from the other side. The Germans, overwhelmed by the Americans suddenly sweeping up from their flanks and rear, began throwing down their rifles and abandoning their machine guns.[46]

MacArthur's men had little time to celebrate their success. The Germans launched two desperate counterattacks to retake the hill. A well-timed artillery barrage by the Field Artillery Brigade broke up one; massed rifle fire from the Iowans and Alabamans drove off the other. By nightfall, Châtillon had been taken. Major Ross had only 300 men and 6 officers left out of 1,450 men and 25 officers.[47] Some of MacArthur's battalions had suffered 80 percent casualties; more than one-third of the Forty-second Division's total riflemen were either dead or wounded.

But Summerall and Pershing had their prize, and MacArthur, who had not slept for nearly four days, sent a terse message to HQ: "I have taken Hill 288," meaning the Côte, and then sank into a dreamless sleep. He remained comatose to the world for the next sixteen hours.[48]

Later, historian Robert Ferrell would question whether MacArthur or Ross or Lieutenant Colonel Bare really deserved the credit for the capture of Côte de Châtillon, and whether capturing the salient was as important as Pershing (and MacArthur) later claimed.[49] Without question, however, as brigade commander, MacArthur could take credit for a victory won by a brilliant bit of soldiering no matter who was the plan's original author. And certainly no one who was there doubted his resolve and courage under fire that had rallied his brigade for three straight days and made final victory possible.

A grateful Summerall, for one, had no doubts; nor did Menoher. "This brigade under the command of Brigadier General Douglas MacArthur has manifested the highest soldierly qualities. . . . With a dash, courage, and fighting spirit worthy of the best traditions of the American Army, this brigade carried by assault the strongly fortified Hill 288 on the Krunhilde Stallung [sic]." He added, "The indomitable resolution and ferocious courage of these two officers"—meaning both MacArthur and Ross—"in rallying their broken lines time and again, in re-forming the attack and leading their men . . . saved the day." Menoher recommended that MacArthur be promoted to major general "for his field leadership, generalcy and determination during three days of constant combat in front of the Côte de Châtillon"—and also recommended the Medal of Honor.[50]

Ironically, it was the same medal his father had won for taking a similar fortified height, Missionary Ridge in 1863—but Douglas did it while facing weapons with a firepower and lethality that Arthur MacArthur could never have conceived. Indeed, in the course of those deadly days of fighting, MacArthur learned many lessons about command that would serve him well later—even though he would sometimes ignore them himself.

He learned, for example, the importance of up-close leadership instead of leadership from miles behind the lines. He learned that "the commander on the spot must have flexibility and a certain power of decision" as Ross and Bare had shown when they convinced him to rescind the bayonet charge order, and that once again there was no substitute for seeing the battlefield in person as opposed to relying on intelligence reports from others.[51]

Above all, as he told Major General Rhodes (destined to be Menoher's replacement), he learned at Côte de Châtillon that a general has to lead his men not just with orders and commands, but with "precept and example." It was that example that the men of the Eighty-fourth Brigade best remembered in their three-day fight. As Reginald Weller, liaison officer of the battalion, later put it, "The courage of General MacArthur was the outstanding feature of the battle . . . he alone made victory possible." Weller remembered how on the fourteenth the sick and shaken MacArthur had gone out at 5:30 to lead his men "and made his way through a heavy interdiction fire of gas and shrapnel" and how he "joined his troop and took command of the line." Those at least were the words Weller wrote down in his personal deposition for MacArthur's Medal of Honor.[52]

In the end, MacArthur did not receive it. It was Pershing, and Pershing alone, who finally blocked the award. When a board of officers from the Forty-second Division unanimously put MacArthur at the head of the list of their men who deserved a Medal of Honor, Pershing turned them down flat.[53] Pershing did, however, approve a second Distinguished Service Cross for MacArthur. He also let the promotion to major general go through.

Later, MacArthur claimed to have been satisfied. He would be the youngest major general in the army's history (another record of his father's had been broken), and he could quote the citation for the Distinguished Service Cross almost from memory, as he did in his memoirs:

> As a brigade commander, General MacArthur personally led his men, and by the skillful maneuvers of his brigade made possible the captures of Hills 288, 282, and the Cote de Chatillon. . . . On a field where courage was the rule, his courage was the dominant factor.[54]

Still, the fact that he had been denied the Medal of Honor, and knowing who had denied it, must have rankled. Pershing's action made their already rocky relationship even rockier. It did nothing to endear MacArthur to his commanding general or to his protégé George C. Marshall, who was about to commit a mistake that brought near catastrophe to the AEF and almost cost MacArthur his life.

After a week of recuperation on the summit of Côte de Châtillon, the Forty-second painfully resumed its forward progress. It had a new commanding general, General Charles Rhodes; Menoher had been promoted to take over VI Corps. Before he left, Menoher wondered seriously if the thinned ranks of gaunt scarecrows he now commanded were up for more fighting. They had taken almost 4,000 casualties; they were 100 officers and 7,100 men short of authorized strength.[55] He held a conference with MacArthur and Reilly, now commander of the Eighty-third, at his headquarters at Neuve Forge Farm near Estremont, to get their opinion.

The meeting wasn't in MacArthur's office but his bedroom, with its built-in bed, red-hot woodstove, and rough plank floorboards. They sat at a rickety table with three wooden chairs, while the small windows let in the fading light of late afternoon.

Menoher told his brigade commanders of Pershing's plan to renew the general advance on November 1. What did they think? Was the Rainbow up for it? MacArthur immediately sprang to his feet and delivered a speech that,

Reilly said later, both he and Menoher agreed it was a shame there was no stenographer present to take it all down.

MacArthur "soon showed that there was no phase of the matter which he had not thoroughly considered from every possible point of view," not just the Forty-second's current state but Pershing's strategy, how it fit into the French and British plans, and how it would fit into the final course of the war. The Kriemhilde Stellung had been the main pivot of the German line in France, he explained, and their last stand. Now that it had fallen, German resistance in the Argonne was bound to collapse.

"It only remains," he exclaimed excitedly, "to gather in the fruits of victory" by pushing the Germans back across the Meuse River. "The 84th," he proudly told his commanding officer, "is fully capable of playing its part in such an advance."[56]

Reilly agreed. His men were not only ready but eager to keep going—and now they had sufficient artillery and machine guns to smother German strongpoints in a November 1 attack.

So Menoher relented, and after a brief respite in reserve under its new commander, the Forty-second joined the rest of the AEF on November 4 in the headlong pursuit of their next goal: the city of Sedan.

Sedan was the critical main juncture for the German army in France, and less than a week before the Armistice, German resistance was steadily crumbling. American units were advancing so fast they found it difficult to keep themselves supplied, as their supply wagons got bogged down in muddy roads and almost incessant rain. They passed long lines of German prisoners who had finally had enough and had thrown down their weapons at the first sight of an American doughboy.

November 5 found the Forty-second just twelve miles south of Sedan. The operation had become a mad chase, as Elmer Sherwood put it, to get to Sedan before anyone else did. "The phrase 'take Sedan' became a sort of fetish," First Army commander Liggett confessed, and "acted as a spur and jaded spirits were stimulated as if dope had been administered." No one, certainly, needed the energizing jolt more than the worn-out men of the Forty-second.[57]

That was when Pershing's HQ made a crucial, potentially fatal mistake.

A memorandum was read that afternoon over the telephone to corps commanders, stating: "General Pershing desires that the honor of entering Sedan should fall to the American First Army." As such he urged continuing the advance through the night. And then, added at the last minute at the bottom of the memorandum were the words "Boundaries will not be considered."

Pershing later stated that he had meant the boundary between the American First and French Fourth Armies, which was also engaged in the frantic rush for Sedan. But the message did not state that: instead it suggested that the boundaries between the various advancing American divisions be disregarded, which meant that troops from two entire corps, division after division, would now be piling into one another along each road and hedgerow leading into Sedan. Pershing's message, as MacArthur put it, "precipitated what narrowly missed being one of the great tragedies of American history."[58]

And the message's author, as it happened, was none other than George C. Marshall.

The confusion the message set off became apparent on the night of November 6, as General Reilly's Eighty-third Brigade, advancing along the road to Sedan, suddenly ran into troops from the First Division, which had been stationed far to the left of I Corps but began cutting clear across the Corps' line of advance—25,000 men in seven separate columns—following their commander's orders "to march immediately on Sedan."[59]

The chaos in the darkness was appalling, and dangerous—the men of the Big Red One were squarely in the Eighty-third's line of fire. By dawn, news of the mess had reached MacArthur. He was preparing to set out from his headquarters at Bulson when he was told an officer from the First Division was waiting for him outside.

"I was very much astonished to hear this," as he described it later. He went out to find it was an officer he knew, Colonel Ericsson of the Sixteenth Infantry.

"What are you doing here, Ericsson?" MacArthur asked.

"Here are my orders," the colonel answered, handing MacArthur a copy of Marshall's memo. MacArthur glanced at it, and said, "Where are your men?"

Ericsson told him they were coming up the river road while others were headed along the Maisoncelle-Bulson road.

"Withdraw your men at once," MacArthur snapped. "This movement is very dangerous and might be disastrous."[60]

Ericsson said he couldn't, it was too late, and he didn't even know where his commanding officer, General Parker, was. It was an angry and exasperated MacArthur who then set out from Bulson to sort out the confusion, after sending messages to his commanders warning them of what was happening and to avoid Americans firing on one another. He was determined to get to the head of his brigade "in order to prevent personally any of these occurrences," he wrote, and was crossing a series of fields near Beau-Menil Farm northeast of Bulson when he suddenly found himself staring down the barrel of a very large service pistol—while he and his aide Major Wolf were ringed by nervous men pointing rifles at the pair.

To his relief they were not Germans but Americans—men of the First Division's Sixteenth Infantry on patrol who had blundered into his sector. But the patrol and the lieutenant in charge, Lieutenant Black, refused to lower their weapons. They had never seen an outfit like MacArthur's before: the rumpled cap, the gray sweater with no insignia, the flowing scarf, and riding crop. As far as they were concerned, they had captured a German officer, maybe even a general.

Black cocked his pistol and ordered MacArthur and Wolf to march down the road.

MacArthur sized up the tired, trigger-happy bunch and speaking softly but urgently, convinced them who he actually was. Black apologized and tucked away his revolver; MacArthur explained what was happening—a midfield collision between two infantry divisions—and told Black he needed to go back to his commanding officer, Colonel Harrell (as it happened, MacArthur's classmate from West Point), and get him to pull his men back.

To show there were no hard feelings, MacArthur offered one of the soldiers in the patrol a cigarette, a Camel. The man took a grateful drag and then said, "I was thinking, if you had just been a Boche general instead of an American one we would all of us got the D.S.C."

MacArthur had to laugh. "If you don't get a medal in any event you do get a package of cigarettes," and passed him the pack of Camels.

The soldier thanked him, and said wistfully, "To tell the truth, sir, I would rather have the cigarettes than the medal."

Black and his men then set off, the soldier holding rear point. As the patrol descended the hill, the soldier turned back to MacArthur and lifted his rifle in salute. "I raised my cap to him," MacArthur recalled, "as he disappeared in the morning mist."

Later MacArthur learned the soldier had been killed in the fighting around Sedan.[61]

In the early evening of November 10, MacArthur was standing on a rise of ground overlooking the city that the American First Army had almost come to blows to reach. Ironically, it was the French, not the Americans, who finally liberated Sedan. But MacArthur knew that while the French might have the town, the Americans had the more valuable real estate, a series of heights facing the Meuse River with commanding views on all sides. In front of him were hundreds of freight cars that the Germans had hoped to use to support their troops, but that now were sitting waiting for grateful and hungry French and American soldiers.[62]

That afternoon he had gotten some more good news. Following General Menoher's recommendation, he had been given command of the entire Forty-second Division, replacing General Rhodes, who had been in charge for less than twenty-four hours. For MacArthur, it was the climax of what had been a spectacular war. He had begun it as a young upstart; he was ending it as an army legend.

That was the other good news. For two days there had been rumors about an armistice ending the fighting, to start at 11:00 A.M. on the 11th. MacArthur was able to pause and reflect on all that had happened in the last year since his arrival in France, and what his division (and now it was *his* division) had accomplished—but also what it had cost.

He summed it up in a bulletin that went out to headquarters a week later:

"The 42nd Division has now been in France more than a year. . . . Out of the 224 days since it first entered the line the division has been engaged with the enemy 180 days . . . The Division has marched by road, by camion and moved by train; it was the only American Division to assist in the decisive defeat of the great German offensive of July 15th . . . From that time on it has taken part in every large American operation."[63]

Although the Forty-second was created from scratch using National Guard troops, even the Germans rated it among the Americans' top two or three divisions. A later study showed that in terms of ground taken in combat, prisoners captured, decorations awarded, and days in combat, the Rainbow counted as the second most effective division in Pershing's army. Only the Second, made up of half regulars and half marines, did better.[64]

But it had cost almost 14,000 casualties: 2,644 battle deaths and 11,275 wounded.[65] MacArthur had risked being among them many times, but somehow emerged unscathed. Soldiers had a nickname to describe him: "Bullet Proof." As MacArthur made clear to others, he believed it was a sign of his destiny, even God's guidance. It had carried him through safely and made him major general at thirty-eight. But would that destiny now carry him forward in peace as it did during war?

Meanwhile, far away in the blue waters of the Pacific, warships were on the move.

They were Japanese warships, part of the navy the island nation had been building over the last decade. Just as Douglas's father had predicted, imperial Japan was the rising new power in Asia, and the war MacArthur and the Rainbow had just fought had completed the modernization and industrialization started there three decades earlier.

In 1914 when the war started, Japan had only eight major steel plants. When it was over, it had fourteen, as well as 166 smaller facilities rolling out steel for Japan's growing navy and army as well as a growing civilian economy. Japan's copper industry grew by almost half, while electric power generation had shot up by 34 percent.[66]

Unlike from the European powers, the war had demanded no great sacrifice from Japan. Just the opposite, in fact. Simply by joining the Allies in 1915 Japan had doubled the size and reach of its Asian empire at almost no cost. First it took over China's Shantung Peninsula from the Germans virtually without a shot. Together with the iron- and coal-rich portions of Manchuria taken in the Russo-Japanese War and the peninsula of Korea annexed in 1910, Japan now had a large and resource-abundant empire on the Asian mainland, as well as a stranglehold on an increasingly feeble China.

Then, gliding like lean, silent greyhounds into the central Pacific, the Japanese navy's vessels seized one chain of islands after another from the retreating Germans: the Marshalls, the Marianas, the Carolines, and the Gilberts. In three decades those names would be engraved forever on American memories. But for now they served as forward bases for Japan's naval presence, extending it to easy striking distance of American bases in Guam and the Philippines, and the horseshoe-shaped port known as Pearl Harbor in Hawaii.

That was just as important. The navy had also looked at the islands off the coast of New Guinea in the Bismarck Sea, the Solomons, and New Britain, for possible bases. But those islands, like New Guinea itself, had passed to Australia in the final peace settlement. No matter, Japanese admirals told themselves. After the humiliation of America negotiating the peace that ended the war with Russia, and despite Teddy Roosevelt's attempts to smooth relations afterward, including ceding control of the Korean peninsula to Japan from 1907 on, wrote Admiral Fukudomi, "the Imperial navy made the United States its sole strategic enemy."[67]

Arthur MacArthur had been right. The emergence of Japan was becoming the key "problem of the Pacific," and "the grim, taciturn, aloof men of iron character and unshakable purpose" that Douglas had so admired on his visit were already preparing the tools to thrust a dagger at America—a dagger whose first target would be the Philippines.

CHAPTER 8

BACK TO WEST POINT

Should serve some years in present grade before
promotion to next higher. Has exalted opinion of himself.

—GENERAL PERSHING ON BRIGADIER GENERAL

DOUGLAS MACARTHUR, 1922

As the fighting ended, Mac's reputation stood on a national pedestal. Secretary of War Newton Baker pronounced him "the greatest American field commander produced by the war." General Gouraud, his old colleague from the desperate Second Battle of the Marne in July 1918, chimed in: "I consider General MacArthur to be one of the finest and bravest soldiers I have ever served with." And Menoher, his old commander, summed up his feelings in a final efficiency report dated August 28, 1919: "One of the most efficient, energetic, and talented officers I have ever known, I consider him an officer of most brilliant attainments."[1]

On March 16, Pershing himself presented MacArthur with his consolation prize for not winning the Medal of Honor: a Distinguished Service Medal to set beside his Distinguished Service Crosses. George Patton and Bill Donovan, who did win a Medal of Honor, were the only other soldiers to be awarded both. And from his fellow officers of the Forty-second he received a gold cigarette case, emblazoned "Bravest of the Brave," which he carried with him the rest of his life.

But what would America's greatest field commander do now that war was done?

At first there was no time to ponder the question. By the terms of the Armistice, the Americans were to take over an occupation zone inside Germany itself. The Forty-second found itself assigned to the area around the city of Coblenz, and MacArthur took as his headquarters a magnificent castle at Sinzig that overlooked the gently flowing waters of the Rhine.

Most Rainbow soldiers, by contrast, were billeted in German homes. Even though Coblenz, like most postwar German cities, was teetering on the edge of starvation, for the survivors of the Ourcq and Côte de Châtillon it seemed like an exotic paradise. No more dawn stand-tos; no more night raids, eyes straining to see through the dark and a throat dry with terror; no more seeing friends torn apart by a hail of machine-gun fire or coughing their lungs out from a phosgene gas attack; no more catching a few hours of sleep in a vermin-ridden foxhole. The Forty-second found occupation duty anything but arduous, and the locals were equally relieved to see the end to the killing. As MacArthur wrote in his memoirs, "The warm hospitality of the population, their well-ordered way of life, their thrift and geniality forged a feeling of mutual respect and esteem."[2]

But for MacArthur the start of occupation also brought disappointment. Two weeks after the Armistice he had to hand over the Rainbow to Major General Charles Flagler. Pershing bluntly told him the reason: his promotion to major general had been blocked. Peyton March had put a freeze on all promotions the day after the Armistice, and that included MacArthur's. Without that second star, he could not retain command of the Forty-second.

Pershing, judging by his later comments, was not heartbroken about conveying the news. For MacArthur, it must have been a bitter moment handing over the division *he* had created, and in his mind carried almost single-handedly to victory, even if it meant returning to his old comrades in the Eighty-fourth.

The disappointment was compounded by the breakdown of his health. The constant gassing at the front led to a severe throat infection, followed by an attack of the so-called Spanish flu that was knocking down and even killing millions across Europe that winter. (Back in the States, one of those laid prostrate by the same flu was MacArthur's new friend, Franklin Roosevelt.) The twin illnesses left him prostrate in bed for weeks. Then in February came a bout of diphtheria. The symptoms were real enough; fortunately, he wrote later, "the doctors pulled me through." But MacArthur hadn't been immune from psychosomatic-related bouts like this in the past. Perhaps part of his erratic health problems was an underlying uncertainty, now that the fighting was done and the rules and red tape of the ordinary army reasserted themselves, about what the future held for him.[3]

Still, as he recovered he had plenty of visitors to distract him. Some came to see the American occupation at work, but most in order to see him, the glamorous Fighting Dude celebrated in newspapers and army reports. MacArthur had learned something important during the war, besides how to command troops in battle. He had learned the value of a self-fashioned persona for standing out from his fellow officers whose personalities, for the most part, tended to be indistinguishable from their drab khaki uniforms. But MacArthur's persona was not a staged pose, or simple playacting: He had proved his courage and skill in battle a dozen times. But his careful self-fashioning did reflect his growing awareness that a characteristic style of dress with accoutrements like a riding crop and a silk scarf—or later his Ray-Ban sunglasses and his enormous corncob pipe—could not only help to rally his men's morale and focus their attention, but could also catch and focus the media's attention on someone whose destiny, as he believed and they would soon realize, was to rise to the top.

One who certainly noticed was Joseph Chase, a portrait artist traveling around the country doing preparatory sketches of American commanders from the war.[4] Chase was intrigued to meet the man whom both French and American colleagues branded the bravest of the brave, and he was not disappointed.

"Young MacArthur looks like the typical hero of historical romance; he could easily have stepped out of the pages of *The Prisoner of Zenda*," he wrote. (Living in a castle once owned by Charlemagne didn't hurt that romantic image, either.) MacArthur agreed to pose for a portrait by candlelight, and Chase had a chance to examine him more closely.

"He is lean, light-skinned, with long, well-kept fingers and is always carefully groomed . . . He is a thorough-going brainy young man, distinctly of the city type, a good talker and a good listener . . . He is quick in his movements, physical and mental, and is subject to changing moods; he knits his brows or laughs heartily with equal facility, and often during the same sentence."[5]

Another who fell under the MacArthur spell was Kansas newspaperman William Allen White. He was there touring the American occupation zone, and his lunch with General MacArthur came almost as a revelation.

"I had never met before so vivid, so captivating, so magnetic a man," White enthused. "He was all that Barrymore and John Drew hoped to be. And how he could talk!" MacArthur was casually lounging in a ragged brown sweater and civilian pants—"nothing more"—as they talked for two hours about the war, the occupation, and MacArthur's anger at the general order forbidding fraternization between American soldiers and German civilians, especially women. "The order only hurt the boys," he told White. He told how the boys of the Forty-second had organized a Christmas party in one of the little towns around Coblenz, complete with Christmas tree, and then had to have a stag dance because no German women were allowed.

"While outside looking in at the windows were two hundred girls," MacArthur exploded. As for MacArthur himself, White noted, his stance and striking features "and good eyes with a 'come hither' in them must have played the devil with the girls."

Their conversation also touched on the German situation. MacArthur expressed his view that the Germans were weary of war and now despised the Kaiser, especially the women who now had the vote. As for the German army, MacArthur asserted it had been virtually demolished at the end, and would pose no threat to the Allies for a long time to come. It was the same view he had expressed to another visitor, the Prince of Wales, when he had stopped by Sinzig and wondered whether MacArthur was worried about a German resurgence.

"We beat the Germans this time," he said in his most decisive voice, "and we can do it again." Especially, he was thinking, if the Americans had General Douglas MacArthur at their head.[6]

William Allen White concluded, "[MacArthur's] staff adored him, his men worshiped him, and he seemed entirely without vanity."[7] That was a judgment on which others were inclined to differ. One of them was General Pershing. Later much would be made of Pershing's comment on MacArthur—

"Has exalted opinion of himself"—in an efficiency report that recommended blocking the younger man's promotion to major general.

But the truth is that in that same efficiency report Pershing noted MacArthur was "a very able young officer with a fine war record," and when Newton Baker's office told *The New York Times* that MacArthur's seniors considered him the most brilliant young officer in the army, Pershing was likely one of them.[8]

All the same, there's no doubt that Pershing and others believed this very able young officer still had some growing up to do. And when MacArthur returned home with the 12,000 Rainbow soldiers and the Eighty-fourth Brigade and divisional headquarters staffs on April 25, 1919, at the New York docks, he quickly learned how fast the glory can fade and mundane reality can take its place.

As the troops disembarked, a small boy was running past and stopped at seeing all the uniforms.

"Who are you?" he asked.

"The famous 42nd," MacArthur answered.

"Were you in France?" the boy asked with some curiosity.

MacArthur grimaced. "Amid a silence that hurt," he remembered, he and his men marched off the dock, saluted and shook hands, and then parted ways. It was over. Everything that they had endured and suffered to win the greatest war in history—the friends they had seen fall and die, the bravery and valor they had all shown in the face of danger—none of it had left any impression on the people they had served. The boy's ignorant reaction turned out to be typical. "No one even seemed to have heard of the war" or seemed to acknowledge the presence of the soldiers who had fought it.[9] America wanted to forget the last two years, just as it wanted to ignore the peace treaty being drawn up in Paris, which, as MacArthur told one of his former comrades, "seem[s] more like a treaty of perpetual war than of perpetual peace." When the Senate failed to ratify the treaty and opted to keep the United States out of the postwar League of Nations, most Americans neither noticed nor cared.

The fact was, America was retreating into its prewar cocoon. If the men who had led the country to intervene in the conflict in Europe had truly but wrongly believed that this was "the war to end all wars," the American people were willing to go along with the illusion. Soldiers and generals, no matter how brave, played no part in the country's postwar agenda.

There was one exception to the general apathy. The New Yorkers of the 165th did get a magnificent parade down Fifth Avenue, followed by a celebratory dance at the Waldorf Astoria Hotel that MacArthur attended. That was a mistake. A manager spotted his boots with riding spurs and told him, "You may not dance in spurs. You might injure the dance floor."

"Do you know who I am?" MacArthur demanded, meaning the most decorated soldier of the war.

"Yes sir, I do," the manager replied. "But I must request you leave the dance floor and remove your spurs." MacArthur spun around, grabbed his date's arm, and swore he would never set foot, spurred or unspurred, in the Waldorf again—a promise he would remember with sheepish good humor four decades later, when he was the Waldorf Towers's most famous resident.[10]

At the time, however, it was a depressed and chastened MacArthur who took the train to Washington, D.C., to be reunited with his mother and to see the army chief of staff to learn of his next assignment. Of course he was staying in the army; any other career was inconceivable. But his future hardly looked bright. The army was undergoing a drastic demobilization, sinking far below even prewar strength. Like his father after the Civil War he would be facing a profound dearth of command opportunities—and when he walked into the chief of staff's office he was already resigned to that bleak reality.

Instead, he got the surprise of his life.

If any single American was responsible for winning World War One, it was Army Chief of Staff Peyton March. Pershing, the commander in France, would grab the glory, but it was March, sitting behind a desk in Washington, who personally manhandled the soldiers, ships, and supplies to put the AEF in the field. By so doing, he had enabled Pershing to provide the Allies with the vital reserve, and then the driving spearhead, that halted the last German advance of the war, shoved the German army back to its borders, and finally forced it to surrender.[11]

Thin, spare, and totally without charm or regard for others, March had been driven during the war by a single goal. That was to make the U.S. Army, and its officer corps, the epitome of a modern fighting force. Now that the war was over, March was determined to continue that development into the future. That meant starting with the center of the army's nervous system, the academy at West Point.

The 117-year-old institution in upstate New York was still very much mired in prewar assumptions and attitudes, just as much of its physical plant dated back to the Mexican War. March had already discussed his plans with Secretary of War Baker for bringing West Point into the twentieth century. But changing the outlook up there, four hundred miles from Washington, was going to require someone tough and resourceful with "a comprehensive grasp of world and national affairs," March had written, "and a liberalization of conception that amounts to a change in the psychology of command."[12] That man would have to be expert in the latest technologies of war, but also sensitive to the sweep of history and the need to preserve tradition while recognizing the need for change—and for obeying General March's wishes.

Then the door opened and Douglas MacArthur, the man Peyton had decided was the one to do it, was standing in front of him.

"Douglas, things are in great confusion at West Point," the chief of staff said. "It's forty years behind the times. Mr. Baker and I have talked this over and we want you to go up there and revitalize and revamp the Academy. It's been parochial in the past. I want to broaden it and graduate more cadets into the army."[13]

March wanted West Point's courses updated, the curriculum modernized, and hazing ended. Even more radically, he wanted its cadets to graduate in three years, not four. That was more than enough time, he had decided, to forge officers for the wars of the future.[14]

MacArthur was stunned. He was still nursing the leg wound he had received just before the Armistice. Now he was back in the States for less than a month and the army's chief of staff was telling him he was going to be superintendent of his beloved West Point, the youngest superintendent in more than a century.

"I'm not an educator, sir," he protested. "I am a field officer. Besides, there are so many of my old professors. I can't do it."

March smiled. "Yes, you can do it."[15]

It was a pleased but somewhat apprehensive MacArthur who went back to his mother to break the news, and say it was time to start packing. He would be reporting to West Point on June 15, and there was no time to lose.

Mac spent the next six weeks tirelessly working to get himself ready for the job. He read over every file on West Point at the War Department; he spoke to fellow officers at the War Department. He also talked to members of Congress about what was happening up at the monastery on the Hudson, and listened as they poured out their doubts and frustrations.

What he discovered was that West Point, his beloved Point, was in a hell of a mess—so much so that some in Congress were talking openly of abolishing it altogether.

The trouble began soon after war broke out, when the academy's regular four-year program was drastically shortened to one year, so that the academy could graduate enough commissioned second lieutenants to meet the needs of a rapidly expanding force.[16] But that left a yawning, and dangerous, gap as each class graduated faster than the last. An institution built around older students molding the character and habits of the younger ones over the course of four years had suddenly come apart.

"The traditional disciplinary system," as MacArthur later wrote, "so largely built around the prestige and influence of the upper classmen was impossible in a situation where there were no upper classmen."[17] Instead, chaos reigned inside the Corps with such rapid turnover and the admission of so many cadets who would never have qualified under peacetime rules.

In fact, six months after the Armistice, there was no longer a Corps at all but three separate corps. The first was the last of the speeded-up wartime Corps, still sporting their traditional gray bell-buttoned dress coats and black-striped trousers. The second group was the next class of plebes who the War Department on November 1 ordered to enter early that winter, and who were forced to wear privates' uniforms in order to keep them distinct from the gray-clad fourth classmen.[18]

If that was not confusing enough, the War Department also ordered returning officers who would have graduated in the class of 1921 back to West Point for an additional half year of training.[19] They wore not cadet gray or a private's olive drab but their commissioned officers' uniforms, complete with

Sam Browne belts and field boots. Many had seen action in France, and some had commanded men under fire—yet starting that spring they would be submitting to the same training, and living under the same discipline, as the rawest, youngest plebe.

It was true class conflict, with all the jealousy and distrust that any Marxist would have wished. Then in May 1919 came the inadvertent coup de grâce. Chief of staff March announced that the "greys" and "orioles" (the returning officers) would all be staying for a full three-year course, instead of graduating in a year, as many had assumed.[20] More than 100 cadets resigned from the Academy; those who stayed were filled with remorse and bitterness—not just toward the army for making a misery of their time at West Point, but toward their fellow classmates. "The Corps had died November 1918," a staff member later wrote. "Not even a miracle could bring it back to life."[21]

Some recent historians of West Point, like Theodore Crackel, disagree. They reject the claim that the tangle of 1918–19 posed any existential challenge, let alone required bringing in an outsider like MacArthur.[22] Those on the ground at the time, however, felt differently. "At the Academy," notes historian Stephen Ambrose, "all was turmoil." The time had come for a radical revision of how West Point functioned and trained its cadets, and Douglas MacArthur was appointed to do it.[23]

So for those instructors and administrators still reeling from the problems of the past year came the worst news of all. The new superintendent was someone with no teaching or academic administrative experience, a mere stripling of thirty-nine compared to the seventy-one-year-old he was replacing.

As for MacArthur, it would be his first test at executive leadership, with no chain of command to rely on. He and his mother drove up to the superintendent's house on June 12, 1919. The iron grille gate opened; a truck loaded with their luggage pulled up in the driveway; soon trunks and cases were being taken through the front door of the large brick house. MacArthur made sure his mother was comfortable, and then set off for the office.

It was June 1919. In two weeks Germany would finally sign a peace treaty in the halls at Versailles, under sullen protest—dissent from which Hitler's

Nationalist Socialists would take their cue. Two months earlier Benito Mussolini had created his new nationalist party in Italy, while Vladimir Lenin launched the Communist Party's Third International in Moscow.

Revolution and discontent were in the air. Not least in West Point, New York.

Colonel William Addleman Ganoe, the academy's official adjutant to the superintendent, was the first person MacArthur met. Ganoe had wearily handled the paperwork associated with the school's administrative meltdown during the past two years. Over the last month he had eavesdropped on conversations among faculty and staff about the new appointment.

"Looks like another effort to wreck the Academy," some said. "The Academic Board will make a monkey out of him," another remarked. "I remember him as a cadet," said one of the wives. "He might have looked and acted all right. But appearances are deceiving." Another said wistfully, "Maybe he'll just sit back and let them run the show," meaning the board.[24]

Ganoe didn't think so. He remembered Cadet MacArthur from the days when he himself had been a plebe, sixteen years before, and could recall a tall, handsome ranking officer of the Corps, "glittering immaculate with maroon silk sash, plumed dress hat, glinting sword and four gold stripes of chevrons."[25] Still, Ganoe had been devoted to MacArthur's predecessor, and had already written out his resignation when he heard the click of shoes on the terra-cotta floor in the hallway, and the door opened and Douglas MacArthur burst in.

Ganoe rose and saluted. MacArthur ignored the salute, then stepped forward and took his new adjutant by the elbow.

"Ganoe, Ganoe," he said slowly, as if reminiscing. "Yes, now it comes back. A girl in bustle and corset singing a love song." He smiled and laughed. "Long time ago."

Ganoe was stunned. The song was one Ganoe had sung in drag at the conclusion of the 1903 version of the amateur theatricals that were staged every year by West Point cadets, a throwaway number Ganoe himself barely remembered—but MacArthur had remembered and had dragged the song up out of his memory to greet him.[26]

From that moment on, William Ganoe was MacArthur's admirer and ally. His reminiscences of MacArthur's brief but decisive tenure as superintendent at West Point are an invaluable guide to those tense years, and give us an intimate picture of the MacArthur who was still to come.

Ganoe noticed at once, for example, that the brigadier from France "wasn't as robust as when he had been a cadet. He had been slender then," Ganoe remembered, "but now his muscles seemed to have shrunk into sinew. There were beginnings of crow's feet at his eyes, and his cheeks just escaped being hollow." A year and a half of trench warfare had taken its physical toll. Yet if MacArthur was not as cool and breezily correct as he had been in West Point days, he was more centered and more at ease with himself. A year and a half of leadership and command had also left their mark.

Most strikingly, there was no evidence of decorations—no sign of the Silver Stars or two D.S.C.s or the D.S.M. This was MacArthur as he would remain until the day he left the army three decades later. Except "for the stars on his shoulders, he might have been taken for any passing officer off duty."[27]

MacArthur also made quick work of Ganoe's letter of resignation. After a series of detailed and direct questions about every aspect of the current setup, from the Cavalry Department and the Officers' Club to the Commissary, Cadet Store, and academic curriculum, MacArthur took the letter and tore it into tiny bits. He also informed Ganoe that his new title would be chief of staff. "Adjutant" wasn't a title worthy of the wide range of tasks and responsibility MacArthur would now expect Ganoe to shoulder.

MacArthur understood the gravity of the task he faced. "The Old West Point . . . had gone," he later wrote. "It had to be replaced." The question was whether what replaced it would prepare the officers it trained—and the United States Army—for the realities of twentieth-century warfare, or simply be a pale, outmoded imitation of what came before.

That in turn depended on how MacArthur handled himself. If he made embracing the future look feasible and attractive, the changes he and Peyton were hoping for would happen. If he offended or alienated possible supporters, and left hostages to fortune potential opponents could exploit, the effort at reform would fail.

Starting that day, MacArthur would transform himself into a visible pillar of strength around which everyone, from generals to privates, could rally, and whose every word and gesture was a source of hope and encouragement. It would complete the process of heroic self-fashioning that he had begun during his years in France. It would last him through the next decade and his years as chief of staff. It laid the foundation for his leadership style during the Second World War and Korea.

And it began with people.

Ganoe noticed at once MacArthur's remarkable and lifelong gift for inspiring confidence from those who worked with him and under him, a characteristic that he would share with two other leaders in the next war, Franklin Roosevelt and Winston Churchill.

MacArthur showed it first when, to everyone's relief, he turned down the invitation to stage a formal review of the Corps as a greeting for the new superintendent. "They'll see me soon and often enough," he told Ganoe. "There are occasions when ceremonial is harassment. I saw too much of that overseas."[28] Instead, there was an easy informality to the MacArthur style of command that allowed him to command without being commanding. He could be as aloof as his father had been, but at West Point under Douglas MacArthur "the air was quickly charged with new vitality that extended from his new chief of staff on down."[29]

The informality also went with his willingness to let people handle tasks and assignments in their own way. As one of his staff during the Korean War noted, MacArthur "judged people [by] what they did best"—and then left them to do it. It would be one of his most attractive features as a general, one that even those who didn't like him came to appreciate. As one officer remarked to another during the Point years, "He makes you feel you're the only man in the only job."[30]

The staff responded with a combination of enthusiastic loyalty and hard work. His commandant of cadets, Major Robert Danford, remembered MacArthur's leadership as "a leadership that kept you at respectful distance, yet at the same time took you in as [an] esteemed member of his team, and quickly had you working harder than you had ever worked before in your life."[31]

MacArthur also built confidence with his easy style of greeting when anyone came into the office. He would rise with a smile, shake hands, turn to the desk to pick up his gold cigarette case, and offer its contents with, "Have a pill?" Then he would sit down and listen with an intensity and focus of those liquid black eyes that some visitors found almost unnerving. "His listening fairly shrieks," one once told Ganoe. "He not only looks through you, but down the back of your neck."[32]

Then he would rise and pace back and forth, repeating what he had heard word for word with the powerful memory Ganoe had first noted. Then he would ask a series of penetrating questions until the visitor was both exhausted and exhilarated—and convinced that the superintendent had made the best and most rational decision possible.

One time in a fit of daring, Ganoe decided to put MacArthur's memory to the test. When a visitor came in, he stationed a stenographer outside the door as the man told a five-minute story. As MacArthur stood and paced and repeated the story, Ganoe and the stenographer went over the notes. To their amazement, his recitation was almost verbatim.[33] No one questioned the superintendent's ability to retain any information passed on to him ever again.

MacArthur also built loyalty by his willingness to cut through red tape in order to see the right thing done or, in the case of a cadet's complaint, justice served. "Rules! Rules!" he would tell Ganoe scornfully.

"Rules are mostly made for the lazy to hide behind . . . Some little thing goes wrong. Instead of mending the situation on the spot, we make a rule," he said.[34] MacArthur's approach, by contrast, was to deal with the situation head-on.

Ganoe found that out in late August when MacArthur came back to the office after a round of inspection. MacArthur said, "Come in, Chief," and then shut the door behind him.

MacArthur started talking almost before he had taken off his cap.

"I'm convinced now of what I opined all along," he said. "The Academy has come to the end of an epoch. We are training these cadets for the past, not the future."

He began pacing the room. "How long are we going to prepare for the War of 1812?"

Ganoe didn't answer. He had learned that when MacArthur was pacing like this, like a tiger in a cage, and speaking to his guest, he was actually "communing aloud with his own mind. He was questioning MacArthur's reasoning in front of a live witness." It was something subordinates would see again and again, at the War Department, in the Philippines, Brisbane, and Tokyo: the sight and sound of MacArthur communing with his own mind.

He went on.

"Chief, I learned certain principles, certain means and methods over there that taught me the changes which have come with warfare." The days of small professional standing armies, including the U.S. Army, were done. Now "whole populations will fight whole populations." That means "the regular soldier no longer plays the role he has played for centuries." In the age of total warfare, an officer must learn to lead soldiers who are also civilians, to understand their thinking, their motivations, and their perspectives on the world.

"He must be trained along broad and humane lines," Mac continued, but a future officer also had to be able to confront the realities of the age of total war, with barbed wire, trenches, and mass death. "The kind of war the world has developed is an endless physical and mental preparation. Why put that off for a minute with the cadet? Why cheat him by our waste and neglect?"

MacArthur finally stopped and turned. "Chief, it seems to be the common belief that what happened to the Academy last year was a calamity. I regard it as an opportunity" to make West Point confront the radical changes in the world—and warfare.

He was going to start that afternoon, with Cadet Summer Camp. "Of what possible benefit is Cadet Summer Camp?" he demanded to know.

Ganoe's memory drifted back to his own days in the summer. The mornings spent doing formal drills in uniforms and formations that a Winfield Scott or Robert E. Lee might have approved of; the afternoons spent lying on their cots in barracks; marching to fife and drum to the mess hall for sumptuous dinners served by white-jacketed waiters; evenings spent reading or at a formal dance at Cullom Hall; while cadet sentries in gray uniforms and white cross belts changed guard as if they were at Buckingham Palace, shouting in unison, "All's well!"[35]

"Sentry duty—sentry duty!" MacArthur said with a wry smile, as if he had been reading Ganoe's mind. "Walking post like that against the Boches! Walking that way at all would have been the man's end."

MacArthur shook his head. "No, it's out of time and out of place. It is not only inappropriate, it's baneful. We bring them up as fashion-plate soldiers in a rich man's vacation spot."

And so Cadet Summer Camp would be no more. Or so it would be if the Academic Board approved so momentous a change. Ganoe had to wince.

Ganoe: "General, you'll meet with a world of opposition."

MacArthur: "Chief, we met more than that in France and won."

But then Ludendorff and the kaiser hadn't sat on West Point's Academic Board.

The Academic Board was, as Clausewitz himself might have said, the *Schwerpunkt* of the West Point establishment.

Besides the superintendent himself and the cadet commandant, the board consisted of the heads of the departments of instruction at West Point. It would be easy, and misleading, to portray them as a band of benighted and superannuated traditionalists.[36] It was true that since the members all had lifetime tenure, and long service as professors, they were inclined to see the prestige of West Point as a direct reflection of their own authority—an authority they were prepared to defend against all challengers, including one, in MacArthur's case, who had been one of their students.

But there were some members, the younger ones, who did see the need for changes at the school, especially after the debacle of the war years. And all of them were as keen as MacArthur to preserve the spirit of the institution for which they had spent their lives, and its motto: "Honor, Duty, Country." Their powers were absolute regarding curriculum, textbooks, methods of instruction, admission and graduation requirements. If Mac could win them over to his side, then his and March's program could go on to victory. If not, it would die in No Man's Land, unburied and forgotten.[37]

As adjutant, William Ganoe attended all Academic Board meetings as a non-voting member. He watched MacArthur attend his first, watched him come in after the other dozen members had taken their seats, and observed how their faces showed "every expression, from tense anticipation by the younger members to resigned endurance by the elders."[38]

Among the younger were Colonel Lucius Holt, head of the English and history faculties and West Point's only Ph.D. (from Yale), and Major Charles Hines, acting professor of ordnance and gunnery, who was just thirty-one years old. They and the Corps Commandant, Major Robert Danford, who was an old friend of MacArthur's from cadet days, were by and large inclined to look favorably on the new superintendent's proposals.

But six of the older Academic Board members, led by Colonel Gustav J. Fiebeger, head of civil and military engineering, and the chairman of the department of modern languages, Colonel Cornelius Willcox, were not. Fiebeger and Willcox had been cadets at West Point before MacArthur was born; both were prepared to oppose anyone trying to impose reforms during a short tenure, which would then leave them and the rest of the permanent staff holding the bag.[39]

It wasn't long before their worst fears were realized. After a breezy, "Well, Chief, what's first on the agenda," to Ganoe, MacArthur began quizzing the individual board members about every aspect of every department, much as he had quizzed Ganoe, and without making comment on the answers. The members were impressed by the breadth and depth of his knowledge but sensed that there was an agenda under the polite but relentless questioning—an agenda that would mean the end of the old West Point way of doing things.

At last one of the senior members (almost certainly Fiebeger) rose and addressed MacArthur directly. He spoke of the recent disasters that had befallen the Point, and how the board members were struggling to restore some semblance of the school's former glory. Any new interference, he implied, would only disrupt things more. Let each department head work out the solution on his own was the request. Stay in your lane and leave us alone was the subtext.

MacArthur smiled and asked a single question. "For my own enlightenment, please tell me: Would there be no advantage to a cadet in knowing the bearing one subject has on another," in other words a more cross-disciplinary approach.

Fiebeger's answer was cold and final. "Unnecessary, in the present scheme."

MacArthur's answer was to ask Ganoe if there was anything else on the agenda, and on learning there was not, he announced the board meeting was at an end.[40]

Afterward, back in his office, Mac shook his head with a puzzled smile.

"Old practices die hard," he told Ganoe. "I wish some of these elderly gentlemen had been with me a little in France." They would have learned the importance of knowing what's happening on your right and left flanks, he said. One's survival depends on it.

"I am unable to declare why the same principle is not applicable to a curriculum," he declared. Right now cadets went from one class to another like a traveler going from one town to the next with nothing tying them together. "It's a lot of loose bricks without mortar," MacArthur concluded, and he was out to see if that could be changed.[41]

And with that, the battle was on.

MacArthur started his war with the West Point establishment with what he called some personal reconnaissance. He began sitting in on classes, the first and only time Ganoe remembered a superintendent actually going to find out what was happening, and visiting professors in their offices. The reaction ran from outrage to surprised delight, but either way MacArthur was unconcerned. He was learning what he had to know in order to do battle, just as he had with trench raids during the war. Once, as he left his office to head for another class, he called out, "I'm getting an education. I don't know yet how liberal!"[42]

It also gave him a chance to meet some of the cadets, whose reactions to the new superintendent and war hero were varied. Some found him rather aloof, "walking across the Diagonal Walk, apparently lost in thought, his nose in the air, gazing at distant horizons."[43] Marty Maher, the legendary athletic trainer at the academy for more than half a century, said cadets "could always count on him for a square deal." There was one embarrassing and potentially humiliating incident involving an editorial in the cadet newspaper, whose student editor casually took it upon himself to criticize aspects of MacArthur's leadership. MacArthur was furious—not just at the insubordination, but also that the paper had leaked the fact that some at

West Point were unhappy with the new superintendent, in a form that might reach higher-ups at the War Department. He ordered every last newspaper confiscated before the issue left the grounds—and personally fired the paper's faculty advisor.[44]

The staff, too, got mixed messages from their new boss. When Army beat Navy in baseball, cadets poured out that night onto the grounds, marching and shouting past MacArthur's quarters to Fort Clinton, where they built an enormous bonfire.

The next morning MacArthur summoned Commandant Danford.

"Well, Com, that was quite a party last night."

"Yes, it was, sir—*quite* a party!" Danford answered.

"How many did you skin?" the superintendent asked, meaning "punish."

Danford shot back, "Not a one!"

"Good!" MacArthur said, banging his fist on his desk for emphasis.

"You know, Com, I could hardly resist the impulse to get out and join them!"[45]

A less pleasant encounter was with a professor who wanted two of his instructors replaced—a request that normally went without question at the Point. MacArthur, however, smelled several rats, as he told his chief of staff—including a lack of due process, tradition or no tradition. When he confronted the professor directly as to why he wanted the instructors fired, he could give no answer except that they were mediocre.

"Sir," MacArthur answered sharply, "we'll always have the mediocre with us. They are in the majority. We have a decided duty to develop them in order to better and leaven the whole. . . . We must not strive for ready-made perfection. We must construct it. I have every confidence," he said with a smile as he showed the man the door, "that with your kind of personality you can elevate these two instructors till they'll be above par."[46]

Request denied. MacArthur may have saved two instructors from an injustice—but he had also made an enemy of their senior professor.

"The professors are so secure, they have become set and smug," he complained to his confidant Ganoe. "They deliver the same schedule year after year with the blessed unction that they have reached the zenith in education."[47]

It was MacArthur's fate that his impatience to reform the curriculum alienated those who would have to carry it out. Change at West Point required careful consensus building; MacArthur's leadership style ran in the opposite direction. Indeed, he was learning that things got done best when he could handpick his staff. Otherwise, he tended to make as many opponents as he did converts to his vision of what must be done.

In the meantime, the battle for hearts and minds kept swinging back to the Academy Board.

It resisted any attempt to overhaul the curriculum and grew increasingly furious at his interference, no matter how well intended or well informed—or well supported from above. He did have his supporters club on the board, like Commandant Danford and Colonel Holt. But the pro-MacArthur party was too small in number, and too inexperienced in the ways of West Point, to make a difference. MacArthur found that suggesting even minor changes in classroom procedure, like introducing the slide rule to science (or natural philosophy) classes, met with a wall of uncomprehending resistance. Even the abolition of Cadet Summer Camp threatened to stir a major revolt, and MacArthur reluctantly had to pull back.

This Côte de Châtillon refused to be taken by frontal assault. So MacArthur reverted to guerrilla warfare. When his aide Lewis Hibbs asked whether he should schedule a board meeting for the usual 11 A.M., MacArthur angrily said no. "Call the meeting at 4:30 pm. I want them to come here hungry— and I'll keep them there till I get what I want."[48]

Still, the battle spilled out into the open only once, when one of the diehard older professors began badgering MacArthur at a faculty meeting. He uttered remarks, Danford remembered, that "bordered on the insubordinate," as the rest of the faculty shifted uneasily in their chairs and stared at their shoes. Finally MacArthur could take it no longer.

"Sit down, Sir," he barked. "I'm talking." Danford, MacArthur's ally, considered it a "wholesome lesson" for the entire faculty. But it's not clear that anything useful came from it, then or later.[49]

In the end, MacArthur's hopes of overhauling the West Point curriculum, with up-to-date offerings in English and history, and the creation of a whole new battery of courses from psychology and sociology to political science and economics, had to wait several more years.[50] Instead, during his short, stormy tenure of less than three years, he had to be content with the smaller victories.

He managed to get only a single combined course in economics and American government, and a few extra classroom hours of English past the board.

But in 1921 it did give way on certain vital points. There was no more Fort Clinton summer camp; cadets spent their summers at Fort Dix instead for more serious military instruction. MacArthur forced the board to liberalize the regulations on the use of leave, which he had seen as important so that cadets could learn about the civilians they would one day lead in battle.

Two other changes were important to MacArthur personally.

One was hazing. MacArthur hoped to see it eliminated, or at least no longer receive any hint of official sanction.[51] On New Year's Day 1919 a plebe named Stephen Bird had committed suicide under the barrage of abuse from upperclassmen; MacArthur called together a meeting of first classmen to discuss possible changes in the system. But even MacArthur's authority and charm, including handing out cigarettes to the classmen (forbidden under regulations), could not get them to budge. Nor could he get Beast Barracks, the three-week boot camp that upperclassmen ran for incoming cadets, abolished—although he and Commandant Danford agreed that its round-the-clock brutality gave cadets entirely the wrong idea of what army discipline was about.

Finally, he and Danford worked out a plan to put Beast Barracks under the command of commissioned officers instead of upperclassmen. "The alumni set up a howl," as Stephen Ambrose noted, but the plan stuck while MacArthur was superintendent.[52]

MacArthur's other big change in cadet behavior was setting up an Honor Committee and a written honor code. The honor system, that a cadet's word is always accepted and that he is expected to tell the truth at all times, had been part of West Point going back to 1817 and the academy's Moses, Sylvanus Thayer. But a written code backed by an Honor Committee that could investigate and adjudicate but left punishment to higher-ups was an innovation that made the system not only more fair but more transparent. It may have been MacArthur's single longest-lasting reform during his years as superintendent, with the possible exception of sports.[53]

MacArthur had adored organized team sports during his cadet years, and he saw it as an important adjunct to training a cadre of military officers. "Nothing brings out the qualities of leadership, mental and muscular coordination, aggressiveness, and courage more quickly," he liked to say.[54] In addition to breathing new life into the official football and baseball programs, MacArthur set in motion a whole new system of intramural sports, including hockey, tennis, golf, and polo. The competition proved so tough that the games were soon known as "Intra-murder" sports. MacArthur was delighted, however, and wrote up four lines of poetry that he had carved on the stone portals leading to the gymnasium:

> *Upon the fields of friendly strife*
> *Are sown the seeds*
> *That, upon other fields, on other days*
> *Will bear the fruits of victory.*

That motto is still there to this day.[55]

In other battles, especially with Congress, MacArthur was less successful.

He pushed hard for more money for new buildings, including a new stadium, and for doubling of the size of the Corps. He lost on both counts.

But as 1922 began, the superintendent of West Point had other things on his mind.

He was getting married.

She was Louise Cromwell Brooks, a wealthy, attractive divorcée who was the stepdaughter of one of America's richest men, Edward T. Stotesbury, and the ex-wife of another rich businessman, Walter Brooks. She had spent the war years in Paris with her two children; there she became a popular party girl in Parisian society and, in the words of historian Carol Petillo, "an early flapper."[56]

At one of those parties she met a handsome American army officer who took an immediate fancy to her vivacious personality and well-rounded physical charms. He was no one less than John J. Pershing, commander of the AEF, and when he returned to Washington, D.C., after the war, she returned to the States as well. She became Pershing's official hostess, and there were even reports that they might get married.[57]

It was not to be. In September 1921 she was in New York City and joined a party of army officers who were driving up to West Point for the day. There she met another handsome officer, the superintendent of West Point, who was seventeen years Pershing's junior and, unlike Pershing, seemed to be interested in something more than a casual relationship.

Indeed, Douglas MacArthur fell hopelessly and helplessly in love, almost at first sight. In October she was back in New York and staying at the Ritz-Carlton, and invited him to come down for a visit. He had to decline, as he had a series of conferences scheduled with the Academy Board that was going to demand his full attention.[58] But from that moment on, he was hooked. His courtship of the wealthy, vivacious divorcée became virtually an obsession for him, and he poured all the yearnings and romantic emotional baggage he had been carrying for decades into the relationship. For the very first time, his mother moved into the background as the most important woman in his life.

"I [have] now come to the end of the Rainbow—to find you," he wrote to Louise on October 15, after she had returned to Washington.

> I have followed that arc of light in childish delight, hoping to find
> at the other end of the bow the way, and the truth, and the light.
> And now face to face with destiny, dazzled and blinded with the
> glory I have come upon, I can but mumble incoherently my
> thanks to a God that guided my faltering steps.

What did Louise, the sophisticated flapper, make of this romantic gush?

We have the answer in her own handwriting, at the bottom of the letter: "After our second meeting and we were engaged!"[59]

What MacArthur's mother made of this whirlwind courtship, this intrusion of another woman into the intimate relationship she enjoyed with her son, is another matter. Douglas himself, it seems, was oblivious to the disruption it represented—or the drastic change that marriage would represent for a forty-one-year-old bachelor. Instead, "Are you really mine, you beautiful white soul," he wrote the first week of November, "you mirth-making child—you passion-breeding woman—you tender-hearted angel—you divine giver of delight . . . You sweet altar of Old Fashioned Roses."[60]

It's not difficult to infer that his relations with Louise involved his first sex with a woman, or at least the first that counted. Louise would later claim that Douglas was a virgin when she met him.[61] It must also have been a strange, if exciting, encounter for her to have this charismatic and virile national war hero all but eating out of her hand—and a sexual novice as well. In any case, she seems to have been as smitten as he was, and plans were made for a wedding in January 1922.

Meanwhile, from her bedroom in the superintendent's house his mother maintained a stony silence.

As preparations got under way, the "mirth-making child" began making inquiries about the man she was about to marry. First she spoke to General Pershing. Whatever sense of disappointment he may have felt at watching his hostess and paramour carried away by a younger rival—one with whom he had rocky relations himself—we can only guess. MacArthur wrote an angry letter when he learned what Pershing told her in response.

"I hate cowardice in a man," MacArthur told Louise, "and this is evidence of just that. He is trying to break your spirit. Don't let him."

What had Pershing said? He had evidently revealed to Louise something that even MacArthur's mother had not known.

Douglas MacArthur had once been engaged to another woman.

To this day no one has found out her last name. We know her simply as Ramona, a young woman MacArthur met in Panama in 1911 when he and a fellow officer were on a brief tour of duty in the Canal Zone. "Ramona was very charming and gracious to us," he told Louise, "and made our stay of four weeks very attractive." A "flirtation" sprang up, he confessed, and after his father died Ramona came to see him in Washington, D.C.

"I was in mourning," MacArthur explained, "not going out and used to drop in on Ramona about twice a week." He thought theirs was a friendship, he said; Ramona, it seemed, had other ideas. She was the "victim of one of those real infatuations which amount almost to a disease."

"I had no love for her but I was shocked at my responsibility," he wrote.

To clear his conscience, he tried to summon up the courage to propose, but "I could not do so." Then on his return from his secret mission to Mexico, he learned to his shock that Ramona was telling everyone they were engaged to be married. He had sent her postcards while in Mexico, and "there might have been letters," but nothing was said that warranted her belief they were about to be bride and groom.

When he went to see her to tell the truth, there was a painful scene.

"She charged that my indifference was due to association with lewd women," he told Louise, hastily adding, "this was untrue. She had by this time become violent with me."[62]

He never gave her a ring, he told Louise, and made no formal proposal. "My part in the affair was characterized by inexperience, vacillation, and weakness. I was young and careless and was plunged into tragedy before realizing it." His one regret was that he had hoped Louise would be spared "this sickening recital."

As for now, "You are the only love of my life, the only woman I have ever coveted or desired to wed," he wrote, "and at the last God will bear me true witness of this in the final day of Judgment."[63]

It was an impressive, if embarrassing, confession to make—especially coming from a man who believed he could never show any flaw or mistake in judgment, on or off the battlefield, without ruining the image of perfection he was supposed to live up to: that of his father. We don't have Louise's reply, but it's obvious that a chill set in on their relationship. And in mid-December Louise sent him a letter that said it was time to postpone the wedding until the following summer.

MacArthur wrote a long, pleading letter in response. She had agreed to marry him in January, then changed it to April. Now came this. He protested. "We can no longer drift." He argued that the summer would be too late; before then he expected to be under orders to leave West Point. "I must pack, must sort our things," and "I cannot do so when everything is so nebulous."

"I pray to God," the letter ended, "that the divine spark will cause you to rise over obstacles—they are really small when analyzed—and give with the generosity of the Queen you are."[64]

Louise acquiesced. On January 15, 1922, they announced their engagement, and they were married on February 14—Valentine's Day. The ceremony wasn't at West Point but in Palm Beach at El Mirasol, Louise's stepfather's estate. It was a chastened bride and a stern groom who marched down the aisle between the two hundred guests. They had had a brief but fierce fight just before the ceremony, when Douglas arrived in his dress whites and medals and found Louise casually standing on a stepladder hanging decorations. She didn't even know where her chiffon dress and diamonds were, but she reacted badly when MacArthur delivered a scolding lecture on the importance of being prompt.

It was, as biographer William Manchester notes, an omen.[65] In any case, the ceremony went off without a hitch and the newspapers carried the headline MARRIAGE OF MARS AND MILLIONS.[66] Of the two hundred guests, however, there was one in particular who was missing. It was Douglas's mother, Pinky. She had flatly refused to attend. Instead, she was back at West Point, supervising the packing.

This was because two weeks after his engagement, MacArthur had learned that General Pershing was removing him as superintendent of West Point.

CHAPTER 9

THE TUMULTUOUS YEARS

With you I live for the first time.
Without you I die for the last time.

—DOUGLAS MACARTHUR

TO LOUISE CROMWELL BROOKS, NOVEMBER 1921

Douglas MacArthur saw his work at the academy as a success.

"My work of reconstruction is almost done," he had told Louise the second week of the previous November. "I have made West Point almost human and in so doing I have turned the enormous resentments that greeted [me] at the end of the war into words of sympathy and praise. . . . Long after I am dead and moulding the Corps will call me Father of West Point."[1]

Later historians like Stephen Ambrose tend to agree. Few thought so at the time, however, and MacArthur seems to have had an inkling that his days as superintendent were increasingly numbered. The fact that the order relieving him of command came from Pershing himself led many to wonder if it was the act of a jilted suitor—so much so that Black Jack had to make a statement to the press denying that the motive was personal. "It's all poppycock," he said, "without the slightest foundation." It was time for General MacArthur to move on for foreign command duty, he explained, and Pershing had found the perfect post for him: the Philippines.[2]

Did Pershing act out of personal as well as sexual spite? No real evidence supports that conclusion; in fact, the bulk of evidence points the other way. In his letter ordering MacArthur's transfer, Pershing expressed his own dissatisfaction with MacArthur's actions as superintendent, especially his agreeing to testify on Capitol Hill about the West Point budget without notifying either Pershing or the secretary of war.[3] In any case, the opposition to what MacArthur was doing at West Point was growing so intense, both inside and outside the academy, that it was inconceivable he would end up serving the usual four-year term as superintendent.

It was in many ways ironic, almost tragic: In trying to carry out Peyton March's wishes for reform, MacArthur had managed to alienate virtually every important constituency at the Point, including many of the cadets themselves. Lacking sufficient support from his superiors, he had seen some of his most important reforms reversed, while others were stuck in abeyance. He also knew his successor, Fred Winchester Sladen, would try to undo as many of the others as he could. "I fancy [Sladen's appointment] means a reversal of many of the progressive policies which we inaugurated," he wrote gloomily.[4]

And so in late June 1922 MacArthur vacated the superintendent's house, while his mother moved into the Wardman Park Hotel in Washington, D.C., with his brother Arthur and his family. Pinky's health was not strong: The few notes she penned during those years that survive show a deteriorating, spidery handwriting.

No one felt she was up to sailing away to the Philippines, and the idea of her, Douglas, and Louise sharing a long voyage across the Pacific was unappealing to all of them.

There is, however, a famous photograph of her from that time, showing her gazing adoringly at a picture of her son that she is holding—no, embracing—in her arms. If her son was determined to make this mistake and marry this woman, she would still think no less of him, the picture says. And if after a few years in the Philippines he did realize he had made a mistake, his mother would stand by him—and give him the support and strength he would need to sever ties with the wife he called his "pulsing, passion flower."

The loving couple sailed from San Francisco on September 25. "My leaving West Point is a matter of complete indifference to me," he had told Louise. "On the ashes of Old West Point I have built a New West Point—strong, virile, and enduring." And indeed, even his fiercest critics have had to agree that what he did at West Point marked a major transformation for the better—and laid the foundations of the academy that trained the officer corps that successfully led the United States Army to victory in World War Two.

All the same, it was not a happy Douglas MacArthur who was returning to the Philippines.

In addition to ending his assignment to West Point on a distinctly sour note, he was also saddled with a less-than-glowing new efficiency report for his personnel file written by his old nemesis, General Pershing.

Pershing's rating of his performance and knowledge was "above average," which in the Army means mediocre. He called MacArthur "a very able young officer with a fine record for courage" but said he "has an exalted opinion of himself." MacArthur was someone whom he had once recommended for promotion to major general. But now Pershing reversed himself. There should be no promotion, he stated, and of the forty-six active brigadier generals in the army, Pershing rated him no better than thirty-eighth—a bitter and as Geoffrey Perret has remarked, unwarranted downgrading.[5]

To what degree personal bitterness over Louise may have influenced Black Jack's judgment is, of course, impossible to determine. But whatever the reasons, Pershing's judgment would have confirmed the unhappy impression that MacArthur had been fired as superintendent. MacArthur must have seen returning to the Philippines as a kind of exile, perhaps even the beginning of the end of his career.

No wonder, then, that his return to the Philippines occupies one of the shortest passages in his memoirs: barely four paragraphs for nearly two and a half years. In many ways, it was the lowest point of his life. Yet it would be crucial to the making of his future and the future of the Philippines.

The presence of Louise did not help his overall mood. MacArthur's professional troubles were increasingly compounded by personal ones. On the voyage out, her children treated their new stepfather with a distant coolness that he returned with interest.

Then there was the luggage issue. Douglas and Louise were traveling with one hundred army officers and forty army wives, including sixteen other newlyweds. Since MacArthur was the ranking officer, his luggage went on the ship first. Unfortunately, Louise had brought so many trunks, hatboxes, and suitcases that the other officers and their wives were limited to one trunk each—and so many automobiles that there was no room in the cargo hold for even a single Model T.[6] Thanks to Louise, Douglas was already the most unpopular American officer in the Philippines before he even stepped off the boat.

Still, there were signs of hope when they landed. The moment he disembarked in Manila Harbor, under "the massive bluff of Bataan and the lean grey grimness of Corregidor," he was amazed at the "the progress that had been made" since he had left Luzon as a lieutenant in 1904. "New roads, new docks, new buildings were everywhere."[7] There was a new legislature, too, the Philippines' first, headed by its energetic, idealistic young president and MacArthur's acquaintance from twenty years ago, Manuel Quezon.

Quezon was preoccupied with charting his own independent course as nationalist leader and avoiding being seen as a tool of American imperialist interests. Indeed, his ultimate goal was full and complete independence, and in 1919 he had gone to Washington to lobby for it. President Wilson and Congress had rebuffed his efforts, but Quezon—and MacArthur—believed the weight of history was on his side.[8]

The other hopeful sign was the presence of MacArthur's old mentor, General Leonard Wood, now governor-general of the Philippines. He greeted his protégé warmly, and then the two of them sat in Wood's office with the electric fan whirring from the ceiling, while the general waxed eloquent on the progress the Philippines had made since MacArthur had last seen it.

"Peace and order reign in every province and archipelago," Wood would have proudly told him. Even the fearsome Moros, the last bastion of resistance during the insurgency that Douglas's father had fought, are "now a peaceful people." Wood was more worried about "the ravages of the business depression" that had descended on the Philippines after the "sudden stoppage of war demands" for Philippine hemp and coconut oil.

Since 1919, Wood stated, the situation had been bad. "Unemployment prevailed, credit deflation continued, monetary circulation fell off, bank deposits decreased, imports diminished, while exports increased." Nor was he very sympathetic to the Quezon-led push for independence. Quite apart from the issue of whether the Filipinos as a people were ready for it, it wasn't clear to Wood how it would help to solve the economic downturn, which he believed ultimately couldn't be overcome without direct U.S. help.[9]

But Wood's biggest headache was the strategic plans being drawn up in Washington, and their implications for the islands. Wood's concerns were shared by Major General William Wright, departmental commander, and then his successor, who arrived shortly after Douglas did, General George Read, with whom MacArthur had served at Leavenworth. The story they told was a woeful one. The Philippine Department was seriously short of men and equipment for the mission it had, especially since planners at the War Department presented them with War Plan Orange.

It dealt with a hypothetical attack on the Philippines by Japan. Washington planners estimated it would be at least six months before any help could arrive from the States. War Plan Orange decreed that in those circumstances, the Philippine Department garrison was to join with native forces to hold Corregidor and Bataan in order to keep the Japanese from using Manila Harbor until help finally arrived—if indeed it ever did.

But how were they supposed to do this, Wright asked, with only 4,100 American soldiers? There were no resources for new, modern fortifications, while the funds needed to maintain, let alone increase the troops there continued to be cut.

Wright and Read could only throw up their hands in frustration. Whenever their protests reached Washington, they were simply told, "The Philippine Department must carry on under the status quo until the time arrives for the establishment of a stable and continuing policy."[10]

Unfortunately, no one could say when that time would be. Indeed, it never came. And neither Wood nor Wright nor Read nor MacArthur himself could know that MacArthur would be the one who would pay the terrible price for a plan for defending the Philippines with American arms that was inadequate from the start.

So America would remain in charge of the Philippines for the foreseeable future, all the while refusing to devote the resources needed to protect the islands or guarantee their security—the very reason the United States claimed it was needed there in the first place. The alternative, cutting losses and abandoning the Philippines to its fate, was not an option. The army's chief planner baldly stated, "Our withdrawal would be encouragement to the pan-Asiatic movement . . . and [leave] our friends of the European nations to bear the white man's burden alone." For the sake of racial superiority, if no other reason, it was important for the Americans to stay.[11]

MacArthur himself had little truck with this kind of thinking. His father had inoculated him against race-based white supremacist arguments; he saw no reason why policymakers in Washington resisted Quezon's call for independence. Then and later, he was convinced that a free and independent Philippines would make a steadfast ally in holding the islands against an armed aggressor—and protecting America's western Pacific flank. But racist "attitudes die hard," he noted years later, "and the old idea of colonial exploitation still had its vigorous supporters," as did those who believed Filipinos were simply incapable of self-rule.[12] It would be another decade and more before MacArthur would have a chance to change American minds on that point.

For now, as brigadier general, he was supposed to head the Military District of Manila, a post created specifically for him. But he had barely five hundred men under his command, and by mid-morning his in tray was largely empty.

So he took to returning home for lunch, to the opulent comfort of 1 Calle Victoria, once the headquarters of the Philippine Constabulary and perched high in the Intramuros. Louise had decorated the villa with ultrachic furnishings while painting the walls jet-black. With virtually unlimited funds at her disposal, she had matching blue naval uniforms made for all the servants, with the letters "MacA" stitched on the breast pocket.

MacArthur taught her son Walter riding, and bought them all a small beach house so they could get away from the summer heat of Manila. Otherwise, it was a life of appalling boredom, especially for Louise. For the woman who had once been the toast of Paris café society, Manila society seemed unfathomably provincial. Their one frequent dinner guest was General Wood, and as the courses came and went she would complain bitterly about MacArthur's exile. Wood would nod and agree, but point out that there was nothing he could do about it.[13]

To relieve her boredom, Louise volunteered to work as a part-time police officer; she even made at least one arrest. So it must have been with some sense of relief for Louise but trepidation for her husband when a telegram arrived from Arthur's wife, Mary, saying that MacArthur's mother was desperately ill. MacArthur announced they were leaving for the States at once.

They returned to America in March 1923 to find Pinky's heart condition worse than ever. Her son Douglas was not overly worried. He had been through this before when he was superintendent and his mother had checked into the post hospital. Doctors then had told him with solemn faces that his mother had days, possibly weeks, to live. He had gone to her bedside, patted her hand, and told her, "I have the finest news in the world. The doctor just told me that you have a strong heart, and you can leave the hospital anytime you want." She checked out in less than a week.[14]

Mary MacArthur's real problem wasn't her heart, but the fact that she was lonely and missed her devoted son. So he found a new army doctor, Howard Hutter, who understood the problem and would be at her side for the rest of her life, even during MacArthur's frequent absences. But while Pinky's physical powers were certainly fading, she remained as sharp and relentless as ever in her quest for her son's future. She even recovered enough to have a meeting with her old friend the army chief of staff, General John Pershing, followed by a long, flirtatious letter.

"It was a real joy to see you on Saturday looking still so young and wonderfully handsome!" it read. "I think you will never grow old." The main purpose of the letter was to urge him to reconsider her son's career. "Can't you find it convenient to give him his promotion during your regime as Chief of Staff?"[15] But the letter brought only silence from Pershing and no relief for MacArthur. He returned to the Philippines with his prospects as frozen as ever.

There was, however, one glimmer on the horizon. In June, MacArthur was given command of a brigade of the brand-new Philippine Division, based at Fort William McKinley. Created in April 1922, the 7,000-man division was the brainchild of Brigadier General Omar Bundy, whom MacArthur had known during his AEF days. It was an effort, admittedly on a shoestring, to make up for the shortfall of American troops by integrating Filipino troops into a divisional organization under American command. These were the Forty-fifth and Fifty-seventh regiments of the Philippine Scouts, the elite corps of Filipino volunteers created during the 1900 insurrection.

For MacArthur, the post meant a welcome return to the routine of commanding an infantry unit, even during peacetime. He also discovered to his delight that the tough, able Scouts generally outperformed their American counterparts in field exercises, especially at marksmanship.[16] Among his other duties was mapping out a defensive perimeter for the Bataan Peninsula in case of attack. It meant mapping more than forty square miles of wilderness with a team of surveyors and engineers. "I covered every foot of rugged terrain, over its trails, up and down its steep mountainous slopes, and through the bamboo thickets," he wrote. He was able to hand over the job to the department's chief engineer the next year with relief. But he also acquired an intimate knowledge of that peninsula that came in handy in much darker and more dire circumstances some eighteen years later.[17]

MacArthur developed a strong respect for the Filipinos under his command—"they were excellent troops," he said years later, "completely professional, loyal, and devoted"—and by most indications they became devoted to him. So it must have come as a considerable shock when on a steamy morning in July 1924 his American officers burst into his office with chilling news.

His Scouts were in mutiny.

The first indication of trouble had come the night of June 27, when Fort McKinley's provost marshal heard a gentle but urgent knock at his door.

It was a Filipino Scout from the Fifty-seventh—the same regiment in which that previous year every company had scored 100 percent in its rifle and machine-gun marksmanship. "I believe this is the first regiment in the Army of the United States to make such a remarkable record," MacArthur's boss, General Read, had written.[18] This nervous Scout informed the provost marshal that there were ongoing meetings at the barracks and in homes outside the fort, and the Scouts were seething.

The Scouts had found out they were drawing less than half the pay of the American troops and had none of their financial benefits, like hardship pay. The disgruntled Scouts were determined to take action, and were preparing to "step out for their rights," the man told the provost marshal. He said the other Scouts would kill him if they knew he was speaking to an American, and then he slipped back out into the night.[19]

Remarkably, the provost marshal seems to have done nothing until July 6, when he broke up one such meeting at the post hospital. Perhaps he thought it was panicky gossip; or perhaps he believed it was impossible that the redoubtable Scouts could waver in their duty.

Everyone was disabused of this hope the next day, when the bulk of two battalions refused to obey orders for drill. The disturbed officers turned to MacArthur, who quickly called the military police to quell the scene. There was no violence, no abuse of white officers or attack on the facilities. The Scouts themselves called it a "strike," not a mutiny. But they refused to form, drill, or obey any orders. In the end, MPs rounded up 222 mutineers and marched them off to the post guardhouse. Although the mutiny spread briefly to another regiment the next day, the entire episode ended almost as suddenly as it had begun.

All the same, the story of the mutiny caused a national sensation—and for American officers in the Philippines, it was an unwelcome wake-up call. They began to wonder what would happen if they found themselves facing an attacking enemy in front, but had an unwilling ally—or even a hostile enemy—at their rear? Contrary to the assertion of some later scholars, American authorities didn't entirely ignore the problem. In fact, one of the steps toward reform was appointing MacArthur in Bundy's place, especially since MacArthur was known to be a supporter of equal status of his Filipino soldiers with whites.

Yet nothing much could be done about the core grievances, which revolved around pay—especially when the Philippine Department had a demonstrably tight budget. As for Filipinos, mutiny meant the Scouts lost their luster as an elite force. Instead, they looked like everybody else: natives deprived of equal status with their American partners. "Whereas in the past, they have applied for enlistment" in such numbers that there was a waiting list for joining the Scouts, Read had to report, "a new and difficult situation confronts this department . . . in which Scout soldiers will have to be recruited."[20]

Then or later, MacArthur revealed nothing about his feelings regarding the mutiny. It doesn't merit even a mention in his memoirs. But if MacArthur had set himself the task of restoring trust, or even equalizing the pay and benefits of his Scouts, he never had enough time to try.

On September 24, less than two months after taking over the division, he got the welcome news he had been waiting for for five years. He was being promoted to major general.

The chief obstacle to his advancement, Pershing, had finally been forced to retire at the mandatory age of sixty-four. His successor, John L. Hines, immediately moved MacArthur to the head of the promotion list, which became effective in January 1925. MacArthur just missed being the youngest major general since the Civil War. But as his press ally, *The New York Times*, noted, he was still the youngest on the active list, and "with good health he stands a splendid chance of some day becoming head of the army."[21]

With the appointment came even more welcome news. He and Louise and the children were going back to the States. He would be heading up the IV Corps Area outside Atlanta, to assume the full duties of an American two-star general in peacetime.

His career was on the move again. As their ship set sail with five Filipino servants and Louise's pile of steamer trunks and furniture, Douglas MacArthur must have wondered if he would ever see those islands again.

Indeed he would, sooner than he thought. But not before he, and the army, had gone through a wrenching series of crises, both personal and professional.

And when he returned, he would be alone.

For the newly minted major general, Atlanta's main attractions weren't the duties of heading IV Corps Area, which included such exciting feats as sending troops from Fort Bragg to help rescue miners trapped in a North Carolina mine explosion and overseeing the summer training of ROTC volunteers and reservists. It was wandering northwest of town to visit the battlefields where his father had served during the Civil War. In his memoirs he says, "They became daily sites to me"—and daily reminders of the price of valor in an America determined to forget about war, suffering, and sacrifice.[22]

One was Kennesaw Mountain, where Major Arthur MacArthur had led the Twenty-fourth Wisconsin on June 24, 1864, in a reconnaissance against Confederate forces. Now his son wandered along the south face of the mountain, where the Wisconsin men had come under withering fire from rebel rifle pits and nineteen-year-old Arthur took a bullet in the chest. He went down at once; his men assumed he was dead. But minutes later he was miraculously on his feet and leading his men again, in an orderly retreat, leaving twenty-five dead and wounded behind.

Back at camp the regimental surgeon examined his wound. Luckily the bullet had been spent and had wedged itself under the skin, directly over his heart, but somehow it hadn't penetrated farther. They all wondered why, MacArthur included. What they found was that a packet of letters in his chest pocket from his father the judge had cushioned the impact and let him escape death with no more than a bad bruise. A good story for a laugh around the campfire, and one to tell his sons years later—but also a reminder of how close and sudden mortality can be on the battlefield.[23]

Then the younger MacArthur wandered through the groves of Peach Tree Creek where Union forces on July 20 met a savage attack by Confederate troops under their new general, John Bell Hood, and again the Twenty-fourth Wisconsin had been in the thick of it. "On the enemy came again and again," a Twenty-fourth veteran, Moritz Tschepe, remembered. "They came without skirmishers and with yells whose volume exceeded any battle shout ever heard," as Union troops poured on volley after volley and fired grapeshot at the charging rebels almost point-blank. The fighting went on until nearly dark, when MacArthur's bone-weary men were finally able to drop to their knees and lay down their rifles. Ringed around them were the bodies of nearly 4,800 Confederate dead and wounded, to 1,710 Union casualties.[24]

The crash of guns, the roar of musketry, faint bugle calls and drums beating the long roll: Mac must have fancied he could hear them all, then could hear them fade to silence. They had fallen silent in his own time; but would the army to which both he and his father had dedicated their lives be ready when the sound of guns returned, this time on a scale no one—certainly not his father—could ever have imagined?

For months he had been expressing his worries to General Wood, who in contrast to Pershing had been a keen supporter of MacArthur's promotion.[25]

Finally the army had listened to Wood, and MacArthur had a major general's two stars. But now MacArthur wondered if there would be an army modern and competent enough for an officer like himself to command. It was a question he would be confronting head-on in only few months, but far away in Baltimore.

This was because his father's deeds had made him a marked man in Atlanta. MacArthur and his staff discovered this the first time they attended Sunday service at a local Episcopal church. As he and his men took their seats, heads swiveled and words were whispered. More heads turned and the buzz of conversation began to drown out the service. Then, one by one, three-quarters of the congregation got up and left.[26]

A furious MacArthur fired off a telegram to the War Department requesting an immediate transfer. It came three months later, to III Corps Area with its headquarters at Fort McHenry in Baltimore, and MacArthur gratefully left the city of Atlanta to the bitter memories of the vanquished.

Baltimore was a double blessing because it was only a twenty-minute drive from Louise's estate at Rainbow Hill, and closer to Washington, where his mother was living, frail and ill but as much a charismatic presence as ever. But it was also the setting for tragedy, because barely he had unpacked his trunks when "one of the most distasteful orders I ever received" reached his desk.[27]

He was to preside at the court-martial of his friend Colonel Billy Mitchell.

On July 21, 1921, Mitchell and fellow pilots at the controls of a Martin B-1 bomber had sunk a confiscated German battleship, the *Ostfriesland,* in waters off Chesapeake Bay—the first time a naval vessel had been sunk by aerial attack, a vessel dubbed by its German builders and American inspectors as unsinkable. Then just to prove it was no fluke, Mitchell did the same twice more in 1923, this time to decommissioned American battleships. In Mitchell's mind, he had proved once and for all that the airplane was now the dominant weapon of modern warfare. No country, no city, and certainly no navy in the world was safe.

Admirals and officials at the Navy Department furiously denied that assertion—and many in the army were just as doubtful. Was the army supposed to shift resources to this new experimental technology, the airplane, versus the tried-and-true military arms that had sustained the army through a world war? Next they'll be telling the cavalry they have to give up their horses, Mitchell's colleagues scoffed after their second Scotch at the officers' club. What they did not realize was that they too had been shown the future—how a new technology in sufficient quantity and in the right hands could bring decisive results on the battlefield. However, they chose to turn their backs on it, and on Mitchell.

When his effort to create an air force that was coequal with the army and navy failed, Mitchell had grown more outspoken and bitter. Finally he was demoted to colonel and shipped off to Hawaii. Instead of fading from the scene, however, he wrote and published *Winged Defense,* predicting that someday bombers would find a way to launch a surprise attack on the Hawaiian Islands, unless the navy and the army recognized the potential value and also the potential threat, of airpower. Both organizations ignored it, although both agreed that the wayward colonel was a painful thorn in their side that they wanted removed.

It was his reaction to the crash of the navy airship *Shenandoah,* however, that finally brought the accumulated rage down on his head. Mitchell told anyone who would listen, including reporters, that the accident, and a similar crash of seaplanes off Hawaii, was "the direct result of the incompetency, criminal negligence, and almost treasonable administration of the national defense. . . . As a patriotic American citizen, I can stand by no longer and see these disgusting performances by the Navy and War Departments."[28]

That did it. With President Coolidge's approval, the army ordered Mitchell court-martialed for bringing "discredit upon the military service" and "conduct prejudicial to good order and discipline"—some even thought his inflammatory comments were an invitation to mutiny by members of the newly formed Air Corps. So Mitchell found himself summoned to Washington in late October 1925 to face the charges before a panel of senior officers who would act as both judge and jury.

One of them was to be Douglas MacArthur.

It put MacArthur in an almost unbearable position. He had virtually grown up with Mitchell in Milwaukee. Mitchell had served under his father in the Philippines, and both served together on the western front. Although

Mitchell usually detested West Pointers as narrow-minded stuffed shirts, he had made a big exception in MacArthur's case, while MacArthur sensed that Mitchell's advocacy of the importance of airpower, if overstated, was largely right. "Neither ground nor sea forces can operate safely," he had said publicly, "unless the air over them is controlled by our own air power."[29]

MacArthur even invited him to speak at West Point on the topic. Then Mitchell came out to the Philippines on a visit, where he pointed out inadequacies of air defenses, as he often did when he visited any military installation, and even gave old Aguinaldo a ride in his plane over the jungle.[30] Certainly MacArthur was one of the judges Mitchell assumed he could count on for the most support.

But MacArthur was the youngest on the panel and only one of eight judges. The rest of the panel included Pershing favorite Frank McCoy and the new superintendent of West Point, Fred Sladen, both of whom were deeply hostile to Mitchell and his ideas. So was the president of the court, MacArthur's old corps commander from the Rainbow days, General Charles Summerall. MacArthur probably realized at this juncture of his career that he would gain nothing by pushing Mitchell's case; it could only cost him the future support of his superiors and peers.

On the other hand, he had nothing to lose by remaining as neutral as possible, to the point of complete self-effacement—no easy task for the Fighting Dude and hero of the Côte de Châtillon. Throughout the trial MacArthur never spoke or made a motion or even questioned a witness. He sat, Mitchell later remembered, with "his features as cold as carved stone."[31]

The one emotion he showed was a smile when Louise showed up every day with a bunch of fresh flowers.

Meanwhile, Mitchell's defense lawyers ran circles around the prosecutors. They even got Summerall removed for bias, with Major General Robert Lee Howze taking his place.[32] Louise herself sat next to Betty, Mitchell's sister, and during the breaks chatted amiably enough. Even old Mrs. MacArthur herself, cane in hand, came to hear his final summation. Everything suggested that MacArthur was in Mitchell's corner, along with, the airman figured, three other judges. In his mind, and in the minds of the public following the trial's headlines, it seemed certain that this case and the cause of airpower would be vindicated for good.

On Thursday, December 17, the last solemn arguments were heard and the jury of generals left the court to deliberate. At 6:35 P.M. the jury door swung open and the generals walked back into the court after four grueling hours. MacArthur, according to witnesses, looked wan and exhausted. To Mitchell, "he looked as if he had been dragged through a knothole."[33]

While Mitchell stood at attention, the verdict was read. It stunned everyone. He had been found guilty on all specifications, by two-thirds of the jury—enough to convict. Mitchell stood motionless as the court adjourned, his face a mask. "Why, these men are my friends," a reporter overheard him saying. He was thinking certainly of MacArthur.

So how did MacArthur vote? Mitchell never learned how any of the generals voted, and to this day no one knows. Mitchell's sister was never convinced that MacArthur voted not guilty; although Mitchell himself later told a disciple, "Some day people will realize how good a friend of mine he was back there in 1925."[34]

MacArthur himself always insisted that his had been the sole not guilty vote, and even persuaded the others not to dismiss Mitchell from the service but let him earn his pension and retirement after a five-year lapse—and since that's what happened, MacArthur's account might be true. One bit of physical evidence did surface that backed his story. Seventeen years later, Mayor Fiorello La Guardia, who had testified at the trial, told a Mitchell biographer that a reporter rummaging through a wastebasket in the jury room found a slip of paper with the vote of not guilty.

The handwriting was MacArthur's.[35]

True or not, years later MacArthur's opinion on the Mitchell case was crystal clear. "It is part of my military philosophy that a senior officer should not be silenced for being at variance with his superiors in rank and with accepted doctrine. . . . When a ranking officer, out of purely patriotic motives, risk[s] his own personal future in such opposition, he should not be summarily suppressed. Superior authority can, of course, do so if it wishes, but the one thing in this world that cannot be stopped is a sound idea. *The individual may be martyred, but his thoughts live on* [italics are mine]."[36]

MacArthur wrote these words twelve years after his own harrowing experience in Korea. He knew the subject of that last sentence might have been himself.

*   *   *

Adding to the pain of those years in Baltimore was the fact that his marriage was falling apart.

Douglas MacArthur tried to adjust to the affluent suburban lifestyle that Louise loved, a lifestyle out of an F. Scott Fitzgerald or John O'Hara novel. The house on Rainbow Hill became the setting for rounds of Jazz Age parties and dinners. MacArthur joined the Green Spring Valley Country Club, spent many hours riding to hounds after the foxes of rural Maryland and attending hunt balls, as well as dutifully discussing investments with the husbands of Louise's friends.

MacArthur was no fool about money; he had married into it. He resisted attempts to draw him and Louise into the current Florida real estate boom, which he correctly predicted was going to end badly. He also resisted calls from his wife and her family to retire from the Army and join a swank law firm like the one owned by her family, the Cromwells of Sullivan & Cromwell. Years before, his mother had tried to tempt him with a lucrative position with E. H. Harriman's Union Pacific Railroad, but she failed. Louise failed as well.

Certainly this marriage was not going as she had planned. Louise had endured the Philippines, almost the way Pinky had endured New Mexico and Texas. She had tried to make the the best of it, even there. Now Louise became disillusioned with a husband stuck in what she saw as a dead-end profession. She was also distressed that the husband she contemptuously referred to in private as "Sir Galahad" was fast losing interest in sex with a woman whose feminine allure was now lost under a layer of middle-aged fat. "The general," she would say years later after a round of drinks, "is a buck private in bed."

Yet despite her pleas, MacArthur was adamant about not leaving the army. But there must have been moments when, at age forty-five and seated at his desk surrounded by meaningless reports and bound to a rigid routine of inspections and meetings, he wondered if he had gone as far in his profession as he could—and whether serving in this peacetime army was really worth the effort. His first tour of III Corps Area found motor transport "in poor condition," with trucks and vehicles built during the world war worn out beyond repair. "Harbor Defenses of the Potomac have been abandoned," he reported, while "Air Corps activities have been devoted almost entirely to the training of the National Guard and Organized Reserves." Meanwhile, "reduction in personnel of the troops under current allotments renders it impossible to supply demonstration units for National Guard camps," while parents were reluctant to send their sons to Corps Military Training camps even for a single month. And the army's own training schedule was impossible to draw up because no one knew whether the funds would be there. The army's budget had been cut to less than $380 million, with fewer than 135,000 men under arms—even as pacifist groups were growing in number, as were the demands for making war "illegal."[37]

A deeply frustrated MacArthur had the opportunity to strike back, at least in a minor way, when he was asked to speak at the Sailors and Soldiers Club banquet at the Ritz-Carlton in New York on April 7, 1927. He chose as his theme the calls across the nation for disarmament, on the very day after French foreign minister Aristide Briand issued a public letter to the American people urging them to support an international treaty outlawing war. MacArthur was determined to disagree.

"Total disarmament is unthinkable," he told his audience. "No one takes seriously the equally illogical plan of disbanding our fire department to stop fires or disbanding our police departments to stop crime. Our country insists upon respect for its rights, and gives due recognition to the rights of all others. But so long as humanity is governed by motives not in accord with Christianity, we are in danger of an attack directed by unworthy impulses. We should be prepared against brutal attack. . . .

"Our nation has shrunk from enforced military service," he continued. "But between the two extremes has been evolved the conception of citizen soldiery," who are called up in a national emergency and trained to fight by a cadre of regular professional officers, commissioned and noncommissioned.

"Upon the successful solution of this problem—the citizen soldier—will depend the very life of our nation," MacArthur emphasized. "And when the bloody test comes, some American chief, on the day of victory, is going to thank God for what this nation is now building up in its citizen soldiery."[38]

Unfortunately, right then there didn't seem to be much building up—it was mostly tearing down. That included his marriage. That summer Louise left him and moved to New York City. So it was with a sense of deep relief as well as expectation, that he asked for and accepted the post of president of the U.S. Olympic Committee.

If the Douglas MacArthur of the 1920s was the father of the modern West Point, one could also argue he was the father of modern American Olympic sports.

It's hard to remember that when MacArthur left West Point the modern Olympic Games were barely a quarter century old. A big question remained about how much time and money the United States should divert—or waste, some thought—to the Olympic effort. When the president of the U.S. Olympic Committee died suddenly, with the 1928 games in the Netherlands less than a year away, MacArthur's name came up as a replacement. It was a natural choice. He was already famous for his advocacy of sports at West Point and amateur sports generally; the previous year he had organized a football game between the Army and the Marine Corps, in which MacArthur's team trounced the leathernecks, much to the delight of his old chief General Charles Summerall.[39]

MacArthur accepted the post with enthusiasm, and threw himself into the task as if he were planning a military campaign. Everything about it suited him, from meeting with coaches, giving inspiring speeches to athletes, and sponsoring committees, to planning the travel and workout schedule. He even took pleasure in contemptuously dismissing sports reporters and other naysayers who questioned his decisions, such as allowing the legendary sprinter Charley Paddock—"the World's Fastest Human"—to play in the games even though Paddock was under investigation for accepting money, which threatened his amateur status. "We won't stand for sniping from the rear," he wrote in a furious telegram to critics—and that, as far as MacArthur was concerned, was that.[40]

When the team arrived in Holland, "the outlook was not bright for our entrants," MacArthur wrote later, "but I was determined that the United States should win at Amsterdam."[41] He became in effect the coach-in-chief, attending every practice he could and meeting with athletes to evaluate their performance and motivate them to a higher level. MacArthur admitted that he rode them hard: "I stormed and pleaded and cajoled." He constantly reiterated the link between American sports and American exceptionalism. He told them that since America was the greatest nation in the world, it deserved to have the greatest Olympic team—and he meant to deliver on that proposition. "We have not come 3,000 miles just to lose gracefully," he thundered. "We are here to win, and win decisively."

When the U.S. boxing team's coach threatened to withdraw the team from further competition after a blatantly unfair decision, MacArthur barked, "Americans never quit."[42] Some coaches and athletes grumbled at the constant badgering and micromanagement, but most, as one steeplechaser observed, admired "MacArthur's earnest efforts and zeal."

It paid off. By the time the games were over, the United States had won twenty-four gold medals, more than the next two countries, Finland and Germany, put together. The U.S. team had set no less than seventeen Olympic records and seven world records. When they returned to the United States, they were feted and celebrated across the country, while MacArthur wrote up a stirring and dramatic report for President Coolidge on their performance. It began, "To portray adequately the vividness and brilliance of that great spectacle would be worthy even of the pen of Homer himself" and ended by urging that the financing of the Olympic Committee be put on a more regular basis with a $2 million endowment fund, so that more time could be devoted to training and coaching than fundraising.

" 'Athletic America' is a telling phrase," MacArthur wrote. "It is talismanic. It suggests health and happiness. It arouses national pride and kindles anew the national spirit. . . . Nothing has been more characteristic of the genius of the American people than their genius for athletics"—and the U.S. Olympic team, MacArthur believed, had to be the summing up of that national genius of a "more sturdy, more self-reliant, a more self-helping people."[43]

The experience, he said, "has made me proud to be an American." Another who was proud was his old commander Charles Summerall, who sent MacArthur a letter the day they returned to New York. "You have not only maintained the reputation that Americans do not quit," it read, "but that Americans know how to win."[44]

But perhaps MacArthur's finest hour came when they were leaving Amsterdam harbor. Two athletes who had failed to make the Olympic team but stowed away anyway to be with the team, found themselves stranded without any money and couldn't pay for passage back to the United States. The entire team lined the ship's rails, looking helplessly down on the hapless pair as the ship prepared to sail. Then suddenly MacArthur ambled down the gangway before it pulled away, spoke a few words to a ship's officer, and then rushed the two men on board. "You should have heard the cheer that went up," one of them, a University of Michigan athlete, remembered. Once the ship was well clear, MacArthur explained that he had struck a bargain with the officer to let the stowaways work off their passage with a few odd jobs around the ship.

They spent the rest of the voyage across the Atlantic on their hands and knees scraping paint.[45]

General Summerall had told MacArthur that he showed the world once again that Americans know how to win. It was a message of optimism and hope that the public was going to need over the next five years, and none more than the U.S. Army. It was even one that would have been welcome to MacArthur himself, as a man trapped in a ruined marriage and a potentially dead-end career.

Yet the truth was that his career was finally beginning to turn around. At the age of forty-eight he was poised for a series of major breakthroughs as well as disappointments. A series of events would decisively shape his character and his national reputation, both for better and for worse—as well as shape the nation. The Douglas MacArthur who would become an American hero during World War Two emerged over these next years, as would the Douglas MacArthur whom Franklin D. Roosevelt would pronounce "the most dangerous man in America."

CHAPTER 10

SAVING THE ARMY

*From Magna Carta to the present day there is little in
our institutions worth having or worth perpetuating
that has not been achieved for us by armed men.*

—DOUGLAS MACARTHUR, ADDRESS TO THE
REUNION OF VETERANS OF THE RAINBOW
DIVISION, WASHINGTON, D.C., JULY 14, 1935

The turnaround began almost as soon as MacArthur returned to the
United States from the Olympic Games. He learned he was being reassigned back to Manila, but this time as commander of the entire Philippine
Department. "No assignment could have pleased me more," he wrote.[1]

The last time he had been in the Philippines it had been at the nadir in his
career and life. This time he would be going without the encumbrance of
Louise; she and her children would remain in the States as their divorce became finalized. He would also be the man who had given America its first
major Olympic triumph. More important, this time he would also have some
executive power as well as responsibility. Now others would be seeking him
out for advice and support—including his friend and now Philippine president Manuel Quezon.

Their friendship had deepened during MacArthur's earlier three years in
the Philippines. Douglas was a frequent guest at the Quezon home, where
the two men would sit on the veranda and discuss the major trends sweeping
across Asia: the growing power of nationalist movements challenging the
white man's colonial rule and "the growing threat of Japanese expansion," as
MacArthur later put it, particularly in the Philippines.

"Thousands of Japanese [immigrants] were pouring into Davao, in the great southern island of Mindanao," where they were becoming an important commercial colony—but also, MacArthur worried, a growing possible security threat. Quezon felt otherwise; he tended to see the Japanese as a boost to the Philippines' economic fortunes.[2] But both agreed that Japan's imperial ambitions in the Pacific posed a danger to peace and stability—and that Asia's European colonial powers would soon find themselves overwhelmed not only by nationalist challengers like Mohandas Gandhi in India and Chiang Kai-shek in China, but by an upsurgent Japan, as well.

"The stage was being set for a vast political and social upheaval, vitally affecting every land and race in East Asia," MacArthur remembered. Both he and Quezon saw "the possibility that the Philippines could easily be caught in the struggle for power" that would engulf the entire Pacific. Yet Americans remained woefully ignorant about the growing threat, and the pitiful lack of preparation for it in the Philippine Department.[3]

During his previous assignment in the Philippines, MacArthur had experienced firsthand the apathy emanating from Washington, and the difficulties in trying to overcome its destructive inertia. This time, from the moment he arrived in Manila in October 1928, MacArthur strove to pull the department's resources up to working speed himself. He was delighted to get the War Department to finally give the Philippine Scouts their pay increase and pensions after thirty years' service, which triggered a marked increase in morale and efficiency in that elite force. It also reinforced MacArthur's reputation among Filipinos, both military and civilian, which would steadily grow. The seeds of the MacArthur who would become a Philippine national hero were planted in these crucial years.[4]

Otherwise, the situation looked bleak. When one of his predecessors, Fred Sladen (ironically, the man who succeeded MacArthur as superintendent of West Point), was asked by *his* successor what the War Department's plan for the Philippines was, Sladen had told the man bluntly, "There isn't any plan, and you won't get any money, so go to it and do the best you can."[5]

In 1928 the Joint Board (predecessor of the Joint Chiefs of Staff) estimated that the Japanese could land 300,000 troops in the Philippines a month after a war started. To face them MacArthur would have 11,000 Regular troops and Scouts, 6,000 Constabulary, and an air force of exactly nine obsolete bombers and eleven fighters.[6] No wonder the board had shrunk the department's mission from conducting offensive-defensive operations on Luzon to keep the Japanese at bay to simply defending Manila Bay, especially Corregidor, in hopes that these paltry forces could hold out with the help of the Asiatic Naval Detachment—although recent cuts in the number of American warships made that support look shaky as well.

The main culprit, in both MacArthur's eyes and the eyes of the U.S. Navy, was the Washington Naval Treaty of 1921–22, also called the Five-Power Treaty. Crafted at the behest of American secretary of state Charles Evans Hughes, the treaty had limited the future construction of naval ships by the five victorious powers in the Great War, including the United States and Japan. In order to meet the 5-5-3 ratio of U.S. and British capital ships compared to their Japanese counterparts the treaty's terms imposed, however, the navy had had to scrap twenty-eight battleships and cruisers, while agreeing not to build more beyond a certain size. The restrictions also included a ban on new fortifications in the Philippines. The treaty's goal was to prevent an international arms race. Its real effect was to make defense of the Philippines almost impossible, and to seriously weaken the U.S. Navy, as even Japan's navy was free to build and build.

Yet the problems went beyond the Washington Treaty. MacArthur had to ask: if keeping the Philippines as an American base in the Pacific was important, where was the commitment of resources to do it? He still believed the Philippines could be "a military asset," but that would entail both more money and a change in the attitude toward the Filipinos, especially on the issue of independence. Here he found a sympathetic ear in the new governor-general, Henry Stimson, whose view on the future of the Philippines differed markedly from that of his predecessor Leonard Wood. Stimson too believed in the white man's burden and the American mission in the Philippines, but he also believed it was possible to evolve a relationship like that of Great Britain with its Commonwealth nations such as Australia and Canada.[7]

This was some distance from MacArthur's belief that independence was the best route to secure the islands' future alliance with the United States—and to dispel growing anti-Americanism among Filipino nationalists. But the two men formed a warm working relationship in the short time Stimson was there (he had come in March 1928 to fill in after General Wood's sudden death) that would serve them both well during World War Two.

With Stimson's departure in 1929, it crossed MacArthur's mind that he himself might be a good candidate for the next governor-general. In addition to a major advance for his career, it would empower him to shape more of U.S. policy toward the Philippines. He even managed to plant that idea with *The New York Times,* which published a story in April saying that "according to highly reliable information, the latest active candidate for the Governor Generalship is Gen. MacArthur, commanding the Philippine Army of the American Army."

The reliable source was, of course, MacArthur himself.[8]

President Herbert Hoover named Dwight Davis, former secretary of war, instead. But since coming into office that March, Hoover had had his eye on MacArthur. Indeed, forces were in motion back in Washington that would land him the job that had eluded his father—a disappointment that had certainly contributed to Arthur MacArthur's death.

In the summer of 1930 Army Chief of Staff Charles Summerall was set to retire. As the issue of who would replace him loomed, his mind turned to the former battalion commander from the Rainbow Division whom he had seen in action more than a decade ago, and who was now struggling to complete the fortification of Corregidor in Manila Harbor some 12,000 miles away.

Looking over the list of active officers, Summerall could see that there was a seniority issue. MacArthur ranked only seventh among the active major generals, but none of those in front of him had more than two years before mandatory retirement at sixty-four, and the typical term for a chief of staff was four years. The others included two other major generals appointed the same year as MacArthur, in 1925. One was Pershing's former operations chief General Fox Conner; the other was the brilliant Major General William Connor, head of the Army War College. But neither of them had MacArthur's wartime record or General Staff service, let alone experience of being in charge of an army corps area at home or a department overseas. And neither was as familiar a name on Capitol Hill as MacArthur, thanks to his service as superintendent of West Point and, one could add, on the U.S. Olympic Committee.[9]

Yet when Summerall proposed MacArthur's name to Hoover's secretary of war, Patrick Hurley, Hurley was unconvinced. Hurley had served in the World War in the Judge Advocate General's Office and the field artillery, and won his own Silver Star for bravery. No doubt he had heard a lot about the Fighting Dude during his time in France; much of it may not have been very complimentary. In any case, Hurley decided he would travel out to Omaha, Nebraska, to talk to Johnson Hagood, commander of the VII Corps Area and a former aide to Leonard Wood, and ask him about MacArthur.

He half expected Hagood to present his own case for being made chief of staff. Instead, Hagood sang MacArthur's praises. Hurley listened with a skeptical ear.

"Isn't he vain?" he insisted. "Isn't he pompous? Intolerant of his superiors' wishes and overbearing toward civilians?"

Hagood shook his head. MacArthur was "the ablest man and the best soldier" in the army. He was the perfect choice for chief of staff.[10]

Hoover, meanwhile, was hearing from two heavyweights who were also keen on MacArthur. One was Peyton March; the other was publisher Roy Howard of the Scripps-Howard newspaper chain, a stronger political supporter of Hoover but also of General MacArthur—whom he secretly saw as possible presidential timber in the future.

One heavyweight came out strongly against MacArthur: Black Jack Pershing. He wanted his protégé Frank McCoy instead and after an unsatisfactory interview with Hurley, who was still convinced that MacArthur was the right choice, the American victor of World War One demanded one last interview with the president himself.

Pershing was adamant, almost desperate. Appoint anyone as chief of staff, he pleaded, as long as it's not MacArthur. Hoover was half inclined to agree. He was miffed that MacArthur had turned down the chief of engineers appointment that Hoover had offered him in July—an appointment that MacArthur refused in part because he sensed the chief of staff job might be coming. No president likes to hear someone say no; it's a privilege he entirely reserves for himself.

So afterward Hoover turned to Hurley. Maybe it's time to find a compromise candidate, he told his secretary of war; maybe MacArthur was just too controversial.

Now it was Hurley's turn to be adamant. He refused to budge on MacArthur, and Hoover reluctantly went along.[11] The president put the best face on things, saying, "I searched the Army for younger blood, and I finally determined upon General Douglas MacArthur. His brilliant abilities and his sterling character need no exposition from me." So did Pershing: "[H]e is one of my boys. I have nothing more to say." Indeed, he didn't.[12]

The radiogram went out to Manila from the acting chief of staff on August 5: "President has just announced your detail as Chief of Staff to succeed General Summerall. My heartiest congratulations."

The news came as no shock to MacArthur. He had known of Summerall's imminent departure for months, and cultivated his relations with Hurley since the spring.[13] The only surprise may have been that it was coming sooner than he would have expected. He was only fifty, the third youngest ever. "I had been in military service for thirty-one years," he wrote long afterward, "years of receiving orders and following policies I had not promulgated . . . Now the responsibility of making decisions and giving the orders was mine."[14] And he was taking responsibility when America, and the world, were on the verge of extraordinary turmoil.

Just eight months earlier had come Black Tuesday and the great Wall Street crash. The last French troops were leaving the Rhineland, the last remaining buffer between their country and Germany. Mohandas Gandhi was starting his Salt March, which would shake British rule in India to its foundations. Josef Stalin's bloody purges of the Soviet Communist Party were poised to begin, and in China the civil war between Chiang Kai-shek and Mao Zedong was taking a new and violent turn in the country's northern provinces.

MacArthur was even planning an official tour of China, Japan, and Korea, much as he and his father had done in 1904–05, including Manchuria, where there was growing tension between the native Chinese and their Japanese occupiers. Now he had to cancel his plan.[15] But it was clear to him that this growing arc of crisis, which included Soviet territory in Asia, would inevitably have a direct impact on American interests in the region, including the Philippines.

But for now it was a moment for celebration, and also reflection.

There was a series of banquets in his honor, attended by Quezon, Manuel Roxas, and other Filipino politicians thanking him for his service and devotion to the Philippine people. The biggest was at the Manila Hotel, where one speaker after another praised MacArthur and wished him luck in his new position. He rose to his feet and, according to a reporter, gave "a more or less extemporaneous address" that lasted some forty minutes.

"Leaving the Philippines is severing the threads of connection that have linked me with this country for thirty years," he said. In that time "the world has changed more rapidly than in any other period," particularly "the shift of the center of interest from the Atlantic to the Pacific."

He continued, "You in this hall are engaged in a momentous task. The Asiatic continent is at present undergoing an adjustment of its Oriental background to an Occidental point of view." The rhetoric may have been old-fashioned, but MacArthur had put his finger on the problem that would haunt Asia for the rest of the twentieth century, and beyond.

"Can this problem be solved?" MacArthur believed it could. Bringing together Asia and the West, including Western economies and technology, would require courage, intelligence, and a sense of balance, "a sense of proportion and relative importance of things" between the energies of the West and the values of the East.

But above all, he said, it would demand a sense of tolerance.

> History teaches us that, when two races are brought by the working of an inscrutable Providence to live together, tolerance, a sympathetic understanding of each other's desires, hopes, and aspirations, is the inescapable necessity. . . . It raises to sublimity him who extends it, and him who by accepting it, shows his readiness to return it in kind.[16]

It was a principle—MacArthur would argue a biblical principle—that he would invoke to guide his policy not only in the Philippines but also, some sixteen years later, in a conquered and defeated Japan.

*   *   *

MacArthur arrived in San Francisco and was formally sworn in as army chief of staff on November 21, 1930. He was exhilarated about his new position, which gratified a lifetime's ambition. Still, there was some trepidation. It was characteristic that before he accepted the job he had summed up his doubts in a telegram to his mother, who wrote back, "[Y]our father would be ashamed if you showed timidity." Also characteristically, she now joined him in the big red-brick house at Fort Myer, No. 1, that would be his home and headquarters. She was now seventy-eight, frailer and less mobile but personally as formidable as ever. MacArthur had a sunporch built across the back of the second floor and he installed an elevator, both for his mother's comfort. Then, "I moved into quarters . . . and prepared to face the music."[17]

It would be louder, and more discordant, than even he imagined.

As the official historian of the Army Chiefs of Staff has noted, "The armed forces of the United States underwent an almost continuous weakening from 1918 onward for a decade and a half."[18]

After initial cuts following demobilization after the world war, the actual numbers of officers and men didn't dwindle much, but there had been a steady decline in funding. This elicited no reaction from a public that had convinced itself that the 1917–18 conflict had been the "war to end all wars," not so much because there would actually be no more wars (although the Kellogg-Briand Pact signed by dozens of nations in 1928, including the United States, swearing off the use of military force may have persuaded some optimists that humanity was ready for that step), but because they believed America would never participate in them.

Pershing himself had offered some pungent comments on this attitude during his chief of staff tenure in 1925, warning, "Under our very eyes there have been serious reductions made by Congress" that ignored the possibility of future threats to the United States and would make it difficult to fight any modern war. "The politician, himself oftentimes uninformed as to his country's history, frequently appeals to the ignorant and unthinking on the score of economy . . . Such demagogues are dangerous."[19]

Dangerous or not, the cuts had continued, and the situation was made worse by the 1929 crash. Hoover browbeat Chief of Staff Summerall into more economizing, and the army budget for 1932 shrank to $351 million, $11 million less than the previous year, while the Bureau of the Budget sliced off another $8 million. At the same time money was added to the one service arm bound to rile many field officers, namely the Army Air Corps. In fact, MacArthur was arriving at Fort Myer just as the battle with Congress over where to spend the army's dwindling funds, not to mention how much, was on the verge of breaking wide open.

MacArthur's job was as difficult as any he would ever undertake, in terms of walking the tightrope between political pressures and realities on the ground. He would be forced to preside over a further deterioration of U.S. Army funding and resources during the current wave of Depression-era economizing as well as pacifism and isolationism both in Congress and among the public at large. At the same time, he had to deal with the opposite problem, congressmen who had certain military hobbyhorses that they believed should be top budget priorities. One was Representative Ross Collins of Mississippi, powerful chairman of the Armed Services Committee. Collins was fascinated, obsessed even, with Major Adna Chaffee's pioneering experimental mechanized force at Fort Meade. Collins believed (rightly) that the tank was the weapon of the future; he also believed (wrongly) that the way to develop an American tank force was to funnel money out of virtually every other branch of the service into Chaffee's array of armored vehicles that were still in the early and uncertain stages of development. Others pushed for more funding for the Air Corps, out of the same twin convictions.

MacArthur had to say no to both groups, and to their lobbyists inside the army itself. Instead, he established a single clear principle while he was chief of staff. At a time of budget stringency, there would be an even distribution of funding across the branches, so that no one branch, not even the cavalry, would be left wanting—or allowed to hog the bulk of the budget, no matter how promising. It was a decision that many would criticize later, in light of the impending shift toward air-supported mechanized warfare and for which the army was woefully unprepared when war finally came in December 1941. But it's hard to see how anyone could have made the prescient decisions needed to prepare America for a style of blitzkrieg warfare that caught every other Western democracy off guard a decade later; or how a chief of staff could have maintained harmony inside the army itself by picking favorites, instead of distributing the meager rations equally—which is what MacArthur did.

As it was, MacArthur backed his approach to funding with a second principle: that the most valuable resource the army had was its manpower, not its materiel. He launched a virtual crusade to preserve the officer corps at its current strength and increase the number of cadets at West Point (an old favorite idea of his), while keeping reserve officers and enlisted men in training. He also pushed for support to increase the budgets for both the ROTC and the National Guard.

America had no need, he asserted, "for maintenance in peacetime of a huge military machine such as exists in almost every other major power." But there was a need for a military command and control structure that would be ready for a general mobilization if war did come—and in September 1931 an event on the other side of the Pacific moved that war one step closer to being a reality.

On the night of September 18 at 10:20 P.M. a bomb went off on a remote section of the South Manchurian Railway near Lake Liutiao. Damage was minor; later a train from Changchun to Shenyang (Mukden) passed without a problem. But this portion of the line had been under Japanese control since the end of the Russo-Japanese War, and when Chinese guards arrived to investigate, they were met by four irate Japanese officers who blamed them for the explosion and accused them of deliberate sabotage. Then early the next morning, September 19, Japanese artillery opened fire on the Chinese garrison at Mukden as Japanese infantry overran the post, killing 500 Chinese, while 200 Japanese lost their lives.

In fact, the Japanese officers themselves had planted the bomb. Their plan was to provoke a violent incident that would serve as pretext for Japan to seize control of southern Manchuria. It worked. Over the next two months, the Japanese army took over virtually all of Manchuria and installed a puppet government, even as the fighting spread steadily south.

MacArthur had been in France on a tour of European military installations when news of the Manchurian incident broke across the world's wires, and he immediately headed for home. American prestige was on the line.

Since the 1920s the United States had made supporting China's territorial integrity a foreign policy priority, as part of its Open Door Policy. Back in Washington, MacArthur was adamant in discussions with Secretary of State Henry Stimson and President Hoover: the United States must impose economic sanctions against Japan and urge other Western countries to do the same.

Hoover, however, worried that this might trigger a war with Japan, refused. Beyond a strongly worded note from the Secretary condemning Japan's actions, the White House did nothing.[20]

But by the end of January 1932 doing nothing was no longer an option. The Japanese army was at the gates of Shanghai, as Japanese aerial bombing killed thousands of residents and threatened to kill thousands more, including Americans living in the city's International Settlement. The American consul general and commander of the Asiatic Fleet, Montgomery Taylor, urged Hoover to order an evacuation of Americans. Stimson and MacArthur persuaded the president to send the Thirty-first Infantry and six hundred marines to Shanghai; bolstered by the strong American response, Britain and France promised to send troops as well.

For two months Japanese and American troops eyed each other uneasily, as relations between the two countries hovered on a knife edge. But then after an initial show of backbone, the Western response to aggression fell apart in a wave of self-doubt, mutual recriminations, and pusillanimity combined with prudence.

The truth was, no Westerners were prepared to die to protect China against the Japanese juggernaut—not least Americans. The League of Nations prepared a report scolding Japan, a member of the League, for the use of military force but not proposing any punishment or sanctions. Japan withdrew from the League in protest anyway. The Hoover administration criticized the League for inaction, but did nothing to suspend American trade with Japan any more than Britain or any other Western powers did.[21]

In May Japanese troops withdrew from Shanghai, and the Thirty-first Infantry and the marines headed home. But the damage was done. Japan was now resigned to its role as international pariah, but since there was no incentive to stop, its behavior in China and elsewhere would become more and more reckless.

It may be going too far to say that World War Two began that day in September 1931. But the pattern of pusillanimity on the part of the Western democracies would repeat itself over the next decade as a new era of international lawlessness was ushered in. Both Italy's Mussolini and Germany's new chancellor, Adolf Hitler, watched events in Manchuria and drew the appropriate lessons for their future aggressions.

Certainly events in China did not bode well for an America that was putting its faith in international treaties, and both oceans, to protect itself from future wars.

It now became MacArthur's mission as chief of staff to wake up the nation, and Congress, to the gathering danger.

He had already set off a national firestorm in June 1931 when a national magazine, *The World Tomorrow,* ran a poll of nearly 20,000 American clergymen and found that 83 percent disapproved of military training in high schools or college. Fully 80 percent wanted the United States to unilaterally disarm; another 60 percent hoped members of their congregations refused to serve in the armed forces if America found itself at war again, while 54 percent said they themselves would not serve. Thirty-four percent said they would not serve even as chaplains.[22]

The magazine editor sent MacArthur a copy of the poll for comment, and MacArthur decided he couldn't let this pass. He wrote back and expressed his surprise "that so many clergymen of our country have placed themselves on record as repudiating in advance the constitutional obligations that will fall upon them equally with all other elements of our citizenship" in the event of war being declared by Congress in the event of national attack.

"That men who wear the cloth of the Church should openly defend repudiation of the laws of the land . . . seems almost unbelievable. It will certainly hearten every potential or actual criminal and malefactor who either has or contemplates breaking some other law."

But MacArthur wasn't done. "It is a distinct disappointment to know that men who are called upon to wield the sword of the spirit are deluded into believing that the mechanical expedient of disarming men will transform hatred into love and selfishness into altruism"—men who, more than anyone else, should know the origins of war, not in social or political systems, but in the sinfulness of man.

Disarming America would invite destruction of not only the country's political and economic freedom, but its religious freedom as well.

"History teaches us that religion and patriotism have always gone hand in hand," he wrote, while it was Jesus Christ Himself who said, *"When a strong man armed keepeth his palace, his goods are in peace"* (Luke 11:21). But MacArthur went further. "It is my humble belief that the relation which He came to establish is based on sacrifice, and that men and women who follow in His train are called by it to the defense of certain priceless principles, even at the cost of their own lives"—like the soldiers who followed his father in the Civil War and the Philippines, or died on the slopes of the Côte de Châtillon, and would in a decade be dying in the jungles of New Guinea.

It was as broad a philosophical basis for MacArthur's understanding of the duties of soldiering as he had ever written. While his response to the *World Tomorrow* poll led to a deluge of angry letters lasting all summer, including one death threat from an anonymous pacifist,[23] Mac would continue for the rest of his life to frame the issues of American defense and military service in forthright religious terms.

"I confidently believe that a red-blooded and virile humanity," he had concluded, "which loves peace devotedly, but is willing to die in the defense of the right, is Christian from center to circumference, and will continue to be dominant in the future as in the past."[24]

It was that future that MacArthur was now fighting for, with every political and rhetorical weapon at his disposal.

His battleground was the War Department, where his chief antagonist was Ross Collins of Mississippi, chair of the House Subcommittee on Military Appropriations. In addition to tanks, Collins was an enthusiast for the kind of strategic airpower Billy Mitchell had advocated, and he saw no reason more funds of the military's already anorexic budget shouldn't be shifted to building fighters and bombers, not to mention tanks. As an amateur strategist, Collins was deeply enamored of the new theories of mass mechanized warfare coming out of Britain and Germany in those years. Let any additional funds go to these future weapons, Collins would thunder at MacArthur as he sat across the table during hearings, instead of ROTC, the National Guard, the Reserves, or maintaining bases at home that had no place in a modern war—or were wasted in training thousands of officers for an army that didn't exist.

It is easy in retrospect to sympathize with Collins's position or the views of others who wanted money shifted to the Army Air Corps, given what planes and tanks would do on the plains of Poland and then France in the next war. But MacArthur's responsibility was not just stockpiling weapons for future wars but maintaining a force structure that could, in the event of war, be rapidly expanded to wield those weapons effectively. That meant, in his mind and in the view of the General Staff, spreading their slender resources as evenly as possible through all the arms of the service—including West Point and the ROTC—in order to cover all contingencies, instead of dumping all appropriations in a couple of as-yet-unproven technologies.

This also meant some hard choices. One was spending no more on the Air Corps than was necessary to build pilot models of new bombers, tanks, and other costly weapons, he told a livid Ross Collins.[25] Another was closing down Major Chaffee's experimental armored unit in the late spring of 1931, and deciding that instead of creating an independent tank force within the army, it was better and more economical to let each service arm, including the artillery and cavalry, develop its own mechanical and armored vehicles. It was a fateful decision.* Yet an army chief of staff starved for funds by both Congress and the Hoover administration had few other options, especially when shutting down outmoded army bases around the country that would have brought paroxysms of rage from every congressional district, including Collins's own.

In May 1931 President Hoover summoned MacArthur and Secretary Hurley to his presidential retreat in Rapidan, Virginia. The national economic slump was deepening, Hoover told them; they had to find ways to cut still more from the military budget. The president suggested imposing a

---

* It meant that the United States would never develop the kind of independent panzer divisions the Germans would deploy as part of their blitzkrieg tactics, and that the advanced tank designs Christie was developing for the U.S. Army would be sold to Soviet Russia instead—and become the basis of its T-34 tank design of World War Two.

round of forced retirements on a military that had already shrunk from 200,000 personnel in 1920 to fewer than 140,000 in 1931. He also urged closing as many as semi-active installations as possible.

Despite MacArthur's misgivings, the War Department acquiesced by announcing it was shutting fifty-three army posts.[26] Soldiers' pay was cut by 10 percent; headquarters staffs of the army's nine corps areas fell by 15 percent, and the army's overall strength was reduced by another 6,000 soldiers and officers—leaving an army that was the sixteenth largest in the world, not much bigger than Portugal's.

But the truly epic fight for the army's survival didn't begin until May 1932, when Congressman Collins released his army appropriations bill for 1933. It was a shocker.

The War Department had asked for $331 million; the president's own Bureau of the Budget had slashed that by $15 million. Ross Collins's final number cut that by another $24 million, but the biggest shock of all was an amendment requiring a reduction in the number of Regular Army officers from 12,000 to 10,000. That was not much more than half of the 18,000 officers the 1920 National Defense Act considered essential for maintaining strength in peacetime. To MacArthur, it seemed as if the very survival of the U.S. Army itself was at stake.

That was the gist of the blistering letter he fired off to House Minority Leader Bertrand Snell. Beyond the numbers and MacArthur's protests over Collins's amendment, the letter offers an illuminating window on MacArthur's thinking about how to maintain an effective fighting force in the face of straitened budgets.

For the education of the House leader, he went back to basics. Prior to 1920, he wrote, "there existed in the world only two general systems under which military forces were organized and maintained." One was a force organized around mandatory conscription or a draft; the other was a force made up entirely of professionals. The United States, however, had elected a third way: "a small professional force to act as a training cadre—a covering force in case of need, and a framework upon which mobilization of our full force could be effected."

To make this system work, "the Regular Army is the bulwark and basis of the whole structure. It is the instructor, the model, and, in emergency, the leader of the whole" as the repository of "the professional knowledge and technical skill capable of accumulating, organizing, training, and leading to victory a national army of citizen soldiers."

The 1933 budget appropriation, he stated, now threatened that vital role. The minimum number of officers required to do the job was 14,000, now down to 10,000. "Trained officers constitute the most vitally essential element in modern war; and the only one that under no circumstances can be improvised or extemporized." An army can get along on short rations, poor housing, even too few or inadequate weapons. However, "it is doomed to destruction without the trained and adequate leadership of officers." Those trained officers form the vital margin between victory and defeat, he warned. Now the Congress was asking the American people to accept defeat as a matter of course.

MacArthur explained that he could understand the need for economy in public expenditures, especially when the rest of the country was in such poor shape. Even so, the United States still ranked number one in the world in wealth compared to size of population, while its army barely ranked sixteenth. "But the Department insists that any retrenchment which destroys or seriously damages a vital element of our already weakened defensive structure is not economy but extravagance of the most expensive kind."[27]

MacArthur had thrown down the gauntlet in what his friend John O'Laughlin, editor of The Army and Navy Journal, was calling the army's most serious fight since the Civil War. Congressman Collins was bound to pick it up. So began a three-month siege, with MacArthur going to Capitol Hill to cajole individual congressmen and twist arms, and Collins following up with individual meetings to untwist them. Collins had an unexpected ally in members of the House who were fans of a strong U.S. Navy, and saw cuts in army appropriations as a way to forestall cuts in the navy's. Their members included the powerful House Speaker John Nance Garner, and so it was no surprise that in the end the House passed Collins's bill 201 to 182.

MacArthur had lost, but he was not about to quit. Instead he went to the office of Colonel Ernest Graves, who was on the staff of the chief of the Army Corps of Engineers. The Corps was in the middle of a massive project, involving the floodwaters of the Mississippi, that covered more than a dozen states—each of which was represented by senators with whom Graves had cultivated strong relations, and MacArthur knew it. He urged Graves to go to see them, lobby them for the army's sake on the appropriations bill and urge them to vote against Collins's dangerous scheme to trim back the officer corps.[28]

It worked. The officer reduction amendment went down to defeat in the Senate. Collins fought furiously to revive it by overriding the Senate veto in the House but lost on a final vote.

MacArthur was jubilant. He sent a telegram to Frederick H. Payne, assistant secretary for procurement: "Just hog tied a Miss. cracker. House voted our way 75 to 54. Happy times are here again."

It was, however, a bittersweet victory. The final appropriation for 1933 was only $305 million, the lowest since 1923. The cut in pay for 1932 remained in place. In addition, money for the War Department's non-military expenditures, like the Corps of Engineers, was actually going *up*—especially since Congress saw these as sources of civilian jobs that were getting harder to find in the broader economy, not to mention sources of political pork.[29]

But it was another military-related appropriation, passed back in 1924 over President Coolidge's veto that would cause MacArthur the most personal pain in the late summer of 1932. It would also earn him the totally unexpected—and totally undeserved—title of "the most dangerous man in the country."

The end of World War One had discharged more than two million men from the armed forces—the largest pool of military veterans, and the largest potential political lobby, since the Civil War. In an effort to placate that lobby, in 1924 Congress passed a law issuing to veterans "adjusted compensation certificates" based on their time of service and redeemable in twenty-one years, in 1945, but with the right to borrow against the bonus certificates up to 22½ percent of their value. President Coolidge didn't think much of this largely unnecessary outlay of federal money (the economy was booming and unemployment at barely 6 percent), and he vetoed the bill. Congress, however, overrode his veto. World War veterans could now look forward to borrowing up to $220 against certificates averaging one thousand dollars per veteran.

Then came the Depression, and suddenly a certificate represented not just a bonus but a lifeline—but not if veterans couldn't borrow more or redeem the certificates now. Congress complied with a law allowing them to borrow up to 50 percent, but veterans' groups decided that was still not enough. And so in late 1931 Representative Wright Patman of Texas proposed a new law ordering immediate payment of the entire bonus and setting aside $2.4 million in the army budget for the purpose.[30]

This aroused the ire of President Hoover, who smelled a political rat (Patman was a progressive Democrat) as well as a whiff of a measure that would fuel inflation. He launched a sharp counterattack, including getting the American Legion to reject a resolution supporting the Patman bill at its national convention.[31] But the veterans' allies in Congress and out rallied, and by the spring of 1932 the Patman bill was inching toward possible passage in the House—and a certain veto at the White House.

It was ex-army sergeant—ironically, who had served in the Rainbow Division's Forty-first Infantry—and unemployed cannery worker Walter W. Waters of Seattle, Washington, who led the first group of 300 jobless veterans on a march to Washington to show their support for the new Bonus Bill. They dubbed themselves the Bonus Expeditionary Force, or BEF, and within days thousands of other vets joined them on a pilgrimage to the nation's capital— a march that would become known ever after as the Bonus March. Many brought along their families and by June an enormous shantytown of tents and makeshift huts housing 20,000 veterans had sprung up along the banks of the Anacostia River south of the District of Columbia.

No one doubts today that the Bonus March was a spontaneous, unplanned movement born of frustration and—in many cases—desperation.[32] In 1932, however, there were many who saw more sinister motives in the restless throngs gathering in sight of the Capitol building—motives bordering on violent revolution. One of them was President Hoover, who, under siege from an economic crisis like no other, was steadily descending from gloom (the writer H. G. Wells, visiting him in the White House, found him "sickly, overworked, and overwhelmed") to paranoia. He was never convinced that the majority of the Bonus Marchers were veterans at all, and he believed, then and later, that they were "organized and promoted by the Communists" while being egged on by his Democratic rivals. In his mind, what was happening that summer was a direct challenge to his authority, perhaps even to lawful governance, and he was prepared to meet force with force.[33]

Another skeptic was Douglas MacArthur. He had encountered protesting veterans at a benefit track-and-field meet in Washington in 1922, and although he had not followed the bonus issue very closely, he was perfectly aware of how radical revolutionary elements like the Communist Party of the USA were poised to promote and take advantage of massive popular protests. Early in 1930, Communists had spearheaded hunger demonstrations in cities including Cleveland, Philadelphia, Chicago, and New York, that had led to violent confrontations with police. In March police had fired on rioting autoworkers at a Ford plant in Detroit, killing four and wounding more than fifty. The funeral procession for the slain had included portraits of Lenin and banners with the hammer and sickle.[34]

In this atmosphere it didn't take much to convince MacArthur that "the [Bonus] movement was actually far deeper and more dangerous than an effort to secure funds from a nearly depleted federal treasury," he wrote later. Like Hoover, MacArthur was convinced that American Communists wanted to use the Bonus March "to incite revolutionary action."[35] It wasn't a bad guess, as it happened, because in fact that was exactly what the CPUSA was trying to do.

Their stalking horse inside the Bonus Army was John T. Pace, a lean, hatchet-faced Communist organizer and former veteran who had come from Detroit with a band of dedicated radical bonus seekers. MacArthur critics would later point out that Waters had specifically sworn that his Bonus March would put up with "no panhandling, no drinking, no radicalism." They also note that Pace and his men numbered fewer than two hundred in a camp of thousands. Yet the truth was, that was all Pace needed to provoke the kind of incident that the Communist Party could capitalize on. As Pace himself confessed years later, "I was ordered by my superiors to provoke riots . . . and to use every trick to bring about bloodshed" that would force the U.S. Army, and MacArthur, to intervene.[36]

They tried several times—even as other Bonus Marchers tore up their propaganda sheets—including trying to establish a picket line around the White House. But relations between the marchers and the authorities remained largely peaceful, even friendly. Police superintendent Pelham D.

Glassford, who had been a brigadier general in France during the war, was particularly sympathetic to their cause. He paid daily visits, arranged for the Salvation Army to offer food and bedding, provided housing in some vacant downtown buildings for veterans and their families, and even at Waters's request handled the Bonus Army's finances—as well as arranging for the Marine Band to serenade them.[37]

MacArthur was more aloof, although he states in his memoirs that he ordered tents, rolling kitchens, and other camp equipment to be provided to the marchers. He met with Waters and reached an agreement that if the army did get called in, the veterans would withdraw without violence. But his doubts about a peaceful end to the massive sit-in were growing. On June 8 MacArthur spoke at the University of Pittsburgh and offered strong words about the threat of "pacifism and its bed-fellow, Communism," which were "organizing the forces of unrest and undermining the morals of the working man." He made it clear that he was including the Bonus Marchers in his indictment, which provoked outbursts from student demonstrators, leading to arrests and fines.[38]

That same day 8,000 members of Waters's BEF staged a march through downtown Washington, as MacArthur returned and ordered his nine corps area commanders to give him any information on Communist groups who might have passed through their areas posing as Bonus Marchers.

A week later, the summer heat was settling over the District as things began to build to a climax. On June 15, the House of Representatives passed Congressman Patman's bill, 209–179. Waters and his people were jubilant, but the real test, the vote in the Senate, remained. Waters and other BEF officials asked to see President Hoover; he brusquely refused. Then on the night of June 17, crowds gathered at the Capitol to hear the final Senate vote.

It was devastating. The Senate rejected the Bonus Bill by a 62–18 margin—an overwhelming defeat. According to eyewitnesses, the veterans tearfully sang a stanza of "America the Beautiful," then fell into formation by platoons and returned to Anacostia. For most, the vote represented the end of the road—and their hopes. A smattering began leaving Washington, but many others stayed, arguing that they had no place else to go. Governor Franklin D. Roosevelt even offered to pay the rail fare for any veterans from New York State who were willing to leave. Then in early July, President Hoover and Congress passed a bill providing funds for returning all the veterans home (although the rail fare would be deducted from their 1945 bonus redemptions). More than 6,000—"the real veterans," as MacArthur liked to think of them—took the offer and left. "But the hard core of the Communist bloc not only stayed, but grew," he grimly wrote in his memoirs.[39]

It was time to prepare for the worst, in case the president ordered a forced evacuation of the rest.

Congress adjourned in mid-July as the army quietly made its preparations. MacArthur was taking no chances and hoped an overwhelming show of force would compel any marchers thinking of resisting to back down. He ordered tanks brought up from the Aberdeen Proving Ground, and a squadron of cavalry under the command of Colonel George S. Patton. Troops underwent anti-riot training at Fort Myer, and cavalry units practiced dispersing large crowds. Meanwhile, MacArthur and General Perry Miles reviewed the War Department's "White Plan," an emergency contingency plan in case of civil disorder in the capital. They agreed that the critical points to protect were the White House, the Capitol, the Treasury building, and the Bureau of Engraving and Printing. Troops would assemble at the Ellipse, behind the White House, for dispersal to any trouble spots.

In their minds, they were preparing for revolution, especially assistant chief of staff General George Van Horn Moseley. An ardent right-winger who had earlier presented the General Staff with a plan to nip radicalism in the bud by expelling all foreign-born aliens from the country, Moseley would be one of the key instigators of a strong army reaction to the growing tension in the Bonus Marchers' camp. There Communists and other radicals were directly challenging Walter Waters's authority, while Waters himself began talking about organizing a "Khaki Shirt" movement made up of veterans to "return government to the masses"—a distinct echo of Mussolini's Blackshirts and Hitler's storm troopers. On July 16, nervous district commissioners told Chief of Police Glassford to use force if necessary to keep any marchers from parading close to the White House.[40]

A point of no return had been reached. On July 21 Glassford got the order from the commissioners to clear the veterans out of buildings they had occupied on Pennsylvania Avenue, and shut down all BEF encampments by noon on August 4. Everyone assumed the police would probably need the assistance of the military, although it was not until July 27 that Hoover called MacArthur, Secretary of War Hurley, and Attorney General Mitchell to his office to get them to agree that the army would be ready to help the police clear the Pennsylvania Avenue corridor if necessary.

The city held its breath the next morning as police arrived at Pennsylvania Avenue between Third and Fourth Streets, and began clearing the buildings, starting with the old armory, where some 1,100 Bonus Marchers were holed up. Glassford had negotiated a deal on evacuation with Walter Waters, and the process was under way when a flying squad of Pace's Communist thugs tried to start a riot, attacking the police line and hurling bricks, one of which hit Glassford. Still, the incident soon passed. There were a few arrests, and Glassford was able to head back to the district commissioners to tell them the situation was well in hand but that they should hold off on any further evictions that day.

So far, then, there was no sign of the army or any need for it. But the district commisioners quickly lost their nerve. At 1:00 P.M. they asked President Hoover for federal troops, saying, "it will be impossible for the Police Department to maintain law and order except by the free use of firearms which will make the situation a dangerous one."[41]

The telephone rang in MacArthur's office. It wasn't Hoover but Commissioner Herbert Crosby, a former major general, who informed him that Glassford "requested that troops should be held in immediate readiness for action." MacArthur ordered General Miles to gather his troops at the Ellipse, and so he wasn't surprised when at 2:55 he got a message from Secretary Hurley stating that "the President has just informed me that the civil government of the District of Columbia has reported to him that it is unable to maintain law and order in the District. You will have United States troops proceed immediately to the scene of the disorder."[42]

At this juncture MacArthur made two decisions—neither of which had any bearing on what was going to happen over the next eight hours but which would reverberate back through the media and shape the popular image of what did happen.

The first was that he decided he would accompany General Miles, the officer in charge, to the scene. Miles was startled at the idea of the chief of staff himself presiding over what was a minor operation (fewer than 800 troops would be involved), but MacArthur reassured him that he was going "not with a view of commanding the troops but to be on hand as things progress, so I can issue [any] necessary instructions on the ground." Besides, he said, "I will take the rap if there should be any unfavorable or critical repercussions"—words that would be uncannily prophetic.

Nonetheless, Miles was not the only officer who thought this an odd proceeding. Another was Major Dwight Eisenhower, who was attached to the General Staff. He told MacArthur he thought the chief of staff showing up in person was "highly inappropriate."

MacArthur shook his head. "This is a question of Federal authority in the District of Columbia," he told Eisenhower, and besides he was worried that "the incipient revolution was in the air." The man who had charged up the Côte de Châtillon unarmed was not going to be absent when his troops confronted what could turn out to be an insurrectionary situation.[43]

His second decision had to do with his clothes. MacArthur was wearing a light summer suit that morning. That seemed inappropriate for a chief of staff attending a military operation, no matter how minor—especially one being held in the nation's capital. He sent his Filipino valet to Fort Myer to find him a uniform. The orderly came back with the most ornate uniform he could find—one that MacArthur's mother usually picked out for formal occasions and dinners, and decorated with every ribbon and medal, including his marksmanship badges. Mac put it on without thinking twice. But it would hurt him later when people saw photographs of him in action that day. To the ignorant (or malicious) eye it looked as if MacArthur thought his full dress uniform, complete with breeches and gleaming riding boots and spurs, was the right garb for putting down unemployed veterans and their families—especially since the same photos showed Eisenhower and Miles in more modest military attire.

Meanwhile, the situation on the ground was deteriorating rapidly.

Police who had pushed their way into one partially demolished building near Fourth and Pennsylvania were met with bricks and clubs. A cop slipped and lost his footing, and in a panic opened fire. In moments there were two dead veterans, killed by gunshots, and three seriously injured policemen. It was news of this incident that had prompted President Hoover into action, and now MacArthur and Miles were driving down Pennsylvania Avenue as infantry and Patton's cavalry hurried up to meet them.

MacArthur jumped out of the staff car to find police chief Glassford, still nursing his head wound but determined to be on the scene.

"I have orders from President Hoover to drive the veterans out of the city," he barked at Glassford. "We are going to break the back of the B.E.F." Glassford, chagrined that his men had lost control of the situation and that the marchers had broken their promise that there would be no violence, said nothing. He and MacArthur had served together at West Point—he was class of '04. The last thing he was going to do was interfere with his former class commandant.[44]

Then he and MacArthur both watched as the next stage of the tragedy unfolded.

First came the cavalry down Pennsylvania Avenue at the trot, clearing the road with sabers drawn. Then the infantry fanned out to empty the buildings one by one. At the first sign of resistance, an officer ordered his men to put on gas masks as they threw tear gas grenades—"by the hundreds," according to one eyewitness—through doors and windows.

In minutes "black smoke and orange flame rose from the shacks constructed between buildings" as veterans poured out and ran in every direction, choking and cursing. Farther down the avenue the troops advanced, as the marchers, pushed back across Maine and Missouri Avenues, continued to fight. "Growing hate and defiance was evident," reported Lieutenant Colonel Kunzig, "from the boos, barrage of profanity, the throwing of rocks and the return of tear gas grenades."[45]

One of those who came under attack from the mob was the driver of MacArthur's own staff car, his aide Captain Thomas Davis. Davis emerged unhurt, but MacArthur's eyes were left puffy and streaming from the clouds of tear gas.

Still, he was pleased. "Not a shot was fired," he would remember in his memoirs. "The sticks, clubs, and stones of the rioters were met only by tear gas and steady pressure. No one was killed"—that is, not by his troops—"and there were no serious injuries on either side." Even so, the black smoke from the burning shacks along Pennsylvania could be plainly seen from the Capitol.

They were still burning at 9:30 P.M. as remaining veterans fled across the Eleventh Street Bridge in the last light and headed back to the Anacostia flats.

"It was a good job," MacArthur told a reporter, "quickly done, with no one injured." That wasn't entirely true: almost thirty people had taken blows from bricks, clubs, bayonets, and sabers used as prods and paddles along their flat edge—"[W]e made a lot of bottoms sore," Patton remembered—and one infant later died from smoke inhalation.[46]

Still, the question now was whether the troops should use the occasion to continue on and clear the Anacostia camps, as Hoover had ordered they should eventually do. Back at the White House, a worried Edward Starling, head of the Secret Service White House detail, raised that very question— but in a worried tone. In the aftermath of the fighting along Pennsylvania Avenue, was the army now going to use gas and bayonets to clear the women and children camped out there?

That made Hoover pause and think. After a few minutes he ordered Secretary Hurley to tell MacArthur and Miles that under no circumstances were troops to cross the Anacostia bridge until all the women and children had been evacuated.

The message was sent—but MacArthur was destined never to see it. The man responsible for that was none other than MacArthur's own assistant chief of staff George Van Horn Moseley. It was he who received Hurley's order; later he claimed in his memoirs that he delivered it to MacArthur, "who was very much annoyed at having his plans interfered with."[47]

That story turned out to be a lie. As historian Geoffrey Perret has pointed out, no fewer than three independent witnesses contradict him. The most damning is Assistant Secretary for Air F. Trubee Davison, who ran into Moseley and Fred Payne the morning after, and found them smiling and congratulating themselves.

"What in the world have you fellows done that's so terrific?" Davison asked.

"Well, the President wrote an order to MacArthur to stop at the Anacostia bridge," they told him, but they had made sure it never arrived. Moseley, who detested the marchers and was convinced, as MacArthur was, that they were only a hotbed of radicals and criminals, wanted them cleared out no matter how it was done. Later, Eisenhower confirmed Davison's story: MacArthur never saw the message. "The result," Davison relates, was that "MacArthur and the whole force went across the bridge" as the second stage of the tragedy took place.[48]

Meanwhile, darkness had fallen. Soldiers stood silently on the Eleventh Street Bridge, arms at rest, staring out to the Anacostia flats beyond.

MacArthur finally turned to Glassford. At this critical point he had decided he was taking over the operation. Miles's men were going forward, he told the police chief, but "we will proceed very slowly. I will stop the command for supper so that full opportunity will be given for everyone to leave without getting hurt."[49]

There was a pause for nearly two hours while Glassford and MacArthur met with intermediaries from the camp to negotiate a peaceful evacuation. Meanwhile at the White House, Herbert Hoover, who had heard nothing about what was happening and was getting worried, sent a second message repeating his order for MacArthur to halt at the bridge.

That message never got through either. Instead, General Moseley again made sure the officer carrying it never arrived in time; "get lost," he reportedly told him.[50] By the time the messenger reached the Eleventh Street Bridge—after covering three miles in three hours—the troops were already moving out.

As they did, the darkness was suddenly split by bursts of yellow, red, and orange. "The whole encampment of shacks and huts just ahead began burning," Eisenhower remembered. We now know it was the marchers who had set fire to the camp in a final gesture of defiance, torching more than 2,100 huts, tents, and lean-tos in a conflagration that filled the night with a dark red glow visible to President Hoover from his bedroom window.

Yet the myth would soon circulate that the fires had been set by the soldiers, and were even set at MacArthur's orders. In fact, MacArthur had already pulled his men back at the entrance to the encampment and left its final clearance to Glassford's blue-coated policemen backed by troops who were brought in by truck to assist, but under the police chief's orders. MacArthur, Miles, and their weary troops then headed back to their barracks. MacArthur went to bed, tired but pleased that the army had carried out the president's orders with an absolute minimum of injury to life and limb—and that his men had very possibly forestalled a revolution and the American equivalent of the storming of the Winter Palace.

Certainly when he appeared at the War Department the next morning before heading for the White House, he was expecting to be greeted by the congratulations of the entire nation. Instead, he was greeted by a very worried Major Eisenhower.

A gaggle of correspondents were waiting to talk to him, Ike warned him. "It might be the better part of wisdom, if not of valor, to avoid meeting them," he said. Let Secretary Hurley and other civilian officials deal with the reporters; after all, the evacuation "had not been a military idea really, but a political order," he later remembered telling MacArthur.[51]

MacArthur dismissed the idea at once. He wasn't afraid of any reporters, and when they gathered around him he poured out a spirited defense of the operation, with Secretary Hurley at his side, as a forest of pencils furiously scribbled down his words.

"That mob down there was a bad-looking mob," he firmly told the reporters. "It was animated by the essence of revolution. Beyond the shadow of a doubt, they were about to take over in some arbitrary way either the direct control of the Government or else to control it by indirect methods."

He plunged on. "There were, in my opinion, few veteran soldiers in the group that we cleared out today; few indeed. I am not speaking by figures because I don't know how many there were; but if there was one man in ten in that group today who is a veteran, it would surprise me."

At last, he concluded: "I have been in many riots, but I think this is the first riot I ever was in or ever saw in which there was no real bloodshed. So far as I know, there is no man on either side who has been seriously injured."[52]

Eisenhower, who knew that at least that last assertion was untrue (two veterans had died, albeit at the hands of the police, not the army), listened and shook his head. He realized that the impromptu press conference would only injure MacArthur's reputation and encourage the public to think "General MacArthur himself had undertaken and directed the move against the veterans," instead of at the orders of Hoover and Hurley.

Ike was proved right. If the Communist Party hadn't been in the forefront of the Bonus Army movement, it did take the lead in describing, and embellishing far beyond the bounds of truth, its violent demise. Communist accounts described how "the soldiers charged with fixed bayonets, firing into the crowd of unarmed men, women, and children." It spread tales of the use of tanks and poison gas; of tents being set on fire with men and women trapped inside; of cavalrymen's sabers dripping blood from slicing off veterans' ears, and even of a small child being bayoneted while trying to save his pet rabbit. And presiding over it all was General Douglas MacArthur, booted and spurred and even—in some accounts—on horseback, leading the final cavalry saber charge on the helpless veterans.[53]

Hence the birth of a new and ugly public perception of the former World War One hero and army chief of staff as the right-wing "man on horseback" who hated the poor and unemployed as much as he did radicals and Communists, and who was prepared to use the pretext of the Bonus March to declare martial law in the nation's capital and perhaps even seize political power for himself. The truth was "there was no cavalry charge," as MacArthur would patiently explain in his memoirs. "There was no fiery white charger. There was no saber"—except to swat recalcitrant bottoms.[54] But it was that image that would grow and persist, and lead the Democratic presidential candidate that year, Franklin D. Roosevelt, when asked whom he considered the most dangerous men in America, to list first Huey Long, the demagogic governor and semi-dictator of Louisiana, and then Douglas MacArthur.

Meanwhile back at the White House, MacArthur was getting a very different reception than he expected. Hoover laid into the chief of staff for taking actions that the president considered a direct breach of his orders—orders that he did not know MacArthur had never received. The president was also furious about MacArthur's unbridled statements to the press that would only raise more questions than they answered. MacArthur listened with growing rage. In his mind, he had only been following orders; in his mind, he had been given discretion in handling the evacuation, and he had done so with a minimum of fuss and bloodshed.

When Hoover was finished, MacArthur offered to resign on the spot—but he would make no apology for what he had done.[55]

Hoover didn't accept the offer, and in his public statements he stoutly backed up the man he had upbraided in private. Later, when he had calmed down, the president came to admit that everything MacArthur had done had been within the scope of his instructions (although neither he nor MacArthur ever learned about General Moseley's role in blocking Hoover's cease-and-desist order from reaching MacArthur in time). As for other officials who had been on the spot, police chief Glassford and General Miles, both believed that MacArthur's actions had been justified and that the criticism was unwarranted, as did Secretary of War Hurley.[56]

But the damage had been done, not just to MacArthur but especially to President Hoover. The Bonus Army debacle of July 28 marked the final doom of his presidential reelection campaign. Subsequent congressional investigations of the episode, which were timed to come before the November 1932 election, all made Hoover look like a liar as well as a monster. It certainly came as no surprise to anyone that the election result would be a Democratic landslide, with candidate Franklin D. Roosevelt carrying all but six states with 477 electoral votes to 59. The Bonus Army—and, one could argue, Douglas MacArthur—completed the destruction of Hoover's reputation that the Great Depression had started, both then and later.

The other man whose reputation was wrecked was MacArthur. The public, and most subsequent historians, never bought his theory that the Bonus Marchers were led by thugs and Communists bent on revolution. It did little good to point out, as both Hoover and MacArthur did, that a large number of the marchers who were arrested had violent criminal records, or that those arrested on the final day of the evacuation included Pace; Emmanuel Levin, a figure in the New York Communist organization; and James Ford, American Communist Party candidate for vice president in 1928.[57]

Nor were there many willing to acknowledge, then or later, the fact that it had been General Miles, not MacArthur, who had been in actual command during the most violent phases of the operation; or that it was the police, not the soldiers, who actually fired on the marchers.

Instead, the image of MacArthur as would-be dictator and trampler of the poor and unemployed took root and spread, first from radical media organs like the Communist *Daily Worker* and *The Nation* and then to liberal newspapers and across the rest of the media. By the end of the summer, even the *Columbus Dispatch* could report that while MacArthur remained popular with the army, he had made too many enemies on Capitol Hill to survive as chief of staff.

His stock with veterans in particular, it seemed, was particularly low. When Josephus Daniels, former secretary of the navy, spoke at various American Legion conventions that fall, he found "the feeling against the General was very strong." He warned that MacArthur's reappointment as chief of staff when his term expired in 1935 would be seen as a "grave reproach" to the Legion and to other veterans.

Certainly the overwhelming consensus was that Mac would never survive as chief of staff under the new Democratic president, Franklin Roosevelt, let alone get appointed to a second term.

Yet FDR would surprise them all. Against all advice and expectation, the man who had described MacArthur as the most dangerous man in the country would spare him from the public lynching that many hoped for. Indeed, he would ultimately thrust him into a position of greater power and responsibility than MacArthur had ever held before—albeit on the other side of the world.

CHAPTER 11

SAVING FDR

General Douglas MacArthur was quite literally "the man on a white horse" for FDR's inauguration.

As the army, navy, and coast guard marched past the parade stand on March 10, 1933, it was MacArthur who led the procession, on a white steed. He wasn't wearing the formal uniform he had worn while "breaking the back of the B.E.F.," as he had put it. Rather he was in his full dress uniform, complete with sword and spurs. As he passed the president and the other distinguished guests on the parade stand, he saluted. Then the army's distinguished chief of staff dismounted, handed his steed over to an aide, and strode to the podium, where he and the new president—the man who had branded him "the most dangerous man in America"—watched the rest of the parade.

They smiled and chatted, and laughed. They pointed out sights of interest as soldiers, airmen, and sailors marched by. Overhead flew the airship *Akron,* the pride of America's dirigible air fleet—the one that was supposed to keep the country safe from attack on either coast. Anyone watching the pair would have assumed they were old friends, even relatives—and in fact they were both.[1] MacArthur and Roosevelt had known each other since 1916, when

Franklin was a hardworking assistant secretary of the navy and Douglas was an equally hardworking member of the General Staff putting together a plan for prewar mobilization.

Both had grown up with strong, domineering mothers; both were intensely ambitious; and both were consummate dramatic actors when the occasion demanded it. One was intensely liberal in the progressive Democratic tradition of Woodrow Wilson; the other conservative in the progressive Republican tradition of Theodore Roosevelt. But both also believed in a strong America, and together they would forge a strange alliance from the moment of Roosevelt's inauguration until his death in 1945. Later MacArthur wrote, "Whatever difference arose between us, it never sullied in slightest degree the warmth of my personal friendship for him"—and he meant it. It was no autobiographical boilerplate. Especially after his experiences with first Truman and then Eisenhower, he would gaze back on the Roosevelt years, even the worst of them, with a sense of nostalgia, almost regret.[2]

For the first year of Roosevelt's presidency, however, they were deeply at odds. Roosevelt considered the army chief of staff's role during the Bonus March to be an abomination, and as a navy man he was bound to see any defense cuts aimed at balancing the budget (it was an election-year pledge) as coming from the army. MacArthur kept his views to himself. At the social festivities following the inauguration, he "shed benign charm on fellow guests," an observer noted.[3]

What he was really thinking, that this "leading liberal of the age" was poised to transform America in ways that MacArthur and his fellow Republicans dreaded, was no secret. What FDR's staff thought of MacArthur was no secret either. They regularly called him a "warmonger" and a "bellicose swashbuckler." When MacArthur came to White House functions or meetings, most kept their cool distance. Roosevelt's interior secretary, Harold Ickes, blasted him in his diary as "the type of man who thinks that when he gets to heaven, God will step down from the great white throne and bow him into His vacated seat."[4]

Virtually everyone assumed that MacArthur would soon be put out on the street, along with the other Hoover holdovers. Josephus Daniels, a leading Democrat as well as MacArthur foe, told Roosevelt's new secretary of war, "Get a new Chief of Staff and a new set up as soon as possible. MacArthur is a charming man, but he was put in by your predecessor and thinks he should run the Army."[5]

Roosevelt's own assessment was more nuanced, despite his "most dangerous man in America" remark. Before the inauguration he revealed his true thinking to one of his Brain Trust of economic advisors, Rex Tugwell. "I've known Doug for years," he said reflectively. "You've never heard him talk, but I have. He has the most portentous style of anyone I know. He talks in a voice that might come from an oracle's cave. He never doubts and never argues or suggests; he makes pronouncements. What he thinks is final."

Still, Roosevelt was not inclined to let him go. As he told Tugwell, "He's intelligent, a brilliant soldier like his father before him. He got to be a brigadier in France." What worried Roosevelt was that MacArthur might one day rally political opposition to Roosevelt, and lead it against him. He was already a hero to millions for defeating the Bonus Marchers, who they had believed were Communist-led. If they really were looking for a man on a white horse, "a man of charm, tradition, and majestic appearance," to lead, even take over, the country, "Doug MacArthur is the man."[6]

So Roosevelt's solution wasn't to fire MacArthur but to beguile and outwit him—as he would beguile and outwit friends and foes alike, from a succession of vice presidents to GM's Bill Knudsen and Winston Churchill. Besides, MacArthur represented the conservative forces that Roosevelt needed to cajole in order to achieve his most far-reaching plans.

"We must tame these fellows," he concluded, "and make them useful to us."

It was a shrewd plan, except that it turned out to be MacArthur who made FDR useful to him and the army, starting with the Civilian Conservation Corps.

The CCC was President Roosevelt's pet project—he had done something like it as governor of New York. The idea was for the government to pay unemployed, unmarried men between the ages of eighteen and twenty-five a basic wage to do unskilled manual labor relating to the conservation of natural resources, such as building roads and recreational spaces in national parks, planting trees (in the end the CCC would plant some 3 billion trees), and digging ditches for flood control. Roosevelt proposed the idea in a speech on March 21, 1933, with the goal of enrolling 250,000 men by July 1. It took Congress only ten days to pass the bill creating the Civilian Conservation Corps, while leaving most of the details to the executive branch to work out.

That suited MacArthur fine. When he heard that FDR's plan included having the War Department recruit enrollees, give them a two-week conditioning course, and then ship them off to the camps where the U.S. Forest Service would take charge, his reaction was not at all like the outrage some soldiers felt at being used to further the New Deal. He was immediately enthusiastic.[7] Though he was in no mood to see the army reduced to doing civilian manual labor, as some officers feared it would be, and although he was adamant that "no military training whatsoever" would take place, in order to reassure those for whom the War Department's involvement smacked of fascism, the idea of having a quarter million young men under canvas, with army officers training and supervising them, appealed to his imagination— as did the idea that only the army could plan, organize, and administer a national program of this size.

He realized that the army's involvement in Roosevelt's pet project would prove its worth to the nation, and to Roosevelt—and give hundreds of officers starved for duties something to do.

On March 24, just three days after FDR's speech, MacArthur showed the surprised and delighted Roosevelt the army's plans and regulations for the training camps. The next day MacArthur sent secret encoded messages to the commanders of the army's corps areas informing them of what they were to do. The same day the bill was signed, March 31, the army was ready and waiting.[8]

MacArthur's unexpected cooperation not only won him points in the White House, it also set the stage for the next big change in the program when the CCC's director, Robert Fechner, decided in May, after seeing the General Staff's projections, that he would never meet the needed enrollment by the July 1 deadline. He recommended that the War Department take over administration of the entire CCC. Roosevelt was willing to go along, and so while Congress was working on a bill entrusting the CCC to the army's care, MacArthur and his staff were working even harder to pull together a comprehensive plan for the agency. It meant mobilizing 200 trains, 3,600 army trucks, supplying tens of thousands of shirts, trousers, and socks, as well as feeding hundreds of thousands of recruits—including, ironically, many army veterans—and housing them in barracks and military receiving areas, while planning it all in less than twenty-four hours.

"It was a momentous day," one of MacArthur's staffers later recalled. "That night, instead of a stray light here and there the War Department's windows were ablaze. The big machine was rolling. . . . The Army was under test, but what a grand opportunity the task offered."[9] The army passed the test. Until the CCC was disbanded at the onset of war in 1942, it proved to be one of the New Deal's most popular programs. The army's involvement also inoculated it from further budget cuts—part of MacArthur's strategy all along. His own contribution was to decentralize the effort, giving local corps area commanders as much latitude as possible in administering CCC efforts in their districts—much as he would with subordinates later.*

But above all, he had found a way for a peacetime army headed for the budget chopping block to keep itself busy and valued, and its officers gainfully employed (the mobilization and logistics of CCC were exactly what MacArthur anticipated would happen in an outbreak of war). As the War Department's representative on the program put it, "mobilization of the CCC . . . has been the most valuable experience the Army has had since the World War."[10] It was such a success that MacArthur began to worry that it was drawing on his officers' time too much, and in 1935 he shifted command over to officers of the Organized Reserve—in terms of future mobilization plans, the next best thing. At one point he even wondered aloud whether CCC recruits might benefit from a basic course in military instruction, but when that idea met with almost universal dislike, he backed down.

Still, an admiring Dwight Eisenhower was able to write in June 1933, as budget talks loomed again, "We will lose no officers or men (at least this time) and this concession was won because of the great numbers we are

---

* One was Lieutenant Colonel George Marshall, who was put in charge of nineteen CCC camps in the IV Corps Area and tens of thousands of young men from Georgia, Florida, and South Carolina. "I'll be out to see you soon," he told one of his officers. "If I find you doing something, I will help you, but if I find you doing nothing, only God will help you."

using on the Civilian Conservation Corps work and of Gen. MacArthur's skill and determination."[11]

Robert Fechner felt a similar gratitude for MacArthur's help at a critical moment in the CCC's birth. "Your personal interest and constant willingness to talk over all problems that have arisen has been of the greatest value to me," he wrote. "I know that your sympathetic interest was the main spring in the work that the Army has performed."

MacArthur wrote back that his connection with the CCC had been "a real inspiration" rather than a burden. "It is the type of human reconstruction that has appealed to me more than I sometimes admit. . . . I think all concerned in this splendid effort have cause for rejoicing in the results it is producing." Like the Olympic Committee that he had supervised five years before, this "human reconstruction" involving civilians taking on the discipline and dedication of mind and body that usually fell to the military was in his mind representative of the "greatest nation in the world."[12]

In any case, MacArthur was able to breathe a brief sigh of relief. He had restored the reputation of the army, at least with New Dealers. Now maybe Roosevelt and his team would think twice about further slashing of the War Department budget. Getting more money was too much to expect, but now he had a standing chance to halt more cuts.

He was wrong. The much-needed money for the army's work with CCC would stay in, but on the rest Roosevelt would double-cross him with a budget that would make the cuts of the last decade look like the fat years in the Bible.

Even after a succession of brutally lean appropriations, the defense budget for 1934—Hoover's last—had been a heartbreaker. It had come to only $277,700,000—$43 million less than what the War Department had asked for.[13] Congress hacked off another half million or so when it passed the appropriations bill for 1934, but the real deathblow came three weeks later. FDR's budget director, Lewis Douglas, had decided that no less than $80 million would have to come out of the nation's military expenditures in order to reach the president's goal of a balanced budget. The army's budget would be cut by more than half, or 51 percent, the National Guard by a quarter, and the Organized Reserves and ROTC by a third each.[14]

On top of that, Congress passed a 15 percent reduction in all federal and military salaries, including veterans' benefits, and offered to give the president power to furlough army officers (3,000 to 4,000 of them) on half pay. Roosevelt said publicly that he would do just that.

MacArthur was enraged. His first reaction was to dub the Roosevelt budget "a stunning blow to national defense," and he personally rushed to the Hill to lobby his allies to halt it in its tracks. He testified to Congress on the folly of the furlough idea: "The foundation of our National Defense system is the Regular Army," he insisted, "and the foundation of the Regular Army is the officer. He is the soul of the system." Reduce his numbers below 12,000, MacArthur patiently explained, and the United States could never turn an army of civilian draftees into an effective fighting force in the event of war.

"If you had to discharge every soldier," he pleaded, "if you had to do away with everything else, I would still professionally advise you to keep those 12,000 officers" as "the mainspring of the whole mechanism"; otherwise, there would be no mechanism at all, no army to defend America.[15]

MacArthur managed to win the furlough fight in the Senate, but Roosevelt was stubbornly committed to his other budget cuts. In his blacker moments MacArthur felt he was locked in a losing battle over the entire future of the U.S. Army. At stake was whether it could temporarily get along as the seventeenth-largest fighting force in the world, smaller than those of Greece or Portugal, but still have the resources to resurrect itself if and when war came—or whether it would lose its effectiveness as a fighting force forever in a misguided effort to balance the federal budget, even while CCC was going to cost $143 million just in its first three months.[16]

In June he gave the graduation address at West Point. In front of rows of seated cadets and their families he spelled out the danger ahead and threw down the gauntlet to the president and Congress. "As the necessity of national defense is sacrificed in the name of economy, the United States presents a tempting spectacle. It is a spectacle that may ultimately lead to an alignment of the nations, which may lead to another World War. . . . It is my conviction that at this moment the Army's strength in personnel and materiel and its readiness for deployment are below the danger line."

He warned the cadets, "History has proved that nations once great, that neglected their national defense, are dust and ashes." Reversing America's decline from greatness was now MacArthur's crusade in his last months as army chief of staff.[17]

Fortunately, MacArthur discovered that he had an unexpected ally in the Roosevelt camp. He was George Dern, secretary of war and former business-man and governor of Utah, who had fought to streamline the department budget but who also understood, as a smart businessman would, how im-portant it was to preserve the foundation for an American military when real trouble came its way. He was also a MacArthur admirer. "He was in thor-ough agreement with army plans," MacArthur remembered later, "and a pil-lar of support for the military. My esteem for him grew daily"—not least because Dern was able to intervene with Ross Collins, who had learned about the indiscreet "Mississippi cracker" comment and wanted MacAr-thur's head until Dern convinced him to ease off.[18]

But could Dern move the president? MacArthur was going to find out, when the pair of them made a trip to the White House in late March 1934. They needed to make the insouciant Roosevelt realize the gravity of the 51 percent cut he had proposed. In his usual quiet, deliberate way Dern led the discussion with a long dissertation on why it would be "a fatal error" to insist on balancing the budget on the back of the army and the National Guard, especially when Nazi Germany was rearming and Japan acting more aggres-sively in the Pacific.

Roosevelt, growing impatient at being challenged, began to strike back. He replied in harsh, bitter words until, as MacArthur later remembered, "the Secretary grew white and silent." It was a bad moment. MacArthur began to feel it was a moment when America's defense would hang in the balance un-less he spoke up.

"I felt it was my duty to take up the cudgels," he wrote almost thirty years later. "The country's safety [was] at stake and I said [so] bluntly."

In retrospect, it's not difficult to reconstruct the scene. Three powerful public men were clustered together in the Oval Office. One of them, Franklin

Roosevelt, was clearly irritated at being bearded in his throne room on an issue he considered irrelevant to the nation's immediate future. Another, George Dern, had been reduced to an angry silence by the president's gift for biting sarcasm and "lashing tongue."

Then there was MacArthur himself, resolved that this moment was as important to the nation, and to his own pride as a soldier, as any since the Civil War, and that he now had to be as forceful as he was eloquent.

It was not a good strategy. "The President turned the full vials of his sarcasm upon me," MacArthur remembered. "He was a scorcher when aroused." The discussion turned warm and intense. "For the third and last time in my life," MacArthur confessed, "that paralyzing nausea began to creep over me"—the nausea that had overwhelmed him at West Point and then after the tongue-lashing by Pershing during the World War.

As the feeling of discomfort grew, he grew more reckless. "When we lose the next war," he finally intoned, speaking in the voice usually reserved for biblical prophets, "and an American boy, lying in the mud with an enemy bayonet through his belly and an enemy foot on his dying throat, spits out his last curse, I want the name to be Roosevelt, not MacArthur!"

Roosevelt's face turned beet red. The color of George Dern's face is not recorded.

"You must not talk that way to the President of the United States!" Roosevelt roared.

MacArthur, to his credit, realized that FDR was right. He had done the unforgivable: he had reamed out an American president to his face. "I felt my Army career was at an end," he recalled later. Stiffly he offered his resignation as chief of staff and rose to go to the door.

The air in the room, if anything, grew more stifling. Then Roosevelt tried to dispel it all by saying, "Don't be foolish, Douglas: you and the budget must get together on this." He said it "with that cool detachment which so reflected his extraordinary self-control," and that earned MacArthur's respect, if not his love, from that moment on.

MacArthur stepped out the door. At his elbow was a jubilant George Dern, who had followed him out.

"You've saved the Army," Dern chortled. But MacArthur felt no such triumph. He felt instead a sense of shame that he had not known since West

Point days—or probably never. "I just vomited on the steps of the White House" was the way he described it many years later.[19]

Whatever MacArthur's misgivings, his dramatic intervention had worked. Begrudgingly Roosevelt agreed to restore the full schedule of training for the National Guard and let the Reserve Officers Association representatives who visited with him at the White House persuade him to allocate additional funds for field training.[20] In the end, he even gave way somewhat on the budget numbers, deciding that the $80 million he had demanded would be only $51 million instead.

Still, the fight over the 1934 budget was a moment of no return for both Roosevelt and MacArthur. In Roosevelt's mind, his showdown with the army's egotistical power-hungry chief of staff had been essential to demonstrate "that he [i.e., Roosevelt] would be no mere nominal Commander in Chief." Indeed, it was the kind of exertion of power over his service chiefs that he would demonstrate again and again during the Second World War, to the point of overruling his most trusted military advisors.

For MacArthur, the episode was his introduction to Franklin Roosevelt in full. This was not the charming, easygoing, rather willowy scion of a patrician dynasty whom he had known during the last war. This was a Roosevelt who "had greatly changed and matured," he decided. A man who was willful but also open to changing his mind; disingenuous to the point of duplicity but absolutely fearless; a president capable of doing great harm but also great good. It was this Roosevelt with whom he would have to contend for the next decade, until the day in April 1945 when an Army caisson would carry Roosevelt's body down Pennsylvania Avenue before a grieving nation and a new president, one less tested and less trusted, took Roosevelt's place.[21]

Together Dern and MacArthur had saved the army from a permanent starvation diet. Congress's appropriation for fiscal 1935 was still dismal in the War Department's eyes: barely $280 million. MacArthur explained in his annual report in mid-1934 that the army and the National Guard were "at considerably less than half the strength contemplated" by the law that Congress itself had passed, the National Defense Act of 1920, and its equipment was "inadequate even for limited forces . . . and manifestly obsolete." The Reserve

Officers' Corps was still "inadequately supported." Even more shockingly, "we have no enlisted Reserve."[22]

But the era of draconian cuts was over. In 1934 a new mood was sweeping over Congress and public opinion now that the worst of the Depression had passed, and people were becoming aware that all was not well with the outside world. In Germany Adolf Hitler was firmly in power, and taking concrete steps to not only rearm Germany but also pull out of the League of Nations. Japan was already out, and later that year announced that it would also be pulling out of the Five-Power Washington Naval Treaty—the treaty that had been the anchor of America's mistaken belief that reducing its navy and army would have no consequences, since other powers, including Japan, were formally committed to limiting theirs or even doing the same. And far off in Africa, Italy's Benito Mussolini was preparing for his boldest overseas venture yet, with an invasion of Abyssinia from Italian Somalia.

In this tense atmosphere, MacArthur felt confident enough to ask for an additional appropriations for fiscal 1936, raising the War Department budget to $361 million—the biggest yet since becoming chief of staff.[23] It was a pipe dream: everyone still assumed that if the world exploded in war, the United States would not have to take any part in it. Indeed, Congress would pass, and Roosevelt sign, the first Neutrality Act that next year, 1935, precisely on the hope that America could steer clear of any future conflicts by refusing to help arm either side.

All the same, no one was willing to risk weakening the American military any further, given the increasingly dangerous world. Under MacArthur's leadership a corner had been turned, and if the army was not yet on the road to recovery, at least it was off the operating table.

Still, as the summer of 1934 drew to a close, MacArthur told Ike he believed his days as chief of staff were numbered, might even be over in a few months.[24]

His position had been made worse by two scandals, the first involving the U.S. mail service. In February, without consulting MacArthur, Roosevelt asked the head of army aviation, General Benjamin Foulois, if the army could take over delivery of U.S. air mail from its commercial carriers, which were being investigated for antitrust corruption. Foulois immediately said yes, thinking it would be great publicity for an Army Air Corps that had barely survived its post–World War One cuts and the Billy Mitchell scandal.

Instead, it was a disaster. Over the first eight days of the flights, the army suffered eight fatal crashes; and three more in March. Roosevelt was furious: he summoned MacArthur and Foulois to the White House and demanded, "When are those airmail killings going to stop?"

Foulois's answer was equally blunt. "Only when airplanes stop flying." He blamed bad weather and poor navigation for the deaths, but the public—and Congress—blamed Foulois and MacArthur. The chief of staff found himself hauled up in front of a Senate investigating committee, before which Foulois, far from trying to pass the buck, pointed out that MacArthur had never been consulted on what was a major reallocation of army resources.

The senators were aghast. "The Executive Order of the President was made before you knew of it?" they asked MacArthur.

"Yes sir," MacArthur replied coolly. "I knew nothing about carrying the mails until I was told of it by [the] Associated Press." His testimony let him off the hook for any responsibility for the tragic crashes, shifting it instead to the White House. But MacArthur was careful to keep himself on the moral high ground. He pointed out that the army always carries out the orders it's given, and that Foulois and the Air Corps were blameless in the deaths that had taken place.* He was also careful not to lay too much blame for the fiasco on Roosevelt himself, which was politically as well as personally astute.

Because he was going to need Roosevelt's help in getting through the next scandal, which involved the goings-on in a certain D.C. apartment building called the Chastleton.

The Chastleton sits on Sixteenth Street north of R Avenue and across from the Scottish Rite Temple belonging to the Masonic Order. Thoroughly renovated today, in 1934 one of the Chastleton's residents was a beautiful young girl named Isabella Rosario Cooper. She was a Filipino dancer and film star,

---

* MacArthur's defense of Foulois turned the general into an unqualified fan. "MacArthur was the kind of man you either deeply respected or hated with a passion," he wrote many years later. "I not only respected him. I believed him to be possessed of almost godlike qualities."

in fact, who had appeared in the Philippines' first on-screen kiss, which earned her the nickname Dimples.

She had lived at the Chastleton since 1930, but never received a single rental bill. That was paid for by Douglas MacArthur, a man thirty-four years her senior who had brought her with him when he had left the Philippines for Washington.

In the summer of 1934 the army chief of staff's secret assignation—so secret that his own mother knew nothing about it—was about to go public. In an age when a movie could not show a man and a woman sitting on the same bed unless they were supposed to be married, MacArthur knew he faced public disgrace as great, if not greater than, the problems that had followed the Bonus Army debacle.

He had met Isabella when he returned to the Philippines in 1928. He was fresh from his divorce from Louise and enjoying the bachelor life in quarters with four other bachelor officers, "a gay and lively group," he admitted years later, with whom he spent evenings and weekends going to the cinema, polo matches, and boxing matches. It was at one of those boxing matches, at Olympic Stadium in 1929, that an exquisite young woman caught his eye. As if in a scene from an Ernst Lubitsch movie, he had his aide Tommy Davis send her a note.

Soon she and MacArthur could be seen all over Manila riding in his chauffeured limousine, which would stop outside her home on Herron Street in the Paco district of Manila.[25] MacArthur would come up to share a cigarette and talk and drink a concoction of Spanish brandy, squeezed mango, and crushed ice that she christened "the Douglas."

She was as unlike Louise as any woman could be. Small, soft-spoken, beautiful, Dimples was charming yet self-effacing—and darkly exotic. Louise had been two years older than he; Isabel was not even eighteen. But when he was recalled to Washington in the fall of 1930, he was determined that she join him when he got settled. He bought her a jade-and-diamond ring as well as a ticket for the States, and the day he sailed, he watched her waving from the dock in her bright green dress until she faded from sight.[26]

Whatever else she was, Isabel triggered something in MacArthur akin to a frantic passion. His letters back to her (at one point he was writing two a day) were filled with his plans for their reunion. In fact, given her flourishing career in the Philippines and her wide circle of admirers, he was pathetically worried that she might not follow him to America. The language of the letters bordered on the erotic, not to say pornographic, as he described how "I kiss your dear lips and press your soft body to my own." His memory of her kept him awake at night, as he found himself "groping for you . . . seeking for you to soothe my fever" and "all the passion of my starving panting body."[27]

It was not until early December that "Darling One" and "My Baby Girl" arrived in the States and took up residence at the Chastleton. It's not entirely clear what Isabel saw in him beyond a handsome and powerful sugar daddy and protector. He did buy her a fur coat, a chauffeur-driven car, a French poodle, and a large collection of French lingerie. MacArthur even provided her an allowance. On the other hand, it may have been that she found his devotion touching, not to say stimulating. Having one of the most powerful and respected men in the United States literally at her feet—even if he was thirty-four years her senior—must have been gratifying to the teenager from Manila.

Certainly she did want something more than clandestine meetings. She began using the name Mrs. Isabel Cooper—a clear hint. But MacArthur would have none of it; indeed, he could not. Quite apart from the absurdity of contemplating marriage to a barely legal girl whom a race-conscious government and army would see as a half-caste, he knew that the revelation of their relationship would become a juicy Washington scandal—especially given his reputation as more marble monument than man.

Then there was his mother. Frail, dressed in widow's black twenty years after Arthur MacArthur's death, and wearing black sunglasses to protect her failing eyesight, she was still a formidable presence in her son's life. When she arrived at Quarters Number One, she had announced she would receive no visitors. But her son was still the center of her life, and the story went out that she checked the weather every day to choose his coat or umbrella for him before he set off for the office. On one wintry day someone saw her standing on the porch as MacArthur boarded his car, and heard her calling plaintively, "Dougee—did you remember to take your overshoes?"[28]

She would have found Isabel *entirely* unsuitable, either as wife or as female associate. And so although MacArthur recognized that the relationship had no future, there was also no way out. Instead, he did his best to keep it a deep secret.

That didn't last for long. And the one responsible was his ex-wife, Louise.

Gross, overweight, addicted to drink, and deeply bitter over the breakup with her husband, the once-elegant Louise was prime fodder for anyone looking for information to discredit an army chief of staff who was largely hated in liberal and New Deal circles.

In the spring of 1934 she met liberal columnists Drew Pearson and Roger Allen, authors of the widely read "Washington Merry-Go-Round" column. They were determined to skewer MacArthur, the evil mastermind of the Bonus Army debacle, any way they could. They were therefore delighted to find in his ex-wife a seemingly bottomless fount of scandalous stories, including—as she would drunkenly wag her little finger—that MacArthur was impotent. "This is Douglas's penis," she would say and giggle. "He thinks it's just for peeing with!"[29]

The impotence story stayed under wraps. But when their column appeared in mid-May flaying MacArthur's supposed "dictatorial, insubordinate, disloyal, mutinous and disrespectful" behavior during the Bonus Army days, MacArthur exploded. He brought a $1.75 million lawsuit for libel, citing seven examples with a $250,000 price tag on each.

None of them, however, involved Isabel. That information came to Pearson and Allen not from Louise—she was terrified into silence by the lawsuit and told the columnists she would never testify under oath—but from MacArthur's old nemesis Congressman Ross Collins, whom they approached for any damaging information they could use to bolster their defense. Collins said (according to Pearson), "You know, MacArthur's been keeping a girl in the Chastleton Apartments." And so the secret was out.

How Collins got the information—whether through private detectives or ordinary War Department scuttlebutt—didn't matter. The irony was that the affair was already over. In 1933 Isabel had met a young law student, her interest in MacArthur steadily faded, and when he found out in the spring of 1934, there had been an ugly scene and they parted ways. That July MacArthur had bought her a steamship ticket to send her back to the Philippines. Instead, short on funds now that her allowance was gone, she cashed in the ticket, moved out of the Chastleton, and went looking for a cheaper place to live—and she demanded more money. Finally, MacArthur sent her a note saying "From the Humane Society. Apply to your Father or Brother for any future help." He also sent her the "Help—Women" classifieds from the *Washington Times*. If anything was calculated to turn Isabel into a spurned lover seething for revenge, that was it.[30]

That was the person Pearson found when he finally located her, and she happily handed over whatever physical evidence she had of their affair—including the bundle of torrid letters.

Unlike Louise, she was more than willing to testify in court, including testifying to hearing MacArthur say, "Hoover was a weakling, but I finally put some backbone into him" and refer to Roosevelt as "that cripple in the White House."

This was interesting, if only because the person who had been advising MacArthur in the lawsuit was Roosevelt himself. He had even advised him as to the exact amount of the suit—$1.75 million—and told his cabinet that he had "authorized" MacArthur to sue that "chronic liar" Pearson, hoping the result would be the end of Pearson's career, even though Pearson was one of the most loyal supporters of his administration.

But now the stakes had changed. Pearson offered a straightforward blackmail deal: call off the lawsuit or I'll make the affair and the letters public. It seems MacArthur sent off his aide Dwight "Ike" Eisenhower to try to talk to Isabel, but she had disappeared (Pearson had her living in hiding with his brother in Baltimore).

So finally he reluctantly agreed to drop the suit and pay his former mistress $15,000 to get his letters back—even though Pearson kept copies of several just in case.

Some wondered why he had caved. Admiral Leahy, who was working as FDR's naval advisor and had gotten wind of the scandal, guessed the reason was "that old woman he lived with in Fort Myer," namely, Pinky, and he was probably right. MacArthur must have known that the revelation of the scandal would have broken his mother's heart—and very likely might have destroyed her already fragile health.[31]

But it's also possible that his own heart had suffered as well—although he was too proud to admit it. Love's young dream had been exposed as a lie; and his private passion, which had seemed so romantic at the time, had come within an ace of being exposed in a crowded courtroom to scorn and ridicule.

So he paid up to make the scandal go away. And it did; Pearson kept his promise not to use the letters during the general's lifetime. Even MacArthur's most thorough biographer, D. Clayton James, never learned the full details.

It was also the end of Isabel. With her cash in hand and her former law student in tow, she headed for Hollywood, where she struggled unsuccessfully to establish a movie career—and struggled unsuccessfully to kick a growing addiction to barbiturates. In 1960 an overdose took her life.

Her last years had been deeply unhappy ones. Some said she spent them trying to convince people that she had once been Douglas MacArthur's teenage mistress. Everyone had simply laughed at the idea.[32]

In January 1935 MacArthur sat in full dress uniform with brightly polished boots in front of the assembled members of the House Subcommittee on Military Appropriations. His personal life might be a mess; the sordid Cooper scandal may have hurt the regard with which some Washington insiders held him, the president included. But that afternoon MacArthur could be happy and confident. The War Department had just announced that in fiscal year 1936 it intended to increase the army's enlisted strength from 119,000 to 165,000—its biggest peacetime strength in fifteen years—and its officer corps from 12,000 to 14,000. At the same time it was looking to increase the West Point corps from 1,374 to 1,960 cadets—again, the biggest peacetime gain in years.[33] All the plan needed was a War Department budget increase to $331,800,000—and what made the army's chief of staff happy was that this time he believed he could get it.

The president's Bureau of the Budget had hacked away $30 million from that figure and eliminated the increase in the enlisted ranks. But this time, instead of accepting the best of a bad deal, MacArthur was going on the counterattack. He urged the appropriations subcommittee to repudiate the bureau's decision. It was one "I think so fundamental and so basic that its application unbalances the bill from the standpoint of reasonable policy," MacArthur intoned, "and may jeopardize the prospect in the case of major operations."

The subcommittee's chairman, and MacArthur's old nemesis, Ross Collins, rebuffed his arguments, but to MacArthur's delight the rest of the subcommittee backed him up. They restored $7 million to the Bureau of the Budget's numbers and empowered the president to raise the enlisted level to 165,000 men. The downside was that the army's request for more officers lost out. For MacArthur, however, it was still a big victory, and when the final appropriations came out of the Senate in late March 1935, where MacArthur's strength was greater, the army's budget was just $6 million short of the department's request; and the increase to 165,000 men was now a matter of law.

The press proclaimed that Congress had "voted MacArthur virtually everything he wanted," and admitted, "General MacArthur has a way with Congressional committees." Even the administration's decision to sequester $9 million of that increase couldn't dampen his sense of triumph, and *The New York Times* had to concede that Mac had won his case not just through personal persuasion but because of the growing talk of war on this side of the Atlantic and the Pacific. Indeed, public opinion in 1935 for the first time showed support for increased appropriations—although Congress still leaned completely the other way.[34]

MacArthur's annual report for 1935 was a deeply satisfying one.

"For the first time since 1922," he wrote, "the Army enters a new fiscal year with a reasonable prospect of developing itself into a defense establishment commensurate in size and efficiency. This year definitely marks the beginning of a long-deferred resumption of military preparation on a scale demanded by the most casual regard for the Nation's safety and security"—and, he might have added, a casual glance at the headlines.

Mussolini was invading Ethiopia; Japan was occupying northern China. Adolf Hitler had taken over the Saar territory on the border with France and was instituting mass conscription in Germany. Mussolini was doing the same in Italy, with the goal of one million men under arms by the end of the year.

Under these conditions, an American standing army of 166,000 men didn't seem that warmongering after all.

In addition, there had been vital steps to increase military aviation. Echoing his old friend Billy Mitchell, who had died an alcoholic, broken man the year before, MacArthur stressed that "a blow that can be delivered by a strong air unit is sudden, and depending on the vulnerability of the target, can be peculiarly devastating." There were also plans for developing a strong mechanized force for the army, including "the possibility of transporting into and even through the vicissitudes of battle itself the infantry of entire divisions." Indeed, "nothing is more important to the future efficiency of the Army than to multiply its rate of movement."

All the same, despite the new technologies the army would be harnessing, there was certainly no cause for complacency. The road to transforming the U.S. Army into a modern and efficient force ready to fight modern battles was still a difficult and long one, MacArthur affirmed. But at least "it is now open and unobstructed. . . . I am happy to have had the opportunity through an additional year to continue the struggle to free the Army of shackles tending to chain it to obsolescence and stagnation." Although much remained to be done, he concluded, "[m]y successor in this office . . . will have the unswerving support of the whole Army—the most able, loyal, devoted, and unselfish body of public servants that this Nation or any other has ever produced."[35]

It was MacArthur's last address to Congress as chief of staff. By ordinary lights, his reference to a successor would have been a matter for regret, after what he and his successor, General Malin Craig, both believed had been a highly successful tenure. But all the evidence suggests that MacArthur was eager to leave: eager to leave behind the poisonous world of Washington politics and the Washington media, Drew Pearson included, as well as President Roosevelt's tangled webs of intrigue.

That included Roosevelt's stringing him, and the army, along on his reappointment for more than a year. His ordinary term had run out in November 1934. The conventional wisdom was that Roosevelt would replace MacArthur, the conservative Republican who was still blamed for the Bonus Army debacle, with someone more in line with the New Deal outlook. But Roosevelt was unhappy with the alternatives. So he startled everyone with an announcement on December 12, 1934: "I have sent a letter to the Secretary of War directing that General Douglas MacArthur be retained as Chief of Staff until his successor has been appointed . . . I am doing this in order to obtain the benefit of General MacArthur's experience in handling War Department legislation" in a Congress that was as headstrong as it was unsure of what to do on national defense matters.[36]

Then the following June Roosevelt extended his term yet again—until October.[37]

By then, however, MacArthur already had his eye on a new job after chief of staff—one he was eager to take on.

In the summer of 1934, MacArthur had a welcome visitor from the Philippines—Manuel Quezon. His old friend was now head of the Philippines' largest political party and about to become the first president of the Philippine Commonwealth in November.

It was Quezon's second trip in two years. He had been in Washington before to lobby hard for Philippine independence; the result had been a bill sponsored by Millard Tydings of Maryland and John McDuffie of Alabama. It was much less than Quezon had hoped for. It offered independence for his country no earlier than 1946, with a gradual shift of governmental responsibility to the Filipinos themselves—more gradual than the political opposition Quezon faced in Manila would have liked. But Quezon put the best face on Tydings-McDuffie, which included provisions for continuing American bases in the islands, and used its passage to win his own election as president.[38]

Worries kept gnawing at Quezon, however. Japan's army was on the move in China; Japan's navy was rapidly expanding. How long would it be before Asia's budding imperial power cast its gaze in the direction of the defenseless Philippines?

When he raised this issue with Roosevelt and members of Congress, he got little more than vague reassurances. The days when Congress worried about the fate of "our little brown brothers" far across the Pacific were long gone; the Depression had focused all attention at home. As for Roosevelt, he "was always too absorbed in other matters to give the Philippines much thought," as one historian has put it. Meetings at the White House were fruit-less.[39] Quezon decided to seek out the one person he thought would care about what happened to the Philippines, his friend Doug MacArthur.

The minute they sat down together, Quezon posed the crucial question. "Do you think the Philippines can be defended"—at least once indepen-dence was achieved in what seemed to be the far-off date of 1946?

MacArthur's first answer was, "I don't think so." He then added, "Any place can be defended if sufficient men, munitions, and money is available—and there's sufficient time to raise all three." The monetary figure he had in mind was $5 million a year for ten years. Obviously the Philippines couldn't expect to create a modern army, complete with air and mechanized forces, even with that kind of time and money. But MacArthur unveiled the idea he had borrowed from Leonard Wood: that of creating a Swiss-style army of civilian reserves, who could be trained in peacetime and led in war by a small and highly motivated force of professionals.

"No country will dare to attack you," MacArthur said, almost certainly with a dramatic sweep of his arm that usually accompanied big bold state-ments of this kind. "The cost of conquest will be more than the expected profit."[40]

Quezon digested this for a moment, and then asked his next question.

"Will you undertake the task?"

MacArthur must have been taken aback by the question, but then he gave his answer almost without thinking.

"Yes, I will," he said, and the two men shook hands.[41]

It was an extraordinary change of direction for a man who had spent his life in the United States Army, and now held its highest post. Yet for MacAr-thur it made sense. It would return him to the country where, for most of his life, he had been happiest.

It would enable him to complete the work his father had set out to do, namely, to bring about the freedom of the Philippine Islands; it would re-unite him with Quezon and people that, unlike those he worked with in Washington, he could count on as real friends. Above all, taking on the job would allow him to remain in the army; he would be going out in the newly created post of military advisor. Instead of his departure as chief of staff marking his retirement, it would just be the springboard to something even more interesting.

Besides, he was fifty-five and a bachelor with no family ties except his mother. If anyone was entitled to start his life over in a new job in a familiar setting thousands of miles away from Washington, it was Douglas MacArthur.

After the meeting he sat down and wrote a letter to Quezon.

"The great work involved as your Military Advisor seems to me to transcend in ultimate importance anything else that is conceivable. I am prepared to devote the rest of my life if necessary to securing a proper defense for the Philippine Nation."[42]

The next stage was breaking the news to Roosevelt and Secretary of War Dern. Perhaps to his surprise, they were enthusiastic—maybe because they would finally have him far, far away from Washington. He wrote to Quezon, "As a consequence I am making definite plans to close my tour as Chief of Staff about June 10 and leave for the islands immediately thereafter."

But nothing was easy with Roosevelt. Instead of smoothing the way for MacArthur's transition, Roosevelt announced he was keeping the general on as chief of staff until October. Then when the pair were having lunch at Hyde Park in September, Roosevelt unveiled his new offer. He wanted to appoint MacArthur as the United States' first high commissioner to the Philippines, once the commonwealth was established and the old post of governor-general was abolished.

For MacArthur, the offer was breathtakingly tempting. It was an opportunity like no other to oversee the Philippines' transition to full self-government; to leave his personal stamp on the democratic experiment unfolding there; and to be the first U.S. senior official defining a new relationship between the United States and the Philippines. But when he returned to Fort Myer, the army's top lawyers warned him that if he took the job he would have to retire from the army. MacArthur wrote a sad note to Roosevelt, saying he was "somewhat dismayed and nonplused" at this development; unless the law was changed to allow him to remain on the active list, he would have to turn the high commissioner post down.[43]

The post of military advisor, on the other hand, kept him very much in the army, with the added bonus that he could continue to draw his army pay ($7,500 a year) in addition to what he negotiated with Quezon, which in the end came to $18,000 annual salary and $15,000 for expenses—more than double his present salary.

In addition, as historian Geoffrey Perret has revealed, MacArthur had an additional deal to receive a percentage of Philippine defense spending up to 1942 as a performance bonus, once the defense plan was approved by the commonwealth government—which, with his friend Quezon at the helm, was virtually guaranteed. By then the $46/100$ of one percent could add up to a quarter of a million dollars—a tidy retirement nest egg.[44]

All of it was not only shrewd business and entirely legal, but it met the approval of the army's adjutant general—as did any changes in compensation and emolument that MacArthur cared to make in his position later. MacArthur would be going to the Philippines with extraordinary carte blanche, not just to make whatever defense plans he deemed necessary but to make him independently wealthy in the process.

On September 18 his appointment as military advisor to the Philippines was announced. That same day MacArthur learned that Quezon had been elected president, as expected. He sent his friend a telegram of warm congratulations, and then turned his attention to deciding what, and who, would be going with him on his latest adventure.

One who was going was his mother. She was now eighty-three, and most doctors would have said her heart wouldn't be able to stand the strain of living in the Philippines. But Pinky was more than game. The sea voyage and the warmth of Manila would do her good, she insisted; Douglas shouldn't miss out on this wonderful opportunity out of concern for her.[45] Besides, nothing would have killed her quicker than saying goodbye to her son, with no hope of ever seeing him again.

MacArthur, however, was not going to let her travel alone. He asked her doctor, Major Howard Hutter of the Medical Corps, if he would accompany them to the Philippines not just as his mother's doctor but as MacArthur's medical advisor on dealing with sanitation and health issues for the new Philippine Army. Hutter enthusiastically said yes.

Then there was Major Dwight Eisenhower, whom MacArthur asked to join him as his chief of staff. Their relationship was something of a puzzle. Born to dirt-poor Mennonite pacifist parents in Kansas, Eisenhower had gone to West Point largely as a way to pay for a college education. Once there, however, "Ike" had proved to be an able soldier and graduated at the top of his class at the Command and General Staff School at Leavenworth. He was a gifted administrator—one reason MacArthur liked him—and was also a gifted writer. He had written General Pershing's memoirs, and most of the official American Battlefields and Monuments guides published accounts of the AEF's combat operations, which had given him an intimate knowledge of the war he hadn't gone to fight, the Rainbow Division's war included.[46]

Ike was a rising star in the army bureaucracy, who understood the power of pushing paper effectively—and attaching oneself to a powerful patron like MacArthur. "Ike got so he could write more like MacArthur talked than the General himself," one General Staff officer remembered.[47]

MacArthur, in fact, had been so impressed by Eisenhower's work on the 1931 Annual Report to the War Department that he put a special commendation into the major's personnel file, and sent a copy to Ike, which his wife, Mamie, had framed.[48]

Privately, Eisenhower's opinion of MacArthur was more mixed. His affair with "Dimples" Cooper and his personal vanity (MacArthur could spend hours examining himself in the mirror) disturbed him. He also believed MacArthur's complacency and arrogance had led him to make crucial mistakes during the Bonus Army fiasco. But when MacArthur called, he was happy to go, and for the next four years they would be in the closest contact MacArthur ever had with any officer.

He allowed Ike to bring an aide. This was Ike's West Point classmate Major James "Jimmy" Ord, who would prove to be a popular officer not just with Americans but with the Filipinos as well. MacArthur's own personal aide, Captain Tom Davis, and Arthur MacArthur's widow, Mary, who came along as female company for Pinky on the long voyage, rounded out their little band.

Then came the final ceremonies for his departure as chief of staff: an Oak Leaf Cluster was added to his Distinguished Service Medal, and the Reserve Officers Association issued him a special citation. The veterans of the Rainbow Division asked him to give the keynote address at their annual convention, which MacArthur delivered to rousing cheers and a standing ovation. The Bonus Army shame, it seemed, was finally behind him.

As one reporter for the *Washington Herald* put it, "Brilliant and magnetic General Douglas MacArthur is going out as Chief of Staff in a blaze of splendid glory."[49]

Media hype aside, how good a chief of staff had MacArthur been?

Certainly he had overseen some major changes in the administration of the U.S. Army, ones that experts and historians agree were crucial for the future. They included creating a four-army system for mobilization, divided into nine corps areas around the country, that streamlined the mobilization process. He had built up the Army Reserves and the ROTC, as well as opening the General Staff College at Leavenworth to lieutenants. He also turned the Army War College into a lively place for serious thinking about tactics and strategy.

In addition, he had overseen the launching of three weapons that would become iconic arms of the U.S. armed forces in World War Two.

The first was the M-1 Garand rifle. MacArthur was its crucial champion in the search for a weapon to replace the .03 Springfield bolt-action rifle. He personally selected the M-1's .30 caliber and had told the president that outfitting the army with a new rifle would put thousands of workers back on the job with a ripple effect throughout the economy, as well as give American soldiers their first semiautomatic weapon. Once in service, the M-1 Garand would become the indispensable rifle for his troops in the New Guinea and Philippines campaigns, as well as in Europe and the central Pacific. If there was one weapon that gave American soldiers and marines the extra edge in World War Two, it was the M-1—and they owed it to MacArthur's foresight and determination.

The second was the B-17 bomber, which was under contract with the Army Air Corps beginning in 1935 and which came into service in 1937. The third was the 105 mm howitzer, which would support army formations in every campaign from North Africa to the Philippines. MacArthur also put into production the army's first light and medium tanks—ancestors of the

Grant and Sherman that would be the key combat vehicles of British as well as American armored formations throughout the Second World War. In addition, he had given the army's medals and ribbons an overhaul and set up the standard system we see on soldiers' chests today, and revived the Purple Heart as the ultimate tribute for wounds received in combat.[50]

But perhaps his most generous action was saving General Pershing's pension. As part of its mania for economizing, Congress had proposed that no retired officer's pay exceed $2,400 a year, which would mean that Pershing's special pension of $21,000, granted when he retired as general of the armies, would be slashed to the bone. MacArthur headed for Capitol Hill—"he could turn his attention on a House committee like a searchlight," Robert Eichelberger remembered—to testify against the bill. He did this by comparing Pershing's retirement with what his British counterpart, Field Marshal Douglas Haig, received upon his retirement. That had included a life trust of $9,000 a year plus a $1 million trust fund yielding $30,000 a year that was perpetual for his children, grandchildren, and great-grandchildren.

Congress got the message; it dropped the bill. Pershing, who was now seventy-two years old and ill, sent MacArthur a message. "Please allow me to send you my warmest congratulations upon the way you have succeeded in overcoming opposition in Congress to the Army. I think you have much to be thankful for, as we all have. And may I also express my appreciation for the way you have defended the Retired List and especially your reference to me."[51] In a single afternoon MacArthur had laid an old grudge, and old ghosts, to rest.

In the end, it's hard to avoid the conclusion that MacArthur had saved the United States Army from dwindling to impotence, in a time when the majority of Americans didn't think about their military, or care. He had also saved Franklin Roosevelt's presidential legacy, by giving him an army that could respond to the sudden challenge of war in December 1941. In that sense, MacArthur was correct when he said, looking back on his service as chief of staff, "we formed the central character of the U.S. Army in World War Two."[52]

Yet the character of the president he had served eluded him. "You are the best general," Roosevelt once told him, "but the worst politician"—evidently thinking of the Bonus Army mess. And although they were ideological opposites, MacArthur had spent many hours in the White House discussing domestic policy as well as foreign policy. He tells us in his memoirs that he finally asked Roosevelt why he kept asking his advice on domestic issues when he seemed to pay no attention to MacArthur's views on what he knew best, the military.

"Douglas," the president said, "I don't bring these questions up for your advice but for your reaction. To me, you are the symbol of the conscience of the American people." If Roosevelt had meant to say "conservatism" instead of "conscience," he was probably right.[53]

When they met for the last time before MacArthur left, MacArthur told friends, Roosevelt's mood was grave. He thanked him for his work both for the country and for Roosevelt himself. Then as MacArthur rose to leave, the president looked up with considerable emotion.

"Douglas, if war should suddenly come, don't wait for orders to return home. Grab the first transportation you can find. I want you to command my armies."[54]

It may have been a typical Roosevelt throwaway line, signifying nothing. Or he may have meant it. With the exception of Pershing, MacArthur was America's greatest living soldier and also the most admired—and Pershing would not be coming back to command anything. If there was a supreme commander that any president, Democratic or Republican, would turn to in time of war, it was Douglas MacArthur.

When they next met that war would be in full swing—and MacArthur would be locked with Roosevelt in a battle of wills that would determine the difference between victory and defeat.

CHAPTER 12
MISSION TO MANILA

The power that rules the Pacific rules the world.

—SENATOR ALBERT BEVERIDGE, 1900

One bright day in the summer of 1935, thirty-seven-year-old Jean Faircloth was having breakfast in her aunt's house in Murfreesboro, Tennessee. She was unmarried, and living with her aunt Myrie, who worked at the local telephone company. It was a relaxed, easygoing existence but also rather dull—especially after the places Jean had seen.

She was gazing out the window, wondering what she could do with herself for another unexciting day in Murfreesboro, when her aunt looked up from the breakfast table and said: "Why don't you go back to the Far East, Jean? You loved it so much."[1]

Those were magic words, ones that would set her niece on a journey unlike any either of them imagined.

Jean Faircloth was a stars-and-bars kind of Southern girl, born in Nashville and raised in nearby Murfreesboro after her father, a prominent banker, and her mother divorced. Barely five feet two and weighing less than one hundred pounds, she was lithe and lively, with bright eyes and a wide, infectious smile—and a taste for adventure.

For some time after the divorce she and her mother had lived in Murfreesboro with her grandparents—the grandfather was a Confederate veteran—from whom she learned strict rules about behavior and deportment, and imbibed a deep patriotism and a love for the military. "If you want to win Jean Marie," local boys were told, "you better get a uniform."[2]

Then after graduating from Soule College in Murfreesboro, Jean got an unexpected break. Her father, with whom she had grown close, died and left her a substantial fortune. She used it to travel around the world with one of her half brothers; then on a South American cruise with her half sister; and finally in 1926 on a voyage to the Orient and the Philippines, where she wandered the streets of Manila before heading back to Honolulu and San Francisco.

She returned to small-town life in Murfreesboro and endured it for nine years before her aunt made her inspired suggestion. Jean immediately arranged to buy tickets on the SS *Hoover* for Manila and back. She intended to be away for six weeks. Instead, the trip would change her life.

While waiting to board their ship in San Francisco, Jean and her friend spotted a large entourage on the dock with a veritable mountain of trunks and suitcases in tow. They were led by a tall, distinguished-looking man with dark hair and a tiny, frail woman dressed all in black and using a cane. Another young woman, with dark hair, followed close behind.

Jean asked someone who they were.

"He's General Douglas MacArthur," she was informed. "He's traveling with his mother out to the Philippines."[3]

Jean had heard his name in Manila on her last trip—he was already well known to Filipinos and Americans out there—and then learned he was bound for Manila to assume a new post, as military advisor to the new president. She subsequently discovered that the younger woman was not the general's wife but his brother Arthur's widow, Mary MacArthur (Arthur, Douglas's beloved older brother, had died suddenly of appendicitis in December 1923).

On leaving San Francisco Jean saw the distinguished-looking general rarely, and his mother never. She had retired to her cabin for virtually the entire duration of the voyage. Night after night Jean and her friend sat at the captain's table, enjoying the food and conversation, but Douglas sat at his own table with his sister-in-law and a group of serious men who looked military in spite of their civilian attire.

One of the other guests on board was former Boston mayor James Curley, who was bound for Honolulu. The night before they docked, the captain suggested that the ladies attend a party for Curley in the captain's quarters. As she and her friend entered the sitting room, they spotted two men in white tuxedos whom they had never seen before. As they stopped to chat, she realized to her shock that she was talking to MacArthur, and that the other man in a white tux was his aide, Major Ord.

They did not talk long before MacArthur excused himself and left early. "Typical general," Jean thought.[4]

But the next day after going ashore in Honolulu, she returned to her stateroom to find a large basket of flowers. Inside was a note: "with the compliments of Douglas MacArthur."

From that point on, for the next two weeks they met frequently, usually for breakfast. MacArthur's formal reserve was what she had grown up with and expected; she had no trouble detecting the considerable charm, even humor, underneath. She was even delighted to learn that his father had been the great Union Army hero at Missionary Ridge; her grandfather, she told MacArthur, had been one of the Confederate officers holding down the ridge. There was a moment of surprised laughter, and then the conversation deepened.

All the same, he was rarely alone with her. The MacArthur entourage, she learned, was like "one big family." Jimmy Ord or Major Eisenhower would be sitting attentively at her elbow along with Tommy Davis, while Mary MacArthur chatted away amiably. Eisenhower, meanwhile, had the cabin next to hers. In the mornings she could hear him singing the Irving Berlin song "You're in the Army now, you're not behind a plow," as he shaved.[5]

There was only one person missing from the charming gathering: Mrs. MacArthur. Pinky remained ensconced in her room, growing increasingly ill. MacArthur would stop by every night—as he had every night they were together for half a century—to give an account of the day's doings. He never mentioned Jean, but his sister-in-law Mary noticed and approved.

In fact, as they neared Shanghai it was Mary who suggested that Jean cut short her visit there and sail on with them to Manila. Jean was delighted to accept.[6] They docked in Manila on October 26. MacArthur, dressed in a white suit with straw boater, was greeted with open arms and a formal ceremony by the soon-to-be-president Quezon and his entourage. The MacArthur entourage had arrived in time to attend his inauguration on November 15; almost a quarter of a million people jammed the streets of Manila to watch the proceedings and the parade afterward. Douglas invited Jean to attend the inauguration as well, and the party afterward at the Wallace Field Auditorium, where couples whirled around the dance floor until the early morning hours while she and the general talked quietly in the moonlight.

Douglas MacArthur was clearly taken by the vivacious young woman from Murfreesboro. But his principal concern in those early days in Manila was his mother's health. Mother and son had moved into the six-room air-conditioned penthouse of the Manila Hotel—his home for the next six years. Two large balconies gave a commanding view of the red-roofed city and Manila Bay. One, which became MacArthur's favorite spot for pacing and thinking, opened out from the dining room and had an excellent view of Bataan and Corregidor.[7]

Pinky moved into one of the bedrooms, with Dr. Hutter close by in another suite of rooms in the hotel. Hutter had okayed the voyage to the Philippines because he had known it would probably not worsen her condition, although it would never make it better. She was fading fast, and it seemed she would never leave the penthouse again.

Now that she was settled in her bedroom and the penthouse, MacArthur could focus on the job at hand.

It was a difficult, some said impossible, one. But with his usual optimism he had reason to be hopeful. He had a highly competent staff, a comfortable income, and would soon be taking on an impressive new title: Field Marshal of the Philippine Army. He also had the complete trust of the new president, and virtual carte blanche to design whatever plan he wished for creating a national Philippine army. Existing Filipino units like the Philippine Scouts would continue to be part of the U.S. forces in the Philippines, and outside his command. Otherwise it was up to him to figure out how to arm and defend these thousand or so separate islands, while working from a blank canvas—and with no established budget.

Fortunately, he had in his hands a defense plan outline by Siguion Reyna of the Philippine Department of the Interior. Dated May 1935, it started with what seemed a dismal premise: that the Philippines was more geographically vulnerable to attack by its more powerful neighbors than Switzerland or Belgium, which the Germans had steamrolled in 1914 and were about to take over again in 1940. Raising and maintaining a modern army large enough to repel such an attack, Reyna had concluded, required a much larger economic base than the islands could boast, while a modern navy large enough to prevent it was similarly out of the question.[8]

Therefore, the report recommended building an effective defense system that would have to rely on a three-tier system of mobilizing manpower.

The first would be a regular professional army nucleus, the second a corps of active reserves, and the third a national militia trained for regular military service if and when the need arose. This would also raise the country's level of civic culture by bringing discipline and a sense of pride to thousands of young male Filipinos.

MacArthur must have smiled as he read Reyna's report. It was almost exactly the same idea that he had outlined to Manuel Quezon when they met in 1934 (something Reyna noted and that made Quezon more willing to accept the three-tier plan) and had hammered out with his staff while they were still in the United States.

MacArthur, Ord, and Ike had worked out the preliminary numbers with help from the Staff College. They would propose a professional force of 930 officers and 10,000 other ranks as the first-tier core. Then each year 40,000 recruits would be trained as reservists, to be responsible for military service for thirty years. Half of those would enter special camps for five and a half months' training each year, followed by the other half.[9] To supplement this force would be a national militia organized according to a decentralized command structure, which seemed the best way to ensure that the Philippines' far-flung islands could respond quickly to any attack.

MacArthur insisted the entire plan had to be revised to cost no more than 16 million pesos—roughly the amount he could expect the National Assembly to give him from its own limited budget. So Ike and Ord cut the projected professional force from 1,500 officers and 19,000 enlisted men to 930 officers and 7,000 men, put off building an independent artillery corps, and deferred the purchase plan for modern munitions from ten years to two decades.

They warned him that they felt the revised plan lacked enough professional personnel to be truly effective. There was also the problem that for the next ten years the Philippine Army would be equipped with essentially World War One–era weapons.

According to Ike, MacArthur waved their concerns away. Douglas MacArthur was here; he had made miracles happen in the States with a deeply straitened budget. He could at least do the same here in the Philippines.[10]

There was, however, a strange incident during Quezon's inauguration that foretold some of the difficulties to come.

The question had arisen of how large a gun salute President Quezon was entitled to receive at state occasions. The standard number was, of course, twenty-one; but the head of the Bureau of Insular Affairs recommended that the number of the gun salute not exceed "that accorded the sovereign head of government," namely President Franklin D. Roosevelt. Cox suggested nineteen guns, the same number as the governors of American states and the outgoing Philippine governor-general.[11]

This set MacArthur off on a tirade. "I disagree utterly," he said. To refuse the full twenty-one-gun "sovereign salute to the elective head of this people will create a sense of resentment and insult in the breasts of all Filipinos." He pointed out that the Filipino government would undoubtedly prescribe the twenty-one-gun salute in its official protocol. This would lead to the strange situation in which U.S. forces in the Philippines would be giving nineteen-gun salutes, and the Philippine army and navy, and other foreign navies, a twenty-one-gun salute, to the same person. "I know of nothing which is more calculated to create friction than such a situation."[12]

The bureau chief was convinced, and forwarded the recommendation to the secretary of war. But when MacArthur's former ally Secretary Dern showed up in Manila for the inauguration, he learned that the ruling had caused rancor among American officials, particularly the new high commissioner, Frank Murphy, who felt the gesture would undermine their authority and "make effective exercise of American sovereignty impracticable."[13]

At this point President Roosevelt weighed in. After "long consideration" he had decided Quezon should get a only nineteen-gun salute, reserving the twenty-one-gun honor for the president of the United States, who "should be accorded special honor because of his direct supervision and control over foreign affairs."

The inauguration was only days away when someone informed Quezon of Roosevelt's decision. He flew into a rage and said he would no longer take part in the inauguration ceremony. It took some work by MacArthur along with soothing words from Dern and a reassuring telegram from Roosevelt himself to finally calm him down. Angrily he acquiesced in the decision; so did MacArthur, although he was shortly to learn that the army's adjutant general had ruled that American forces in the Philippines would accord no salutes or honors to his position as field marshal, since the Philippine Army "is considered analogous to the National Guard" rather than to the armed forces of a sovereign nation.[14]

It was galling, even maddening. But if MacArthur was paying attention, it was also an indication of just where MacArthur and the Philippines stood in the minds of his former colleagues and the administration.

They were nowhere.

In the meantime, his mother died.

It wasn't her heart but a cerebral thrombosis, or blood clot in the arteries of the brain, that finally took her life. Dr. Hutter and MacArthur watched her slowly sink, until finally she fell into a coma. On the morning of December 3 she rallied enough to say some soothing words to her son. Then she was gone.

She had been the central character in his life, even before his father's death, certainly much more so than his wife, Louise—whom Pinky had increasingly come to despise. She had been tough and charming, practical yet sentimental, an incurable romantic yet wise to the ways of the world— character traits that she had passed on to her son.

Although Mac had watched her strength wither over several years, it was still devastating. "Our devoted comradeship of so many years came to an end," he later wrote in his memoirs.[15] To his friend Charlie O'Laughlin, he wrote days after her death, "Mother's death has been a tremendous blow to me and I am finding the greatest difficulty in recoordinating myself to the

So they elected to pursue a policy of calculated hypocrisy that would last for more than six years. As for MacArthur, it's hard in retrospect to blame him for pressing his belief that the Philippines could be defended, and *would* be defended by Uncle Sam, even if help didn't come right away. It's also hard in retrospect not to blame him for failing to realize that if a Japanese invasion did come, more likely than not he'd be on his own.

Still, as 1936 dawned, the first training camps were being built and the prospect looked hopeful. The same was true of his personal life.

Jean Faircloth had taken rooms at Manila's Bayview Hotel at the MacArthur party's suggestion, and had even received a ticket for President Quezon's inauguration. It was the general's car that picked up her and Ike and Captain Davis and Major Ord to take them to the big party afterward at the Malacañan Palace, where the general's father had presided over the country and which was now the presidential residence. As the crowds swept into the ballroom and glasses of champagne appeared on silver trays, Tommy Davis came up to her side.

"The general," he said softly, "is waiting for you on the terrace."[26]

There she found him in his white tuxedo, talking to President and Madame Quezon, as well as Governor-General Frank Murphy. If she was expecting to be led away for a more intimate conversation—under the trees in the garden, for example—she was mistaken. After MacArthur introduced her to his friends and Murphy, the conversation veered away to official topics, and she drifted back to the house, where she spent most of the evening talking to Dwight Eisenhower.

But after his mother died and Jean moved into the Manila Hotel for the winter, MacArthur found that she was becoming a natural part of his inner circle—she and Ike had lunch almost every day and she played bridge and golf with the rest of the entourage. Eventually, MacArthur began asking her out, first to movies or the theater, and then to dinner.

"Ready, Jean?" He would say promptly at 8:45 when the heat of the day and the sun had faded, and then they would head off. MacArthur insisted in sitting in the first row of the loge—Manila theaters were still segregated in those years, with Americans sitting in the balcony and Filipinos on the main floor—and he often fell asleep during the showing. But together they sat through one Hollywood classic after another, from *A Tale of Two Cities* to *Mr. Deeds Goes to Town*, virtually six nights a week.[27]

The routine became so firmly established that one night Jean threatened to break it by throwing a cocktail party in her hotel room. MacArthur couldn't attend, but her plan was to end the party by 8:30 so they could make their movie date. To her dismay, the guests were having such a good time they weren't leaving. Jean turned to Sid Huff, a U.S. Navy officer stationed in the Philippines.

"What do I do?" she asked in a whisper, then explained the situation.

"Just go ahead and leave," was Huff's advice.

"I couldn't leave my guests! Or could I?"

"Certainly," Huff said. "It's an old Manila custom."

As he watched her surreptitiously slip out the door and join the general in his car waiting at the curb, Huff realized that the relationship between the two had solidified into something significant.[28]

It wasn't difficult to see what she saw in Douglas MacArthur. In addition to being the biggest celebrity figure in Manila, except for President Quezon himself, as well as the most powerful, he was a man who prided himself on his gallantry and considerable charm, especially with the ladies. He also gave "clean cut" a new level of meaning. He was fastidious in his dress and manners, almost to the point of obsession. He could spend an hour in front of a mirror examining himself for flaws or a stray hair or whisker. The big wardrobe in the penthouse held twenty-three uniforms and suits, which he changed three times a day. Tall and slim—one observer said he carried his paunch like a "military secret"—with clear skin and hair that was still dark brown, he looked more like a man in his midforties than someone approaching sixty.[29]

He was also a man of moderate drinking habits—"I'll have a gimlet," he would invariably say at a cocktail party, and by the time he left, the drink had barely been touched. He ate moderately as well. It's likely that the indigestion problems and reflux esophagitis that would plague him during his years in Korea had already started.[30] His pipe smoking, which became iconic later on, was supplemented during a workday by a procession of lit cigarettes and slim brown Manila cigars that he would take from a box at one end of his desk, offering one to a visitor before lighting one himself. Yet no one described him as a chain smoker; more often than not, after a puff or two the cigar or cigarette would remain in the ashtray as MacArthur paced and talked, gesticulating energetically as the flow of words swept over the subject at hand, pausing now and again, with the only sounds breaking the silence being the whir of punkah fans overhead and the clatter of typewriters in the outer room.[31]

For all his power and prestige, however, he was, as his friend William Ganoe once observed, "the loneliest man in the world," even before his mother's death. "When a man gets to be a general officer, he has no friends," he once confided to his aide at West Point.[32] So it also wasn't difficult to see what he saw in Miss Jean Faircloth. She bore no physical resemblance to Pinky or to his first wife, Louise Brooks, but she combined the vivacity of the latter with the strong moral character of the former, together with the same willingness to devote her time and energies to his needs. He no doubt sensed that here was a woman who could fill the spiritual void left by his mother, but without the dominating, sometimes dogmatic tone—or the unspoken comparisons to his absent father.[33] A companion he could treasure, perhaps for life; certainly one he needed as the world around him grew more complicated and shadows began to fall over the project he had taken on with such expectations of success.

On August 24, 1936, came the moment MacArthur had been waiting for, his installation as Field Marshal of the Philippine Army.

There was a solemn ceremony at the Malacañan Palace attended by virtually every important personage in Manila, both American and Filipino. MacArthur walked to the podium dressed in a uniform of black sharkskin trousers and a white coat covered with gold braid, stars, and his American army decorations. There President Quezon presented him with a gold-handled marshal's baton, as the crowd politely applauded.

Dwight Eisenhower watched with a deeply skeptical eye. He considered the whole occasion "rather fantastic" and something of a joke considering that Field Marshal MacArthur still didn't have an army to command.[34] The uniform also drew considerable comment from the American press, most of it unfavorable; later the story would circulate that MacArthur had designed the uniform himself. If anything was needed to confirm the view of MacArthur as a man with dictatorial aspirations, a would-be "man on a white horse," the whole event served perfectly.[35]

It was not true that MacArthur had designed the uniform, although he, not Quezon, had selected the title of Field Marshal. There was also some method to this madness. MacArthur was firmly convinced that this traditional rank of supreme command in European armies would enable him to be treated with the same precedence and protocol as a Field Marshal Foch of France or a Field Marshal Hindenburg of Germany, including gaining him additional leverage in Washington for getting the supplies and munitions he would need to create a genuine army.

In this he was mistaken. Washington began rebuffing nearly every request he and his staff presented for arming the Philippine trainees who would soon be full-fledged soldiers.

In a July entry in his diary Ike noted they had been sending urgent messages to the War Department recommending that it ship Enfield rifles, Lewis machine guns, Stokes mortars, and 75 mm field guns from its surplus warehouses to bolster the existing stock of Filipino war supplies. "From the standpoint of the American army all this equipment is obsolete or obsolescent," he wrote.[36] Yet the War Department refused to budge.

MacArthur himself took up the fight over the rifles, offering to buy 400,000 of the elderly firearms (older even than the '03 Springfield, which was still the standard shoulder arm for the American soldier) at two dollars apiece. A straight answer was not forthcoming; a decision on the arms was postponed, then postponed again. Part of the problem, as it turned out, was that Commissioner Murphy, a committed pacifist, didn't believe in MacArthur's scheme to create a Philippine army under any circumstances. He passed news of MacArthur's war materiel requests on to his colleague in the Roosevelt cabinet, Interior Secretary Harold Ickes, who led a one-man, three-year campaign to keep MacArthur from being able to arm the Filipinos with any weapons, let alone modern ones.[37]

The new field marshal did have an ally in Major General Lucius Holbrook, commander of the army's Philippine Department, who saw the value in what MacArthur was trying to do—including creating a Philippine army that could help his own forces if the islands faced invasion. But Holbrook himself had no resources to spare. He had 10,000 men in the Thirty-first Infantry Regiment, the two regiments of Philippine Scouts, two regiments of Filipino artillery under American command—and precious little else. No airplanes, no tanks or armored cars, and a total of 20,000 men to protect a country covering a thousand separate islands.[38] He was also alarmed as MacArthur kept raiding his staff to build up his own, until the Philippine Army GHQ consisted of thirty officers, all Americans, and fifteen enlisted men. Holbrook finally prevailed upon the War Department to require MacArthur to ask approval before he carried out any further shifts of personnel.[39]

But MacArthur found himself in a tough predicament. On the one hand, Washington recognized that he would be making all key decisions in defending the islands from attack, and gave him all the leeway he needed to make those decisions. His instructions in September 1935 called on him to "use your own judgement" and to feel free to call on the War Department for anything he needed. "Your mission must be accomplished—ways and means are left to you." On the other hand, the War Department was doing all it could to withhold those means—while the only reliable troops for defending the island were not under his direct command.

Yet MacArthur refused to be discouraged—or, despite the charges of later critics, overly optimistic. His speech after his installation as field marshal, one observer noted, "was a powerful piece of realism" on defending the Philippines. He said his plan was to build up a Philippine army that would "give pause even to the most ruthless and powerful," while admitting that if war came the country would have to be held through "the furthermost retreat left available." No place, he affirmed later, was indefensible. "Any place can be defended, any place can be taken, provided superior forces can be assembled." He later told a *Collier's* magazine correspondent, "We're going to make it so very expensive for any nation to attack these islands that no nation will try it."[40] But until he had the resources, such statements were meant more to intimidate eavesdroppers in Tokyo than to express the arrogant overconfidence that critics later accused him of showing.

MacArthur's chief problem was that those resources simply weren't materializing, either from the United States or from within the Philippines itself. The first wave of inductees for the training camps were a disaster. The

20,000 or so who showed up at the start of 1937 spoke eight different languages and eighty-seven different dialects. Twenty percent were totally illit-
erate, including men designated as sergeants and company clerks.[41] In
addition, there was already talk in the Philippine parliament of cutting the
defense budget, and using its slender funds for other domestic projects. "Ours
was a hopeless venture," Ike admitted later, "the Philippine government
simply couldn't afford to build real security from attack."

As for the American government, Eisenhower began to sense that its resistance to helping the Filipinos arm themselves was less ideological or financial than race-based. To many in Washington, Filipinos were an inferior
and dangerous race with a history of rebellion. Giving them modern weapons was a terrifying prospect—and would, many thought, serve only to an-
tagonize the Japanese. In the end, MacArthur was able to persuade the War
Department to send along a quarter of the surplus Enfield rifles it had available, but to reach this deal he had to argue that not only were the weapons
not a threat to Americans but they were too old to be a threat to anyone—not
exactly the kind of statement a military leader wants to make about the forces
under his command.[42]

Still, Eisenhower wrote later, "General MacArthur's amazing determination and optimism made us forget these questions at times, [even though]
they kept coming back in our minds."[43] MacArthur remained convinced that
with the right kind of training and the right equipment, he could create an
effective army in spite of the doubters and "defeatists," as he called them.
"The Philippine Army represents one of the most heroic efforts a liberated
people has ever made to maintain independence and national integrity," he
told a group of reporters. "It deserves the complete support of public opinion
in the United States and wherever freedom is the guiding spirit of men's
lives."[44]

MacArthur's plea touched on the heart of the matter. In the end his vision
for the Philippines depended entirely on support from Washington, and as
1936 ended Eisenhower increasingly urged him to return to the States and
try to persuade the powers that be to release the resources he required to
adequately defend the Philippines. MacArthur would have to deal directly
with Franklin Roosevelt, who had been privately critical of his plans and
who had just won reelection in a landslide. On the other hand, Roosevelt's

more secure position might make him more conciliatory, and more willing to confront the gathering threat of Japan by shoring up America's first line of defense in the Philippines.

Finally, MacArthur agreed—and decided to bring Quezon along to make their appeal. But before he left, he had one matter he wanted settled once and for all.

Jean Faircloth was in her hotel room one morning late in 1936 (later she couldn't recall the exact date or even the month) when the phone rang. It was Dwight Eisenhower. MacArthur wanted to see her, he said. The general was sending around his car to take her to his headquarters.

It sat high up on the walls of the Intramuros, a great stone building filled with splendid Spanish furniture. A Filipino sergeant who had been with MacArthur since his chief of staff days showed her into his office. Behind his desk was a stand with the flags of every one of his previous commands, from the Forty-second Rainbow Division and superintendent of West Point to army chief of staff and now field marshal of the Philippine Army.[45]

They sat together and talked quietly for a while. Then the car whisked her back to the Manila Hotel. Some days later she announced to friends that she was planning to return to the States.

"But when will you be back?" people kept asking.

"I have no idea," she would answer. "I'm just going to Murfreesboro."

Sid Huff saw her off as she boarded Pan Am's China Clipper. He remembered watching her tiny figure in a dark dress and stylish tricorne hat walking up the gangplank. He must have wondered if they would ever see her again.[46]

The ship she would be sailing on back to San Francisco was the liner *Lurline,* and she had to wait in Honolulu several days for its arrival. When it did, a friend gave her a ride out in a navy launch belonging to the friend's father, the navy commandant at Pearl.

The friend dropped the bombshell as they sped across the harbor in a veil of spray.

"Well, you'll be seeing your general on board," she said with a chuckle.

Jean was shocked. "What do you mean? You're fooling me!"

But the friend wasn't. MacArthur and Quezon had set out from Manila on the *Empress Canada* days before; but on seeing the *Lurline* in harbor, they had sought to transfer to the other ocean liner in order to arrive in San Francisco one day earlier.[47]

It was sheer coincidence, although Jean guessed that gossip would have it that she had planned the rendezvous all along. She also wondered what MacArthur would think. But he and Quezon were very pleased to see her, and they had a pleasant voyage the rest of the way to California.

They parted in San Francisco as Quezon and MacArthur prepared for their trip to Washington, and Jean sailed on to Los Angeles to catch the Twentieth Century Limited on her return trip to her home in Murfreesboro—her first visit in a year and a half.

As she hustled through the Los Angeles train station and down the red carpet to board the Limited, she saw a figure in white standing at the far end of the platform. It was MacArthur, resplendent in a gleaming white tuxedo—the same tuxedo he had worn when they first met.[48]

He had driven down from San Francisco alone to surprise her. There was no kissing or hugging. Only the usual bow from MacArthur as he took her arm and helped her up the step to board the Limited. He waved from the platform as the train pulled away; she smiled and waved from the window. She was returning to Tennessee, with a secret she had sworn to tell no one until MacArthur gave her the word. He meanwhile was setting off for Washington, on the visit that both he and Quezon hoped would change the future of the Philippines forever.

Despite all their high hopes, the trip was not a success. Although MacArthur did not realize it at the time, it probably sowed the seeds of later misunderstandings, as well as future disaster.

The troubles began in Los Angeles. Quezon insisted on staying several weeks, much to MacArthur's annoyance. The Philippine president wanted to visit Hollywood, where he met Clark Gable and other stars, before finally agreeing to travel on to New York. There he made a disastrous speech at the Foreign Policy Association. Quezon had hoped to speak to an audience who was sympathetic to the defense of the Philippines and to Philippine independence; instead he was hit with hostile questions about whether the creation of a Philippine army would needlessly provoke Japan; whether he was squandering the country's wealth on weapons of war; even whether he was comfortable teaching Filipino children "to kill."

Quezon was incensed. At one point he retorted in a bellowing shout, "If I believed the Philippines could not defend itself, I would commit suicide this afternoon." Afterward he reproached MacArthur for leading him into a roomful of "liberal pacifists" and not explaining the threats the Philippines faced. MacArthur did not fare much better. He was feted at a dinner where the lead speaker, a retired army general, made a jocular remark about the new Philippine field marshal's uniform resembling that of a washroom attendant. The audience laughed appreciatively while MacArthur sat white-faced, staring into space.

In Washington, MacArthur later remembered, "Quezon was practically ignored." Quezon wandered the halls of Congress trying to extract promises for his most important goal, his country's independence. Most were unsympathetic; some were overtly hostile. Even those who supported the idea of independence could not foresee it happening before 1946.[49] MacArthur went to the War Department to get some munitions for his fledgling army, and here, too, he met a wall of resistance and incomprehension. "My request for supplies and equipment went unheeded," MacArthur remembered.[50]

Worst of all, the White House refused to receive President Quezon. Stunned, MacArthur asked why. There was no response; possibly Roosevelt decided a foreign dignitary who preferred to spend several weeks in Hollywood and then New York City probably wasn't in a hurry to see Roosevelt, so why should Roosevelt be anxious to see *him*? Finally, though, he relented—sort of.

He was willing to clear five minutes on his schedule to meet MacArthur to discuss the matter.

MacArthur was outraged, but agreed.

The five-minute meeting actually lasted two hours. The two men smiled and laughed and argued, then argued more heatedly, then laughed and smiled. The upshot was that Roosevelt agreed to meet with Quezon at a luncheon in the next two weeks, although he assured MacArthur that he had no plans to grant the Philippines independence. MacArthur took what he could get, and they parted amicably.

The luncheon was as unsatisfactory as anyone would have expected. Quezon demanded FDR's support for independence by December 31, 1938; Roosevelt said no. He added he couldn't see granting independence in 1939 either. It was a tight-lipped, deeply disappointed Quezon who left the White House luncheon, disappointed but also disillusioned by the lack of support he was able to wring from his American supposed protectors—including MacArthur.

In April he set off for Mexico City; he would go on to a tour of Europe, not returning to the Philippines until August.

MacArthur, meanwhile, headed back to Manila with his aide, Captain Davis. The trip had been a bitter disappointment for him, as well. Even worse, the 1937 trip had driven an unexpected wedge of distrust between him and Quezon, which would grow until it reached chasmlike proportions.

There had been only two highlights for MacArthur. The first was the decision by the navy to send him help. He could have a flotilla of patrol torpedo or PT boats, they said; they hoped they would come in handy. MacArthur was grateful; it was better than nothing at all.

The other came after a phone call he made to Murfreesboro, Tennessee.

The call came as no surprise to Jean. They had spoken by phone almost every day since getting back to America. That Friday morning, however, MacArthur had a special request.

"Quezon has finally made his plans," he said, "and I have to go back to Manila. Can you get to New York City?"

Jean said yes, and then waited until her sister Angie came home from her job at the Murfreesboro Power and Light Company for lunch before dropping a bombshell of her own.

"Angie," she exclaimed, "I'm going to New York City to marry General MacArthur!"[51]

It was true. They had been secretly engaged for almost five months, after that quiet conversation in his Intramuros office when he had proposed. There was "no bended knee, or anything," she remembered afterward—just a solemn request that she marry him, and then an equally solemn request that she keep it secret until he could return from his trip with Quezon and organize his affairs so that she could come out and join him in the Philippines.

Now the moment had come. Jean packed her bags, and her sister and aunt saw her off to the train station. They would not see her again for fourteen years.[52]

Arriving at Penn Station in New York, she was met by Tommy Davis, who took her to the Astor Hotel, where the general had rented a suite for her to change, and then they set off together for City Hall.

There was no elaborate church wedding, no display of pomp and circumstance, no double row of officers in dress uniforms holding swords on high for the bride and groom to pass under.

There were just the four of them: Jean, MacArthur, Tommy Davis, and Dr. Hutter, his mother's former physician. Afterward they adjourned for breakfast at the Astor. But the press still got wind of what was up, and a clutch of reporters and photographers had gathered outside the hotel lobby.

"This is going to last a long time," MacArthur told them. And so it did. Later MacArthur said, "[I]t was probably the best decision of my life."

It was April 30, 1937. Jean and Douglas MacArthur would remain virtually inseparable for the next twenty-seven years. She would be his constant companion in war and peacetime. He would arrange to have her by his side throughout the entire Second World War, as well as the war in Korea. He had at last found the intimate advisor and emotional prop he had been missing since the death of his mother. Someone who would make his every need her need; someone to reassure him through every crisis and moment of self-doubt, and support him through every difficult decision; someone who could advise him on how to handle perplexing people, and could even handle them herself.

But someone who was also a wife and sexual companion, and mother of his children. It was a moment of personal triumph at a time of growing professional frustration, a pledge of future happiness no matter what else happened.

Meanwhile, events were unfolding that ensured he was going to need that pledge.

* * *

In July 1937 fighting broke out between Chinese and Japanese forces on either side of the Marco Polo Bridge in Manchuria. Although no one knew it yet, the Second World War had just begun.

As the fighting increased, the balance of victory quickly shifted in Japan's favor. Chinese Kuomintang armies were sent reeling in retreat while their foes, the Chinese Communists, retreated deep into the mountains. Meanwhile the Japanese unleashed all the terrible furies of modern war, including the indiscriminate bombing of cities and civilians, as well as the fury of a racist imperialist rage.

In December 1937 they occupied the Chinese capital, Nanking, as Japanese soldiers went on an orgy of killing, rape, and unspeakable bloodlust. More than 300,000 Chinese civilians were murdered, many of them women after being repeatedly and brutally raped. Even the Nazi ambassador in Nanking was horrified, and wrote a letter protesting what he called "the work of bestial machinery."

Roosevelt had already bracketed Japan with the other international aggressors, Germany and Italy, in his "quarantine" speech in November, setting the stage for economic sanctions against the island empire. But there was no stopping the Japanese military juggernaut now. In March 1938 the Japanese parliament, or Diet, was dissolved; Japan's generals and admirals were now in full control of the country as the last vestige of the rule of law disappeared from the political scene.

On October 21 Japanese troops swept into Canton, and on the 25th into Hankow. They had taken Shanghai the previous November after a four-month siege. Foochow on the Taiwan Strait had already fallen; Swatow, the port city east of Hong Kong, was clearly next. Chinese forces were now virtually cut off from their east coast, and although Roosevelt pledged $50 million in aid to support Chiang Kai-shek, if Swatow fell it was not clear how that aid, or any other help, could reach him.

The occupation of China's coastline as far as Foochow also meant that Japanese forces were now closer than ever to Luzon and the Philippines.

If war did come, only a few miles of ocean would protect its inhabitants now.

*   *   *

For MacArthur, 1938 opened with the gathering threat to the Philippines from the west, but also deteriorating relations with those he relied upon for his plans for the defense of the Philippines, starting with Dwight Eisenhower.

He had returned to Manila with his bride in May, to take up married residence in his penthouse apartment. Virtually everybody who was anybody in Manila already knew Jean; the verdict regarding their betrothal was overwhelmingly positive. But she found her plush new surroundings a bit trying. Like a true Southerner, she loved the heat and found the penthouse's central air-conditioning far too cold for her taste. She wound up installing a series of hidden electric heaters around the apartment, so that she could secretly warm her feet and toes while visitors complained how hot Manila was, and how they cherished the air-conditioning running full blast.[53]

They had barely recovered from the first blush of married bliss when the bad news began to pour across MacArthur's desk. The first 20,000 reservists had graduated from the first five-month training program. While MacArthur pronounced the men fit and the program a success, Eisenhower and Ord knew otherwise. Almost none of the graduates could do even the minimum tasks the program was supposed to prepare them for, largely because most of the training had been spent doing remedial work like getting the men used to living in barracks, using bathrooms and other modern facilities, and learning how to read rudimentary English—while even basic supplies and equipment had been entirely missing.[54]

In any case, the training budget of 16 million pesos was clearly too low. MacArthur told Eisenhower that they had been promised another 30 million pesos to finance the mobilization, but neither he nor Ike really believed the money would ever be forthcoming.[55]

Then had come disconcerting news from Washington. It had been decided that MacArthur should return to the United States at the end of 1937 to assume a new army command. The order came from Chief of Staff Malin Craig, but it was obvious the real force behind the move was MacArthur's critics, especially Murphy and Secretary Ickes. They wanted to short-circuit any further moves by MacArthur to build up the defenses of the Philippines; even his ally General Holbrook would not be against removal of the man who had become an increasing source of friction over men and resources.[56] Pershing and others in the army also thought if MacArthur was no further along in organizing his vaunted Philippine army, it was time for him to come home.

That left MacArthur with a painful choice. He could uproot himself and Jean and abandon his great project by returning to the States; or he could quit the army—or to put it more accurately, retire. After much soul-searching, that was the choice he made. He sat at his desk and composed a letter he had never imagined he would have to submit. He wrote that since his health was failing (a total lie), and it was time to make way for younger, more deserving officers (also clearly a contradiction of his own view of things), he had decided to retire from the army after thirty-four years of unbroken service. On October 11, 1937, Craig told MacArthur that President Roosevelt had accepted his request.[57]

It had been a gut-wrenching decision. To leave the United States Army, to abandon the institution to which first his father and then he himself had dedicated his life, required a decision he could never have made a year before. There is no doubt that if it hadn't been for his marriage to Jean, he would never have made it. She had given him the confidence to make the most crucial career choice he had made since he had been superintendent at West Point—to take risks he had never dared to take before. He was leaving the most powerful institution in his life, in order to forge a new future.

Still, across the water there must have been many who celebrated the choice he had made, not least Franklin Roosevelt. The man whom he had once feared as a political rival had not only exiled himself in the Philippines; MacArthur had now voluntarily severed the formal ties between himself and the United States. It was a happy yet magnanimous president who sent a message from the White House to Manila:

> Dear Douglas: With great reluctance and deep regret I have approved your application for retirement, effective December 31. Personally, as well as officially, I wish to thank you for your outstanding services to your country. Your record in war and in peace is a brilliant chapter of American history. . . . I count on seeing you as soon as you get back.[58]

Of course, Roosevelt assumed Douglas MacArthur would never come back. He was sure, as they all were at the War Department and the State Department, which had labored hard to deny him any support, that they would never have to see him again—or that they would only when he had had enough of his failed experiment of creating a genuine Philippine army.

Yet MacArthur would fool them all. He wasn't prepared to declare failure by a long shot. Instead, he was about to dig himself in deeper, in order to fulfill a promise—even though those to whom he made the promise were also losing faith in him.

One was President Quezon. MacArthur's resignation from the United States Army should have been a sign of his unqualified commitment to helping the Philippines arm for war. Douglas MacArthur was now all in, as the phrase has it, and no one should have been more appreciative than his friend Quezon.

Yet Quezon drew the opposite conclusion. On the last day of 1937, he reappointed MacArthur as military advisor to the president. Deeply moved, MacArthur answered, "This is a call of duty I cannot fail."[59] But to Quezon, MacArthur's resignation meant the end of his usefulness to the Philippines. As an active army officer, he had been Quezon's link to the powers in Washington. Now he was no more than field marshal of the Philippine Army—or more cruelly, a glorified drill instructor for Philippine Army trainees. A thought began to take root in the deep recesses of Quezon's mind: perhaps giving his friend command as military advisor had been a mistake.

The other was Dwight Eisenhower. The issue broke in January 1938 when MacArthur decided that what his new Philippine Army needed was a parade.

It was time, MacArthur told Eisenhower and Jimmy Ord, to demonstrate to the Philippine people—which really meant the residents of Manila—that their hard-earned investment in a fighting army had been worth the money. The way to do that was with a parade through the streets of the capital by the men he and Eisenhower had trained—a kind of Grand Army of the Republic parade of the sort that his father had been part of after the Civil War, and that Bill Donovan's Fighting Sixty-seventh had led down Fifth Avenue in New York, to cheers and fanfare and the promise that a new future had dawned.

Eisenhower was not convinced. It would be expensive and chew up a military budget that was shrinking, he said. He did not add that the budget was bound to shrink further now that MacArthur no longer had any active ties to the War Department or the United States Army—indeed, his former friend General Holbrook was all too happy to cut him loose. MacArthur overruled him. But when Quezon learned of the plan, he was furious.[60] "The president was horrified to think that we were ready for a costly national parade in the capital," Eisenhower remembered. Quezon saw it as a perfectly fruitless waste of public money, and castigated MacArthur for even suggesting it.

Then MacArthur did something extraordinary for him, and egregious for anyone. He told Quezon it wasn't his idea anyway, and publicly lambasted both Ike and Ord for coming up with the idea in the first place. "General MacArthur denied that he had given us an order," Ike remembered, "which was certainly news to us."[61]

There was a scene, an ugly one.

"General, all you're saying is that I'm a liar, and I am not a liar," Eisenhower remembered saying. "So I'd like to go back to the United States right away."

MacArthur tried to placate his irate lieutenant. According to Eisenhower, he threw an arm around Ike's shoulder and said, "It's fun to see that Dutch temper take you over. It's just a misunderstanding, and let's let it go at that."[62]

But Ike could not. For him, the string of misadventures in the Philippines had finally run their course. Likewise for Tommy Davis, who with Ike's help transferred back to the States.[63] Jimmy Ord had no choice in the matter. Later that same January he was killed in a plane crash. "From then on most of the planning fell on my shoulders," Eisenhower later remembered. Nothing had essentially changed, "but without my friend, all the zest was gone"—especially when he had lost his respect for his commanding officer.[64]

So there it was. While MacArthur looked for a replacement for one key subordinate, the competent, popular Ord, he had to digest the fact that, rightly or wrongly, his decision to shift the blame for an idea that had triggered a violent reaction from Quezon had now alienated his other key subordinate. These were not happy times for his command.

Eisenhower was headed back to the States anyway, to make one last desperate plea for money and equipment. On the one hand, he and MacArthur had needed a break from each other, and it was a relief to see his wife, Mamie; on the other, it was obvious that as the drums of war beat louder not only in Asia but in Europe as well, the War Department was reluctant to yield up materiel to the Philippines that it might need itself in the event of war.

Ike toured various munitions companies and plants, including Beech Aircraft in Wichita, Kansas, which assured him that its planes could be modified for military use (Ike was more dubious).[65] But without pesos to buy the planes and guns and mortars that the Philippine Army would need, the trip was largely an exercise in futility. He had toyed more than once with the idea of arranging for a new posting stateside, but finally decided to head back to the Philippines and MacArthur. He did not return to Manila until November 5, to find the Philippine Army training program in a shambles and his chief under siege from all sides, including from President Quezon and his inner circle.

The Philippine National Assembly had decided to cut defense's share of the Commonwealth budget from 25 percent to 14 percent; while the number of those registering for the national draft was steadily dropping, from 155,100 in 1936 to fewer than 91,000 in 1940. The number of trainees completing the five-month active duty training was tumbling too, from 36,600 in 1936 to 29,500 in 1939—well below the 40,000 figure Ike and MacArthur had counted on. In some districts those summoned for service simply disappeared into the mountains.[66]

If there was one person who was not alarmed by what was happening, it seemed to be President Quezon. The Japanese offensive in China had sent shock waves through the Philippine upper class, Quezon included.[67] MacArthur's retirement from the army drained away whatever faith Quezon still had that the Philippines could defend itself on its own—or even that American help would ever arrive. Things came to a head that summer of 1938, as Dwight Eisenhower headed to Washington to present MacArthur's case for more resources and support, and Manuel Quezon headed the opposite way, to Tokyo for talks with the Japanese government. Significantly, his military advisor did not go with him.

Officially on what was deemed a "vacation," Quezon was in fact feeling out the chances of Japan's leaving the Philippines off its list of future conquests, if its new president declared the country officially neutral. He came back reassured—but not if his military advisor's defense plan was still being implemented. Bit by bit he began to hack away at its underpinnings. Within weeks he persuaded the National Assembly to reverse MacArthur's plan to integrate his Philippine Army with the Philippine Constabulary, a move that slashed the army's budget further. Throughout 1939, in fact, "Quezon continued to work at cross purposes with MacArthur."[68] He established a Department of National Defense separate from MacArthur's authority as military advisor, setting off a bureaucratic turf war; he cut funding for ROTC training and public school military training (already under heavy criticism from liberal circles in the United States as well as the Philippines), eventually terminating the program altogether.

As the clouds of war steadily gathered in Europe over Danzig and Poland, and Japan began preparing to attack Swatow in July, the Philippines' political elite, including Quezon, were more convinced than ever that only a policy of passivity combined with independence as soon as possible would keep them out of the path of destruction.

Yet MacArthur continued to soldier on, squeezing whatever he could from whatever resources he could find. He was focused, for example, on trying to get the Philippine air force off the ground, quite literally. He oversaw the organization of its first squadron, with twenty-one pursuit and observation planes, in early 1939, and began training Filipino pilots at the American air base at Clark Field. Eisenhower, in fact, became so interested in the fledgling air arm that he took up flying himself, and graduated with his pilot's license at age forty-nine. Jimmy Ord was not so lucky. His death in late January 1938 had come on a training flight to Baguio with one of the Filipino airmen.[69]

MacArthur's other interest was building up the Philippines' coastal defense—no easy task when Luzon alone had 250 miles of beaches suitable for a Japanese landing. But MacArthur put much faith in his original plan for acquiring fifty patrol torpedo (PT) boats by 1946, and called in his ex-navy military advisor, Sid Huff, for a talk.

"Sit down, Sid," he said, and then began immediately pacing the room, a cigarette dangling from his fingers.

"I want a Filipino navy of motor torpedo boats, Sid," he said. "If I get you the money, how many can you get built in ten years?"

Huff remembered that the question felt "like a punch in the gut." He stammered, "General, never in my life have I seen a torpedo boat."

MacArthur waved the objection aside. "That's all right, you will. But I want you to start work on plans for a navy. You're a navy man and you should know what to do. . . . Work on it. Let me know how you do."

Outside, Huff realized he had just been given the assignment of creating a full-blown Philippine navy, starting with PT boats. He wondered if he had even done the right thing in taking the assignment. But "I began to think I could do it, perhaps because it was MacArthur who told me to do it."[70]

It was a feeling that many on MacArthur's staff would share over the years. MacArthur's confidence was like a boost of vitamin D, making ordinary people believe they could do extraordinary things, even the impossible—and MacArthur often demanded exactly that.

In the end, only two PT boats would be purchased for the Philippine Navy, bought from the Norwegians. Efforts to build the boats in the Philippines were a flop. Yet it was MacArthur who would make the PT boat famous—American boats, not Filipino—on a dark March night miles off the coast of the Bataan Peninsula, in a moment of fear and dread but also nautical skill that cost an army its commander but ultimately saved a general for future victory.

The only other bright spot of that increasingly dismal year was the birth of Arthur MacArthur IV, seven pounds, eight ounces, on February 21, 1938.

There had been some worry that, because of Jean's slight build, the birth might have to be cesarean. But the baby and mother came through fine; a friend wired Douglas, "I didn't know you had it in you." He wired back, "You know, I didn't know it myself." At almost sixty, he had chosen to become a father. It was a decision he never regretted. "With my little family I would be lonely no more."[71] Just as he indulged Jean's every whim and showered her with affection and love, he would spoil his son, Arthur, with presents and attention. Together his son and wife would form a corner of private comfort in the midst of the growing storm.

*   *   *

On September 1, 1939, German tanks invaded Poland as the world war broke out in Europe. Quezon's morale plummeted to rock bottom. He went to the National Assembly and told the stunned representatives of the Philippine people that there was no way the islands could be effectively defended "for many years to come." In November he added dramatically: "The Philippines could not be defended even if every last Filipino were armed with modern weapons."[72] The only hope the Philippine president could see now for his country was neutrality and immediate independence, which he demanded again from the American Congress, with no result.

MacArthur continued to pretend that his relationship with Quezon was secure and that the Philippines would be in no danger once his defense plan was finished. "It would cost the enemy, in my opinion," he told reporters, "at least a half million men as casualties and upwards of five billions of dollars to pursue such an adventure with any hope of success." Besides, he said, "no rational reason exists why Japan or any other nation should covet the sovereignty of this country."[73]

What he neglected to say was, no reason unless war broke out between the United States and Japan. Then a Japanese move to seize America's most westward military base in the Pacific would be inevitable, especially a base that was so vulnerable and poorly defended. That is, unless MacArthur could somehow build up a credible deterrent in the meantime.

But time, as well as money, was running short. As 1940 began, the War and Navy Departments realized that war with Japan was a growing possibility. In April the Pacific Fleet was ordered to remain indefinitely in Hawaii.[74] The previous summer Washington began revisions of War Plan Orange; planners admitted that the old assumption that the Philippines could hold out for six months until relief arrived was overly optimistic. "It is highly improbable," they were forced to conclude, "that expeditionary forces will be sent to the Philippines in the early stages of an Orange war." The best advice they could give any commander of the Philippine Department was to hold on tight and make do with what he had on hand. The same applied, by extension, to Field Marshal MacArthur and the nascent Philippine Army.[75]

Yet without explicit approval from Quezon and his new minister of national defense, MacArthur could not order munitions, enroll recruits, or sign contracts for new military construction. The projected budget for his army was cut again for 1940, by 14 percent from the 1939 figure; another round of spending cuts was coming in fiscal year 1941.[76] The one hope MacArthur had left was help from America.

So far the United States had shipped him 1,220 three-inch trench mortars, 87,550 automatic rifles, 900 British-model 75 mm guns, 3,500 other 75 mm guns, 65,000 .30-caliber machine guns, and almost 200,000 Enfield rifles. Those numbers looked impressive—until one realized that they were meant to equip an army that had thousands of square miles to defend and that ammunition was in chronic short supply.[77] MacArthur repeatedly urged the United States to send more, on the understanding that all such munitions and weapons were subject to immediate American recall if a national emergency demanded it. "The responsibility . . . for the defense of the Philippines," he wrote, "as long as it remains an integral part of the United States, is federal and devolves upon the American government," just as it would if New York or the District of Columbia were attacked.

Yet American forces in the Philippines were clearly inadequate to the task, and "until the basic plans of defense of the American government are known, no detailed, intelligent program for the civil or military population of these Islands can be made."[78]

But no detailed plan from the States was forthcoming, and no arms either. In the summer of 1940 the U.S. government finally began mobilizing for war, as munitions orders poured into factories, plants, and shipyards. Yet every new airplane, every new tank and machine gun and artillery piece, was going to be needed by the U.S. Army itself, to prepare for the war it was expecting in Europe, not the Philippines. The Philippine Department could expect little more than scraps from the table—and MacArthur the scraps of the scraps.[79]

"From every angle," writes historian Carol Petillo, "the Field Marshal of the Philippine Army found himself disappointed, and under heavy criticism."[80] Early in 1940 President Quezon even asked the new American Commissioner for the Philippines, Francis Sayre, to send MacArthur back to the States. Startled, Sayre asked the president to put the request in writing. Quezon hesitated, then backed down. But it was a sign of how thoroughly he had lost trust in his friend and military advisor.[81]

It wasn't just Quezon who had let MacArthur down. In late 1939 after

Germany and the Allies settled into war, Eisenhower asked MacArthur that he be relieved of duty in the Philippines so he could return to the States. They wound up having a bruising interview in MacArthur's office.

"In my opinion the United States cannot remain out of this war for long," Ike said. "I want to go home as soon as possible. I want to participate in the preparatory work that I'm sure is going to be intense."

MacArthur made it clear that he considered Eisenhower's decision a mistake. You've spent four years here in the Philippines, he said; the work they were doing was far more important than taking up some post as a lieutenant colonel in the army.

Eisenhower reminded MacArthur that he had already missed one war, spending the First World War as an instructor at Camp Meade in Maryland and then in Pennsylvania. He was determined not to miss this one.

President Quezon was more demonstrative in his effort to retain Ike's services. He offered to tear up Eisenhower's current contract with the Philippine government and to let him write in any pay amount he wanted.[82] But it wasn't money that was at issue. He and MacArthur were already being paid far more than officers in the U.S. Army could expect to make. MacArthur's salary stood at $3,000 a month; Ike was making $980 a month, while an American major general made $666.[83] The issue was that he had lost faith in the mission, and in his former mentor.

There was a farewell luncheon at the Malacañan Palace for Ike, Mamie, and their son John. Then the Eisenhower family headed for the Manila pier. Ike and MacArthur spoke before he boarded the ship that would carry them to Hawaii. "We talked of the gloominess of world prospects, but our foreboding turned toward Europe—not Asia."[84] Eisenhower sailed on to take up duties at Fort Lewis in Washington State, before becoming chief of staff for the Third Army under Major General Walter Krueger. MacArthur remained in the Philippines, without an army, without money, without trust from the president who had hired him or the one (Franklin Roosevelt) who had let him leave for virtual exile in the Philippines.

In March he wrote to a friend stateside: "Conditions in the Far East are in a state of flux. A man would be a fool or a knave who pretended to predict with accuracy what the future holds . . . I have been doing everything that I can during the last four years to strengthen this very weak outpost . . . Much progress has been made but nothing compared to what I had visualized."[85] His one remaining hope was that the U.S. Navy would go ahead with plans to build a new naval base on the island of Guam, which could be used to reinforce the Philippines in case of war. But in February 1939, Congress turned down the $5 million request. The closest base for supporting the Philippines remained Pearl Harbor, more than 5,000 miles away.[86]

Yet in many ways, as MacArthur and Eisenhower had seemed to agree, the possibility of war seemed to have passed the Philippines by. Japan was busy consolidating its gains in China; the major fighting had shifted to Europe and Germany, where Nazi panzer divisions swiftly overran Belgium and France, forcing France's capitulation on July 22 and a British evacuation from Dunkirk. Planners in Washington were now convinced that Germany posed a more immediate and dangerous menace than Japan; Admiral Harold Stark was pushing for a forward strategy for the navy in the Atlantic and a far more defensive posture in the Pacific.[87]

The new commander of the Asiatic Fleet, Admiral Thomas Hart, found this out when he arrived in Manila in October. Tommy Hart had been a close friend of MacArthur's navy brother Arthur, and he and Douglas had known each other for forty years. He was able to tell Douglas that with the exception of his heavy cruiser flagship USS *Houston,* the fleet he had inherited consisted of World War One–era vessels, fit for not much more than coast guard duty. "All my ships are old enough to vote," he used to joke.[88]

MacArthur, however, refused to give in to doubt or despair. "I am holding myself in readiness," he told Theodore H. White when the young, bespectacled correspondent for *Time* stopped off in Manila in December on a tour of military installations in the Far East. He found the general looking hale and hearty at nearly sixty-one. MacArthur may have been dressed casually in his gray bathrobe with the West Point A stitched on the back, but the conversation was deadly serious, about the future of Asia and the certainty that war with Japan was coming. White, who had been in China, had to agree, much to MacArthur's surprise and delight.

"It was destiny that brought us together, White, destiny!" he exclaimed. "By God, it is destiny that brings me here now."

MacArthur had one final prediction for the *Time* correspondent. "I will command the American expeditionary force in the Far East when war comes," he said. Even White had to wonder about that one. When he had stopped by the office of the new commander of the Philippine Department, Major General George Grunert, he had been told by Grunert's press officer not to bother interviewing MacArthur.

"He cuts no more ice in the U.S. Army than a corporal," the man had said contemptuously.[89]

Yet in less than six months the ice would begin to break.

CHAPTER 13
WAITING FOR THE ENEMY

This is a call of duty I cannot fail.

—DOUGLAS MACARTHUR

At nine o'clock in the morning on October 24, 1941, U.S. Army Private Paul Rogers stepped out onto the deck of his troopship and gazed at the mountains flanking Manila Bay.

"There was a sudden swoosh and a roar," he remembered, as two fighters came out of nowhere and swept over the deck from stem to stern.

Soldiers ducked and ran for cover. The planes weren't hostile, however. They were American P-36s engaged in a little stunt flying, as they rolled up in a steep climb and then came back amidships, "shaking the ship under us, the wind from the props blowing off our caps." Then they returned to fly on either side of the ship, their wingtips almost touching the bulwarks, before abruptly climbing and disappearing into the sky.[1]

The ship soon passed Corregidor Island, its massive concrete gun emplacements standing out clearly in the sunlight, and then docked that evening in Manila. An army band played a welcome salute as the American soldiers marched down the gangplank.

"Rogers," someone shouted.

"Here," he answered. It was a sergeant.

"Step over here. You're going up to General MacArthur's headquarters."

Paul Rogers was from Iowa and when his draft board called him up in August, he had volunteered for service in the Philippines. It sounded interesting and exotic, and he had turned down the chance for a deferment to go. "Son, I admire your courage," the recruiting sergeant had said. Neither of them knew how true those words would end up being.

On the way out on the army transport *Tasker Bliss,* Rogers had been pressed into service as stenographer for a shipboard court-martial because he knew shorthand. That in turn led Colonel Clyde Selleck to put his name down on the Detached Enlisted Men's List, Headquarters Philippine Department, which meant he would be performing special duties when he arrived in the Philippines. Once they docked, Rogers learned to his astonishment that he was now official stenographer for the new commander of the United States Army Forces Far East, General Douglas MacArthur himself.

At USAFFE headquarters, a stocky grim-faced lieutenant colonel summoned Rogers into his office. It was MacArthur's new chief of staff, Richard K. Sutherland, who explained to the awed Rogers that he would be working for "one of the biggest men in the United States Army," and then dictated a long dispatch that Rogers transcribed. Sutherland examined the memo, and nodded. By the time Private Rogers went back to his barracks, he had secured the job he would hold for the next four years.[2]

It was a stunning turnaround for the young man from Iowa, and a stunning turnaround for Douglas MacArthur. Just five months earlier, in June 1941, the military advisor to the Philippine Commonwealth and field marshal of the Philippine Army had seemed more forlorn and forgotten than ever. Now MacArthur had become, as his chief of staff Sutherland noted, one of the most important men in the U.S. Army. The reinstated MacArthur was commander in chief of all army forces in the Far East, and the man Roosevelt had personally appointed to turn the Philippines into the first line of defense against a Japanese attack that both Washington and Manila now believed was inevitable.

This turnaround was in part a reflection of MacArthur's undaunted belief that destiny had not meant for him to be sidelined in "these monumentally momentous days," as he had put it in a letter to President Roosevelt the previous April. But it was also a reflection of events first in Europe, then in Asia, that improbably put Douglas MacArthur back in the spotlight—and back in command.

Indeed, by the spring of 1941 even MacArthur's confidence in the value of his mission in the Philippines had been shaken. When rumors circulated that Commissioner Francis Sayre might soon be returning to the States, MacArthur fired off a letter to Washington asking for the job. "I will probably close out my work with the Philippine Army within the year," he explained to one of Roosevelt's aides, and even claimed that the mission had been a great success (MacArthur himself knew otherwise). He even added a brief encomium to Roosevelt as "our greatest statesman . . . our greatest military strategist"—a clear sign of how desperate he was.[3]

The rumors were wrong. Sayre was not leaving Manila. But MacArthur did get back a letter from Roosevelt's chief military aide, Brigadier General Edwin Watson. It was short, but in the circumstances, sweet. "The President asked me to write," it read. "[H]e wished me to tell you that he wants you there in your military capacity rather than any other."

To the approval-starved MacArthur, the request was manna from heaven. He wrote back that he was "delighted that the President desires to utilize my services . . . I shall therefore plan to continue to develop the Philippine Army for an emergency."[4]

He had already sent a note to Roosevelt press secretary Steve Early (they had known each other when Early worked for the AP and MacArthur was the army's media spokesman). Now he suggested that Early suggest to the president that MacArthur would be the man for the job of uniting the Filipino and American commands, if war came. He had already told another American correspondent, John Hersey, that "if Japan entered the war, the Americans, the British and the Dutch could handle her with about half the forces they now have deployed in the Far East"—especially if his twelve Filipino divisions were thrown into the mix, and particularly (it was implied) if the Allies had the right general in charge, namely, himself.[5]

He waited for several weeks; there were no further messages from the White

House. Tired of the delays, MacArthur made plans to shut down the advisory office and even ordered his chief of staff to book passage back to the States. He sent a copy of the order to Steve Early, hoping it would prompt some action on Washington's part. And indeed this time the wheels began to turn.

Ironically, it was the Nazi blitzkrieg victories in Europe that swiveled the attention of first Roosevelt, then the War Department, back to the Pacific. The serial defeats of France and Holland had left the fate of their Asian colonial possessions in serious doubt. The Japanese were now poised to help themselves to French Indochina and particularly the Dutch East Indies, which were a valuable source of rubber as well as oil. If they did, a war for control of Europe's Asian empires would be almost certain—and the United States and Philippines would be caught in the middle of a Pacific-wide conflict.

The United States might not have a battle-ready army in the Philippines, but it did have a battle-ready general, one only recently retired. Washington seized on MacArthur like a drowning man grabbing on to a spar. On May 21 Henry Stimson noted in his diary, "[George] Marshall told me that in case of trouble out there, they intended to recall General MacArthur into service again and place him in command."[6] The "they" in this case included not just the army but the president himself. Marshall himself then composed a letter to MacArthur on June 20, 1941, stating that closing the Advisory Mission might be premature, to say the least.

> *Both the Secretary of War and I are much concerned about the situation in the Far East. During one of our discussions about three months ago it was decided that your outstanding qualifications and vast experience in the Philippines makes you the logical selection for the Army Commander in the Far East should the situation approach a crisis. . . . It is my impression that the President will approve his recommendation.*[7]

So MacArthur was coming back; his career in the army was about to restart. Marshall warned it was too early to make the appointment "as he does not feel the time has arrived for such an action." But all MacArthur had to do was to wait until something broke loose on the international scene, to make that time arrive.

That something came two days later. On June 22, 1941, Hitler's armies invaded Russia. For the Russians it was a disaster, as one city after another was buried in the German onslaught, and Red Army groups began surrendering en masse. But for Japan, it was a hell-sent opportunity. The war with Germany relieved Tokyo of the possibility of Russia interfering with its imperial ambitions across Asia.

On July 21 the emperor's new prime minister, Hideki Tojo, penned a note to the French Vichy government, demanding access to its airfields in Indochina and to Cam Ranh Bay, the best natural harbor on the South China Sea. American observation planes flying from Clark Field in the Philippines had already spotted Japanese troop transports en route south.[8] On July 23 Vichy gave way. In a matter of twenty hours 50,000 Japanese soldiers were disembarking at Cam Ranh, and Japanese fighters and bombers were landing on airfields that were now French in name only—and were only a few hours' flight from Manila.

Roosevelt's usual response to a crisis was to avoid any quick decision, preferring to wait until either the problem went away on its own accord or until a decision could no longer be put off without inviting disaster. This time, however, the president's response to the news from Indochina was immediate. He ordered a freezing of Japanese assets in the United States. It was a major, even decisive step, since it meant that Japan could not tap American sources to buy the oil and natural gas it needed to keep the war machine humming.

He also sent an urgent message to Manila. MacArthur was having breakfast when two aides burst in and presented him with the decoded version.

"You are hereby designated as Commanding General, United States Army Forces in the Far East," it read, a command consisting of both American and Philippine Commonwealth forces on air, land, and sea. "You are also designated as General Officer United States Army . . . effective July 26, 1941. Report assumption of command by radio."[9]

MacArthur glanced at the calendar on his desk. It was July 27. He had now been back in the United States Army for almost twenty-four hours (later that same day a bulletin came in confirming his appointment as temporary lieutenant general). He sent a message to his chief of staff, Richard Sutherland, who was about to tee off for a morning golf game, and ordered him back to the office.

Sutherland had had the difficult job of replacing Jimmy Ord, the able and lovable major who had been MacArthur's aide and Eisenhower's best friend. No one had ever called Sutherland lovable. Hard-faced and emotionally distant with an abrasive temper, he was a graduate of Yale, where he won a second lieutenant's commission by competitive examination and served in the AEF during the war before making the army his permanent profession. He had first met MacArthur at the War College in 1932–33, and was serving in China with the Fifteenth Infantry when MacArthur called him to the Philippines in March 1938.

Sutherland sailed with his wife and daughter on a ship filled with Japanese soldiers and officers coming from Shanghai. It was a miserable trip. "Our room was next to two Japanese girls," his daughter, Natalie, remembered. "Every night the Japanese officers got drunk" and one night [they] tried to assault the two Japanese girls, banging on their door and yelling, while the two girls cowered inside and sobbed. Sutherland didn't dare intervene for fear of causing an international incident. But it was a glimpse at the dark underside of the Japanese warrior code, *bushido,* that he would not soon forget.[10]

Sutherland's timing was good. Jimmy Ord was dead; Eisenhower was about to embark on his tour of the States. When Ike returned on November 5, he found that Sutherland had largely displaced him as MacArthur's chief of staff. MacArthur had written a glowing report to an officer-friend: "Sutherland has proven himself a real find. Concise, energetic and able, he has been invaluable in helping me clarify and crystallize the situation."[11]

Sutherland was helpful in two other ways as well. The first was an instinct for understanding MacArthur's thinking down to the last nuance, even when it went unstated, which he could communicate to others with unambiguous clarity. The second was a willingness to be disliked, even hated, by subordinates in order to get the job done. This allowed him to play "bad cop" to his boss's "good cop." MacArthur hated personal confrontations or berating members of his staff in public. He was now able to leave that unpleasant task to Sutherland, who thrived on it.

In any case, over the next seven years Sutherland would become closer to MacArthur than any other human being, with the exception of Jean. Sutherland's rising status almost certainly encouraged Eisenhower's decision to leave the Philippines and return to the States for good, leaving Sutherland a vast area of responsibility when MacArthur took on his new role as commander in chief.

That same afternoon of July 27, 1941, they immediately set to work, studying every way to integrate the army of the Philippine Commonwealth, which MacArthur had built up from nothing, with the American forces of the Philippine Department, including naval and air assets—and do it all in time to ready the Philippines for an eventual Japanese invasion.

At one point Sutherland looked up from the piles of papers on the desk and said, "You know, General, it adds up to an almost unsurmountable task."

MacArthur was examining a map. He looked up at Sutherland over his reading glasses and said, "These islands must and will be defended. I can but do my best."[12]

It *was* an insurmountable task. But as commander in chief MacArthur had certain advantages that he had never had as a mere military advisor.

The first was the full faith and confidence of his superiors in Washington, who now bowed to the fact that Douglas MacArthur was America's top soldier. In the final analysis, in fact, there really was no other choice for USAFFE commander general. No one else had the seniority of rank: the current chief of staff, George Marshall, who was the same age as MacArthur, had received his first star as brigadier general almost twenty years after MacArthur won his. No one else had the depth of experience, not just in the Philippines and Asia but also both in combat *and* behind a desk as army chief of staff.

Also, no other serving general had his political clout on Capitol Hill, built over years and particularly with Republicans, on whom Franklin Roosevelt had to keep a wary eye as he readied the nation for the possibility of war. Finally, no one else in the army had the kind of personality that would allow him to take a job that any other officer would say was impossible and then say not only that it could be done, but that it *will* be done—and then devote every atom of energy and determination toward completing the task.

Certainly MacArthur was thrilled with the appointment, and with returning to the institution to which both he and his father had dedicated their lives. "I feel like an old dog in a new uniform," he shyly confessed to Jean. In public he was more strident. "I am glad to be able to serve my country at this critical time," he told the press. "This action of the American government in establishing this new command can only mean that it intends to maintain, at any cost and effort, its full rights in the Far East. . . . To this end both the American and Filipino soldiery can be expected to give their utmost."[13]

It was a commitment that in MacArthur's own case was total and unbreakable. "I will not be taken alive," he later said, speaking of what would happen if the Japanese took the Philippines—and he meant it.

His second advantage was the renewed support of President Quezon, as well as other political parties in Parliament, including the Communists. The mercurial president who had been ignoring MacArthur and undermining his authority only months before now began calling him "my brother" again, and penned a personal note of congratulations: "I am fully confident that you will attain in this difficult assignment the same success that has crowned your every endeavor in the past."[14]

The appointment proved to Quezon's satisfaction that now the United States would not abandon him or the Philippines, and that this was just the first step in a major buildup of U.S. military and financial support for the islands. All thought of neutrality, or striking a deal with the Japanese, vanished. "All we have, all that we are, is yours," he jubilantly told MacArthur.[15]

But MacArthur's single biggest advantage was the American Regular Army troops he now commanded in the Philippines and their facilities, especially Clark Field. They were just over 22,000 men, manning barracks in Intramuros; Corregidor and the Manila Harbor defense system; Fort Stotsenburg near Clark Field; and a handful of fighter airfields on Luzon (only token forces were scattered on the other islands). "American troops" was something of a misnomer, since more than half of them were actually Philippine Scouts grouped into two regiments, the Forty-fifth and MacArthur's old favorite, the Fifty-seventh.

Indeed, the only completely American infantry unit in the entire Philippines was the Thirty-first Infantry, consisting of just 1,729 men. But all of them were solid professionals, men serving long enlistments with the discipline and training to match. The Thirty-first and the two Scouts regiments, plus some field artillery battalions, constituted the Philippine Department's core unit, the Philippine Division. It was 10,000 strong when MacArthur assumed command, and was led by a tall, lean, tough-as-hardtack brigadier general named James Wainwright.

MacArthur and Wainwright hit it off immediately when they met to discuss the future, and MacArthur explained his plans. He told Wainwright he was assuming command of all U.S. troops in the Philippine Department, including the Philippine Division, coastal defense units, the Twenty-sixth Philippine Scout Cavalry regiment, and other field artillery and military police units, as part of a single unified command, dubbed United States Army Forces Far East or USAFFE. All operational control of American units would pass on to his USAFFE staff, just as his staff would exercise all operational control over the army of the Philippine Commonwealth.

In short, the Philippine Department of the U.S. Army was now transformed into a service command, MacArthur explained, "an administrative echelon analogous to a Corps area."[16] Its principal task would now be training and supplying the Philippine Army.

That was going to be an enormous task. Over the last four years MacArthur had put together on paper a Philippine army of 4,000 regular troops and officers with 616 Reserve officers on active duty, and ten Reserve divisions of 7,600 men each.[17] In reality, almost none of these men had proper training, let alone modern weapons. The American regular officers who were training the Filipinos found it a tough challenge. Colonel Glen Townsend, commander of the Philippine Eleventh Infantry Regiment, soon found out that about half his force consisted of Christian Filipinos, mostly from the Ilocos provinces and the Cagayan Valley, and half were pagans from the mountains.

"There were representatives of nearly all the former headhunting tribes, including Bontocs, Hugaos, Kalingas, Ilongots, Beuguets, and Lepantos," he remembered. None of them spoke the others' languages, which meant that every order had to be translated into a dozen different dialects before it could be obeyed.[18] Most had no boots or even shoes; there were no blankets or mosquito nets; disease and poor hygiene were rampant.

Yet somehow MacArthur expected his officers to pull this polyglot horde together into a fighting army in a matter of months, not years. He was still confident that he had time: MacArthur believed Japan could not possibly attack before the spring of 1942. In those precious months he believed he could build up a Filipino defense force, backed by more U.S. reinforcements, that would be sufficient for him to hold Luzon and the capital, Manila, against all comers, starting from the beachhead.

This beachhead defense strategy would be the most controversial, and most criticized, aspect of MacArthur's plan to hold the Philippines as it unfolded over the hot late summer and early fall of 1941. His biographer Clayton James has even said that MacArthur "must bear a large share of the blame" for events "that would soon lead to military disaster."[19] In retrospect, it's hard to disagree. But at the time no one had tried to meet a seaborne invasion of islands like the Philippines, or thought about how to repel such an invasion. It was impossible for any commander to predict how a military operation that had no precedent, and that involved the engagement of forces that had never been tested in combat, would turn out—unless he was confident he would have the men and resources to do it.

And MacArthur *was* confident. That confidence wasn't based on sheer ego—at least not entirely. He believed an American ramp-up in the Philippines would give his strategic plan its crucial edge—and a buildup *was* in progress. Reinforcements promised on August 16 were on their way by September 12. An antiaircraft artillery regiment, a tank battalion of fifty-four tanks, and supplies had left from San Francisco. Another thirty tanks and fifty self-propelled mounts for 75 mm guns—plus the arrival of the 200th Coast Artillery Regiment with a dozen new three-inch guns and more machine guns—would reach Manila before the end of September.

Then there were the troops, more than 18,000 of them, as well as 1,321 officers and twenty-five American nurses.[20] The officers included Air Force Second Lieutenant Sam Grashio, who sailed from San Francisco on November 1 to join an American fighter squadron of brand-new Curtiss P-40s. His ship was a former luxury liner turned troop transport, and on board was a clutch of senior officers fresh from the National War College.

"To a man they were convinced there would be no war with Japan," he remembered, "because the Japanese would not be so stupid as to start a war they would be certain to lose within a few weeks." In short, MacArthur's confidence was not limited to himself and his staff.[21]

Indeed, MacArthur wrote in a letter to his friend John O'Laughlin, editor of the *Army and Navy Journal,* that news of his appointment had left Tokyo "dumbfounded and depressed," while the rest of Asia, including the Dutch East India and Chiang Kai-shek's China, greeted it with "complete jubilation." President Roosevelt had "completely changed the picture and an immediate and universal feeling of confidence and assurance resulted"—a sure sign that MacArthur had read Quezon's enthusiasm as a region-wide response.[22]

MacArthur figured that by the spring of 1942 he would have a Philippine army of 200,000 men, even though so far not one regiment or company had reached full authorized strength. Most were at half that level.[23] Yet in August MacArthur demanded that Washington ship him an additional 84,500 M-1 Garand rifles, 330 .30-caliber and 326 .50-caliber machine guns, 450 37 mm and 288 75 mm guns, as well as 8,000 vehicles of all types, to equip his as-yet shadow army for a full-out battle on the beaches.[24]

MacArthur still believed that when push came to shove the Filipinos would rise to the call of their fatherland, and that the spiritual courage of his troops would overcome any numerical or material disadvantage they faced in fighting the Japanese. It was the same faith in mind over matter he had seen fulfilled with Americans in the Forty-second Rainbow Division. If it was misplaced (and when war came, many Philippine units surprised their American officers with their courage and fight, including Colonel Townshend's Eleventh Regiment) one can note that it sprang from a lack of racist feeling rather than otherwise.

But MacArthur's conviction that his forward strategy would work rested on more than sentiment. It also rested on American airpower, specifically the B-17 heavy bomber. He had authorized its initial development as army chief of staff. With four engines, a crew of ten, and bristling with .50-caliber machine guns, the B-17 could fly 200 miles with a 6,000-pound bomb load. Neither the Germans nor the Japanese had an airpower weapon that could compete. In late August the army's Air Corps chief, Hap Arnold, had decided to ask for four heavy bombardment groups, some 272 B-17s with another sixty-eight waiting in reserve, to be sent out to the Philippines, along with two fighter groups of 130 planes each.[25]

Once they arrived, the expert consensus held, they could pound any Japanese landing force into submission from the air, and make life for Japanese naval support impossible. And in early October 1941 the first new B-17s landed at Clark Field, sixty-five miles north of Manila. Soon afterward the first fifty P-40s were uncrated in Manila, ready for assembly and flight. The promise of American airpower saving the Philippines seemed on the verge of being fulfilled.[26]

In the event of war with Japan, MacArthur's final asset, in his mind, was his USAFFE staff. They were men in the prime of their careers: with one exception, none was more than fifty years of age, and the youngest was forty-three. In addition to Sutherland and Sid Huff, there was Deputy Chief of Staff Richard Marshall, a VMI grad who switched from the artillery to the Quartermaster Corps after service in France in the last war. Marshall (no relation to George Marshall) was Sutherland's equal as a hard-charging workaholic, but without the abrasive temper. In MacArthur's view, Marshall had "no superior as a supply officer in the Army."[27] If Sutherland was the overseer at USAFFE GHQ, Dick Marshall was the workhorse, supervising procurement and storage of supplies, organizing the Philippine Army's logistics supplies, and handling all the work for planning mobilization of the Philippine economy.[28]

Charles A. Willoughby had come to Manila in 1939 and had acted as the liaison between MacArthur and the then-head of the Philippine Department, General Grunert, and President Quezon. No easy task, handling three such eccentric personalities; and Willoughby was something of an eccentric himself. Born in Germany to a German father and American mother, he had changed his family name from Tscheppe-Weidenbach to the more English aristocratic-sounding name Willoughby before becoming a second lieutenant during the First World War. He still spoke with a German accent and examined papers wearing pince-nez dangling from a silk cord.[29]

But he also had a penetrating intelligence and inquiring mind. He had taught at the Infantry School and Leavenworth, and had even written a book, *Maneuver in War*, which he claimed was based on MacArthur's own operational doctrines developed while army chief of staff. He had been promoted to lieutenant colonel the same day as Sutherland, and when USAFFE HQ was set up, MacArthur brought him over as his intelligence officer or G-2— a position in which Willoughby would repeatedly be a source of controversy, as well as insight, with regard to Japanese strengths and intentions.[30]

Rounding out the key positions were William "Billy" Marquat, a specialist in coast and antiaircraft artillery; LeGrand Diller, whom Sutherland re-cruited from Wainwright's Philippine Division over a game of golf to become MacArthur's aide-de-camp ("you're a member of my family now," MacArthur told him when Diller agreed to join); Lieutenant Colonel Hugh Casey, engineering officer; and Colonel Spencer Akin, signal officer. They would form the core of what would become known as "the Bataan Gang." As time went on, critics would dismiss them as a gang of incompetent sycophants who never told MacArthur news he didn't want to hear; or alternately, as a gang of competent sycophants who did the thinking and legwork for which MacArthur liked to claim all the credit.[31]

Neither characterization is accurate or even insightful. The truth was, MacArthur demanded loyalty from his staff as most egoistical, powerful men and women do, but he also gave loyalty back. That meant he sometimes overlooked mistakes, even blunders that would have cost less loyal staffers their jobs. But mistakes in MacArthur's USAFFE headquarters were few, es-pecially on the logistics and planning side. As time went on, MacArthur learned to give a few verbal instructions to Sutherland to pass on to the rest of the staff, who would then hammer out the details in time for MacArthur to read their findings, then approve—which he could do, because the results were perfectly coordinated with his ideas and vision. It wasn't an approach to staff work that suited everybody; his successor in Korea, General Matthew Ridgway, would choose a very different, more hands-on, approach.[32] But it worked for MacArthur through two wars—and it made the Bataan Gang es-sential to his brand of generalship.

The lowliest of the group was Private Paul Rogers, stenographer to both MacArthur and Sutherland, and his memoirs give a vivid picture of the rou-tine at 1 Calle Victoria in those tense months of September and October 1941.

Rogers's day began promptly at 7:30 A.M., with Colonel Sutherland usually already at his desk. It ran without interruption until lunch, followed by a brief return to the office until Master Sergeant Turner, the man in charge of the typewriting pool, would signal that Rogers was free to leave and wander the streets of Intramuros for an hour or two when MacArthur was hosting a late luncheon and Rogers was left with little to do.[33] It was a 7:30-to-5:00 workday, seven days a week (with alternate Sundays off), while Sutherland and the rest of the staff tried to get the Philippines ready for war.

Rogers never forgot the first time he was called in to take dictation from the general himself. One of MacArthur's Filipino sergeant orderlies leaned in through the door. "Rogers, the General wants you. Bring your pad."

Rogers walked into the long office with its display of flags from MacArthur's former commands. MacArthur was already pacing back and forth, and simply said, "Rogers, sit down and take this message." He began dictating a message to General Marshall in Washington. Rogers was impressed with how MacArthur's thoughts "rolled out with the precise, consistent, logical order that one expects of highly trained troops on review." Later, as MacArthur was going over the typed transcript, Rogers had a chance to examine him more closely.

"I noticed his black hair combed carefully over the thin spot on top of his head. His right hand trembled as he pointed to the letter"—already the slight tremor had appeared that MacArthur sought to hide but that plagued him for the rest of his life, and that some observers would mistake as fatigue or even shell shock.

"His voice was husky with a slight guttural rasping," Rogers later remembered, "pleasant but decisive. Handsome, poised, in perfect command of himself, yet gentle and benevolent in speech and manner," this was the general to whom Rogers would dedicate the rest of his army career. He was also the one to whom Washington had entrusted the fate of the American effort in the Philippines, on the grounds that not only was he experienced and knowledgeable about the islands and the Far East, but was also, as commanding officers go, blessed with luck.[34]

For the trial that was coming, he would need both, especially when he learned in October what Washington had planned for him.

That was when MacArthur first learned of the details of Rainbow Five, the new overall Allied plan for war with Japan in the event of a simultaneous war with Germany, as now seemed likely. It ordered withdrawal of all U.S. naval forces from the Philippines and ordered MacArthur's forces to pull back for a last-ditch defense of Manila Bay. There was no word of when the navy might return; the implication was clear that it probably never would before the Philippines fell to the enemy.

MacArthur was indignant, feeling almost betrayed. This was even worse than the limited defense of the Philippines that War Plan Orange had envisaged. That at least had offered the hope of relief, even if the six-month timetable was too optimistic. Rainbow Five, he felt, would deliver an even more bitter blow to Filipino morale if word leaked out. MacArthur composed a long letter back to Marshall, arguing that the new Philippine Army was up to the job of defending the islands alongside his American troops, and that with his new air force and new air force commander, whose arrival he expected imminently, they could hold out against the Japanese until relief came.

It was in this message that he outlined his idea of a forward defense of the entire archipelago, especially the southern islands, where, if the Japanese managed to establish air bases, air bombardment would make retaining control of Manila Bay almost impossible.

"The wide scope of enemy operations," he wrote, "especially aviation, now makes imperative the broadening of the concept of Philippine defense, and the strength and composition of the defense forces here are believed to be sufficient to accomplish such a mission"—that is, if he had enough munitions to supply an army that would grow to 200,000 by early 1942, and especially if those promised B-17s arrived.[35]

MacArthur's bold forward strategy had a strong supporter who knew the terrain and the difficulties involved: Jim Wainwright. The commander of the Philippine Division had considered War Plan Orange a disastrous, even cowardly course of action; he deplored Rainbow Five even more. "Defense must be active, damn it, not passive," he told MacArthur. "It must involve counterattacks." He endorsed MacArthur's counterplan of preventing the establishment of a Japanese bridgehead instead.[36]

So MacArthur forged ahead with establishing tactical commands for North Luzon, South Luzon, and the Visayan-Mindanao area, including sending munitions and supplies to the dispersed commands and sending almost half the Philippine Army to the islands south of Luzon.[37] On November 21 General Marshall wired Washington's answer to MacArthur's proposals. It was full authorization to defend the entire Philippines from enemy attack. Marshall also warned him that in the event the navy became involved in intercepting Japanese shipping or coordinating operations with the British Navy, MacArthur's bombers would be expected to join in the fight.

Permission was given; the die was cast. In retrospect, Washington's expectations—and MacArthur's—have an air of wishful thinking, not to mention unreality. But Marshall and the War Department believed MacArthur's glowing accounts of how the Philippine Army was progressing. They also believed the conventional wisdom about the omnipotence of airpower, especially the B-17. So the critical issue now was how MacArthur coordinated with his air and naval counterparts—and what resources, including leadership, they could bring into the picture.

MacArthur's new air force commander was General Lewis Brereton, who arrived from Hawaii in November—and presented himself at the Manila Hotel. MacArthur told him to come straight up.

To Brereton's surprise, the commander in chief of USAFFE met him in an ancient dressing gown that had faded to rose or violet or even salmon—visitors who caught MacArthur in the midst of his dressing routine found it hard to tell. He greeted Brereton like an old friend as they reminisced about the Great War (Brereton had been in an aerial observation squadron serving with the Forty-second in 1918).

"Lewis, you are as welcome as the flowers in May," MacArthur said the next day, when Brereton showed the list of planes Hap Arnold was planning to send to the Philippines. He called Sutherland into his office. "Dick," he said excitedly, "they've given us everything we've asked for." They could now expect the imminent arrival of some 170 heavy and medium bombers, including B-17s, and 86 light bombers—a heady prospect.[38] He soon set his new chief engineering officer, Hugh Casey, scouting for new airfield sites in central and southern Philippines, especially for the big B-17s.[39]

Brereton was still an unproven quantity, but MacArthur's relations with his air chief were certainly off to a good start. Relations with his navy commander, Rear Admiral Thomas Hart, were not so good. Hart and MacArthur, of course, had known each other for years; Hart had served with his brother Arthur. But Hart found his dead friend's brother more "apart," more distant, and as his seniority grew, less approachable. He also found MacArthur's restless pacing and nonstop oratory in his husky, sometimes tremulous voice, unnerving. Once he plaintively asked, "Douglas, can't we just relax and talk?"[40]

But there was no time to relax. So MacArthur would find himself shifting to a phony bonhomie and enthusiasm that bordered on high-handed condescension. After one encounter, Hart wrote to his wife only half-jokingly: "Douglas is, I think, no longer altogether sane . . . he may not have been for a long time."[41] It was an unfair, exaggerated comment. But it underlined how far apart MacArthur and Hart stood on how to defend the Philippines—and even as commander in chief of USAFFE, MacArthur had no formal authority to get Hart to do anything.

Indeed, Thomas Hart knew that his options were limited with only twelve submarines, a light and heavy cruiser, and a baker's dozen antiquated destroyers.[42] Yet MacArthur thought the navy could do more. The pair quarreled constantly over coordination of army and navy air patrols; MacArthur once told Hart bluntly he did not want his air arm directed by a naval force "of such combat inferiority as your Command."[43]

They even quarreled over navy shore patrols supervising American soldiers visiting bars and nightclubs in far-off Shanghai, where the navy personnel were fearful of any potential incident now that China's biggest commercial city was under Japanese occupation. As commander of USAFFE, however, MacArthur had jurisdiction over army personnel in Shanghai. He considered the navy's action a serious violation of army procedures, so serious that his protests went all the way up the ladder to Admiral Harold Stark himself in Washington.[44] MacArthur's vigorous defense of a soldier's right to get drunk when and where he wanted, earned plaudits from his grateful GIs—but none from Hart.

In the final analysis, the real source of friction between them was not based on personalities or interservice rivalry or even different views of the use of seapower—something that would get MacArthur into trouble with admirals in Washington later.[45] It was a matter of divergent orders. In the event of war, MacArthur would have to stay put and fight. Hart, by contrast, was under orders to sail away to join up with other Allied naval forces in the defense of Singapore or the Dutch East Indies. There was nothing MacArthur could do to convince Stark, Admiral Ernest King, and the other naval brass back in Washington that they should leave him a naval force that could

The boy soldier: Arthur MacArthur, Jr., Douglas MacArthur's father, as a lieutenant in the Twenty-fourth Wisconsin. He ended the war as a Medal of Honor winner, and with a love of the U.S. Army, which he passed on to his son. *Wisconsin State Historical Society*

Captain Arthur MacArthur; his wife, Mary "Pinky" MacArthur; and sons, Arthur III and Douglas, in white and gold curls, c. 1886. *General Douglas MacArthur Foundation*

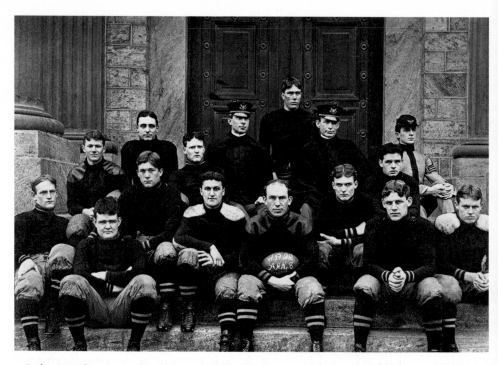

Cadet Douglas MacArthur, far right in gray uniform, as manager of the West Point football team, c. 1900. The faraway, visionary look in his eyes was one colleagues and subordinates learned to get used to. *USMA Library*

Captain Douglas MacArthur in highly irregular gear during the Veracruz campaign (1914). He thought his secret mission deserved a Medal of Honor. The army thought otherwise. *MacArthur Memorial Archives*

otain MacArthur as the War Department's press relations officer in Washington, D.C., 1916. The job ght him a lot about handling the press that he put to good use throughout his career. *U.S. Army Signal* *ps*

neral John J. Pershing pins a second Distinguished Service Cross on Colonel MacArthur, 1918. cArthur ended the First World War as the most decorated soldier in the U.S. Army. *U.S. Army Signal* *ps*

"I never met so vivid, so captivating, so magnetic a man." Editor William A. White, on visiting MacArthur at his headquarters in occupied Germany, 1919. *U.S. Army Signal Corps*

MacArthur as superintendant of West Point, c. 1920. His plans to modernize the military academy never bore full fruit, but set the agenda for the future of the Point. *U.S. Army Signal Corps*

MacArthur with his first wife, wealthy heiress Louise Cromwell Brooks, in 1925. Their storybook romance ended in a bitter divorce two years after this picture was taken. *International News Photo*

...ky MacArthur gazes fondly at her ...'s photograph, c. 1925. She was the ...ar of strength in his life until her ...th in 1935. "Like mother like son, is ...ing so true / The world will judge ...ely of mother by you." *Underwood ...d Underwood and Brown Brothers*

Army Chief of Staff Lt. General MacArthur supervises eviction of Bonus Marchers in Washington, D.C., 1932. His choice of uniform that day would haunt him later. *MPI/Getty Images*

MacArthur and President Franklin Roosevelt with Secretary of War George Dern (center), 1934. The laughter belied the uneasy rivalry between these two titans that lasted until FDR's death in 1945. *Brown Brothers*

cArthur arrives as military advisor to the Philippines, 1935. Standing behind him, on his right, is his ef of staff, Colonel Dwight D. Eisenhower. *U.S. Army Signal Corps*

Jean Faircloth before her marriage, c. 1935. *General Douglas MacArthur Foundation*

The Philippines campaign: MacArthur and General Jonathan M. Wainwright, c. December 1941. *U.S. Army Signal Corps*

The Philippines campaign: MacArthur and Chief of Staff Richard Sutherland in Malinta Tunnel, Corregidor, early 1942. MacArthur assumed he would die on Corregidor fighting the Japanese. FDR had other plans. *U.S. Army Signal Corps*

at least harass and hamper, if not defeat, a large Japanese landing when it came.

Lack of control over what the navy did was a severe disadvantage to MacArthur's plans—not as crucial as he later liked to complain, but still a drawback. All the same, as November wound down he found every reason to be confident about the future. The American buildup was under way; he now had thirty B-17s in the Philippines, with more promised and on the way. American ground forces had swelled by 8,000, including more than 1,000 officers; while the Philippine Army, still gun- and training-poor, numbered more than 100,000 men.[46]

Sid Huff's effort to arm a Philippine navy with PT boats had not panned out. But a squadron of PT boats under Commander John Bulkeley, a red-haired, barrel-chested veteran salt, was ready to patrol Manila Bay—and would play a crucial part in the saga of MacArthur in the Philippines later on.

By the end of November 1941, there was still plenty to do. There were airfields being built, and airfields to be built. There was Del Carmen south of Manila, and Del Monte, for example, and Nielson Field and Nichols Field. Nichols at least had a paved runway, yet Clark Field with its soft green turf was the only field large enough to accommodate the big B-17s. At times it crossed MacArthur's mind that if something happened to Clark . . . Yet his masters in Washington were still convinced that war, when it came, would not be before spring 1942. It was the operative assumption, a mantra almost, so convincing and reassuring that MacArthur was able to repeat it to his staff and subordinates with such confidence that many concluded it was actually his own prediction. Critics would bitterly repeat it back to him later.[47]

Because very suddenly time ran out.

"Boom Boom Boom!"

At 7:30 every morning, the door to the office of the commander of USAFFE would burst open and a tiny dark-haired figure in an army sergeant's uniform would toddle in.

Douglas MacArthur immediately jumped up from his desk and snapped to attention. It was his three-year-old son, Arthur, in a uniform specifically tailored to be an exact replica of a United States Army sergeant's.

She asked him what he thought about a purely defensive strategy for the Philippines.

"Defeat," MacArthur said.[51]

Clare Luce went home with her interviews and pictures of the general posing on the ramparts of the Intramuros, gazing across Manila Bay. Her answer for her husband, and the readers of *Life,* was that MacArthur was indeed a genius, and not a fraud. MacArthur, despite his assurances to her about the strength of his position, knew that the facts didn't bear them out. He knew the training program run by the Philippine Department was not going well. "In my inspections to date," he wrote to General Grunert at about the time she visited, "I have found large groups of trainees and their officers standing around and doing nothing. . . . [A] pall of inactivity was evident."[52]

He also had a report by a USAFFE aide named Harold George, a former World War One fighter pilot, which told the sobering truth about his situation in the air even before General Brereton arrived. The Japanese would use 1,000 land-based bombers and 1,000 fighters in an air war over the Philippines, George concluded. Given a standard reserve of 25 percent for planes being refitted or maintenanced, defending the Philippines would require no fewer than 1,500 combat aircraft operating from fifty-six airfields.[53]

In fact, as November drew to a close MacArthur had less than a quarter of that number, even with his 33 B-17s and 100 or so P-40Es, the most advanced fighter in the U.S. Army Air Force, which was no possible match for the Japanese Zero.[54] Instead of fifty-six airfields, he had five, with Del Monte slated to be finished by early December.

Then on November 27 came the message from the War Department that MacArthur had been dreading.

"Negotiations with Japan appear to be terminated . . . hostile action at any moment. If hostilities cannot, repeat cannot, be avoided, The United States desires that Japan commit the first act."

That was cold comfort for MacArthur and his commanders. Still, he sent the alert on to Wainwright, who was now commander of all American forces in USAFFE after Grunert's departure earlier in the month, and to his other field commanders. "Under existing circumstances, it is not possible to predict the future actions of the Japanese. Take necessary action to insure immediate readiness for any eventuality."[55]

That Sunday the Army-Navy football game was scheduled to be broadcast. Although it was taking place 12,000 miles away, the game was a Manila ritual for the American garrison. Army and navy officers would gather on the lawn in front of the Philippine Division's barracks in the Intramuros, drinks in hand, and listen to the game, broadcast in the early-morning hours. Whenever Army scored a touchdown, a mule would be ceremoniously escorted around the lawn. When Navy scored, a goat was led around the same circuit.[56]

That Sunday, MacArthur, a keen footballer, ordered the broadcast canceled. It was a sure sign to everyone, military and civilian, American and Filipino, that something serious was about to happen.

On December 1, the Fourth Marine Regiment arrived from Shanghai, and on December 2, another seven hundred marines docked with the *President Harrison* at Olangapo. They were MacArthur's final reinforcements, and very welcome ones. But they knew no more about fighting a modern war than his army troops did. In some ways, they were no better prepared for battle against the Japanese than his Filipino trainees. In fact, the only time the marines arriving on the *President Harrison* had fired a weapon had been during basic training in the States.[57]

That same day crews working at dawn on Clark Field spotted a lone plane passing high in the sky. It was a Japanese reconnaissance plane, but no one bothered to scramble to try to intercept it. A few days before, there had been some reports of long-range patrol planes spotting Japanese troop transports in the South China Sea, bound for somewhere. Most assumed it was Indochina.[58]

To any sensible observer, the possibility of war seemed to be growing to a certainty. As tensions mounted, MacArthur grimly went ahead with his preparations. He told Washington that a full alert was in effect for all American installations in the Philippines. All stations were manned on a twenty-four-hour basis; aircraft on airfields were dispersed as much as possible to foil any surprise air attack; and the guard was doubled at all installations. With more than 18,000 Japanese living on Mindanao and elsewhere, MacArthur was taking no chances.

He had also ordered General Brereton to increase daily and nightly reconnaissance flights. On December 4 a fighter patrol encountered Japanese planes fifty miles out at sea, but the Japanese pilots turned back as the Americans approached. MacArthur was also conducting regular radar sweeps for unidentified aircraft. But he had only one radar set, at Iba Field, eighty-five miles northwest of Manila, and the only communication with headquarters was by landline telephone.

Then, on December 5, MacArthur had an unscheduled visitor. It was British admiral Sir Tom Phillips, on his way to assume command of the battleship HMS *Prince of Wales,* which would now headline the British naval squadron based in Singapore. Great Britain was as unprepared for a war in the Far East as America was; with London's attention firmly focused on the war with Germany, even less so. The hope was that the arrival of *Prince of Wales* and the battle cruiser *Repulse,* would make the Japanese think twice about starting a conflict with the British Empire, scattered and undermanned though its forces were.

Phillips found MacArthur in a grim but cautiously optimistic mood. On the basis of Washington's warnings, he had now drastically telescoped his timetable for a Japanese attack. "General MacArthur thought the attack would come sometime after January 1," Phillips told reporters after the meeting. Phillips's meeting with Hart also went well. He explained that his ships were increasing their activity at sea, to be on lookout for any approaching Japanese vessels, and that "he was optimistic about the striking power of his subs"—all seventeen of them. They all made preliminary plans to coordinate British and American naval operations in defending the Malay Barrier, once war came.

They never got the chance. One week later Phillips would be dead, while his great battleship and the *Repulse* lay at the bottom of the ocean—even as the mighty British Empire in Asia teetered on the brink of collapse.

As for the Philippines, everything now depended on how fast the Americans could detect the first Japanese move. The radar set at Iba kept picking up unidentified craft off the coast of Luzon appearing as dots on the screen, but they kept disappearing. Back at Clark, Colonel Harold George solved the mystery.

"It's my guess they're getting their range data established," he said, "possibly a rendezvous point from Formosa." When the dots didn't appear the next day, "they've got all they need now," George remarked sourly. "The next time they won't play. They'll come in without knocking."[59]

Fortunately, MacArthur had on hand a better resource for detecting a Japanese attack than blips on a radar screen.

The War Department had been cracking Japanese naval and diplomatic ciphers as far back as the 1920s. The crucial breakthrough came in 1940 when, eighteen months after Tokyo introduced the machine code-named PURPLE for enciphering diplomatic codes, the army's Signals Intelligence Service managed to reproduce the same results with a machine of its own.[60] The U.S. Army proceeded to build eight duplicate PURPLE machines. Four were kept in Washington, where they carefully monitored the mounting tensions in the Far East by reading the diplomatic cables running back and forth between Tokyo and Washington. Three found their way to London. The navy had a similar machine ensconced in its annex on Corregidor, but MacArthur did not—and he had no direct access to the navy's.

Still, in the summer of 1941 MacArthur personally requested that Spencer Akin, one of the masterminds of reading encrypted Japanese radio traffic, be sent out as his chief signal officer. Although MacArthur was no cipher expert, then or later, and although Akin himself had not been personally involved in reading PURPLE decrypts, MacArthur soon had his army working round the clock on intercepted radio traffic at a small hut outside the gate at Fort McKinley, which became known as Station 6.[61]

The presiding genius at Station 6 was Major Joe Sherr. From his arrival in July 1940, he began deciphering Japanese diplomatic codes by hand, which he could do faster than the navy's PURPLE machine was doing from Corregidor's Monkey Point. The work became so intense that it began affecting Sherr's eyesight.[62]

But it was vital to know what, if anything, might give away a Japanese move in advance. The drawback was that Station 6 had to send the copies made of decrypted messages to the navy signals intelligence people on Corregidor for translation, loading them into a mailbag that went on a PT boat plying the waters between Manila and Corregidor, otherwise known as the

CHAPTER 14

RAT IN THE HOUSE

The history of failure in war can be summed up in two words: Too late.

—DOUGLAS MACARTHUR TO

THEODORE H. WHITE, 1940

It was 3:40 in the morning when the phone rang in MacArthur's penthouse apartment.

Sutherland was on the other end. "Pearl Harbor's been attacked," he said curtly. Sutherland had learned the news from Major Diller, who learned it from a correspondent who learned it from a commercial news broadcast.[1] Sutherland added that the U.S. fleet had been caught unawares.

"Pearl Harbor!" MacArthur exploded. "It should have been our strongest point."

He recovered from the shock long enough to throw on some clothes and tell Jean the news. Then he picked up his mother's Bible, read a chapter or two, and prayed.[2]

Minutes later he was ensconced at No. 1 Calle Victoria, surrounded by his staff. Sutherland was still on the phone, demanding more news on what was happening in Hawaii. Admiral Hart was wringing his hands nearby, warning MacArthur that he needed to get his ships out of the way in case there was a similar attack on the Philippines.

That was the question all of them were asking in the inky blackness of the early morning, besides how badly the fleet at Pearl had been hit. Would they be next? MacArthur had spoken by phone to Brigadier General Leonard Gerow in Washington, who told him to expect an air attack soon.[3] But when and where? One way to find out would be to send out some air patrols, which meant talking to Lewis Brereton.

Brereton had had a rough night, and an even rougher morning. He had been attending a birthday party with his fliers until the early hours. In between rounds of drinks Sutherland had informed him that war might be days, even hours, away. He later remembered how Brereton's face fell at the news, but Brereton had stayed on to party. When he showed up at 1 Calle Victoria, he may have been drunk; accounts differ. He probably still had liquor on his breath. That could be one reason that Sutherland insisted he stay in the outer office while MacArthur talked to Admiral Hart.[4]

Alcohol-befogged or not, Brereton was worried, as they all were, but also angry. He wanted to do something. His pilots had been alerted about the same time as Sutherland got the news. They were already in their P-40s with engines running and standing by on their radios.[5] Their chief now told Sutherland he wanted to conduct a raid on Japan-occupied Formosa—which was also the location of the airfields that any long-range attack on the Philippines would come from. Here again accounts differ, but Sutherland seems to have given Brereton tentative permission but wanted to confirm the order with MacArthur before anything happened.[6] Brereton headed back to Clark to alert his B-17 crews there and at Del Carmen that they would be leading the strike on Formosa.

Years later Brereton would insist that he kept pressing Sutherland and MacArthur to give him permission to launch an attack. MacArthur would insist with the same vehemence that Brereton never pressed him to do any such thing. When he read a later newspaper account stating that his air chief had approached him with the idea of a preemptive raid on Formosa using his B-29s, MacArthur announced that it was news to him and that he didn't even see Brereton that day.[7]

There is, however, one indisputable fact. Neither MacArthur nor Brereton spoke directly to each other for almost five hours. Instead it was left to Richard Sutherland, who had plenty else to do on that chaotic morning, to communicate the one's intentions to the other.

For example, according to Sutherland, Brereton had no clear idea what, if anything, he would be bombing on Formosa. Brereton's plan was far too vague to present to his chief. "What targets? What airfields?" Sutherland kept asking him. That made him reluctant to press the plan to MacArthur, even after Brereton drove back to 1 Calle Victoria to renew his plea. On the other hand, MacArthur still believed he was under orders from Washington not to take any offensive action until he had been attacked himself.

"My orders were explicit," he later told army historian Louis Morton, "not to initiate hostilities against the Japanese," although it's difficult to know what the attack on Pearl was except an initiation of hostilities demanding some kind of response from MacArthur. At the same time, orders modifying war plan Rainbow Five had been issued on November 19, 1941, explicitly requiring MacArthur to fly air raids on Japanese targets within range of his Philippine airfields in such an event. Yet if MacArthur had been left free to disregard Rainbow Five, he might have decided to disregard this order, as well.[8]

Or did MacArthur believe not inititating hostilities referred to the Philippine area? Did he believe he was supposed to wait until the Japanese struck at forces under his direct command before taking action? In retrospect, this seems to have been how MacArthur interpreted his orders from Washington. Either way, Sutherland seems to have conveyed to General Brereton a message of caution in a phone call at 8:30 A.M. And it was a furious Brereton who turned to his staff, who were working out the details of the Formosa raid, to say, "No, we can't attack until fired upon"—words that tend to reinforce MacArthur's account of the constraints he felt he was under at the time.[9]

It was a confusing moment, in the midst of greater confusion. While MacArthur claimed years later in his memoirs that "we were as ready as we possibly could be" on December 7, when "every disposition had been made, every man, gun, and plane was on alert"—there can be no doubt that the proverbial fog of war was settling thickly over 1 Calle Victoria. Eyewitnesses later stated that MacArthur "looked grey, drawn and exhausted."[10] He had no reliable information of what the enemy was doing and no reliable communications with his forces in the field, including at Clark Field, and they had none with one another—the phone system kept breaking down, due to either sabotage or poor maintenance or both. Radio communication was intermittent at best.

Perhaps for the first and only time in his life, MacArthur was uncertain what to do next. Above all, he had no adequate plan for what to do until Japanese intentions were made plain. That uncertainty may have sprung from the belief, already mentioned, that Washington wanted him to wait until the Japanese struck the first blow before retaliating. That in turn fed absurd rumors later that MacArthur may have secretly hoped that the Philippines could remain neutral in a U.S.-Japanese conflict, and that the Japanese would pass them all by if he did nothing.

The only thing that is plain is that he and Sutherland decided it was better to sit tight until they had more accurate information on which to act. MacArthur tells us in his memoirs that he was still unclear how badly the United States had been damaged at Pearl Harbor, or indeed even whether it was the Japanese, not the navy, who had come out the worse for the attack.[11]

Brereton, at least, was under no such illusions. He had received a phone call from Hap Arnold in Washington. The head of the Army Air Forces told him in no uncertain terms that the air force on the ground in Hawaii was all but wiped out. Make sure your fighters and bombers are in the air, he warned the head of the Fifth Air Force, or dispersed on the ground.

At 8:50 (Brereton later claimed) he called Sutherland back, still asking for permission to attack. Sutherland still told him, "Hold off for present."[12]

Only minutes later, something happened that got everyone's attention. A radio bulletin came in saying that Japanese bombers had been spotted over Lingayen Gulf, headed for the Philippines. It was that report that spurred Brereton into taking unilateral action. He sent a radio message to Clark Field ordering the planes and bombers there into the air, so that they would not be caught in any air raid. At ten Brereton put in another call to HQ, in which, he said later, he warned Sutherland that "if Clark Field were attacked successfully we would be unable to operate offensively with the bombers."[13]

Sutherland, meanwhile, had passed the Lingayen Gulf report on to Washington, and on to MacArthur. Then he got back to Brereton with the first suggestion from 1 Calle Victoria that the Formosa plan might be in the works. Get some planes aloft to take aerial reconnaissance photos of Formosa, Sutherland said, so we can find worthwhile targets.

But it was already too late.

* * *

The men at Clark Field weren't the only ones listening in on Brereton's radio message to his pilots ordering them to take to the air. So were the Japanese on Formosa.

Five hundred Japanese bombers and fighters had been poised to attack the Philippines since before dawn. A dense fog kept most of them on the ground for nearly six hours, while they heard reports that the strike on Pearl Harbor had been a success (shrill shouts of "Banzai!" echoed across the airfields) and that planes assigned to hit northern Luzon had taken off from bases farther east that were clear of fog.

Then came the intercepted message, which the Japanese could interpret only one way: B-17s were headed to attack them. Hitting Clark was now an urgent priority for the Japanese air force. Finally after another hour of tense waiting, the fog slowly lifted. Still, it wasn't until 10:45 that morning that the fifty-three bombers and forty-five Zero fighters, led by future fighter superstar Saburo Sakai, finally took off and set their course for Clark Field.[14]

At 11:00 MacArthur finally telephoned Brereton, and the two men spoke for the first time. Brereton told the commander of USAFFE that he had three planes headed for Formosa to reconnoiter, and that the rest of his bombers were already in the air. MacArthur approved, but added that he should wait for those reports on Formosa before launching his attack.[15]

They were going to need it. Information and charts were poor, certainly without the bomb target maps and bomb release lines for speed and altitudes that European air forces like the Luftwaffe, or even the RAF, had.

But Brereton's report that his planes were in the air was mistaken. In fact, after circling Clark for almost two hours, and with no hostiles in sight, the B-17s began to land back at the field, along with the P-40s.[16]

By now the men at Clark had learned that the first wave of Japanese bombers spotted by Americans had struck at Tuguegarao and Baguio, but then turned north and headed for home. As the news spread, so did relief that Clark had been spared. At 10:30 the all-clear had sounded. Sometime between 11:00 and 11:30 most of Clark's P-40s and B-17s were back on the ground.

Their relief and lack of caution were unjustified. At almost the same time when planes were landing back at Clark, the American commander of the Eleventh Infantry Regiment, on patrol near Iba, heard aircraft engines.

Looking up, he and his men counted no fewer than eighty-four Japanese bombers passing overhead. Minutes later the radar installation at Iba sent out a frantic alert to all Air Corps bases that a large formation of planes was coming in from the China Sea. They were vectored in the direction of Clark Field.

It was the last communication Iba ever made. Bombers at 28,000 feet unloaded a wave of destruction that knocked out the only radar installation in the Philippines and destroyed every building.

The loss of Iba left Clark Field—and MacArthur—sitting blind. The only other source of information was the Philippine phone system, which wasn't very reliable in the best of times. At noon, it went stone dead, either from sabotage or from technical problems—to this day, no one knows which.[17]

At 11:30 the air raid Klaxons at Nichols Field south of Manila began to sound. The Twentieth Air Group stationed there had picked up word of an incoming second Japanese strike and guessed (correctly) that it might be headed for Clark. Nichols scrambled its three flights of P-40s, in hopes of intercepting the attack.

One of those scrambling was the newly arrived Lieutenant Samuel Grashio. "After the initial alert [that morning], we cut our engines, got out of the cockpits and sat under the wings and waited as seemingly endless hours dragged by," he remembered later. Then at 11:30 came an alert to go into action, "though just what action was unspecified."[18]

It wasn't until 11:50—twenty minutes after the initial warning—that the P-40s were actually in the air, and two had to turn back due to oil leaks that covered their windshields so thickly they couldn't see. Grashio and his three remaining planes lost track of the other fighters. They finally radioed down to Nichols to say they were going to pass over Clark Field.

At the same time Nichols sent a final warning to Clark by teletype and by radio about an impending attack. Neither message ever made it.[19]

Back in Manila, MacArthur rang up Sutherland at almost that same time, 11:50. Check with Brereton, he ordered, concerning reports about Japanese air operations during the past two hours. On the phone General Brereton confirmed that there had been two groups of Japanese bombers seen over Luzon, but he had no other information. The vital point was, however, that Japan had attacked the Philippines. Brereton could now go ahead with the attack on Formosa, which, he told Sutherland, would go out "this after-noon."[20]

The clock in MacArthur's office struck twelve noon. He may have glanced at his watch as well. This was the hour designated for Brereton's photo recon mission to take off. But something happened to delay the flight: the assigned B-17 crews realized they had the wrong cameras. So there had been a long wait for the right cameras to be flown over from Del Monte field.

Despite the tension, no one seemed to be in much of a hurry. After all, the last reports they had received indicated that the most recent Japanese air operations were passing them by. Soon everyone at Clark stopped work to grab a quick lunch, while Brereton's staff went over their final plans for the raid on Formosa.

At 12:20, Lieutenant Gashio and his three companions were directly over Clark Field. They saw nothing amiss, so they decided to set off to the west for a further look.

Finally at 12:30, the right cameras arrived and the photo recon planes were revving their engines as they waited for the signal to start. In prepara-tion for providing escort, the Twentieth Pursuit Squadron's P-40s were al-ready taxiing to the runway, their propellers whirring and pilots making their last-minute check before takeoff. Bombs, meanwhile, were being loaded on the sixteen other B-17s.

At 12:31, one of the B-17 pilots, Lieutenant Fred Crimmins, had just pulled loose a .50-caliber machine gun that needed replacing and was carry-ing it over to the hangar when one of his mechanics said wide-eyed that a radio report said Japanese bombers were right overhead. Crimmins barely had time to hand the machine gun over before the Klaxon sounded.

By then the first bombs were falling.

At 12:32, Grashio's radio suddenly crackled: "All P-40s return to Clark Field. Enemy bombers overhead!" It was Clark's tower operator, and he sounded as if he were in pain. Grashio could hear the sound of bombs ex-ploding back where Clark was.[21]

Two tight vee formations of Japanese bombers led by Saburo Sakai's fight-ers dropped their bombs on Clark in a wide pattern, setting up destruction all across the field. The B-17s on the runways were soon smashed and burn-ing. Parked P-40s exploded, sending propellers and parts of wings high into the air, and every building was hit. Clark's antiaircraft batteries belatedly blazed away, hoping to hit some of the bombers, but their ammunition was old and defective. Only one in every six 3-inch shells actually fired.[22] Four of Clark's nine P-40s managed to get into the air in the confusion. The others, and their pilots, were blown to bits.

Lieutenant Grashio, meanwhile, who had banked back and was now passing overhead, was astounded at the inferno raging below him. "The whole area was boiling with smoke, dust, and flames," he would remember, "in the middle a huge column of greasy black smoke from the top of which red flames billowed intermittently." Grashio tried to attack some Japanese dive bombers strafing the field, but he was jumped by two Zeros and had to dive and veer away without firing a shot.

In just forty-five minutes it was all over. Not a single plane that had been on the field when the attack started could fly. Craters pocked every runway, and fires consumed hangars and buildings. Fifty-five men were dead; more than one hundred were wounded. Half of the B-17s, the ones MacArthur had ordered sent to Del Monte, were still intact. The P-40s of Twentieth Pursuit that had managed to take off shot down three or four Japanese fighters, and even the obsolete P-35s of Thirty-fourth Pursuit based at Del Carmen caught up with the fleeing Japanese and downed three without a single loss.[23]

But otherwise, literally in one fell swoop, MacArthur's air force had been cut in half.

The recriminations began almost at once, and they continue to this day. Many still blame MacArthur for the debacle at Clark. Many then and later blamed Brereton, who, evidence suggests, may have surreptitiously altered the Clark daily log in order to suggest that he was more ready to take off at MacArthur's orders than he actually was.[24] And certainly almost everyone blames Sutherland for not making MacArthur's orders clearer to Brereton and not making Brereton's actions clearer to MacArthur.

All the same, once the historian takes into account Brereton's woeful lack of preparation for a sudden Japanese attack, and his going against MacArthur's express orders, and Sutherland's failures in coordinating command and control, and MacArthur's failure to keep better track of what was happening to his air force in those confusing but crucial hours on December 8—even after that exercise in retrospective judgment, it's hard not to conclude that the real problem was a combination of bad luck and a broken communication system, including communication among the various Far East Air Force bases that might have gotten the news to Clark in time that the Japanese were coming.

For those eager to point the finger of blame at MacArthur, however—and for those just as eager to deflect the blame in another direction—the events of December 8 remain a matter of bitter controversy. Yet it was MacArthur who said the history of failure in war could be summed up in two words, "Too late." It may be the only suitable epitaph for the men who died in those forty-five minutes of shock and awe on Clark Field and during the rest of MacArthur's campaign in the Philippines.

MacArthur, meanwhile, received the devastating news by phone, even as Jean and little Arthur were watching the smoke rising up from Clark from their balcony at the Manila Hotel. For five minutes MacArthur berated his air chief for not moving out the B-17s as he had ordered (allowing them to land that morning all at once was also a blunder, one that MacArthur didn't mention).

He slammed down the phone, still in a rage. When he looked up, a grim-faced Sutherland was standing before him.

He told the general that a Lieutenant Howard Brown of the Signal Corps was here with a top-secret message. MacArthur agreed to see him.

Brown saluted and handed him an envelope, which he immediately tore open. It was a secret decrypt from Washington sent the day before, informing MacArthur that Japan was now at war with the United States and Great Britain.

As MacArthur glared in disbelief, an abashed Lieutenant Brown explained it had taken hours to get this message from the Navy decrypt office to USAFFE GHQ because of the long, slow bureaucratic trail involved. MacArthur took the cruel trick that fate had played without much comment.

"Thank you, son," was all he said. Brown saluted, turned, and left MacArthur sitting alone, his face a mask.

As General Gouraud, his mentor from the World War, might have said, *il ne manquait que cela.* The belated message was the final insult in what was turning into a very long and disastrous day.[25]

The losses at Clark were more than a shock and a setback to his strategy of using his bombers to keep the Japanese off the beaches. They were proof that he faced an enemy with more resources, better discipline, and a more effective strategy than his own. If that required further proof, it came that afternoon when he got the full report of the devastation at Pearl Harbor, including the destruction of the fleet that was supposed to come to rescue them in the Philippines.

"Sixty Japanese carrier borne dive bombers attacked airfields and Pearl Harbor Oahu at 8:00 A.M., damaging hangars and planes on the ground. Three battleships reported sunk and three others seriously damaged. Second air raid at 11:00. . . . Reports of attacks on Wake and Guam . . . Reports received that Singapore attacked by air. . . . Limit this information to essential officers."[26]

MacArthur then spoke with Admiral Hart, who had received the same report. Their conversation was somber, as the full weight of the disaster at Pearl sank in (in fact it was even worse than the report indicated: no fewer than nine battleships had actually been either sunk or crippled). Commissioner Sayre arrived at 5:30. He found MacArthur "pacing the floor" with a deeply troubled expression on his face. He read Sayre the radiogram "telling of the tragic losses at Pearl Harbor" and then filled him in on the disaster at Clark Field.[27] They knew that any chance of a quick dispatch of naval forces to help protect the islands was now gone.

But there was worse to come. MacArthur was losing his own navy as well.

Clark Field was bombed on Monday, December 8. On December 10 the Japanese took off again, this time aiming for the other American airfields in the Philippines, including Del Carmen, Nichols, and Nielson Fields near Manila. The rain of bombs on Nichols was so intense that for a time the aircrews on Nielson two miles away thought their own field was under attack (they took their own pounding a few minutes later).[28] That day the Japanese achieved full air superiority over the Philippines—and that same day, the Japanese hit the naval base at Cavite, eight miles southwest of Manila, leaving a trail of destruction and burning docks. More than five hundred men were killed or wounded in the raid.

Tom Hart watched in outrage from his hotel balcony—ironically only one floor down from MacArthur's own penthouse suite. As he watched, a yeoman presented a message. Japanese planes had sent the British navy's *Prince of Wales* and *Repulse* to the bottom, taking Admiral Tom Phillips with them.

Hart had had enough. He went to see MacArthur. He announced that he was pulling his naval forces out. It didn't come as a complete shock to MacArthur. They had had a similar conversation before, at the end of October when they received the revised war plan, Rainbow Five, ordering the Asiatic Fleet to withdraw to the Indian Ocean in case of hostilities. Hart told him he now intended to follow those orders.

MacArthur tried to cajole him into following his, instead. "I'm counting on you to keep the sea lanes open," he told Hart, so that transports from Pearl and the States could get through. For example, he had learned that very day that a seven-ship convoy led by the cruiser *Pensacola,* with 5,000 troops, 18 new P-40s, and other munitions, had diverted from Brisbane to the Philippines.[29]

Hart's next words were like a dagger to his heart.

"The *Pensacola* convoy," he predicted darkly, "will never reach Manila." The Japanese had the islands blockaded, he said; no ships from the outside would be able to get through. MacArthur scoffed at the idea. It was only "a paper blockade," he said.

Besides, "The Philippine theater of operations is the locus of victory or defeat. IF THE WESTERN PACIFIC IS TO BE SAVED IT WILL HAVE TO BE SAVED HERE AND NOW." Those at least were the words he was sending to Washington, and to General Marshall.[30] But Hart was adamant. He told MacArthur bluntly that the Philippines was "doomed." He already had Chief of Naval Operations Admiral Harold Stark's approval to withdraw, and except for eleven submarines, the six-boat PT squadron under Commander Bulkeley, and some PBY flying boats, Hart was preparing to move the rest of his forces south to the Dutch East Indies. Marshall, and the army, did nothing to stop him.

Hart's decision came on December 13, a Friday, as it happened. Three days earlier MacArthur had had news that was almost as bad: Japanese troops were already landing on Luzon.

* * *

The very first Japanese to land in the Philippines had actually disembarked at Batan Island in the Luzon Strait on December 8.[31] But the first serious invasion forces were scheduled to arrive at Aparri, on the northern tip of Luzon, and Vigan, on the western coast. There they would seize airfields to provide fighter cover for the main event: a major amphibious landing farther south at Lingayen Gulf. Now that MacArthur's air forces had been reduced by half, that part of the plan, at least, seemed assured.

All the same, the Aparri and Vigan landings did meet some unexpected opposition. The minute MacArthur learned of them, he ordered what was left of his air force to strike.[32] As Japanese troops began disembarking, two B-17s from Del Carmen, whose crews had spent a harrowing night on the damaged Clark Field sleeping in their planes, came lumbering over the beach and began unloading bombs. One of the bombs hit one of the transports; the other, piloted by Captain Colin Kelly, struck what he assumed was a Japanese battleship, the *Haruna*. The triumphant moment was cut short when a Zero fighter ambushed Kelly's plane as he was headed back to base. Kelly was shot down and killed, earning him the war's first posthumous Distinguished Service Cross—and the first decoration for a West Point graduate. Meanwhile, P-35s from Lieutenant Samuel Marrett's squadron sprayed the beach with machine-gun fire in several strafing passes, as Japanese soldiers scattered and tried to fire back. Marrett himself managed to blow up an ammunition ship before he, too, was shot down and killed, earning the second posthumous DSC of the war.[33]

Unfortunately, the army wasn't in a position to match the persistence and valor of the Americans in the air. The troops never got a chance to fire a shot. Wainwright's men were stretched so thin on the ground that he had only a single company around Aparri to oppose some 2,000 Japanese landing there, and no one at all at Vigan. And so they withdrew without even seeing the enemy, although MacArthur did order Wainwright to destroy all the bridges running south toward Manila in the Cagayan Valley, and to block Balete Pass, which Wainwright believed could be held by a single battalion.[34]

Still, to Wainwright none of this mattered. Like MacArthur and Willoughby, he believed the main landing would take place at Lingayen Gulf, where the bulk of his forces were stationed, especially the Eleventh Division.

All the same, there was no denying, as Wainwright put it, "the rat is in the house." The question now was how to keep him in the basement—in other words, away from Manila and Manila Harbor.[35]

It was while he was still digesting all this news that MacArthur was hit with Hart's decision to pull out. The navy's decision may or may not have been the result of panic, as MacArthur believed then and later (they had been "terrorized" by Pearl Harbor, he always insisted), but Hart was right about one thing: the *Pensacola* convoy was never going to arrive. The day war was declared, the convoy turned around and headed back to Hawaii—even though Washington continued to assure MacArthur that it was still on its way.

MacArthur's painful Friday the 13th meeting with Admiral Hart was followed the next day by an equally painful meeting in Washington between General Marshall and Dwight Eisenhower, MacArthur's former chief of staff who was now head of the War Plans Division. It was Ike's first day on the job, but if he was expecting an introductory tour of the War Department and staff followed by lunch, he was disappointed.

When Ike entered Marshall's office, the army chief of staff was standing at his desk, his face a grim mask. In a few quick sentences he spelled out the disaster steadily growing in the Pacific, especially in the Philippines.

"We have got to do our best in the Pacific," he concluded, even though he and Eisenhower knew Europe would be the central focus of the American war effort. "How are we going to do it?"

"Give me a few hours," Ike answered without hesitation and adjourned to his office.[36]

When he came out, he had a handwritten, three-hundred-word statement titled "Assistance to the Far East." Its first heading was to build up Australia as a base of supply for reinforcing the Philippines. Since "speed was essential," Ike recommended using the navy's aircraft carriers and fast merchant ships to ferry planes and supplies to keep the Philippines, and MacArthur, in the war.

"It will be a long time before major reinforcements can go to the Philippines, longer than any garrison can hold out without direct assistance . . . but we must do everything for them that is humanly possible. The people of China," he added, "the Philippines, of the Dutch East Indies will be watching us. They may excuse failure but they will not excuse abandonment."

"I agree with you," Marshall said. "Do your best to save them."

Secretary of War Henry Stimson also agreed. An old Philippines hand, he too believed that abandoning the islands would wreck American credibility. He showed Roosevelt MacArthur's cable of his conversation with Admiral Hart.

Both men agreed that Hart's actions showed "the usual Navy defeatist position" and that it should be stopped. "We cannot give up the Philippines this way," Marshall had told Stimson, and Roosevelt told Admiral Stark that if he, as president, was pledged to defend the Philippines, so was the navy.

Stark bowed to the president's orders. But he vigorously opposed MacArthur's idea of sending aircraft carriers east to attack Japanese shipping around the islands, and did nothing to stop Hart's departure. The discussion ended around 6:00 P.M. that evening with no clear decisions made.[37]

All the same, on that day the American policy toward MacArthur and the Philippines was set. There would be no withdrawal, but also no emergency reinforcement. Certainly there would be nothing that might reach Manila in time to save the situation—that is, unless a miracle happened and MacArthur and the Armed Forces of the Far East managed to hold off the Japanese long enough for Admiral Stark to decide the navy had recovered sufficiently from Pearl Harbor to make sending help "practicable."

So there was no *Pensacola* convoy headed for Manila, no carriers headed at flank speed to fly new P-40s off to Clark Field, no countermanding Hart's decision to withdraw to the East Indies. Instead, the support MacArthur would receive from Washington over the next weeks and months would be entirely moral.

"My personal and official congratulations on the fine stand you are making," read one cable from President Roosevelt himself. "All of you are constantly in our thoughts. Keep up the good work."

Marshall's messages were in a similar vein all that December. "Your reports and those of press indicate splendid conduct of your command and troops. The President and Secretary of War and quite evidently the entire American people have been profoundly impressed with your resistance to Japanese endeavors."[38]

Marshall also promised MacArthur a fourth star, and on December 18 Roosevelt sent President Quezon a check for $10 million for war relief. Two days later came promotions for Sutherland to major general, and Marshall, Casey, and Akin became brigadier generals.[39]

Otherwise, MacArthur, his men, and the Philippine people were on their own.

Over the next week, MacArthur and his staff supervised the closing of schools and began the evacuation of Manila residents to the countryside. There were trenches and air-raid shelters to be dug; food and medical supplies to be shipped to new locations; there was even the dispatch of bulldozers to construct new airfields on Manila and Mindanao where MacArthur could put the new planes he still believed Washington would be sending him.

Many on his staff must have pondered their commander's mood. In MacArthur's own mind, his chief duty was to project an unruffled optimism and a Churchill-like defiance of the enemy. When an aide suggested taking down the Stars and Stripes from the HQ, since it made it an obvious target for Japanese bombers, MacArthur shook his head. "Take every normal precaution," he said, "but let's keep the flag flying."[40]

One evening a pair of reporters, one of them John Hersey, caught him standing out in the veranda of 1 Calle Victoria, hatless and feet spread apart, watching a flight of Japanese Betty bombers passing over Manila. A nervous aide asked, "Don't you think you'd better take cover, General?"

MacArthur ignored him. He turned to one of his aides, saying "Give me a cigarette, Eddie," as he continued to watch the planes. One morning another reporter saw him looking the picture of "serenity and confidence," with "his gold-braided cap tilted jauntily . . . and swinging a cane." To someone else, he confided with a slight smile: "You know, I feel Dad's presence here"—a clear source of comfort to the commander of USAFFE and, he must have hoped by saying it, to others.[41]

But there was no disguising the fact that their situation was increasingly desperate. He had only one resource left for saving the Philippines. That was his beloved army, and General Joseph Wainwright's North Luzon Force.

To prevent the Japanese from landing more troops, and to keep those already landed bottled up in the north of the island, Wainwright had exactly three Philippine Army divisions, with 3,000 Americans interspersed with native soldiers who had little training and even less experience, plus a Philippine Scout Cavalry regiment and infantry battalion, a field artillery battery, and a quartermaster depot unit. This was the force that was supposed to hold thousands of square miles of territory and 250 miles of beaches—while the Japanese enjoyed air superiority and complete freedom of movement at sea.[42]

The enemy demonstrated this on December 12 when, again without warning, fresh Japanese troops staged another landing, this time in southeast Luzon near Legaspi. Once again Japanese timing proved superb, while luck told against the Americans. The capture of Legaspi gave the Japanese a rough but usable airstrip, where they installed fighters just in time to intercept three B-17s that were flying up from Del Monte in a valiant effort to beat the Japanese back. Instead, only one bomber made it home, badly shot up; the other two crash-landed in the jungle. MacArthur and Brereton had another grim meeting and agreed that their remaining Flying Fortresses should pull back to Darwin, Australia, before any more were lost.[43]

MacArthur had now lost his entire bomber force—the force that was supposed to be the decisive key to keeping the Japanese from taking the Philippines. Instead, the B-17s had proved far more vulnerable, on the ground or in the air, and far less effective, than anyone predicted. As Richard Marshall sardonically pointed out to Sutherland after the Clark Field disaster, "If we hadn't lost them on the ground at Clark today, we would have lost them later."[44] All the same, it was one more resource gone—and one more sign that nothing could stop the Japanese now.

Outwardly at least, MacArthur did not let the news from Legaspi ruffle his demeanor. He told astonished journalists that he was still waiting for the right moment to strike back. "The basic principle in handling troops," he explained, "is to hold them intact until the enemy has committed himself in force." He had even more far-reaching plans. On December 10, in the midst of digesting the Clark Field disaster, he had sent a message to General Marshall that "a golden opportunity now exists for a master stroke while the enemy is engaged in overextended initial air effort." The master stroke MacArthur had in mind was enticing the Soviet Union to join the fight against Japan, which, he suggested, was "Japan's greatest fear." Marshall never bothered to respond.[45]

The truth was, Russia or no Russia, MacArthur still assumed that the decisive battle for the Philippines would take place in Lingayen Gulf, where his intelligence chief, Colonel Willoughby, predicted the Japanese wouldn't be able to conduct an amphibious landing until December 28, more than two weeks away.[46] But the day after the Appari-Vigan landings, December 13, he suddenly sent a message to President Quezon and to Commissioner Sayre. It instructed them to be ready to leave for Corregidor on four hours' notice.

Quezon in particular was stunned. He had believed MacArthur's earlier promises that the Philippines would be able to hold out against the Japanese. He never imagined he would have to leave Manila or, despite the news about Japanese landings and the daily air raids, that the campaign was already going so badly. That evening he headed out to meet MacArthur at the Manila Hotel.

Because of the threat of Japanese air raids, the building was blacked out and plunged into darkness. But MacArthur met him at the service entrance to the penthouse, and the pair walked down to the garden, where they conversed in whispers.

Quezon could barely contain his anxiety. Did MacArthur really think he should leave Manila? MacArthur hastily explained no, it was just a precaution in case of the worst.

Quezon drew himself up. "I shall stay among my people," he said stoutly, "and suffer the same fate that may befall them."

MacArthur tells us he was moved. "Mr. President," he said, "I expected that answer from such a gallant man as I know you to be." But he had his own duty to fulfill, which was "to prevent you falling into the enemy's hands."

Besides, there was another plan he was also considering. He would declare Manila an open city, meaning that it and all its residents would be neutral in the coming fight and make no resistance to the Japanese.

Quezon was aghast. "Do you mean, General, that tomorrow you will declare Manila an open city and that sometime during the day we shall have to go to Corregidor?"

Again, MacArthur had to reassure him it was only a contingency plan. They simply had to be ready, he said, in case the Japanese managed to land in strength, and the rest of Luzon couldn't be defended.[47]

He did not like to admit it, but that contingency was looking more real every day, especially when the Filipino soldiers under his command were clearly not up to the job. In fact, the very day he received his fourth star from Washington, December 20, the Japanese staged a landing on Mindanao, near Davao—the city with the substantial Japanese colony, but also home to the Philippine 101st Infantry Division.

Corporal Mays was a machine gunner on Davao who had been seconded to the 101st from the U.S. Thirty-first Infantry, in order to stiffen the Philippine troops' fighting morale. As the Japanese came ashore shortly before dawn in four large landing boats, "packed like sardines poured into a can," he and the other Americans guarding the harbor realized that they were on a futile mission. Mays opened up as the Japanese boats got within two hundred yards. "I leveled off all four of them," but the Japanese kept coming and Mays and his Filipino gun crew fell back along with the other troops— eventually getting a ride with an American lieutenant in his Oldsmobile sedan while Japanese planes buzzed overhead and the piers and other buildings caught fire.

Asked by his commanding officer about casualties, Mays answered, "It's hard to say. So many ran." Out of the 1,900 men in his regiment, he figured, there were only 200 still around when they reorganized—and of those missing, not more than 200 had been killed or wounded.[48]

Needless to say, the Japanese secured Davao.

On the evening of December 21 a weary MacArthur sent a radio message to Washington:

> *Aggressive attempts at infiltration increasing both north and south. Enemy air raiding over Luzon, Cebu, and Mindanao. Indications point to progressive building of forces. His naval units move with complete freedom which makes it possible for him to concentrate in force at one or at many points.*

The bulletin concluded with a request that the navy "make some naval threat" to force the Japanese to pull back. Secretary Stimson showed the bulletin to President Roosevelt and Commander in Chief of the U.S. Fleet Admiral Ernest King. All three shook their heads and agreed that something should be done, but nothing was done.[49]

Then MacArthur got the worst news of all. Forty-eight hours earlier, the submarine *Stingray* had spotted a large convoy of Japanese troop transports, escorted by several heavy cruisers, fifty miles off the coast of north Luzon.

They were headed straight for Lingayen Gulf.

In fact, the Japanese landing force under Lieutenant General Masaharu Homma included eighty-five troop transports, together with two battleships, six cruisers, and two dozen destroyers.[50] In the predawn hours of December 22 some 12,000 Japanese soldiers began landing on the beach, while the battleships and cruisers pounded the shore. A few artillery rounds were fired as the landing craft neared the beach, none of which hit their targets; four B-17s passed overhead, strafing and firing on the boats as they tossed in the surf. But they had no bombs to drop. Those had been dropped on Davao, far to the south. They were reduced to being helpless spectators to the debacle now unfolding.[51]

Facing Homma's troops were four Filipino divisions—the Twenty-first, the Seventy-first, the Eleventh, and the Ninety-first—and a battalion of Philippine Scouts backed by a few tanks. The Scouts fought bravely, even charging Japanese tanks on horseback; the other Filipinos fired a few shots and then dropped their rifles and ran. The Seventy-first Division simply disintegrated as a fighting unit. They "were never organized," their commander later commented, "never adequately equipped, and the training was so meager" that their collapse was foreordained.[52]

By 10:30 the Japanese had secured the beaches and were moving inland, toward Route 3, the cobblestone road that led directly to Manila.[53]

That afternoon a grim-faced MacArthur heard the first reports on the course of the fighting in Lingayen Gulf—or more accurately, nonfighting. Sutherland heard him mutter, "What an opportunity for submarines!" But the three American submarines operating in the gulf—*Stingray, Saury,* and *Salmon*—had fired torpedo after torpedo into the massed Japanese ships only to have them fail to explode, thanks to the Mark XIV torpedo's defective detonators.[54] In the end, only two transports were sunk, while swarming Japanese destroyers chased the subs out of the area.

MacArthur had also hoped to persuade Admiral Hart to mine the gulf before withdrawing his ships, but Hart had done nothing. Instead, he had to sit helplessly as—two weeks into the war and before most of his troops had fired a shot—the campaign for the Philippines was virtually decided.

That afternoon MacArthur sent his aide Sid Huff into Manila to buy presents for his wife and son. It was three days before Christmas, but MacArthur told Jean, "We must pretend it's Christmas Eve." Jean opened the boxes with scarves, dresses, and embroidered blouses.

"Sir Boss, they are beautiful," she exclaimed. "Thank you so much."

She carefully rewrapped them and put them away in her closet.

She would never see them again.[55]

This was because MacArthur's mind was already made up. He spoke to General Henry Casey about the demolition of installations and bridges to the north of the city, and at 3:20 he ordered that a call be made to the staff on Corregidor ordering them to prepare the island for becoming his headquarters.

MacArthur then made two fateful decisions that would determine the direction of the rest of the campaign—and haunt him for years to come.

The first was to declare Manila an open city starting on the day after Christmas.[56] The second was to abandon his beach defense plan, on which he and his army had focused all their efforts over the past year, and revert to War Plan Orange. In short, all his forces, including Wainwright's, would now withdraw to the Bataan Peninsula for a last stand.

MacArthur's decision to declare Manila's status as an open city—meaning his troops would not use the city for military purposes and therefore the Japanese should not bomb or attack it—came from the best humanitarian motives, but its initial result was to trigger confusion, not to say panic. For tens of thousands of Manila residents, including American civilians, it meant their war was effectively over, without their having seen a single Japanese soldier. For the military personnel in the city, it induced a mad scramble to pack up and leave—either to join the forces headed for Bataan or to join MacArthur on Corregidor.

One of the most disconcerted by the announcement was Admiral Hart. He and his staff had cached barges of fuel, torpedoes, and other supplies all around the Manila area, in order to keep his submarines running. Now all that would have to be abandoned, along with the navy's piers. He polled his staff about the wisdom of remaining in the Philippines; everyone agreed that without Manila it was pointless. On Christmas Day Hart handed over command of what was left of his Asiatic Fleet to Admiral Francis Rockwell, and left aboard the submarine *Shark*.[57]

MacArthur himself was still in his office supervising the destruction of the army's storage depots and storage tanks. Sutherland reminded him of a nearby warehouse containing war supplies—but also where some 4,000 books of his father's library were stored.

MacArthur's face was expressionless. "Blow it," he said.[58]

For the next two days explosions took place all around Manila, even as Japanese planes continued to rain death and destruction from the sky, bobbing and weaving over the city. Anxious crowds roamed the streets, while shopkeepers boarded up their store windows and others tried to escape into the mountains, or simply sat and wondered what would happen next. Looters began breaking into warehouses along the waterfront, as the possibility of law and order vanished—until the Japanese came.

At the Malacañan Palace, Quezon's private secretary, Jorge Vargas, and Judge Jose Laurel said their good-byes to the Philippine president. "Keep your faith with America," he told them, his voice choking and his eyes brimming with tears. "You two will deal with the Japanese." Then he stood outside, quietly awaiting the arrival of MacArthur's Packard.

MacArthur was saying his own goodbyes. One was to General Brereton. His Air Force commander told him he had ordered all remaining planes, except four P-40s, flown out to Darwin. There was no point in keeping them in the Philippines anymore. They could do nothing to prevent further Japanese landings. MacArthur said he understood.

There was an awkward moment, then MacArthur and Brereton solemnly shook hands.

"I hope you will tell the people outside what we have done and protect my reputation as a fighter," MacArthur said.

Brereton's answer was prompt, and heartfelt.

"General, your reputation will never need any protection." Then he turned and he was gone.[59]

Probably no one person had done more damage to MacArthur's chances in the Philippines than Brereton, by allowing his planes to be caught on the ground on that fateful December 8. Yet MacArthur never once attacked Brereton for the events of that day, not then or later. Our planes "were completely overwhelmed by the enemy's superior forces," he wrote in a press release in 1943. "I attach no blame to General Brereton or other members of the command for the incidents of the battle. Nothing could have saved the day for them."[60]

When Brereton left, MacArthur cleared his desk as he always did before going home, then told an orderly to pick up his personal belongings and take them to the courtyard. There was a growing bonfire of papers as the sun was setting, while trucks were being loaded for the trip to Corregidor.

MacArthur stepped out of his office into the anteroom. "Rogers," he called abruptly. His stenographer, now a corporal, jumped up and found MacArthur looking around at the many mementos of his Philippine years, first as a lieutenant, then as brigadier general, and finally as military advisor, all which would now have to be left behind.

Then MacArthur's eye fell upon a staff in the corner, with a red pennant with four white stars. It was the pennant he had flown from his car when chief of staff.

He pointed. "Rogers, cut off that flag for me."

Flustered, Rogers didn't have scissors or even a knife. So when MacArthur repeated the order, he painstakingly untied the thongs and rolled it up, handing it to his general.

"Thank you." MacArthur tucked it under his arm. He sighed and turned to Sutherland. "Well, Dick, I guess it's time to go. There isn't anything left to do here."[61]

Down in the courtyard were two Packard sedans, their engines panting in the darkness. MacArthur and Sutherland stepped into one, with two privates as guards and escorts following. Rogers climbed into the second, alone, and had to time to admire the plush seats and pull-out bar as they moved out into the deserted street.

They stopped briefly to pick up Jean and little Arthur and his ayah, a stern-faced Chinese lady with the strangely onomatopoeic name of Ah Cheu. They then proceeded to the pier, where they met President Quezon and Commissioner Sayre and a hundred other passengers waiting for the steamer *Don Estaban* to take them to the Rock. Jean had only one suitcase with her, a relic from her traveling days. It still sported a faded travel sticker: GRAND HOTEL—YOKOHAMA.[62]

As they stood waiting they were surrounded by the constant sound of explosions. Ammunition dumps and fuel depots were being blown all around the city. The air around them smelled of burned cordite and gasoline. Arthur grabbed his mother's hand and whimpered, "I want to go home."

Suddenly a figure in a naval uniform stepped out of the gloom. He extended his hand to MacArthur.

It was Admiral Hart. He was there to tell MacArthur that he was handing over command to Rear Admiral Francis Rockwell and leaving on his last remaining warship, the submarine *Shark*. For MacArthur it must have been an awkward moment, exchanging words with the man who he believed had let the Japanese land in Lingayen Gulf without lifting a finger—and had generally let him and his troops down. But even after the *Don Estaban* pulled up along the dock, they continued to talk in low, earnest voices. Then Hart saluted and, like Brereton, was gone.[63]

The passengers trudged up the gangplank, MacArthur being the last. He took a final glance back at Manila before stepping on deck. But there was a delay as a truck pulled up, unloading the Philippine government's supply of gold and silver bullion.[64]

At last they set off. Everyone was standing shoulder to shoulder on the crowded steamer. There wasn't even room for the general to pace. Behind them Manila was bathed in light and smoke, and explosions—while the sky, Paul Rogers remembered, was filled with stars. Off the port bow was a bright glow, as the piers of Cavite continued to burn.

It was Christmas Eve. Some officer started to sing, "Silent Night." At first no one joined in. Then MacArthur and Jean and others in their party took it up, and they continued to sing one carol after another for the rest of the journey.[65]

For MacArthur and everyone else on board, it was a desperate journey into the complete unknown.

Somewhere ahead lay Corregidor, the fortified island that few on the *Don Estaban* had ever visited, and that now was blacked out and invisible in the darkness.

CHAPTER 15
WHEN MEN MUST DIE

Some officers consider the whole thing already lost.

—SGT. PAUL ROGERS'S DIARY,

JANUARY 8, 1942, ENTRY

Never in history was so large and gallant
an army written off so callously.

—DOUGLAS MACARTHUR TO

COL. WARREN CLEAR, FEBRUARY 4, 1942

Evacuating Manila and declaring it an open city was the first of MacArthur's fateful decisions on December 23. The other was to abandon Rainbow Five, which had centered on defending Manila and Subic Bay from the landward side, and revert to War Plan Orange.

In some ways the decision was already made for him, with the revised version of Orange, designated War Plan Orange Three, issued in July 1941.[1] It made the principal mission for American—and by extension Philippine— land forces to deny a Japanese invader use of Manila Bay, by holding Corregidor and the Bataan Peninsula. Although army planners may not have agreed with MacArthur that the Philippines was "the key to the Pacific," they understood that if the Japanese could operate supplies and fleets in and out of Manila, they would have a huge advantage in denying American forces access to the western Pacific—and a tremendous jumping-off point for pushing their forces southward toward Australia.

War Plan Orange Three involved a simple and limited mission. But implementing it now, after MacArthur had dispersed his troops across Luzon, required one of the most difficult maneuvers in warfare: a fighting retreat and

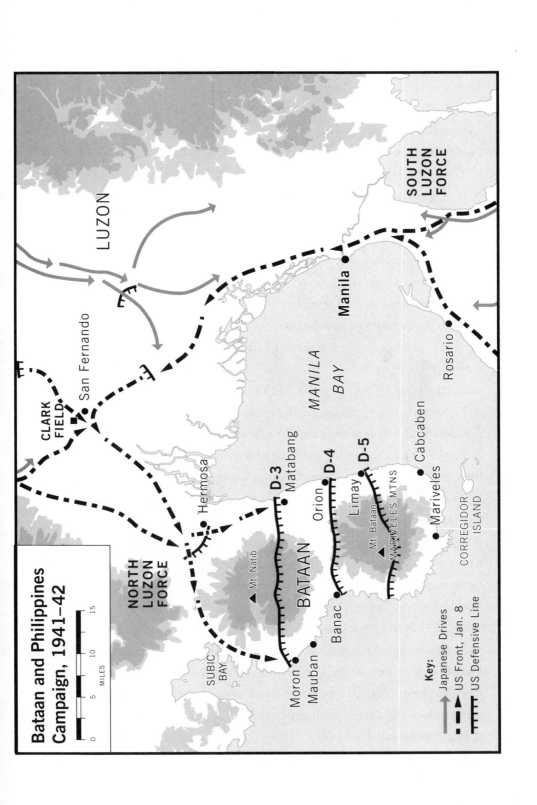

Bataan and Philippines Campaign, 1941–42

MILES
0 5 10 15

LUZON

San Fernando

CLARK FIELD

SUBIC BAY

NORTH LUZON FORCE

Hermosa

Moron
Mauban

▲ Mt. Natib

BATAAN

Banac

Matabang

D-3

Orion

D-4

Limay

D-5

▲ Mt. Bataan

MARIVELES MTNS

Cabcaben

Mariveles

CORREGIDOR ISLAND

MANILA BAY

Manila

Rosario

SOUTH LUZON FORCE

Key:

Japanese Drives

US Front, Jan. 8

US Defensive Line

simultaneous withdrawal, by not one but two forces, Wainwright's North Luzon Force and Major General George Parker's South Luzon Force, now combined into Bataan Force. Either phase could quickly degenerate into a rout, especially if the troops involved lost heart or their commanders failed to maintain contact with each other's moves, or failed to maintain a schedule based on pinpoint timing.

Changing plans in this way involved no hasty decision on MacArthur's part. It was clearly on his mind the minute he learned of the first Japanese landings, and implicit in his warnings to Quezon and Sayre to be prepared to evacuate to Corregidor. On the 22nd, in fact, he had alerted General Marshall of his intention to revert to WPO-3, and Marshall approved.[2]

It was also a plan well known to everyone involved. When headquarters fired off the message on December 23, "WPO-3 is in effect," everyone knew what to do. A series of five defensive positions would be held, to delay the Japanese advance along the central Luzon plain while Bataan itself made ready for defense. To buy extra time, the revised plan used Wainwright's men, backed by 192nd and 194th Tank Battalions made up of National Guard units, to hold off the Japanese north of the city of San Fernando where Route 8, the main highway into the Bataan Peninsula, started, until January 8, while Parker's South Luzon Force would head west and north to San Fernando and then cut south to Bataan. The Calumpit Bridge over the Pampanga was the all-critical juncture: it had to be held at all costs until the last of Parker's men had gotten across.

On December 24 the Twenty-first Division started its withdrawal.[3] By 4:00 A.M. on Christmas Day most had reached Aguilar, although it was not until afternoon that most had reached North Luzon Force's first defensive line, D-1. Army trucks, soldiers, animal-drawn carts, civilian cars, and thousands of Philippine civilians followed in their wake.

The term "defensive line" was a misnomer. The positions that MacArthur, his staff, and officers on the ground had sketched out on their maps actually stretched for miles over a wide variety of terrain—farther, in fact, than their thin forces could defend against determined attack. Each line was to be occupied before dawn and held during the day; then the exhausted troops would pull back under the cover of night to the next line, and the entire process would start again.[4]

Meanwhile, a mad scramble was on to get supplies that had been moved out to support the beach defenses during MacArthur's original plan back into Bataan, by truck, rail, boat, even oxcart. Many officers, however, knew that many of the supplies would never make it.

One of the biggest depots on Luzon was Fort Stotsenburg near Clark Field. As part of the evacuation, its nearly 300,000 gallons of gasoline as well as high-octane aviation fuel had to be blown up—and tons of food, clothing, and military supplies abandoned. Meanwhile huge stockpiles of food set aside in the central Luzon plain, including more than one million pounds of rice, could find no transport and had to be left behind.[5] Even more valuable stockpiles of ammunition fared no better.

Reverting to War Plan Orange Three made strategic sense. But the men defending Bataan were going to find themselves short on food, supplies, and ammunition even before the battle started.

At 8:30 P.M. the *Don Estaban* finally chugged to a halt at Corregidor's North Dock.

The passengers, including MacArthur and his party, disembarked from the boat in inky darkness. Corregidor's commanding officer, Major General Moore, was there to meet him. Their destination was the 1,400-foot-long, 30-foot-wide Malinta Tunnel that American engineers had dug into the rock of Malinta Hill, rising 400 feet above the sea. In the eerie gloom cast by blue mercury vapor lights they followed the railroad track running down its main shaft past the tunnel's twenty-five 400-foot-long lateral branches, along with another network of tunnels that would serve as the island's field hospital.

The Quezons would be bunked in the hospital section, Moore explained. Though the president's tuberculosis left him often helpless with hacking coughing fits, he would have to endure the dank, damp air of the tunnel.

"We've partitioned off another section for women," Moore said apologetically. "We've never had women around here before, and things may be a little crude."

MacArthur looked around him, then announced that he would never live in this dank cavern.

"Where are your quarters?" he asked Moore.

"Topside," Moore answered, meaning the flat northern part of Corregidor, with barracks, officers' quarters, and offices, rising from cliffs more than six hundred feet above the water.

"We'll move in there tomorrow morning."

Moore tactfully pointed out that Topside, and his own quarters, were exposed to almost daily Japanese air attack.

"That's fine," MacArthur replied. "Just the thing."[6] At midnight President Quezon and his fellow Filipinos celebrated Christmas Mass in the tunnel.

The next morning Sid Huff had scarcely settled down in his new billet on Topside when he was ordered to see MacArthur. The general had assigned everyone on his staff quarters on Topside despite the threat of Japanese air raids, while a small cottage nearby became home to Jean, MacArthur, and little Arthur. From the veranda MacArthur could admire the view of Bataan, just two miles away. During the day, however, he shared an office with Sutherland at the end of Lateral Tunnel No. 3, and that's where Huff found the general.

"I need you to go back to Manila," MacArthur announced to Huff. "There's some documents I need there."

As Huff recovered from his shock and surprise, the commander of USAFFE added, "While you're in my apartment look in the bedside table, where you'll find my Colt .45—the one I carried in the First World War. Bring that. And if you look in the cupboard you'll see my old campaign hat. I'd like to have that."

Huff nodded, saluted, and made ready to go. Then MacArthur had a final thought.

"I think if you look in the dining room you may see a bottle of Scotch. Just as well bring that too. It may be a long cold winter over here."[7]

Huff set out that night in one of Commander Bulkeley's torpedo boats to evade enemy planes. At the Manila Pier he found a city on the verge of moral and civic dissolution. Marshall's demolition teams were still continuing their work, as the moist night air was punctuated by the sounds of explosions and the sky was lit on all sides by bonfires of supplies and stockpiles of ammunition.

Crowds of looters continued to roam the streets night and day, as Huff found out when he set out the next morning to round up the general's things and buy some additional supplies for Jean and little Arthur. Yet stores remained open, in a brave show of normalcy. There were two forlorn Santa Clauses out on the Escolta; one of them was grimly piling sandbags in front of his store. Huff came back to Corregidor under cover of darkness, laden with MacArthur's hat and gun, oranges and jars of baby food for little Arthur—and General MacArthur's bottle of Scotch.[8]

MacArthur's new headquarters were on the ground floor of the artillery barracks on Topside. It occupied three rooms in the southeast corner of the building, sheltered by a veranda that faced the parade ground. MacArthur took over a corner office, with Sutherland next door. Willoughby, Sutherland's aide Lieutenant Colonel Francis Wilson, and some clerks and Rogers, shared the third.[9]

From the veranda MacArthur could look out over the 2.75 square miles of the island, with a golf course adjoining the parade grounds. Next to Topside sat Middleside, with more quarters for officers and noncoms, a hospital, a white clapboard service club, and schools for service families' children.[10] From there the land fell away to the east almost to sea level, where a strip of land six hundred yards wide dubbed Bottomside offered docks, warehouses, a small barrio, and the island's power plant—the plant that generated electricity not only for the island's wells and refrigeration plant, but also powered the electric railroad that supplied Corregidor's military installations.

Those were formidable, at least by the standard of the First World War. Corregidor bristled with massive coastal artillery pieces, most housed in impregnable concrete bunkers, while three smaller adjoining islands—Fort Hughes, Fort Frank, and Fort Drum—sported similar heavy artillery. Fort Drum itself, which guarded the southern entrance to Manila Bay, was built like a concrete battleship with twenty-foot-thick walls and fourteen-inch guns, while antiaircraft batteries ringed the island's principal peaks, including Topside and Malinta Hill.

No enemy ship could pass in or out of Manila Bay without coming under withering fire from Fort Drum's guns, or the other batteries. No wonder MacArthur could confidently tell his staff that the Japanese might "have the bottle" by occupying Manila and the surrounding bay, but "I have the cork."[11]

There was only one problem. While Corregidor might be impregnable from the sea, no one had considered what would happen if it came under determined attack from the air, especially if bombs knocked out its vital power plant. The island had a tiny airstrip, but no warplanes—and the anti-aircraft guns were old, with second-rate ammunition.

That day they had their first air raid. Antiaircraft fire drove off the bombers, which then headed on to pound Manila and Cavite. Some of MacArthur's staff breathed a sigh of relief; maybe they were invulnerable to air attack after all.

Others who knew better said nothing. They knew the optimists would learn the truth soon enough.

The next day Manila was officially an open city. Little changed on the ground. People continued to stream out of the city into the hills. Conventional haunts like the Yacht Club and hotel bars "looked like funeral parlors," according to one eyewitness. But there were some changes. American officers still completing their demolition jobs passed without sidearms; American flags disappeared from flag poles. Japanese prisoners of war were set free and, unarmed, wandered the streets like tourists.[12]

The biggest change was the night the blackout ended. From Corregidor the defenders could see the bright glow—although not as bright as before the war. MacArthur would have watched as he smoked a last cigarette before heading for bed. The island was quiet; for a few hours the war must have seemed very far away. The only indication that it was still on was the arrival of men from the Fourth Marines, who had come to Corregidor from their positions on the opposite side of the bay, as part of the last evacuation of American forces.

The marines would be part of the island's last-ditch defense, if or when Bataan fell. MacArthur hoped, and perhaps even believed, that would not happen. He was still convinced that help from America and Hawaii would arrive in time.

"I can give you anything but time," Napoleon used to tell his generals. Yet that was what MacArthur was asking for now; not just from Wainwright and Jones, his commanders on Bataan, but from himself. Time for Washington to order a relief convoy, to send help, to redeem its promise to the Philippine people—and to save its most distinguished general from inevitable defeat and capture.

Soon after the war, a reporter asked MacArthur if he really believed Washington would send help in time to save him and his army. "By God, I did believe it," MacArthur exploded. "And you know, those messages didn't say yes, but they didn't say no. They [were] full of meanings that could be interpreted two ways.

"I see now," he added sadly, "I may have deluded myself."[13]

One such message came from General Marshall on December 27. It was in response to what Marshall called the "splendid conduct of your command and troops through trials of Christmas Day. . . . Your reports on arrangement of your command setup and disposition of your air forces are acknowledged." It added, "The president again personally directed the navy to make every effort to support you. You can rest assured [the]War Department will do all in its power in Far East to completely dominate that region."[14]

MacArthur radioed back: "The following is my present strategic concept of the situation. Enemy penetration of the Philippines resulted from our weakness on the sea and in the air," especially the withdrawal of Admiral Hart and the navy. "The enemy has utter freedom of naval and air movement," and this, he predicted, would give them complete freedom for air operations from Mindanao to assist the conquest of the Dutch East Indies. MacArthur was reiterating his most intimate fear: that the fall of the Philippines would have a domino effect, threatening the entire region. It was, he stressed, essential that the United States Navy act. "Strong naval forces must seek combat with the enemy," he wired. It was an optimistic view that the navy itself, with its biggest battleships sunk or crippled at Pearl Harbor, was not inclined to endorse. That didn't matter to MacArthur. "I wish to emphasize the necessity for naval action," he concluded, "and for rapid execution by land, sea, and air."[15]

Combined operations on the scale MacArthur envisioned had never existed before in the U.S. military—or indeed in most other militaries around the world.

More importantly, there were no resources to be had. Instead, while the navy nursed its wounds and cleared up the debris from the December 7 attack, there was only a shortwave radio message. It came from President Roosevelt to the Philippine people. The refugees jammed in the tunnels and on Topside of Corregidor could eavesdrop as the familiar sonorous voice with its mid-Atlantic accent voiced these confident words:

> News of your gallant struggle against the Japanese aggression has elicited the profoundest admiration of every American. The people of the United States will never forget what the people of the Philippine Islands are doing this day and will do in the days to come. I give to the people of the Philippine Islands my solemn pledge that their freedom will be redeemed and their independence established and protected. The entire resources, in men and in materials, of the United States stand behind that pledge . . . The Philippines may rest assured. . . . The United States Navy is following an intensive and well planned campaign against the Japanese forces which will result in positive assistance to the defense of the Philippines.[16]

That was on December 28. The next day saw the first serious Japanese air raid on Corregidor.

It began at 11:45 when the air-raid siren blasted a warning, just as MacArthur's forward echelon staff on Topside was starting to think about lunch. The officers quickly left their desks and headed for the veranda to check the number and type of aircraft.

MacArthur was there, of course. He was carrying a brown curved-handle walnut cane under his arm, with his cap pushed back on his head, and a Lucky Strike stuck in his black cigarette holder. He was casually counting off the Japanese bombers as they came in, "as coolly as if keeping [a] baseball score," an eyewitness remembered, and muttering to himself, "seventy-one, seventy-two, seventy-three . . ."

There were in fact more than eighty, plus ten dive bombers, and as the first bombs dropped the spectators realized that this was no idle raid. This was meant to annihilate MacArthur and his command as decisively as they had overwhelmed Pearl Harbor.

"I guess we're in for it," Sutherland muttered as he watched. Most were too paralyzed with shock to nod and agree.[17]

The bombs hit the water first, throwing up great geysers, then began exploding on Topside as dirt and smoke flew in all directions. MacArthur told Jean to take shelter at once. She grabbed little Arthur and dashed into a bomb shelter, whose iron door refused to shut behind them so that with each bomb burst it banged and clanged from the blast. Shortly afterward, a bomb hit the cottage where they had all been standing, destroying the structure.

MacArthur continued to watch, standing in the open on the veranda. Then a bomb exploded close, almost too close, throwing shrapnel in every direction. MacArthur stooped behind a hedge, and his orderly, Sergeant Domingo Adversario, stripped off his own tin helmet and shoved it on MacArthur's head. Just then a shard of shrapnel ripped past them both, tearing open Adversario's hand and denting the helmet, but leaving the general unharmed. MacArthur wrapped up his sergeant's hand himself as the bombs kept falling. Later he made sure Adversario got the Purple Heart.

In the midst of the pandemonium, Sutherland was still working at his desk—even though a chunk of shrapnel had killed a Marine standing in MacArthur's office. Corporal Rogers, like the others, curled up under his desk when the first wave of bombers passed and the buzzer sounded.

Rogers then trotted down the hall with his steno pad in hand. Sutherland had just begun dictating another memo when they heard a second wave of bombers passing overhead. Outside there was another deafening clatter as explosions rocked the room. Japanese bombs delivered direct hits on the station hospital and the barracks. Army doctor Captain John K. Wilson was outside searching for casualties as planes continued to pass overhead, bombing and strafing. He ran into MacArthur out there, and MacArthur stopped counting planes long enough to ask Wilson about casualties.

Between explosions, the doctor gave the commander of USAFFE his best-guess answer. In the end there would be twenty-two dead and eighty wounded. The two men spoke for only two or three minutes, but Dr. Wilson remembered later it was more like two or three hours.[18]

Finally, after bombing Corregidor continuously for three hours and fifty minutes, the planes faded into the distance. Topside was a smoking ruin, with a circle of bomb craters ringing the headquarters end of the barracks, which had virtually collapsed. Power was out all across the island; the power generator on Bottomside had taken a direct hit. Meanwhile, soldiers and civilians were scrambling to retrieve the wounded and put out the scattered fires.

MacArthur was standing outside, impervious to the destruction around him. When Jean found him, he was adjusting the bandages on Sergeant Adversario's arm. The general smiled ruefully at his wife and gestured toward the debris. "Look what they've done to the garden," he said.[19]

That evening they reluctantly moved out of Topside.

In the end his staff found a small house for the MacArthurs down on Bottomside, not far from the damaged power plant. The place was entirely unfurnished, and Sid Huff and others had to scrounge around to find everything from beds and an overstuffed armchair to a refrigerator, complete with a bullet hole through the door.[20] For a couple of days until the power plant was repaired, everyone had to drink brackish water and read reports by candlelight. Meanwhile, Doc Wilson was using a flashlight to work on the wounded at the hospital.

MacArthur's disappointment and chagrin were lightened somewhat by reports from Wainwright. The withdrawal was proceeding as planned; the North Luzon Force had pulled back to the Bamban-Arayat line in front of San Fernando, the last stop before crossing to the Bataan Peninsula. The South Luzon Force was expected to clear San Fernando on January 1. Within forty-eight hours the two halves of his army would be united and ready to defend Bataan.[21]

Before the day was over MacArthur paid a visit to Quezon in the tunnel. The president's tuberculosis was bad, made worse by the damp conditions in his tunnel quarters. He was barely able to get words out between agonizing fits of hacking coughing. But he got out enough words to make it clear that he was furious about MacArthur's remaining out in the open during the raid like that.

The general drew himself upright. "Don't you know," he said in his sonorous voice, "the Japanese haven't yet made the bomb with my name on it?"

He smiled, then said seriously, "Of course, I understand what you mean, and I have no right to gamble with my life, but it's absolutely necessary [that] at the right time a commander take chances." Then the men under his command, MacArthur said, when "they see the man at the top risking his life, the man at the bottom says, 'I guess if that old man can take it, I can, too.' "[22]

In a few weeks the men on Bataan would have a very different perspective on MacArthur and his future prospects for mortality.

The day after the big raid, December 30, a solemn ceremony took place at the mouth of the Malinta Tunnel. It was the second inauguration of President Quezon.

The first had been a magnificent affair, with U.S. Vice President John Nance Garner in attendance and whirling couples dancing in the candlelight at Malacañan Palace. This time a team of marines had hammered together a wooden platform on an outdoor cooking site. Two wooden folding chairs were set on the crude dais, one for MacArthur and one for Quezon, as a chaplain's organ played "Hail to the Chief."[23] Then Quezon took the oath of office and spoke to the small throng assembled there. He spoke of the future of the Philippines as an independent country, then turned to MacArthur.

"No words in any language," he said between bouts of coughing, "can express to you the deep gratitude of the Filipino people and my own for your devotion to our cause, the defense of our country, and the safety of our population." Quezon sat down, and then MacArthur spoke in tones so low that even those closest to the dais had to strain to hear him.

"Never in all history," he said, "has there been a more solemn and significant inauguration. An act, symbolical of democratic processes, is placed against the background of a sudden, merciless war. The thunder of death and destruction, dropped from the skies, can be heard in the distance. Such is the bed of birth of this new government, of this new nation."

His final words were these: "Through this, its gasping agony of travail, through what Winston Churchill called 'blood, sweat, and tears,' from the grim shadow of death, oh merciful God, preserve this noble race." Then he turned away, his face wet with tears.[24]

That same day in Washington, Roosevelt fired off a memorandum to Secretary of War Stimson and Secretary of the Navy Henry Knox. "I wish that War Plans would explore every possible means of relieving the Philippines," it read. "I realize great risks are involved but the object is important."[25]

It was a vain, if not fatuous, hope. The new commander of the Pacific Fleet, Chester Nimitz, was in Pearl Harbor surveying the damage from the air raid three weeks earlier. The air still smelled of burned oil and scorched metal and wood. In his pocket were his operational orders from the commander of the U.S. Fleet, Admiral King. They were to secure a sea communications and supply line between the West Coast, Hawaii, and Midway Island, and a second sea link between the West Coast and Australia via Samoa, New Caledonia, and Fiji. Nothing more.[26]

This was a navy operating on an emergency shoestring, and on the defensive. Relieving MacArthur in the Philippines could play no part in its plans.

Meanwhile, the evacuation of Manila continued until New Year's Eve.

The city was still burning, not just from American demolition but from constant air attack. The open city declaration made no impression on the Japanese; their planes continued to bomb and strafe anything that moved in and around the city. "To the native population," wrote one eyewitness for the *Saturday Evening Post*, "encircled by fires, bewildered, panic-stricken . . . it seemed like the end of the world."[27]

Another eyewitness remembered "heaps of wreckage and crumbled ruins were everywhere" while bombed ships burned brightly in Manila Bay.[28] At the docks enormous piles of goods sat ready to be shipped out—all too late to make it to Bataan or Corregidor. Instead, scores of beggars and priests, children and old men, were combing through the piles "like flies on a dung hill," remembered one of the last Americans to leave, civilian engineer Robert Cartwell. "Filipinos who had never owned more than a loin-cloth and bolo in all their lives, saw laid before them a fortune"—and took what they could.[29]

For almost forty years Manila had been the key outpost of American civilization in the Far East. Now it was a smoldering ruin, wreathed in smoke and fire.

Far off in Washington, Henry Stimson sat at his desk and wrote in his diary.

"The last day of the old year, and a pretty gloomy one, for the Japanese are encircling Manila and the fall of the city is very imminent. MacArthur seems to be making a successful and skillful retreat to the peninsula of Bataan and Corregidor. But the psychological effect on the Filipinos is very bad, coming after the defeat at Hawaii, the effect here in this country is also very bad . . . I think and trust our people will have enough steadfastness to carry through the work of driving the invaders out and reestablishing our effort in the Philippines, but I foresee many difficulties . . . and a long strain."[30]

Back in the Philippines, as the last day of 1941 turned to New Year's Day 1942, General Wainwright was standing in the blackness on the Calumpit Bridge. Beneath him were two 8,000-pound dynamite charges that had been suspended underneath the steel bridge's double spans.

Nicknamed "Skinny" since West Point days, Wainwright was tall, thin, and rawboned. He was a born cavalryman who had successfully made the transition to modern warfare with its planes and tanks, and had become MacArthur's most able field commander. Wainwright was also known for an overfondness for the whiskey bottle, which sometimes worried MacArthur.

He was stone-cold sober now. A team of engineers, led by Colonel Harry Skerry, were crouched nearby around a detonator plunger. They were waiting for Wainwright's signal to blow up the bridge, which would seal off Bataan Peninsula from the Japanese.

If Wainwright had a moment to reflect in the sticky darkness, his "fighting withdrawal" that was supposedly one of the most difficult of all military operations, had gone very well, all things considered—so well that it would later become a textbook case.[31] With MacArthur meticulously issuing orders at every stage, North Luzon Force's pullback had managed to stay ahead of the Japanese advance without becoming a rout, all in time to rendezvous with General Albert Jones's South Luzon Force retreating westward with Manila at their backs.

There had been nasty moments. On December 29 General Homma—who understood exactly what MacArthur and Wainwright were up to—had tried to break North Luzon Force's next-to-last defensive line, dubbed D-4, by driving through the center, hoping it would cut Wainwright's command in half. Instead the Japanese attack ran into stiff resistance from the Philippine Eleventh Division as it held fast at a key roadblock, but on the right Wainwright's line began to sag, and he had been forced to order a full retreat before everything gave way.[32]

The truth was, all the lines that North Luzon Force had to hold existed more on maps than they did in reality. "Not a single position was really occupied and organized for defense," MacArthur's overall intelligence estimate said later. "Troops were barely stopped and assigned defensive sectors before they stampeded into further withdrawal, in some instances without firing a shot."

Yet somehow it had worked, just as somehow Jones's command, South Luzon Force, had managed to find its way west toward San Fernando.[33] In this fighting withdrawal MacArthur had been helped by two things. The first was that the bulk of Homma's troops were moving toward taking the capital, Manila, not pursuing the Philippine Army. The other was that even though the Japanese enjoyed complete air superiority, they had directed their air attack at targets in and around Manila instead of the long drawn-out convoys of trucks, oxcarts, footsore soldiers, and terrified refugees that marked the North Luzon Force withdrawal. "Had the [Japanese] bombers struck the jammed columns with bombs and strafing," noted Colonel James Collier, "our withdrawal would certainly have been seriously crippled"—and probably would never have succeeded.[34]

Also fortuitously, the Japanese had never bombed the Calumpit Bridge, an action that would have cut off South Luzon Force—which was slated to clear the bridge by New Year's Day.

That was what Wainwright was waiting for when suddenly he heard the rumbling of tanks in the darkness.

With a knot in his stomach, Wainwright wondered whether he should give the signal to blow the bridge at once, to keep any Japanese tanks from grabbing the objective. But then he breathed a sigh of relief. They were American tanks, National Guardsmen with Company C of the 192nd, who had blocked the Japanese advance at Baliuag, as Japanese and American tanks chased each other up and down the narrow streets.[35] Company C had managed to knock out eight Japanese tanks with no losses of their own, while heavy and accurate artillery fire had covered their withdrawal and the last elements of South Luzon Force. By the time the Japanese recovered and surged forward past Baliuag, the Americans and Filipinos were gone.

Hour by hour, Wainwright watched the exhausted men of South Luzon Force trudge out of the darkness and cross the bridge. By 5:00 A.M. the last rear-guard unit, the Fifty-first Infantry, made it across. That left only a platoon of Filipino demolition engineers under Lieutenant Colonel Narciso Manzano on the road south of Calumpit. They waited until 6:15, when Wainwright decided he could wait no longer, and with a rumble and a roar, the charges went off as the remains of the Calumpit Bridge tumbled into the deep, unfordable Pampagna. Manzano and his men would have to find some other way back. For now, MacArthur's army—or what was left of it—was safe.[36]

There was no denying their numbers were sadly depleted—Wainwright had left Lingayen with 28,000 men and now had barely 16,000—as men became lost, or simply ran away, in the jungle. But the troops who were left were fitter, more motivated, and more cohesive than before the Japanese had landed. Still dressed in their old-fashioned coconut-style helmets, blue tunics, and white trousers, the Philippine Army had become, as one participant remembered, "a fighting force."[37]

But there was also no denying that they were starting the defense of Bataan with supplies at a low ebb. The original War Plan Orange had envisaged enough food and ammunition to keep a fighting army of 43,000 in the field for six months. They had nowhere near those supplies now—and the numbers of troops who had to be fed and armed were closer to 80,000, including airmen and sailors who had lost their planes and ships. There were also 26,000 civilians, American and Filipino, who were taking shelter on Bataan and who would have to be fed as well.

But for now MacArthur could take pleasure and pride in the operation. Not a single major unit had been lost or even cut off during the two-week pullback, despite constant pressure from the enemy. It was, in the words of the official army historian, "a tribute to the generalship of MacArthur, Wainwright, Jones, and to American leadership on the field of battle."[38] That afternoon back on Corregidor he got the final message from Wainwright: withdrawal completed without major loss of men or materiel. The final defense of Bataan was about to begin.[39]

The next day, January 2, MacArthur looked out with his binoculars clear across Manila Bay and saw something peculiar flying from his penthouse roof atop the Manila Hotel. His face twisted into a strange crooked smile.

It was a flag with a large red sunburst. The Japanese were in Manila.

That next day in Washington, Marshall met with his staff at the War Department. The picture they drew was sobering. To relieve the Philippines would require at least 1,500 aircraft of all types, seven to nine battleships, five to seven carriers, fifty destroyers, and sixty submarines—plus auxiliary and support ships. Even if it were possible, they concluded, it would "constitute an entirely unjustifiable diversion of forces from the principal theater—the Atlantic."[40]

The final nail in the coffin for any plan to relieve the Philippines came from General Gerow, who had commanded the Philippine Department before MacArthur took over. Gerow recognized that MacArthur had been right—the Philippines was indeed "the key to the Far East position" of the Allied Powers, and that if Japan took the Philippines, the Dutch East Indies and Singapore would soon follow. China would be isolated, and Australia threatened.

All the same, the best the Allies and the United States could hope for now was to hold a line from Australia and the Malay Barrier to Burma while "projecting operations northward to provide maximum defense in depth." Gerow recommended that "operations for the relief of the Philippines not be undertaken."[41]

Marshall bowed to Gerow's judgment, and his staff. But he would never tell MacArthur. Instead, for the next month and a half he and the president would continue to send messages that would encourage hope of coming relief without actually lying to the commander of U.S. Armed Forces Far East.

It was not a comfortable decision. Stimson in particular felt the dilemma acutely. In late December, Marshall and Secretary Stimson met with Winston Churchill. The joint Anglo-American decision to win the war in Europe first had already been made, but when Roosevelt proposed shipping the supplies slated for MacArthur to Britain instead, Stimson angrily rebuffed the idea. He even threatened to resign.[42] The supplies remained where they were, at the San Francisco docks, waiting for ships to carry them west to Asia— ships that would never arrive.

Now Stimson and Marshall had to tell Churchill the truth: there was no hope of saving the Philippines and no plan for evacuation. Astonished, Churchill asked what the Americans intended to do. Stimson said simply, "There are times when men have to die."

Unless a miracle happened, it would be the epitaph for the U.S. Armed Forces Far East—and for MacArthur.

Miracles, of course, do happen, especially in wartime. And certainly if God Himself decided to create a place where a small defensive force could hold off a much larger army for an indefinite time, Bataan would be it.[43]

Twenty-five miles long, and twenty miles across at its widest point, the peninsula was covered with jungle, deep ravines, and only two roads suitable for motor vehicles. One, Route 110, ran down the east coast to Mariveles at the southern tip and up the west coast to Morong, a small town two-thirds of the way up the peninsula. The other ran east to west like a waist belt, passing between the Mariveles Mountains to the south and the towering peak of Mount Natib rising 4,111 feet in the center of the peninsula—suitable, at least in theory, for shifting troops east to west to meet attackers trying to come down Route 110 on either side.

Any attacker was at a severe disadvantage in every respect. He had a lack of roads for moving troops and supplies, a lack of room for moving around a defender's flank, and no way forward except along the coast or across jungle so thick, especially on the western side, that a man couldn't advance a step without a compass and a machete or bolo in his hands. In addition, the thick jungle canopy, in Colonel Skerry's words, "concealed the works of the defender even when the enemy had constant air superiority and air observation."[44]

The Japanese were facing an impossible task. No wonder morale in Bataan Force was looking up despite the long retreat since before Christmas. "We have run far enough," one officer confidently noted, "now we'll stand and take 'em on."

For MacArthur, taking the Japanese on meant splitting Bataan Force in two. Wainwright himself would be defending the west coast approaches with I Corps, consisting of three Philippine Divisions: the First, Thirty-first, and Ninety-first, with some detached combat units, including the Twenty-sixth Cavalry of Philippine Scouts, and a couple of field batteries—22,500 men in all. Holding the other side of Mount Natib along a line running east to Abucay was General Parker's II Corps, with four Philippine Army divisions, the Fifth-seventh Infantry of the Philippine Scouts, and some artillery—about 25,000 men in all. Eight miles back, still finishing dispositions for a final line of defense when all else failed, was an operational reserve consisting of the crack Philippine Division, MacArthur's remaining tanks, and some self-propelled artillery.[45]

Opposing them would be more than 80,000 Japanese, plus multiple squadrons of bombers and fighters and a Japanese navy now in full control of every seaward approach. As the new year of 1942 dawned, General Homma and his staff were as confident of an easy victory as MacArthur's men were of making that victory as tough and bloody as possible.

And here the Japanese made a mistake. So confident was Tokyo that Homma was facing a demoralized force on the run and short on rations, that it pulled away his best troops for operations in the Dutch East Indies. Homma protested, but to no avail. Instead he was left with the Sixty-fifth Brigade to spearhead the attack on Bataan, an occupation unit of overage veterans "absolutely unfit for combat duty."[46]

Whatever his inner doubts, on January 4 Homma ordered the Sixth-fifth Brigade to take up their main battle position. It would take them four days to reach their destination. By then MacArthur had been forced to make a fateful decision. On January 5 the supply situation was already so dire that he ordered everyone on Bataan on half rations—roughly 2,000 calories a day, enough to keep civilians from going hungry but hardly enough to keep active soldiers working and fighting in the jungle eighteen to twenty hours a day. "Each day's combat, each day's output of physical energy," as one officer wrote in his diary, "took its toll of the human body—a toll which could not be repaired."[47]

The first shot had not been fired, and yet a specter already haunted MacArthur's forces on Bataan—the specter of starvation.

*   *   *

Still, it was MacArthur's job to keep the Bataan Force upbeat and motivated, so on the evening of January 9 Sutherland sent a message to both Parker and Wainwright: Have all general officers assemble to receive an important visitor. MacArthur was leaving the Rock to visit his troops on Bataan.

Events were already moving ahead of him. On that very day, January 9, the Japanese began their preliminary assault on II Corps with a massive bombardment that "shook the northern portion of the Bataan peninsula." Parker's 155 mm artillery replied with a ferocious barrage of its own, as shells thundered down on the advancing Japanese column. It was a signal that the American and Filipino forces weren't running away; they were there to stay. There was no direct contact between infantry units as yet, but that would change very soon.

On the 10th a PT boat pulled up at the Mariveles pier with MacArthur and Sutherland on board. A car carried them up to Parker's headquarters, where he met his principal officers and inspected the lines. "I had to see the enemy or I could not fight him," MacArthur later wrote in his *Reminiscences*. "Reports, no matter how penetrating, have never been able to replace the picture shown to my eyes." Then he took the east-west Pilar-Bagac road until he met Wainwright and his waiting officers.[48]

"Jonathan," MacArthur said, "I'm glad to see you back." He congratulated Wainwright on his successful withdrawal, saying it was "as fine as anything in history." For that, he was recommending Wainwright for permanent major general in the Regular Army—not just the USAFFE. Very pleased and flattered, Wainwright then offered to show MacArthur his 155 mm emplacements.

"I don't want to see them," MacArthur said stoutly. "I want to hear them"—in other words, hear them pounding the enemy.[49]

Then he turned to the other officers. One of them was Cliff Bluemel, commander of the Philippine Thirty-first Division.

"Help is definitely on the way," he told them. "We must hold out until it arrives. It can arrive at any time. Parker is fighting the enemy on the Manila Bay side and he'll hold them. He'll throw them back. We've just got to hold out until help arrives."[50]

MacArthur, of course, was mistaken. Help was *not* on the way, although he did not know it yet. But he was right about one thing, at least. Parker *was* throwing them back, all the next day when the Japanese Sixty-fifth Brigade renewed its attack along the Abucay line. A blizzard of artillery fire once again sent them reeling in retreat, but by late that night the Japanese had managed to reach a sugarcane field in front of the Fifty-seventh Infantry. The Sixty-fifth's full-scale attack would be met by the Philippine Scouts in their first combat experience.

Around midnight "a great shout of 'Banzai' came from the front," Lieutenant Colonel Philip Fry, commander of Second Battalion, remembered, "and the Japs started a Civil War charge. I got [Captain] Haas on the phone and told him to sweep I Company's front with his machine guns. It was slaughter." When the attack faded and died, Fry's men had suffered fewer than five wounded. The Scouts whooped with triumph. Fry sternly warned them to expect another serious attack soon.

It came at 1:00 A.M., preceded by small-arms and mortar fire. This time the Scouts and Americans opened with everything they had, including 75 mm artillery, as wave after wave of screaming Japanese headed for the barbed wire in front of the Fifty-seventh's I Company, some throwing themselves on the wire as human bridges for the Japanese soldiers following them.[51]

Firing furiously, I Company tried to stand its ground as first light came up. When its commander was seriously wounded, however, the men began to fall back. Fry threw L Company in to plug the gap, but when this failed, the Fifty-seventh's commander, Colonel Clarke, sent in a company of his reserve battalion. The line was still holding when Japanese tanks arrived, but many Japanese were infiltrating around the ends of the Second Battalion's lines and opening up with light machine guns on the exposed flank. All day teams of volunteers had to ferret out the snipers one by one. The most effective group was led by a junior lieutenant, Alex "Sandy" Nininger, who had arrived in the Philippines back in November, as part of reinforcements. With a Garand rifle, a Japanese submachine gun, and an armful of grenades, Nininger brought down one Japanese infiltrator after another like a hunter on safari.

Then on one of his ventures into the thicket, he didn't come back. His men later found him propped up against a tree, dead. Three Japanese soldiers who had charged with bayonets were dead at his feet. Nininger would win the first posthumous Medal of Honor of the Second World War.[52]

The fighting dragged on all that day and night, as the Scouts counterattacked again and again until they found themselves back at their original line. At dawn on January 12 the scene that greeted the surviving Scouts "was one of utter chaos and devastation," the regiment's adjutant, John Olson, remembered. "Broken and bloody bodies were sprawled all over the foxholes and open ground throughout the I and left of K Company sectors. . . . Mangled Japanese bodies were strung on the barbed wire like dirty laundry." It was a scene MacArthur had witnessed dozens of times during his war in France, but it was new to these young Americans and Filipinos. Occasionally the quiet was broken by shots as the Scouts rooted out the last resistance. But no one, least of all the Japanese, seemed eager to resume the battle.[53]

The Fifty-seventh had lost more than a hundred men in the battle of the cane field, and the Japanese had left between two hundred and three hundred dead behind. Their total casualties were considerably more.[54] It had been an American-Filipino victory, but there had also been problems that were harbingers of trouble to come.

Lieutenant Colonel Fry, for example, discovered that the ammunition for his heavy mortars was World War One vintage, and six out of every ten shells had been duds—and the ammo for the new light mortars had never arrived, forcing them to abandon their guns. When the Fifty-seventh's executive officer tried to get additional ammunition and supply to replace what had been lost, those in charge said no: his request exceeded their standard replacement schedule. In desperation he went over their heads to Sutherland, who overruled them. Sutherland also began a search for a new commander for the Fifty-seventh, since the current commander had been slow to respond to the crisis going on around him on the 10th and 11th, and had become, according to his executive officer, "phobic" about air attack.[55]

The other problem was that the Japanese, despite their losses and proof that the Americans and Filipinos were going to stand and fight, were not going to let up. That same day a determined attack tore a hole through the Fifty-first Infantry sector to the left of the Scouts, and plugging it up required a counterattack by an entire battalion.[56]

By nightfall it was evident that the Japanese were shifting their effort against II Corps to the west. That would spell eventual disaster, although there was only one person on the Rock who had already guessed it.

That person was *not* MacArthur. He had returned from his ten-hour tour of Bataan with a renewed sense of confidence. He went down into the tunnel to convey his enthusiasm to President Quezon, who was now virtually confined to his cot by his constant hacking fits.

"There's no reason to worry," MacArthur told him. "I can hold Bataan and Corregidor for months; the morale of our forces is high." The Filipino reservists, with their five and a half months of training, he said proudly, "have become veterans in less than one month of actual fighting against a determined and superior force."[57] He almost certainly showed Quezon the letter that had reached him while he was on Bataan.

"You are well aware you are doomed," it read. "The end is near."

It was a surrender ultimatum from General Homma, arriving by sheer coincidence even as MacArthur was touring his troops.

"The question is how long you can resist. You have already cut rations in half. I appreciate the fighting spirit of yourself and your troops. . . . However, in order to avoid needless bloodshed and to save the remnants of your divisions and your auxiliary troops, you are advised to surrender."

MacArthur's only reply had been to increase the artillery fire from II Corps sector.[58] Surrender was out of the question, especially when his men were fighting so splendidly—and so much depended on standing firm both on Bataan and on Corregidor.

The man who did guess the truth, that the shift of fighting to the II Corps sector could signal disaster, was MacArthur's chief of operations, Dick Marshall. But by the time he and Sutherland could convince MacArthur to take measures to stave off defeat, it would already be too late to save the men on Bataan.

Mac's life on the Rock began every morning before dawn with a shave that left his face clean but rubbed raw, since the water he—like everyone else—

used for shaving was seawater. His orderly, Sergeant Adversario, would present him with polished shoes and his general's uniform neatly pressed, except that the uniform now hung in folds. MacArthur lost twenty-five pounds during his first eight weeks on Corregidor.[59]

Then he would leave the small Bottomside cottage, trying not to wake Jean, and walk with a deliberate stride around the house several times to gather his thoughts before setting off, jauntily swinging his walnut cane, a cigar or cigarette holder (the famous pipe would come later), jammed in his mouth on the one-mile walk to the tunnel and his office.

The office, General Headquarters USAFFE, was in Lateral No. 3, where MacArthur, Sutherland, Willoughby, and the others shared a row of desks illuminated by huge drop lights that would sway eerily whenever an air raid took place overhead—which after December 29 became an almost daily occurrence. Pieces of cardboard had to be put over stacks of documents to keep them from getting soaked by the damp that dripped down the limestone walls. On one side was a large mounted map of the Philippines on which an orderly would occasionally move pins representing USAFFE and Japanese units, especially on the section showing the Bataan Peninsula—pins that were usually remorselessly headed south.[60]

Telephones bolted into the walls would ring constantly while MacArthur paced the narrow corridor, his hands "clasped behind him," a Filipino officer remembered, "his head bowed a little, his hawk like face cast in bitter lines."[61] What that face tried but failed to disguise, was a growing rage at his own helplessness in a war, and in a crisis, that was rapidly running beyond his control.

The lack of supplies was dire. On January 10, and again on January 17, he fired off warning messages to Washington explaining the seriousness of the situation. He pointed out that his men were now on half rations, and "the result was becoming evident in the exhausted condition of the men."[62] New supplies could reach them only by submarine or the occasional intrepid steamer that was willing to run the ever-tightening Japanese blockade.

One of the latter was the *Legaspi,* a small craft of less than a thousand tons piloted by a Filipino captain, Lino Conejero, that made the run from Corregidor to the Visayan province coast to load up on food for the garrison on the Rock. *Legaspi* came back a week later to Corregidor under cover of darkness and unloaded 1,400 sacks of rice, eggs, chickens, sugar, and salt from its hold even as the Japanese pounded the pier with artillery fire. Captain Conejero and his first mate were being interviewed in the tunnel by Captain Carlos Romulo when MacArthur burst into the room.

He "spoke to me as though I were his son," the astonished Conejero told a questioner later, and praised him for "risking his life for his country" in order to feed the beleaguered garrison. "I'm going to decorate you both," MacArthur kept saying, barely choking back the tears.

When Conejero left MacArthur, the commander in chief of USAFFE "was crying like a baby." On her next smuggling run to Corregidor, the *Legaspi* was caught by a Japanese gunboat, ran aground on rocks off Mindoro, and sank. Conejero and his crew managed to escape into the hills.[63]

Corregidor did not undergo the half-ration regime—a source of some anger on Bataan, where soldiers had bitter fantasies of the Corregidor garrison dining on eggs, fruit, and other delicacies. In fact, meals on Corregidor consisted mostly of rice and tinned salmon, Paul Rogers later recalled, served twice a day at a field kitchen set up at the east entrance of the tunnel. Once in a great while there was a special treat, as when wieners appeared on the menu or mule steak when five were killed by Japanese artillery fire.

Still, "rice was the basic ingredient of our meal," Rogers remembered, "with fish or other bits of meat that must have included carabao"—although no one inquired too closely, since they knew that in the Philippines dog was considered a delicacy. A dog named Duke made the rounds at each meal, begging for scraps and Rogers would sometimes share his meager meal, even his spoon with the animal, knowing full well that at some point he might be eating Duke himself.[64]

The daily routine on Corregidor was punctuated by air raids—and after February 5 by Japanese artillery on the mainland—and while the sound of warning sirens sent everyone scurrying into the safety of the tunnel, including Jean and little Arthur (it was a ninety-second car ride from their Bottomside cottage to the entrance of the tunnel—and she had it timed precisely), there was always one person coming out—MacArthur himself. Some thought his determination to be present at every raid, even count the planes, an unnecessary risk; others, since he refused to wear a helmet, viewed it as foolhardy madness. Still others wondered if he half believed what he had said in jest to Quezon after the air raid on the 29th: that destiny would choose when and where he would die, so why not meet fate head-on instead of retreating from it?

Most, however, found his courage awe-inspiring, even unworldly. Artillery Captain Godfrey Ames caught sight of him once at the Topside battery, "standing tall and never taking the field glasses from his eyes" as a flight of Zeros came in low to drop their bombs. Ames pleaded with his commander in chief to take shelter or at least put on a helmet; Mac ignored him and simply said, "The bombs will fall close." They did, less than one hundred yards away. MacArthur was unmoved, watching impassively as the planes circled wildly overhead.

President Quezon, even after his trust in MacArthur was revised downward, summed up the feelings of many when he wrote: "On the rock of Corregidor, Douglas MacArthur was a rock of strength."

MacArthur knew what he was doing. "There was nothing of bravado in this," he wrote years later. "It was simply my duty. The gunners at the batteries, the men in the foxholes, they too were in the open. They liked to see me with them at such moments"—which, he believed, helped tamp down feelings of panic, or just plain exhaustion.

"Leadership is often crystallized in some sort of public gesture," he wrote in a powerful and revealing passage. "In war, to be effective it must take the form of a fraternity of danger welded between a commander and his troops by the common denominator of sharing the risk of sudden death."[65] It was a leadership principle that MacArthur would give himself many opportunities to practice.

Still, if there was a member of the MacArthur family who was a hero to the common soldier and civilian on Corregidor, it was probably Jean. Her spare, lively figure was seen everywhere, and everyone got a beaming smile and a kind word even in the tensest hours of a Japanese air raid or power failure. People would remember her sitting with her knitting outside the tunnel as soldiers and officers walked in, sometimes wearing sunglasses and sometimes not, and greeting every passerby as if it were a casual Murfreesboro Sunday.

The social highlight of the Corregidor siege was little Arthur's fourth birthday. The MacArthurs were joined by the Sayres' fifteen-year-old stepson, Billy, the only other child on the island. Mrs. Sayre managed to procure some cans of orangeade and enough flour, sugar, and other ingredients to bake a small cake. Jean and the general gave Arthur two presents that they had salvaged from the wreck of the post exchange store, a toy iron motorcycle and a flyswatter.

Arthur's ayah, Ah Cheu, came up with a more elaborate present. She had found a tailor on the base who made up a miniature overseas garrison cap. Sid Huff's gift, a fake cardboard cigarette holder made to resemble his father's, completed the outfit. Arthur was delighted, and paraded around the tunnel in his new finery.

The cap and cigarette holder became an inseparable part of Arthur's outfits. Once a soldier ventured to salute him and call him "general." Arthur was furious.

"I'm not a general," he said in a hurt voice. "I'm a sergeant."

"Why a sergeant?"

"Because sergeants," the boy promptly replied, "get to drive automobiles."[66]

At other times, Jean spent hours at the hospital, tending to the wounded. Often MacArthur would come in to find her, and kneel down at the foot of the hospital bed to talk to her quietly.

Evenings were a trial. They usually consisted of gathering around the radio to catch whatever news broadcast could be interpreted or picked up on shortwave. The news was uniformly bad. Hong Kong had fallen to the Japanese on Christmas Day. America's remaining outpost in the western Pacific, Wake Island, fell a few days later. One Japanese army was bounding down the Malay Peninsula for Singapore, while another was advancing into Burma. Thailand had been overrun as well as Indochina, and the Dutch East Indies were next. Meanwhile, a large force of Japanese infantry and engineers was headed for Rabaul, to turn that island into a fortress-base, giving the Japanese navy and air force complete command of the South Pacific.

As MacArthur's troops were digging in on Bataan, imperial Japan controlled one-quarter of the earth's surface.[67] And no one had yet found a way to stop it from acquiring more.

Then there was news from the States, of senators and congressmen speaking of MacArthur's heroic defense on Corregidor, and of the heroes on Bataan whom the country would not abandon or allow to die in vain. MacArthur would listen with an expressionless face. Then once came news that a Japanese submarine had shelled Santa Barbara, California. MacArthur broke off to say with a straight face, "I think I'll send a wire to the California commander, and tell him if he can hold out for thirty more days, I'll be able to send him help."[68]

Then, before retiring, MacArthur would walk out into the night air for a final smoke, as Jean swung along beside him, but sometimes following behind while MacArthur walked with his head bowed, thinking, planning, then shaking his head and thinking some more.

In those moments Jean would listen to the rumble of the PT boats in the harbor and the boom of Japanese artillery far off on Bataan, and think, "This is hopeless."[69]

It was not long before everyone would learn how right she was.

CHAPTER 16
BACK TO THE WALL

Tell the president I will never surrender.
Tell him I will stay here with my men til we rot. Tell him.

—DOUGLAS MACARTHUR TO DEPARTING

U.S. ARMY OFFICER, MID-DECEMBER, 1941

On January 16 things on Bataan began to come apart.

The trouble started in II Corps sector on the right flank, where at dawn the Fifty-first Division counterattacked the Japanese to regain vital ground lost in fighting on the previous day. The commander of the Fifty-first, General Jones, had fought against General Parker's order to advance. He insisted his position was too weak, and his troops too exhausted and depleted, for an effective counterstrike. Parker, however, overruled him, and at first it looked as if he had been right. The advance went well—too well, in fact, as the division's lead regiment shoved the Japanese so far back that a dangerous gap appeared in the Fifty-first's line.[1]

The Japanese at once pounced from three sides. The regiment disintegrated as a fighting unit, and the entire line might have collapsed if Jones hadn't stationed an emergency reserve force 4,000 yards behind the point at which the attack had started. Still, by that evening, Homma's commander on the scene, General Akira, was in a position to turn the entire II Corps line.[2]

On the 17th, Parker sent in his one American regiment, the Thirty-first Infantry, and the Forty-fifth Philippine Scouts to retrieve the situation. They fought hard and bravely, but their attack was piecemeal. Japanese resistance was fierce, and a day later the Japanese were still holding their ground and the line was still in danger.[3] Another attack on the 19th proved just as useless and just as costly, as did attacks during the next couple of days. Parker's men, worn out, sleepless, pounded by incessant Japanese air attack, and seriously underfed, could stand no more as the defense of Bataan on the eastern side verged on collapse.

On the other side of the peninsula, the situation was also deteriorating fast.

The entire plan for holding Bataan depended on maintaining a defensive line that cut across both coastal highways, with Mount Natib in the middle. Holding that line depended in turn on the assumption that Natib and surrounding peaks were impassable to Japanese troops, and could be left largely undefended. Dick Marshall, for one, thought this was a mistake. He believed the line of defense should have started farther up the peninsula in order to protect the northern approaches to Natib from an enemy who, "were he in possession of Mount Natib," Marshall warned Sutherland, could turn both lines while cutting I and II Corps off from each other.

Sutherland and MacArthur, too, saw the risk, but neither was willing to overrule the commanders on the ground. That meant the opportunity was available for any Japanese unit that was intrepid enough to take on the steep slopes, thick jungle terrain, and supposedly impassable peaks around Natib, to drive a wedge between Wainwright to the west and Parker to the east.[4]

On January 20 a Japanese battalion did just that, descending into Wainwright's rear and onto the one major road used for transporting heavy equipment and supplies, even as Japanese forces swept through the village of Morong and secured the high ground overlooking the I Corps lines. Attempts to dislodge the Japanese, like those of II Corps days earlier, proved futile, and soon Wainwright's troops had to fall back along the beach, abandoning their artillery.[5]

The result was that by the January 22, disaster was staring the Allies in the face along the entire line. Sutherland took a PT boat over from Corregidor to pay a personal visit and see firsthand how close to catastrophe MacArthur's army really was. At once he told Wainwright and Parker to order a full withdrawal, which MacArthur also agreed to on the 23rd. By that morning columns of weary American and Filipino soldiers were tramping down both coastal roads toward Mariveles, as Japanese planes constantly harassed the II Corps retreat by bombing and strafing, Zeros swooping in and firing at untrained Filipinos soldiers, who scrambled "like sheep in a slaughter pen."[6]

"It was impossible to do anything but keep the mass moving to the rear," Colonel Miller, commander of a tank battalion, remembered. "It was a nightmare."[7]

The last to pull out of II Corps sector were the Americans of the Thirty-first. An eyewitness saw them on the road, "walking like dead men" with "a blank stare in their eyes," and "their faces, covered with beards, lacked any semblance of expression."[8] They looked more like hobos than soldiers; yet together with the Scouts they were slated to be the heart and soul of any successful defense.

On the 24th the first units of I and II Corps were stumbling into the reserve battle position, a line running from Bagac in the west to Orion in the east. "With its occupation," MacArthur grimly told George Marshall, "all maneuvering possibilities cease. I intend to fight it out to complete destruction."[9]

But to his troops and personnel, he intended to remain stoutly upbeat, and so he issued a statement that would haunt him the rest of his life—and his reputation ever afterward.

"Help is on the way from the United States," it read. "Thousands of troops and thousands of planes are being dispatched. The exact time of their arrival is unknown [but] it is imperative our troops hold until those reinforcements arrive."

He went on, "We have more troops on Bataan than the Japanese have thrown against us. Our supplies are ample. A determined defense will defeat the enemy's attack." Still, "no further retreat is possible."

"If we fight we will win; if we retreat, we will be destroyed."[10]

It was here at the tip of the peninsula, his statement implied, with 90,000 soldiers and civilians occupying some 200 square miles of brush and jungle, that the defenders of Bataan would make their final stand.

MacArthur had meant his words to be upbeat. He had hoped they would be inspiring; he knew the phrase about troops and planes "being dispatched" was ambiguous (most, he knew, would be headed not for the Philippines but for Europe), and the truth behind the remark about supplies being "ample" was flimsy at best.

But there are good reasons to believe that he didn't mean to mislead the men of Bataan—although many who heard him had already concluded that only a direct act of God could save them now.

They had learned this the night before, on January 22, when over the scratchy reception of hundreds of radio sets the residents of Bataan and Corregidor heard the familiar drawling voice of President Roosevelt speaking from thousands of miles away, about the war. The president spoke sternly of the need to free Europe from the domination of Rome and Berlin; he spoke of the need to defeat Tokyo and the Japanese; he spoke of America's and its Allies' final victory.

But as they turned their radios off, the listeners realized there was one problem.

Roosevelt had never mentioned the Philippines.

As one American officer on Bataan put it, "Plain for all to see was the handwriting on the wall, at the end of which the President had placed a large and emphatic period. The President had—with regret—wiped us off the page and closed the book."[11]

Deep in the bowels of Corregidor and the Malinta Tunnel one of those listening had been President Quezon. Although now confined almost constantly to a wheelchair, he flew into a violent rage. "Come, listen to this scoundrel," he cried out in a shriek that echoed through the tunnel. "*Que demonio!* For thirty years I have worked and hoped for my people. Now they burn and die for a flag that cannot protect them. . . . Where are the planes they speak of? America writhes in anguish at the fate of a distant cousin, Europe, while a daughter, the Philippines, is being raped in the back room."

Furious and desperate, he sent a message to MacArthur. "Why don't I go to Manila," he pleaded with his friend when MacArthur arrived, "and become a prisoner of war?"

MacArthur had to shake his head. This was his worst nightmare. Once interned back on the mainland at Malacañan Palace, he explained, Quezon would become only a hapless Japanese puppet. If he refused to sign the declarations they ordered him to sign, they would simply forge his signature.

Besides, MacArthur hinted, the Filipinos still fighting and dying on Bataan would remember him not as a patriot but a traitor.

So Quezon relented, but he still insisted on sending a personal cable to FDR. "This war is not our making," he wrote. No government could expect the loyalty of citizens it cannot defend. "It seems that Washington does not fully realize our situation nor the feelings which the apparent neglect of our safety and welfare have engendered in the hearts of the people here."[12]

Roosevelt's soothing reply arrived the next day, filled with the rolling tones of personal reassurance. "Although I cannot at this time state the day that help will arrive in the Philippines," the president of the United States wrote, "vessels . . . have been filled with cargo of necessary supplies and have been dispatched to Manila. A continuous stream of fighter and pursuit planes is traversing the Pacific . . . while extensive arrivals of troops are being guarded by adequate protective elements of our navy."[13]

It was a warm message of reassurance, and of much-needed hope. Yet the picture Roosevelt painted of docks piled high with American supplies and lines of American soldiers loading onto ships destined for the Philippines, was a lie. Roosevelt knew that nothing was being done, and that the only reinforcements that would be coming from the States were verbal ones.

Because it wasn't just FDR who was in on the deception. So was Chief of Staff George Marshall, who had told MacArthur back on January 4 that the War Department was steadily building up its airpower in order to cut off Japanese supply lines south of Borneo, in order "to permit an assault in the southern Philippines"—when his own staff had told him the day before there was no hope of relieving the Philippines. It was also George Marshall who on January 17 told MacArthur that his friend and former secretary of war Pat Hurley was being dispatched to Australia "to organize blockade running measures on a broad front for your supply of food and critical munitions . . . and lend his energetic support to efforts to reach you with supplies."[14]

Yet Marshall knew his words of encouragement were empty, as did Henry Stimson. "I stood in Washington helpless," he wrote later, "and had to simply watch their glorious but hopeless defense." In order to keep the Philippines in the fight as long as possible, however, he and Marshall had to keep sending "news that would buck General MacArthur up"—just as they knew that

MacArthur, in order to do his duty, would pass that encouragement on to his troops and personnel.

It was a cruel, though perhaps necessary, deception. Some were not fooled; others, like Madeline Ullom, a nurse who had made her escape from Manila to Corregidor on that nightmarish evening of December 29, still believed. Later she recalled how, after MacArthur's stirring statement on January 23, "every morning before breakfast I walked to the top of Malinta Hill to see if the promised convoy was arriving."[15]

Sadly, it wasn't just MacArthur who had misled her, however inadvertently. The brass in Washington, and her own president, were doing the same.

Meanwhile, the Japanese pressure on the new American-Filipino positions began even before Bataan Force had settled into their foxholes.

It started on the 22nd, not from the front lines but from the sea, with a series of amphibious landings on the peninsula's west coast. It involved only a battalion or so of Japanese troops, and was hastily organized. Some of the landing barges ran afoul of John Bulkeley's PT boats in the dark, and took a hail of .50-caliber bullets that sank two barges, one of which Bulkeley himself boarded before it sank, taking two prisoners whom he held in the water until his PT crew picked him up. The others came ashore, where they ran into a scratch force defending Mariveles naval base consisting of grounded airmen, Philippine Constabulary, and beached sailors.

Although they had no infantry training, these eager volunteers managed to rout their Japanese attackers, and by nightfall of the 24th they had secured the major points where the Japanese had landed—although it was not until February 8 that the last Japanese soldier was finally killed.[16]

By that date, more-conventional Japanese attacks along the Bagac-Orion line had failed too, and now it was the Japanese army's turn to find itself in a desperate situation. Homma's army had paid a terrible price in the advance down the peninsula. It had suffered more than 7,000 battle casualties, with 2,700 killed, while another 10,000 to 12,000 had been laid low by dysentery, malaria, and beriberi. His Sixty-fifth Brigade, which had taken the brunt of the fighting, was down from 6,500 men to barely 1,000, while the Sixteenth Division, once a proud force of 14,000 soldiers, had 712 men left who were able to carry a rifle.

Their supply situation was, if anything, even worse than MacArthur's. Daily rations for Japanese soldiers had to be cut from sixty-two ounces to just twenty-three—barely two cups of rice a day.[17]

In fact, Japanese sources point to an inevitable conclusion, that the Japanese Fourteenth Army had all but ceased to exist as a fighting force.[18] General Homma, who had hoped to declare victory by the end of January, had to call a halt to the entire proceedings—even order a temporary withdrawal. The army on Bataan, for all their inexperience, poor supplies, and bad luck, had fought the Japanese to a standstill. Homma would later claim that if MacArthur's men had taken the counteroffensive, "they could [have walked] to Manila without encountering much resistance on our part."[19]

But the Bataan Force wasn't going anywhere. Wainwright's surgeon general reported that almost half his men were incapacitated by some dread tropical disease or general malnutrition. Every battalion hospital was full to overflowing. The quinine had run out, and so had virtually every other medicine, as well as the food. Rations had to be cut from sixteen ounces to eight and then four—with a twice-a-week ration of carabao, mule, or horse meat (one of the first horses to be eaten was Wainwright's own charger, Joseph Conrad, which he shot himself). There was no flour, no sugar, no vegetables. Major Harold Johnson, of the Fifty-seventh Regiment, saw his men "sitting beside trails, boiling a piece of mule hide or carabao hide in a tomato can and chewing away at the hide."[20]

Some units were so reduced in numbers by casualties and disease that they took to propping the dead up in their foxholes, rifles pointing to the front, to fool the Japanese. Wainwright and his naval aide, Lieutenant Norman Champlin, visited one ghastly trench filled almost completely by dead "sentries," all bloated and covered in flies from the feces at the bottom of the trench.[21]

Even if Wainwright had somehow pulled his troops together for a desperate advance, their ammunition was all but running out—and much of what was left was either defective or too old to be of much use. One veteran remembered about throwing his World War One–era grenades, "if two out of ten went off, we'd be lucky."[22]

And while the Japanese still controlled the air and sea, and were able to resupply their sick and exhausted troops, the defenders of Bataan could not. All the successful efforts to run the blockade barely added 100,000 tons to Bataan's slender resources, and like the *Legaspi,* more runners were caught than succeeded.[23]

All the same, for almost six weeks—from mid-February to the end of March—fighting on the Bataan Peninsula virtually came to a halt. "The enemy has definitely recoiled," MacArthur told TAG on February 26. "[H]is attitude is so passive as to discount any immediate threat of attack."[24]

Yet while stalemate reigned on Bataan, over on Corregidor events were quickly building to a climax. For MacArthur himself, in fact, the endgame was closer than he could have thought.

It started when Quezon decided he had reached his limit in dealing with the Americans.

On February 4 there was a conversation between MacArthur and a Lieutenant Colonel Warren Clear, who had come over to the Philippines from Singapore on an intelligence-gathering assignment. Clear had been ordered to return to Honolulu on the submarine *Trout,* which was also carrying away $10 million in gold and silver bullion from Corregidor. MacArthur kept asking the intelligence officer about what Washington was thinking, and whether the war chiefs and Secretary Stimson were serious about relieving his army. Clear said he had been told by Stimson and presidential press secretary Early that Roosevelt had said, "very emphatically that England and Russia had priority in all things."

MacArthur was furious. "Never before in history," he said in a tremulous voice, his face flushed, "was so large and gallant an army written off so callously."[25]

Listening in the shadows, as it happened, was President Quezon.

"To hell with America," he told Carlos Romulo afterward. "The fight between America and Japan is not our fight. We must try to save ourselves."[26]

On February 8—three days after Japanese artillery on the mainland began shelling Corregidor, in addition to the almost daily air attacks—Quezon assembled the members of his cabinet in his tunnel sanctuary, where he drafted a letter for President Roosevelt.

"After nine weeks of fighting," Quezon's message began, "not even a small amount of aid has reached us. . . . The British and American Navies, the two strongest fleets in existence, have seemingly pursued a strategy that excludes any attempt to bring aid to the Philippines. Consequently, while perfectly safe itself, the United States has practically doomed the Philippines to almost total extinction in order to secure a breathing space."[27]

What followed was a proposal that the Philippines be granted immediate independence so that he, President Quezon, could begin negotiations with Japan for Philippine neutrality.

MacArthur did his best to dissuade his friend from sending the cable. He told Quezon there "was not the slightest chance" that the United States would agree to Philippine neutrality, but when Quezon insisted, MacArthur sent his own evaluation of the situation separately to Roosevelt.

"The temper of the Filipinos is one of almost violent resentment against the United States," it read. "Every one of them expected help, and when it was not forthcoming, they believe they have been betrayed in favor of others." For MacArthur in particular it must have been an especially bitter moment. The nation that his father had been determined to help to emerge as a modern nation, and the country for which MacArthur himself had thrown over his military career in order to organize its defenses, had turned against America. His PT commander Bulkeley estimated that 80 percent of Filipinos were now either anti-American or neutral. Above all, Quezon and colleagues watched and listened on the radio as politicians on the mainland, like Jorge Vargas and Manuel Roxas, were adjusting to Japanese rule—while they choked on mold and dust in a dark, dank tunnel.

In the final analysis, MacArthur did not think Roosevelt should agree to Quezon's proposal (interestingly, commissioner Sayre did, and sent his own cable to that effect). But he did not mince words about the state of affairs on Bataan. "There is no denying the fact that we are near done," he told the president. "Troops have sustained practically fifty percent casualties . . . they are capable now of nothing but fighting in place in a fixed position. . . . All our supplies are scant and the command has been on half rations for the past month. Nothing . . . can prevent their utter collapse and their complete absorption by the enemy."[28]

To George Marshall, MacArthur was even more blunt. The current Allied strategy against Japan was "a fatal mistake." Instead of acting defensively and building up forces along Japan's front, now was the time for a bold thrust— "not at the enemy's strengths but at his weakness." With Japan's lines of communication stretched across 2,000 miles of ocean, "a great naval victory on our part is not necessary to accomplish this mission; the threat alone would go far toward the desired end."

MacArthur added, "[F]rom my present point of vantage I can see the whole strategy of the Pacific perhaps clearer than anyone else." What he foresaw was a Japanese victory—not just in the Philippines but across Asia— unless the United States retook the initiative.[29]

Meanwhile, "since I have no air or sea protection," MacArthur concluded in his memorandum to Roosevelt, "you must be prepared at any time to figure on the complete destruction of this command. You must determine whether the mission of delay would be better furthered by the temporizing plan of Quezon, or by my continued battle effort."

Quezon's message, and MacArthur's, hit Washington like a "bombshell," according to Dwight Eisenhower. He himself was getting fed up with MacArthur's refusal to take his situation stoically, and confessed as much to his diary after getting MacArthur's unsolicited advice "extolling the virtues of the flank offensive. Wonder what he thinks we've been studying all these years. His lecture would have been good for plebes." Now came this "long wail" from Quezon, "I think he [i.e., Quezon] wants to give up."[30]

As for Roosevelt, few could remember him being so furious. "We can't do this at all," he raged, slamming his hand on his desk with emphasis as Stimson and Marshall sat stone-faced in his office. There would be no declaration of neutrality, no accommodation with Japan, and no pullout of American troops. He ordered Marshall and Stimson to prepare a draft statement to that effect, for both MacArthur and Quezon.

"American forces will continue to keep our flag flying in the Philippines," it read, "as long as there remains any possibility of resistance. I have made these decisions in complete understanding of your military estimate that accompanied President Quezon's message to me. The duty and necessity of resisting Japanese aggression to the last transcends in importance any other obligation now facing us in the Philippines."

Stimson was deeply impressed by FDR's resolution, as was Marshall, who said later that day "I decided he was a great man."[31] Quezon's immediate reaction, however, when Roosevelt's reply arrived on February 10, was blind fury.

"Who is in a better position, Roosevelt or myself, to judge what is best for my people?" He kept saying, and threatened to resign. MacArthur let him rant. He knew Quezon would calm down and change his mind (in twenty-four hours, he did).

But that still left the fact that Washington had no strategy for the Philippines, except to let the mission die. There were no plans for relief, no plans for a countermove, no plans for anything beyond trying to send an occasional ship or sub through the ever-tightening Japanese blockade. And at last, in the final part of his message to MacArthur, Roosevelt made that clear.

The last paragraph from Roosevelt read, "I therefore give you this most difficult mission in full understanding of the desperate nature to which you may shortly be reduced. It is mandatory . . . that the American determination and indomitable will to win carries down to the last unit. . . . The service that you and the American members of your command can render to your country in the titanic struggle now developing is beyond all possibility of appraisement."[32]

As MacArthur read the cable standing in front of his desk, the full import hit home. So that was it. He and his command were to die fighting. His reply was immediate:

"I have not the slightest intention in the world of surrendering or capitulating the Filipino forces under my command. I intend to fight to destruction on Bataan and then do the same on Corregidor."

He certainly was personally prepared for a last stand. "They will never take me alive," he told Huff matter-of-factly. Jean felt the same. Her refusal to leave when George Marshall on February 2 suggested she could be taken away by submarine, signaled that. "We drink of the same cup," she reportedly told MacArthur. "We three are one."[33] [34]

For MacArthur himself, there would be no surrender and no retreat. He told two reporters who were about to leave Corregidor, the AP's Clark Lee and *Life* photographer Melville Jacoby, "if we don't get reinforcements, the end here will be brutal and bloody"—which also included himself.[35] He had sent a message to General Marshall on January 23 that was a kind of last will and testament. It paid tribute to his troops on Bataan—"no troops have ever done so much with so little"—and went on to say that "in case of my death" he was naming Richard Sutherland as his successor in command of USAFFE. "Of all my general officers," he wrote, "Dick has the most comprehensive view of the situation," and would be the one most likely to prevent an overall collapse.[36]

MacArthur had once told Francis Sayre, who had complimented him on his incredible bravery during the air raids, "death will take me only at the ordained time." Now as the second week of February began, he was ready to meet that moment on Corregidor.

But those back in Washington had other plans.

The reason had nothing to do with the Philippines, nor the overall American strategy in Asia. It had a lot to do with what MacArthur, and a handful of reporters on Corregidor, were saying about what was happening out there.

After three months of uninterrupted bad news, Americans were looking for a hero. In the cold late winter of 1942, they found him in Douglas MacArthur. Official dispatches from Corregidor, many of them written by MacArthur himself, had created a military and political drama in which he was single-handedly defying the entire might of the Japanese empire—and he alone of the opponents the Japanese had faced was getting the better of them.

"When the hordes of the north swept down on the south like wolves the legend of Japanese military superiority had preceded them," read one dispatch. "The initial successes of the enemy seemed to bear this out but the legend is now shattered. The superiority of the Japanese military machine has been reduced in the crucible of war. Filipinos and Americans shoulder to shoulder and greatly outnumbered have stopped and thrown back the Japanese infantry. The Japanese soldier emerges from the shattered legend as a man with feet of clay."[37]

Another went out on Roosevelt's birthday:

"Today January 30, your birth anniversary, smoke begrimed men covered with the murk of battle, rise from the foxholes of Bataan and the batteries of Corregidor, to pray fervently that God may bless immeasurably the President of the United States."[38]

They were masterpieces of verbal pyrotechnics, combining a strong dose of poetic license—or, one might say, heroic license—with artistic ego. Of the 142 official communiqués sent from the Philippines from the start of the war until early April, 109 mentioned only one name, that of General Douglas MacArthur.[39]

Americans soon got the message. There was one American standing foursquare against the Japanese hordes despite the odds, and the embattled men on Bataan were both his instrument of resistance and the nation's trust.

Already by the end of January 1942 the press was regularly comparing the defense of Bataan to that of Valley Forge and Yorktown, and MacArthur to America's finest soldiers. On his birthday, January 26, the stream of praise swelled to a flood.

The front page of the *Washington Post* paid tribute "to an American soldier who spent his sixty-second birthday shaming the prophets of disaster . . . there was no way yet for millions of hungry Americans to tell Gen. MacArthur fighting his last ditch fight in the bamboo jungles of Bataan of the hope and pride he has fanned to flame in their hearts . . . [and] strengthened the will of every man and woman and child back home."[40]

The *Baltimore Sun* enthused, "General MacArthur is not only a professional soldier. He is something in the nature of a military genius."[41] The Associated Press dubbed his fortress at Corregidor "MacArthur's Gibraltar." The *New York Herald Tribune* devoted half a page to photos emblazoning his military career. The *Philadelphia Record* started serializing MacArthur's life, and proclaimed that he had celebrated his sixty-second birthday "by proving anew that he is one of the greatest fighting generals of this war or any other war."

On Capitol Hill, Representative Lee O'Daniel found time to suggest that Luzon be renamed MacArthur Island, while another congressman wanted the TVA's Douglas Dam to be renamed MacArthur Dam. Still another pushed for him to be given the Congressional Medal of Honor, while Senator Scott Thomas of Utah declared, "Seldom in all history has a military leader faced such insuperable odds. Never has a commander of his troops met such a situation with greater and cooler courage, never with more resourcefulness of brilliant action."[42]

Seventy years on, it's easy to scoff at this histrionic, even hysterical praise—and to frown at the bulletins MacArthur saw fit to fire off across the Pacific to his fellow Americans. It's true that like Napoleon's in an earlier age, they were often inaccurate, like the one describing the sinking of the battleship *Haruna* by Medal of Honor winner Clark, when the *Haruna* wasn't even in the theater. Sometimes they were deliberately incorrect, like the claim about being "greatly outnumbered," when it was Homma and the Japanese who had the smaller, although better-equipped and more experienced force. One bulletin in particular that has come under harsh condemnation from later biographers reported that General Homma, despairing of victory, had actually committed hara-kiri in Mac's old suite at the Manila Hotel, and described the general's funeral rites the next day.

Yet the fact was that MacArthur did get a report of Homma's suicide, and although it was untrue, it was not deliberate misrepresentation. "I hope he didn't mess up my carpet," was MacArthur's comment when he first heard the story.[43]

Then, when the USAFFE's last remaining quartet of P-40s managed to launch an attack with some 500-pound bombs on Japanese craft in Subic Bay and hit some ships, MacArthur managed to turn the incident into a magnificent air-to-sea battle in which seven Japanese transports were sunk, while "innumerable motor launches and other small craft, and thousands of Japanese soldiers had gone down in [Subic's] waters." He also reported that "we lost no planes by enemy action," even though official reports showed one P-40 shot down and no record of any enemy vessels sunk.[44] No wonder the *Los Angeles Times,* among other papers, kept reporting that "MacArthur's stand in Philippines, judged by every military standard, has inflicted grievous defeat on attackers who have failed to reach objectives, suffered heavy losses, and are now dangerously behind schedule."[45]

What was MacArthur thinking? There was purpose behind his license with the truth, and his self-dramatization of the ordeal, that went beyond pure ego. It was to convince the American people, and Washington, that their stand in the Philippines was worth supporting, and worthy of whatever help the United States could send. He also knew that the Japanese were listening—and that the more convinced they were that American and Filipino morale was high and their spirit indomitable, the less likely they were to launch the all-out attack that would undoubtedly spell the end of the command.

"The distillate of forty years—Filamerican," began a MacArthur communiqué on March 6. "The word was coined in the thick of battle. Filamerican troops, Filamerican spirit. Filamerican grit! This perfect union of two races began early in this century. . . . But the fire of war brought forth the perfect and pure understanding."[46]

By then, however, it was all too late.

The soldiers on Bataan were not feeling the Filamerican spirit in the first week of March.

> *Dugout Doug MacArthur lies ashaking on the Rock*
> *Safe from all the bombers and from any sudden shock*
> *Dugout Doug is eating the best food on Bataan*
> *And his troops go starving on.*
>
> *Dugout Doug's not timid, he's just cautious, not afraid*
> *He's protecting carefully the stars that Franklin made*
> *Four-star generals are as rare as good food on Bataan*
> *And his troops go starving on.*

Colonel Ernest B. Miller, one of Wainwright's tank commanders, found a copy of this anonymous ditty circulating around his men, and saw them "laughing quite heartily over the verses."

Chorus: Dugout Doug, come out from hiding
Dugout Doug, come out from hiding
Send to Franklin the glad tidings
That his troops go starving on.

The song stated "with clarity," Miller remembered, "just what went on in the minds of the men on Bataan" in the grim days of that spring of 1942.[47]

The attack was scurrilous and unfair, of course; far from hiding, MacArthur was displaying a reckless courage when the Japanese air raids came daily over Corregidor. Far from eating like a king, he ate the same diet as his men. The official army historian of the Bataan campaign, Louis Morton, who was no MacArthur devotee, had to conclude that most defenders who were close to him on Corregidor held him in high esteem, especially the Filipinos. Quezon's description of him as a "rock of strength" was not far wrong in the minds of everyone who was caught in close proximity with him on that embattled island.

But the men on Bataan felt otherwise. An occasional visit might have made a marginal difference to morale. The sole one, on January 10, was not repeated. MacArthur later claimed that Quezon urged him not to risk his life unnecessarily by going across to Bataan—a strange request, given MacArthur's reckless performance during air raids on Corregidor. All the same, it was true that slipping across Manila Bay ran the risk of a Japanese destroyer snaring the launch containing the USAFFE commander—or a dive bomber blowing it out of the water. There was also the issue of MacArthur wanting to stay on the Rock in order to keep track of the latest developments in Washington—although again, that was a task his right arm, Richard Sutherland, was more than able to handle.

There may, in fact, have been another reason why MacArthur never went to Bataan after his initial visit: he could not look them in the eye. Having led them to this place and situation, with the certainty that they were doomed and that he was responsible—and that he still had to encourage them to hope for help while knowing in his heart that Washington had written them off—may have been too much for him.

He would never admit to that implicit sense that he, not Washington, had betrayed their trust. But it certainly drove his desire later to liberate the Philippines, and rescue the survivors of Bataan, as the fulfillment of an inner vow. As he admitted to Jean, the memory of their stares that January 10 when he did visit haunted him almost every day for the rest of the war. And it may have been what kept him gazing toward the peninsula during his morning and evening walks, knowing: *They are waiting for me there but I cannot bring myself to go.*

As for the garrison on Bataan, if they felt bitterness at their desperate situation, they were justified—but it was not in fact Douglas MacArthur who had let them down. He made a convenient target, and the legend of Dugout Doug would linger on, long after his death.

> *Dugout Doug is ready with his Kris Craft for the final flee*
> *Over bounding billows and the wildly raging sea . . .*
> *And we'll continue fighting after Dugout Doug is gone*
> *And still go starving on.*

On February 11 MacArthur told Roosevelt he was arranging for Quezon's evacuation. He let Marshall know that Quezon had refused several times to leave by submarine because he felt too frail and feared the voyage would kill him.[48] Sutherland figured it would take six days to make the necessary arrangements.

But before he left, MacArthur had some business to do—and Quezon had a special gift for his old friend.

Two days later, on February 13, MacArthur came down to Lateral Tunnel No. 3 and motioned to Sutherland to join him for a talk "about highly secret matters of policy." Sutherland listened, then returned to his desk and his yellow pad. He began writing; three and a half hours later he was still at it. When it was done, he handed Paul Rogers a memorandum to type up, which read at the top "Special Executive Order from President Quezon."

The order was an award of $500,000 to MacArthur for his service to the Philippine Military Mission; as well as $75,000 to Richard Sutherland and $45,000 to Richard Marshall, while Sid Huff found himself richer by $20,000. To Rogers's surprise, the memo was dated January 1, which implied that the agreement for the payment had been reached beforehand, with implementation to begin when it was time to evacuate.[49]

No single document from the MacArthur files has caused more controversy than Executive Order #1, since scholar Carol Petillo discovered it in 1978. Many, if not most, have treated it as nothing less than a bribe. As Geoffrey Perret points out, "Most scholars have treated it as a corrupt transaction."[50] MacArthur critic Michael Schaller has taken it to mean that MacArthur was planning to cut and run, and was lining his pockets before he left. One writer has even suggested that MacArthur had blackmailed Quezon into paying up before letting him leave Corregidor.[51]

MacArthur did nothing to help his case, since he never mentions the incident in his memoirs or in Charles Willoughby's laudatory biography which MacArthur largely coauthored. That silence isn't surprising, since accepting the money would have been a technical, albeit clear, violation of the American military code that he had sworn to uphold.

In fact there was nothing secret about the deal at all. Paul Rogers even mentioned it in his diary, although he revised the numbers downward, since he had been told not to record MacArthur's financial affairs.[52] And certainly Marshall and Stimson and FDR all knew about it, since no transfer of funds from Philippine treasury certificates to Chase National Bank could take place unless it was authorized by the Treasury Department, which means Roosevelt.

Why did Marshall and the army let it happen? Geoffrey Perret points to a September 1935 letter from the adjutant general to MacArthur giving him complete discretion in how much money he received from the Philippines government, and in what form—all with the permission of the secretary of war.[53]

It was suggested to Roosevelt in 1937 that he should revoke the authorization, but Roosevelt chose to let it stand. Marshall and Stimson may not have liked the transaction and its conspiratorial overtones, but there was nothing they could do to stop it.

More importantly, why did Quezon do it? Carol Petillo herself supplies the most compelling answer. The gift of money, Quezon believed, would draw MacArthur more closely to him as his advocate, and would serve as a symbol of, rather than a reward for, the bond of loyalty existing between them—and the bond between the Philippines and the United States. A Renaissance monarch like Henry VIII of England or Charles V of Spain would have understood the transaction; Douglas MacArthur, who was something of a Renaissance prince himself, no doubt understood it that way. The notion that somehow he knew he was accepting something dishonorable—even contradictory to his character as an American officer—simply flies in the face of who MacArthur was or, even more important, who he thought himself to be.

Yet this begs the most crucial question of all. Why did MacArthur accept the money? Certainly he had financial reasons for doing so. Far from having enriched himself during his stay in the Philippines as critics claimed, MacArthur was overheard saying the half million dollars didn't even cover the financial losses he had incurred by staying with the military mission.[54]

Yet the best explanation may be the simplest. As Geoffrey Perret points out after having gone over the evidence, MacArthur accepted the money because he never expected to spend it. He assumed he would die on Corregidor, along with his command. Most of the other recipients guessed they would never live to see their money either. The whole business "was no great affair," Corporal Rogers noted, compared to the constant bustle and hurly-burly of matters on Corregidor, including preparing for the final siege and death.[55]

They could not guess how wrong they were.

It was a chilly night in Boston on Lincoln's birthday, February 12, 1942, where the main speaker at the annual Republican event to commemorate the occasion was the man Roosevelt had defeated in the 1940 election, Wendell Willkie. Willkie's speech surveyed the sorry state of America's defenses two months after Pearl Harbor. Everywhere the country was on the defensive; everywhere the enemy, both Japan and Nazi Germany, had the upper hand. Willkie demanded that one man was needed "to bring about effective cooperation" among the armed services and the Allies; one man empowered to "direct military services" in order to retrieve a desperate situation before it was too late.

"The last two months have proved we have that man," Willkie said, "the one man in all our forces who has learned from first-hand, contemporary experience the value and proper use of Army, Navy, and Air Forces fighting toward one end: the man who on the Bataan Peninsula has accomplished what was regarded as the impossible by his brilliant tactical sense; the man who alone has given his fellow-countrymen confidence and hope in the conduct of this war—General Douglas MacArthur."

After the stunning roar of applause died down, Willkie went on.

"Bring Douglas MacArthur home. Place him at the very top. Keep bureaucratic and political hands off him . . . Put him in supreme command of our armed forces under the President."[56]

With Willkie's speech the cavalcade of praise and adulation of Douglas MacArthur began that would eventually carry him away off Corregidor—and nearly to the gates of the White House.

It wasn't just Republicans who began to rally around this idea. George Marshall first brought up the idea of MacArthur leaving Corregidor on February 4. If the forces on Bataan were doomed and only defense of Corregidor were left, he wrote to MacArthur, "under these conditions the need for your services there will be less pressing than other points in the Far East."[57]

Then after Quezon's "bombshell" letter of February 8 prompted Washington to propose evacuating the president and his family before he came to harm—or caused more mischief—Marshall urged MacArthur on February 14 to reconsider his decision to stick it out on Corregidor, and to consider Marshall's two earlier options: moving his command to Mindanao, which was still, incredibly, largely free of Japanese soldiers, or, alternately, going directly to Australia.[58]

MacArthur acknowledged the message, but did not reply. Instead he told the staff that while they should start preparing for Quezon's and Sayre's departure, he would want to stay as long as possible if he thought his presence helped with defense.[59]

The change of tone is significant. MacArthur was becoming aware that whatever happened, Washington at least was not about to leave him to die.

On February 15 the news arrived at Corregidor that Singapore had fallen. Almost 80,000 men capitulated to the Japanese commander General Yamashita. It was the greatest mass surrender in British history—in spite of Winston Churchill's admonition to the British commander, Lieutenant General Arthur Percival, that he and the Singapore garrison should die to the last man.[60] The possibility that MacArthur and the men on Bataan would be asked to make the same sacrifice that Percival had refused to make, was fading fast.

The next day MacArthur sent a message to Washington:

> "The unexpectedly early capitulation of Singapore emphasizes the fact that the opportunity for a successful attack upon the [Japanese] lines of communication is rapidly vanishing. . . . A determined effort in force made now would probably attract the assistance of Russia who will unquestionably not move in this area until some evidence is given of concrete effort by the Allies. The opportunity still exists for a complete reversal of the situation. It will soon however be too late."[61]

MacArthur was desperate. He was playing the Russian card again. But he found no takers. What was happening in Washington, however, was something very different: a growing fear that leaving MacArthur to die would do more harm than good.

Dwight Eisenhower, for one, was for leaving him exactly where he was. He had become thoroughly disillusioned with his former mentor's refusal to take Washington's failure to help lying down—MacArthur and Quezon "are both babies," he wrote—and it was reflected in his diary entries for those crucial weeks in February and March.

"He's doing a good job where [he] is," Eisenhower told his diary on February 23. "Bataan is made to order for him. It's in the public eye; it has made him a national hero; it has all the essentials of drama: and he is the acknowledged king on the spot." If he's brought out, Ike worried, he might be given a command that would prove too difficult for him. "Public opinion will force him into a position where his love of the limelight may ruin him."[62]

No one was listening to Eisenhower. Roosevelt's military aide Colonel Edwin Watson believed that bringing MacArthur back to the States would be worth "five army corps"—and not just in military terms. The very fact that MacArthur was a national hero, especially among Republicans, was precisely why the White House couldn't abandon him. Roosevelt didn't want accusations that he had abandoned MacArthur haunting him in the 1942 midterm elections, or the next presidential race in 1944. Watson also pointed out that bringing MacArthur out would make it look like Roosevelt was finally taking decisive action against Japan, if only in bringing home his top field general to "live to fight another day."

Still, Eisenhower and others, including military historian Gavin Long, could and have argued that recalling MacArthur didn't necessarily require finding him a new command. Given his serial mistakes during the Philippines campaign, from his failed defense-on-the-beaches strategy to the Clark Field debacle, the best option would have been to bring him home, relieve him of all command, and put him safely behind a desk in Washington.[63]

But this overlooked the fact that MacArthur's mistakes had also been Washington's mistakes. To relieve him of command would present the White House with the worst of both worlds: a national war hero being unaccountably put on the bench, one who could use his intimate contacts with the opposition political party and the press to argue that he could have saved the Philippines if Washington had not misled him about sending support—who would go on to proclaim he could still win this war if President Roosevelt hadn't pushed him into retirement.

So the idea to pull MacArthur off Corregidor was born.

Interestingly, the first person to act on the idea was not an American at all, but an Australian, Prime Minister John Curtin, fifty-two years old and a tough ex–union activist. From his desk in Canberra, Curtin had watched his country coming under a growing threat of invasion from Japan, including air raids on the country's northern cities—one on Darwin sank a navy destroyer and four merchant vessels—while at the same time being all but abandoned by Great Britain after the sinking of the *Prince of Wales* and the *Repulse.*

The surrender of Singapore was the final straw. The loss of 80,000 soldiers—15,000 of them Australians—seemed to him an "inexcusable betrayal," and it was necessary, he wrote to Winston Churchill, to do something to correct it without relying on Britain for help.

"The Australian Government therefore regards the Pacific struggle as primarily one in which the United States and Australia have the fullest say in direction of the Democracies' fighting plan," Curtin wrote in a *Melbourne Herald* editorial at almost the same time. "Without any inhibitions of any kind, I make quite clear that Australia looks to America, free of any pangs as to our traditional links with the United Kingdom."[64]

It was a stunning declaration of independence. As part of it, Curtin demanded that Great Britain return the three Australian divisions that Curtin had sent to join the fighting in Europe and secretly ordered the Australian Sixth and Seventh Divisions en route to Burma to help the British to return home.[65] From the United States, he asked for dispatch of an American general to assume supreme command of all Allied forces in the Southwest Pacific. It was easy to guess whom he meant: General Douglas MacArthur.[66]

It was an idea that had now ripened in Washington as well. On Roosevelt's desk on February 21 was a long memorandum from his special envoy to Australia, an old MacArthur friend, Brigadier General Patrick J. Hurley.

It stated that Australia was now "extremely vulnerable" to the Japanese, in part because preparations for defense were so lax. Hurley believed an American contribution to the defense effort was essential since "[t]he United States' contributions to the defense of the Southwest Pacific [will] enormously exceed the total output and resources of the combined British Dominions in ships, tanks, planes, equipment and manpower." For that reason, "it is logical and essential that the supreme command in the southwest Pacific should be given to an American."

Hurley also had a clear idea as to who that should be. So did General Archibald Wavell, the British commander in the Southwest Pacific region, who "frankly stated that he would like to have MacArthur with him."

Hurley had to explain that getting MacArthur out of the Philippines would be difficult, and "that it would be necessary for the President to definitely order MacArthur to relinquish command and proceed elsewhere and that even if such orders were issued, MacArthur might feel that he had destroyed himself by leaving his beleaguered command—that I knew MacArthur well enough to realize that his most treasured possession is his honor as a soldier."[67]

That was enough for Roosevelt. The same day Stimson and Marshall were coming around to the idea of not leaving MacArthur on Corregidor, Roosevelt was realizing that ordering him to Australia would solve a number of problems at once. It would save a national war hero; it would bolster Australian confidence and prepare the way for a robust defense of the continent with American help; it would deprive Japan of an enormous propaganda victory in capturing or killing America's greatest active soldier.

It would also keep Douglas MacArthur far away from Washington, far from where he was bound to disrupt war plans already made and develop grandiose ones of his own that would be spread to the media, all of which would center on winning the war in Asia, and avenging Pearl Harbor, instead of saving America's European ally Great Britain.

At the same time, Roosevelt understood only too well that "the departure of MacArthur from Corregidor would be a grievous blow to the heroic men of his command" on Corregidor and Bataan, his speechwriter and advisor Robert Sherwood later recalled. "It was ordering the captain to be the first to leave the sinking ship."[68]

But the decision was made. Late that day Marshall sent a radiogram to MacArthur warning him that the president was considering ordering him off the Rock.

A day earlier, on February 20, a single car drove through the Malinta Tunnel toward the jetty on the island's eastern end. When it stopped, MacArthur got out, and then Sutherland. Together they helped a frail President Quezon out of the backseat. To Quezon's longtime admirer journalist-turned-MacArthur-aide Carlos Romulo, Quezon looked like a ghost in the moonlight. Before Quezon boarded the small navy tender that would take him out to the submarine *Swordfish,* MacArthur embraced the old man one last time.

"Manuel," he said, "you will see it through. You are the father of your country and God will preserve you."

"I am leaving you with a weeping heart," Quezon said in a note he had left behind for MacArthur. "You and I have not only been friends, we have been more than brothers. . . . I am leaving my own boys, the Filipino soldiers, under your care." At the quay he slipped a signet ring from his finger and gave it to MacArthur. It was the signet he had used to seal letters of state.

"When they find your body," he said in a breaking voice, "I want them to know that you fought for my country."[69]

MacArthur saluted as the tender headed out to the bay and into the darkness. Waiting for him when he returned was Quezon's note, along with the

Distinguished Service Star of the Philippines, presented by Quezon with this citation: "The record of General MacArthur's service is interwoven forever in the history of the Philippines and is one of the greatest heritages of the Filipino people."[70]

On the 22nd of February there was a major meeting at the White House. Besides Roosevelt, Stimson, and George Marshall, Secretary of State Cordell Hull, Admiral King, and Roosevelt advisor Harry Hopkins were present. Australia, and MacArthur, were the items on the agenda. The day before, Australian prime minister Curtin and his cabinet had sent a formal request to Roosevelt that MacArthur be sent out as commander in chief of a reconstituted American, British, Dutch, Australian Command, or ABDACOM, to be dubbed Southwest Pacific Area.

Curtin wasn't limiting himself to polite messages. Roosevelt had also learned from Churchill that Curtin had told him he wanted all Australian units pulled out of the Middle East unless something was done to reassure Australia it wasn't being abandoned to Japanese invasion. The entire strategy that Roosevelt and Churchill had agreed to, to fight the war—rallying the Allies, including Australia, to winning the war in Europe first—was in jeopardy.[71]

So it was, ironically, that in order to save the Europe-first strategy, Roosevelt finally agreed: MacArthur would have to be asked to leave the Philippines.

Early the next day Roosevelt and Stimson met to figure out how to phrase it. If it were put as a suggestion, the commander in chief USAFFE would reject it out of hand; if it were presented as a personal plea, it would leave MacArthur worrying about his honor.

Finally, Stimson threw up his hands. "Make it an order," he said. Roosevelt nodded agreement. And so that morning, February 23, FDR issued a direct order to MacArthur to leave Corregidor for Australia to assume command of a new Southwest Pacific theater.[72]

The one lingering question was, would MacArthur obey it?

*   *   *

On the morning of February 24, MacArthur strode into the Malinta Tunnel, a crumpled cablegram clutched in his hand. In Lateral Tunnel No. 3 he found Sid Huff packing a locker full of records that were supposed to be taken away by submarine before the Rock surrendered.

Huff glanced up. "I looked at the General's face," Huff later wrote, "and I knew something had happened."

MacArthur asked in a harsh voice, "Where's Jean?"

"She's in the other tunnel, General," Huff answered. Dick Sutherland, who was also there, stood up.

"Come on, Dick," MacArthur ordered in the same harsh tone. He grabbed his cap and headed for the other tunnel, with Sutherland following.[73]

When they found Jean, MacArthur showed them both the crumpled cable.

"The President directs that you make arrangement to leave Fort Mills and proceed to Mindanao," it read. "You are directed to make this change as quickly as possible." At Mindanao, MacArthur was to "take such measures as will insure a prolonged defense of that region," but his sojourn there was to last no more than a week. His real destination was to be Australia, "where you will assume command of all United States Troops" and where Washington would arrange for the British and Australian governments to receive MacArthur as commander in chief of all Allied forces in the area.[74]

As he and Sutherland and Jean set off for the gray bungalow, MacArthur's mind was a firestorm of conflicting emotions. Despite his reputation, he was only human. One emotion had to be relief that Washington had not abandoned him, at least, or his family; when the final curtain came down on the drama of Bataan and Corregidor, they would not be there. But to leave before that final curtain—that he was not prepared to do.

For weeks "I fully expected to be killed," he told reporter and friend Frazier Hunt later. "I would never have surrendered. If necessary I would have sought the end in some final charge." But he knew the law of averages would have worked against that last-stand heroism. "I would probably have been killed in a bombing raid or by artillery fire. . . . And Jean and the boy," he paused, his eyes shaded, "might have been destroyed in some final debacle."[75]

Now, at the house that afternoon, he and Jean sat on the porch as he agonized. "I am an American—Army born and bred," he said finally, "and accustomed by a lifetime of discipline to the obedience of superior orders. But this order I must disobey."

Then he bowed his head and wept.[76]

When he returned to the tunnel, someone who saw him said he looked old and ill, and "drained of the confidence he had always shown." To his assembled staff, he read aloud the presidential order and spoke of his dilemma. If I disobey, I'll be court-martialed, he told them. If I obey, I'll be guilty of deserting my men. He suggested that maybe the best course of action was to resign. Then he could volunteer to go to Bataan as a private citizen, and be with his men until the end.

"But Sutherland and my entire staff would have none of it," he wrote later.[77]

They pushed hard for MacArthur to agree to go to Australia (not forgetting that they, as his staff, would have to go too). There a concentration of men, arms, and transport would be amassing for a rescue operation in the Philippines, and MacArthur was clearly the man to lead it.

MacArthur's resolution wavered. Nonetheless, that evening he drew up a formal letter of resignation, though Sutherland convinced him to wait until morning before sending it. After a sleepless night, MacArthur saw that his staff was right. He would leave the Philippines; but he and only he would decide when.

His radiogram to Washington went off on February 24. "Please be guided by me in this matter," it read in part. "Unless the right moment is chosen for so delicate an operation a sudden collapse might result"—that is, if the beleaguered bastards on Bataan felt that they were being abandoned by their commander.[78] He asked for time to choose his own departure. As for his men, "any idea that might develop in their minds that I was being withdrawn for any other reason than to bring them immediate relief, could not be explained"—and he wanted Washington to commit to that rescue mission.

So there was still that inner conviction that somehow, he would get Wainwright, Parker, and their men out of this mess, even if it meant going to Australia to summon up the men, ships, and planes to do it. It was that belief that, in the final analysis, sustained his decision, and what sustained him in the days afterward.

Meanwhile, two days later Marshall gave his answer:

"Your message [of February 24] has been carefully considered by the President. He has directed that full decision as to timing of your departure and details of method be left in your hands since it is imperative that the Luzon defense be firmly sustained." The phrasing was ambiguous; it could have suggested to MacArthur that the commitment to sustaining the defense of Luzon, meaning Bataan, included a future relief mission.[79]

As it happened, on the day MacArthur's message arrived in the morning, FDR had a press conference in the afternoon, where someone asked about the situation in the Philippines, and whether MacArthur was "at odds with the high command" in Washington over the issue of relief and reinforcement.

For once, Roosevelt was nonplussed. With reporters gathered around his desk, he gave a long, incoherent, stuttering reply:

"I wouldn't do any—well, I wouldn't—I am trying to take a leaf out of my notebook. I think it would be well for others to do it. I—not knowing enough about it—I try not to speculate myself."

Still, Roosevelt was pleased that MacArthur was leaving Corregidor. The president had dodged a major political bullet. What would happen when he reached Australia—when he realized just how thin the resources would be when he got there—was something the president, Marshall, and Stimson would have to deal with when it came up.[80]

By then, it would be too late for MacArthur to turn back.

Commissioner Sayre and his family were the next to leave. The *Swordfish* returned the night of the 24th to pick them up, only to find that in addition to the three Sayres another ten people who were part of his staff were also going. They were MacArthur's codebreakers (the navy had pulled its team and their PURPLE machine on February 4), who were beginning a long and fascinating journey—not just for themselves, but for MacArthur once they set up their operation in Australia.[81]

Once again the tender went out in the darkness to the sea, and once again MacArthur and his party saw them off and then returned to the Malinta Tunnel. "They are leaving us one by one," Carlos Romulo wrote in his diary that night—not knowing yet, but perhaps sensing, that MacArthur would soon be one of them.[82]

CHAPTER 17
I SHALL RETURN

How the hell can we win this war unless we can crack some heads?

—DWIGHT EISENHOWER, MAY 6, 1942

The only question for MacArthur now was not whether he'd leave, or why, but how.

The others had gotten out by submarine; Washington assumed MacArthur would too. MacArthur himself, however, would have none of it. He sensed that the trip to Australia might be perilous, with Japan having complete control of the seas. "It is a long run to Australia," he told his staff one evening, "most of it through seas that are not well charted or not charted at all."

He was in the living room of the house, with blankets nailed up to black out the windows. He paced up and down and smoking one of the cigars President Quezon had left him, while his staff sat and listened under the dim light of a single overhead bulb.

They knew they were all going with him. There would be a total of eighteen in addition to MacArthur, Jean, Arthur, and his ayah, Ah Cheu. The rest of the list included Sutherland, Marshall, Rear Admiral Francis Rockwell and Rockwell's chief of staff, Captain James Ray; MacArthur's naval aide, Sid Huff; Hugh Casey, the engineering officer, and his G-2, Charles Willoughby. There was also Billy Marquat, in charge of antiaircraft, and Colonel Paul Stivers of army personnel; and the man who would prove to be perhaps the most significant of the group: Brigadier General Spencer Akin of the Signal Corps.

In all, there were eighteen persons chosen to escape certain death or capture, for a new lease on life and the war in Australia—*if* they made it out alive. And few thought they would, especially when MacArthur announced the way he was planning to leave.

"I had a talk with Lieutenant Bulkeley," MacArthur was saying as he paced. Bulkeley was the commander of the PT squadron on Corregidor who had arrived shortly before Pearl Harbor—the navy's last vessels in the Philippines. "He tells me we have a chance to get through the blockade in PT boats. It wouldn't be easy. There would be plenty of risks. But four boats are available and, with their machine guns and torpedoes, we could put up a good fight against an enemy warship if necessary. And of course the boats have plenty of speed."[1]

MacArthur's plan wasn't to go all the way to Australia in the seventy-foot-long plywood boats, of course. It was to land on Mindanao and then get to Del Monte airfield, where an escort of B-17s could pick up the entire party and ferry them by air to Darwin, Australia.

The rest of the group listened in tense silence. They said nothing about the general's plan, but to some, if not most, it must have seemed daylight madness. The idea of the lightweight boats taking to the open seas, and then encountering a Japanese destroyer or cruiser would have appealed to anyone's sense of the absurd—not to mention mortal danger.

But MacArthur's mind was made up. He gave his last terse orders. Sutherland then told Huff, Bulkeley, and Ray to work out the details.

The date set for their departure was March 18.

Meanwhile back on Bataan, ironically, morale was higher than it had been since the start of the war.

Rations were just as short, disease just as rampant, and men were still venting their frustration with occasional choruses of "Dugout Doug." But the victories in February—wiping out the last pockets of Japanese infiltrators from the last week in January, one of which alone cost the enemy 450 dead, and foiling a series of unexpected amphibious attacks the first weeks in February—had left the Japanese "badly mauled," as MacArthur said in his report for Marshall, and turned his Filipino frontline troops on Bataan into tough, seasoned veterans. "The opinion here," wrote a naval intelligence officer who was usually skeptical of the Philippine Army's competence, "is that the army has improved by many discharges and thousands of desertions, by the realization that it has to fight its own battle with little if any substantial aid"—and made them eager for battle.[2]

As February turned into March, increasingly confident Philippine and American troops boldly ventured into the no-man's-land of marsh and jungle between the two lines of defenses, seeking out combat with their enemy. At times HQ had to put the brakes on efforts to take the offensive northward in hopes of retaking lost ground.[3]

The Japanese were not idle either. General Homma had been given a new chief of staff, Lieutenant General Takeji Wachi, and when Wachi toured the Japanese positions on Bataan he was shocked by what he found. He bluntly told the high command in Tokyo, "The Japanese Army [has been] severely beaten." Morale was low, and the army's disposition in chaos. The high command immediately set about correcting that problem. Night by night massive new reinforcements poured in, including the 4,000-strong Nagano Infantry Regiment from China and the veteran Fourth Division, some 11,000 strong. No fewer than five artillery regiments arrived from Hong Kong, as well as sixty-two twin-engine bombers—while big new guns were sent to pulverize MacArthur's remaining defenses on Bataan as well as Corregidor.

The Japanese knew nothing, of course, of MacArthur's evacuation plans; nor did he know the details of Homma's intense preparations, although he and Wainwright could easily guess. Reinforced and reinvigorated, Homma's army would soon be ready to take the offensive. The full-scale bombardment of the Allied positions was set for March 24; the final Japanese push would follow on April 3.[4] Afterward Homma would take on the toughest nut of all, Corregidor; but by then the Rock would be without its commander in chief or his staff.

MacArthur had ridden in PT boats before, but Jean hadn't, and so he arranged a demonstration for her with Lieutenant Bulkeley. They met one afternoon at the dock. Bulkeley was easy to spot. The hero of the Battle of the Points in February when his PT boats had taken on and sunk several Japanese amphibious transports, he wore a long, unruly beard and two enormous pistols holstered at his side. His eyes were red-rimmed from a chronic lack of sleep and constant night missions, but his immense nervous energy gave him an impressive swagger. "A swashbuckling pirate in modern dress" was a standard description of Bulkeley, who was a MacArthur favorite.[5]

They roared around the island a few times—hardly a fair test for traveling in open seas, but it gave Jean a sense of the little boat's pitch and power, with the spray coming over the deck at every turn.

For security purposes, Bulkeley still did not know where they would be going (the night they left, even his crews still did not know their final heading). Sutherland had simply ordered him "to prepare his squadron for a trip over 500 miles to an undisclosed location." Over several days he made fuel consumption and speed runs with a fully loaded boat and checked the boats' compasses for deviations. He also made sure that each boat had a rubber dinghy and a deckload of gasoline, as well as plenty of emergency provisions.[6]

Meanwhile Admiral Rockwell's aide Captain Harold Ray, Bulkeley, and Sid Huff were working out the final logistical details. They agreed that MacArthur and his family would be aboard Bulkeley's boat, PT-41, with the others distributed on the three other boats. The first night out they would head for the Cuyo Islands, a group of uninhabited clumps of sand and rock northwest of Mindanao. There they would sit out the daylight, to evade Japanese air and naval patrols. Then when the sun set, the four boats would start out for Mindanao; a submarine would join them just in case the boats couldn't make the last leg of the journey.[7]

Even with these preparations, MacArthur's plan looked outlandish and risky. Supposing they somehow managed to reach Mindanao, they would still have to rendezvous with the bombers coming in from Australia to Del Monte field, and then take off again, evading Japanese navy and air force planes, which by then would have guessed the truth and would be hot on their trail. Navy officers were thinking that MacArthur had barely one chance in five of making it out alive.[8]

But now there were no alternatives. It was, as the saying goes, the best bad plan they had. And on March 1 a signal went out to General George Brett, the new head of United States Army Forces in Australia (USAFIA):

Request detail best pilots and best available planes be placed in top condition for trip. B-24's if available otherwise B-17's. Ferry mission only. Desire if possible initial landing on return to be south of combat zone. Anticipate call for arrival Mindanao about 15.

The message began: "You have probably surmised purpose of mission." If Brett hadn't, he would soon be getting his instructions from Washington, as well as Fort Mills.[9]

Every morning for the next ten days MacArthur met with Bulkeley to work out the final details of the evacuation.

Even so, MacArthur hesitated.

On March 6 a cable arrived from Washington: "The situation in Australia indicates desirability of your early arrival there." There was no answer from Lateral Tunnel No. 3, no setting of a date for departure, no date for landing in Australia. There was only MacArthur, pacing relentlessly and smoking his cigars. Carlos Romulo, who had moved into the house next door to the general and Jean when Quezon left, could almost feel the physical weight of MacArthur's decision. He would be "breaking, in his own mind, his pledge to die with his men on the Rock," Romulo realized. Far from allowing MacArthur to feel relief at going, it involved a betrayal of a vow that would haunt MacArthur the rest of his life.[10]

Another cable came on March 9—just as the Japanese resumed their regular bombardment of Corregidor.[11] By now MacArthur's mind was fully made up. It was just a matter of choosing a final date of departure. He replied to Washington that he expected to leave on March 15—"the Ides of March," as he sardonically told his staff—and planned to be in Australia on the 18th.

But there were still security worries. The longer MacArthur put off the trip, the more likely it was that the Japanese would learn his plans—and by March 9 it seemed they had. The number of navy patrols around Corregidor had tripled. Philippine lookouts reported that a Japanese destroyer division was headed for the southern Philippines at flank speed, and there was increased activity in Subic Bay, northwest of Bataan.[12]

Bulkeley, for one, was convinced that the Japanese knew MacArthur was leaving and were determined to intercept him. Speed was now of the essence. They could not wait for the submarine USS *Permit* to show sometime after March 13; they had to leave "as soon as preparations [can] be completed," preferably on March 11 when the moon was still on the wane.

On March 10 a grim-faced Sutherland handed Bulkeley his orders.

They stated that Motor Torpedo Boat Squadron would be taking a party of twenty-one passengers (there were three last-minute additions to the original roll of eighteen) "to a southern port to be designated later." They would be leaving the next night, March 11, in time to rendezvous at the turning buoy at 8 P.M. They were to take fuel for a 510-mile journey and food for five days. "Enemy air and surface activity will be expected along the route."[13]

Before leaving, however, MacArthur had one last unpleasant duty to perform.

At noon a fast Elco cabin cruiser, marked *J-230* on her prow, pulled up at Mariveles dock on Bataan. Three U.S. Army officers climbed aboard and the *J-230* quickly roared away from the pier, headed for Corregidor.

"Wonder what he wants, General?" one of the officers asked General Jonathan Wainwright.

"Wish to God I knew," Wainwright replied wearily, his eyes focused on the growing bulk of Corregidor on the boat's prow. "All I know is that Sutherland phoned last night and told me to come over, the General wanted to see me."[14]

Week by week, Wainwright had watched his command deteriorate. They were nearly out of food, nearly out of ammunition, and despite the lull in the fighting since mid-February, nearly out of hope as well. Some units were down to one tin of canned salmon for every fifteen men.

Unless a regular shipment of supplies arrived from somewhere, Jim Wainwright had resigned himself to watching his men slowly starve and waste away—although he, and they, were still committed to fighting to the end. Wainwright felt strongly that MacArthur had made some serious mistakes, but the friends were too close to argue about it. In fact, he was the only person who ever called the commander in chief of USAFFE Douglas, and

MacArthur was the only one who called him Jonathan. Although they were friends, they had clashed over the MacArthur plan for defending Luzon, then over abandoning the plan and reverting to WPO-3, and over the fighting withdrawal strategy.

On one thing, however, they were in agreement. There would be no retreat, no surrender. Perhaps that was why, when Wainwright reached the island, it was Sutherland, not MacArthur, who broke the news.

"General MacArthur is going to leave here and go to Australia," he said gruffly. "He's up at the house now and wants to see you . . ."

They were standing in the half-gloom of Lateral Tunnel No. 3 as Sutherland filled him in. How the White House had been pressuring MacArthur for days, but MacArthur had kept refusing. How MacArthur was now planning to leave tomorrow evening by PT boat for Mindanao. And how Wainwright was to tell no one—"no one," Sutherland sternly repeated—until the morning of the 12th.[15]

Wainwright said nothing as the shock of the news settled in. Instead, he listened as Sutherland outlined some of the command changes MacArthur would be making before departing for Australia. Wainwright would now assume command of all troops on Luzon; General Jones was getting a promotion to take over Wainwright's I Corps; General Moore would keep command of all harbor defenses and fortified islands in Manila Bay, including Corregidor; and MacArthur himself was retaining overall command from his new headquarters in Australia.

They made the quarter-mile walk to the general's house, and as they arrived, the door opened and MacArthur stepped onto the porch.

In his mind, he had a clear conscience. If Wainwright felt MacArthur had made mistakes, MacArthur had similar private doubts about Wainwright. He felt Wainwright hadn't been aggressive enough in defending Bataan; he felt Wainwright had missed opportunities in fighting the Japanese; he also believed Wainwright drank too much. But they were old friends and there could be no hard feelings, MacArthur believed. Besides, he was leaving the new Luzon commander with enough supplies and a ration plan that he thought would be enough to enable the remaining men to hold on until July 1, by which time he'd be back with relief and reinforcements.

All the same, he couldn't disguise his shock at Wainwright's appearance. The general, already nicknamed "Skinny," had lost so much weight on half rations that he looked like a living skeleton.

"Jonathan," MacArthur said after the two generals shook hands, "I want you to understand my position very plainly." He went over his arguments with the president over the past several days, and ended with, "Things have gotten to such a point that I must comply with these orders or get out of the Army."

MacArthur especially wanted Wainwright to make sure that the men on Bataan understood this, understood that he was not running out on them. Wainwright said he would.

"If I get through to Australia you know I'll come back as soon as I can with as much as I can," MacArthur said. "In the meantime you've got to hold."

Wainwright said that for him and his men, holding Bataan was "their one aim in life."

They discussed particulars and tactics briefly, and then Wainwright said, "You'll get through."

"And back," MacArthur said with fierce determination.[16]

Wainwright rose to go. MacArthur gave him a box of his cigars and two jars of shaving cream as a parting gift.

"Goodbye," MacArthur said as they shook hands. "When I get back, if you're still on Bataan I'll make you a lieutenant general."

"I'll be on Bataan if I'm alive," Wainwright replied with a wry smile. He walked back alone to the Malinta Tunnel, and the painful parting interview was over.

MacArthur went back into the house, his face flooding with emotion. "I was to come back," he wrote many years later. "But it would be too late. Too late for those battling men in the foxholes of Bataan, too late for the valiant gunners at the batteries of Corregidor, too late for Jim Wainwright."[17]

March 11 dawned bright and clear.

Private Rogers was seated at his typewriter as usual when Sutherland handed him a copy of Special Order 66. It was the summary of orders for leaving Corregidor; Rogers was to type copies for every officer selected to go.[18]

As Rogers typed, he noticed at the bottom of the list Sutherland had written "M/Sgt Paul P. Rogers," with his serial number. Rogers wasn't just going with MacArthur, he realized with a jolt. He was getting a promotion.[19]

"I looked around the room," he remembered later, "at the men who would be left behind with a feeling of shame, guilt, and regret. God knows, I would be glad to leave," he realized, but also he could perform one last service for those left behind. He told two friends what was happening, and that if they had anything they wanted sent out with him, he would take it along.

By three o'clock his barracks bag was full of last letters to loved ones and friends.[20]

Dick Marshall then appeared at his desk, looking gaunt and grim (he had been struck down by extreme dysentery and had learned from MacArthur only the night before that he was leaving Corregidor). "Rogers, it's time to go."

Rogers grabbed his barracks bag and headed out of the tunnel, not daring to look at the men being left behind, who were still working, or pretending to work, at their desks. Silence reigned. Then they went out to the west entrance to meet the jeeps that took them to the North Dock.

Jean MacArthur, meanwhile, was busy. She and Sid Huff spent the day stuffing four duffel bags with K rations, one for each PT boat: Bulkeley had told them he had no food he could spare for his passengers. There was also the question of what else she should bring, both for her and for little Arthur. Finally she decided she would leave everything except two dresses—one of which she would wear—a dressing gown, and a pair of straw shoes, while Arthur was allowed to bring his teddy bear and the gift from his fourth birthday, his six-inch-long cast-iron motorcycle. His ayah and his mother dressed him in a blue zipper jacket, khaki pants, and the overseas cap that Ah Cheu had had made for him. Ah Cheu's own belongings fitted into a single folded handkerchief.

At 7:00 P.M. the general appeared at their side. "Now we go, Jean," he said. "We have to go now."[21]

As for MacArthur, he was traveling with nothing, absolutely nothing, not even a razor (he would borrow Bulkeley's). He was not even in uniform, just a nondescript suit and some brown wing tips. The one personal item he did insist on was his four-star license plates. "We may not be able to replace them in Australia," he said sensibly. It was also his first direct reference to his future command after the Philippines.[22]

Still, given the number of people going, it took three staff automobiles to load all the baggage in the tunnel. The general stepped into the first car "and left the tunnel in a kind of stunned silence." Jean, Arthur, Ah Cheu, and Sid Huff followed him as the little caravan made its way down to the North Dock—the South Dock had been pounded to pieces by Japanese air attacks— where a rather battered-looking PT sat tied up, with a nervous Lieutenant Bulkeley waiting for them.[23]

MacArthur's face had turned a ghostly white, and a muscle in his cheek was twitching constantly. Some thought it might be nerves, but Jean knew the truth. "He was just heartbroken, you know just heartbroken," she said many decades later. A small crowd of soldiers and officers had gathered in the dusk. Jean heard someone mutter, "He hasn't a ghost of a chance."[24]

One of the officers present was General Moore, who commanded the harbor defenses. He and MacArthur discussed what to do if Corregidor finally fell, how to destroy all the artillery and fortifications so the Japanese couldn't use the fortress as a base to repel an American retaking of the Philippines.

But MacArthur was convinced that Corregidor would *not* fall. "Hold Corregidor until I return," Mac said. "George, keep the flag flying. I'm coming back." Sid Huff heard him say distinctly, "I shall return," and so a legend was born.[25]

MacArthur exercised his privilege as commanding officer to be the last to board. For a moment he stood, looking back at the fortress from which he had run the campaign to save the Philippines for nearly two and a half months, framed against a black sky with no moon—a good omen.

Then he raised his braided cap over his head. It was both a salute, and a signal to the commander of artillery Colonel Paul Bunker—who had been an all-American halfback at West Point when MacArthur was superintendent— to open his diversionary bombardment to draw away Japanese attention (meanwhile, on the other side of the bay Philippine Q-boats were staging a diversionary attack on Subic to draw Japanese naval vessels). The guns boomed, the air was filled with sound and flashes, as MacArthur stepped onto PT-41.

"You may cast off, Buck, when you are ready," he said to Bulkeley.

The PT's engines roared to life, the nervous crew threw off the mooring line, and PT-41 headed out into the moonless night toward the turning buoy. This marked the beginning of the outer mine-free channel through Manila Bay—and the rendezvous point with the three other PT boats, which had picked up their passengers earlier and had been anchored at Mariveles.

The rendezvous went like clockwork—no one knew it would be just about the last item on the agenda that *did* go according to plan. The four PT boats circled for a moment, then set off in single file through the mine channel into Manila Bay. They were sailing into the South China Sea, bound for Cabra Island, which lay to the southwest. Once clear of the mine channel, three boats dropped back, as the flotilla sped forward in a diamond-shaped formation.[26]

Almost everyone on PT-41, including the general, was instantly seasick as the boat bounced around in the wake from the other boats. The only exceptions were the navy men and the unsinkable Jean, who sat with the general at the bow on chairs facing each other. Jean wasn't seasick, but she didn't feel like eating anything either, as she clutched a thermos of hot cocoa. Meanwhile wave after wave swept over them, and "the flying spray drove against our skin like stinging pellets of birdshot," as MacArthur later described it.[27]

As they sped along, they passed several silent shapes in the dark, Japanese ships flashing lights to each other as a signal that someone had broken the blockade. Fortunately no Japanese naval vessels tried to intercept them. But then their their luck ran out. Just as they were leaving Apo Island to aft, the magnetos of PT-41's worn-out engines became soaked with spray and had to be shut down for repairs. The other boats experienced similar difficulties and, bobbing in the wash, soon lost contact with one another.

No one had sighted any Japanese ships or patrol boats. But there was every reason to believe that that blessing wouldn't last for long. After endless hours in the dark, first light began to appear on the eastern horizon, and Huff and Bulkeley began to look around for land.

But there was none. The island they were supposed to rendezvous at by dawn was nowhere to be seen. Nor were the other boats. It took a moment for the situation to settle in.

Douglas MacArthur, commander in chief of U.S. Armed Forces, Far East, and soon to be Supreme Commander, South West Pacific Area, was lost in the South China Sea.

On Bataan, news of MacArthur's departure hit like an emotional battering ram.

Alvin C. Poweleit, a doctor, wrote in his diary, "This morning we learned General MacArthur had left Corregidor via PT boat. Several men were upset by this. However, most of them felt he could do a better job in another area like Australia."

"Of course, there was a great deal of resentment among those left behind," noted Irv Alexander, quartermaster officer of the Seventy-first Division. "[T]he expression 'ran out on us' was on many tongues." Alexander himself was one of those who had been given two hours' notice to leave for Corregidor in order to join the general's departing staff. The call, however, never came.[28]

"I think it hurt morale all the way down to the front-line people," remembered General Bluemel. "There are always soldiers who say it's nice to fight under a lucky commander," and MacArthur was considered one of those. "I said to some of the American officers, 'we've lost our luck' and I think we did."

General Brougher, commanding the Eleventh Division, was bitter at what he called this "foul deception . . . played on a large group of Americans by a commander-in-chief and a small staff who are now eating steak and eggs in Australia. God damn them!"

MacArthur's former classmate Paul Bunker, stationed on Corregidor, was more philosophical. He knew where the real blame for their predicament lay. "We have been at war almost four months now and so far as we can see, not the slightest effort has been made to help us," he wrote in his diary. Bunker was now convinced that the higher-ups in Washington who had concocted both Plan Orange and Rainbow Five had planned to sacrifice the army in the Philippines from the start.

"Now, if anybody can help us it is MacArthur," he wrote. "He is our only chance."[29]

Anyway, the troops on Bataan had other things to think about. They were now living on twenty ounces of food a day. Rice had replaced wheat and potatoes, and meat was now whatever they could find in the fields and the forest. "Iguana is fair," one veteran later remembered. "Monkey I do not recommend. I never had snake."[30]

Besides that, there were more ominous developments. The Japanese were reinforcing their artillery. "Every day or so a new battery would appear in my area," one artillery officer, Alva Fitch, remembered. Other observers spotted heavy movement of supplies into Bataan from the north, while the surrounding jungle was alive with Japanese troops moving across the Pantingan River toward the east side of Bataan.

A major attack was coming. The battling bastards of Bataan had been waiting for a final Japanese onslaught. Their waiting was almost over.

Meanwhile, no one in MacArthur's party was eating steak and eggs.

For the passengers and crew on PT-32, it had been a rough and sleepless night at sea. This was the boat carrying Spencer Akin and Hugh Casey, the head engineer. When dawn came up on the 12th they found themselves completely alone near some islands in the Cuyo group. They were idling on one engine, rolling from side to side in the rough sea as Ensign Vincent Schumacher, the boat's commander, scanned the horizon with his binoculars.

His head pivoted as "a strange, unidentified craft" appeared dimly in the distance. It grew closer, zeroing in on their boat. Fearing it might be a Japanese destroyer, Akin was preparing to throw a sack filled with invaluable coding devices overboard, when Schumacher realized it was actually one of their missing PT boats—with a familiar figure in a battered field jacket and gold-braided cap standing at the prow.[31]

The first feeling at the sight was jubilation. To celebrate, the cook on PT-32 whipped up some hotcakes for the crew and passengers on both vessels, and little Arthur had a hilarious morning cavorting with the cook's pet monkey, known as General Tojo. [32] But then reality set in. The other two PT boats were still missing, the ones with MacArthur's top staff officers, and they all were highly vulnerable to being spotted by a passing Japanese plane or patrol boat. "We were still an hour or two short of the island where we had planned to take cover," Sid Huff remembered, namely, Tagauayan. Meanwhile, when the skipper of PT-32 thought the other PT boat was a Japanese vessel, he had ordered the extra fuel it needed for the trip to Mindanao dumped overboard for a quick getaway. Now it would never make it without help.

MacArthur paced up and down the deck and finally asked Captain Ray, "What would you think of trying to go on to the rendezvous island by daylight," where the other two PT boats might be waiting.

Ray shook his head and advised against it. They were too exposed; best to wait until dark before shoving off. So MacArthur asked General Casey to join him on PT-41 while they worked out what to do next as Bulkeley passed some of his own precious fuel on to the hapless Schumacher.[33]

The cautious choice was to wait. But MacArthur grew increasingly nervous and suggested they should set off for Tagauayan. At 2:30 both vessels weighed anchor and set their course for the rendezvous island. The ride was, if anything, worse than the night before, as saltwater spray swept the decks of both boats, soaking everyone to the skin. Bulkeley and Ray literally had to hang on to the stub mast to avoid being washed overboard.

MacArthur and Jean were hunkered down in the lower cockpit, perched on a dirty mattress. MacArthur later compared the sensation to riding inside a concrete mixer: rising up on a wave "to hang free in space," then plunging down the other side with a crash, with water flying in all directions.[34]

At about 4:00 P.M. they approached Tagauayan Island with, as Bulkeley put it to Captain Ray, "the wettest bunch of generals I've ever seen." There they found a welcome sight: PT-34, which was carrying Admiral Rockwell, as well as others of MacArthur's staff. The fourth boat, with Marshall and Willoughby, was still missing. But by now "all of us had decided we didn't want to see a torpedo boat again," Huff remembered, and MacArthur was one of them. He had overcome his misgivings about traveling by submarine, and suggested to Ray and Bulkeley that they wait for the *Permit* to carry them all to Mindanao.

Bulkeley, however, was adamantly opposed. Who could say when the *Permit* could show up—they had no means of radio contact—and by then the Japanese could have spotted and rounded up the entire group. He did not mince words; the next leg of their journey could be even more dangerous than the first. But Sutherland and Rockwell agreed it was best not to wait for the *Permit*.

"We'd better get the hell out of here fast," the admiral urged. Besides, he promised, the seas would be calmer and the weather better.

MacArthur listened and sighed, and finally agreed.[35]

The only casualty was PT-32. There was not enough fuel to take Ensign Schumacher's boat, and so his passengers were transferred to the other two. After being told by Bulkeley to "make out as best you can," Schumacher stayed back to contact the *Permit* when and if the sub arrived, and then head for Iloilo City—which, ironically, was where MacArthur had supervised the building of docks forty years before.

Darkness was coming on fast as the two PT boats sped away from Tagauayan Island. PT-34, under the command of Lieutenant Robert B. Kelly, took the lead, with PT-41 following. Rockwell's assurances about the weather turned out to be mistaken. The sea was as rough as anything the party had seen, and soon everyone was once again soaked in spray.

Then suddenly at 7:00 P.M. PT-41's engines cut back. Bulkeley gave tense orders to his crew and spun the helm for a new course, due west.

MacArthur, still lying in the lower cockpit, listened. He soon grasped the situation: a lookout had spotted a Japanese cruiser headed on an intercept course. Turning into the setting sun had managed to hide the two PT boats from the cruiser's lookouts. In a few minutes it was pitch-black, again with no moon. They were safe.

Meanwhile, Jean began to worry about housekeeping in their cramped little space. The mattress they were lying on was soaked, not just with water but with cocoa, since a rough wave had shattered the thermos, covering her dress and the mattress with hot liquid as well as glass shards.

Without thinking, she switched on a flashlight.

"PUT OUT THAT DAMNED LIGHT!" It was Bulkeley shouting at the top of his lungs. Jean did so immediately. They were going to have to sleep on a wet mattress that night.[36]

There was one more bizarre incident that night. As they passed an island, the sound of their engines aroused the Japanese garrison there. But they mistook the sound of the PT engines for airplane engines, and for long minutes after the boat sailed past, searchlights continued to probe the night sky, long white fingers reaching up for American planes that never came.

Huff decided he was exhausted. "None of us had slept ten minutes in the past forty-eight hours," he recalled. So he found a semi-comfortable position in the lower cockpit and was almost instantly asleep—until he suddenly heard a voice.

"Sid? Sid?"

It was MacArthur.

"I can't sleep," the general said.

"Sorry, sir."

"I want to talk."

"Yes, sir. What about?"

"Oh, anything. I just want to talk," MacArthur replied.

"Yes, sir."

And so began what Huff later described as "a couple of the strangest hours of my life."[37] As they plunged along through the darkness with Bulkeley at the helm and the boat slamming through the waves, MacArthur "in a voice slow and deliberate and barely distinguishable above the high whine of the engines," spoke of what had happened in the past four years and more.

He spoke of being forced into retirement in 1937; of his efforts to arm the Philippines in time for the country's independence in 1946 and to protect it from the growing Japanese danger. He spoke of the failed campaign just past, trying to analyze what had gone wrong and why. He spoke of his epic bouts with Washington, including the most recent, over the order to leave Corregidor.

His voice choked as he spoke of that. Huff realized that he was listening to a man who had sunk just about as far down as a man could get; a man who had lost all his possessions not once but twice; a man who had lost the battle and the campaign, and now his command.

A man who had almost lost his own self-respect.

MacArthur may not have used the words he wrote to Bonner Fellers more than a year later: "A merciful God has miraculously brought me through so far, but I am sick at heart at the mistakes and lost opportunities that are so prevalent," but he certainly felt them that night on PT-41.[38]

But Huff also realized that although MacArthur "was in the trough of the wave at the moment, he had no intention of staying there. His jaw was set. His face was grim. When he said he was planning to return to the Philippines, he meant it, and he was already planning how to do it."[39]

MacArthur made one last pledge. "Sid," he said, "if we ever get to Australia, the first thing I'm going to do is make you and [Major LeGrand Diller, his aide-de-camp] lieutenant colonels."

Huff thanked him and then, as the general fell silent, tried to sleep. His mind, however, was racing with all that MacArthur had said—including the fact that Diller was on the PT boat that was still missing. If Diller didn't make it to Australia, who was to say that any of them would?

And so they sailed on into the night.

Cagayan de Misamis was a small settlement, facing onto the sea. In the early morning of March the rector of the tiny Jesuit college there, Father Edward Haggerty, thought he heard aircraft engines passing over as he prepared for Mass. Instead, they were the engines of PT-41 and PT-34 as they limped into Cagayan harbor.[40]

They had traveled 560 miles through Japanese-controlled waters—with Bulkeley continuously at the helm for thirty-five hours—before sighting landfall shortly before 6:30 A.M. Bulkeley then guided both boats into the harbor to find a Colonel William Morse waiting for him with a hastily assembled honor guard of American soldiers.

The first person Morse saw was MacArthur, standing at the prow looking like "Washington crossing the Delaware," Morse remembered later. Jean was standing behind him, clutching her belongings in a red bandanna—her purse had been lost overboard—as MacArthur stepped down and helped her off the boat. He returned Morse's salute and the honor guard's, and turned back to the captain of PT-41 one last time.

"Bulkeley," he said, "I'm giving every officer and man here the Silver Star for gallantry. You've taken me out of the jaws of death, and I'll never forget it."

Then he turned to Morse and asked where he could relieve himself.[41]

Three hours later he was standing in the office of the commander of the Mindanao garrison, General William Sharp, when Sharp introduced the astonished Father Haggerty. A Japanese air raid started moments later, and after the commander of USAFFE excused himself and took his wife, little Arthur, and Ah Cheu to a bomb dugout, he came back to Haggerty.

"Would you like to go to a shelter, Father? There are only two planes; I never bother about so few."

"No, your calmness makes me feel brave," the padre stoutly said.

So they sat in General Sharp's office as bombs and antiaircraft guns went off outside, and talked.

MacArthur explained that he was going to Australia at President Roosevelt's order to start an offensive to retake the Philippines. "Bataan cannot be taken if food holds out," MacArthur affirmed. "The men on Bataan are splendid. . . . They have proven their valor far beyond my expectations—beyond the expectation of friends and, especially, the enemy."

It took five minutes for the all clear to sound. MacArthur went to find his family. It still wasn't clear to Haggerty if MacArthur's mention of "the enemy" referred to the Japanese or to Washington, or both.[42]

Over a breakfast of fresh pineapple—the first fresh fruit any of the group had had since they left Manila—MacArthur learned from General Sharp that their troubles were far from over.

There had been a mix-up on the dates when planes were supposed to arrive from Australia. Four B-17s had taken off on the 12th instead of the 13th to meet them. Two of the planes had developed engine trouble and turned back, while a third had crashed into the sea. The fourth had similar engine difficulties but managed to limp in to Del Monte airfield that evening. But since it couldn't remain on the ground in the daylight without attracting Japanese bombers and fighters, and had no functioning brakes or superchargers, Sharp had ordered the pilot to take off and head back to Australia that morning. MacArthur had just missed him.

No planes on Del Monte; no planes on the way. MacArthur had to send a sharp order to General Brett summoning three more Flying Fortresses. "This trip is most important and desperate and must be set up with absolutely the greatest of care"—which, the message implied, it had not been so far.[43]

There were two bits of good news. Around noon the remaining lost PT boat, PT-35, pulled up at Cagayan pier with a tired but relieved group of passengers that included Colonel Willoughby, Diller and Wilson, and newly minted Master Sergeant Rogers. It turned out they had gotten separated from the others during that black night of the 11th and completely missed the assembly point at Tagavayan by several miles. Instead they had tied up alongside a deserted island all day on the 12th, expecting any minute to be spotted by the Japanese.[44]

The other good news was that eight of the crew of the ditched B-17 had managed to swim to shore, and were now in safekeeping at the plantation. Sutherland spoke to them and introduced the pilot, Henry Godman, to MacArthur.

"Anyone as lucky as you are," Mac swore, "can serve with me." And so Godman became the GHQ's first staff pilot and was added to the list of people headed for Australia.[45]

Now there was nothing to do but sit and wait.

On the day MacArthur arrived in Cagayan, March 12, the commander of Japanese forces on Java accepted the surrender of his British, Australian, and American counterparts and their 60,000 troops—the Dutch army on the island having surrendered days before. It marked the ignominious end of ABDACOM, the first effort to organize joint Allied resistance to Japan—and the last until MacArthur would arrive on the scene.

Meanwhile, on March 8, Japanese soldiers had landed unopposed on the island of New Guinea, at Lae and Salamaua overlooking Huon Bay. Their mission was to build an airfield for launching air attacks on Australia, even as a Japanese submarine, I-25, was using a floatplane to reconnoiter strategic points in New Zealand.

The Japanese noose on the Western powers was tightening—and not just in the Philippines. It would be up to MacArthur to figure out how to loosen it, and reverse the tide of war—that is, if he ever reached Australia.

Because the noose was tightening around Cagayan, as well. Japanese patrols were operating only thirty miles away—while Del Monte's 500 air force personnel could not have held off a determined attack, had the local Japanese commander known what an incredible prize was just beyond his grasp. Sergeant Rogers was shown a cave where he was told MacArthur and his party could take refuge if the Japanese did attack. Since MacArthur had just escaped one set of underground tunnels, it's not clear what he would have said about having to hide in another.[46]

So there really was nothing to do but wait. Quarters were tight—MacArthur's staff had to find cots and sleep in the plantation clubhouse—and daily Japanese air attacks sent everyone scrambling for bomb shelters. But after the deprivations of Corregidor, Del Monte seemed a veritable paradise. One could walk the fields and pick fresh bananas, pineapples, and oranges; the officers' club offered tea, coffee, and other refreshments, "and most of all a great sense of freedom and release."

Still, there was no denying that every day of delay increased the chances that the Japanese would find out where they were. And as they waited, the Japanese raids intensified.

Then on Monday, March 16, the welcome news came by radio: the Flying Fortresses were coming in that night. The field had no lights, so they used car headlights and flares to guide the planes in just before midnight.

There was still one problem. Only two bombers had made it. If everyone in the party of twenty-one was going, the pilots said, they would have to leave everything, absolutely everything, behind if the B-17s were to take off.

No one was in the mood to argue. All baggage was thrown aside as the group divided in two and hastily boarded the planes. The base ordnance officer found a mattress for the general and his family to sleep on in the navigator's compartment.[47]

One by one, the engines came to life—although one of them coughed and sputtered and showed every sign of conking out. As the plane rumbled down the runway, the passengers wondered if they would ever get in the air, but slowly, painfully they did. Then they wheeled east until they were completely clear of the Mindanao coast—and any stray Japanese night air patrols—before heading south for Darwin, Australia.

The miles melted away in the darkness, mile after mile and hour after hour. Passing thousands of feet below them were Japan's latest conquests. First Java and the Dutch East Indies, then Timor, and finally northern New Guinea.

What was MacArthur thinking as he flew off into the night and left the

Philippines, the island he had sworn to defend even to the death of himself and his family?

No eyewitnesses tell us, but just before leaving, MacArthur had penned a long letter to President Quezon that reveals as much about his state of mind as any document from that period.

"An entirely new situation has developed," it read. "The United States is moving its forces into the southern Pacific area in which is destined to be the great offensive against Japan. The troops are being concentrated in Australia which will be used as a base for the offensive drive to the Philippines. President Roosevelt has designated me to command this offensive and has directed me to proceed to Australia for that purpose. . . . As a matter of fact I had no choice in the matter, being preemptorily ordered by President Roosevelt himself. I understand forces are being rapidly accumulated and hope that the drive can be undertaken before the Bataan-Corregidor situation reaches a climax."[48]

In his mind, at least, three points were as bright and clear as the sunrise coming through the cabin windows as they approached Australia.

First, he had not deserted his men on Bataan and Corregidor; he had been ordered to leave by his president, the commander in chief.

Second, on arriving in Australia he would set to work assembling the army he needed to relieve the forces he had left behind in the Philippines, which were still under his command, and to liberate the islands from their Japanese invader.

Third, once the Philippines was liberated, he would devote himself to leading the final great offensive that would crush Japan and set Asia free.

CHAPTER 18

TAKING SUPREME COMMAND

They are strong, I tell you very strong. With it all,
we shall have them.

—WINSTON CHURCHILL

TO PAUL MAZE, SUMMER 1939

There's a photograph of Jean and Douglas MacArthur in the dining car of a train to Adelaide, taken hours after they had arrived in Australia from the Philippines. Jean looks well dressed but bleary. Sir Boss is drawn and pensive, with a nervous and subdued smile.

There was reason for them to be subdued: black flies that were swarming throughout the cabin. As MacArthur's aide Sid Huff snapped pictures for posterity, Jean—who had a horror of flies—had grabbed a piece of toast and popped it into her mouth. She was suddenly frozen in horror: there had been a black fly on the toast she was swallowing.

MacArthur laughed. "It's all right, Jeannie," he said. "Just swallow it. A fly won't kill you."[1]

It was but one bizarre incident among many that had befallen them in the last twenty-four hours, hours when they had suddenly passed from being desperate refugees to celebrities and would-be saviors for a nation, namely, Australia, that was hungry for both.

The first incident came as they were approaching Darwin in their B-17, in the growing light of dawn. A radio report warned them that Darwin was under Japanese air attack. Instead they would have to land at an emergency strip called Batchelor Field, fifty miles from Darwin.[2]

For the passengers, including Sid Huff, being back on land was nothing less than a miracle, as they unwound their weary bodies from the plane's cramped interior and finally found their feet standing on solid ground.

"Never, never again, will anybody get me on an airplane!" Jean exclaimed with real vehemence. "Not for any reason!" She appealed to Huff to find some way to get them to Melbourne without having to fly.

Huff inquired, but Jean's wish wasn't going to happen. Even as the stiff and tired group were finishing a meager breakfast, they heard a new report: Japanese bombers were headed for Batchelor Field next.

Dick Sutherland acted fast. Their bombers would have to refuel and take off for Alice Springs, 800 miles away. It was a two-hour flight at most, Sutherland calculated; then they could find other, non-aerial transport the rest of the way to Melbourne.

"You get Jean on that plane," Sutherland warned Huff in a voice that brooked no opposition.[3]

In fact, the commander in chief and his wife were too tired to argue. But as they boarded the plane and stood in the aisle, the plane began to rumble down the runway. MacArthur lost his balance and barked furiously at Huff: "Sid, get that pilot's name!" It was only then that he learned that the airfield was about to be bombed, and that it was leave now or possibly never leave at all.

They flew over one of the most barren regions in Australia, empty desert punctuated by rows of rugged, impassable mountains—"the end of civilization," Huff remembered. His dismal thoughts were reinforced as they landed in Alice Springs. A few clapboard houses, a few shops and stores, a blast of stifling heat, and a constant cloud of biting, snarling black flies. But there was also a railroad track that headed out across the horizon toward Melbourne.

Jean finally put her foot down. There would be no more air flights; no more reliance on the resources of the U.S. government. When MacArthur's old friend Patrick Hurley unexpectedly flew in by chartered plane, and after happy greetings offered his plane's services to carry everyone to Melbourne, Jean said:

"No, thank you, no. We're going by train."[4]

At that moment, the army finally came through. There was a regular passenger train once a week, but the army had arranged for a special train to leave that afternoon, March 18. It wasn't much to look at: it was an old-fashioned smokestack engine with a cowcatcher in front and a coal car behind. There were two passenger coaches but no plush seats, only wooden benches on either side of the aisle. Yet once Jean MacArthur walked onto the train, Douglas, little Arthur (who was excited to be on a train for the first time in his life), and the rest of the staff followed.

The moment they left Alice Springs, MacArthur began to relax and unwind. Dinner was tedious, since the engineer had to stop the train, allow everyone to disembark and then board the dining car, where people had to climb over the benches to find their place at the long dining table.

Afterward MacArthur returned to his bench seat and watched the Australian desert landscape slip by with hypnotic monotony. His head began to nod, his eyes to close. Slowly he began to tip in the direction of Jean, who was seated next to him. A few minutes later his head was in her lap and he was fast asleep.

"I knew this train trip would be best," Jean murmured to Sid Huff. "This is the first time he's really slept since Pearl Harbor."[5]

For more than six hours MacArthur slept the sleep of the dead.

It took three days to get to Adelaide. Three days in which the outside world—the Philippines, Japan, and the United States—was shut out while the black flies were shut in, and MacArthur could finally sleep, adjust, and become the fearless intrepid commander once more, just as Jean had planned.

Tubs of ice held the food they were to eat on the trip. There was no sleeping car at first, but they picked up one later on the journey—and both Jean and Ah Cheu made up the bunks every morning.[6]

On the third day they bade goodbye to their old-fashioned train and switched to the governor of South Australia's special train for the overnight trip to Melbourne. Dick Marshall met them in Adelaide, having made the flight with Hurley that Jean had refused, and he and MacArthur paced the train talking as the reality of their situation settled in.

It was grim. There was no army in Australia to relieve Corregidor. At most there were 25,000 American troops in Australia. Not one was a rifleman. Most were engineers or aircrews and maintenance. There were no tanks and no artillery. There was no navy. There was no air force. There was no way to ferry troops and supplies to the Philippines even if Washington wanted to do so; the majority of the navy's big ships were still at the bottom of Pearl Harbor, and the rest were bracing for a possible Japanese attack on the West Coast.

For MacArthur it was a low moment in a year that had presented him with many low moments. According to Marshall, the color drained from MacArthur's face and his knees shook. He muttered, "God have mercy on us!" In Marshall's judgment it was the worst shock MacArthur experienced during the entire war, worse than Pearl Harbor.[7] Then afterward he and Jean paced the train almost all night while he sorted out the options, weighed the consequences, thought about the future. When Jean grew tired she would plop down in a chair and rest, while MacArthur continued to pace and talk and think.[8]

On the platform in Adelaide he had told the crowd of reporters watching him leave that Roosevelt had recalled him from Corregidor for the express purpose "as I understand it, of organizing the American offensive against Japan, the primary object of which is the relief of the Philippines. I came through and I shall return."[9]

"I spoke casually enough," he remembered years later, "but the phrase 'I shall return' seemed a promise of magic to the Filipinos"—and to the Americans still on Bataan and Corregidor. Now, however, he realized, although he could barely bring himself to admit it, that the hope was fading, and fading fast.[10]

Whatever else he and Jean said that night, he pledged to himself that somehow, some way, he would make that promise stick. He would make the return to the Philippines—and to the men he had been forced to abandon—the centerpiece of any strategy he evolved here in Australia.

But there was little time to think. He barely had time to catch a nap before the long, sleek train pulled into Melbourne station at 10:00 a.m. and Douglas MacArthur descended to the platform.

What greeted him was a roar of approval from a crowd of between 4,000 and 6,000 Australians, and a swarm of Australian officials, including Minister of the Army Francis M. D. Forde, plus an honor guard of 360 American soldiers and 60 reporters from Australian, American, and Dominion news sources.

MacArthur looked regal, as usual, "his jaunty garrison cap, glinting in the sun with golden oak leaves," as one reporter described it, with "an old bush jacket, like a wind breaker, open at the throat and bare of his four shiny stars." It was cold in Melbourne, much colder than he and Jean and the others were prepared for. Jean was shivering by the time they reached their hotel, despite the fur-trimmed coat she had carried in her luggage and a silk scarf Willoughby had given her.[11]

All along the way there were crowds, waving and screaming: "[I]t was their first taste of such boisterous demonstrations and it was a bit frightening," Sid Huff remembered. Jean clutched Arthur close to her as the caravan made its way through the adoring throng. MacArthur said to Sid Huff, "take care of the family," and then headed off for the first round of meetings that would introduce him to his Australian hosts, and introduce them to the MacArthur way of doing things.

Australians in March 1942 found themselves in a terrible fix, as they themselves might say. The Japanese attack on British possessions in Asia had been all too successful. Malaya, Singapore, Burma: one by one the bastions of empire had fallen, leaving Australia and New Zealand, the twin dominions in the Southern Hemisphere, dangerously exposed. The sinking of the *Repulse* and the *Prince of Wales* back in December signaled the end of any British naval deterrence in that part of the world. Australians were on their own, and had no resources to counter the steady, inexorable Japanese advance in their direction—or the bombs falling on northern cities like Darwin.

Then came news of MacArthur's arrival, along with only a vague picture of what had happened in the Philippines, or of MacArthur's ongoing battles with Roosevelt and Washington. Far from being "Dugout Doug," or a general rescued by presidential order from a failed campaign, to Australians he seemed a paladin, a savior even, in a time of desperate need.

The *Brisbane Courier* wrote that his arrival "was stirring news, the best news Australians have had for many a day." The *Melbourne Herald* wrote:

"[T]he United States would not send its greatest contemporary soldier to a secondary war zone, and the fact that it regards Australia as a sphere of supreme importance is by far the most heartening circumstance which the Commonwealth ministers have encountered since Japan entered the war." Minister Forde himself (later a severe MacArthur critic) was convinced that "MacArthur was the man who would influence his government along the right lines."[12]

What MacArthur did not understand then or later was that his presence represented far more than the arrival of a great military leader on Australian soil (a fact that Douglas MacArthur would never deny). In his memoirs he would describe how he met with worried Australian military officials who showed him maps with three-quarters of the country abandoned to the Japanese, while a last-ditch defense was prepared behind the so-called Brisbane Line, all of which MacArthur dismissed with a swipe of his hand. "The concept was purely one of passive defense," he recalled, "and I felt it would result only in eventual defeat."[13]

In fact, the Australians were never quite so timid, or so naive. What they were really getting with MacArthur was an American pledge of unlimited support, the kind of outpouring of men, planes, ships, and war materiel that was already hurtling across the Atlantic to Britain; through the Arctic Circle to Russia; and over the Himalayas to China. Now they would be safe—and not just because General Douglas MacArthur had graced them with his presence.

But he did also grace them with his presence, both in his mind and theirs, starting that afternoon at the train station when he read a short statement.

"I am glad indeed to be in immediate cooperation with the Australian soldier," he proclaimed. "I know him very well from the World War days and admire him greatly. I have every confidence in the ultimate success of our joint cause: but success in modern war requires something more than courage and a willingness to die; it requires careful preparation."

He was telling them that it would be a long war and, given the paucity of war materiel he had and could expect, it would be a war of logistics as much as fighting and strategy. America and Australia would prevail, but "my success or failure will depend primarily upon the resources which the respective governments place at my disposal."[14]

Meanwhile, it was clearly going to be a long, hard journey from Melbourne to Manila.

On March 26 MacArthur had his real coming-out party.

Henry Godman flew him to Canberra, the nation's capital, for a lavish dinner in his honor hosted by Prime Minister John Curtin. It was the first time the two men had met. Curtin, who had risked everything in suggesting that MacArthur come to Australia to assume command of the combined American-Australian forces, was captivated by his charisma and confidence. MacArthur told the premier's Advisory War Council that he didn't think the Japanese had the strength to take North Australia (some might have pointed out that he hadn't thought they could take the Philippines either) and that he believed the Germany First strategy that Roosevelt and the War Department had taken on was a mistake. Nonetheless, the chief job of the Allies was "to make Australia secure," and he was going to do it.

But that would be only the first step toward a counteroffensive to retake the Philippines, he said. Since Prime Minister Curtin was also minister of defense, MacArthur suggested that they personally coordinate the joint Australian-American planning.[15]

Although Curtin had no military experience, he agreed, while the Advisory War Council became, in effect, Australia's War Cabinet. As they left the meeting, MacArthur threw his arm over the prime minister's shoulder and said, "You take care of the rear and I'll take care of the front." From that point on, Curtin would be MacArthur's biggest fan outside his own staff, and he would defer to MacArthur's judgment on everything, including war mobilization, far more than he would to his own military.[16]

The highlight of the dinner that night was a stunning announcement from the American ambassador. General MacArthur had just been awarded the Medal of Honor.

"For conspicuous leadership in preparing the Philippine Islands to resist conquest," read the citation (George Marshall had drafted it himself), "for gallantry and intrepidity above and beyond the call of duty in action against invading Japanese forces . . . He mobilized, trained, and led an army which has received world acclaim in men and arms. His utter disregard of personal danger under heavy fire and aerial bombardment, his calm judgment in each crisis, inspired his troops, galvanized the spirit of resistance of the Filipino people, and confirmed the faith of the American people in their armed forces."[17]

The crowd rose to their feet and applauded. MacArthur must have been amazed, and chagrined. For once the impetus for America's highest military honor had not come from him, but from General Marshall—and Congress. MacArthur's fans in Congress had passed a resolution calling on President Roosevelt to give him the Medal of Honor—the first time Congress had ever prompted a president to make such an award.

Marshall had agreed. Marshall saw the Medal of Honor as a way to bolster the confidence of the American people as well as MacArthur. It was to make them feel that the eventual fall of the Philippines was a matter of heroic sacrifice rather than a humiliating loss, and to counter Axis propaganda that portrayed MacArthur as a coward who had abandoned his command.[18]

That was in fact the way MacArthur himself felt about what had happened. In his mind, he had won a Medal of Honor for deserting his command under orders. This was not what he would have wanted, not after Mexico twenty-eight years earlier, and certainly not after the Côte de Châtillon. But MacArthur accepted the award with a stoic face (interestingly, he doesn't even allude to the incident in his memoirs) and then gave an emotional speech to the assembly that left few dry eyes, and no doubt that a great change had come to Australia's situation in the war.

"There can be no compromise," he told the guests in a voice thick with emotion. "We shall win or we shall die, and to this end I pledge the full resources of all the power of my mighty country and all the blood of my countrymen." In fact, it was not a pledge that he had any authority to give. But it reassured Australians: come what may they were not going to lose or be conquered. And for Douglas MacArthur, the meetings and the dinner on March 26 marked his rebirth as commander and strategist after the Bataan debacle.[19]

"MacArthur is out of Philippine Islands," Dwight Eisenhower wrote in his diary for March 19. "Now supreme commander of 'SouthWest Pacific Area.'"

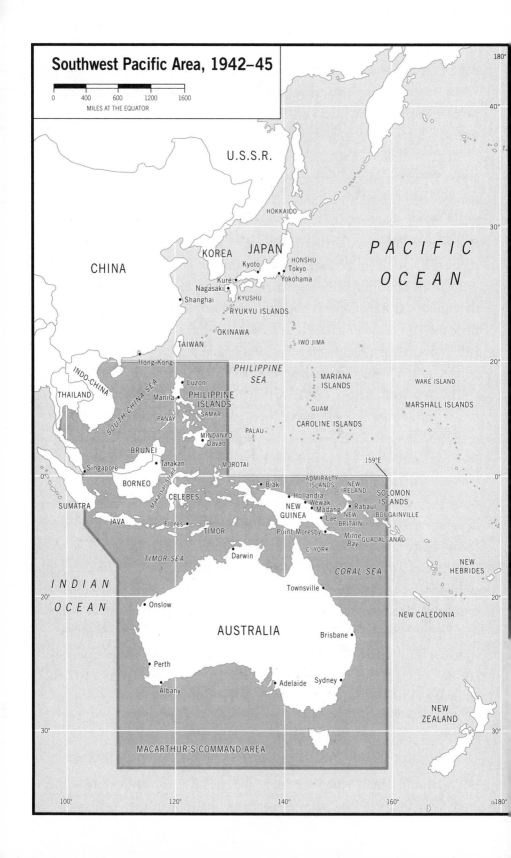

Southwest Pacific Area, 1942–45

0   400   600   1200   1600
MILES AT THE EQUATOR

U.S.S.R.

PACIFIC

OCEAN

CHINA

HOKKAIDO

KOREA   JAPAN
         Kyoto   HONSHU
         Kure   Tokyo
Nagasaki   Yokohama
• Shanghai   KYUSHU
         RYUKYU ISLANDS
              OKINAWA
TAIWAN   ○ IWO JIMA

Hong Kong

PHILIPPINE
SEA   MARIANA
                    ISLANDS   WAKE ISLAND

INDO-CHINA
THAILAND   • Luzon
            Manila • PHILIPPINE   MARSHALL ISLANDS
SOUTH CHINA SEA   ISLANDS
         PANAY   SAMAR   GUAM
                           PALAU   CAROLINE ISLANDS
            MINDANAO
BRUNEI   • Davao

• Singapore • Tarakan   MOROTAI   159°E
BORNEO   ADMIRALTY NEW
         CELEBES   • Biak   ISLANDS IRELAND SOLOMON
SUMATRA   • Hollandia   ISLANDS
                             NEW   • Wewak • Rabaul
JAVA   Flores •   GUINEA • Madang NEW   BOUGAINVILLE
                TIMOR   • Lae BRITAIN
                        Point Moresby •   Milne GUADALCANAL
                                          Bay
TIMOR SEA   Darwin •   C. YORK

INDIAN   CORAL SEA   NEW
                                                       HEBRIDES
OCEAN   • Onslow   Townsville •

                                              NEW CALEDONIA
         AUSTRALIA   Brisbane •

• Perth

      • Adelaide Sydney •
Albany   NEW
                                              ZEALAND

MACARTHUR'S COMMAND AREA

100°   120°   140°   160°   180°

180°
40°
30°
20°
0°
20°
30°

The newspapers acclaim the move—the public has built itself a hero out of its own imagination. I hope he can do the miracles expected and predicted; we could use a few now."[20]

Ike's gloom was understandable. By the end of the month Japan had captured every objective for which it had gone to war. Malaya, Singapore, Hong Kong, the Dutch East Indies, and northern Borneo were in Japanese hands. The fall of Burma and the Philippines was only a matter of time.

For the Allies, especially the British and the Americans, the past five months had been one defeat after another. In addition to lost territory and the disaster at Pearl Harbor, British naval losses (taking into account ships lost in the European theater since November 1941), had left the once-great Royal Navy with only one modern battleship, the *King George V,* and two fleet carriers.[21]

Neither Britain nor America had ever fought a major war in the Pacific, nor had either ever fought an enemy who had better air *and* sea power. The old prewar planning assumption that still prevailed when Churchill and Roosevelt met in Washington on December 12, 1941, and American and British military leaders met at the so-called Arcadia Conference, that Britain and America could hold off the Japanese while fighting their main battles in Europe, was now clearly—perhaps fatally—out of date.

It was now apparent that three things would have to happen if the Allies were going to somehow reverse the tide of defeat.

First, there would have to be a massive reinforcement of ships, troops, and warplanes to prevent any further Japanese advance. Second, the United Kingdom and the United States would have to coordinate their operations in the Pacific and work out a common strategy—something that no one had attempted so far.

Third, the United States was going to have to take the lead in both, including in the Southwest Pacific. Britain had neither the industrial resources nor the bases in the region any longer to act as anything but a deputy to the Americans. Washington had always thought of that vast area of ocean as part of Britain's global responsibility, including defending Australia. Now that was clearly impossible. The United States would have to step in, not just to halt any Japanese invasion of Australia but to take leadership of the entire Pacific war.[22]

That suited MacArthur. He saw himself as the man poised to assume both roles. Meanwhile, the generals and admirals back in Washington, the very ones he blamed for his recent debacle, were working around the clock to give him the power to make it happen.

How was America going to fight a war thousands of miles away in the Pacific? That was the problem the Joint Chiefs of Staff in Washington were pondering. Everyone understood the basic principle of unity of command, of having a single commander in chief. But the services couldn't agree on who should get the nod. The navy was clearly going to dominate any strategy in the Pacific. Its ships and aircraft carriers would be essential to defeating Japan. By the same token, there was no way the navy would allow any army general to take command of its ships, and certainly not MacArthur. He had permanently poisoned his relationship with the navy brass during the Philippines campaign, with his constant complaints about their lack of support—lack of courage even.[23]

Likewise, there was no way that Army Chief of Staff George Marshall was going to agree to let an admiral, no matter how experienced or senior, tell the army what to do. Eisenhower's view of Navy Chief Admiral Ernest King—"he's the antithesis of cooperation, a deliberately rude person, which means he's a mental bully . . . one thing that might help win this war is to get someone to shoot King"—was shared by many in the army, and was not too far removed from Marshall's.[24]

So in the end the Joint Chiefs arrived at a compromise, and a split of command. Admiral Chester Nimitz would assume command over the vast reaches of the central Pacific, including the eastern approaches to Japan, with his headquarters at Pearl. MacArthur was picked to be supreme commander in what was dubbed the South West Pacific Area, or SWPA, including Australia and New Zealand, the Philippines and Dutch East Indies, Sumatra, and Borneo, in addition to the Solomon Islands and New Guinea—and an arc of ocean equal to the size of twenty-five Texases.[25]

Commanding and coordinating military campaigns in a theater this large was going to be a logistical nightmare, especially when the bulk of navy and civilian shipping was being directed across the Atlantic to Europe. At the same time, MacArthur would have to share what was left with Nimitz's Pacific Oceans Area. In addition, Nimitz would retain overall control over *all* naval operations in both areas, even when they occurred in MacArthur's backyard (only a small token force was under MacArthur's direct command).[26]

This would be a constant source of friction and difficulty as the war went on—as was the fact that both MacArthur and Nimitz had to defer on matters of overall strategy to Washington, where the Joint Chiefs of Staff retained final say. This is in fact a vital point: at no time during the entire war was MacArthur allowed to plan and carry out strategy by himself. Everything had to pass through Washington for discussion and debate, including his plans for liberating the Philippines—and now his plans for organizing the defense of Australia.

In one sense, MacArthur didn't care. For him, supreme command of the South West Pacific Area was the call of destiny as well as a personal crusade. The logistical problems, the lack of troops and resources, especially airplanes, and his divided, truncated authority—all these challenges paled in comparison to what he saw as his number one priority: defending Australia so he could launch his campaign to save the Philippines.

To do this, he decided, he would need three or four combat infantry divisions, a brace of aircraft carriers, and a marine amphibious division, in addition to a lot more aircraft than the 12 B-17s, 27 dive bombers, and 177 fighters he had on hand. Most of those fighters were either out of date or unserviceable, as were many of the planes in the two Royal Australian Air Force combat squadrons operating out of Darwin and the three based in New Guinea.[27] But Washington had nothing to send. At the beginning of April 1942 only four army divisions had embarked for the entire Pacific theater, two of which were incomplete—and only one of those, the Forty-first, was headed for Australia.

That meant that whatever MacArthur was going to do that spring and summer, he would have to rely on his Australian allies. They were commanded by General Sir Thomas Blamey, a rotund, square-headed man who looked more like a pub owner than the Down Under version of Douglas MacArthur. Blamey had earned plaudits in World War One first as a combat officer, taking part in the Gallipoli campaign during the bloody landings at Anzac Cove on April 25, 1915, then as a staff officer, both during the Gallipoli campaign and on the western front. Like MacArthur, he ended the war as a brigadier general; like MacArthur, he liked to lead midnight trench raids even as a staffer.

Also like MacArthur, Blamey had a keen interest in any new military innovations, like the tank, of which he was an early supporter, and he helped to form the Royal Australian Air Force between the wars. Finally, like MacArthur, Blamey knew the face of defeat against a technically superior, better-prepared enemy. After serving in the Western Desert commanding an Australian division, he had transferred to the debacle in Greece in 1941 where his soldiers' subpar performance led him to organize an overhaul of Australian troop training. He then returned from the Middle East in March 1942 to take over as commander in chief, Australian Military Forces.

On paper, certainly, it was a sizable force of seven infantry divisions, one armored, and two motorized divisions—more than 104,000 soldiers in addition to 265,000 trained militia.[28] For the SWPA, Blamey was prepared to supply three soldiers to every one of MacArthur's Americans. He must have assumed he would have a major say in how they operated and where, while on April 9 George Marshall urged MacArthur to make sure that senior positions on his SWPA staff were given to Australian officers, on whom he would have to rely to do most of the fighting.[29]

Both Blamey and Marshall fully understood MacArthur's need to rely on his own handpicked staff, especially in times of uncertainty. But both also underestimated his skill in outmaneuvering any possible rival for directing overall strategy. He had already taken the first step by becoming fast friends with Prime Minister John Curtin. The second came with co-opting Australian Defence Department head Fred Shedden. Indeed, Shedden's diary provides a revealing record of MacArthur's steady courtship of the prime minister and his War Cabinet, until in the end Curtin relied more on MacArthur for advice on how to run the Australian war effort than he did on his own generals.

Shedden began meeting regularly with MacArthur in April. "Anyone who has had close relations with General MacArthur," he wrote later, "cannot come away without [sic] any other impression than that he has been in the presence of a great masterful personality" with "a broad and cultured mind and a fine command of English," although Shedden admitted that some might be put off by "a certain demonstrative manner and his verbosity."

Still, Shedden found "he has great enthusiasm for his work, but becomes depressed at the political frustrations which, in his view, shape world strategy, to the detriment of the Southwest Pacific Area." It was a considerable shock, for example, to hear MacArthur openly lament his lack of resources in Australia and say that he had "lost heart and wanted to give his job up."[30]

If his cri de coeur was meant to rally a nervous prime minister, and an equally nervous cabinet, to MacArthur's cause, it succeeded perfectly. Shedden presented Curtin with a letter—it may have been written by MacArthur himself—endorsing the plan to commit all Australian forces to MacArthur's command. "You have come to Australia to lead a crusade," the letter enthused, "the result of which means everything to the future of the world and mankind. At the request of a sovereign State you are placed in supreme command of its Navy, Army, and Air Force, so that with your great nation, they may be welded into a homogeneous force and given that unified direction which is so vital for the achievement of victory."[31]

No more was heard about incorporating Australian officers into MacArthur's evolving South West Pacific strategy, let alone admirals. He now had the tiller in his hands and his only—except for the permission he needed from the Joint Chiefs in Washington, and except for what Admiral Nimitz and his boss, Admiral King, were willing to assign as naval assets to carry out their plans.

Then, just as MacArthur was regaining his confidence and gaining political purchase for the campaigns to come, the worst news of all emerged.

Bataan had surrendered.

When MacArthur had left, Homma's Japanese forces had still been regrouping and resupplying for the final assault. On April 2 they were ready. That night the skies over Bataan opened with an air and artillery bombardment that rivaled World War One.

When the sun rose on the next day the peninsula was literally on fire. "The artillery fires were reinforced periodically by the heavy thumps of bombs," an eyewitness said, "which shrieked in clusters from dive bombers which flew with almost complete impunity back and forth across the lines."[32]

After five hours of relentless pounding, the Japanese had blown a hole through the jungle where the Forty-first Philippine Division was situated. "The defenders had been reduced to a dazed, disorganized, fleeing mob," John Olson, an American officer with the Fifty-seventh Philippine Scouts, observed. Elsewhere Japanese tanks punched holes in lines and the Americans had no chance of plugging them.

Back on Corregidor, Paul Bunker got the news. "It appears that our Philippine Army Bataan Force had crumpled and run, letting the Japs penetrate our center and roll up our right," he confessed to his diary. On April 7 Japanese troops had reached Mount Samat, the 2,000-foot promontory overlooking the entire peninsula.

General Clifford Bluemel and his men were steadily falling back as their flanks collapsed. On the night of April 8 they halted by a quick-rushing stream, and General Parker reached Bluemel by field telephone to order him to form a new line of defense.

"I have no staff, I have no transportation, no communications except the phone I hold in my hand," Bluemel bellowed. "My force consists of the only units that have fought the enemy, not run from them. . . . Where is the food we need to revive our starving bodies? Where is the ammunition we need to fire at the enemy? . . . I'll form a line, but don't expect it to hold much past daylight. OUT!"[33] Back on Corregidor, Wainwright sent a desperate message to MacArthur. "I am forced to report that the troops on Bataan are fast folding up." He listed three divisions that over the past forty-eight hours had ceased to exist. "The troops are so weak from malnutrition that they have no power of resistance."

But from his office in Melbourne, MacArthur was still not writing off Luzon Force. He knew, following FDR's directive, that there was no possibility of surrender. So he drafted a last-minute three-part plan, with I Corps on the left staging an artillery bombardment, II Corps on the right launching a surprise attack, followed by I Corps doing the same on the left. If II Corps could reach Subic Bay, MacArthur reasoned, there was a slim chance they could get supplies and make a fresh stand. If the attacks failed, the survivors, "after inflicting important losses upon the enemy, could escape through the Zambales Mountains and continue guerrilla warfare" with partisan forces operating in northern Luzon.[34]

It was a wild, desperate plan. Historians, conveniently forgetting about Roosevelt's order, have had a field day criticizing MacArthur's vision of American and Philippine soldiers, 80 percent of whom were crippled by malaria and/or dysentery, carrying out a formal surprise attack, then conducting an orderly withdrawal into the mountains. But in MacArthur's mind, this was all that was left. Washington had no better ideas, but refused to endorse his plan.

To the end of his life MacArthur was convinced it could have gotten at least some of the American and Filipino soldiers into the relative safety of Luzon's hinterlands. Whatever deprivations awaited them there, they would be better than the humiliation of the biggest mass surrender in American history—and the horrors of what came afterward.[35]

Skinny Wainwright, on the other hand, was closer to realities on the ground. He was seeing surrender as the last remaining option to avoid wholesale massacre. But he could not disobey Roosevelt's order *not* to surrender. So in the end he left the question up to the commander of I Corps, General Edward King.

It was a gross abdication of the responsibility of command—almost exactly what MacArthur would be wrongly accused of doing for years afterward. But no one can dare blame Wainwright for exercising it. He and King spoke by field telephone on April 8. When he hung up, King explained to his staff that while Wainwright could not authorize a surrender, he would not interfere if King decided on his own authority to surrender.

Hungry and exhausted, many of them began to weep.

"If I survive to return home I fully expect to be court-martialed," he told them. "History won't deal kindly with the commander who surrendered the largest force the United States had ever lost."[36]

The next day two officers from King's staff set out toward the front line with a white flag. They were charged and nearly killed by a platoon of Japanese infantry, until frantic waving of the flag made it clear that the Americans had had enough and wanted to see the Japanese commanding officer.

After a ninety-minute meeting with General Kameichiro Nagano, commander of the Twenty-first Infantry Group, King reluctantly accepted unconditional surrender. During the talks fighting was still going on—including for Bluemel's Thirty-first Philippine Division, who may have fought the last engagement on Bataan. Meanwhile, the air was punctuated with the sound of ammo dumps being blown up across the peninsula. Finally, on April 10, orders came for the garrison on Bataan to stack arms and put out white flags.

The news came to MacArthur in Melbourne like a bolt of lightning. He canceled all appointments and retreated to his office. Captain Ray found him there, relentlessly pacing like a caged panther. When MacArthur turned, tears were streaming down his face.

To make it worse, the same day he received a message from FDR. The president had decided to rescind the official No Surrender order he had issued to MacArthur on February 9 and to Wainwright on March 23, and left it up to Wainwright to decide what to do—but "only if you concur both as to substance and timing," he said in an aside to MacArthur.[37]

What MacArthur wanted was now irrelevant; Bataan had surrendered. In its final days MacArthur had adhered to his president's wishes, and now looked like the coldhearted villain for leaving his men behind. To some, including some Bataan veterans, he still does. What MacArthur didn't realize was that Roosevelt had only wanted the appearance of an Alamo on Bataan, to rally public opinion. MacArthur, in his literal-minded way, had given him the reality.[38]

Now only Corregidor still held out—although it was obvious that nothing could save its tiny garrison once the Japanese brought their full weight to bear.

After April 10 MacArthur's plans focused on a new objective, once he had secured Australia. It was the biggest Japanese base in the region, and the key to the entire South West Pacific Area: Rabaul.

Since the Japanese had captured Rabaul during the last week of January, they had turned this easternmost tip of the island of New Britain into one of the most lethal pieces of real estate in the Pacific. More than 100,000 troops were garrisoned there, while engineers cleared six airfields with 166 concrete revetments for bombers and 265 revetments for fighters. Rabaul was also a major naval airbase and had anchorages for seaplanes, while forty massive coastal guns backed by twenty powerful searchlights earned it the nickname "Pearl Harbor of the South Pacific."

Rabaul not only gave Japan air superiority for a thousand miles in every direction. It could also serve to block seaward access to Australia from the east, including from the United States, and to protect new Japanese conquests to the west, including Borneo and the Philippines. Finally, it was the perfect jumping-off point for a fresh wave of Japanese invasions, aimed right for the capital of New Guinea, Port Moresby, and even Australia itself.

But before MacArthur could begin planning his routes to Rabaul, the U.S. Navy carried out three operations that began to shift the balance of power away from the Japanese for the first time, and would give MacArthur breathing space to transform looming disaster into a springboard for taking the offensive.

The first came on March 10, when planes from the aircraft carriers *Yorktown* and *Lexington,* en route for a raid on Rabaul, caught a number of Japanese ships landing troops on the coast of New Guinea at Lae and Salamaua in the Huon Gulf (the first Japanese arrived on the 8th). The planes sank two large transports and two other ships, and pounded nine others, including a light cruiser and two destroyers. It was the U.S. Navy's first big success in battle, and proof that the American carriers could be as effective as their Japanese counterparts had been at Pearl Harbor. The raid also spurred the Japanese to decide that if they were going to conduct bigger operations against Australia and MacArthur's forces there, they would need a more forward air base from which to operate—namely, Port Moresby on the southeastern tip of New Guinea.[39]

News that a Japanese invasion fleet was aimed at Moresby, under the protection of no fewer than three aircraft carriers, prompted the navy's second big success, as Admiral Nimitz sent the *Yorktown* and the *Lexington* to meet them. On May 7 the two forces tangled over the skies of the Coral Sea, in the first carrier-on-carrier conflict in history. The *Lexington* took a pounding from the Japanese planes, then fell victim to a submarine, leaving Nimitz with just one carrier, the damaged *Yorktown,* and forty pilots. But the Americans managed to take out one Japanese carrier, the *Shoho,* and damage another so severely that it had to head back to its base on Truk for repairs.

Overall, the Japanese lost so many planes and pilots in the Battle of the Coral Sea that the invasion fleet had to turn back.

Even though the battle had been squarely in the middle of his Southwest Pacific Area, MacArthur himself had played no part in the fight, except to send a small force of Australian and American cruisers and destroyers under his naval commander, Australian rear admiral J. G. Grace.[40] Yet the action in the Coral Sea had stopped a Japanese invasion of New Guinea cold, before MacArthur would have been prepared to meet it, and it set the stage for the navy's third and most decisive contribution to leveling the playing field in the Pacific, the Battle of Midway on June 4, 1942.

News of the impending Japanese invasion had come from navy code-breakers who had penetrated the Japanese navy's most secret plans (MacAr-thur's codebreakers in Australia, by contrast, were still baffled by the Japanese army's ciphers).[41] During the last week of May the codebreakers learned the date, time, and locations of a far bigger Japanese operation than the invasion of Port Moresby: a simultaneous strike on the Aleutian Islands and on the remaining U.S. possession in the central Pacific, Midway Island, backed by no fewer than six aircraft carriers and nine battleships hoping to entice the U.S. fleet out for a final decisive battle.

The mastermind of the Midway operation, Admiral Yamamoto, got more of a battle than he bargained for. When it was over, Nimitz's carriers *Hornet, Enterprise,* and *Yorktown* had sunk the four Japanese carriers headed for Midway along with a heavy cruiser, while damaging another. American losses—the carrier *Yorktown* and a destroyer—seemed miraculously light compared to the crippling blow they had delivered to the Japanese navy and to Yamamoto's reputation as the reigning naval genius of the age (he had also masterminded the attack on Pearl Harbor).

Very suddenly the entire picture of the war in the Pacific had changed. The possibility of Japan's using its naval strength to gain the upper hand across the two areas of command, Nimitz's and MacArthur's, had dimin-ished almost to the vanishing point. Never again would the Japanese navy be able to mount large-scale offensive operations, and certainly not against Australia. This meant the next phase of the war against Japan was going to be a land war, retaking Japan's Pacific conquests one by one. And Coral Sea and

Midway together had bought MacArthur the time he needed to build up his forces for taking on that vital task.

By June 1942 MacArthur's American forces, which had seemed so pitifully thin on the ground in March, had steadily built up. The core was the men of the Thirty-second Division, now joined by large elements of the Forty-first Division, as well as new air and artillery units. All the same, the bulk of MacArthur's forces in SWPA would be Australian, even though MacArthur made sure that the Australians played no role in the shaping of overall strategy.[42]

This was strange, since his very first order for the organization of SWPA, issued on April 18, assigned as his immediate subordinates two Australians, General Blamey in charge of Allied Land Forces and Vice Admiral Herbert Leary in charge of Allied Naval Forces, along with Major General Julian Barnes in charge of United States Forces in Australia and Wainwright commanding United States Forces in the Philippines (a command that soon ceased to exist). Yet none of this mattered, since all his senior staff who did the SWPA planning and supervised execution of the plans were Americans, and all except three had been with him in the Philippines, the group that posterity branded the Bataan Gang.

The gang included the usual suspects such as Sutherland as chief of staff; Dick Marshall, deputy chief of staff; Charles Stivers, personnel (G-1); Charles Willoughby, intelligence (G-2); Hugh Casey, engineer; Billy Marquat, anti-aircraft; and LeGrand Diller, public relations.[43] The newcomers were Stephen Chamberlin, head of planning (G-3); Lester Whitlock, head of supply (G-4); and Adjutant General Burdette Fitch, chief administrative officer.

As a cohesive team, they soon found themselves enmeshed in the personal and turf battles that were typical of any large command staff, and especially MacArthur's at SWPA. Sutherland was as abrasive as ever; Chamberlin proved to be a fatherly man with a great capacity for hard work and an almost hero-worship attitude toward MacArthur. But he also suffered from almost-fatal caution when it came to planning military operations that his chief constantly had to battle against. Willoughby's affectations, including his polished, Prussian-like manners, continued to irritate many on the staff. His inconsistent and sometimes wildly off-the-mark intelligence estimates irritated them more, although MacArthur never seemed to lose faith in the man who was, above all, dedicated to MacArthur officially and personally.

The outstanding figure on MacArthur's staff over the next two years, however, would be former Lieutenant Colonel, now Brigadier General, Spencer Akin, officially chief signal officer but in fact MacArthur's leading code-breaker.

Tall and gangly with a pencil neck and Lincolnesque features, Akin had served in the office of the army's chief signal officer, in charge of signal intelligence from August 1939 until April 1941. Then MacArthur had personally asked to have him sent out to the Philippines to head his own intelligence unit, which Akin set to work intercepting Japanese radio traffic.[44]

Nothing they did had helped in any way to learn of the attack on the Philippines, but MacArthur never lost his personal interest in Akin's activities. When Akin and his team evacuated to Australia in March 1942, MacArthur ordered the creation of the Central Bureau in April, combining American and Australian intelligence gathering and code breaking under one roof, literally, in offices on Henry Street in Melbourne.

Akin was in charge, and put his team to work sifting daily through Japanese radio traffic and translating and deciphering whatever they could find. What Akin produced, Willoughby as head of G-2 analyzed (together with whatever deciphered messages the navy passed along from its code breaking or Operation ULTRA), while it was up to Sutherland to decide whether MacArthur would see the results or not.[45] It was a grueling, frustrating job. For months, Akin and the men on Henry Street struggled to turn Morse code dots and dashes in Japanese into actionable intelligence, an almost impossible task, given the fact they had no way to decipher the various codes. But increasingly they would provide MacArthur with a situational awareness, if only by showing where and when Japanese military traffic was increasing, that would gradually strip away the mystery from the enemy's moves on the SWPA chessboard—until by 1944 Central Bureau could give MacArthur and his staff almost unlimited insight into every Japanese move before it happened.

For now, however, MacArthur felt confident enough after the victory at

Midway to unveil his own plans for surrounding the Japanese on New Guinea, and pressing on to capture Rabaul. He knew that by taking the fortress on New Britain, he could wipe out any Japanese air superiority over the entire region—and drive any Japanese shipping back to the island of Truk, more than 700 miles to the north. On June 8 he wrote to Marshall, emphasizing that the victory at Midway had created a situation that should be "exploited at once." He proposed sending a task force of two carriers with an amphibious division to strike at Rabaul. Marshall was convinced, and did MacArthur one better by adding three infantry divisions to MacArthur's amphibious force—even if it meant diverting troops from the buildup in Europe—and putting in a third carrier to the supporting task force.[46]

The navy, however, killed the plan cold, and in the end, it was a good thing they did. The plan called for three carriers more than King and his colleagues were willing to commit to a venture that would expose them to round-the-clock land-based air attacks—and certainly not a venture commanded by the likes of Douglas MacArthur. Even more, the resources that MacArthur and Marshall were committing to a ground attack would have been woefully inadequate in the face of the forces the Japanese had built up in Rabaul. Any amphibious landing in 1942, given the Japanese advantages in Rabaul and American inexperience with assaults of this sort, would have been a slaughter. So MacArthur's idea died a merciful bureaucratic death, as planners in Washington scrambled to find other ways to take the initiative away from imperial Japan.

The navy veto of the Rabaul plan revealed something else as well. Nimitz had thought nothing of sending two carrier task forces during Coral Sea operations without seeking MacArthur's permission, yet his superiors thought nothing of vetoing MacArthur's plan inviting carriers into the same area. And when earlier on April 24 MacArthur had begged for carriers to be part of SWPA naval forces, with Prime Minister Curtin personally signing on, the navy had said no—even as *Yorktown* and *Lexington* were steaming toward the Coral Sea, which sat in the middle of MacArthur's jurisdiction.

Historian H. P. Wilmott, hardly a MacArthur partisan, has pointed out that the treatment of MacArthur on this occasion was "dishonest."[47] Secretary of War Henry Stimson, meanwhile, complained bitterly of the navy secretary's and the president's seeming inability to rein in their admirals, especially Ernest King, in their detestation of MacArthur. While "the extraordinary brilliance of that officer was not always matched by his tact," Stimson noted, "the Navy's astonishing bitterness toward him seemed childish."[48]

The truth was, not only was MacArthur a lower priority than winning the war in Europe. He was also a lower priority than supplying and equipping Nimitz's forces in the central Pacific. In an area as large as the continent of North America, from San Francisco to New York, and from Alaska to Guatemala, MacArthur and his generals would be chronically starved for ships and planes and men. Prime Minister Curtin noted it too. He wrote to Churchill, "[T]he commander in chief . . . is bitterly disappointed with the meager assistance promised for the Southwest Pacific Area for the performance of the tasks imposed upon him by his directive."[49]

Yet Churchill had passed the Australian problem on to Roosevelt, and washed his hands of it—while Roosevelt and General Marshall acquiesced in the navy's takeover of overall strategy. This was maddening for MacArthur, who blamed George Marshall for letting it happen. "The complete absorption of the national defense function by the Navy," he exploded at one point, had left the army "relegated to merely base, training, garrisoning, and supply purposes."[50]

MacArthur set out to change that. On May 8 he had even sent a letter to Roosevelt insisting that the SWPA was now the real second front to help the Soviet Union, and should receive its share of resources accordingly. Even Winston Churchill had to tell FDR that with this letter MacArthur had crossed the line that separated military responsibility from political authority, and had to be admonished not to do it again.[51] It was not the first time MacArthur had trod close to that line, and it would certainly not be the last.

So there was no Big Push coming from the SWAP, and no big buildup in men or materiel for MacArthur. But one thing was clear. With the victory at Midway, he and Curtin agreed on June 17 that the threat of immediate invasion had lifted. Now it was time to take the initiative.[52]

That meant MacArthur's attention was now riveted to the north and west, on the green expanse of the island of New Guinea.

Roughly the size of California, Papua New Guinea is the second-largest island in the world after Australia. A sprawling 175,000 square miles of jun-

gle, swamp, and volcanic mountains, it is split across the center by the Owen
Stanley Range running from the northwest to the southeast. The Owen Stanleys rise to 13,000 feet at certain points, and are virtually impenetrable except across two or three passes.[53] Every place else on the island is covered by
a thick canopy of jungle and inhabited by a bewildering variety of tribal
people who speak one-fifth of all the languages spoken in the world. In 1942
it had no roads or infrastructure; no real towns except its capital, Port
Moresby; and was home to mind-destroying heat and humidity, and every
tropical disease known to humanity.

But New Guinea was vital to Japanese plans—and now to MacArthur's.
The Japanese had already occupied the western part of the island, along with
Lae and Salamaua farther east. Their original plan had been to seize Port
Moresby as a forward base for attacks into northern Australia and to halt any
Allied buildup in the Southwest Pacific Area from moving north, especially
in the direction of Rabaul—the linchpin of Japan's entire empire in the South
Pacific.

That plan had been foiled at Coral Sea. But only days later the threat from
Rabaul had taken a dangerous new twist, when on May 18 MacArthur received a message from his new naval commander, Vice Admiral Arthur
Carpender. MacArthur didn't have any better relations with Carpender than
he had had with Thomas Hart; he was just as convinced that the navy saw its
job in SWPA as undercutting his authority, and limiting support for his operations, as much as possible.[54]

But in this case Carpender's help was vital, because it was a message from
the navy's ULTRA decrypt office in Melbourne, which Nimitz ordered the
admiral to share with MacArthur. It predicted that by June 15 the Japanese
would attempt an overland invasion of Moresby from Lae and Salamaua, just
200 miles northwest of Port Moresby, by using the Kokoda Trail over the
Owen Stanley Mountains.[55]

At first MacArthur was not overly alarmed. He didn't imagine the Japanese could pull such an invasion off. He knew the Owen Stanley terrain was
murderously rugged; it seemed impossible anyone could get across those
mountains, certainly not a large force. Yet he had seen the Japanese do something similar on Mount Natib on the Bataan Peninsula. So he sent a mina-
tory message to Blamey that there was a possibility that "minor forces" might

make a stab at Port Moresby from the Law-Salamaua area, and telling him to put his forces on the lookout.[56]

Meanwhile, MacArthur was focused on his own plans for using New Guinea as the stepping-stone for his advance running in the opposite direction as the Japanese, toward New Britain and Rabaul. That meant first building an adequate airbase at Milne Bay, one that could knock out any seaborne attack on Port Moresby, and also stationing troops at Buna, farther up the northern coast, where there was already an airstrip. A survey had revealed that the Buna strip was not suitable for large numbers of combat aircraft, but engineers could build another strip at Dobodura, ten miles to the south, that would do the job.[57]

MacArthur was getting excited at the possibilities of going on the offensive, even with his severely slender resources. Starting on June 25, two Australian army brigades set to work at Milne Bay building and protecting an airfield, while the American Thirty-second and Forty-first Divisions were moved north to Queensland from their bases in Adelaide and Melbourne.[58]

Then on July 2 he received the revised plan for SWPA from the Joint Chiefs. They had finally decided MacArthur was right; the capture of Rabaul should be the essential goal for the entire campaign. How to accomplish that, however, had triggered a tumultuous week of meetings and arguments between General Marshall and Admiral King, who insisted that taking the island fortress would be impossible without the navy in charge, while Marshall pointed out that since taking Rabaul was entirely in MacArthur's theater of operations, MacArthur and the army should be in charge.

The result was a three-phase compromise, all spelled out in the July 2 directive to MacArthur. Phase or "Task" One would involve an assault on the island of Tulagi in the southern Solomons, as a way to both neutralize any Japanese effort to sever communications between the United States and Australia and also prepare a staging area for the attack on Rabaul. This assault was tasked to Nimitz and the navy by the simple expedient of moving the previous boundary between his theater and MacArthur's one degree west (MacArthur's feelings when he learned that can be imagined).

Task Two, however, was entirely MacArthur's. This involved advancing along the northeast coast of New Guinea with a simultaneous westward move up the Solomon Island chain, until the two forces met in preparation for Task Three, the final assault on Rabaul itself.[59]

MacArthur was less than pleased with the new plan, dubbed WATCH-TOWER. He told Marshall and King he was fine with the three-phase time-table; he had simply hoped to be in charge of the entire operation—and the Joint Chiefs were reserving for themselves the authority to decide who would be in charge of the final Task Three.[60] Also he and Admiral Robert Ghormley, the man in charge of Nimitz's naval forces protecting New Zealand, thought the August 1 deadline was premature. They sent a joint communiqué on July 8, pointing out their lack of ships, materiel, and port facilities and asking for a postponement.

Washington abruptly turned them down.[61] Indeed, the navy had discovered that the assault on Tulagi might be hampered by a Japanese airfield being built on a large, jungle-covered island to the south of Tulagi called Guadalcanal. So Task One orders were altered to include landing marines on Guadalcanal. It would be the start of one of the most epic battles of World War Two; and for MacArthur, it would be a source for more bitter recriminations as men and resources that he needed for his advance in New Guinea were diverted instead to Guadalcanal.

Still, at least there was a plan, and a call to action. MacArthur set August 10 as the date for the move on Buna, dubbed Operation PROVIDENCE, to be led by Brigadier General Robert Van Volkenburgh and the soldiers of the American Fortieth Artillery Brigade, an antiaircraft outfit at Port Moresby. Then Australian troops would move up to begin securing the site as Buna Force dug in, until by the end of August MacArthur expected to have no less than 3,000 soldiers in place.[62]

Five days later, on July 20, MacArthur began the move of his headquarters up from Melbourne to Brisbane, to oversee the entire operation. Their train pulled into Brisbane on July 21, where MacArthur was met by chagrined members of his intelligence staff.

They had bitter news. The Japanese had gotten to Buna first, and were there in force.

*　　*　　*

In fact, they had landed that same day, July 21, and how MacArthur and everyone else were caught flat-footed was a tale of missed communications and misread intelligence, including by his own ULTRA people.

In June Allied analysts picked up radio messages suggesting the Japanese were assembling amphibious forces for a strike somewhere in New Guinea, while a navy decrypt in early July actually disclosed the possible destination as Buna. It even named the landing date: July 21. But there is no indication that the bulletin ever reached MacArthur's chief of staff, Richard Sutherland, or that anyone else at SWPA headquarters ever saw it.[63]

Even so, Charles Willoughby was reading other ULTRA sources, and concluded on July 15 that the enemy destination was Buna or perhaps Milne Bay, and suggested that Chamberlin as G-3 start concentrating air reconnaissance efforts over those areas. Then suddenly, three days later, Willoughby reversed himself, and backed away from predicting an invasion threat. The new Japanese movements were to reinforce existing positions on New Guinea, he decided, not to establish new ones.[64]

It was not the first, or last, time Willoughby's penchant for second-guessing himself would have dire consequences. MacArthur chose to accept his G-2's revised judgment—especially when he had few resources with which to watch where, along New Guinea's 3,000-mile coastline, any Japanese attacker might be headed.

Not even a frantic phone call from General Van Volkenburgh on the 17th, reporting that the navy had spotted a large assembly of transports at Rabaul that he was convinced were headed for Buna, could disturb MacArthur's inclination to stick to his original timetable.[65] Willoughby told him the ships could just as well be headed for Lae or even Guadalcanal. And how was he going to pull together the transports he would need for landing at Buna two weeks ahead of schedule, even if he had wanted to?

It may have been an inevitable delay, but it was a costly one. On July 19 navy decryptologists had evidence of Japanese warships escorting four troop transports off Salamaua and bound for—destination unknown. The hope was that Allied planes at Port Moresby might be able to get a quick strike in, but heavy rains were sweeping over the area, grounding every plane.[66] By the time the weather cleared, some 16,000 Japanese had splashed ashore at Buna

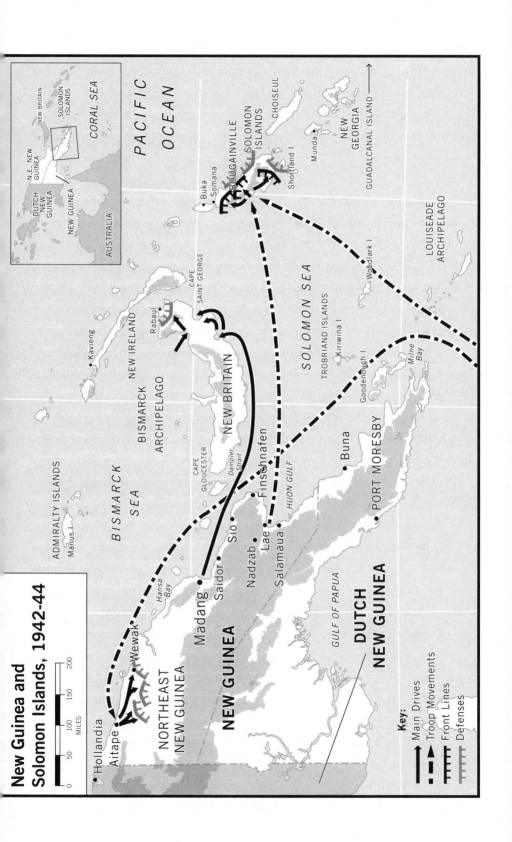

New Guinea and Solomon Islands, 1942-44

Key:
- Main Drives
- Troop Movements
- Front Lines
- Defenses

MILES
0 50 100 150 200

PACIFIC OCEAN

CORAL SEA

NEW BRITAIN

SOLOMON ISLANDS

N.E. NEW GUINEA

DUTCH NEW GUINEA

NEW GUINEA

AUSTRALIA

CHOISEUL

BOUGAINVILLE

SOLOMON ISLANDS

NEW GEORGIA

Buka

Somana

Shortland I

Munda

GUADALCANAL ISLAND

Woodlark I

LOUISEADE ARCHIPELAGO

CAPE SAINT GEORGE

Rabaul

Kavieng

NEW IRELAND

BISMARCK ARCHIPELAGO

NEW BRITAIN

SOLOMON SEA

TROBRIAND ISLANDS

Kiriwina I

Goodenough I

Milne Bay

BISMARCK SEA

ADMIRALTY ISLANDS

Manus I

CAPE GLOUCESTER

Dampier Strait

Finschhafen

HUON GULF

Buna

PORT MORESBY

Hansa Bay

Madang

Saidor

Sio

Nadzab

Lae

Salamaua

GULF OF PAPUA

DUTCH NEW GUINEA

Hollandia

Aitape

Wewak

NORTHEAST NEW GUINEA

NEW GUINEA

and were beginning to probe their way toward the Kokoda Trail, the first step on their overland advance on Port Moresby.

Overnight the first phase of Task Two had turned into the battle for Buna. Australian and American forces that were supposed to use Buna as the jumping-off point for the recapture of New Guinea would now have to scramble to plug the Kokoda Trail. That "trail" was only a narrow track through some of the most inhospitable terrain on earth, winding through steep gorges, across torrential streams, and over mountains that required men carrying forty-pound packs and a rifle or machine gun on their backs to crawl on their hands and knees—all the while facing poisonous snakes, malaria-carrying mosquitoes, and a sniper's unexpected bullet.

By the 29th the Japanese were in Kokoda, which the first Australian arrivals briefly retook on August 8. Over the rest of the month Australian units were fed piecemeal into the fighting under the overall command of Lieutenant General S. F. Rowell, while two brigades of Australians also beat back a second Japanese landing on Milne Bay on August 25—the first time any Allied troops had ever defeated a Japanese amphibious force.[67]

MacArthur was unimpressed. In general, he and his staff did not appreciate the difficulties of fighting along the trail, where 75 percent of Allied casualties never even saw a Japanese soldier before being cut down by malaria, dysentery, or a particularly virulent form of typhus. Sutherland paid one visit to Port Moresby and met with Australian commanders.[68] But he never took a trip to the interior to see the conditions under which outnumbered, sick, underfed, and exhausted men were struggling to halt an enemy who seemed as impervious to the tropical conditions as he was to the idea of defeat. Needless to say, neither did MacArthur.

As August turned into September, MacArthur's mood darkened. His New Guinea campaign was entirely stymied; the growing battle for Guadalcanal was consuming more and more resources that he believed should be going to him; and if the Australians were looking poorly prepared for battle, his men of the Thirty-second and Forty-first Divisions were even more in need of additional training. Even worse, the Japanese advance from Kokoda was starting to remind him of Bataan, or even Malaya.

By mid-September, General Horii Tomitaro's troops were on the Imita Ridge overlooking the last defensible barrier before Port Moresby.[69] A week or so later an unnamed member of MacArthur's staff (probably Sutherland) personally told Admiral Nimitz that "the Australians won't fight" and that New Guinea was "gone."[70]

Yet the man who was about to turn the war—and MacArthur—around had been in Australia more than a month.

CHAPTER 19
GREEN HELL

There is hardly any celebrated enterprise in War which was not achieved
by endless exertion, pains, and privations; and as here the weakness
of the physical and moral man is ever disposed to yield, only an
immense force of will, which manifests itself in perseverance admired
by present and future generations, can conduct us to our goal.

—CARL VON CLAUSEWITZ, *ON WAR*

The new commander of the Air Forces of the Far East was General George Kenney. A short, strutting gamecock of a man who bore a striking resemblance to the actor Humphrey Bogart, with an air of contained insolence to match, he had been born in 1889 in Nova Scotia, and had been a fighter pilot in World War One. He had gone on to serve as U.S. air attaché in France in 1940 when the Germans unleashed their devastating blitzkrieg tactics of fast-moving tank columns backed by interdiction bombing from the air. The experience taught him valuable lessons about the use, and misuse, of airpower that he brought back with him to the States. When he was told he was going to relieve General George Brett as MacArthur's air chief, Kenney was determined to bring those lessons with him when he arrived in Brisbane at the end of July 1942.

George Kenney made an unlikely addition to MacArthur's inner circle. Yet they soon established a close cooperative relationship; indeed, Kenney would become closer to MacArthur than any other individual except Jean. It was far more than an attraction of opposites. Each man instinctively understood that he needed the other in order to achieve his goals; the bond of trust that resulted would sustain them both for the remainder of the war.

Bonds of trust were hard to find when Kenney made his first visit to SWPA headquarters, and his diary entries paint a fascinating picture of MacArthur and his court that late summer of 1942. His first meeting was with Sutherland, who immediately blasted Kenney's predecessor as responsible for "the terrible state the air [force] is in," and also blamed Brett's predecessor General Brereton for the December 8 debacle at Clark Field.

Kenney called on MacArthur the next day just before noon, and for more than an hour heard a heated lecture on what a mess the air force and AAF/SWPA was in. "I have no use for anyone in the organization," MacArthur said flatly, from Brett on down (Brett had shown Kenney into MacArthur's office but refused to stay around). Brett in particular had been "disloyal," and MacArthur used terms like "scatterbrain" to describe most of his subordinates.

Kenney finally stepped in. "I'm here to take over the air show," he said, "and I intend to run it. If it's a matter of loyalty, if for any reason I can't work with you or be loyal to you, I'll tell you myself and will do everything in my power to get relieved."

MacArthur was taken aback. Then he grinned, put his hand on Kenney's shoulder, and said, "I think we're going to get along all right."[1]

They settled into a more comfortable talk, as MacArthur gave Kenney his views on the course of the war.

He thought the entire Europe-first strategy was a mistake. "He feels Washington has let him down and will continue to do so," Kenney wrote.

"In general, he acted quite depressed over the whole show," especially now that the Japanese had stolen a march on him at Buna. But Kenney had to admit, MacArthur "looked good" for a man of sixty-three.[2]

Kenney's private meeting with his predecessor was predictably bitter.

Brett "was almost boastful when he told me he hadn't spoken to MacArthur for a month and only to Sutherland on the telephone." Brett was particularly furious with Sutherland, whom he described as "primarily an egotist with a smatter of knowledge pertaining to air operations." He warned Kenney that MacArthur was prone to making all operational decisions himself without consulting with any other services chiefs.

"General MacArthur has a wonderful personality when he desires to turn it on," Brett told him. "He is, however, bound up in himself. I don't believe he has a single thought for anybody who is not useful to him." Above all, MacArthur didn't understand airpower or the miserable conditions in which his men, particular his airmen, were forced to fight.

"The lads at the front," Brett concluded gloomily, "are beginning to wonder when this is going to end."[3]

It was Kenney's intention to turn this situation around, starting with the morale among his aircrews. He had met them at Port Moresby for the first time, and found the whole setup "chaotic" and morale at rock bottom.

All the mission briefings were being done by Australian personnel, whom the Americans often couldn't understand, and no group or squadron organization was in place, and there were no formation leaders. Weather reports were prepared from the previous year's data; meals were cooked in the open without mosquito netting or any other pest control, so it wasn't surprising that after two months' duty most units had to be relieved because of losses from malaria and dysentery.[4]

When he got back to Brisbane, Kenney had a two-hour sitdown with MacArthur. He outlined his impression of what was wrong and how he intended to correct it, both in Australia and in New Guinea. But he would need authority to make heads roll, he said.

"Go ahead," MacArthur told him. "You have my enthusiastic approval."

In Kenney's mind, his number one mission was "take out Jap air strength until we own the air over New Guinea." There was no possibility of checkmating the advance on Port Moresby, or kicking the Japanese off the island, until air superiority had been established.

"There's no use talking about playing across the street until we [get] the Nips off the front lawn," Kenney said, and MacArthur again agreed. The effort against the Japanese airdromes on New Guinea had to be continuous until the runways were so damaged that "they even stop filling in the holes." That meant almost round-the-clock bombing, a much bolder and more comprehensive operation than the air force had tried so far. Six B-17s per mission seemed to be the current limit. Kenney wanted to increase that to sixteen or eighteen, or more.

MacArthur "looked as though he was about to kiss me," Kenney wrote in his diary. "I don't care how your gang looks," was how MacArthur wrapped up their meeting, referring to complaints about the sloppy appearance of the air force boys. He could remember similar complaints about the men of the Forty-second Rainbow, including from Pershing himself.

"I don't care whether they raise the devil or what they do," he continued, "as long as they will fight, shoot down Japs, and put bombs on the target."[5]

Kenney and his flyboys. MacArthur was going to need them if he was going to turn the battle for the Kokoda Trail around.

He was finally getting help in the fighting department, as the first experienced Australian units began to move up into the line. By the end of September, Rowell had a formidable force with which to hit the Japanese, consisting of the Australian Sixth and Seventh Divisions, who relieved the battered regular troops who had been holding the Japanese back, along with two other brigades and the U.S. 128th Regiment, the first Americans to go into battle. Other units from the Thirty-second and Forty-first Divisions were on the way. On October 1 MacArthur declared it was time to go on the offensive. The next day he visited New Guinea for the first time, and to the commander of the Australian Sixteenth Brigade, John E. Lloyd, spearheading the assault, MacArthur said, "Lloyd, by some act of God, your brigade has been chosen for this job. The eyes of the Western World are upon you and your men. Good luck and don't stop."

A worried General Blamey warned MacArthur that in a land without roads or any form of wheeled transport, his 7,000 troops and 3,900 native bearers on the ground would have to be supplied by air.[6] Kenney assured him he now could do that. His bombers had been pounding Japanese airfields on a regular basis, first at Vunakanau on August 7 with the sixteen B-17s that Kenney had promised. He had also convinced General Marshall back in Washington that he should reorganize the existing personnel, planes, and facilities in Australia and New Guinea as the Fifth Air Force, with the units at Moresby under the one air force officer who had impressed Kenney, Brigadier General Ennis Whitehead, serving as commander of the Fifth Air Force Advanced Echelon.[7]

Kenney was also experimenting with new bombing techniques, like the use of fragmentation bombs attached to parachutes, the brainchild of an eccentric former Philippine Air Lines pilot named Irvin Gunn, known to the crews at the base at Charters Towers near Brisbane as "Pappy" on account of his very advanced age of thirty-three. Gunn would introduce other important innovations with the two-engine bombers like the A-20 and B-25, such as multiple packages of .50-caliber machine guns for ground strafing, which would eventually make the Fifth Air Force one of the most fearsome tools in MacArthur's arsenal.

Kenney himself was proving to be a fearsome tool. On August 4 he had a showdown with Sutherland. "I'm running the Air Force because I'm the most competent man in the Pacific," he said in an explosive meeting after the chief of staff rescinded some orders Kenney had made. Kenney even pulled out a piece of paper and made a pencil mark. "This piece of paper represents what I know about air operations," he went on. "[T]hat dot represents what you know."[8]

The two men were shouting at each other when Kenney finally said, "Let's go in the next room and see General MacArthur and get this straightened out." At that, Sutherland backed down, confirming Kenney's suspicion that he was an interfering bully and nothing more. From that point on it was clear who was in charge of what the Fifth Air Force did, and who was not.

The Fifth Air Force now began a massive supply operation from Australia to the troops along the Kokoda Trail—some 50,000 pounds a day. The soldiers never got all they wanted; they complained when drops went astray or when enemy planes appeared and the unarmed C-47s and DC-3s had to bank away without dropping their loads of food, medicine, and ammunition. But in the end the air supply train from Brisbane was a game changer, as was Kenney's steady bomber offensive.

After thirty days of hard, often savage fighting, the Australians had pushed the Japanese back up the Kokoda Trail as far as Eora Creek, joined by the American Thirty-second Division pushing up from trails to the south. The last fight in the mountains was just below Kokoda, where some 600 Japanese were killed and their commander, General Horii, drowned trying to cross the treacherous Kumusi River.

Kokoda fell on November 2, and the first of Kenney's supply planes was able to land on the airstrip there two days later.

As MacArthur's pincers began to close, the Japanese survivors were steadily falling back to a tiny triangle of villages: Gona, Sanananda, and Buna itself. MacArthur ordered the new Australian commander, General Edmund Herring (MacArthur had preemptorily ordered the removal of General Rowell, probably unfairly, for not being aggressive enough), to prepare an offensive on the Buna beachhead for November 15. Lloyd's Sixteenth Brigade was slated to take Sanananda; the Twenty-fifth Brigade was to take Gona; and Buna, the southernmost Japanese position, was assigned to the Americans, under Major General Edwin Harding, with the 128th Regiment advancing north along the coast with the 126th Regiment on its left. They had arrived by air, flown in by Kenney over Sutherland's objections, on October 19—proof that the Fifth Air Force could not only supply MacArthur's army by air, but move them where he needed them as well.

On November 19 the GIs of the Thirty-second Division moved toward Buna, expecting to find maybe 500 starving and battle-weary Japanese defenders. Instead, they ran into 3,500 fresh and battle-seasoned veterans, who poured out a torrent of fire that cut down the Americans where they stood.

What no one knew was that the Japanese at Buna had been turning every bunker into a veritable fortress, with logs reinforced with concrete and even armor plating sometimes ten or fifteen feet thick, over which natural vegetation had regrown, providing perfect camouflage for the Japanese to bring converging machine-gun fire over the four approaches through a swamp.[9]

With no covering artillery (Sutherland had decided that transporting guns over the Owen Stanleys was too dangerous, and vetoed General Harding's request for them), and no flamethrowers, the Thirty-second Division actually had less firepower than MacArthur's men had had on Bataan. The attack soon ground to a halt. Meanwhile, the Australians fared no better. At Gona the Australian Twenty-fifth Brigade took a heavy mauling at the hands of the Japanese, then ran out of food and ammunition and stopped dead. At Sanananda the Sixteenth Brigade met the same frustrations, with similar casualties. Then the skies opened up and rain poured down on the tired, discouraged troops as they crouched in the mud and swamps and counted their wounded and dead.

Meanwhile, MacArthur had now moved his headquarters to Port Moresby. He set up his staff in Government House, a rambling bungalow with a long veranda where he could pace and think to his heart's content. He was watching the advance at Buna with intense interest, but also the fighting on and around Guadalcanal, where the American and Japanese navies were engaged in a deadly duel, each striving to cut the other's ground forces off from all help or relief. MacArthur feared that if Guadalcanal fell and the Japanese could use its airfield for launching bombers and fighters over the New Guinea coast, any hope of driving out the Japanese would vanish.

It made him anxious about the fighting in front of Buna, impatient for victory—and impatient with anyone who threatened not to deliver it.

Attempts to resume the attack on Buna the next day were a disaster. Major David Parker, an engineer with the 128th, was equally appalled at how well camouflaged the Japanese were and at the lack of American preparation for a hard, grinding fight. "The first opposition from the enemy . . . was a surprise and shock to our green troops," he reported. "The enemy habitually allowed our troops to advance to very close range—sometimes four or five feet from a machine gun post—before opening fire . . . It was impossible to see where the enemy fire was coming from . . . Snipers were everywhere."[10] Men began turning, running, fleeing. Machine-gun crews threw down their weapons and headed for the rear.[11]

Kenney had spent the day with "Pappy" Gunn yanking everything including the bombardier's position out of the North American Aircraft Company's B-25 bombers, the ones that had hit Tokyo in the Doolittle raid back in April, and filling the plane with .50-caliber machine guns with five hundred rounds each. The idea they had worked out was to create a plane that could shoot up Japanese shipping more effectively than bombing could, and thereby give the Allies a decisive advantage in the war at sea around New Guinea.

That day Kenney had finally shipped the third 105 mm gun from Brisbane to Port Moresby. The first two were already in action east of Dubodura, against the Japanese—and against Sutherland's wishes. But no troop carriers had gotten through in three days because of the miserable weather, and no supply drops—which meant the troops around Buna were eating their last meal.

Kenney wasn't worried; the weather would clear and the supplies would be delivered. He was (according to his own account) whistling when he strolled into MacArthur's office at Government House. MacArthur looked up and said, "Hullo, George, let's go for a walk."

They went into the garden and sat on a bench. Then MacArthur began.

"George, you know there's a lot of men over there"—meaning around Buna—"eating their last meal tonight."

"Yes, General," was Kenney's response, "but tomorrow we serve breakfast at 6:30 and by noon I'll have five days' chow over to them."

Kenney explained the problems with the weather, and how his new organization of the Fifth Air Force meant these problems would be solved, permanently.

MacArthur listened. Then he told Kenney about the meeting with his entire staff earlier that morning, how they lashed into MacArthur for "his foolhardy endorsement of this nutty airborne show" and how "they recommended throwing in the towel and pulling out although," MacArthur added, "where the troops were to go I don't know."

Kenney looked up and MacArthur smiled.

"George, the Fifth Air Force hasn't failed me yet and I'll never doubt them again. We'll get this show across. I'm not worried any more about it."[12]

Kenney went back to his bungalow and wrote in his diary: "The General stuck by me today. I'll stick by him in spite of hell or high water and I think he knows it."

The next day, November 21, the weather broke. Kenney's pilots delivered 300,000 pounds of supplies, mostly rations, enough to sustain Harding's men for an entire week.[13] Now it was up to Harding and the commanders on the ground to break the deadlock.

The next attack was scheduled for November 22. It was Sergeant Roland Acheson of the Thirty-second's twenty-first birthday. "They was all dug in at Buna," as he later put it, meaning the Japanese, "pillboxes, redoubts." Acheson and his buddies soon learned that "Japan-man," as they called him, "was very smart. Lot of their equipment was stuff they had captured from the British, Lewis or Vickers machine guns. They'd turn it right around and use it on you." On the other hand, "dumb Americans like we are, we did our supply during the day. Japan-man would always barge at night. Their planes sank about five of our barges." One of them even contained General Harding and his staff, who had to swim ashore.[14]

"From then on everything was by air," which meant every supply or reinforcement came in from the new Fifth Air Force. Despite the vaunted air-drops, the men of the Thirty-second Division were living on C rations and dried crackers and powdered milk. Officers could not get their men to advance into the Japanese furnace of fire. If we don't shoot at them, went the rationale, they won't shoot at us. Discipline had collapsed. Americans at Buna had lost all will to fight or win.

That at least was Dick Sutherland's report to MacArthur after a brief visit to the Buna front, almost a month after the battle had begun. Sutherland blamed the problem on a failure of nerve among the Thirty-second's commanders, conveniently ignoring the fact that he and MacArthur had sent General Harding with inexperienced troops into an unexpectedly tough fight, with no fire support and little backup. MacArthur was already hearing snide remarks from Blamey about the failure of U.S. troops in combat; it seemed only fair after Sutherland's remarks about how Australian troops "won't fight."

MacArthur began pacing the Government House veranda with increasing fury. He was remembering World War One, when despite the mud and bad weather and hunger, Americans from National Guard units still pushed themselves forward, forward, crawling at night and taking on every challenge, in order to achieve victory. Now, it seemed, they were stalling out and quitting.

"Dick," he said one morning to Sutherland, "I think you better bring Bob Eichelberger up here. We're going to need him."[15]

Robert Eichelberger, from Ohio, was three years older than Kenney. Like MacArthur, he came from a divided family; his father was a prominent Union officer during the Civil War, and his mother's family was from Mississippi. He himself was West Point, class of '09, and first met MacArthur at the Command and General Staff College at Leavenworth. Later he served on the General Staff when MacArthur was chief of staff. He was awed by the general's powerful personality and "unconventional hours," as Eichelberger remembered—and now was assisting his old mentor by commanding

I Corps, consisting of Thirty-second and Forty-first Divisions, both originally National Guard units—which must have made MacArthur's disappointment all the sharper.

Eichelberger arrived at Government House on November 30, and found
MacArthur agitated and furious at the news that the attacks at Buna were
stalling out. "Never did I think I'd see American troops quit," MacArthur
raged. "I can't believe that those troops represent the American fighting man
of this war."

MacArthur was marching back and forth, his voice trembling, his eyes flashing. He made it clear to Eichelberger that Buna was of crucial importance to
the campaign, far more than the numbers going in showed. MacArthur was
convinced he had the manpower to win. One more concerted push at Buna
would do it, he insisted; it only required the right man for the job.

"I believe they need leadership to go on," he went on. "They are sick but,
Bob, a leader can take those men and capture Buna." MacArthur had decided
it was time to relieve Harding and every battalion commander if necessary:
"If you don't relieve the commanders, I will."

His staff told him that Eichelberger needed three or four days to get ready.
MacArthur couldn't give them to him. The Japanese might land reinforcements any night. He must go forward in the morning.

MacArthur wound up dramatically: "Time is of the essence! If you don't
take Buna I want to hear that you and Byers [Brigadier General Clovis Byers,
Eichelberger's second-in-command] are buried there."[16]

That story would become famous, even notorious. What didn't become famous was that the next day at breakfast, MacArthur put his arm around
Eichelberger with a wan smile: "Don't get killed, Bob. You're no use to me
dead."[17]

Eichelberger and Harding had been West Point classmates. Eichelberger
was uncomfortable with the task of relieving his friend; but he had a job to
do, and his staff had concluded that Harding's entire staff had to go as well.

His immediate superior, Australia's General Herring, saw Eichelberger's arrival as "a very pure breath of fresh air" that "blew away a great deal of the impurities that were stopping us getting on with the job."[18]

But nothing could be done until artillery arrived. That reached Buna the second week in December; now Eichelberger could launch his heaviest attack, shortly after the Aussies had finally taken Gona on December 9 after taking 750 casualties in the assault on the last stronghold.[19]

At Sanananda, by contrast, the Australians were bogged down completely. So were Eichelberger's hopes of forward progress along the Buna front. What Eichelberger soon realized, but MacArthur had not, was that the core problem wasn't a lack of troops but a lack of firepower. Besides a shortage of artillery, there weren't enough rifle company troops at the front. Heavy machine guns and mortars proved useless in that dense jungle terrain, where men couldn't advance five yards without some sort of protection.

On December 5 Eichelberger persuaded the Australians to lend him five tracked armored vehicles known as Bren gun carriers, but each was blown to bits by Japanese artillery. Eichelberger was there personally that day to push his troops forward, but then a sniper took out the sector commander, General Albert Waldron. The lead detachment lost half its troops to withering Japanese machine-gun and mortar fire, then dropped to the ground and halted.[20]

Failure.

Over the next week troops from the detachment known as Urbana Force hammered away at the Japanese positions around Buna.[21] The first tanks arrived on December 12, but if Eichelberger and MacArthur expected them to create a breakthrough, they were disappointed. Since they were Australian tanks, Australian troops came up to support them. The minute they rolled into view, however, Japanese antiaircraft began taking them out one by one, and the Australians fell back.

Failure again.

Back at Government House, meanwhile, nerves were raw and MacArthur's patience was at the breaking point. He sent a terse note to Eichelberger:

"Time is fleeting and our dangers increase with its passage. . . . Your mission is to take Buna. All other things are subsidiary to this. No alchemy is going to produce this for you."

But that same day, December 14, alchemy did work. Overnight on the 13th–14th the Japanese cleared out of Buna, and Urbana Force marched in as Eichelberger and his staff broke open liquor bottles to celebrate. Their elation was premature; the fighting for a nearby coconut grove took several more days, and General Byers fell wounded at Eichelberger's side—almost fulfilling MacArthur's grim ultimatum. MacArthur sent a congratulatory note to Eichelberger, but he was still worried. The strongest part of the Japanese line still lay ahead, from Buna Mission to Duropa Plantation. The Americans would need help, again from the Australians, but this time MacArthur wondered if even stronger medicine was needed.

On the 15th MacArthur sent Sutherland off to talk to Eichelberger once more, but this time with a different agenda. "If Eichelberger won't move," MacArthur barked, "you are to relieve him and take command yourself. I don't want to see you back here alive until Buna is taken."

It was a tense and very nervous Sutherland who set off for Buna that morning. Later in the day General Blamey stopped by to talk with MacArthur.

Sergeant Rogers in the next room could hear their voices, as MacArthur paced, saying, "I relieved Harding. I sent Sutherland over today to get Eichelberger moving. I told him to relieve Eichelberger if necessary. If I have to, I'll relieve Sutherland!"[22]

Sutherland never took over from Eichelberger; it was a command he neither wanted nor felt comfortable in assuming. In the end, he told MacArthur that Eichelberger should stay. Still, the conversation was a sign of how far the situation had deteriorated, and whom MacArthur was willing to sacrifice in order to get the job done.

Eichelberger had tanks for reinforcements along with a battalion from the Australians' Eighteenth Brigade, and by December 18 they were ready. He planned a double pincer move, with his Warren Force led by the tanks and the Aussies attacking Duropa Plantation, while Urbana Force pushed through the final Japanese strongholds in front of Buna Mission and then reached the sea at last.[23]

The attack started well, with the tanks and the confident Australians surging forward through the plantation groves. Then a Japanese antiaircraft gun opened up, and the tanks halted, unable to advance under the punishing fire. The men of the Eighteenth Brigade had to move forward on their own, taking out the bunkers one by one with grenades.

The next day two tanks renewed the assault, but both got mired in swampy ground and one had to be abandoned. The tanks made one more try on Christmas Eve, but this time Japanese fire was even deadlier. It knocked out three tanks at once, and the Australian commander announced there would be no more tank attacks until the Japanese guns were silenced. That meant a slow, bloody series of infantry assaults again, yard by punishing yard, even as Japanese planes, despite Kenney's steady pounding of their airfields, still managed to swoop in and hit Eichelberger's exhausted forces.[24]

Eichelberger wrote to MacArthur that the failed attacks were "the low point of my life." He even wondered if the entire Buna operation might not turn out to be "an American military disaster."[25]

MacArthur had already experienced one American military disaster, on Bataan. He was not about to endure another. He was already thinking ahead about how to remedy the situation, and he unburdened himself to General Herring on a visit to Government House on Christmas Day. Herring had already agreed to send the rest of the Eighteenth Brigade and more artillery up from Milne Bay, but wondered if it would do any good.

"Well, we're not getting on very fast, are we?" MacArthur growled. "If we don't clean this position up quickly, I will be finished and so will your General Blamey, and what will happen to you, young man, I just don't like to think."[26]

In the end, he didn't have to relieve Eichelberger. During the last days of December the stubborn resistance of the Japanese, who were maddened by heat and hunger and disease, finally began to crack. Allied troops pushed through to Simemi Creek, and on January 2 they killed the last Japanese soldiers at Buna Mission. There were still survivors to track down; several Japanese soldiers were shot trying to swim away into the surf. Sanananda, the last Japanese holdout, did not finally fall until three weeks later. But MacArthur, and Eichelberger, had their victory and they were determined to make the most of it.

MacArthur's dispatch on January 8, 1943, read:

"The Papuan campaign is in its final closing phase. . . . One of the primary objects of the campaign was the annihilation of the Japanese Papuan Army . . . This can now be regarded as accomplished."

Considering that nearly half of the Japanese Papuan Army was still in action around Sanananda, MacArthur's triumphalism seemed premature.[27]

But congratulatory telegrams poured in from Stimson and Marshall, Australian prime minister Curtin, and even Winston Churchill. MacArthur might pretend that all had gone smoothly and according to plan. But his letter back to Marshall hinted at his truer feelings, that the difficulties at Buna were the result of a lack of support back in Washington: "However unwarranted it may be, the impression prevailed that this area's efforts were belittled and disparaged at home, and despite all my efforts to the contrary the effect was depressing. Your tributes have had a tonic effect."[28]

With his staff at Port Moresby, he shared a rare celebratory glass. One of them remembered him quoting Robert E. Lee: "[I]t is a good thing that war is so terrible or we might learn to love it."[29] Buna veterans might have missed the point of the bon mot.

The same day, before leaving for Brisbane, he sent a note to Eichelberger:

"I am so glad that you were not injured in the fighting. I always feared that your incessant exposure might result fatally. With a hearty slap on the back, Most cordially, MacArthur."

Eichelberger, exhausted and elated, yet with hard fighting still going on a mile or two away, brooded over MacArthur's delayed congratulations. "The boys tell me that last night San Francisco radio carried word of what troops are here and that I have been in command . . . The Big Chief . . . returned to the mainland and he evidently released the information after his arrival." It was the first time one of MacArthur's communiqués had ever mentioned Eichelberger, or the Thirty-second. Until then, it had been "I" and "my command."[30]

Eichelberger was sore about being ignored in the communiqués, and justifiably so. What he didn't know was that MacArthur had been a thread's width away from stripping him of his command, and that his fiercest critic, Dick Sutherland, had saved him. On the contrary, Eichelberger believed until his death that it was *MacArthur* who had saved him from being relieved, not Sutherland.[31]

As for MacArthur, he had his win at last. Yet he knew it couldn't go on like this. Buna had been a World War One–style yard-by-yard slog, of the kind MacArthur had seen many times. But he didn't have the resources or the manpower of an American Expeditionary Force, and the tropical conditions took their own toll. Approximately 14,500 Americans were in action for barely six weeks, yet 930 had been killed, 1,918 wounded, and no fewer than 8,700 struck down by disease—a total loss rate of more than 70 percent.[32]

MacArthur could console himself with the fact that the Japanese had suffered worse. The entire Buna command, 13,000 men, had been wiped out; in kill ratio terms, the Allies were beating the Japanese almost five to one, even with the Japanese on defense. That ratio would only grow as time went on, as MacArthur and his forces, including Kenney's flyboys, learned their trade better.

All the same, the capture of Buna ended a grim year for MacArthur—and a frustrating one for his foe. On New Year's Day 1943 stalemate had settled over the Southwest Pacific. Despite their larger numbers and superior strength, the Japanese couldn't figure out how to oust the Allies from New Guinea or Guadalcanal. At the same time, the Allies were a very long way from driving the Japanese out of the Solomons and the Bismarcks, including Rabaul, let alone freeing the Philippines.

It would have taken a bold prophet indeed to predict that MacArthur was about to start the road back.

As 1943 began, Japan still held the advantage in the Southwest Pacific, in terms of air, naval, and ground strength. The Japanese high command had reached a momentous decision, to abandon the exhausting fight for Guadalcanal and to focus instead on making eastern New Guinea and the Bismarcks an impregnable barrier to U.S. and Australian operations. Starting in February they would be on the defensive, but it was a defense that looked unbeatable.

The hub of the Japanese plan was their base at Rabaul. Its harbor, airfields, and seaplane anchorages would serve as the hub's spokes, from which troops, supplies, and air support flowed in every direction, almost with impunity. As MacArthur wrote later, his war was not going to advance unless and until he could neutralize Rabaul.[33]

Planners back in Washington understood that too.[34] At the Casablanca Conference that January, Admiral King and General Marshall proposed that henceforth 30 percent of all Allied resources be devoted to the war in the Pacific, instead of the 15 percent that King claimed was currently being spent. In the end, British planners and Prime Minister Churchill balked at this division of labor, although they did pledge that once Hitler was beaten, Britain and America could turn all their attention, and direct all their forces, to the defeat of Japan.

That left MacArthur struggling to find the shipping, bombers, and landing craft he would need to launch any effort at Rabaul, especially when Admiral King was planning his own offensive thrust in the central Pacific, along the lines of the old War Plan Orange, which would devour troops and equipment that MacArthur believed rightfully were his.

Nonetheless, MacArthur forwarded his plan for taking Rabaul on to Washington in February, at the request of General Marshall. It was not for the faint at heart. It involved nothing less than a five-stage operation for enveloping and destroying Japan's biggest base in the Pacific.

First, MacArthur's forces would seize the Huon Peninsula of New Guinea, for air support against Japanese strongholds in New Britain as well as Rabaul.

Then Admiral William Halsey, commander of the Third Fleet, would land Marines to grab airfields on New Georgia in the central Solomons, in order to do the same thing.

After that, MacArthur's forces would take airfields in western New Britain while Halsey and his marines overran Bougainville. Halsey's final move would be to seize Kavieng Airfield on New Ireland, as he and MacArthur prepared for the final advance on Rabaul itself. All in all, MacArthur surmised, the entire operation would involve five additional infantry divisions and 1,800 more planes, in forty-five air groups.[35]

Once they caught their breath, the Joint Chiefs were inclined to say no. MacArthur was asking for more resources than either the army or the navy was prepared to devote to the entire Pacific, not just to MacArthur's theater. MacArthur, however, pushed to send Sutherland to Washington to explain the details of his plan, dubbed Elkton I. The Joint Chiefs, somewhat surprisingly, agreed, but also insisted that representatives from both Nimitz and Halsey join them, as well, in a wide-ranging discussion of Pacific war strategy, to commence on March 12, 1943.

Perhaps Marshall and King thought that bringing in the other commanders' views would force MacArthur to modify his views of what was possible and what was not. In any case, MacArthur swiftly agreed to the meeting. He decided he would send Generals Kenney and Chamberlin, in addition to Sutherland, to take up the cudgels for Elkton I.

There was still a war to be won on New Guinea. But at least now he had an overall strategy, an operational team he trusted, especially Kenney, and hopes of fresh new troops and equipment, including the long-range P-38 Lightning fighter.[36]

But he still needed a new tactical approach, something to replace the grinding head-on attack that had been so costly at Buna. Fortunately, the man who would find it for him had touched down by seaplane in Brisbane Harbor on a rainy, blustery January 10, even as the fighting for Buna was still going on. Together with Kenney and Spencer Akin, Rear Admiral Daniel Barbey, creator and commander of the new Seventh Amphibious Force for MacArthur's SWPA, would give MacArthur's war a fresh new lease on success.

A warm, rather rotund and avuncular man, Barbey was born and raised in Portland, Oregon. He graduated from the Naval Academy in 1912 and was a junior grade lieutenant on the destroyer USS *Lawrence* during the American occupation of Veracruz, while Captain Douglas MacArthur was tracking down locomotives in the Mexican interior.

But after World War One and the interwar years, which had been almost as lean for the navy as they were for the army, Barbey had transferred his interest from engineering to the new military art form known as amphibious warfare. In 1940 and 1941 he had overseen the training of the First Marine Division and the First U.S. Army, the Big Red One, in fleet landing exercises, as well as taking charge of the design and construction of the navy's bewilderingly diverse series of new amphibious craft like the Higgins boat, the drop-ramp shallow-draft boat that would carry the men of the Big Red One onto Omaha Beach; the LCT, or Landing Craft Tank, capable of carrying medium-sized tanks or equivalent vehicles directly onto the shore; and the LCI, or Landing Craft, Infantry, that could take on 188 infantry and drop them directly on the beach.

Above all, there was the Landing Ship, Tank or LST, a 4,000-ton, 328-foot-long cargo ship that had a shallow enough draft that it could come up to shore, lower its ramp, unload up to 20 medium tanks or 1,000 men and their officers, and then head back out to sea.[37] Barbey had not only overseen the ships' design and construction but had tried them out at sea personally. He knew their strengths and their weaknesses—what they could do and what they couldn't, under the right conditions and with the right kind of commander.

As early as November MacArthur foresaw the advantages that these amphibious haulers would give him and his men along the harborless shores of New Guinea, and requested as many as the navy could offer him. Fortunately for MacArthur, the decision had just been made to postpone the cross-channel invasion of France, which had been slated for 1943, for another year. That not only freed up the boats and vessels that had been designated for Europe for service in SWPA; it also meant MacArthur received, in addition to Barbey's amphibious fleet, Barbey himself, now promoted to rear admiral.[38]

Barbey set out for Australia with some trepidation. MacArthur had a reputation in Navy Department offices only slightly better than that of Lucifer himself; he had already fired one naval commander, Admiral Hart, and was about to fire another. A Navy Department friend quipped as Barbey packed up his office, "So you are leaving the United States Navy to join MacArthur's Navy. God help you. No one else will."[39]

Instead, MacArthur turned out to be a pleasant surprise.

When Barbey walked into the SWPA chief's Brisbane office for the first time, he was taken aback, as most visitors were, by its spartan starkness. Its furnishings consisted of some straight-backed chairs, a single black leather couch, a desk completely devoid of papers, and a single map on the wall. The conversation was entirely one-sided, with MacArthur providing a nonstop monologue on his strategy in the Southwest Pacific, including the capture of Rabaul, and of his desire to make sure that the liberation of the Philippines remained the single top U.S. priority, not just as a moral commitment but as a way to give heart to guerrilla movements all across Southeast Asia. He lamented at length his lack of material support from Washington, the lack of planes, ships, and men, and the terrible casualties his men had suffered at Buna. He did not intend to allow similar casualties for the rest of the war in New Guinea, or later in the Philippines.

"Your job," he said finally, with deadly seriousness, "is to develop an amphibious force that can carry my troops in those campaigns."

Then he paused, and asked Barbey his first question of the meeting: "Are you a lucky officer?"[40]

The question took Barbey aback, but he soon realized what MacArthur was driving at. Technical skill was one thing, but men could be led willingly into a new and dangerous enterprise if they believed the man leading them was not just knowledgeable and experienced, but had that indefinable quality that instinctively brought his troops success. MacArthur had had it until Bataan; he was looking to recover it, and he would need men like Barbey to help him do so.

Still, Barbey left MacArthur's office with some misgiving. He wondered how things would work out with someone who had no touch of small talk or humor, none of the camaraderie or informality of Nimitz's headquarters. In the event, "General MacArthur proved to be the finest commander I ever worked for," Barbey later wrote. "He delegated authority far more than do most commanders. He gave his subordinates a job and then left to them the details of how it was to be done." That suited Barbey fine, since there really was no one else in the armed forces who understood amphibious tactics better.

Barbey ("Uncle Dan" to his subordinates) would turn the Seventh Amphibious Fleet into the best ship-to-shore operating force in the war—especially with the help of the Army Engineer Amphibious Brigade, commanded by General William Heavy, which specialized in unloading a fighting force on a hostile shore. Indeed, MacArthur's campaigns over the next two years would have been almost unimaginable without Barbey—or "Dan the Amphibious Man"—at his side.

Still, MacArthur knew his resources were distressingly meager. He had less than 10 percent of the one million army and air force personnel serving outside the United States, and less than 1 percent of the air force's planes. In terms of naval forces in ships and personnel compared to the U.S. Navy's total, he had an even smaller share—even though his theater area extended over almost two million square miles of ocean.[41]

But he was going to fight with what he had—and in January 1943, even before the fighting at Buna was over, he learned that the Japanese were planning to turn up the heat on his positions in New Guinea.

He learned this from Akin's Central Bureau codebreakers, who sent General Kenney a warning that a Japanese transport convoy was setting out from Rabaul. The cryptographers were finally having some success in penetrating the meaning of Japanese naval radio traffic—although the Japanese army's messages were as baffling as ever—and had picked up indications that the convoy was set to sail on January 6. Navy radio interceptors were getting even more menacing news from the traffic they were picking up from their station in Melbourne. Veteran Japanese units from China, the Philippines, and the home islands were heading into the SWPA from their staging areas in the Palau Islands northwest of New Guinea.[42]

The Japanese commander on Rabaul was preparing a hot reception for MacArthur if he tried to venture forth from his newly won position at Buna, starting with fresh reinforcements for the Japanese garrison at Lae and capturing the island of Wau, 150 miles northwest of Buna, the perfect place from which to send fighter and bomber squadrons to threaten MacArthur's seaward lines of supply.

When Kenney got word of what was happening, he immediately sent his bombers into the air, in the direction of Rabaul. "I'm having an interesting time inventing new ways to win a war on a shoestring," he told a fellow air force officer, and he and Pappy Gunn showed their pilots and ground crews how to do the same thing. Planes that crash-landed in the jungle were immediately hunted down by salvage parties for parts and ammunition. Airdrome crews learned to jerry-build repairs and equipment, for example inserting Australian sixpence pieces into engine magnetos and substituting Kotex tampons for air filters.[43]

In this way, although the Fifth Air Force's total number of planes barely increased from September 1942 through December, the total number of missions jumped dramatically, from 1,000 to 4,000, including raids on the dreaded defenses on Rabaul. Then on January 6 Kenney's reconnaissance planes picked up the Japanese convoy and for the next two days pounded the transports—although Japanese Zero escorts fought them off so that only one transport was hit and set adrift, as Japanese destroyers had to rescue some six hundred survivors.

So Kenney shifted his tactics. He moved his Eleventh Air Fleet away from the convoy to Lae itself. When the transports arrived on January 8 they found the remains of Japanese fighters that had been destroyed on the airfield, and they themselves were soon under constant air attack as they tried to disembark their troops. "Bombs come down like rain and explode around the ships," one awed Japanese survivor remembered. "Several tens of planes coming in rapid succession made their intensive attacks which were utterly indescribable," was how he put it.[44]

MacArthur learned the final results from ULTRA. Two Japanese transports had been sunk and another damaged; six hundred Japanese soldiers had died. Less than one-third of Rabaul's reinforcements had reached Lae, and only half of its equipment. Still, the commander on Rabaul, General Imamura Hitoshi, pressed ahead with his plan.

ULTRA and the Central Bureau missed the next convoy departure of 10,000 Japanese troops from the Palaus to Wewak in western New Guinea. An unexpected change of Japanese cipher keys delayed decoding until ten days after the transports sailed. But the success of the landings on Wewak encouraged Hitashi to go ahead with his next troop move on February 14, ordering the entire Fifty-first Division under General Adachi Atazo to Lae, even though his own planners predicted that the move only had a fifty-fifty chance of success given Kenney's growing command of the air around New Guinea.[45]

That same day an American reconnaissance plane snapped a photograph over Rabaul, showing the harbor choked with shipping, some seventy-nine vessels. They were clearly headed somewhere—but where? Another photograph on February 22 showed that the number of merchant ships had grown from forty-five to fifty-nine, almost 300,000 tons. Since nothing was happening in the Solomons, Charles Willoughby issued a warning: this could be readying reinforcements for New Guinea including Lae, where a new navy decrypt revealed there were plans to send new troops.

On the 24th came the final confirmation of Japanese plans, again from ULTRA in Washington. A six-ship convoy would be landing at Lae on March 5, carrying the Japanese Fifty-first Division. The message had been dated February 21. But when would it sail, and what route would it take? There was no time to lose; they had to find some answers.

The next day MacArthur and Kenney spent the afternoon in front of the map in the SWPA chief's office, going over the ULTRA report. Kenney decided the convoy would sail the first week in March. "The weather will be bad along the west coast of New Britain," he remarked. "I'll bet they'll use it for cover."

He announced that he would head over to Port Moresby the next day to make final plans. He was supposed to be going to Washington for the big Pacific Military Conference in March, but he would wait until "this show is over."

MacArthur asked, "Are you calling off all other air operations except this?"

Kenney said yes—everything, that was, except reconnaissance flights and supply planes to keep the Australian garrison on Wau going, which had landed on January 29 and had been fighting there ever since (the fighting was so close and intense that some Australian troops were hit by enemy fire as they stepped off the plane). He would also be spending the next several days rehearsing a simultaneous low- and high-altitude attack, going out as far as a combined air operation could reach.

When Kenney arrived at Moresby, Ennis Whitehead and his staff had already worked out contingency plans in case the convoy didn't land at Lae but went on to Madang, or split apart to go to both. On the 27th his bombers and fighters ran a full-dress rehearsal so realistic that one aircraft crashed and two others were badly damaged.[46]

"The Japs are going to get the surprise of their lives," Kenney told his men and headed back to Brisbane.

Kenney went over his plan for the Japanese convoy one last time with MacArthur, and told him, "The kids are hot for it," meaning his crews.

"I think the Jap is in for a lot of trouble," was MacArthur's final judgment. "Don't forget to keep me informed as fast as any news comes in."[47]

Late the next day, March 1, a lone American reconnaissance plane off the northern coast of New Britain spotted wakes in the water illuminated by the setting sun. It banked and saw a collection of ships, sixteen in all, but then lost the convoy in the gathering darkness.

It was a tense dawn and early morning on March 2 as the Eighteenth Air Group waited for reconnaissance planes to reacquire the convoy. At 8:30 they finally did locate it, but then rain and a series of squalls blanketed Port Moresby, making takeoff impossible. It wasn't until 10:00 that Kenney's B-17s and B-24s were able to reach the convoy and begin their deadly high-altitude attack.

The first wave of B-17s managed to sink one transport; a second wave of eleven bombers took out another. Then darkness fell again, as the rest of the convoy sailed on, bound for the Dampier Strait between New Britain and New Guinea.

The morning of March 3 brought the convoy within reach of Kenney and Whitehead's medium-range bombers and fighters, as the Japanese well knew. Their lookouts watched with relief as Japanese fighters moved in, to protect the transports from another high-altitude attack.

Then by 10:00 relief turned to alarm. Out of the western sky came a cloud of more than one hundred Allied planes, not at high altitude but flying almost at mast height.

They were American A-20s, Australian Beaufighters, and thirty B-25s modified by Pappy Gunn to bristle with .50-caliber guns that sprayed death in all directions as they skimmed over the Japanese transports—while the A-20s and other bombers practiced another technique that Gunn and Kenney had invented, of skip-bombing: dropping bombs that literally skipped once on the water before hitting their targets' hulls. Some planes came in so low that Japanese sailors thought they were torpedo bombers.[48]

Bombs blew holes through the hold that continued down into ships' engine rooms, as soldiers scrambled onto the deck, where they were machine-gunned down in droves. Japanese soldiers and sailors who made it into the water and tried to climb onto rafts or rubber dinghies were also fair targets. Planes swooped in to strafe lifeboats again and again, and then strafed survivors floating in the water.

> The water was whipped into a bloody froth, the blood mixing with chunks of flesh and the oil from the sunken ships. There was no respite for the survivors, who now floated defenseless, naked and exposed to machine gun fire. The grisly business continued into the night. When nothing was seen to move in the water, the strafing runs ended.

During the last hours of what would come to be called the Battle of the Bismarck Sea, some Allied pilots and crews became sick and vomited at the low-level sight of the carnage their bullets and cannon shots were causing.[49]

Back in Brisbane, MacArthur grew more and more excited as the news of the battle began to come in. Jean MacArthur remembered him pacing back and forth in their dining room, the latest dispatches in his hand. "Mitchell! Mitchell!" he kept saying over and over. It was the name of his former friend and martyr Billy Mitchell, whose predictions of what airpower could do were finally, horribly, being realized in the waters of the Bismarck Sea.

When Kenney came over to the apartment at 3:00 A.M. with the final tally, he said, "I have never seen such jubilation." He sent off his own jubilant telegram to Ennis Whitehead before his plane left for Washington at 6:00 A.M.: "Congratulations on that stupendous success. Air Power has written some important history in the past three days. Tell the whole gang that I am so proud of them I am about to blow a fuze."[50]

In his press release MacArthur claimed twenty-two ships sunk (fourteen transports and eight destroyers) with 15,000 Japanese soldiers confirmed dead. The numbers were wild fantasy, as air force brass in Washington well knew.[51] The reality, however, was stunning enough. Eight Japanese transports had been sunk, together with four destroyers—without a single Allied vessel in sight. Almost 3,000 Japanese soldiers had been killed. More than half of the 7,000 men of the Fifty-first Division managed to survive the savage attack, but only 1,000 actually reached Lae. The rest had been rescued at sea and sent back to Rabaul, where they had started. The Battle of the Bismarck Sea was not the holocaust MacArthur and Kenney at first thought, but it had rendered Japan's effort to reinforce New Guinea a failure. Emperor Hirohito himself, when he heard the news, warned his generals to learn the lessons for future landings.

Even worse for Hirohito, the virtual destruction of the crack Fifty-first Division severely weakened Japan's southeastern defenses of Rabaul. It was no longer enough just to reinforce existing garrisons and confidently wait for MacArthur to exhaust himself pounding on the gates. A new, more offensive strategy was going to be needed, one that shifted resources from the Solomons to New Guinea, where the fate of Rabaul would now be decided.

Meanwhile, the fate of MacArthur's own strategy was being decided in far-off Washington.

The minute Kenney's plane touched down at Wright Field in Ohio on March 9, he learned that he and MacArthur were the talk of the nation.

News of the Battle of the Bismarck Sea had spread across America's newspapers. Many people, including many in the air force, couldn't believe it was possible; Kenney, however, was able to fill them in on the details (later he and MacArthur would bitterly dispute the attempts to roll back the final numbers of Japanese ships and soldiers destroyed). "It was the best news to come out of the Pacific for some time," Kenney later remembered, and it was the perfect setup for establishing MacArthur's credibility at the Pacific conference over the next two weeks.[52]

He and MacArthur had discussed the upcoming conference in Washington before he left. "Help keep Dick out of trouble," MacArthur said bluntly, speaking of Sutherland. "He's unpopular and sarcastic and might get us in Dutch if you don't help smooth things over"—and come back, SWPA's chief stressed, with plenty of extra planes. MacArthur sensed they were going to need them.[53]

Sure enough, the first week of the conference became an arm-wrestling match between Sutherland and the Joint Chiefs, including General Marshall, over the details of MacArthur's master plan. Kenney could sense the hostility toward the Elkton strategy, especially from King and the navy brass, but he also thought Sutherland was "obsessed with the idea that everyone in Washington is out to get him." Kenney felt that as long as MacArthur was winning in New Guinea, "he is bound to get support. If I can get some airplanes, he will keep on winning."[54]

Surprisingly to some, two of MacArthur's biggest supporters were Admiral William "Bull" Halsey and Halsey's air chief, General Millard Harmon. They didn't agree that Elkton would overstretch their resources; in fact, Halsey, the navy's most innovative fighting admiral, Kenney, and MacArthur were finding their way toward a mutual respect and support that would ultimately be enormously beneficial to the Pacific war effort.

They would prove a lethal combination against the Japanese, but they could not move Admiral King and his chief strategist, Rear Admiral Charles Cook. They and Marshall knew the American larder didn't have on hand nearly the resources needed for the MacArthur plan, and probably never would.

So in the end there was a compromise. The Joint Chiefs asked what the Pacific representatives thought they could accomplish in 1943 with the best reinforcements Washington *could* deliver. Sutherland and Halsey's representatives all agreed they could carry the original Task Two that Washington had assigned: the taking of northeastern New Guinea and the Madang-Salamaua-Huon Gulf triangle, along with Bougainville, New Georgia, and Cape Gloucester on New Britain. All these islands and airfields would tighten the noose on Rabaul, they said, but there wouldn't be enough left over for them to take Rabaul itself.[55]

The Joint Chiefs finally said, in effect, let's forget about Rabaul for now, and focus instead on giving Allied forces complete control of the Bismarck Archipelago, as a prelude to any final push. MacArthur wrote from Brisbane that he thought the plan was a mistake. "We are already committed to the campaign in New Guinea. . . . If at the same time we enter upon a convergent attack on the New Georgia group, we have committed our entire strength without assurance of accomplishment of either objective." So Halsey said he was willing to wait to launch his attack on New Georgia until MacArthur had achieved his first round of objectives, the islands of Kiriwina and Woodlark in the Trobriand Islands.[56]

The deal was done. To nearly everyone's amazement, Admiral King accepted the revised MacArthur plan with very little complaint or modification. The final directive went out on March 28, canceling the earlier three-stage drive on Rabaul. Instead, the objectives for 1943 would be first Woodlark and Kiriwina, to provide new airfields for extending the range of American airpower; then the Madang-Salamaua-Finschhafen triangle as well as western New Britain; and finally the Solomon Islands, including the southern part of Bougainville. The exact sequence of moves, and the exact timetable, remained to be set by the Joint Chiefs, not MacArthur or Halsey. But for the first time in the Pacific war, there was an agreed-to strategy for winning in the Southwest Pacific, and if MacArthur didn't get everything he wanted in terms of objectives (nothing had yet been said about the Philippines), he now had an achievable plan and overall "strategic direction"—and a steadfast navy ally in Bull Halsey.

After lengthy conversations with both Roosevelt and Hap Arnold about air reinforcements, Kenney reckoned he would have five hundred additional airplanes before 1943 was over.[57]

He was going to need every one of them. As he boarded a plane for the trip back to San Francisco on the 29th, the Japanese were finalizing plans to take MacArthur and the Fifth Air Force out of the strategic picture for good.

CHAPTER 20

DOING CARTWHEEL

Mine eyes have seen MacArthur with a Bible on his knee,
A-typing out communiques
For guys like you and me.
'Our heavy bombers hit Rabaul
And God is filled with glee'!
While Mac goes marching on.

—ANONYMOUS NAVY POEM BASED ON
"BATTLE HYMN OF THE REPUBLIC"

When MacArthur had arrived in Melbourne, he had told his aide Sid Huff to buy him a civilian hat. He hoped he might wear it if he went out for a movie when time permitted. In fact, the hat never left its box. Over the next three years, MacArthur had no time for his favorite entertainment. Running SWPA consumed all his time except for the handful of hours he snatched away for Jean and his son—while Jean and little Arthur had to adjust to their strange new surroundings of Australia largely by themselves.

For Jean, the first few weeks after arrival had meant a dizzying round of social engagements, starting with luncheons with various prominent ladies, and continuing on to cocktails and dinner virtually every night. After a time she began to complain of headaches until one day MacArthur came home for lunch and found her in bed, feeling overwhelmed by the blur of social obligations.

"What'll I do? What'll I do?" she kept asking him in a plaintive voice.

MacArthur called the doctor, who pronounced her physically fit. After he left, MacArthur gently closed the door and said, "If you don't stop worrying about these things, we'll have to write 'What'll I do' on your tombstone."

That was the end of the social whirl.[1] Even after they moved to Brisbane and settled into the Lennons Hotel, a short walk from the nine-story office building that was SWPA headquarters, Jean and Douglas settled into the more serene domestic routine they had established in Manila, with Jean preparing the general's lunch every day as he came back from the office to eat and enjoy a short nap, then returning to the office until early evening.

There were other headaches. For a time, they received anonymous letters threatening to kidnap little Arthur, or hinting that others were planning to do so. MacArthur refused to let it disturb their regular routine, although Sid Huff did start traveling with a revolver every time he and Jean and the boy went out. Arthur had a spell of eating troubles, sometimes taking more than an hour to finish his meals. Jean also argued that the general spoiled his son shamelessly, presenting him with gifts and little rewards no matter the occasion or how badly Arthur behaved.

Once an old friend of Sid Huff's who owned a toy and sporting goods company sent two enormous crates for Arthur filled with everything from balloons and toy airplanes to lead soldiers and boxing gloves—with ten specimens of each.

"We mustn't let the General know about this," Jean told Huff in a dismayed tone. "He would give them all to Arthur tomorrow morning."[2] From then on, all toys and gifts were stored in a "secret closet" to which only Jean had the key—and from which both Arthur *and* Douglas MacArthur were barred.

MacArthur had his own peculiar eating habits. His sensitive stomach kept him away from most spicy foods, as well as alcohol, and while their three-floor suite at the Lennons had a kitchen, most dinners were brought up from the hotel restaurant. He rarely commented on what was served, beyond an occasional, "no more cauliflower" or "no more Brussels sprouts" when the appeal of that particular vegetable had begun to wane. But as he began coming home later and later to find his dinner cold, Jean took up cooking his dinner herself, as well as his lunch.

They were a tight-knit group, in the midst of a foreign country and a world at war. Along with Ah Cheu and the Bataan Gang who had survived the escape from Corregidor, no outsider understood what they had been through, or the bond that held them together—certainly not Australians. Virtually the only public appearance that Jean made in Brisbane was christening a new Australian Royal Navy destroyer, the *Bataan,* and the only public speech was the one she gave on that occasion:

"I christen thee Bataan, and may God bless you."[3]

MacArthur's friendship with Prime Minister Curtin was genuine, as well as the source of his political leverage over SWPA. Yet he never built a warm relationship with his Australian hosts—certainly nothing like the bond that developed with the Japanese after the war. The adulation from every sector of Australian opinion that had greeted him on his arrival faded. The Australian armed forces in particular resented doing a major part of the fighting—and taking the greater burden of casualties—while having little say over where or when they fought.

Jean herself found few friends in Melbourne. She yearned for prewar Manila, and would from time to time pack and unpack footlockers for the day when they would be heading back.[4] So did little Arthur. He had few memories of their lives in the Philippines but would sometimes tell his parents he wanted to go back to their penthouse in the Manila Hotel, just so "we don't have to go by PT-boat," he would quickly add.

As for the general, whatever he was doing, no matter how focused we was on the fighting in New Guinea or getting more planes for George Kenney or more LSTs for Dan Barbey or bracing himself for the next round of bruising communications with the Joint Chiefs, the Philippines were never far from his thoughts—nor were the men he had left behind.

He would remember in his mind's eye "their long bedraggled hair framed against gaunt bloodless faces" and the tattered clothes and "hoarse wild laughter." The battling bastards of Bataan were only a memory to most Americans, but they were real and present to MacArthur for more than three years. "They were filthy," he wrote, "and they were lousy, and they stank. And I loved them."

The truth was, though, that in their prison camps, they did not love him—just as they mistakenly blamed him for their miserable fate.[5]

The Japanese plan to wreck MacArthur's plans was code-named Operation I.; it was simple and brutal. The Japanese army and navy would join their air forces for a massive bombing campaign of Allied airfields and shipping in the Solomons, including Guadalcanal, which by the spring of 1943 was firmly in American hands, and then New Guinea.

The goal was to so cripple MacArthur's air and sea assets that he would be unable to launch any fresh offensive for a year or more. By then, Operation I's mastermind hoped, Japan would have consolidated its position in the Solomons chain, and Rabaul would be an impregnable fortress.

The mastermind of Operation I was Japan's greatest war hero, Admiral Yamamoto. He had assembled 350 aircraft, both fighters and bombers, to do the job, and on April 3 he flew to the naval base at Truk in the Caroline Islands, to direct the operation himself.

Meanwhile, General Kenney was back in Brisbane and sat down with MacArthur to review his Washington trip. He found MacArthur more excited about the future than he had been at any point since arriving in Australia.[6]

For good reason. The promised air reinforcements hugely increased the chances of a successful offensive in 1943. Barbey's amphibious fleet was still pitifully small: just four aging destroyers turned into transports, six of the big LSTs, and thirty other landing vessels. But the Fifth Air Force now numbered 1,400 planes in addition to Australian and Dutch air units, while Halsey's command brought on six battleships, five carriers, and thirteen cruisers, plus another 500 aircraft.

As for troops on the ground, General Blamey had under his command two U.S. Infantry divisions, the Thirty-second and the Forty-first, one marine division, and no fewer than fifteen Australian divisions. With Halsey's seven divisions thrown in, this was beginning to look like an army ready to take on anything the Japanese could throw at it.[7]

Still, the numbers were deceptive. Kenney and MacArthur agreed that "we were at low ebb right then as far as any decisive action was concerned," the air force chief remembered later. Blamey's ground forces were exhausted after the rigors of the Buna campaign; so were many of Halsey's troops after the fierce fighting for Guadalcanal. Two regiments of the Forty-first were still working their way west along the north coast of New Guinea, but wouldn't reach their objectives for some time. Kenney's air forces were worn out and flying on spare parts and skimpy maintenance; instead of three fighter groups of seventy-five planes each, he was lucky if there were seventy-five fighters total that were operational.[8]

All in all, it would be two or three months before MacArthur could be on the move again, first against Lae and Salamaua and then west toward Madang. In the meantime, Kenney's bombers were hitting Japanese convoys as far east as Kiriwina and as far north as Kavieng on the island of New Ireland. It was only a few days after their meeting, on April 11, that Kenney and MacArthur realized something big was up, and it was headed right for Port Moresby.

After relentlessly attacking the Solomons from April 5 through April 10, Yamamoto now shifted his attention to New Guinea. This time naval intelligence let MacArthur down. They had managed to get advance warning of Yamamoto's raids on the Solomons and Guadalcanal, but missed the timing of the "Y Phase," or the turn to New Guinea.[9] But Kenney's instinct had already told him to shift his main fighter strength to protect Dobodura and Milne Bay. He made only one mistake. The main target wasn't Milne Bay itself but his own headquarters at Port Moresby, and he had barely eight P-38s and twelve older P-39s to guard the harbor and airdromes.[10]

At about nine o'clock in the morning on the 12th, radar picked up a large Japanese air formation coming out of Rabaul and heading for Milne Bay. Kenney's Lightnings hit in a head-on pass and began shooting down bombers while the P-39s tangled with the Japanese fighters. The Japanese bombers dumped their bombs over Port Moresby, including several on Laloki airfield, then banked away and headed back toward Lae with the P-38s pursuing. Damage was light, as the bomb pattern had been hasty and indiscriminate. It only reinforced Kenney's low opinion of the Japanese air force commanders as "a disgrace to the airman's profession," as he put it in his diary.[11]

Despite heavy losses, Admiral Yamamoto was exhilarated. His pilots had brought back a wildly fanciful account of the damage they had done in the raids, claiming they had sunk an American cruiser, two destroyers, and twenty-five Allied transports besides shooting down 134 aircraft.[12] Yamamoto was so delighted that he decided to take a victory tour and visit his intrepid airmen.

The message about the admiral's visit went out on April 13. Yamamoto didn't know it, but he had just signed his death warrant.

∗   ∗   ∗

Dawn on April 18 brought a misty morning under a turbulent sea as two Mitsubishi Betty transport planes carrying Admiral Yamamoto and his staff made their way from Rabaul toward the western edge of Bougainville, while half a dozen navy Zeros provided escort and cover overhead.

It was around three o'clock that the pilot of Yamamoto's plane spotted a plane on the horizon. It was a P-38 Lightning in dark khaki coloring with white stars set against dark blue circles, and it was circling over the rendez-vous point assigned for the Yamamoto party. Then it was joined by another; then another and another, followed by still another.

In minutes there were eighteen P-38s clustered in the air, as if they had been lying in wait. The Japanese Zeros dove in vain to provide cover for the transports while some of the American planes rose to meet them and others, led by Captain Thomas Lanphier, swept in toward the two lumbering Bettys.

One Betty bomber swerved and crashed in the jungle, killing most of Ya-mamoto's staff. The one carrying the admiral himself tried to bank and weave to avoid Lanphier's blazing .50-caliber machine guns almost at treetop level. Then a burst from Lanphier's plane tore open the Betty's port engine; the plane dipped and rolled and smashed into the ground in a blaze of fire and flying debris.[13]

The communiqué detailing Yamamoto's entire itinerary had been inter-cepted by ULTRA three days before the trip. Torn between possibly shooting down the man who masterminded the Pearl Harbor attack and possibly re-vealing to the Japanese that their most sensitive codes had been uncovered, the Office of the Secretary of the Navy hesitated. Finally it passed the mes-sage on to SWPA, and MacArthur gave the go-ahead to intercept.[14]

The P-38s had come from Halsey's command; later there was debate as to whether Lanphier or another pilot from the same squadron had pulled the fatal trigger—hardly unexpected. The death of Yamamoto sent shock waves through the Japanese high command and Imperial Navy. Yet "for whatever reasons, the Japanese navy refused to consider that the Allies had broken the five-digit mainline naval operations code," writes Edward Drea, the chief his-torian of decryption analysis in the Pacific war.[15] Together with the discovery of a Japanese army list with the names of 40,000 active Japanese officers in a lifeboat that washed ashore after the Battle of the Bismarck Sea, enabling Akin's cryptographers to match personal names to radio signals from Japanese army units, this refusal ensured that MacArthur's intelligence remained as operationally up to date as it could be, for the foreseeable future.

In the meantime, while one admiral exited MacArthur's life—"one could almost hear the rising crescendo of sound from thousands of glistening white skeletons at the bottom of Pearl Harbor," MacArthur wrote years later—another admiral, an American this time, entered.

William Halsey was the navy's version of MacArthur.[16] They met in Brisbane on April 15, and they hit it off at once. MacArthur found the South Pacific commander "blunt, outspoken, dynamic," while Halsey remembered MacArthur this way:

> Five minutes after I reported, I felt as if we were lifelong friends. I have seldom seen a man who makes a quicker, stronger, more favorable impression. He was then sixty-three, but he could have passed as fifty. His hair was jet black; his eyes were clear; his carriage erect. . . . My mental picture poses him against the background of these discussions; he is pacing his office, almost wearing a groove between his large, bare desk and the portrait of George Washington that faced it; his corncob pipe is in his hand (I rarely saw him smoke it): and he is making his points in a diction I have never heard surpassed.[17]

Halsey and MacArthur hammered out a plan on April 26 that they released as Elkton III. The code name, however, was CARTWHEEL, and that is the name by which it's been known ever since.

It consisted of thirteen amphibious landings in just six months, with MacArthur and Halsey providing maximum support to each other's efforts.

The first would take place in June, when everyone was ready and rested, with the islands of Woodlark and Kiriwina in the Trobriands, and then New Georgia in Halsey's sector. Salamaua, Lae, and Finschhafen would be next, severing eastern New Guinea from Japanese-controlled western parts of the island.

Once Madang was in Allied hands, and the southern end of Bougainville, landings would take place at Cape Gloucester on New Britain as Halsey's forces would knock out Japanese air bases on Buka, the island off the northern coast of Bougainville, while MacArthur's prepared to clear Japanese resistance in the northwestern half of New Guinea.

These were insignificant operations compared to the big landings being planned in Sicily and Italy that fall, or Normandy a year later. But they added up to the step-by-step process by which Japan's empire in the South Pacific would be dismantled. By January 1944, MacArthur and Halsey figured, they would be ready for the final assault on Rabaul—the ultimate objective for victory.

MacArthur resisted sending details of their joint plan to Washington—perhaps for fear that the Europe-obsessed Joint Chiefs would veto their ambitious thrust.[18] He told them only that he anticipated that the first move toward Woodlark and Kiriwina would start in June. But that was too slow for Admiral King. King wanted his protégé Admiral Nimitz to begin a thrust into the central Pacific through the Marshall Islands in November, and proposed shifting the Marine First and Second Divisions, the one under MacArthur's command and the other under Halsey's, to help the Marshall offensive, along with two bomber groups promised to Kenney.

MacArthur's rage boiled over in a caustic message to George Marshall, damning the entire central Pacific strategy as an unnecessary, even "wasteful" diversion from what should be the main Pacific strategy, MacArthur's own.

"From a broad strategic viewpoint," he wrote, "I am convinced that the best course of offensive action in the Pacific is a movement from Australia through New Guinea to Mindanao." He added that "air supremacy is essential to success" for the southwestern strategy, where large numbers of land-based aircraft are "utterly essential and will immediately cut the enemy lines from Japan to his conquered territory to the southward." He told the Joint Chiefs that pulling in those additional heavy bomber groups, "would, in my opinion, collapse the offensive effort in the Southwest Pacific Area. . . . In my judgment the offensive against Rabaul should be considered the main effort, and it should not be nullified or weakened" by some quixotic thrust into the central Pacific.[19]

King, however, was adamant. There would indeed be a central Pacific thrust led by the navy, with its main axis passing through the Marshalls and Marianas toward Japan itself, while bypassing the Philippines altogether. It was a strategy entirely at odds with MacArthur's. Moreover, Marshall supported King, as did the other Joint Chiefs. Yet in the end King relented on the transfer of the two marine divisions, and the bomber groups. Now it was time for MacArthur to put up or shut up—that is, reveal his timetable for CARTWHEEL.

So MacArthur told them he planned to take Kiriwina and Woodlark in the Trobriand Islands on or around June 30. The advance on New Georgia would start on the same date, and in September the First Cavalry and three Australian divisions would commence operations on the Madang-Salamaua area. Meanwhile, MacArthur's Forty-third Division would start the conquest of southern Bougainville on October 15, while the First Marines and the Thirty-second Division would take on Cape Gloucester on the southern tip of New Britain, on December 1.

In retrospect, it seems a long time to take a handful of tropical islands and jungle outposts, without even getting within striking distance of Rabaul. But MacArthur and his staff knew that the Japanese would fight them like wounded tigers at every step. The battle for Buna had shown them that the Japanese soldier was prepared to fight to the death, even for the tiniest sliver of territory. They knew that despite the blow to morale with Yamamoto's death, the enemy still had formidable air and sea forces in the area that could strike at every move MacArthur's forces made.

But MacArthur believed he could make CARTWHEEL work. He now understood how airpower could isolate the enemy from support by land or sea. Given enough bombers, it could neutralize the port and the airfields at Rabaul while CARTWHEEL got under way. He also foresaw how Barbey's amphibious fleet could give his troops decisive mobility to jump from island to island with the support of Kenney's air force and Halsey's carriers and cruisers. And he had the battlefield commander he needed to carry out CARTWHEEL, the fourth crucial member of his team who had joined him in Brisbane in February, General Walter Krueger of the United States Sixth Army.

Krueger's presence was part of an administrative shakeup that MacArthur had set in motion after the Papua operation, in order to give himself more direct control over the flow of troops, supplies, and other logistics for his Elkton offensive, and now CARTWHEEL. MacArthur's USAFFE headquarters was now the administrative nerve center for all American army commands in the area—Kenney's Fifth Air Force, the Sixth Army consisting of the Thirty-second and Forty-first Divisions, the First Marines, two antiaircraft brigades, a paratroop regiment, and a field artillery, soon to be joined by the First Cavalry and a new infantry division, the Twenty-fourth; and Army Services of Supply (MacArthur made sure it performed according to his orders, not Washington's).

MacArthur made Krueger not only head of the Sixth Army but head of something called Alamo Force, a special tactical force that would carry out CARTWHEEL under MacArthur's ultimate authority—and that also happened to include the exact same units as the Sixth Army. It was a subtle change, but it was not lost on General Blamey. By a bit of administrative sleight of hand, MacArthur had given Krueger and American ground forces their own independent command as Alamo Force. The redesignation of the Sixth Army as Alamo Force rendered Blamey's title of Commander, Allied Land Forces effectively meaningless.[20]

It was a bitter blow to Blamey, although it took him two years before he registered a formal complaint about his decapitation by flowchart.[21] The commander in chief of SWPA, however, was determined to have a free hand for himself and his officers to develop the new combined operation formula as they saw fit. Blamey and the Australians would have their own force, New Guinea Force, to carry out the overland conquest of New Guinea as far west as Madang. But it was Alamo Force that, in MacArthur's mind, would revolutionize modern warfare, starting in the Trobriand Islands at Woodlark.

Australian Navy Lieutenant P. V. Mollison was asleep when villagers suddenly burst into his hut. Mollison was assigned to Woodlark Island as a "coastwatcher," and the natives had alarming news. A flotilla of ships was headed into Guasopa Bay on Woodlark's eastern side. Mollison hastily drew up his native militia force into a skirmish line one hundred yards from the beach, gleaming pure white in the darkness. They watched as the first boats landed and began to pull up on the beach. One by one, ramps dropped, and armed men began to spread out. With a sigh, Mollison signaled his men not to fire. The armed men were Americans, he realized with relief, who were landing where there were no Japanese to fight.[22]

The men of the Eighteenth Regimental Combat Team were relieved to be there, as well. They had spent hours being seasick as waves tossed their tiny boats around on the way into Guasopa Bay; it was later determined that almost half the force had been so incapacitated by seasickness they could not have fired a rifle if they had had to fight their way onto the beach.[23] But fortunately there were no Japanese on Woodlark or on Kiriwina, the bigger island to the northwest, where another combat team came ashore that same early morning after an even stickier landing (every single landing craft got stuck on coral reefs as they approached the beach and had to be tugged out).

Within a few days, engineers blew a channel through the reef, and Barbey's sailors began ferrying over supplies from Port Moresby to build its first pier, then airfields on both islands. In just three weeks, by July 24, fighters were ready for operations on Woodlark; by August 18 the Seventy-ninth RAAF Squadron was flying from Kiriwina. By November the Seabee construction battalions would complete airstrips large enough for Kenney's heaviest bombers, all within 350 miles of Rabaul.[24]

MacArthur's Alamo Force also did the Australians a favor with a landing at Nassau Bay, which was also unopposed. Troops then began pushing inland to hook up with a bigger Australian force holding the village of Wau, site of a major airstrip twenty miles southwest of Salamaua—a strip that would be essential for the landward push to Salamaua in September. Now they had a way to supply the Australians by sea, and to stage more shore-to-shore strikes on their march up the New Guinea coast.[25]

At the same time, a hundred miles away, Halsey's forces were landing on New Georgia, northwest of Guadalcanal. Their objective: the big Japanese airfield at Munda, which couldn't be approached by large naval vessels and would have to be taken by the advancing American soldiers, marines, and New Zealanders, one jungle clearing at a time.

CARTWHEEL had started, and MacArthur followed its progress that summer from his map in Brisbane. The joint American-Australian drive for Salamaua, in his mind, was really only a feint. The main objective was Lae, to be taken by both overland and amphibious assault, and then Finschhafen, the small port on the tip of the Huon Peninsula, while Halsey completed the reduction of New Georgia and Munda.

Then "both prongs," as MacArthur described it, "the Southwest and South Pacific, covered and supported by the newly won bases, would push on to strike simultaneous blows against New Britain to the west and Bougainville to the east"—all with the goal of cutting off Rabaul and rendering it helpless to halt MacArthur's advance to the Philippines.[26]

To do all this, however, was going to require more complete control of the air, and for that MacArthur turned to George Kenney. His chief objective that summer was the Japanese air base at Wewak, 500 miles south of the Allied airdrome at Dobodura—the one the Japanese had been trying to knock out for months.[27] Starting on August 17, bombers with P-38s in support reduced Wewak to a wreck, with 175 Japanese planes destroyed on the ground.[28]

The Allies now had air superiority over the entire Huon Gulf region. At last, CARTWHEEL could begin to roll.

By the first week in September, Salamaua and Lae were virtually isolated, thanks to a series of coordinated air, ground, and sea operations. Barbey's amphibious force landed fresh Alamo Force troops northeast of Lae, cutting the Japanese line of communication with the port at Finschhafen. Then Kenney dropped troopers of the 503rd Parachute Regiment and an Australian artillery battery into Nadzab, northwest of Lae. That town and Salamaua fell to the Allies at the end of the month, and on October 2 MacArthur's men had taken Finschhafen. At the same time Australian troops had marched up the Markham Valley in central New Guinea, giving MacArthur complete control of the Huon Peninsula—while Nadzab became another air base for raids on Hollandia, Rabaul, and the hapless Japanese who were still stuck on Wewak.[29]

It was a spectacular success. Kenney and Dan Barbey had their disagreements over the kind of air support the Third Amphibious Force wanted. Barbey wanted more or less continuous fighter and bomber coverage for his ships and landings, like an airborne umbrella. Kenney thought this tactic a waste of time, and preferred to pound Japanese airfields in advance to render them useless, so that an air umbrella would be unnecessary—while keeping his fighters in reserve to smother any Japanese air counterattack.[30]

But the man who really brought airpower into its own was the SWPA commander, MacArthur, who saw at last that Billy Mitchell had been half-right. Wars couldn't be won by airpower alone, but they couldn't be won without it.

One person who understood that was the supreme air chief, Hap Arnold, who wrote to Kenney from Washington: "I want to tell you that I don't believe the units could possibly perform in the manner they are doing without the most sympathetic support from General MacArthur. It requires complete understanding between General MacArthur and you. In this respect, our Air Forces are very, very fortunate."[31]

However spectacular Kenney's expert use of airpower had been, and Barbey's skilled amphibious moves, once the troops moved from the beach into actual fighting, the going got agonizingly slow, as the fighting degenerated into vicious, no-quarter combat between companies and platoons that ground out the casualties one by one in the most inhospitable environments God ever created.

The 503rd Parachute Regiment found this out after their jump into Markham Valley to secure Nadzab, the first major parachute drop of the Pacific war. MacArthur had insisted on going along, in spite of the danger that his plane might be intercepted by Japanese fighters (this was only months after Yamamoto had suffered a similar fate). "I decided that it would be advisable for me to fly in with [the troopers]," he remembered later. "I did not want them to go through their first baptism of fire without such comfort as my presence might bring to them."[32]

MacArthur watched from a B-17 as the 503rd made the jump, their delicate white parachutes floating down into the lush green jungle. Hugh Reeves was one of those who jumped, and he was knocked unconscious by a tree limb as he fell. When he came to, a medic orderly was standing over him with a submachine gun.

"Lager," the orderly said in a warning tone.

"Label," Reeves quickly answered. They had chosen that word as the counter password because it was believed the Japanese couldn't handle the L sounds. Reeves looked up and saw his chute hanging above him, entangled in a vine with one-inch needlelike thorns sticking out.

His comrade Rod Rodriguez wasn't so lucky. "I landed in a tall tree and drove a branch as sharp as a spear through my thigh," barely missing the main artery. For two days medics fed him morphine to hold back the agony, until they could get him evacuated from the airfield they had just secured.[33] The rest of the 503rd, along with the Australian Ninth Division, were soon bogged down in the hard fighting in front of Lae until the town finally fell on September 13.

The XIV Corps found out the same hard truth on New Georgia, where for weeks the 169th and 172nd Regiments of the Forty-third Division tried to advance on the Munda airfield without success. The Americans had a new weapon, the flamethrower, introduced into combat for the first time on New Georgia. Under the relentless assault of flamethrower teams backed by mortar and artillery fire while parties of riflemen and light machine guns cut down any Japanese trying to escape the fierce jets of flame, Japanese resistance began to crumble. By August 5 the Munda airfield was declared secure—although it took two more weeks of mopping operations to clear the last Japanese defender from the island.[34]

And the First Marines, "The Old Breed," conducted their first landing under MacArthur's command, on Cape Gloucester on the day after Christmas, in the last major operation of CARTWHEEL. Kenney and the Fifth Air Force had prepared the way all October, with a series of punishing raids on Rabaul, dropping bomb loads that daily set Pacific war records. Many of the marines were veterans of the hard slogging on Guadalcanal, but few had seen terrain as harsh and unforgiving as this, the extreme western tip of New Britain—the watchtower overlooking the Dampier Strait that connected the Solomon Sea with the Bismarck Sea, and which would serve as the vital passageway for any further American progress west.

After a fierce air and naval bombardment, Barbey's landing craft got them on the beach virtually unopposed, but the marines faced an even more formidable obstacle in their advance on the unfinished airfields in the middle of the cape. It was the weather, a virtually constant monsoon that soaked everything and everyone—while seething out giant trees whose roots had been destroyed by shell fire, that fell and crushed men underneath them.[35]

After clearing out Japanese positions around the airfield, the weary and soaked marines planted an American flag on the last day of 1943. Yet the real fight still lay ahead: securing the two large hills overlooking the airstrip. The last two hundred feet or so were virtually perpendicular rock.

A Seventh Marines battalion under Lieutenant Colonel Lewis Walt dragged a 37 mm gun up the jagged, rain-slimed slopes and used it to batter the Japanese off one of the summits. A Japanese counterattack couldn't dislodge them; instead they pushed on to the next hill, where mortar fire forced them to halt. Sherman tanks and artillery gave them cover the next day to wind around through the jungle until they found a path leading to the top. The fighting raged another two days in the mud and among the rocks until finally Cape Gloucester was declared secure on January 16, twenty-one days after the operation began. It had cost the marines 248 men killed (25 of them crushed by falling trees) and 772 wounded to take a position barely fifteen miles wide. Virtually every veteran of Guadalcanal swore that Cape Gloucester had been far worse, because of the constant rain.

Things were not going much better for Halsey's men on Bougainville. To everyone's surprise—especially MacArthur's—CARTWHEEL was stuck, as all forward movement seemed to cease. Even after the striking successes on the Huon Peninsula, in twenty months MacArthur had advanced only some 300 miles, barely one-third of New Guinea's northern coast, and the most formidable objectives still lay ahead. The Australians were faring no better. The day the marines landed at Cape Gloucester, the Seventh Division struck at Japanese positions near Dumpu in the Ramu Valley, where the Aussies, toting Enfield rifles and Bren guns, promptly got stuck in brutal fighting around a 4,900-foot-high line of hills known as Shaggy Ridge.[36]

So far, 11,000 Americans had been killed and wounded in 1943 on MacArthur's watch, in addition to 4,000 Australians. CARTWHEEL had cost the Japanese much more: some 50,000 soldiers and sailors; 150 merchant ships and 75 warships, and some 3,000 aircraft.[37] Yet General Adachi's Eighteenth Army, despite numerous defeats, remained intact and in charge in northern and western New Guinea. And MacArthur was still a very long way from Manila.

MacArthur was still convinced that the problem was not his strategy but a lack of resources with which to carry it out. He wrote to his friend General George Moseley, "Out here I am busy doing what I can with what I have, but resources have never been made available to me for a real stroke. Innumerable openings present themselves which because of the weakness of my forces I cannot seize. It is truly an Area of Lost Opportunity."[38]

Just days before the twin offensives on the 26th, General George Marshall had wound up his first and only tour of the Southwest Pacific Area, including a stop in Brisbane, where he told MacArthur the facts of life from Washington.

"Admiral King [has] claimed the Pacific as the rightful domain of the Navy," Marshall said. "He seems to regard the operations there as almost his own private war; he apparently feels that the only way to remove the blot on the Navy disaster at Pearl Harbor is to have the Navy command a great victory over Japan."

King felt a personal resentment toward MacArthur, Marshall said, and he encouraged other navy officers to feel the same resentment. King's strategy of a concerted push across the central Pacific, from the Gilbert Islands to the Marianas, had the strong support of Navy Secretary Knox, Chief of Staff Admiral Leahy, and even Roosevelt himself.[39] For MacArthur, it must have been cold comfort to know his belief that the navy had a vendetta against him wasn't just paranoia—or at least George Marshall didn't think so.

Yet the truth was, despite MacArthur's carping, the resources allocated to the war in Japan were nearly equal to those allocated to the fighting in Europe (7,900 aircraft were stationed in the Pacific, for example, compared to 8,800 in Europe), and MacArthur himself now commanded the biggest land-based air force and one-third of all U.S. ground forces—their numbers had doubled from December 1942 to December 1943, to nearly 700,000.[40]

Yet even as MacArthur wallowed in the Slough of Despond, the Japanese were about to leave him a treasure trove that would make up for lost opportunities and change the course of the war.

On January 2, 1944, shells began falling around the headquarters of the Japanese Twentieth Division at Sio. They were Australian artillery shells as the Ninth Division sought to cut the Twentieth Division off from their comrades to the west. The final phase of the battle for eastern New Guinea was under way.

General Hatazo Adachi, the general in charge of the defense of Lae and Finschhafen, was now engaged in a desperate rear-guard action to cover his retreat to Madang, which he believed was MacArthur's next objective. The

8,000 troops holding Lae had barely escaped the enclosing Allied trap; more than 2,000 starved to death on the twenty-six-day trek over the 12,000-foot-high Sakura mountain range. Adachi didn't want the retreat of his Twentieth Division from Siop to be as desperate or disorderly; he came over on January 4 to personally supervise the pullback.

In fact, the weather made it worse, as cascading rains soaked everyone and everything in sight and reduced visibility to a few yards. Meanwhile, the Twentieth's thoroughly drenched headquarters staff were destroying whatever they couldn't take with them. What they couldn't burn they decided to bury near a streambed, hoping the steadily rising waters would cover the traces of their hasty efforts. Then they disappeared into the mountains.

A few days later an Australian advance party moved into Siop, using mine detectors to look for possible booby traps the Japanese had left behind.

One young Australian engineer heard a shrill sound in his earphones and froze. He had found something metal, but something much bigger than a booby trap or a land mine. He called out to his mates, and in a few minutes they were using shovels and pickaxes to dig it out.

It was a steel trunk, a large steel trunk with an already rusting lock, which they quickly knocked away. Inside were piles of books with the covers torn off, and some of the pages still dripping wet. One of the Australians realized at once that they were codebooks that the retreating Japanese had buried, hoping that the river waters would complete the books' destruction.

Instead, the books were shipped off to Central Bureau in Brisbane. Major Joseph Richard and his team gingerly hand-dried the mildewing pages one by one, including putting some in a gas oven. When they started reading, they realized that what they had was the entire cipher library of Adachi's Twentieth Division, including codebooks, key registers, and substitution tables. When they were done, they had a complete version of the four-digit, mainline Japanese army code.[41]

They sent the bulk of the documents off to the main ULTRA decryption center, Arlington Hall in Washington, where IBM technicians made punch card entries for each codebook and began decoding the Japanese documents—decoding so fast, in fact, that the Japanese translators couldn't keep up.

Meanwhile, back at Central Bureau the codebreakers were facing the same problem: they were solving the Japanese army coded messages so quickly that a veritable stack of untranslated decrypts was piling up in the corner. MacArthur immediately put in a request for two crackerjack translators from the navy, who decided upon their arrival that they should start translating the latest decrypts first. One of them, Lieutenant Commander Forrest "Tex" Biard, grabbed the first document on the pile. It turned out to be a thirteen-part report of major decisions on New Guinea strategy made at a conference for Japanese admirals and generals only weeks before—all ready for MacArthur's morning reading.[42]

It was as if a thick cloud cover had been lifted from the South West Pacific Area, revealing every detail of Japanese army operations. By early spring the U.S. Army and MacArthur were monitoring the Japanese army's moves almost as closely and accurately as the Japanese themselves.

MacArthur said nothing in his memoirs about this unbelievable intelligence gift at the start of the 1944 fighting season—the single greatest intelligence breakthrough of the entire Pacific war. Likewise, still-classified sources kept his standard biographers, including Clayton James and William Manchester, largely ignorant of the role that decryption of the Japanese army codes had in changing the tempo and direction of the war in the Southwest Pacific, and in saving MacArthur's entire strategy.

Saving it, indeed, not just from the Japanese but from the decision makers in Washington who were having serious second thoughts about how to conduct the war against Japan.

Admiral Nimitz, for one, was never convinced that the central Pacific thrust was the best strategy compared to joining MacArthur in the push for Mindanao. Nimitz's first serious amphibious operation, on the island of Tarawa in November 1943, had been a near disaster. The Joint Chiefs, however, were still stuck on the double-prong, double-command concept. But now they were willing to push the timetable forward a bit. They were looking for landings on Mindanao for end of March 1944, instead of January 1945. They were thinking about imposing a naval and air blockade on Japan's home islands instead of a final head-on invasion—that is, until the war in Europe was won. Until then, it seemed, they were content to let the action in MacArthur's South West Pacific Area drift along as a strategic backwater.[43]

MacArthur, however, was not. He had entered a firm protest in January not to let the Pacific war dwindle away to "two weak thrusts" instead of one strong one—namely, his. On February 2 he sent Dick Sutherland back to Washington to plead his case one more time. But this time he had something new to offer the Joint Chiefs: a far bolder plan that meant bypassing the next objective after Mandang fell, namely, the well-endowed but also well-defended Hansa Bay, in favor of a fresh series of objectives two hundred miles north of the New Guinea coast: the Admiralty Islands.

On February 2, MacArthur was given a detailed appreciation of the Japanese Eighth Area Army's situation in New Guinea and the surrounding islands, dated January 19. What made this document different from similar analyses drawn up by Willoughby and his G-3 staff was that this was the Eighth Army's own chief of staff's report for his superiors in Tokyo, all decrypted and translated by Akin's Central Bureau team.[44]

The report contained much fascinating and detailed information that was invaluable for evaluating past, present, and future operations in the SWPA, but it also contained one priceless piece of intelligence gold. It revealed a crucial gap between the Japanese Eighteenth Army, stationed at Wewak, and the forces gathering to repel a future MacArthur attack at Hansa Bay, and the garrison farther west at Sarmi. This was at Hollandia, a long, broad stretch of coast overlooked by mountains and jungle, with a splendid harbor.

The question MacArthur now had to face was how to land forces there, and split the Japanese Eighteenth Army in two. That was when George Kenney appeared in his office with some interesting data about the collection of islands in the Bismarck Sea known as the Admiralties. Located north of the New Guinea coast, but parked midway between Sarmi and Hansa Bay, the two biggest of the Admiralty Islands, Manus and Los Negros, shared a fine anchorage for ships, Seeadler Harbor.

The Admiralties had been on the Joint Chiefs' shopping lists of places to be captured in isolating Rabaul, along with Hansa Bay, but the intelligence from Akin and Kenney's report from Ennis Whitehead's command gave them a sudden burning importance. Whitehead's B-25s had flown clear across the island chain without any sign of a single plane, or any enemy activity. The enemy air base at Momote on the eastern end of Los Negros, they said, looked "completely washed out."

Willoughby had already weighed in on the matter. Given the fresh intelligence, he believed that a leap at poorly garrisoned Hollandia was now a distinct possibility.[45] Clearly the Admiralties and Seeadler Harbor in particular would make perfect staging areas for such a pounce. But Willoughby wasn't buying the story that the islands were deserted. He estimated there could still be 3,000 Japanese garrisoned there, maybe more. A slapdash amphibious landing could find itself bogged down in a long, hard slog against a fanatical enemy.[46]

"So let's try a reconnaissance in force," Kenney urged. Let's find out if there really are Japanese on those islands, he was saying, and then deal with what we know for sure—not what we think is going on.

MacArthur paced up and down the office for a while, nodding, then stopped.

"That will put the cork in the bottle," he said with firmness—meaning the capture of the Admiralties would keep the Japanese from reinforcing their troops in the Bismarck-Solomons area from points farther west.

The isolation of Rabaul would be virtually complete.

"Get Chamberlin and Kinkaid in here," MacArthur ordered, referring to his new naval commander, Vice Admiral Thomas Kinkaid, who had arrived in Brisbane on November 23 to replace Carpender and was already proving to be a no-nonsense, hard-charging sea officer—and a MacArthur favorite.[47]

Preparations for a landing on Los Negros went into frantic high gear: Chamberlin and his operations staff had less than four days to put together the force that would be at sea by February 29. Code-named Brewer Task Force, it would be led by Major General Innis Swift, commander of First Cavalry Division.

One thousand cavalrymen would do the landing, while another 1,500 and 400 Seabees would be ready to sail from Finschhafen forty-eight hours after D-Day if the reconnaissance showed that Los Negros was ripe for the taking.[48]

As the aides scattered and the paperwork began, a plan was starting to take shape in MacArthur's mind. With the Admiralties and Seeadler Harbor in his grasp, there would be no need to take the heavily fortified Kavieng on New Ireland or any other base in the New Britain area—or anywhere else under Halsey's command. Instead, Alamo Force would be poised to strike anywhere along the New Guinea coast, starting with Hollandia. Very suddenly, the route to Mindanao didn't seem so dim and distant after all.[49]

There was one additional twist. In addition to escorting the three APDs (assault destroyers) carrying Brewer Task Force, Kinkaid and the cruiser *Phoenix* would be carrying a special passenger to the Los Negros landing: General MacArthur.

MacArthur had decided he would make the crucial decision of whether to press ahead or pull out from Los Negros himself, from the bridge of the *Phoenix*. Kenney thought this a mistake. You'll just get seasick on the *Phoenix*, he told MacArthur.

"I'll fly you over in one of my B-24s," Kenney urged. "You can even pull the bomb release lever yourself," he added with a smile.

But MacArthur was deadly serious. "I've been taking the chance of being shot at all the years I have been in the Army. I am going to continue taking that chance when it's advisable."[50]

General Krueger was equally shocked. All it would take was one stray Japanese plane dropping a bomb on the *Phoenix*, or a stray artillery blast from shore, and the commander in chief SWPA would be gone. MacArthur could not be moved. "I have to go," he said, and that was that.[51]

On the 27th MacArthur and Kenney flew to Milne Bay, where they boarded the *Phoenix*, under the command of Captain Albert Noble. MacArthur showed an almost boyish curiosity about the workings of the ship, its sailors' and officers' routines, and he talked easily with the sailors who asked him for autographs—a ritual that he would go through many more times as the war wore on.

His eager good humor helped to cover the bad news they had received earlier that day. A six-man team of scouts that snuck over to Los Negros the night before had come back with a report that the island was "lousy with Japs." Kinkaid, Barbey, and Kenney's staff back at the air base at Nazdab wondered if the prudent course wasn't to cancel the operation. MacArthur shook his head. He wasn't going to cancel out on such an imprecise report. The landing would go ahead as planned.[52]

That night MacArthur was too excited to sleep. At 1:30 in the morning a marine guard awakened MacArthur's doctor, Roger Egeberg, who had been base surgeon at the army hospital in Melbourne before reporting for duty as

MacArthur's private physician just the month before. Egeberg had been a little taken aback on February 23 when he learned he would be sailing into his first battle with the general at his side; now he was taken aback at being woken up to see the general hours before the landing would take place.

Egeberg dressed quickly and went to MacArthur's cabin, where he found his patient "restless" and "excited in a peculiar way." MacArthur wanted to talk to someone, like the night he had talked to Sid Huff on the PT-47, except that MacArthur didn't want to talk about the battle the next day or the campaign or the course of the war. He wanted to talk football—*his* football at West Point, the games they won and one they should have won but lost, and about playing baseball at the Point as well as his early days in the Philippines when he was a shavetail lieutenant. Nothing else—certainly not the current war—seemed on his mind, and as MacArthur talked, Egeberg took his pulse. It was strong and slow and regular, so Egeberg sat back and simply listened.

Finally, after half an hour, MacArthur announced he felt like going back to sleep, thanked Egeberg, and lay back down on his bunk. The next morning the general made a joking reference to his insomnia, saying that after Egeberg left he discovered the bed was pitched so that his feet were higher up than his head. MacArthur simply reversed his position, he said, and then slept soundly until morning.[53]

"Morning" was a relative term, Egeberg realized, looking around. It was now 5:00 A.M. and pitch-black. But once out on deck, "we noticed a lessening of the intense blackness of night and later a uniform grayness and a drizzle. The cruiser's engines quieted down and we seemed almost to drift slowly in the water parallel to a shore which gradually appeared as the grayness lightened," until the first palm trees were visible, some five or six miles away.[54]

Also visible were two destroyers and Barbey's LCIs loaded with First Cavalry Division troops. Then an orderly passed out cotton for everyone's ears: the naval bombardment was about to start, including the guns of the *Phoenix.*

The gunfire came not in a continuous roar but in a series of short, loud explosions, as MacArthur and his staff watched the six-inch shells fly away from the cruiser into the jungle, and then watched for the blasts on shore. It was MacArthur's first experience of a naval bombardment, and he found it fascinating and exhilarating. Then a Japanese shore battery opened up, bracketing the *Phoenix* with shells that exploded less than 200 yards away. "Their next salvo could be expected to land on the deck," Egeberg realized.

Kinkaid said something to MacArthur, who stood very tall and rigid at the rail, staring hard at a point on the shore. Then the ship's gunnery officer vectored in on the Japanese guns, and a simultaneous broadside from all the *Phoenix*'s six-inchers silenced the shore battery once and for all. "This performance so thoroughly converted MacArthur into a naval gunfire enthusiast that he became more royalist than the king," Admiral Kinkaid remembered later.[55]

Small Higgins boats or LCVPs (Landing Craft, Vehicle, Personnel) were now pulling alongside the LCIs and taking on parties of thirty or forty troops for the ride in to shore. It was a dangerous ride; Egeberg watched the coxswain of one and several troops be hit by machine-gun fire as they weaved toward the beach. Then one of the LCVPs peeled off and pulled up alongside the *Phoenix*. Egeberg realized with a lump in his throat that this was the craft that was going to take him and the general to shore.

MacArthur was wearing no helmet or protective gear, just khakis and his customary scrambled-egg cap. He stood at the prow of the LCVP as they swept in, despite the machine-gun fire and occasional 20 mm gun bursts all around them.

On the beach MacArthur passed soldiers digging foxholes and clearing away enemy emplacements and gear. He was eager to see the condition of the Momote landing strip and insisted on walking its entire length even though it was still under fire from Japanese mortars and snipers. At one point an officer pointed at the line of trees just fifty yards away.

"Excuse me, sir, but we killed a Jap sniper in there just a few minutes ago."

"Good," MacArthur replied. "That's the best thing to do with them."[56]

The Dugout Doug myth was finally buried, if not forever, certainly for the duration of his command in the Pacific.

On the strip itself, MacArthur himself measured the craters American bombs had left behind and told an aide, Colonel Lloyd Lehrbas, to help him dig into the coral bed that made up the strip to see if its surface was deep enough to support Kenney's heavy bombers. The layer of coral, in fact, was only a couple of inches deep—not deep enough to handle B-24s and B-25s.

"I'm afraid General Kenney isn't going to like this," he told Lehrbas and

Egeberg. He stood up and surveyed the scene. The gunfire was letting up, and MacArthur had time to pin a Distinguished Service Cross on the first man ashore, Second Lieutenant Marvin Hinshaw. "You have all performed marvelously," he told their commander, General Chase. "Hold what you have taken, no matter against what odds. You have your teeth in him now. Don't let up."

Indeed, casualties had been light. The Americans had suffered just four dead and six wounded, while only five Japanese had been killed, with the rest fleeing into the jungle. But before he returned to the *Phoenix,* MacArthur warned Egeberg that the cavalrymen would be seeing a banzai charge as soon as night fell (sure enough, there was one that night). He also warned his doctor to wear a helmet next time instead of his cloth officer's cap.

"You probably took a look at me and didn't put it on," he said as they were sitting down to lunch in the admiral's cabin on the *Phoenix.* "Well, I wear this cap with all the braid. I feel in a way I have to. It's my trademark . . . a trademark that many of our soldiers know by now, so I'll keep on wearing it, but with the risk we take in a landing I would suggest that you wear a helmet from now on."[57]

It was the closest anyone ever came to hearing MacArthur talk about the visuals of leadership, the idea he had embraced during his days as the Fighting Dude in World War One. The cap and corncob pipe had become in effect his heraldic crest, like that of a knight of the Middle Ages, the sight of which told his men that their commander was with them and that, whatever dangers they faced, victory would eventually be there as well.

It was reassurance they were going to need. It turned out the reports about Los Negros being "lousy with Japs" were correct. After the beach landings and the predawn banzai attack, casualties steadily mounted. Captured Japanese mess tables became operating tables; wounded were ferried back to the destroyers offshore. It was a hellish day and night as the destroyers used illumination shells to light up the beachhead with a garish glow as naval shells rained down on the Japanese.[58]

But the next morning at dawn reinforcements arrived in the form of six LSTs, including Seabees to clear and repair the airfield. By March 3 enough additional troops had arrived to bolster Chase's men through a final banzai charge that left the Japanese too weak to mount another—and to relieve the

First Cavalry men who had been in combat for four continuous days and nights without any letup.

A week later an additional cavalry brigade under General Vernon Mudge took over Seeadler Harbor and by March 18 they had overrun the last Japanese defenses on Manus. The Admiralty Islands were secure. American fighters were flying off the Momote field, a new strip for bombers was being built at Lorengau, and Seeadler Harbor saw its first American ships—the first of many that would be preparing for the invasion of Hollandia.

Back in Brisbane, MacArthur was delighted. Now he was nearly ready for the showdown with the Japanese in northern New Guinea, and more than ready for a showdown with the Joint Chiefs.

CHAPTER 21

STEPPING-STONES TO VICTORY

Military strategy is based on speed—come like the wind,
go like lightning, and opponents will be unable to resist you.

—ZHANG YU, CHINESE STRATEGIST,

SUNG DYNASTY

William Halsey and his staff got a foretaste of what was up when they arrived in Brisbane on March 3, 1944, the very day the First Cavalry on Manus was bracing for the final banzai attack.

MacArthur had radioed Halsey to come at once, and when he arrived, "even before a word of greeting was spoken, I saw that MacArthur was fighting to keep his temper." The SWPA chief delivered a long tirade "in which he lumped me, Nimitz, King, and the whole Navy in a vicious conspiracy to pare away his authority."

At issue was the newly won naval base at Manus. It turned out that Admiral King wanted it transferred to his and the U.S. Navy's authority. MacArthur insisted that since his troops had taken it, it was his; he had given orders that the only ships allowed into Seeadler would be Kinkaid's and the Royal Navy's, which were due in a few weeks. Everyone else, even American ships, would be kept out.

Halsey was appalled, and said so. "If you stick to this order of yours, you'll be hampering the war effort." MacArthur's staff were shocked at Halsey's bluntness—but it worked.

After two more days of argument, MacArthur finally yielded. "You win,

Bill!" he said with an enormous smile, and no more was said about Seeadler.[1] Instead they discussed the base at Kavieng—MacArthur wanted it taken, Halsey said it would be too costly—and Rabaul, which Halsey's carrier planes had blasted, as well as Truk, the other major Japanese naval base set in the Carolines in the central Pacific.

But in fact MacArthur's interest in Rabaul had faded—if it had existed at all. Historian Eric Bergerud's hunch is that his push to attack the big base was a means to an end, to get Washington to free up some of the resources earmarked for Europe and send them to him instead.[2] In any case, his inclination now was, in his words, to "let 'em die on the vine" as the noose he had originally designed for Elkton and then CARTWHEEL took real shape. With Manus and the Admiralties firmly in control, he had the bases he needed for the descent on northern New Guinea. Except this time, instead of heavily defended Hansa Bay, his calipers were pointing on the map at Hollandia.

All that was left was convincing the Joint Chiefs and their Joint Strategic Survey Committee that Halsey and MacArthur should now combine forces along the lines that MacArthur and Sutherland had outlined in their so-called Reno IV plan, a sweeping movement to capture the remainder of New Guinea and the Solomons, "sever sea communications between Japan and the vital Borneo-N.E.I. [i.e., Dutch East Indies]-China Coast area" by mid-September, then be ready for an invasion of Mindanao by November 5.[3]

With Halsey's approval, Richard Sutherland presented the plan in Washington, where the response was at first surprise and resistance, then judicious doubt, followed on March 12 by reluctant surrender—with some provisos. The first was that MacArthur had to give up on making the SWPA line of advance the axis of the entire Pacific theater. A two-pronged thrust from both MacArthur and Nimitz was still the rule. All the same, the capture of the Admiralties had caught the Joint Chiefs completely by surprise. It seemed to demonstrate that MacArthur's overall strategy outlined in Reno IV might be fruitful after all.[4] So they approved the campaign for making Hollandia instead of the Vogelkop Peninsula, at the far western end of New Guinea, the main staging base for the invasion of the Philippines. The deadline for the latter was now set as November 15, 1944.[5]

The Joint Chiefs also agreed to MacArthur and Nimitz now sharing their resources as their respective drives up from the South Pacific and across the central Pacific began to converge. MacArthur would retain control of the harbor at Manus as he requested, but he would have to share the anchorage with the Pacific Fleet and provide air support for Nimitz's push into the Marshall and Palau Islands. Likewise, Nimitz would offer naval support, including carrier air support, for MacArthur's move on Hollandia and then Mindanao.

There was, however, one bitter disappointment for MacArthur, and for George Kenney. They would be getting none of the new B-29 superbombers that the Air Force would soon have available, with their 20,000-pound bomb load capacity, 6,000-mile range, and 350-miles-per-hour cruising speed. Kenney's mouth watered at the thought of having a squadron or two of these fast, well-armed monsters to demolish what remained of Japanese airpower in the SWPA.[6] But those not being sent to the India-Burma-China theater were reserved for the air war over Japan, to be launched from bases in the Marianas—another reason why Nimitz's drive to take islands like Saipan, Tinian, and Guam was viewed as crucial to the entire Pacific war.

In the end, the loss of the B-29 made no appreciable difference to the outcome of the fighting in the SWPA. Given the major headaches that the plane gave pilots and air force commanders, with a tendency for engines to catch fire and with "more bugs than the Smithsonian Museum," as one B-29 pilot grumbled, Kenney may have been lucky not to have to rely on the temperamental aircraft—or to have to build airfields to accommodate its mammoth size.[7]

All the same, MacArthur could be satisfied. His war in the Pacific had reached a major turning point. The way was now open and a deadline set— November 15, 1944—for launching the campaign that mattered most to him next to defeating Japan: liberation of the Philippines. And the faster he completed the conquest of New Guinea, the faster Nimitz's and Admiral King's chances of stopping him in order to shift everything over to the push through the central Pacific faded away like a Papua sunset.

*   *   *

That conquest would start with the capture of Hollandia.

On March 8, even before the end of the last Japanese resistance in the Admiralties, MacArthur revealed his plan to the Joint Chiefs for an attack on the Japanese base set for April 15. Almost 80,000 men and 217 ships would be involved, bypassing the enemy still ensconced at Wewak, by 1,000 miles. Another, smaller force would land at Aitape, midway between Hollandia and Wewak, to grab the fighter field there.[8] Meanwhile, Kenney and naval air support would relentlessly pound the Japanese airfields around Hollandia, and intercept any Japanese attempt to reinforce Aidachi's Eighteenth Army as MacArthur's move left it divided and isolated.[9]

It was the kind of broad, bold offensive operation that appealed to MacArthur—the first real exercise in "bypassing the enemy" that he would become famous for—but when Admiral Nimitz came to Brisbane for a joint summit on March 25, he expressed grave doubts. He thought the Hollandia operation a reckless gamble, and worried that his big carriers would be exposed to attack from Japanese ground bases when they came in to support the Hollandia landings.

MacArthur knew better. The priceless gift of being able to decrypt the Japanese army codes made him aware that far from being reckless, he was hitting the enemy at his weakest point, the Eighteenth Army's vulnerable back door.

Further decrypts had also revealed the enemy's exact plans for reinforcing Hollandia and Wewak by sea, which Kenney's airborne commerce destroyers would intercept and destroy. As for the air bases Nimitz was concerned about, Kenney told him point-blank that he would have those rubbed out by April 5, thanks to his new air bases on Los Negros.[10]

The head of the Fifth Air Force was as good as his word. By the time the invasion forces arrived in Humboldt Bay in front of Hollandia, there was no Japanese airpower left in the area. There was no way MacArthur was going to miss the Hollandia landings, so he set off on the cruiser *Nashville* on April 19. On the way, he made his one and only stop at Cape Gloucester, where the First Marines, still bogged down in the island's mangrove swamps, were furious at being left to fester. The marine band members who were assembled to greet him even refused to play, claiming they were out of practice.

But MacArthur performed his brief tour without self-consciousness and passed among officers and men, shaking hands as if they were old friends.[11] Then he reboarded the *Nashville*. Hollandia was beckoning.

Doc Egeberg was in awe at the size of the invasion force that a hot and muggy dawn revealed on April 22. "There were cruisers, destroyers everywhere," along with aircraft carriers and a fleet of LSTs, LCIs, and other large landing craft loaded with tanks, trucks, and personnel. An excited MacArthur watched the preliminary bombardment of the Hollandia-Pim beaches, then the Twenty-fourth Division poured ashore three miles south of Hollandia, while the 186th Regiment moved up to take Pim, four miles south of the objective.

"The ease of the landings exceeded even my expectations," MacArthur later wrote. "No withering fire met us at the beach. Instead, there was disorder—rice still boiling in pots, weapons and personal equipment of every kind abandoned."[12]

They had achieved complete and utter surprise. Indeed, the first time the Japanese at Hollandia learned that an invasion was imminent was when they woke up to see MacArthur's ships in Humboldt Bay.

At 11:00 A.M. MacArthur insisted on going ashore to see what was happening. He and Generals Krueger and Eichelberger toured the battlefield around Pim, as the sixty-four-year-old led his staff on a three-mile hike along the beach that left everyone else out of breath. Back on the *Nashville*, they celebrated with chocolate ice cream sodas. The day was almost unbearably hot, and the sodas were an unexpected treat. Eichelberger remembered wolfing his down before the others had barely started. MacArthur "grinned and gave me his own untouched, frosted glass."[13]

Then they sailed to Tanahmerah Bay, the other assault landing zone. MacArthur disregarded warnings of approaching enemy planes, and insisted that his landing craft get them to the beach. They arrived at 3:00 P.M. for another busy march along the narrow beach, with dense jungle rising up behind. After two hours, they re-embarked—with MacArthur as usual not even breaking a sweat.[14]

On the 24th he learned that the operation at Aitape had also been a success, and that evening he sent a jubilant communiqué back to Washington:

"Complete surprise and effective support, both surface and air, secured our initial landings with slight losses," it ran. MacArthur described the enemy's Eighteenth Army as completely surrounded. "To the east are the Australians and Americans; to the west the Americans; to the north, the sea controlled by our Allied naval forces; to the south untraversed jungle mountain ranges; and over all our Allied air mastery." While the Japanese could be expected to try to break out of their isolation with desperate attacks, "their ultimate fate is now certain. *Their situation reverses Bataan.*"[15]

It was a stunning, if deeply satisfying, sentence for MacArthur to write. Only three Americans had been killed at Aitape, compared to 625 Japanese killed and 27 captured. The fall of Hollandia brought an even bigger bag of 600 Japanese POWs, the largest number ever captured in the entire SWPA. It was a sign of the surprise that MacArthur had achieved, as was the fact that while some 3,300 Japanese had been killed, only 159 Americans died in the entire operation.[16]

It was just the kind of battle MacArthur liked, and the kind he would later claim was his specialty. An unexpected and decisive strike that resulted in low casualties, while leaving an enemy overwhelmed and in headlong retreat (more than 7,000 Japanese had to flee Hollandia west to Sarmi, and thousands never made it). He had scored a big triumph, not just against the Japanese but against the doubters in Washington.

It remained to be seen what he would do with it.

Fortunately, the Japanese had left behind at Aitape another gift for MacArthur. A careless Japanese radioman failed to destroy 147 pages of decryption worksheets along with key and indicator tables.[17] They were swiftly shipped off to Arlington Hall in Washington, where IBM machines allowed the codebreakers to crack the latest version of the Japanese army's top secret codes. The breakthrough didn't last long; on May 10 the Japanese stopped using the code. But a search through backlogged encrypted messages, which were now easily read, revealed something even more important. A barge that Kenney's planes had sunk off Aitape had actually been carrying a cargo of new key registers.

Spencer Akin and Central Bureau sent a diver over from Brisbane who found the barge in relatively shallow water.[18] The steel box in which the books were contained was intact, and once each page was painstakingly extracted, remounted, and daubed with rubbing alcohol (a suggestion from one of the Australians working at Central Bureau), the books began to reveal their secrets.

Almost 85 percent of the key register was recovered. Since General Adachi's only method of keeping in touch with his 60,000 troops scattered across New Guinea was by radio, it meant MacArthur was learning about Japanese troop movements on the island at almost the same time as the Japanese officers in charge. And not just troop movements on New Guinea. In June General Marshall sent a message to MacArthur suggesting that since Adachi's decrypted radio messages were supplying so much information on Japanese plans all across the Pacific, the SWPA chief might want to avoid wrapping up the New Guinea operations too quickly. "Will advise when this advantage ceases."[19]

There is no record of MacArthur's reaction to this suggestion that he not win the war against Japan—or at least not the war in New Guinea—too fast.

Meanwhile, the buildup of Hollandia as MacArthur's main base on New Guinea was under way.

"Sides of mountains were carved away," General Eichelberger remembered, "bridges and culverts were thrown across rivers and creeks, gravel and stone fill was poured into sago swamps to make highways as tall as Mississippi levees."

Swarms of Seabees and army engineers built roads, docks, and 135 miles of aviation fuel pipeline over the rugged hills overlooking Humboldt to feed the hundreds of airplanes that would soon be taking off from both Hollandia and Aitape airdromes. "Where once I had seen only a few native villages and an expanse of primeval forest," Eichelberger wrote, "a city of 140,000 men took occupancy"—along with one of the biggest bases of the Second World War.[20]

There was still one problem with Hollandia: none of the airfields was fit for heavy bombers. MacArthur would need them to fulfill his promise to support Nimitz in the upcoming assault on Saipan. So to do that, there was still one more island to be taken, one more stepping-stone to the Philippines: Biak Island.

It was part of the Shouten island group 300 miles west of Hollandia and just west of the Vogelkop Peninsula at New Guinea's westernmost end. Virtually uninhabited, Biak was covered with twelve-foot-high jungle springing up from its coral outcroppings. There were few sources of fresh water, and temperatures regularly ran higher than one hundred degrees. For all its unattractive features, it had one redeeming virtue: its three solid, well-cleared airfields, all built and maintained by the Japanese, with the biggest and best at Mokmer.

ULTRA had told MacArthur that Japanese resistance on Biak would be "stubborn but not serious, and that the enemy had no ground reserve to move in to support the island." That would be wrong, as it turned out; and ULTRA failed to disclose either the exact size of the Japanese forces on the island or the fact that they included tanks. Instead, Willoughby and his intelligence staff anticipated that they would find the bulk of the Eighteenth Army's defenders gathering at Sarmi on the coast or even on the nearby island of Wakde, as every other reserve was being drained away to reinforce Japanese strongpoints on New Guinea proper.[21]

The situation called for caution, and Willoughby said so. But the truth was MacArthur was in a hurry; he needed to take advantage of the confusion that his advance was causing the Japanese. His codebreakers had revealed how his antagonist General Adachi was desperately scrambling to catch up with the new realities on the ground, in the air, and at sea, especially after the fall of Hollandia. The danger was that if he did, Adachi and his still formidable forces could turn western New Guinea into the kind of network of mutually supporting strongholds that made Halsey's advance through the Bismarcks so harrowing and slow, the same kind of situation that MacArthur had narrowly avoided at Buna.

So MacArthur disregarded his G-2's advice and pressed ahead with the invasion of Biak, set for May 27, 1944.[22]

There was also another reason for speed: the Imperial Japanese Navy. ULTRA was enabling him to keep track of Japanese fleet movements.[23] As it happened, there were two sizable units within striking distance of Biak, one at Davao and the other at Tawitawi, just sixty sailing hours from Biak. If either one moved in force beyond the Malacca Strait, MacArthur reasoned, that could make landings at Biak or anywhere else, difficult or even impossible.

The risk of tempting the Japanese navy to intervene was made obvious, paradoxically enough, when ULTRA scored one of its biggest triumphs. Its decrypts revealed the dispatch of a major Japanese convoy headed from Manila to the Dutch East Indies and western New Guinea, with no less than 12,784 troops of the Japanese Thirty-second Division and an unknown number from the Thirty-fifth Division, all in nine transports with seven escorts.

The decrypts revealed not only the size of the convoy but its exact route, speed, and daily noon position, so that when the convoy entered the Celebes Sea an American submarine, the USS *Gurnard,* was waiting for it. Within ten minutes on May 6 the *Gurnard* had sent three transports and 3,954 soldiers to the bottom of the sea. Another 6,800 soldiers were rescued, but all their heavy equipment had been lost. The rest of the convoy turned back. There would be no Japanese reinforcement for New Guinea from the Philippines.

Everyone breathed a strong sigh of relief, including the Central Bureau when its deciphering of radio traffic revealed that the Japanese were blaming the disaster on spies in Manila, not the breaking of their codes.[24] But the lesson was clear, including to MacArthur. The sooner the Allies made their move on Biak, the less likely there would be interference from the sea. The resistance on land would be bad enough.

"The Hollandia invasion initiated a marked change in the tempo of my advance westward," MacArthur wrote later. "I was determined to reach the Philippines before December, and consequently concentrated on the immediate utilization of each seized position to spark the succeeding advance."[25]

But Biak was important for another reason. By taking it and putting heavy bombers on its airstrips, MacArthur would prove his bona fides in support of Nimitz's offensive in the Marianas, which would start with Saipan on June 15—less than three weeks away.

MacArthur ordered his amphibious team to strike first at the island of Wakde, a few short miles from the New Guinea coast. Wakde would serve as a useful staging area for the final assault on Biak. George Kenney was also delighted by the decision. He needed Wakde as a forward air base, but he too knew the other danger of waiting too long. His reconnaissance flights over Biak suggested the Japanese might finish and equip their airstrips there before the United States could capture them.

On May 18, 1944, the landings at Wakde took place. There was only a small Japanese force to greet them, but it still took two days of fighting to clear the island. Even before it was over, Kenney had the captured airstrip up and running. In less than two weeks his B-24s would be flying their first reconnaissance missions over Mindanao. MacArthur's return to the Philippines was starting to take shape.[26]

Biak was next, and the Japanese knew it. They had built up formidable defense lines with bunkers and pillboxes, connected by caves cut through the coral, with additional defenses overlooking the seven-mile-long coastal road to Mokmer. They then put 12,000 defenders inside the fortified complex, and waited.

On May 27, lead elements of the Forty-first Division came ashore after a sweeping air and naval bombardment. Watching from their transports, the divisional commander Major General Horace Fuller and his soldiers wondered, as they always did, how anything could survive the savage onslaught of waves of Vought Corsair ground attack fighters and A-20s in addition to the five- and twelve-inch naval guns, as the glare from explosions and clouds of smoke rose up almost to blot out the sun.

The shelling, however, had done nothing to disturb the Japanese, who waited it out in their coral caves. As the Third Battalion, 162nd Infantry moved from the beach down the coastal road toward Mokmer, the Japanese opened up with machine guns and mortars. Another Japanese battalion swung out to cut off the American line of retreat. It was a grim afternoon's fighting until the Third's sister battalion, the Second, moved up and covered the Third's withdrawal.

The next day, as a blood-red sun rose over the haze, a tank battle opened, as Japanese nine-ton tanks clashed with Fuller's Shermans. Three times the men from the Second Battalion drove back the Japanese, under a broiling sun with stupefying humidity. After sundown the survivors were pulled back by amphtracs dodging through the inky darkness. Fuller ordered up two fresh battalions for an encircling movement, while more troops backed by artillery and air support pushed forward to the Mokmer road.[27] A week later they were still pushing, as the casualties mounted and the enemy kept the Americans pinned down.

This was not what the swift capture of Hollandia and Wakde had led Krueger's men to expect. Back in Brisbane, MacArthur was blissfully unaware of what was happening. The very day the Japanese tanks launched their counterattack he was telling the world, "[Biak] marks the practical end of the New Guinea campaign." On June 3 came his dispatch that "mopping up is proceeding," even though Fuller was still readying himself for his main attack.[28]

On June 5 MacArthur finally became aware of how the fighting on Biak was bogged down. He composed a stern note to Krueger. "I am becoming concerned at the failure to secure the Biak airfields. Is the advance being pushed with sufficient determination?" Stung as well by Fuller's slow progress, Krueger wrote back that he had "seriously considered" relieving Fuller, but he would get out a full report once his chief of staff, Brigadier General George Decker, visited Biak to find out what had gone wrong.

What Decker found was a writhing, living hell. Weary American soldiers were reduced to one canteen of water every twenty-four hours as they tried to fight their way uphill through a network of pillboxes and foxholes occupied by a well-supplied, determined enemy who had been reinforced by another 1,000 men slipping through the navy's cordon of the island at night.

On the 13th, Fuller demanded his own reinforcements. Krueger reluctantly sent elements of the Twenty-fourth Division along with General Robert Eichelberger with a mission: take over Hurricane Task Force on Biak, relieve Fuller, and get the job done. Douglas MacArthur desperately wanted that airfield, and Walter Krueger was hell-bent on giving it to him.

Eichelberger arrived on the 15th to find the battle area in chaos, and a discouraged and disgusted Fuller. Krueger had ordered him to give up high ground he had taken to devote himself to a full frontal assault on the Mokmer airfields, even though those fields were useless as long as the Japanese could fire down from their fortified positions above—and even though that meant more casualties in a futile cause. Fuller told Eichelberger, "I do not intend to serve under a certain man [i.e., Walter Krueger] again even if I have to submit my resignation every half hour by wire."

As Eichelberger took charge, the men of the Twenty-fourth arrived to find "the smell of death and war was all over the place." Where the tank battle had taken place two weeks before, there were "bodies blown apart; human parts laying about the area" and rotting in the high heat. Captain Eric Diller wrote, "As we moved forward to relieve a company engaged in a firefight, the walking wounded were moving slowly to the rear. . . . I saw men in bloody bandages becoming a deeper shade of red since the crude first aid administered was not enough to stem the flow of blood." After another round of bitter fighting, the easternmost airfield was secured on June 22, but only for Kenney's single-engine fighters. The other strips weren't finally safe for use by his bombers until August 5.[29]

As Captain Paul Austin of the Twenty-fourth and his company patrolled Biak, he remembered later, "Some places were just engulfed with the smell of death. The decaying human body puts out a fierce odor that permeates the area," including their clothes. Because the island was literally made of coral and rock, his men couldn't bury the dead Japanese bodies. Instead they had to find a sump hole in the coral, soak the bodies with gasoline and set them alight. The flames got rid of tens of thousands of the blue flies feasting on the dead flesh, but thousands more survived to contaminate everything they touched, including the food, with dysentery. "It got to me so badly I passed out," Austin remembered. He had to retreat to a first-aid station until he recovered after a few days.[30]

Still the fighting ground on. On August 20 Eichelberger finally felt he could declare the entire island secure; by then MacArthur's deadline was past and useless. The same was true at Noemfoor, sixty miles east of Biak, where MacArthur and Kenney had thrown in some 8,000 tons of bombs to soften up the island before the 158th Regimental Combat Team, the same men who had overrun Wakde, waded ashore to meet the enemy, while paratroopers of the 503rd made a mass jump onto a coral airfield lined with trees and strewn with wreckage. Almost one in ten troopers broke a leg and smashed an ankle or an arm without the enemy firing a shot. Other troopers on patrols found ample evidence that the Japanese on Noemfoor had been reduced to cannibalism, and had butchered American prisoners for food.

Nothing was said to the media, then or later, because "the story would have a negative effect on home front morale," one of the troopers, Paul Rodriguez, was told by MacArthur aides.[31]

Certainly the news from the Biak operation was bad enough. In addition to the injured paratroopers and those killed on Noemfoor, Hurricane Task Force had lost 400 men killed and 2,000 wounded. The Japanese had suffered 4,700 killed and 200 captured, but then some 7,400 Americans had also been taken out of action by injury and illness. Almost two months had been required to take an island that was supposed to fall in a few days.[32]

But there was no denying that MacArthur's campaign was working. The 7,400 sick and injured troops would return to duty; the 4,700 dead Japanese were never coming back and would never be replaced. For Japan's Eighteenth Army, cut off and surrounded, time was running out; on July 10 General Adachi brought things to a quick conclusion. MacArthur's intelligence people had lost track of Adachi's forces after he evacuated Sarmi; in fact, his units were moving piecemeal through jungle and mountain, advancing on Hollandia and the airstrip at Aitape for a final attack to reverse MacArthur's progress. For most it was a harrowing journey, with thousands starving and dying while thousands of others, living skeletons but battle hardened, finally reached the banks of the Driniumor River, and waited for the final command to attack.

Central Bureau got the first wind of preparations for the attack on May 28, and after painstakingly piecing together decrypted radio messages, issued a warning to troops defending Aitape that a Japanese assault was coming on July 4. Nothing happened. MacArthur's codebreakers issued another warning for the night of July 9–10 (they were actually eavesdropping on Adachi and his staff debating which night would be better).[33] Again nothing happened, and soldiers began to wonder if the rear echelon wasn't getting spooked.

In fact, the Japanese were now lining the riverbank in strength. Just as Willoughby had all but given up and concluded in a briefing for MacArthur that "present patrol activity would not seem to point that attack imminent," men on night patrol from the 128th Infantry heard noises from across the Driniumor barely one hundred yards away.

A soldier raised his M-1 and fired a shot at the sound. At that instant 10,000 Japanese poured out of the jungle, with a shrill scream of *"Banzai!"*

A hail of bullets from Browning Automatic Rifles and M-1s slammed them back, then artillery opened up while Japanese mortars barked their sharp replies. The heavier American shells smothered the attack, while machine guns fired until the barrels glowed red hot. Flares lit up the night sky as the desperate Japanese refused to quit, surging over piles of fallen bodies, until the Americans, overwhelmed, fell back.[34]

General Charles Hall of XI Corps, commanding the task force defending Aitape, ordered his troops to counterattack. XI Corps eventually retook the Driniumor line and held it, while Adachi tried various outflanking maneuvers, which only added more casualties to both sides. Fighting dragged on for several more weeks, until Hall's force had suffered 440 killed and 2,500 wounded, while Adachi's Eighteenth Army had lost more than 10,000 men in battle and thousands more from starvation and exposure. The Eighteenth Army had virtually ceased to exist.

"Make the supreme sacrifice, display the spirit of the Imperial Army," Adachi had exhorted his men before the battle, and they had, but to no purpose other than to destroy what was left of their own effective resistance on New Guinea.

MacArthur sent a congratulatory message to Hall, expressing his "admiration for the splendid conduct of the campaign ... The operations were planned with great skill, were executed with great determination and courage, and were crowned with great success"—all of which ignored the fact that the Americans had almost been caught flat-footed, and that if Adachi had indeed retaken Aitape MacArthur's whole campaign would have been in very serious straits.[35]

Yet nothing succeeds like success, and MacArthur now moved to finish up operations in New Guinea. After the bloody fighting at Aitape, Japanese resistance faded and the rest of the Vogelkop Peninsula fell almost harmlessly to the Americans, first at Sansapor and then at Mar. On September 15 soldiers from the Thirty-first Division would be landing on the island of Morotai, the last stepping-stone to Mindanao and the Philippines.

It had been amazing progress, despite the missteps and near-fatal blunders. In less than three months MacArthur had come 1,400 miles, and opened up the Southwest Pacific from Finschhafen to the Moluccas.

He was now only a few hundred miles away from Mindanao, the southern gateway to Luzon and Manila—and freedom for the Filipino people and the American POWs he had been forced to leave behind. Only three men could prevent that from happening. All three were in Washington, and MacArthur prepared a grim, ruthless campaign to get them on his side—or to push them out of his way.

The first was President Franklin Roosevelt.

It was with a mixed sense of surprise and irritation that MacArthur received a bulletin from General Marshall on July 23 summoning him to a meeting at Pearl Harbor on the 26th with the president, who was arriving on the cruiser *Baltimore.*

"Purely political," was how MacArthur described Roosevelt's visit, which included key speechwriters but didn't include the Joint Chiefs of Staff—his first-ever tour of an American overseas theater of war without them.[36]

Nineteen forty-four was an election year, and Roosevelt was running for an unprecedented fourth term. Most observers, even his own advisors, assumed the visit was a chance to burnish his image as commander in chief. Being seen with one of America's most celebrated generals and heroes wouldn't hurt Roosevelt's reelection chances, either—especially if that general was a popular *Republican* hero.

Still, MacArthur felt free to complain about the trip all the way to Hawaii, as he paced up and down the aisle of the plane, "disgruntled and angry at being called away from his war duties." At one point he exclaimed in disgust: "The humiliation of forcing me to fly to Honolulu for a political picture-taking junket!"[37]

But as he paced, he was also thinking. This would be his first meeting with Roosevelt in almost ten years. During those ten years Roosevelt had gone from being "Mr. New Deal" to being "Mr. Win-the-War," as the president quipped to a reporter in 1942. He had been transformed from a politician whose urgent focus was domestic matters to a commander in chief holding together the greatest wartime coalition ever seen, and presiding over the greatest war machine in history that was outproducing Japan in ships by a factor of sixteen to one, and in planes by thirty to one.

MacArthur had undergone his own metamorphosis, from the Bonus Army–tainted retired chief of staff sent into virtual exile to be field marshal in a remote foreign country, to the most celebrated war leader in America, with the exception of Roosevelt himself—indeed, poised in a few short months to possibly challenge FDR for the presidency.

Running for president had crossed MacArthur's mind more than once. First in 1936 after retiring as chief of staff; briefly also in 1940 when his fortunes in the Philippines were at low ebb and returning to America to challenge Roosevelt in his bid for a third term seemed a fleeting possibility.

It wasn't until October 1943, when a Mutual Broadcasting System radio report mentioned that MacArthur "has definitely agreed" to be a candidate in the 1944 election, that the idea gained a genuine public airing (although an SWPA spokesman quickly warned the general had no plans for leaving for the States to run a political campaign: "General MacArthur's ambition is still to fly the American flag on Bataan as soon as he can"). But over the next several months the rumors grew, and MacArthur for President clubs began to spring up around the country—especially in Wisconsin, an important primary state, with SWPA GHQ staffer Colonel Philip La Follette, son of the famous Wisconsin senator Robert "Fighting Bob" La Follette, acting as unofficial campaign chairman.

The rumors became so rife that General Kenney took it upon himself to sit down in the living room of the MacArthur apartment in Lennons Hotel and read him and Jean the facts of life.

"I don't think anyone can defeat Roosevelt while the war is going on," he said. "I hope you don't listen to those politicians in or out of the service"— Kenney knew that La Follette and some others on MacArthur's staff wouldn't have minded running his presidential campaign—"who may try to persuade you to throw your hat in the ring."

MacArthur smiled and reassured his air force chief, "Don't worry. I have no desire to get mixed up in politics." His number one priority, he said, was to fulfill his and America's pledge to set the Philippines free. "Then I want to defeat Japan." That, it seemed, was the end of the matter.[38]

All the same, there were those who disagreed with Kenney. They believed the two top contenders for the Republican nomination, Wendell Willkie and Thomas E. Dewey, would likely deadlock in the convention, opening the way for MacArthur as a compromise candidate. They believed that if he were nominated, MacArthur could decline to campaign in order to remain at his post—or alternately, accept a vice-presidential candidacy and remain in the Pacific while his running mate ran the campaign.

They also believed the best way to win the war was to have a man with military experience in the White House. One reason the war had been dragging on for so long, they believed, and would continue to drag on until 1946 at the earliest, was that the country didn't. MacArthur himself wasn't about to disagree with that conclusion, especially when so many wanted him to be that man.

In January, for example, Republican congressman Albert L. Miller of Nebraska had written a letter to MacArthur, saying, "You owe it to civilization and to the children yet unborn" to run for president, to prevent Roosevelt from "dooming" the country and the war. "If this system of left-wingers and New Dealism is continued for another four years," Miller wrote, "I am certain that this Monarchy that is being established in America will destroy the rights of the common people."

MacArthur wrote a polite letter back, thanking Miller for his views and adding, "Your description of the conditions in the United States is a sobering one, indeed. . . . [But] Like Abraham Lincoln, I am a firm believer in the people, and, if given the truth, they can be depended upon to meet any national crisis," especially with the right man at the helm. MacArthur didn't exactly suggest himself, but he did clearly imply that the right man *wasn't* Franklin Roosevelt.[39]

And so MacArthur graciously allowed his name to be placed on the Republican ballot that spring, and had the inexpressible pleasure of winning the Illinois primary, securing 550,000 votes against his nearest competitor's 35,000. Things, however, went quickly downhill from there. In Wisconsin MacArthur suffered from a poorly organized campaign and came in third behind Dewey and Harold Stassen (who was actually serving in the Pacific as a staff officer), while Wendell Willkie did so badly that he withdrew from the race entirely.

That was one nail in the sarcophagus of MacArthur's presidential hopes, since it ended any chance of a deadlocked convention. The second was when Representative Miller made the mistake of making his letter public, as well as MacArthur's reply, which set off a "furor," as MacArthur later wrote, with critics both in and out of the GOP suggesting that the supreme commander of SWPA had somehow been disloyal to his own commander in chief in his unguarded remarks—not the last time a MacArthur letter to a congressman would land him in trouble.[40]

In the end, MacArthur brought the entire matter to an end by issuing a statement from Brisbane. "I can only say what I have said before, I am not a candidate for the office [of President] nor do I seek it. I have devoted myself exclusively to the conduct of the war. My sole ambition is to assist my beloved country to win this vital struggle by the fulfillment of such duty as has been or may be assigned to me."

Thus the door to the White House in 1944 was firmly shut—if indeed it was ever open. Roosevelt could rest easy that he would not be meeting with a future political rival, but only with one of his two supreme commanders in the Pacific theater. Indeed, the other, Admiral Nimitz, would also be arriving for a summit discussion of strategy both present and future, for defeating Japan.

That fact set MacArthur to thinking as their plane landed at Hicks Field in Honolulu. Political junket or not, what was said in the next few days might determine the entire course of the war—especially if he could make his strategic vision clear to the man who had so far denied him what he had wanted most, supreme leadership of the war in the Pacific.

The two men greeted each other on the 26th like old friends—but friends who had undergone transformations that caught the other by surprise. Roosevelt, for example, was surprised by MacArthur's flamboyant new appearance, with his leather flying jacket, his Filipino field marshal's cap, sunglasses, and enormous corncob pipe.

"Hello, Doug," the president said. "What are you doing with that leather jacket on—it's darn hot today."

"Well, I've just landed from Australia, it's pretty cold up there" was MacArthur's reply, and from there they set off in the president's car.[41]

MacArthur, in turn, was shocked at Roosevelt's emaciated, weakened appearance. In fact, the president was deathly ill with cancer and had less than a year to live. Yet the man was as shrewd and cunning as ever. It slowly began to dawn on MacArthur that the conference may have been called to deliver the growing consensus in Washington that retaking the Philippines would be a mistake.

That night Roosevelt hosted a dinner for MacArthur, Nimitz, Halsey, and Admiral Leahy, the chief of naval operations. After they had eaten and chatted, Roosevelt moved everyone into a conference room with an enormous map of the Pacific.

"Well, Doug," the president asked, "where do we go from here?"

MacArthur strode to the map and picked up the pointer.

"Mindanao, Mr. President," he said, slapping the pointer on the island. He slapped the next island: "Then Leyte." Finally the last one: "Then Luzon." He explained that retaking the Philippines was as much a moral as a strategic goal.

"They look on America as their mother country," he explained, and then paused before adding, *"And promises must be kept."*

Everyone in the room knew the remark was aimed at Roosevelt, and his failed promises to MacArthur and his men in 1941–42. Roosevelt, however, acted as if nothing had happened, and gestured to Nimitz to start his presentation.

Nimitz laid out the new thinking among the brass in Washington. After completing the capture of the Marianas and Palaus—so the thinking went—the combined Allied forces would now strike at Formosa and the China coast instead of the Philippines, and then launch attacks on Japan's outer islands, Iwo Jima and Okinawa. Finally, Nimitz proposed, a series of coordinated naval and air campaigns would compel Japan's surrender before Allied soldiers would have to do a D-Day–style invasion.

MacArthur's reply was cold and prompt. "I don't think we could ever justify liberating the Chinese on Formosa and abandoning millions of Filipinos on Luzon." Roosevelt pointed out there were half a million Japanese soldiers in the Philippines. "Mr. President," MacArthur replied, "my losses would *not* be heavy, any more than they have been in the past. The days of frontal assault should be over," because the casualties were too heavy. Yet that was exactly what Nimitz and Admiral King were planning to do on Iwo Jima and Okinawa.

MacArthur argued, cajoled, jabbed his pointer and his pipe at the map for the better part of two hours. He explained how capturing the Philippines would cut Japan's remaining supplies of oil and iron and copper; how the Japanese were too thinly dispersed across the Philippines' 2,000 islands to offer any solid resistance; and how he had the ships and troops he needed to complete the reconquest of the Philippines in less than six months. He also wrung two important concessions from Nimitz: that Manila's harbor would be invaluable for an invasion of either Formosa or Japan, and that bomber bases on Luzon would be better able to provide essential air support for any assault on Formosa than bases in the Marianas.[42]

Those at least were the arguments he presented to Roosevelt, in front of Admirals Nimitz and Leahy and assembled staff and news photographers, in a meeting that dragged on after midnight. The next morning after lunch MacArthur asked for ten minutes with the president alone.

As the door closed behind Nimitz and the others, MacArthur was brief and to the point.

"Mr. President," he said, "the country has forgiven you for what took place on Bataan. . . . But the nation will never forgive you if you approve a plan that leaves 17 million Christian American subjects to wither in the Philippines under the conqueror's heel . . . Politically, it would ruin you."[43]

Roosevelt blinked. Thomas E. Dewey was now the Republican nominee. Polls showed he was giving FDR the closest election he had ever faced. MacArthur's words were as much a threat as a prediction: if the president gave up on the Philippines, the general would make sure the country gave up on him.

Later that day they inspected more military installations on Oahu, and chatted amicably. When MacArthur returned to Australia, he told his staff that Roosevelt was backing his plan. Roosevelt confirmed it by letter a few days later. "I am convinced that as a whole it is logical and can be done. . . .

Some day there will be a flag raising in Manila—and without question I want you to do it."

Roosevelt also told his doctor after his meeting with MacArthur to give him an extra aspirin. "In all my life nobody has ever talked to me the way MacArthur did."

Did MacArthur's dramatic intervention really turn the president against the navy plan, and lead him to re-embrace the return to the Philippines? Historians argue otherwise. They point out that the final decision dragged on for another month and a half, and no final communiqué was made until September 15. Nonetheless, Roosevelt was someone who took his title as commander in chief very seriously, overseeing virtually every aspect of strategy and even operational command. If he had been for the navy plan of bypassing the Philippines, without question it would have become war policy. On the other hand, the meeting with MacArthur may have dissuaded him from interfering in a process that was heading back to the Philippines option, anyway, as the Joint Chiefs gathered in Washington in mid-September with Richard Sutherland acting once again as MacArthur's advocate.

The truth was, the plan of delivering a single thrust to Formosa had a sole champion, Admiral King, while nearly everyone else, including Nimitz himself, saw the logic of the MacArthur plan. MacArthur had the bulk of land and air forces in the Pacific under his command already; he had proved his ability to perform logistical miracles over long distances and under primitive conditions. The Philippines would be an invaluable base for further operations, especially against Japan; it would also seal off any Japanese hope of reinforcing their imperial conquests farther west, from Borneo and the East Indies to Burma and India.

Still, deadlock on further plans reigned until Nimitz pointed out that once the Marianas were secure, no further operation could start until the Joint Chiefs reached an agreement. So on September 9 they did. They issued MacArthur instructions to conduct his landing on Mindanao on November 15; Leyte on December 15; then secure Luzon and Manila by February 1945.

MacArthur had won—but he soon found that the timetable would be seriously accelerated.[44]

On September 13 Halsey reported excitedly that his flyers had made several passes over the Philippines as far north as the Visayas without finding any opposition. Forget about Mindanao, he urged MacArthur and the Joint Chiefs; speed up the timetable by going directly for Leyte instead.

The Joint Chiefs thought it a feasible plan; so did Nimitz, who said he could send his Third Amphibious Force and XXIV Army Corps to help with the landings. Now they all wondered what MacArthur thought. MacArthur, however, could say nothing. He was sailing from Hollandia for Morotai and was maintaining radio silence. For making the most important decision of the entire war in the SWPA, its commander was out of the loop.

It fell instead to Sutherland to make it. Although he knew his boss's mind better than anyone, he didn't want to do it alone. He assembled Generals Kenney, Chamberlin, and all his senior staff at SWPA GHQ. They had the intelligence reports showing that far from being "wide open" as Halsey claimed, there were 21,000 Japanese on Leyte, and that Japanese airpower in the Philippines was still formidable. The dilemma was that if they said no to moving on Leyte, that would leave the door open for Admiral King to push on to Formosa.

So with a lump in his throat, Sutherland sent the following message: "Subject to completion of arrangements with Nimitz, we shall execute Leyte operation on 20 October. . . . MacArthur."

The deed was done, and Nimitz and the Joint Chiefs never knew they were communicating not with MacArthur at all, but with his chief of staff.[45]

It took just ninety minutes for the military chiefs assembled in the Quebec Conference to issue the definitive orders to MacArthur and Nimitz. There would be no more intermediate stepping-stones. The invasion of Leyte was moved up from December to October 20.

That was the message relayed to MacArthur on September 15, as he stood on the bridge of the cruiser *Nashville* watching the men of the Twenty-first Division descend into their landing craft. He had been busy over the last two weeks setting up his new forward headquarters at Hollandia, then set off with the Twenty-first for the landing on Morotai.

Once more Spencer Akin and ULTRA had come to his rescue. The original plan had been to stage a landing on nearby Halmahera, but the Japanese had guessed that the latter island was all too suitable for an Allied air base and had surreptitiously been building up forces there until they numbered 40,000 ill-fed, ill-equipped Japanese soldiers—soldiers who nonetheless could be counted on to fight to the death to hold on to Halmahera.

So MacArthur chose Morotai instead, which ULTRA said was lightly defended.[46] The landings would be under General Hall with some 60,000 troops. Dan Barbey was in charge of naval forces, as usual, with six fast carriers from Admiral Clifton Sprague's Task Force 78 in support, as well as Fifth Air Force bombers rumbling off runways on the new bases around Vogelkop and Geelvink.

It was the kind of combined land, air, and naval forces that MacArthur could only dream about two years before. Yet now it represented only a sizable fraction of the total SWPA forces under his command, while the invasion of the Philippines would give him still more resources in men and materiel, making him the single most powerful American general in history.

Even so, the Morotai landings were a mess. The amphibious ships ran into undetected coral reefs, which forced soldiers to unload far from shore. Troops sank up to their armpits in the mudflats, but fortunately there were no Japanese to take advantage of their vulnerability. Most had fled into the mountains after the first bombardment; the only serious fighting involved beating back a hasty banzai attack that night and then mopping up the rest until the 21st, when the island was declared secure.[47]

MacArthur, as usual, insisted on landing on the beach less than two hours after the first soldiers arrived, around 10:30. He was in a lighthearted mood. Sutherland's message had reached him about the change of plans for Leyte, which meant the liberation of the Philippines was now definitely a lock. Sutherland's ruse had paid off. The SWPA chief had defeated the last doubters and naysayers and that was all that mattered.

MacArthur and Doc Egeberg along with Dan Barbey went ashore near the Pitoe airfield. MacArthur inspected the field and shook hands with a party of mud-covered GIs. "You have done well. You now dominate the last stronghold which barred our way to the Philippines. The enemy, as usual, was not in the right place at the right time." He did not say that was because he had known the enemy's plans in advance almost as well as the enemy did.

Then he turned to a group of officers on the beach. "We shall shortly have an air and light naval base here 300 miles from the Philippines," he told them. He turned and stared out to sea, toward the far shore where Bataan and Corregidor lay. "They are waiting there for me," Egeberg heard him mutter. "It's been a long time."[48]

He was about to fulfill his vow, made in a spur-of-the-moment remark more than two years earlier: "I shall return." In fact, that return would be harder, and bloodier, than MacArthur at that moment could imagine.

CHAPTER 22
LIBERATION

Let every arm be steeled. The guidance of divine God
points the way. Follow in His name to the
Holy Grail of righteous victory!

—DOUGLAS MACARTHUR, OCTOBER 20, 1944

In late September 1944, it was hard to find a busier place in the Pacific Ocean than Hollandia harbor. The anchorage that MacArthur had seized with his brilliant stroke in April had blossomed into the staging ground for the impending invasion of the Philippines.

The number of cargo vessels alone docked there soared from 70 in January 1944 when the Japanese still occupied it, to 120 by May, and would soon approach 200. Teams of engineers supervised the building of tents for tens of thousands of troops, while Hollywood stars like John Wayne and Bob Hope arrived to meet and entertain the throngs of sailors and soldiers. Even actress Judith Anderson came out, to perform Shakespeare in the steamy haze of New Guinea and under the stern gaze of 7,000-foot Cyclops Mountain.

Any visitor could spot the headquarters of the SWPA's commander, Douglas MacArthur, from the Hollandia harbor. It sat on top of a hill about eight hundred feet high overlooking Lake Sentani and the airdrome area along its shores, some ten miles south of Hollandia village. Hostile reporters described it as a New Guinea version of Shangri-La. George Kenney knew better. "The house was made of three Army-type prefabricated houses joined together and was quite comfortable," he wrote later. "To make it look better,

I had several striking aerial photographs enlarged, framed and hung up on the walls. From MacArthur's office in Brisbane had come a few rugs and furniture." To the north of Lake Sentani sat Cyclops, its blue mountain mass hovering over the lake's deep blue waters, with its five-hundred-foot waterfall shrouded in perpetual clouds. It was a magnificent setting for the greatest invasion the Pacific war had ever seen.

As he trudged up the hill, Kenney knew he had a vital role to play in what was coming. MacArthur had carved out a new position for him as head of SWPA Army Air Forces, while passing his old command of the Fifth Air Force to his brilliant subordinate, Ennis Whitehead. MacArthur felt secure with his air chiefs, and Kenney's ability to isolate the battlefield and to bring victory. "Of all the brilliant air commanders of the war," MacArthur later wrote, "none surpassed him in those three great essentials of combat leadership: aggressive vision, mastery of air tactics and strategy, and the ability to exact the maximum in fighting qualities from both men and equipment."[1]

If Kenney was MacArthur's strong right arm, his strong left arm was Walter Krueger. Nine years younger than MacArthur, he had a reputation as a soldier's soldier who shared every hardship with his men, eating the same rations and living in the same tent. He believed officers had to pay a price to build the bond of trust that enabled them to lead in battle. During the savage fighting for Lone Tree Hill on Noempoor, Krueger asked about casualties among officers. His chief of staff admitted they had been heavy. "Good," was Krueger's comment.[2]

Krueger had only thirty-five more days to ready his forces for the invasion. He decided the landings on the eastern coast of Leyte would require a two-corps landing force, with the Tenth Corps sweeping in on the town of Tacloban and its vital airfield, then pushing on to Carigara. Meanwhile the Twenty-fourth Corps, made up of the Seventh and Ninety-sixth Infantry Divisions, would take Balog, then aim for Burauen. Two more divisions, the Thirty-second, which had borne the brunt of fighting at Buna almost two years before, and the Seventy-seventh, would form his reserve.[3]

Thomas Kinkaid and his Seventh Fleet, together with Barbey's amphibious forces and Admiral Halsey's Third Fleet, would provide the essential naval support for MacArthur's and Krueger's landing. A veteran cruiser commander of both Coral Sea and Midway like Kenney, Kinkaid found MacArthur's principle of non-interference with subordinates liberating and refreshing. And like both Kenney and Krueger, he also found that the best way to proceed was to ignore or bypass Dick Sutherland and the rest of the Bataan Gang and deal with MacArthur directly. "He said his door is always open to me," he wrote to his wife after their first meeting. "I could not have asked for a more cordial reception."

Despite their differences over naval strategy (MacArthur always wanting his navy men to take more risks, Kinkaid always wanting to take fewer), they had worked out a relationship that belied claims that MacArthur had a built-in bias against the U.S. Navy, or that he had no understanding of maritime strategy.[4]

Together they had supervised the steady buildup of the Seventh Fleet in Hollandia harbor, until it consisted of 471 ships of all kinds, from cruisers and escort carriers (grouped together as Task Force 3 under Rear Admiral Clifton Sprague) to amphibious landing ships and troop transports and cargo vessels acting as floating warehouses.

It had been a logistical nightmare. Even after the invasion force sailed, eighty-seven cargo ships were in harbor every day, "12 discharging, 3 loading, 24 awaiting call to Leyte, 33 waiting to discharge, 5 waiting to load, and 10 miscellaneous."[5] Fortunately MacArthur had appointed his trusty engineer Hugh Casey to head up his SWPA Army Service Command, in order to get everything ready and loaded for invasion day, while Kinkaid and Barbey knew their landing craft and escort warships would be ready.

The real issue, however, as Kenney had pointed out from the beginning, was air cover. From Hollandia to Leyte was 1,300 miles. For the first time MacArthur was extending himself beyond normal air protection. If Kenney's air forces couldn't get bases established on Leyte in time, then the whole liberation of the Philippines would be in jeopardy. Getting the troops there to secure those bases now depended entirely on Halsey's and Sprague's carriers. Yet Halsey's principal brief from his commander, Admiral Nimitz, wasn't to protect the beachhead but to destroy the Japanese fleet. In nominal terms, he would be free to pull his carriers out if that opportunity presented itself. MacArthur was gambling that Halsey wouldn't, and that Kenney would get his bases on land in time.[6]

MacArthur meanwhile was still in Brisbane, determined to put in as much time with his son as he could before the invasion pulled him away. Barely six years old, little Arthur was evolving into a precocious musician. He could pick out Gilbert and Sullivan tunes on the piano, and his teacher discovered he could play almost anything by ear instead of reading the music. That summer, before moving to Hollandia, MacArthur rarely got home before the boy was in bed. All the same, he would stop at his son's room and watch him sleeping—sometimes sitting and thinking for fifteen or twenty minutes.[7]

Soon after the establishment of the Hollandia headquarters, he went to see Jean.

"I won't be back," he said—meaning he wouldn't return until the landings on Leyte were successful.

"You've got to send for me the minute you think it's safe for me to come to Manila," she said. Then Sid Huff heard her tease her husband: "When I go to Manila I want you to fix it so I can stop off in Hollandia. I want to see this mansion you built—the one that I'm supposed to have been living in luxury!"[8]

They laughed, then MacArthur was off. He was flying on his new plane, a brand-new B-17E outfitted with tables and leather chairs—one of only three that had been converted into passenger planes. Until November 1943 MacArthur had flown in standard transport planes like the C-47 and DC-3, although he also used Kenney's custom B-17, nicknamed "Sally," for flights over the ocean. Then in November he had taken delivery of the new plane, along with a new pilot: Weldon Rhoades, inevitably nicknamed "Dusty."

Extraordinarily for MacArthur's staff, he was a civilian—although MacArthur arranged for him to have a major's rank, and be attached to his general staff. A tall, gangly man with sad eyes, Rhoades had an aviator's instinct for getting a plane full of passengers wherever it needed to go despite the risks. The plane carried only one .59-caliber gun in its Plexiglas nose. If attacked by a flight of Zeros it was more vulnerable than Yamamoto's ill-fated transport plane—that is, if Kenney's fighter escorts weren't sticking like flypaper to its tail.

The plane's name was emblazoned on its port nose: *Bataan*. It was as much a pledge as an aircraft's nickname; and now in the fall of 1944 it had become for MacArthur almost a public sacrament.[9]

Before going to Hollandia, MacArthur had one stop to make. He landed in Canberra, the Australian capital, to pay a brief visit to Prime Minister John Curtin, who was dying of heart disease.

For more than two years they had been constant and fierce allies in the battle not just against the Japanese but against the consensus view in Washington and London that the war in Europe must have top priority, and that men and resources shipped to the SWPA were, in effect, men and resources wasted. In the end, they had even been allies in the struggle against Australia's own high command, who had their own ideas about how the war in the Southwest Pacific was to be fought and who should be in charge.

Curtin's trust in MacArthur has not earned him plaudits from Australian historians.[10] But it had been indispensable to MacArthur's success as SWPA commander. He paid public tribute to Curtin in a message to the Australian people: "[H]e was one of the greatest of wartime statesmen, and the preservation of Australia from invasion will be his immemorial monument." But MacArthur also knew he himself had pushed things to this point, the verge of liberating the Philippines, without having to rely on Curtin's help.[11]

The Australians had been instrumental to driving the Japanese out of New Guinea. But the transformation of SWPA from a sideshow into a dagger directed at the heart of Japan's Pacific empire was entirely the result of MacArthur's relentless effort. Now MacArthur arrived back in Hollandia only days before the invasion was to be launched. He had left the overall planning to Kenney, Barbey, Kinkaid, and Krueger, all of whom were a ten-minute jeep ride from one another and sat down often to work out the details. This was, of course, typical of MacArthur's approach to operational planning. Once he and his chief of staff had worked out what they wanted done, and when, they would draft up a plan to circulate with his service chiefs. Then they and their staffs would chew on it, work out and modify the details, then send it back to headquarters for final discussion and MacArthur's approval.

This is exactly what happened in the planning for the landing on Leyte, so that when the *Bataan*'s wheels touched down on Hollandia's main airfield on October 16 MacArthur was as fully briefed on the details as Kenney, Kinkaid, and the rest—and given his prodigious memory, undimmed at age sixty-four, perhaps more so.

The one flaw in the process, and MacArthur's biggest disappointment in readying for the invasion of the Philippines, was his chief of staff, Dick Sutherland.

Since Sutherland's promotion to lieutenant general, it was as if something had broken down in his sense of courage, integrity, and judgment. It led eventually to a breach of trust with the man to whom he had been the intimate subordinate through five stormy and crisis-laden years, a breach that would widen until the two barely spoke.

It had to do, improbably enough, with a woman.

Her name was Elaine Clark, an Australian whose mother was Australia's top socialite, and whose father, Norman Brooks, the country's most famous tennis player.[12]

She was married to an English steel tycoon named Reginald Bessemer-Clark, who had been captured by the Japanese in Malaya. While he was starving and languishing in Singapore's Changi prison, Elaine struck up an acquaintance, then an affair, with MacArthur's chief of staff. When Sutherland and GHQ moved to Brisbane, she moved with him. Indeed, Sutherland's attention grew into an infatuation as he arranged for his paramour to get a commission in the Women's Army Corps (WAC) in early 1943.

This was not entirely unusual, and MacArthur—who was infallibly faithful to Jean—could say little about the nepotistic arrangement. After all, both Sutherland's deputy Dick Marshall and General George Kenney himself made similar arrangements for their Australian mistresses. The problem was that Captain Elaine Clark became a source of friction with other members of his staff. Sutherland installed her as assistant to the headquarters commandant, where she felt it appropriate to supervise the guards and issue passes to GHQ staff. In a high-handed way she took to rewarding those she liked with favors and perks, and punishing those who crossed her (a steadily growing number) with the opposite. When Dusty Rhoades's predecessor, Henry Godman, secured his own jeep, Captain Clark claimed it as her own when he was away on a flight. When Rhoades dared to complain, Clark insisted that

Sutherland send Godman back into combat—which Sutherland, somewhat shamefacedly, did.

MacArthur was furious when he learned what had happened. But he hesitated to overturn his chief of staff's decision. When he learned that Sutherland had planned to move her to Hollandia, however, he read Sutherland the riot act. What Sutherland did on his own time was his business, MacArthur told him. But the relationship with Clark must never again interfere with staff business. Above all, when GHQ moved to Hollandia, Captain Elaine Clark was to remain in Brisbane. Permanently.

Sutherland had agreed, so it was with some considerable anger that MacArthur learned in July that Elaine Clark was not only in Hollandia but was acting as unofficial hostess at cocktail parties and receptions for visiting generals and admirals. There was a specific order against allowing women, American or Australian, to serve anywhere north of Port Moresby; not even Jean was allowed to come to Hollandia. Sutherland had violated that order, as well as his promise. In a towering rage MacArthur told Sutherland to send her back. In a rare burst of defiance, Sutherland said he would rather be relieved or transferred.

MacArthur refused, and instead drafted a direct written order to his chief of staff stating that Captain Clark was to return to Brisbane and remain there. When he returned from the Morotai landings, he asked and was told that Clark was gone.[13]

Problem solved, or so MacArthur thought. He did know that he was underestimating Clark's deviousness, and Sutherland's. When the final blowup came, it would send reverberations throughout the whole of GHQ and all the way back to Australia.

Apart from Sutherland, however, MacArthur was at the top of his game. He would soon be leading the second-biggest amphibious landing in history, second only to D-Day itself in Normandy earlier that June. He now had not only Kinkaid's and Halsey's forces under his command, but Nimitz doing his bidding as well.

Above all, everything was now green-lighted not only for the invasion of

Leyte but for the liberation of Luzon as well. The prospects for an invasion of Formosa were sinking fast. The last series of central Pacific landings—Guam, Saipan, followed by Peleliu and the Palaus—had been bloody, costly in lives but also in time lost. MacArthur's proven bypass strategy was looking better and better, especially when he proposed that he could now move up the invasion of Luzon to December 19. Then had come a report from the Pentagon that a prospective invasion of Formosa would involve thousands of men and tons of shipping that Nimitz's forces didn't have—not, that is, until the war in Europe was over.

It was the end of any central Pacific–to-Formosa strategy. Admiral Leahy, chairman of the Joint Chiefs, signed on to the new MacArthur plan, as did Marshall and Hap Arnold. Admiral King, the final holdout, found himself outvoted three to one, and threw in the towel. The last fight in his long battle against MacArthur was lost.[14]

Soon after Washington relayed its decision to MacArthur, there came more good news. Halsey's ten-day cruise off the Philippine Islands as well as Formosa, Okinawa, and the Ryukyus starting on October 10 had all but wiped out Japanese naval air strength, destroying more than five hundred planes, crippling thousands of tons of shipping, and completely wrecking two major base facilities. A forceful Japanese intervention to support or reinforce its garrisons in the Philippines was looking less and less likely. And while the Japanese were getting weaker and weaker, MacArthur was getting stronger and stronger. Indeed, by January he would have no fewer than six army divisions installed on Luzon for the final liberation of Manila.

The only discordant note for MacArthur's plans was that Manuel Quezon would not be there to see them unfold. On August 1, at Saranac Lake, New York, the Philippine president had finally died of the tuberculosis that he had been battling for almost a decade. "I felt a stab in the heart" at the news, MacArthur later remembered, and to the press he commented, "He was the very apotheosis of the aspiration of the Filipinos for the higher things of life . . . I mourn him."[15]

They had been friends, then virtual enemies, then friends again for more than forty years. Quezon had put his nation's trust in MacArthur, and in America, twice, and both times he and America had let Quezon down.

MacArthur was determined not to let it happen again. This time he would prevail—and by returning, he would fulfill a personal as well as a national pledge of honor.

Everything depended on how the Japanese army would perform in the Philippines. It would be their last chance to win a decisive victory over MacArthur, and Central Bureau and ULTRA were warning him that they were planning a red-hot reception—including appointing Japan's finest general to bring it off.

Spencer Akin and his team had spent weeks gleaning intelligence about the Japanese buildup in soldiers and planes on both Luzon and Leyte, since the Japanese had no doubt that MacArthur would have to take that large island to the southeast of Luzon first. By October 10, Akin and Willoughby estimated there were more than a quarter of a million Japanese in the Philippines, with 20,000 or so on Leyte, concentrated around Tacloban, and the bulk of the remainder installed on Luzon. Meanwhile, the navy was reporting large numbers of planes staging from Japan to the islands. If Halsey thought he had all but wiped out the air forces in the Philippines, the Japanese were making sure they were back in strength.[16]

Then came the news that Lieutenant General Tomoyuki Yamashita, "The Tiger of Malaya," had been appointed the new commander of Japanese forces in the Philippines. Yamashita had masterminded the seventy-day blitzkrieg that had captured Manila and Singapore against a numerically stronger foe; Japan's high command obviously hoped that he could engineer a similar miracle in the Philippines.

Yamashita took only a few days to decide that his best course of action was to concentrate his forces on Luzon, to meet MacArthur's main assault there. This would also facilitate the main Japanese strategy for defeating the United States in the Philippines: to draw the Americans into a decisive naval engagement, a repeat of Admiral Togo's defeat of the Russian fleet at Tsushima in 1904, that would leave MacArthur's army stranded and cripple the U.S. war effort once and for all.

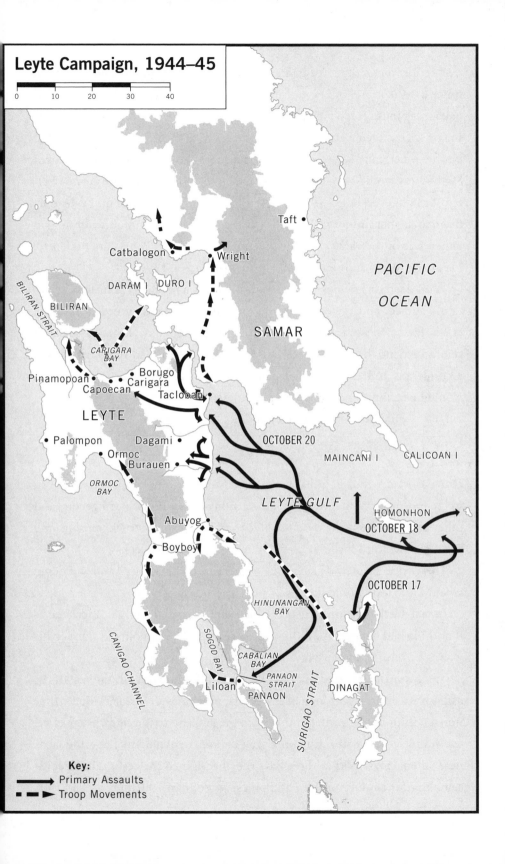

Leyte Campaign, 1944–45

0   10   20   30   40

Taft

Catbalogon

Wright

DARAM I   DURO I

BILIRAN STRAIT

BILIRAN

CARIGARA BAY

SAMAR

PACIFIC

OCEAN

Pinamopoan

Capoecan

Borugo

Carigara

Tacloban

LEYTE

Palompon

Dagami

Ormoc

Burauen

ORMOC BAY

OCTOBER 20

MAINCANI I   CALICOAN I

LEYTE GULF

HOMONHON

OCTOBER 18

Abuyog

Boyboy

OCTOBER 17

HINUNANGAN BAY

CANIGAO CHANNEL

SOGOD BAY

CABALIAN BAY

PANAON STRAIT

Liloan

PANAON

SURIGAO STRAIT

DINAGAT

Key:
→ Primary Assaults
▪▶ Troop Movements

But Tokyo had other ideas, and overruled him. When the high command looked at the island of Leyte, they failed to see an underequipped and inadequate Japanese force facing inevitable defeat. They saw on their maps the major anchorage on the western side of Leyte, at Ormoc; clearly this would be the Americans' key objective. To get there, however, General Krueger's Sixth Army would have to fight their way across the broad, wide Ormoc Valley. It might even be possible to fight the main decisive battle on Leyte, they decided, by hemming in Krueger's advance from the mountains running on either side of the valley. So they preemptorily ordered Yamashita to deplete his Luzon forces and reinforce the troops he had on Leyte.

With deep misgivings that the new plan was a mistake, Yamashita reluctantly agreed, and in compensation the high command agreed to shift the crack First Division from Manchuria to Ormoc Bay. It was a delayed reinforcement that ULTRA completely missed.[17] Instead of facing 20,000 second-rate and unprepared Japanese troops on Leyte, Krueger's troops would be facing some of Japan's finest soldiers.

They would be walking into an inferno.

Douglas MacArthur boarded the cruiser *Nashville* on October 16, at eleven in the morning. With him were Sutherland, Kenney, his doctor Egeberg, and other aides. As he stepped off the ladder a sudden wave struck the ship, and as a final awkward insult tossed him headlong onto the deck.

There were gasps and glances, as soldiers and sailors stared and wondered what MacArthur would do.

In fact, he did nothing. He got to his feet, returned the salute, and acted as if nothing had happened. Nothing, not even nature, was going to stand in his way as he returned to face his destiny.[18]

The *Nashville* steamed out of Hollandia harbor along with the rest of the assembled ships. It was "one of the greatest armadas in history," MacArthur noted. "Ships to the front, to the rear, to the left, and to the right, as far as the eye could see"—all steaming on zigzag courses to avoid any lingering Japanese submarines. Within three days they had joined the rest of the fleet assembling for assault on the Philippines. More than 700 ships and 140,000 soldiers were ready to fulfill MacArthur's vow—and to take revenge for the humiliations of Bataan and Corregidor.

"I had no illusions about the operation," MacArthur wrote later. "I knew it was to be the crucial battle of the war in the Pacific. On its outcome would depend the fate of the Philippines and the future of the war against Japan"— a perspective that Nimitz and his admirals and marine generals fighting in the Palaus might not have endorsed. Still, "Leyte was to be the anvil against which I hoped to hammer the Japanese into submission in the central Philippines"—and the springboard for the first landings on Luzon.[19]

On the trip out, MacArthur spent his mornings reading and writing telegrams, and his afternoons reading reports and talking to General Kenney or Colonel Courtney Whitney, his new head of the Philippine section of G-2, who had joined the staff in the late summer of 1943. Whitney would watch the supreme commander, SWPA, drift from time to time to the rail, to see the endless parade of ships stretching to the horizon on every side.

Whitney ventured to say, "General, it must give you a sense of great power having such a mighty armada at your command."

Mac surprised him by saying, "No, Court, it doesn't." His mood was somber, not triumphant. "I cannot escape thinking of those fine American boys who are going to die on the beaches tomorrow morning."[20]

It was a dark moonless night when the *Nashville* and the rest of the armada entered the Gulf of Leyte on October 21. "I knew that on every ship nervous men lined the rails or paced the decks," MacArthur wrote later, "peering into the darkness and wondering what stood out there beyond the night waiting for the dawn to come." MacArthur at least had an inkling of what was there. As it happened, he had done an official survey of the Tacloban coast where the Twenty-fourth Division would be landing, on his first army assignment after leaving West Point, more than forty years before. He knew that the ground this time of year was soft from the rains, and that the Tacloban airfield might not be solid enough to hold bombers taking off and landing—although he had reassured his own engineering staff that such a miracle was possible.

MacArthur adjourned to his cabin. He wrote a letter to be sent to FDR from the beach, dated October 20. Then he wrote a brief letter to Jean, saying he was "in good fettle and hope to do my part tomorrow and in the days that followed." He signed it "Sir Boss."[21] He reread favorite passages from the Bible to steady his nerves.

> Give me, O Lord, that quietness of heart, that makes the most of labor and of rest. Save me from passionate excitement, petulant fretfulness and idle fear.
>
> Teach me to be alert and wise in all responsibilities, without hurry and without neglect. When others censure, may I seek thy image in each fellow man, judging with charity as one who shall be judged.

Then "I prayed that a merciful God would preserve each one of those men on the morrow."[22]

At four o'clock the troop transports accompanying the *Nashville* came to life. Captain Paul Austin of F Company, Thirty-fourth Regiment, Twenty-fourth Division, was awakened for "the usual pre-landing breakfast, steak and eggs. This was the only time we ever got that kind of food," Austin later remembered. He and his men had fought through the horror of Biak. Now they would be part of the second wave on Red Beach, the main objective of Tenth Corps—the capture of Tacloban.[23]

Moments later sailors on the battleships scheduled to cover the landing were scrambling to their stations, stowing gear, clearing decks, and loading their great naval guns. The battleships were six in number, all survivors of the Pearl Harbor attack, and all ready to take their revenge, along with three heavy cruisers, four light cruisers including the *Nashville,* and twenty-one destroyers. In the predawn light the gun turrets of every ship slowly swiveled, and readied to fire.

At precisely 6:00 A.M. American naval guns opened up along an eighteen-mile stretch of the Leyte coastline. On the *Nashville*'s deck, MacArthur watched and later remembered, "Thousands of guns were throwing their shells with a roar that was incessant and deafening. Rocket vapor trails crisscrossed the sky, and black, ugly pillars of smoke began to rise. High overhead, swarms of airplanes darted into the maelstrom. And across what would have been a glinting, untroubled blue sea, the black dots of the landing craft churned towards the beaches."[24]

Han Rants was a phone linesman with the Twenty-fourth's Second Battalion Headquarters company. He remembered the landing barges going over the side by crane and cargo nets being lowered down the side of the ships before the bombardment started. Men descended by groups of fifteen, and if one stepped on another's hand on the net ropes (as happened with exhausted men after a sleepless night and with frayed nerves) they could fall twenty to thirty feet to the bottom of the boat as it rose and fell in the waves.

He also remembered men being sick in the bobbing boats, with the smell of diesel fumes making everyone choke. At 10:00 a.m. the boats spread out and started in. "The beach seemed to be one big explosion," Rants later wrote. "We got to feeling confident that there couldn't be anything alive in there with all of this."[25]

It was the usual confident prediction troops made watching a massive naval bombardment prior to an amphibious landing, and as usual, they were wrong. The Japanese were firing on the boats all the way to the beach. "I looked out at sea and saw a landing boat take a direct hit," Rants wrote. "That boat literally disappeared, nothing left except a few pieces of scrap and steel helmets." Other boats, including two LSTs and LCIs, were blazing wrecks.

As their boat hit the sand, Paul Austin and his men bailed out. Although his company was supposed to be part of the second wave, they were shocked to find that the first wave was still there. Machine guns and snipers and mortars were keeping them pinned down, as the men and their officers clung to every bit of cover, including the thousands of palm trees blasted down by the bombardment.

The fire "was coming in pretty heavy," Austin remembered. "Our Captain Wye from regimental headquarters was killed a minute after he set foot on the beach. Another company commander from the 1st Battalion was killed very near Colonel Red Newman."[26]

It was on that same beach that MacArthur was now planning to land with his staff and the exiled president of the Philippines and Quezon's successor, Sergio Osmeña.

*   *   *

On the voyage from Hollandia, MacArthur spent his evenings drafting and redrafting the two speeches he planned to give, one on the beach and the other when he restored the government of the Philippines, and after putting down his pencil he would read them both aloud to Egeberg and Lehrbas, who made constant corrections and comments. "That's a worn-out cliché," one of them would say at a particular phrase, or even "It stinks," and MacArthur would start over.[27]

In his mind, however, it was vital that he and Osmeña be seen, heard, and photographed on Filipino soil as soon as possible, to make it clear to the millions of Filipinos that their government and MacArthur were back—and that the Americans would never abandon them again.

Now he brought to his cabin the four correspondents who would be accompanying him in the landing craft. It was 11:00 and the third wave was going in; the sky was filled with pillars of smoke from the beach ten miles away, as flights of navy planes roared overhead to continue pounding Japanese positions. After his somber mood the night before, MacArthur was ebullient and upbeat, sucking on his corncob pipe and assuring the reporters that everything was going according to plan. It was forty-one years ago, he told them, when he had first been here as a shavetail second lieutenant and crossed to Tacloban in a tiny interisland steamer. Now, he didn't need to tell them, it would be at the head of the biggest invasion force the Pacific had ever seen.[28]

At 1:00 P.M. MacArthur and his party set out for the rail and began descending the ladder to the LCM that would take them to the beach.

There were Kenney and Kinkaid, followed by Whitney and Sutherland, as well as Dr. Egeberg and Lehrbas, the journalists, and MacArthur's Filipino orderly. The last to board was engineer Pat Casey. He was supposed to inspect the Tacloban airfield once it was captured, to see if it was up to handling large bombers, but he had severely injured his back falling into a hole on Hollandia; Egeberg concluded it was probably a slipped disk. Casey shouldn't move with that back, Egeberg told MacArthur.

"Doc," MacArthur finally told Egeberg, "I don't think I have ever called anyone indispensable, and at this time Pat Casey is indispensable. So you get him ashore." And so Casey went on board the LCM strapped to a stretcher, with an armful of painkillers.[29]

The LCM roared off. They stopped briefly beside the transport ship *John Land* to pick up President Sergio Osmeña. They were not friends the way MacArthur and Quezon had been; during the two months Osmeña had been at Hollandia they had barely spoken. But now he and MacArthur would be landing at the same time to restore a free government to the Philippines, and rouse the Philippine people to rise up against their occupiers.

The rest of the way in, MacArthur sat on the engine housing, Osmeña on his left, Sutherland on his right, as they crashed through the waves. On the ninety-minute trip they passed dozens of landing craft heading back, some damaged and others carrying dead and wounded from the first three waves. One of them was a barge from one of Kinkaid's battlewagons.

"Hail that barge," Mac ordered the coxswain.

The barge came about as the LCM pulled alongside.

"Son," MacArthur called out to the helmsman, "where is the hardest fighting going on?" The helmsman pointed to Red Beach, where the Twenty-fourth Division was still pinned down.

MacArthur turned to the coxswain. "Head for that beach," he ordered, and they roared off again.[30]

As they got closer, they passed four big landing craft that had been hit by Japanese mortars, "and one was burning nicely when we landed," Kenney remembered. Another had just capsized and sunk.

MacArthur turned to Sutherland. "Dick, believe it or not, we're back."

It was now 2:30 and while the men of the Twenty-fourth Division had managed to advance inland 300 yards, there was still plenty of fighting as they tackled a line of Japanese pillboxes. Kenney could hear the snap of sniper bullets whizzing overhead as the LCM's engines reversed and the craft came to a halt and dropped its ramp.[31]

At that moment a MacArthur icon, and a legend, were born.

The LCM had come to rest on a shallow sandbar, and as the four reporters, including two photographers, went down the ramp they found themselves in water up to their knees. MacArthur did not hesitate; he descended, followed by Osmeña, Kenney, and the rest. The cameras rolled, and the image of Douglas MacArthur, sternly wading ashore in his field marshal's cap and Ray-Bans, became stock footage for newsreels and appeared on the front page of newspapers around the country.

The photo, one of the most iconic of World War Two, also started a rumor that quickly circulated among MacArthur critics, and would live on in two opposite myths. The first was that the whole thing had been staged and even rehearsed before being played out in front of the cameras.* The second was that MacArthur had been furious and berated everyone for so undignified an arrival. But as biographer Geoffrey Perret points out, he had waded ashore at Morotai in even deeper water.[32] Douglas MacArthur didn't mind getting his feet wet, and besides, that afternoon there were other things to think about.

One was the sniping along the beach. Jan Valtan, a rifleman and reporter with the Twenty-fourth, was one of the first to see the little cluster of khaki-clad men wading up from the water's edge. "You stare, and you realize that you are staring at General Douglas MacArthur. . . . He walks along as if the nearest Jap sniper were on Saturn instead of in the palm tops a few hundred yards away."[33]

The party also passed troops clustered behind fallen palm trees and firing ahead, as Kenney overheard one flustered soldier say to another, "Hey, there's General MacArthur." The other didn't bother to turn around as he surveyed the fighting in front of him. "Oh, yeah?" he drawled. "And I suppose he's got Eleanor Roosevelt along with him."[34]

A steady rain began to fall. MacArthur prowled around for nearly an hour, talking to officers and soldiers and getting a "feel for the fighting," as he told his divisional commanders, Generals Irwin and Sibert, who had pulled up in their landing craft a few moments before MacArthur had arrived. What he was really waiting for was a radio transmitter, which finally showed up on a tracked weapons carrier. It was to broadcast his message in several frequencies in hopes that it would reach Filipino guerrillas and anyone in Manila or other towns who still had radios.

Then at two o'clock MacArthur lifted the microphone and began to speak.

"People of the Philippines, I have returned! By the grace of Almighty God, our forces stand again on Philippine soil . . . Rally to me! Let the indomitable

---

* General Yamashita, who managed to see copies of the photograph, assumed the scene had taken place back in New Guinea.

spirit of Bataan and Corregidor lead on. . . . Rise and strike! For your homes and hearths, strike! Let no heart be faint. Let every arm be steeled. The guidance of divine God points the way. Follow in His name to the Holy Grail of righteous victory!"

Mac's hands were trembling as he handed over the microphone to Osmeña. Onlookers had noted that his voice had "taken on the timbre of deep emotion." When Osmeña finished a ten-minute address to his people, the technician had to tell MacArthur the recording device had not worked. Could the general possibly read the speech again? MacArthur did, and then he and Osmeña sat under some trees for a while and talked, even as Japanese bombers swooped in and dropped their bombs.[35]

MacArthur made one last visit to Irwin's command post when some Japanese mortar shells began to land nearby. MacArthur's pilot, Dusty Rhoades, had followed the general every step but now he began to edge away to find the shelter of a tree trunk.

MacArthur looked up. "What's the trouble, Dusty, are you worried?"

Rhoades said he was going to be less worried the closer he was to a large tree.

"Well," MacArthur said, reassuring him, "the Almighty has given me a job to do and he will see that I am able to finish it."

"I'm just not convinced that God is equally interested in *my* survival," Rhoades promptly answered.

MacArthur said nothing, just broke into a broad grin.[36]

The last thing he did at the command post was write a message to President Roosevelt.

"This note is written from the beach, near Tacloban, where we have just landed," it began. "It will be the first letter from the freed Philippines and I thought you might like to add it to your [stamp] collection."[37]

Then the landing craft took everyone back to the *Nashville* for the night—but not before a Japanese Kate bomber flew low over their heads and dropped a torpedo that crashed smack into the cruiser *Honolulu*, leaving her badly damaged and listing.

When MacArthur got back on the ship, he found a message waiting for him. It was from FDR: "I know well what this means to you. I know what it cost you to obey my order to leave Corregidor."[38]

Did the message lift at last the sense of resentment, and of shame, that Roosevelt's order had brought MacArthur for more than two and a half years?

His memoirs give no indication. More significant, he says, was a very old Filipino man who greeted him on the beach and said, "Good afternoon, Sir Field Marshal, glad to see you. It's been many years—a long, long time."[39]

He had returned. And now nothing, and no one, would get him to leave again.

The soldiers and officers who been there on the beach that afternoon knew they had witnessed history. Some were miffed that MacArthur had said "*I* have returned" instead of "*We* have returned," and some in the States thought the speech was overblown and, with its frequent references to God, even "sacrilegious." Others thought the references to Bataan and Corregidor were poor salesmanship.

MacArthur, however, had known what he was doing, The speech was not for Americans, but for the Filipinos; MacArthur had made his return to the islands a matter of both personal and national honor. By making good on his promise, he had proven not only his own good faith but that of his country as well.

Phil Hostetter learned that the next day. He had been busy patching up GIs at his first-aid station on the beach, when someone said, "Do you know who was just here? General MacArthur and some admiral!" He was told the general and his party had watched him at work, but then moved on without disturbing him.

The next day a radiantly happy Filipino guerrilla soldier showed up, asking, "Where is General MacArthur?"

"He was here yesterday, we all saw him," Hostetter replied, lying slightly.

"Oh, I cannot believe it," he answered with great joy. "This means you are here to stay."[40]

Even the nonadmirers were impressed. "We really didn't have a lot of love for MacArthur," Han Rants remembered, "because as a general he wanted to win wars fast." But even Rants conceded, "While seeming to be a kind of grandstand thing . . . it really took some courage for a man at that level to be there. . . . As much as we disliked the guy," he concluded, "we knew there was no one who knew the Philippine Islands better, and we knew if we had landed somewhere else, we probably would have had a lot more people killed than we did."[41]

And casualties *were* light—fewer than 50 killed and only 192 wounded—but not just because MacArthur and his staff had chosen the right beach. Japanese naval intel had given their army counterparts no warning about the Leyte invasion, and by chance the landings had caught the Japanese in the midst of a change of command and communications networks, making it almost impossible to coordinate resistance.

Instead, the Japanese found themselves steadily shoved back until by nightfall Krueger's Sixth Army held two large beachheads more than a mile deep, with the First Cavalry and Twenty-fourth Division holding the Tacloban airstrip and a hill dominating the northern beaches, and the Twenty-fourth Corps closing on the airfield at Dalog.[42] More than 50,000 troops had landed, and some 4,500 vehicles.

The advance resumed the next morning, as MacArthur continued his tour of the battlefield, this time with the First Cavalry. With fighting intensifying just two miles away, he held a ceremony at Tacloban signifying the return of the Philippine president and government in exile to their homeland. American and Philippine flags were flown in profusion, while Filipinos lined the streets and cheered MacArthur and his men. The town would now serve as SWPA headquarters for the rest of the operation.

That operation was going well. Within a week Krueger's men had all but secured the eastern part of Leyte, and the Japanese were sent reeling back into the hills of the interior. The only disappointment was that the Tacloban and Doga airfields were, as MacArthur had feared, unsuitable for heavy bombers to provide adequate air cover. They were going to need support from Halsey's carriers a little longer.

Unfortunately, out at sea events were unfolding that would strip away that support, and even put the entire invasion of the Philippines at risk.

*   *   *

A little after one o'clock on the morning of October 23, the U.S. submarines *Dace* and *Darter* spotted a large Japanese naval force off the southern end of Palawan Passage, and immediately attacked.

They fired torpedoes at three cruisers and sank two. But what they had spotted was a much bigger force than anyone imagined, including the super-battleships *Yamato* and *Musashi*—and it was headed straight for Leyte.

What was unfolding was the Japanese plan to finally defeat MacArthur by land and sea, and reverse the course of the war by decisively crushing his naval support. It involved a three-pronged thrust with the Imperial Navy's remaining warships into Leyte Gulf. One prong, the biggest, would navigate through the San Bernardino Strait under Admiral Kurita, who would be commanding not only the *Musashi* and *Yamato* with their eighteen-inch guns, but also three other battleships, ten heavy cruisers, and more than a dozen destroyers.[43]

The second prong, Admiral Shoji Nishimura's so-called Southern Force with two battleships, a heavy cruiser, and four destroyers, was to pass into the gulf through Surigao Strait. Then both forces would converge and with luck catch the Americans in their trap, crushing the Seventh Fleet and leaving Krueger's Sixth Army stranded.

The one obstacle was what to do with the Americans' overwhelming naval air strength, with no fewer than twelve carriers under the command of Admiral Halsey. That job fell to the plan's third prong, Japan's four remaining large carriers under Admiral Jisaburo Ozawa, the battered but still unbowed loser of what became known as the Marianas Turkey Shoot in the Philippine Sea in May. There was no question of engaging Halsey's powerful force even on unequal terms: Ozawa had barely twenty planes per carrier. Instead, he was to act as bait, to allow himself to be spotted and then with luck draw Halsey's forces far off to the north, where he would be destroyed—while Kurita and Nishimura destroyed the rest of MacArthur's naval support.

For once, ULTRA missed the entire operation. It was American subs like the *Dace* and *Darter*, rather than the navy's codebreakers, that ended up providing the best information on what the Japanese were up to.[44]

But even with the element of surprise, the Japanese plan, Sho 1, required precision coordination among three widely separated fleets, all the while evading American attacks from the air. It also required that the wily Bill

Halsey and his task force commanders fall for Ozawa's bluff. In the greatest naval battle of World War Two, the odds were against the Japanese from the start.

But by a combination of bad luck and bad decisions, the U.S. Navy would unexpectedly put victory within reach of the Japanese—and with it the doom of MacArthur's army.

It was shortly after dawn on October 24 that a U.S. Navy Helldiver bomber radioed the message "Enemy in sight," to Halsey's flagship, the battleship *New Jersey*. An hour later Nishimura's Southern Force was also spotted, and planes from the carriers *Enterprise* and *Franklin* dropped bombs and torpedoes on the Japanese ships as they steamed for the Surigao Strait. But the full devastating air attack that Nishimura expected never came. Instead, Halsey's carriers focused their effort on Kurita's big battleships and cruisers in the Sibuyan Sea.

Torpedo-carrying Avengers from the *Intrepid* scored at least four hits on the massive *Musashi* by midday, while the *Yamato,* the cruiser *Myoko,* and other ships took heavy hits from successive waves of dive bombers and torpedo planes. By three o'clock the one-sided battle was all but over. The *Musashi* was virtually dead in the water (that evening she rolled over and sank, taking more than a thousand sailors with her) and the *Myoko* was too badly injured to continue. Kurita ordered his ships to reverse course, and jubilant American aircrews reported back to the *New Jersey* that the Japanese were fleeing the scene.

With Halsey's planes tied up farther north, it had fallen to Kinkaid's Seventh Fleet to deal with the next prong in the Japanese attack, Nishimura's Southern Force. MacArthur, as usual, insisted on being part of the action.

Kinkaid's plan was straightforward: to bottle up Nishimura in the Surigao Strait with his own formidable surface force, which included six battleships. Kinkaid wanted to use the *Nashville* to help increase the odds, but admitted he was reluctant to ask the commander in chief to give up his flagship.

"Great," MacArthur answered. "When do we start?"

"I'm afraid you cannot come along, General," Kinkaid answered firmly. "The Seventh Fleet is my fleet, and this is my flagship. I have to go and I cannot take the risk of your being aboard, so I shall have to ask you to transfer to another vessel if you will, right now."

MacArthur was inclined to argue. He admitted he had never been in a major naval action and he was eager to see one. But he finally saw reason.

"You're right," he said with a rueful smile. "We'll get off."[45]

MacArthur and his staff transferred to Krueger's command ship, the *Wasatch*, as Kinkaid and the *Nashville* sailed away. With six battleships and supporting cruisers, the Seventh Fleet had more than enough firepower to overwhelm Nishimura's ill-fated fleet.

A picket line of PT boats were the first to pick up Nishimura's approach on radar around 10:30 that night. At 12:26 A.M. Kinkaid's battleships, led by Admiral Jesse Oldendorf, learned the Japanese were coming, and radioed Kinkaid and the *Nashville* with the news. By then Kinkaid and MacArthur had also learned two pieces of important news from farther up the gulf. The first was that Kurita's force had been beaten and was headed away from Leyte.

The second was that Halsey had received confirmation around 4:40 that afternoon of a large formation of Japanese carriers and escorting vessels approaching from the north, and that after considerable deliberation, Halsey had decided to set out with his full carrier force to catch and destroy them. The Seventh Fleet could expect little or no help from his planes in the upcoming fight.

Although no American knew it, the carriers were, of course, Ozawa's decoy fleet, and Halsey had swallowed the bait in one bull-like gulp.

Halsey's departure left the Seventh Fleet exposed and helpless, just as the Japanese had hoped. Kinkaid did have at least sixteen aircraft carriers in his fleet, but they were small escort carriers called "baby flattops," each of which carried eighteen or so planes equipped for providing air cover against troops on the ground—but certainly not enough to protect a naval armada from attack. Indeed, the thin-skinned baby flattops would themselves be sitting ducks for any big Japanese warships that got into Leyte Gulf, as would the nearly six hundred cargo and landing ships huddled together in the gulf, on which the future of the liberation of the Philippines depended.

But Halsey did assure Kinkaid by radio that a group of battleships and cruisers "will be formed as Task Force 34" to guard the San Bernardino Strait in case Kurita tried to come back. So Kinkaid's battleships went into battle with no worries about the remainder of the fleet; even without Halsey's carriers, they would be safe. And Nishimura's pair of aging battleships, the cruiser *Mogami,* and quartet of destroyers were now sailing to their doom.

The two fleets spotted each other around 2:00 A.M. Aboard the *Wasatch* MacArthur watched as the night sky came alive.

"Small flashes, big flashes, lightning-like flashes, the sound of guns, and the explosions of hits," Egeberg remembered. "[S]ome tremendous explosions, magazines going up. When one thought of the meaning of those sounds, it was horrifying."

MacArthur was pacing, more quickly than usual, with more pipe-lighting than usual. Then they noticed small lingering lights dancing far off on the horizon, and MacArthur learned that the Japanese were using magnesium flares to illuminate the dark.

He became intensely excited. "If they're using flares they can't have radar," he said, clutching his pipe, "and without radar we'll get them in the dark. We'll get them!"[46]

He was right. The *West Virginia, Tennessee, California, Maryland,* and *Pennsylvania*—all survivors of Pearl Harbor—were able to take their revenge in an almost continuous hailstorm of fourteen- and sixteen-inch shells, with cruisers *Louisville, Portland,* and *Minneapolis* joining in. Admiral Nishimura went down to the bottom of Leyte Gulf with his fleet; one lone destroyer escaped.

Kinkaid and his commanders were relieved and elated. The admiral ordered one final staff meeting in the last dark hours before dawn, and turned to his chief of staff to ask if there was anything left to do.

"Admiral, I can think of only one thing," he said. "We never directly asked Halsey if Task Force 34 is guarding San Bernardino Strait."

"Well, let's ask him," Kinkaid promptly answered. A radio message went out.

IS TF 34 GUARDING SAN BERNARDINO STRAIT?

An hour passed, then another hour without an answer. Thanks to poor handling and delays, it wasn't until 7:00 A.M. the next morning that Kinkaid got his reply. It turned his stomach to ice.

NEGATIVE TF 34 IS WITH ME PURSUING ENEMY CARRIER FORCE.

Twenty minutes after that came a frantic message with even worse news. It came from the baby flattops and destroyers guarding the landing forces in Leyte Gulf.[47]

They were under heavy attack from Kurita's battleships and cruisers. It was going to take something extraordinary, possibly even a miracle, to save MacArthur's invasion fleet.

To his credit, MacArthur had never believed Halsey's air support would last. "Get the Fifth Air Force up here as fast as you can," he had told Kenney on the very day of the invasion. "I'm never going to pull another show without land based air, and if I even suggest such a thing, I want you to kick me where it will do some good."[48]

The problem was airfields. After inspecting the captured field outside Tacloban, Kenney had concluded that with work it might be able to handle a group of P-38s, but nothing heavier. Dogan was no better. Until they found new strips deeper inland, MacArthur and his Sixth Army were entirely dependent on the navy for any air cover. And now, thanks to Halsey's blunder, the bulk of that cover was gone.

As if on cue, Kurita had spent the night of the 24th regrouping his ships to continue through the San Bernardino Strait, despite their losses, and as dawn broke on the 25th they were steaming into open sea.

An alert Avenger pilot soon spotted the fleet and radioed back to Clifton Sprague, commander of FT3 or Taffy 3, the northernmost group of baby flattops. Sprague dismissed the report at once; the kid must be wrong, he decided. He must have seen part of Halsey's carrier fleet on its way north and gotten confused. So Sprague, along with his five carriers and seven destroyers and destroyer escorts, paid no attention.

Sprague's first indication that something was truly wrong came around 7:00 A.M., when strange, multicolored splashes began to appear around his flagship *Fanshaw Bay* and another escort carrier, *White Plains*. Sprague looked to the northwest to see, to his horror, the top masts of a large enemy fleet appearing on the horizon. The splashes had been shells from Kurita's battleship *Yamato*, the yellow, green, blue, and red dye colors telling Japanese gunners where their shells were falling. Sprague's entire task force was under direct attack from the most powerful battleship in the world, along with three other battleships and half a dozen cruisers.[49]

Clifton Sprague sprang into action. He ordered every ship to lay down a smoke screen to cover a hasty retreat to the southwest, while ordering his carriers to come into the wind so their planes could take off. By now shots from the battleships *Kongo* and *Haruna* were zeroing in on the carriers; one near miss on the *White Plains* sent men flying across the flight deck and sent one plane colliding with another, its whirring propeller slicing off the other plane's wingtip. The carrier *St. Lo* suffered similar near misses, with shrapnel from the Japanese ships, still more than fifteen miles away, cutting men down on deck.

Meanwhile, a series of frantic messages went out to Halsey: Send help, we're under attack. Sprague remembered thinking that "it did not appear any of our ships could survive another five minutes."

Then Sprague, and MacArthur, received their miracle.

It came in the form of a sudden rain squall, which cast a heavy mist that hid the carriers from Japanese view. The Japanese continued to fire, blindly, in the direction of Taffy 3, but the squall had bought Sprague and his ships precious time to put some distance between themselves and Kurita's battleships, and to get all their planes aloft and out of range of the *Yamato* and her mammoth eighteen-inch guns.

Sprague's only real fighting ships were three destroyers—*Johnston, Hoel,* and *Heerman*—and they now swung back to take the fight to the enemy. Their cause was hopeless. They had only five-inch guns to take on the *Yamato*'s eighteen-inchers and *Kongo*'s and *Haruna*'s fourteen-inchers—but the sudden squall gave them time to close the gap and launch a series of torpedo attacks. One from the *Johnston* blew off the prow of a Japanese cruiser, the *Kumano,* and left her dead in the water, and while the others did little damage, they nevertheless caused the Japanese ships to swerve away from the attack, buying Sprague's helpless carriers still more time.

All the while, Taffy 3's planes were also trying to carry the fight to the enemy, even though most had only small general-purpose bombs and some none at all—they could still make "dry runs" over the Japanese cruisers to confuse and distract, even as tracers and antiaircraft shells swept wildly around them. Then torpedo planes from Taffy 2 arrived and had a more deadly effect, wounding and eventually sinking three of Kurita's cruisers.[50]

All the same, the Americans' odds in the battle were swiftly turning from slim to nonexistent. The carrier *Kalinin Bay* was on fire, destroyers *Hoel* and *Johnston* were heavily damaged although still fighting, Sprague's own ship had sustained four hits by fourteen-inch shells but was somehow still afloat, while the *White Plains, St. Lo,* and *Gambier Bay* were constantly dodging near misses.

Then at 9:10 the next miracle happened. Admiral Kurita suddenly ordered his fleet to turn around and head back up the San Bernardino Strait.

To this day no one knows exactly why. It was true Kurita had been convinced that he was actually engaged with Halsey's big *Essex*-class carriers and that he was facing a far larger and deadlier force than Taffy 3, one that could administer fierce punishment from the air if he drew too close. It was also true that his ships were now scattered across the ocean, with the *Yamato* trailing far behind, and would be vulnerable to any counterattack on the surface like the one that sent Nishimura and his fleet to the bottom. Or it may be that the fierce American resistance had simply stunned the Japanese commander, who had been on his feet for forty-eight sleepless hours, into a state of panic.

In any case, the order went out, and one by one the Japanese ships turned away and the shell fire ceased. "Godammit boys," one of the signalmen on the *Fanshaw Bay* shouted jubilantly, "They're getting away!" Sprague stared out in disbelief. "At best I expected to be swimming by this time," he later wrote. "I could not believe my eyes . . . I could not get the fact to sink into my brain."[51]

The ordeal of Task Force 3 was not over. Later that morning it became the target of a new deadly threat, Japan's first kamikaze suicide attacks of the war. Planes screamed in and crashed into the *St. Lo,* setting off the bombs and torpedoes in her hold and blowing up the ship. Two other of Kinkaid's escort carriers, *Santee* and *Suwanee,* also took kamikaze hits.

As for Task Force 3's pilots and aircrews, their ordeal had also just begun—and MacArthur on the *Wasatch* was a horrified witness. They were now out of fuel and had nowhere to go. Their carriers were either under attack or, like the *Gambier Bay* and the *St. Lo,* already on fire and sinking. The planes had no choice but to crash-land on the primitive airstrip at Tacloban. MacArthur and his staff had to watch helplessly as the Hellcats and Avengers came in, more than a hundred in all, some spiraling out of control as they landed, others flipping over. A few of the staff, like Doc Egeberg, actually wept at the sight. MacArthur did not.

"There was only a look of deep sadness on his face," Egeberg remembered, as he and the doctor gripped the rail and thought of the young airmen's lives needlessly sacrificed—and the terrible risk they had all run, thanks to Halsey's carelessness.[52]

Yet the fact remained that the Seventh Fleet, and the landing force, were safe. And although Kurita managed to get his remaining battleships and cruisers, including the *Yamato,* back to home waters, the Imperial Japanese Fleet was finished as a fighting force. MacArthur would be able to complete the rest of his operations in the Philippines without interference from that quarter.

Yet MacArthur knew how close he had come to disaster, and he knew who had almost let it happen. The next night when he and his staff gathered for dinner there was considerable talk about that "stupid son of a bitch" and "that bastard Halsey."

MacArthur slammed the table with his fist. "That's enough," he ordered. "Leave the Bull alone. He's still a fighting admiral in my book."[53]

And that was the end of that.

CHAPTER 23

ON TO MANILA

Mac never blamed Halsey for what had happened in the Leyte Gulf, then or later. Instead, blame "can be placed squarely at the door of Washington," he wrote years later, and the decision to keep Halsey operating in support of, but also entirely independent from, MacArthur and SWPA. "I believe it was the first time a ground commander ever placed his complete trust in naval hands"—and that trust had been let down. Three times, MacArthur said after the war, he sent messages to Nimitz asking him to order Halsey to come back, but received no answer.[1]

The lesson in his mind was clear. If he couldn't fix Washington, he could fix his own airpower. That same night Kenney dropped by and found MacArthur reading the biography of Robert E. Lee by one of his favorite historians, Douglas Southall Freeman.

"You know," MacArthur remarked, "both Lee and Stonewall Jackson's last words were, 'Bring up A.P. Hill's light infantry'"—the fighting force that had saved the Confederate army at Antietam and both generals relied on in a tight spot.

He looked at Kenney. "If I should die today, tomorrow, next year, anytime, my last words will be, 'George, bring up the Fifth Air Force.'"[2]

The first arrivals of that air force came two days later at his new HQ at Tacloban, at Price House.

When MacArthur had finally gone ashore on Leyte on the 26th, he had taken up occupancy of a large two-story colonial building called Price House, which had served as the Japanese commander's headquarters. When they arrived, Sutherland, Rogers, and the other staff were amazed to discover the desks covered with files and papers, even pots of tea.[3]

MacArthur was still settling in at his Price House offices and lunching with General Kenney on the 27th when he heard the roar of engines.

"Hullo, what's that?" he wanted to know.

"That's my P-38s from the Forty-ninth Fighter Group," Kenney promptly said. The pilots included ace Richard Bong, and when Kenney and MacArthur drove out to the airfield to meet the fighter group the general called out, "Bong, get over here."

The fighter ace got his first meeting with the SWPA commander, as did the other Forty-ninth Group pilots, to whom MacArthur simply said, "You don't know how glad I am to see you."

The warm fuzzy feeling didn't last more than a couple of hours, since at five o'clock Japanese planes swept to hit Tacloban airfield. The Lightnings jumped aloft to catch them and shot down several. But the raids continued over the next twenty-four hours, and the relentless Japanese attacks shot down half of Kenney's P-38s. Kenney hastened to send up more, but still Price House and the sector around the airfield were in the Japanese crosshairs and the raids continued to take their toll.

And it wasn't just the Japanese; the liberator of the Philippines sometimes had to look out for friendly fire. At one point an American antiaircraft shell smashed through the wall of the room adjacent to MacArthur's; another landed in his bedroom but failed to explode. MacArthur saved it until his antiaircraft expert, Bill Marquat, arrived for dinner, then set it down on the table along with the first course.

"Bill," he said with deadpan sangfroid, "ask your gunners to raise their sights a bit higher."

Then one night a Japanese light bomber passed overhead and opened up with its machine guns. MacArthur all but ignored bombs that dropped outside his office window or on the lawn outside, but this time .30-caliber shells ripped past his head and embedded themselves in the rafter eighteen inches from his desk.

MacArthur immediately summoned his aide Larry Lehrbas.

"Larry," he said, pointing to the bullet holes, "dig those out."

"Thank God, General, I thought you had been killed."

MacArthur said nothing, just ordered the spent slugs to be sent to his son in Brisbane. With them went this note:

"Dear Arthur—Papa is sending you two big bullets that were fired at him and missed. He misses you and Mama and sends you both his love. Poppie."

It was impressive bravado. But it couldn't cover up the fact that a week into the invasion of Leyte, if the Japanese didn't have air superiority, neither did the Americans. The other grim news came from the other end of the island. After Krueger's initial success, which cleared the eastern half of the island, Japanese resistance was growing, and the fighting on Leyte was getting bogged down.

That was not how the invasion was supposed to play out. Part of the problem was the arrival of Japanese reinforcements that no one had counted on—the crack First Division. Akin's and MacArthur's ULTRA people had failed to identify the force's ultimate destination as Leyte. So instead of 26,000 Japanese on hand when the invasion came, there had been more than 70,000, with 45,000 sneaking in by boat despite constant air attacks by Kenney and the Seventh Fleet.[4] Still, it was the arrival of the Japanese First Division, "more than any other," as the official U.S. Army history has it, that "was responsible for the extension of the Leyte operation."

The truth was beginning to dawn on MacArthur, as well. As he wrote to Kinkaid, "[T]he enemy has decided to make a decisive stand in western Leyte in order to delay our further advance in the Philippines." It was time to break the bottle, and soon.

His cause was not helped by Krueger's own serious miscalculation. He had captured Carigara, on the northern edge of the island, on November 2 virtually without a shot. The next move for General Franklin Sibert's X Corps was across the rugged line of mountains west of Carigara and then south to Ormoc and the tempting anchorage at Ormoc Bay. But Krueger also worried about a seaborne attack on Carigara and ordered Sibert to dig in there and wait until it was secured before pushing for Ormoc. The delay was crucial; by the time Krueger was satisfied and told Sibert to "advance vigorously to the south," the Japanese First Division had dug in along the steep, rugged slopes and were patiently waiting for the Americans.

Military historians have debated the wisdom, or the lack thereof, of Krueger's move ever since. Wise or not, by the time Sibert's weary troops of the Twenty-fourth Division arrived in Ormoc Valley on the 5th, they met a firestorm and all advance ground to a halt. The next two weeks brought some of the bloodiest fighting of the campaign, as Americans and Japanese attacked and counterattacked, scrambled up and down the rocky slopes and through the cogon grass of Breakneck Ridge, throwing hand grenades and mortars and meeting death hand to hand—and going for days with no supplies except what Kenney's C-47s could drop by parachute.

MacArthur was not pleased. He was frustrated not only by Krueger's lack of forward progress on Ormoc, but also by the continuing failure to get any airfields on Leyte up and running. Despite every effort by his engineers, the runways at Tacloban and Dulag couldn't be turned into effective airfields. When the monsoons hit in early November, they became virtual lakes, almost unusable. That meant no air support for the men fighting for their lives on Breakneck Ridge. It also meant that MacArthur had no means of attacking the kamikaze bases on Luzon that continued to wreak havoc on the Seventh Fleet.

Finally there was a meeting, on November 8 at Krueger's headquarters at Tanauan, and another on the 12th. They talked about "the progress of the battle, the frustrating effect of the continuous rain, and the disappointing condition of the Leyte airfields."[5] MacArthur promised that he would send Krueger every replacement the entire SWPA region received—yet in the end that would come to barely 5,000 troops. The next day news reached the Sixth Army HQ that still more Japanese reinforcements had reached Ormoc. Krueger told MacArthur that he couldn't possibly clear the Leyte valley and take Ormoc without fresh combat units.[6]

MacArthur agreed to send along the Thirty-second Division and the 112th Cavalry Combat Team, the first elements of which started showing up five days later, as well as the Eleventh Airborne and the Seventy-seventh, a division that had been part of the retaking of Guam and was now under MacArthur's command. But in addition to this embarrassment of reinforcements, as it were, MacArthur also had another, more-loaded card up his sleeve. It was General Robert Eichelberger and his newly formed Eighth Army. MacArthur broadly hinted that if Krueger couldn't complete the conquest of Leyte, it would be Eichelberger and the Eighth who would—and very likely would then lead the Luzon invasion.

Krueger got the message. He knew MacArthur was quick to replace officers who he felt weren't up to the job, and he had no intention of joining that growing list—or to have the combat reputation of the Sixth Army sullied.

So he begged his boss to give him an extra three weeks, and to give him the Seventy-seventh Division for the kind of bold move he knew MacArthur would approve: a swift surprise seaborne landing on Leyte's west coast, just south of Ormoc itself.

MacArthur was delighted with the Ormoc landing—so much so that years later in his memoirs he would claim credit for it.[7] But now a new obstacle loomed in front of his goal of completing the conquest of Leyte. This time it was his Seventh Fleet commander, Thomas Kinkaid.

At the start of November MacArthur's biggest disappointment was General Krueger—"I expected him to be a driver," he confessed privately to Eichelberger. By the end of the month Admiral Kinkaid had become the other source of MacArthur's disappointment. Kinkaid was daily haunted by a fear of kamikazes, and the prospect of exposing his ships to sustained attacks by moving them clear around Leyte was not only distasteful, but seemed to court disaster.

Even more, MacArthur's plans to stage a further landing on Mindoro to create large airfields for the Luzon invasion, code-named L-3 and set for December 5, made still less sense. His two top invasion force commanders, Admirals Arthur Struble and Theodore Roddock, were dead set against it. "I do not consider L3 sound at this time," Struble told Kinkaid forthrightly, and on

November 30 Kinkaid brought the unwelcome news to MacArthur at Price House.

It was a stormy meeting. Only four days earlier, Kinkaid had told MacArthur he *could* do the operation, using six escort carriers, three battleships, three light cruisers, and eighteen destroyers.[8] Now MacArthur felt cheated, betrayed almost by Kinkaid's volte-face, only days before the invasion was supposed to take place—and just hours after he had relayed those plans to a group of reporters, including *The New York Times*'s C. L. Sulzberger.[9]

For two hours MacArthur paced up and down his cramped combination office-bedroom, his arms working like windmills as he and Kinkaid argued the point back and forth. Japanese airpower is weak, he kept telling Kinkaid; it'll cause little trouble. Kinkaid described how a single kamikaze hit was enough to disable or even sink his escort carriers, but MacArthur wouldn't listen.

Finally a frustrated Kinkaid told MacArthur, "I intend to tell Admiral King that you are rejecting my professional advice." MacArthur's temper roared to rage, forcing Kinkaid to lean against the bedstead, as if for support.[10]

At that moment, as a Kinkaid biographer has put it, "the admiral's career hung in the balance."[11] He returned to the *Wasatch* dazed and angry, and immediately drafted a letter for King that read, "General MacArthur declines to accept my evaluation that the Mindoro operation be not, repeat not, conducted now." He stated his forthright opinion that such a move would be "disastrous." It ended, "I regret the necessity for sending this dispatch but as COM 7th Fleet it is my duty to do so. I can find no alternative. I request immediate action on this dispatch."[12]

The "alternative" that Kinkaid actually was considering, but did not mention in his dispatch, was resigning. But then a message arrived for MacArthur from Nimitz that made resigning unnecessary—and largely saved the Mindoro operation. It spelled out Admiral Halsey's problems with trying to get his fast carriers ready for action against Japanese air bases in Formosa, in order to give MacArthur more freedom from air attack during the Luzon landing. Halsey needed at least ten more days, Nimitz explained. By delaying both Mindoro and Luzon to give him that extra margin, Nimitz believed, Halsey could race back in time to make both landings a sure success.

Kinkaid now felt more confident about arguing for not launching the attack on the 5th; his staff were also telling him that they felt better about the Mindoro operation as long as Halsey's carriers were there to support it. He returned to Tacloban that afternoon—his angry letter to King still unsent. Kinkaid and MacArthur had another set-to over the wisdom of sending the Seventh Fleet's carriers to Mindoro without adequate air support (even the usually optimistic Kenney had said his bombers couldn't cover a predawn landing that far out in the Sulu Sea).

MacArthur still refused to budge, but then put his arms on Kinkaid's shoulders like a Roman emperor, and said, "But, Tommy, I love you still. Let's go to dinner!"[13]

They were just starting dessert when Halsey's dispatch from the 29th, forwarded on from Nimitz, arrived at Chief of Staff Richard Sutherland's elbow. It asked for a ten-day delay in the Luzon and Mindoro operations, promising that his carriers would then be more effective. MacArthur and Sutherland adjourned to another room for a brief conference. When they came back they told a highly relieved Kinkaid that the Mindoro operation would be postponed until December 15, giving Halsey his ten-day margin, and delaying the Luzon landings until January 9, 1945—a full twenty days away.

That night Kinkaid returned to the *Wasatch*. He stuck his unsent letter to King in a file in his desk. Neither King nor MacArthur or Nimitz would ever know how close to a major crisis the original L-3 had brought them all.

The landings on December 15 were a complete success. MacArthur had fully intended to sail with the landing force, but at the last moment his staff persuaded him not to. It was a good thing, too, because kamikazes caught up with Admiral Strubel's fleet as it entered the Sulu Sea on the 13th. One smashed into the *Nashville*, killing 133, including Strubel's and General William Dunckle's chiefs of staff, and wounding 190 others. Strubel had to transfer his flag to a destroyer. Then another kamikaze struck the destroyer right next to his, killing or wounding another 40 sailors.[14]

It was not a good start. But after that, Strubel found that his passage to Mindoro was virtually incident-free. Halsey's carriers, back from their missions over Formosa, spent three days smashing or shooting down anything that flew or moved on Mindoro or in central and southern Luzon. On the 15th more than 27,000 troops quickly poured ashore, pushing aside the Japanese, whom they outnumbered more than twenty-five to one, and securing the island. It took only five days to get airfields built and the first of Kenney and Whitehead's squadrons ready for future operations—including protecting the future landings at Lingayen Gulf.[15]

By then Krueger had also gained the upper hand on Leyte. As MacArthur pointed out to Kinkaid, now that the Seventh Fleet no longer had to land at Mindoro, they were free to do the Ormoc landings instead. That came on the third anniversary of Pearl Harbor, December 7, 1944, as the Seventy-seventh Division stormed ashore with hardly any opposition. As with the Mindoro operation, MacArthur had caught the Japanese completely by surprise: some furious kamikazes managed to sink a destroyer and a destroyer escort as they lay at anchor, and a group of Japanese bombers sank a landing craft and hit some other vessels. But otherwise the Ormoc operation was a complete success.[16]

The truth was, the Japanese on Leyte had no troops left to fend off the threat to their main supply port, and despite desperate efforts to land troops to save Ormoc (including some 500 paratroopers who successfully dropped on a nearby airfield), they could do nothing to prevent the Seventy-seventh from taking the town on December 10. The Seventy-seventh Division commander wired Krueger exultantly, "Rolled two sevens in Ormoc." Then, referring to the Seventh Division and the Eleventh Airborne, still fighting their way eastward toward the coast, "Come seven, come eleven."[17]

There was still plenty to do. There remained 40,000 Japanese soldiers on Leyte, prepared as always to fight to the death. Krueger's resupply situation was still precarious; and he still had no adequate air cover (the airfields on Mindoro some 400 miles away were being readied for the invasions to come). What MacArthur's men had to endure was driven home to him when two privates from the Eleventh Airborne's 511th Regiment who had been wounded in the fighting in the Leyte valley came back to Tacloban to recuperate and found themselves in front of Price House. Impulsively they asked a general standing outside if they could meet General MacArthur. They wanted to ask him why the Eleventh Airborne wasn't getting the battlefield credit it deserved, and kept getting left out of official communiqués.

The general told the two men, PFC R. J. Merisiecki and PFC Charles Feuereisen, absolutely not, the general was too busy. But MacArthur had heard them through the open window and ordered the privates to come in. He showed them on his own operational maps just where the Eleventh was located, and the part it was playing in the fighting, and explained that he was leaving the Eleventh out of official communiqués in order to conceal its presence from the enemy, until he judged it the right time to reveal the role it was playing in the fighting.

He asked them to show him where their companies were on the map, and then asked them to carry a message back to their comrades and their commander, Major General Joseph Swing.

"Tell them I know of their great fight against the enemy," he told the two awed privates, "as well as the terrain and the elements, and that as soon as I can I will give the 11th Airborne the full credit it deserves."

Merisiecki and Feuereisen left Price House "with a mixed feeling of eminence and satisfaction," as the Eleventh's official historian put it, and the knowledge that their outfit was indeed not forgotten. As far as they were concerned, "General MacArthur was beyond reproach" from that day on, and they let every man in their company, and General Swing, know it as soon as they got back.[18]

There was still fighting ahead, but for all intents and purposes the battle for Leyte was over. MacArthur knew it, although he did not officially declare the island secure and the campaign ended until December 26; his attention was now entirely focused on Luzon—and what he and his men had accomplished in just a year.

"A year before the assault on Leyte," he wrote later, "my forces had been deep in the tangled jungles and swamps of New Guinea, almost 1500 miles from the Philippines. Now we were in the very heart of the islands—in a position to become masters of the archipelago . . ." Then he added dramatically, "The dark shadow of defeat was edging ever faster across the face of the rising sun of Japan. The hour of total eclipse was not far off."[19]

On his desk at the time was a message from George Marshall in Washington: "Congratulations on the great success of your operations." So was a telegram announcing that he had been promoted to the nation's highest military rank, general of the army (Marshall had received the same title two days earlier). From now on his collar and the flag on his jeep would carry five stars instead of four.

For MacArthur the lifetime soldier, someone who understood the full value of promotions, awards, and the other glittering measures of success, it was a powerful moment. His was a rank that only three men in American history—Grant, Sherman, and Sheridan—had ever held, and one even that General Pershing had never attained. It was certainly one his father could never have imagined reaching.

He sent a telegram to Jean. It made no mention of his promotion, however; it was instead a greeting to be delivered on December 27, her birthday. "Many happy returns of the day," it read. "The entire command joins me in saluting our staunchest soldier."[20]

The fact was that "the old thrill of promotions and decoration was gone," he confessed many years later. "Perhaps I had heard too often the death wail of mangled men—or perhaps the years were beginning to take their toll." Perhaps, also, there was the apprehension of what was to come.

Because if MacArthur knew the Leyte campaign was over, so did his opponent, General Yamashita. He sternly sent a message to his commander on Leyte on the 17th, warning that there would be no more reinforcements. Yamashita had already spent nearly 100,000 men defending the island—he would have said "wasted"—including his elite First Division and the Sixteenth Division—the same one that had taken the Philippines from MacArthur in 1942.

But he still had 275,000 left for the defense of Luzon. They were undersupplied and underfed, and deeply hated by the local population, who would greet the Americans as liberators. They also had no more naval protection and, thanks to Halsey's incessant pounding, barely 150 planes still operational on the entire island.[21]

But Yamashita also had a plan, one that he had devised and would personally supervise, unlike the one on Leyte. The Japanese cause in the Philippines might be doomed, but General Yamashita was sure he could make the American retaking of Luzon a living hell.

During the last two weeks of December 1944, meanwhile, MacArthur had other things on his mind besides the Philippines.

MacArthur revealed this to a group of reporters who gathered on the porch at Price House a few days before his promotion to general of the army. He began talking about his vision of what would happen after Japan was finally defeated, of his fears about the deteriorating situation in the China theater (the Japanese had launched a fresh offensive in eastern China, threatening both the Chinese Nationalist capital at Chungking and Kunming, the terminus of China's Ledo Road), and the failure of leadership in Washington to recognize the importance of the Pacific theater.

"The history of the world for the next thousand years will be written in the Pacific," he intoned.

Japan had understood that, he explained, when she launched her Greater East Asia Co-Prosperity Sphere before the war, and saw that if she could control China, she could control the entire future of Asia. Stalin also understood it, and MacArthur predicted that the Communist dictator would soon try to reverse the losses that Russia had suffered during the Russo-Japanese War of 1904–5. Russia still wanted a warm-water port facing onto the Pacific, as well as the mineral-rich lands bordering Manchuria. If Chiang Kai-shek collapsed, MacArthur warned, then China's future as a free nation would be at risk—and the real winner would be not Japan but Stalin's Soviet Union.[22]

The only power that could prevent that outcome, MacArthur believed, was the United States. The attack on Pearl Harbor had roused his country from its lethargy and was forcing her realize her destiny in Asia—the destiny (although he did not say so) that his father had foreseen more than sixty years before. The first part of that destiny was protecting the Pacific world from the tyranny of Japan; the second would be protecting it from the tyranny of Russia—again, much as his father had predicted.

The future shape of the balance of power was clear in MacArthur's mind at least. The struggle against Japan was now reaching its climax. When it was over, the struggle against Russia would begin.

Five years later MacArthur's words to those reporters would seem prescient almost beyond imagining.

On Christmas Eve, soon after his explosion with Sutherland, MacArthur was keeping his lonely vigil on his veranda when a small cluster of GIs appeared outside the hedge that bordered the porch. They began to sing, softly at first, then gathering volume as they sang a series of traditional Christmas carols.

"We wish you a Merry Christmas, we wish you a Merry Christmas, we wish you a Merry Christmas, and a Happy New Year!"

Suddenly there was the sound of an airplane engine. Searchlights went up and the singing stopped. The light caught a Japanese plane swooping in on an attack before one short burst of antiaircraft fire sent it crashing into the jungle in flames.

The soldiers cheered. MacArthur stared out in the darkness, very pleased.

"Thank you, gentlemen, for your singing," he said, and resumed his pacing.[23]

What was he thinking about? Possibly his birthday greeting to Jean.

This was the longest they had been separated since their marriage, almost three months. They had left Corregidor together two years and eight months ago; now he would be returning with an army of more than 200,000 men and a fleet of 850 ships—the biggest ever assembled.

But in his mind, he was returning alone. He would always be alone until Jean was again with him in Manila, and until the nightmare of the past three years was finally past and the Philippines was finally free—and he was finally free of the shame that went with it.

Sergeant Vincent Powers was attached to the chief regulating officer's section at GHQ, and had become used to the sight of MacArthur at Price House.

"The General could be seen at all hours walking up and down the veranda, smoking his elongated corncob pipe, strolling alone, or with an aide or conferring with high-ranking military leaders. When he walked alone, every few steps, he would look out into the clear air, his sun glasses hiding his deep thoughts. Then there were times we would see him racing back and forth, an aide at his side, talking rapidly, gesticulating with quick nods, sucking his pipe with deep, long draughts. Suddenly he would take the pipe in hand, ask a rapid, short question, jam the stem back between his teeth as he listened to the answer."

Powers remembered, "[W]e grew to know his mood from the way he walked, how he smoked and whom [*sic*] his pacing companions were. Watching him, some claimed they could surmise the turn of history."[24]

On the evening of January 3, 1945, Powers and his fellow clerks were indeed watching history.

"We went to the office to gather final odds and ends," Powers remembered. It was the night before the armada for the Luzon invasion was to sail; GHQ personnel at Tacloban were going too, since Mac was intent on establishing SWPA's presence as soon as the beachhead was secured.

That night they noticed, to their surprise, that the veranda was deserted. It wasn't until after 10:00 P.M. that they saw that "there on the porch was the same familiar figure pacing silently."

Tonight his demeanor was different, Powers remembered. "He wasn't smoking. His famous Bataan hat was missing. With head bared, he walked, hands clasped behind. The pace was measured, reverently slow. He was alone."

They suddenly felt self-conscious, and hurried on. They ran into the general's guard coming off duty, who offered to join them on the way home.

They had walked half a block when the guard turned and said, "You know what he was doing as we left? He was conferring with God. On the eve of all major operations, the moment he is notified that the assault troops have sailed, he . . ." His voice trailed off.[25]

The clerks and guards went home to catch a few hours' sleep, but the solitary figure continued to pace.

The landing on Luzon was about to happen.

The plan, he knew, was a good one. He and Krueger and their staffs had spent weeks hammering it out. It involved putting four infantry divisions on two stretches of beach on Lingayen Gulf on Luzon's west coast—the same Lingayen Gulf where General Homma's Japanese troops had landed almost exactly three years earlier. This was almost inevitable. That stretch of water gave the best access to the Sixth Army's real objective, the central plains leading southward to Manila and Manila Bay, and access to the island's best railroad and road network.[26] Manila remained MacArthur's ultimate objective, and not just because it was the Philippines' capital or because it had been his home for ten years. Manila would also have to be the principal port for unloading American supplies and reinforcements, as the campaign shifted

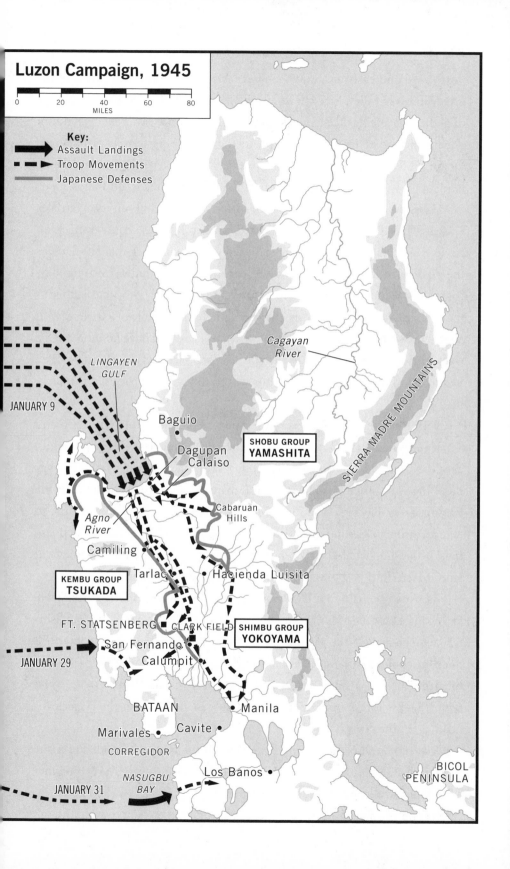

Luzon Campaign, 1945

0 20 40 60 80
MILES

Key:
→ Assault Landings
--▸ Troop Movements
— Japanese Defenses

JANUARY 9

JANUARY 29

JANUARY 31

LINGAYEN GULF

Cagayan River

SIERRA MADRE MOUNTAINS

Baguio

Dagupan
Calaiso

SHOBU GROUP
YAMASHITA

Agno
River

Cabaruan
Hills

Camiling

Tarlac

Hacienda Luisita

KEMBU GROUP
TSUKADA

FT. STATSENBERG   CLARK FIELD

SHIMBU GROUP
YOKOYAMA

San Fernando

Calumpit

BATAAN

Manila

Marivales   Cavite

CORREGIDOR

NASUGBU
BAY

Los Banos

BICOL
PENINSULA

northward and eastward, into the Sierra Madre and the steep ridges of the Cagayan River valley. Mac's newest staff officer, Courtney Whitney, in charge of gathering intelligence from Filipino guerrillas since 1943, had given him a grim picture of Japanese strength in the forbidding terrain of northern Luzon.[27] MacArthur knew it would be a hard and bitter fight clearing the island, but it would be much harder until Manila was back in his hands.

He also knew that the thrust south from Lingayen Gulf ran its own risks. Krueger had told him he fully expected a sharp Japanese counterattack on his left, and planned for a strong armored group to anchor that left flank as the push for Manila got under way. The beach at Lingayen was also too narrow to allow for a major buildup. Once all of Krueger's army was landed—more than 200,000 men in six divisions, including the First Cavalry, with another division, the Twenty-fifth, in reserve—it would have no more than a week or two before it started to run short on supplies and ammunition. They *had* to get to Manila first, MacArthur was thinking, as he paced in the darkness.

Everything he had done, everything he had planned, in the past two and a half years had come down to this. He had thought about every option and about everything that could go wrong. They had launched diversionary bombing runs on targets in southern Luzon; photo recon missions over the Batangas-Tayabas region south of Manila; and even sent transport planes to fake an airborne assault: everything to convince Yamashita and the Japanese that the landing would be anywhere but Lingayen Gulf.[28] And once they did land, MacArthur had to wonder, what would Yamashita do then?

His usually reliable ULTRA intelligence did tell him the Japanese were expecting a landing at Lingayen Gulf, but left him in the dark as to Yamashita's own plans.[29] If the Japanese commander decided to counterattack at once, he could tie up the Americans in the rice paddies and swamps that led off from the Lingayen beaches, costing them lives and time. Or he could withdraw his forces up into the mountains, or try to meet the Americans head-on in the central plains.

One terrible thought came to him: What if the Japanese decided to make their final stand in the city of Manila itself, and tried to turn the capital into a Stalingrad-style graveyard for the Americans?

No one on his staff had any good answers if that happened, although

MacArthur himself believed Yamashita would abandon the city and take to the mountains for a final defense. Other staffers were still thinking the Luzon invasion should wait until they had more troops or more armor or until they had complete air supremacy, but MacArthur had pointed out that they could wait until they were stronger, but the Japanese would get stronger too.

"The time to attack is now," he had told them. "The largest pot I ever lost in a poker game was when I held four kings in my hands."[30]

Now in the early-morning darkness, a glance at his watch told him that he would be embarking in a couple of hours. There remained one other imponderable: Could the kamikazes on their own bring the entire invasion to a halt? In fact, even as he was preparing himself for battle, Japanese suicide pilots were making life for the Seventh Fleet a fiery nightmare.

The combat formations of the invasion fleet had set off for Lingayen starting on January 2, and they became a kamikaze magnet almost from the first day.

It was a fleet of 160 battleships, cruisers, escort carriers, destroyer transports, and minesweepers under the command of one of Kinkaid's most redoubtable lieutenants, Admiral Jesse Oldendorf, and it was that same afternoon that a pair of Japanese bombers picked out the minesweepers for attack but missed. The first kamikazes turned up at first light on the 3rd, when one hit an oil tanker but fortunately did little damage. Another tried to hit one of Oldendorf's baby flattops but was shot down and crashed a couple of hundred yards short.[31]

Their aim got better the next day. One crashed into the carrier *Ommaney Bay* and sank her, and on the 5th they managed to smash into two cruisers, another carrier, a destroyer escort, and a landing craft.[32] On the 6th as the force entered Lingayen Gulf no fewer than sixteen of Oldendorf's ships took kamikaze hits. One was the battleship *New Mexico*, where Winston Churchill's British liaison, Lieutenant General Herbert Lumsden, was killed as he descended a ladder from the navigation bridge. MacArthur and Lumsden had become good friends, and he wrote a brief personal note to Churchill, "His general service and usefulness to the Allied cause was beyond praise. . . . My own personal sorrow is inexplicable."

By the 6th, MacArthur himself was under way in the cruiser *Boise* (the

Nashville was still under repairs from an earlier kamikaze strike) along with the amphibious portion of the invasion fleet. That was, as always, under the command of the redoubtable Daniel Barbey, on board his own flagship, the *Blue Ridge*. The kamikazes and other Japanese planes swarmed in, but in fewer numbers. One crashed into a destroyer, and another dropped two bombs on the *Boise,* but both missed.

"Again and again," MacArthur remembered later as he stood and watched beside an antiaircraft battery near the *Boise's* quarterdeck, "with vicious plunge and whirling propellers, enemy planes would dive, only to be cut down in the blazing barrage of antiaircraft fire as every ship opened in a deafening blast of flak."[33]

Then came a new threat. "Midget submarines, looking for all the world like dripping black whales," suddenly appeared in the water, carrying out their suicide missions with torpedoes instead of bombs. One fired two torpedoes at the *Boise,* but MacArthur "calmly watched the action" as the cruiser turned sharply away from the white wakes in the water. Then a destroyer came along on the port side and rammed the submarine, sending it and its crew to the bottom.

The next day, even as the kamikaze attacks were reaching their climax, wrecking two escort carriers, a transport, and an LST, no one could convince MacArthur to leave his post on deck. Besides, the first sight of land appeared off the starboard bow. Suddenly "there they were, gleaming in the sun far off on the horizon—Manila, Corregidor, Marivales, Bataan."

All at once the kamikazes were forgotten. "I could not leave the rail," he wrote later. "One by one the staff drifted away, and I was alone with my memories. At the sight of those never to be forgotten scenes of my family's past, I felt an indescribable sense of loss, of sorrow, of loneliness, and of solemn consecration."[34]

As night fell, the suicide attacks came to an end. A lone Japanese destroyer tried to slip out of Manila Bay under the cover of darkness and immediately met a hail of gunfire. On the *Boise* MacArthur could see the stabs of light and the tremendous explosion when one of the destroyer's magazines was hit and the ship went down in a fierce fireworks display.[35]

First light on January 9 revealed a vast panorama unfolding in Lingayen Bay. Almost a thousand ships lined the gulf from every horizon, the biggest armada in the history of the Pacific. As if on cue, the first kamikazes appeared, but far fewer than on the days before. They still managed to wreak destruction on another battleship and a pair of cruisers (for one, the *Australia,* it was the fifth kamikaze hit since leaving Leyte).[36] But otherwise the rows of LSTs and landing craft—2,500 in all—collected their GIs and their equipment, as a ferocious naval bombardment was unleashed on the landing beaches, including thousands of rockets fired from LCMs.

At 9:00 the assault craft were off. One of them contained Lieutenant Stanley Frankel of the Thirty-seventh Division, a nearsighted native of Dayton, Ohio, who had wound up being drafted and then, at a colonel's recommendation, signed as a Jungle Warfare Officer Candidate at a training base on Fiji Island. He had served on Bougainville and risen to staff officer before joining the Thirty-seventh in time for its landing on Dagupan beach as part of the Luzon invasion.

Congratulations, his colonel told Frankel before they boarded their landing craft. "You will have the honor of commanding that part of our regiment which will have the hardest time."

Frankel thought that was the one honor he could do without. "I also made certain I carried a GI shovel with me so that the moment I hit the beach, I could start digging a foxhole to protect myself from enemy fire."[37]

Leaving thousands of white wakes through the bright blue water, the landing craft made their way toward shore as the bombardment, including the *Boise,* reached its climax and then shifted farther inland to cut off and isolate any Japanese on the beachfront.

The first amphtracs growled up onto the beach at about 9:30. "I was apprehensive as were most all the way," remembered the gunner on one of them, "but I think after so many months of training and waiting they were glad to start fighting."

The firing was still intense when Stanley hit the beach, and the moment he did he began shoveling furiously. "I was almost underground," he recalled, "frantically throwing the wet sand all around the hole." Then he noticed the shelling had almost stopped, and he was hearing voices coming from higher up the beach, jubilant voices saying, "Veectorie! Veectorie!"

He looked up. "I recognized the friendly faces of a dozen Filipinos, who were then swarming all around us. 'Where are the Japanese?' I asked. 'All gone . . . two days ago . . . running to Manila.'" Frankel's astonishment was shared by everyone else in the Thirty-seventh as, except for the firing of a few mortar shells, there was no sign of the enemy.[38]

It was the same all along the rest of the beaches. The landings went far better than anyone had expected; in the end the GIs suffered fewer than 120 killed. The navy offshore was still catching hell, but the kamikazes too had largely fired their bolt in the days before the invasion. By the 9th, the same day as the landing, there were fewer than 50 Japanese planes left on the entire island, instead of the 250 that MacArthur's intelligence people had anticipated.

MacArthur arrived on the beach four hours after the first wave, and found "a scene of immense activity." Amphtracs, tanks, trucks, and wheeled amphibious "ducks" or DUKWs were swarming across the sand and revving up beyond the shore, as soldiers shouldered rifles, machine guns, and mortars and took off to follow them. "Now and then an enemy Zero would whine down over the beach, but . . . almost a solid wall of fire would go up, and swarms of fighters from the carriers offshore would dive in to take care of the intruder." Otherwise, there were still no Japanese in sight.[39]

That was a good thing, the Americans were discovering. As they moved only a few yards inland, they found an entangling mass of rice fields, swampy marshes, and fishponds. If the Japanese had set up a line of resistance there, they could have made things very tough going for the men of I and XIV Corps. Instead, apart from having blown up the principal bridges (as MacArthur discovered when he tried to drive his jeep to Dalugan and found the bridge there gone), there was almost no sign the Japanese had been there at all.

By nightfall on the 9th, some 68,000 men had established a beachhead seventeen miles wide and, at some points, four miles deep.[40] After returning to the *Boise* for the night, MacArthur was back on the beach the next morning, visiting all four divisional sectors. Overnight the Japanese had sent several dozen suicide motorboats on a desperate raid, but they did little damage and were all but wiped out by dawn.[41] Otherwise, there was everywhere the same strange lack of any Japanese resistance.

Strange, that is, to everyone but MacArthur. He sensed that the Japanese would pull back inland to find the best ground for resistance; when he had gone over Krueger's original invasion plan, he had scoffed at the notion that they would have to fight their way off the beach. "There aren't many Japanese there," he declared.

"Well," the briefing officer said, "most of this information comes from your headquarters."

"Not from me," Willoughby bellowed back.

Afterward, MacArthur took the briefing officer aside. "Sit down," he said. "I want to give you my idea of intelligence officers. There are only three great ones in the history of warfare—and mine isn't one of them."[42]

If the Japanese didn't put in an appearance on the Lingayen beach, there were plenty of Filipinos who did. Hundreds had greeted him as he stepped ashore the first time, shouting his title in Tagalog: "Mabulay!" Many more swarmed his jeep when he finally reached Dagupan. "[T]hey would crowd around me, try to kiss my hand, press native wreaths around my neck, touch my clothes, hail me with tears and sobs. It embarrassed me to no end."[43] It also helped to peel away some of the shame of having abandoned them, as well as his own troops, during those dark days in March 1942.

Now, as he set up his HQ in Dalugan, his mood was optimistic. The situation in the air was also looking up as well, thanks to General Kenney's chief airstrip engineer, Brigadier General Lief "Jack" Sverdrup. He had bet Kenney a bottle of Scotch he'd have a runway up and working seven days after the landing, but when he arrived at Lingayen a battalion of tanks threatened to roll through the one piece of hard ground his engineers could use.

Sverdrup leapt from his jeep, pulled out his .45 and threatened the armored battalion's commander, saying he'd shoot if he didn't back off. He did, but complaints about the incident wound up in MacArthur's lap.

He was unfazed. "I'll promote Sverdrup," he told Kenney, "and I'll give him the DSC." Sverdrup got his DSC, pinned to his chest by MacArthur personally just as the field was being finished, and he got the Scotch from Kenney. The head of Army Air Forces got a fighter group into Lingayen a day later, and had his B-24s lumbering down the strip a day after that.[44]

Then things began to bog down.

First there was the weather, which had been perfect on January 9th, but began to whip up the next day. The surf off Lingayen turned into eight-foot waves and landing craft and pontoon bridges carrying supplies inland were swamped, as the masterminds of the Sixth Army's logistics realized that the sooner everyone got down to Manila the better.

That, too, became more problematic, thanks to General Krueger. He was worried, not elated, about the lack of Japanese resistance. Every step his troops took, he grew more worried. The Japanese passivity defied logic; it defied common sense; it defied the intel—even as MacArthur urged him to press forward while the opportunity was ripe.

"Where are your casualties?" he asked Krueger in an interview on board the *Boise* on January 12. "Where are they?" He firmly believed Yamashita would not fight to hold Manila (he was right, as it turned out) and that the city was ripe for the taking.

Even though "Krueger almost worshiped MacArthur," in the words of one of his staff officers, he refused to be rushed.[45] He had lost 2,888 killed and 9,858 wounded in the fighting on Leyte, and he was in no mood to go unprepared up against a far stronger and more cunning enemy on Luzon—or leave his left flank unprotected as he turned south from the beaches to advance toward Manila. Then as I Corps under General Swift began their move forward, they found themselves running straight into what Krueger had feared—and into the teeth of Yamashita's defenses.

Yamashita, meanwhile, had been ready for the Americans. He had split his troops into three regional defense zones, each bounded by mountains and easily defendable terrain, which he figured would make MacArthur's advance as costly and painful as possible.[46] The smallest, the Kembu Group under General Rikichi Tsukada, held the rough mountainous area west of the central plains, overlooking Clark Field, which Yamashita guessed, correctly, would be a key American objective. The second, General Yokoyama's Shimbu Group with 80,000 men, would be stationed east of Manila controlling the city's water supply, after it had pulled everything Yamashita needed out of the capital. As MacArthur guessed, Yamashita had no intention of fighting a losing battle for control of Manila.

The third group, the biggest, under Yamashita's personal command, extended itself across the rugged wilderness of northern Luzon, and the Cagayan Valley. Consisting of some 150,000 soldiers, Yamashita's Shobu Group was short on ammunition, heavy equipment, food, and rice—everything except guts and a determination to die for their emperor, and strong defensible positions in which to carry out that wish. It was this force that Swift's I Corps now brushed up against as they moved inland to guard the Sixth Army's left flank. Instead of an easy passage, they found their way blocked by miles of intricate tunnels, interconnecting caves, concrete pillboxes, and other fortifications, all of which would be impossible to take out except at close range—which meant days, or possibly weeks, of bloody fighting.[47]

This was what Krueger had most feared. What he saw was more than just a formidable defensive line. It was a possible staging area for Japanese counterattack on his left flank as he advanced southward. Krueger decided there could be no significant forward advance until that flank was safe, and so he ordered Swift to pivot and shove the Japanese back.

To MacArthur, this plan made no sense. The storms on the 9th made it clear that getting to Manila and opening the bay to American shipping was more imperative than ever. Swift's brief encounter with Yamashita's stronghold doubly convinced MacArthur that Krueger would meet little resistance if he simply pushed on to the capital. Any Japanese counterattack would have to descend into the western plains, where the Americans' overwhelming advantage in artillery, armor, and airpower would be devastating.

Besides, the kamikazes were back, making the landing force on Lingayen more precarious than ever. They had already sunk four ships and damaged 43 others, with 2,100 sailors and soldiers killed or wounded. The longer it took to get to Manila, the longer MacArthur's logistic lifeline lay exposed to suicide attack from the sky.

"Go to Manila," he urged Krueger. "Go around the Nips, bounce off the Nips, but go to Manila!"[48]

The more MacArthur pushed, however, the more stubborn Krueger seemed to get. At their conference on board the *Boise* on the 12th, he told the SWPA chief, as he later remembered it, "I considered that a precipitate advance toward Manila would probably expose it to a reverse and would in any case cause it to outrun its supply." MacArthur was unconvinced, but in the end did not interfere with Krueger's overall plans.[49]

But a new idea was germinating in MacArthur's mind. This was to have the liberation of Manila take place on his birthday, January 26. That, plus a possible victory parade like a Roman triumph, would be the final personal vindication of the humiliation the Japanese had imposed on him and the Philippine people.

But events, and Krueger, weren't keeping up with that timetable. Swift and the I Corps continued to take their time pushing up against Yamashita's line in the Cabaruan Hills. It was the usual bitter, bloody hand-to-hand fighting over rough terrain that the Sixth Army was used to—even though it was a fight that MacArthur considered completely unnecessary.

As for Griswold's XIV Corps, his advance couldn't have gone smoother. By the 17th he was some twenty-seven miles from Lingayen and had crossed the Agno River at Camiling. Huge crowds of Filipinos gathered to cheer the Americans on as they passed into the town. They were now only thirty-some miles from Clark Field, the next big objective for getting Kenney's air force up and establishing air supremacy over the entire island.[50]

There were only nine days until MacArthur's birthday. Again he urged Krueger forward, with a message on the 17th saying the drive must be speeded up. On the 18th he sent another message. He confided to Krueger that General Marshall had asked him who should be considered for promotion. MacArthur was going to put Krueger's name down, he said, for promotion to four stars. The flattery may have worked because the next day Krueger told Griswold it was time to take Clark Field without delay.[51]

But this time it was Griswold who refused to be rushed. He was more and more worried that he was being drawn into a trap, and when his troops started to run into stiff resistance around the town of Bamban off Highway 3, he pulled up and prepared for a series of short, probing attacks to see what he was up against.

The army way of fighting the Japanese also took time, compared to the marines or the Australians, who usually rushed any strongly held objective, then let mop-up squads clean out any lingering resistance. Krueger's men preferred to wait until the artillery came up to blast away anything that stuck out aboveground. Then squads would crawl up any exposed hole, throw in an explosive satchel or a grenade or two, and cut loose with Browning Automatic Rifle fire or M-1 volleys as the charges went off. That might be followed by another grenade; then when the soldiers were convinced there was no one left alive inside they would move on to the next hole.

"It saved many American lives and got better results although it took longer," as one American divisional historian put it.[52] It also meant that MacArthur was going to have to wait while Swift's I Corps inched their way forward, as XXIV Corps cautiously advanced on the crucial Clark Field.

The last hurry-up message to Krueger went out on January 23. By now MacArthur had given up on any victory parade on his birthday. Instead, he had told Krueger he wanted to be in Manila by February 1. The chances of making his timetable for taking Manila were quickly shrinking. Thus far, since landing at Lingayen Gulf the Sixth Army had suffered barely 250 men killed, of which only 30 were XIV Corps. MacArthur couldn't understand why his generals were so reluctant to push forward: a meeting with Krueger on the 19th hardly went any better than the previous one on the *Boise.*

Finally on January 25, the day before his birthday, MacArthur made a desperate change of strategy—not for defeating the Japanese but for dealing with his generals. He shifted his entire SWPA headquarters inland to Hacienda Luisita, miles ahead of Krueger's own HQ at Calasiao. It was an obvious attempt to make Krueger feel like he had to step up and be more aggressive. The mood at Hacienda Luisita was grim. Sutherland was thoroughly convinced that Krueger should be "sent home" and told his boss as much. MacArthur said he was "very impatient" and "disgusted" with Krueger's dawdling, but decided to keep him on anyway.[53]

Part of his hesitation, perhaps, were his own growing doubts about the man who would have to replace Krueger if he were relieved, Robert Eichelberger.

Eichelberger had been the hero of the Buna operation and deeply grateful to MacArthur for the Distinguished Service Cross it had earned him (although he never knew how close MacArthur had come to replacing him at the eleventh hour or that MacArthur had vetoed his citation for a Medal of Honor).[54] But Buna had made Eichelberger a cautious man in fighting the Japanese, and now the commander of the new Eighth Army was caught off guard when MacArthur suggested revising a plan for sending one of his divisions, the Eleventh Airborne, into action on Luzon as a reconnaissance in force, Los Negros style, at Nasugbu Bay, forty-five miles southwest of Manila.

Sutherland bluntly told Eichelberger, "General MacArthur would like you to capture Manila if possible." What the SWPA commander envisioned was a swift and sudden airborne drop on Nichols Field, just three miles from downtown Manila, instead of the Nasugbu Bay operation. And as he had with Krueger, he dangled the possibility of promotion to four stars if Eichelberger signed on.[55]

MacArthur had high hopes that Eichelberger would do so. "He told me I'm his Jeb Stuart, his Stonewall Jackson, to MacArthur's Robert E. Lee," Eichelberger once eagerly told his wife.[56] Now Marse Douglas expected his Stonewall to see that this bold plan could shorten the Luzon campaign by days, even weeks.

But Eichelberger didn't sign on. Instead, he saw only the risks, not the opportunities, of an unsurveyed airdrop on Nichols. Instead he opted to stick with Nasugbu Bay, the sort of safe, predictable operation he and his men could handle. MacArthur was bitterly disappointed but said nothing. He was realizing that his top field commanders were careful, methodical men whose reluctance to surge ahead regardless of the casualties, might unintentionally be blazing a path to disaster.

MacArthur and Krueger had another meeting on the 26th, which also happened to be their joint birthdays, but again MacArthur refused to override his commander on the ground. Instead, he patiently allowed Krueger to move up fresh reinforcements before launching his two-pronged drive on Manila itself on February 1.

Meanwhile, it was not until the 28th, after several days of probing attacks, that Griswold felt strong enough to launch his XIV Corps into the Clark Field complex. By then, Swift had at last cleared out most threatening positions and was even approaching Yamashita's HQ at Baguio. MacArthur had personally gone to watch the 161st Infantry—"its commander, Colonel James Dalton II, was one of my finest field commanders"—repel and destroy an enemy tank attack by Yamashita's Second Armored Division, which ended with what was left of Yamashita's armor wiped out. Dalton was promoted to brigadier general, and MacArthur won his third Distinguished Service Cross.[57]

On the 31st Griswold was able to secure Clark Field and begin the reconstruction for Kenney's airplanes. There were still plenty of Japanese left in the hills to the west, but now he could move his main force together with First Cavalry to join in the final big push on Manila, with the First Cavalry driving down Highway 5 and the Thirty-seventh Division moving from Clark Field down Highway 3.

For the next three days MacArthur was everywhere. He had driven up to inspect Clark Field even before the last shots were fired in the battle for the airfield; now his jeep forged ahead of the columns of troops as if he were on point himself in a Sherman tank, instead of in an exposed jeep with a scared driver and an equally scared Doc Egeberg sitting beside a supreme commander whose scrambled eggs cap and corncob pipe made him the most valued sniper target in Asia.

At one point they drove into the middle of a fierce firefight. "Fifty or sixty yards to our right was a battery of 105 millimeter cannon firing point-blank at three Japanese machine guns emplacements," a stunned Egeberg remembered. "The Japanese were pouring a heavy fire from both sides. We were literally under fire from both sides." The driver offered to go forward, but MacArthur had sense enough to order him to back up into a nearby cane field.[58]

Another time MacArthur was scouting ahead as artillery slammed the area around the road ahead. Suddenly MacArthur yelled, "Stop!" Their driver, a large, resolute Swede, slammed on the brakes. MacArthur got out and led Egeberg over to a large block of concrete in which was set an ancient muzzle-loading cannon with worn lettering on its barrel.

"On that spot, Doc, about forty-five years ago," MacArthur announced, "my father's aide-de-camp was killed standing at his side."

Behind the Ray-Ban sunglasses, MacArthur's eyes were full of excitement at the memory. The only excitement Egeberg felt was an intense desire to get back in the jeep and avoid joining Arthur MacArthur's aide on the roll of the honored dead.

"I was fighting on ground that witnessed my father's military triumphs," MacArthur remembered. "I knew every wrinkle of the terrain, every foot of the topography. I was able to avoid many a pitfall, to circumvent many an enemy trap." Now the final prize beckoned: Manila.

"Three years ago I was driven out of there," he told Egeberg, "made it an open city to save it. I want to be the first to get in there."[59]

He remembered too the thousands of prisoners and civilians still in Japanese hands. "I knew that many of these half-starved and ill-treated people would die unless we rescued them promptly," he recalled. Stories of their horrible deprivation and horrible treatment by the Japanese had reached

GHQ in Brisbane. They were there because of him; they had had to wait while MacArthur pulled together the forces he needed to set them free. The time had come to finally right that wrong.

By dusk on the 1st, elements of First Cavalry were just ten miles from the outskirts of the city. The Thirty-seventh Division was edging even closer. The day before, Eichelberger's landing at Nasugbu had gone according to plan. Krueger now ordered Griswold to take the city, while troopers from the Eighth Cavalry were heading down from the north of the city, close to the University of Santo Tomas, where it was known that at least 4,000 internees were being held.[60]

Victory finally seemed within reach—and the liberation of Manila. But then disaster struck, thanks to a fanatical Japanese officer who decided to turn the ancient city into a holocaust.

General Yamashita originally had no plans to hold Manila. On the contrary, the city's large perimeter and the logistics of holding a potentially hostile city of 800,000 inhabitants made defending the capital look more like a strategic liability than an asset—especially since Manila's thousands of wooden struc-tures and thatched-roof houses made it a natural tinderbox.[61]

Rear Admiral Sanji Iwabuchi, on the other hand, had his own ideas. He had no effective fleet left, only a few ships stuck in Manila Harbor. But he did have some 16,000 soldiers and sailors under his command, and he was deter-mined to make a last-ditch stand in the city—his own version of the banzai charge or kamikaze suicide mission. He also had plenty of ammunition and weapons, and so he began barricading Manila for a fight to the death.

When Yamashita got word of what Iwabuchi was going to do, there was nothing he could say to stop him. He would much rather have had those 16,000 men and mounds of weapons and ammunition to use for his own plan, but under the command arrangements of the Japanese military, he had no authority to countermand the admiral's orders. So Yamashita made the best of a bad situation. He ordered his own general there, who had already blown up bridges connecting northern and southern Manila in preparation for evacuation, to add his three battalions of troops to Iwabuchi's forces, and then Yamashita, still safe and secure in his headquarters at Baguio, waited to see what would happen.

Meanwhile, Iwabuchi and his men blocked city streets with barricades; streets were mined, buildings booby-trapped, naval guns stripped from ships in the harbor and installed inside buildings and houses for the final fight.[62]

The Americans assigned to liberate Manila were going to be in for a very nasty surprise.

CHAPTER 24

BATTLEGROUND

Every soldier must expect to sacrifice his life in war,
Only then has his duty been done;
Be thankful that you can die at the front,
Rather than an inglorious death at home.

—GENERAL SOSAKU SUZUKI,

JAPANESE COMMANDER ON LEYTE

Yalta is a resort town in Crimea facing onto the Black Sea, with a warm, subtropical climate that supports vineyards and fruit orchards around the city.

On February 4, 1945, hundreds of officials and diplomats were gathering in Yalta for the last summit conference of the Big Three leaders of the Allies, Josef Stalin, Winston Churchill, and Franklin D. Roosevelt, as MacArthur and the First Cavalry were racing to complete the envelopment of Manila.

The war in Europe was nearly over. Nazi Germany was on its last legs; Adolf Hitler had only two months more to live. The Big Three had gathered to decide on how to arrange the postwar settlement in Europe, and complete the war in the Pacific—even though one of the Big Three, Stalin, had still not entered the fighting against Japan.

Now Stalin shrewdly used that fact as diplomatic leverage. In exchange for agreeing to declare war on Japan within three months after the surrender of Nazi Germany, he was able to reclaim almost all the territory Russia had lost during the Russo-Japanese War, including the Kuril Islands and Sakhalin peninsula. Stalin also won major concessions of territory in Mongolia and

Manchuria from China, even though China had no representative at the conference.

But there was one piece of territory in East Asia on which Stalin agreed to make no claims. This was the peninsula of Korea, annexed by imperial Japan in 1910, which Stalin now agreed with Roosevelt and Churchill—and later President Truman—would come under four-power trusteeship (Russia, China, Great Britain, and America) after Japan's defeat. All agreed that no matter what happened, Korea would remain intact, a single sovereign nation once it was ready for independence.

And so, even before the current war in Asia was over, the stage for the next global conflict was being set.

In the race into Manila, the Eighth Cavalry Regiment beat the Thirty-seventh Division into Manila by a curled lip.

A tank from the Eighth's Forty-fourth Battalion, B Company, "Yankee," was the first to enter the city. The tanks of B Company arrived buttoned up, expecting trouble, but instead what stood out in the mind of B Company's Private John Hencke as his Sherman rumbled forward, were the church bells. "The ringing of bells, church bells, out across the fields. Filipinos out there started running toward the road, waving their arms. It was a very pleasant sight to see."

People were cheering but also looking for food. "They were starving and didn't have much [to offer], jewelry, rings, clothing." But B Company had no food to give, so they pushed on, "until we reached a large, open boulevard. It was like a parade without tickertape, the people yelling, hollering, climbing up on the tanks . . . Then some Japanese snipers fired a few shots and everyone disappeared. We fired back into the upper stories and rooftops of building to discourage anyone pointing a gun at us and continued down the boulevard."[1]

Their goal was the University of Santo Tomas, now an internment camp where some 3,500 people, most of them Americans, had been held for more than two years. It was just turning dark when the men of the Forty-fourth found themselves outside the large campus. The university was pitch-black.

The Japanese guards had cut off all electricity, and now began firing away into the night.

Inside the darkened compound terrified civilians and prisoners could hear only shooting and the rumble of tanks. The only warning they had received that rescue might be on the way was late in the afternoon on the 3rd when an American plane buzzed the camp and dropped a pair of aviator goggles. People picked them up before guards noticed. A note attached, "Roll out the barrel. Santa Claus will be coming Sunday or Monday." Few figured out what it could mean, and even fewer dared to think it might be true.[2]

Now it was Sunday night, around 8:30 under pitch-black skies. The firing suddenly ceased. People near the windows heard a welcome American voice calling out: "Where the hell's the front gate?"

There was a pause, then one of the Forty-fourth's light tanks, nicknamed "Battling Basic," smashed through the entrance of the university compound. Another followed, and then another, as the Japanese sentries gave up and scattered.[3]

John Hencke's was one of those first tanks driving through the university gate. He used his searchlight to sweep the darkened buildings, looking for pillboxes. "When we got to within ten or fifteen feet of the first building I saw a doorway that had a bamboo screen covering part of it. Beneath it I saw some feet. I yelled, 'We're Americans! Come on out!' A boy and girl, teenagers, scared to death, came out. Once they saw who we were it didn't take long for them to be happy."[4]

Other inmates then began venturing out, still in a daze about what was happening. But most refused to leave: they couldn't believe Americans were actually here. It had to be a trick or a trap. One of those who did go out was Betsy McCreary, who had grown up with American parents in Iloilo. She was almost nineteen. At the sound of American voices she and a friend had raced down the stairs into the open plaza, but then had second thoughts.

"We were still under curfew," she recalled, "and all I could see was the silhouette of a man with a gun."

It turned out to be an American soldier, holding an M-1. "He was huge," she remembered with awe. "Compared to the more recent uniformed men in our lives," meaning the Japanese, "he seemed gigantic." Betsy gingerly touched his sleeve, not believing he could be for real. "I put the palm of my hand on his sleeve and I felt the sweat that had come through. He was real. He handed out cigarettes and I took one."

Betsy had no doubts now. She brought the cigarette back to the other people in her room who still refused to believe their rescuers were here. "Look at this," she said, "an American cigarette. The blue letters on it say Camel." Three or four had to examine the cigarette for themselves before they were convinced.

MacArthur and the Americans had come back, just as he had promised.[5]

It wasn't until the next morning that the last Japanese resistance in Santo Tomas gave up. Sixty-three Japanese held 266 prisoners hostage in a small building and refused to release them until they were allowed to leave the camp under safe passage. After they fled, the internees were finally safe and free. By then, the Thirty-seventh Division had also carried out its own mission of mercy, nearby at Bilibid Prison.

They had entered Manila shortly before dark on the 4th, the 148th Infantry moving southward through the Tondo and Santa Cruz Districts, west of Santo Tomas.[6] By eight their Second Battalion had reached the northwest corner of the notorious prison where at least 800 Allied POWs were believed to be held, as well as 500 civilians. There was an intelligence report that the Japanese were planning to set off an ammo dump on the premises if American troops showed up, so Sergeant Ray Anderson and the others of F Company moved up cautiously, in spite of the crowds of grinning Filipinos slapping them on the back and offering them small gifts. They were greeted by a burst of machine-gun fire and scattered rifle shots; eventually Sergeant Anderson and his men managed to kill two Japanese sentries and shoot off the lock on the prison's side entrance.

They pried the slats off some boarded-up windows, and looked in. "There were about fifty people huddled together in the room," he remembered, looking terrified. He and his men urged them to come out, but they refused. The Americans inside had never seen soldiers like these, soldiers with round helmets instead of the World War One–era tin hats that MacArthur's men had worn when they were defending Bataan.

They had never seen soldiers carrying M-1s and "grease guns" (the army's

M20 machine pistol) instead of the sturdy '03 Springfield they had last seen army troops carrying. They had never seen soldiers carrying bazookas and driving tanks and half-tracks, which hadn't even existed when the war had ended for them back in April 1942. The soldiers of the Second Battalion looked as strange as men from Mars, and the Bilibid inmates were firmly convinced that these men were there to kill them.

Even when Anderson and his men sang a couple of choruses of "God Bless America," they refused to budge.

Then Anderson tossed in some Philip Morris cigarettes. Like Betsy McCreary's Camels, they finally convinced the inmates that these were indeed fellow Americans and they were there to rescue them, not execute them. Soon the entire battalion followed up to sweep the buildings clear and free the rest of the Bilibid prisoners, many of whom were on the verge of death from starvation and malnutrition (at Santo Tomas, where conditions were not as harsh, prisoners were down to half a cup of rice per day).[7]

Just three blocks away came the sound of shooting. They were troops from the Eighth Cavalry, who had also hoped to reach the prison—but they were busy with the first serious firefight since Americans had come into the city.[8]

As the Eighth Cavalry's tanks and troopers had headed down Quezon Boulevard toward the Pasig River that afternoon, they were met by a firestorm of machine-gun and rifle fire from the three-story concrete buildings of Far Eastern University, as well as 47 mm artillery fire.

Tanks began backing up, slamming into vehicles advancing from behind. In the ensuing chaos they could have been perfect sitting ducks, but Filipino guerrillas guided them off onto side streets and back to Santo Tomas to regroup and reinforce, and wait to renew the fight the next day. Meanwhile, the Fifth Cavalry, ordered to take Quezon Bridge at the foot of Quezon Boulevard, also ran into heavy fire from Far Eastern University and a huge roadblock, complete with mines, steel rails driven upright in the roadbed, and trucks lashed together. They too had to pull back and await reinforcements even as the Japanese blew the bridge.[9]

Until now the Americans had found going into Manila fairly easy. But now the battle for the city had begun. Yamashito hadn't planned on it;

MacArthur hadn't expected it. But it was real and here and now, with every broad street blocked or barricaded, every intersection set to be a death trap of machine-gun crossfire, and every large structure a major fortress that would have to be taken floor by floor, room by room, closet by closet.

It was the first time in the entire Pacific War that Americans would have to take a major fortified urban center, and neither MacArthur nor his men were prepared for it.

Indeed, at first MacArthur refused to believe it was happening. The drive into Manila had been so straightforward, and the ease and efficiency with which the final trap had been sprung so impressive, that on February 6 he launched one of his famous victory communiqués:

"Our forces are rapidly clearing the enemy from Manila. Our converging columns . . . entered the city and surrounded the Japanese defenders. Their complete destruction is imminent."[10] Congratulatory telegrams poured in from the usual suspects: George Marshall, Henry Stimson, Churchill, FDR. MacArthur's biggest priority wasn't rushing to supervise the fighting but visiting the Americans and Filipinos he had let fall into captivity, and now had finally set free.

He started at Bilibid. These were veterans of Bataan and Corregidor, the men who had followed his orders in the hopeless weeks after the Japanese invasion and cursed him as Dugout Doug. Colonel Paul Bunker, MacArthur's classmate who had been part of the final resistance on Corregidor before the Rock surrendered on May 6, was not there. He had died in 1943 in a prison camp on Luzon. Sam Grashio, the P-40 pilot who had witnessed the destruction of Clark Field, was not there. He managed to escape to Mindanao after the fall of Bataan, and was one of the handful of Americans who had joined the anti-Japanese insurgents. Jim Wainwright was not there; he was reportedly still alive in a distant camp, but no one knew where.

What MacArthur did find were men who had been too ill to be marched off to work camps in Japan, Korea, and Manchuria, but who somehow managed to pull themselves into "some semblance of attention" in front of their lice-ridden cots.

The first to greet him was a virtual skeleton who saluted and said softly, "Welcome to Bilibid, sir." He introduced himself as Major Warren Wilson, an army doctor now in charge of the prison hospital.

MacArthur could barely speak. "I'm glad to be back" was all he said as he shook hands with the ghostly figure.[11]

He first visited the hospital, where hundreds of men too weak to stand stared out from their beds and tried to smile and shake his hand. Some simply stared in disbelief: "You're back," they whispered, or "You made it," or sometimes simply "God bless you."

"I could only reply, 'I'm a little late but we finally came.'" MacArthur moved along to the barracks and looked around at the debris of prison life, the tin cans the prisoners had eaten from and the filthy old bottles they had been allowed to drink from. "It made me ill just to look at them."[12]

Then came Santo Tomas, which was still under fire (Betty McCreary remembered an artillery shell crashing through a window and maiming two girls in her dormitory) but where inmates still had enough energy to raise a cheer and pull off his coat and throw their arms around him.

"I entered the building and was immediately pressed back against the wall by thousands of emotionally charged people," he remembered. "In their ragged filthy clothes with tears streaming down their faces, they seemed to be using their last strength to fight their way close enough to grasp my hand." He remembered a woman trying to lift her son up to touch their savior: "I took the boy momentarily and was shocked by the uncomprehending look of deprivation in his eyes."

For MacArthur, it was an unforgettable if harrowing moment, to be extolled as "a life saver, not a life taker." But as he left Santo Tomas, surrounded by crowds of Filipinos as "men and women literally danced in the streets," shouting and reaching out to touch him, it still hadn't dawned on him that his role as life taker was not yet over.[13]

Then his jeep was stopped by his own troops. They had captured the San Miguel brewery barely an hour before. They brought their general a beer, which he drank and pronounced good. They drove on to Malacañan Palace, a place filled with memories, where to his amazement he found his Cadillac limousine, which the Japanese military governor had used and kept intact. It wasn't until he tried to get down to Manila Bay and was met with a curtain of sniper and machine-gun fire that the reality sank in.

All the same, his mood was exultant. "The fall of Manila marks the end of one great phase of the Pacific struggle," he wrote in a communiqué, "and sets the stage for another. We shall not rest until our enemy is completely overthrown. We do not count anything done as long as anything remains to be done.

"We are well on the way, but Japan itself is our final goal . . . On to Tokyo! We are ready in this veteran and proven command when called upon. May God speed the day!"[14]

Meanwhile, outside in the streets the Japanese were now being pressed from three directions at once. The Thirty-seventh Division was still attacking from the north along the Manila waterfront; First Cavalry was still driving down from the north and northeast. But now the Eleventh Airborne was finally in position to start pushing up from the south.[15]

First Cavalry probably had the easiest job, at least at first. In addition to continuing the advance south from Santo Tomas, they were also assigned the task of clearing the enemy away from the dams, reservoirs, and other facilities northeast of the city. The Japanese were certainly thick on the ground there, but the operation involved less urban fighting. They could use heavy artillery and even air support, to clear resistance—something MacArthur resolutely forbade inside Manila itself. Indeed, by the morning of February 7 the men of First Cavalry were done and ready to tackle the next big objective.

Meanwhile, the men of the Thirty-seventh could only depend on their tanks to take out Japanese strongholds, while rifle and heavy machine-gun fire poured down from every building as they moved on toward the Pasig. Teams sprinted forward, spraying BAR and .30-caliber fire, while they waited for the tanks of 754th Battalion to catch up. Gunner Tom Howard was with the 754th's Company A. He remembered how they got a short briefing on "city streets and names of principal intersections and landmarks . . . so that when we enter the city proper we can get around without getting lost."[16]

Moving in, Howard and his crew found a phantasmagoria of macabre scenes. On one side of the street Filipinos danced and sang and handed out drinks (one man gave Howard an entire bottle of Three Feathers Whiskey that he had been saving since the Japanese occupation began). On the other, people were going through garbage cans looking for food, and running away with their children from the intense crossfire a few blocks ahead.

Then great clouds of smoke rose up as they neared the river. Fires set by Japanese defenders were sweeping through the city. They spread across the far side of the Pasig, then quickly jumped across the river and begin setting alight anything flammable, including blocks of thatched-roof houses. The thick smoke made it hard for attacker and defender alike to see each other until they were in close proximity. Then it was brutal hand-to-hand combat with grenades tossed through windows and bursts of Thompson and BAR fire to clear one room before moving on to the next.

By evening, the tanks of the 745th had reached the Commonwealth Life Insurance Building overlooking the Jones Bridge, the main crossing over the Pasig from north to south Manila. Their orders were to hold the span no matter what the cost. Howard stood guard all night with a grenade in his hand with the pin pulled out and his thumb on the release, so he could respond fast to any threat—and to keep himself awake.[17]

That same evening, GIs of the Thirty-seventh fought their way through the raging inferno around them, which included enemy pillboxes, sniper fire, and collapsing buildings, to the banks of the Pasig River. As darkness fell, they and the First Cavalry had cleared the Japanese from the entire city north of the river. Troops of the 148th had even crossed the river in assault boats after an intense artillery barrage of the Japanese-held opposite bank. They took more than 150 casualties, but managed to set up a bridgehead to start clearing neighborhoods east of the Intramuros the next day. That still left nearly half the city in the enemy's hands, with the most formidable obstacle of all, the citadel of the Intramuros, looming ahead.[18]

MacArthur had watched the landing of the 148th through binoculars, even as clouds of smoke rose up from the growing inferno that was his beloved city. He returned to Hacienda Luisita that night, exhausted by the emotional scenes with the freed prisoners and in a somber and chastened mood. It might be some time, he informed his staff, before they would be moving their headquarters into Manila. That victory parade would have to wait.

*   *   *

Fierce fighting continued on the 8th and 9th, with the Americans still trying to figure out where the Japanese strongpoints were, and their heaviest concentrations of troops. Gunner Howard and the tanks of the 745th repulsed several attacks as the carnage grew. "Bodies of civilians and Japanese were strewn over the streets, in gutters, on lawns and in the middle of the pavement," he remembered. Japanese snipers were everywhere; when he and his men entered any building they found mounds of dead Japanese, some of whom were actually snipers pretending to be dead. The tankers soon learned to shoot every Japanese soldier in the head, whether he was clearly dead or not, to make sure no one sprang to life the second their backs were turned.

From their observation post overlooking the Pasig, they also had to endure the sight of Japanese soldiers across the river dragging Filipino women out, raping them, and shooting them dead. They were under strict orders not to fire, in order to avoid revealing the American positions. "There was no way to describe the emotion of hatred for the Japanese," Howard later said, "and the anguish of not being able to help . . . but orders were orders."[19]

On the 9th MacArthur reluctantly lifted the order on the use of heavy artillery and the full weight of XIV Corps Artillery poured forth, leveling entire buildings as the Thirty-seventh Division continued its block-by-block advance westward, and both Japanese soldiers and Filipino civilians were buried under the rubble. It was the civilians who suffered worst throughout the battle. Starved and driven from their homes by flames and gunfire, thousands were murdered by desperate and demented Japanese soldiers.

Their bodies soon filled the streets in parts of the city east of the Intramuros. It was impossible to bury them because of Japanese sniper fire; American combat teams learned the only thing they could do was to dump quicklime over the bodies to make them decompose faster and reduce the stench of decaying flesh.

For MacArthur, February 10 was crucial. For the first time First Cavalry had moved across the Pasig and was now pounding steadily southwest toward the suburb of Pasay on Manila Bay. That day, too, control over the Eleventh Airborne passed from Eichelberger's Eighth Army to the Sixth Army. Since the 4th the paratroopers had been battering fruitlessly away on the line of powerful defenses the Japanese had set up to keep the Americans away from Nichols Field. The XIV Corps commander General Griswold now brought his corps artillery to bear in support of Swing's troopers. Howitzers, tanks, and tank destroyers turned their fire loose on Iwabuchi's naval troops and their entrenched positions. MacArthur's mood began to brighten.

But not for long. Four days of intense, rugged fighting were needed before Nichols Field was finally cleared of all but the last two hundred or so Japanese defenders. It turned out that Iwabuchi's heaviest artillery, including six-inch naval guns, and steel-reinforced emplacements outside the Intramuros had been installed in the Parañaque–Nichols Field sector.[20]

"General MacArthur came down in a jeep yesterday to see what we had been doing," Swing wrote to Peyton March. "Think he was a little surprised at the opposition we encountered. . . . Said I had done a fine and grand job." Now the Eleventh and the First Cavalry had made contact, closing the noose on the Japanese that were still left in Manila. Iwabuchi's warriors were now completely surrounded, trapped in the area around the Intramuros and the waterfront to its south.[21]

For Iwabuchi, who had withdrawn to the Intramuros on the 11th, the final hope was a sudden attack by the Japanese Shimbu group, in the hopes he might break out while they tied up the Americans. Instead, they were utterly destroyed by the combined power of MacArthur's air and artillery.

For every Japanese soldier, the only options left were surrender or death.

MacArthur and his staff drove in every day to supervise the fighting. But theirs was an intense frustration at being only spectators to the growing slaughter and having no control over its course.

Starting on the 14th, the First Cavalry began scouring out resistance from Pasay. For two days they fought yard by yard through Rizal Stadium and the baseball diamond at Harrison Park. Flamethrowers and Sherman tanks had to fire directly into the dugouts, and sandbagged positions under the grandstand, to get the last Japanese out.[22] As troopers crept through the outfield, posted signs reminded them not to pick the flowers.

Farther west, outside the city, things were going well. The retaking of Bataan Peninsula proceeded better than anyone had expected. After an initial series of bloody repulses at Zig Zag Pass, XI Corps managed to clear the pass by the 14th and was moving steadily south. Thanks to MacArthur's earlier decision to put the cork in the Bataan bottle, there were never enough Japanese troops to make the fighting for the peninsula a major headache, let alone the turning point of the battle.

Instead, that was going to be the taking of the Intramuros, and already by the 16th plans were complete and the artillery and troops were ready.[23] But before the storming of Manila's last fortress, there was one more operation to go.

That was retaking Corregidor.

The Rock was crucial for MacArthur's strategy.

Quite apart from the symbolic value of the fortress that had been his HQ and the Americans' final stronghold until the last ragged American and Filipino defenders had surrendered on May 6, 1942, there was also the fact that the Japanese garrisoning the island, few in number though they were (Willoughby's estimate was that there could not be more than 850), were still enough to harass any American ships entering or leaving Manila Bay. They could throw the whole objective of securing the bay for the next phase of the campaign into doubt. The mighty fortress had to be taken by force, and the question was how to do it.

Kenney's airplanes had kept Corregidor under steady bombardment since January 22, and stepped up their efforts at the start of February so that by the 16th they had dropped more than 3,000 tons of bombs.[24] At the same time, MacArthur and his staff had come up with a dual plan for taking the Rock, either amphibious or airborne assault or both. Everything depended, he told Krueger, on the results of the aerial bombardment.

An airdrop on the Rock looked wildly risky. Only three and a half miles long and one and a half miles wide, the Rock has only one feasible drop zone, barely 250 yards wide and 325 yards long. Yet Krueger proposed putting 2,000 men in by parachute, and at an unprecedented low level at that. In fact, one reason MacArthur and his staffers figured they would gain the advantage of surprise was that the Japanese would think the Americans were out of their minds to try such a plan.[25]

Yet an amphibious assault on the island, with its narrow beaches and forbidding cliffs, was even more risky. So the airborne plan moved forward, even though it would take five hours to get all 2,000 men onto the landing area known as Topside, the same place where MacArthur had set up his headquarters more than three years before.

At dawn on February 16, the C-47s rumbled off the runways on Mindoro loaded with paratroopers from the 503rd Regimental Combat Team. One of them, Rod Rodriguez of G Company, had made both of the previous combat jumps at Noemfoor and the Markham Valley. He felt even more nervous about this one, and began walking the length of the plane. Then he looked out the window.

All around them were C-47s with flights of P-38s above providing escort. Below on the azure sea, there were LCIs carrying 1,000 of the Thirty-fourth Infantry toward the beaches, where they would initiate an amphibious assault to distract and divert the Japanese from the parachute drop. Even farther out was a formation of cruisers and destroyers, their guns glistening in the sun. "It was an inspiring sight," Rodriguez later admitted.[26]

They would need some inspiration. Rodriguez and his fellow troopers didn't know that MacArthur's intel was seriously flawed. Instead of the 800 or 900 Japanese guarding the fortress, there were actually 5,000.[27] They were flying into a death trap.

At 8:40 A.M. they were over the Rock. The buzzers rang and the troopers stood and clipped up. Then at the green light, one by one they headed out the door into the void.

"We jumped at four hundred feet," Rod remembered. "Since it takes about 175 feet for the parachute to open, it meant the average trooper had about 225 feet for the parachute to open, not very long." At that height, opening too early might mean drifting seriously off course, tumbling into the cliffs or even into the sea. Opening too late might mean death.

Meanwhile, the Japanese were waiting for them.

Back on the mainland, MacArthur rose early and was on the road at 6:00 A.M. to visit the recaptured areas on Bataan. His jeep sped past Abucay, where Wainwright and General George Parker had held their first defensive line in 1942, and Balanga, where they held the last.[28]

A little farther along they came upon a company of soldiers who had just beaten off a desperate banzai attack. Fresh Japanese bodies were strewn across the road and along the ditches; so were American bodies. As the GIs gingerly pulled the wounded out for the trip to the first-aid station, MacArthur stopped, got out, and talked to the officers and men, wounded and un-wounded. "We soon passed our forward point, a man on either side of the road stealthily proceeding down the ditch," Egeberg recalled. "What had ear-lier been a rather large cavalcade of jeeps had dwindled down to six," of them the SWPA commander's. They had entered enemy territory, which "certainly took the edge off my enthusiasm."

But MacArthur was of another mind. "Go on," he ordered the driver. "This is my personal patrol." Half a mile ahead they found two scouts and spoke briefly. The men admitted that they had heard some Japanese up ahead but weren't sure how many.

"You are the forward point?" MacArthur wanted to know. "None of our men ahead of you?"

They said, "None of our men ahead of here, sir. No, sir!"

"Larry, Doc, get your carbines unlimbered," MacArthur said, as the jeep edged forward at fifteen miles an hour, its engine growling in low gear, as the other five vehicles, carrying soldiers with rifles and BARs, other officers, and correspondents and photographers, followed.

Then they came to an acre of clearing. It was an abandoned Japanese camp, with pots of rice still sitting on fires and a machine gun pointing men-acingly down the road at them—but with no gunner. He and his fellow sol-diers had clearly fled in a hurry.

As they came to another campsite, again abandoned, the walkie-talkie squawked. There was a report that some one hundred Japanese soldiers had just landed from the Manila Bay side of Bataan and were crossing the road behind them.

That caused something of a sensation among the group, but MacArthur waved it off.

"Just a group of frightened and demoralized soldiers," he said, "retreating from Manila and coming across to head for the hills to join their comrades." It turned out MacArthur was right. That was the last they saw, or heard, about the hundred soldiers.[29]

MacArthur's hope was that he could meet up with American troops coming north from Mariveles, but it was not to be. At a turn in the road they came upon a large stream where the bridge had been blown apart by an air strike. MacArthur got out and inspected the blasted bridge ruefully. At that moment, another P-38 turned up and dove for a strafing pass, then at the last minute pulled up and peeled away. MacArthur had ignored him, then simply signaled that they should head back. He wasn't getting to Mariveles this day.

When they were back behind American lines, MacArthur said, "Doc, it's been a long time since I led a patrol into no-man's-land. Makes you tingle a bit, doesn't it?"

Egeberg wisely said nothing. MacArthur had stopped, and was thinking of the fact that he had finally won the battle for Bataan—three years too late to save his old command, but a matter of deep satisfaction nonetheless.

"You don't know what a leaden load this lifts from my heart," he finally said. "This day has done me good."[30]

Still, he was disappointed. He had hoped to make it to the bay so he could watch the airdrop over Corregidor.

"I was just little over the treetops that lined the golf course" on Corregidor's Topside, Rod Rodriguez remembered, "when my parachute blossomed. I came crashing down on the edge of the course. The other guys of the platoon landed around me." They were the lucky ones. He could see troopers being hit in midair by machine-gun fire and antiaircraft batteries as they descended. Others fell far off course. In the end, there would be almost 300 casualties from bad falls and accidents. In the first wave, in fact, almost one out of every four troopers of the 503rd was disabled or out of action before he could unsling his rifle.

But then they got lucky. A cluster of troopers who were blown off course completely missed Topside but fell by sheer chance into the Japanese observation post overlooking the beaches. There Captain Akira Itagaki was busy staring out at the approaching landing craft when suddenly the view from his binoculars was filled with white parachutes and olive drab–clad Americans.

The Japanese had no time to react, as the paratroopers poured on the fire with their M-1s and Thompsons. Captain Itagaki was dead almost before he realized he was under attack, and his entire outpost was wiped out.[31]

The Japanese defenders still outnumbered their attackers by more than two to one, but they were now leaderless. Doors on the first LCIs dropped at 10:30, and the soldiers of the Thirty-fourth Infantry Regiment swarmed ashore almost unopposed. They ran into heavy machine-gun fire as they came inland, but within half an hour they were on the top of Malinta Hill—while Rodriguez and other paratroopers set up their firing posts and counted their dead and wounded.[32]

The fighting went on the rest of the day, with the Americans steadily gaining the advantage over the disorganized Japanese. Some defenders tried a breakneck counterattack that night to clear the Americans off the beach, only to run into the murderous fire of the paratroopers' machine guns overhead.[33]

Most, however, retreated deep into the island's caves and tunnels, including the Malinta Tunnel. There would be another two weeks of ugly fighting before the last of them was dead.

But as dawn broke on February 17, the Americans had effective control of the island at a cost far lower than anyone could have expected. The cork in the bottle of Manila Bay was back in MacArthur's hands, after almost three years.

But there were still Manila and the Intramuros to deal with.

The same day the 503rd was securing Topside, MacArthur watched with his heart in his mouth as the bombardment of the old walled city was set to begin. He still forbade the use of any bombers—"I can't do it, George, and that's final" was what he told General Kenney—but he had finally relented on allowing the heaviest artillery that the XIV Corps could bring to bear. Only overwhelming firepower was going to penetrate a sixteenth-century stone wall that was as much as fifteen feet thick in some places and forty feet at its base. The decision to go forward broke MacArthur's heart. It also doomed the Intramuros, every civilian, and the 16,000 Japanese still inside its walls.

Sergeant Rogers was there the morning of the bombardment. "The huge guns were jacked up on their supports," he remembered, "to permit point blank fire."[34] At 7:30 A.M., 130 artillery pieces, ranging from 75 mm tank guns to 240 mm howitzers, opened up. The old city vanished in a rising cloud of smoke as more and more guns rained death on Japanese and Filipinos—the Japanese had refused to let the pitiful remaining residents leave. The bombardment went on and on, not ending until 8:30 A.M., *six days later,* on February 23, when the Thirty-seventh Division began to creep in through the handful of holes blasted through the walls.

Almost at once the artillery opened up again, this time with smoke and white phosphorous shells to keep the Japanese from spotting where the Americans were passing through the gas walls, and where they were advancing—as well as more high explosives to widen the breaches after already having fired some 8,000 rounds.[35]

The fighting was savage, even primitive, with American and Japanese meeting bayonet to bayonet in cellars, including in the dungeon of the old fort, while grenades and flamethrower tanks rolled into action. Desperate, angry Americans even resorted to pouring gasoline down into holes and crannies and setting them alight to finally get the last enemy fighters out.

There was a brief pause as MacArthur's men closed on the last redoubt, a series of fireproofed government buildings. They were about to attack when suddenly the doors of nearby churches burst open and some 3,000 Filipino women and children—the men had all been executed by the Japanese—came running out. The startled Americans held their fire until they understood: the civilians were hostages, released by the Japanese at the last minute, just as they prepared to fight to the death. It was a strange, almost medieval scene, as priests and nuns in white and gray robes gathered up the survivors of their butchered flock and led them to sanctuary, and silence filled the nearby streets. Then the fighting resumed and continued to its inevitable end.

As the GIs inched their way through alleyways and basements, they found thousands upon thousands of dead Filipinos. Some had been killed by the American artillery fire, but many more had been murdered by the Japanese, hundreds of them dying with their hands tied behind their backs before being shot or having their throats severed.

It was not until March 3 that the final Japanese soldier was cleared out of the shattered, burned-out remains of the Intramuros. By then it was clear who had won and who had lost one of the epic urban battles of the Second World War, but also one of the most forgotten—and who had paid the most terrible price, namely, more than 100,000 innocent Filipinos.

Tom Howard and his fellow tankers had been there at the end. They had started at the Lingayen landing with seventeen tanks. They still had eleven, but they had only enough surviving crewmen to man eight at a time.

"We who were left were a motley looking crew, unwashed, unshaven, clothes in tatters. I existed as the rest did by stripping dead Japs of their jackets and pants and stockings . . . I had forgotten when I had last eaten a hot meal, instead of picking on a cold can of C ration, had a full night's sleep, had taken a crap," said Howard. Totally overwhelmed, "I remember I sat and cried for no apparent reason, uncontrollably, unashamed, and not cold, but spent[,] exhausted."[36]

But even as the fight for the Intramuros ground to its horrible end, the last battles raged for control of the last portions of the city, and they included personal tragedy for MacArthur.

He had been there personally, as usual, coming up right on the heels of the soldiers who were fighting inch by inch up key streets, at one point being pinned down with his staff for half an hour while the Japanese and a platoon of the Thirty-seventh Division exchanged shots and grenades.

He also couldn't resist joining the fighting for the Manila Hotel on February 22, where he watched the First Cavalry push up Dewey Boulevard and then lob 75 mm shells into the building. In moments flames engulfed the structure, and spread up toward the penthouse—which had been the home for his family for almost a decade.

"Suddenly, the penthouse burst into flame," he wrote later. "They had fired it"—meaning the Japanese. "I watched, with indescribable feelings, the destruction of my fine military library, my souvenirs, my personal belongings of a lifetime"—and the lifetimes of his mother and father.

It wasn't until nightfall that the fires were put out. MacArthur slowly walked up the stairs (with no power, the elevators were out) to the shattered penthouse.

Sprawled across the doorway he found a dead body. It was a Japanese colonel; the penthouse had been his last command post. Scattered around the body were tiny shards of porcelain, from the two enormous vases that had guarded either side of the doorway and were now shattered into a thousand pieces.

MacArthur grimaced. The vases had been given to his father by the Japanese emperor himself. They had been priceless mementos of a different era. Now, MacArthur thought, their shards made a grim shroud for the colonel's bloody corpse.

A young lieutenant of the First Cavalry stepped up, his carbine still smoking.

He grinned at MacArthur, his face flushed with success. He evidently thought MacArthur had shot the colonel himself, and congratulated him with a confident "Nice going, chief!"

MacArthur could only shake his head. "There was nothing nice about it to me," he later recalled. "I was tasting to the last acid dregs the bitterness of a devastated and beloved home."[37]

And a devastated and beloved city.

"Manila Is Dying."

That was the headline being carried by several American newspapers, and when MacArthur saw it he flew into a fury.

"MacArthur was shattered by the holocaust," Sergeant Paul Rogers remembered. "[H]e had gone to great lengths in 1941 to prevent needless destruction of the city he loved. Now his own forces were killing it ruthlessly and methodically, a bit at a time."

His "habitual self-control," after sixty days of fighting, was at an end.

"He growled an order to [public relations officer Brigadier General LeGrande] Diller to censor the offending phrase out of all copy written by any correspondent . . . [Reporters] were permitted to report the facts of the destruction on condition that no one would ever say, 'Manila is dying.'"[38]

In MacArthur's mind, the city—and the Philippines' freedom—were being reborn, despite the destruction. And there two ceremonies that, for him, would make that process complete.

The first came on February 27. Since landing at Leyte, MacArthur had wanted to reinstall the legitimate government of the Philippines in its true capital. In February 1942, in the darkest days of the fighting, in the darkest recesses of Malinta Tunnel, he had made a promise to President Quezon. "I will put you in the Malacañan," he had sworn, "on the point of my bayonets." Now Quezon was dead; the promised bayonet point turned out to be napalm and gasoline. All the same, the time had come to fulfill the vow.

That morning full constitutional government was restored to the Filipinos, in a city without lights or power, four-fifths of which lay in rubble—the worst-hit Allied capital in World War Two, with the exception of Warsaw. "I passed through streets," MacArthur said later, "with their burned out piles of rubble, the air still filled with the stench of decaying unburied flesh." Once-famous buildings were now twisted piles of rubble. Only Malacañan survived: unlike virtually every other public or large private building in the city, it had survived intact. "Its stained glass windows, elaborate carvings, and even its richly embroidered hangings and large crystal chandeliers were still there."[39]

MacArthur marched up the steps, as soldiers saluted and Filipino officials, many of them ex-guerrillas, stood at attention. Inside the state reception room was President Osmeña. They were never destined to be friends, and in a few days MacArthur would make a decision that would drive a permanent wedge between them.

But for now Osmeña and his staff were grateful for MacArthur's help. "For me, it was a soul-wrenching moment. Nearly every surviving figure of the Philippines was there, but it was the ghosts of the past—the men who used to be—who filled my thoughts: my father, Quezon, Taft, Wood, Stimson, Davis, Theodore Roosevelt, Murphy. In this city, my mother had died, my wife had been courted, my son had been born; here before just such a gathering as this, not so long ago, I had received the baton of a Field Marshal of the Philippine Army."

There was a microphone, and not a sound in the room. MacArthur cleared his throat and began:

"More than three years have elapsed; years of bitterness, struggle, and sacrifice—since I withdrew our forces and installations from this beautiful city that, open and undefended, its churches, monuments, and cultural centers might, in accordance with the rules of warfare, be spared the violence of military rampage."

They were awkward words, more heartfelt than crafted eloquence, but he plunged on.

"The enemy would not have it so, and so much that I sought to preserve has been unnecessarily destroyed by his desperate action at bay. . . . That struggle was not in vain. God has indeed blessed our arms. The girded and unleashed power of America, supported by our Allies, turned the tide of battle in the Pacific . . . My country has kept the faith."

He turned to Osmeña and the other expressionless officials.

"On behalf of our government I now solemnly declare, Mr. President, the full powers and responsibilities under the constitution restored to the Commonwealth. Your country, thus, is again at liberty to pursue its destiny . . . Your capital city, cruelly punished though it be, has regained its rightful place—citadel of democracy in the East. Your indomitable . . ."

Then MacArthur's voice trailed off. He could not continue. "To others it might have seemed my moment of victory and monumental personal acclaim, but to me it seemed only the culmination of a panorama of physical and spiritual disaster." He asked the assembled to join him in the Lord's Prayer, then left almost immediately afterward, shaken to the core.

"It had killed something inside me to see my men die" and so many Filipinos die with them in a battle that had seemed so unnecessary, and so unnecessarily cruel.[40]

The second ceremony came six days later.

On February 26 the last Japanese survivors on Corregidor had set off a massive explosive charge deep in the underground arsenal. The explosion hurled debris as far as Topside, a mile away, and threw rocks and shards on the deck of a destroyer 2,000 yards from shore. The blast and resulting landslide killed 50 paratroopers and wounded another 150—as well as exterminating the Japanese in the adjoining tunnel.[41]

But the blast signaled the end of Japanese resistance. Two days later Corregidor was declared secure. Taking it had cost more than 1,000 Americans killed and wounded. Of the 5,000 Japanese, only nineteen had been captured alive.

On March 2 MacArthur journeyed by PT boat to see the flag-raising ceremony on the Rock. It was his second great emotional moment in a week: for him, returning to Corregidor was almost a religious rite.[42] Nevertheless he chatted amiably with thirty-four-year-old Colonel James Madison Jones, West Point class of '35, commander of the 503rd's paratroopers, and with the men who had been part of Rock Force assigned to take the fortress. As he toured his old hideout in Malinta Tunnel and his old office on Topside, now a complete ruin, his face remained a stoic mask. The stench of death was present everywhere and he could barely breathe as he approached the parade ground and its solitary flagpole, "a slightly bent, shell and bomb scarred ship's mast with twisted rigging and ladders still hanging from its yardarm."[43]

As the paratroopers and infantry drew to attention, Colonel Jones marched up and saluted.

"Sir, I present you Fortress Corregidor."

MacArthur gave a brief speech, calling the capture of Corregidor one of the most brilliant operations in military history and thanking Jones and his men for their courage and skill—and presenting their commander with the Distinguished Service Cross.

Then, his voice trembling with emotion, MacArthur went on.

"I see the old flagpole stands. Have your troops hoist the colors to its peak, and let no enemy ever haul them down."[44]

A moment of deep personal satisfaction, unforgettable to those who attended it. MacArthur had also received a personal message from President Roosevelt:

"Congratulations to you personally and to your commanders and troops on the liberation of Manila. This is an historic moment in the reestablishment of freedom and decency in the Far East, and the celerity of movement and economy of force involved in this victory add immeasurably to our appreciation of your success."[45]

Yet the fight for Luzon, and final defeat of Japan, still had a long way to go.

* * *

Manila was battered beyond recognition, but free. Manila Bay was now firmly under MacArthur's control, and open to American shipping.

But there were still 172,000 Japanese on the island, including 50,000 ensconced in the mountains east of Manila, close enough to lob long-range artillery shells into Manila itself. It was against this force that Krueger decided he would launch his first effort.[46]

It wasn't going to be easy. MacArthur had informed him that, in addition to clearing Luzon, some of Krueger's units were going to be detached for operations in southern and central Philippines, including Mindanao. And the timetable would be tight. MacArthur needed to secure southeast Luzon in order to open a quick sea route through the straits, for what would be his last mission of the war: the full-scale invasion of Japan.[47]

The joint staff planners had been working on this mammoth task since November 1944. The result was a plan code-named Operation OLYMPIC, which would begin with an assault on Kyushu scheduled for September 1, 1945, and then an invasion of Honshu, set for December 1, 1945—code-named Operation CORONET.

Both involved massive numbers of troops and ships, employing nearly all of the twenty-one army and six marine divisions already in the Pacific, with another fifteen shipped over from the United States and Europe, once Hitler was finally defeated. Twenty-two of those were to be staged in the Philippines by November 1945, while an invasion fleet of staggering size, with 42 aircraft carriers, 24 battleships, and 400 destroyers and destroyer escorts, was being assembled.[48]

Then in the spring of 1945 the planners in Washington decided to postpone preparations for Olympic and Coronet. Indeed, they wondered if they could be staged at all.

The reason was that although the noose around the Japanese home islands was growing steadily tighter, only MacArthur's theater showed any sign of staying on schedule.

On February 19 three divisions of marines hit the beaches on Iwo Jima,

775 miles from the Japanese mainland. It was only after weeks of savage combat, and grinding American casualties, that the relatively tiny island finally fell. On April 1 a similar assault began on Okinawa, just 350 miles from Japan, with 180,000 marines and soldiers led by some 1,200 ships, including more than 40 carriers and 18 battleships. By the second week of June, more than three months later, the battle for the sixty-mile-long island was still going on, while U.S. casualties were climbing past the 20,000 mark.

Although the navy still favored a plan that focused on the push through the central Pacific—indeed, even argued that seizing positions on the South China coast combined with a massive naval blockade and aerial bombardment of the home islands would make a full-scale invasion unnecessary—it seemed highly unlikely that Nimitz's forces would now be ready for a December 1 deadline. MacArthur, by contrast, was moving ahead. Between February 28 and June 25, SWPA conducted no fewer than fifty-two amphibious landings on islands in the central and southern Philippines, with Krueger and five divisions focused on clearing out the last Japanese resistance on Luzon and Eichelberger's Eighth Army running all operations south of Luzon.[49]

The fighting was sometimes intense, even though Japanese resistance was disorganized and their cause hopeless. As military strategist Basil Henry Liddell-Hart observed, "Loss of hope rather than loss of life is what decides the issues of war."

In this case, the loss of life was also lopsided: clearing the Sulu chain, which began on March 16, cost 40 American lives versus some 2,000 Japanese.

Still, a veteran of the Twenty-fourth Division remembered the fighting for Mindanao after the fall of Davao, as "the hardest, bitterest, most exhausting battle of their ten island campaigns." Bob Eichelberger remembered the going was tough "for GI's who had no newspapers to tell them that everything was well in hand."[50]

Yet that was the impression MacArthur was able to convey to his masters in Washington. So they had little useful to say or object to when he proposed his own preparation for invasion by taking the battle in an unexpected direction. It would not only generate controversy with his Australian allies, but it would leave historians scratching their heads ever after.

CHAPTER 25

DOWNFALL

Jean will be here in just over two weeks," MacArthur quietly announced to Doc Egeberg one day in late February. He had not seen her for more than five months, the longest they had ever been separated. But they had written back and forth constantly and on his birthday, his sixty-fifth, she had sent a letter:

> Dearest Sir Boss—
> For your birthday, I send you all my love to you and may it help to form a mantle of protection for you. I love you more than you will ever know. May we be able to share in peace many more of your birthdays together.
>
> God bless you,
> Jeannie

Now came the news that she was leaving for Manila on a refrigeration ship and would be arriving on March 6. MacArthur sent her a sad note describing the destruction of their beloved penthouse in the Manila Hotel, and all their possessions. "Do not be too distressed over their loss," he wrote. "It was a fitting end for our soldier home."[1]

In the meantime, he had found another, a large whitewashed house inevitably called Casa Blanca in the exclusive Santa Mesa District, less than a mile from the Malacañan Palace. Its owner, Mr. Bachrach, had been a wealthy car dealer in the Philippines and had been murdered by the Japanese; his wife had escaped and joined the guerrillas up in the hills.[2] After liberation, Mrs. Bachrach had heard that George Kenney was looking for a house to live in while he was ensconced in Manila, and offered him Casa Blanca. Kenney checked it out and told her agent, "OK, put my name down for it."

The next day he described its beauties to MacArthur: the solid concrete-block construction, the four large bedrooms, the huge swimming pool with a massage room and steam bath in the basement. MacArthur silently listened; then the next morning missed his usual breakfast with Kenney.

When he came back that afternoon, he was smiling sheepishly.

"George, I did a kind of dirty trick on you. I stole your house."

"I know," Kenney told the astonished MacArthur. He had guessed immediately why the SWPA commander had missed breakfast, and he had called the Bachrach agent to see if there was another house available if he didn't want Casa Blanca. The agent said there was, a house belonging to Mrs. Bachrach's sister, who had told the original contractor, "I want an even better house than my sister's."

Kenney took it at once, and relayed the story to the new occupant of Casa Blanca, who was somewhat relieved he hadn't thrown his air force commander out in the street.

"So where is it?" MacArthur wanted to know.

"No, I'm not going to tell you," Kenney said firmly. "I made one mistake, and I'm not going to repeat it."[3]

Casa Blanca suited the MacArthur family very well. When Jean and Arthur arrived on March 6 after sailing into war-smashed Manila Harbor, MacArthur was finally able to relax into the domestic routine that suited him best. Above all, he had Jean with him, who had become the advisor-cum-confidante that his mother had always been, and with whom he could speak frankly about his worries and the war, the constant clashes with Washington, and his concerns about the future.

Once after a long evening of far-ranging conversation with Egeberg, MacArthur had gotten up and said, "Good talk, it was bit like talking with Jean." His doctor took it as the highest compliment, and realized how important the partnership between the pair was.[4]

Now in Manila she took on another important duty for her husband, visiting army hospitals. MacArthur had confessed to Egeberg that he never could; it was far too painful for him and, "a handshake or a pat on the shoulder seems a paltry gesture" for what he had asked them to sacrifice. But "why don't you take Jean to visit the hospitals? The men would rather see her anyway."

And so Egeberg did, as she toured one hospital after another over the next months, meeting and greeting doctors and nurses and then going bed to bed, saying, "I am Jean MacArthur and I am so sorry you are in the hospital. Are they taking good care of you?" With many patients she would linger for several minutes, talking and asking where in the country they came from. It wasn't unusual for her to visit and talk with a hundred or more of the wounded, before going on to the next facility.

Eventually and inevitably, she insisted on going up closer and closer to the front lines. Egeberg consented, and took her to a small field hospital northeast of Manila that had been under enemy mortar fire the night before. She visited tent after tent, often talking to soldiers who had been hit in the field less than an hour before; when Egeberg and she left, he remembered, her eyes were glistening with excitement as well as deep emotion. Like her husband, she would have been happy to go up to the front itself.

When MacArthur heard what had happened, he was furious.

"You cannot, you mustn't expose her like that" to possible enemy fire, he bellowed, slamming his fist on his desk. "You know what Jean means and how I need her . . . Don't do that again!"

A chastened Egeberg didn't. But it made him more aware than ever of the powerful bond between Jean and the SWPA supreme commander, "Sir Boss." It was the only time Egeberg ever got a dressing-down from MacArthur. He later reflected that, considering she was the wife of the boss, he probably deserved it.[5]

Meanwhile on April 12, 1945, Franklin D. Roosevelt died, after twelve years in office and six months of battling cancer. His death plunged the nation, and the nation's armed forces, into mourning. Most of the teenagers or twenty-year-olds serving in MacArthur's command, or in the central Pacific or in Europe, couldn't remember a U.S. president other than FDR. MacArthur's own reaction was muted; for more than a decade the pair had been rivals, almost enemies. Their professional partnership since MacArthur's tenure as army chief of staff had been deeply strained; any friendship had been far more a matter of necessity than choice. But six days before he died, Roosevelt had made his last important decision as commander in chief. He handed over to MacArthur command of all ground forces in the Pacific.

That decision resulted from an uneasy compromise among the Joint Chiefs in Washington. There still could be no agreement on a single unified command that would satisfy all parties; indeed, there were now more independent commands than ever, including the newly formed Twentieth Air Force with its B-29 superbombers under the personal supervision of General Arnold, which had launched its air offensive over Japan with the spectacular firebombing of Tokyo on March 6, killing more than 85,000 people.[6]

Yet as the two great area commands came closer and closer to converging, it was apparent that some new overall arrangement was necessary. So as Nimitz took command of all naval forces, including Kinkaid's Seventh Fleet, MacArthur now assumed command of all army ground forces except those in Hawaii, including the American troops in Okinawa.

But where would they be going and what would they do? King still held out for a blockade and aerial bombardment plan, without an invasion. MacArthur pointed out, not unreasonably, that strategic bombing alone hadn't defeated Germany, so why assume it would work with Japan?[7]

In the end, it was Nimitz again who broke the deadlock. He opted for the invasion-of-Japan idea and, facing opposition from his own inner circle, King was forced to acquiesce. On May 25 Nimitz flew out to Manila to discuss the plan with MacArthur, while MacArthur's staff threw themselves with enthusiasm into revising the details of OLYMPIC and CORONET, the two parts of the overall defeat of Japan, code-named DOWNFALL.

OLYMPIC, or the assault on Kyushu, would now begin sometime in the autumn of 1945; CORONET's landings on Honshu would take place in March 1946. Walter Krueger and his Sixth Army would carry the brunt of OLYMPIC, which would beef up to eleven army and three marine divisions—almost 650,000 ground troops.

Three corps of three divisions each would land at three different objectives in southern Kyushu while General Charles Hall's XI Corps would stage a diversionary strike at Shikoku.[8] Only when the southern portion of Kyushu was secure would preparations for the Honshu invasion begin, using airfields and staging areas on Kyushu for the final decisive push.

Even then, just the southern portion of the island would be occupied, but MacArthur and his staff understood only too well that the fighting for Kyushu would be indescribably bloody. No one could be sure that the fanatical Japanese wouldn't fight literally to the last man, woman, and child. Using casualties on Okinawa as his benchmark, Admiral Leahy estimated that the OLYMPIC invasion force would take 35 percent casualties. With 760,000 Americans involved in the attack, that meant more than a quarter million killed or wounded.

It would take a supreme optimist to enter into an invasion plan like this lightly, and MacArthur was no supreme optimist. It was not surprising, then, that he was determined to take one more decisive step toward cutting off Japan's war-making resources, by seizing its last remaining source of oil and gasoline: the Dutch East Indies via Tarakan in eastern Borneo.

To planners back in Washington—not to mention historians—MacArthur's decision to launch a major offensive in Borneo in May seemed inexplicable, an unnecessary diversion of soldiers and resources away from the principal goal, namely, the conquest of Japan.[9]

But to MacArthur it made good strategic as well as political sense. The soldiers involved would not be Americans but Australians; indeed, employing the Australian I Corps in Borneo under American leadership would prevent Lord Louis Mountbatten's Southeast Asian Command from using them to recapture Burma and Malaya, as part of returning the British Empire to Asia.

Here MacArthur and Admiral King were in rare agreement. Once the British were allowed back in the Southwest Pacific, they felt, it would be tough getting them out again. The future of Asia involved pushing the British and the other old European colonial empires out and planting the American flag in their place—as a prelude to granting independence to the indigenous peoples there.[10]

For once, however, the Australian high command dug in its heels at doing MacArthur's bidding. He and General Blamey had a huge fight—not so much over the wisdom of launching an offensive in Borneo and the Dutch Indies, but over whether SWPA GHQ was free to take command of Australian troops without Blamey's consultation or approval. "I think the time has come," Blamey angrily wrote to Prime Minister Curtin, "when the matter should be faced quite squarely, if the Australian Government and the Australian Higher Command are not to become ciphers in the control of the Australian military forces"—since that control was now being ceded to MacArthur and the Americans.

MacArthur's reply on March 5 was tart and unambiguous. Since the Lae operation, he wrote, ground forces had been organized under task force commanders responsible to him. There was no possible way Australian troops in Borneo could be under the command of an Australian officer already burdened with command of troops in New Guinea and Australia, namely Blamey. "Any other course of action would unquestionably jeopardize the success of the [Borneo] operation and impose a risk that could not be accepted."[11]

Blamey replied that MacArthur's memory was faulty, at the very least. He had always been in charge of any and all Australian forces in the field; the First Army was operating according to that standard even as they were writing back and forth. He reminded MacArthur he had said there would be no move from New Guinea until the last Japanese resistance on the island had been crushed. If MacArthur was determined to clear the enemy from the Philippines in order to protect his rear, Blamey and the Australians should be allowed to do the same in New Guinea.[12]

It took a meeting between MacArthur and Blamey on March 14, and a personal intervention by the desperately ill Curtin, to end the crisis in command. Curtin insisted that the operation in Borneo go forward; Australian newspapers were not unhappy that their troops were once again active in the final assault against Japan, no matter how remote from the center of action.[13] Yet, in historian Gavin Long's words, "Resistance to the Borneo operation, which had been disapproved by Marshall in February, adopted by the Joint Chiefs in March, objected to by the British chiefs in April and May, continued even after the opening of the first phase when an Australian brigade group was landed on Tarakan on 1 May."[14]

MacArthur was there, of course, to watch the Australians in action. As for the kerfuffle with Blamey, he could not have cared less. Now at last he could smell final victory, and it didn't matter whom he offended in pursuing it. He had already set off a political land mine in late April when he learned that Manuel Roxas, a Philippine politician and a close friend of his as well as of the late President Quezon, was being held at Sixth Army headquarters in Pampanga, and ordered Roxas released.

There was one problem. Roxas had been a member of the Japanese puppet government since late 1944, and the news of his release sent shock waves through the Filipino press and sparked a controversy that rocked the new government of President Osmeña as well as the American occupation.

The fact that Roxas was a MacArthur pal as well as an Osmeña antagonist, and as former Treasury secretary was the one legal witness to the $500,000 transaction between MacArthur and Quezon on Corregidor, has fueled speculation among historians and anti-MacArthur partisans ever since.[15]

Those who speculate that the release was some form of payback or even a way of buying Roxas's silence don't know the facts (far from the Quezon deal's being a guilty secret, all of MacArthur's superiors in Washington had approved it) and don't know MacArthur. He was completely dismissive of the controversy that Roxas's release had set off, especially on the political left.

"I have spoken with a number of people who [were in Manila] during the occupation," he told Doc Egeberg, "and I spoke with him [i.e., Roxas] several times. I have decided that the work he did with, or under, the Japanese was of a positive help to the Philippines and the Filipino people, and I urged the

Philippine government not to look on him as a collaborator." It was also true that Roxas had been active in the Japanese opposition, and even in touch with the resistance, when the puppet regime in Manila begged him to help them reach out to their domestic foes.

"The Philippines need him as a leader, and you mark they will soon use him," MacArthur barked at Egeberg, poking him in the chest with a forefinger.

"The people love him, and I have confidence in him as a man."* And that was enough, as far as MacArthur was concerned.

He and Egeberg were having this conversation as they sailed in the USS *Boise* on their way to Borneo. Despite the ill will with Blamey, MacArthur was determined to watch the Australian troops, whom he still thought of as *his* troops, in action. On June 9 they were off the coast of Brunei Bay, Borneo, as the usual massive naval bombardment went off and then Australians of the First Division poured ashore.[16]

There was not much action to see, so the next day MacArthur insisted on going ashore again, this time in the marshlands below Brunei Bay. There he, Kenney, and Whitney had to wade through calf-deep mud until a jeep picked them up and ran them and the rest of the landing party closer to the action. They drove as far as the town of Brunei, where the Australians were busy rousting out Japanese resistance. Someone pointed out a pair of dead Japanese nearby, snipers who had been hunted down and killed. MacArthur walked over to look at the bodies; one of the photographers with him snapped a picture. Another standing next to him was just then hit in the shoulder by another sniper's bullet.[17]

Kenney and the others now insisted it was time to go. But MacArthur said no; he wanted to keep going. Finally a flustered Australian colonel came up and said in no uncertain terms that MacArthur, five stars or not, had to leave. He couldn't assume responsibility for the life of SWPA's commander in chief. MacArthur reluctantly agreed to go, and they returned to the *Boise* for MacArthur and his staff's favorite treat after a brush with death, a chocolate ice-cream sundae.

---

* In fact, Roxas would go on to become president of the Philippine Commonwealth and the first president of the new republic in 1946.

At one point his doctor had to ask MacArthur if he wasn't taking one too many chances with his own life, with these frontline visits. He shook his head.

"Don't forget I had a lot of combat experience in World War One," he said, "certainly more than any of our present general officers—and as you live through such experiences you learn things. You learn to see things that are dangerous or that are reassuring, and you get a sense of timing."

Besides, he added, "it does help morale, you know, when they see a major or colonel or general with them. Something happens to the men."[18]

Running risks is the price of leadership, he was saying. By doing so a general can make things happen—if his timing is right, it might even turn a war around.

As MacArthur's staff continued the final planning for DOWNFALL, poring over maps and charts of Kyushu and Honshu and calculating how many thousands of tons of supplies and ammunition the mammoth operation would take, and how many hundreds of planes and bombers, planners in Washington were looking over a pile of recent ULTRA decrypts and getting very worried.

Everyone, including MacArthur's headquarters, had understood that with the fall of the Philippines and Okinawa, Japan would now shift all its remaining troops and resources to the defense of the home islands, especially Kyushu, the inevitable choice for a MacArthur-led amphibious landing. Likewise, every American decision maker knew not only that every Japanese soldier would fight to the death but virtually every civilian too—more than 200,000 had died in the taking of Okinawa.

But no one until May realized how many soldiers and planes Japan was actually cramming onto the island in preparation for the final battle, even as Kenney's aircrews were bombing and shooting up every Japanese vessel they could find crossing between Kyushu and Honshu, while the B-29s of the Twentieth Air Force were firebombing one Japanese city after another into smoldering ruins, starting with the capital, Tokyo.

What the ULTRA decrypts revealed to both the Joint Chiefs and MacArthur's G-2, General Willoughby, was a deeply alarming picture of between eight and eleven infantry divisions committed to the defense of the island. In addition, there were more than 1,000 planes available as kamikazes to hammer an invading fleet, with at least 1,200 more from the Japanese navy—and tens of thousands of pilots being trained for the final suicide ride that would end by crashing into the deck or the bridge of an American ship.

All through May and June the numbers kept growing. Willoughby concluded that Japanese mobile infantry strength alone had increased from 80,000 to 200,000 troops between April and July. "This threatening development," he finally had to report, "may grow to a point where we attack on a ratio of one (1) to one (1) which is not the recipe for victory." In other words, the Americans landing on Kyushu as part of OLYMPIC could find themselves outnumbered the moment they hit the beach—with many more Japanese waiting for them once they fought their way inland.[19]

On June 18, 1945, a very worried new president, Harry Truman, and the Joint Chiefs met to discuss the situation. Marshall asked MacArthur's GHQ to provide an estimate of American casualties in the first ninety days of OLYMPIC. The reply that came back—105,050 battle and 12,600 non-battle casualties—left Truman gasping. Marshall wrote back to MacArthur that those numbers were too high to contemplate an invasion of Kyushu.

MacArthur quickly replied to reassure Marshall and the president that those numbers were "purely academic and routine," and he had every expectation that successful landings would be far less costly. Besides, weren't the Russians about to enter the war in Manchuria? That would divide and distract the Japanese, and take away any hope of any further reinforcements for Kyushu. "I most earnestly recommend no change to OLYMPIC."[20]

The men locked in the conference room at the White House were not so sanguine. Truman had watched U.S. casualties on Okinawa swell to 70,000 in less than eighty days; this conflict would be against a much more numerous and more desperate foe. He wanted a reassurance from the Joint Chiefs that the invasion of Kyushu wouldn't degenerate into a bloody race war, pitting white American soldiers against Japanese civilians in an endless fight to the death. None could give it.

Marshall, meanwhile, was making his own calculations based on MacArthur's experience on Luzon, and guessed that casualties would run about 1,000 a day, assuming that the Japanese had eight divisions on the island.

Admiral Leahy was also doing his numbers, which pointed to a quarter million casualties overall.

There was dead silence in the room. Every person was thinking, *Even after we complete the conquest of Kyushu at that bloody rate, there will still be Honshu.* This, in fact, had been the most chilling revelation from ULTRA: far from being discouraged by defeat after defeat, the Japanese war chiefs were determined to fight on. In the words of historian Kenneth Drea, ULTRA "showed that [Japan's] military leaders were blind to defeat and were bending all remaining national energy to smash an invasion of their divine islands."[21]

If MacArthur had been there, of course, he would have exerted all his remaining energy to lift the growing veil of gloom. He would have called Leahy's estimates absurdly high; he would have pointed out that intelligence strongly suggested that the Japanese were only strong enough to try to blunt one prong of his offensive on Kyushu. The other two were bound to get through.[22] Besides, he would have reminded them, the goal wasn't complete conquest of the island, only enough to provide airfields and staging areas for the final push to Honshu and Tokyo. Given the Allies' complete air and naval supremacy, the Japanese would be helpless to prevent the next and last stage of DOWNFALL.

What MacArthur did not know was that Truman already had another option.

Everything hinged on what happened on a stretch of New Mexico desert near a former convent known as Los Alamos. On June 28 MacArthur announced that all of Luzon had been liberated. Eighteen days later Truman learned that the test at Los Alamos had been successful. On July 25 he gave his approval to dropping one atomic bomb on the Japanese city of Hiroshima, and if Japan did not then surrender, another on the city of Nagasaki.

There were many strategic reasons behind Truman's decision. But the steady buildup of Japanese forces on Kyushu, MacArthur's next destination, was one of the most important. Even as the *Enola Gay* was taking off from Tinian with its deadly cargo, a new ULTRA decrypt confirmed two more new divisions on Kyushu, raising the final estimate of the number of Japanese soldiers on the island to 560,000.[23]

That final report was dated August 7. The day before, the entire war—indeed, the entire history of warfare—had changed at Ground Zero at Hiroshima.

MacArthur learned what had happened from a copy of *Stars and Stripes* that same day. He had been in Manila almost a month, overseeing the United States' occupation and the transition to Philippine rule—and preparing for OLYMPIC in the autumn. A hospital had been set up in Manila of 30,000 beds, including a large psychiatric unit (troops on Okinawa had suffered more than 25,000 mental breakdowns). It was a chilling reminder of what the ultimate cost of the landing might be.[24]

The last days in June, he had gone off to watch the Australians in action one last time—the last amphibious landing of World War Two. It had been at the big oil terminal at Balikpapan, where the Australian Seventh Division splashed ashore in a nightmare landscape, with exploding oil-storage tanks filling the sky with belching black smoke and fiery red flames. It was a fitting Wagnerian scene with which to end the war in the Southwest Pacific, and the operation that achieved MacArthur's objectives of cutting Japan off, at last, from its vital supply of oil.

But it came too late to make a strategic difference. MacArthur was still operating under the assumption that he would be launching OLYMPIC in a few weeks, when he saw the headline in *Stars and Stripes:* ATOM BOMB DROPPED. His staff watched as he read over the story, slowly and carefully, then mounted the stairs to his office. On the way, he took the paper and read the story again.

"That's far beyond anything you can imagine," he murmured to his staff.[25]

"The development of nuclear weapons had not been revealed to me until just before the attack on Hiroshima," MacArthur wrote in his memoirs.[26] To his credit, his first thoughts were not about how he had been left out of the loop (although later he expressed anger that General Eisenhower had been informed of the Manhattan Project weeks before he was told of it), but what the impact would be on the Japanese war effort. He told an informal gathering of reporters that same day: "The war may be over sooner than some think. Things are in such a state of flux that anything can happen. The Japanese already are beaten, but their leaders hang on in the hopes of some break that will save them." Now the biggest break of all had doomed those hopes.

His remarks had been off-the-record, but to Doc Egeberg he was more direct.

"This will end the war," he said confidently. "It will seem superhuman— almost supernatural—and will give the Emperor and the Japanese people a face-saving opportunity to surrender. You watch, they'll ask for it pretty quick."[27]

Six days later his prediction proved correct. A Manila radio broadcast announced that Japan had accepted the Allies' terms for surrender. Hundreds of jubilant GIs gathered outside MacArthur's second-story office window and called for him to come out.

The MacArthur who appeared at the window was visibly moved, barely able to speak to the men he had led on the 3,000-mile journey from Brisbane through New Guinea and the Solomons to Manila.

"I hope from the bottom of my heart that this is the end of the war," he finally said. "If it is, it is largely due to your own efforts. Very soon, I hope, we will all be going home." Then he left as abruptly as he had appeared.[28]

The next day, August 12, MacArthur learned that he had been appointed by Truman—with Attlee, Stalin, and Chiang Kai-shek's approval—as supreme commander of the Allied powers in Japan or (SCAP), which meant he would oversee the occupation of Japan. He would also be the presiding officer at the formal surrender ceremony in Tokyo. Once again, there was no possible other choice. And perhaps it was compensation for the man who had just been denied the chance to command the greatest seaborne invasion in history.

On August 19 a delegation of Japanese arrived to negotiate the final terms of occupation. MacArthur refused to meet them; instead he left negotiations to Sutherland, Marshall, and the others on his staff. That took most of the night and a good deal of the next day. The Japanese were particularly miffed that the surrender document treated Emperor Hirohito without sufficient dignity. This was a matter of "extreme importance" to the Japanese people, they insisted; it might make the difference between the Japanese resisting the occupation, in spite of the surrender, rather than "enduring the unendurable," as the Emperor had asked them to in his post-surrender radio broadcast.

Sutherland took the matter to MacArthur. He agreed. "I have no desire whatever to debase him in the eyes of his own people," he told Sutherland. "[T]hrough him it will be possible to maintain a completely orderly government."

Already a strategy for dealing with a completely defeated nation, and its hitherto divine leader, was taking shape in his mind.[29]

It was also agreed that the first Americans would land at Atsugi air base, fifteen miles west of Yokohama, and that MacArthur himself would arrive there after a stopover on Okinawa, on August 26 (a series of typhoons sweeping through the area later forced them to change that date to August 30). There was no other location in Japan, the Japanese implied, where they could ensure MacArthur's safety—and even there, where thousands of kamikaze trainees were stationed, there was no guarantee there wouldn't be trouble.

MacArthur waved those worries aside. He had little to say that evening on the way home. His mind was filled with the plans for occupation, for demobilizing the Japanese army and beginning the process of rebuilding a shattered land and a defeated people. As he and Egeberg got out of the car, he simply remarked:

"No more shooting, Doc, no more shooting. Good night."[30]

Then he went in to tell Jean the news.

It was time to fly.

August 30, 1945, dawned clear and bright on Okinawa as MacArthur, Sutherland, and the others boarded *Bataan II,* the Douglas C-54 Skymaster successor to the B-17 that MacArthur had flown since 1942. At 9:00 A.M. precisely they took off and headed north. They were flying toward the Japanese mainland, with no more protection than a pair of B-17s escorting them. They were headed directly into what had been, barely two weeks before, the heart of the enemy's homeland—a trip three weeks before would have been unimaginable.

They were supposed to fly in the day before, with plans to land at Atsugi air base outside Yokohama. The Japanese had put them off and pleaded bad weather, but the truth was there had been a dustup. Atsugi had been a principal training base for kamikaze pilots; there were more than 30,000 of them still at the base or nearby. Army officials worried that some or all might rebel at the arrival of Americans, their mortal enemy for nearly four years—a rebellion that might trigger a national catastrophe.

The scenario was not so far-fetched. The very day that Hirohito had made his surrender speech, a team of army fanatics had swept into the Imperial Palace grounds, determined to cut off the broadcast. They had even killed the commanding general of the Imperial Guard, General Takeshi Mori, and burned down the prime minister's house before they were finally subdued.[31]

As it was, officials at Atsugi had to deal with nearly the same thing. They tried removing the propellers from the kamikaze planes to prevent them from taking off to intercept MacArthur. The fanatical young kamikazes fought back. Japanese troops had to open fire to put down the revolt.[32]

For all these reasons, Japanese officials had insisted that MacArthur mustn't land at Atsugi. So did his staff. As they pressed their case, MacArthur paced back and forth listening and thinking. He knew the stakes were high if something went wrong. In addition to the rebellious kamikazes at Atsugi, there were more than 150,000 Japanese soldiers in the Kanto plain of Tokyo, close to Yokohama. At the slightest outbreak of an incident—or a last-minute order from an officer they trusted—they would descend on the Americans and wreak havoc.

But MacArthur refused to budge. All the same, his doctor, Egeberg, could see he was ill at ease, thinking through the issues of postponing his arrival.

"For the supreme commander," as he summed it up years later, "a handful of his staff, and a small advance staff to land unarmed and unescorted where they would be outnumbered by thousands to one was foolhardy. But," he went on, "years of overseas duty had me well versed in the lessons of the Orient." Not to go would be a major loss of face; in addition, "what was probably more important," he had to reinforce the perception that he took the Japanese surrender at its word and would not back down no matter how many soldiers were still there.[33]

They were going forward.

At least the flight from Okinawa was on schedule.[34] In minutes they were airborne, banking up and north, toward Japan.

The mood was tense, alternately ebullient and anxious. Only a short time after takeoff the ocean dropped away, and land began to appear first on their port side, then straight ahead. Then MacArthur roused himself and began pointing out landmarks along the southern beaches of Honshu.

He knew this terrain well, if only from maps. If it hadn't been for the atomic bomb, troops from Eichelberger's Eighth Army and Lieutenant General John Hodge's XXIV Corps would have been landing on these beaches just eight months from that very day, as part of Operation CORONET.

Was MacArthur grateful for the atomic bomb? In fact, then and later MacArthur believed use of the bomb "was completely unnecessary from a military point of view," and that if the Potsdam July 26 ultimatum had included assurances that the emperor would not be removed or harmed, the Japanese would have capitulated there and then.[35]

Historians are free to disagree; but if the Japanese had *not* surrendered after Hiroshima and Nagasaki, MacArthur was quite prepared to go ahead with his DOWNFALL invasion plan, heavy casualties and all.

"Let me know when we get close to Mount Fuji," he told his pilot, Dusty Rhoades, and then headed aft.

Time for a nap, MacArthur had decided. It was going to be a long day, and he wanted to be as fresh as possible.[36]

As he dozed, the staff talked quietly among themselves. The land swept away below them, as they drew nearer and nearer to Yokohama and their destination. What was going to be awaiting them as they landed? MacArthur had heard reports that when the first U.S. troops arrived, 150 engineers and technicians, the "reception by Japanese was entirely correct." There were even pitchers of orange juice and rice wine to greet the first representatives of the American forces.[37]

But what would be the greeting for the American supreme commander once he was on Japanese soil—and completely cut off from his forces? "The war had started without a formal declaration," Courtney Whitney was thinking. "The usual rules of war had not been complied with; deadly traps had frequently been set. Here was the greatest opportunity for a final and climactic act," the assassination of the SCAP himself as he arrived at the Atsugi airport.

If that was the Japanese plan, there would be no Americans to prevent it from happening.

"I held my breath," Whitney remembered as they banked toward Yokohama, adding with only the slightest exaggeration, "I think the world held its breath."[38]

Dusty Rhoades came back from the cockpit and woke MacArthur up. Something you should see, sir, he said with a reassuring grin. MacArthur went forward.

There dead ahead was a great blue cone rising up from the landscape, capped with white. It was Mount Fuji.

"Beautiful!" Mac murmured. There wasn't far to go now.[39]

As the plane approached the mouth of Tokyo Bay, the passengers on *Bataan II* could glimpse an even more breathtaking sight.

It was the entire American Pacific Fleet, 280 ships drawn up in formation, waiting for the formal surrender ceremony. There were carriers by the dozen, battleships, cruisers, and destroyers: without doubt the single greatest armada in modern history.

Somewhere down there was Chester Nimitz, MacArthur realized. Nimitz had been his rival for command, and for a winning strategy, along with Nimitz's boss, Admiral King. In fact, Nimitz and MacArthur had gotten on better than many in the navy had expected. It was King who had retained the most bitter feelings toward MacArthur personally and had been his principal opponent in more than three and a half years of war.[40]

Yet on two of the most crucial decisions of the Pacific war, the encirclement of Rabaul and the invasion of the Philippines, King had given way to MacArthur and Marshall, and allowed his judgment to be overruled. Now they were all partners in the final defeat of Japan. And in a few days, MacArthur knew, they would be standing side by side as friends at the Japanese surrender ceremony—just as he and Dick Sutherland had planned it.

His mind, meanwhile, was racing with the job he now had to do. Courtney Whitney could hear him muttering to himself as he paced the length of the plane, planning in his mind the agenda to transform Japan.

"First destroy the military power . . . then build the structure of representative government," he was saying. "Enfranchise the women . . . liberate the farmers . . . Establish a free labor movement . . . Encourage a free economy . . . Develop a free and responsible press . . . Liberalize education . . ."[41]

Bataan II steadily lost altitude as the ground rushed up toward them. They slowly circled Atsugi at little more than treetop level. Whitney could plainly make out antiaircraft batteries scattered around the field, which only increased his worries. All it would take was one deadly accurate burst, and the whole adventure would be over.

Then it was wheels down as *Bataan II* swooped down toward the field. The landing was unsteady—"rubbery," one eyewitness said—but then the plane came to a halt and Dusty shut down the engines one by one.[42]

The cabin door opened. Steel steps with a railing clattered down to the concrete runway. MacArthur calmly lit his pipe and stepped out.

Overhead the sky was bright blue, with a few splotches of cloud. A beautiful day. It was the first time MacArthur had set foot on Japanese soil since he had visited the country as a young lieutenant forty years earlier—but now setting that foot was like satisfaction of a vow, and as sweet as victory.

There was no time to savor the moment in solitude. Cameras started clicking and whirring from the instant he emerged from the plane, and standing in front of him was General Eichelberger, along with the marching band of the Eleventh Airborne Division. They and a couple of thousand paratroopers had flown in a few hours earlier, just to secure the landing site, and now as the band struck up a march, Eichelberger strode forward and saluted.

"Bob, this is the payoff," MacArthur said with a grin. "From Melbourne to Tokyo is a long way, but this seems to be the end of the road."[43]

Eichelberger gave back a tense smile. He knew it could be the end of the road in more ways than one. Although he had full faith in his paratroopers and although the Japanese had behaved well so far, he knew standing on that runway he and MacArthur and the other Americans were outnumbered thousands to one. All it would take was "one undisciplined fanatic" to "turn a peaceful occupation into a punitive expedition," he remembered later, and MacArthur's triumphant landing into a bloodbath.[44]

But MacArthur wasn't worried. He smiled as the band played on. "Thank you very much," he called out to the bandleader. "I want you to tell the band that's about the sweetest music I've ever heard."[45]

The crowd of onlookers, Americans for the most part, but also some curious Japanese on the edge of the scene, continued to grow. The first of MacArthur's B-17 escorts landed, followed by the second three minutes later. Out of one stepped George Kenney and his staff; out of the other came General Carl Spaatz, head of the U.S. Strategic Air Force, and his aides.

Everyone was shaking hands and relaxing, even laughing, when MacArthur noticed something. Both Spaatz and Kenney were carrying sidearms, .45 pistols as a standard part of combat dress.

MacArthur shook his head. "Better leave the pistols behind," he cautioned. "There are fifteen fully armed Jap divisions within ten miles of us. If they decide to start something, those toy cannons won't do any good."[46]

Both generals put their guns back on their planes. Now all of them were standing, completely unarmed, on the runway surrounded by photographers, reporters, the Eleventh Airborne musicians, and a growing horde of curious passersby.

Now what? Sutherland and Marshall looked at each other. The agreement reached in Manila was that the Japanese would provide MacArthur's escort into Yokohama.

Then from the edge of the airstrip there appeared the strangest assortment of antique automobiles that MacArthur, Kenney, and the others had ever seen. They looked like the car pool from a Harold Lloyd silent movie. In fact, they were practically the only drivable civilian transport left in Yokohama, but MacArthur had been insistent that no military vehicles were to be used in the lead-up to the surrender ceremony, either Japanese or American. The war was over. He and his staff would be arriving as guests of the Japanese people, not as conquerors.

Still, someone pointed out, there was protocol to be observed. How about an honor guard for the supreme commander? So after a few minutes twenty troopers from the Eleventh Airborne were hustled up to act as honor guard, and they and MacArthur and the rest boarded the twelve-car motorcade.[47]

MacArthur's was an ancient Lincoln touring car, the one vehicle the staff judged the safest for him to drive. A rickety old fire engine led the way as the bizarre motorcade coughed and sputtered to life and finally drove off.

It was a long trip. The road into Yokohama was heavily cratered from the incessant American bombing, and the cars in the motorcade constantly broke down. It took almost two hours to travel thirty miles.

All around them was an empty landscape, an eerie silence, and an even eerier sight. The entire route to Yokohama was lined by Japanese soldiers—two divisions' worth, some 30,000 men—standing stiffly erect at present arms at hundred-foot intervals, but with their backs turned to the road. At first Egeberg and the others were puzzled, but the explanation slowly began to dawn. The soldiers were there to make sure that no one took a potshot at the motorcade, including the soldiers themselves.[48]

But there was also something happening, something that they learned about only later. This ceremonial salute was the kind of formal presentation of arms that the Japanese army usually reserved for the emperor himself.

For the first time Egeberg, Sutherland, and the others felt sure they were going to live to see the end of the day.

Indeed, there was no untoward incident, at the airport, on the way to Yokohama, or later. MacArthur's gamble was paying off.

"General MacArthur knew he had the Emperor's word and he trusted it," Egeberg would write later, "trusted it as the Emperor's honor and trusted the strength of the Emperor's word to control the Japanese people, including their army."[49]

The trust was also starting to flow the other way. His decision not to arrive with sidearms had not gone unnoticed, and the Japanese responded to his gesture of faith with a sigh of gratitude and relief. Winston Churchill's later verdict was that MacArthur's arrival at Atsugi was the single most courageous act of the war. But the new head of SCAP knew what he was doing.

"It was an exhibition of cool personal courage," the Japanese historian Kazuo Kawai wrote later. "[I]t was even more a gesture of trust in the good faith of the Japanese. It was a masterpiece of psychology which completely disarmed Japanese apprehensions."[50]

The danger of a mass Japanese uprising against the American occupiers vanished from that moment on.

* * *

The destruction that MacArthur and his entourage found in Yokohama was shattering. Eighty percent of the city had been destroyed by Curtis LeMay's B-29s, yet they could still clearly make out the streets and intersections. It turned out that most of Yokohama's bombed buildings hadn't had time to fall across a road; the mostly wooden structures had simply been scorched away in the firebombing, along with tens of thousands of their inhabitants.

Even MacArthur was shaken. "It brings in to you the horror of war," he told Egeberg, "total war. Those were civilians working and living there"—and now there was only a lifeless void.[51]

Considering the obliteration surrounding it, their destination, Yokohama's Grand Hotel, was remarkably intact. Built on a ridge along the waterfront, it had miraculously escaped the worst of the bombing. It was a square-built edifice in the European Art Deco style, with a dark, narrow lobby. Inside, the owner, an elderly Japanese gentleman in batwing collar and swallowtail coat, greeted his new tenants with a deep bow and offered the supreme commander a suite of rooms on the third floor. He also offered MacArthur a private room in which to dine (it was now early evening), but MacArthur said no, he would eat with his fellow officers.

The meal was simple: beans, bread and butter, and some cold meat. Whitney wondered if MacArthur shouldn't have someone taste the meat first, preferably someone Japanese. The general only laughed as he reached for his plate: "No one can live forever."[52]

That, too, was not lost on the Japanese who watched. Word got back to the hotel's owner, who rushed to reappear at MacArthur's elbow. He had heard from the hotel staff what had happened, he said, and he was "honored beyond belief." MacArthur, too, was secretly pleased. The news of his small gesture of trust, like that of the sidearms, would get around. He knew they had done good work that day, building the bond on which the American occupation would be secured.[53]

He was able to take another step in building that trust that next morning. They all woke up to a day of pouring rain. General Swing of the Eleventh

Airborne had to report that his men had found exactly one egg in the entire Yokohama area. MacArthur responded, It's all right. From now on, he ordered, American forces will live on their own rations, not from civilian sources.

"Willoughby tells me this country is close to starvation," he told Egeberg. "They sorely need meat or fish or soybeans." Instead of the Japanese having to feed their occupiers, as the orders from Washington had implied they should do—as was done with armies of occupation for centuries, even when MacArthur was in Germany in 1919—MacArthur was going to make sure the occupiers shared what they had with the Japanese. One of his top priorities, in fact, during the early days of the occupation would be steering army food stockpiles left over from the war to Japan to keep the country alive.[54]

That next day, September 1, they drove into Tokyo.

If anything, the destruction there was even more overwhelming and appalling. "Between seventy and eighty percent of the buildings had been destroyed, burned, bombed," Egeberg remembered years later. Amid the ruins they spotted large water-tank affairs, also smashed and blackened. When Egeberg asked what they were, a foreign service officer said they'd been built and filled with water so that Tokyo residents could jump in them during firebombing raids. They hadn't worked, the officer said. The people in them had simply been boiled to death in the intense heat.[55]

They stopped at the American embassy, which was still habitable and almost exactly as Ambassador Joseph Grew had left it when it closed that Sunday in December 1941. Most impressive of all was the Imperial Hotel built by Frank Lloyd Wright in the twenties and standing out stark and straight from the surrounding moonscape. Not far away was the Dai-ichi insurance building, also still largely intact. It was there that MacArthur and his team decided they would set up his headquarters as Supreme Command of the Allied Powers, or SCAP—what would be the nerve center of the American occupation.

They didn't stop to see the Imperial Palace or pay a call on Emperor Hirohito. That, MacArthur had decided, could wait for another day. Instead they headed back to Yokohama for an event that, in his mind, was more important than confronting the broken deity who had led his people into a calamitous war and catastrophic defeat.

Dinner that night at the Grand Hotel was more sumptuous than the previous night's meal. There was a long table lined with Allied officers—Americans, British, Australians, Canadians, even a couple of Soviets—who were trying to chat amiably in this strange, foreign ambience, made stranger by uniforms they had never seen and talk about battles in places others had never known existed. At least the food was good: rice, fish, soup, vegetables, and steak. Egeberg was surprised at the steak. "We hadn't brought it with us," so it was clearly a Japanese gesture of hospitality.[56]

Then suddenly an officer appeared at MacArthur's side and murmured in his ear. All eyes became riveted on the door, as the general leapt from his seat and dashed for the lobby.

There he found him.

"He was haggard and aged," MacArthur remembered later. "His uniform hung in folds on his fleshless form. He walked with difficulty and with the help of a cane. His eyes were sunken and there were pits in his cheeks. His hair was snow white and his skin looked like old shoe leather. He made a brave effort to smile as I took him in my arms, but when he tried to talk his voice wouldn't come."[57]

It was Wainwright. After V-J Day no one, not even the Japanese, had any idea exactly where he was. Finally the Russians had located him in a prison camp near Mukden in Manchuria. When he heard the news from Henry Stimson, MacArthur was frantic to get Wainwright to Japan in time for the surrender ceremony.[58] Getting him there had originally been George Marshall's idea, but MacArthur enthusiastically signed on and suggested that British General Percival, who had surrendered Singapore to the Japanese a month before the fall of the Philippines, be there too.

A CBS reporter was watching as the two men now met in the lobby of the Grand Hotel. "Without waiting for the formality of a salute," as he described it, "General MacArthur grabbed Wainwright's hand and put his arm around his shoulder in a half embrace." There was more emotion in Douglas's face than the reporter, who had covered him since New Guinea, ever remembered seeing there before.

"Jim . . . Jim," was all the usually eloquent MacArthur could say. It was the first time MacArthur had called him by his nickname, instead of Jonathan. "I'm glad to see you." He held him to look at, hands on both shoulders and eyes moist, then embraced him again. A camera caught the moment. MacArthur with his arm around the friend and colleague he had been forced to abandon in the Philippines; Wainwright overcome with emotion at the sight of his former commander in chief.

Then the moment was over. MacArthur led him into the dining room, where everyone rose and cheered and eyes teared and there were even shouts of "Skinny!"—Wainwright's West Point nickname—under the circumstances a nickname tinged with sardonic, even grotesque, humor.

They all sat down, with Wainwright at MacArthur's elbow. MacArthur kept gazing at his long-lost subordinate; Wainwright conveyed a similar affection for his rescuer. Those who expected him to be bitter or distant toward the commander who had "abandoned" him and his men were due to be disappointed.

They talked all through the meal. For four years, Wainwright confessed, he had expected a court-martial upon his release, for disobeying orders by surrendering. He certainly didn't expect this, to be welcomed like a returning hero. He told MacArthur that he had never thought he'd be allowed a command again.

"You can have any command you like," Colonel Mashbir overheard MacArthur say. "What would you like?"

"I want command of a corps," Wainwright said in a barely audible voice. "Any one of your corps."

MacArthur said, "You can have any one you want. Why, Jim," he said reassuringly, "your old corps is yours when you want it."[59]

Sadly, it wasn't to be. Wainwright's days in active service were numbered. His health broken, he was headed for retirement, not command. There was talk about a Medal of Honor—not for Bataan but for his endurance during four years of captivity. The fact that MacArthur had blocked the initial MOH recommendation would be conveniently forgotten.[60] But for MacArthur, the reappearance of his old subordinate and that of General Percival, who had also been released from captivity, changed the mood. By ten o'clock he had left the party. The next day he moved into a large house near the harbor, where he could pace and think.

The coming surrender ceremony weighed heavily on his mind. Everything had been planned down to the last detail, by Sutherland and a team from the United States Navy.[61] But the speech he would give when it all was over would be his own. "I had received no instructions as to what to say or what to do," even though it would be broadcast all around the world. "I was on my own . . . with only God and my own conscience to guide me."[62]

We know MacArthur wrote and rewrote the speech many times. We know he sought advice from a wide range of people, including his doctor, and surprisingly, took much of it.

He knew that in some ways it would have to transcend his usual eloquence—an eloquence some found overblown. In some ways, it would have to be even bigger than he was. This speech would have to not only end a war but begin a peace—and a new era of reconciliation with Japan. It would be a major piece in the strategy at which his every move since arriving at Atsugi had aimed: helping to create a new Japan—even a new Asia—that acknowledged the value of the past, but also set a firm new direction for the future.

The man who stood at the center of that strategy was the Japanese emperor, Hirohito. Nearly everyone in the Allied camp thought the man should be deposed; the British and Russians thought him a war criminal, and wanted him tried and executed as such. MacArthur had other plans for him. Hirohito would not be at the surrender ceremony; as he had been throughout the war, the emperor remained silent and ensconced in his Imperial Palace. But the two men would have to meet at some point in order for the American occupation—and the creation of a new destiny for Japan and Asia—to proceed. MacArthur was determined that he would have the upper hand at that meeting; and that it would set the tone for everything that unfolded afterward.

Until that happened, however, there was still the surrender itself.

CHAPTER 26

BRIEF ENCOUNTERS

Though I had defeated the Japanese in battle, I intended,
by means of the concepts of a free world, to win them in peace.

—DOUGLAS MACARTHUR

MacArthur rose before five to sit down with his staff for a breakfast of bacon and eggs, toast and jam. There was a discussion of possible last-minute glitches and missing people and what to do if that happened. But as a whole, every movement in the next six hours had been meticulously choreographed by MacArthur and his staff, and at 7:20 they drove off in MacArthur's car to see it done.

It was a gray, overcast day and they drove in silence. MacArthur's mind seemed far away, not just on the meaning of the surrender and what they had all been through, but on the next great drama to come.

"Dick," he asked suddenly, "are you meeting a representative of the emperor this afternoon?"

Sutherland said he was.[1]

Things were cold between them. After years of trust, Sutherland had ruined their relationship by his dalliance with Captain Clarke. When MacArthur discovered that Sutherland had brought her to Tanuan against his express orders, he had exploded in a rage at a level that no one had ever seen—even ordering Sutherland's arrest.[2] Captain Clarke had been sent packing back to Australia on *Bataan II*; Sutherland had been allowed to keep his job. But his days as part of MacArthur's staff were numbered.

Today, however, he had a vital role to perform, in overseeing the formal Japanese surrender ceremony on board the USS *Missouri*.

At the pier MacArthur and Sutherland were met by an honor guard and a military band; then everyone boarded the destroyer *Buchanan,* where they met the others who were assembling like the cast of characters in a play. Jim Wainwright was there, looking happy but subdued. Ennis Whitehead and General Thomas White of the Fifth Air Force were there also, along with General Kenney and General Jimmy Doolittle, who had last been on the scene in a B-25 flying hell-for-leather at a low level over Tokyo Bay in April 1942—the first indication to the Japanese that this war was not going to go all their way.

On their way out, there was a second breakfast and then everyone headed for the rail to watch as they approached the *Missouri*. Planes were constantly flying and circling overhead. The air seemed light and free despite the overcast skies, and then off the port side there appeared America's most advanced battleship.

It was "the most startling warship I had ever seen," Wainwright remembered as they gazed up at the gray hull looming above them. "I simply could not believe anything could be so huge, so studded with guns."[3] MacArthur had chosen the battleship as the scene for the surrender in honor of the new president, Harry Truman, whose home state was Missouri.

One by one they mounted the *Missouri*'s steps. Wainwright suddenly found himself greeted by a lusty cry of "Skinny!" He looked up. It was Admiral Bull Halsey, whom he had known since the early thirties and who now was pumping his hand and helping him up the ladder.

In a few minutes the atmosphere on deck became that of a happy class reunion. A great circle of men in starched khakis were standing and chatting, men who came from thousands of miles apart to be together at this moment. There were Halsey and Admiral John McCain; Bob Eichelberger and Walter Krueger; and General Percival, the former British commander at Singapore, looking almost as drawn and emaciated as Wainwright himself.

And there was Chester Nimitz. He was piped aboard the *Missouri* from another destroyer, and he and MacArthur had their first face-to-face meeting since the Japanese surrender in the admiral's cabin.

MacArthur's manner was friendly and matter-of-fact with everyone, but his face was tense. His doctor could see that he wanted to be alone. MacArthur had another, more pressing mission. He caught Dusty Rhoades's eye, signaled him to follow him, and left for the captain's head, or bathroom. With Rhoades guarding the door, MacArthur entered and closed the door. Rhoades could hear him retching inside. That old nervous reaction was back, the one that had nearly paralyzed him before his entrance exam for West Point and had him throwing up on the steps of the White House as army chief of staff.[4]

Rhoades asked him if he wanted a doctor.

"No, I'll be all right in a moment," MacArthur firmly replied.

Then he walked out, turned, and strode toward the deck.

There was history to be made.

The surrender was set to take place on the *Missouri*'s veranda deck, number two gun turret. The assemblage included British, Dutch, Chinese, Russian, and American officers, all in a bewildering variety of uniforms—while the battleship's entire complement, some 1,100 men, watched from every turret, stair, and vantage point they could find. There was also a microphone, where MacArthur would speak as he oversaw the ceremony—and explain to Americans everywhere by radio hookup not just what was happening, but what it meant.

"Was the day beclouded by mists or trailing clouds?" MacArthur wrote later. "I cannot remember but this I do—the all embracing pride I felt in my country's monumental victory."

Overhead was the flag that had flown from the United States Capitol on December 7, 1941. MacArthur had arranged that another flag be there as well: Commodore Matthew Perry's pennant from his visit to the same Tokyo Bay in 1853. MacArthur was a direct descendant of Commodore Perry's family, a distant cousin of the American who ninety-two years earlier had first tried to change Japan's ways at the point of a gun. Perry's "purpose was to bring to Japan an era of enlightenment and progress, by lifting the veil of isolation to the friendship, trade, and commerce of the world," MacArthur would say later. "But alas the knowledge thereby gained of western science was forged into an instrument of oppression and human enslavement."[5] MacArthur was determined not to let that happen again.

The tide of world affairs may ebb and flow, he was thinking, old empires may die, new nations be born; alliances may arise, thrive, wither, and vanish. "But in its effort to build economic growth and prosperity, an atmosphere of hope and freedom, a community of strength and unity of purpose . . . my own beloved country now leads the world."[6] After all the sacrifice in two world wars, MacArthur could embrace that proposition with pride.

Then everyone's excitement turned to high tension. The word was out: the Japanese officials were arriving on board. Heads swiveled to watch the ladder where they would be coming up from the deck below.

"Suddenly the major part of a silk hat appeared," Doc Egeberg remembered, "then almost disappeared." Then the hat again, this time with a face: that of Foreign Minister Mamoru Shigemitsu, in formal hat and cutaway coat.[7]

No senior Japanese official had wanted to be there. All of them considered signing the surrender document a humiliation; they would rather die, they said, than be part of it. So at the last minute the emperor had to give the order to Shigemitsu, who had accepted as an act of duty and honor to his emperor regardless of the humiliating circumstances. "We must endure the unendurable," Hirohito had told his people the day he announced Japan's surrender. For Shigemitsu, this was his part.

Then came General Yoshijiro Umzedu, chief of the general staff. He had threatened to commit hara-kiri rather than go to the ceremony on the *Missouri* until the emperor's express order forced him to suppress his feelings.[8] Coming with him were six other officers and two civilians.

Both of the civilians were foreign ministry officials. One, Katsuo Okazaki, had been consul general of Hong Kong when the war broke out. The other was Toshikazu Kase, who happened to be a graduate of Amherst and Harvard and had been added to the entourage at the last minute.

It had not been a pleasant journey for them. First, they had had to thread their way through the devastation of Tokyo, then sail through the harbor past line after line of American warships, "the mighty pageant of the Allied navies," Kase remembered in a flight of poetry, "that so lately belched forth their crashing battle, now holding in their swift thunder and floating like calm sea birds on the subjugated water." Nearly two hundred and sixty warships, to be exact, but no aircraft carriers. Those were on alert farther out at sea, in case the Japanese changed their minds at the last minute.

There was a strange moment as the Japanese delegation, all now on deck, moved toward the dais. Foreign Minister Shigemitsu spotted a Canadian doctor in the crowd—the same doctor, as it happened, who had saved his life in Shanghai in the1930s when a bomb had cost the Japanese diplomat his leg. Shigemitsu smiled and almost waved. Then he caught himself, and moved on.

All stood solemnly as a navy chaplain read a brief prayer. Then a windup phonograph played a tinny rendition of "The Star-Spangled Banner" with the crew and officers of the *Missouri* all watching from every deck and gallery.

As the music played, Toshikazu Kase glanced at his fellow Japanese. He thought they looked like penitent schoolboys waiting for the stern headmaster. "There were a million eyes beating us in the million shafts of a rattling storm of arrows barbed with fire," he remembered. "I felt their keenness sink into my body with a sharp physical pain. Never have I realized that the glance of glaring eyes could hurt so much."[9]

Then MacArthur stepped forward to the microphone and the mood changed.

"We are gathered here, representatives of the major warring powers," he began in his dark, husky voice, "to conclude a solemn agreement whereby peace may be restored." His hand was shaking, his forehead sweating. The moment was heavy on everyone's mind, so much so that few noticed at first the words he had chosen. Not "unconditional surrender of Japan" but "restoration of peace." But Kase, who understood English, did.

"It is my earnest hope," MacArthur went on, "and indeed the hope of all mankind that from this solemn occasion a better world shall emerge out of the blood and carnage of the past. . . . As Supreme Commander for the Allied Powers, I announce it my firm purpose, in the tradition of the countries I represent, to proceed in the discharge of my responsibilities with justice and tolerance, while taking all necessary dispositions to insure that the terms of surrender are fully, promptly and faithfully complied with."

Peace restored; justice and tolerance; also faith and understanding. It seemed a very unusual way to proclaim victory after the bloodiest, bitterest conflict in history, especially one in which Japanese and Americans had hunted each other like jungle animals in the mountains of New Guinea, the caves of Peleliu and Iwo Jima, and the alleyways of Intramuros. It had been a war without mercy, without pity or understanding, or so it seemed.

Then the ceremony began.

The Japanese delegates stepped forward to the table to sign the surrender documents. One set was bound in dark green leather. That was the American copy. The other was in a cheap black binding. That was Japan's. Shigemitsu put his silk hat and white gloves on the table, but then seemed confused what to do next.

MacArthur's voice rang out like a shot. "Sutherland, show him where to sign."[10]

A grim-faced Sutherland did, with an extended forefinger. Then General Umzedu signed for the Japanese military, and MacArthur called on Wainwright and Percival to step forward and bear witness as MacArthur himself signed.

He sat at the table and from his pocket extracted six pens. Six pens to sign, six pens to remember the moment forever.

One for the National Archives. One for West Point. One for the Naval Academy at Annapolis, a gesture to the navy.

One was for Jim Wainwright, and one for Percival, emblems of the final removal of the shame of surrender.

The last one was a small red pen with an inscription in gold letters that read simply, "Jean."

MacArthur then rose, and it was the turn of the other Allied representatives. Chester Nimitz was first, then representatives of China, the United Kingdom, the USSR, Australia, Canada, France, the Netherlands, and New Zealand.

When all had signed, MacArthur had the last word. "Let us pray that peace be now restored to the world and that God will preserve it always," he intoned.

"These proceedings are *closed.*"

Then a roar went up—not cheering, but hundreds of planes, including 400 B-29s in formation overflight and 1,500 navy planes, the greatest overflight in history. The day had started under a heavy overcast; planners had wondered if the overflight would have to be canceled. But as the signing ceremony ended, the skies mysteriously cleared and the sun peeked out over Tokyo Harbor. And so the American planes, the instruments of final victory, flew over the scene, the shadow of their wings passing over the blackened remains of Tokyo.[11]

"Today the guns are silent. A great tragedy has ended. A great victory has been won."

It was MacArthur speaking to the American public in a radio broadcast from the deck of the *Missouri* after the signing ceremony had ended. He was finally delivering the speech he had written and rewritten in the days after the fighting had ended.

"A new era is upon us," he said. "Even the lesson of victory itself brings with it profound concern, both for our future security and the survival of civilization. The destructiveness of the war potential, through progressive advances in scientific discovery, has in fact now reached a point which revises the traditional concept of war."

Peace, MacArthur said, could now be attained only by a change of heart and spirit, as well as alliances and balance of power. Then he spoke of Japan.

"We stand in Tokyo today reminiscent of our countryman Commodore Perry ninety-two years ago. His purpose was to bring to Japan an era of enlightenment and progress by lifting the veil of isolation to the friendship, trade, and commerce of the world." Now, MacArthur believed, in the aftermath of total victory America had that chance to set Japan's and Asia's hearts and minds free from a brutal, oppressive past.

The dream of America's role in Asia that his father had unveiled more than sixty years earlier would finally be realized.

"We are committed by the Potsdam Declaration of Principles to see that the Japanese people are liberated from this condition of slavery. It is my purpose to implement this commitment . . . If the talents of the [Japanese] race are turned into constructive channels, the country can lift itself from its present deplorable state into a position of dignity."

That was why MacArthur had brought Perry's flag to the surrender ceremony, not as a banner of triumph but as a pledge of hope—a pledge, he believed, that extended not just to Japan but to all the peoples of Asia, whose "unshackled peoples are tasting the full sweetness of liberty, the relief from fear," he concluded.[12]

But he would start in Japan. His model would be what his father and others, including himself, had tried to do for the Philippines. The fostering of democratic institutions, the inculcation of the idea of individual rights and equal opportunity, of the rule of law, even the encouragement and spread of Christianity—in MacArthur's mind these would be the hallmarks of his work with the Japanese people. He was firmly convinced he and the Americans would replace iniquity and fanaticism with the spirit of charity and truth.

How would the Japanese themselves react? In Toshikazu Kase's case, standing on deck in his morning suit and listening and watching behind his thick glasses, his mood had undergone a radical shift.

"Is it not a piece of rare good fortune, I asked myself, that a man of such caliber and character should have been designated as the Supreme Commander who will shape the destiny of Japan? In the dark hour of our despair and distress, a bright light is ushered in, in the very person of General MacArthur."[13]

MacArthur's last words, however, were for his soldiers, sailors, and airmen.

"Their spiritual strength and power has brought us through to victory. They are homeward bound—take care of them."

Many, of course, were *not* going home. They would be the occupation forces under MacArthur's command, who would see to the dismantling of the still-formidable Japanese war machine in Japan and across its former empire—and to maintaining peace and order if civil society collapsed.

That seemed likely, if not certain. The Japanese and the people they had conquered had suffered death, starvation, and epidemic disease during the course of this war, the most destructive Asia had ever witnessed. An estimated seventeen million people had died at the hands of the Japanese, almost all of them noncombatants. Japan itself had lost nearly five million people. In addition, there were deep resentments and social divisions within Japan itself—between rich and poor, workers and industrialists, Western-educated urbanites and a Japanese army drawn from poor rural areas—which had been kept under iron clamp by the military regime for decades, but which were now free to surge to the surface.

"After this terrible fury," as historian John Dower states, "Japan entered a strange seclusion"—one from which it could emerge whole or bitterly resentful toward the victors, much as Germany had done after World War One.[14]

In short, if MacArthur and the Americans made a single serious misstep, the result could be chaos—and not just in Japan.

Five days after the *Missouri* ceremony, the port of Inchon on the Korean peninsula had a visitor. He was a lean, hard-faced man dressed in starched fatigues and a battered American officer's cap. Lieutenant General Hodge and his troops of XXIV Corps had been ordered there to disarm Japanese troops on the peninsula and to maintain law and order.

Despite the ecstatic cheers that greeted Hodge and his men as they marched from Inchon to the city of Seoul, he sensed that his task was not going to be easy. Korea's last independent government had ended in 1910, when it had been swallowed up by the Japanese empire. Now with the Japanese surrender, virtually every trace of civil authority had collapsed. Nationalist groups of all political stripes were surging around Seoul, the old Korean capital, all claiming to represent the Korean people and all demanding that they, not their rivals, be put in charge of a future independent Korea.

Koreans could be tough, outspoken, and brusque. Now they were also seething with impatience. Behind the ecstasy of liberation was a tense atmosphere of latent violence, even civil war.

Hodge was a soldier's soldier, who had fought his way from Guadalcanal and Bougainville, where he had commanded a division before leading the XXIV Corps in the fierce fighting on Leyte and at Okinawa. Now he had a very different job: governing a foreign people after their liberation from a brutal colonial ruler. He was going to have to be part statesman, part judge and arbitrator, part economist, and part policeman—all the skills that had come naturally to the MacArthurs, father and son, but for which Hodge was in no way prepared.

Still, as he gazed at the American flags waving at him from the happy throngs in Seoul, he knew there was one headache he didn't have to deal with. A month before he arrived and days after Russia declared war on Japan in August, thousands of Russian troops had poured into Manchuria and Korea. They had ruthlessly hacked their way down the peninsula and had gotten as far as Seoul and then Inchon, before the Japanese surrender. Postwar planners back at the Pentagon had worried that this left no clear line of jurisdiction between American and Russian occupation forces—and also worried that if the Russians overran the entire peninsula, the Americans would never get in at all.

For administrative purposes "we have got to divide Korea," one of them, a brigadier general said. "Where can we divide it?"

They were all gazing at a map of a country thousands of miles away that none of them had ever visited—none, that is, except one of the colonels standing around the table. He had visited Korea several times and protested that no one could really divide the country. Geographically, linguistically, culturally, and economically, it formed a single unit.

The harassed general answered, "We've got to divide Korea, and we've got to do it by four o'clock this afternoon."

Then a young captain who had recently come back from the China-Burma theater had a suggestion. He pointed to the line of latitude that ran through what looked like the narrowest point of the peninsula.

The map designated it the 38th parallel. Everyone nodded; that would work. They alerted the Russians, who, somewhat to the Americans' surprise, agreed. Within days of the XXIV Corps' arrival they marched back across the 38th parallel and gathered their forces around the city of Pyongyang, north of the demarcation line but still less than forty miles from Seoul.

And there they were going to stay, Hodge knew. He was now free to get on with disarming the Japanese soldiers still south of the 38th parallel, and securing order and peace.

In idle moments, Hodge may have wondered who the army captain was who had come up with that line of demarcation.

His name, as it happened, was Dean Rusk.[15]

Douglas MacArthur was now the most powerful American in history.

He was the sole ruler of a country of eighty million people whose entire governing structure had been shattered along with its major cities: Almost 700,000 homes had been obliterated in Tokyo alone. He was also Japan's first foreign ruler in more than two thousand years.

But MacArthur's powers extended far beyond Japan. As head of AFPAC he led no fewer than six major military commands. There were the Sixth and Eighth Armies acting as occupation forces in Japan, commanded by his old colleagues Walter Krueger and Robert Eichelberger, respectively; the U.S. Army Forces in the West Pacific, which comprised the Philippines and the Ryukyu Islands, including Okinawa; U.S. Army Forces in the Middle Pacific, and General Hodge's U.S. Army Forces in Korea. MacArthur was also head of Pacific Air Command, U.S. Army, with Ennis Whitehead in charge, which included planes, bases, and bomber and fighter squadrons both in and around Japan, like Atsugi, in the Philippines, islands in the central Pacific, and even as far away as Honolulu.

Altogether MacArthur was supreme commander of almost 1.7 million Americans under arms, and although that number would be sharply reduced before 1945 was out, it made him the undisputed master of an area even larger than the one he had commanded as SWAP, albeit far more populous, and more vitally strategic to the rest of the world.

Only the U.S. Navy remained outside his control. He angrily rebuffed efforts to unify army and navy commands into two separate West Pacific and Central Pacific theaters, a plan urged by both Eisenhower and Chester Nimitz, who became chief of naval operations in Washington in November 1945.[16]

This was precisely the kind of unification of command in the Pacific that MacArthur had been advocating since 1942, but now he turned it down. In the aftermath of war, he was happy to sacrifice unity to make sure that no one interfered with his power to use the army when, where, and how he and he alone wanted to shape the future of Japan.

That also included America's erstwhile allies. In MacArthur's mind, now that the war was over, he owed nothing to the historic alliance that had won it. He fully bowed to the authority of the declaration signed by Truman, Stalin, and Attlee at Potsdam in July—the one to which he owed his supreme position. All the same, this occupation was going to be a United States show, and no one else's. In 1946 he eventually allowed a token force of 36,000 ANZAC, British, and even Indian troops to join the occupation forces, but they always remained under MacArthur's operational control and under General Eichelberger's direct command.[17]

There was one ally, however, whom MacArthur would never allow to set foot on Japanese soil, and that was Russia.

He had understood the logic of having Russia enter the war against Japan—if events had forced an invasion, Russia would have provided a useful second front. But the fact that Stalin had entered the war only two days before the bomb dropped on Hiroshima, and used it to snatch Manchuria, the Kuril Islands, and the Sakhalin peninsula away from Japan, did not in MacArthur's mind entitle the Soviet Union to any role in shaping the future of a country that so many Americans had sacrificed their lives in order to defeat.

Stalin and his foreign minister, Molotov, saw things differently. They pushed for the kind of joint four-power occupation that was taking place in Germany, and assumed that the joint declaration on the future of Japan made at the Potsdam conference in July would provide the framework for it—including the installation of Soviet occupation forces.[18]

Although Washington was as suspicious of Stalin's motives as MacArthur was, it reluctantly conceded the principle of a joint occupation. It even set up a four-power Far Eastern Commission in Washington to oversee the process. MacArthur, however, was adamant. There would be no Soviet troops in Japan, ever.

That led to a head-on confrontation with Lieutenant General Kuzma Derevyanko, the Soviet liaison in Tokyo, who asserted Russia's right to occupy Hokkaido, Japan's northernmost island. MacArthur said no. The discussion grew heated and Derevyanko became "abusive," according to

MacArthur's later account. He began shouting that he would see to it that MacArthur was fired and that Soviet troops would arrive in Hokkaido, whether MacArthur wanted them to or not.

"If a single Russian soldier enters Japan without my permission," MacArthur thundered, "I will at once throw the entire Russian mission, including yourself, in jail."

Derevyanko sat back, stunned. Then he muttered, "By God, I believe you would," and walked out. No Soviet troops ever landed on Hokkaido or anywhere else in Japan, and MacArthur heard nothing more about it.[19]

Nor did he pay much attention to what the Far Eastern Commission in Washington said or did in the four years of its existence, until the final signature of the peace treaty with Japan brought it to an end. "Not one constructive idea to help with the reorientation and reconstruction of Japan ever came from the Far Eastern Commission," he later wrote, or its satellite body, the Allied Council, of which he said, "its sole contribution being that of nuisance and defamation."[20]

MacArthur intended to be in total charge, and he soon made it clear that he would brook no opposition—even from the highest levels in Washington.

There the decision to entrust all this power to MacArthur had not been uncontroversial.

Feelings toward MacArthur in the Truman White House and the cabinet ranged from distrust to hatred and contempt. As New Deal Democrats, they were bound to view an unabashed Republican and a conservative with misgiving, but then so had Roosevelt. With Truman the antagonism ran deeper, even though the two of them had never met. Truman minced no words in describing his feelings toward MacArthur, then or later: "Mr. Prima Donna, Brass Hat, Five Star MacArthur. He's worse than the Cabots and Lodges: they talked with one another before they told God what to do. MacArthur tells God right off."

Much of the problem was bitter feelings over the Bataan debacle. Most believed the "Dugout Doug" myth: Senator Tom Connolly, the powerful Senate majority leader, referred to MacArthur as "Dugout Doug" even in private conversations. Like Eisenhower, Truman privately bemoaned the fact that it was Wainwright who had been left behind and MacArthur who had been rescued, rather than the other way around. "We'd have had a real General and a fighting man if we had Wainwright," Truman said, "and not a play actor and a bunco man."[21]

Both ignored the fact that no general, no matter how bold or skilled, could have held on in the Philippines or that MacArthur had then proceeded to destroy Japan's empire in the South Pacific, and liberate the Philippines, with proportionately fewer casualties than his Central Pacific rival, Admiral Nimitz. On the contrary, Truman and Secretary of the Interior Harold Ickes, another MacArthur hater, blamed FDR for having burdened America with "Mr. Prima Donna" in the first place, both by rescuing him from the Philippines and by then putting him in command of the Japan invasion forces. They never wavered in their belief that Roosevelt's decision to stick with MacArthur had been political rather than strategic, as a way to defuse Republican criticism and to sideline a possible presidential rival.

"FDR was always afraid of MacArthur," Truman told Kenney's former airfield builder Jack Sverdrup, who was now based in Washington, "and seemed to think he might have tremendous political power." Now it was Truman's turn to be nervous about what MacArthur might do, since the war was over and a presidential election was looming in 1948.[22]

All in all, the consensus within the postwar Democratic Party and the Truman administration was that appointing MacArthur supreme commander of SCAP was a mistake. But as Harold Ickes admitted to Truman, the decision was probably unavoidable. Deny him the appointment, Ickes grumbled, and the GOP would make a martyr out of him and a candidate for president. By sticking him out in Japan and the Pacific, preoccupying him with matters of demobilizing and reforming Japanese society, both men reasoned, MacArthur would be marginalized and have no input about policy where it really counted: dealing with the menacing Soviet presence in Europe. Given MacArthur's outspoken anti-Communist proclivities, it made sense not to have him casting public pronouncements on how to handle Stalin and his allies.

In any case, strict rules had been drawn up to govern the occupation, in a comprehensive plan from the Joint Chiefs of Staff. It had reached MacArthur on August 29 as he was about to leave Okinawa. The plan reflected the agreement that Truman, Churchill, and Stalin had reached at Potsdam, allowing for "the eventual establishment of a peaceful and responsible government" in Japan, but through democratic means by the Japanese people themselves and not by forcible imposition at the point of a bayonet.

The document also dictated the terms for disarmament and demobilization of Japan's armed forces of 6.9 million men; for disbanding of military and secret police, and trying of Japanese accused of war crimes; the establishment of the rule of law and the freedom of worship; protection of civil liberties and civil rights, including for women; legalization of unions and the reform of Japan's agriculture; and the breakup of the military-industrial complex that Japan's massive *zaibatsu* corporations had set up and overseen.

MacArthur approved the plan. He already had the basic outline in his head when they left Okinawa for Tokyo; he had recited it to Courtney Whitney on the way over on the plane. But he also took to heart the directive in Part II of the plan, that "the policies of the United States will govern" all matters through the supreme commander, who will be free to exercise "his authority through Japanese governmental machinery and agencies, including the Emperor."[23]

The Joint Chiefs instructed MacArthur, "The plight of Japan is the direct outcome of its own behavior, and the Allies will not undertake the burden of repairing the damage." Instead, "Japan will be expected to provide goods and services to meet the needs of the occupying forces."[24]

At the end of the day, MacArthur had all the authority he needed to do as he wished because Washington had given it to him. He would not hesitate to wield his absolute power, even if it meant collision with the administration.

That actually didn't take long. Just nine days after arriving in Tokyo, MacArthur set off a major explosion revolving around the size of the occupation force itself. What seemed an elementary issue actually had potentially huge political implications, as MacArthur soon discovered.

Japan's sudden surrender in August 1945 had caught policymakers at the War Department by surprise. By then there were more than 8 million Americans in army uniform, and while the draft had been sharply curtailed in anticipation of final victory, no one assumed they were going to finish the year with standing forces of anything less than 6.8 million men.[25]

A week after Nagasaki those numbers looked absurdly high. Even with American forces occupying the two major ex-belligerents, Germany and Japan, the pressure to demobilize as soon as possible was "terrific," as General Marshall noted to Ike as early as August 14—as was the nation's desire to end the draft now that peace had finally broken out.[26]

To the War Department, and to Army Chief of Staff Marshall, however, the future looked less sanguine. They weren't so eager to shrink U.S. forces by half or even two-thirds, as some were urging. The global situation was still unstable: chaos in Asia, massive devastation across Europe, and above all the looming threat of the Soviet Union. Showing strength through numbers looked attractive.

One way to impress upon the public the need for maintaining American military strength, they decided, would be to call for a big occupation force in Japan. Department planners thought 400,000 troops would be about right; possibly even 500,000. Numbers like that, and similar ones for Europe, would also require maintaining a peacetime draft—another War Department goal that was deeply unpopular with the public. The Pentagon and President Truman were anxious for MacArthur to go along with this strategy, and told him so.

But MacArthur supporter and West Point classmate Robert Wood of Sears, Roebuck, saw something else at work. He warned MacArthur that supporting such a large occupation army would actually make him the target of hostility back in the States. It certainly would "put the burden of blame on you if you should demand a very large army of occupation, which would have to be maintained through a draft. . . . The commander who demands an exorbitant army will later be pilloried, in my opinion, in the eyes of the public."[27]

That was what Democrats who were worried about MacArthur's presidential aspirations in 1948 would prefer, Wood suggested, and why they were proposing the idea in the first place.

Deliberate trap by his enemies or not, MacArthur was in no mood to fall for it. Wood in his letter suggested that 300,000 or even 200,000 troops might be enough, and MacArthur came to agree. So on September 17 he shocked everyone—including the Japanese—by stating that the occupation would require far fewer than half a million men. By using the Japanese government itself, he said, to help maintain order, reestablish essential services, and prevent possible starvation and outbreaks of epidemics, "Within six months the occupational force, unless unforeseen factors arise, will probably not number more than 200,000 men." Then once the military phase of occupation was over, MacArthur averred, the full integration of Japan back into the community of nations, with the help of the United Nations, could begin. Either way, he was implying, the timetable was a lot shorter than anyone, especially anyone in the War Department, ever expected. One of his subordinates even stated that the entire occupation might be over in just a year.[28]

When MacArthur's words hit the news wires, Washington exploded. Truman raged that the statement was contrary to policy and "was wholly uncalled for" and would do a "great deal of damage." He had an even more volatile outburst in the presence of his assistant press secretary.

"I'm going to do something about that fellow," the usually tight-lipped president muttered, "who's been balling things up. I'm tired of fooling around." When someone suggested using the crisis as an excuse to fire MacArthur, however, Truman drew back. Instead, his own public statement was supportive: "I'm glad to see the general won't need as many [troops] as he first thought. He said first 500,000, later 400,000, and now 200,000"—conveniently suggesting that it was MacArthur, not the administration, who had pushed the higher number and was now backing away from it.[29]

Even so, the diplomatic blowback was considerable. Australia, Great Britain, and the other Allies all wanted reassurance that the changing numbers didn't reflect a softening on policy toward Japan. Marshall sent a sharp telegram off to MacArthur telling him that the effect of his statement was to "embarrass or prejudice War Department efforts" to handle the postwar situation, including Selective Service, and admonishing him to henceforth "coordinate" all public statements and press releases regarding demobilization and garrison requirements with the War Department.

After catching an earful from the embassies of America's allies, Truman's acting secretary of state also issued a statement denying that "anybody can see at this time the number of forces that will be necessary" to keep order and security and adding tartly, "the occupation forces are instruments of policy and not the determinants of policy."[30]

MacArthur was completely unruffled. "There was not the slightest thought that my statement . . . would cause the slightest embarrassment," he told Marshall. As far as he was concerned, his September 17 statement had been perfectly in line with War Department policy, and he intended for things to stay that way. In MacArthur's mind, that was the end of it. All the diplomatic upheaval it was causing, and all the gnashing of teeth at the White House, mattered to him as much as doings on the moon.[31]

As for the acerbic public rebuke from the acting secretary of state, MacArthur never replied, but he would remember the man's name: Dean Gooderham Acheson. They were never destined to be friends; over the next half decade they would prove to be more than a match for each other in assertiveness, egotism, and pride—and in articulately defending policy preferences that, as time went on, would drift further and further apart.

The result was a clash of wills that would reach a crescendo on Korea's snow-covered slopes south of the Yalu River.

For now, however, MacArthur didn't care. No one in Washington, not even the president, was going to interfere with the role destiny had carved out for him in Japan.

One of his first official visits was to the American embassy in Tokyo, which, considering that the rest of the city had been firebombed into nonexistence, was remarkably intact. Only the chancellery roof had been damaged; the rest of the embassy was almost exactly as Ambassador Joseph Grew had left it in December 1941. There was even a portrait of George Washington still hanging on the wall. MacArthur stopped to look at it, drew himself to full attention, and saluted.

"Sir, they weren't wearing red coats," someone heard him say, "but we whipped them just the same."[32]

The stage was now set for the American occupation of Japan, and for MacArthur's leadership in reshaping that country into a peaceful member of the world community, symbolized by the newly formed United Nations, as well as molding it into a friend, rather than a foe, of the United States. MacArthur knew that there was one man, and one man only, who would determine whether that goal was realized, and whether his leadership of the occupation proved a success or failure.

That man was Emperor Hirohito, still hidden and aloof in the Imperial Palace. But unbeknownst to MacArthur, he had already made a favorable impression on the Japanese ruler's consciousness. Even as MacArthur, Acheson, and Truman were arguing over future troop levels, the emperor had pored over a document in Japanese that was lying on his desk. It was Toshikazu Kase's description of the surrender ceremony, and of the shift in mood from humiliation and despair to optimism and hope, after MacArthur's words on the deck of the *Missouri*.

It contained this description of the new commander of SCAP:

"He is a man of peace. Never has the truth of the line 'peace has her victories no less renowned than war' been more eloquently demonstrated. He is a man of light. Radiantly, the gathering rays of his magnanimous soul embrace the earth; his footsteps paving the world with light . . . General MacArthur [is] a shining obelisk in the desert of human endeavor that marks a timeless march onward toward an enduring peace."[33]

These were words of praise that were usually reserved for the Tenno himself. Hirohito might have been justified in being miffed. Instead, he was relieved. There might be hope for an opening, after all.

Yet for three weeks the two men did not meet.

MacArthur was unperturbed. Ordering Hirohito to visit "would be to outrage the feelings of the Japanese people and to make a martyr of the Emperor in their eyes," he told his staff. "No, I shall wait, and in time the Emperor will voluntarily come to me." Then he smiled sardonically. "In this case, the patience of the East rather than the haste of the West will best serve my purpose."[34]

Instead, he would begin with the foreign minister, Shigemitsu.

Their meeting on September 2 after the surrender ceremony, was intense. MacArthur told him three proclamations were to be put into effect immediately. The first imposed SCAP's military control over all Japan. The second ordered that any Japanese who violated the terms of surrender or "does any act calculated to disturb the public peace" would be tried by military court. The third imposed a new military occupation currency to replace the Japanese yen.

Shigemitsu was "stunned." Word of these proclamations would set Japanese-American occupation relations on the wrong foot, he told MacArthur bluntly. He pointed out they were addressed "to the people of Japan," thus completely bypassing the cabinet and existing government. This would shake what was left of the ruling order loose from its foundations. Instead, he urged MacArthur to look for ways to set up close cooperation between the Japanese government, broken and discredited though it was, and SCAP.

"Should the government fail to fulfill its duties, or should the occupation authorities feel the government's policies are unsatisfactory," Shigemitsu said, "then direct orders could be issued by the occupation officials." But not before, he pleaded.

MacArthur listened, and then said, "I have no intention of destroying the nation or making slaves of the Japanese people." The purpose of the occupation was getting the Japanese people back on their feet. "If the government showed good faith, [then] problems could be solved easily." MacArthur then turned to Sutherland, and told him all three proclamations were to be scrapped.[35]

It was a major step forward in occupation relations. To Japanese officials, MacArthur now appeared to be someone amenable to reason, a force to be feared and obeyed but also one willing to listen. Here was a man they could deal with. For MacArthur, it was a lesson in the exercise of absolute power. Three days later, he received a directive from the Joint Chiefs reminding him "our relations with Japan do not rest on a contractual basis, but on an unconditional surrender" and "the authority of the Emperor and the Japanese government to rule the State is subordinate to you as Supreme Commander for the Allied Powers," and "you will exercise your authority as you deem proper to carry out your mission."[36]

Yet there was a difference in having supreme authority over 80 million people in a formal sense, and how it was exercised. MacArthur was determined not to repeat the mistakes that had been made in Germany after World War One; his goal was not just occupation of a defeated nation, but the transformation of its entire culture and society. He decided from the start that it would have to be done with Japanese cooperation, including that of former power-wielders in the old imperial government.

Still, he was also determined that no one, including those in the United States, mistake restraint for weakness. "I have noticed some impatience in the press based upon the assumption of a so-called soft policy," MacArthur told a klatch of reporters on September 14. "The surrender terms are not soft and they will not be applied in kid-gloved fashion." When he learned that Shigemitsu had leaked details about their meeting to the Japanese media, MacArthur refused to have any more dealings with him. The foreign minister was forced to step down from the cabinet.[37]

And still the emperor did not come.

The Dai-ichi Life Insurance Company's home office was a massive granite building erected just before the war. It had survived the firebombing of Tokyo; even its air-conditioning system still functioned. MacArthur installed himself and his staff on the building's top floor, while Jean and Arthur moved into the MacArthurs' personal residence on Renanzaka Hill inside the U.S. embassy compound, just five minutes away by car.

Like all his offices, MacArthur's new one was spare. There were two comfortable leather couches in front of a large green-baize-covered desk. On the desk he kept a wooden in-and-out tray, pencils and a notepad, and not much more. MacArthur disliked having a telephone on his desk or an intercom system. He preferred a small buzzer he could use to summon his chief of staff or an aide, depending on the number of buzzes.

Along the wall were a glass-enclosed bookcase, some upholstered chairs, and a stand with the flags of his various commands, including that of SCAP. Behind his desk hung two portraits, George Washington and Abraham Lincoln, and in the middle a framed quotation from the Roman historian Livy that read in part:

I am not one of those who think that commanders ought at no time to receive advice; on the contrary, I should deem that man more proud than wise, who regulated every proceeding by the standard of his own single judgment.

Balancing that rather humble sentiment was a quotation from Abraham Lincoln mounted under the picture of the sixteenth president:

If I were to try to read, much less answer, all the attacks made on me, this shop might as well be closed for business. I do the very best I know how, the very best I can, and I mean to keep doing so until the end. If the end brings me out all right, what is said against me won't amount to anything. If the end brings me out wrong, ten thousand angels swearing I was right would make no difference.

For the next six years this office would be the center of MacArthur's universe. He never traveled to see the rest of Japan; outside of some government officials and some distinguished visitors, he hardly ever ventured out to meet any Japanese people—a source of criticism then and later. Even Jean and Arthur were little more than occasional diversions from the task that confronted him every day on the sixth floor of the Dai-ichi building: how to reconstruct a broken nation almost from scratch.

The scale of the task was only beginning to sink in; so was the scale of the justice that would have to be meted out to punish Japan for the war crimes it had committed. With the collapse of Japan's empire had come more and more evidence of hideous atrocities, not only against Asia's civilians, such as the mass gang rapes and murders in the capture of Nanking in 1937, but also against Allied prisoners of war. Under the Japanese the death rate among British and Dutch POWs was one in four.

By contrast, the death rate of all Allied soldiers captured by the Germans and Italians was one in four hundred. Among Australians and Americans in Japanese captivity, the death rate was an appalling one in three.[38]

MacArthur had seen for himself the horrors inflicted on his men who were captured on Bataan. He had learned how 76,000 American and Filipino prisoners had been force-marched one hundred miles without food or water to POW camps infested with dysentery, typhus, and malaria. The 18,000 prisoners who couldn't make the Bataan death march had been either shot or beaten to death along the way. At one point Japanese guards herded 150 POWs into a bunker, doused them with gasoline, and set them alight.

A similar march in Thailand had seen 3,500 POWs starved, beaten, or shot. At Sendakan prison camp in Borneo hundreds were shot or decapitated or even crucified in the last days of the war. There was also shocking documentary evidence of medical experiments on Allied prisoners, including injections of anthrax and other deadly infectious diseases.[39]

All this, and much more, demanded a reckoning. Many wartime Japanese leaders knew it, and feared it. General Hideki Tojo, Japan's premier at the time of Pearl Harbor, was one of forty people that MacArthur ordered arrested for trial as war criminals (General Masaharu Homma, MacArthur's old antagonist and the man responsible for the Bataan death marches, was another). On September 24, Tojo attempted suicide. American army doctors saved his life.

Many Japanese were shocked and disgusted that the premier who had issued the order urging that soldiers "not live to incur the shame of becoming a prisoner" had allowed himself to be a prisoner at all, then attempted suicide with a pistol instead of the traditional samurai sword—and managed to botch it.[40]

And still the emperor did not come.

MacArthur waited three weeks.

Then on September 27 a large Daimler limousine, flanked by two motorcycle outriders and four other cars pulled out of the Imperial Palace grounds. Inside was a slim middle-aged man in a morning coat, striped trousers, and silk top hat, wearing what one Japanese eyewitness called "an extraordinarily somber expression."[41]

The car crossed the moat and mounted the hill toward the city of Tokyo.

At the Toranomon crossroad witnesses saw the limousine do something extraordinary.

When the light turned red, the car stopped. No one had seen the emperor stop for a traffic light before; his motorcades had always traveled after the route had been cleared of all traffic, an imperial process without halting or pausing.

Soon the car arrived at the entrance to the American embassy. MacArthur had known Hirohito was coming, and he kept the visit top secret so there were no press or photographers. But he was not there to greet the emperor—another unforgivable breach of imperial protocol in the old days, but now a somber reality of Japan under American occupation.

Guards opened the Daimler's doors and Hirohito stepped out. He had a strangely bewildered and forlorn expression, until General Bonner Fellers stepped up with hand extended.

"Welcome, sir." It was General Bonner Fellers, who had acted as MacArthur's chief advisor on things Japanese even before the surrender. Indeed, it was Fellers who had ensured that Hirohito wasn't at that moment sitting in a prison cell.

Fellers escorted the emperor upstairs. The imperial retinue of nine officials remained below, looking anxious and surrounded by unsmiling American faces.

Upstairs, Fellers took the emperor's top hat and noticed his hands were trembling. He looked "frightened to death," Fellers remembered.[42]

There on the threshold of the drawing room stood MacArthur. He wore his usual khakis, with five stars on the collar and no tie. This casual appearance was another breach of imperial protocol, even an insult—and MacArthur knew it. The Japanese press, when they saw the photos afterward, were horrified. But it sent another vivid, unmistakable message: America was now in charge.

Hirohito greeted the supreme commander with a deep bow, very low, "a servant's bow," Fellers noticed. MacArthur noticed also, and also saw the emperor's strain. "He was nervous and the stress of the past months showed plainly. . . . [I] tried to make it as easy for him as I could, but I knew how deep and dreadful must be his agony."[43]

MacArthur then dismissed everyone except the interpreter and directed Hirohito toward chairs near the fireplace.

He offered the Tenno a cigarette, which Hirohito took with thanks—although his hands shook as MacArthur lit it.

MacArthur noted with a sardonic coyness, "You know, we've met before." Hirohito's head cocked in mild curiosity. The general explained. It was when he had been visiting his father, Arthur MacArthur, at the close of the Russo-Japanese War, and he had been introduced to the five-year-old prince.

There was an awkward pause. Clearly Hirohito was not interested in revisiting the remote past. It was the more recent past he was focused on, as he made clear in his first opening sally.

"I come to you, General MacArthur," he said, "to submit myself to the judgment of the powers you represent as the one to bear sole responsibility for every political and military move taken by my people in the conduct of the war."

Even on this most extraordinary of days, it was an extraordinary thing to say, and MacArthur was startled. Hirohito was taking responsibility for the terrible crimes committed in his name by Japanese soldiers throughout the war, including those against MacArthur's own men during the death marches from Bataan. Hirohito obviously knew that his former prime minister Tojo was under arrest; would he himself be arrested now? Japan's divine emperor had no way of knowing.

The British and Russians, for example, had been clamoring to see him arrested and tried as a war criminal. A congressional resolution to that effect was already circulating in Washington.[44] But MacArthur was of a different opinion—and Hirohito's willingness to take the fall, even on these broad terms, broke the ice.

MacArthur's attitude changed from astonishment to relief. "A tremendous impression swept me," he wrote later. "This courageous assumption of a responsibility implicit with death, a responsibility clearly belied by facts of which I was fully aware"—namely, that Hirohito had largely acquiesced in policies imposed by the military and its allies, rather than vice versa—"moved me to the marrow of my bones. He was an Emperor by inherent birth, but in that instant I knew I faced the First Gentleman of Japan in his own right."[45]

Others were far less sure. Later some would wonder if Hirohito, by his seeming candidness in this first meeting, hadn't actually dodged a bullet—or at least a hangman's noose. But MacArthur had no more doubts. He felt he now had a partner in remaking Japan, one who would make sure that what MacArthur was about to do would be sanctioned and obeyed by the Japanese people.

Then they spoke of the war's end. MacArthur praised Hirohito's personal intervention in forcing a surrender—at the risk of his own life. "The peace party did not prevail until the bombing of Hiroshima created a situation which could be dramatized," Hirohito explained—in other words, that the only alternative to peace was the extinction of Japan itself. On the other hand, Hirohito refused to say that he regarded going to war in the first place as a mistake. "It wasn't clear to me that our course was unjustified." Again, his statement showed an astonishing candidness when addressed to the representative of the country whose ships and planes had been attacked at Pearl Harbor.[46]

MacArthur, however, was willing to move on. He laid out to Hirohito what he believed would be the overall principles of the American occupation, including the establishment of democracy. "I found he had a more thorough grasp of the democratic concept than almost any Japanese with whom I talked," MacArthur marveled. Others would be more skeptical.

They said nothing more about the war. Both were thinking about the future, although no one knows whether MacArthur raised the ticklish subject of the emperor renouncing his own divinity—another of the nonnegotiable demands that the Allies had made and that MacArthur was determined to impose.

Then the meeting was over. They stepped into MacArthur's office for photographs. Then the two men headed downstairs, where Hirohito's retinue waited, enormously relieved to see him safe and alive. MacArthur took the courteous step of escorting the emperor to his car—but did not shake hands, and turned to leave before the imperial motorcade had driven away.

Back upstairs he met both Jean and Arthur. MacArthur was starting to tell her how the emperor looked, but Jean burst out laughing. "Oh, I saw him," she confessed. "Arthur and I were peeking behind the red curtains."

MacArthur laughed and they left the study. Servants cleared away the remains of the meeting, emptied the ashtrays and stirred the fire.

One coffee cup stared up at them. It was the emperor's, still full. MacArthur had poured, but the emperor had left the cup untouched. Was it nerves? Or perhaps fear of being poisoned? Some in his retinue had worried that the Americans might make it happen. Did Hirohito worry as well?

To this day no one knows. But it was a sign that the bond of trust that MacArthur and Hirohito had started to forge still had a very long way to go.[47]

CHAPTER 27

BEING SIR BOSS

Asia may yet be destined to exhibit the greatest of political wonders.

—ARTHUR MACARTHUR,

"CHINESE MEMORANDUM," 1882

The photograph taken in MacArthur's office appeared in both Japanese and American papers the next day. It shows a defeated but still-divine emperor in his morning coat and trousers, looking like someone about to undergo heart surgery with no anesthesia, and a victorious general in casual khakis with his hands on his hips, looking cool and collected with a slightly disrespectful slouch. Some Japanese were shocked by the picture; more-traditionalist ones were outraged. But no one could deny that something totally unprecedented had happened. "It seemed the Son of Heaven had stepped down to a very earthy earth," wrote one source. "As nothing else could, the imperial homage to MacArthur told the people that Japan was truly beaten."[1]

They were also learning who was now the undisputed master of their country.

Certainly his instructions from Washington had told MacArthur that. "Your authority is supreme," Truman's own brief to him had read. "You will exercise our authority as you deem proper to carry out your mission." The emperor's visit had only put the final stamp on it. Now MacArthur and his team could get down to business.

To any ordinary person, even a five-star general, it would have seemed a gargantuan task—single-handedly running an entire nation of eighty million people—but MacArthur approached it, as he did everything else, with supreme confidence rooted in a faith in his own competence.

For one thing, military occupations were nothing new to him. "I garrisoned the West Bank of the Rhine as commander of the Rainbow Division at the end of World War One," he could remind any visitor to the Dai-ichi building. He had also seen his father do the same in the Philippines.

"At first hand I saw what I thought were basic and fundamental weaknesses" of past American occupations, he wrote. One was the reliance on military instead of civilian authority to get things done, which failed to allow ordinary organs of government to resume or take on functions. Another was "the loss of self-respect and self-confidence by the people [and] the lowering of the spiritual and moral tone of a population [ruled] by foreign bayonets."

A third was "the deterioration of the morale of the occupiers themselves," as the disease of power infiltrated their ranks and bred "a sort of race superiority"—as had happened to the Japanese themselves in China, Manchuria, and the rest of their former empire.[2]

MacArthur was determined not to let that happen to Americans in postwar Japan. Of course some degree of racial tension was always present during the American occupation. Given the racist overtones of much anti-Japanese propaganda during the war, which had portrayed the Japanese as virtually subhuman "yellow monkeys," MacArthur's GIs were not inclined to greet the Japanese as their racial equals—especially when Japanese atrocities committed on the battlefield, as well as on POWs and civilians alike, seemed proof that this was a people lacking in basic human feelings.

Thanks to his father, MacArthur felt no such sense of race superiority. A sense of cultural superiority, however, was another matter. What he saw of traditional Japan was a culture distorted by primitive superstition, pernicious myths such as the divinity of the emperor, and moral values that discounted human feeling and compassion and celebrated violence over peace.

Here MacArthur firmly believed that part of his mission was to reshape Japanese culture toward a greater respect for ordinary human life, for the dignity of the individual, and for basic human rights. To this end, he hoped to encourage the spread of Christianity among Japan's population, "to fill the spiritual vacuum left in Japanese life by collapse of their past faith." In his mind, this development was the spiritual complement to the resurrection of material life in a broken Japan.

In sum, he would publicly announce on the second anniversary of V-J Day, "The opportunity here afforded to bring to a race, long stunted by ancient concepts of mythological teaching, the refreshing uplift of enlightenment and truth and reality, with practical demonstrations of Christian ideals, is of deep and universal significance." It was a mission that MacArthur at least took deeply seriously, and it was why he insisted many times that the most important principles he used for creating "a Japan reoriented to peace, security, and justice" were those of the Sermon on the Mount.

In facing the weakness of past armed occupations, MacArthur wanted to avoid above all the tendency to centralize authority rather than relying on local powers and the principle of self-help. "If any occupation lasts too long," he noted, "one party becomes slaves and the other masters." The study of history had convinced him that the careers of Napoleon, Alexander, and Caesar had all suffered serious setbacks because of foreign occupations. He was not going to make the same mistake. He fully intended that acting as Japan's supreme master would not mark the end of his career and reputation, but the culmination of it.

"Sometimes my whole staff was lined up against me," he wrote years later in his memoirs. "But I knew what I was doing. . . . My doubts were to be my best safeguard, my fears my greatest strength."[3] So was an unspoken hope of where success in Japan could lead: possibly even to 1600 Pennsylvania Avenue and the White House itself.

Whatever later detractors may say—and their criticisms are many and often penetrating—one undeniable fact about MacArthur's years in Japan remains. He is still the one occupier of a foreign country in modern history, to emerge with his reputation enhanced rather than diminished.

Certainly he was undeterred by the fact that this was by far the largest administrative task the U.S. Army had ever undertaken.

He and his staff loved nothing more than hashing out a large bureaucratic logistics challenge, especially one involving lots of unknown factors, and this was no exception. They first worked out the broad outlines of what they, and the authorities in Washington, wanted to achieve. From there it was just a matter of figuring out how the vast military machinery he had put together to win the war would turn itself to democratizing and transforming the country of Japan.

MacArthur's solution was straightforward, if not exactly simple. It was to transfer most of the functions formerly performed by AFPAC directly into the administration structure of SCAP. On October 2 AFPAC's military government formally dissolved and GHQ, SCAP took its place. But little had changed. The standard sections of military command—G1, G2, G3, and G4—simply blossomed into the channels through which Mac's authority became enforced in Japan. Every original AFPAC division chief became his SCAP counterpart.[4]

The staff was in many cases the same as the group who had steered MacArthur to victory in the Philippines, with one major exception.

Richard Sutherland, now a lieutenant general, formally stepped down in the autumn of 1945. MacArthur had recalled him from vacation in Washington to help organize the surrender ceremony on the *Missouri*. Afterward he had finished his vacation in Australia, and returned to Tokyo expecting some kind of assignment. MacArthur gave him nothing. The bond of trust that had existed between them had been shattered forever by what MacArthur saw as Sutherland's poor judgment and bad faith over the Clark incident.

Finally Sutherland, who suffered from severe hypertension, went to see MacArthur to tell him he wanted to be relieved as chief of staff so he could return stateside. MacArthur said he thought that was a good idea. Sutherland saluted and left, without so much as a thank-you from his old boss.[5]

One of the closest and most productive working relationships of the Second World War was over. On the fifty-hour flight from Tokyo back to Washington, Sutherland complained bitterly about his treatment at the hands of the supreme commander. "Nothing I could do seemed totally to please him," he kept saying. Rhoades, one of the very few on MacArthur's staff who actually liked the crusty, caustic Sutherland, listened politely as Sutherland voiced his disappointment mile after mile, hour after hour.

Sutherland also said that MacArthur had never explained why he had fallen into disgrace—although both he and Rhoades knew why. Sutherland ended up, Rhoades wrote later, "a bitter and disappointed soldier." He lived until 1966 without ever mending the relationship with his former chief—the only one of the old Bataan Gang who never spoke to MacArthur again.[6]

Sutherland's place as chief of staff was taken for the next four years by Richard Marshall, MacArthur's old G-1, but the man who would take Sutherland's place as MacArthur's chief confidant—alter ego, almost—was Brigadier General Courtney Whitney. They had known each since Manila days in the thirties when Whitney was a prosperous attorney; then he had handled liaison with guerrilla groups in the Philippines and civil affairs in post-liberation Manila.

Like Sutherland, Whitney was aloof and abrasive; like Sutherland, he had a gift for making enemies. "A stuffed pig with a mustache," was how one detractor described him, "with a pointed nose and small eyes."[7] But MacArthur trusted him implicitly. Whitney would head up SCAP's Government Section starting in December, and transform it into the most important bureaucratic division of the occupation—in fact, into the equivalent of the Constitutional Convention of Japan.

One old Bataan Gang member who did not leave—although some may have wished he had—was Charles Willoughby, now Major General Willoughby. He remained MacArthur's G-2 or head of military intelligence, but in May 1946 he persuaded his boss to give him control over the Civil Intelligence Section, as well.

He would become MacArthur's J. Edgar Hoover—"my lovable fascist," MacArthur would disarmingly tell visitors—devoted not just to running down Japanese war criminals, occupation profiteers, and ex–military intelligence officers (some of whom he incorporated into G-2) but also to spying on domestic Communist groups and Communist sympathizers.

Sometimes described as "the second most powerful man in Japan," Willoughby also occasionally dabbled in Japanese politics by undercutting politicians through leaks regarding corruption or subversive activities—at one point even allegedly authorizing the kidnapping of a Communist intellectual, Kaji Wataru.[8] Willoughby's domestic surveillance efforts don't win him many plaudits from liberal-minded historians, American or Japanese. But they kept MacArthur closely informed of how those who were his enemies, particularly on the Japanese left, were reacting to his policies—and kept Communist-led unions and other groups from opening a possible subversive fifth column with the outbreak of war in Korea.

William Marquat, now also a major general, took over the Economic and Scientific Section of SCAP, which oversaw sensitive matters such as exports and imports, labor unions, and cartels and antitrust, including the vast Japanese industrial corporations, or *zaibatsu,* which MacArthur was dedicated to breaking up. Steve Chamberlin remained on as G-3, and Hugh Casey as chief engineer officer. Spencer Akin remained chief signal officer, including monitoring other people's signals, and was head of SCAP's Civil Communication Section. LeGrande Diller was still head of public relations, and a place was even found for Sid Huff to stay on—while MacArthur's chief advisor on Japan, Bonner Fellers, served as military secretary of GHQ.

Probably the busiest section at GHQ, at least in the early days of the occupation, was Public Health and Welfare, headed by Colonel Crawford F. Sams (who because of his indefatigable efforts to stamp out infectious diseases across the islands became known to the Japanese as Doctor Lice).[9] But by far the most important was Whitney's Government Section, which oversaw virtually every major political reform in Japan until the formal end of occupation in 1951.

Whitney was soon joined by Charles Kades, a liberal New Dealer whose views on what to do about Japan, far from alienating MacArthur, steadily won his support and respect. The Whitney-Kades team was exactly the balance MacArthur was looking for, as they all embarked on the most extraordinary bureaucratic adventure of the twentieth century, transforming a proud but defeated Asian nation with ancient feudal roots into a modern functioning democracy—in MacArthur's words, turning Japan into "the world's greatest laboratory for an experiment in the liberation of a people from totalitarian military rule and for the liberalization of government from within."[10]

No expert, including experts on Japan, thought they would succeed. Some still insist they failed, and that too much of Japan's rigid social system and traditional elitist culture survived the American occupation. But without doubt the emergence of modern Japan would have been impossible without them—and without MacArthur driving hard at the helm. In the words of one distinguished Japanese historian, "in a profound and basic way, it set the course of Japanese history in the second half of the twentieth century."[11]

Washington did not make the job easy. As during the war, there was a constant frustrating tug-of-war, not with the Joint Chiefs this time but with the State Department and various other government agencies trying to oversee policy in Japan, at first because MacArthur's policies seemed too radical, especially regarding Japan's military, but later because they were not radical enough.

MacArthur thoroughly believed the problem was that the administration, including Secretary of State Marshall and his deputy Dean Acheson, saw everything that happened in Asia through a Eurocentric lens. They seemed too focused on what was happening in Germany and Europe; Marshall and his aides, MacArthur warned one visitor, "paid heed" only to "Wall Street whose main holdings were in Europe."[12] From his desk in the Dai-ichi building he would always feel that the Truman men treated Asia and Asians with a mixture of condescension and cultural chauvinism—and therefore treated him in much the same way.

In the end, however, MacArthur managed to prevail in virtually every major dispute by a combination of persuasion, guile, sheer willpower, and outright bullying. He had key advantages. He was, after all, the man on the scene, with the authority to override directives he disagreed with—or ignore those he couldn't override. He was a leading figure in the opposite political party, the Republicans, who could summon allies on the Hill and even a former president, Herbert Hoover, when he needed them. MacArthur was a cherished hero at home, the most widely recognized victor of World War Two. He would soon be a cherished hero in Japan as well.

So although some critics would later claim that MacArthur's major changes were all dictated from Washington and he was only following orders, the fact remains that he left his own personal stamp on everything that happened, from votes for women to a new Japanese constitution—and did it in ways that made Jean's nickname for him, Sir Boss, after the Mark Twain character who single-handedly tries to transform a medieval society into a modern industrial one, ironically appropriate.

There were, however, two other people who were indispensable to the process.

The first was Bonner Fellers, former planning section chief for G-3 for SWPA, and then MacArthur's military secretary and chief of his psychological warfare group. One of his key duties there was figuring out how to convince more Japanese soldiers to surrender rather than fight to the death. Fellers had studied Japan while at Leavenworth's Command and General Staff School from 1933 to 1934, with a particular focus on the Japanese soldier's fanatical devotion to the emperor even to the point of suicide. Fellers had even predicted the emergence of kamikaze tactics.

Yet he also deplored the American habit during the war, after long bitter experience, of refusing to take Japanese prisoners who all too often would use a white flag to draw Americans out and then open fire, or would turn out to have a grenade hidden in their underwear.

Taking prisoners was a matter of breaking down that fanatical devotion, Fellers believed, by risking compassion, and as "a matter of national honor we make good our word" when urging Japanese to surrender.[13] Now, after the war, it was also Fellers who convinced MacArthur that the emperor should not only be retained but be the central pivot for the reform of Japanese society.

"As Emperor and acknowledged head of state," Fellers wrote frankly, "Hirohito cannot escape war guilt." Still, "the hanging of the Emperor to [the Japanese] would be comparable to the crucifixion of Christ. . . . But the mystic hold [that] the Emperor has on his people and the spiritual strength of the Shinto faith properly directed need not be dangerous. The Emperor can be made a force for good and peace . . . Once the Tokyo gangster militarists are dead, once the armed forces are destroyed, and the liberal government formed under the Emperor, the Japanese people—sadder, fewer, and wiser— can begin the reorientation of their lives"—under American leadership and based on American values.[14]

MacArthur agreed. His desire to turn Japan into a laboratory of democracy and liberty needed a powerful ally on the scene, and from first to last he would work to make Hirohito his ally in that process.

The other key figure was new to the MacArthur team. William Sebald had been a corporate lawyer working in Japan in the twenties before he entered the United States Foreign Service, and in 1945 was made the State Department's point man in Tokyo in dealing with Japan—and with MacArthur. Although often ignored in most accounts of the occupation, Sebald's relationship with MacArthur and their almost daily conversations, with MacArthur talking and Sebald listening, became one of the most important points of coordination, and reduction of friction, between SCAP and Washington. Indeed, very often plans that MacArthur had "thought out loud" with Sebald in his office would appear later as implementable policy in official pronouncements.

Sebald knew that MacArthur viewed Washington's interference as ignorant and unwarranted. MacArthur treated the State Department as a foreign, even hostile entity—and the Far Eastern Commission, with its Russian and British members, even more so. Sebald also understood that MacArthur saw himself as simultaneously moving forward on the transformation and fighting a bitter rear-guard action against any dilution of his authority. "Never before in the history of the United States," Sebald wrote of the first months of occupation, "had such enormous and absolute power been placed in the hands of a single individual." It served as a great burden but also a great temptation to abuse. Yet the system worked well, Sebald later acknowledged, thanks to "the personality, experience, assurance, image, and—for lack of a better word—the wizardry of MacArthur."[15]

But even MacArthur had the sense to know that although he could beat Washington into submission, and even the emperor and his advisors, he could not bend the Japanese people themselves to his will. Even in abject defeat, they were going to exert their power to shape events and deflect any changes that cut too much against the Japanese cultural grain. Part of MacArthur's success over the next six years was his recognition of that reality—and of the limits, as well as the possibilities, of reform.

From the start, however, the biggest problem he faced was simply keeping the Japanese alive.

Food shortages had already begun to appear before Pearl Harbor, and by the time of surrender most Japanese were seriously undernourished. Lack of food had disrupted the war effort, pulled apart the social and cultural fabric (in Osaka Prefecture in 1944 almost half of all "economic crimes" involved the theft of food). Wheat and even rice had become virtually nonexistent and the imperial government had been forced to do things like encourage people to use acorns, tree bark, and sawdust as substitutes. One schoolgirl remembered thinking, when she heard the emperor's surrender broadcast on August 15, 1945, that the end of the war would mean she wouldn't have to go to the river every night to catch frogs for the family supper.[16]

Now with the war over but most of Japan's merchant marine sunk by Allied submarines, the possibility of making up the difference by means of imports from its former empire (one out of every three sacks of rice the Japanese ate had to be imported) looked alarmingly dim. Hirohito's minister of agriculture warned him on the day of surrender that there were barely three days' worth of rice mixed with soybeans left in Tokyo. In the three months after the surrender there were more than a thousand deaths from malnutrition. The minister of finance predicted that another ten million would die if food was not forthcoming.[17]

It was MacArthur who saved the situation. He set up army food kitchens to feed hundreds of thousands of Japanese. He also seized some 3.5 million tons of food stockpiled by the U.S. Army in the Pacific, and shipped it all to Japan to see the country through the winter.

Some Americans were horrified. There were those, like Mississippi senator Theodore Bilbo, who thought one of the war's goals should be "almost total elimination of the Japanese as a race." Gallup polls showed that 13 percent of Americans believed every Japanese should be exterminated. Why should they care if the Japanese starved—and why confiscate the food set aside for our boys overseas to prevent it?

MacArthur's terse reply was that "the Japanese people are now our prisoners," no less than the men in Bataan had been Japan's. How can America claim to punish those responsible for starving and mistreating them if Americans do it themselves? "To cut off Japan's relief supplies in this situation would cause starvation to countless Japanese," he told Washington, "and starvation breeds mass unrest, disorder, and violence. *Give me bread or give me bullets.*"[18]

MacArthur got the bread—plus rice, powdered milk, tinned corned beef, and mountains of K and C rations that Japan needed to stay alive, while GHQ made sure it was properly distributed across the country. In the end, more than $2 billion worth of food, medicine, and relief goods came to Japan during MacArthur's tenure, most of it during the critical first year of 1945–46.

To the Japanese, it seemed a miracle. MacArthur's relief efforts were "like a merciful rain during a drought," one Japanese yearbook stated at the end of 1945, and "kindled a light of hope" in Japan's beaten, often homeless masses.[19]

Food shortages would continue down to the end of the occupation. But after the initial crisis, American aid prevented further outbreaks of malnutrition— or of any civil disturbance. It also sowed the seeds of a new respect for Americans, and especially for the man at their head.

He was going to need it. In October the hammer began to fall on the remains of Japan's prewar totalitarian order.

The first, and most massive, task was demobilizing what remained of the Japanese army. It still amounted to some seven million individuals, grouped in 154 divisions, including 57 divisions inside Japan itself. This could have been a complex, even potentially dangerous job—unlike in Nazi Germany, where at surrender there was virtually no organized army left.

But thanks to the breaking of the Japanese army code, Willoughby's G-2 had extensive knowledge of where the units were and who commanded them, and both he and MacArthur had had the experience of overseeing the Japanese surrender in the Philippines. They knew that the individual members of this army were largely broken men, bitter and disillusioned toward their former leaders, who had little reason or incentive left to fight on. By October, the peaceful extinction of the Japanese army in Japan was all but complete.[20]

On the 16th MacArthur could report, "Today the Japanese Armed Forces throughout Japan completed their demobilization and ceased to exist as such . . . I know of no demobilization in history either in war or peace, by our own or any other country, that has been accomplished so rapidly or so frictionlessly."[21]

Repatriating Japanese soldiers from abroad, as well as Japanese POWs and millions of civilians who had been sent out as colonists to places like Korea, Manchuria, and the South Sea Islands but who were now hated and homeless, was a more laborious task. In the end, it required the cooperation of virtually every Allied country, including the Soviet Union. But again the administrative wheels of SCAP took on the task, and by the end of 1945 almost a million Japanese had returned home, including half a million former soldiers—the first wave of a repatriation process that would still be going on three decades later.[22]

For the Japanese in Soviet hands, the process would be particularly brutal. Perhaps as many as half a million Japanese, both soldiers and civilians, would die in Soviet detention camps. Almost a quarter million of those perished in the Manchurian winter of 1945–46.[23] Together with Stalin's seizure of the Kuril Islands and the Sakhalin peninsula, it was an atrocity that didn't bode well for Communism's popularity in postwar Japan—while the prestige of MacArthur and Americans, who sent their own LSTs and former Liberty ships to bring back Japanese, rode correspondingly high.

The next blow to the old order fell on October 4, when MacArthur promulgated a civil liberties directive. The Japanese government was henceforth to abrogate all laws restricting freedom of speech, religion, assembly, and freedom of the press, as well as ending all laws involving discrimination on the basis of race, creed, or political ideology (including Communism); and release from prison all persons who had been incarcerated on the basis of those laws. At the same time, the minister of home affairs, his police chief, and some 5,000 police officials across Japan were dismissed from their jobs.[24]

This "Magna Carta" for postwar Japan was too much for the sitting prime minister and his cabinet, who resigned en bloc on October 5. MacArthur later insisted that his new ally the emperor had fired them; the truth was they simply could not stomach changes this radical.[25] The State Department, on the other hand, wanted the former prime minister arrested as a suspected war criminal. MacArthur said no; in dealing with Japan's cabinet he was pushing ahead to the future, not settling scores from the past.

The new prime minister, Baron Shidehara, found this out when he was summoned to MacArthur's office on October 11, where the supreme commander read to him a seven-point memorandum on the reforms he wanted the new government to implement. These included creating free labor unions, the end of child labor practices, "the opening of schools to more liberal education" so that the Japanese people would learn that the government was there to serve them, rather than vice versa, and the end of Japan's oligarchic economic system.

But the most radical change of all, the one that headed the list, was votes for women.[26]

This last point must have made the old baron's glasses steam up and his mustache curl. For Japanese traditionalists, the notion of women having the vote, let alone legal equality, flew in the face of centuries of de jure as well as de facto patriarchalism. But MacArthur was adamant.

It was part of a larger scheme of his, not only to enfranchise women but to transform their status in Japanese life. They would have an important role in reshaping Japanese culture, moving it away from its militarist past and toward a democratic future. That had been one of MacArthur's goals in Germany in 1919, when he told journalist William Allen White that he saw German women armed with the vote as the principal obstacle to an imperial German revival.

He felt the same way about Japan, and no doubt having strong female role models of his own like his mother and Jean gave him the confidence that when Japan's women got the vote, it would "change the entire complexion of Japanese political life" for the better. As he wrote in his memoirs, "Of all the reforms accomplished by the occupation of Japan, none was more heartwarming for me than [the] change in the status of women" he had set in motion.[27]

The other related duty he expected Shidehara to carry out was the writing of a new constitution, one that cleared away the worst authoritarian features of the Meiji constitution drawn up in 1889. The government had already called for a general election by April 1946. Very well, MacArthur told him, it would have to take place under a constitution that embodied the key democratic principles encapsulated in his seven-point memorandum, as well as ending the emperor's divine status and position as absolute ruler.

Shidehara promised it would, and appointed a committee to oversee the process headed by Dr. Joji Matsumoto, a seventy-year-old former law professor at the University of Tokyo. It was not until early February 1946 that the committee presented its handiwork, and this time it was MacArthur's spectacles that steamed up. "It turned out to be nothing more than a rewording of the old Meiji constitution," MacArthur wrote. "The power of the Emperor was deleted not a whit." The old phrase describing the Tenno's powers as "sacred and inviolable" was changed to "supreme and inviolable"—hardly a significant difference. Even worse, most of the new rights granted to the Japanese, like freedom of speech and religion, were made subordinate to statutory law, which meant they could be taken away by passing new laws or by simply changing the constitution.

MacArthur declared the new constitution unacceptable. The Japanese had tried and failed; now it was the Americans' turn.[28]

They did not have a lot of time. The deadline for registering to vote in the April election was looming. On February 4 twenty members of the Government Section were called together in a conference room, where Courtney Whitney read them their orders. They had ten days, he said, to draft a new Japanese constitution. The stunned Kades, head of GS, had already told Whitney it was impossible; his section had far too much to do already.

"Lock the doors," was Whitney's grim response. "We're just going into executive session—the whole Government Section."[29]

Whitney also passed along to Kades MacArthur's detailed instructions on what this new constitution would have to look like. First, there was to be a truly representative legislature, elected on the principle of popular sovereignty; second, all titles of nobility and feudal privileges were to be abolished; third, although the emperor was to remain as head of state through dynastic succession, all his powers were to be subordinate to the constitution, while "the budget was to be patterned after the British system." Finally, "[n]o Japanese Army, Navy, or Air Force will ever be authorized and no rights of belligerency will ever be conferred upon any Japanese force," meaning the constitution would make renunciation of war a matter of fundamental Japanese law.

All of these were provisions of a new constitution that the State Department had outlined in a memo forwarded on to MacArthur via the Joint Chiefs on January 9. In that sense, the claim that "it was a State Department document that MacArthur put into effect" is perfectly true—except for one provision. That memo (SWNCC 228) includes no mention of making the Japanese renounce war, now and forever. That was entirely MacArthur's doing; and however understandable, it was the one constitutional provision that would cause the most friction with the powers back in Washington.[30]

Meanwhile, the GS men went to work in a frenzy. They set up separate committees to draft provisions on the emperor, on civil liberties, on local government, and so on—all of which contributed to those sections of the final constitution. MacArthur's instruction about British-style budgets caused some head-scratching until someone pointed out that it simply meant the Japanese Diet or legislature was to have full power of the purse, and hence ultimate control over the executive—including the emperor.

Kades and his team had to scramble to find English-language copies of the U.S., Weimar, and French constitutions to serve as models. Someone found a book with extracts from Abraham Lincoln's speeches; another found a book on constitutions in the University of Tokyo law library. Someone else discovered a copy of the writings of one of the original authors of the 1789 French constitution, the Abbé Sieyès.[31]

At the end of nine days, the exhausted team had finished. They handed in their draft on April 12. At ten o'clock in the morning on April 13, General Whitney appeared at the home of Japanese foreign minister Shigeru Yoshida, where Dr. Matsumoto and two other officials were also waiting.

In the minister's study Whitney insisted on sitting with his back to the sun, so he could see every detail of the Japanese reaction. He told them bluntly that the Matsumoto draft "was wholly unacceptable to the Supreme Commander as a document of freedom and democracy." He then handed them fifteen copies in Japanese of the new draft constitution and left the room.

He wandered down into the garden, where an American plane was passing overhead. He and his assistant turned around to see Matsumoto's secretary coming to join them.

"Ah," Whitney said, "we are out enjoying the warmth of atomic energy." The secretary's face went dead white as he spoke. It was a cruel, but meaningful reference to Hiroshima—and a reminder of who was in charge and who was not.

At ten minutes to eleven Whitney returned to the house and read the Japanese officials the riot act. Unless the government adopted the SCAP draft, two things were going to happen. First, the case of trying the emperor as a war criminal would be reopened. Second, SCAP would submit the draft to a national referendum, which would mean that the current clique of politicians running postwar Japan would lose control of the constitutional process, possibly even the future of the country.

Matsumoto's secretary "straightened up as if he had sat on something," Whitney remembered. "Dr. Matsumoto sucked in his breath. Mr. Yoshida's face was a black cloud." All of them "acted as though they were about to be taken out and shot."[32]

Still, they did as they were told. Prime Minister Shidehara made one last try on February 21 in a personal meeting with MacArthur to get him to relent on some of the more radical provisions, especially Article 9, renouncing war, which would in effect leave Japan with no military, but MacArthur would not be moved. Shidehara reluctantly gave in and on March 4 submitted the committee's draft, beginning with "We, the Japanese people," of the new constitution for SCAP's, and MacArthur's approval. They got it; and on March 6 it was unveiled to the world with an eloquent endorsement from the prime minister (few knew that he and his entire cabinet had wept bitter tears as they signed it) and a statement from Emperor Hirohito: "It is . . . my desire that the constitution of our empire be revised drastically upon the basis of the general will of the people and the principle of respect for the fundamental human rights."[33]

On April 10, 1946, Japan had its first modern democratic election— "a true plebiscite," as MacArthur later wrote—choosing the legislature that would go on to approve, with minor changes, the full constitution on November 3, to go into effect on May 3, 1947.

MacArthur hailed the constitution for showing "how far we have come since hostilities ended. It represents a great stride forward toward world peace and good will and normalcy." He made no mention of the fact that it had been almost entirely written by a team of Americans sitting in a conference room; although most Japanese, seeing the contrast between Matsumoto's original draft and the final version, guessed as much. MacArthur was particularly proud of two aspects of the new Japan that the constitution and the election represented. The first was Article 9's renunciation of war—

although that would soon cause almost as much worry back in Washington, which might need an armed ally like Japan if the growing tensions with Communism in Asia became too hot, as it did in Tokyo.

The other was the huge turnout of women, more than thirteen million, for the April 10 election. MacArthur saw it as the first major step forward in their status in Japanese society—although others found in the election results a matter for worry.

"Something terrible has happened," one Japanese legislator told MacArthur in a crash visit to the Dai-ichi building. "A prostitute, Your Excellency, has been elected to the House of Representatives."

MacArthur asked, "How many votes did she receive?"

The legislator sighed and said, "256,000."

"Then I should say," MacArthur replied with a straight face, "there must have been more than her dubious occupation involved."

The legislator quickly changed the subject.[34]

Meanwhile, MacArthur was taking on a far less pleasant task: the purging and punishing of former Japanese officials, starting at the top.

On October 29, 1945, a large crowd had gathered in Manila, outside the high commissioner's residence near the waterfront. In plain sight were the ruins of the Intramuros, where the rubble still held remains of the tens of thousands of Filipinos murdered by the Japanese during the siege of the city.

A car pulled up and guards leapt out. A rear door opened, and the guards helped a stocky figure in cast-off fatigues step onto the pavement. At once the crowd let out a collective howl of rage, pouring torrents of insults on the man's head. The Manila police held back the crowd of yelling, fist-shaking Filipinos with difficulty, as American soldiers watched silently until the man was inside.

The man in the fatigues was General Yamashita, "the Tiger of Malaya," whom MacArthur had bested in the battle for Luzon. Now he was a prisoner of war on trial for what his soldiers had done during the Philippine occupation, in the first of the big Japanese war crimes trials that MacArthur and the victors had set in motion.

His trial was a national sensation in the Philippines. Some Filipino officials were thankful to have Yamashita as a welcome distraction from the
postwar problems that were piling up, including charges of corruption, a
long-standing problem in the islands which MacArthur's liberation had no
way of resolving.[35]

For MacArthur himself, the trial of General Yamashita represented a stern
call to justice in the name of the innocent. "Rarely," he remarked later, "has
so cruel and wanton a record been spread to public gaze." But the trial itself
became steadily muddied by the public outcry against it, the ceaseless parade
of witnesses testifying to horrific crimes that no one could trace to Yamashita
himself, and MacArthur's own actions in trying to speed up justice.

His first was personally drawing up the twenty-two rules under which the
trial would proceed, even though he was no criminal lawyer—and even
though they included rules permitting entry of hearsay evidence and affidavits from persons not living, as well as evidence that "would have probative
value in the mind of a reasonable man" rather than evidence beyond a reasonable doubt.[36]

Then when the defense asked in November for more time to prepare
Yamashita's case, MacArthur refused, saying he was disturbed at "reports of a
possible continuance." And later, after Yamashita's guilty verdict was reviewed
and sent to MacArthur for final approval, the Japanese general's lawyers appealed to the U.S. Supreme Court. The Court issued a decision in February
upholding the conviction, although dissenting justices Wiley Rutledge and
Frank Murphy, MacArthur's old rival when Murphy had been Philippines
high commissioner, wrote a scathing criticism of the entire proceedings.

MacArthur, however, refused to budge. He may not have been a lawyer,
but he did understand the issue of responsibility of command. He wrote in
his final review opinion in February:

> The soldier, be he friend or foe, is charged with the protection
> of the weak and unarmed. It is the very essence and reason of
> his being. When he violates that sacred trust, he not only pro-
> fanes his entire cult but threatens the very fabric of international
> society.

MacArthur went on:

> The traditions of fighting men are long and honorable. They are based upon the noblest of human traits—sacrifice. This officer [i.e., Yamashita] of proven field merit, entrusted with high command involving authority adequate to responsibility, has failed this irrevocable standard; has failed his duty to his troops, to his country, to his enemy, to mankind; has failed utterly his soldier faith.

The soldier faith: it was an extraordinary statement of MacArthur's most cherished belief, that the soldier's calling was a sacred calling based on the willingness to sacrifice one's own life for one's fellow human beings. From MacArthur's perspective, the taking of other lives in battle was secondary; and the taking of innocent life was beyond the pale.

"Peculiarly callous and purposeless was the sack of the ancient city of Manila," he continued, "with its Christian population and its countless historic shrines and monuments . . . which with campaign conditions reversed had previously been spared."

So there it was. Someone had to pay for the destruction of Manila, and its concomitant loss of Filipino lives, and that someone was to be Yamashita. He was free to argue—and did—that he had ordered the city evacuated, not destroyed, and that the decision to fight to the last man in the Manila streets had been taken by Admiral Iwabuchi, now dead. But if Yamashita had not ordered the city's destruction, he had allowed it to happen; and that forgoing of responsibility, in addition to other crimes committed by his troops, were "a blot upon the military profession, a stain upon civilization and constitute a memory of shame and dishonor that can never be forgotten"—or expunged except by the death of the man responsible.

Therefore, "I approve the findings and sentence of the Commission," MacArthur concluded, and ordered the execution of "the judgement upon the defendant, stripped of uniform, decorations and other appurtenances signifying membership in the military profession."[37]

A petition arrived on MacArthur's desk signed by 86,000 Japanese citizens asking him to either give Yamashita clemency or allow him to commit hara-kiri. MacArthur ignored it, and ordered an account of the trial by one of the defense attorneys, A. Frank Reel, to be banned from being translated into Japanese.[38] Instead, on February 26, 1946, the "Tiger of Malaya" mounted the gallows.

Yamashita's conviction and death sealed the fate of MacArthur's other opponent in the Philippines, the one who had bested him in battle, General Masaharu Homma.

MacArthur had wanted Homma tried by an army tribunal, not the International Allied War Crimes Commission like Yamashita, as befitted someone whose actions against U.S. and Filipino troops, especially the Bataan death marches, were among the most heinous of the Pacific war.

As the trial proceeded, however, the heinous story grew more and more ambiguous. It turned out Homma had had a plan to get U.S. and Filipino POWs safely and humanely into camps and to keep them fed; but instead of the 25,000 captives he had anticipated, he ended up with 75,000, most of them too sick or weak for the kind of march the Japanese had in mind.[39] In addition, the supplies of rice and food for the Allied POWs turned out not to be ready because Wainwright's surrender had come three weeks earlier than expected.

Instead, the original plan collapsed and local commanders had to improvise. Homma's argument in court was that he had been too preoccupied with the imminent siege of Corregidor to pay attention, and didn't learn about what had happened, including at hellholes like the notorious POW center at Camp O'Donnell, until it was too late.

It was a clever argument, but it drew no sympathy from the judges. There was no doubt in anyone's mind, least of all MacArthur's, that Homma had given his troops license to engage in sadistic brutality, including such treatment of Filipino civilians during the occupation of the Philippines.

"Soldiers of an army invariably reflect the attitude of their General," was how MacArthur stated it in his review of the final verdict. "The leader is the essence." In this case, Homma had allowed his troops to brutalize and wantonly kill soldiers who had laid down their arms after a valiant and heroic struggle; "of all fighting men of all time none deserved more the honors of war." That Homma had denied them that was "a violation of a fundamental code of chivalry" among fighting men, and "will forever shame the memory of the victorious troops."[40]

But there was another, more personal reason MacArthur believed Homma should pay the ultimate price.

He disclosed it to Averell Harriman, FDR's formal special envoy and now Truman's, who arrived after a tour of American-occupied Korea and was on his way back to Washington. They discussed the Yamashita trial, and MacArthur read out his order that Yamashita be put to death, "with considerable emotion." But when the conversation turned to General Homma, MacArthur's mood grew even darker.

He explained that when Wainwright offered to surrender Corregidor, Homma had threatened to shoot every American in the fortress if Wainwright didn't order all the other American commanders in the Philippines to surrender as well, including Mindanao, to which Wainwright's authority did not extend.

It was a violation of the elementary rules of war, MacArthur said in a shaking voice, and "absolutely indefensible." He rose and went to the table to pour a glass of water. But an astonished Harriman noted that tears were streaming down MacArthur's cheeks.[41]

In any case, there was no doubt as to what the ultimate verdict would be. On February 11 Homma was sentenced to death, although in a last-minute concession he was sentenced to be shot instead of hanged. There was another appeal to the U.S. Supreme Court, but this time the Court refused to hear the case: its ruling on the Yamashita case, it said, was the final word on the subject of war crimes trials (Murphy and Rutledge again furiously dissented).[42]

So Homma was set to die for his crimes. Yet the story took still one more bizarre twist. On March 11 a somber MacArthur entered his office at the Dai-ichi building to learn that he had a visitor. It was Homma's wife, Fukijo Homma, together with a defense attorney.

MacArthur agreed to see them, although he later admitted it was "one of the most trying hours of my life." She was not there to plead for her husband's life, she told him. She wanted to thank him for letting her visit her husband during his imprisonment in the Philippines. At the same time, she hoped MacArthur would "consider carefully all the facts in the case" as he reviewed the final verdict. MacArthur said he would, and that he "understood and sympathized with her position."

There was an awkward pause. Then she said, "It's a very hard job for you, I suppose."

According to her subsequent account of the meeting, MacArthur replied brusquely, "Never you mind about my job," words that showed his tension and pent-up anger for the first time.

She rose to leave. "Please remember me to your wife."

MacArthur said nothing as she and the attorney left.

"No trial could have been fairer than this one," MacArthur wrote in his final review eleven days later. "No accused was ever given a more complete opportunity of defense, no judicial process was ever freer from prejudice." He had also reviewed the evidence against Homma and the circumstances. "I can find no extenuation although I have searched for some instance upon which to bear palliation." Failing to punish "such acts of criminal enormity" as the Bataan death marches would "threaten the very fabric of world society," MacArthur concluded. Therefore, "I approve the finding of guilt and direct the Commanding General, United States Army Forces in the Western Pacific, to execute the sentence."[43]

Seven days later, on April 6, Homma died by firing squad at Los Banos.

On New Year's Day 1946, MacArthur had issued the following pronouncement:

A New Year has come. With it, a new day dawns for Japan. No longer is the future to be settled by a few. The shackles of militarism, of feudalism, of regimentation of body and soul, have been removed. Thought control and the abuse of education is no more. All now enjoy religious freedom and the right of speech without undue restraint. Free assembly is guaranteed . . . The masses of Japan now have the power to govern and what is done must be done by themselves.[44]

At that date there was still no finished constitution, and no elected government. The Tokyo war crimes trials, which traumatized the Japanese public and triggered recriminations against the American occupiers, were still in the offing. Yet when MacArthur said he had brought freedom to Japan, the Japanese believed him, then and later, and they loved him for it.

In 1946 MacArthur had emerged as more than a proconsul, or "American shogun." He had become the object of admiration, even veneration, to millions of Japanese who saw in the seventy-year-old supreme commander the kind of awe-inspiring reverence once reserved for Hirohito himself.

Every morning crowds would gather outside the Dai-ichi building hoping to catch a glimpse of MacArthur as he arrived in his 1941 Cadillac at around 10 or 10:30 to begin his day, and the same scene occurred when he left in the evening. Letters poured in from every post, heaping accolades on their American conqueror. Some writers praised his "exalted and godlike benevolence," while others spoke of him as a "living savior." One man wrote describing how he worshiped MacArthur's portrait every morning and evening as he used to worship the emperor's portrait.[45]

Others saw him in a variety of religious and semireligious lights. One cultural group in Kobe sent him a commissioned painting of Christ delivering the Sermon on the Mount, with a letter comparing his leadership to that of the Son of God. Hundreds of ordinary Japanese wrote letters confessing their misdeeds during the war, as if he were a Catholic priest; others compared him to Buddha and the "friend from afar" mentioned in the Confucian Analects. Still more simply thanked him for giving them hope and happiness when they had feared what might happen under foreign occupation.

He was daily showered with gifts, from dolls, elaborate scrolls and paintings, lacquered boxes, and miniaturized bonsai trees to freshly caught fish from local fishermen, live chickens from humble farmers (a dozen hens virtually became part of the American embassy staff), boxes of tea, lotus roots, dried chestnuts, and even a deerskin and antlers sent by a remote tribe of Ainu on the island of Hokkaido, with a note: "a token of our grateful appreciation for what he [i.e., MacArthur] has done to secure land for our people and give to Japan a democratic society, based on law and order."

One ten-year-old had grown a pumpkin from seeds he had received from the United States, and kept a journal of its progress, which he copied and sent to MacArthur, while the boy's father sent along a painting he had made of the pumpkin. Someone else presented MacArthur with a fan on which he had written in tiny characters the entire text of the constitution. As historian John Dower points out, "These gifts were offered as simple expressions of gratitude to the supreme commander, not as the more calculated ritual gestures of reciprocity and dependency that characterized gift giving in the purely Japanese context."[46]

MacArthur brought to the process certain traits that fed into his virtual cult following during those heady years in Japan. He stood five feet ten, hardly towering, but he always looked taller because of his erect posture—and in a country where the average male was five four it gave him the physical aura of power and authority. He was also in his midsixties when he took over the occupation of a country that respected age as an emblem of wisdom and emotional gravitas.

In addition, he conducted himself with an imperial aloofness that was one part deliberate and another part pure MacArthur, as the Dai-ichi building assumed an imperial solitude. Until the outbreak of war in Korea, he left Tokyo only twice in five years. Someone estimated that during his entire tenure in Japan, "only sixteen Japanese ever spoke to him more than twice, and none of these was under the rank, say, of Premier, Chief Justice, president of the largest university."

Above all, MacArthur believed that "the Oriental mind," as he put it, would "adulate a winner," and a supreme commander who projected himself as such—roles that came naturally to Douglas MacArthur. He understood that the prestige of this new institution in Japan, democracy, would depend on *his* prestige, and he was determined to play the invincible, all-knowing, but ever-compassionate leader to the hilt—even if it meant shutting himself away from the country he was governing.[47]

He would need that prestige and power to take on the other mammoth task of the American occupation: the purge of old regime officials.

The 1945 Potsdam conference had ordered the elimination "for all time the authority and influence of those who have deceived and misled the people of Japan," from government officials to teachers and businessmen. MacArthur was of two minds about this. On one side, he definitely believed in clearing away those Japanese officials who might undermine his new, enlightened democratic order. On the other, "I doubted the wisdom of this measure as it tended to lose the services of many able government individuals" who would be difficult to replace—although the truth was that he later resisted the National Security Council's efforts to reduce the scale of the wholesale purge he had been ordered to carry out.[48]

The first step was a blanket ban on ultranationalist and militaristic groups like the Black Dragon Society and the Bayonet Practice Promotion Society, followed by a ban on the participation in government of individuals belonging to such groups, enacted on January 4, 1946. That meant that 90 percent of the old Japanese Diet were barred from reelection, while almost anyone who had served in Japanese public office for the past decade found himself out of a job. Thousands more lost their positions in business organizations, the press, and academic life. It was a far less thoroughgoing purge than the one taking place in post-Nazi Germany, where 2.5 percent of Germans in the American zone were affected, compared to only 0.3 percent of Japanese.[49]

Nonetheless, it represented a considerable shakeup of Japanese society. One hundred eighteen senior officials lost their posts in Hirohito's imperial household (a cousin, Prince Konoye, chose to commit suicide rather than face further scrutiny). Virtually everyone in the country had to fill out a questionnaire detailing past military record, his or her membership in societies and organizations, and job history—often going back as far as 1931. Sometimes family members suffered removal or disbarment as well.

By 1947, however, no one was required to complete a questionnaire. Evasion became the norm, and by October 1948 the process had begun to run in reverse, with Washington ordering the reinstatement of people who had previously been seen as too collaborationist—and over MacArthur's strenuous objections. In the end, as British historian Robert Harvey notes, "Denazification in Germany was a much more thorough and lasting process."[50] Yet whether Japan's postwar recovery, both politically and economically, would have been as smooth if there had not been a radical rooting out of the old order is open to question.

That is particularly true when it came to the *zaibatsu,* the great oligarchic companies like Mitsubishi, Mitsui, and Sumitomo that had dominated the imperial Japanese economy and had been central pillars of its authoritarian order—and supplied the military with arms for conquest.

Most experts on Japan, including economist Thomas N. Bisson, assumed that a democratic order would require breaking up the *zaibatsu*, just as they assumed it demanded the removal of the emperor. MacArthur had defied them on the emperor issue, but he was wholeheartedly in support of an end of the *zaibatsu*.

Creating a new democratic Japan required "tearing down the traditional pyramid of economic power which has given only a few Japanese families direct or indirect control over all commerce and industry, all raw materials, all transportation, internal and external, and all coal and other power re- sources," MacArthur told a Democratic senator, Brian McMahon. "The Japa- nese people fully understand the nature of the forces which have so ruthlessly exploited them in the past."

They understand, he explained to McMahon, that if "this concentration of economic power is not torn down and redistributed peacefully," "its cleans- ing will eventually occur through a blood bath of revolutionary violence."[51]

Some then and later expressed surprise that MacArthur, the conservative anti-Communist, would be so forthright a foe of the Japanese version of big business. But he was also a progressive Republican of the Teddy Roosevelt variety, who had fought to break up monopolies like Standard Oil and other "malefactors of great wealth." In MacArthur's mind, the *zaibatsu* were more a species of socialism than capitalism.[52] Their breakup would actually be a step toward "an economic system based upon free private competitive enter- prise Japan has never known before." Like the laws pushing land reform and permitting the formation of labor unions, the war on the *zaibatsu* would be indispensable for creating a new order of "competitive enterprise to release the long suppressed energies of the people towards the building of that higher productivity of a society which is free."[53]

As historians Meirion and Susie Harries note, "MacArthur's ambition was to develop a laissez-faire economy in the American tradition, in which small and medium-sized enterprises would compete freely in an open market."[54] In August 1946 MacArthur gave the Japanese ninety days to break up all trade control associations and cartels and set up the Holding Company Liquidation Commission to oversee breakup of the interlocking directorates that made the *zaibatsu* so powerful. At the same time, some 2,200 *zaibatsu* loyalists were thrown out of top jobs in Japanese business and industry by mid-1947.[55]

How effective were MacArthur's reforms? Most critics on the left then and now saw them as ineffectual, or even a sham. One SCAP economist, Eleanor Hadley, acidly noted in September 1947 that out of sixty-seven designated holding companies only two had been dissolved—while in another 1,100 subsidiary companies, "not a single stock reorganization plan had as yet been set in motion."[56]

On the other hand, a leading article in *Newsweek* back in the States condemned MacArthur's reforms as going too far. It argued that "25,000 to 30,000" Japanese businessmen were faced with pink slips, along with their relatives to the third degree: "thus making a total of 250,000 victims." How was Japan expected to recover economically if its ranks of business, industry, and finance were being thus weeded out? the article asked, and called for a congressional investigation as to "why American capitalist principles are being undermined by American occupation authorities."[57]

MacArthur fired off a furious counterblast defending the purges. "It is fantastic that this action should be interpreted or opposed as antagonistic to the American capitalist economy," when of course in MacArthur's mind the *zaibatsu* were in truth state socialists, and feudal ones at that.

"It was these very persons, born and bred as feudalistic overlords, who held the lives and destiny of the majority of Japan's people in virtual slavery." They deserved no place in the development of Japan's future, and even if their removal hurt Japan's economic recovery, which MacArthur very much doubted, then that was the problem of the Japanese who had supported their power for so long.

That same year, 1947, saw two of the most sweeping anti-*zaibatsu* reforms ever envisioned. The Anti-Monopoly Law in April outlawed interlocking directorates and mergers and established the Fair Trade Commission, with enforcement powers. In July MacArthur ordered the breakup of the two biggest

Japanese megacompanies, Mitsubishi and Mitsui—so big that each spawned more than two hundred separate corporations.[58]

All the same, the *Newsweek* article signaled a change in the wind for American policy toward the occupation, and toward MacArthur. It would crystallize more than a year later when a plane touched down at Tokyo airport, bearing news that the days of MacArthur's free hand were almost over.

CHAPTER 28

HEADWINDS

We have known the bitterness of defeat and the
exultation of triumph, and from both we have learned
there can be no turning back. We must go forward
to preserve in peace what we won in war.

—DOUGLAS MACARTHUR, SEPTEMBER 2, 1945,

ON THE DECK OF THE USS *MISSOURI*

On September 2, 1947, the head of SCAP issued a statement from the Dai-
ichi building.

It began: "Two years have now passed since the fateful September 2, on
the *Missouri,* when the Allies on the one hand and the Japanese on the other
entered into the solemn commitments underlying surrender conditions."

MacArthur then reminded his readers of all that had been accomplished
in those two years. The establishment of peace, the demobilization of Japan's
military forces, and the first stirrings of the nation's postwar economy. "The
industrial output has now risen to over 45 percent of pre-war normal, and
the improvement can be expected to continue," he noted, while also herald-
ing the prospect of a final peace treaty between the Allies and Japan, which
he had been pushing for months. At the end of the message, MacArthur
pointed out that "Japan today stands out as one of the few places in a dis-
traught world where, despite an economy of critically short supply, there is a
minimum of fear, of confusion, and of unrest."[1]

The rhetoric may sound overblown, but in very profound ways MacArthur was right. Japan under his aegis was fast becoming the still point in a
turning, churning world, particularly in Asia.

Europe was in growing turmoil even as Stalin's grip relentlessly tightened over Soviet-occupied countries, first with a pro-Communist coup in Hungary and then in Czechoslovakia in 1948. China had redissolved into civil war in 1946, with Chiang's Nationalist forces steadily losing ground to Mao Zedong's Communists as the United States dithered about sending more aid. India, too, seemed on the verge of civil war as Hindus turned against Moslems and the prospect of a violent struggle for independence and partition loomed larger. On the Korean peninsula efforts to arrange an Allied withdrawal were swept up in the mounting tension between competing nationalist groups; in Indochina Communist-led insurgents were on the brink of full-scale war with their French colonial masters.

In August 1946 MacArthur had returned briefly to the Philippines to find that country in turmoil as well. A month earlier, on July 4, the United States had finally recognized Philippine independence. The man that both MacArthur and Quezon had envisioned as leader of the country, Manuel Roxas, was now president despite his brief collaborationist past. Yet there were many in the Philippines who saw Roxas as a puppet, first of the Japanese and now of the Americans. Accusations of corruption were rife as postwar Filipino politics turned out to be an ugly and bitter cockpit for the struggle for power, rather than a cradle of democracy as MacArthur had hoped.

MacArthur was there, however, to celebrate a hero of the past, not to fight the feuds of the present. The body of former president Quezon was being brought home from the United States to be reinterred in Manila, and MacArthur was to speak at the ceremony.

"Of all men of all time, none more truly merited the appellation of patriot-statesman," MacArthur said on August 1. "Few could, as did he, replace the uniform of the soldier with the mantle of statecraft." It was not difficult for Douglas MacArthur, the son of Arthur MacArthur, to forget that when the guerrilla leader Aguinaldo had surrendered to the Americans, the one disciple who turned away from his master in rage and bitterness had been Manuel Quezon. Trust in the Americans had been a hard struggle for Quezon; the relationship with the son, Douglas, had been crucial in that process.

What Quezon had thought of his old friend, at the very end, no one knows. He had sensed that MacArthur had betrayed him, and the Philippines, with promises of armed support in 1941–42 when none had been forthcoming, though he rightly blamed Roosevelt and the decision makers in Washington more.

Still, MacArthur owed his career, and his future fortune, to Quezon. It was Manuel Quezon who in 1935 had brought MacArthur, then the retired chief of staff, out to the Philippines to build the defenses of a new nation. It was Quezon who made him, for better and worse, the man of the hour when Japanese planes passed over the Philippines and plunged both countries into war.

MacArthur continued:

> Throughout his long years of public service, never did he compromise the principle he thus espoused—never did he divert his gaze from the goal which he thus resolutely sought. . . . That his native land now stands as one of the free and independent nations of the world is responsive, more than to all else, to the indomitable will by which he developed in the conscience of his people a firm belief in their destiny as a race. . . . Father of his infant Republic, which he planned but never saw, he has returned. He has come home forever.[2]

As MacArthur returned to the airport for the flight back, he was determined never to break the bond of trust that he had built with the Japanese people, as he and America had with the Philippines.

Indeed, in 1947 MacArthur's influence and popularity in Japan was at its height. The new constitution had been promulgated to everyone's acclaim; and in July the Far Eastern Commission had endorsed MacArthur's plan for the permanent demilitarization of Japan.[3] New educational reforms had been launched, with the purge of more than six thousand ultranationalist teachers and officials from schools and universities. A new liberalized national curriculum had been created under the twin measures of the Fundamental Law of Education and the School Education Law, both of which passed in 1947. Both laid the foundation of the education system of modern Japan, and the intellectual foundations of the future Japanese economic miracle.[4]

Another foundation was laid by GHQ's Scientific and Technical Division.

There a group of American and Australian scientists and engineers worked with Japanese counterparts to create a series of new national bodies to oversee scientific and technical research. Freed from the need to serve the old imperial military-industrial complex, Japan's scientists found new areas for research in a wide range of areas from medicine and physics to engineering and industrial development. One of those research sites was the Ministry of Commerce and Industry—later to become the Ministry of International Trade and Industry or MITI. SCAP's contribution to Japan's economic future also included inviting American quality-control guru W. Edwards Deming to speak to Japanese business managers and engineers. Those speeches and Deming's writings would become virtually Holy Writ for a generation of Japanese industrialists, who would lead companies like Toyota, Toshiba, and Sony into the forefront of the global economy.[5]

There was, however, one scientific area where MacArthur's efforts were completely frustrated. That was the fate of Japan's four cyclotrons, two at the Institute of Physical and Chemical Research and one each at Kyoto University and Osaka University. Allied investigators were shocked to discover how far along the Japanese had gotten in the development of an atomic bomb. Given Japan's wartime record, Washington quickly decided that the four cyclotrons needed to be destroyed.

MacArthur vehemently disagreed. One of the principal architects of the American bomb, Dr. Karl Compton, had come out to visit and inspected two of the Japanese cyclotrons. He and MacArthur were of one mind: the existing cyclotrons posed no military threat, and they were useful scientific instruments "inadequate to a very large factor, to produce explosive quantities of anything." They should be preserved. The War Department, however, said no. When MacArthur protested, the department overruled him. When American scientists, including Compton, raised their objections, officials in Washington put them off by implying it was MacArthur's decision, not theirs.

So the machines were destroyed. "It was an unhappy affair," MacArthur wrote later, "and the attempt of the War Department to falsely shift the blame left a bad taste in my mouth."[6] In fact, we now know that the decision to destroy the cyclotrons was largely the result of a miscommunication between General Leslie Groves's Manhattan Engineer District office and the War Department. Whether saving them would have made a major contribution to science is hard to say; whether the incident further embittered relations between Washington and GHQ is not.[7]

Things were better at home.

The day at the MacArthurs' began at 7:30 A.M., when little Arthur had his breakfast and Jean would join him and sip a cup of coffee. Then at 8:00 A.M., four dogs would gather at the foot of the hill below the residence. They were Uki, a white Akita dog; a Japanese Shiba terrier named Brownie; a cocker spaniel named Blackie after a stray dog MacArthur had found during the advance on Manila and had adopted until Doc Egeberg found the dog so ridden with illness he had to be put down; and Koko, a cocker belonging to Bataan Gang aide Sid Huff.

Promptly at 8:00 the dogs would charge up the hill at a servant's whistle, to join the general for breakfast. He was in his ever-faithful gray dressing gown with its West Point "A," and would feed scraps to the dogs while Arthur played with them until finally the boy's tutor had to get a bell that rang loudly at 8:30 to summon him to his lessons.[8]

Then the dogs trotted along to watch the general do his calisthenics. They involved a series of muscle and bending exercises, done every day, and when he came to the last one, deep knee bends, the dogs would leave the room—all except Blackie, who would follow MacArthur into the bathroom while he washed and shaved.

Then four times a day, seven days a week, policemen across Tokyo would switch the traffic lights so that MacArthur's Cadillac limousine would pass from one green light to the next, until he reached the Dai-ichi building by 10:00 or 10:30. He would pass the door, ignoring the crowds that gathered outside (especially on Sundays when hundreds of American soldiers and sailors joined the throngs of Japanese to watch MacArthur mount the steps), and head for the elevator to the sixth floor.[9]

The Cadillac reappeared in time to whisk him back to the embassy for lunch at 1:30 or even 2:00, where he would entertain a round of guests until 3:00. Then he would nap. Like Winston Churchill, MacArthur used his afternoon nap to recharge and preserve his energy; like Churchill, he took a long nap of an hour or more. When he awoke, the limousine would return him to the Dai-ichi building for another three or four hours of work.

It was a twelve-month, seven-days-a-week schedule. His staff, of course, kept very different hours. They were expected in the office by 8:00 A.M. and did not dare leave until Sir Boss headed home in the evening. But MacArthur scoffed at the idea of vacations—just as he scoffed at telephones and typewriters. Both of those were tools for office personnel, who answered calls and typed up memos that he wrote out in longhand on a legal pad. Letters from others, on the other hand, he answered conscientiously, starting at breakfast, when he and Jean would sort through the mail and decide what to write to whom.

Indeed, it was a rare correspondent that didn't get a personal letter back from MacArthur, no matter how humble or how exalted—or even an invitation to lunch. "The general is from this point of view extremely accessible," noted a member of his staff. "All anybody needs to do to gain his attention is to write a letter."[10]

William Sebald remembered "there was always a touch of drama" when a visitor entered MacArthur's inner sanctum. "The quick bounding from his leather desk chair; the strong handclasp; the hearty words of welcome, always personal and warming; the penetrating eyes." MacArthur would seat the visitor on the leather divan, then plunge into the chair next to him or her. But not for long: in a moment or two he would be pacing back and forth, "restless and eager," talking and breathing confidence in the mission of SCAP and the future of Japan—and America's mission in Asia.

MacArthur hated formal dinners, and avoided cocktail parties and other social functions. The main form of entertainment for the many guests and visitors who flocked to Tokyo during the MacArthur years was luncheons at the American embassy. MacArthur would usually appear after all the guests arrived—American senators or Japanese politicians or European ambassadors, it didn't matter. He would go first to Jean, who would have been talking and charming the guests, saying "Hello, my dear!" and kissing her. Then he would greet each visitor with a handshake and personalized welcome, usually some minute detail of the last time they had met, even if it had been when he was superintendent of West Point or when he had testified on the Hill as army chief of staff.

Then MacArthur would take the guest of honor by the arm, announce that everyone must be hungry, and lead the party into the dining room.

There was little formal protocol; once six ambassadors found themselves shoved together in the middle of the table, the distinctly junior position for lunch.[11] Once coffee was served, the MacArthurs would depart. "The party was over"—and the second half of the workday had just begun. Sebald remembered being summoned to MacArthur's office at seven or even eight in the evening to discuss an important topic.

Other times he would get an early-morning call on some urgent matter; for a man who despised the telephone in the office, MacArthur used it extensively to set the day's agenda before leaving home in the morning.

"He was a general in every action," Sebald remembered, "with the naturalness of a lifetime in positions of command," exuding an air not just of confidence but serenity. Only two things regularly got under MacArthur's skin: adverse decisions by the multinational Far Eastern Commission or its advisory arm, the Allied Council for Japan, and criticism in the press of the SCAP mission. Commission pronouncements he could safely ignore, since his power was unchallengeable, but the press comments made his eyes flash with anger, especially since many were repeated in official State Department telegrams.

Sebald would point out in vain that foreign service officers were only doing their duty in summarizing press views in their respective countries, without in any way taking sides. MacArthur was not mollified. "Have the State Department stop this criticism of the Occupation and SCAP!" When Shanghai newspapers launched a vicious attack on the American occupation in early 1948, MacArthur personally ordered Sebald to compile a lengthy press release in rebuttal, which he did—even though Sebald knew the stories were pure Communist propaganda and needed no answer.[12]

Yet nothing prepared MacArthur for the critical storm that broke out when an airplane bearing diplomat George Kennan and General Cortlandt Schuyler touched down at Haneda Airport on March 1, 1948.

Kennan was a key advisor to Acheson and Truman's foreign policy team, and author of the 1947 article in *Foreign Affairs* that became known as "the Long Telegram," which charted a bold new course for dealing with the Soviet Union in the growing Cold War, called containment. Kennan's views on how to conduct a similar containment policy in the Far East were explicit. "We are greatly overextended" in the current model, he argued, and although he

nt MacArthur arrives in Melbourne, Australia, March 21, 1942, to a cheering throng. They thought
come to save them from the Japanese; he intended to make good on his promise to the Filipinos
s men on Bataan and Corregidor, "I shall return." *Underwood Archives/Getty Images*

Jungle warfare: American in[
trymen on New Guinea, c. 1[
The soldier with the M-1 [
(left) owed his indispens[
weapon to then–Army Chie[
Staff Douglas MacArthur. [
Army Signal Corps

MacArthur, Roosevelt, and Admiral Chester Nimitz meet in Honolulu, July 26–28, 1944, to discuss[
egy in the Pacific. "In all my life, nobody has ever talked to me the way MacArthur did," FDR to[
doctor afterward. *U.S. Navy*

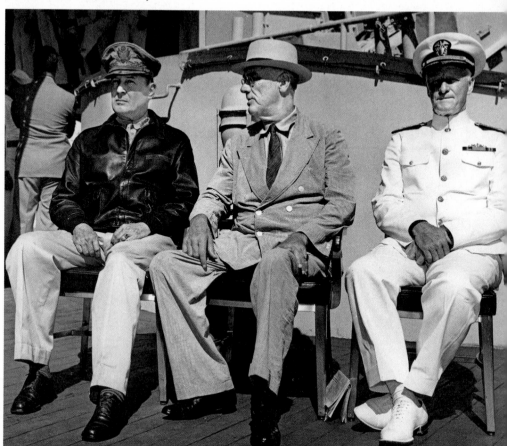

to me," MacArthur addresses the Philippine people on the beachhead at Leyte, October 20, 1944. *al Douglas MacArthur Foundation*

arthur greeted by liberated internees at the University of Santo Tomas, Manila, February 7, 1945. *U.S.*

"The pity of war": American soldiers advancing into the ruins of the Intramuros. Of all Allied capi[tals of] World War II, only Warsaw saw more devastation than Manila. *U.S. Army Signal Corps*

August 30, 1945: MacArthur desc[ends] from Bataan II to the tarmac at A[tsugi] Airfield, Japan. Winston Chur[chill] called MacArthur's action that day [one] of the most heroic of the Second W[orld] War. *ACME*

Jim," MacArthur greets General Wainwright after the latter's release from Japanese captivity. Many hat Wainwright deserved a Medal of Honor for his suffering, but MacArthur vetoed the idea. *U.S. Signal Corps*

"Today the guns are silent. A great tragedy has ended." MacArthur signs the Japanese unconditional surrender, September 2, 1945. Wainwright and General Arthur Percival, commander of the defeated British garrison at Singapore, stand behind him. Admiral William Halsey in cloth cap can be seen standing behind MacArthur; General George Kenney stands at the right. *U.S. Army Signal Corps*

MacArthur meets Emperor Hirohito, September 27, 1945. The photograph sent shock waves across Japan and confirmed MacArthur's role as the "American shogun." *U.S. Army Signal Corps*

Crowds gathered every day to watch MacArthur leave his headquarters in the Dai-ichi Insurance building, Tokyo. *U.S. Army Signal Corps*

The power of supreme command: MacArthur during the Inchon landings, September 15, 1950. *General Douglas MacArthur Foundation*

"It has been said in effe[c]
I was a warmonger. N[o]
could be further fro[m]
truth." MacArthur add[ing?]
the joint session of Con[gress,]
April 19, 1951. *U.S. Arm[y Sig-]
nal Corps*

Norfolk, Virginia, April 11, 1964. Front row, left to right: Courtney Whitney, nephew Douglas MacA[rthur]
II, Jean, son Arthur MacArthur, Jean's brother Colonel Harvard Smith. *U.S. Army*

agreed with MacArthur that Japan and the Philippines should be "the cornerstones of a Pacific security system" conjoined with American interests, he disagreed strongly on how to accomplish it.

Kennan believed the steps MacArthur had taken to revive Japan's economy had been too slow—and the limits he had imposed on its military potential too harsh. Like Germany, Japan needed to brought back to life as quickly as possible in order to help contain the Communist advance in both Europe and Asia. If that meant slowing its transformation into a fully democratic society, so be it.[13]

The attack on MacArthur's democratizing policies had gotten started the previous year, first with the *Newsweek* article, then in September 1947 with a Policy Planning Staff secret document calling for a major change in Japan policy. The "idea of eliminating Japan as a military power for all time is changing," it stated. "Now, because of Russia's conduct, [the] goal is to develop Hirohito's islands as a buffer state"—and a bulwark against Communism both politically and economically. MacArthur's policies had made it more difficult to do both.

As it happened, the head of the Policy Planning Staff was George F. Kennan.[14]

Kennan was a Russia expert, not an Asia expert. He epitomized the State Department viewpoint that MacArthur had always criticized, of seeing everything through Eurocentric eyes—indeed, racist eyes (as the release of Kennan's white supremacist diary entries after his death makes obvious). But his criticism of MacArthur's policies had not gone unnoticed in the Dai-ichi building. MacArthur had already delivered a fierce counterattack in January against critics who said he was moving against the *zaibatsu* too quickly and with too many radical reforms (critics on the left, and later revisionist historians, would argue that he wasn't radical enough). He had already told the British head of mission that the reason "America's tycoons" attacked his anti-*zaibatsu* legislation was that they were afraid it would damage their own business interests.[15]

Now as Kennan arrived early that March morning, MacArthur was determined to set him straight.[16]

Things kicked off with a luncheon at MacArthur's residence. Kennan and Schuyler, who had not slept in forty-eight hours, were surprised to see that

Jean and a MacArthur aide were the only other guests. MacArthur spoke one of his usual monologues, occasionally thumping the luncheon table for emphasis, stressing that the Japanese were "thirsty for guidance and inspiration, it was his aim to bring them both democracy and Christianity." He thundered that there was no danger of Japan going over to Communism; they were tired of slavery and wanted only freedom. Kennan sat immobilized by lack of sleep, wishing he could take notes but mostly struggling to stay awake.[17]

The next day a refreshed Kennan faced a barrage of briefings by MacArthur's staff. The only one he found at all interesting and informative was Willoughby's (largely because Kennan did most of the talking). The main event—a one-on-one interview with MacArthur himself—did not come until a day or two later. Somewhat to Kennan's surprise, it went very well. "He gave his views freely and encouraged me to do likewise," Kennan recalled later. They covered almost every aspect of the occupation policy, and found that they agreed on many points. MacArthur's biggest worry was that the multinational Far East Commission, including the Soviets, might try to meddle in his reforms. Kennan assured him this would not happen; the commission's duties had to do with the Japanese surrender and implementation of the broad framework agreed to at Potsdam. Apart from that, Kennan saw no reason MacArthur should have to consult with the Far East Commission at all.

This pleased MacArthur greatly. He even slapped his thigh in approval, and "we parted with a common feeling, I believe, of having reached a general meeting of the minds." Once again, it seemed that MacArthur's ability to disarm a critic with a personal meeting had prevailed; for one brief moment it seemed that SCAP and State were on the same page regarding Japan.[18]

It didn't last long. Immediately after returning to Washington, Kennan penned a forty-two-page diatribe against SCAP and all its works. He insisted that MacArthur's reforms had generated "a high degree of instability in Japanese life generally" and that the general's trust-busting approach to the *zaibatsu* was imperiling the country's economic recovery, especially its ability to conduct foreign trade. To the suspicious Kennan, MacArthur's policy even smacked of Soviet views about the evils of "capitalist monopoly." Kennan was also worried that SCAP's sweeping away of Japan's old guard had gone too far. It was hampering Japanese society's functioning by imposing a system of "dogmatic impersonal vindictiveness" and "wholly unfathomable complexity," Kennan wrote. Yet "I doubt in fact whether many persons in SCAP could explain [SCAP's] history, scope, procedures, and purpose."[19]

Above all, Kennan believed MacArthur's policies had left the island nation largely defenseless. The occupation forces now numbered fewer than 87,000, far too small in the event of a major conflict and far too many not to be a financial burden (Kennan noted that the Japanese government had had to pay for more than 17,000 housing units for American personnel and their families). The Japanese themselves had been totally disarmed, thanks to MacArthur, and Kennan hinted that it was time to revisit that policy as well.

Kennan, in short, recommended that the reforms that had been implemented since 1945 be cut back, if not halted. It was time for a new policy of economic and political revival, he concluded, directed from Washington, not from the Dai-ichi building—which would necessarily involve reining in MacArthur's personal power.

The hammer fell in October, when the National Security Council issued a new directive, NSC 13/2, ordering MacArthur to institute no new reforms, and to ease current measures that affected the economy. The reform phase of the occupation of Japan was officially over; now the country would be treated as an important ally, one on the glide path to a final peace treaty.

MacArthur was deeply chagrined when the NSC order arrived on his desk. He realized that Kennan (who personally drafted a large portion of NSC 13/2) had done a classic bait and switch in their interview. Kennan had assured him he would no longer be accountable to the dictates of the Far East Commission. Now he was locking him into the dictates of Washington instead. Indeed, he was being double-teamed. While Kennan was overthrowing his reform policies from the State Department, General Kenneth Draper was arguing from the newly minted Defense Department that it was high time to start arming the Japanese again in order to provide for their own defense—and to serve as bulwark in what was being called a "great crescent" of anti-Communist containment extending from Japan across Southeast Asia to India.[20]

MacArthur hit back hard. When he received the NSC draft of Kennan's report, he wrote a furious reply on June 12, arguing that any effort at rearming Japan—even the limited step of establishing a maritime safety board or a Japanese coast guard—would face the immediate opposition of the Far Eastern Commission: in effect trying to play one of his nemeses off against the other. Later, he wrote another memorandum saying that he did not understand the thinking behind NSC 13/2 and arguing that, if implemented, it would contradict certain directives of the commission—as well as his mandate as "sole executive authority in the occupation of Japan."[21]

It did no good. Washington had made up its mind: Japan would now be guided to becoming a steadfast ally in containing Communism, not in spreading the gospel of democracy in Asia by example. The final document was approved on October 7, 1948, and Truman signed it on October 9. Plans were soon under way to develop Japan's fledgling new police force into a kind of civil militia—an important step toward creating a Japanese army. MacArthur pointed out that this plan was not only politically undesirable but militarily absurd—again, in vain.

Although few besides MacArthur realized it, the days of his virtually unlimited authority as American shogun were over. So were his hopes that he could, by sheer force of will and law, transform Japan into a society embodying his own rather utopian hopes for mankind, including renouncing the use of military force forever.

In fact, although no one knew it yet, the shift in the American policy toward Japan was coming just in time.

MacArthur made only two trips outside Japan in his first four years as head of SCAP. The first was to the Philippines, for Quezon's reinternment. The other was in the midst of his titanic battle over the final version of NSC 13/2, in September 1948, when he journeyed to Seoul, South Korea, for the inauguration of the country's first postwar president, Syngman Rhee.

He arrived on September 9, a bright clear day. Photographs show a relaxed MacArthur wearing a lei as he stood beside the two men of the hour, President Rhee and General Hodge. If Rhee looked tense but triumphant, Hodge was troubled and defeated. It had not been a happy three years since he had arrived as head of United States Forces in Korea (USFIK).

It was back in 1943 in Cairo when President Roosevelt, Winston Churchill, and Chinese president Chiang Kai-shek had pledged that once Japan was defeated, "in due course Korea shall become free and independent." The instruments for the liberation of Korea were to be the American and Red Armies.

Six days after Stalin declared war on Japan, Russian troops had poured across the border from Siberia into northern Korea. Three weeks after that, General Hodge and advance elements of his XXIV Corps had landed in the south.[22] Once Japan surrendered, both sides had agreed to disband Japanese forces in Korea according to the boundary drawn up by Captain Dean Rusk and his colleagues, with the Soviets accepting surrender of Japanese forces north of the 38th parallel and the Americans doing the same south of the line.

Then in the midst of this chaotic situation there arrived in Seoul Korea's elder statesman, Dr. Syngman Rhee.

Rhee was a lot like Douglas MacArthur: a man driven by a strong ego and a strong sense of destiny mixed with an imperious manner that some found admirable and others found overbearing. Five years older than MacArthur, he had been active in Korean nationalist movements for four decades. He had been present in Portsmouth, New Hampshire, when Teddy Roosevelt brought the Russian and Japanese ambassadors together to sign the treaty ending the Russo-Japanese War. Rhee had tried to persuade Roosevelt to guarantee Korea's independence in the treaty even as Japan was closing in on the peninsula, but failed.

For the next forty years Rhee lived as a wandering exile, first in the United States, then in China as head of the anti-Japanese provisional government of Korea. The war over, he returned to Korea in October on MacArthur's *Bataan II,* poised in his own mind and those of his supporters, to become the natural first president of the new Korean republic.

That required some doing. In December 1945, Russia, the United States, and Great Britain tried to set up a joint commission that would establish a trusteeship over Korea for a period of up to five years, as the first step to forming a provisional government and granting independence—Rhee's great dream.[23] The dream became a nightmare five months later, as the Communists closed the border between the two halves of Korea and the issue of Korean independence became caught up in the early rumblings of the Cold War.

For the next two and a half years there was frantic activity on either side of the 38th parallel, but in two very different directions. The Soviets on their side began building up a Communist-led Korean army and eliminating any anti-Communist opposition, while Hodges and the Americans in the south struggled to repatriate Japanese soldiers and civilians to their homeland and restore some semblance of law and order.

Everything that MacArthur excelled at totally eluded Hodge, including juggling different administrative tasks such as establishing law courts, a working police force, and bus and sanitary services, while also securing the trust and cooperation of leading political groups. Unlike MacArthur, who had won Japanese hearts with his obvious respect for Japanese culture and people, Hodge did not get along with Koreans. He had been overheard saying that Koreans were a "similar breed of cat" to the Japanese—not a remark geared to endear him to Koreans who had suffered from thirty-five years of brutal Japanese colonial rule.[24]

Hodge made things worse by having to rely on Koreans who had cooperated with Japanese occupiers in the civil administration of Korea, especially the hated police. In the minds of many, Hodge ruled Korea using a cabinet of quislings of widely differing political stripes (the Soviets, of course, installed only trustworthy, obedient Communists and dealt with political differences via a firing squad). Above all, he had a hard time negotiating with the tense, brittle Syngman Rhee. By that fateful August day, the pair were barely speaking to each other.

The result was an increasingly Soviet-style totalitarian state in the north, led by Stalin's willing puppet Kim Il Sung, whom Stalin supplied with a Communist army of 187,000 men complete with Russian-built artillery and tanks and planes. Violence and disaffection reigned in the south, however, much of it engineered and encouraged by Kim's Communist agents sneaking across the border. The first real trouble broke out in the autumn of 1946, when a Communist-led railway strike in Busan in South Korea spread to Daegu, and then to other southern towns. The strike turned violent, and General Hodge and USFIK had to establish an armed Korean constabulary—the ancestor of the Republic of Korea army, or ROK army—to put it down.

In the meantime, both the United Nations and the State Department, which oversaw the American part of the Korean Trusteeship Commission, maintained the fiction that the granting of independence to a united Korea was still possible. In 1947 the General Assembly even passed a resolution setting the stage for elections of a national Korean government, and withdrawal of all occupying forces, American and Soviet.

MacArthur was firmly in favor of the idea. He confessed to William Sebald that he thought the peninsula was militarily indefensible, and would be a distraction in the event of any future conflict with the Soviet Union or with Communist China's Mao Zedong. "I wouldn't put my foot in Korea," MacArthur allegedly said after a meeting with General Hodge. "It belongs to the State Department," which was technically true, since the administration of American occupation forces there fell to Foggy Bottom's jurisdiction, not MacArthur's SCAP. "They wanted it and they got it. I wouldn't touch it with a ten-foot pole."[25]

The problem was that while the Americans were eager to leave Korea, the Soviets were not. They were still consolidating the power of their puppet, Kim Il Sung, who by the start of 1948 had purged or assassinated the last of his Communist rivals and was now undisputed ruler of northern Korea from his capital at Pyongyang. When the UN-appointed commission requested permission to send representatives to supervise elections in the north, the Soviets and Kim refused. The elections in the south proceeded anyway, in May 1948. Syngman Rhee emerged as the clear winner, although the regime in the north refused to recognize the result.

The Communists' goal was becoming clear: to turn Korea into a Soviet satellite by imposing military rule in the north and fomenting revolution in the south. In response, the State Department did little or nothing. Its attention was diverted by the deteriorating situation in China, where Chiang's forces were retreating to a small remaining enclave along the coast. When Congress passed a $10 million military assistance package for Rhee's new government of South Korea, Foggy Bottom dithered over the export permits so that barely a trickle ever reached Seoul.[26]

But if Washington had lost interest in what was happening to Korea, MacArthur and Bill Sebald had not. Sebald traveled to Korea six times between 1947 and 1948, paying visits to Syngman Rhee's American advisors and to President Truman's special advisor on Korea, John Muccio, who stopped in Tokyo for a week in August 1948 to brief MacArthur on what was going on.

As theater commander of American forces in East Asia, MacArthur knew he would be involved if something truly awful happened on the peninsula. But the American Army mission in South Korea, the Korean Military Advisory Group or KMAG, and its commander, Brigadier General William Roberts, assured him the fledgling Republic of Korea army he was building would be able to handle any threat from North Korea. One night at dinner, Roberts spoke boastfully of "my army" and "my forces," and assured both Sebald and MacArthur, "I can handle the Commies."[27]

So it was with a reassured and calm mind that MacArthur landed in Seoul, and spoke to the assembled crowd at the ceremony inaugurating the new president of the new Republic of Korea, Syngman Rhee.

"I am profoundly moved to stand on the soil of Korea in this historic hour," he began, "to see liberty reborn, the cause of right and justice. For forty years I have observed with admiration the efforts of your patriots to cast off the oppressive bonds of foreign power." He went on to describe how the growing ideological conflict between East and West, between Communism and democracy, "may well determine the issue of a world at war or a world at peace." But none of this should influence the future of Korea as a free and independent country: "[Y]our national rebirth today is living proof that the concept of human freedom is far too deeply rooted in human society to ever perish."[28]

But MacArthur was wrong, at least in part. On September 9, 1948, the spirit of freedom was finally extinguished above the 38th parallel, as Kim Il Sung declared his People's Democratic Republic of Korea, headquartered at Pyongyang, while claiming sovereignty over the entire peninsula. The question now was whether freedom could survive in South Korea without American help.

Events soon made the answer an urgent one. Guerrilla fighting had already broken out along the border between North and South in April. In

October the Fourteenth Regiment of the ROK army broke out in mutiny and seized the cities of Yosu and Sunchon. No one doubted who had inspired the revolt, and what the objective was. With Hodge gone, along with virtually every American soldier, it took the South Korean constabulary three days to retake Yosun, and almost as long to reclaim Sunchon. Altogether, some 30,000 Koreans were killed, both soldiers and civilians. American advisors like Lieutenant Robert Shackleton were sickened by the sight of Communist atrocities, including cold-blooded mass killings. "Henceforth the terms Communist and butcher were to me synonymous," he remembered afterward. Yet Shackleton estimated his own Korean troops killed at least 300 Korean civilians through indiscriminate machine-gun fire.[29]

It was a grim foretaste of the slaughter to come. Yet only days before, on September 20, the Joint Chiefs of Staff had released a study that concluded, "[T]he best interests of the Korean people would be served by the withdrawal of all occupying forces from Korea at the earliest practicable date."[30] The Soviets agreed; in December they announced that their troops would be leaving after the New Year. There was no reason for them to stay. By now Kim Il Sung had a well-equipped army of nearly a quarter million men, and a 200-plane air force.[31] He was poised to take South Korea anytime he chose. Once his master, Josef Stalin, gave the go-ahead, the unification of Korea by military force would be a reality.

Without realizing it, MacArthur, the Americans, and Syngman Rhee were sitting on a time bomb. All it would take was a nod from a man in the Kremlin to set it off.

The man in the Kremlin and his allies were flexing their muscles in Japan as well. A revived Japanese labor movement, with strong Communist Party participation, was intent on disrupting industrial relations through protests and strikes. The Soviet representatives in the Allied Council for Japan became more and more obstructionist, until they finally walked out.[32]

But MacArthur's attention was largely focused on what was unfolding in a Tokyo courtroom in the early days of November 1948.

November 4 marked the conclusion of the war crimes trial of prominent

Japanese war leaders that had begun in January 1946, and that ended, in the words of one historian, as "the most disgraceful and least important achievement of the American occupation."[33]

MacArthur, for one, would have agreed with that judgment. He had no qualms about trying and executing military officers who violated the international laws of war, including Yamashita and Homma. But "the principle of holding criminally responsible the political leaders of the vanquished in war was repugnant to me," he later wrote. "I felt that to do so was to violate the most fundamental rules of criminal justice."[34]

That had been MacArthur's view since the earliest days of the occupation. The other leaders of the victorious Allied powers disagreed, however. They envisaged a Japanese equivalent of the Nürnberg trial of Hitler's henchmen for war crimes, and called together the International Military Tribunal of judges and prosecutors to try to convict Japan's wartime leadership, including former prime minister Tojo. The tribunal opened proceedings on January 19, 1946, to great fanfare in both the Western and the Japanese press.

MacArthur washed his hands of the entire affair; indeed, the tribunal's organizers had relieved him of any role in or responsibility for the tribunal before it began. But as the Tokyo trial dragged on month after tedious month, with witness after evasive witness, he began to sense that it was acting as a heavy undertow obstructing what he was trying to accomplish in creating a new Japan, and even sabotaging the bond of trust between Japanese and Americans that he was trying to build.

There was a prelude to the trouble to come when Prince Konoye, who had been a key advisor to Hirohito during the war, got wind of the fact that he was considered a possible defendant. Konoye, in fact, had spent months before the war trying to avert it; he even believed the Americans would see him as someone to be entrusted with a major leadership role in postwar Japan.[35] Instead, he was stunned to discover that he had been added to the list of potential war criminals, including Tojo and General Matsui, the officer in charge of Japanese forces during the Rape of Nanking. He was even ordered to report to Sugamo Prison on December 16, 1945, for questioning.

The order made MacArthur's staff deeply uncomfortable. "The understanding between us [i.e., General MacArthur and investigators] was that we would get word to Prince Konoye that we did not regard him as a war criminal like the others, that we only wanted him as a material witness," Robert Fearey, a SCAP official, remembered. "I am afraid that word of this did not get to Prince Konoye in time. Someone forgot to tell him."[36]

Instead, Konoye took a cyanide capsule the day before he was supposed to surrender. It was a bitter blow to MacArthur, and to Bonner Fellers, who had befriended Konoye and who had hoped Konoye could help draft a reform constitution. But fortunately for those who insisted that the vanquished Japanese leaders had to be punished, there were still plenty of other defendants. "They must have blood," Douglas MacArthur said, echoing his father's words during the Philippine insurgency, "and so there will be blood."

The "trial of the century," as it was termed by the media, was held at Ichigaya, the former headquarters of the Japanese army during the war. There were judges from eleven Allied nations, including the Soviet Union, more than 400 witnesses called, and some 779 affidavits from other witnesses entered in evidence against twenty-two defendants. Total documentation ran to more than 30,000 pages.[37] The British prosecutor, Sir William Comyns Carr, had pieced together a complicated indictment that ensured that the trial would drag on for two and a half years—twice as long as the trial's German equivalent at Nürnberg.

Yet as the proceedings wound along, they confirmed MacArthur's prediction that their impact would be the reverse of what the instigators had hoped. Far from convincing the Japanese public (more than one thousand spectators were in the courtroom at any given time) that their past was steeped in war crimes, they instead tarnished the image of the American occupation as fair-minded and nonvindictive. To the defendants, especially former premier Tojo, the trial offered a chance to present their decisions during the war in the best possible light—indeed, to whitewash Japan's aggressive war intentions. Tojo in particular was in fine fettle—arguing with prosecutors, contradicting witnesses, and presenting himself as a heroic leader and imperial Japan as a country that had been sinned against more than it had sinned.

The Allies, especially the United States, had provoked Japan into going to war, he said. Japan's aims in China, for example, had included "neither territorial ambition nor the idea of economic monopoly." Its empire overseas, the Greater East Asia Co-Prosperity Sphere, had been established to "secure political freedom for all peoples of Greater East Asia," not to exploit its subject peoples for Japan's gain. As for Tojo himself, he claimed he had not known that the Japanese fleet had set sail for the attack on Pearl Harbor, and "neither gave orders for, tolerated, nor connived at any inhuman acts," including massacres of civilians or prisoners of war. A prosecutor asked him if he wasn't ashamed of Japan's alliance with Adolf Hitler. "No, I do not entertain any such cowardly views," Tojo indignantly replied.[38]

But probably the most damaging admission came when Tojo was being cross-examined on the decision to go to war. He related that Emperor Hirohito had not been informed of the details of the Pearl Harbor attack plan, but had known of the decision to go to war. Hirohito had "assented, though reluctantly, to the war," Tojo told the court. "[N]one of us would have dared act against the Emperor's will."[39]

It was a grim moment of truth, both for the Tokyo trial and for the entire rationale of the American occupation. The framework for postwar Japan had been built around the idea of retaining the emperor as head of state, on the grounds that he was blameless for Japan's going to war—indeed, had even secretly opposed it. Tojo's admission shattered that illusion. There would have been no war if Hirohito hadn't approved of it, "though reluctantly." And if others who had approved of the decision to attack were now on trial for waging aggressive war, then why wasn't the emperor?

That became the unanswered question during the rest of the Tokyo trial—unanswered because the prosecution refused to let it be asked. In fact, prosecutors worked hard to keep any evidence showing Hirohito's war guilt from surfacing—or at least to bury it in the growing mounds of documentation. The fiction that Hirohito was blameless for the decisions made by his cabinet during seven years of war in Asia, costing some seventeen million lives, had to be maintained even at the expense of the truth, or—as some would argue afterward—justice itself.

By the time the trial finally ended, on November 4, 1948, the verdicts were almost an anticlimax. The formal judgment took eight days to read, from November 7 until November 12. No fewer than forty-five of the fifty-five charges against the accused were thrown out, although every defendant was found guilty of something. More strikingly, the judges themselves were sharply divided on who was guilty of what. The Indian justice, Radhabinod Pal, acquitted everyone in a judicial opinion that was almost as long as the original indictment. Another found five defendants not guilty, while two judges, Webb of Australia and Henri Bernard of France, were upset that Hirohito had escaped indictment and wrote scathing critiques of the proceedings that to this day hold up under expert scrutiny.[40]

Yet, as MacArthur himself had argued, the real problem had been in the very conception of the trial. The idea that one could organize a war crimes trial in Japan based on the Nürnberg model was misconceived from the start. In Japan there had been no inner circle or camarilla of devoted followers like the one Hitler had mobilized in the thirties. Likewise, there was no national party like the National Socialists; and there were no elite organizations like the SS and Gestapo, controlling and directing the course of government. In short, there was no Japanese Hitler, and no Japanese Himmler either. There were only self-interested, self-deluded men making decisions without regard to consequences—not unlike politicians anywhere. They had been driven by a brutal, inhumane ideology infused by illusions of racial superiority, but there was no organized campaign of genocide, or even collective war guilt, that a team of lawyers could unearth from the surviving documents.

So the sentences, when they came, were piecemeal and supported by only a majority of judges—in some cases a slender majority. Seven were sentenced to death; sixteen to life imprisonment. Former prime minister Koki Hirota was sentenced to death by the vote of only six of the eleven justices. MacArthur had been right: the trials proved to be a travesty. Some branded it "victor's injustice"; back in Washington George Kennan had to agree that the trials were "ill-conceived, psychologically unsound." It "would have been much better received and understood," he concluded, "if we had shot these people out of hand at the time of surrender."[41]

That still left the question of how to carry the sentences out. That responsibility, as it happened, fell on MacArthur as head of SCAP, leaving the irony that the man who had most opposed the trial now had to execute its verdicts. His solution to his dilemma was to summon each of the representatives of the eleven Allied powers involved in the trial, including the Philippines, and ask each for his view of the verdicts. One by one, the diplomats entered the office in the Dai-ichi building and went over the sentences with MacArthur. Only two, Chakravarty of India and Baron Lewe Van Aduard of Holland, recommended any reduction in sentences. Two others, one of whom was

Patrick Shaw of Australia, said they were not opposed to any changes, but would not go on the record opposing the sentences imposed.[42]

MacArthur called in Bill Sebald to witness his review of the final sentences.

He had decided to make no changes; he upheld every one of the tribunal's sentences, reading each one in a low, intense voice that, Sebald said later, "affected me deeply" with a reaction of "sadness, sympathy, admiration, and impending doom." He recommended that there be no photographers at any hanging.

MacArthur agreed; it "would violate all sense of decency." He would order the new commanding general of the Eighth Army, Walton Walker, to carry out the sentences one week after November 25. MacArthur set no definitive date, however, on which they were to be executed.[43]

Sebald watched MacArthur's composure crumple as they sat opposite each other in the Dai-ichi office. "Bill," MacArthur finally said in a low voice, "that was a difficult decision to make." Now it was in Walker's hands, and the United States Supreme Court's. The justices in Washington heard appeals from seven of the Tokyo trial defendants, including Tojo and Hirota, and on December 20 denied them all, saying "the military tribunal sentencing these petitioners has been set up by General MacArthur as the agent of the Allied Powers" and that "under the foregoing circumstances the courts of the United States have no power or authority to review, to affirm, set aside or annul the judgments and sentences."

The hangings were set to begin at Sugamo Prison at 12:01 A.M., December 23. Sebald attended the hangings, along with diplomats of the members of the Allied Council for Japan. MacArthur refused to go; if the Allied Council must have blood, he reasoned, they could do without him present.

In his mind the issue was closed. "I was pleasantly surprised at the attitude of the Japanese people during the period of trial," he wrote afterward. There were no public disturbances, no disorderly petitions on behalf of the condemned. On the contrary, "the prisoners and their families made it a point to write letters to me and to the tribunal after their conviction to express their thanks for our impartiality and justice."[44]

Yet he knew the trials had not helped the American cause in Japan. It had all been so unnecessary, including the revelations about the emperor's role in the war. MacArthur and Feller's stand on Hirohito had been clear from the start: it was impossible to move forward without him, and any calculation of his status had to depend on what he would do in the future, not what he had done in the past. And so Hirohito remained in power; Japan's political establishment had been rocked but not overthrown.

Meanwhile, seven men had died for crimes they may or may not have committed—crimes they may or may not have been able to prevent. Some observers, including India's justice Pal, had wondered aloud whether American leaders on trial for the firebombing of Japan or the dropping of atomic bombs on Hiroshima and Nagasaki would have fared as well. It's a debate that still goes on today.

In the end, the outcome of the Tokyo war crimes trial was another sign that MacArthur's awesome authority as head of SCAP was fading. First there had been Kennan's visit, and the promulgation of NSC 13/2; then came fresh pro-Communist labor demonstrations in the spring of 1950, surrounding May Day, that threatened to disrupt the new social compact MacArthur had wanted for Japan.

But the real forces that would rip apart MacArthur's hope that the American occupation of Japan pointed the way to a peaceful future, were gathering on the Korean peninsula 400 miles away.

By the spring of 1950, the containment policy that Truman, Kennan, and Secretary of State Acheson had developed was working well in Europe. The Atlantic Alliance, anchored in NATO, provided a military shield against Soviet expansion; the Marshall Plan was reviving Western Europe's society and economy.

An emergency aid program to Greece and Turkey had halted the Soviet threat to the eastern Mediterranean, while the Berlin Airlift had forestalled a major crisis—while assuring Europeans that the United States would stand by its commitments.

In Asia, however, containment had not fared so well. In addition to the rise of the new Soviet satellite North Korea, the collapse of nationalist China and Mao's takeover of the Chinese mainland in early 1949 had sent shock waves through the region but also through Washington. The question of how the Truman administration had managed to "lose China" would animate the first critics of containment on the right, who questioned whether containment of the Soviet Union was really a sufficient policy when tens of millions remained enslaved behind the Iron Curtain—and when Communism seemed to be steadily advancing on the other side of the world, in the Pacific. The first test of a Soviet atomic bomb, in September 1949, only intensified the debate on Capitol Hill as to who was really winning the Cold War and who was losing.

The policy of containment suffered from a major flaw. It assumed that Stalin and his allies would stand by while the United States and its allies enveloped them with a broad network of diplomatic and military alliances, and remain passive while the internal contradictions of Communist rule—as Kennan had postulated in his Long Telegram—led to Communism's final collapse.[45] Kennan and the other architects of containment never considered what would happen if Communism decided to break the deadlock, and chose as the point of breakout not where American forces were unambiguously committed, like Western Europe, but a place where political and strategic realities militated against U.S. action.

That place was Korea, and the man who would have to save containment from its major strategic flaw would be Douglas MacArthur.

CHAPTER 29
WAR AGAIN

No lack of resolve here.

—GEORGE F. KENNAN, LATE JUNE 1950

It was before dawn on Sunday, June 25, 1950, when the phone rang in MacArthur's bedroom in the American embassy in Tokyo. It was the duty officer at GHQ on the line, and his voice was tense and urgent.

"General, we have just received a dispatch from Seoul, advising that the North Koreans have struck in great strength south across the 38th Parallel at four o'clock this morning."

MacArthur's reaction was "an uncanny feeling of nightmare." Nine years earlier a similar Sunday phone call had come to him in his Manila Hotel penthouse, with the dreadful news of Pearl Harbor. Now, he realized, a similar policy of weakness and neglect had allowed North Korea, backed by its Soviet and Chinese allies, to try to overrun its southern neighbor—and there was little or nothing MacArthur or U.S. forces could do to stop them.[1]

Of course, Korea was a pot that had been coming to a boil for years.

There were the disagreements over elections in the North and the South, with the Soviets ultimately closing the border. There were the strikes and revolts in 1948, culminating in the army mutiny in October that year that had claimed some 30,000 lives.

In the end, the military balance of power in Korea had coalesced not around the United States and the Soviet Union, but around their two proxies: Kim Il Sung and his Communist People's Democratic Republic of Korea north of the 38th parallel, and Syngman Rhee and his Republic of Korea to the south, with a growing Republic of Korea Army, or ROKA, trained and equipped by the United States. Although the two leaders were ideological opposites, both Kim and Rhee were fervently committed to the same goal, the unification of the peninsula by force if necessary, under their own government.

Kim had the better tools to do it. While the Americans had supplied Syngman Rhee with arms to defend his country from attack, they steadfastly refused to give him weapons for going on the offensive across the border. As a result, the Republic of Korea's "army" was hardly more than a glorified police force. By contrast, when the Soviets left the peninsula in January 1949, they had left behind tons of equipment for Kim's Korean People's Army or KPA, including late-model T-34 tanks—the same tanks that had spearheaded the Russian advance into Berlin in 1945. In addition, any Communist force advancing south would find a ready and willing fifth column, consisting of thousands of North Koreans who had infiltrated across the 38th parallel over the past four years, in anticipation of an invasion by Pyongyang.

But would such an invasion take place, and if so, when? Those were the key questions that had bedeviled Kim Il Sung for almost two years. He had sensed American and South Korean weakness from the start, but when he had approached Stalin about the possibility of an attack, Stalin had hesitated. The Soviet dictator was not ready yet for an enterprise that could lead to a full-scale confrontation with the West.

All the same, Kim's case was immensely helped by the fall of China to Mao Zedong. As 1950 dawned, the Communist victory was complete, with Mao's massive army available to support his North Korean neighbor. Besides, if the United States had been unwilling to intervene to save a major ally like China from a Communist takeover, how likely was it that Washington—or MacArthur in Tokyo, for that matter—would intervene to save a minor ally like South Korea?

MacArthur had already given his answer to that question in March 1949 during an interview with *The New York Times,* on America's strategic position in Cold War Asia since the fall of China. At one time the United States had seen the Pacific Ocean as a geographic barrier against potential enemies. Now, MacArthur had averred, Americans had to realize that the ocean had become "the avenue of possible enemy approach," requiring a clear line of demarcation at which defense in Asia automatically becomes defense of the United States.

Today "our line of defense runs through the chain of islands fringing the coast of Asia," he told reporter G. Ward Price in that 1949 interview. "It starts from the Philippines and continues through the Ryukyu Archipelago, which includes its main bastion, Okinawa. Then it bends back through Japan and the Aleutian Islands chain to Alaska."[2]

There was no mention of Korea, and no wonder. MacArthur had no resources to defend the peninsula even if he had wanted to. There was only one small American combat team left in South Korea, after SUFIK came to a formal end. His and General Walker's Eighth Army in Japan had now shrunk to barely 87,000 men—of which only 27,000 were in combat units. His Far Eastern Air Force had 34,000 men and 1,172 planes, with more than thirty bases scattered across the western Pacific, including Japan. But only half were fighters and bombers, and MacArthur had vetoed using Japanese funds to build longer airstrips for the new jet-powered P-80 fighters that the air force was now developing.[3]

Even more important, the man who had been his architect of airpower, General George Kenney, had long ago gone back to the States. So had his successor Ennis Whitehead. The new head of the FEAF was General George Stratemeyer, an able airman and keen MacArthur admirer. But he did not have the imagination or personal clout that Kenney had brought to the job, which demanded doing more with less; and since V-E Day and V-J Day, less was now the rule in the U.S. military establishment. The U.S. Army had shrunk to just ten incomplete divisions (with two in Germany and four in Japan). The FEAF's fighter and bomber force was the biggest anywhere outside the United States. As for the navy, its global commitments meant that only eighteen of its surviving fighting ships were available in the western Pacific—this, from a navy that had supplied MacArthur with more than 700 combatant vessels in 1945.[4]

If there were any lingering doubts about whether the United States considered defending South Korea a matter of pressing interest, Assistant Secretary of State Dean Acheson had laid them to rest in a speech at the National Press Club on January 12, 1950.

It was a speech about America's future role in Asia as a carrier of freedom—a favorite MacArthur theme. It also repeated MacArthur's description of America's vital defensive perimeter in Asia down to the last detail, with no mention of Korea or even of Formosa, Chiang Kai-shek's last remaining stronghold. Then Acheson added two more fateful sentences:

> So far as the military security of other areas in the Pacific is concerned, it must be clear that no person can guarantee these areas against military attack. . . . Should such an attack occur . . . the initial reliance must be on the people attacked to resist it and then upon the commitments of the entire civilized world under the Charter of the United Nations.

In the Kremlin as well as Beijing and Pyongyang, this passage was immediately interpreted as meaning that America would not intervene unilaterally to defend areas outside that defensive perimeter, including South Korea and Formosa. As if to reinforce that interpretation, President Truman had already declared that no more military aid or assistance would be given to the Chinese Nationalists in Formosa.[5]

How much of this represented an open invitation for Kim to invade South Korea can be a matter of debate. In fairness, when Acheson and Truman's foreign policy team thought about American grand strategy, they were thinking of a *general* war with the Russians. This would come, they believed, with either a surprise Soviet attack on the United States or a Soviet invasion of Western Europe.[6] No one contemplated a limited invasion of a small country in Asia as part of Soviet plans.

But MacArthur and his G-2, Charles Willoughby, did. Cross-border raids and skirmishes between ROKA troops and the KPA had become almost daily occurrences. Willoughby began circulating intelligence estimates in June 1950 that an attack on South Korea was in the offing—or then again, it might not be (this was Willoughby carefully hedging his bets again). MacArthur was not overly worried; on his and William Sebald's visits with GMAC commander General Roberts they kept getting the general's assurances that he and the ROKA could "handle the Commies." Sebald recalled, "I can hardly imagine a more vociferous advocate of South Korean military prowess"—or, as it happened, a more mistaken one.[7]

Because this time Willoughby was right the first time. Kim Il Sung had been ready to strike the south since early spring. As Soviet records would later reveal, Kim had been hectoring Stalin since 1949 to allow him to launch a full-scale invasion of the south in order to unite the peninsula under Communist rule. That May his army got its first modern T-34/85 tanks; between October and November another eighty-seven were added to the initial sixty-four, plus eighty-six combat aircraft. Meanwhile, Soviet advisors convinced Mao to transfer two ethnic Korean divisions from his forces to the North Korean army.[8]

Then after Acheson's National Press Club speech, in February and March 1950 Stalin sent a 150-man elite training mission of Red Army veterans to Pyongyang, bringing the total number of Soviet military personnel in the north to more than a thousand. At the same time, American officers and men in the south numbered less than two hundred.[9]

Yet what finally tipped Stalin's hand was Kim's trip to Moscow on April 25, when he announced that their Chinese Communist ally, Mao Zedong, was willing to provide logistical support for an invasion. Again he reassured the Soviet dictator that the Americans would not intervene—certainly not in time to save South Korea.

Stalin needed no more persuasion, and on May 14 Kim Il Sung went to Beijing to make final plans with Mao. A month later North Korean units were in position, and on June 15 Stalin's ambassador was told that all was ready.[10]

Ten days later the artillery sounded and the tanks rolled.

Given the months of preparation in the Communist north, Willoughby had had a strong inkling that something was up. He had numerous reports of North Korea's steady buildup. Based on Korean assessments on the ground,

FECOM had sent Washington warnings of a possible invasion in March and April 1950. Those turned out to be false; Stalin wasn't yet convinced, and the North Korean army wasn't ready.[11]

The final warning that Willoughby issued in June was more accurate and should have carried more weight. But Willoughby had convinced himself that the final decision to attack would be Stalin's, not Kim's, and that Moscow would wait until the geopolitical situation in Asia was more propitious. In addition, Willoughby refused to believe reports from South Korean military intelligence that weren't backed up by his own agents.

Instead, he was content to predict an imminent invasion, without assessing when it would come. By so doing, he failed to make MacArthur aware that FECOM faced a major crisis, one that would reverberate far beyond Korea to Communist China, Japan, and Formosa—and indeed around the world.[12]

Once again Willoughby had let MacArthur down, as he had many times in the past. Yet this time MacArthur's skill in improvisation, and his confidence that he would eventually come out on top no matter what the enemy did, would be put to the supreme test—even more so than in the Philippines in December 1941. It would take every ounce of willpower and stamina that the seventy-year-old supreme commander had, to turn around what was unfolding as a major disaster on the Korean peninsula.

Fortunately, help was at hand in the person of John Foster Dulles. The Republican Party's most senior diplomat, he was in Tokyo by sheer coincidence: Dean Acheson had sent him there as special envoy to discuss a Japanese peace treaty with MacArthur. Even more coincidentally, only two days before, he had been on a fact-finding trip in Korea. FECOM officers had taken him up to the 38th parallel, separating North and South Korea, and assured Dulles, just as they had assured MacArthur, that there were no signs of any imminent attack and that the South Korean army was more than ready to deal with it if and when it came.[13] Indeed, if Dulles had stayed in Seoul another week, he would have been right in the heart of the fighting.

Although Dulles was a Republican himself, his word carried weight in the Truman White House and with people like Acheson and Marshall. That

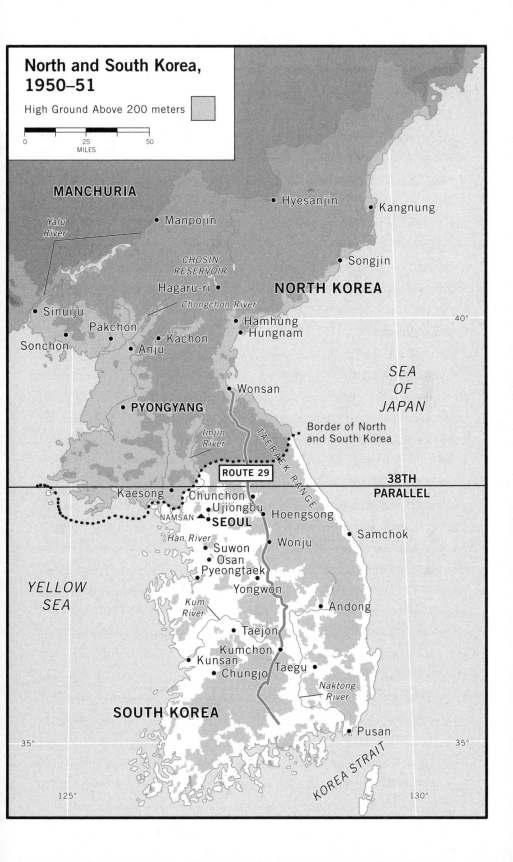

North and South Korea, 1950–51

High Ground Above 200 meters

0   25   50
MILES

MANCHURIA

Yalu River

MANPOJIN •

• Hyesanjin

• Kangnung

CHOSIN RESERVOIR

Hagaru-ri •

Chongchon River

NORTH KOREA

• Songjin

• Sinuiju

Pakchon •

• Hamhung
• Hungnam

Sonchon •

• Kachon
• Anju

40°

• Wonsan

SEA
OF
JAPAN

• PYONGYANG

Imjin River

TAEBAEK RANGE

Border of North
and South Korea

ROUTE 29

38TH
PARALLEL

Kaesong •

• Chunchon

• Hoengsong

Ujiongbu •

NAMSAN ▲ SEOUL

Han River

• Wonju

• Samchok

• Suwon
• Osan
Pyeongtaek •

YELLOW
SEA

Kum River

• Yongwon

• Andong

• Taejon

Kumchon •

• Kunsan

Chungjo •

Taegu •

Naktong River

SOUTH KOREA

• Pusan

35°   35°

KOREA STRAIT

125°   130°

made him the perfect ally for MacArthur to get the message across that the situation in Korea meant war, and that the United States had to act.

In the late afternoon of June 25 Dulles and MacArthur had a long meeting. They were in complete agreement. To sit by while South Korea was overrun would set off "a disastrous chain of events leading most probably to world war," was the way Dulles put it later to Truman. MacArthur's dispatch called the North's attack "serious in strength and strategic intent" and "an undisguised act of war." The implication was that it was aimed at the United States and the West, not just South Korea, and demanded a strong response.[14]

MacArthur seemed "very calm," according to Bill Matthews, a reporter for the *Arizona Daily Star* who saw the general that evening. He told Matthews the attack "was an act of international banditry: inexcusable, unprovoked aggression."

Despite his conviction that the United States had every reason to react unilaterally, MacArthur's dispatch to Washington also urged summoning the United Nations to take a hand; so had Dulles's. MacArthur realized that there was immense propaganda value in having the United Nations back the use of force to expel Kim Il Sung's forces from the south. All the same, he was convinced that only prompt action could reverse the situation and avert a major crisis, and that meant the United States.

"I hope the American people have the guts to rise to this occasion," he told Matthews, especially since it was coming so soon after the end of the biggest war in American history. He still believed General Roberts's optimistic view that the South Koreans could hold their ground against Kim's forces, at least temporarily. Even so, he had already ordered the evacuation of all American and United Nations personnel from Korea.[15]

Then in the early morning of June 26 MacArthur was called to the phone again. This time it was President Syngman Rhee.

"You have to save Korea," he sobbed into the phone. MacArthur promised to send ten P-51 Mustang fighter-bombers, seventy-one howitzers, and antitank rocket launchers from FECOM's inventory.[16] Still, the decision to do more, he knew, rested with Washington. He had made his recommendation; it was up to Truman and his people to decide whether America would stand and fight, or let Korea be overrun.

For once Washington did not let him down. When word of the North

Korean attack reached President Truman in Independence, Missouri, he had flown back to Washington early the next morning. He told his secretary of state that he had been thinking about Hitler and Mussolini; this time the totalitarians would not get away with aggression. America would send in troops at once.[17]

The problem was, there were no troops—or very few. In 1945 America had spent $50 billion on defense; in 1950 it spent a tenth of that amount, barely $5 billion. Its 8.25-million-man military had shrunk to fewer than 600,000, and most of those were still in Europe. The Eighth Army's four undermanned, underequipped divisions would somehow have to stem the massive Communist tide on their own.

Meanwhile members of the UN Security Council (minus the Soviet Union, which was boycotting the council—in retrospect a fatal mistake) passed a resolution ordering both Koreas to "cease hostilities" and North Korea to return its forces north of the 38th parallel, opening the door to U.S. intervention to enforce the resolution. With the unanimous agreement of the Joint Chiefs, Truman authorized MacArthur to provide military assistance to the ROK army; to use U.S. and naval forces to protect U.S. and UN personnel evacuating Korea, and to send a military survey team to Korea. Meanwhile, the Seventh Fleet would set out from Okinawa to protect Formosa, in case the Communists made a move there.[18]

"No lack of resolve here," George Kennan chortled—and indeed, it was more resolve than America had shown in Asia in years. Still, "I don't want to go to war," Truman said the next day. He certainly didn't think the American people would stand for it without more advance persuasion by their political leaders, including Truman himself. Moreover, his mind, like almost everyone else's in Washington, was on what the Soviets were up to in Europe—or alternately the Middle East, where Truman anticipated a similar lightning strike on Iran.[19]

But the head of SCAP and FECOM was thinking in Asian, not Eurocentric terms. MacArthur hoped the crisis in Korea would spark the formation of an American-led grand anti-Communist coalition involving the Philippines, Japan, and Nationalist China. He would be bitterly disappointed when he learned that Truman had dismissed an offer from Chiang Kai-shek to send two of his infantry divisions to Korea.[20] But at least on June 28, as reports came in of fierce fighting around the South Korean capital, MacArthur got permission to authorize American air strikes anywhere in Korea north of the 38th parallel.

MacArthur was delighted. Ever since George Kenney had mobilized the Fifth Air Force into a decisive instrument of victory during the campaigns in New Guinea, MacArthur had believed that airpower could turn defeat into victory—and his new air chief, General Stratemeyer, encouraged him to think that something similar could happen in Korea, as long as he could take out airfields in North Korea and gain air superiority in the south.[21]

But first MacArthur was going to fly to Seoul to see the situation for himself.

It was a cold, rainy morning on June 29 when he set out in *Bataan II* under its new commander, Lieutenant Colonel Anthony Story. MacArthur lit his customary corncob pipe, which, he tells us in his memoirs, he hadn't lit during all his time in Japan. "Haven't seen you smoke that pipe, General, for years," someone on the staff pointed out.

"Don't dare smoke it back there in Tokyo," MacArthur growled. "They'd think I was nothing but a farmer. The Peers Club would surely blackball me."

But now he was back into a major shooting war, his third in a little over three decades. "Once again I was being thrust into the breach against almost insuperable odds," he remembered. "Once again it looked like a forlorn hope."[22]

The remark sounded dramatic, but it was hardly an exaggeration. When he landed at Suwon, twenty miles south of Seoul—the capital was under fierce attack—he found a South Korean army outnumbered, outgunned, and overrun, and a South Korean government in disarray. Yet the general collapse that the Communists had anticipated (Kim had expected to be in Seoul in less than a week) hadn't happened. The armored cars of the ROKA Cavalry Regiment were smashed to pieces by advancing T-34s but refused to retreat in the face of the superior firepower. Other ROKA units fought with suicidal determination, officers dying alongside their soldiers.

Still, the Communist tide was unstoppable. President Rhee had been forced to move the capital from Seoul to Taegu, while the American embassy set bonfires of confidential papers as the city prepared for the end.

On June 27 the first North Korean tanks rolled into Seoul, where some

South Korean units continued to fight until the last man was killed or wounded. The North Koreans began shooting hundreds of POWs, while radical students greeted them with cheers and songs even as Communist security teams began rounding up "class enemies" trapped in the city.[23]

But still South Korea did not collapse. This was something as worrying to the Soviets as it was heartening to the Americans—and MacArthur. Perhaps there was still a way to save the country, if he could figure out how to get his forces on the peninsula in time.

Seoul fell exactly one day before MacArthur and *Bataan II* touched down at Suwon airport, twenty miles to the south of the capital. He climbed out onto the tarmac, along with Willoughby; Brigadier General John Church, who was head of the fifteen-man survey team MacArthur had set up to liaison with the ROK chief of staff; and Colonel R. K. "Pinky" Wright, MacArthur's new G-3 in charge of planning. All around them were planes burning from a North Korean air raid minutes before they landed. So MacArthur ordered Story and *Bataan II* to fly back to Japan before there was another air raid—and told his staff to find some ground transport.

The staff finally rounded up a convoy of seven or eight jeeps and an old Dodge sedan. MacArthur climbed into the back of the sedan and they drove off. They rolled past long columns of ROK troops and civilians fleeing the destruction in Seoul. There were "retreating, panting columns of disorganized troops," MacArthur later wrote," the drab color of their weaving lines interspersed here and there with the bright red crosses of ambulances filled with broken, groaning men," and hordes of civilians, "carrying all their worldly belonging on their backs, and leading their terror-stricken but wide eyed, uncrying children" away from death at the hands of the Communists.[24]

MacArthur had told his nervous staff he wanted to drive to the Han River, where an ROK army unit was making a final stand at the last bridge leading out of Seoul. When they reached the bridge, it was under heavy artillery and mortar fire. They were only one mile from Seoul: "I could see the towers of smoke rising from the ruins of this fourteenth-century city," MacArthur remembered. He insisted on climbing to the top of a small hill overlooking the Han, oblivious to the constant clump of Red mortar fire, before returning to the jeeps and heading back to Suwon.

On the way, North Korean planes began passing overhead, engaged in dogfights with American P-51s. The planes swooped so close that Wright could hear spent .50-caliber cartridges from their guns bouncing off the hoods of the cars. One jeep after another pulled off the road as everyone took cover—everyone, that is, except MacArthur. When Wright looked back, he saw the general still sitting calmly in the back of the Dodge, quietly smoking his pipe.

Wright dashed back to the car, keeping a wary eye on the planes overhead.

"General, don't you think you should get out?" he asked.

"Aw, no," MacArthur answered. "These things aren't going to hit me."[25]

On the plane ride back to Japan late that afternoon MacArthur began to draw up his report in his mind.

"The scene along the Han was enough to convince me that the defensive potential of South Korea had already been exhausted," he remembered later. "Even with air and naval support, the South Koreans could not stop the enemy's headlong rush south . . . All Korea would then be theirs"—that is, until the Americans stepped in.

"The South Korean forces are in confusion," his report to Washington began. "It is essential that the enemy advance be held or its impetus will threaten the over-running of all Korea. The South Korean army is incapable of counteraction. . . . The only assurance for holding the present line and *the ability to regain later the lost ground* [emphasis added] is through the introduction of United States ground combat forces into the Korean battle area."

American air and naval support would not be enough, MacArthur said bluntly. It was time to put boots on the ground, as many as possible.[26]

As this first radiogram revealed, already in the midst of chaos and imminent defeat, MacArthur was thinking of how to go on the offensive to retrieve the situation.

MacArthur's report arrived on Truman's desk on June 30 and set off another storm of argument and decision making.

Truman and Secretary of Defense Louis Johnson were still not convinced that going to war was necessary, or that the Republican-dominated Congress would go along with authorizing war without using the vote as a platform for attacking Truman's botched China policy. Johnson had overseen drastic cuts in America's military posture as part of a return to peacetime "normal"; he was in no mood to reverse direction even now, after North Korea's invasion.

So MacArthur's quick series of requests for reinforcements—first for troops to raise the Eighth Army's four divisions back to full strength; then for another four and a half combat divisions, a Marine regimental combat team and Marine aircraft group along with no fewer than fifteen battalions of heavy howitzers and self-propelled artillery and one medium tank battalion for every division—sent successive shock waves through the Pentagon and Blair House. Everyone saw at once that supplying this kind of buildup would mean returning America to wartime mobilization, as well as a draft. Truman and the Joint Chiefs turned MacArthur down. At Acheson's urging, they also turned down the idea of asking Chiang Kai-shek for troops. The general feeling was that if Korea was indeed part of a general Communist offensive and Formosa was next, Chiang would need all his troops to defend the island.[27]

They could, however, authorize sending two divisions that MacArthur already had in the area, both in Japan and in Okinawa, to South Korea. These troops could help to stiffen ROK resistance along a line they were desperately fighting to hold, on the banks of the Han River. Three tank battalions in the States were released for dispatch to Korea. Washington also allowed MacArthur to compose a fourth out of light tank companies already in the theater.[28]

Congressional leaders assembled at Blair House went along with the plan.

"We were then fully committed," Dean Acheson noted in his memoirs.[29] With a wary eye still fixed on Europe, America was sending ground troops into Korea. Now it was up to MacArthur to make sure they weren't too little too late.

The first Americans to arrive were part of a tiny combat team known as Smith Force, after its commander Lieutenant Colonel Charles B. "Brad" Smith. They were two rifle companies from the Twenty-fourth Division and a 105 mm howitzer battery.

All told, there were 540 men, although other eager volunteers joined in as the group formed up on July 1 at Kumamoto, Kyushu. By now Stratemeyer's bombers had slowed the North Korean offensive to a crawl, and had taken out key bridges across the Han. But the Communists had somehow managed to ferry some of their T-34s across the river, and by the time Colonel Smith and his men were ready to go into action, ROK resistance along the Han had crumbled and soldiers and more refugees were streaming toward the rear.

Smith Force took up position on a hill three miles north of Osan, twenty-five miles south of the Han River. Their commander thought he could at least slow down the North Korean force headed toward him, the KPA's elite Fourth Division. But with only a handful of howitzers, some outdated bazookas, and just six modern anti-tank HEAT rounds—plus a steady heavy rain that made air support impossible—the Americans didn't have a chance.[30] When the North Koreans plowed into their line on July 5, Smith's men still managed to cripple four of the KPA T-34s in a desperate seven-and-a-half-hour battle before abandoning their weapons and taking to the hills.

By the time Smith rallied his men, he had lost 40 percent of his command. But their sacrifice had bought valuable time. Now other American troops were arriving, battalion by battalion, even as North Korean troops and tanks pushed through another American-held position farther south, at Pyeong-taek, the next day, sending men from the newly disembarked Thirty-fourth Infantry reeling to the rear.[31]

Over the course of the next week, July 5 through July 12, the same pattern repeated itself. Small groups of GIs armed with bazookas, rocket launchers, some machine guns, and a couple of field howitzers took on wave upon wave of North Korean tanks and infantry, laying down lethal, punishing fire before having to fall back, sometimes in such haste that they had to leave their weapons behind. Eventually they would arrive, spent and exhausted but still alive, at the next American line of defense, where they got new weapons and started all over again. Some observers, especially reporters, blamed the poor performance on MacArthur and the American occupation of Japan, claiming that it had made his men soft and sloppy and unprepared for combat on the barren plains and harsh mountain ridges of South Korea. The image of Americans panicking and running away in the early days of the Korean War has passed into legend.

But as historian Allan Millett has pointed out, that image is untrue and unfair. No infantry formation was going to hold the battlefield by itself without tanks and strong air and artillery support, while enemy armor was driving at its front and enemy infantry kept surging around its flanks to surround and cut off any line of retreat. So the Americans found themselves being shoved steadily down the peninsula, as casualties mounted—sometimes precipitously. The Thirty-fourth Infantry, for example, which had arrived on July 3 with 640 men, had only 175 left on July 8.[32]

Yet their heroic resistance against fierce odds was slowing the North Korean offensive to a crawl, and bolstering South Korean morale. Above all, it was buying time for MacArthur to pull together the combined forces he needed to bring the Communist advance to a halt.

That effort started with the air force. Even before he landed back in Tokyo on June 29, MacArthur had ordered General Stratemeyer to start bombing Communist air bases north of the 38th parallel, even though he was still authorized to use American airpower only *south* of the parallel. "Take out North Korean airfield immediately," was Stratemeyer's terse message to his Fifth Air Force commander. "[N]o publicity. MacArthur approves."[33]

Stratemeyer's Far East Air Force started the war with 1,100 aircraft, including B-29 heavy bombers left over from the air war on Japan. That number quickly swelled over the next several months as air force planes, backed by navy and marine aircraft operating from carriers, pounded the North Korean advancing columns and supply lines, took out bridges and railroad junctions in both the north and the south, and scrubbed the skies clear of Communist aircraft. By July 10 the air force had established clear air supremacy over Korea and the North Korean air force was virtually wiped out. By then the navy together with British warships was setting up a blockade around the entire peninsula, and Australian, Canadian, New Zealand, and Dutch warships were on their way to join in.[34]

This was one of the novel aspects of the escalating conflict both for the United States and for MacArthur. He and his men now had allies to help out at the very start of the fight, instead of midway through (as with the British and Russians in World War Two) or at the tail end, as with MacArthur's losing fight for Bataan. Thanks to a United Nations resolution authorizing the use of force to expel North Korea from south of the 38th parallel, soldiers and ships from a dozen nations would soon be lending aid and support.

And on July 8, MacArthur was appointed commander in chief of all of them, as Commander-in-Chief, UN Command, in addition to retaining his position as SCAP. Six days later, President Rhee gave him overall command of ROK forces as well.[35]

Whatever Truman's personal misgivings about MacArthur, he didn't hesitate to approve the Joint Chiefs' recommendation to give him the supreme UN post. In the words of the official history of the JCS, "There was only one conceivable choice."[36] Others were not so sure. While *The New York Times* itself endorsed the appointment ("fate could not have chosen a man better qualified to command the unreserved confidence of the people of this country"), one of its rising columnists, James Reston, noted that MacArthur was "a sovereign power in his own right, with stubborn confidence in his own judgment." How likely was it that the seventy-year-old, who had already authorized air attacks on North Korea without the president's go-ahead, would display the "diplomacy and a vast concern for the opinions and sensitivities of others [that] are the political qualities essential to his new assignment"?[37]

To MacArthur, of course, critics like Reston were no more than chihuahuas snapping at his heels. Of course he would know how to handle a multinational coalition. He would propose a plan, and they would approve it. He also knew that, as in the Southwest Pacific, the United States would provide the overwhelming bulk of forces. American officers would head the bulk of commands; American boys would do the bulk of the dying. It was only fitting that he, as the United States Army's most experienced and decorated officer, with half a century of active service—more than a quarter of that spent in foreign countries—plus a long record of handling desperate situations, should take overall charge.

He wrote a grateful note to President Truman that concluded:

"I can only repeat the pledge of my complete personal loyalty to you as well as an absolute devotion to your monumental struggle for peace and good will throughout the world. I hope I will not fail you."

The 40,000 or so American troops now in Korea and their South Korean counterparts hoped so too.[38]

The first phase of MacArthur's strategy had been to slow the North Korean advance and prevent a South Korean collapse. It had meant throwing in troops and equipment piecemeal, but "I had hoped by that arrogant display of strength to fool the enemy into a belief that I had greater resources than I did."[39]

By July 19 that display of strength had come down to a desperate stand at the city of Taejon, south of the river Kum. Some half a million refugees choked the city streets as American and ROK forces prepared for a determined Communist assault. The Americans now had tanks—the first had gone into action on the 11th—and modern 3.5-inch tank-busting bazookas, but not nearly enough of them. A relentless tidal wave of T-34s swept into the city on the 20th; units from the Twenty-fourth Division mounted a hard but hopeless fight, knocking out twenty of the enemy tanks. But then resistance gave way as the Communists once again swept around the underdefended flanks. Men dropped their weapons and took to their heels; the Twenty-fourth's commander, Major General William Dean, was taken prisoner.

"There was a spirit of hopelessness and confusion" among the survivors as they fell back to the south and east, a reporter noted, that "must have created a black and defeatist atmosphere."[40]

By now MacArthur had shipped three of the Eighth Army's divisions to Korea, including the First Cavalry Division, which had spearheaded MacArthur's drive to retake Manila in February 1945. Now it arrived on the battlefield from Japan confident that it could do something similar in turning the battle around here. Instead, the men of the First Cav soon found themselves flying backward in full retreat, as the North Korean advance seemed unstoppable.

Yet Taejon proved to be the apogee of Communist dominance on the battlefield. The second phase of MacArthur's strategy was about to begin: creating a stable and secure defensive line that would halt the Communists cold. Once that was done, MacArthur explained to the Joint Chiefs, he could "fully exploit our air and sea control, and, by amphibious maneuver, strike behind his mass of ground forces." That memo had been written on July 7. Already, even as the situation on the ground had never looked bleaker, the outline of what would happen in the next two months was clear in his mind.[41]

The place MacArthur chose, and circumstances dictated, for that defensive line was around the port city of Pusan, on South Korea's southeastern coast. The terrain around Pusan was ringed by high hills, highly defensible from their eastern slopes; there would be no room for any more Communist flanking movements. The port itself would be useful for resupply—it could handle up to 10,000 tons a day—and shipping in more reinforcements. At worst, it would be vital for evacuation if a final enemy assault proved too much to contain.

On August 1 MacArthur and his Eighth Army commander, General Walton Walker, ordered all American and ROK units to fall back to the Pusan perimeter, as it was now designated, an area extending eighty miles from north to south and fifty miles from east to west. Three days later, every bridge leading to the perimeter was blown up. Some 47,000 U.S. Army and Marine troops, and 45,000 South Korean troops, now began digging in as North Korean units quickly moved up to occupy the rest of the peninsula. Walton set up his Eighth Army headquarters at Pusan, as did Syngman Rhee's government. It was now an island of resistance, in a land submerged under the Communist flood.

From MacArthur's office in Tokyo, there must have been times when the retreat to Pusan seemed hauntingly like the retreat on Bataan. The long, losing, fighting withdrawal down a foreign peninsula against a ruthless enemy; the endless lines of refugees and weary troops; the final last-ditch perimeter from which there was no retreat. Certainly many who were there, like Marshall and Willoughby and Hugh Casey, could remember those harrowing days and the sense of inevitable hopelessness they brought.

But in fact the two situations were completely different. MacArthur now had effective control of the air and sea; and while his position at the perimeter was only going to get stronger thanks to supplies and reinforcements, his enemy's was only going to get weaker.

MacArthur's pleas for reinforcements were finally being met. The Joint Chiefs had agreed to bring the Eighth Army's divisions up to full combat strength, including the Seventh Infantry Division, and were shipping two more army divisions, the First and the Second, as well as the First Marine, plus two infantry regiments. The Truman administration also finally resurrected the draft, which meant a steady supply of replacements was now guaranteed. Walker's forces would never have enough artillery; and a shortage of support and supply troops was always a problem.[42] But together with military units from other UN nations, most notably Britain, MacArthur's army was starting to look like a real fighting force.

At the same time, the war had cost the North Koreans some 58,000 casualties—far more than the Americans estimated at the time. Kim's formidable tank force had dwindled to barely a few dozen, and his air force had all but ceased to exist. As reports from the battlefield poured into Pyongyang, Stalin's ambassador was beginning to sense that time was running out for conquering Korea—if not for the Korean People's Army itself.[43]

Still, the KPA had plenty of fight left. General Walker discovered that on August 7, when the Twenty-fourth Infantry tried a counterattack from the Masan sector, the perimeter's southwestern anchor, and had to pull back to meet a new Communist threat from the north at Taegu. The next two weeks brought a series of confused and confusing battles, as defense of the perimeter hardened and the North Koreans increased their pressure on its outposts, but never achieved a breakthrough.

Then, after August 25, the fighting petered out and reached a stalemate. The North Koreans were too worn out, and their supply lines too thinly stretched, to try to break in; the UN forces (the Americans and ROK troops had now been joined by 2,000 men of the British Twenty-seventh Infantry Brigade, the first of the foreign contingents to join under the powder blue UN flag) were still too weak to break out. There were still not enough tanks, especially M-24 Pattons, to meet the Communist armored threat on equal terms. Machine guns, mortars, field artillery pieces, trucks, and jeeps had to be cannibalized for parts. Keeping the 180,000 men inside the perimeter fed was a constant problem. There was very little food to be foraged from nearby farms, and most of the rations were World War Two surplus. More seriously, there was a severe shortage of drinking water. Most groundwater was contaminated; soldiers who didn't boil their canteen water or use iodine or halazone—and too few did—came down with diarrhea, or worse.[44]

Yet already by August 7 MacArthur was sensing that the moment was coming to reverse the tide of war, and he was making plans accordingly. Those plans should have made him the hero of the hour. Instead, just a week earlier—less than a month after his warm letter to President Truman, and Truman's equally warm response—he had set off a firestorm with Washington, which prefigured a coming reversal in his relationship with the White House.

It had to do with his decision on July 31 to visit the island of Formosa and meet with Generalissimo Chiang Kai-shek.

In MacArthur's mind, his motives were innocent enough. Since the perimeter of his new command included Formosa as well as the Pescadore Islands, "I felt it necessary, at the end of July, to visit the island in order to determine its military capabilities." The Joint Chiefs were worried about his decision too. They sent him what Omar Bradley said "amounted to a war warning" showing intel that Red China might be planning an invasion of Formosa, and that Chiang Kai-shek, who had declared himself the legitimate ruler of China in March, was in the crosshairs.[45]

The Joint Chiefs therefore authorized MacArthur to conduct overflights on the mainland coast opposite Taiwan, and to send a survey team to see what Chiang might need to repel an attack. They even recommended that Chiang be authorized to launch preemptive air strikes if an invasion fleet sailed (Acheson, worried about a major incident, stopped that idea cold).[46]

There was certainly nothing untoward in MacArthur's deciding to head the survey team himself, especially when the Joint Chiefs, after suggesting that he might hold off going on his own, nonetheless said he was "free to go" if he chose. So MacArthur did, on July 31, flying over with Stratemeyer and fourteen other senior officers.

They spent two days talking with Chiang in Taipei and touring Nationalist military installations. "It was a great pleasure for me to meet my old comrade-in-arms of the last war," MacArthur later wrote of Chiang. Like many Americans, he felt that the Nationalist leader had been unfairly abandoned by the Truman administration, thus letting the mainland fall into the hands of the Communists. He was also still angry that Truman had rejected Chiang's offer of two divisions for the fight in Korea—two divisions that MacArthur and Walker would have immediately put to use. Still, the meetings were warm and cordial. "Arrangements were completed for effective coordination between the American forces under my command and those of the Chinese nationalists," MacArthur later wrote. Before returning to Tokyo, MacArthur also decided that three squadrons of F-80 jet fighters should be sent to Taiwan to help bolster Chiang's defenses.[47]

The result was panic and consternation in Washington, followed by anger and rage. When Secretary Acheson learned of MacArthur's plans for sending jets to Taiwan, he was told (wrongly) that the general had already given the order—thus making a major foreign policy decision that belonged with the president, not with MacArthur.

The Truman administration's position had always been that while the United States would act to protect Formosa if the Communist Chinese attacked, Formosa and the United States were not formal allies. MacArthur's action implied that they were. To say that Acheson and Truman were furious would be a pathetic understatement (the Joint Chiefs were less than pleased, as well, at MacArthur's overstepping their instructions). The president's acerbic comments on MacArthur's presumption "evoked the admiration and envy of us all," Acheson later wrote.[48]

The Joint Chief fired off a stern warning to MacArthur letting him know that such a decision involved "political" issues and required approval from the government's "highest levels"—which by implication did not include MacArthur. Still another, even sterner message came from Defense Secretary Johnson: "No one other than the President as Commander-in-Chief has the authority to order or authorize preventive action against concentrations on the 'Chinese' mainland . . . The most vital national interest requires that no action of ours precipitate general war or give excuse to others to do so."

By now, MacArthur was too old and too experienced to be dismayed by this kind of thing. He waved off Johnson's objections (the idea that he intended to start a war with China was in his mind beyond absurd) and sent along a soothing note saying he understood his limitations as theater commander; and he told Truman's special assistant Averell Harriman when he came to Tokyo that while he disagreed with Truman's China and Formosa policy, "I'm a good soldier and know how to obey orders."[49]

But MacArthur was not finished. On August 7 he sent his report on his Formosa visit to the Joint Chiefs, urging a reappraisal of U.S.–Nationalist China military ties. He argued that "there is real potential in the Armed Forces on Formosa," but said they needed additional equipment and training, especially in joint operations like seaborne landings and air interdiction.

He also urged setting up a Far East Command communications center in Taipei; setting up more American overflights and naval patrols in the Taiwan Straits separating Formosa from the mainland; and taking steps for "immediate coordination in the defense of Formosa" between American and Chinese senior air and naval commanders.[50]

The recommendations were hardly radical. Some were proposals that the Joint Chiefs themselves had made; except for the joint coordination planning, most were unobjectionable from a larger policy and security standpoint. But coming after the uproar over MacArthur's visit with Chiang, the report seemed to be a direct challenge to Truman's stated policy—even insubordination in the face of written warnings to stay away from the Formosa issue. That was compounded on August 17 when, at the invitation of the Veterans of Foreign Wars, MacArthur sent a statement for their national convention that warned "Formosa in the hands of . . . a hostile power could be compared to an unsinkable aircraft carrier and submarine tender ideally located to accomplish offensive strategy" against U.S. forces in Okinawa and the Philippines, and concluded, "Nothing could be more fallacious than the threadbare argument by those who advocate appeasement and defeatism in the Pacific that if we defend Formosa we alienate continental Asia. . . . They do not grant that it is in the pattern of Oriental psychology to respect and follow aggressive, resolute and dynamic leadership [and] to turn on a leadership characterized by timidity or vacillation."[51]

The reaction at Blair House and the State Department was pyrotechnic. "All of us were outraged at the effrontery and damaging effect at home and abroad of MacArthur's message," Acheson later wrote. They were particularly furious about the last sentence implying that the administration was being timid and vacillating on China and Formosa. Yet the fact was that millions of Americans, including many in the VFW, firmly believed Truman and Acheson *had* been timid and vacillating—and that the events in Korea were the result of it.

Even so, it was above even MacArthur's pay grade to put that out publicly, so Truman ordered Secretary Johnson to order MacArthur to withdraw the message.[52]

Now it was MacArthur's turn to be outraged. "My message was most carefully prepared to fully support the President's policy position," he wrote back to Secretary Johnson. "My remarks were calculated only to support his declaration [on June 27] and I am unable to see wherein they might be interpreted otherwise"—although hardly anyone who read his VFW statement reached the same conclusion.[53]

But MacArthur's attention was moving on to other, more pressing matters. Things were building to a head in the Pusan perimeter; MacArthur now had a plan to break the deadlock—and destroy North Korea's army in one blow.

He had already hinted at his strategy in a meeting with Truman's special envoy Averell Harriman and the Joint Chiefs' two personal representatives, General Matthew Ridgway and the air force's General Lauris Norstad, in Tokyo on August 6. Pacing back and forth in front of the map of Korea, he stressed his need for two more American divisions and whatever other forces the United Nations countries could provide. The war in Korea had reached a critical stage, he kept saying. The KPA was at the breaking point; "Their leadership has been vigorous . . . their tactics have been skillful," but he was sure they had used up their last reserves. With additional forces he could win a decisive victory before any Chinese or Russian troops could intervene to save the North Koreans—something he thought unlikely in any event.

MacArthur told them that winning the war would not only safeguard Japan, and cement the U.S. relationship with its fledgling democratic government. It would be a convincing global triumph for a U.S.-led coalition to "save the world from Communist domination and so would be recorded in history." Harriman and Ridgway were impressed; in their conversations with Walker at Taegu they found him less sanguine about victory. But at this point even Walker may have had no inkling of what MacArthur was thinking of doing to reverse the course of the war, or the risks he was willing to run in order to do it.[54]

The idea of a surprise amphibious landing deep in the rear of North Korea's advancing armies to cut off their supplies and line of retreat probably occurred to MacArthur after his visit to Korea on June 29. We know that on July 2 he ordered his new chief of staff, Lieutenant General Edward Almond, his G-3 Pinky Wright, and the staff of Wright's Joint Strategic Plans and Operations Group to draw up plans for an amphibious landing involving the First Cavalry and a Marine regimental combat team he had just requested. MacArthur wanted the operation ready in just twenty days, for July 22, but the plan was canceled when the First Cavalry and marines had to be sent in to shore up the crumbling American position south of the Han instead.[55]

In any case, MacArthur told his joint planning staff, known by the unlovely acronym JSPOG, to keep working on a later and larger amphibious operation, which got the code name CHROMITE. ("Pinky, let's think of a couple of end runs around each coast," was the way he put it to Wright.)[56] We also know that by July 10 MacArthur had a good idea of where he wanted the landing to take place. The head of Fleet Marine Force, Pacific, General Lemuel Shepherd, was in Tokyo for a visit and found MacArthur pacing back and forth in front of a map of the Far East.

"I wish I had the entire 1st Marine Division under my command again," MacArthur said. "I have a job for them to do."

"What's that?" Shepherd wanted to know.

MacArthur stopped and struck the map with his pipe. He was pointing to a port city 150 miles northwest of Pusan and 30 miles east of Seoul.

"I'd land 'em here," MacArthur said, his face grim, "at Inchon." It was also the city he told Wright would be his first choice for a landing.[57]

Inchon was a large seaport, capable of handling considerable amounts of United Nations shipping once the landing had been achieved. It was also tantalizingly close to the Communist-controlled South Korean capital and Kimpo airfield, as well as the KPA's supply lines from the north. Grabbing Inchon would put the cork in the bottle, to use MacArthur's favorite metaphor, trapping the North Koreans even as they imagined they had the Americans trapped at Pusan.

Then with MacArthur pushing down from Inchon, and Walker pushing out from Pusan, they could destroy the North Korean forces in detail.

On July 27, he let the Joint Chiefs in on the CHROMITE plan, although he did not release many details. He even had a date for D-Day: September 15. Reaction at the Pentagon was mixed, to say the least. MacArthur's experience with amphibious landings in New Guinea and the Philippines made him optimistic about the success of the plan; Omar Bradley's experience at Omaha Beach, and General Lawton Collins's knowledge of what happened at Anzio, where an American army had nearly been destroyed, made them correspondingly pessimistic. At one point in 1949 Bradley had even told the House Armed Services Committee that large-scale amphibious operations would never happen again.[58]

Now here was MacArthur proposing just such an operation—and outside a port where, as navy analysts at the Pentagon had discovered, there was an abnormally deep tide of thirty-three feet, which meant there would be only a very brief period twice a day when assault craft could get close to shore. There were other geographic drawbacks as well. Rivers in the Inchon area emptied into low, flat basins where at low tide landing craft could get stranded and become helpless targets for defenders on the shore. Navy planners also didn't care for Inchon's port facilities, which were old and not suited for a bridgehead port. There was also an island, Wolmi-do, dominating the approaches to Inchon harbor the way Corregidor dominated the Manila approaches. Taking Wolmi-do would require its own operation, thus eliminating any hope of surprise.

"We drew up a list of nearly every natural and geographic handicap" that an amphibious assault might face, one naval staff officer later remembered, "and Inchon had 'em all."[59]

The Joint Chiefs began trying to dissuade MacArthur from pursuing CHROMITE. If he didn't want to give up the amphibious landing altogether, then at least choose a different spot for it, they urged him, preferably one closer to Pusan for the final linkup with Walker. MacArthur, however, was adamant. It would be Inchon or nowhere. His only worry was making sure he had all the troops he needed for a breakout south from Inchon to connect with Walker and then push east to retake Seoul. Above all, he had to have the full First Marine Division, he told them, not just one or two combat teams. He made his most eloquent plea for more troops to Averell Harriman when he visited on August 6, and they sat down for a private man-to-man meeting.

"I cannot believe that a great nation such as the United States cannot give me these paltry reinforcements," he told Harriman. "Tell the president that if he gives them to me, I will, on the rising tide of the fifteenth of September, land at Inchon and between the hammer of this landing and the anvil of the Eighth Army, I will crush and destroy the army of North Korea."[60]

Harriman had known MacArthur for almost thirty years—they had played polo against each other when MacArthur was West Point superintendent—but he had never seen or heard him as passionate as this. He wrote back to Truman, urging him to give MacArthur what he wanted. And on August 10, the Joint Chiefs informed MacArthur that he would have the First Marine Division, all three regiments.[61]

MacArthur now had the forces he needed: the marines to make the breakout from Inchon and retake Seoul, and the Seventh Infantry Division under Major General David Barr to make the linkup with Walker and the Eighth Army. There were still the numbers of ships and transports to be worked out, and air cover: but Almond, Wright, and the staff of JSPOG did a brilliant job of bringing together senior naval and air force officers to flesh out the final plan.[62]

There were just two centers of resistance to overcome, and neither one involved the North Koreans. The first was from the two commanders in charge of the operation itself, Marine General O. P. Smith, who would lead the First Marine Division, and Rear Admiral James Doyle, who would command the amphibious phase of CHROMITE. After arriving in Tokyo on the morning of August 22, Smith conferred with Doyle and both agreed that the entire plan should be scrapped. They didn't like the choice of Inchon any more than the Pentagon did; they decided the whole operation should be put off a week and staged at Posung-Myon, twenty miles south of Inchon, instead.[63] That afternoon Smith had a meeting scheduled with MacArthur. Whatever his respect and admiration for the man, it was time to tell him the bad news and get him to change his mind.

When he entered MacArthur's office at the Dai-ichi building, he was surprised, as most visitors were, by its starkness. The bare furnishings and lack of formal display seemed to contradict the media image of MacArthur as a man with a towering ego and a flair for the dramatic. Even more surprising was the man himself. For a man over seventy, he was still ramrod straight and tall, with an almost youthful glow to his skin.

"My God, how does he do it?" another amazed visitor, Assistant Secretary of War John McCloy, commented during a visit at the end of 1945. "He's in better health than when I saw him before the war." Reporter John Gunther happened to have lunch with MacArthur just before the North Korean invasion and noted that the general's appearance "was that of a man of fifty, not seventy, moreover a man of fifty in the very best physical condition and at the top of his form." Another regular MacArthur follower said, "I never saw him look so fit and well, so alert and youthful and full of color and mental vigor."[64]

MacArthur was going to need that vigor in the next twenty-four hours. First he had to deal with General Smith's resistance to CHROMITE. After greeting Smith warmly, he sat down and listened carefully to Smith's objections, one by one. Then he waved his hand as if he hadn't heard them. The Inchon landing will be decisive, he told the general. The war will be over in a month.

It was a stunned marine who left MacArthur's office. "It was more than confidence," he said later of MacArthur's attitude. "[I]t was supreme and almost mystical faith that he could not fail."[65] Even though Smith did not quite share that faith, he would break the news to Doyle that CHROMITE was going ahead.

That is, unless the visitors arriving the next day were to stop MacArthur.

They carried far more weight than Smith or Doyle—and far more prestige, including back in Washington. If MacArthur couldn't persuade them that the landing in Inchon would succeed, it would never take place.

The fate of CHROMITE, and the entire course of the war, hung on what happened in the next twenty-four hours.

CHAPTER 30
INCHON AND BEYOND

The history of the world for the next thousand years
will be written in the Pacific.

—DOUGLAS MACARTHUR, DECEMBER 1944

On the morning of August 23, three uniformed men stepped off their plane at Tokyo Airport, looking tense and somber. They were General Lawton Collins, Chief of Naval Operations Admiral Forrest Sherman, and Lieutenant General Idwal Edwards, chief deputy to the head of the U.S. Air Force, Hoyt Vandenberg.

They were soon joined by another party of top brass who had flown in from Pearl Harbor two days before, including Commander in Chief, Pacific, Admiral Arthur Radford and MacArthur's friend Marine General Lemuel Shepherd.

All of them knew the outline of MacArthur's plan; all of them had different reactions. Shepherd was CHROMITE's keen supporter; Collins was completely convinced it was a mistake. Edwards's attitude was more wait-and-see, depending on MacArthur's presentation. As for Sherman, MacArthur himself believed the admiral's vote would be the most decisive.[1] If he could sway the old veteran of half a dozen campaigns in the Pacific war, MacArthur reasoned, the navy chief would carry the others with him.

That afternoon they all assembled at SCAP GHQ in the late afternoon in a small conference room—too small for the number of important people there. Besides the guests from Washington and Pearl and MacArthur himself, there were also his chief of staff, General Almond; his G-3, Pinky Wright; General Stratemeyer; naval commanders Strubel and Doyle; and a flock of staffers and briefing officers. For reasons that are still obscure, two people were missing from the room: MacArthur's most skeptical critic, Marine general Smith, and his fiercest supporter, Marine general Shepherd. If MacArthur did manage to sway the Joint Chiefs, he would have to do it without Shepherd's help.

MacArthur sat silently fingering his pipe as Wright laid out the basic plan of CHROMITE. Then Doyle's naval briefers took over, outlining the naval and amphibious aspects of the plan; their analysis was, as the official account of the meeting puts it, "decidedly pessimistic." Then came Admiral Doyle himself, speaking of the immense difficulties of sailing ships up the main channel leading into Inchon, which might be mined or covered by heavy batteries, or both—no one knew. One American ship sunk in a channel that narrow could doom the whole operation.

Admiral Sherman then interjected, "I wouldn't hesitate to take a ship up there."

MacArthur smiled and spoke for the first time. "Spoken like a Farragut!"

Doyle ignored the outburst. He concluded by saying that in his opinion the Inchon landing was "not impossible"—hardly a ringing endorsement.[2]

Then it was Lawton Collins's turn. He outlined his objections as MacArthur again sat silently, his pipe gripped tightly in his teeth. Collins pointed out that the Inchon plan meant stripping the Pusan perimeter of the First Marine Brigade, which would leave General Walker's men unnecessarily exposed to a sudden North Korean attack. Even supposing that the Marine landing succeeded and MacArthur managed to drive on to Seoul, it was Collins's personal belief that MacArthur would be too far away to link up with Walker, and that if the Communists counterattacked he could easily find himself trapped with no hope of relief.

He strongly urged considering a landing instead at Kunsan, one hundred miles south of Inchon, which was closer to the Eighth Army's position. Otherwise, if MacArthur failed to make "a quick junction" with Walker, the result in Collins's opinion would be a "disaster."

The conference room fell silent. MacArthur's chief of staff, Almond, shifted uneasily in his chair. The tension and the temperature in the small space rose steadily.

MacArthur said nothing, barely moved, for an entire minute. Then he rose and began walking back and forth. What followed was classic MacArthur, with the fate of an entire war hanging in the balance.

"The bulk of the Reds are committed around Walker's defense perimeter," he began. "The enemy, I am convinced, has failed to prepare Inchon properly for defense."

He plunged on to say that the very argument that critics like Collins and Doyle were advancing was precisely why the North Koreans would not expect a landing at Inchon. "Like Montcalm," he said, referring to the French general who failed to defend Quebec during the French and Indian War against a surprise assault by British general Wolfe, "the North Koreans would regard an Inchon landing as impossible. Like Wolfe, I could take them by surprise."

As he warmed to his subject, MacArthur's pacing became more animated, his gestures more grandiloquent.

"The Navy's objections as to tides, hydrography, terrain, and physical handicaps are indeed substantial and pertinent," he said, even as he waved those objections aside. "My confidence in the Navy is complete, and in fact," he said without glancing at Admiral Doyle, "I seem to have more confidence in the Navy than the Navy has in itself."[3]

He had now spoken for forty-five minutes without a single note. Every eye in the room was riveted on him.

"The only alternative to a stroke such as I propose will be the continuation of the savage sacrifice we are making at Pusan, with no hope of relief in sight. Are you content to let our troops stay in that bloody perimeter like beef cattle in the slaughterhouse? Who will take responsibility for such a tragedy?"

There was silence.

"I certainly will not. The prestige of the Western world hangs in the balance. Oriental millions"—that racial reference would make later historians cringe—"are watching the outcome. It is plainly apparent that here in Asia is where the Communist conspirators have elected to make their play for global conquest."

His peroration brought the issue back to operational reality.

"If my estimate is inaccurate and should I run into a defense with which I cannot cope, I will be there personally and will immediately withdraw our forces before they are committed to a bloody setback. The only loss then will be my professional reputation. But Inchon will not fail. Inchon will succeed. And it will save 100,000 lives."

According to witnesses, he then spoke of the ticking clock of destiny, as his eyes grew wide and more determined. "I realize that Inchon is a 5000-to-one gamble, but I am used to taking such odds. We shall land at Inchon and we shall crush them."

Everyone in the room was stunned. Even Collins, his biggest critic, sat immobilized as he watched MacArthur "gradually building up emphasis with consummate skill." Finally Forrest Sherman broke the silence by standing and saying, "Thank you. A great voice in a great cause."[4]

MacArthur had thought that Sherman was one of the doubters he had to win over. In fact, unbeknownst to him, on August 21 Sherman had confessed to Admiral Arthur Strubel, who had served under MacArthur during the Philippine campaign and who now had overall responsibility for CHROMITE, "I'm going to back the Inchon operation completely. I think it's sound." But even after MacArthur's impassioned presentation, the navy chief told a staffer, "I which I could share that man's optimism."

Lawton Collins found himself in a more difficult situation. He knew MacArthur's own generals opposed the plan. Even though he had to admit he had been deeply impressed by MacArthur's presentation, he still worried that everything would go wrong. Together with Smith, Doyle, Radford, and even Shepherd, Collins remained convinced that Inchon was the wrong place for a landing, and that Posung-Myon was the right place. After listening, Admiral Sherman agreed and revisited the Posung-Myon idea again with the commander in chief, United Nations Forces, the next day. Shepherd, his devoted fan, took up the same refrain.[5]

But MacArthur refused to budge. Why was MacArthur so adamant? There can be only one explanation. Inchon was closer to Seoul, and MacArthur believed that when American forces liberated the Korean capital it would change the entire direction of the war. As with the Philippines and Manila, freeing a nation's capital transcended matters of strategy. In MacArthur's mind, it was a decisive act in the nation's destiny, a turning point in its future and for its people. To have American soldiers and marines carry it out would shape America's future in Asia, MacArthur believed. As with Japan, a new future was dawning—and here in South Korea he would be destiny's instrument, as he had been in Japan.

So on August 30 MacArthur nailed down his final operational orders for CHROMITE with virtually no changes. Meanwhile, a chastened Sherman and Collins had returned to Washington recommending that MacArthur's plan be endorsed, with two provisos. The first was that he have "alternative plans" for a landing at Kunsan or some other beach south of Inchon if things went awry, and the second was that he keep the Joint Chiefs better informed in future "as to your intentions and plans for offensive operations."

A happy MacArthur accepted the provisos without a grumble. He had won his fight; even the fiercest doubters had reluctantly gone along. Now there was only the preparation, and the waiting.

In the meantime, the North Koreans were on the move again.

They struck on the night of August 31–September 1 in an all-out attack on the Pusan perimeter. The KPA assault was aimed at a worn-out, over-extended Eighth Army, one that was reduced by disease, fatigue, and hunger to lashing out at the multiple attempts at a breakthrough, instead of carrying out an overall strategic plan. Jim Edwards, battalion commander of second battalion, Twenty-third Infantry, watched as his men gradually became dispirited even though their line did not fall apart.

North Korean officers personally led the human wave assaults; Edwards saw one shot seventeen times before he finally went down. After two days of fighting off the attacks without sleep, Edwards's men began to collapse; some cried, some sat paralyzed, some tried to shoot back but shook so violently they couldn't hold a weapon. Artillery barrages sprayed Edwards's sector with KPA body parts, on which the rats feasted after dark.[6]

Yet somehow the perimeter held. General Walker told his men there was no retreat, because there was nowhere to go.

"We must fight to the end." If they had to die, he said, "at least we die fighting together."

Then on September 3 Walker began a counterattack with MacArthur's authorization, including the First Marine brigade that soon would be withdrawn to become part of the Inchon landing. The marines fought hard and well; they lost 200 men in retaking the so-called Naktong Bulge. When they finally left Pusan, they had lost more than 900 effectives since August. Jim Edwards's battalion's weapons company had suffered 70 percent casualties.

All the same, by September 7 the North Korean offensive was spent. The Pusan perimeter was safe for now. But if MacArthur was going to rescue the men of the Eighth Army and their South Korean allies, it had to be soon.

On September 12 MacArthur climbed aboard the amphibious command ship USS *Mount McKinley,* as he had so many warships just before amphibious landings on Los Negros, Hollandia, Morotai, Leyte, Luzon . . . This would be his last. The *Mount McKinley* was Admiral Doyle's flagship, moored at Sasebo harbor in Japan. Joining him were Almond, Wright, and Whitney, as well as Lemuel Shepherd. On the drive over from Tokyo they had noticed a rainbow breaking through in the leaden evening sky.

"That's my rainbow!" MacArthur excitedly told Shepherd. "I commanded the Rainbow Division in the first war. That's my lucky omen. Lem, this operation is going to be a success."[7]

On board the *Mount McKinley* they shook hands with Doyle and General Smith, and then at midnight set sail for Inchon.

The seas were heavy during the early-morning hours. They were passing through the edge of a typhoon, "one of the worst storms I ever met," Doyle recalled later. It packed winds of up to 125 miles per hour but then moved off to the east, missing the main body of invasion ships. MacArthur's luck was still holding.[8]

He himself did not hold up so well. Doyle later admitted he had steered into the typhoon's edge deliberately, to give his commanding general "a taste of ocean warfare." It also brought MacArthur a bout of seasickness—together with the nervous stomach he usually got just before a crisis. Whitney found him in his cabin huddled in his "A" bathrobe, looking and feeling miserable. Whitney and Pinky Wright convinced him to have a dram of Scotch to steady his stomach. MacArthur did so, immediately felt better, and after chatting a while, went to sleep.[9]

By the afternoon, the seas smoothed out and that evening MacArthur took a walk on deck, dressed in his leather aviator's jacket. He watched the sun set beyond China on the ship's port side. "I had made many landings before," he recalled thinking, "but this was the most intricately complicated amphibious operation I had ever attempted."

Around him were 260 ships from six nations—America, Britain, Australia, New Zealand, Holland, and France. They were loaded with some 70,000 personnel, including the First Marine Division and the Seventh Infantry Division, which now had some 8,000 Korean troops integrated into its ranks to beef up its numbers.

CHROMITE had been a triumph of logistical and administrative skill. Now they would find out if it was a triumph of military strategy as well.

Yet even after MacArthur's dramatic conference on the 23rd, it almost didn't happen. On September 7—less than a week before the invasion armada was supposed to sail—he received a message from the Joint Chiefs asking him once again to consider calling off the landings. They urged him to think about sending the troops to reinforce Walker's hard-pressed forces on the Pusan perimeter (they did not know that the North Korean attacks had already failed).

The message "chilled me to the marrow of my bones," MacArthur admitted, and he quickly penciled a polite but firm reply: "I regard the chance of success of the operation as excellent. I go further in belief that it represents the only hope of wresting the initiative from the enemy and thereby presenting the opportunity for a decisive blow." There was also no chance that the Pusan perimeter would collapse. Once MacArthur landed in the north, he predicted, the North Koreans would collapse instead.

The alternative was a long, grinding war of attrition on the Korean peninsula, he said. He was telling the Joint Chiefs in stark terms: it's this, or nothing.[10]

On the 8th the Chiefs gave up. They officially authorized the operation, just days before the marines were supposed to hit the beaches. Privately, MacArthur believed it was the president who tried to block his plan at the last minute. He was determined not to let him or the Joint Chiefs interfere again. He sent a copy of CHROMITE's detailed instructions to Washington as requested, but made sure it arrived too late for anyone to order the landings stopped.[11]

Now the waiting was almost over.

"Next morning we would have to thread our way over the shifting bars of 'Flying Fish Channel,'" MacArthur was thinking in the gathering darkness. That was the main channel leading into Inchon. Then "under the guns of Wolmi-do" island, they would have to "skirt the edges of the deadly mud banks that stretched for 2 miles across the harbor."

That night he could barely sleep. At quarter to two he took another turn around the blacked-out ship, and watched the phosphorescent seas breaking across the *Mount McKinley*'s prow. "Within five hours," he realized, 40,000 men would be landing at Inchon, in order to save 100,000 still trapped in the Pusan perimeter.

"I alone was responsible for tomorrow, and if I failed, the dreadful results would rest on judgment day against my soul."[12]

Suddenly a light flashed out of the darkness.

Startled, MacArthur wondered what it was, just as it flashed again. It couldn't be a ship; every ship in the fleet was blacked out. Then he realized: the channel navigation lights had been left on. The North Koreans still didn't know what was about to hit them. The Inchon invasion force had achieved complete surprise.

He went back to bed with a lighter heart than he had felt for days.

But he didn't have much time for sleep.

A roar like distant thunder woke him up. "Our guns had opened up on Wolmi-do," he wrote later. He hastily dressed and went up on deck. Ten American and British cruisers and destroyers were pounding the 335-foot hill that dominated the island. The North Korean guns had fired back at first, then ceased. As MacArthur watched, dark-blue marine Corsair fighter-bombers "swooped down from the clouds and added their strafing to the destruction." Some were also unloading napalm in bright spectacular bursts as thousands of marines boarded their landing craft from their mother ships.

MacArthur, Doyle, and the rest watched through binoculars as the first landing craft carrying troops from the Fifth Marines, made their way to the north end of Wolmi-do. It was 6:30 A.M. The marines landed to little resistance. By 7:00 they had run up the American flag on Wolmi-Do.

That was one obstacle out of the way. Then marines swarmed over the other island in the channel, Sowolmi-do. The garrison there fought harder, but soon also threw up their hands and surrendered. So far the marines had not suffered a single fatality. They had killed more than 200 of the enemy and taken 140 prisoners, at the cost of 17 wounded.[13]

When word got back to the *Mount McKinley,* MacArthur turned to Doyle.

"Please send a message to the fleet," he said, and to Admiral Strubel on board the cruiser *Rochester.* "The Navy and Marines have never shone more brightly than this morning. MacArthur." Then he turned to Shepherd, Smith, and Almond. "That's it. Let's get a cup of coffee."

They headed below. The main landings still had hours to go, but MacArthur felt certain now that success was assured. After breakfast he dictated an update for the Joint Chiefs.

"First phase landing successful with losses slight. Surprise apparently complete. All goes well and on schedule."[14]

It was good that MacArthur was so confident, because there was still plenty that could go wrong.

With Wolmi-do captured, the invasion fleet now had to wait for hours while the deep tide ebbed, leaving great exposed mudflats that would have trapped the marine landing craft if they had arrived a few hours later. The fleet itself would have been in serious trouble if the North Koreans had laid a large batch of new Soviet magnetic anti-ship mines that had arrived in Inchon a week or so before; but the North Koreans hadn't. It was MacArthur luck yet again.[15]

The North Koreans, however, were beginning to recover from the shock and surprise of the attack, and started tattooing the Marines on Wolmi-do with artillery fire from the mainland. There were several tense hours until 5:30 P.M. when the tidal flow finally allowed the two main assaults to get under way, one headed for the northwest edge of Inchon, code-named Red Beach, and the other for Blue Beach, south of the main part of town.

The Fifth Marines landing on Red Beach had to use ladders to scale the steep seawall; if its North Korean garrison had been positioned to meet them on the wall, it might have been a slaughter. But Inchon's 2,500 or so defenders were disorganized, confused, and badly led. After several brief but deadly hand-to-hand encounters, the marines cleared the seawall and by midnight held key points overlooking the city.[16]

On Blue Beach there was a bigger mixup. Commander of the First Marines Colonel Lewis "Chesty" Puller pushed his men onto the beach too fast and too soon. The first wave of marines discovered that the naval bombardment hadn't broken down their seawall and they had to pause while successive waves crowded in behind, or had to circle in their LCVPs until the beach was cleared. It was Iwo Jima all over again—except that the marines were fighting stunned and dispirited North Koreans instead of disciplined Japanese. By midnight the marines on Blue and Red Beaches had suffered 200 casualties and had taken roughly one-third of Inchon, while nearly every KPA defender had been either killed or captured, or had fled.

Strubee, Almond, and Shepherd took an evening boat ride to see the action (MacArthur for once chose to stay on board). Shepherd counted thirteen fires in the city area, and just as the sun set another rainbow appeared, this time over Inchon.

"It was a terrific sight," Shepherd remembered. He returned to the *Mount McKinley* to find a delighted MacArthur firing off another brief report to the JCS.

"Our losses are light," he told them. "The command distinguished itself. The whole operation is proceeding on schedule."

He had done it. He had defied the critics, the naysayers, the odds, even nature herself in the shape of tides and typhoons. The Inchon landings had succeeded. He went to bed that night in a mood of vindication as well as triumph. But now would come the most critical phase of the operation, the double breakout east toward Seoul and south toward Suwon, for the eventual hookup with Walker and the Eighth Army.

The next morning the marines cleared out the last remaining North Koreans from Inchon and began their advance eastward. It was, as one historian has put it, a textbook operation, with tanks, rocket-armed infantry, and waves of attacking marine Corsairs doing devastating damage to the Communist forces in front of them, crippling T-34s and sending the remaining KPA defenders fleeing for the rear. By the 19th the marines had reached the banks of the Han River.[17]

On the way MacArthur paid them a frontline visit. He stopped at one position where an attempted North Korean ambush had just been beaten back. Several of the North Korean tanks were still burning when he walked through and shook hands with his victorious marines. What he did not know was that five North Korean stragglers were hiding in a culvert underneath his parked jeep. The marines found them only when MacArthur climbed back in the jeep and drove away.[18]

The next day, MacArthur spotted an old friend in Inchon harbor. It was the battleship *Missouri,* which had joined in the final bombardment. He boarded her for a quick tour, and found a plaque on the quarterdeck commemorating the surrender ceremony of five years earlier.

MacArthur was suddenly overcome with emotion. Tears began to roll down his cheeks as he stood without speaking for several minutes. Then he turned to the ship's captain and said, "You have given me the happiest moment of my life." Whether he was referring to the plaque or the success at Inchon wasn't clear.

That day he also presented Marine General O. P. Smith with the Silver Star. His sharpest critic was now his dedicated friend; MacArthur praised him as the "the gallant commander of a gallant division." Lem Shepherd won a Silver Star as well, with MacArthur saying, "You have served your country with great distinction." They were standing on the tarmac at Kimpo field, which the marines had recaptured on the 17th. Then MacArthur boarded *Bataan II,* waved to his generals and the large gathering of photographers and reporters, and flew back to Tokyo.[19]

He had reason to feel proud and confident about what he and his men had achieved—and were about to achieve. Because the prediction that he had made about the North Korean army's disintegrating after the Inchon landing was coming true.

Meanwhile, right on cue, General Walker had begun his breakout from Pusan.

To serve as the "anvil" to MacArthur's "hammer," MacArthur had instructed him, Walker should begin his offensive on the 16th from the northwest side of the Pusan perimeter, where Walker had massed four army corps, including two South Korean corps. The attack immediately ran into stiff resistance, and Walker's men didn't cross the Naktong River until the 19th, when the marines had already finished clearing Inchon.

Then the tide of battle around Pusan suddenly changed. The North Korean forces began moving headlong for the rear, as thousands of KPA soldiers began shedding their uniforms and donning civilian clothes. Thousands of others evaporated into the hills to the north and west. A peremptory order to withdraw had been issued from Pyongyang, ostensibly to help defend Seoul but in fact to save whatever forces were left before they were completely trapped.[20]

The First Cavalry Division surged forward on the 23rd, finding little resistance until it reached Osan on the 26th. There, on the other side of the hill, scouts spotted soldiers in American uniforms. They were advance elements of the Seventh Infantry Division, which had disembarked at Inchon on the 18th and had been moving steadily forward after taking Suwon. The long-anticipated "junction" of the Eighth Army and X Corps, as the Inchon landing force was dubbed, had been achieved. All that was left was mopping up the thousands of KPA prisoners who were throwing down their weapons and surrendering, when they weren't running headlong for the 38th parallel.

The toughest fighting would be for Seoul itself. On the 20th the Fifth Marines crossed the Han River and by evening on the 21st, they were at the city gates.[21] Smith and Almond discovered that the city was held by fresh, albeit green, KPA troops determined to fight to the death. The marines had a hard go of it when they advanced toward the city on September 23, taking on defenders who outnumbered them three to one. Once again, it was marine artillery, tanks, and Corsairs flying close air support that made the difference, at several points fighting battles that reached the intensity level of Iwo Jima.

Almond wanted Smith to take the city using the First and Fifth Marines in an enveloping movement from south of the city. Smith didn't like the idea, and said so. Almond, "with the curtness that was his hallmark," told the marine general he had another twenty hours to take Seoul. Otherwise he would send in the Seventh Army Division. Smith, like his fellow marines, thought of the Seventh as a second-rate, scratch outfit—especially with its large Korean contingent. Losing the honor of taking the city to that particular division would have been a bitter blow—so the marines pressed on.

They still missed Almond's deadline, so Almond devised a plan to put Seventh Division troops across the Han and occupy South Mountain, in the enemy's rear. With Smith still objecting, the operation got under way on the 24th.

Almond's young staffer Captain Al Haig led the crossing of the Han in a marine amphibious vehicle under cover of a massive artillery barrage, and the next day South Mountain was captured.[22]

After that, Communist resistance quickly crumbled, and by September 26 the First Marine Division had cleared the central city all the way to the capitol. By then two battalions of the Fifth Marines had lost five of six original rifle commanders since Inchon, and seventeen of eighteen rifle platoon commanders. For every ten men MacArthur's forces had lost in the Inchon-Seoul campaign, seven were marines who suffered 364 dead and more than 2,000 wounded.[23]

But it was all over. On the 28th, the last fighting in the streets of Seoul had all but died away. By Almond's count, there weren't any active KPA units left in South Korea. United Nations forces had taken more than 7,000 prisoners and inflicted upwards of 14,000 casualties—adding to the 50,000 troops North Korea had already lost in the campaign to subjugate the south. The entire effort had cost MacArthur and the Americans some 3,500 killed and wounded, but it had also turned the war inside out.

Now it was time to restore the antebellum status quo, in MacArthur's mind, and return President Syngman Rhee to his capital. The Joint Chiefs urged him to wait, saying the authority to do so was not his. MacArthur fired back a terse "Message Not Understood" and went ahead with his plans anyway.

On September 29 a convoy of jeeps and trucks led MacArthur and President Rhee through the battle-scarred streets of Seoul. MacArthur had brought Jean with him, along with Courtney Whitney and General Stratemeyer; his personal plane had brought Rhee and his entourage to Kimpo from Pusan. The trip forcefully reminded MacArthur of driving through Manila in the grim months of March 1945, to restore the Filipino government to power. The same smashed buildings, downed power lines, broken vehicles scattered along the streets, windows and doorways hollowed out by small-arms fire.

The Communists had also left their special mark. Rummaging through the hotel that Kim Il Sung's Soviet advisors had used during the occupation of the city, Captain Haig discovered that the Russians had defecated in the center of every room they had occupied, as a farewell gesture to the advancing Americans. "This bestial insult made a lasting impression on me," he later remembered.[24]

The Americans also found something else when they liberated the city, something also reminiscent of Manila 1945. These were the bodies of thousands of civilians who had been murdered by Kim's secret police, some 26,000 up and down the peninsula; most had died for the simple crime of being "class enemies" or working for the Rhee regime. Walker's men had also discovered mass graves containing the bodies of American prisoners that the Communists had killed on their advance to Pusan; most had been shot in the head, their hands tied behind their backs—sometimes with barbed wire.

It was a grim reminder of what a final Communist victory would have meant for thousands more Koreans—and what South Korea had been freed from. Whatever doubts some back in Washington had about Dr. Rhee, MacArthur was thinking, his government was certainly better than this—although some ROK troops took their own revenge on North Korean troops, with American soldiers quietly looking the other way.

The convoy reached Seoul's capitol building, and precisely at noon the ceremony began in its National Assembly Hall. The place was packed with South Korean officials and civilians, as well as dozens of ROK, American, and British officers who had participated in the campaign, many of them carrying sidearms and most except MacArthur wearing steel combat helmets.

MacArthur strode to the podium and spoke for five minutes. He thanked "the grace of a merciful Providence" for the moment of restoration of South Korea's government and freedom, and thanked "our forces fighting under the standard of that greatest hope and inspiration of mankind, the United Nations." He spoke of his confidence "that from the travail of the past there may emerge a new and hopeful dawn for the people of Korea."

Then MacArthur led the entire assemblage in what one eyewitness said was "the most dramatic recitation of the Lord's Prayer I have ever heard."[25]

Our Father who art in Heaven
Hallowed be Thy Name

Far off in the distance the audience could hear artillery fire and even the occasional snap of rifle fire, as the last mopping-up operations around the city were still under way.

Thy Kingdom come

A louder artillery blast and resulting thud shook the building. Broken glass rained down from the ceiling, and those, like Captain Al Haig, who were still holding their helmets hastily put them on.

MacArthur, of course, did not even pause:

Thy will be done
On Earth as it is in Heaven.
Amen.

The echoes of "Amen" died away and then MacArthur turned to Syngman Rhee standing beside him and said:

"Mr. President, my officers and I will now resume our military duties and leave you and your government to the discharge of civil responsibilities."

Rhee stepped forward and gripped his hand. Tears were streaming down his face; soon they were running down MacArthur's as well. Two elderly men, who had seen much pain and suffering in their lives, now together in a moment of unexpected happiness and triumph. Yet one seemed bowed and almost broken by the ordeal of the last three months, while the other looked young enough to be his son.

"We admire you," Rhee was telling MacArthur in a husky voice. "We love you as the savior of our race. How can I ever explain to you my own undying gratitude and that of the Korean people?"

MacArthur knew he didn't have to, as he boarded *Bataan II* for the trip back to Japan at 1:30 that afternoon. He knew he had not only freed the Korean people but had scored one of the most amazing victories in military history—and had reversed not just the war but the Communist cause in Asia.

Back at his office in the Dai-ichi building he found an anxious message from the Joint Chiefs. They had heard that MacArthur had allowed the American flag to be flown at the restoration ceremony next to that of the Republic of South Korea.

They believed this was a serious mistake; it should have been the flag of the United Nations instead.

MacArthur grimaced and contemptuously shoved the radiogram aside. Then he focused on the pile of other telegrams and messages that had come in.

There was one from President Truman: "I know I speak for the entire American people when I send you my warmest congratulations in the victory which has been achieved under your leadership . . ."

One was also from the Joint Chiefs: "You have given new inspiration to the freedom-loving peoples of the world. We remain completely confident that the great task entrusted to you by the United Nations will be carried on to a successful conclusion."

Another came from Secretary of Defense Marshall: "Accept my personal tribute to the courageous campaign you directed in Korea . . ."

Prime Minister Yoshida in Japan wrote: "The bold stroke in your strategy has changed overnight the whole picture of the Korean situation. To you, the indomitable and inspiring Commander-in-Chief, the world owes an infinite debt of gratitude."

Dwight Eisenhower, now the president of Columbia University, also chimed in: "I cannot stay the impulse to express the conviction that you have again given us a brilliant example of professional leadership."

Still another telegram was from Bull Halsey: "Characteristic and magnificent. The Inchon landing is the most masterful and audacious strategic stroke in all history."

The man who, next to MacArthur, had done the most to prevent a collapse of leadership and morale in the immediate Korean crisis, John Foster Dulles, wrote: "Congratulations—you have done it again."

And buried toward the bottom of the pile was a terse tribute from Winston Churchill: "A perfect job."

Douglas MacArthur was standing at the apex of his prestige and his career. Côte de Châtillon, the island-hopping campaigns in New Guinea and the Solomons, the Philippine landings: they all paled to a dismal memory in comparison with what he had achieved that September of 1950. Every critic was struck silent; every doubter was now eager to win his approval.

In his mind, however, there was no time to enjoy the accolades or the deep glow of inner satisfaction. There was still a war to be won, despite the end of the fighting in South Korea. "The golden moment to transmute our victory at Inchon had arrived," he wrote later, to defeat the Communists once and for all.[26]

He would now commit all the prestige and authority he had earned with Inchon to making that happen.

Despite the warm telegrams that had been sent, in Washington news of MacArthur's success brought amazed relief, mingled with chagrin that so many had been so wrong about the Inchon operation and MacArthur had been so right.

MacArthur had been wrong about one thing; it wasn't President Truman who had tried to block CHROMITE at the last minute. Virtually everyone in the administration and the Pentagon who heard the plan, or weighed the circumstances, thought it wouldn't work—everyone *except* Truman. The man who had persuaded the president that it could succeed was none other than Averell Harriman, who after his Tokyo visit in August believed MacArthur could do what he said he could, regardless of the so-called experts. Defense Secretary Louis Johnson was furious that Harriman managed to convince Truman to disregard Johnson's advice and that of the Joint Chiefs, and to endorse the invasion.

"What have you done to the president?" Johnson had asked Harriman bitterly. He thought Truman had made the worst mistake of his presidency, as did nearly everyone else.[27]

Instead, "[t]he Inchon counteroffensive succeeded brilliantly," Dean Acheson would concede in his memoirs.[28] He and the other MacArthur skeptics had to admit that the general had won his victory, and fulfilled his mandate to drive the North Koreans out of the south. The question was, now what?

Two schools of thought sprang up. The first, led by George Kennan, held that MacArthur's UN forces should remain in South Korea and not cross over the 38th parallel. This group had the firm backing of most of America's UN allies, including Great Britain. They feared a violent Soviet reaction if the border into North Korea was crossed.

The other group, supported by two key figures in the State Department's Far Eastern division, Dean Rusk and John Allison, believed the 38th parallel was an entirely arbitrary dividing line (Rusk would have known, having drawn the line himself). They argued that crossing it in order to force a North Korean unconditional surrender shouldn't be ruled out. Indeed, "peace and stability would not exist while the country was divided," they insisted—thereby hinting that this might be the moment for the peninsula to be united under President Rhee, rather than the Communists.[29]

The Joint Chiefs went further. They believed that MacArthur should be *ordered* to cross the parallel, defeat what was left of the enemy's forces, and occupy the entire country. They contended that America and its allies had more than enough resources to finish the job and to declare a free, independent Korea under UN mandate. They also confidently believed the Soviets would choose not to intervene, either in Asia or in Europe. It was time to wrap this operation up, and MacArthur had proven he was the man to do it.

MacArthur was in total agreement. The road to Pyongyang, the Communist capital, was now open. According to Willoughby's intelligence estimates, the KPA could not muster any force larger than corps strength. Moreover, President Rhee had announced that *he* was not paying attention to any arbitrary dividing line. South Korean troops were going to pursue the enemy across the border, regardless of what the UN said. An American officer then told the press that if the South Koreans did cross the parallel, American forces would be there to stop them—which made the State Department mad, since it implied there was a firm policy regarding what to do about the 38th parallel, when there was not.

After much heated discussion, the Far East hands and the Joint Chiefs won out—almost. On September 26, two days before MacArthur flew to Seoul, the JCS were able to send him a directive by cable on how he was to carry out future operations in Korea.

"Your military objective is the destruction of the North Korea armed forces," it read. He had complete freedom to operate throughout North

Korea, as long as no "major" Soviet or Chinese forces entered the country. It warned MacArthur that only South Korean units should be used in areas close to the Chinese-Soviet borders, on the assumption that they would be less likely to provoke a Communist response, and that he was not to conduct any air or sea operations in Manchuria or Soviet-occupied territory. Once the North Koreans were finally defeated, ROK units were to take the lead "in disarming remaining North Korean units and enforcing the terms of surrender"—the most important goal of all. It was only after North Korea had formally surrendered that the United States and the United Nations would decide the final fate of Korea, not before.[30]

The directive concluded with a final requirement: "You will also submit your plan for future operations north of the 38th parallel to the JCS for approval."

MacArthur didn't care for that last order. He was planning for a fast-moving American-led blitzkrieg that would crush North Korea's remaining forces and clear the country of the stench of Communism. He chafed at having to get permission for winning the war beforehand. He also worried that if Washington got nervous about a possible Chinese or Russian move, it might stop him before he completed his job. After all, if he had listened to them in August, Inchon would never have happened—and they'd all be stuck back at Pusan.

In any case, the push northward was gathering momentum. More than 350,000 UN troops were on the move against a fast-retreating enemy. There was no way they weren't going to pursue him across the 38th parallel. And George Marshall, who was the new defense secretary, had sent him a personal message on the 28th: "We want you to feel unhampered strategically and tactically to proceed north of the 38th Parallel." To MacArthur that sounded like carte blanche to send his forces anywhere in North Korea he wanted.

Nonetheless, he did as told and gave the Joint Chiefs the window onto his thinking.

"Briefly, my plan is," he told them, "(a) Eighth Army as now constituted will cross the 38th parallel with its main effort" being the capture of Pyongyang; "(b) X Corps"—meaning the Inchon invasion force—"as now constituted will effect amphibious landing at Wonsan," which sat on North Korea's east coast, "making juncture with the Eighth Army." Finally, only ROK units would proceed north of the Chungjo-Yongwon-Hungnam line, roughly two-thirds of the North Korean peninsula. He envisaged the Eighth Army's attack getting under way October 15—certainly no later than October 30.[31]

The Joint Chiefs gave their approval, and on October 5 the United Nations General Assembly passed a resolution authorizing the plan. Four days before that, the ROK Third Division was already across the 38th parallel. The war was going north, into uncharted territory in political terms, if not geographic terms. No one, not even MacArthur, could estimate where it would finally end.

There was one man, however, who did have a clear idea of where events were headed.

He was Mao Zedong, Communist China's newly minted ruler. Sitting in the former imperial Forbidden Palace in Beijing, he didn't like the news that was coming up from the country to his south, and he was now determined to do something about it.

When Kim Il Sung had approached him asking for support for his invasion of South Korea back in March, Mao was still flush with triumph from his victory over the Nationalists and was inclined to be generous. Like Stalin, he assumed that Kim would win with only token help from his Communist allies; like Stalin, he had become increasingly alarmed when the Americans intervened after Kim had said they wouldn't. News of Inchon and the recapture of Seoul had badly shaken both Beijing and Moscow, but the two Communist dictators chose two very different responses.[32]

Stalin had no desire to be drawn into a direct conflict with the Americans on the Korean peninsula. His support for Kim had never gone beyond providing equipment, military advisors, and sending the 151st Fighter Air Division with sixty-two new M-15 fighters to Manchuria. Yet to Kim's frustration, those new MiGs and their Soviet pilots spent their time flying training missions with their Korean and Chinese counterparts, instead of venturing south to take on the Americans.[33] Moreover, MacArthur's fast-moving successes on the battlefield made Stalin even less inclined to intervene.

By contrast, Mao was eager to take action. He had convinced himself that the American intervention in Korea was only a prelude to a much bigger American intervention in China—all evidence from the Truman administration's abandonment of Chiang Kai-shek notwithstanding. As soon as MacArthur's first reinforcements started arriving in Korea in July, he and chief advisor Zhou Enlai began gearing up for a full-scale war with the United States.

Starting that July, division after division of the People's Liberation Army began deploying in Manchuria. By early August a quarter million were in place along the Yalu River. Plans were under way to equip and supply a force of half a million. Yet when on August 4 Mao pressed his top generals to send a large expeditionary force into Korea to destroy the Americans, they still demurred.

They would not be ready to intervene until October, they told him; American firepower, airpower, and sea power presented challenges that the PLA had never before faced. They would need almost overwhelming numbers of men and materiel before taking on the American colossus, they said.[34]

Mao was unfazed. He was already telling the Chinese people to prepare for total war against the Western imperialists; he even said they never had to worry about a nuclear attack. The Americans no longer had the guts to use the bomb against civilian populations, since it would prompt the immediate condemnation of the United Nations and the rest of the capitalist world.[35]

Meanwhile, the ominous Chinese buildup in Manchuria continued.

The Americans did have some inkling of what was going on. By August 31, while MacArthur was preparing to launch CHROMITE, U.S. intelligence was saying that nine PLA armies, or thirty-seven divisions of Chinese troops, were in Manchuria. They also concluded that Mao had already sent 40,000 to 80,000 troops into North Korea. Even Willoughby in Tokyo, cautious as ever, estimated that there were at least sixteen PLA divisions ready for action in Manchuria, commanded by Mao's intimate Lin Biao.[36]

The CIA even predicted that Mao's forces would enter the war first as Chinese volunteers of Korean origin, together with Japanese POWs volunteering to serve as mercenaries. It also knew that Chinese agents were impressing civilians of Korean ethnicity into the army. Yet no one seemed to draw the correct conclusion, including MacArthur: the Chinese were committed to war the moment the first Americans set foot in the Korean peninsula. Contrary to critics then and later, it wasn't MacArthur's advance across the 38th parallel into North Korea that provoked the Chinese into action—let alone his advance toward the Yalu. Those moves only trip-wired the offensive that Mao had conceived in July. His plan was to let the Americans advance up the peninsula, then strike in order to bring on a general war—and with it a Chinese victory in Korea.

Mao's generals had told him they would be ready by October. By coincidence so was MacArthur. On October 1, 1950, he sent a message authorized by President Truman to Kim Il Sung, commander in chief of North Korean forces, calling on him to lay down his arms unconditionally.

"The early and total defeat and complete destruction of your armed forces and war-making potential is now inevitable," MacArthur said. "As the United Nations Commander-in-Chief, I call upon you and the forces under your command . . . forthwith to lay down your arms and cease hostilities . . . and I call upon you at once to liberate all United Nations prisoners of war and civilian internees under your control [while] North Korean forces, including prisoners of war in the hands of the United Nations Command, will continue to be given the care dictated by civilized custom and practice and permitted to return to their homes as soon as practicable."[37]

In MacArthur's mind and Washington's, they were preparing for the end-game. In Mao's, however, the game was just beginning.

At 5:35 A.M. on October 3, Dean Acheson was awakened by an urgent cable. Since the government in Washington had no diplomatic relations with Communist China, India's ambassador in Beijing, K. M. Panikkar, often served as unofficial go-between for the two capitals. The cable revealed that Mao's deputy Zhou Enlai had bluntly told Panikkar that if U.S. forces pressed north across the 38th parallel, China would have to intervene. Back in Tokyo, Ambassador William Sebald got the same message. Because it came through army channels, he knew MacArthur had gotten it as well.[38]

What did MacArthur think when he read it, assuming that he did read it (we have no clear indication that he did)? Certainly the prediction was in line with his own thinking about Chinese intentions, and Willoughby and the FECOM G-2's. They knew that Chinese forces were grouped close to the Manchurian border; there was even a solid consensus that they could enter the war at any time.[39]

But would they? The general view at the State Department, and among military intelligence officials in Washington, was that the Chinese would not. When State's delegation at the UN nervously asked around among other Asian delegations to gauge the reaction, most seemed to think the Chinese were bluffing.

Only the Burmese seemed to think the statement was serious; and Panikkar himself believed that any Chinese intervention would be on a small scale and could be localized. Secretary Acheson was inclined to take Chou's words as simply a warning, not to be disregarded but, on the other hand, not to be viewed as an authoritative statement of policy.[40]

The overwhelming consensus was that the Chinese would enter the conflict only as part of a general Communist offensive, including in Europe—or only if MacArthur did something rash to provoke them. Even then, the CIA's prediction that it would be Chinese volunteers who would be sent in, only encouraged the prevailing perception that if China *did* intervene it would be in a piecemeal fashion, which would give the Americans—and MacArthur—time to decide on a counterstrategy. MacArthur himself was confident that he could avoid a provocation by steering clear of the Yalu River boundary. And if he had known that Mao's top military and policy advisors all thought intervening in Korea would be a mistake that would drag China into an unwinnable war, he would have been even more confident—not to say complacent.

But if it was complacency, it was shared by every other American policymaker and analyst. The upshot was that no one in Washington or in the Dai-ichi building or at Turtle Bay in New York understood that Chou's words were neither a warning nor a prediction, but a simple statement of fact. At the moment when American troops entered South Korea, Mao had prepared for war; at the moment when Americans crossed the border into North Korea, Chinese forces would be ready to attack. For Mao, all that remained was choosing the right moment to strike.

In retrospect, these issues would weigh heavily on the historical record, and what was about to happen on the ground. That first week in October 1950, however, the Chinese were the last thing on MacArthur's mind. He was getting ready for the climactic stage of the Korean campaign. This would be the double envelopment of North Korea, with the Eighth Army continuing its thrust toward the North Korean capital at Pyongyang, while the X Corps under the command of William Almond—now Lieutenant General Almond—did another Inchon-type landing at Wansun on North Korea's east coast.

MacArthur's decision to divide his forces in the face of the enemy, even a disintegrating one, has left military strategists and historians shaking their heads ever since. Admiral Strubel, General Walker, his own G-3 Pinky Wright—all thought it a serious mistake at the time. One distinguished military historian has even dubbed the decision "markedly maladroit generalship."[41]

Why MacArthur did it, instead of sticking to a single axis of advance up the peninsula, remains one of the mysteries of the Korean War. Speculation abounds as a result, that it was done as a favor to General Almond, by giving him independent command of X Corps in reward for his loyalty and success with Inchon. It was also no secret that Almond and Walker, both hard chargers, did not get on well. A chain of command that put X Corps under the head of the Eighth Army would have bred considerable friction; far better, MacArthur reasoned—so the theory goes—to give each a separate command on either side of the North Korean peninsula.

But there may be a far simpler, and less devious, explanation for MacArthur's thinking. He had been here before, eight years earlier in the first Philippine campaign. The northern end of the Korean peninsula is split down the middle by the treacherous Taebaek Range, just as the Bataan peninsula had been bisected by a tangle of jungle-covered mountains. In 1942 he had handed one half of the peninsula over to Jim Wainwright and the other, eastern side to General Turner. MacArthur's mistake then had been not to insist that the two forces stay in constant contact over the mountain range that separated them. Now he insisted that Almond and Walker establish regular communication, even link up their forces, across the Taebaek Range.

Besides, in 1942 MacArthur had been on the desperate defensive. Now he was on the attack against a demoralized and defeated enemy. He believed that throwing a two-fisted punch at the Communists, instead of a single line of advance, would only hasten the collapse of resistance. Capturing Wonsan would also sever Kim's main Russian supply line from the seaport of Vladivostok. MacArthur's memoirs provide an additional explanation (or rationalization). "It was essential to secure the eastern corridor of the peninsula," he would write, as well as bring flank pressure to bear on the advance on Pyongyang. In any case, Inchon could barely handle 5,000 tons of supplies a day. Given his vastly expanded force, a new port of supply in the north was needed, and Wonsan was it.[42]

Rationalization or not, the net result of MacArthur's decision was to tie up Inchon harbor even more. Even as supplies and equipment were being unloaded, other troops and equipment were being reloaded for Wonsan, starting with the First Marines. Inchon became a logistical nightmare, while the Seventh Division had to head back to Pusan to embark for the voyage north. On October 11 the ROK Third Division entered Wonsan. By then Strubel's naval forces had discovered more than 3,000 mines in the city's harbor, all of which had to be painstakingly cleared out while the marines sailed back and forth for days—and while Walker's men were starved for supplies and transport that were being diverted to Wonsan harbor and X Corps.

It was a classic SNAFU—very unusual for MacArthur. Maybe he was showing his age at almost seventy-one; maybe his sense of invincibility, reinforced by Inchon, was getting the better of him. Or perhaps his hunger for seeing the Korean War end in as comprehensive and as decisive a victory as possible was propelling him to take strategic risks that a commander with shorter horizons wouldn't have taken. Whatever the reasons, his main focus now was on the push for Pyongyang, with Walker's four American divisions, four ROK divisions, and a brigade of British Commonwealth troops striking first toward Sariwon some twenty-five miles due south of the Communist capital, then moving on the capital itself.

The Eighth Army offensive jumped off on October 7, but the first division across the 38th parallel, the First Cavalry, ran into unexpected heavy resistance along a string of hills between Kaesong and Kumchon. Dug in on the hills were three KPA divisions backed by fresh Soviet-made T-34 tanks and SU-76 self-propelled guns. It took three days of hard fighting before the North Koreans, pounded relentlessly by artillery and from the air, finally pulled back. But their retreat now opened the way north, and by the 14th the First Cav and First ROK divisions were marching up the highway to Pyong-yang. The general in charge of the First ROK was particularly anxious to get there; Pyongyang was his hometown.[43]

But MacArthur was not there to see the advance; he was not even in Tokyo. Much to his frustration, he was two thousand miles away on tiny Wake Island, impatiently waiting to meet his commander in chief.

The October 12 message from Defense Secretary Marshall asking MacAr-thur to meet Truman had come as an unpleasant surprise to SCAP and his entire staff. MacArthur neither liked nor trusted Truman, and he knew the feeling was mutual. The last thing he wanted to do was to be pulled thou-sands of miles off course just when the invasion of North Korea was reaching its most critical juncture. He also suspected that the meeting was a political stunt on Truman's part and—despite the protestations of Truman admirers and his latest biographer—he seems largely to have been right.[44]

Truman's job approval ratings had steadily plummeted in the two years since his reelection in 1948, in large part due to the twin fiascoes of the Com-munist takeover of China and the Communist invasion of Korea, while MacArthur's ratings had steadily climbed. Democrats were looking to take a beating in the November elections. Truman hoped that some of MacArthur's exalted standing in the minds of American voters might rub off in a face-to-face meeting; photographs and newsreel shots of the two of them beaming and shaking hands might make Inchon look like a brilliant victory devised by two military geniuses, not just one.

Still, MacArthur was hardly in a position to refuse a request from his commander in chief. The one question was where to meet. Truman origi-nally proposed Honolulu, but Wake was closer to Tokyo and involved less of a flight for the UN's commander in chief in the middle of a war, so it was there that the two men agreed to meet for the first time, on October 15.

MacArthur's plane touched down on Wake about twelve hours before the president's. He had spent most of the flight pacing up and down, cursing his fate at being dragged away from the war just so Truman could get some extra votes in November. His staff wanted him there twelve hours early so he could get some rest before the big summit meeting. MacArthur, however, was too mad to sleep.

He had only one resolution in his mind. If this was a meeting solely for the politics and the photo op, he was going to beat Truman at his own game.[45]

At 6:30 the next morning, the 15th, a large plane could be seen approaching the island. MacArthur was sitting in a jeep near the edge of the tarmac. Protocol demanded that the most senior military officer be present at the foot of the ramp whenever a president steps off a plane or ship or train. MacArthur, however, refused to move even as the president's plane circled and then landed.

As the plane came to a stop, the ground crew wheeled a ramp up to the door. The plane was just opening when MacArthur ordered his driver to drive. The result was that President Truman was starting down the ramp when MacArthur's jeep stopped and the general jumped out. MacArthur then timed it perfectly, so that he and the president both reached the bottom step at the same time—thus fulfilling protocol while putting himself on an equal footing, almost literally, with his commander in chief.[46]

He also did it by not saluting but instead offering to shake hands—which Truman, after a moment's confusion, did. The cameras caught the beaming smiles and the happy clasp, but now it was MacArthur, not Truman, who again had the upper hand.

"How are you, General?" Truman said. "I'm glad you are here. I have been a long time meeting you."

"I hope it won't be so long next time," MacArthur graciously replied. In fact, they would never meet again.[47]

A small Chevy sedan took them over to a building where they could have a private chat. Meanwhile, MacArthur's team and the twenty-four members of Truman's entourage boarded a bus to take them to the site of the main conference.

The makeup of that entourage also confirmed MacArthur's suspicions about the motives for the meeting. Neither Marshall nor Dean Acheson was there; if it had been a serious strategy session they would have been. "I wanted no part of it," Acheson simply wrote later, "and saw no good coming from it."[48] Instead, there were Chairman of the Joint Chiefs Omar Bradley and Secretary of the Army Frank Pace. Dean Rusk and Philip Jessup led the delegation from the State Department. Averell Harriman was also there, having arrived early like MacArthur. Tucked under his arm was a five-pound box of chocolates for Jean.

"What's this meeting about?" MacArthur had asked his old friend. Harriman told him it was to see how to win a political victory in Korea, now that MacArthur had won a military one. MacArthur, Harriman remembered, seemed relieved at the answer. He took Harriman's arm and confessed he had taken "an awfully big risk" at Inchon. Harriman reminded him that Truman had taken an equal risk in backing MacArthur.[49]

Truman and MacArthur sat alone for forty minutes in one of the most celebrated face-to-face meetings of the twentieth century—and one of the least satisfying. Neither man's account of what was said is trustworthy (Truman's account of the Wake visit is more disingenuous, and sprinkled with what can only be described as falsifications of known facts), especially their mutual assurances later that they took a liking to each other. The story that MacArthur apologized for getting into politics in 1948—"they made a chump out of me," he said regarding his GOP supporters—is probably true, as is the story that Truman told him not to worry about it. Beyond that and some discussion of the future of the Philippine government, neither man would venture close to the sensitive issues at hand without witnesses—which came when they were driven over to the building with the other conferees.

The public meeting was, if anything, less satisfactory than the private one.

Five small folding tables had been pushed together to create one long oblong, around which the participants sat. Dean Rusk in particular was shocked at the superficiality of the questions Truman put to MacArthur—and at the rudeness with which MacArthur answered them. MacArthur did little to hide his conviction that the meeting was a sham, while Truman, incensed at the general's rudeness and wanting to end the meeting as soon as possible, fired off one question after another without bothering to listen to the answers.

Some were significant. When Truman asked about the impending peace treaty with Japan, MacArthur answered, "[A]ll occupations are failures," and urged that the treaty—and the American mission—end soon. Omar Bradley worried that the bulking up of MacArthur's army in Korea had depleted

America's reserves, especially if there was a Soviet move in Europe. MacArthur promised to release a division, the Second, which was one of his best, in January.

Everyone in the room assumed that the war was rapidly drawing to a close, and several questions about rebuilding South Korea, about dealing with prisoners of war, and punishing North Korean war criminals, reflected that.

Then Truman raised the question that got the most significant answer of all.

"What are the chances of Chinese or Soviet interference?"

"Very little," MacArthur replied, puffing on his pipe (he had forgotten to ask the president for permission to smoke until the very last moment). "Had they interfered in the first or second months it would have been decisive. We are no longer fearful of their intervention." Only 50,000 or 60,000 Chinese could get across the Yalu River, he said; China also had no air force. "If the Chinese tried to get down to Pyongyang there would be the greatest slaughter." Even with Russian-provided air support (and "I believe Russian air would bomb the Chinese as often as they would bomb us"), a Chinese intervention would be a failure, where it wasn't unlikely in the first place.

Truman nodded and moved on. It was an important moment; in retrospect, even a milestone in American policy in Asia. Yet no one spoke up with a follow-up question; just as importantly, no one in the room spoke up in MacArthur's support, even though his views were broadly the same as the consensus of the intelligence community, the Pentagon, and the State Department—a fact that critics of MacArthur's performance on Wake conveniently forget. Dean Rusk was the only one who was worried that the meeting was running too fast over this and other crucial issues. He quietly slipped a note to Truman, urging him to slow down the questions. "Hell, no!" Truman scribbled back. "I want to get out of here before we get into trouble!"[50]

Instead it was MacArthur who would get into trouble for his overconfident prediction. Even though every knowledgeable person in the room agreed with his opinion that the Chinese wouldn't intervene and if they did, they'd lose, he was the only one who stated it out loud. In less than eight weeks, those words would come back to haunt him—so much so that conspiracy-minded biographers Courtney Whitney and William Manchester have accused Truman of deliberately asking the question in order to trick MacArthur into making a gaffe. They would even accuse Truman of posting a secret unseen stenographer behind a half-closed door to record his answer. In fact, there was a stenographer, one of Jessup's staff members named Vernice Anderson, but the claim that she was a secret plant is untrue.

The truth is very different—and as usual in these cases—more banal. MacArthur's complacency about a Chinese intervention sprang from the same intelligence reports the others had seen. It also sprang from the same belief that the Chinese were weaker, and Mao Zedong more dependent on Stalin's control, than reality warranted. Events would prove them all wrong, but a combination of myth weaving, historical revisionism, and furious buck passing by others, including Truman, would come to fix the blame on MacArthur alone.

In any case, the ninety-minute meeting was over. Truman asked MacArthur to join them for lunch. The general demurred, saying he had to return to Tokyo at once—another slap in the face of his commander in chief. After the president presented him with his fourth Distinguished Service Medal, MacArthur was on board *Bataan II* and safely in the air.

He breathed a deep sigh of relief. From his perspective, the Wake meeting had gone well. No one had challenged his capacity to wage the rest of the war as he saw fit; after Inchon, no one dared. He had also warned the president that his views on Chinese intervention were speculative (a warning that Omar Bradley's final report on the meeting left out) and that understanding what they would do necessarily fell to State and the intelligence community, not to his military staff. As far as he was concerned, all of North Korea was still his battleground and he could range as far and as wide as he pleased.[51]

He could also be gratified that he had managed to make Truman look second-rate and foolish without revealing his underlying contempt for the man—or hurting America's image abroad. MacArthur didn't much care for the new, more cautious stance in Washington, the current president included. "The defiant, rallying figure that had been Franklin Roosevelt was gone," he wrote later. This president "seemed to be swayed by the some of the more selfish politicians in the United Nations," especially Europeans worried that an American victory in North Korea might provoke the Soviets into striking west across the Iron Curtain. "[Truman] seemed to be in the anomalous position of openly expressing fears of over-calculated risks that he had fearlessly taken only a few months before"—and MacArthur didn't like the change.[52]

The truth was the Truman team was nervous, and MacArthur's confidence made them more nervous. George Marshall could remember MacArthur's unqualified reassurances about defending the Philippines, and how that turned out. So could General Pace and Omar Bradley. In a strange sense, it was a group who knew one another almost *too* well, but with no resultant sense of trust.[53] Each expected, and was waiting for, the other to make a misstep, and all were focused on how they could correct the error when it came.

But it was already too late to go back and reassess the strategy that had gotten them this far with such unexpected success. As MacArthur's plane touched down back in Tokyo, the endgame in Korea was already under way.

They were now left with only one unknown. How far they could go before the rest of the Communist world realized what a threat American victory in Korea really would be.

CHAPTER 31

REVERSAL OF FORTUNE

Invincibility is in oneself, vulnerability is in the opponent.

—SUN TZU, *THE ART OF WAR*

On October 19 Pyongyang fell.

The First Cavalry and First ROK took the town with little fighting, as Kim Il Sung and his government fled northward to Anjun. The next day MacArthur, Pinky Wright, Whitney, and Stratemeyer took off to witness the first airdrop of the war by the 187th Airborne Regimental Combat Team, in a bid to seal the gap between Sukchon and Sunchon, some thirty miles north of Pyongyang. Most North Korean troops had already escaped farther north; the paratroopers captured fewer of the enemy than MacArthur had hoped. But from the air this was not apparent, so MacArthur was jubilantly telling reporters, "It looks like we closed the trap. . . . This very definitely is coming to an end." Later that day, MacArthur took a drive through a deserted Pyongyang, where portraits of Stalin and Kim Il Sung still hung in the streets and on the walls of government offices.[1]

The value to capturing Pyongyang was for MacArthur as much symbolic as strategic. "Aggressive Communism had been decisively defeated at a time and place of its own choosing," he wrote later. "The prestige of the United Nations, and especially the United States, was again high in all Asia."[2]

But MacArthur's forces had paid a steep price for the victory. MacArthur reviewed F Company of the Fifth Cavalry Regiment, the first Americans to enter the Communist capital. He asked how many had been with F Company when it first entered combat ninety-six days before. Five men raised their hands. They were the only ones left of the 200 men who had first come to Korea as F Company.

The rest were all replacements; even more sobering, of the five original survivors, only two were still unwounded.[3]

Walker made Kim Il Sung's own office his headquarters; Stratemeyer pinned a Distinguished Flying Cross on MacArthur for his "outstanding heroism and extraordinary achievement" in participating in the air jump (though of course MacArthur hadn't jumped with the others but had stayed in his plane), as well as his other low-level flights across Korea under "precarious" conditions. Then the commander in chief Far East (CINCFE) returned to Tokyo, where he penned a triumphant note to the Joint Chiefs the next day. He was preparing for the departure of the Eighth Army from Korea, he said, which "would start before Thanksgiving and be completed before Christmas."

Indeed, it really did seem as if all of North Korea was now in United Nations hands. Kim and his henchmen had to flee the advancing ROK and American forces again, evacuating Sinuiju near Anju for a spot deeper in the mountains. On the 26th, the Sixth ROK Division sped ahead of the rest of Walker's army until one of its platoons reached the banks of the Yalu River near Chosan and could look across into China. That same day the marines of X Corps began landing at Wonsan. They didn't anticipate doing much fighting. MacArthur had already informed them that two of First Marine's regiments would soon be headed home, and the third for Japan.[4]

Yet the imminent end of hostilities only made the men sitting back in Washington more anxious. Their worries were still centered on the risks of triggering a wider war, either with China or the Soviet Union. News that one hundred new Soviet-built fighters had been spotted by an American reconnaissance flight near Antung, Manchuria, made them particularly jumpy; so did a CIA report that Chinese volunteers might be sent into action to defend the Suiho hydroelectric plant near Sinuiju if MacArthur made a move in that direction.[5]

MacArthur reassured the Joint Chiefs that he had no plans to attack the Suiho plant; he added he wouldn't hesitate to destroy it if he found out it was being used for military purposes like manufacturing munitions. Indeed, his plans for wrapping up this war involved more military operations, not fewer, especially from the air.

His principal objective was bombing the massive North Korea supply center at Rocin, which was used to unload supply trains coming in from the Soviet Union. The Joint Chiefs, however, said no; it was too close to the Chinese border. They also nixed any plans to bomb hydroelectric dams along the Yalu—again, too close to the China border.[6]

MacArthur could only throw up his hands in frustration at what he saw as Washington's timidity. But that timidity was fast turning into anger when the Truman team learned that MacArthur had moved the northernmost line for UN action even farther north along a new Sonchon-Songjin axis on October 19, and then on October 24 abolished any demarcation line altogether—all without their permission or prior consultation. Instead, MacArthur was ordering his forces "to drive forward with all speed and full utilization of their forces," even to the Yalu if necessary, in order to "secure all of North Korea."

"Your action is a matter of some concern here," the Joint Chiefs wrote archly. They pointed out that MacArthur's directive was clearly contradictory of their directive on September 27 setting the non-ROK unit boundary. "While the JCS realize you undoubtedly had sound reasons for issuing these instructions, they would like to be informed of them."

With a perfectly straight face, MacArthur wired back, "There is no conflict that I can see." The JCS themselves had said at the time that the September 27 directive was provisional and might need modification. Then he played his trump card, the message "dated 30 September from the Secretary of Defense [George Marshall] which stated: 'We want you to feel unhampered tactically and strategically to proceed north of the 38th Parallel.'"[7]

Certainly Marshall never meant his personal cable to MacArthur to be a blank check for any and all operations north of the parallel, but MacArthur now felt free to use it as such. The Joint Chiefs were stung into silence—for now. But their patience with what seemed to be MacArthur's high-handedness bordering on insubordination was wearing thin. A sentiment was growing, at both the Pentagon and the State Department, that someone needed to rein him in before something disastrous happened. But in the shadow of Inchon and now the collapse of North Korea, no one was willing to.

Besides, everyone had a more urgent issue to worry about. The very day that MacArthur's reply reached Washington, the Chinese entered the war.

They entered first in the sector around Onjong, forty miles north of Anjung.

The Sixth ROK Division suddenly found itself engaged with an enemy in unknown uniforms carrying old Japanese rifles and using bugle calls and drums to launch troops into battle. They were the 120th Division of the Chinese Fortieth Army, and in a matter of hours they overran two battalions—and inside of two days virtually annihilated the Sixth ROK. Two more South Korean divisions ran head-on into the Chinese onslaught and rapidly collapsed, leaving the Eighth Army's entire right flank wide open.[8]

General Walker immediately alerted MacArthur of the South Korean rout and the Chinese presence; suddenly Korea had become, as MacArthur put it somewhat later, "an entirely new war."

Still, MacArthur wasn't too worried. He and Willoughby were still operating within the consensus of American intelligence, both military and the CIA, that the Chinese entry into the war was provisional, possibly just a symbolic gesture to keep United Nations forces from getting too close to the Yalu and China's hydroelectric grid along the river.[9] Willoughby's sources said that no more than 16,000 Chinese troops might be in North Korea (the actual number was closer to 200,000). That confident estimate was Willoughby's biggest blunder in his career—with the most fateful consequences for his beloved commander in chief.

The Chinese troops were positioned as part of Mao's master plan: to set up a grand ambush of the Eighth Army. Mao had been waiting since early August for this moment; now it had finally arrived. His principal general, Peng, and the first Chinese "volunteer" forces had already sprung the trap on the South Korean divisions; if MacArthur had failed to advance beyond the Pyongyang-Wonsan line, Mao was ready to use the winter to train and equip his armies for a general assault in the spring. No one on the American side understood it at the time, but the widening war in Korea was a Chinese operation from the beginning. What MacArthur did, or didn't do, didn't matter. He was determined to fight against the American imperialist aggressors, and Kim Il Sung's impending defeat was merely the excuse for doing it.[10]

MacArthur, of course, believed there was every reason to assume the Chinese entry into the war could be contained: no one in Washington at that point was prepared to suggest otherwise. His primary focus was still his plan for annihilating North Korean resistance before the Chinese could make any further aggressive moves and before the bulk of his forces reached the Yalu River. Walker's corps commander pushed the First Cavalry Division to fill the gap on the right flank; the Twenty-first Infantry pushed its way to within twenty miles of the Yalu on the 31st—its lead commander, ironically enough, was Lieutenant Colonel Brad Smith of the original Smith Force. MacArthur was already conjuring up his plan to finish the war. The Chinese volunteers threading their way to the south only fed his certainty that it would work.[11]

Then on November 1 everything changed.

Chinese troops poured overnight into action against the First Cavalry Division and the Eighth Cavalry Regiment in particular, smashing through the lines and destroying tanks, artillery, trucks, and everything that stood in their way. For three days the Eighth Cav had to fight their way back through a series of Chinese roadblocks; first one and then the second battalion held out against the encircling Chinese until they were overwhelmed. The last survivors fell back to the Nammyon River on November 6; they were barely 200 out of a command of 1,000. All the rest were dead or POWs; the Eighth Cavalry gave up twelve tanks, twelve howitzers, fifty-six mortars, and ninety-two jeeps. The regiment had ceased to exist as a fighting force. Some called it the cavalry's worst defeat since Little Bighorn.[12]

On the other side of the Taebaek Range, Almond's X Corps had also made its first contact with the new enemy. The Seventh Marine Regiment fought Chinese units that had pounded to pieces a South Korean division, the Third, on November 2. The fight lasted five days until the Chinese unexpectedly broke off—as they were mysteriously breaking off everywhere and heading for the hills. Australian and British troops fought a hard, desperate hand-to-hand battle with Chinese troops at Pakchon until they too vanished from the battlefield.

Captain Al Haig accompanied Almond on a visit to meet Chinese prisoners taken in the fighting on the 30th. They were "young, well fed, and showed every sign of good training and excellent morale," Haig remembered. He also remembered their uniforms, which would become iconic in the next climactic stage of the war: quilted goose-down uniforms and "fleece-lined hats—but no gloves or overcoats—and, instead of boots, a sort of rubber sneaker." The Chinese soldiers had crossed the Yalu River at Manpojin two weeks before, they told interrogators, then headed southeast with their equipment loaded on horses and mules. The prisoners were happy to be out of the war; but it was clear there were many more Chinese who were poised to come in.[13]

American commanders, including MacArthur in Tokyo, were thoroughly confused about what was happening. Despite the devastating losses to the Eighth Cav, the line on both sides of the Taebaek Range was holding. Walker's Eighth Army, however, was at the end of its strength. His South Korean divisions had been all but wiped out. Almond's X Corps appeared less vulnerable because it could hug closer to its supply base at Wonsan, and had been joined by the fresh Third Infantry Division. But it was still dangling on the edge of the unknown, with no clear picture of the enemy it faced, or how many he was.

On November 3 the mystified Joint Chiefs asked MacArthur for his assessment of the situation. MacArthur gave them his best estimate, although he did not tell them it rested on very spotty intelligence (some of his field commanders still thought the Chinese they were capturing were North Koreans). Of all the possibilities, he considered a full-scale Chinese intervention the least likely. Either the Chinese were giving Kim covert help; or they were trying to buck up North Korean resistance; or they thought they could intervene in force only as long as they encountered South Korean forces.

He considered any of those three options more likely than assuming that America was now in an all-out war with Communist China. "I recommend against hasty conclusions," he wrote. "A final appraisal should await a more complete accumulation of military facts."[14]

But MacArthur himself was in no mood to wait. By November 5, he had made up his mind. It was time to strike against the Chinese who were already in Korea, this time from the air. He ordered Stratemeyer to draw up plans for a two-week bombing offensive to "destroy every means of communication and every installation, factory, city, and village" in North Korea between his troops and the border. Only Suiho Dam, the hydroelectric plants on the Yalu, and the supply center at Rocin were to be spared; and bridges were to be bombed on their North Korea side. Those were MacArthur's only concessions to the sensitivities of the Joint Chiefs and State Department.[15]

Otherwise, it was total war from the air, starting with the twin bridges linking Antun and Sinuiju, which MacArthur believed were the key conduit for keeping Kim and his North Koreans supplied and still in the war—and which were now conduits for Chinese reinforcements.

When Marshall and the Joint Chiefs learned what was happening, their rage was considerable. Deputy Defense Secretary Robert Lovett consulted with Dean Acheson, and they agreed that the bombing mission had to be halted at once; it was too risky, and might endanger a UN resolution calling on China to cease all operations in Korea. From his home in Independence, Missouri, Truman assented. Even as Stratemeyer's B-29s were warming their engines the Joint Chiefs ordered MacArthur to cease and desist, and attack no targets closer than five miles from the Chinese borders.[16]

Now it was MacArthur's turn for rage. He ordered his acting chief of staff, General Hickey, to draft up a letter of resignation so MacArthur could sign it. Hickey persuaded him not to send it, saying it would demoralize the army. MacArthur had to agree, and tore the letter up. Whether the letter was a serious gesture, or just a way of letting off steam, is anyone's guess; but he did fire off a blistering note to the Joint Chiefs, calling the Chinese intervention "one of the most offensive acts of international lawlessness of historic record" and warning of the consequences of not acting now.

"Men and materiel in large force are pouring across all bridges over the Yalu from Manchuria," he wrote. "The movement not only jeopardizes but threatens the ultimate destruction of the forces under my command.... Every hour that this is postponed will be paid for dearly in American and other United Nations blood."[17]

So which was it? On the one hand MacArthur said he was unworried about Chinese intervention; on the other he was saying it threatened his army with annihilation. The Joint Chiefs asked Truman's opinion and he, against all his own instincts, came again to MacArthur's rescue. Since MacArthur was the commander on the ground, his call prevailed. Let the bombing begin.

Later, Omar Bradley said MacArthur's dispatch of the 6th—so pessimistic and dire in tone from the one that had come two days earlier—should have been a warning that he needed to be stopped, even relieved. "Right then— that night—the JCS should have taken firmest control of the Korean War" away from the CINCFE in Tokyo, he complained, since MacArthur seemed to have lost any stability of judgment.[18]

In fact, MacArthur's views had not changed at all from the 4th to the 6th. The explanation for the difference in tone was MacArthur's unlimited faith in airpower. What the Fifth Air Force had done under General Kenney, the Air Forces Far East could do under Stratemeyer: isolate the battlefield, shatter the enemy's supply lines and ability to sustain the fight. Willoughby was telling him that the Chinese had no more than 45,000 men in North Korea— again, a pitiful underestimate—but another 350,000 were poised on the other side of the river.[19] Knock out the bridges, MacArthur assumed, and they'll have to stay there. Then he, Almond, and Walker would destroy the rest.

On the other hand, vetoing an aggressive air campaign would leave the Chinese advance unchecked. Once the Chinese had the full advantage of superior numbers, the overextended, divided UN command *would* be in real danger—and MacArthur would have no choice but to pull back.

But this time MacArthur was mistaken. Unleashed airpower did not change the situation on the ground. More than seventy B-29s rained death and destruction on Sinuiju; 60 percent of the city burned to the ground, but the approaches to the bridges were barely damaged. Intense antiaircraft fire from North Korean batteries manned by Russian crews kept the bombers and U.S. fighters from coming in close enough to do much damage to most of the other bridges; and the Joint Chiefs' rules of engagement made it impossible to take out the bridge at Namsan, because a final bombing run had to come from the forbidden Manchurian zone.

In the end, only half of the Yalu bridges were damaged, while Russian-piloted MiG 15s brought down two B-29s and damaged three more.[20]

In fairness, Stratemeyer had told MacArthur it couldn't be done, anyway— not under Washington's rules of engagement. MacArthur later claimed that one bomber pilot who had lost an arm during one of the raids and was near death asked him, with blood pouring from his mouth, "General, which side are Washington and the United Nations on?"[21]

But there was another, more urgent issue puzzling MacArthur, Willoughby, and G-2 analysts. Where did all the Chinese go?

In more specific terms, what had happened to the Chinese troops inside the border? After the intense battles from October 31 to November 2, they had simply vanished. No one, not Willoughby, not the British or American military intelligence, and certainly not the CIA, could provide any helpful information as to where they had gone.

A logical assumption, and a convenient one, was that they had headed back to China. Their presumed pullback meant that the United Nations forces had prevailed, and now controlled the battlefield. No wonder MacArthur felt that the day was his, and that the United Nations forces, after a brief crisis, had regained the advantage.

What no one knew, least of all MacArthur, was that Mao had pulled them back on purpose. What he dubbed his First Offensive against the American imperialists and their Korean stooges was over; it had been a disastrous slaughter of his soldiers, but he personally rated it a success. Now he was gearing up for a Second Offensive, with more than half a million Chinese descending upon the unsuspected American and UN forces.[22]

When it came, MacArthur and his generals would be fighting not just an enemy that outnumbered them two to one, but the forces of nature itself.

In the first two weeks of November, a series of storms roared across both North and South Korea, opening the way for an icy Siberian front to descend on the peninsula. On November 15–16 temperatures dropped below zero. In the words of one historian, by November 20 "Korea became a frigid land of blowing snow, plunging temperatures, cutting winds, blinding dust, thickening clouds, heavy ground fog, and 'white outs.'" Even worse, Stratemeyer's air force intelligence had disturbing news. The frigid temperatures meant that the Yalu would freeze so thick that troops, trucks, and even armored vehicles would be able to get across. Further bombing on the Yalu bridges was now useless; Communist China could reinforce its army in North Korea at will.[23]

The fog of winter as well as war had fallen over the battlefield, obscuring everything. Yet from his office in Tokyo, MacArthur refused to be daunted.

"There were but three possible courses of action," he later wrote. "I could go forward, remain immobile, or withdraw." He decided to go forward. If he did, "there was a chance that China might not intervene and the war would be over." If he stayed put and waited out the weather, the Chinese might use the opportunity to descend on him in overwhelming numbers and destroy his army. If he withdrew, "it would be in contradiction to my orders and would destroy any opportunity to bring the Korean war to a successful end."[24]

Blessed with the inestimable gift of hindsight, later historians and commentators almost unanimously condemn MacArthur's decision to advance to the Yalu as a disastrous one. Some have even compared MacArthur to a character in a Greek tragedy, overcome by hubris and possibly even declining mental and physical health. They have portrayed MacArthur's progress from the victory at Inchon to the push to the Yalu as a final death ride—in General Lawton Collins's words, "like a Greek hero [marching] to an unkind and inexorable fate."[25]

It is important, however, to remember that MacArthur had good reason to believe that the tools of victory were still in his grasp. Despite the appearance of the Russian and Chinese MiG 15s, he enjoyed overwhelming air superiority. He also had complete control of the seas on either side of the Korean peninsula, with ample port facilities for resupply. Even more, he had a battle-tested army on the march against a devastated North Korean enemy and a primitively equipped Chinese foe in worrisome but still (he believed) manageable numbers.

In his mind the only things that stood in the way of final triumph were the doubters in Washington and the naysayers at the United Nations, especially the British, who were pushing a plan to establish a demilitarized zone along the border between Manchuria and North Korea (a plan that we now know neither Mao nor Stalin would ever have accepted). There was no reason for a confident MacArthur not to assume that one final decisive push would get his men to the Yalu and make the Chinese think twice before trying to cross.

Furthermore, his assurances to the Joint Chiefs that Stalin had no inclination to intervene, either in Korea or in Europe, would also prove correct. We also know from secret Soviet archives that the Soviet dictator believed the war in Korea now belonged to two persons and two only, Kim Il Sung and Mao. It was theirs to win or lose. He was not about to commit Soviet troops to save the Korean peninsula, or his Asiatic allies, from the Americans, let alone provoke a second front in Europe.

MacArthur's confidence also sprang from the one other insuperable advantage that he enjoyed over all his critics. He had a plan; no one else did. And so, after long, intense debate and with deep foreboding, the Joint Chiefs, Defense Secretary Marshall, State's Dean Acheson, and with Averell Harriman representing the president, signed on to his plans for a large new offensive to begin on November 24. Assuming that the Chinese entered the war in force, their instructions read, "you should continue the action as long as, in your judgment, action by forces now under your control offers a reasonable chance of success." Then, "on the assumption that your coming attack will be successful," the president and his team would want to make sure certain steps were taken for the unification of the Korean peninsula and disengagement of remaining Chinese forces by diplomatic means.

Other than that, the war was his to win.[26]

MacArthur took up the offer with enthusiasm. On November 21 the first unit of Almond's X Corps reached the southern bank of the Yalu. One eyewitness could see on the other bank "Chinese sentries walking their rounds and other soldiers coming and going" with "their breath vaporized in the frigid air."[27] Yet the Chinese on China's soil never fired at the Americans. It seemed to prove MacArthur's point: once the United Nations controlled all of North Korea, the Chinese would back down.

More important, arriving at the Yalu meant that Almond's forces had completed the preliminaries for MacArthur's November 24 offensive, a "massive compressive envelopment," as he called it, that would catch the Chinese and remaining North Koreans in its jaws. The Eighth Army, some 240,000 strong (although half were the often unreliable ROK army) would thrust northward, while the X Corps' 102,000 Americans, Koreans, and British, would push to the northwest to close the trap, with a series of massive bombing raids that would seal off the enemy from his supply lines.

Although he and Walker had drawn up a fallback plan for withdrawal in case the Chinese did in fact intervene in large numbers, MacArthur was supremely confident of success. Unfortunately, so was the Chinese general opposing him, Peng Dehuai. At almost the same time MacArthur was driving his armies forward, General Peng would be hurling 388,000 Chinese soldiers straight into the heart of Walker's army.[28]

On the morning of November 24, MacArthur's plane landed on the frozen tundra outside what was General Walker's headquarters on the Chongchon River.

He and Walker agreed that the supply situation for the Eighth Army was still unsatisfactory, but there was no time to waste. They had already put off the offensive once, when it was set for November 15. Now the time had come to strike, before any more Chinese troops filtered across the Yalu.[29]

MacArthur toured the lines for five hours, with the press following eagerly behind. He met with General Milbourne, ironically nicknamed "Shrimp" on account of his enormous height, commander of the Twenty-fourth Infantry Division, in a large tent together with some other officers. Milbourne began showing him on a map how much ground they had covered in the past week, despite the Chinese resistance and the atrocious weather.

MacArthur was impressed. He said, "If we can keep this up, we will have some of these people home by Christmas."

Outside the tent, reporters' ears perked up; pencils scratched the phrase down on notepads. In newspapers across the country MacArthur's coming offensive was redubbed the "Home by Christmas Drive."[30]

For MacArthur, the operative word was "some." He told the officers that if the Red Chinese didn't intervene further, General Bradley had already slated two divisions to head back to the States by that date. But the words "home by Christmas" would haunt him in less than twenty-four hours.[31]

Meanwhile, "I decided to reconnoiter" the Yalu River line and "try to see what was going on." He particularly wanted to see the Chinese airstrips that were supposed to be on the opposite bank. Since he couldn't do it on foot, he decided he'd do it by airplane, on Story's Lockheed Constellation with its name emblazoned its nose: *SCAP.*

His staff looked at one another. "Everyone was appalled," Pinky Wright later remembered. They knew the big, lumbering Constellation would instantly draw all kinds of fire from the ground—and probably send Chinese jets scrambling to shoot them down.

But MacArthur shook his head.

"I don't care. I don't want to get right over this airstrip. I just want to get close enough so that I can see it."

Once they were in air and headed for the river, MacArthur explained his real mission: to do an aerial tour of the entire Yalu, from the mouth at Antung clear across to Hyesanjin in the east and the Siberian border. Even if the Chinese troops remained invisible, he felt it would still give him a sense of the terrain over which his men would be fighting the next several days.

Since American fighters could follow for only fifteen minutes before their fuel began to run out and they had to head back to base, MacArthur, *SCAP*, and his staff flew at 5,000 feet for the next four hours without any protection or fighter escort. His staff all assumed these were their last hours on earth. MacArthur was too absorbed in staring out the window to notice.

"All that spread before our eyes was an endless expanse of utterly barren countryside, jagged hills, yawning crevices, and the black waters of the Yalu locked in the silent death grip of ice and snow," he later wrote dramatically. Those lines of jagged hills would be a problem; troops advancing up one set of ravines would barely notice what was happening in the valleys on either side. It was a perfect setting for ambushes and sudden counterattacks, as the Americans were about to find out.[32]

At last MacArthur told a relieved Colonel Story to turn around and head back to Tokyo. When they came back to earth, General Stratemeyer was waiting with a reward for his chief's daring flight: a Distinguished Flying Cross. Pinned to it was an honorary pair of pilots' wings. Stratemeyer, at least, had not lost faith in the CINCFE; the men in Washington were still uncertain. What happened in the next day or two would determine whether they had made the right choice in backing MacArthur, or the wrong one.

From GHQ in Tokyo came a press release from MacArthur himself:

> *The United Nations massive compression envelopment in North Korea against the new Red armies operating there is now approaching its decisive effort. . . . If successful this should for all practical purposes end the war, restore peace and unity to Korea, enable the prompt withdrawal of United Nations military forces, and permit the complete assumption by the Korean people and nation of full sovereignty and international equality. It is that for which we fight.*[33]

In fact, MacArthur was now fighting for a much larger goal than the unification of Korea. He had never accepted the argument that his move toward the border would trigger a Chinese reaction, although posterity (wrongly) would claim otherwise. From the beginning, he stressed to the Washington men that Mao's entire approach to the war had been proactive, not reactive. In an extraordinary personal memorandum sent to Secretary Marshall on November 8, MacArthur revealed his thinking in response to the question of what he thought the Chinese were up to.

"Their activities in Korea throughout have been offensive, never defensive," he wrote, starting with the Communist invasion of North Korea. What was on display in Korea, he said, was a Chinese nationalism "of increasingly dominant aggressive tendencies" that was spawned fifty years before during the Boxer Rebellion, and "has been brought to its greatest fruition under the present regime."

The result has been the creation "of a new and dominant power in Asia which for its own purposes is allied with the Soviet Union, but which in its own concepts and methods has become aggressively imperialistic with a lust for expansion and increased power."

He added, China's "interests are at present parallel to those of the Soviet Union." But to MacArthur, "the aggression shown in Korea as well as Indo-China and Tibet" suggested that Peking was following its own line of expansionist conquest—and not the Soviet line. On the one hand, it showed the Chinese were not automatically Soviet satellites, doing Stalin's bidding. On the other hand, MacArthur concluded, "When they reach the fructification of their military potential, I dread to think what may happen."[34]

George Marshall was an intelligent, insightful man but no egghead. He was slightly puzzled by the entire historical-cultural disquisition, and wrote back that MacArthur might have misunderstood his question. But MacArthur's remarks revealed a prescient insight into what was actually taking place in Asia, and what might happen in the future. While the conventional wisdom in Washington held that Mao was only Stalin's stooge, MacArthur was anticipating the possibility of a future Sino-Soviet split—even the future direction of Chinese foreign policy sixty years later.

What was at stake was far more than victory in Korea, in MacArthur's mind. It was putting the brakes on an incipient Chinese conquest of East Asia before it was too late.

* * *

It was in the dim morning light on November 24 that Walker's I and IX Corps—four American divisions and a British brigade—began their advance toward the Yalu, with the ROK II Corps on their right. Farther east, Almond's Third Infantry Division and First Marine Division, which had reached the Yalu at Hyesanjin on the 21st, wearily resumed their march to join up with the Eighth Army. Although they had faced little opposition over the past two weeks, the marines were cold, tired, and footsore. They were suffering acutely from frostbite; temperatures on the eastern side of the Taebaek Range were on average thirty degrees lower than where Walker was advancing, and during the day hovered around twenty degrees below zero.[35]

Although they were advancing slowly—too slowly to make Walker happy—the men of X Corps weren't meeting much opposition now either, as the marines reached the south end of the large body of water known as the Chosin Reservoir and turned northwest. Nor were Walker's men, who covered twelve miles that first day of the offensive and into the next.

Everything was going according to plan, and not just MacArthur's plan.

When he returned to Tokyo on November 24 there had been a message waiting for him from the Joint Chiefs. It expressed concern about "a general conflict" if his advance to the Yalu brought on a major clash with the Chinese. But it still urged "there should be no change in your mission" and that MacArthur make plans for "the establishment of a unified Korea" as well as "reducing the risk" of a bigger conflict with the Chinese.[36]

Then suddenly MacArthur's strategy lay in ruins, almost overnight.

The black, frozen night of November 25 was shattered by a massive barrage of mortar, artillery, and rocket fire. Then tens of thousands of soldiers from the Chinese Thirty-eighth and Forty-second Armies surged over the ROK II Corps in a human tsunami, while others swept around the South Korean flanks. Only one ROK regiment, the Seventh Division's Third, managed to evade the Chinese encircling pocket by marching west to join up with the American Second Division.

Then it was the Second Division's turn, along with a brigade of Turkish infantry. They made a heroic sacrifice over the next day and night with appalling losses, but managed to slow the Chinese advance long enough for Walker to stanch his bleeding right flank. By daylight on the 27th, four Chinese armies—180,000 men—were now hammering the Eighth Army back, while two more armies struck south along the Taedong River, trying to cut off the United Nations force's access to the road back to Pyongyang.[37]

That night it was X Corps that took a mauling from the Chinese.

Almost 120,000 of them swept down on the First Marine Division and the Twenty-seventh Infantry Division as they moved west of the Chosin Reservoir. It was the same tactic the Chinese were using in their assaults on the Eighth Army. Once darkness fell, there would be a "frightening uproar of noise. Bugles, whistles . . . cymbals . . . drums . . . the crowing of cocks . . . shouting, laughing, chattering." When the noise stopped, the attack would begin, a human battering ram of one massed infantry regiment following another on a narrow front, heedless of casualties as the Americans poured on everything they had: rifle fire, machine-gun fire, artillery firing nearly at point-blank range.[38]

Then slowly, inevitably, the Americans would give ground, gathering up their casualties, and fall back to the next line of hills as the Chinese would regroup and begin the attack again. Farther to the west, Walker's troops had managed to evade the expanding Chinese pocket, but they were falling back to the southeast bank of the Chongchon River, along the Anju-Kachon-Kunuri Road at a rate that more resembled a rout than a fighting retreat. The Eighth Army was in serious trouble, and it was up to MacArthur and his commanders to figure out how to save it.[39]

MacArthur's reaction to the events since the 25th had been slow, largely because his commanders, Almond and Walker, were slow to catch on to the size and extent of the Chinese offensive. This in turn happened because of the confusion and the cold, and as with most battles being fought at night, it was difficult to understand where their own troops were, let alone the Chinese. But by the morning of November 28 all three men realized this was indeed "an entirely new war," as MacArthur put it. A 300,000-strong enemy was battering steadily at their front and their flanks, and they faced a looming disaster unless they reacted swiftly.

But what to do? On the 28th MacArthur summoned Almond and Walker to Tokyo for a quick war conference—an unusual move for him, and a sign that he was deeply worried about what was happening. They gathered late that night: MacArthur, Walker, Almond, Stratemeyer representing the Air Force, and Admirals Joy and Arleigh Burke sitting in for the navy. MacArthur's staff was there—Hickey, Wright, Willoughby, and Whitney—but for once they didn't have a preconceived plan. Neither did MacArthur. Everything short of a total withdrawal from Korea was on the table.

When they finally adjourned at 1:30 the next morning, they knew what to do. There was no alternative to dropping back; it was just a matter of deciding how far. In the end, they agreed that the Eighth Army would leave the Chongchon Valley and retire to a line just north of Pyongyang; MacArthur told Walker he could even abandon Pyongyang if he had to.[40]

On the other side of the peninsula, the navy would pick up the X Corps at Hungnam on North Korea's east coast and carry them back to Wonsan while keeping supplies flowing to both Walker's and Almond's men. The air force would continue its bombing runs up the Yalu and try to slow the Chinese advance, but the threat of meeting Stalin's MiGs diminished the airmen's confidence that they could stop it. MacArthur's faith that airpower could be decisive in the Korean conflict had been wrong. This was an infantry slugging match from start to finish. He might have drawn more lessons from his experiences with the Rainbow Division in World War One than from what he and Kenney had achieved in the battles for the Solomons and New Guinea.

As the meeting broke up and Almond and Walker flew back to Korea, MacArthur was left alone with his thoughts. He doesn't reveal them in his account of those days in his memoirs. But later he would fix the blame for the debacle they had just suffered squarely on Washington and the Joint Chiefs, for failing to allow him to destroy the Yalu bridges. In his memoirs he would even darkly hint that someone had leaked his plans to the Chinese in advance, and they had known that "they could swarm down across the Yalu without having to worry about bombers hitting their Manchurian supply lines."[41]

The truth was that the Yalu bridges were the least of his problems. The people who had really let him down were the ever-erratic Willoughby, the CIA, and the army's own G-2 units for not detecting the arrival of Chinese "volunteers" in Korea, and their massive numbers, sooner. He had been led to believe he was playing a minor-league ball club, as it were, when he was actually in the World Series.

Now it was up to him to do something to save the two halves of his army. Fortunately, the marines fighting along the banks of the Chosin Reservoir bought him the time to save the X Corps half. The Fifth and Seventh Marines started a cautious, phased pullback from Yudam-ni to the perimeter around Hagaru-ri. There was no panicky, desperate flight as sometimes happened during the Eighth Army's withdrawal; or even in some of Almond's army units. But there was plenty of fighting. The marines pushed their way through no fewer than thirty-seven Chinese roadblocks and firesacks in subzero temperatures, with gunners from artillery batteries and even marine typists and truck drivers filling the rifle platoon ranks when their numbers got too thin. During the day they got air support from their Corsair fighter-bombers; at night they cut down the waves of attacking Chinese with artillery, tank, and massed infantry fire.[42]

Men stayed alive by eating Tootsie Rolls when their food ran out; they also used Tootsie Rolls to plug bullet holes in truck radiators. Others used their own urine to keep their weapons' bolts working. Any body part exposed to the air immediately froze, which medics learned meant that men with severe gunshot wounds could be kept from bleeding to death by letting the wound freeze until it could be treated at an aid station.

By the time the last marines made it to Hagaru-ri, they were a shadow of their former selves. Company B, First Battalion, Seventh Marines started the fight with seven officers and 215 marines; they finished it with one officer and 26 marines.

But when General Smith watched one of the last battered battalions form up to march and heard them sing "The Marines' Hymn" in lusty, cracked voices, he knew his men's fight back from Chosin Reservoir had written one of the epics of the Korean War—and an immortal chapter in the history of the Marine Corps.[43]

On the other side of the Taebaek Range, the army's Second Division was not so lucky when on the retreat back to Pyongyang they entered a long mountain pass between Kunu-ri and Sunchon—what would later be remembered among the survivors as "the Gauntlet." For forty-eight hours they had to fight their way through Chinese roadblocks, ambushes, and a withering crossfire from the hills on either side. Wrecked vehicles filled with dead GIs often clogged the road, while the men behind were sitting targets for Chinese riflemen and machine gunners. Close air support and infantry-tank counterattacks couldn't break the Chinese grip on the Gauntlet. Only one combat team from the Second Division managed to break out intact. By December 1, the division had lost 5,000 men, abandoned all its engineering and most of its artillery and radios, as well as hundreds of jeeps and vehicles.

The marines' calvary at Chosin had inspired Almond's command with hope; the Second Division's inspired General Walker to abandon the strategy he and MacArthur had agreed to. He gave up on the idea of holding on to the Pyongyang-Wonsan line—or any other line north of the 38th parallel. He would pull his forces back into South Korea. As he explained to MacArthur, he had suffered some 10,000 casualties; he had lost massive amounts of artillery. He had no choice but to pull back to a line he could protect with the artillery he had left.

So on December 2 he closed his headquarters in Pyongyang, and by December 6 the Eighth Army had cleared the city while engineers prepared to blow the bridges connecting the road from Pyongyang to Seoul—bridges that the Eighth Army had crossed in triumph less than six weeks before.

The speed of the Eighth Army's withdrawal caught the Chinese by surprise.

It was not until December 20–21 that their advance battalions caught up with Walker's new front line just north of Seoul.[44]

That precipitous retreat should have left X Corps totally exposed at Hungnam, but they were no longer there. On November 30 MacArthur had already ordered their departure from North Korea; he was going to need them in the south. Almond, even with his thinned and bedraggled forces, managed to set up a twenty- or thirty-mile perimeter at Hungnam, protected on each side by massed artillery. When the Chinese tried to break through, their losses were even greater than they had been in the fighting for Chosin Reservoir. Almond's aide, Captain Alexander Haig, believed X Corps could have held out indefinitely.[45] But on December 12 the navy began loading up its transports with sick, frozen, and battle-weary marines and soldiers—some 105,000 men plus 91,000 Korean refugees, 17,000 vehicles, and more than 90,000 tons of stores and munitions.

It was Inchon in reverse. By Christmas Eve they were disembarking at southern Korean ports, to get ready for the next stage of the battle.[46]

The evacuation of Hungnam had been a brilliant logistical success. But as Winston Churchill said about Dunkirk, wars are not won by evacuations— nor is public opinion. News of the Chinese offensive, and the retreat from North Korea, hit American newspapers with express-train impact. Suddenly all of MacArthur's assurances about "coming home by Christmas," and of the Communist advance in Asia not only halted, but broken, vanished in a steady outpouring of bad news from the front.

Except for MacArthur's stalwart supporters like the Hearst and McCormick newspapers, the media in America and Western Europe painted a picture of defeat comparable only to Napoleon's retreat from Russia. Men and vehicles frozen in the snow; panicked Western troops fleeing the irresistible Oriental tide; a reckless power-mad general whose thirst for glory had led his forces to irrevocable disaster: these were the images of the situation in Korea that were conjured up in the American public's mind by papers like the *New York Herald Tribune, The New York Times,* and the *Washington Post.*

The mood in Washington was, if anything, even gloomier. Among State Department officials, there was an element of Schadenfreude at seeing Douglas MacArthur finally getting his comeuppance. But everyone in the president's new National Security Council understood that this was a disaster of the first order.

On December 3 meetings at the Pentagon deepened the gloom. The Joint Chiefs announced that they might have to consider the complete evacuation of Korea.[47] Truman was alarmed enough to send Army Chief of Staff General Lawton Collins directly to Tokyo to take stock of the situation—and of MacArthur's state of mind. There were stories circulating of MacArthur being in a blue funk and on the verge of a breakdown, and alternately, stories of his towering rage and his lambasting the administration for not letting him bomb the Yalu bridges. There was even an interview in *U.S. News & World Report* in which he was quoted as saying that his advance to the Yalu had actually saved the situation in Korea by exposing the Chinese presence before it became overwhelming, and that the restrictions Washington put on his command had been "an enormous handicap, without precedent in history."[48]

Truman and Acheson were understandably furious about the *U.S. News & World Report* interview. But then Truman was no stranger to the habit of shooting off his mouth in front of reporters, even in the midst of this crisis. On November 30 he had even suggested to them that atomic bombs might be used to stop the Chinese attacks. That revelation set off alarm bells in the capital of every country that had troops in Korea; British prime minister Clement Attlee bustled over to Washington from London to make sure the remarks weren't meant for real. If MacArthur's staff was learning to cringe every time a reporter came near him during this crisis, so was Truman's.

General Lawton Collins arrived in Tokyo on December 4, 1950, and then toured the battlefront in Korea. He visited Walker and Almond while the Eighth Army was retreating from Pyongyang, and while the Marines and X Corps were still trying to break out for Hungnam—not exactly propitious days for the UN forces or their commander. But in Tokyo Lawton found that MacArthur, far from being reduced to a cowering wreck by the disasters in Korea, or "defeatist" as some historians have claimed,[49] was planning a comeback.

He told Collins he estimated that he faced half a million Chinese (the real number was closer to 300,000) and 100,000 North Koreans, backed by Soviet advisors—with hundreds of thousands of other Chinese poised to move across the China–North Korea border. He grimly showed him a map of South Korea with nine different withdrawal lines in case they were forced all the way back to Pusan.

All the same, MacArthur believed the situation could still be saved—but he would need three things. The first was a naval blockade of Red China; the second was a free hand to strike targets in Manchuria; the third was reinforcements from Nationalist China. If those couldn't be guaranteed, he told Collins, then it would be time to evacuate Korea altogether.

Collins was shocked. His tour hadn't suggested to him that the UN command's position was anywhere near as bad, or that Seoul would have to be evacuated as MacArthur suggested (though MacArthur would turn out to be right). But he declined to argue the point with the CINCFE. When he returned to Washington, he told his Joint Chiefs colleagues that if the United

States and the United Nations weren't prepared to make "an all-out effort in Korea," then MacArthur should be authorized to do what he needed to do to prevent the complete destruction of his forces, including an evacuation of the peninsula.[50]

To their credit, Truman and his advisors vetoed any talk of evacuation. "We all agreed . . . we could not in good conscience abandon the South Koreans to their Chinese–North Korean enemies"—although MacArthur, to *his* credit, had suggested no such thing. He had seen evacuation not as abandonment but as a regrouping in order to renew the fight at a later date. Still, it's not difficult to see looming behind MacArthur's ultimatum (if that's what it was) a darker inner fear: that if the Chinese overran UN forces in Korea, he would be blamed again for abandoning a command to their doom and doing nothing to save them.

Besides, Truman's people had another, even more disastrous plan that they had to block. This was a proposal from the British, backed by other nervous UN countries, to negotiate an immediate cease-fire. Marshall, for one, rejected the idea out of hand. He felt strongly that the Chinese and Soviets would only use a cease-fire to rearm Mao's forces and the North Koreans; Acheson and others believed that any price Red China demanded in return for agreeing to a cease-fire would be far too high.

A long series of meetings with Attlee and his advisors between December 4 and 11 finally laid the British proposal to rest.[51]

Despite the disastrous retreat, the Chinese offensive, and the deteriorating relationship between MacArthur and Washington, the way was actually open for a fresh start in fighting the Korean War. MacArthur would have agreed with one deputy chief of staff for the army who remarked during the December 3 meeting, "We owe it to the men in the field to stop talking and act."[52]

Improbably enough, in less than three weeks he and MacArthur would be partners in command. His name was Matthew Bunker Ridgway.

On December 23 General Walton Walker decided he was going to take a driving tour of his command as they were organizing for the defense of the sector north of Seoul. He had just won a major bureaucratic victory: MacArthur had agreed that X Corps, led by MacArthur's former chief of staff, would now be subordinate to Walker's command of the Eighth Army.

Maybe the news made Walker more reckless than usual on the Korean roads. Lawton Collins had warned MacArthur that Walker was too inclined to run risks that might cost him his life.[53] In this case it wasn't enemy fire but a ROK army truck. Walker's jeep collided with it on the road between Seoul and Uijongbu, and Walker was killed instantly.

The news couldn't have come at a worse time—or a better one, depending on one's perspective. Walker was not MacArthur's favorite general. He felt his leadership of the Eighth Army since Pusan had been halting, even hesitant; he worried that Walker's slow advance toward the Yalu before November 25 might have weakened the United Nations position, even tempted the Chinese to strike sooner and harder than they did (no one would have disagreed more than Walker himself).

Nonetheless, Walker was gone. Who would take his place? General Almond, MacArthur's protégé, would have done anything for the job. But instead MacArthur wired to Washington with one name on his list: Matthew Ridgway.

Ridgway's life and career had been much like MacArthur's. Born in 1895 at Fort Monroe, Virginia, he was the son of an artillery officer. Like MacArthur, his earliest memories were of bugles blowing reveille and sounding taps after dark. Like MacArthur, he attended West Point to please his father, although he missed seeing combat in World War One. He made up for that in World War Two, organizing and then personally leading the Eighty-second Airborne on airdrops in Sicily, Normandy, and in Operation Market Garden in Holland.

Just as importantly for his new position, Ridgway had been athletic instructor at West Point when MacArthur was superintendent. A bond of friendship and trust developed that culminated twenty-eight years later when Walton Walker's jeep met destiny in the shape of a South Korean truck, and MacArthur finally found the commander he needed to turn the war in Korea around.

Thanks to the briefings at the Pentagon over the last several weeks, Ridgway was primed and ready. He boarded a plane for Korea on Christmas Eve, and thirty-seven hours later was in MacArthur's presence in Tokyo.

"My meeting with MacArthur [and Hickey] began at nine thirty" that evening, he later wrote. "I had known MacArthur since my days as a West Point instructor but, like everyone who had ever dealt with him, I was again deeply impressed by the force of his personality." As MacArthur outlined their situation on the Korean peninsula, Ridgway realized that although MacArthur had the actor's gift for invoking the dramatic, "so lucid and so penetrating were his explanations and his analysis that it was his mind rather than his manner or his bodily presence that dominated his listeners."[54]

Yet despite the theatrics, Ridgway understood MacArthur's main point, and his assignment.

"Hold as far as possible in the most advanced possible positions in which you can maintain yourself," CINCFE said. MacArthur thought it essential to hold on to Seoul for psychological as well as strategic reasons, but not if it became another Stalingrad, "a citadel position."

MacArthur wanted to restore a war of movement; then, he felt, the Chinese would be too slow to respond—and American airpower would have a second chance at winning the day. He warned Ridgway that the Chinese "were a dangerous foe," but that if the United Nations could regain the initiative, it would fill what he called "the mission vacuum." The diplomats would have to yield to the military men and their success; as during World War Two, victory in the field would dictate its own terms.

Ridgway sat on the long brown couch and digested all this.

"Form your own opinions," MacArthur finally said. "Use your own judgment. I will support you. You have my complete confidence."

Ridgway hesitated. He was used to having his own way in commanding troops; he was no sycophant. He respected MacArthur, but he was not afraid of him as some others, including Generals Almond and Stratemeyer, head of the air force, were inclined to be.

His last question was: "If I find the situation to my liking, would you have any objections to my attacking?"

MacArthur gave a broad grin and said, "The Eighth Army is yours, Matt. Do what you think is best."

It was, Ridgway realized, the best order he had ever received.[55]

CHAPTER 32

ENDGAME

*You are only remembered and become
famous because of your mistakes.*

—DOUGLAS MACARTHUR

Ridgway would emerge as the most admired figure of the Korean War—for many because he was not Douglas MacArthur. He would also be seen as the man who turned the war around almost overnight. The usual story is of how MacArthur's missteps and then defeatist attitude created an Eighth Army devoured by self-doubt and "bug-out fever": "the staring eyes of soldiers who had become accustomed to defeat," was how one reporter described it.[1] Then instantly and miraculously—the story goes—this broken army was turned into a magnificent fighting force thanks to the intrepid former leader of the 101st Airborne. Certainly no one contributed more to the legend than Ridgway himself in his memoirs.[2]

Yet the truth is that General Lawton Collins had been right. The Eighth Army's position was never as dire and desperate as critics, including sometimes MacArthur, were inclined to believe. Its losses had been painful—more than 7,700 killed, wounded, or taken prisoner. Most of those, however, had been in the Second Division, and as MacArthur himself later pointed out, taking Iwo Jima had cost twice as many men, while Okinawa had cost five times as many.[3] It was also true that combat casualties weren't the army's only problem. Fourteen thousand soldiers and marines were laid low by frostbite.

All the same, combined American, UN, and ROK forces still had 443,000 men on the South Korean peninsula. They probably could have held the Pyongyang-Chungchon line if MacArthur had ordered them to. It was Walker, not MacArthur, who had sent his forces reeling back over the 38th parallel—and Walker, not MacArthur, who abandoned North Korea to the Communists.[4]

Indeed, if anyone had "bug-out fever" it was the United Nations. On December 14, its General Assembly decided that it "viewed with grave concern the situation in the Far East," and passed a resolution asking the assembly president, Iran's Nasrollah Entezam, to appoint a commission for determining the basis of a cease-fire in Korea. Beijing turned the proposal down flat.[5] But the next phase of the war would take place against a backdrop of American allies, not American GIs, steadily losing heart in the struggle and desperately pushing for a cease-fire rather than victory.

Moreover, if it had been a brutal winter so far for the Americans and their fellow UN troops, it had been far worse for the Chinese. They had suffered more than 72,000 casualties. They were badly equipped for winter fighting, with shoes instead of boots and down jackets instead of overcoats. They had been issued no gloves, and most had been issued only enough rations to last them five or six days. By December most had been fighting in Korea for a month.

Theirs was a war of frostbite, starvation, and disease, as well as sudden death from American bombs and artillery. MacArthur's men got firsthand glimpses into what the Chinese were suffering. One Seventh Marine platoon at Chosin reported discovering a Chinese position with fifty soldiers sitting bolt upright but too frozen to move, let alone shoot back. The Chinese were still alive but had to be lifted out one by one as the marines loaded them onto stretchers and carried them away—after prying their rifles loose from fingers frozen like claws around the triggers and barrels.[6]

And while UN forces were in constant resupply, especially heavy artillery, thanks to their control of the sea, the Chinese had seen barely a trickle of fresh weapons and ammunition, almost all of which had come by primitive horse and mule train. Plus the Americans had a new player over the battlefield, the F-86 Sabre. It would steadily reassert American air superiority, and eventually clear the skies of Communist opposition.

So contrary to the standard myth, the Eighth Army was indeed an army poised to resume the offensive. It just needed a commander ready to do it, and MacArthur had found the one who could.

Ridgway shook up the command the moment his plane touched down in Korea. A tour of corps, division, regiment, and even battalion headquarters revealed a deepening pessimism among his senior command. After listening to their defensive plans, he wanted to know their offensive plans. None had any. Ridgway would gruffly tell them to start drawing up some, and then he would move on to the next command post.

When he saw maps posted showing the terrain behind frontline positions, as preparation for withdrawal, he would rip them down.[7] This army was going forward, he was telling his officers; stop planning where we're going to retreat and start thinking about where we're advancing next.

But even Ridgway couldn't hold back the tide when the Chinese launched their third, and biggest, offensive of the war.

As darkness fell on the last day of 1950, six Chinese divisions crashed through ROK army positions on the far bank of the Imjin River. The two divisions facing them had been considered first-rate; now they folded like a wet blanket. Men and officers streamed for the rear. Ridgway himself was nearly run over when he tried to stop a panic-stricken ROK army convoy.[8]

Ridgway ordered his Twenty-fourth and Twenty-fifth Divisions, along with the Turkish and British brigades, to try to build a new defensive line north of Seoul but the Chinese were too fast for him. Three more South Korean divisions melted away as the Communist onslaught continued; soon the entire line from Chunchon northeast of Seoul to the sea was poised to give way.

A sober reality was staring the Eighth Army's new commander in the face. He would have to abandon Seoul.

Ridgway sensed that this could trigger a humanitarian, as well as a military, disaster. Some 600,000 Koreans had returned to their homes in and around Seoul after the capital had been captured the previous September.

Now they joined the panicked flood southward, jamming the roads and threatening to jam the all-important bridges across the Han, which Ridgway needed to move troops and supplies away from the surging Chinese. ROK military police and American military engineers had to keep herding the streaming thousands down to the banks of the Han, which was fortunately frozen over, so they could cross on foot, slipping and sliding on the ice. Thousands of others, however, died of exposure in the subzero cold, leaving a dismal trail of frozen men, women, and children sprawled along the roads as the Eighth Army began its pullback.

Ridgway was unhappy with the withdrawal. Many units ignored his orders to stay in fighting contact with the Chinese as they fell back; others displayed the "bug-out fever" that reporters had talked about and he had discounted. Army engineers were all too eager to blow up Kimpo airfield, including 9,000 tons of engineering supplies, and the bridges across the Han—again!—before taking to their heels themselves.[9]

Still, the Eighth Army managed the retreat without it becoming a rout. By January 4 they had abandoned Seoul to the triumphant advancing Chinese, and on January 7 they established a new line roughly seventy miles south of the 38th parallel, running from Pyongtaek in the west to Samchok in the east.[10]

As far as Ridgway was concerned, this was as far as the retreat would go. He alerted the Joint Chiefs that as soon as the line stabilized and the Chinese attacks were checkmated, he would be going on the counterattack.[11]

Now for the first time, the men back in Washington thought they had found someone who grasped the situation in Korea better than the aging patriarch in Tokyo. They were still pondering MacArthur's reply to their December 29 directive ordering him to stand fast, in which he reiterated the three choices the United Nations faced: massive reinforcement, evacuation, or annihilation. President Truman even sent him a personal message on January 13 to buck him up, explaining why withdrawal or relying on Chinese Nationalist reinforcements was unacceptable. It ended: "The entire nation is grateful for your splendid leadership in the difficult struggle in Korea, and for the superb performance of your forces under most difficult circumstances."[12]

MacArthur's reply was terse: "We shall do our best." To his GHQ staff he said simply, "There will be no evacuation."[13]

Yet what Truman and his people saw as their stand-fast determination to stay in Korea, MacArthur read as a catastrophic "loss of the will to win," since they had rejected his overall strategic plan. The Joint Chiefs' directive of December 29 had told him, "We believe that Korea is not the place to fight a major war." MacArthur believed they were already fighting that war, and he was determined to win it.

The men in Washington, on the other hand, saw MacArthur's all-or-nothing plan as alarmist, even "defeatist" (interestingly, the same word MacArthur was using about them). They also saw his recent boasts that his advance to the Yalu had actually been a *success* because it had forced the Chinese to launch their attack before they were fully ready—"we had reached up, sprung the Red trap, and escaped it," was how he put it in his *Reminiscences*—as self-justifying braggadocio. All the same, at least one top-level commander in Korea thought MacArthur's diagnosis was correct. "If the Chinese had waited for us to deploy along the Yalu and then attacked," he would write later, "they would have destroyed us with ease. MacArthur was correct in saying he had to feel out the enemy, and that by forcing their hand he averted a great disaster."[14]

In any case, now there was the commander on the ground, Matthew Ridgway, saying he could hold the Chinese back and retake the initiative without any additional reinforcements or blockade of Red China. As the bonds of trust between Washington and the CINCFE steadily frayed, both sides would turn to Ridgway as the man to save their credibility: the man who could win the war (MacArthur's main objective) without widening it (Washington's).

All that both sides needed was proof that Ridgway was right. And starting on January 7, 1951, that proof came at the village of Wonju.

Wonju sat at the crossroads of the main road leading east from Seoul and Route 29, the north-south highway running all the way to Pusan. In their New Year's Eve push, Wonju had fallen to the Communists—except the Communist units were North Koreans, not Chinese. Mao's divisions fighting the marines at Chosin had taken such a mauling that Soviet and North Korean planners had moved newly reconstituted North Korean divisions into the line instead. The capture of Wonju was part of their next envelopment strategy. Five KPA divisions would overwhelm Wonju; another five would swing southeast, forcing the Eighth Army into yet another fighting withdrawal. But they ran afoul of General Almond and the Second Infantry Division instead.

On January 8 Almond ordered the men of the Second to retake Wonju; after intense fighting it was still in North Korean hands, but the Americans took up position on a hill dubbed Hill 242 overlooking the village and, with the help of the French and Dutch battalions, and with ROK divisions protecting their flanks, they held on through the storm.

For the next five days the North Koreans hurled one division after another to take Hill 242 but failed to dislodge the UN position as artillery and air support pounded their attacks to pieces. Almond moved up the U.S. Seventh Infantry Division to hold the critical towns overlooking Route 29, while the ROK commander rallied his divisions to hold their ground, which they did. It was, as one historian notes, Almond's finest hour; at one point the battle raged forty miles from Wonju to Andong on the Naktong River. It was also the finest hour of the ROKA, as they proved at last that they could dig in and fight without fleeing to the rear under Communist attack.[15]

By January 13—the same day Truman sent his message to MacArthur explaining why evacuation was impossible—Wonju was in ruins, reduced to rubble by American artillery. Almond's counterinsurgency force, the Special Activities Group or SAG, was still rooting out North Korean troops who had tried to slip behind the UN lines to raise havoc as insurgency guerrillas. The last were killed or captured on the 15th. But the battle for Wonju had been fought, and won, by the X Corps. Two American divisions, backed by three ROK divisions, had fought ten North Korean divisions to a draw. From that point on, the initiative in Korea belonged to Matt Ridgway.[16]

He was now infusing the Eighth Army and United Nations forces with a new spirit of drive and enthusiasm for battle. MacArthur's staff usually found him not at army headquarters, but at some regimental or battalion command post, exhorting anyone who would listen that they were there for a purpose, and that purpose was killing Chinese. He once asked a startled lieutenant colonel what tanks were for.

"To kill Chinese," the man blurted after a moment's thought.

"That's right," Ridgway shot back, as he strode outside.[17]

They called him Iron Tits because he wore two grenades on his chest, attached to his utility harness. He hated reporters and the media, and told his staff that every story going out from Korea was subject to censure—a very un-MacArthur-like attitude. He also had a quick and savage temper—again un-MacArthur-like. Ridgway didn't hesitate to drive his jeep over anyone's tail if it gave him the freedom to do what he wanted.

The one person he never crossed, however, was MacArthur. MacArthur himself was delighted with Ridgway, the man he "held in highest esteem," he later told a congressional committee, "as a cultured gentleman and one of the most magnificent characters I have ever been acquainted with."[18] And as Ridgway began slowly to turn the tables on the Communists, MacArthur was determined to be part of the action, and identified with the turnaround.

On January 12 he flew over to Korea—the first of eight trips he would make in the next three months. It was a revived MacArthur, exuding confidence and optimism. "There has been a lot of loose talk about the Chinese driving us into the sea," he told reporters. "No one is going to drive us into the sea. This command intends to maintain a military position in Korea just as long as Washington decides we should do so."[19]

Then, MacArthur wrote later, "I ordered Ridgway to start north again." In his copy of MacArthur's *Reminiscences,* Ridgway wryly wrote in the margin, "There was never any such order."[20] But it didn't matter. Although new defensive positions were being prepared near Taegu and Pusan, there was nowhere to go but forward; MacArthur and the UN forces couldn't leave Seoul to the Communists even if they had wanted to. Moreover, Ridgway was of the same mind as MacArthur: this had become a war about defeating Communism in Asia. America, not just the United Nations, had to win it. MacArthur later said, "There is no substitute for victory" in Korea. Ridgway wholeheartedly agreed.

And so on January 15, even as the entire peninsula lay blanketed under Arctic-like conditions, Ridgway ordered his I Corps forward in Operation Wolfhound. Their orders were to find and destroy any Chinese formations they encountered; and as the I Corps inched along the road to Suwon, they found plenty. Most dropped back under the Wolfhound attacks and more than a thousand air sorties. The Chinese took up new positions south of the river Han and waited for an opportunity to envelop the advancing Americans. But the way was now open for the first decisive UN offensive since the fighting along the Yalu two months before.[21]

"The Eighth Army has plenty of fight left," Ridgway wrote to MacArthur, "and if attacked will severely punish the enemy. [But] this command, I am convinced, will do far more," and he intended to prove it in Operation Thunderbolt.[22]

This was what Ridgway dubbed his division-size reconnaissance in force, a massive probing operation that started on January 25 and ran along the entire length of the peninsula. Each American division was backed by a ROK division as part of Ridgway's plan to stiffen the South Koreans' spine by showing them more fighting, not less—but with coordinated U.S. support. Thunderbolt worked. By January 28, UN forces had punched through Chinese resistance at Osan, and reoccupied Suwon. The Chinese commander's hopes of enveloping the Eighth Army's flank died, as Ridgway insisted on keeping an unbroken line of advance across the peninsula.[23] Instead, the Chinese were steadily falling back under the relentless onslaught of air and artillery attacks, naval gunfire from offshore, and Ridgway's terse orders to his troops: they were to kill Chinese, nothing else. "Keep throwing scrap iron at them."

And so they did, surrounding Chinese troops by night, and then pulverizing their positions by day—while strafing planes slaughtered those who tried to break and run from the lethal pockets the UN forces made. MacArthur made another visit to the Eighth Army, shaking hands and getting briefings from all his commanders. When he returned to Tokyo, Ridgway wrote him a note: "We are all deeply grateful that you gave us of your time this Sunday. All were inspired by your visit."[24]

On the last two days of January, Chinese People's Volunteer Army (CPVA) resistance stiffened; Ridgway's advance shrank to a few hundred yards a day. Then very suddenly on February 9, the Chinese pulled back to the far bank of the Han River, letting UN forces come right to the river's edge. The next day I Corps took back Inchon and Kimpo airfield without firing a shot.[25] On the 9th another operation, dubbed Punch, left more than 4,200 Chinese dead on the battlefield as the Han River now became the boundary between UN and Communist forces.

A jubilant Ridgway wrote to MacArthur on February 3, reporting that his forces had inflicted maximum casualties on the Chinese while sustaining minimum casualties themselves, and stating his intentions to close the line along the Han, although he felt that retaking Seoul was not yet feasible. MacArthur wrote back saying he was in complete accord with Ridgway's plan, but Ridgway shouldn't feel he should stop at the Han. "If you reach the river without serious resistance," Ridgway should keep going until he found some.

MacArthur was as anxious as Ridgway to keep the momentum going; and while retaking Seoul had less military value than diplomatic and symbolic importance, retaking Kimpo and Inchon were vital (which Ridgway did on the 9th). "Your performance of the last two weeks in concept and execution has been splendid," MacArthur wrote at the end, "and worthy of the highest traditions of a great captain."[26]

That great captain was about to undergo his most intensive test. What he and MacArthur did not know was that the Chinese had dropped back to re-supply and prepare for Mao Zedong's fourth and greatest offensive.

The attack began at night on February 11 and fell first on three hapless ROK divisions sitting just north of Hoengsong. The Chinese broke through, and poured into Ridgway's rear, setting up roadblocks and ambushes as Ridgway and his men struggled to recover. There were several days of confused fighting, with the UN abandoning Hoengsong and falling back toward Wonju.

The night of the 13th proved the turning point. The Chinese Thirteenth Army Group threw themselves on Almond's Second Infantry Division and the French Battalion, who had been in the thick of the fighting at the first Battle of Wonju and now proved their skill and bravery once again in what became known as the Battle of Chipyong-ni. Almond's men were cut off; Ridgway told Almond to stand fast. He would resupply the Second Infantry by air, he said, while blasting the surrounding sector with bombs and artillery fire.

It was a risky order, one that depended on American airpower to win the day—and American airpower came through. For three murderous days one wave of Chinese attackers after another crashed against the UN troops, who held firm as ceaseless napalm strikes rained down on the Chinese, decimating their formations. By the 16th it was all over. The French and Americans held the grim, smoldering battlefield. Farther east, similar Chinese attacks failed to dislodge the rest of X Corps.[27]

The UN line stabilized and Ridgway moved forward with a combination of what he called "good footwork with firepower." His troops would beat back one Chinese counterattack after another as the artillery and air strikes pounded Chinese positions, until his soldiers were ready to move in. Then, once the Chinese broke and scattered, massed tanks would move in to complete the kill.

This lethal process, which Ridgway and his men came to call "the meat grinder," repeated itself over and over, until by the 18th Ridgway's forces were in line with the entire south bank of the Han River. Meanwhile, the First Marine Division and ROK security forces had reduced the Chinese and North Korean guerrillas operating behind his lines—some of whom had escaped during the first Battle of Wonju—to manageable proportions. When Ridgway ordered another cautious probe forward, his men found only abandoned foxholes and weapons. The fact was, the Chinese army in Korea was all but beaten; its supplies had run out, its ranks had shrunk by a third, not just from U.S. firepower but by typhus, frostbite, and trench foot as well.[28]

Now Ridgway and MacArthur could at last take the offensive, and drive the Communists back across the 38th parallel in three rapid strokes.

First came Operation Killer on February 21, as seven UN divisions pushed forward to destroy as many CPVA as possible. The first big thaw of the year had started, providing a major relief to men who had suffered three and a half months of subzero temperatures but also a major hamper to mobility, as streams overflowed their banks and became unfordable while Korea's roads turned to mud.

Still, Chinese resistance proved lighter than anyone expected. Sometimes troops found just a line of empty trenches with a long, shallow grave dug behind them and lined with corpses killed days before. Stratemeyer's planes dropped thousands of leaflets on the retreating CPVA with a message in Chinese for every officer: "Count your men"—a message aimed at destroying the morale of the Chinese command as well as that of their soldiers.[29]

By the 28th Ridgway had retaken Hoengsong, and every Chinese unit south of the Han had either pulled back or been destroyed. By one count, the

Chinese may have suffered almost half a million casualties in just six weeks of fighting.

Then, after a one-week pause to rearm and refit, Ridgway launched Operation Ripper on March 7.

It was intended to outflank Seoul and split the Chinese off from North Korean formations farther east. It commenced with a head-on assault across the Han preceded by the heaviest artillery bombardment of the war. The Chinese on the north bank held on for three bloody days; it was estimated they lost 21,000 men in the first twenty-four hours of fighting. But by the 10th the U.S. Twenty-fifth Infantry Division was across the river, and elsewhere the Chinese were falling back, sometimes standing and fighting in suicidal defiance of the inevitable, sometimes simply turning and running—and running.

By the 13th troops from I Corps crossed the Han River on the western flank, and were in the outskirts of Seoul. Two days later they moved into the city's deserted streets as Seoul changed hands for the fourth—and final—time. The rest of the Eighth Army was completing its move across the Han River. Farther east a successful ROK attack drove the North Koreans northward toward the 38th parallel, while in the center IX and X Corps had to blast the enemy out of a series of deep bunkers before reaching the line that Ridgway had established as the foremost limit of the Operation Ripper advance. It was dubbed Line Idaho, and extended from Seoul to just north of Kangnung in the east, and in the center to just south of the 38th parallel.

The tide of war was now running fully in the UN's favor. Meanwhile, Communist forces had completed their pullback to just *north* of the parallel, into a complex of forts, tunnels, and shelters dug out of the rock by tens of thousands of North Korean peasants and reinforced with concrete.

What to do next? MacArthur, for one, had no doubts. It was time to cross the 38th parallel again and finish the Communists off, this time for good.

The men in Washington, however, had other ideas.

"While General Ridgway was fighting the enemy, General MacArthur was fighting the Pentagon."[30]

That at least was Dean Acheson's assessment of the situation in late February and March 1951, as the disagreements over why and how the war in Korea was to be fought reached their final climax.

Since late December the consensus at the Pentagon, State, and Blair House was that if by some miracle MacArthur could survive the Chinese onslaught and turn the fighting around yet again, the best goal the United States and the United Nations could hope for would be to reestablish the 38th parallel as an international boundary with South Korea as a free independent country. All thought of freeing the entire peninsula from Communist rule, outlined in NSC 81/2, was now out.[31] And as Ridgway's success on the battlefield encouraged the belief that the worst was now over, the Truman administration began making arrangements for adopting the British plan and instituting a cease-fire once the Communists were driven back across the parallel and a twenty-mile demilitarized zone was established on either side of the border.

It was a strategy that Truman had ordered his national security team to start on as early as December 11; it came together with Truman, Acheson, and Marshall all acceding on December 26, and was the basis of the directive sent to MacArthur on December 29, and the president's message to the CINCFE on January 13.[32]

It was a sensible, realistic strategy; one that most later observers have suggested was the best option left to the United States in the spring of 1951. It also reflected a consensus, including the Joint Chiefs, of what should *not* happen. Nothing should be done that might provoke a Soviet reaction in Europe or encourage a wider Chinese intervention. Under no circumstances were sites in Manchuria to be bombed; under no circumstances were United Nations forces to cross the 38th parallel again in sizable force.

Yet these last two points were essential to MacArthur's own alternative strategy—not just to achieve a satisfactory stalemate but to win the war, including, if possible, the total destruction of Communist China.

Instead of the plan presented to him by the Joint Chiefs, which he considered too timid by half, he conceived a four-point plan in mid- to late February, while his forces were still slightly south of Seoul. It would take advantage of what he reckoned was China's overextended and overstretched position in Korea, with its supply lines vulnerable to air and naval attack, and the unwillingness of the Soviet Union to be dragged into a general war, even if it meant sacrificing its Chinese client.

The first step would be to use twenty to thirty atomic bombs to take out Chinese air installations and supply bases in Manchuria. The second would be to lay a radioactive belt of nuclear-contaminated material across the northern neck of the peninsula, thus severing North Korea from Red China.

The third was to put half a million Nationalist Chinese troops from Formosa plus two marine divisions into Korea with simultaneous amphibious landings on both the east and the west coasts of North Korea, who would then join up and cut off the million or so Chinese that MacArthur's intelligence people estimated were still on the peninsula.

The fourth and final stage would be moving a reinforced Eighth Army (MacArthur had asked for four National Guard divisions) northward across the 38th parallel to finally crush the CPVA and its remaining North Korean allies.

MacArthur estimated that it would take ten days to force the complete surrender of Chinese forces in Korea, with as few casualties for the UN as possible. It might even trigger the fall of Mao himself.

It's not clear that MacArthur ever submitted his plan to the Joint Chiefs; most of its details did not emerge until years later, and in MacArthur's own memoirs. Certainly they would have rejected it out of hand; it might even have led some in the Pentagon to question his sanity (among Dean Acheson and his State Department colleagues, there were no remaining doubts). The reaction of MacArthur's biographers to The Plan, as it's sometimes called, has been correspondingly harsh. Clayton James called it "grandiose" and utterly "fantastic."[33]

But other analysts, including British military historian Edgar O'Ballance, have suggested that MacArthur's plan was not so ill-conceived. It certainly was not unprecedented. President Truman himself had first raised the specter of using nuclear bombs to halt the Chinese advance; so had the Joint Chiefs in December, although they had concluded that the mountainous terrain of North Korea would nullify the impact. They had even asked MacArthur's advice on potential *Soviet* targets for nuclear attack if Stalin decided to enter the war.[34]

Likewise, MacArthur's idea of using twenty to thirty bombs seems a strategic extravagance until one realizes the enormous advantage that the United States enjoyed in its atomic arsenal in 1951 vis-à-vis the only other nuclear power in the world, the Soviet Union. The Strategic Air Command's ability to deliver nuclear weapons anywhere in the world, including the far northern portion of North Korea, would have made the plan feasible, even at the cost of exhausting America's existing nuclear arsenal—albeit (MacArthur would have argued) as the price for achieving final victory.

The idea of using radiological warfare to defeat an enemy was also nothing new. In early June 1950 then Secretary of Defense Louis Johnson had released a study on how to create a deadly radioactive belt, using atomic pile waste, to deny an enemy areas on the battlefield—a study that MacArthur had read.[35]

Instead, it is the idea of Nationalist Chinese troops toppling the mainland's Communist regime that has drawn the most scorn from readers of MacArthur's plan. It's led to many detractors then and later to see his concept of "unleashing Chiang Kai-shek" as unbridled fantasy. But in the circumstances of early 1951, it was not so far-fetched as hindsight suggests.

The truth was, Mao's forces *were* overextended; his best armies and military equipment were in Korea, not guarding the mainland—and they were being systematically destroyed. As Edgar O'Ballance has pointed out, "The Red Chinese regime was still unsteady, bewildered, and more than slightly surprised at its victory over the Nationalists"—which had as much to do with the cutoff of American support for the Nationalists as it did with Communist battlefield skill. In addition, "the Chinese Red Army had been diluted by huge infusions of turn-coat Nationalist soldiers" whom a Chiang-led invasion might have persuaded to turn coats again, while there were still sufficient Nationalist guerrillas fighting in the interior to tie up more than a million of Mao's forces.[36]

An American-supported Nationalist invasion, with or without nuclear weapons, would have certainly wreaked havoc on Mao's regime. If it didn't actually topple the Red leader, it would have led to a serious resumption of the civil war—possibly even the partition of China. All of this would have crippled Chinese resistance against advancing UN forces, and North Korean resistance along with it. Only Stalin's entry into the conflict could have saved the Communist cause; and almost every analyst now agrees that he was not prepared to start World War Three. Indeed, the prospect of a long, drawn-out war between China and the United States might have served his strategic purposes very well.[37]

All that being said, no one in the Truman administration, not even MacArthur's supporters in Congress, was prepared to endorse such a plan on such a scale. Truman and his advisors were keenly interested in winding down the war; MacArthur's plan would substantially widen it, although with the laudable goal of victory rather than stalemate and cease-fire.

And here the differences among MacArthur, Acheson, and Truman grew into a yawning chasm. For all his faulty calls and overconfidence alternating with overpessimism, MacArthur still believed that decisive victory was possible—indeed, sending American troops into battle to fight and die without that possibility seemed unfair, even obscene. To those who argued that he would then draw Red China fully into the war, as he wrote later, "How could Red China have been more at war against us? . . . How can one reasonably say it is not war when approximately 150,000 Americans [*sic*] and many times that of our ally, South Korea, were killed or maimed" by Red Chinese forces?[38]*

Nor was MacArthur alone in believing that engaging Red China head-on in a wider war was the route to victory. We know now that in early March he requested the Joint Chiefs activate contingency plans in case more Chinese forces, and even Soviet forces, crossed the Yalu; and that the Joint Chiefs sent at least nine unassembled atomic bombs to Guam—just in case.[39] The move suggests they at least understood MacArthur's strategic concerns, and his willingness to take extreme measures to prevent a Communist takeover of the Korean peninsula.

But MacArthur also saw other geopolitical forces at work in the Korean conflict, forces that would ricochet around the Pacific Rim. To give up the goal of victory would encourage would-be Communist regimes in other parts of Asia, while dealing a "catastrophic blow to the hopes of the free world," he wrote. That included other Asian governments such as Indonesia, Malaysia, and India, which would have drawn closer to the United States

---

* Actual U.S. casualties in the Korean War were 133,409 killed, wounded, and missing.

after a forthright display of power and resolve—but which, as Korea eventually ground to a stalemate, chose to withdraw into neutrality or even tacit acceptance of Chinese hegemony, instead.

Nothing that happened in the next decade—the Communist insurgency in Malaya, Mao's armed clash with India and his invasion of Tibet, America's growing involvement in the fighting in Indochina—would have come as a surprise to MacArthur. His former G-3, Pinky Wright, later agreed. As he told Clayton James in a personal interview long after the war, The Plan might have triggered a full-scale confrontation with China, and even the Soviet Union. But it was a confrontation that the United States would have decisively won.

"If this had happened," Wright said in 1970, "we wouldn't be in Vietnam." It's difficult to see how that judgment was wrong, then or later.[40]

From the perspective of Washington, however, the risks of such a confrontation were too great. That was why it still forbade MacArthur to conduct any air operations along the Yalu even though the Yalu remained the Chinese force's chief line of support; and why it rejected using Nationalist troops out of hand. It was also why, as the Chinese pulled back in March and MacArthur saw the prospect of pushing across the 38th parallel as a way to open the next decisive stage of the war, the Truman people had already decided that Korea was, in Omar Bradley's famous formulation, "the wrong war at the wrong place at the wrong time with the wrong enemy." They had also decided that MacArthur was the wrong commander, at least for the next phase of the war they had in mind.

The decision to remove MacArthur as CINCFE was a long time coming— Omar Bradley later said he thought he should have been removed as early as the previous October. In fact, no one was less surprised than MacArthur. Pinky Wright later said he knew for some time he would be relieved.[41] Certainly when a theater commander realizes that what he thinks about the conduct of the war no longer matters to the commander in chief, it is time to go.

In addition, the statements that MacArthur began issuing to the media were increasingly critical of Truman's policy. Those statements would later serve as the justification for his removal. Yet it might be better to read them not as the hubristic outbursts of a power-crazed tragic hero but as the last gestures of a man who sensed his time was up.

The first was his interview with Hugh Baillie of *U.S. News & World Report,* complaining of "the limitations which prevent unlimited pursuit of Chinese large forces and unlimited attack on their bases" as being "without precedent in history," and castigating the "somewhat selfish though most[ly] short-sighted viewpoint" of Western European leaders who were reluctant to take on Red China. MacArthur did not name, but clearly implied, that France and Great Britain were those selfish and shortsighted allies.

Truman was furious. "I should have relieved General MacArthur there and then," he wrote later, but Truman didn't want to swap out commanders in the midst of the Chinese offensive. He contented himself instead with fir-ing off a directive on December 6 stating that all U.S. government personnel, civilian or military, clear "all but routine statements with their departments" and "refrain from direct communication on military or foreign policy with newspapers, magazines, or other publicity media."[42] The directive was duly noted by MacArthur, who naturally assumed it did not apply to him.

The second incident came on March 7, when MacArthur gave a press con-ference at Suwon airfield and predicted that the "savage slaughter" would continue and the Eighth Army would face a stalemate if it did not get reinforcements, or if he did not get more leeway in striking at the enemy. "Vital decisions have yet to be made," he warned, "decisions far beyond the scope of the authority vested in me" on how to end "Red China's undeclared war in Korea." But he left no doubt as to what he thought those decisions should be, that is, all-out war. The Truman team were upset at what they saw, rightly, as direct criticism of the rules of engagement the president had im-posed, and also a blatant violation of the earlier December directive. But again they chose to take no action.[43]

The third provocation came a little more than two weeks later, on March 24. Ridgway was mopping up isolated Chinese and KPA units trapped below Line Kansas, and preparing to shift his focus eastward, where IX and X Corps would launch Operation Dauntless. This northward advance would give the Eighth Army control of the Chorwon-Kumhwa-Hwachon area south of

Pyongyang and well above the 38th parallel, at the base of Communist defensive positions known as the Iron Triangle. On the 22nd MacArthur instructed Ridgway, "Do not cross the 38th parallel. I expect new directive from Washington shortly."[44] In the meantime, MacArthur decided to issue a call to the Communist Chinese to admit they were defeated and to either negotiate a peace or face a widening war.

"The enemy," he stated, "must by now be painfully aware that a decision of the United Nations to depart from its tolerant effort to contain the war to the area of Korea, through an expansion of our military operations to his coastal areas and interior bases, would doom Red China to the risk of imminent collapse." China could give up now or give up later, was the implied message; "I stand ready at any time to confer in the field with the Commander-in-Chief of the enemy forces" on how to realize "the political objectives of the United Nations in Korea, to which no nation may take just exception, might be accomplished without further bloodshed."

In his memoirs, MacArthur described the bulletin as "routine." When it hit Washington, however, Dean Acheson described it as "a major act of sabotage of a Government operation."[45] He, Dean Rusk, and others had been engaged in a delicate diplomatic balancing act of polling the other participating UN countries on the idea of announcing that the UN command was prepared to accept a cease-fire as the first step to a broader settlement. On the 21st a draft under Truman's signature had gone out for final approval. The Joint Chiefs had even given MacArthur a warning of what was up, that the hope was to propose a halt to the fighting before troops crossed the 38th parallel.[46]

Now MacArthur's statement seemed to doom the proposal in advance. The consensus was that taunting Communist China this way would kill any chance that Beijing would listen to Truman's offer. Acheson remembered that Robert Lovett, the new defense secretary, who replaced Marshall on March 1, was "angrier than I had ever seen him" (MacArthur later claimed he had prepared his assessment of China's military situation before he had read the Joint Chiefs' March 20 communiqué).[47]

"MacArthur must be removed," Lovett said firmly, "and removed at once." Acheson read the statement and agreed. It seemed to him "insubordination of the grossest kind to his Commander-in-Chief." The next morning, March

24 (MacArthur's statement had reached them the previous evening), Truman summoned everyone to the White House. In the presence of Acheson, Lovett, and the other key principals, Truman dictated a message to MacArthur:

> The President has directed that your attention be called to his order as transmitted 6 December, 1950 [stating that CINCFE was to make no statements of policy to the press without prior approval]. In view of the information given you 20 March 1951 any further statements by you must be coordinated as prescribed in the order of 6 December.
>
> The President has also directed that in the event Communist military leaders request an armistice in the field, you immediately report that fact to the JCS for instructions.[48]

Given the size of the provocation in the minds of Truman and his team, this seems a remarkably weak response. Certainly MacArthur was unimpressed. Since he believed his statement had been "a routine communiqué," the December 6 directive clearly didn't apply anyway.

Besides, he scoffed later, the claim "that I had disrupted some magic formula for peace" was "utter nonsense." "No such plan was even in draft form," and MacArthur in 1951 had guessed what we in fact now know was true. Far from being tempted by a cease-fire offer, Mao was getting ready for yet another, fifth offensive. In fact, MacArthur had warned Ridgway to mount "strong patrol action" to stay in constant contact with an enemy who, intelligence suggested, was gathering his forces for a major attack.[49]

The weather over Korea was starting to thaw as April began. Southern winds were driving the clouds lower as the snow turned into soft rains. On April 3 MacArthur paid another visit to Ridgway and the troops—his fifteenth since the war had begun and, although no one knew it, his last. He flew to Kangnung and traveled by jeep along the coastal road to Yangyang, where he watched the ROK Capital Division take up its new position fifteen miles north of the 38th parallel. Across the parallel Ridgway's troops were surging forward in strength, readying for an attack on the formidable Iron Triangle. Back in Tokyo, MacArthur told the press, "Our strategy remains unchanged and is based on maneuver and not positional warfare." As far as he was concerned, the 38th parallel "has never had any military significance." His job and Ridgway's was to fight the enemy wherever he was.[50]

In fact, it would be Ridgway's fight alone. MacArthur's fate was about to be sealed—not by his enemies in Washington, of whom he had taken full account, but disastrously and unexpectedly, by one of his closest supporters.

On April 5 Joseph Martin, Republican congressman from Missouri, strode to the podium of the House. The Republicans had scored a massive victory at the polls in November—mostly due to disgust with the way the war in Korea was proceeding—and Martin was the new Speaker of the House, the first Republican to hold that post in almost two decades. Martin and his Republican colleagues were determined to hold the Truman administration accountable for its major failures in Asia, including the loss of China and the ongoing bloodshed in Korea, and Martin had in his pocket what he thought was the means to do it.

At the podium he pulled it out and began reading. It was a letter Martin had received from the general he revered, Douglas MacArthur, on March 20, in response to a letter Martin had sent. That missive had contained a speech Martin had made about America's mishandled policy toward Formosa, and urged the United States to help Chiang Kai-shek open "a second Asiatic front" with Red China.

"I would deem it a great help if I could have your views on this point," Martin had written, "either on a confidential basis or otherwise."

MacArthur probably should not have written back. He should have realized that in a leak-obsessed Washington anything he sent to the Speaker of the House, confidential or otherwise, would eventually make its way into the nation's headlines—especially if it could be read as harshly critical of the current administration.

But he couldn't help himself. The national melodrama that had become Truman versus MacArthur since their meeting on Wake Island was about to take a major turn as MacArthur sat down and wrote to Martin, in part:

It is strangely difficult for some to realize that here in Asia is where the Communist conspirators have elected to make their play for global conquest . . . that if we lose this war to Communism in Asia the fall of Europe is inevitable; win it and Europe most probably would avoid war and yet preserve freedom. As you pointed out, we must win. There is no substitute for victory.

As Martin finished reading the general's letter and left the House chamber, he did not realize that he had destroyed MacArthur's career. Neither did MacArthur. When he got wind from one of his staff that one of his letters had set off a firestorm in Washington, MacArthur later testified, "I had to go back into the files. I didn't even recall what the circumstance was."[51]

In one sense, MacArthur had no reason to be alarmed. There was nothing he had said in the letter about his views on China and Formosa that he hadn't told the administration before; certainly nothing about his views on the larger stakes in Korea, including in his communiqué with then Secretary Marshall.

Still, only someone who had not set foot in Washington in more than fifteen years could have been so obtuse as not to realize that such a letter, if made public, would be widely taken as an attack on the administration and the president. Making it worse was the release the same day of an interview in the British newspaper the *Daily Telegraph* quoting MacArthur as saying he "found himself in a war without a definite objective" and that "the situation would be ludicrous if men's lives were not involved," while the conservative magazine *The Freeman* ran an article saying that MacArthur had told them the reason South Korea's army had not grown to larger numbers had to do with "basic political decisions beyond my authority," and putting the blame squarely on the Truman administration.[52]

Truman's personal rage at this sudden barrage of MacArthur "shooting off his mouth," as the president put it, was real and understandable. "This looks like the last straw," he wrote in his diary. "Rank insubordination." Acheson called it "a declaration of war." Truman called Acheson, Marshall, and Averell Harriman, as well as Chairman of the Joint Chiefs Omar Bradley. Ironically, the previous day the Joint Chiefs had issued MacArthur approval to attack air bases in Manchuria and the Shantung peninsula if Communist planes tried a large attack on his force—just the loosening of the rules of engagement that MacArthur had been begging for.[53] But that order was quickly shelved as Bradley huddled with the others to decide what to do about the president's insubordinate subordinate.

What followed was either a tragedy or a triumph of administrative finesse, depending on one's perspective. Acheson's view, and Harriman's, was that MacArthur should be given the shove at once. Marshall and Bradley were more circumspect; they worried that MacArthur's dismissal would draw the ire of the Republican Congress, and make getting military appropriations that much harder. Acheson had to agree. It would "produce the biggest fight of your administration" to fire the general who was not only the Republicans' hero in Korea but the hero of Bataan and the war in the Pacific—a war that many Americans imagined MacArthur had won single-handedly (MacArthur would not have disagreed). But it had to be done; and it was necessary to get the unanimous agreement of the Joint Chiefs before doing it, to provide as much political cover as possible.[54]

And so the discussion ran on, through the afternoon and into April 7 and the weekend. The question was no longer whether MacArthur had to go, but how to deliver the coup de grâce. Truman wrote in his diary on the 7th, "It is the unanimous opinion of all that MacArthur be relieved. All four so advise."

Someone suggested relieving MacArthur of the Korean command only, and leaving him in charge of the occupation of Japan. This idea went nowhere when General Collins pointed out, correctly, that the two commands were so intermingled administratively that it wouldn't be possible to separate them out. Besides, it wouldn't remove the real source of friction, MacArthur himself.

On Saturday Marshall and Bradley wrote a personal confidential letter to MacArthur pointing out that he had put the president in an untenable position.

Perhaps they hoped it might prompt MacArthur to apologize, but it was never sent. Instead, the Joint Chiefs met on Sunday and after two hours of deliberation Bradley told Lovett that "if it should be the President's decision to relieve MacArthur, the JCS concurred."[55]

That night the president and Acheson attended a dinner sponsored by

Latin American foreign ministers and a reception at the Pan American Union that dragged on late into the night. Neither man said a word to anyone about what was about to take place—certainly nothing to anyone who could possibly leak the word back to Tokyo.[56]

On Monday morning the Big Four conclave gathered again, this time with General Bradley and JCS's formal endorsement of the relief of MacArthur in hand. Everyone's views were now the same: MacArthur must be relieved of all his posts and a successor appointed. Bradley proposed Matt Ridgway; Truman happily agreed. The group would return the next day, April 10, to draw up the final orders for dispatch to Korea and Tokyo.

On April 11 MacArthur was just finishing lunch at the American embassy in Tokyo. The guests were Senator Warren Magnuson of Washington, a Democrat, and William Stern, the executive vice president of Northwest Airlines. MacArthur was in a relaxed but thoughtful mood. He was planning to fly to Korea that afternoon, to meet again with Ridgway on the growing threat of another Chinese attack.

It was the overall impression in Washington that General Ridgway was on the same page as Truman and the rest on the need for a cease-fire, and for stabilizing the front line at the 38th parallel "as the first step in ending the aggression and the war."[57] Nothing could have been further from the truth. Ridgway was as impatient as MacArthur in wanting to push the war forward into the north, to finish off their vicious, hated enemy once and for all—even to the border of Communist China again, if it came to that. A MacArthur-Ridgway conference that evening would no doubt have drawn up fresh plans for extending the war, not winding it down.

As the three men talked and joked, the phone rang in the outer office. Jean got up and went to answer it.

Someone who knew her would have said she looked wan and emaciated. People had noticed the physical change that had come over her during the war in Korea, especially since the crisis in December. She ate little and lost weight; she had trouble sleeping at night. Sid Huff advised her to take sedatives; she refused. When the general's plane took off for Korea she would pace for hours, watching and waiting until he returned. Then she would turn up at the airport, where MacArthur would deplane, and his first words were "Where's Jean?"

They would drive back in the dark to the embassy, holding hands in the backseat. Jean would then tuck him into bed and insist on staying up until she knew he was asleep. She would head for her bedroom, draw the shades, and lie in bed. But sleep would rarely come.[58]

Then in February the worst of the crisis had passed, and Jean MacArthur began to regain her old spirit. With guests and visitors she was again the same charming, ebullient person as she was that afternoon when she went to the study and picked up the receiver.

It was Sid Huff, and he sounded shaken. He had just heard on the radio a news bulletin. It said: "President Truman has just removed General MacArthur from his Far Eastern and Korean Commands and from the direction of the occupation of Japan."

Jean couldn't believe it. There had been no word, nothing, from Washington. Yet, Sid Huff said, there was no doubt it was true.[59]

MacArthur looked up as his wife came back to the table, her face ashen. She bent down to whisper the news. MacArthur listened without expression, and sat silent for a moment or two. Then he turned to Jean and said in a loud but gentle tone, "Jeannie, we're going home at last."

The now somber luncheon finished without rushing; MacArthur wouldn't be going to the airport after all. Instead, when the guests left, he quietly phoned Courtney Whitney and asked him to meet him at the Dai-ichi building.

They had a lot to talk about.[60]

MacArthur, of course, had sensed something was coming.

On April 9 General Almond, who had been in Tokyo for a week of family leave, stopped by his office on his way back to Korea. MacArthur seemed unusually quiet, almost disconsolate.

He told his favorite field commander, "I may not see you anymore, so good-bye, Ned."

Almond was startled. He pointed out that MacArthur frequently came over to visit the commanders and troops in Korea. Surely he wasn't going to stop now.

"That isn't the question," MacArthur then said. "I have become politically involved and may be relieved by the President."

Almond dismissed the idea. "Well, General, I consider that absurd and I don't believe the President has the intention of taking such a drastic action. We'll expect to see you in X Corps headquarters very soon."

"Well, perhaps so" was all MacArthur said, and then they parted ways.[61]

It was also possible that MacArthur had gotten word of what was brewing when he spoke to a team of army brass arriving that day from Washington for a conference, headed by Secretary of the Army General Frank Pace. We know Pace briefed him in private for more than two hours, very likely over the trouble that was brewing over his letter to Speaker Martin, and how it wasn't going away.[62]

Or perhaps MacArthur simply knew that if *he* had been Bradley or Lawton Collins and one of his generals had behaved as MacArthur had done, he would have ordered him dismissed. It wasn't a question of if but when—and how.

Certainly what seemed to bother him most then and later was not the firing, but the manner of it. The fact that he first learned about it from someone who had heard it on the radio deeply rankled, understandably so. "No office boy, no charwoman, no servant of any sort would have been dismissed with such callous disregard for the ordinary decencies," he wrote in his memoirs.

Why this had happened is not clear. In reconstructing what went wrong, Dean Acheson insisted that an official order *had* been sent as Truman instructed, via cable to Ambassador Muccio in Seoul, who was to pass it along to General Pace, who then would head back to Tokyo with the order in hand to present to MacArthur. If that seemed unnecessarily roundabout, Acheson wrote, they thought this would spare CINCFE the embarrassment of having the news leak through normal army communications. That seems less than convincing, since it was exactly what happened. When the cable company failed to deliver the message to Muccio on time, Pace only got the orders the next day while in Ridgway's command tent. Hail was streaming down on the canvas so hard he could barely hear the message.

But by then it was too late. The orders had been resent by normal army channels, the word leaked out to the press, and so MacArthur was, if not exactly the last to know, certainly the last major principal to get word of the president's decision.[63] Was it a deliberate snub? Almost certainly not. Was Truman disappointed that MacArthur found out about his dismissal by third hand? Probably not.

In any case, most observers that day and the next agree that MacArthur took the news very well. "MacArthur wanted only to discuss the problems that would confront *me* after his departure," Whitney remembered with amazement.[64] Matt Ridgway, when he learned that he was to be not only the new UN commander but CINCFE and lead the occupation forces in Japan, flew the next day to Tokyo to meet with his predecessor.

He was naturally curious to learn how MacArthur was handling the blow. But "he was entirely himself," Ridgway remembered, "composed, quiet, temperate, friendly, and helpful." MacArthur made some remarks about Truman's health, about how "he wouldn't live six months" because he had malignant hypertension, some doctor had told MacArthur: it was an allusion to the possibility that when Truman had fired him the president may not have been in his right mind. In any case, MacArthur had "no trace of bitterness or anger in his tone" and seemed to have accepted calmly "what must have been a devastating blow to a professional soldier at the peak of his career."[65]

But perhaps it was not so strange. Perhaps underlying his stoic calm was a sense of profound relief. For almost ten years—since December 8, 1941—he had been in a state of constant alert and tension, shouldering one major burden after another with bigger and bigger consequences for any misstep, including now calculating the possibility of triggering a nuclear World War Three in Korea. It had been a decade of a steady war of nerves and constant physical strain for a man in his sixties, together with a constant seesaw of emotions, from utter defeat and humiliation to triumphant return and final victory in 1945.

Instead of returning to the States to a well-deserved retirement, however, he had found himself sole ruler of eighty million Japanese, charged with the mammoth task of rebuilding his broken foe. Then suddenly in the last week of June 1950 came a surprise attack all too reminiscent of the one in December 1941, followed by the exhilaration of victory at Inchon that gave way to crushing defeat yet again. Finally, just as he managed to reverse the course of the war again, Washington had cut him off at the knees—and all in less than ten months.

It would have demanded a heavy price from anyone, let alone from a seventy-one-year-old. It already had. Of all America's leaders at the start of World War Two, he was the only one except George Marshall still standing. All the rest had retired or died. After fifty years of active service MacArthur was more than ready to take on more. But perhaps he was also willing to walk away. Perhaps his exclamation to Jean when he heard the news—"we're going home"—was less the expression of stoic calm or resignation to the inevitable than a heartfelt expression of relief.

Because he *was* going home—but not before the Japanese people had their say.

The day the announcement of MacArthur's dismissal was made public, the liberal Japanese newspaper *Asahi Shimbun* published "Lament for General MacArthur":

> We have lived with General MacArthur from the end of the war until today . . . When the Japanese people faced the unprecedented situation of defeat, and fell into the kyodatsu condition of exhaustion and despair, it was General MacArthur who taught us the merits of democracy and pacifism and guided us with kindness along this bright path. As if pleased with his own children growing up, he took pleasure in the Japanese people, yesterday's enemy, walking step by step toward democracy, and kept encouraging us.[66]

Over the next four days until MacArthur's scheduled departure on April 16, similar tributes poured in from all across Japan, including from Japan's other major newspaper, *Mainichi Shimbun*. The Japanese Diet passed a unanimous resolution praising MacArthur for his accomplishments; so did the Korean National Assembly. Japan's prime minister, Yoshida, sent a personal message to MacArthur expressing regret at his departure and thanking him for all he had done for Japan; Syngman Rhee sent a similar note, thanking him for saving South Korea.

On the Sunday before, April 15, a regular procession of GHQ staff and wives came to the embassy to say their farewells to Jean MacArthur. Some were emotional; Marshall and Willoughby and Sid Huff had been with her every step since the outbreak of war in 1941. The MacArthur home was now bare; the furniture had been all but packed up in preparation for shipping to the States. Jean and the general received them all with grace and friendliness "as usual," as William Sebald remembered, "without the slightest hint of bitterness and resentment."[67]

Sebald's last interview with MacArthur at the Dai-ichi building was more difficult. "I was so keyed up that I was unable to speak," Sebald recalled. "A tear rolled down my cheek." They had been constant intimates for more than five years; they had negotiated their way through a seemingly endless series of hurdles, from the war crimes trials and the Soviets on the Far Eastern Commission, to the outbreak of war in Korea—not to mention the hurdles thrown up by the policymakers in Washington.

It was hard saying goodbye.

Finally Sebald said, "The present state of Japan is a monument to you and I would hope that everything possible could be done to preserve it." MacArthur offered Sebald a cigarette as they sat down. They were discussing whether MacArthur should issue a statement urging the Japanese people to support and cooperate with the new head of SCAP, General Ridgway. MacArthur shook his head. He knew the statement was unnecessary; the Japanese would continue on the constructive path they were already on and needed no encouragement.

He was more somber about the war in Korea. He had no doubt that a cabal had engineered his dismissal, perhaps one inspired by Communist agents; he feared it "would result in the eventual crumbling of the entire United States position in the Far East." He also warned Sebald as they parted: "Bill, the weakness of your position is that you have been too loyal to me. You may have to pay for that loyalty."[68]

But without a doubt the visit that mattered most to MacArthur was the one by the emperor himself—"the first time in history," a Japanese historian noted, "that a Japanese monarch had called upon a foreigner who held no official capacity."[69]

Hirohito's staff had advised him against it. It was MacArthur's duty, they said, to visit the emperor. But Hirohito went anyway, and the two men spoke for more than an hour. It was the eleventh time they had met and this time, for the first time, MacArthur accompanied the emperor back to his limousine and watched it drive away.[70]

The biggest surprise of all, however, came as dawn broke on April 16, 1951. Douglas, Jean, and little Arthur had risen shortly before 5:00 A.M. in order to get ready. Now, as their limousine hurtled down the road to Haneda airport, they were jammed on all sides between half a million and a million Japanese who had been standing there in the predawn darkness for a final glimpse of the man they still called *Makassa Gensui,* or Field Marshal MacArthur.[71] With them were also tens of thousands of American soldiers, sailors, and airmen, waiting to see off the man who had been their supreme commander.

At the airport MacArthur's honor guard was drawn up, standing stiffly at present arms, as flags snapped in the brisk early-morning breeze. At precisely 7:00 A.M. the familiar green Cadillac limousine pulled up and the MacArthurs stepped out.

Waiting for them were Sebald, Ridgway, Vice Admiral Turner Joy, the senior American naval officer; commander of the British Commonwealth forces Sir Horace Robertson; MacArthur's old friend General Stratemeyer; and a large party of other American officers and officials.

MacArthur reviewed the guard of honor with his usual impassive scrutinizing gaze and then, as usual, shook hands with the guard's commander.

Then he walked up to shake hands with the senior officers, smiling and thanking them for their service. Some of their wives were sobbing openly; men like Stratemeyer found their eyes had suddenly gone misty.

MacArthur stepped up to the Japanese officials in attendance. Naotake Sato, president of the Japanese Upper House, held back tears as he and MacArthur shook hands for the last time. Prime Minister Shigeru Yoshida's voice choked as he said final words of farewell.[72]

After fifteen minutes Jean and Douglas MacArthur turned and headed for the airplane. Lining the airport fence they could see thousands upon thousands of Japanese, some waving, some in tears, all of them wondering what would happen now that the man on whom they had come to rely for everything for six years was leaving their lives.

There was a quick nineteen-gun salute that briskly reverberated through the chilly morning air, and an honor flight of jet fighters and B-29 bombers passed overhead. As the sound of the engines faded, the honor band struck up "Auld Lang Syne." Then MacArthur took his wife's arm and guided her onto the plane ramp. They were not going alone: the ever-loyal Sid Huff, Courtney Whitney, Colonel Bunker, and of course Arthur and Ah Cheu were flying with them back to the country that thirteen-year-old Arthur had never seen—and that MacArthur himself had not seen in nearly a decade and a half.

The plane door shut; Anthony Story throttled the *Bataan II*'s engines and the plane quickly taxied away. The crowd watched as it roared off the runway, banked, and then headed up into the clear blue sky until it became a speck that finally vanished.

"The accomplishments of General MacArthur in the interest of our country are one of the marvels of history," Prime Minister Yoshida had said in his radio broadcast of farewell to MacArthur. "No wonder he is looked upon by all our people with the profoundest veneration and affection. I have no words to convey the regret of our nation to see him leave."[73]

In truth, Japan owed MacArthur more than it knew at the time. By turning occupied Japan into his major logistical base for operations in Korea, MacArthur had resurrected Japan's economy. As historian Michael Schaller has noted, "war orders benefited the textile, construction, automotive, metal, communications, and chemical industries. At the peak of the Korean conflict, nearly 3000 Japanese firms held war-related contracts while many others arranged with U.S. companies and the Defense Department to acquire new technology." In 1950–51 alone, procurements for the U.S. military totaled 40 percent of all Japan's exports—and in 1952 that amount more than doubled.[74] Truck sales for Toyota Motor Company, for example, shot up from barely 300 vehicles a year before the war to 5,000 a year later—almost all to the U.S. Army. It can truly be said that MacArthur had laid the foundations of Japan's "economic miracle" in the sixties and seventies, first during the occupation and then during the Korean War, by turning America's former enemy into its military-industrial workshop.

The importance of all this lay in the future. At the time everyone's attention was consumed by MacArthur's dismissal and what the political repercussions would be. There was, however, one American who understood all that MacArthur had accomplished not just in Japan but in Korea. This was John Foster Dulles, who had been with MacArthur when the war first broke out that disastrous Sunday. As it happened, Dulles was now flying back to Japan, and high over the Pacific his plane passed MacArthur's and the two men talked—not by radio but by Morse code.

"I asked him for advice," Dulles later told Congressman Walter Judd of Minnesota, "and he gave me concrete suggestions as to what it would be most useful for me to do and say when I got to Tokyo. His whole concern was for the success of his mission there," and "there was not one word of bitterness."

Then Dulles told Judd soberly, "I never had greater admiration for a man. Under such provocation, he still uttered not a word of personal bitterness; he considered only the cause of his country."

Dulles paused, and added: "As long as America can produce men of that stature and caliber it will be safe."[75]

The question now was how many in the United States would understand the same thing.

CHAPTER 33

FADING AWAY

War's very object is victory—not prolonged indecision.
In war, indeed, there is no substitute for victory.

—DOUGLAS MACARTHUR, APRIL 19, 1951

The crowds were bigger than anything he had ever seen in his life.

The moment the MacArthurs stepped down the ramp at the San Francisco airport on April 18 at 8:30 P.M., tens of thousands of cheering yet anxious Americans broke through the police barriers surrounding the field. News of his removal from command had spread like quicksilver across the United States. Newspapers from Boston to Los Angeles proclaimed the news in banner headlines: MACARTHUR DISMISSED. The overwhelming public consensus that April was that Truman's action was a blunder, even a catastrophic one. A Gallup poll on April 14 showed that two out of three Americans disapproved of MacArthur's removal; in the Republican-dominated Congress the feeling against Truman ran even higher.[1]

Congressional leaders who weren't shocked at the sudden dismissal were outraged. Some, like Republican Styles Bridges of Maine, tried to get Truman to reconsider. Others simply sat in stunned dismay. Perhaps surprisingly, the president's own party was probably the most upset. They knew this would give the majority Republicans, including their rising paladin in the Senate, Joe McCarthy, the excuse to do what they had wanted to do since the fall of China to Communism: tear into the Truman foreign policy record. They doubted it would win more Democratic votes.

Indeed, both Senate and House Republicans soon assured the public that there would be hearings—long, probing hearings—into why MacArthur had been fired, with plenty of time for the general to defend himself—and to refute his foes.

Senator Richard Nixon introduced a resolution calling for MacArthur's reinstatement. William Jenner of Indiana took it a step further, calling for Truman's impeachment and proclaiming that "this country today is in the hands of the secret inner coterie which is directed by agents of the Soviet Union." Joe McCarthy went even further, calling the decision "a great Communist victory" that "may well have condemned thousands of American boys to death, and may well have condemned Western civilization."[2]

MacArthur's stalwart supporters in the Hearst, McCormick, and Scripps-Herald newspaper syndicates echoed the same themes, though Truman found support on the editorial pages of *The New York Times* and the *New York Herald Tribune*. In general, the overwhelming majority of journalists and reporters, including those in Japan and Korea, thought the dismissal had been the right thing to do. The media in Britain and Europe agreed—as did, of course, the press in Communist countries.

For most ordinary Americans, however, the situation was clear. To them, MacArthur was the great hero of Bataan and World War Two, and the architect of victory—or near victory—in Korea. Now, suddenly and without warning, he had been fired just as he had reversed the Red Chinese tide and final victory seemed within America's grasp. Millions of Americans wanted to know why, and they would demand that Congress find out who was responsible. But for now they were content to show their support for the man they believed had been shamefully, possibly treasonously, treated—the man who, many believed, was all that stood between victory and defeat over international Communism.

On the fourteen-mile drive from the airport to the St. Francis Hotel in downtown San Francisco, some half a million people lined the road in the darkness to greet their returning hero. The next day an even bigger crowd watched a ticker tape parade for the general and his family through the streets of San Francisco, while 100,000 jammed themselves in front of city hall to hear MacArthur deliver a short impromptu speech before waving to the roaring throng and returning to his hotel.

For MacArthur, the massive show of public approbation was naturally gratifying, but also surprising. He had been out of the country for nearly fifteen years; he had last been there when Franklin Roosevelt was president and pro–New Deal feeling was running high, as was a blatant isolationism. This was a more conservative, even more religious America, one much more worried about threats from the outside world after the traumas of Pearl Harbor and World War Two. Even in the fading shadow of total victory, American public opinion had become highly suspicious of their former ally the Soviet Union and *its* allies, including Communist China. The sudden attack on South Korea in 1950 had confirmed the widespread sense that those, like MacArthur, who had warned of a vast conspiracy to undermine America's position in Asia had been right—even that some in the Truman administration might be part of it, or at least woefully blind to the danger.

When Truman tried to explain his decision to a national radio audience the evening of April 11, even Dean Acheson had to concede that the result was "a complete flop." Truman said almost nothing about why MacArthur had been fired, which seemed doubly mysterious. Instead, he spent his time on the air reiterating the administration's policy in Korea, which most listeners thought was a failure anyway. As a result, Truman's always brittle approval ratings began to collapse. Polls soon showed that 66 percent of Americans thought dismissing MacArthur was a mistake. Mail to congressmen showed the pro-MacArthur supporters running ten to one.[3]

In the meantime, supporters swamped MacArthur's motorcade everywhere it went.

"My welcome through the entire land defies description," MacArthur later wrote. "America took me to its heart with a roar that will never leave my ears." In New York, Chicago, Boston, Cleveland, Detroit, Houston, Austin, and a dozen other cities it was the same rapturous scene: the drive down the main avenue, waving from the open limousine to the cheering throngs, the ticker tape, the massive police escorts, the waving American flags, and other paraphernalia associated with the greeting of returning heroes like Charles Lindbergh or, later, returning astronauts.

All his life he had been used to receiving praise, honors, rewards, even adoring admiration when he first arrived in Australia or in the days after the liberation of the Philippines. But never had Douglas MacArthur received adulation like this—certainly not from his fellow Americans. It was bound to turn anyone's head, and it turned his.

"Men, women, and children," he reflected later, "rich and poor, black and white, of as many different origins as there are nations on the earth, with their tears and smiles, their cheers and handclaps, and most of all, their heart-lifting cries of 'Welcome home, Mac!' "[4]

It would be rash to suggest that it affected MacArthur's judgment. He had been determined for some time to defend himself and his record when he returned to America, and what he would say and how he would say it had been on his mind long before his plane touched down in San Francisco. But the rapturous receptions he met, including those from some of America's most powerful politicians, did give him hope that if Truman's decision on removing him could not be reversed, perhaps MacArthur himself would soon be in a position to affect the crucial decisions on Korea and on fighting Communism in Asia, from his own desk in the Oval Office.

President Douglas MacArthur. Was it really so far-fetched a dream? After he had toyed with the idea briefly in 1944 and then again in 1948, that ultimate reward for a half century of heroic public service must have seemed closer to reality than ever, in those heady days of late April 1951. That was especially true when he arrived in Washington, D.C., to deliver what would be the climax of his nationwide tour: an address to a joint session of Congress on April 19.

MacArthur had worked on the address almost from the moment the invitation had arrived from House Minority Leader Joe Martin—ironically, the man more responsible than any other for MacArthur's dismissal—and the Senate Majority Leader, Ernest McFarland. He had worked on it on the plane across the Pacific, despite a bout of airsickness; he had tried to find time to work on it when they touched down in Hawaii, where he got his first glimpse of the adulation that was coming when a crowd of more than 100,000 greeted him in Honolulu and the university presented him with an honorary doctorate of law.[5]

For MacArthur, the address would be the most important speech he would ever make. It was an opportunity to summon all his knowledge, all his oratorical powers and flair for the dramatic, not only to justify his actions and policies in Korea but to awaken Congress and the nation to what he conceived to be America's long-term interests in Asia. It was his moment to spell out the promise and perils awaiting the world's most powerful democracy in the Pacific Rim.

In effect, the grand vision of America's future in the Pacific, which, seventy years earlier, his father had painfully typed out to his own army superiors in a forty-page memorandum, Douglas MacArthur would now take to center stage in a joint session of Congress.

The plane landed at National Airport at a quarter after midnight on April 19. President Truman was not there to greet him, of course; nor was Dean Acheson. But George Marshall, the Joint Chiefs, and Truman's military aide, Major General Harry Vaughan, did show up and were waiting for MacArthur on the darkened tarmac. Someone spotted Jim Wainwright in the crowd, and he was asked to join the tiny greeting party.[6] As the MacArthurs descended from the plane and briefly shook hands with Marshall and the others, the crowd, more than 12,000 strong, charged forward. The police had difficulty restoring order; it took more than half an hour just to get the MacArthurs to their car. Courtney Whitney was pushed to the ground in the crush; at one point the general didn't even know where Jean was as the people surged between them, cheering and reaching for his hand or just to touch his sleeve.

Finally, with police sirens wailing and lights flashing, they set off for the Statler Hotel. "It looked like the entire District of Columbia greeted our arrival," MacArthur wrote later.[7] The normally thirty-minute drive took hours, as they crept past the swarming crowds and the traffic snarls, until finally the exhausted party reached their destination.

The landing on Leyte; the surrender ceremony on the deck of the *Missouri;* the first meeting with Emperor Hirohito; the landing at Inchon. These had all been moments of personal triumph as well as great landmarks in history. But on this day he believed he would chart a new course not just for the nation and the world, but for himself. The era of Douglas MacArthur, American soldier, was over. The era of Douglas MacArthur, American statesman—American president, even—was about to begin.

At noon the representatives and senators and members of the Supreme Court began to arrive in the Capitol's House chamber and take their seats. One row of seats, however, was conspicuously empty—those usually reserved for the president's cabinet, all of whom were conspicuously absent. Undismayed, Speaker Martin arranged that those seats be given to Jean MacArthur, Arthur, and the other members of the MacArthur party instead. One of them was the always loyal Sid Huff. They had come a long way together since they had escaped together from Corregidor, sharing a wave-soaked mattress in the well of a speeding PT boat. Now Sid was there to hear MacArthur speak to America.

Every American television network would be showing the speech live; more than twenty million Americans would be listening in on their radios. A sudden thought crossed Huff's mind, something MacArthur had said when they had stared out the windows of *Bataan II* at the tremendous crowd waiting for them at the San Francisco airport, with the beacons of light flashing through the blackness.

"I hope," MacArthur had muttered, watching the throng, "that they are not cheering because they feel sorry for me." He and Sid and Jean were about to find out.[8]

At 12:31 P.M., the door of the House creaked open and the House door-keeper announced in a deep voice, "Mister Speaker, General Douglas MacArthur."

The chamber exploded in a roar of sound. MacArthur strode in, escorted by a phalanx of Republican congressmen, as the cheering echoed up from the House floor and down from the packed visitors' gallery. House Speaker Sam Rayburn introduced him and then Douglas MacArthur stepped to the podium.

He wore no medals or ribbons. Only a trim waist-length military jacket with five gold stars attached to the collar. He stood tall and somber for three minutes as the applause went on and on. Then the audience was seated, silence fell, and the general began.

"Mister President, Mister Speaker, and distinguished Members of the Congress: I stand on this rostrum with a deep sense of humility and great pride—humility in the wake of those great American architects of our history who have stood here before me; pride in the reflection that this forum of legislative debate represents human liberty in the purest form yet devised."

The chamber exploded again in massive applause. In fact, the entire thirty-seven-minute address would be interrupted by applause more than fifty times. MacArthur, however, never let the standing ovations throw him off his pace—or off message. "From his first words," one observer noted, "it was clear that he was in complete command of the situation."[9] And that message would be that there could be no surrender to Communism in Asia, and that stalemate in Korea would be as bad as surrender.

America's relationship with Asia past, present, and future was uppermost in his thoughts and words. "While Asia is commonly referred to as the gateway to Europe, it is no less true that Europe is the gateway to Asia, and the broad influence of the one cannot fail to have its impact upon the other . . . [To] consider the problems of one sector, oblivious of those of another, is but to court disaster for the whole."

That in truth is what MacArthur saw happening to the country's current approach to the global Communist threat. Failing to check its advance in East Asia, including Korea, would only guarantee its future victory elsewhere, including in this new globally interconnected world in which America now found itself.

Then he spoke of the Asia he had known since his first visit with his father almost forty years before. "Long exploited by the so-called colonial powers, with little opportunity to achieve any degree of social justice, individual dignity, or a higher standard of life such as guided our own noble administration of the Philippines, the people of Asia found their opportunity in the war just past to throw off the shackles of colonialism and now see the dawn of new opportunity, a heretofore unfelt dignity and the self-respect of political freedom" for half the world's population and 60 percent of its available resources.

America had a vital destiny to play in kindling that freedom and helping to foster that social justice and individual opportunity—and not just for altruistic reasons. At one time the Pacific had seemed a protective barrier to America's western approaches, he explained. After Pearl Harbor and during the Second World War, however, America had come to realize that its forward western flank, running from Hawaii and Midway to Guam and the Philippines, was "not an outpost of strength but an avenue of weakness along which the enemy could and did attack." In short, fostering freedom and democratic allies in Asia was the best way for America to defend itself in the future.

America had achieved that goal in the Philippines, he said, and was doing so in Japan, its former enemy. "The Japanese people since the war have undergone the greatest reformation recorded in modern history. . . . Politically, economically, and socially, Japan is now abreast of many free nations of the earth and will not again fail the universal trust." That the world owed this massive turnaround to one man, himself, he did not have to add.

With China, by contrast, the United States had failed in its historic mission.

There, American weakness had permitted a Soviet satellite to take shape and threaten its neighbors. Instead of a free democratic China, America's failed policies had left behind a militarized China that "has become aggressively imperialistic, with a lust for expansion and increased power normal to this type of imperialism." MacArthur had no doubts that this China would soon follow its own destiny without regard to its current ally the Soviet Union (it was not a view shared by many in Washington, but in a few short years his prediction would prove correct). But it would nonetheless threaten America's strategic position in Asia, and the independence of its postwar allies, including Japan.

For that reason, MacArthur insisted, America now had to stand by Chiang Kai-shek and Formosa more than ever, as a vital hub of the "protective shield for all the Americas and all the free lands of the Pacific Areas." Likewise, the Pacific itself would become "a vast moat to protect us as long as we hold it" by land, air, and sea. "Indeed," he went on, "it acts as a protective shield for all of the Americas and all free lands of the Pacific Ocean area. We control it to the shores of Asia" itself, thanks to a island chain linked together by U.S. naval and air bases extending from the Aleutians to the Marianas, from which "we can dominate with sea and air power every Asiatic port from Vladivostok to Singapore"—and keep the Soviet Union and its allies from making any hostile moves into the Pacific Ocean.

Now in Korea, he concluded darkly, America was again failing in its mission to protect Asia from Chinese expansionism—and to protect America from any future Communist threat.

"While I was not consulted prior to the President's decision to intervene in support of the Republic of Korea," he added, "that decision, from a military standpoint, proved a sound one." MacArthur and the United Nations forces had been able to throw back the North Korean invader and decimate their armies.

"Our victory was complete and our objectives within reach when Red China intervened with numerically superior ground forces."

MacArthur vehemently cast aside the accusation Dean Acheson and others were making, that he himself had somehow triggered the Red Chinese intervention by his advance into northern North Korea—possibly even deliberately in order to widen the war into China itself. "No man in his right mind would advocate sending our ground forces into continental China and such was never given a thought," he thundered.

Still, "the new situation did urgently demand a drastic revision of strategic planning if our political aim was to defeat this new enemy as we had defeated the old."

But in fact, as MacArthur had soon discovered to his sorrow, that was not the aim of the president and his advisors at all. He had presented to them his four-point plan to secure victory, including a naval blockade of China and releasing Chiang's forces on Taiwan to join the fight, and they had turned him down. He had even been severely criticized for drafting a plan designed "to bring hostilities to an end with the least possible delay and at a saving of countless American and Allied lives."

In short, the Truman administration had rejected all his calls for a decisive end to the war by military action. "I have been called a war-monger," he noted with scornful indignation. "*Nothing* could be further from the truth." Few in the current armed services had seen firsthand as much of the horror and destruction of war as he had, starting in the First World War. His views on the future of war had been made clear on the deck of the USS *Missouri* in September 1945, when he said that with the new destructiveness of nuclear war, mankind had no alternative to peace.

"But once war is forced upon us, there is no other alternative than to apply every available means to bring it to a swift end. War's very object is victory, not prolonged indecision. In war, there can be no substitute for victory."

At that moment the chamber exploded in a storm of applause and approbation. Those words from his letter to Joe Martin had become a catchphrase around the country—words that were either immortal or misleading and dangerous, depending on one's political stance. But at that moment they seemed to sum up a lifetime of one man's achievement—and the hopes of an America desperate to escape an ongoing quagmire in Korea.

"The tragedy of Korea is further heightened by the fact that as military action is confined to its territorial limits," he added, "it condemns that nation, which it is our purpose to save, to suffer the devastating impact of full naval and air bombardment, while the enemy sanctuaries are fully protected from such attack and devastation" in Red China. At the same time, "my soldiers asked of me, why surrender military advantages to an enemy in the field? I could not answer."

Then he said, "I have just left your fighting sons in Korea. They have met all tests there and I can report to you without reservation they are splendid in every way. . . . Those gallant men will remain often in my thoughts and in my prayers always."

Finally he talked about himself.

"I am closing my fifty-two years of military service. When I joined the Army even before the turn of the century, it was the fulfillment of all my boyish hopes and dreams. The world has turned over many times since I took the oath on the Plain at West Point, and the hopes and dreams have long since vanished. But I still remember the refrain of one of the most popular barrack ballads of that day which proclaimed most proudly that—

"'Old soldiers never die, they just fade away.'"

By now there were few dry eyes left in the chamber.

"And like the old soldier of that ballad, I now close my military career and just fade away," he said with a wry smile. "An old soldier who tried to do his duty as God gave him light to see that duty."

Then he finished with a halting "Goodbye."

* * *

His biographer Clayton James, no fan of the speech or this phase of MacArthur's career, wrote that it must be ranked "as one of the most impressive and divisive oratorical performances of recent American times"—although James himself found its basic proposition "faulty" and even "downright dangerous." Dean Acheson dismissed the speech at once as "demagogic."[10] Most recent historians of the Korean War and the Truman-MacArthur controversy have expressed similar negative sentiments.

MacArthur partisans, on the other hand, have generally agreed with former president Herbert Hoover's remark after the speech, that MacArthur was "the reincarnation of Saint Paul into a great General of the Army who came out of the East." Representative Dewey Short of Missouri did Hoover one better: "We saw a great hunk of God in the flesh, and we heard the voice of God."

Yet in retrospect, it is hard to find much in MacArthur's speech to disagree with—including his views on Communist China. That Mao would eventually split from his Soviet ally was something MacArthur already sensed but that even the Acheson-Kennan team hadn't realized; and that China would become an aggressive military imperialist power in East Asia was a sound strategic judgment, the truth of which seems more relevant today than ever.

As for MacArthur's views on the growing Communist threat in Asia, those too seem prescient in light of events in Indochina and Vietnam that were unfolding at the time, and that would grow in significance in less than a decade. Even the theme of "no substitute for victory" would carry forward in the so-called Powell Doctrine of the 1990s. In that sense, MacArthur's views take on fresh, hard relevance in the light of recent conflicts in Afghanistan and Iraq.

Finally, MacArthur's remarks about the folly of allowing an enemy sanctuaries from which to freely operate, along with his view that "history teaches with unmistakable emphasis that appeasement begets new and bloodier wars . . . like blackmail, [appeasement] lays the basis for new and successively greater demands, until, as in blackmail, violence becomes the only alternative" seem remarkably sane, rather than demagogic or dangerous.

So then what was the real quarrel critics had, and continue to have, with MacArthur's speech? Without a doubt, it was publicly questioning the strategic assumptions of the Truman-Acheson team—the assumptions that led them to decide that MacArthur's policy on Korea was no longer in sync with their own and that he should be removed.

The key assumption was that Korea was a no-win proposition. Once China intervened, they concluded, the best outcome that could be hoped for was a negotiated cease-fire along the 38th parallel, followed by a voluntary Chinese withdrawal and a permanently divided Korea. To point out that this is in fact what happened—as most MacArthur critics do—does *not* imply that Truman and Acheson were right and MacArthur was wrong. It simply recognizes that once MacArthur had been removed, no other options existed. Even though General Ridgway's views on driving the Chinese out of Korea were similar to MacArthur's, including using chemical weapons, which MacArthur had to veto, he was not the man with the power to carry it out alone—or a man with the larger geopolitical vision in which drawing out the war with Mao's China would make sound strategic sense.

The truth was that, far from opposing MacArthur's strategy for winning in Korea, Truman, Acheson, George Marshall, and the Joint Chiefs had been on record endorsing, even encouraging, him up to the point that China massively intervened—that is, until the going got difficult, and MacArthur's forces found themselves on the defensive. Then the administration quickly reversed itself. In a matter of weeks, it came to accept the viewpoint of its European allies that the war was unwinnable without a drastic expansion of its size and scope, including the use of nuclear weapons, and that it was time to cut a deal.

From that moment, MacArthur's aggressiveness ceased to be an asset and became a liability. That he refused to adjust himself, and his public statements, to the new strategy, was perfectly true; but that it *was* a new, even unprecedented, change in American military policy was also true.

In that sense, MacArthur's removal was inevitable—not for insubordination or because he had dared to challenge civilian leadership of the military, as some critics charged then and later. It was because he was an inconvenient reminder of the Korea strategy that the president had endorsed, until it struck a reef. Starting over with Ridgway as CINCFE meant for everyone a clean break from an embarrassing past—and from relations with a proud, overbearing officer that none of the White House team could stand, anyway.

Yet MacArthur had put his finger on the fatal flaw of containment. If not victory, then what? Stalemate? It was difficult to imagine America's military leadership devoting themselves to a strategy that involved denying objectives to an enemy, for example preventing a Communist takeover of a foreign country, while resigning themselves to achieving none of their own aims, for instance, destroying that Communist power's forces and their ability to fight. But what if the foe chose not to accept stalemate and decided to fight on? Then the alternative was endless war, with American forces and their allies constantly blocking enemy attacks and taking casualties, and having only momentary respites as the enemy regrouped and refitted before trying again. This kind of endless war would become all too familiar to the American military and public in the coming years, from Vietnam to Afghanistan and Iraq, not to mention the constant knife-edge tension of the Cold War itself. It would become the long, bitter legacy of containment, even after the Cold War: an America resigned to fighting wars that its political leadership is determined not to win, until the public finally loses patience and insists that its leaders call it quits.

By rejecting the MacArthur alternative of no substitute for victory, Washington had committed the nation to maintaining a world in which if there were no more wars among the great powers, there certainly would never be peace.

There was, however, one statement in MacArthur's address that was false and misleading. It was when he said his plan was now "just to fade away."

Nothing could have been further from his mind. His goal was now to use his vast, unchallenged popularity to galvanize the country in a new direction for dealing with Korea and the global Communist threat, as well as its future direction *as* a country.

In San Francisco, a reporter asked if he had any political plans. "I do not intend to run for any political office. . . . The only politics I have is contained in a simple phrase known to all of you—God Bless America!" This was less than ingenuous. MacArthur had every intention of now making himself a major figure on the American political scene. And as the last rousing cheers in the House chamber died away on April 19, and the last handshakes with his friends and political allies both old and new were over, he must have wondered just where his new preeminence might take him.

Yet his national preeminence had just crested, and his ability to influence events would steadily slip away until in less than a decade he would become a largely forgotten figure and a virtual hermit.

It certainly didn't seem that way the next day, as he and Jean and Arthur now wrapped up their visit in Washington in preparation for heading to New York City.

After a triumphant luncheon with Congressman Martin and forty of his colleagues, MacArthur gave brief speeches at Constitution Hall and then to an immense throng on the National Mall before setting off again for National Airport.

The motorcade down Pennsylvania Avenue drew a crowd of more than a quarter million; in New York the crowds were even greater during a nineteen-mile parade through Manhattan. When he arrived at the Waldorf Astoria Hotel, mailbags containing 150,000 approving letters and 20,000 telegrams were waiting for him—many of them arranged by his Republican allies on the Hill. Over the next weeks more bags of fan mail arrived almost daily.[11]

The Waldorf Astoria would now become his home in retirement, as he and Jean took an immense ten-room penthouse suite in the next-door Waldorf Towers for their permanent residence. For MacArthur it must have been a moment of sardonic triumph, to be living in the hotel from which he had once been expelled for wearing spurs at a victory dance. Eventually room after room would become filled with mementos, books, pictures, Asian art, and furniture from their years in Japan. Almost nothing survived from their years in the Manila Hotel, and even less from his life in America or with his parents. But in the Waldorf Astoria he and Jean made a new life for themselves and their son, Arthur; one reflecting his status as America's greatest living soldier.

For now, however, there was only travel, to virtually every major city in the United States, where the crowds, speeches, and parades became almost indistinguishable from one another.

"It is with a sense of high honor that I appear on this rostrum to address you," he told the assembled legislature at the state capitol in Austin, Texas, on June 21, "a State which has contributed so abundantly to American progress and in which I feel so sincere a personal interest." He told the Massachusetts legislature on July 15 that "in this historic forum I recall vividly and reverently the memory of those great architects and defenders of liberty who immortalized the Commonwealth of Massachusetts. To this section of the country men point as the cradle of our freedom."[12]

And so on. In each city, in front of every legislature or august group, the message was the same: the danger of appeasement; the needless sacrifice of men in Korea without a clear goal of victory; the threat from within of Communism and Communist sympathizers (without naming names) who "have already so drastically altered the character of our free institutions—those institutions which formerly we hailed as something beyond question or challenge—those institutions we proudly called the American way of life."

If he wasn't a presidential candidate, he was certainly sounding like one—and officials in the Republican National Committee were carefully making sure that every speech and press interview got plenty of coverage in local newspapers and the national media. From the perspective of Democrats in Washington it must have looked grim. Truman for one, though, wasn't worried. One of his staffers recorded in his diary: "The President did not seem too upset by the uproar that has resulted throughout the country from his recall of General MacArthur from Tokyo. He has suggested that within the Administration nothing be said to keep the fire going."[13]

Perhaps Truman wasn't worried because he sensed Republicans would blow this opportunity, as they did every other time. He was right. The MacArthur juggernaut would begin to break down almost from the moment the joint congressional hearings on Korea began on May 3, with MacArthur as the first witness.

MacArthur's three days of testimony should have been the capstone of his popular comeback, an opportunity to expand on his views from the April 19 speech and further explain his larger strategy for winning in Korea. MacArthur himself had seen his testimony that way. "The concept that our forces withdrew in disorder [in December 1950] or were badly defeated is one of the most violent prevarications of the truth that was ever made," he stated baldly. He continued to insist that the source of the difficulty had been the failure to adequately bomb the bridges over the Yalu, and that his four-point plan for winning after China's intervention could still prevail, if only the administration would give up its defeatist attitude.

He also rejected the notion, current in Democratic and liberal circles, that any strong response to Chinese aggression would trigger World War Three. He said his strategy would "tend to not precipitate a world war, but to prevent it," because the risk of global conflict would increase if the war were allowed to go on, or "if we practice appeasement" of Mao's China. He even suggested that Stalin would prefer to see China not become too powerful, and might be pleased to see "this new Frankenstein" that he had helped take power in Beijing come a cropper in Korea—something that Truman's architects of containment, who assumed that Moscow called the shots and Beijing and Pyongyang only moved in lockstep, had never considered.[14]

All in all, MacArthur's testimony contained many intelligent, even perceptive observations on the future of the Cold War, but they got lost in the furor over the rest of the hearings. Here the Republicans made two mistakes. First, instead of focusing on strategy in Korea and fighting the Cold War, they became obsessed with showing that MacArthur's dismissal was the result of a deliberate pro-Communist conspiracy—something they couldn't prove because it didn't exist. The removal of MacArthur had been nothing but a legitimate act of executive authority, however misguided.

The second was that while MacArthur got three days and 300 written pages of testimony to prove his case, the administration got twenty-eight days and 772 pages to refute it—almost half the entire testimony of the hearings. It was a steady parade of administration heavyweights led by Dean Acheson, General Marshall, Omar Bradley, Lawton Collins, and General Vandenberg—a display of military uniforms and medals as well as executive branch power and prestige.

Their message was coherent, compelling, and unified. General MacArthur had made a series of disastrous military decisions culminating in the attack from China and the retreat south of the 38th parallel; he had disregarded specific instructions from the Joint Chiefs regarding his advance into North Korea that triggered the Chinese intervention; and above all, his actions and words had challenged the fundamental principle of civilian leadership of the American armed forces.

"It became apparent that General MacArthur had grown so far out of sympathy with the established policies of the United States that there was grave doubt as to whether he could any longer be permitted to exercise the authority in making decisions that normal command functions would assign to a theater commander," General Marshall told the senators. "In this situation, there was no other recourse but to relieve him" once he began publicly voicing his disagreements with the policies of the commander in chief.[15]

That indeed is the charge that has continued to stick with regard to MacArthur's dismissal, that he had challenged the president's authority and so had to go. Otherwise, so goes the argument, the principle that America's soldiers follow the bidding of their elected civilian superiors rather than the other way around would be irrevocably and disastrously overthrown.

MacArthur's own view of the subject was made clear in his memoirs.

"The legal authority of a President to relieve a field commander, irrespective of the wisdom or stupidity of the action, has never been questioned by anyone. The supremacy of the civil over the military is fundamental." But, MacArthur asserted, that "was not an issue in this case." The real lesson is that MacArthur was removed "without a hearing, without an opportunity for defense, with no consideration of the past," including the fact that Truman had been praising MacArthur's strategy and efforts almost up to the day he was removed.[16]

We now know at one level that this was not true. The discontent over what MacArthur was doing, and had been saying, had been brewing for weeks. Yet MacArthur's larger point was correct. There had never been a full and frank exchange of differing views on Korea between the president or the Joint Chiefs and their theater command, followed by an ultimatum: carry out our new strategy, or we will find someone who will. That very likely would have led to MacArthur's resignation, which Truman could have accepted—and which could have spared the country a major uproar and very possibly have spared the Democrats a humiliating defeat in the presidential election of 1952.

But now that was not to be. A Republican *was* destined to take the White House the next November—but it would not be Douglas MacArthur. Instead, he would be outmaneuvered and upstaged by the man he still considered his subordinate and protégé, but who was increasingly his rival as soldier-statesman: Dwight D. Eisenhower.

Meanwhile, removing MacArthur hadn't helped the war effort in Korea. After he left, in fact, things went rather badly.

Even as *Bataan II* was leaving Japan for the States, Mao Zedong launched his fifth great offensive of the war, backed by some 700,000 troops. I Corps had to take the brunt of the attack, in a series of bloody slogging matches in which Ridgway's superior firepower with aircraft and artillery beat back the numerically superior Chinese attackers, who kept regrouping and attacking to receive the same punishment. From the 22nd of April to the 25th, 1951, battles at Imjin River and Kapyong finally drove the Chinese offensive to ground along a line just north of Seoul.

Undaunted, Mao's forces struck again in May, this time against X Corps and a reorganized ROK army. Again, initial Chinese gains were erased in a hailstorm of bombs and artillery fire, with UN troops grimly pressing home counterattacks until they drew up at what came to be known as "Line Kansas." There Ridgway's forces would stay, for all of the rest of the year and until December 1952.

It was stalemate, World War One style—almost exactly what the Truman people had wanted. Except that casualties kept mounting, as one effort to negotiate a cease-fire after another failed and Beijing continued fighting, oblivious to the slaughter of its own troops. The Battle of Bloody Ridge (August 18–September 5, 1951); the Battle of the Punchbowl (August 30–September 21, 1951); the Battle of Heartbreak Ridge (September 13–October 15, 1951); the Battle of Old Baldy (June 26–August 4, 1952); the Battle of White Horse (October 6–15, 1952); the Battle of Triangle Hill (October 14–November 25, 1952): forgotten fights in what was coming to be known as the Forgotten War, except by those families who received telegrams regarding the death of another son or brother or husband, in a conflict that seemed without purpose or end point. America was learning that there might not be a substitute for victory after all—certainly not one that could stop the killing.

Eventually the man the public turned to, to end it, was Eisenhower. He had been primed for the presidency since 1948—except as a Democrat then rather than a Republican. By the time MacArthur was ready to enter the political arena, he had been out-spent, out-organized, and out-caucused by both Eisenhower and his principal opponent, Robert Taft.

The irony was that Ike owed a large part of his push into the presidency to MacArthur. According to Eisenhower in an interview in 1967, when he visited his former chief in Tokyo in 1946 all MacArthur could talk about, from after dinner until 1 A.M., was why Ike should run for president. It was a MacArthur full-court press; the man of destiny—"He was a man who sincerely believed he was a man of destiny," Eisenhower told his interviewer, "above others and unique"—speaking to someone who could fulfill America's mission when MacArthur himself felt he could not. Ike asked why MacArthur himself didn't run. "I'm too old for the job," he said, dismissing the idea out of hand. Six years later, he may have regretted he pressed Ike so hard— and that he had eliminated himself from the running on the basis of an advancing age he neither showed nor felt.[17]

But it was too late for regrets. He did have the honor of delivering the keynote address at the Republican National Convention, which opened in Chicago on the Fourth of July, 1952. He spoke as he had for the past several months, of "those reckless men who, yielding to international intrigue, set the stage for Soviet ascendancy as a world power and our own relative decline" at Yalta and Potsdam, and "the tragic weakness of our leaders reflected in their inability to rebuild our strength and restore our prestige, even after our commitment to war in Korea more than two years ago dramatically emphasized the inadequacy of our security preparation."

But it was an anticlimax after the drama of the joint session speech the year before. For once, he was ill at ease and seemed hesitant as the words poured out into the amphitheater and over the airwaves to eighteen million television viewers.

"That party of noble heritage"—meaning the Democrats—"has become captive to the schemers and planners who have infiltrated the ranks of leadership to set the national course unerringly toward the socialistic regimentation of a totalitarian state."[18]

Did he really believe it? It's hard to say—he was certainly more conservative in his domestic views than he had been when he left America in 1935, and his audience was more conservative as well. But the man who had brought sweeping top-down social and economic reforms to Japan in a progressive program that many had attacked as socialistic, made a strange prosecuting attorney against Truman's Democrats.

When he left the podium, there was applause—but hardly the thunderous ovation that had usually greeted him over the previous year. His political star had already faded; he was already a figure from the past rather than the future. Republicans were looking to new heroes to lead them. There was Joe McCarthy, "Tail-gunner Joe" and scourge of the Democrats' tolerance for Communists and crypto-Communists in their ranks; Robert Taft, the prophet of economic laissez-faire and cutting back on the New Deal welfare state; and now Dwight Eisenhower, whose entire presidential campaign that year hinged on a single promise: "I will go to Korea."

In the end, Eisenhower's solution to the Korean quagmire came ironically close to the one that MacArthur had proposed two years earlier, in December 1950. He let it be known that he was prepared to use nuclear weapons to break the deadlock on the battlefield. The Soviets got the message; the message got to both Mao and Kim Il Sung. By March 1953, UN and Communist forces agreed to an armistice, and the fighting was over. The war was not, however; no final peace treaty was ever signed, and American troops, 30,000 strong, continue to guard the border along the 38th parallel to this day.

When MacArthur heard the news of the Armistice, his worst fears were realized. Communism, and Red China, now had their secure foothold in East Asia; it would embolden, he believed, every Communist insurgency across the region, from Indochina and Vietnam to Malaya. Less than a year later would come the defeat of the French by Ho Chi Minh's forces at Dienbien Phu and the agreement at Geneva establishing yet another Communist government in Asia, this one headquartered in Hanoi. Ike's advisors warned him that Laos was next. The dominoes were starting to fall, even before anyone had used the term as a metaphor for Communist expansionism in Asia.

MacArthur had been thinking about these matters for many months when his friend John Dulles, then secretary of state designate, arranged a private meeting between Ike and MacArthur in New York City on December 17 to discuss what should be done about Korea.

"A successful solution to the problem of Korea involves political as well as military considerations," the former CINCFE wrote in a secret memo he prepared for Ike on the basis of their discussions. He noted the growing strength of North Korean and Chinese forces since his departure in April 1951: the growth of a Communist-led jet-powered air force prepared to challenge, if not actually overturn, American air superiority; growing artillery and motorized capacity on the part of the Chinese and their KPA allies; better communications on the battlefield.

In short, the advantages that United Nations forces had possessed when MacArthur had been in charge were slipping away. The issue, he now believed, could no longer be resolved on the battlefield (Ike was inclined to agree, as his subsequent bid for a cease-fire proved). Instead, he advocated cutting through the entire Gordian knot of East-West relations by proposing a head-to-head summit between Ike and Stalin. "To that end our consideration of the Korean problem should be broadened in the search of peace," he urged, not just in East Asia.

The proposal should include: the unification of both Germany and Korea by popular referendum, with the declaration of neutrality of both countries along with Japan and Austria (which was still occupied by Russian troops in 1952); withdrawal of all foreign forces from both Europe and East Asia, including U.S. forces in Japan; a mutual agreement between the United States and the Soviet Union to end war as an instrument of national policy.

If Stalin failed to agree to these terms, MacArthur wrote matter-of-factly, he should be told that the United States was prepared to use nuclear weapons "to clear North Korea of enemy forces"—and to "neutralize Red China's capacity to wage modern war," as well. America's advantage in nuclear weapons would fade fast, he warned Dulles and Eisenhower; it was time to use it for the best possible leverage—not just to end the war in Korea but to bring a peaceful end to war as an institution.[19]

Needless to say, Eisenhower did not take MacArthur's sweeping advice.

He did use America's nuclear leverage to end the fighting in Korea, but the larger goal of ending war altogether was not on his agenda, or anyone else's in the administration.

It was on MacArthur's, however. Perhaps surprisingly, over the next five years he would take up the cause of international disarmament with the passion of a new convert—albeit a strange one for a former five-star general. He told frequent audiences that "war has become a Frankenstein to destroy both sides" and "no longer is it the weapon of adventure whereby a short cut to international power and wealth—a place in the sun—can be gained." If you lose, you are annihilated. If you win, you stand only to lose later.

"The great question is," MacArthur told one such audience, the American Legion of Los Angeles, in 1955, "does this mean that war can now be outlawed from the world? If so, it would mark the greatest advance in civilization since the Sermon on the Mount."[20]

It was the inspiring, even quixotic, hope that would inspire his declining years, along with a passionate belief that America's cause in Asia was still not lost, in spite of Korea. It was a subject that he would hold forth on for anyone who cared to listen, and in April 1961 one of those listeners was John F. Kennedy.

The president was paying a courtesy call on the eighty-one-year-old MacArthur at his penthouse in the Waldorf Towers. Kennedy found himself spellbound. He later told his aides that the old general was one of the most fascinating conversationalists he'd ever met, "politically shrewd and intellectually sharp." In fact, their two-hour conversation was engaging enough that the pair became friends, with a later luncheon visit to the White House that lasted all afternoon.

"You're lucky to have that mistake happen in Cuba," the general said, referring to the abortive invasion at the Bay of Pigs, "where the strategic cost was not too great." He warned Kennedy not to make the same mistake in Asia, and above all in Vietnam. He reminded the president of the importance of Asia to America's future, and how the loss of China to Communism had been not only a betrayal of a wartime ally but a dramatic shift in the balance of world power.

He also warned him that American involvement in the growing conflict in Indochina would backfire, and advised against sending any troops to Vietnam. Neither Kennedy nor his successor Lyndon Johnson would heed MacArthur's parting words: "Anyone who gets in a land war in Asia should have his head examined." Certainly if anyone knew the bitter truth behind those words, it was MacArthur.

President Kennedy also provided MacArthur and his family with the plane that took him on his last trip to the Philippines in 1961, to commemorate the twentieth anniversary of Bataan and Corregidor. There MacArthur received the miles of cheering crowds and the unquestioning mass adulation from officials and the media that he had always craved from his fellow Americans but had never quite gotten. To Filipinos he was still a national hero without peer—and for the octogenarian MacArthur, that was now enough. "When I saw the happiness in their faces, as I saw the prosperity of the community," he wrote, "a great weight was lifted from my heart, and I thanked God that I was one of those who had helped them to freedom."

He returned home ill and frail, and when he went to West Point that next year to accept the academy's Sylvanus Thayer Award, many realized that it would be his final public appearance.

But not his last word. That would come in his memoirs, *Reminiscences*, which he would begin writing in October 1962 in a firm, confident hand on hundreds of legal pads (they survive, without a single crossing-out or erasure). It wasn't until he was finished, in August 1963, that MacArthur and publisher Henry Luce reached an agreement to publish seven installments in *Life* magazine, with the complete publication in book form, for a sum of $900,000.[21]

It seems strange that MacArthur hadn't written more about his life before.

He had, however, prepared the way with a two-volume work, *The MacArthur Record*, which he and Courtney Whitney organized as their own official history of the war in the Pacific after the United States Army's version proved disappointing and (they felt) unfairly critical of MacArthur's record, especially in the Philippines.

There is also every indication that Whitney's own biography of MacArthur was largely written by MacArthur himself—which goes a long way to explain why it resembles *Reminiscences* in many key passages.

The goal of *Reminiscences*, however, was neither self-vindication nor to supply information on his life that others had forgotten or left out. Indeed, what makes it fascinating reading is what MacArthur himself decided to omit (the events of his first marriage, for example, and his winning of the Medal of Honor).

Instead, the book was "merely my recollection of events," as MacArthur explained in the preface, many of which took place beyond the memory of many still living, so that "it may assist the future historian when he seeks to account for the motives and reasons which influenced some of the actions in the great drama of war."

The other audience, he stated, was "the rising generation, who may learn therefrom that a country and government such as ours is worth fighting and dying for, if need be."[22]

It was that rising generation that a bent and gaunt Douglas MacArthur met on the Plain at West Point on May 12, 1962, as he arrived to inspect the 2,200-strong Cadet Corps—more than twice the size of the Corps from the days when he had been superintendent. There to meet him was the current superintendent, who would go on to have his own controversial career: Major General William Westmoreland, later supreme commander in Vietnam—ironically, the very same ground war MacArthur had warned against.

As he walked down the aisle of Washington Hall, leaning on Jean's arm, with the cadets standing at attention on every side, it must have seemed as filled with ghosts as with young cadets. Ghosts of the cadets with whom he had served as upperclassmen and the cadets he had commanded as superintendent; of the soldiers he had commanded in the Rainbow Division at Côte de Châtillon and a dozen other battles; of soldiers on Bataan and then at Buna, Leyte, and Luzon; at Pusan and Inchon and Taekon; the ghosts of Pershing and Peyton March and Frank Funston; the ghosts of his mother and father.

In a low but steady voice, he told the young cadets of their illustrious past, their confident present, and their boundless future as officers in the United States Army.

"The long gray line has never failed us," he said.

> Were you to do so, a million ghosts in olive drab, in brown khaki, in blue and gray, would rise from their white crosses, thundering those magic words: Duty, Honor, Country. This does not mean that you are war mongers. On the contrary, the soldier above all other people prays for peace, for he must suffer and bear the deepest wounds and scars of war. But always in our ears ring the ominous words of Plato, that wisest of all philosophers: "Only

the dead have seen the end of war." The shadows are lengthening for me. The twilight is here. My days of old have vanished—tone and tint. . . . In my dreams I hear again the crash of guns, the rattle of musketry, the strange, mournful mutter of the battlefield.

But in the evening of my memory I come back to West Point. Always there echoes and reechoes; Duty, Honor, Country.

He looked around the hall. In the words of one eyewitness, "there were tears in the eyes of big strapping Cadets who wouldn't have shed one before a firing squad."[23]

"Today marks my final roll call with you," he concluded. "But I want you to know that when I cross the river my last conscious thoughts will be of the Corps—and the Corps—and the Corps. I bid you farewell."

On April 5, 1964, he did indeed cross the river, at Walter Reed Hospital.

Having been born in one military hospital, he died in another, as America's warrior lost his final battle.

CONCLUSION

Your guidepost stands out like a tenfold
beacon in the night: Duty, Honor, Country.

—DOUGLAS MACARTHUR TO
WEST POINT CADETS, MAY 12, 1962

For Filipinos and Japanese, MacArthur's death was a day of national mourning. His state funeral in Washington, D.C., on April 8 and 9 was as grand and solemn as any president's, with 150,000 people filing past his bier as it lay in state in the Capitol Rotunda before traveling to Norfolk, Virginia, for final burial. When Jean died in 2000, at age one hundred and one, she was laid to rest beside him, the couple together again at last.

Among the many tributes to pour in in 1964 was, ironically but fittingly, MacArthur's own to himself. His *Reminiscences* was published just months after his death. Although the book was an instant bestseller, the reaction from critics and historians was largely negative. The title of the review in *Harper's* was "Egoist in Uniform." In it the reviewer concluded, "He was always his worst enemy, and his autobiography will add nothing to his reputation. He should be remembered by his deeds, not his words."

But would he be?

The great figures in history live on as legends, which historians and biographers revisit from time to time. Sometimes they bring new evidence to light that forces a reexamination of why he or she made some important decision, or chose to ignore a crucial factor that might have influenced that same decision, for better or worse. But more often they bring their own prejudices and assumptions to the subject, which enables them to rewrite the legend in a new positive or negative light.

Washington, Lincoln, Theodore Roosevelt, Franklin Roosevelt, Winston Churchill, Napoleon, even MacArthur's nemesis Harry Truman: all have gone through this reexamination process. Certainly MacArthur belongs in that exalted company; but how have historians dealt with his legend, and how has the making of the legend obscured the truth, and the man, underneath?

In 1945 the MacArthur legend was of a storybook hero and military genius who towered over America's other living war leaders, almost over the memory of FDR himself. It was a legend largely manufactured by the press during the crisis in the Philippines, and not a little by MacArthur himself. Of course it ignored certain mistakes, blunders even, that MacArthur had made during that campaign, and mistakes later in New Guinea as well as during the retaking of the Philippines. It also discounted the contributions made by others, such as George Kenney and Daniel Barbey, to MacArthur's success. Yet it also sustained the nation during one of its darkest times, in the months following Pearl Harbor. As the war proceeded, the MacArthur legend only gathered strength until when war broke out again in June 1950, America saw him as the obvious choice to reverse the tide of battle and bring its forces to victory once again—not only once but twice when the Communist Chinese unexpectedly intervened.

Then in April 1951 something happened that shook that legend to its foundations. America's greatest war hero found himself dismissed by America's least popular president, in the midst of a war that most Americans believed could turn global at any time, and at the high tide of a campaign that seemed on the brink of final victory. Truman and his supporters needed to show that firing MacArthur was not only desirable but inevitable, that the general had brought this on himself, and that his reckless actions had endangered not only the course of the war in Korea but the nation itself.

And so, almost from the moment he was dismissed from command in Korea, the attacks on his reputation began, the goal being to justify both President Truman's action and the Truman policy in Korea. Works like *The General and the President*, coauthored by Democratic Party stalwarts Richard Rovere and Arthur Schlesinger, propounded the dubious thesis that

MacArthur's behavior in Korea constituted not only an attack on the principle of civilian leadership over the military but even an attack on the Constitution itself. They also raked over his record in World War Two, looking for ways to imply that recklessness, misjudgment, and incompetence were the hallmarks of MacArthur's entire career. The "Dugout Doug" myth took hold once again, as did the "man on a white horse" charging the Bonus Marchers. The story of his escape from Corregidor in the dead of night became embellished until it seemed he had left his command almost in defiance of the president's orders, instead of in obedience to them—and the bitterness that many Bataan veterans felt toward what they saw as an act of betrayal and cowardice became the narrative that explained MacArthur's actions from the moment bombs fell on Clark Field.

As time went on, historians like Stanley Falk and Gavin Long came to question virtually every decision MacArthur made in World War Two, including the decision to liberate the Philippines at all. The myth that his dramatic splashing ashore on Leyte was staged, even rehearsed, became so widely accepted as fact that the MacArthur Memorial had to publish a short book refuting it. I have even been asked if it's true that the reason MacArthur chose to land first at Leyte rather than Luzon was that he had a mistress living in Tacloban.

Then came attacks on MacArthur's record in the American occupation of Japan by Cold War revisionist historians like Michael Schaller, who cast "the American shogun" as an arrogant autocrat more obsessed with battling Communists and left-wingers than with building a democratic Japan. In the aftermath of Vietnam, MacArthur's reputation as commander in Korea sank to new lows, as well, as every move he made—including Inchon—was largely dismissed as either incompetent, ill-conceived, or (as in his refusal to take the possibility of massive Chinese intervention seriously) divorced from reality. Even otherwise sympathetic biographers like Clayton James and William Manchester were affected by the negative consensus. Both would treat MacArthur's war in Korea as the nadir of his career, and his famous speech to the joint session of Congress as a matter of embarrassment rather than triumph.

By the 2000s the impulse to debunk the MacArthur legend would even include questioning his record in World War One, with historians hinting that the cluster of medals he carried away from that conflict owed more to old-boy-network connections than to actual skill or valor on the battlefield.[1]

That cumulative negative judgment is not only unfair but distorting of his larger significance both as military leader and as American hero. In the end, the flaws that detractors pointed out sprang from the same larger-than-life frame as the virtues that admirers celebrated. The same man who could make some of the most monstrous mistakes in the history of American arms was also capable of some of the most inspired. The man whose vanity and thirst for adulation knew almost no bounds was also capable of touching acts of charity, and unshakable courage under fire.

His spectacular successes were always haunted by his equally spectacular failures, while the sacrifices he imposed on his soldiers would be questioned and requestioned even during his lifetime. Some would never forgive him, including many in his profession. Indeed, in many ways, the American military tradition since the Korean War has involved a conscious turning away from the MacArthur model of leadership: that of the charismatic, even glamorous, supreme commander, aloof and all-knowing, who demands unquestioned obedience from his men and unlimited freedom of action from his superiors, including his commander in chief. It's a Napoleonic model that MacArthur shared with George Patton as well as George Pershing and his own father. It's one that accepts casualties as inevitable and high casualties as sometimes necessary; it sees a soldier's primary role as fighting and killing the enemy, not winning hearts and minds—at least, as in MacArthur's experience with Japan, until the fighting is over and the enemy has lost.

Above all, it is a military tradition that resolutely refuses to embrace any war strategy that does not include a plan for final victory. The post-MacArthur military has proven more willing to operate without that precondition, despite the so-called Powell Doctrine; it's certainly more mindful of minimizing combat deaths, both the enemy's and its own. Yet after the experiences of Vietnam, Iraq, and Afghanistan, it seems debatable whether the U.S. military, and the world, is truly better off for rejecting the MacArthur model— not to mention the example of today's Korean peninsula, where soldiers are still occasionally killed along the DMZ and the threat of North Korean nuclear-armed ballistic missiles hangs over all of East Asia.

MacArthur's reputation as a war leader has suffered, compared to men he thought of, and often treated, as junior subordinates, such as Marshall and Eisenhower and Ridgway. Even his success at Inchon is more often treated as a matter of luck than brilliant vision and flawless operational planning. Nonetheless, the most trenchant chronicler of MacArthur's military mistakes, Australian historian Gavin Long, has had to acknowledge MacArthur's "courage, his patriotism, his ability to inspire his subordinates and others," including Australians and his fellow Americans in 1942, and millions of Filipinos, Japanese, Koreans, and other Asian nations during and after World War Two. And no one ever doubted his sense of duty to flag, service, and country—although in the end it led him to challenge a sitting president to a duel of wills, and to trigger what seemed to be a political crisis in the midst of war.

Probably nothing has contributed as much to the decline of MacArthur's reputation as his confrontation with Truman over Korea—a confrontation that has been as much misrepresented by historians, even military historians, as it has been misunderstood. As we have seen, there is very little in MacArthur's actions that can be characterized as deliberate disobedience, let alone a challenge to civilian leadership of the military.* At the very most, MacArthur can be accused of insubordination: publicly criticizing a policy and strategy *he was actually carrying out* even though he thought it (to paraphrase Omar Bradley) the wrong strategy at the wrong time in the wrong war. Yet the reaction from the White House, which had seen him proven more right than wrong throughout the Korean conflict, was one of rage, even panic.

The turning point should have been the meeting between MacArthur and Truman at Wake in October 1950. It should have been the moment when both men could put aside their separate agendas and find a way to communicate more directly on what really mattered: how to win in Korea. Instead, both men—and here MacArthur is as much to blame as Truman—looked for ways to score off the other, and to express their mutual distrust (twenty years later, Truman was still at it, with his disingenuous version of what happened,

---

* The closest MacArthur came to contradicting declared policy was in his March 21 directive offering to meet with his Chinese counterpart to arrange an end to the fighting. Yet as he states in his memoirs, he drew up the memorandum before he learned that there was another peace plan in the offing—one that his March 21 communication supposedly disrupted (no evidence, incidentally, currently supports that latter contention).

and what they said to each other, in Merle Miller's *Plain Speaking*). The result was a tragedy, not just for America but for Korea and East Asia. The meeting at Wake ranks as one of the great missed opportunities in history.

Yet even after Wake, the possibility of coordination, if not cooperation, between Washington and Tokyo GHQ still loomed. But instead, Washington was prepared to fire MacArthur and was looking for an excuse to do so—just as MacArthur, we now know, had braced himself to be dismissed. The White House found the excuse it was looking for, with Congressman Martin's release of a letter that had been a private communication, and which MacArthur neither knew about nor had endorsed. But in the end these were irrelevant trifles. The Republican congressman's action was merely a pretext, first for a Truman administration eager to rid itself of a general whose presence reminded everyone of strategic decisions that, in hindsight, looked foolhardy; and for a general who sensed he had nothing left to contribute and for whom it was, as he remarked to Jean, time to go home.

Nonetheless, in the long view, for all his faults and his virtues, both as a soldier and warrior, MacArthur has to stand apart. No one served his country longer as a military commander, and certainly none loved his profession and its way of life more. It is safe to say that MacArthur's life transcended the profession in which he served. Of all Americans, only Franklin Roosevelt left so personal a stamp on the history of the twentieth century—and none over so many years, including in three global conflicts. Taken as a whole, the only other world figure who begins to compare is his distant cousin, Winston Churchill. Both men shared many of the same virtues and many of the same faults, including a willingness to take risks that nearly torpedoed both men's careers. Indeed, without Truman's dismissal, MacArthur's name might loom as large in history as Churchill's—just as, if one or two events in 1940 had turned out differently, an entire publishing industry of Churchill hero worship might not exist.

In sum, MacArthur's life reveals three aspects of the man that stand out from the legend and require acknowledgment.

The first is the degree to which Douglas MacArthur's story was also his father's. Arthur MacArthur was not only the mentor and personal inspiration for his son's career. The old general's basic stance on how to win wars and then win the peace; how to uphold the values of duty, honor, and country; and how America's destiny lay westward to the Pacific and Asia, all underlay Douglas MacArthur's most fundamental beliefs and attitudes.

The second is the degree to which his life was decisively shaped by the women in his life, beginning with his mother. Mary Hardy, Louise Brooks, Jean Faircloth, even Isabel Rosario Cooper: all revealed different aspects of the inner man that he otherwise kept hidden from view. The self-doubting son, the chivalrous romantic lover, the spouse in need of unconditional love and support: these were the other sides of Douglas MacArthur that the women in his life exposed to view, if only in private.

He was not the first famous general who appeared so stern and impervious in the presence of other men, but was in fact the most comfortable and relaxed, even vulnerable, in the presence of women. England's Duke of Wellington, Horatio Nelson, and even Andrew Jackson shared the same characteristic. It was in fact, perhaps, a part of MacArthur's Victorian nineteenth-century temperament—and one which modern biographers find the most baffling but which, in many ways, is the easiest to understand and even admire. It would even surface in his pride in what he considered the most important of all his reforms in Japan: securing the vote for women.

The third was MacArthur's brilliance as a grand strategist—perhaps the most incisive the American military has ever produced. As a general and military commander, he had peers, even superiors. But as a thinker about the purpose of war, and the conduct of the strategy underlying America's military campaigns from World War One to Korea and beyond, it's hard to point to an equal. Some may disagree with the conclusions MacArthur came to, as with his Pacific-first strategy in World War Two and on the Cold War and Korea. As a combination of vision, intellectual reach, and innovative thinking, however, they are unique.

It was MacArthur who pioneered the concept of all-arms combined operations in World War Two; who showed how to coordinate ground operations with an overall maritime strategy in the Pacific; and who illustrated how to transform a war-fighting army into a peacekeeping force in postwar Japan. Above all, it was MacArthur's belief that "there is no substitute for victory" that persists as the most basic lesson in the history of American warfare—although too often it has proved the hardest for politicians to absorb.

Indeed, the great debate that MacArthur launched during the war in Korea, on what constitutes victory and why, persists to this day. So does his belief in the future of Asia and America's role in that part of the world.

"Today we stand on the threshold of a new life," MacArthur once told an audience soon after he returned from Korea. "Its limits are as broad as the spirit and imagination of man."[2] As soldier, statesman, and supreme commander, MacArthur's lifelong goal had been to secure that future, both for America and for its allies. In its pursuit, MacArthur's actions were never immune from criticism, but no one can doubt that his motives were always noble.

ACKNOWLEDGMENTS

M y thanks go to the MacArthur Memorial Archives in Norfolk, Virginia, especially its archivist, James Zobel, and its director, William Davis. Jim Zobel not only patiently pulled boxes of files and hunted down rare photographs, but was a sure and shrewd guide to the many treasures lurking in the archive shelves—and to understanding Douglas MacArthur as a soldier and as a man. Conversations with Bill Davis helped me to gain additional perspective on the career of someone who led and shaped the United States Army in not one but three wars, and if the U.S. Marine Corps doesn't appear in this book as often as it should, I know Lieutenant Colonel William Davis, USMC (retired), will understand.

Thanks are also due to the staffs of the following libraries: the Library of Congress; the National Archives in College Park, Maryland; the Library of New South Wales in Sydney, Australia; the Franklin D. Roosevelt Presidential Library; the Harry S. Truman Presidential Library; the United States Army Historical Center in Carlisle, Pennsylvania; and the libraries of the University of Virginia, Virginia Commonwealth University, the Virginia Military Institute, and the Cosmos Club.

I'd also like to thank my colleagues at the Hudson Institute, who were fully supportive as I completed work on the manuscript, who cheerfully listened as I discoursed on various aspects of MacArthur's career, and who offered useful suggestions and insights that have made their way into the final book. Hudson Institute President Kenneth Weinstein; John B. Walters, Christopher DeMuth, Lewis Libby, William Schneider, William Luti, Seth Cropsey, John Lee; Ambassador Hussein Haqqani; John Fonte, and everyone else: It's impossible to imagine a better set of friends and intellectual companions. In addition, my research assistant, Idalia Friedson, provided invaluable help with the book's maps and photographs.

Two other figures deserve special mention for having had a decisive impact on the shaping of the book and its themes. One is Kenneth Drea, who has given every MacArthur scholar fresh perspective on the role of intelligence-gathering for understanding MacArthur's strategy in World War Two. The other is Henry Kissinger, who decisively shaped my thinking about the issues surrounding MacArthur's dismissal in April 1951, and who has encouraged my work on the theme of military versus civilian leadership in America's land wars in Asia in ways that have left a permanent imprint on this book.

The list of friends with whom I discussed key aspects of the book, historians who selflessly offered help and advice, eyewitnesses to key events in the book with whom I had the privilege to speak, and others who encouraged me to write this book the way I wanted to write it, is really too long to include here, but I can mention a few who stand out: Andrew Roberts, Richard Frank, Carlo D'Este, Walter Borneman; Mark J. Reed, Ivor Tiefenbrun, Sacha Jensen, Alex Pollock, Keith Urbahn, Matt Latimer, Bob Brown, Al Haig, Philip Anns, Brandt Pasco, Farhad Jalinous, Yoshihisa Komorio of the Sankei Shimbun, Toshiyuki Hayakawa of the Sekai Nippo, Seiichiro Mishima of Nikkei Asian Review, Kyosuke Matsumoto, President of Asian Forum Japan; Kin-Ichi Yoshihara, Ambassador Kenichiro Sasae, and prime minister Shinzo Abe of Japan.

Thanks also go to my editor, Molly Turpin, and the production staff at Random House, especially Dennis Ambrose, for their persistence and patience in seeing this book to execution, and to my parents, Arthur and Barbara Herman.

Finally, my greatest debt is to my wife, Beth, who endured three years of MacArthur madness, including changes of editor and agent. You have been my rod and staff, the true love of my life. Thank you, honey; the dedication says it all.

NOTES

CHAPTER 1: SON OF THE FATHER

1. Kenneth Ray Young, *The General's General: The Life and Times of Arthur MacArthur* (Boulder, CO: Westview Press, 1994), 4–5.
2. "Proceedings Attending the Reception and Banquet to Major General Arthur MacArthur," quoted in Young, 87.
3. United States War Department, *The War of the Rebellion: A Compilation of the Official Records of the Union and Confederate Armies* (Washington, D.C., 1880–1901), 38:327–30.
4. Young, 109.
5. Quoted in Young, 97.
6. Record Group 94, MacArthur Memorial Archives (cited henceforth as MMA), Letters Adjutant General to MacArthur, August 6, 8, 12, 1866; September 20, 1866.
7. Office of the Center for Military History, 228.03 Permanent HRC File, Arthur MacArthur.
8. Douglas MacArthur, *Reminiscences* (New York: McGraw-Hill, 1964), 12.
9. MMA RG 94, National Archives, Document File, Officers Individual Report from May 1, 1890; quoted in Young, 127.
10. *Reminiscences*, 13.
11. Young, 130–31.
12. *Reminiscences*, 14.
13. Young, 138.
14. Young, 140.
15. W. N. Chambers, *Old Bullion Benton, Senator from the New West* (Boston: Little Brown, 1956), 353.
16. Robert S. Thompson, *Empires in the Pacific: World War II and the Struggle for the Mastery of Asia* (New York: Basic Books, 2001).
17. Quoted in *Stars and Stripes*, "Remembering U.S. Grant's Visit to Japan," April 8, 2004.
18. Letter to Badeau, quoted in Joan Waugh, *U.S. Grant: American Hero, American Myth* (Chapel Hill: University of North Carolina Press, 2009), 161.

19. J. F. Packard, *Grant's Tour Around the World* (Cincinnati, OH: Forshee & McMakin, 1880), 756.
20. Packard, 756.
21. Young, 143.
22. "Chinese Memorandum" and Notes [1882], MMA, RG 20, Microfilm Collection, 6–8.
23. Memorandum, 13.
24. Memorandum, 18.
25. Memorandum, 22, 25.
26. Young, 144.

CHAPTER 2: TURNING POINTS

1. Young, *General's General*, 145.
2. Carol Morris Petillo, *Douglas MacArthur: The Philippine Years* (Bloomington: Indiana State University Press, 1981), 14–15.
3. *Reminiscences*, 14.
4. Quoted in Petillo, 18–19.
5. *Reminiscences*, 15, 16.
6. Petillo, 254, n. 27.
7. *Reminiscences*, 3, 4, 8.
8. Young, 161–62.
9. Quoted in D. Clayton James, *The Years of MacArthur*, Vol. 1, *1880–1941* (Boston: Houghton Mifflin, 1970), 29.
10. *Reminiscences*, 16–17.
11. James I, 58; "West Texas Academy," Wikipedia.
12. *Reminiscences*, 17; James I, 60.
13. James I, 60.
14. James I, 61.
15. Allen Burlsen to AG, June 1, 1898, Record Group 94, National Archives, Adjutant General's Office (AGO)-DF 38122; quoted in James I, 60.
16. Young, 168.
17. *Reminiscences*, 18.
18. Frazier Hunt, *The Untold Story of Douglas MacArthur* (New York: Devin-Adair Company, 1954), 18.
19. James I, 63.
20. James I, 64.
21. James I, 65.
22. Hyman Rickover, *How the Battleship Maine Was Destroyed* (Annapolis, MD: Naval Institute Press, 1994); Edward Marolda, ed., *Theodore Roosevelt, the United States Navy, and the Spanish American War* (London: Palgrave, 2001).
23. E.g., Geoffrey Perret, *Old Soldiers Never Die: The Life of Douglas MacArthur* (New York: Random House, 1996), 25.
24. A. Beveridge, "The March of the Flag," September 1898.
25. Young, 175; James I, 30–31.
26. Max Boot, *America's Savage Wars of Peace: Small Wars and the Rise of American Power* (New York: Basic Books, 2002), 103.
27. Young, 178.
28. *Reminiscences*, 18.
29. *Reminiscences*, 18; James I, 67–68.
30. Hunt, 18.
31. Hugh Johnson, *The Blue Eagle from Egg to Earth* (Garden City, NY: Doubleday, Doran 1935), 24–25.
32. William Manchester, *American Caesar* (Boston: Little, Brown, 1978), 62.
33. James I, 67–68.

CHAPTER 3: GLORY DAYS

1. Jesse George, *Our Army and Navy in the Orient, Giving a Full Account of the Operations of the Army and Navy in the Philippines* (Manila, 1899), 54.
2. Boot, *America's Savage Wars*, 104.
3. Young, *General's General*, 200.
4. Quoted in Margaret Leech, *In the Days of McKinley* (1956; Westport, CT: Greenwood Press, 1975), 345.
5. Fredrick Funston, *Memories of Two Wars* (1911; Lincoln: University of Nebraska Press, 2009), 177–78.
6. Wood, "An Upperclassman's View," *Assembly* 23 (Spring 1964).
7. James I, 70; Perret, *Old Soldiers*, 33.
8. Hunt, *Untold Story*, 25.
9. James I, 70.
10. *Reminiscences*, 25.
11. Stanley Karnow, *In Our Image: America's Empire in the Philippines* (New York: Random House, 1989).
12. Quoted in Gates, *Schoolbooks and Krags: The United States Army in the Philippines, 1898–1902* (Westport, CT: Greenwood, 1973), 198.
13. Young, 257.
14. Brian Linn, *U.S. Army and Counterinsurgency in the Philippine Wars, 1899–1902* (Chapel Hill: University of North Carolina Press, 1989); Young, 263.
15. Mark Moyar, *A Question of Command: Counterinsurgency from the Civil War to Iraq* (New Haven, CT: Yale University Press, 2010).
16. Young, 263.
17. Boot, 116.
18. Boot, 119; Young, 288.
19. *Reminiscences*, 25–26.
20. *Reminiscences*, 26.
21. Hunt, 22–23.
22. Donald Smythe, *Guerrilla Warrior: The Early Life of John J. Pershing* (New York: Scribners, 1973), 13; Perret, 31.
23. Hunt, 31.
24. Hunt, 31.
25. Quoted in Hunt, 33.
26. James I, 72, 74.
27. Perret, 34–35.
28. Perret, 39.
29. *Reminiscences*, 26.
30. Quoted in Boot, 116.
31. Petillo, 55–56; Young, 302.
32. *Official Register of Officers and Cadets of the United States Military Academy*, June 1903 (Washington, D.C.: Government Printing Office, 1903), 10; James I, 77–78.
33. Perret, 43; James I, 77.
34. Hunt, 27.
35. Arthur Hyde, "Douglas MacArthur," *Assembly* I (October 1942), 3; Hyde, "MacArthur—His Barracks Mate Reminisces," *Hudson Views* (1964).
36. Quoted in Petillo, 37.
37. Douglas MacArthur, *A Soldier Speaks: Public Papers and Speeches of General of the Army Douglas MacArthur* (New York: Praeger, 1965), 358.

CHAPTER 4: YOUNG MAN GOING EAST

1. *Reminiscences*, 28.
2. *Reminiscences*, 29.

3. Arthur Herman, *Gandhi & Churchill: The Epic Rivalry That Destroyed an Empire and Forged Our Age* (New York: Ballantine Books, 2008), *l.*
4. John Hersey, *Men on Bataan* (New York: Alfred A. Knopf, 1942), 76.
5. Theodore Friend, *Between Two Empires: The Ordeal of the Philippines 1929–1946* (New Haven: Yale University Press, 1965), 264.
6. *Reminiscences,* 29.
7. Hunt, *Untold Story,* 37.
8. MacArthur to COS, National Archives; quoted in Perret, *Old Soldiers,* 51.
9. Frank Vandiver, *Black Jack: The Life and Times of John J. Pershing* (College Station: Texas A&M University Press, 1977) vol. 1. See also Pershing Papers, Library of Congress, Military Attaché, box 324.
10. Young, *General's General,* 318.
11. Yuki Tanaka, *Hidden Horrors: Japanese War Crimes in World War II* (Boulder, CO: Westview Press, 1996), 72–73.
12. Young, 319.
13. *Reminiscences,* 30–31.
14. Quoted in Mark Perry, *The Most Dangerous Man in America: The Making of Douglas MacArthur* (New York: Basic Books, 2015), 137.
15. *Reminiscences,* 31.
16. Documents relating to the tour, including itinerary, can be found MMA, RG 30.
17. *Reminiscences,* 32; Young, 323.
18. James, *Years of MacArthur* I, 92.
19. Young, 325; James I, 93.
20. *Reminiscences,* 32.
21. Young, 326.
22. Petillo, *Douglas MacArthur,* 92.
23. *Reminiscences,* 32.
24. Young, 327.
25. James I, 94.
26. Petillo, 96–97; James I, 94.
27. *Reminiscences,* 32.
28. James I, 95.
29. *Reminiscences,* 33.
30. Quoted in Petillo, 101.
31. James I, 100–101.
32. Petillo, 102.
33. The handwritten poems are in MMA, RG 15; Petillo, 103–4.
34. Manchester, *American Caesar,* 83.
35. *Reminiscences,* 35.
36. John Gunther, *The Riddle of MacArthur: Japan, Korea, and the Far East* (New York: Harper, 1951), 32–33.

CHAPTER 5: COUNTDOWN TO WAR

1. Young, *General's General,* 338.
2. Young, 331; James, *Years of MacArthur* I, 42–43.
3. William J. K. Beaudot, *The 24th Wisconsin Infantry in the Civil War: The Biography of a Regiment* (Mechanicsburg, PA: Stackpole Books, 2003), 7.
4. Beaudot, 6.
5. Beaudot, 7–8.
6. Young, 340.
7. *Reminiscences,* 36.
8. Young, 340–41.
9. Petillo, *Douglas MacArthur,* 110.

10. James I, 108–9.
11. *Reminiscences,* 39.
12. The best account is still Robert Quirk, *An Affair of Honor: Woodrow Wilson and the Occupation of Veracruz* (New York: Norton, 1967).
13. James I, 116.
14. *Reminiscences,* 40.
15. James I, 117.
16. James I, 118.
17. National Archives, RG 94, War Diary Brig. Gen. Frederick Funston, May 3, 1914.
18. James I, 118.
19. Hunt, *Untold Story,* 54; *Reminiscences,* 41. Hunt's version of MacArthur's report omits the reference to the Bible.
20. *Reminiscences,* 41.
21. Hunt, 54; *Reminiscences,* 41.
22. Hunt, 56; *Reminiscences,* 42.
23. Letter Cordier to Wood, quoted in James I, 120; also in Hunt, 51.
24. James I, 123.
25. Funston to AG, January 13, 1915, in James I, 123–24.
26. James I, 125.
27. Quotations are from Petillo, 114–15.
28. James I, 129.
29. James I, 129–30.
30. Diana Preston, *Lusitania: An Epic Tragedy* (New York: Berkeley, 2003).
31. James I, 130.
32. *Reminiscences,* 43.
33. See Jack McCallum, *Leonard Wood: Rough Rider, Surgeon, Architect of American Imperialism* (New York: NYU Press, 2005).
34. R. Ernest Dupuy, *Men of West Point: The First 150 Years of the United States Military Academy* (New York: Sloane, 1951), 131; James I, 131.
35. Perret, *Old Soldiers,* 74. John Buchan, *John MacNab* (Boston: Houghton Mifflin, 1925), 103.
36. Hunt, 62–63.
37. Arthur Herman, *To Rule the Waves: How the British Navy Shaped the Modern World* (New York: HarperCollins, 2004), 511.
38. *Reminiscences,* 46–47.
39. *Reminiscences,* 45.
40. MMA, RG 14, Box 4, E. K. Wright interview, 43.
41. Henry J. Reilly, *Americans All: The Rainbow at War. The Official History of the 42nd Rainbow Division in the Great War* (Columbus, OH: F. J. Heer, 1936), 26.
42. Reilly, Introduction; *Reminiscences,* 46.
43. *Reminiscences,* 46.
44. Francis X. Duffy, *Father Duffy's Story* (New York: George Doran, 1919), 17–18.
45. 42nd Division: Summary of Operations in the World War (Washington, D.C.: GPO, 1944), 1–2.
46. James I, 140.
47. Quoted in James I, 142.
48. MMA, Wright interview, 31.
49. *Reminiscences,* 51–52.
50. James I, 143–44.
51. Manchester, *American Caesar,* 91.

CHAPTER 6: INTO THE FIRE

1. James, *Years of MacArthur* I, 149.
2. *Reminiscences,* 53.

3. Reilly, *Americans All,* 99.
4. C of S, AEF, to CINC, AEF, November 25, 1917, *The United States Army in the World War, 1917–1919* (Washington DC: Center for Military History, 1988), 669–70.
5. *Reminiscences,* 53.
6. Walter Wolf, *A Brief Story of the Rainbow Division* (New York: Rand McNally, 1919), 8–10.
7. MMA, RG 26 DM 201 File, Efficiency Report, August 28, 1919.
8. Albert Ettinger, *A Doughboy with the Fighting Sixty-Ninth: A Remembrance of World War I* (New York: Pocket Books, 1993) 101–2, 135.
9. MMA, RG 12, World War One photo album.
10. Hersey, *Men on Bataan,* 114.
11. *Reminiscences,* 54.
12. Quoted in Anthony Cave Brown, *The Last Hero: Wild Bill Donovan* (New York: Times Books, 1982), 44.
13. *Reminiscences,* 54.
14. *Reminiscences,* 54; James I, 157.
15. Ogden Diary, quoted in Perret, *Old Soldiers,* 84.
16. MMA, RG 26, DM 201 File.
17. For details, see J. A. Swisher, *MacArthur and Iowa Troops* (Iowa City, 1942).
18. *Reminiscences,* 55.
19. *Reminiscences,* 55–56.
20. John Taber, *The Story of the 168th Infantry* (Iowa City: State Historical Society of Iowa, 1925), 1:126.
21. Quoted in Perret, 84.
22. Boyle to DM, May 31, MMA, RG 10.
23. Ettinger, 92.
24. Mary Hardy MacArthur to Pershing, James I, 160.
25. James I, 160.
26. John Keegan, *The First World War* (New York: Alfred A. Knopf, 1999), 396.
27. James I, 161.
28. *Reminiscences,* 56; James I, 165.
29. James I, 165.
30. Reilly, Introduction.
31. Hunt, *Untold Story,* 74–75.
32. Mary Hardy MacArthur to Pershing, James I, 171.
33. Mary Hardy MacArthur to Pershing, James I, 169–71.
34. Perret, 93–94.
35. Duffy, *Father Duffy's Story,* 119–20.
36. Keegan, 408.
37. James I, 177.
38. Duffy, 130.
39. Reilly, 253.
40. *Reminiscences,* 181.
41. Reilly, 255–56.
42. *Reminiscences,* 58.
43. James I, 180.
44. James I, 178.
45. James I, 180.
46. *Reminiscences,* 58.

CHAPTER 7: FIGHT TO THE FINISH

1. MMA, RG 15, General Order No. 48, July 20, 1918.
2. Reilly, *Americans All,* 323.
3. Letter, William Donovan to Ruth Donovan, August 7, 1918, in Brown, *The Last Hero,* 49.

4. MMA RG 15, Box 13, Summary of Intelligence 113, July 27–28, 1918, Second Section, General Staff, 42nd Division, AEF.
5. Reilly, 333.
6. *Reminiscences,* 59.
7. Letter, William to Ruth Donovan, August 7, 1918, in Brown, 52.
8. Cooke, *The Rainbow Division,* 133.
9. MMA RG 15, Box 13, Intelligence Bulletin 115, Second Section etc., July 29–30, 1918.
10. Letter, William to Ruth Donovan, August 7, 1918, in Brown, 54.
11. *Reminiscences,* 60.
12. Duffy, *Father Duffy's Story,* 205–6.
13. *Reminiscences,* 61.
14. MMA, RG 26, DM 201 File, Menoher evaluation report, October 30, 1918.
15. Quoted in James, *Years of MacArthur* I, 190.
16. Brown, 55; James I, 191.
17. James I, 195.
18. James I, 196–97.
19. Hunt, *Untold Story,* 85.
20. Robert Ferrell, *America's Deadliest Battle: Meuse-Argonne, 1918* (Lawrence: University of Kansas Press, 2007), 35.
21. Reilly, .
22. Quoted in James I, 202.
23. George S. Patton to his wife, September 20, 1918, quoted in Carlo D'Este, *Patton: A Genius for War* (New York: HarperCollins, 1995), 236.
24. Hunt, 84; *Reminiscences,* 63.
25. George C. Kenney, *The MacArthur I Know* (New York: Duell, Sloane and Pearce, 1951), 17.
26. Ferrell, *Deadliest Battle,* 35.
27. *Reminiscences,* 64.
28. Ferrell, *Deadliest Battle,* 36–37.
29. Ferrell, *Deadliest Battle,* 31–32.
30. Quoted in James I, 211.
31. Ferrell, *Deadliest Battle,* 75–78.
32. Hunt, 96.
33. *Reminiscences,* 70.
34. *Reminiscences,* 66.
35. Hunt, 88–89.
36. Brown, 63.
37. American Battle Monuments Commission, *42nd Division: Summary of Operations in the World War* (Washington DC: Government Printing Office, 1944), 59; Robert Ferrell, *The Question of MacArthur's Reputation: Côte de Châtillon, October 14–16, 1918* (Columbia: University of Missouri Press, 2008), 47–48.
38. 42nd Historical, RG 120, Box 11, Entry 1241.
39. Reilly, 680–81.
40. Ferrell, *Question of Reputation,* 49.
41. Reilly, 679.
42. *Reminiscences,* 66.
43. William Ganoe, *MacArthur Close-up* (New York: Vantage, 1962), 143–44.
44. Hunt, 89.
45. *Reminiscences,* 67; account by Lieut. Royal Little, Company K, 167th Infantry, in MMA,RG 615, Box 75.
46. Ferrell, *Deadliest Battle,* 108.
47. *Reminiscences,* 67.
48. Perret, *Old Soldiers,* 107.
49. Ferrell, *Question of Reputation*; James I, 223.

50. MMA, RG 26, DM 201 File, Menoher's description of the battle for Côte de Châtillon, dated October 26, 1918.
51. Hunt, 84.
52. MMA, RG 26, DM 201 File, deposition.
53. Perret, 109.
54. *Reminiscences*, 67.
55. James I, 224.
56. Reilly, 747; James I, 224.
57. Hunter Liggett, *A.E.F.: Ten Years Ago in France* (New York: Dodd, Mead, 1928), 227.
58. *Reminiscences*, 68.
59. Liggett, 228; James I, 231.
60. Reilly, 800; James I, 232.
61. Reilly, 800; *Reminiscences*, 69.
62. Hunt, 93–94.
63. Bulletin of Information 21, November 18, 1918, MMA, RG 15, Box 75.
64. Perret, 110–11.
65. George Clark, *The American Expeditionary Force in World War I: A Statistical History* (Jefferson, NC: MacFarlane, 2013), 180.
66. Robert Harvey, *American Shogun: MacArthur, Hirohito, and the American Duel with Japan* (London: John Murray, 2006), 91.
67. Harvey, 78.

CHAPTER 8: BACK TO WEST POINT

1. MMA, RG 26, DM 201 file, General Menoher, efficiency report, August 28, 1919.
2. *Reminiscences*, 71–72.
3. James, *Years of MacArthur* I, 253.
4. Manchester, *American Caesar*, 126.
5. *World's Work*, April 1919.
6. Manchester, 125.
7. William Allen White, *The Autobiography of William Allen White* (New York: Macmillan, 1946), 572–73.
8. James I, 172.
9. DM to Weller, May 13, 1919, in *Reminiscences*, 72–73.
10. Faubion Bowers, "The Late General MacArthur, Warts and All," *Esquire 67* (January 1967), reprinted in William Leary, ed. *MacArthur and the American Century: A Reader* (Lincoln: University of Nebraska Press, 2001).
11. Edward Coffman, *The Hilt of the Sword: The Career of Peyton C. March* (Madison: University of Wisconsin Press, 1966).
12. Quoted in Manchester, 129.
13. *Reminiscences*, 77.
14. Coffman, 186.
15. Interview with Douglas MacArthur, December 12, 1960, in Coffman, 186.
16. James I, 262.
17. *Reminiscences*, 80.
18. Ganoe, *MacArthur Close-up*, 13.
19. James I, 263.
20. James I, 263.
21. Ganoe, 20.
22. Theodore Crackel, *West Point: A Bicentennial History* (Lawrence: University of Kansas Press, 2002), 188.
23. Stephen Ambrose, *Duty, Honor, Country: A History of West Point* (Baltimore: Johns Hopkins University Press, 1966), 258–59.
24. Ganoe, 21.

25. Ganoe, 21–22.
26. Ganoe, 24.
27. Ganoe, 24.
28. Ganoe, 25.
29. Blaik, in James I, 266.
30. MMA, RG 49, Box 91, Wright "Oral Reminscences," 31; Ganoe, 30.
31. Quoted in James I, 269.
32. Ganoe, 49.
33. Ganoe, 50.
34. Ganoe, 47.
35. Ganoe, 33.
36. A sympathetic account is in Robert Nye, "The United States Military Academy in an Era of Educational Reform 1900–1925," Ph.D. diss., Columbia University, 1968.
37. Crackel, 188.
38. Ganoe, 37.
39. James I, 266–67.
40. Ganoe, 37–39.
41. Ganoe, 40.
42. Ganoe, 41.
43. Wilbur Nye, quoted in James I, 269.
44. Crackel, 192.
45. Ganoe, 60–61.
46. Ganoe, 62–63.
47. Ambrose, 266.
48. James I, 268.
49. James I, 270.
50. Crackel, 189–90.
51. *Reminiscences,* 81.
52. Ambrose, 278.
53. Ambrose, 279.
54. *Reminiscences,* 82.
55. *Reminscences,* 82; Ambrose, 275.
56. Petillo, *Douglas MacArthur,* 123.
57. Manchester, 142.
58. MMA RG Letter DM to Louise Brooks, postmarked October 3, 1921.
59. Letter DM to LB, October 15, 1921, MMA.
60. Letter DM to LB, postmarked November 8, 1921, MMA.
61. Petillo, 124–25.
62. Letter DM to LB, November 15, 1921, MMA.
63. Letter DM to LB, November 15, 1921, MMA.
64. Letter DM to LB, postmarked December 16, 1921, MMA.
65. Manchester, 143.
66. *The New York Times,* February 15, 1922.

CHAPTER 9: THE TUMULTUOUS YEARS

1. DM to LB, postmarked November 10, 1921, MMA.
2. *The New York Times,* February 10, 1922.
3. James, *Years of MacArthur* I, 290.
4. Crackel, *West Point,* 194.
5. DM 201 File, MMA.
6. Perret, *Old Soldiers,* 130.
7. *Reminiscences,* 84.
8. Friend, *Between Two Empires,* 4–5.

9. James I, 295–96.
10. James I, 298.
11. Friend, 7–9; James I, 299.
12. *Reminiscences,* 84.
13. Leonard Wood Papers, Library of Congress, Leonard Wood Diary, February 26, 1923.
14. Hunt, *Untold Story,* 115.
15. James I, 304.
16. James I, 301.
17. *Reminiscences,* 84.
18. James I, 301.
19. James I, 303–5.
20. James I, 302.
21. *The New York Times,* September 23, 1924.
22. *Reminiscences,* 84.
23. Young, *General's General,* 90.
24. Beaudot, *The 24th Wisconsin Infantry,* 321–22.
25. Leonard Wood Papers, Library of Congress, L. Wood to Weeks, May 9, 1924.
26. Perret, 135–36.
27. *Reminiscences,* 85.
28. Douglas Waller, *A Question of Loyalty: General Billy Mitchell and the Court-Martial That Gripped the Nation* (New York: HarperCollins, 2004), 21–22.
29. *Reminiscences,* 85.
30. Burke Davis, *The Billy Mitchell Affair* (New York: Random House, 1967), 164–65.
31. Waller, 323–25.
32. Davis, 242–43.
33. Davis, 327.
34. Quoted in James I, 310.
35. Davis, 327n.
36. *Reminiscences,* 85.
37. James I, 312–13.
38. James I, 318.
39. Perret, 138.
40. Robert Considine, *General Douglas MacArthur* (Greenwich, CT: Fawcett, 1964), 58; James I, 326–27.
41. *Reminiscences,* 86.
42. *The New York Times,* August 10, 1928.
43. *Soldier Speaks,* 26–27.
44. Hunt, 121.
45. James I, 329.

CHAPTER 10: SAVING THE ARMY

1. *Reminiscences,* 87.
2. James, *Years of MacArthur* I, 338.
3. *Reminiscences,* 88.
4. Petillo, *Douglas MacArthur,* 142.
5. Sladen to Weeks, quoted in Petillo, 142.
6. James I, 335.
7. Stimson diary, February 14, 1932.
8. *The New York Times,* April 21, 1929.
9. James I, 343.
10. Hugh Johnson, *The Blue Eagle, from Egg to Earth* (Garden City, NY: Doubleday, Doran, 1935), 372–73.

11. Don Lohbeck, *Patrick J. Hurley* (Chicago: H. Regnery, 1956), 101–2.

12. Herbert Hoover, *Memoirs* (New York: Macmillan, 1951–52) II, 339; *The New York Times,* August 7, 1930.

13. Hunt, *Untold Story,* 125.

14. *Reminiscences,* 89.

15. Petillo, 150–51.

16. James I, 346.

17. *Reminiscences,* 89–90.

18. Mark Watson, *The United States Army in World War II: Chief of Staff: Plans and Preparations* (Washington, DC: Government Printing Office, 1950), 15.

19. Watson, 18.

20. James I, 374.

21. A. J. P. Taylor, *Origins of the Second World War,* second edition (New York: Fawcett, 1961), 64–66.

22. *The World Tomorrow,* May 16, 1931.

23. James I, 377.

24. "Privilege Without Responsibility," Letter to the Editor of *The World Tomorrow,* June 2, 1931, in V. E. Whan, ed., *A Soldier Speaks: Public Papers and Speeches of General of the Army Douglas MacArthur* (New York: Praeger, 1965), 36–40.

25. James I, 357.

26. James I, 358.

27. Letter DM to Bertrand Snell, May 9, 1932, quoted in James I, 360–61.

28. MMA. Ernest Graves, Brower interview, 1–2.

29. James I, 364.

30. Paul Dickson and Thomas B. Allen, *The Bonus Army: An American Epic* (New York: Walker, 2004).

31. James I, 385.

32. Dickson and Allen.

33. Quoted in Paul Johnson, *Modern Times* (New York: Harper & Row, 1983), 24; Hoover, *Memoirs.*

34. James I, 384; 386.

35. *Reminiscences,* 93.

36. John T. Pace testimony, House Un-American Activities Committee hearing, 82nd Congress, 1st Session, July 13, 1951.

37. James I, 389.

38. James I, 390.

39. *Reminiscences,* 94.

40. James I, 394.

41. James I, 396.

42. *Reminiscences,* 94.

43. James I, 399.

44. MMA, RG 10, Glassford to DM, April 25, 1951.

45. Quoted in James I, 400–401.

46. James I, 401.

47. Perret, *Old Soldiers,* 159.

48. Dwight Eisenhower, *At Ease: Stories I Tell My Friends* (New York: Avon Books, 1968), 217–18.

49. James I, 402.

50. Perret, 160.

51. Eisenhower, 217–18.

52. Quoted in James I, 404.

53. Johnson, *Modern Times,* 249–50; *Reminiscences,* 96.

54. *Reminiscences,* 96.

55. Hoover, *Memoirs* III, 226–27.
56. Perret, 161.
57. *Reminiscences*, 95.

CHAPTER 11: SAVING FDR

1. Arthur MacArthur's great-grandmother, Sarah Barney Belcher of Taunton, Massachusetts, was also an ancestor of Franklin Roosevelt, making them sixth cousins, once removed. She was also an ancestor of Winston Churchill, making him and MacArthur eighth cousins. Manchester, *American Caesar*, 32.
2. *Reminiscences*, 100.
3. James, *Years of MacArthur* I, 416.
4. Perry, *Most Dangerous Man*, 3.
5. James I, 443.
6. Tugwell, quoted in Perry, xv–xvi.
7. James I, 418.
8. James I, 419.
9. Colonel Duncan Major to Fechner, June 30, 1933, OF 268, FDRL, quoted in James I, 420.
10. Quoted in James I, 421.
11. Quoted in Perry, 10.
12. MMA, RG 18, Fechner to MacArthur, September 26, 1935; MacArthur to Fechner, September 27, 1935.
13. James I, 426.
14. *Reminiscences*, 100.
15. James I, 428; *Reminiscences*, 100.
16. James I, 428.
17. *War Department Annual Report*, 1933, I, 49.
18. *Reminiscences*, 100.
19. *Reminiscences*, 101.
20. James I, 429.
21. *Reminiscences*, 99.
22. *War Department Annual Report*, 1934, I, 94.
23. James I, 434.
24. MMA, RG 49, Interview with Dwight Eisenhower, August 29, 1967, 70.
25. Petillo, *Douglas MacArthur*, 151.
26. Harry Ransom Research Center Papers, University of Texas, Austin; MMA, RG 15, File 9.
27. MMA, RG 15, File 9.
28. Perret, *Old Soldiers*, 146; Allen Julian, *MacArthur: The Life of a General* (New York: Army Times Publishing, 1963), 38.
29. *The Secret Diary of Harold L. Ickes*, Vol. 4 (New York: Simon and Schuster, 1954), September 25, 1943.
30. Perret, 168–69.
31. Perry, 25.
32. Petillo, 166.
33. James I, 428, 431. Watson, *Chief of Staff*, 16.
34. Watson, 15–17.
35. *Soldier Speaks*, 53, 55, 65–66.
36. Press conference, December 12, 1934, quoted in James I, 446.
37. Perry, 43.
38. Petillo, 168.
39. Friend, *Between Two Empires*, 138.
40. *Reminiscences*, 102; M. L. Quezon, *The Good Fight* (New York: Appleton Century, 1946), 153–55.
41. Quezon, 155–56.

42. MMA, RG 17, MacArthur to Quezon, June 1, 1935.
43. Franklin D. Roosevelt Library, FDR Papers, MacArthur to Roosevelt, September 9, 1935.
44. Perret, 188.
45. Hunt, *Untold Story,* 170.
46. Perret, 149.
47. Hunt, 171.
48. Dwight D. Eisenhower Library, Eisenhower Diary, December 1, 1931.
49. Quoted in James I, 454.
50. Robert Seals, "The Western Way of 'Peace': General Douglas MacArthur as Chief of Staff," MilitaryHistoryOnline.com.
51. *Reminiscences,* 92.
52. *Reminiscences,* 91.
53. *Reminiscences,* 101.
54. Hunt, 171.

CHAPTER 12: MISSION TO MANILA

1. MMA, RG 13, Papers of Jean MacArthur, 1898–2000, Folder 2, 15.
2. Cornelius Ryan and Frank Kelley, *MacArthur: Man of Action* (Garden City, NY: Doubleday, 1951), 53.
3. MMA, RG 13, 16.
4. MMA, RG 13, 20.
5. MMA, RG 13, 23.
6. MMA, RG 13, 24.
7. Manchester, *American Caesar,* 179.
8. Petillo, *Douglas MacArthur,* 177.
9. Hunt, *Untold Story,* 181.
10. Robert Ferrell, ed. *The Eisenhower Diaries* (New York: Norton, 1981), December 27, 1935 entry, 10.
11. James, *Years of MacArthur* I, 497.
12. MMA, RG 107, SecWar Records, MacArthur to Dern, August 20, 1935.
13. James I, 499.
14. James I, 500.
15. Hunt, 180; *Reminiscences,* 103.
16. Library of Congress, O'Laughlin Papers, MacArthur to O'Laughlin, December 9 and December 18, 1935.
17. James I, 495.
18. Hunt, 181–82.
19. James I, 503.
20. James I, 94.
21. Friend, *Between Two Empires,* 177.
22. James I, 504.
23. Quoted in Friend, 167.
24. Petillo, 180.
25. Stimson Diary, March 30, 1935.
26. MMA, RG 13, Folder 2, 28.
27. Sidney Huff, *My Fifteen Years with General MacArthur* (New York: Paperback Library, 1964), 15–16.
28. Huff, 17.
29. Manchester, 180.
30. Huff, 16.
31. Manchester, 181.
32. Ganoe, *MacArthur Close-up,* 129–31; Hunt, 107.
33. Petillo, 187–88.

34. MMA, RG 49, Eisenhower interview, 71.
35. James I, 506–7.
36. *Eisenhower Diaries,* July 1, 1936 entry, 21.
37. Perry, *Most Dangerous Man,* 55.
38. Perry, 53.
39. James I, 515.
40. *Collier's,* September 5, 1936.
41. Manchester, 185.
42. Perry, 55.
43. MMA, RG 49, Interview of President Dwight Eisenhower, August 29, 1967.
44. James I, 508; *Reminiscences,* 105.
45. MMA, Jean MacArthur interview, Folder 3, p. 3.
46. Huff, 19.
47. Huff, 20.
48. MMA, Folder 3, p. 24.
49. James I, 512.
50. *Reminiscences,* 106.
51. MMA, Folder 3, p. 28.
52. MMA, Folder 3, pp. 3–4; Huff, 23.
53. Huff, 24.
54. Petillo, 188–89.
55. *Eisenhower Diaries,* June 28, 1937 entry, 25.
56. James I, 523.
57. MMA, RG 10, Craig to MacArthur, October 11, 1937.
58. Hunt, 189.
59. Hunt, 191.
60. Petillo, 191.
61. James I, 526.
62. Eisenhower, *At Ease,* 226–27.
63. Perret, *Old Soldiers,* 214.
64. *At Ease,* 226–28.
65. *Eisenhower Diaries,* July 28, 29, 30, 1938 entry, 30.
66. James I, 527.
67. Friend, 190–95.
68. Petillo, 193.
69. James I, 532.
70. Huff, 27–28.
71. *Reminiscences,* 107.
72. James I, 537.
73. James I, 537.
74. Ronald Spector, *Eagle Against the Sun* (New York: The Free Press, 1985), 64.
75. James I, 547.
76. James I, 537.
77. James I, 547.
78. MMA, RG 1, DM to Quezon, October 12, 1940.
79. Arthur Herman, *Freedom's Forge: How American Business Produced Victory in World War II,* (New York: Random House, 2012).
80. Petillo, 192.
81. Friend, 193–94.
82. *Eisenhower Diaries,* 37–38.
83. James I, 530.
84. MMA, Interview with Eisenhower; *At Ease,* 230–32.

85. MMA, RG 10, MacArthur to William Harts, March 2, 1940.
86. *Chicago Sun* article, 1942: MMA, RG 15, Box 75.
87. Spector, 66.
88. Quoted in Perret, 223.
89. Theodore H. White, *In Search of History* (New York: HarperCollins, 1978), 108–9.

CHAPTER 13: WAITING FOR THE ENEMY
1. Paul Rogers, *The Good Years: MacArthur and Sutherland* (New York: Praeger, 1990), 8.
2. Rogers, 10–11.
3. FDRL, Letter DM to Stephen Early, March 21, 1941.
4. FDRL, Letter Edwin Watson to DM, April 15, 1941; letter DM to Watson, May 11, 1941.
5. James, *Years of MacArthur* I, 583–84.
6. Stimson diary, May 21, 1941.
7. Marshall to DM, June 20, 1941, OCS 20850-15.
8. James I, 588.
9. Marshall to DM, July 26, 1941, OCS 18136-35.
10. Quoted in Rogers, 18.
11. Quoted in James I, 566.
12. Courtney Whitney, *MacArthur: His Rendezvous with History* (New York: Knopf, 1955), 8.
13. *Army and Navy Review,* August 2, 1941, in James I, 591.
14. Quoted in Petillo, *Douglas MacArthur,* 198.
15. Hunt, *Untold Story,* 210.
16. Louis Morton, *The United States Army in World War Two: The Fall of the Philippines* (Washington, DC: Government Printing Office, 1953), 23.
17. Report General Gerow to George Marshall, July 30, 1941, in James I, 594.
18. James I, 598–99.
19. James I, 609.
20. Morton, 34.
21. Gerald Astor, *Crisis in the Pacific: The Battles for the Philippine Islands by the Men Who Fought Them* (New York: Donald I. Fine Books, 1996), 25–26.
22. Petillo, 199.
23. James I, 601.
24. Morton, 35.
25. Morton, 37.
26. Hunt, 213.
27. Morton, 19.
28. James I, 567.
29. D. M. Horner, *Crisis of Command* (Canberra: Australian National University Press, 1978), 125.
30. Perret, *Old Soldiers,* 231.
31. Examples of the first include Perret, *Old Soldiers Never Die,* and Michael Schaller, *The American Occupation of Japan: The Origins of the Cold War in Asia* (New York: Oxford University Press, 1985). Examples of the second are L. Morton, *Fall of the Philippines,* and Michael Schaller, *American Occupation of Japan.*
32. MMA, RG 49, Wright interview, 31.
33. Rogers, 10–11.
34. Rogers, 15–16.
35. James I, 595.
36. Perret, 234.
37. James I, 595.
38. Rogers, 73.
39. Perret, 241–42.

40. Rogers, 71.
41. Perret, 243; quoted in James Leutze, *A Different Kind of Victory* (Annapolis: Naval Institute Press, 1981), 218.
42. John Gordon, *Fighting for MacArthur: The Navy and Marine Corps' Desperate Defense of the Philippines* (Annapolis: Naval Institute Press, 2011).
43. Perret, 243.
44. Rogers, 72–73.
45. See Clark Reynolds, "MacArthur as Maritime Strategist," in Leary, ed., *MacArthur and the American Century*, 210–27.
46. Morton, 50.
47. Rogers, 83.
48. Kelley and Ryan, *MacArthur*, 55.
49. Quoted Wilfrid Sheed, *Clare Boothe Luce* (NY: Berkley, 1982), 87.
50. Clare Boothe Luce, "General Douglas MacArthur," *Life*, December 8, 1941, 126–27.
51. Luce, "General Douglas MacArthur."
52. MMA, DM to Grunert, September 7, 1941.
53. MMA, George memo, "Study of the Air Force for USAFFE," September 11, 1941.
54. Table 3, Morton, 42.
55. Perret, 245.
56. Spector, *Eagle Against the Sun*, 106.
57. James I, 615; Astor, 30.
58. James I, 617.
59. Richard Rovere and Arthur M. Schlesinger, Jr., *The General and the President* (New York: Farrar, Straus and Young, 1951), 98–99.
60. Edward J. Drea, *MacArthur's ULTRA* (Lawrence: University Press of Kansas, 1992), 8–10.
61. Drea, 11.
62. MMA, RG 79, Spencer Akin Papers, "Reminiscences of Lt. Harold Brown," 13.
63. MMA, RG 79, Brown, 15.

CHAPTER 14: RAT IN THE HOUSE

1. Rogers, *The Good Years*, 94.
2. Clark Lee and Richard Henschel, *Douglas MacArthur* (New York: Holt, 1952), 70.
3. Perret, *Old Soldiers*, 248.
4. Lewis Brereton, *The Brereton Diaries* (New York: William Morrow, 1946), 68.
5. Astor, *Crisis in the Pacific*, 39.
6. Rogers, 95.
7. James, *Age of MacArthur* II, 8; Manchester, *American Caesar*, 232.
8. Horner, *Crisis*, 40; Richard Connaughton, *MacArthur and Defeat in the Philippines* (Woodstock, NY: Overlook, 2001), 173.
9. Astor, 40.
10. *Reminiscences*, 114.
11. *Reminiscences*, 117.
12. Brereton, 82–83.
13. Perry, *Most Dangerous Man*, 73.
14. Connaughton, 167, 169.
15. Perry, 73.
16. Astor, 41.
17. Astor, 43.
18. Samuel Grashio and Bernard Norling, *Return to Freedom* (Tulsa, OK: MCN Press, 1982); Horner, 42.
19. Rogers, 95; Morton, *Fall*, 85.
20. Rogers, 96.

21. Astor, 43.
22. Astor, 44.
23. Morton, 87; Horner, 47.
24. Perret, 253–54.
25. MMA, RG 79, Akin Papers, Reminiscences Lt. Harold Brown, August 4, 1945.
26. Rogers, 99; MMA, MacArthur War Diary, entry December 8, 1941.
27. Francis Sayre, *Glad Adventure* (New York: Macmillan, 1957), 223.
28. Morton, 94.
29. Morton, 145–46.
30. Quoted in Manchester, 239.
31. Morton, 100.
32. Morton, 104.
33. Astor, 60.
34. MacArthur to AGWAR, Dec. 10 1941, AG 381.
35. Morton, 104.
36. Dwight D. Eisenhower, *Crusade in Europe* (New York: Doubleday, 1948), 17–19.
37. Stimson Diary, December 14, 1941.
38. Quoted in *Reminiscences,* 127.
39. Rogers, 100.
40. Manchester, 240.
41. Hersey, *Men on Bataan,* 34.
42. Astor, 57.
43. Morton, 110–11.
44. Rogers, 99.
45. *Reminiscences,* 122.
46. James II, 27–29; Morton, 122.
47. Courtney Whitney, *MacArthur: His Rendezvous with History* (New York: Knopf, 1956), 15.
48. Rogers, 102–4.
49. John Jacob Beck, *MacArthur and Wainwright: Sacrifice of the Philippines* (Albuquerque: University of New Mexico Press, 1984), 31–32.
50. Rogers, 106.
51. Rogers, 108.
52. James II, 25.
53. Manchester, 243.
54. Astor, 66.
55. Huff, *My Fifteen Years,* Manchester, 249.
56. Rogers, 111.
57. Astor, 70.
58. Rogers, 113.
59. Brereton, 61–62.
60. MMA, RG 5, SCAP GHQ press release, June 25, 1943.
61. Rogers, 119.
62. Manchester, 250.
63. Huff, 39; MMA, RG13, Jean MacArthur interview, Folder 5, 17–18.
64. Manchester, 251–52.
65. MMA, RG 13, Jean MacArthur interview, Folder 5, 19.

CHAPTER 15: WHEN MEN MUST DIE

1. Morton, *Fall,* 62–63.
2. Morton, 163.
3. Morton, 165–69.
4. Morton, 168.

5. Bluemel, in Astor, *Crisis in the Pacific*, 75.
6. Manchester, *American Caesar*, 252; Huff, *My Fifteen Years*, 35–37; Quezon, *The Good Fight*, 195–98.
7. Huff, 41.
8. Huff, 42.
9. Rogers, *The Good Years*, 127.
10. Astor, *Crisis*, 91.
11. Astor, 91–92.
12. Carlos Romulo, *I Saw the Fall of the Philippines* (New York: Doubleday, 1943), 73–74, 77.
13. Lee and Henschel, 151.
14. Beck, *MacArthur and Wainwright*, 44.
15. Beck, 44–45.
16. Perry, *Most Dangerous Man*, 112.
17. Rogers, 114.
18. Beck, 47–48.
19. Manchester, 255.
20. Huff, 44.
21. Morton, 201; Beck, 51.
22. Quezon; Manchester, 255.
23. Manchester, 258.
24. Hunt, *Untold Story*, 248–49; Beck, 49–50.
25. FDR to Stimson and Knox, Dec. 30, 1941: Philippine File, 45, FDR Library, Beck, 51.
26. Walter Borneman, *The Admirals: Nimitz, Halsey, Leahy, and King—The Five-Star Admirals Who Won the War at Sea* (New York: Little, Brown, 2012), 221.
27. Charles Van Landingham, "I Saw Manila Die," *Saturday Evening Post*, September 26, 1942, 70.
28. Madeleine Ullom, *Memoir* (USACMH); Horner, 72–73.
29. Quoted in James, *Age of MacArthur* II, 31.
30. Stimson diary, December 31, 1941.
31. Perret, *Old Soldiers*, 263.
32. Morton, 183–84; Perry, 112.
33. Perry, 114.
34. Collier, *Notebooks*, I, 74; quoted in Morton, 211.
35. Morton, 207.
36. Morton, 210.
37. Rogers, 116.
38. Morton, 230.
39. Jonathan Wainwright, *General Wainwright's Story: The Account of Four Years of Humiliating Defeat, Surrender, and Captivity* (Garden City, NY: Doubleday, 1946), 48.
40. Spector, *Eagle Against the Sun*, 114.
41. Memorandum Lt. Gen. Gerow for Marshall, January 3, 1942; in Beck, 63.
42. Beck, 42.
43. Morton, 245.
44. "Comments on Engineers History," No. 10, in Morton, 245.
45. Morton, 247–48.
46. Spector, 112.
47. Mallonée, *Bataan Diary*, photostat, Office of the Center for Military History, II, 16.
48. *Reminiscences*, 130.
49. Frazier Hunt, *MacArthur and the War Against Japan* (New York: Scribner's, 1944), 52–53.
50. Bluemel, in Astor, 85.
51. Morton, 270.
52. Astor, 81–82.
53. Astor, 84.
54. Morton, 270.

55. Astor, 80, 81.
56. Morton, 271.
57. Quezon.
58. Morton, 269.
59. Manchester, 256.
60. Rogers; Huff.
61. Romulo, 61.
62. *Reminiscences,* 128.
63. Connaughton, 240–41.
64. Rogers, 132.
65. *Reminiscences,* 131.
66. Kelley and Ryan, *MacArthur,* 56.
67. Perry, 120–21, 139.
68. Manchester, 263.
69. MMA, Jean MacArthur interview, RG 13, Box 15, Folder 5, p. 29.

CHAPTER 16: BACK TO THE WALL

1. Morton, *Fall,* 275.
2. Morton, 277.
3. Morton, 286–87.
4. Morton, 274.
5. Spector, *Eagle Against the Sun,* 113.
6. Henry Lee, *"Nothing But Praise"* (Culver City, CA: Murray & Gee, 1948), 25.
7. E. B. Miller, *Bataan Uncensored* (Long Prairie, MN: Hart Publications, 1949), 156.
8. Morton, 294.
9. DM to Marshall, 23 January 1942.
10. Astor, *Crisis,* 99.
11. Perry, *Most Dangerous Man,* 124.
12. Quezon, *Fight,* 259.
13. Rovere and Schlesinger, *General and the President,* 57–58.
14. Beck, *MacArthur and Wainwright,* 74.
15. Astor, 99.
16. Astor, 108–9.
17. Morton, 412.
18. Morton, 349–50.
19. Connaughton, 272.
20. Astor, 121.
21. Connaughton, *MacArthur and Defeat,* 274.
22. Donald Knox, *Death March: The Survivors of Bataan* (New York: Harcourt, 1981), 76.
23. Manchester, 277.
24. Morton, 348.
25. Beck, 90.
26. Romulo, *I Saw,* 102.
27. *Reminiscences,* 138.
28. DM to FDR, February 8, 1942.
29. DM to Marshall, February 4, 1942, in *Papers of George Catlett Marshall,* vol. 3, 101–2.
30. *Eisenhower Diaries,* February 8, 1942, 47.
31. Forrest Pogue, *George C. Marshall* (New York: Viking, 1963).
32. *Reminiscences,* 139.
33. Perret, *Old Soldiers,* 271.
34. Huff, *My Fifteen Years,* 49.
35. Beck, 119–20.
36. DM to Marshall, January 23, 1914, MMA.

872 NOTES

37. Bulletin of March 3, 1942, quoted in Connaughton, 285.
38. Quoted in Connaughton, 258.
39. Manchester, 261.
40. *Washington Post,* January 27, 1942, quoted in Connaugton, 257.
41. Connaughton, 258.
42. Connaughton, 257.
43. Rogers, *The Good Years,* 137.
44. Connaughton, 285–86.
45. Radiograms from Coordinator Office of Information, Washington, D.C., pertaining to General MacArthur, MMA.
46. Romulo, 217.
47. James, *Age of MacArthur* II, 66.
48. USAAFE 30; Secret File, 2-11-42, Rogers, 164.
49. "By the President of the Philippines, Executive Order #1," Fort Mills, Corregidor, January 3, 1942; Petillo, *Douglas MacArthur,* 204–5; Rogers, 165.
50. Perret, 271.
51. Nigel Hamilton, *The Mantle of Command: FDR at War, 1941–1942* (Boston: Houghton Mifflin Harcourt, 2014).
52. Rogers, 165.
53. Perret, 271.
54. Rogers, 166.
55. Rogers, 168.
56. *The New York Times,* February 12, 1942.
57. Marshall to MacArthur, February 4, 1942, Quezon File, National Archives; quoted in Beck, 89–90.
58. Secret File, 2-11, 2-14; Beck, 117.
59. Sutherland diary, Rogers, 184.
60. Arthur Herman, *Gandhi & Churchill: The Epic Rivalry That Destroyed an Empire and Forged Our Age* (New York: Bantam, 2008).
61. MMA Secret File, 2-16-42.
62. *Eisenhower Diaries,* 49.
63. Gavin Long, *MacArthur As Military Commander* (London and Princeton: Van Nostrand, 1969).
64. Lloyd Ross, *John Curtin: A Biography* (South Melbourne: Macmillan, 1977), 270–73.
65. Curtin to Winston Churchill, February 22, 1942, A816, 52/302/142, National Archives of Australia.
66. Perry, 143.
67. Hurley to FDR, February 21, 1942, quoted in Beck, 121–22.
68. Robert E. Sherwood, *Roosevelt and Hopkins: An Intimate History* (New York: Harper, 1948), 505, 509.
69. Beck, 116.
70. Connaughton, 267.
71. Curtin to Winston Churchill, February 22, 1942, A816, 52/302/142, National Archives of Australia; Beck, 122–23.
72. James II, 98.
73. Huff, 50.
74. Radiogram Marshall to DM, February 22, 1942, in Beck, 124.
75. Hunt, *Untold Story,* 257.
76. Lee and Henschel, *Douglas MacArthur,* 72.
77. *Reminiscences,* 140.
78. *Reminiscences,* 141.
79. Marshall to DM, February 25, 1942, MMA, Secret File.
80. Beck, 127.

81. Drea, *MacArthur's ULTRA,* 15–16.
82. Romulo, 141.

CHAPTER 17: I SHALL RETURN

1. Huff, *My Fifteen Years,* 51.
2. James, *Age of MacArthur* II, 59–60; Morton, *Fall,* 351.
3. Morton, 352.
4. Morton, 416.
5. Beck, *MacArthur and Wainwright,* 135.
6. Beck, 135.
7. Huff, 54.
8. Manchester, *American Caesar,* 291.
9. Rogers, *The Good Years,* 187.
10. Romulo, *I Saw the Philippines Die,* 131.
11. Astor, *Crisis in the Pacific,* 135.
12. Beck, 136.
13. Operation Order, The Commandant, Sixteenth Naval District, to The Commander, Motor Torpedo Boat Squadron Three, 10 March 1942, in Beck, 137.
14. Wainwright, *Wainwright's Story,* 1–2.
15. Wainwright, 2–4.
16. Wainwright, 4–5; Beck, 139.
17. *Reminiscences,* 142.
18. Beck, 141.
19. Rogers, 187–88.
20. Rogers, 188.
21. MMA, Jean MacArthur interview, folder 6, p. 5.
22. Huff, 55.
23. Huff, 56.
24. MMA, Jean MacArthur interview, folder 6, p. 6.
25. Beck, 144; Huff, 56.
26. Beck, 145.
27. MMA, Jean MacArthur interview, folder 6, p. 9. *Reminiscences,* 144.
28. Irwin Alexander, in *Memoirs of Internment in the Philippines,* 132.
29. Bunker Diary, in Astor, 132–33.
30. Astor, 133.
31. Beck, 146–47.
32. Beck, 147.
33. Beck, 147.
34. Beck, 147.
35. Beck, 148.
36. MMA, Jean MacArthur interview, Folder 6, p. 14; Huff, 17.
37. Huff, 63.
38. Quoted in James II, 88.
39. Huff, 64.
40. Beck, 152–53.
41. Manchester, 301.
42. Beck, 153.
43. MMA, DM to Brett, March 13, 1942, quoted in Beck, 154.
44. Rogers, 190–91.
45. Rogers, 191.
46. Rogers, 192.
47. Huff, 67.
48. MMA, DM to Quezon.

CHAPTER 18: TAKING SUPREME COMMAND

1. Huff, *My Fifteen Years,* 72.
2. Huff, 67.
3. Huff, 68.
4. Huff, 70; MMA, Jean MacArthur interview, folder 7, p. 15.
5. Huff, 72; MMA, Jean MacArthur interview, folder 7, p. 16.
6. Huff, 71.
7. Perret, *Old Soldiers,* 283.
8. Huff, 75.
9. James, *Age of MacArthur* II, 109.
10. *Reminiscences,* 145.
11. Huff, 78.
12. David Horner, "MacArthur: An Australian Perspective," in *MacArthur and the American Century,* 110.
13. *Reminiscences,* 152.
14. James II, 110.
15. Long, *MacArthur as Military Commander,* 42.
16. Horner, 111.
17. General Order No. 16, War Department, April 1, 1942.
18. Pogue, *Marshall* II, 353–54.
19. *Sydney Morning Herald,* March 27, 1942, 4.
20. *Eisenhower Diaries,* 51.
21. H. P. Wilmott, *The Barrier and the Javelin* (Annapolis: Naval Institute Press, 1983), 123, 144.
22. Wilmott, 127.
23. Borneman, *The Admirals,* 240–42.
24. *Eisenhower Diaries,* entry March 10, 1942, 50.
25. Rogers, *The Good Years,* 223; Richard Frank, *MacArthur* (London: Palgrave, 2007), 65.
26. Spector, *Eagle Against the Sun,* 144–45.
27. Long, 94.
28. Long, 90.
29. Dudley McCarthy, *South-West Pacific Area—First Year, Kokoda to Wau* (Canberra: Australian War Memorial, 1959), 28–29.
30. Frederick Shedden, Impressions of General MacArthur (January 1943), National Archives of Australia: Shedden interview with Gavin Long, January 31, 1946; in Horner, 116, 113.
31. MMA, RG 3, Curtin to MacArthur, April 15, 1942.
32. Astor, *Crisis in the Pacific,* 136.
33. Astor, 139.
34. *Reminiscences,* 146.
35. Astor, 140.
36. Irwin Alexander, *Memoirs of Internment;* quoted in Astor, *Crisis,* 141.
37. Beck, 193.
38. Rogers, 215–16.
39. Spector, 150–51.
40. Spector, 158.
41. Drea, *MacArthur's ULTRA,* 33.
42. Horner, 119.
43. Rogers, 243.
44. MMA, RG 79, Akin Papers, S. B. Akin, "Mass Signal Intelligence Service," 2–6.
45. Drea, 16.
46. Long, 100.
47. Willmott, 186.
48. Henry L. Stimson and McGeorge Bundy, *On Active Service in Peace and War* (New York: Octagon, 1971), 280–81.

49. Quoted in Rogers, 257.
50. Hayes, *Pearl Harbor Through Trident,* 208–9.
51. Willmott, 186.
52. Perret, 295–96.
53. Samuel Milner and Kent Roberts Greenfield, *U.S. Army in World War Two: Victory in Papua* (Washington, D.C.: GPO, 1957).
54. Rogers, 241.
55. Drea, 37.
56. Drea, 40.
57. Perret, 297.
58. Long, 103.
59. Ronald Spector, *Eagle Against the Sun: The American War with Japan* (New York: Free Press, 1985), 186.
60. James II, 190.
61. Louis Morton, *Strategy and Command: The First Two Years* (Washington, D.C.: GPO, 1962), 306–7.
62. Milner and Greenfield, 51.
63. Spector, 188.
64. Drea, 41.
65. James II, 191–92.
66. Drea, 42.
67. Long, 103–5.
68. Rogers, 307.
69. Spector, 190.
70. Nimitz File, meeting from September 25, 1942.

CHAPTER 19: GREEN HELL

1. Kenney diary, July 28/29, 1942.
2. Kenney diary, July 29, 1942.
3. Kenney diary, August 2, 1942.
4. Kenney diary, July 30, 1942.
5. Kenney diary, August 3, 1942.
6. Long, *MacArthur as Military Commander,* 110.
7. Kenney Diary, August 7/9, 1942.
8. Quoted in Spector, *Eagle Against the Sun,* 213.
9. Quoted in Spector, 214–15.
10. Quoted in Drea, *MacArthur's ULTRA,* 52.
11. Rogers, *The Good Years,* 335.
12. Kenney diary, November 20, 1942.
13. Kenney diary; George Kenney, *General Kenney Reports: A Personal History of the Pacific War* (Washington, D.C.: Office of Air Force History, 1937).
14. Astor, *Crisis in the Pacific,* 184–85.
15. Rogers, 336.
16. Robert Eichelberger, *Our Jungle Road to Tokyo: America's Hard-Fought Battle for the South Pacific* (1950: Uncommon Valor Press, 2014); Perret, 322–33.
17. *General Kenney Reports,* 158.
18. J. Luvaas and J. F. Shortal, "Robert L. Eichelberger," in William Leary, ed., *We Shall Return!: MacArthur's Commanders and the Defeat of Japan* (Lexington: University Press of Kentucky, 1988), 162.
19. James, *Age of MacArthur* II, 264.
20. Rogers, 338.
21. James II, 268.
22. Rogers, 341.

23. James II, 269.
24. Rogers, 341.
25. James II, 269.
26. James II, 269–70.
27. James II, 271.
28. MMA, DM to Marshall.
29. MMA, Diller interview.
30. James II, 271.
31. Rogers, 341–42.
32. Eric Bergerud, *Touched with Fire: The Land War in the South Pacific* (New York: Viking, 1996), 438–39.
33. *Reminiscences,* 168.
34. Spector, 220.
35. JPS to JCS, February 15, 1943; James II, 306.
36. E.g., Kenney diary, August 7/9, 1942.
37. Daniel Barbey, *MacArthur's Amphibious Navy: Seventh Amphibious Force Operations, 1943–1945* (Annapolis: U.S. Naval Institute, 1969), 18–19.
38. Barbey, 20.
39. Barbey, 20, 25.
40. Barbey, 21–22.
41. *Reminiscences,* 172.
42. Drea, 64.
43. Thomas Griffith, *MacArthur's Airman: General George C. Kenney and the War in the Southwest Pacific* (Lawrence: University of Kansas, 1998), 98.
44. Drea, 65.
45. Drea, 67.
46. Kenney diary, February 25; Griffith, 105.
47. Kenney diary, Feburary 28, 1943.
48. Spector, 227–28.
49. Drea, 71.
50. *General Kenney Reports,* 205–6.
51. Drea, 71.
52. *General Kenney Reports,* 210–11.
53. Kenney diary, February 28, 1943.
54. Kenney diary, March 13, 1943.
55. James II, 308.
56. MMA, RG 4, DM to JCM, March 25, 1943.
57. *General Kenney Reports,* 218.

CHAPTER 20: DOING CARTWHEEL

1. Huff, *My Fifteen Years,* 81–82.
2. Huff, 84.
3. Huff, 87.
4. Manchester, *American Caesar,* 366.
5. *Reminiscences,* 135–36.
6. *General Kenney Reports,* 224.
7. James, *Age of MacArthur* II, 311.
8. *General Kenney Reports,* 236–37.
9. Drea, *MacArthur's ULTRA,* 72.
10. *General Kenney Reports,* 227.
11. Griffith, *MacArthur's Airman,* 115.
12. Drea, 73.
13. *Reminiscences,* 174–75; Griffith, 115.

14. Drea, 73.
15. Drea, 73.
16. Borneman, *The Admirals,* 111.
17. William F. Halsey and J. Bryan, *Admiral Halsey's Story* (New York: Da Capo, 1976), 154–55.
18. James II, 316–17.
19. MMA, RG 4, DM to GCM, June 20, 1943; DM to GCM, June 12, 20, 24, 1943.
20. James II, 312–13.
21. Horner, "MacArthur and Blamey," in Leary, ed., *We Shall Return!,* 42.
22. Spector, *Eagle Against the Sun,* 233.
23. Barbey, *MacArthur's Amphibious Navy,* 67.
24. *Reminiscences,* 177.
25. Spector, 233.
26. *Reminiscences,* 177.
27. *General Kenney Reports,* 253.
28. Quoted in Herman Wolk, "George C. Kenney, MacArthur's Premier Airman," in Leary, ed., *We Shall Return,* 104.
29. Wolk, 104.
30. Griffith, 120.
31. Arnold to Kenney, September 25, 1943; quoted in Wolk, 104–5.
32. *Reminiscences,* 179.
33. Astor, *Crisis,* 194–95.
34. Spector, 237.
35. Samuel Eliot Morison, *History of United States Naval Operations in World War II,* vol. 6, *Breaking the Bismarcks Barrier* (Annapolis: Naval Institute Press, 2001), 388.
36. Philip Bradley, *On Shaggy Ridge: The Australian Seventh Division* (Melbourne: Oxford University Press, 2004).
37. "Employment of Forces in the Southwest Pacific Area," quoted in Drea, 95.
38. Quoted in James II, 349.
39. Quoted in *Reminiscences,* 183.
40. James II, 349–50.
41. Drea, 91–92.
42. Drea, 93.
43. Spector, 239.
44. Drea, 97.
45. Drea, 97.
46. James II, 381.
47. *General Kenney Reports,* 360.
48. James II, 380.
49. *Reminiscences,* 137–38.
50. Kenney diary, February 26, 1944.
51. Quoted in Perret, *Old Soldiers,* 375.
52. *General Kenney Reports,* 361; James II, 383.
53. Roger Egeberg, *The General: MacArthur and the Man He Called "Doc"* (New York: Hippocrene Books, 1983), 25.
54. Egeberg, 26.
55. Egeberg, 27; James II, 383.
56. James II, 385.
57. Egeberg, 33.
58. Barbey, 154.

CHAPTER 21: STEPPING-STONES TO VICTORY

1. Halsey and Bryan, *Halsey's Story,* 186–90; James, *Age of MacArthur* II, 390; Perret, *Old Soldiers,* 378.

2. Bergerud, *Touched with Fire,* 247.
3. James II, 392, 393–94.
4. James II, 391.
5. MMA, RG 4, JCS to DM, March 12, 1944.
6. *General Kenney Reports,* 341–42; 371.
7. Herman, *Freedom's Forge,* 300.
8. *Reminiscences,* 189.
9. Drea, *MacArthur's ULTRA,* 105–6.
10. *General Kenney Reports,* 377.
11. James II, 450.
12. *Reminiscences,* 190.
13. James II, 452.
14. Barbey, *MacArthur's Amphibious Navy,* 173; Egeberg, *The General,* 53.
15. MMA, RG 4, GHQ communiqué, April 24, 1944.
16. James II, 449.
17. Drea, 120.
18. MMA, S. Akin, "MacArthur's Signal Intelligence," 15; Drea, 120–21.
19. MMA, RG 4, Box 14, Chief of Staff Files, "For MacArthur from Marshall," June 11, 1944.
20. Eichelberger, *Jungle Road,* 121–22.
21. Drea, 135.
22. James II, 455–56.
23. Drea, 137.
24. Drea, 130–31.
25. *Reminiscences,* 192.
26. Spector, *Eagle Against the Sun,* 290.
27. Spector, 292.
28. Perret, 398; MMA, RG 4, SWPA GHQ commos May 28 and June 3, 1944.
29. Astor, *Crisis in the Pacific,* 209.
30. Ibid.
31. Astor, 211.
32. James II, 460–61.
33. Drea, 145.
34. *Reminiscences,* 194; Drea, 150.
35. *Reminiscences,* 194; James II, 485.
36. James II, 526.
37. MMA, RG 32, Interview Bonner Fellers.
38. G. Kenney, *MacArthur: The Man I Knew,* 249–50.
39. Quoted in James II, 434–35.
40. *Reminiscences,* 184.
41. Rosenman, quoted in James II, 528.
42. Perry, *Most Dangerous Man,* 271.
43. *Reminiscences,* 198; Byers diary, quoted in Perret, 406.
44. Richard B. Frank, *MacArthur* (New York: Palgrave Macmillan, 2007), 104.
45. James II, 538–39.
46. Drea, 153.
47. James II, 488.
48. MMA, RG 32, Interview, Egeberg.

CHAPTER 22: LIBERATION

1. *Reminiscences,* 157.
2. William Leary, "Walter Krueger," in Leary, ed., *We Shall Return!,* 70.
3. Walter Krueger, *From Down Under to Nippon: The Story of Sixth Army in World War II* (Washington, D.C.: Combat Forces Press, 1953), 142–43.

4. See Clark Reynolds, "MacArthur as Maritime Strategist," in Leary, ed., *Douglas MacArthur and the American Century*, esp. 211–16.
5. James, *Age of MacArthur* II, 501.
6. *General Kenney Reports*, 426–27.
7. Huff, *My Fifteen Years*, 94–95.
8. Huff, 94–95.
9. Rhoades, diary entry, December 14, 1943, in Weldon E. (Dusty) Rhoades: *Flying MacArthur to Victory* (College Station: Texas A&M University Press, 1987), 165.
10. E.g., David Horner, "MacArthur: An Australian Perspective," esp. 126–29.
11. *Reminiscences*, 258.
12. Perret, *Old Soldiers*, 364.
13. Rhoades, 285; Egeberg, *MacArthur and the Man*, 59.
14. Spector, *Eagle Against the Sun*, 419–20.
15. Quoted in James II, 515.
16. Drea, *MacArthur's ULTRA*, 158–59.
17. Drea, 169.
18. William Dunn, *Pacific Microphone* (College Station: Texas A&M University Press, 1988), 143.
19. *Reminiscences*, 212.
20. Whitney, *MacArthur*, 154.
21. MMA, RG 10, Letter DM to JM, October 19, 1944.
22. *Soldier Speaks*, 131; *Reminiscences*, 215.
23. Astor, *Crisis*, 227.
24. *Reminiscences*, 215.
25. Rants, "My Memories of World War Two" (unpublished manuscript) in Astor, 224.
26. Astor, 228.
27. Egeberg, 66.
28. Dunn, 148.
29. Egeberg, 80–81.
30. Dunn, 6.
31. *General Kenney Reports*, 448.
32. Perret, 421.
33. James II, 556.
34. *General Kenney Reports*, 448.
35. James II, 558; Kenney, 449.
36. Rhoades, 298.
37. Mac to FDR, October 20, 1944, Franklin D. Roosevelt Library (FDRL).
38. FDR to DM, October 21, 1944, James II, 560.
39. *Reminiscences*, 218.
40. Quoted in Astor, 239.
41. Rants, "My Memories"; Astor, 238.
42. Stanley Falk, *Liberation of the Philippines* (New York: Ballantine, 1971), 35.
43. Donald MacIntyre, *Leyte Gulf: Armada in the Pacific* (New York: Ballantine, 1970), 17–18.
44. Drea, 161.
45. Egeberg, 73.
46. Egeberg, 74.
47. Spector, 435–36.
48. Kenney diary, October 20, 1944.
49. MacIntyre, 99–100.
50. Spector, 437.
51. MacIntyre, 110.
52. Egeberg, 74.
53. Kenney diary, October 26, 1944.

CHAPTER 23: ON TO MANILA

1. Hunt, *Untold Story,* 348.
2. *General Kenney Reports,* 464–65.
3. Egeberg, *MacArthur and the Man,* 76.
4. MacIntyre, *Leyte Gulf,* 66.
5. James, *Age of MacArthur* II, 576.
6. Leary, *MacArthur and the American Century,* 76.
7. *Reminiscences,* 232.
8. Gerald Wheeler, "Thomas C. Kincaid: MacArthur's Master of Naval Warfare" in William M. Leary, ed., *We Shall Return!,* (Lexington, KY: The University of Kentucky Press, 1988), 145.
9. James II, 606.
10. Kenney diary, November 30, 1944.
11. Wheeler, 145.
12. Wheeler, 146.
13. James II, 607.
14. James II, 606.
15. *General Kenney Reports,* 494–95.
16. Stanley Falk, *Liberation of the Philippines* (NY: Ballantine, 1971), 75.
17. Falk, 76.
18. James II, 589.
19. *Reminiscences,* 234.
20. MMA, RG 10, DM to JM, December 25, 1944.
21. Falk, 84.
22. Hunt, 355.
23. James II, 590.
24. James II, 618.
25. James II, 617–18.
26. Robert Ross Smith, *Triumph in the Philippines* (Washington, DC: GPO, 1963), 19.
27. Long, *MacArthur as Military Commander,* 162.
28. *Reminiscences,* 239.
29. Drea, *MacArthur's ULTRA,* 192.
30. MMA, RG 49, Middleman Interview, June 29, 1971, 22–23; Drea, 188.
31. Falk, 85.
32. James II, 619.
33. *Reminiscences,* 240; Barbey, *MacArthur's Amphibious Navy,* 298.
34. *Reminiscences,* 240.
35. Barbey, 299.
36. James II, 620.
37. Quoted in Astor, *Crisis,* 355.
38. Astor, 356.
39. *Reminiscences,* 241.
40. Falk, 89.
41. James II, 622.
42. MMA, RG 49, Middleman interview, June 29, 1971, 22–23.
43. *Reminiscences,* 241–42.
44. Egeberg, 105–6.
45. MMA, RG 49, Middleman interview, 24.
46. James II, 625.
47. Smith, 88–91.
48. Quoted in Falk, 103.
49. Krueger, *From Down Under,* 228–29.
50. Smith, 167–68.
51. James II, 623.

52. Long, 157.

53. James II, 625.

54. Luvaas and Shortal, "Eichelberger," 166.

55. Kenney diary, January 23, 1945; James II, 628.

56. Robert Eichelberger, *Dear Miss Em: General Eichelberger's War in the Pacific, 1942–1945,* Jay Luvaas, ed. (Westport, CT: Greenwood, 1972), 203–4.

57. *Reminiscences,* 244; Long, 167.

58. Egeberg, 122–23.

59. Egeberg, 131.

60. Long, 167.

61. Spector, *Eagle Against the Sun,* 523.

62. Smith, 246–48.

CHAPTER 24: BATTLEGROUND

1. Astor, *Crisis,* 384–85.

2. Hunt, *Untold Story,* 366.

3. Hunt, *Untold Story,* 366.

4. Astor, 385.

5. Astor, 386–87.

6. Smith, *Triumph in the Philippines,* 254.

7. Astor, 397.

8. Smith, 254.

9. Smith, 253.

10. James, *Age of MacArthur* II, 637.

11. Egeberg, *MacArthur and the Man,* 135.

12. *Reminiscences,* 248.

13. *Reminiscences,* 247.

14. Hunt, *Untold Story,* 371.

15. Falk, *Liberation,* 108.

16. Astor, 397.

17. Astor, 398.

18. James II, 640.

19. Astor, 400.

20. Astor, 401.

21. Astor, 402; Falk, 108.

22. Smith, 278.

23. Falk, 109.

24. Smith, 340.

25. Smith, 337.

26. Astor, 403.

27. Drea, *MacArthur's ULTRA,* 199–200.

28. James II, 649.

29. Egeberg, 147–48.

30. Egeberg, 149–51.

31. Astor, 403.

32. Falk, 114.

33. Astor, 404.

34. Paul P. Rogers, *The Bitter Years: MacArthur and Sutherland* (New York: Praeger, 1991), 264.

35. Smith, 295–97; Falk, 108.

36. Astor, 410.

37. *Reminiscences,* 247.

38. Rogers, *Bitter Years,* 263.

39. *Reminiscences,* 251.

40. *Reminiscences,* 252; Petillo, *Douglas MacArthur,* 226.
41. Falk, 115.
42. Hunt, *Untold Story,* 368.
43. James II, 652.
44. *Reminiscences,* 250.
45. Quoted in *Reminiscences,* 249.
46. Falk, 120–21.
47. Falk, 120–21.
48. James II, 765.
49. James II, 740–41.
50. Quoted in James II, 747.

CHAPTER 25: DOWNFALL

1. James, *Age of MacArthur* II, 660.
2. *General Kenney Reports,* 542.
3. James II, 657–59.
4. Egeberg, *MacArthur and the Man,* 186.
5. Egeberg, 190–91.
6. Long, *MacArthur as Military Commander,* 172.
7. Spector, *Eagle Against the Sun,* 541–42.
8. Spector, 542.
9. E.g., Spector, 526.
10. Maurice Matloff, *Strategic Planning for Coalition Warfare 1943–1944: United States Army in World War II, The War Department* (Washington, DC: GPO, 1959), 495.
11. MMA, DM to Curtin, March 5, 1945.
12. Long, 175.
13. James II, 715.
14. Long, 175.
15. Petillo, *Douglas MacArthur,* 230.
16. Egeberg, 172–76.
17. James II, 760.
18. Egeberg, 153.
19. Quoted in Drea, *MacArthur's ULTRA,* 316.
20. MMA, RG 4, DM to Marshall, June 19, 1945.
21. Drea, 209–10, 204.
22. Drea, 218.
23. James II, 772–73; Drea, 219.
24. James II, 774.
25. Egeberg, 102.
26. *Reminiscences,* 262.
27. Egeberg, 192.
28. James II, 775.
29. James II, 779.
30. Egeberg, 194.
31. Harvey, *American Shogun,* 295–97; *Reminiscences,* 269.
32. Hunt, *Untold Story,* 301–2.
33. *Reminiscences,* 270.
34. Rhoades, *Flying MacArthur,* 446.
35. James II, 775.
36. Egeberg, 197.
37. James II, 784.
38. Quoted in *Reminiscences,* 270.
39. Rhoades, 446; Egeberg, 197.

40. Borneman, *The Admirals*, passim.
41. Whitney, *MacArthur*, 213.
42. *Reminiscences*, 270.
43. *Reminiscences*, 270–71.
44. James II, 785.
45. Manchester, *American Caesar*, 521.
46. *General Kenney Reports*, 575.
47. *General Kenney Reports*, 575.
48. Egeberg, 201.
49. Egeberg, 198.
50. Quoted in Harvey, 309.
51. Egeberg, 202.
52. *Reminiscences*, 271.
53. Manchester, 524.
54. Egeberg, 202.
55. Egeberg, 205.
56. Egeberg, 205.
57. *Reminiscences*, 271–72.
58. James II, 787–88.
59. *Reminiscences*, 272.
60. Ibid.
61. Perret, *Old Soldiers*, 476.
62. Details are in MMA RG 15, Box 81, folder 3, "Papers of Colonel H. B. Whipple." Whipple was MacArthur's liaison with the U.S. Navy for the USS *Missouri* ceremony.

CHAPTER 26: BRIEF ENCOUNTERS

1. Egeberg, *MacArthur and the Man*, 209–10.
2. Egeberg, 93.
3. Quoted in Manchester, *American Caesar*, 525.
4. Rhoades, *Flying MacArthur*, 452.
5. *Soldier Speaks*, 153.
6. *Reminiscences*, 278.
7. Egeberg, 212.
8. Harvey, *American Shogun*, 310.
9. Quoted in *Reminiscences*, 274.
10. *General Kenney Reports*, 577.
11. Perret, *Old Soldiers*, 479.
12. *Soldier Speaks*, 152.
13. Quoted in *Reminiscences*, 277.
14. John Dower, *Embracing Defeat: Japan in the Wake of World War II* (New York: Norton, 1999), 22.
15. Dean Acheson, *Present at the Creation: My Years in the State Department* (New York: Norton, 1969), 449.
16. James, *Age of MacArthur* III, 70.
17. James III, 69.
18. *Reminiscences*, 279–80.
19. *Reminiscences*, 285.
20. *Reminiscences*, 285.
21. Harry S. Truman, *Off the Record: The Private Papers of Harry S. Truman*, Robert Ferrell, ed. (New York: Harper & Row, 1980), 47; Leary, ed., quoted in Robert Harvey, *American Shogun: MacArthur, Hirohito, and the American Duel with Japan* (London: John Murray, 2006).
22. Leary, 290–91.
23. James III, 12–13.

24. James III, 14.
25. James III, 17.
26. James III, 17–18.
27. MMA, RG 10, Wood to DM, September 4, 1945, quoted in Hunt, *Untold Story.*
28. James III, 18.
29. James III, 18–19.
30. James III, 18.
31. DM to Marshall, September 17, 1945, FRUS 1945 vol VI, 717–18.
32. Mashbir, *I Was an American Spy,* 315.
33. Quoted in *Reminiscences,* 277.
34. Quoted in Harvey, 14.
35. James II, 38–39.
36. JCS Directive to DM, September 6, 1945, in SCAP, Political Reorientation, II, 327.
37. James III, 38–39.
38. Tanaka, *Hidden Horrors,* 2–3.
39. Tanaka, 135–59.
40. Dower, 492.
41. Harvey, 15.
42. Harvey, 15.
43. *Reminiscences,* 288.
44. James III, 105.
45. *Reminiscences,* 288.
46. Harvey, 18.
47. *Reminiscences,* 288; Harvey, 16–17.

CHAPTER 27: BEING SIR BOSS

1. James, *Age of MacArthur* III, 323.
2. *Reminiscences,* 282.
3. *Reminiscences,* 282.
4. Takemae Eijii, *Inside GHQ: The Allied Occupation of Japan and Its Legacy* (New York: Continuum, 2002), 103–5; James III, 41.
5. Rhoades, *Flying MacArthur,* 523.
6. Rhoades, 523.
7. Quoted in James III, 43.
8. Eijii, 164–65.
9. James III, 277.
10. *Reminiscences,* 282.
11. Ikuhiko Hata, "The Occupation of Japan, 1945–52," in Leary, ed., *MacArthur and the American Century,* 315.
12. Quoted in Schaller, "MacArthur's Japan: The View from Washington," *American Century,* 297.
13. Quoted in Dower, *Embracing Defeat,* 285.
14. Dower, 282–83.
15. William J. Sebald, *With MacArthur in Japan: A Personal History of the Occupation* (New York: Norton, 1965), 103–4.
16. Dower, 91–93.
17. Dower, 92.
18. James III, 156.
19. Quoted in Dower, 93–94.
20. Hiroshi Masuda, *MacArthur in Asia: The General and His Staff in the Philippines, Japan, and Korea* (Ithaca, NY: Cornell University Press, 2013), 202.
21. *Soldier Speaks,* 155.
22. Masuda, 202.

23. See Richard Frank, *MacArthur: A Biography* (London: Palgrave Macmillan, 2009), 134.
24. James III, 111.
25. *Reminiscences*, 293.
26. James III, 114.
27. *Reminiscences*, 304–5.
28. *Reminiscences,* 300.
29. Oral interview with Charles Kades, quoted in Masuda, 214.
30. James III, 124–25.
31. Harvey, *American Shogun,* 360.
32. Quoted in Harvey, 361.
33. Quoted in Dower, 384–85.
34. *Reminiscences,* 305.
35. James III, 94.
36. James III, 94.
37. Quoted in *Reminiscences,* 295–96.
38. James III, 95, 97.
39. John Toland, *The Rising Sun: The Decline and Fall of the Japanese Empire, 1936–1945* (New York: Random House, 1970), 294.
40. *Soldier Speaks,* 160.
41. Averell Harriman, *Special Envoy to Churchill and Stalin, 1941–1946* (New York: Random House, 1975), 544.
42. James III, 100.
43. *Soldier Speaks,* 161–62.
44. *Reminiscences,* 295.
45. Dower, 229.
46. Dower, 231.
47. Dower, 206.
48. James III, 117.
49. Frank, 136.
50. Harvey, 347.
51. Quoted in James III, 225.
52. *Reminiscences,* 308.
53. James III, 25; Harvey, 368.
54. Quoted in Harvey, 357.
55. James III, 170.
56. James III, 170.
57. *Newsweek,* January 27, 1947.
58. James III, 172.

CHAPTER 28: HEADWINDS

1. *Soldier Speaks,* 191–93.
2. *Soldier Speaks,* 175–76.
3. See his comments in *Soldier Speaks,* 187–89.
4. Masuda, *MacArthur in Asia,* 220–21.
5. Bowen Dees, *The Allied Occupation and Japan's Economic Miracle* (Richmond, Surrey: Curzon Press and Japan Library, 1997), esp. 227–34.
6. Dees, 32; *Reminiscences,* 286–87.
7. Charles Weiner, *Bulletin of Atomic Scientists,* April 1978.
8. Huff, *My Fifteen Years,* 112–13.
9. James, *Age of MacArthur* III, 61.
10. James III, 61–62.
11. Sebald, *With MacArthur,* 104, 107–8.
12. Sebald, 111–12.

13. Harvey, *American Shogun,* 385.
14. Quoted in Harvey, 386.
15. Harvey, 389.
16. George Kennan, *Memoirs 1925–1950* (New York: Pantheon, 1983), 383.
17. Kennan, 384.
18. Kennan, 386–87.
19. Kennan, 388–89.
20. James III, 235.
21. Masuda, 236–37.
22. Hunt, *Untold Story,* 445.
23. Sebald, 178–79.
24. James III, 392.
25. Sebald, 179; Bowers, "The Late General MacArthur," *MacArthur and the American Century,* 255.
26. Hunt, *Untold Story,* 446–47.
27. Sebald, 181.
28. *Soldier Speaks,* 199–200.
29. Allan Millett, *Their War for Korea* (Washington, D.C.: Brassey's, 2002), 159–60.
30. Sebald, 179.
31. Hunt, *Untold Story,* 447.
32. Sebald, 142.
33. Harvey, 365.
34. *Reminiscences,* 318.
35. Harvey, 367.
36. Quoted in Harvey, 367.
37. Dower, *Embracing Defeat,* 450.
38. Harvey, 371, 373.
39. Quoted in Harvey, 374.
40. Dower, 459.
41. Foreign Relations United States State Department (FRUS), 1948, 6:707–9, 794.
42. Sebald, 168–69.
43. Sebald, 169.
44. *Reminiscences,* 319.
45. Henry Kissinger, *Diplomacy* (New York: Simon & Schuster, 1994), 474.

CHAPTER 29: WAR AGAIN

1. *Reminiscences,* 327.
2. *The New York Times,* March 2, 1949, 22.
3. James, *Age of MacArthur* III, 80–81.
4. James III, 399–403, 412.
5. Acheson, *Present at the Creation,* 356–57; Hunt, *Untold Story,* 449.
6. See, e.g., General Omar Bradley testimony, U.S. House of Representatives, Subcommittee of Committee on Appropriations. . . . Hearings, 80th Cong., 2nd sess., Part 3, p. 3.
7. Sebald, *With MacArthur,* 182.
8. Allan Millett, *The War for Korea 1950–1954: They Came from the North* (Lawrence: University Press of Kansas, 2010), 46.
9. Kathryn Weatherby, "New Russian Documents on the Korean War," *Cold War International History Project Bulletin* 6–7 (Winter 1995–96), 36.
10. Millett, *War for Korea,* 49–50.
11. Millett, *War for Korea,* 42.
12. Millet, *War for Korea,* 43.
13. *Reminiscences,* 324.
14. Millett, *War for Korea,* 99.

15. Millett, *War for Korea,* 99; *Reminiscences,* 328.
16. Millett, *War for Korea,* 100.
17. Acheson, 404–5.
18. Acheson, 405.
19. Millett, *War for Korea,* 117, 116.
20. Millett, *War for Korea,* 116.
21. Millett, *War for Korea,* 130.
22. *Reminiscences,* 332.
23. Millett, *War for Korea,* 105.
24. *Reminiscences,* 333.
25. MMA, Wright Oral reminiscences, RG 15, Box 91, 21–22.
26. *Reminiscences,* 334.
27. Acheson, 412.
28. Millett, *War for Korea,* 133.
29. Acheson, 413.
30. Millett, *War for Korea,* 137.
31. Millett, *War for Korea,* 138; Edgar O'Ballance, *Korea: 1950–1953* (London: Faber and Faber, 1969), 36.
32. Millett, *War for Korea,* 137–38, 139.
33. James III; Millett, *War for Korea,* 130.
34. O'Ballance, 36.
35. O'Ballance, 37.
36. James F. Schnabel and Robert J. Watson, *The History of the Joint Chiefs of Staff and National Policy: 1950–1951, The Korean War: Part One* (vol. III), 135.
37. *The New York Times,* July 9, 1950.
38. James III, 436.
39. *Reminiscences,* 356.
40. O'Ballance, 40.
41. *Reminiscences,* 337.
42. James Schnable, *U.S. Army in Korea: Policy and Decision, the First Year* (Washington, DC: GPO, 1992).
43. Millett, *War for Korea,* vol. III: 107–8; 148.
44. Millett, *War for Korea,* 165.
45. *Reminiscences,* 339; James III.
46. James III, 453.
47. *Reminiscences,* 339.
48. Acheson, 422.
49. Acheson, 423.
50. James III, 455.
51. *Soldier Speaks,* 221.
52. Acheson, 423.
53. *Reminiscences,* 341–42.
54. James III, 456–57.
55. James III, 465.
56. MMA, Wright interview, 57.
57. Robert Heinl, *Victory at High Tide: The Inchon-Seoul Campaign* (London: Leo Cooper, 1972), 19.
58. James III, 465.
59. O'Ballance, 49–50; Heinl, 24.
60. Vernon Walters, *Silent Missions* (NY: Doubleday, 1978), 197.
61. James III, 466.
62. MMA, Wright interview, 7–8.
63. James III, 467.

64. Bowers, "The Late General MacArthur," 244; James III, 359.
65. James III, 467.

CHAPTER 30: INCHON AND BEYOND

1. James, *Age of MacArthur* III, 467.
2. James III, 468.
3. *Reminiscences,* 349.
4. James III, 470.
5. James III, 468.
6. Millett, *War for Korea,* 227.
7. Shepherd interview, quoted in Perret, *Old Soldiers,* 548.
8. James III, 474.
9. Millett, 249.
10. *Reminiscences,* 352.
11. James III, 473, 475.
12. *Reminiscences,* 353.
13. James III, 476.
14. MMA, RG 4, DM to JCS, September 15, 1950.
15. James III, 475.
16. Millett, 250.
17. Millett, 251.
18. James III, 479.
19. James III, 478–79.
20. O'Ballance, *Korea,* 52.
21. *Reminiscenses,* 359–60.
22. Alexander Haig, *Inner Circles: How America Changed the World: A Memoir* (New York: Warner Books, 1992), 44–46.
23. Millett, 255.
24. Haig, 47.
25. *Korean War: Our Time in Hell* (film), Questar Studio, 2001.
26. *Reminiscences,* 371.
27. Harriman interview, Truman Library.
28. Acheson, *Present at the Creation,* 447.
29. Acheson, 451.
30. James III, 488.
31. James III, 489; *Reminiscences,* 358.
32. Millett, 291.
33. Millett, 232.
34. Millett, 234.
35. Millett, 235.
36. Millett, 236.
37. *Soldier Speaks,* 225–26.
38. Sebald, *With MacArthur,* 200.
39. Millett, 298.
40. Acheson, 452.
41. Frank, *MacArthur,* 155.
42. *Reminiscences,* 359.
43. Millett, 281.
44. David McCullough, *Truman* (New York: Simon & Schuster, 1992). John Edward Wiltz, "Truman and MacArthur: The Wake Island Meeting," Leary, ed., *MacArthur and the American Century,* 357–75, esp. 361–62.
45. James III, 503.
46. Perret, 554.

47. *Reminiscences,* 347–48.
48. Acheson, 456.
49. Harriman Oral History, Truman Library.
50. Dean Rusk, *As I Saw It* (New York: Norton, 1990), 168–69.
51. James III, 508.
52. *Reminiscences,* 363.
53. Peter Rodman, *Presidential Command* (New York: Knopf, 2009), 23.

CHAPTER 31: REVERSAL OF FORTUNE

1. James, *Age of MacArthur* III, 496.
2. *Reminiscences,* 364.
3. James III, 496.
4. James III, 497.
5. James III, 498.
6. *Reminiscences,* 365.
7. MMA, RG 6, DM to JCS, October 24, 1950.
8. James III, 518.
9. Millett, *War for Korea,* 297–98.
10. Millett, 295.
11. Millett, 298, 303.
12. Millett, 304.
13. Haig, *Inner Circles,* 56.
14. James III, 520.
15. *Reminiscences;* James III, 520.
16. Acheson, *Present at the Creation,* 463.
17. Mac to JCS, November 6, 1950, MMA.
18. James III, 523.
19. James III, 522–23.
20. Millett, 310.
21. *Reminiscences,* 369.
22. Millett, 317–18.
23. Millett, 306. George Stratemeyer, *The Three Wars of Lt. Gen. George E. Stratemeyer: His Korean War Diary,* (Washington, D.C.: Air Force History and Museums Programs, 1999), 267–98.
24. *Reminiscences,* 371.
25. J. Lawton Collins, *War in Peacetime: The History and Lessons of Korea* (Boston: Houghton Mifflin, 1969), 141–42.
26. James III, 530.
27. Haig, 58.
28. Millett, 335.
29. *Reminiscences,* 372.
30. Wright, *Oral Reminiscences,* 23; James III, 534.
31. *Reminiscences,* 372.
32. *Reminiscences,* 378.
33. MMA, RG 4, Communiqué No. 12, November 24, 1950.
34. TOP SECRET, November 8, 1950, RG 16, Box 4, MMA.
35. James III, 532.
36. *Reminiscences,* 373.
37. Millett, 336–37.
38. James McGovern, *To the Yalu: From the Chinese Invasion of Korea to MacArthur's Dismissal* (New York: Morrow, 1972), 107.
39. Millett, 337–38.
40. Millett, 342.

41. *Reminiscences,* 375.
42. Millett, 342–43.
43. Millett, 343.
44. Millett, 347.
45. Haig, 65.
46. O'Ballance, *Korea,* 73.
47. Acheson, 475.
48. James III, 541.
49. E.g., Millett, 360.
50. James III, 538.
51. Millett, 362–63.
52. Acheson, 475.
53. James III, 545.
54. Matthew Ridgway, *Soldier: The Memoirs of Matthew B. Ridgway* (New York: Harper, 1956), 201.
55. Ridgway, Memo of conference with DM, December 26, 1950, Ridgway Papers in Matthew Ridgway, *The Korean War: How We Met the Challenge* (Garden City, NY: Doubleday, 1967), 81–83.

CHAPTER 32: ENDGAME

1. Millett, *War for Korea,* 317–19.
2. For a good example of the myth, see David Halberstam. *The Coldest Winter: America and the Korean War* (New York: Hyperion, 2007).
3. *Reminiscences,* 374.
4. Millett, 372.
5. Hunt, *Untold Story,* 498.
6. Haig, *Inner Circles,* 64.
7. Lee and Henschel, *Douglas MacArthur,* 221.
8. Millett, 381.
9. Millett, 386.
10. *Reminiscences,* 383.
11. James III, 549.
12. MMA, HST to DM, January 15, 1950.
13. *Reminiscences,* 382.
14. Quoted in Lee and Henschel, 215.
15. Millett, 387.
16. Millett, 387.
17. Lee and Henschel, 221.
18. Lee and Henschel, 220–21.
19. *Reminiscences,* 383.
20. Perret, *Old Soldiers,* 566.
21. Millett, 390.
22. MMA, RG 16a, Box 4, Folder 9, Ridgway to DM, January 26, 1951.
23. O'Ballance, *Korea,* 83.
24. MMA, RG16a, Box 4, Folder 9, Ridgway to DM, January 28, 1951.
25. O'Ballance, 84.
26. MMA, RG 164, DM to Ridgway, February 4, 1951.
27. Millett, 406–8.
28. O'Ballance, 87.
29. O'Ballance, 87.
30. Acheson, *Present at the Creation,* 517.
31. Millett, 365.
32. Millett, 365.

33. James III, 578.
34. James III, 579.
35. James III, 578–79.
36. O'Ballance, "The MacArthur Plan," in Leary, ed., *MacArthur and the American Century,* 378–79.
37. O'Ballance, 377–78.
38. See Richard Bernstein, *China 1945: Mao's Revolution and America's Fateful Choice* (New York, Knopf, 2014).
39. E. Drea, "Military Intelligence and MacArthur 1941–1951: A Reappraisal," in *MacArthur and the American Century,* 202.
40. MMA, Wright interview, 53.
41. Wright interview, 54.
42. James III, 541–42.
43. Acheson, 518–19.
44. Millett, 418; MMA, RG 16a, DM to Ridgway, March 22, 1951.
45. *Reminiscences,* 387–88; Acheson, 518.
46. *Reminiscences,* 387.
47. James III, 587.
48. Quoted in Acheson, 519.
49. Millett, 418.
50. James III, 583.
51. James III, 590.
52. James III, 590–91.
53. James III, 591.
54. Acheson, 521–22; James III, 592.
55. James III, 594.
56. Acheson, 522.
57. Acheson, 518.
58. Huff, *My Fifteen Years,* 135–36.
59. Huff, 6–7.
60. James III, 600.
61. USAMHI. Interview, Almond, part 5, p. 43.
62. James III, 599.
63. Acheson, 522–23.
64. Whitney, 472.
65. James III, 601; Ridgway, *Soldier: The Memoirs of Matthew B. Ridgway* (New York: Harper Bros, 1956), 223.
66. Quoted in Dower, *Embracing Defeat,* 548–49.
67. Sebald, *With MacArthur,* 234.
68. Sebald, 229–30.
69. Quoted in James III, 603.
70. Dower, 549.
71. Sebald, 234.
72. Huff, 139.
73. Quoted in *Reminiscences,* 396.
74. See Michael Schaller, *Altered States: The United States and Japan Since the Occupation* (New York: Oxford University Press, 1997).
75. Quoted in Harvey, *American Shogun,* 427.

CHAPTER 33: FADING AWAY

1. James, *Age of MacArthur* III, 608.
2. Arthur Herman, *Joseph McCarthy: Reexamining the Life and Legacy of America's Most Hated Senator* (New York: Free Press, 2000), 155.

3. Herman, *Joseph McCarthy,* 154–55.
4. *Reminiscences,* 405–6.
5. James III, 609.
6. James III, 612.
7. *Reminiscences,* 400.
8. Huff, *My Fifteen Years,* 140.
9. James III, 613.
10. James III, 613; Acheson, *Present at the Creation,* 528.
11. *Reminiscences,* 406.
12. Representative Speeches of Douglas MacArthur, 20, 27.
13. James III, 608.
14. Quoted in James III, 626–27.
15. James III, 633.
16. *Reminiscences,* 393.
17. MMA, Rg 46, Eisenhower interview, 73.
18. *Speeches of Douglas MacArthur,* 66–67.
19. MMA, RG 16, Box 4, "Memo to Ike," December 14, 1952; also *Reminiscences,* 410–12.
20. *Soldier Speaks,* 315.
21. James III, 684.
22. *Reminiscences,* v.
23. James III, 678.

CONCLUSION

1. E.g., Robert H. Ferrell, *The Question of MacArthur's Reputation: Côte de Châtillon, October 14–16, 1918* (Columbia: University of Missouri Press, 2008).
2. Address to the Congress of American Industry, December 5, 1952, in *Soldier Speaks,* 300.

INDEX

DM = Douglas MacArthur
FDR = Franklin Delano Roosevelt

Acheson, Dean, 644, 660, 688, 748, 784, 820
 accidental leaking of DM's dismissal, 811
 on China, 828
 DM and, 724, 822
 DM insubordination, 804–5, 807–9, 847
 DM refutes accusation about triggering
  Red Chinese intervention in Korea,
  826
 DM's dismissal from Korea and, 833
 Korean War and, 717, 753, 754, 769
 National Press Club speech (Jan. 12,
  1950), 708, 709
 Truman and DM, 758
 Truman's Korean cease-fire plan, 798
Acheson, Roland, 453–54
Adachi, Hatazo, 488–89, 501, 504, 505,
  510–11
Adelaide, Australia, 418, 419
Admiralty Islands, 491–97
 Allied victory in, 497
 Brewer Task Force, 492, 493–96
 DM at odds with Halsey and, 498–99
 Los Negros, 491, 492, 493, 501
 Manus, 491, 497, 498, 499, 500

 Momote landing strip, 495–96, 497
 Seeadler Harbor, 491, 492, 497, 498
Adversario, Domingo, 347, 348, 361
Aguinaldo, Emilio, 35, 39–41, 44, 45, 58, 59,
  189, 683
Air Forces of the Far East (AAF), 446, 447,
  449, 450, 453, 454, 770. *See also*
  Kenney, George
 Kenney as commander, 446–60
 morale problem, 448
Aitape, 501, 502, 503
 codebreakers warn of Japanese assault,
  510–11
 Japanese secret codes left at, 503–4
 XI Corps defense of, 511
Akin, Spencer, 328, 436
 Bataan Gang member, 300
 Central Bureau codebreakers and, 436,
  462, 465, 479, 491, 503–4, 519
 escape from Corregidor, 396, 407
 as USAFFE GHQ signal officer, 300, 311,
  436
 intel about enemy on Luzon and Leyte,
  530

Akin, Spencer (*cont'd*):
    Japanese reinforcements at Leyte missed,
        552
    as SCAP chief signal officer, 659
Akira, General, 366
Alexander, Irv, 406
Alexander the Great, 656
Alice Springs, Australia, 417–18
Allen, Roger, 240
Allison, John, 749
Almond, Edward "Ned," 5, 727, 730, 733–34,
        786
    Battle of Wonju and, 792
    Chinese Fourth Offensive and, 795
    Chinese POWs and, 767–68
    DM's dismissal from Korea and, 810–11
    as DM's protégé, 785
    finest hour, 792
    Hungnam evacuation, 781–82
    Inchon-Seoul Campaign, 737, 740, 741,
        743, 744
    Special Activities Group or SAG, 792
    war conference (Nov. 28, 1950), 779
    X Corps and, 755, 756, 764, 767, 768, 770,
        772, 781–82, 792, 795–96
    Yalu River advance and retreat, 772,
        777–80
Ambrose, Stephen, 159, 170, 176
*American Caesar: Douglas MacArthur
    1880–1964* (Manchester), xii
Ames, Godfrey, 363
Anderson, Ray, 581
Anderson, Vernice, 761
Annapolis, U.S. Naval Academy at, 28, 30
Arnold, Hap, 298, 303, 317, 472, 485
    firebombing of Tokyo, 605
    invasion of the Philippines and, 529
    Twentieth Air Force, 605
Arthur, Chester A., 18
Atazo, Adachi, 466
Atlanta, Georgia, 187
Atlantic Alliance, 703
Atsugi, Japan, 615, 616, 618, 619, 621
Attlee, Clement, 783
Austin, Paul, 509, 534–35
Australia, 385, 420. *See also* Brisbane,
        Australia; Curtin, John; Melbourne,
        Australia; South West Pacific Area
        (SWPA)
    Advisory War Council, 422
    as Allied base in the Pacific, 415
    Allied troops in (1942), 419
    Brisbane Line defense, 421

defense of, 421, 427
DM and command of troops, 607–8
DM and Prime Minister Curtin, 387, 388,
        390, 391, 392, 422, 428
DM arrives in (1942), 416–18
DM assesses military readiness in, 419
DM in (1943), 474–75
DM's escape from Corregidor and, 396
expectations of DM and the U.S. in,
        420–21
Japanese threat to, 387, 413, 421
Korean War and, 719, 738, 756, 767
Pacific Islands granted to, 150
U. S. Army Forces in Australia (USAFIA),
        399
Australian Military Forces (World War II),
        428, 483
    Borneo offensive and, 606–7, 609–10
    control of, 422, 429, 607
    fighting in Europe, 388
    first defeat of a Japanese amphibious force,
        444
    last amphibious landing of WWII by, 613
    New Guinea Campaign and, 526
    Papua and, 444, 449, 450, 451

Baillie, Hugh, 803
Baker, Newton
    accolades for DM, 151, 155
    DM and National Guard, 96, 97, 104
    tour of the front (March 19, 1918), 113–14
    as Wilson's Secretary of War, 90, 91, 93,
        94, 101, 118, 157
Barbey, Daniel, 462–65, 844
    Admiralty Islands offensive and, 493
    Admiralty Islands reconnaissance, 494
    amphibious landing craft and, 462–63,
        476
    Battle of Morotai Island, 520
    DM and, 463–65
    flagship *Blue Ridge,* 566
    Operation CARTWHEEL (Elkton III),
        483–86
    Philippines Campaign (1944–45), 523–24,
        526
Bare, Colonel, 138, 139, 140, 141, 143
Barnes, Julian, 435
Barr, David, 730
Bataan Peninsula, 56, 58, 180, 344, 845
    ammunition problems, 359, 372–73
    Bataan Campaign, 340–41, 348, 355–60,
        366–69, 371–75, 392, 396–97
    Bataan Campaign, army historian for, 381

Bataan Death March, 648–49, 651
  casualties, 359, 374–75
  civilians on, 353, 356
  DM and visiting, 357, 381–82
  DM escape to Australia and, 393,
    400–402, 406
  DM misleads soldiers on, 368–69, 371,
    382
  DM's last plan for, 430–31
  "Dugout Doug" song, 380–81, 382, 395
  fate of the men, 475
  FDR abandons DM's forces, 369
  food and supplies shortages, 341, 353, 356,
    361, 362, 372–75, 396, 407
  I Corps (Philippine Divisions), 356, 357,
    366, 367, 368, 401, 430
  II Corps, 356, 357, 358, 360, 366, 367, 368,
    430
  Japanese casualties, 371–72, 396
  Japanese offensive, 397
  Japanese opponents, 356, 366, 371–72,
    397, 439
  Philippine Scouts, 356, 358, 359, 366, 430
  retaking (1945), DM returns, 588–89,
    590–92
  success against Japanese, 371–72, 396–97
  surrender to the Japanese, 429–32
  troops on, 353, 356, 357, 359, 366, 372,
    406, 430
  troops taken ill on, 372
  twentieth anniversary of, 840
  Wainwright's last stand on, 333
  War Plan Orange Three and, 338–41, 353,
    367
  withdrawal from II Corps sector, 367–68
Bazelaire, Georges de, 108–9, 110
Bell, J. Franklin, 71–73, 76, 79
Bergerud, Eric, 499
Bernard, Henri, 701
Bessemer-Clark, Reginald, 527
Beveridge, Albert, 19, 34, 64, 69
Biak Island
  battle for, 505–10
  casualties, 508, 509, 510
  Eichelberger and, 508–9
  Hurricane Task Force, 508, 510
  Imperial Japanese Navy and, 505–6
  Japanese fortifications on, 507
  Wakde Island assault and, 506–7
Biard, Forrest "Tex," 490
Bilbo, Theodore, 663
Bird, Stephen, 170
Bismarck Islands, 460, 471

Bismarck Sea, Battle of, 466–70
  list of Japanese officers recovered by
    Allies, 479
Bisson, Thomas N., 679
Blamey, Sir Thomas, 427, 454, 457, 458
  Allied Forces of, 427–28, 435, 476
  DM's command of troops kerfuffle, 607–8
  New Guinea Force, 482
  Papua and, 439–40, 449
Bliss, Tasker, 101
Bluemel, Cliff, 357, 406, 430, 432
Bong, Richard, 551
Bonus Army scandal, 212–25, 244, 249
  DM's image and, 217–18, 222–25, 845
Booz, Oscar L., 43
Borneo, 414, 426, 433
  DM offensive, 606–7, 609–10
Bradley, Omar, 4, 728, 762
  criticism of DM's Korean strategy, 769–70
  DM's dismissal and, 807–9, 811, 833
  Korean War and, 774, 802, 847
  Wake Island meeting with DM, 758–60,
    761
Brereton, Lewis, 303, 308–9
  B-17s pulled back to Australia by, 329
  Japanese bombing of Clark Field and,
    318–22, 335, 447
  Japanese interception of message, 318
  leaves the Philippines (1941), 334–35
  P-40s flown out to Darwin, 334
  preemptive raid on Formosa and, 315–18
Brett, George, 399, 412, 446, 447–48
Briand, Aristide, 192
Bridges, Styles, 818
Brisbane, Australia
  Elaine Clark in, 527, 528
  Lennons Hotel as family quarters, 474,
    525
  SWPA HQ in, 441, 459, 462, 463, 469,
    474, 476, 483, 523
Brooks, Walter, 171
Brougher, General, 406
Brown, Howard, 312, 322
Brown, Robert A., 99
Buhite, Russell, xii
Bulkeley, John, 305, 342, 371, 374, 398
  Corregidor evacuation, 396–400, 404–6,
    408, 411
Bundy, Omar, 182, 184
Bunker, Paul, 404, 406, 430, 583, 816
Burke, Arleigh, 779
Burke, John C., 27
Burleson, Allen, 29, 30

Burma, 364, 388, 414, 607
    DM in (1905–1906), 65
Butler, Benjamin, 13
Byers, Clovis, 455

Caesar, 656
Cagayan de Misamis, 411–14
Camp Mills, Long Island, 99–101
Canberra, Australia, 422, 526
Cape Gloucester, New Britain, 471
    Battle of, 480, 481, 486–87, 501
    DM visits, 501–2
    U.S. Marines at, 481, 486, 487, 501
Caroline Islands, 150, 499. See also Truk
    Island
Carpender, Arthur, 439, 492
Carr, Sir William Comyns, 699
Cartwell, Robert, 350
Casey, Charles, 111
Casey, Hugh, 300, 303
    escape from Corregidor, 395, 407, 408
    as GHQ engineer, 435
    landing at Leyte, 536–37
    as SCAP chief engineer, 659
    SWPA Army Service Command, 524
Central Intelligence Agency (CIA)
    on China entering Korean War, 752–53,
        754
    faulty intelligence and losses at Yalu,
        779–80
Chaffee, Adna, 204
Chakravarty, Judge, 701
Chamberlain, John, xii
Chamberlin, Stephen, 435, 442, 462, 492, 519
    as SCAP G-3 intelligence head, 659
Champlin, Norman, 372
Chase, General, 497
Chase, Joseph, 152
Chiang Kai-shek, 197, 201, 262, 275, 298, 560,
        683, 695, 703, 708, 717
    Cairo conference, 693
    DM meeting (July 31, 1950), 724–25
    DM's position on U.S. support for, 825
    DM's "The Plan" and, 799, 800
    FDR promises aid, 275
    Truman refuses aid, 708, 752
China. See also Chiang Kai-shek; Korean War;
        Mao Zedong
    Boxer Rebellion, 67
    Canton, 67
    civil war, 201, 683
    Communism and, 275, 560, 703
    DM in (1906), 67

DM's predictions and, 800–801
DM's strategy on Communist China,
        798–802
DM's urging for U.S. in war with, 800–802
DM's view of U.S. failure in, 825, 833
expansionism and, 776, 802, 826, 828, 837
Grant brokers peace treaty with Japan, 18
Japan attacks Shanghai, 206
Japanese advances in, 262
Japanese threat to, 560
Japanese victories in, 275
Japan occupies north, 243
Japan takes Manchuria, 205–6
Japan takes Shantung Peninsula, 149
Korean War and, xiii, xiv, 751–53,
        766–806
Korean War casualties, 788, 794, 796, 797,
        835
Korean War stalemate and, 835
Kuomintang, 275
Mao Zedong's victory, 706
nationalism in, 197
Peking, 67
Rape of Nanking, 275, 648, 698
revolution, 67
Soviet planes for, 770
Soviet claims in Mongolia/Manchuria,
        578–79
U.S. Fifteenth Infantry in, 293
U.S. support for territorial integrity of, 206
U.S. trade agreement with, 17
war threat to U.S., 752, 801, 812, 833
World War II, 560
World War II begins and, 275
"Chinese Memorandum" (A. MacArthur),
        19–22, 23, 54, 56
Chulalongkorn, King, 66–67, 66n
Church, John, 715
Churchill, Randolph, 65
Churchill, Winston, 37, 65, 349, 416
    Australia and, 438
    Boer War, quip about being shot at, 58
    Cairo conference, 693
    DM as Allied supreme commander in the
        Pacific and, 387–88, 390
    FDR and, 228
    liaison killed on USS New Mexico, 565
    message to DM after liberation of Seoul,
        747
    naps and, 686
    Papuan Campaign and, 459
    Potsdam Declaration, 641
    stature of, and DM's, 848

told U.S. is abandoning the Philippines, 354–55
Yalta Conference, 578–79
Civilian Conservation Corps (CCC), 228–31, 230n, 232
Civil War, xiv, 5
    Battle of Atlanta, 8
    Battle of Franklin, 9, 26, 27
    Battle of Fredericksburg, 99
    Battle of Kennesaw Mountain, 8, 26, 185–86
    Battle of Missionary Ridge, 8, 26, 27, 75, 76, 98, 143, 255
    Battle of Murfreesboro, 27
    Battle of Peach Tree Creek, 186
    DM visits battlefields of, 185–86
    draft riots, 92
    Eleventh Mississippi, 28
    First Bull Run, 99
    Hardy family and, 13
    heroism of Arthur MacArthur, 8–10, 26, 27
    surrender of the Confederacy, 10
    Twenty-fourth Wisconsin, 8–10, 32, 35, 75–78, 98, 186
Clark, Mark, 379
Clarke, Elaine, 527–28, 627–28
Clausewitz, Carl von, 165, 446
Clear, Warren, 338, 373
Cleveland, Grover, 31
Coblenz, Germany, 152, 154
Cocheu, George, 52
Cold War, 3, 694, 704, 833
    containment policy, 688, 703
    New York Times interview with DM, 707
Collins, Lawton, 4, 5, 728–29, 732–35, 782, 787
    DM meeting with (Dec., 1950), 783
    DM's dismissal and, 808, 811, 833
    on Walker's risk-taking, 785
Collins, Ross, 204, 208–12, 233, 240, 243
Communism, 6, 214, 683, 745. *See also* China
    American anti-Communism, 820
    Bonus Army and, 213–16, 217, 223, 224
    containment of, 688, 691, 703, 704, 830, 833
    DM and halt of spread in Asia, 747
    DM learns lesson about appeal to Asians, 65
    DM's position on, 215
    DM's view of threat, 824, 828
    domino theory and, 837
    in Europe, postwar, 683

    in Japan, 697
    in Korea, 694–97
    Korean War and defeating spread in Asia, 793
    U.S. Communist Party, 214, 224
    U.S. wants Japan as buffer against, 689, 691
Compton, Karl, 685
Conejero, Lino, 361–62
Conner, Fox, 199
Connolly, Tom, 639
Connor, William, 199
Cook, Charles, 471
Coolidge, Calvin, 188, 194, 212
Cooper, Isabella Rosario, 237–42, 249, 849
Coral Sea, Battle of the, 433–34, 437, 439
Corbin, Henry Clark, 34
Cordier, Constant, 82, 85–86
Corregidor, 179, 180, 198, 199, 288, 295, 430, 432
    air attacks on, 344, 346–48, 361, 374
    battle for, 338–94
    Bottomside, 343, 348, 361, 362
    casualties, 347, 348
    DM and family arrive at, 341
    DM and family escape, 395–400, 403–6, 845
    DM and family's quarters, 342, 348, 361
    DM gets orders to leave, 391–93
    DM haunted by breaking his vow to stay, 399
    DM prepares for a last stand, 376–77, 384
    DM's codebreakers evacuate, 393
    DM's forces withdraw to, 333–37
    DM's headquarters, 342, 343, 361
    DM's orderly, 347, 348, 361
    DM's routine, 360–61, 364–65
    DM's weight loss, 361
    DM waits for help from Washington, 344–46
    fortifications, 343
    Fourth Marine Regiment, 344
    gold and silver bullion removed from, 373
    Japanese artillery shelling of, 362, 374
    Japanese offensive, 397
    Legaspi and, 361–62
    list of those escaping with DM, 395–96
    Malinta Tunnel, 341–42, 349
    PURPLE cipher machine at, 311
    Quezon and wife on, 341, 348, 349, 360
    Quezon cables FDR with neutrality proposal, 374–75
    Quezon evacuated, 382, 385, 389

Corregidor (*cont'd*):
 Quezón's inauguration and, 349
 reporters and groundswell for DM,
  377–80
 "Special Executive Order from President
  Quezon," 382–83
 Special Order, 66, 402
 supply shortage, 361
 surrender to the Japanese (1942),
  589
 Topside and Middleside, 342, 343, 347
 translations of decrypted messages at,
  311–12
 twentieth anniversary of, 840
 War Plan Orange Three and, 338–41
 Wilkie starts movement to save DM,
  384–85
Corregidor Campaign (1945), 589–93
 bad intel on Japanese strength, 589, 590
 casualties, 592, 598–99
 DM witnesses flag-raising, 599
 Japanese blow up underground arsenal,
  598
 Japanese commander on, 592
 Japanese wiped out, 593, 598
 Malinta Tunnel, 593, 599
 paratroopers drop into, 590, 592–93
Coulter, John B., 100
Crackel, Theodore, 159
Craig, Malin, 244, 276
Crimmins, Fred, 320
Crosby, Herbert, 217
Crowder, Enoch, 60, 92
Cuba, 33, 35, 40, 79
Curley, James, 255
Curtin, John, 387, 390, 526
 Blamey-DM kerfuffle and, 607–8
 DM and, 422, 428, 475, 526
 military strategy and, 438
 Papuan Campaign and, 459
Curzon, Lord, 66
Cushing, Caleb, 17
Custer, George Armstrong, 49

Daily Telegraph, 806–7
Dalton, James, II, 574
Danford, Robert, 162, 166, 168, 169
Daniels, Josephus, 225, 227–28
Davis, Dwight, 199
Davis, Jefferson, 24
Davis, Tommy, 53, 219, 238, 249, 255, 264,
  273, 274, 279
Davison, Trubee, 220

Dean, William, 721
Decker, George, 508
Deming, W. Edwards, 685
Democratic Party, 227, 679, 757, 809. *See also*
  Roosevelt, Franklin Delano; Truman,
  Harry
 Arthur MacArthur and, 51
 Bonus Marchers and, 213, 223
 DM criticizes, 836–37
 DM's appointment as SCAP commander
  and, 640
 DM's dismissal from Korea and, 818–19
 DM's image attacked, 844–45
 DM's presidential ambitions worrying,
  642
 presidential election, 1952, loss of, 834
Derevyanko, Kuzma, 638–39
Dern, George, 233–34, 235, 247, 258
Dewey, George, 35, 39
Dewey, Thomas E., 514, 515, 517
Diller, Eric, 509
Diller, LeGrand, 300, 411, 413, 435, 596, 659
Djakarta, Indonesia, DM in (1905), 64–65
Donovan, William "Wild Bill," 109, 115
 Irish Battalion, Ourcq, 124, 125, 126, 127,
  128
 Medal of Honor, 126, 151
Doolittle, James, 452, 628
Douglas, Lewis, 231
*Douglas MacArthur: Statecraft and Stagecraft
  in America's East Asian Policy* (Buhite),
  xii
Douglas MacArthur: The Far Eastern General
  (Schaller), xii
Douglas MacArthur: The Philippine Years
  (Petillo), xii
Dower, John, 635
Doyle, James, 730, 733, 734, 735
 flagship *Mount McKinley,* 737
 landings at Inchon, 737, 739
Draper, Kenneth, 691
Drea, Edward, 478, 612
Duffy, Father Francis X., 99, 116, 118, 120
Dulles, John Foster, 710, 712, 747, 817, 837
Dunckle, William, 556
Dupuy, Ernest, 92–93
Dutch East Indies, 291, 298, 356, 414, 426
 Asiatic Fleet moves to, 324
 DM in (1905), 65
 DM offensive in Borneo, 606
 Japan invades, 364
 Java, 413, 414
 surrender of Allied forces, 413

Early, Steve, 290, 291, 373
Edwards, Idwal, 732
Edwards, Jim, 736, 737
Edward VIII, Prince of Wales, 154
Egeberg, Roger "Doc," 686
    Admiralty Islands campaign and, 495, 496
    arrival in Japan (1945), 621
    battle for Manila and, 575
    dinner at the Grand Hotel, Yokohama, 624
    as DM confidant, 602, 604
    DM on Japanese surrender, 614, 615
    as DM's private physician, 493–94
    DM's reaction to destruction in Japan, 622
    at Hollandia, 502
    invasion of the Philippines and, 536–37, 545
    Japanese surrender ceremony and, 629, 630
    Jean MacArthur and, 604–5
    at Morotai, 520, 521
    occupation of Japan and, 616
    retaking Bataan and, 591–92
    Roxas's release and, 608–9
    weeping at planes lost at Leyte, 549
Eichelberger, Robert "Bob," 73, 74, 251, 454–55
    battle for Manila, 573–74, 576, 587
    Biak Island and, 508–9
    Distinguished Service Cross, 573
    DM arrives in Japan and, 619
    Eighth Army of, 554, 573, 587, 601, 617, 637
    Hollandia and, 502, 504
    Japanese surrender ceremony and, 628
    occupation forces, 637
    Papua and, 455–60, 573
    relieves Harding, 455
Eisenhower, Dwight David, 236
    America's nuclear leverage and, 838
    background, 249
    believes DM should get a desk job, 387
    as chief of staff, Third Army, 285
    command in the Pacific and, 426
    deteriorating relations with DM, 276, 278–80
    DM and the Bonus Army, 218, 221, 222
    DM and the CCC, 230
    DM as SWPA supreme commander, 423, 425
    DM encourages presidential run, 836
    DM meeting with, on Korean solution, 837–38
    DM proposes Ike-Stalin summit, 838

    DM's Chastleton Apartments scandal and, 241
    as DM's chief of staff, Philippines, 249, 255, 257–58, 261, 266, 269, 293
    on DM's reaction to his mother's death, 260
    DM's situation in Corregidor and Bataan and, 375, 386
    flying in the Philippines, 281
    Jean MacArthur and, 264, 270
    Korean strategy, including atomic bomb, 837
    Korean War and, 836, 837
    leaves the Philippines (1939), 284–85
    leaves the Philippines (1941), 294
    message to DM after liberation of Seoul, 747
    nuclear weapons and, 613
    opinion of DM, 249
    Ord and, 249, 293
    Pershing's memoirs written by, 249
    plan to defend the Philippines and, 326–27
    post-World War II and DM, 637–38
    presidential election, 834–35, 836
    statement of May 6, 1942, 395
    World War I and, 285
    as writer, 249
Eisenhower, John, 285
Eisenhower, Mamie, 249, 285
Entezam, Nasrollah, 788
Ericcson, Colonel, 146
Ettinger, Albert, 106, 113

Falk, Stanley, 845
Fearey, Robert, 699
Fechner, Robert, 229, 231
Fellers, Bonner, 410, 650, 659, 661, 699, 703
Ferrell, Robert, 142
Feuereisen, Charles, 557–58
Fiebeger, Gustav J., 166
"Fight of the General Armstrong, The" (Roche), 30
Finschhafen, 472, 479, 484, 488, 492
Fitch, Burdette, 435
Flagler, Charles, 152
Foch, Ferdinand, 123, 132, 267
Ford, James, 224
Forde, Francis M. S., 420, 421
Formosa, 311, 516, 518, 528, 529, 708, 713, 717. See also Chiang Kai-shek
    DM offers jet fighters to, 725
    DM's position on U.S. support for, 825

Formosa (*cont'd*):
DM's VFW statement on, 726, 727
DM's visit to, 724
preemptive raid on, 315–18
threat of invasion, 724
Truman policy on, 724, 725, 726
Fort Myer, VA, 216, 218
Foulois, Benjamin, 236–37, 237n
France, World War I, 103–49. *See also*
MacArthur, Douglas, 1917–1918
Fourth Army, 116, 118–19, 123, 146
Marne salient, 123, 127
U.S. troops and DM at Château-Thierry,
123–24
U.S. troops and DM at Ourcq, 124–27
U.S. troops and DM at Souain, 119–22
France, World War II, 286, 292
Frankel, Stanley, 567–68
Franz Ferdinand, Archduke of Austria, 75
Franz Josef, Emperor, 75
Freeman, The, 807
French Indochina
Cam Ranh Bay, 292
Chinese expansionism and, 776
Communist insurgency in, 837
DM in (1906), 67
Japan invades, 364
Japan's aggression and, 291, 292
Saigon, 67
Fry, Philip, 358
Fukudomi, Admiral, 150
Fuller, Horace, 507, 508–9
Funston, Frederick, 46, 80–81, 82, 86, 87,
94

Galula, David, 44
Gandhi, Mohandas, 197, 201
Ganoe, William Addleman, 160–61, 266
Garner, John Nance, 211, 349
Garrison, Lindley, 81
General and the President, The (Rovere and
Schlesinger), xii, 844–45
George, Harold, 308, 310–11
Germany. *See also* MacArthur, Douglas,
1917–18; World War I; *specific battles*
Berlin Airlift, 703
denazification of, 678
Fourth Guards, 125
Nüremberg trial, 698, 701
Treaty of Versailles and, 155, 159–60
U.S. declares war on (1917), 93
World War I, 89, 93, 103–49
Germany, World War II

Belgium, Holland, and France taken, 286,
290
blitzkrieg tactics, 209n, 291
conscription instituted (1935), 243
DM billeted at Coblenz, 152, 154
French troops leave the Rhineland (1930),
201
Hitler becomes chancellor, 206
Hitler in power, 236
Hitler's expansionist goals, 243
invasion of Poland, 283
invasion of Russia, 292
Nationalist Socialists begin, 160
panzer divisions, 209n
pulls out of the League of Nations, 236
Gerow, Leonard, 315, 354
Ghormley, Robert, 441
Gilbert Islands, 150, 488
Glassford, Pelham D., 214–17, 219, 221–22,
224
Glenn, George, 140
Godman, Henry, 413, 527–28
Gouraud, Henri, 116, 118–22, 322
accolades for DM, 151
Grace, J. G., 434
Grant, Ulysses S., 16–18, 49, 559
Arthur MacArthur and China posting, 18,
19, 21
art of war, 123
Asia and, 16–18
Hawaii reciprocity treaty and, 17
world tour, 16–18
Grant, Ulysses S., III, 38
Grashio, Sam, 297, 319, 320, 321, 583
Graves, Ernest, 211
Great Britain. *See also* Churchill, Winston
abandoning of Australia, 387
Arcadia Conference, 425
colonizing Asia, 19–20, 65–66, 201, 607
Fifth Army, 114, 121
Korean War and, 719, 723, 738, 739, 745,
756, 767, 771, 772, 773, 777, 783
naval losses (1941–1942), 414
propose Korean ceasefire, 784
sinking of the *Prince of Wales* and the
Repulse, 310, 324, 387
surrender of Singapore, 385
U.S. leadership in Pacific War and, 425
war declared on Japan, 322
Washington Naval Treaty of 1921–1922
(Five-Power Treaty), 198
World War I and, 104, 114–15, 119
Great Depression, xv, 209–10, 212–24, 236

Grew, Joseph, 623, 644
Griswold, Oswald, 572, 574, 576, 587–88
Groves, Leslie, 685
Grunert, George, 287, 299, 308
Guadalcanal, 427, 441, 442, 444, 452, 460, 476, 486, 487
Guam, 150, 286, 500, 528, 554
Gunn, Irvin "Pappy," 449–50, 452, 465, 468
Gunther, John, 730

Hadley, Eleanor, 680
Haggerty, Father Edward, 411, 412
Hagood, Johnson, 200
Haig, Al, 744, 745, 746, 767–68, 781
Haig, Douglas, 251
Hall, Charles, 511, 520, 601
Halsey, William "Bull," 461, 462, 471, 472, 478, 492
    Admiralty Islands and, 498–99
    air power of, 542–43
    CARTWHEEL and, 479–80, 483–84, 487
    DM and, 479
    DM doesn't blame for Leyte Gulf, 549, 550
    Essex-class carriers, 548
    FDR summit, Pearl Harbor (1944), 516
    Japanese naval air power destroyed by, 529, 530
    Japanese surrender ceremony and, 628
    Japanese trap set for, 542–47, 549
    message to DM on Inchon, 747
    Mindoro operation and, 555–56
    Philippines Campaign (1944–45), 523–24, 542
    Reno IV plan, 499
    shelling of Luzon, 559
    surveillance of Philippines and, 518–19
Handy, Thomas, 109, 110
Harbord, James, 104–5
Harding, Edwin, 451, 453, 454, 455–56
Hardy, Thomas (maternal grandfather), 13
Harmon, Millard, 471
Harrell, Colonel, 146
Harries, Meirion and Susie, 679–80
Harriman, Averell, 674, 724, 727, 729–30, 748
    DM's dismissal from Korea and, 807–9
    Wake Island meeting with DM and Truman, 759
Harriman, E. H., 54, 71
Hart, Thomas, 286, 303–5, 310, 314, 332, 439, 463
    evacuates Manila on submarine, 334, 336
    withdraws fleet, 324, 326, 327, 345
Harvey, Robert, 678

Hay, John, 34
Hearst, William, 33
Heavy, William, 464
Hencke, John, 579, 580
Herring, Edmund, 451, 456, 458
Hersey, John, 290, 328
Hibbs, Lewis, 169
Hickey, Doyle Overton, 769, 779, 786
Hindenburg, Paul von, 267
Hines, Charles, 166
Hines, John L., 185
Hinshaw, Marvin, 497
Hirohito, Emperor of Japan, 75, 470
    demand that he renounce his divinity, 652, 666
    DM and, 626
    DM and occupation, 614–15, 645–47
    DM arrival in Japan and, 621
    DM recalls meeting him as child, 651
    farewell to DM, 814–15
    Kase's report on surrender ceremony and, 645
    kept out of war crimes trials, 700, 701
    meeting with DM (Sept. 27, 1945), 649–53, 654
    new constitution for Japan and, 669
    as partner in remaking Japan, 652, 661–62, 703
    surrender speech, 616, 630
    takes responsibility for war crimes, 651
Hirota, Koki, 701, 702
Hitler, Adolf, 159–60, 206, 236, 243, 578, 700
HMAS Australia, 567
HMS King George V, 414
HMS Prince of Wales, 310, 324, 387
HMS Repulse, 310, 324, 387
Ho Chi Minh, 837
Hodge, John, 617, 635–37, 692, 693, 694, 695
Holbrook, Lucius, 267–68, 276
Hollandia, 484, 491, 492, 497, 524
    battle for, 501–3, 506
    DM on cruiser Nashville and, 501
    Hollywood stars visit, 522
    huge base built on, 504
    Japanese banzai attack, 510–11
    Japanese POWs, 503
    Reno IV plan, 499, 500
    staging ground for Philippines, 522, 523, 526
    SWPA HQ on, 519, 522–23, 525
Holmes, Oliver Wendell, 9
Holt, Lucius, 166, 169
Homma, Fukijo, 674–75

Homma, Masaharu, 332, 351–52, 356, 360,
 366, 371–72, 397, 429, 562
   Bataan Death March and, 649, 673, 675
   casualties at Bataan, 371–72
   DM's personal anger at, 673
   false report of suicide, 379
   trial and execution of, 649, 673–75, 698
Hong Kong, 364, 414
Honshu invasion (CORONET), 601, 606, 610,
 617
Hood, John Bell, 186
Hoover, Herbert, 199, 828
   Bonus Army and, 213–17, 219–21, 223–24
   DM calls for sanctions on Japan, 206
   Great Depression and, 213, 224
   military cuts and, 209–10, 231
   Pershing opposes DM as Chief of Staff,
    200
   recommendations for DM as Chief of
    Staff, 200
   reelection scuttled, 224
   retreat, Rapidan, VA, 209
Hopkins, Harry, 390
Horii, Tomitaro, 444, 450
Hostetter, Phil, 540
Howard, Roy, 200
Howard, Tom, 585–86, 587, 595
Howze, Robert Lee, 189
Huerta, Victoriano, 80
Huff, Sid, 265, 270, 282, 299, 305, 306, 333,
 408
   arrival in Australia, 417, 418
   on Corregidor, 342, 348, 364
   Corregidor escape, 395, 398, 403, 404, 410
   DM addresses Congress (1951) and, 823
   DM's conversation aboard PT-41, 410–11,
    494
   DM's family in care of, 474, 525
   DM sends to Manila for personal items,
    342–43
   dog, Koko, 686
   on GHQ staff, Japan, 659
   Jean MacArthur and, 809, 814
   in Melbourne, 420
   news of DM's dismissal and, 810
   Quezon and, 382
   return to America with DM, 816
Hughes, Charles Evans, 198
Hull, Cordell, 390
Hull, Gertrude, 32
Hunt, Frazier, xii
Hurley, Patrick J., 125, 200–201, 209–10, 217,
 220, 222, 223, 224

meets DM in Australia, 417–18
   as special envoy to Australia, 370, 388
Hutter, Howard, 182, 248, 256, 274

Ickes, Harold, 267, 640
Imperial Japanese Navy
   Battle of Biak and, 505–6
   Battle of the Coral Sea, 433–34, 437
   Battle of Leyte Gulf, 542–49
   Battle of Midway, 434–35, 437
   finished as fighting force, 549
   Halsey destroys naval air power, 529, 530
   Southern Force, 542, 543
   super-battleships, 542, 543, 547, 549
Imanura, Hitoshi, 466
India, 65–66, 197, 683, 801, 802
   DM in (1906), 65
Indonesia, 801
Influence of Sea Power Upon History (Mahan),
 19
Irwin, General, 538
Itagaki, Akira, 592–93
Italy, 160, 206, 236, 243
Iwabuchi, Sanji, 576, 672
   last stand in Manila, 576–77, 582–88,
    593–96
Iwao, Oyama, 61
Iwo Jima, 517, 600–601, 741, 787

Jackson, Andrew, 849
Jacoby, Melville, 377
James, D. Clayton, xii, 242, 297, 490, 799, 802,
 828, 845
Japan
   Arthur MacArthur as military attaché in,
    60–62
   Arthur MacArthur's concerns, 68, 69, 150,
    261
   attack on Shanghai (1932), 206
   Commodore Perry and, 16
   dissolving of parliament, 275
   DM arrives in (1905), 63
   expansionist foreign policy, 196, 560
   Grant brokers peace treaty with China,
    18
   Grant visits, 17–18
   Greater East Asia Co-Prosperity Sphere,
    560
   growth of military, World War I, 149
   Manchurian takeover (1931), 205–6
   Meiji reforms, 17
   military discipline, 63–64
   navy of, 149, 150, 245

occupation of northern China, 243, 245, 262

Philippines and, 196–97

as "the problem of the Pacific," 68, 150, 261

pulls out of the League of Nations, 236

territorial expansion, World War I, 149, 150

treatment of POWs, 61

U.S. brokers end of Russo-Japanese War, 62, 150

U.S. seen as enemy (1907), 150

Washington Naval Treaty of 1921–1922 (Five-Power Treaty), 198, 236

weaponry developed (1905), 60

—1938–1945 (World War II), 288–615. See also MacArthur, Douglas, 1941–1945; specific battles

advances (1942), 364, 385, 413, 414, 425

air power, 308

Allied invasion planned, 600, 606, 610, 611–12

atomic bombing of Hiroshima and Nagasaki, 612–13

atrocities by, 275, 587, 593–95

beginning of war, 275

cannibalism, 509–10

deaths caused by, 635

destruction of the Eighteenth Army, 510–11

DM's resistance on Bataan and Corregidor, 338–94

Doolittle's raid on Tokyo, 452

Dutch East Indies and, 291

firebombing of Tokyo and other cities, 605, 610

French Indochina and, 291

glory of death in battle, 578, 610

Great Britain surrenders Singapore, 385

Halsey destroys naval air strength, 529

kamikaze attacks, 548–49, 553, 555, 556, 557, 565–66, 567, 571, 611

midget submarines, 566

naval losses, 433–34

Operation I, 475–76

Pearl Harbor attack, 312, 314–15, 317

Philippines attacked and invaded, 318–77

PURPLE cipher machine, 311

Rape of Nanking, 275, 648, 698

sinking Prince of Wales and Repulse, 310, 324

surrender, xi, 614–15

treatment of POWs, 648–49

warrior code, bushido, 293

war strategy (1943), 460–61

—1945–1951 (Occupied Japan), 615–92

Allied Council for Japan, 688

American Pacific Fleet in Tokyo Bay, 618

Anti-Monopoly Law, 680

Communists in, 697

Constitution, 666–70

Constitution, Article 9, 667–70, 692

convincing soldiers to surrender, 661

cultural change, 655–56

demilitarization, 684, 691

demobilization of army, 664–65

destruction from war, 637

DM allows token Allied force, 638

DM and Japanese government, 646

DM and "Magna Carta," 665

DM arrival in Japan, 615–21

DM as "American Shogun," 692, 696, 845

DM as Founding Father, xv

DM as national hero, 660, 676–77

DM establishes trust, 621, 622–23, 653, 698

DM keeps Soviet Russia out of, 638–39

DM popularity in, 684

DM's dismissal, reaction to, 813–16

DM's goal, 647

DM's New Year's Day, 1946, pronouncement, 675–76

DM's power in, 637, 641, 646, 654, 662, 688, 691, 692, 703

DM's success in, 825

DM statement (Sept. 2, 1947), 682

DM's strategy for occupation, 615, 618–19, 626, 627, 643, 644–45

DM supplies food and medicine, 623, 662–64

DM's vision for, 626, 633–34

economic recovery and political stability in, 682, 816–17

economic reforms, 678–81, 685

educational reforms, 684

emergence of modern Japan, 660

end of occupation (1951), 659

Fair Trade Commission, 680–81

Far Eastern Commission, 638–39, 662, 684, 688, 690, 691, 692

fate of Japan's four cyclotrons, 685–86

Fundamental Law of Education and the School Education Law, 684

government of, 646, 677–78

—**1945–1951 (Occupied Japan)** (*cont'd*):
Hirohito and, 645–47, 649–53, 654,
661–62
Holding Company Liquidation
Commission, 680
Joint Chiefs plan for, 640–41
kamikaze pilots and, 615, 616
Kennan's attack on DM's democratizing
policies, 688–92
Korean War and resurrection of economy,
816
largest administrative task of U.S. Army,
656–57
NSC order 13/2, 691–92
occupation forces, 637, 642–44, 691
political reforms, 665–66, 675–76
Potsdam Declaration and, 617, 633–34,
638, 641, 677
purge of old regime officials, 677–78
racial tensions and, 655
repatriating POWs and civilians abroad,
665
SCAP headquarters, 623 (*see also* Tokyo,
Japan)
scientific and technical research, 685
shift in American policy, 691–92
social divisions in, 635
surrender ceremony and DM's speech,
625–33, 682
Trade and Industry (MITI), 685
war criminal trials, 648–49, 670–75,
697–703
women enfranchised, 666, 670, 849
zaibatsu corporations, 641, 659, 678–81,
689, 690
Jenner, William, 819
Jessup, Philip, 759, 761
Johnson, Andrew, 10
Johnson, Harold, 372
Johnson, Hugh, 37, 92
Johnson, James Steptoe, 28, 29
Johnson, Louis, 716–17, 724, 727, 748, 800
Johnson, Lyndon, 839
Joint Chiefs of Staff
atomic bombs sent to Guam "just in case,"
801
DM's return to America and, 822
report on Japanese military buildup
(1928), 197–98
Sutherland and, 470–71, 518, 519
—**Japan's occupation and DM**
directive on "unconditional surrender,"
646

DM and policy for, 660
rules for, 640–41
—**Korean War and**
bombing near Chinese boarder nixed, 765
Chinese and, 768, 769
complaint about DM flying American flag,
747
DM and, 3, 4, 5, 6
DM defies directive on non-ROK
boundary, 765–66
DM directed on Truman ceasefire effort,
798, 804
DM directed to cease bombing North, 769
DM dismissed from command, 808, 809,
834
DM must submit operations plan to,
750–51
DM ordered to attack North Korea,
749–50
DM's Inchon (CHROMITE) plan and,
728–29, 730, 732–36, 738, 740, 741
DM's "Message Not Understood" reply,
744
DM urges ties with Nationalist China,
725–26
message to DM after liberation of Seoul,
747
okays DM's trip to Formosa, 724
Pyongyang offensive and, 764
Pyongyang retreat and, 783–84
recommends DM for Commander-in-
Chief, UN Command, 720
South Korean assistance authorized,
713
South Korean reinforcements denied,
717
"stand-fast" directive, 790, 791
troops sent to Korea, 722
warning to DM on Formosa aid, 724
withdrawal of occupying forces, 697
Yalu River advance and, 777
—**World War II and**
Admiralty Island campaign, 491, 499
Borneo operation and, 608
DM granted Pacific ground forces
command, 605
DM's clashes with, 132
DM's push for Mindanao and Hollandia,
490, 500, 501
Europe-first strategy, 480
final say on DM's war plans, 427, 429,
475
intel on Japan's defending forces, 610–11

New Guinea Campaign, 470–72, 480–81, 497, 499
   Philippines Campaign, 518–19, 529
   Rabaul plan, 440–41, 461–62
   Reno IV, 499–500
   splits command between Nimitz and DM, 426–27, 490
   Truman and Japan invasion, 611
Jones, Albert, 344, 351, 352, 353, 366, 401
Jones, James Madison, 599
Joy, Turner, 779, 815
Judd, Walter, 817
Judson, William V., 70–71

Kades, Charles, 659, 667–68
Kase, Toshikazu, 630–31, 634, 645
Kavieng, New Ireland, 461, 477, 482, 498
Kellogg-Briand Pact, 203
Kelly, Colin, 325
Kennan, George, 688–92, 701, 828
   containment policy, 688, 703, 704, 830, 833
   Korean War and, 705, 713, 748–49
   Long Telegram article, 688, 704
Kennedy, John F., xiii, 839–40
Kenney, George, 446, 491, 707, 844
   Admiralty Islands and, 492, 493
   air cover for Philippines Campaign, 524–25, 526
   airfield at Dalugan, 569
   appointed head of SWPA Army Air Forces, 523
   arrival in Japan (1945), 620
   Australian mistress, 527
   Battle of the Bismarck Sea, 466–70
   Battle of Hollandia, 501
   Battle of Leyte, 519, 536, 546
   bombardment of Corregidor, 589
   confronts problems with aircrews, 448
   DM and, 446, 447, 448–49, 453, 493, 522–23
   DM's plan for (Elkton I), 462
   DM's praise for, 523
   DM's presidential hopes and, 513–14
   DM "steals" his house, 603
   Far Eastern Air Force (FEAF) and, 707
   Fifth Air Force and, 449, 450, 453, 454, 465–66, 476–77, 486, 501, 523, 546, 550–52, 770
   Japanese surrender ceremony and, 628
   loss of B-29 superbombers, 500
   Mindoro airfields, 557
   new bombing techniques, 449–50

New Guinea Campaign, 477
   operation CARTWHEEL, 483, 484, 485
   Pacific Military Conference, 467, 470–72, 476
   Papua and, 448–60
   Philippines Campaign and, 533, 550–52
   plane, "Sally," 525
   Sverdrup's bet with, 569
   Wakde Island assault and, 507
Kilmer, Joyce, 127
Kim Il Sung, 694, 695, 696, 697, 706, 708, 745
   DM calls for unconditional surrender, 753
   flees into the mountains, 764
   flees to Anjun, 763
   Korean armistice and, 837
   Mao Zedong and, 709, 751
   preparing for attack on South Korea, 709
   Soviet tanks and aircraft for, 709
   Stalin and, 709, 751
King, Charlie, 77–78
King, Edward, 431–32
King, Ernest, 304, 332, 350, 426, 429, 438, 461, 471, 555
   animosity between DM and, 488, 498, 618
   DM's Rabaul campaign and, 437, 471, 472
   European colonialism and, 607
   Formosa plan, 518, 519
   invasion of Japan and, 605
   invasion of the Philippines and, 529
   Japanese surrender ceremony, 618
   Marshall Islands offensive and, 480–81
   Pacific offense, 461
   pulling DM off Corregidor and, 390
   Rabaul plan and, 440–41
King, Hamilton, 66
Kinkaid, Thomas, 492, 493, 495, 524
   baby flattops, 544, 565
   Battle of Luzon and, 565–67
   Japanese naval attack on Leyte, 543, 548–49
   Japanese trap set for, 545–46
   kamikaze attacks on ships of, 548–49, 553, 555, 556, 557, 565–66, 567
   landing at Leyte, 536
   Mindoro operation (code-named L-3), 554–56
   Philippines Campaign (1944–45), 523–24, 526
   relationship with DM, 556
   Seventh Fleet, 543–45, 549, 552, 565–66, 605
Kitchener, Lord, 66
Knox, Henry, 349, 488

Knudsen, Bill, 228
Konoye, Prince of Japan, 678, 698–99
Korea, 683
   annexed by Japan (1910), 149
   Communism and, 694–95
   Communist atrocities in, 697
   control ceded to Japan (1907), 150
   Dean Acheson and, 644
   division at the 38th parallel, 636–37, 693
   DM's opinion as militarily indefensible,
     695
   DM visit (Sept., 1948), 692
   General Hodge and disarming Japanese,
     635–36
   internal hostilities break out, 696–97
   Kim Il Sung, 694, 695, 696, 697, 706
   Korean Military Advisory Group
     (KMAG), 696
   Korean Trusteeship Commission, 579,
     693, 695
   liberation of, from Japan, 693
   Mao Zedong's victory in China and, 706
   North Korea, 703
   People's Democratic Republic, 696, 705
   proxies for U.S. and Soviet Russia in, 706
   Republic of Korea, 696, 705
   Soviet Union in, 636, 693, 694, 695
   Syngman Rhee, 692, 693, 694, 695, 696,
     706
   totalitarian state in the north, 694
   United States Forces in Korea (USFIK),
     692, 695, 707
   USFIK withdrawn by Joint Chiefs, 697
Korean War, 705–813. *See also* MacArthur,
   Douglas, 1950–1951
   airpower, F-38 Sabre and, 789
   airpower and, 714, 768–69, 770, 772, 779,
     786, 792, 795–96
   Allied warships blockade the peninsula,
     719
   American, UN, and ROK forces in, 788
   American military personnel in, 709
   arming of North Korea, 706
   armistice (1953), 837
   atomic bombing considered, xiv, 799–800,
     829, 837
   Battle of Bloody Ridge, 835
   Battle of Chosin Reservoir, 780, 791
   Battle of Han River, 717–18
   Battle of Heartbreak Ridge, 835
   Battle of Old Baldy, 835
   Battle of the Punchbowl, 835
   Battle of Taejon, 721

   Battle of Triangle Hill, 835
   Battle of White Horse, 835
   Battle of Wolmi-do and Sowolmi-do,
     739–40
   Battle of Wonju, 791–92, 796
   Battles of Imjin River and Kapyong, 835
   bombing of Sinuiju, 770
   "bug-out fever," 787, 788, 790
   China and, xiii, xiv, 751–53
   Chinese casualties, 788–89, 794, 797, 798
   Chinese enter war, 766
   Chinese Offensives, 767–72, 789–90,
     795–96, 805, 835
   Chinese People's Volunteer Army (CPVA),
     794, 796
   DM authorized to aid South, 713–14
   DM's accomplishment in, 746–48
   DM's belief in himself and, 97
   DM's defense of his position in, 826
   DM's dismissal, xiv, 802–3, 807–9
   DM's strategy to end war vs. Truman and
     advisors, 798–802, 826, 829, 835
   DM visits Ridgway (Apr. 3, 1951), 805–6
   DMZ (demilitarized zone), 772, 798, 846
   early fighting around Seoul, 714–15
   Eighth Army, 713, 721, 722, 750–51, 755,
     756, 764, 766, 768, 773, 777–79, 780,
     785, 786, 789, 792, 794, 796, 803–4
   Eighth Army, casualties, 787
   Eighth Army, retreat from Pyongyang,
     781
   Eighth Army, retreat from Seoul, 789–90
   Eisenhower strategy, 837
   events leading to war, 708–10
   first airdrop, 187th Airborne, 763
   First Cavalry Division in, 3, 721, 728
   Forgotten War, 835
   Home by Christmas Drive, 774, 782
   Hungnam evacuation, 779, 781–82
   Inchon-Seoul campaign, xv, 3–6, 727–36,
     737–42
   Inchon-Seoul campaign, casualties, 740,
     741, 744
   Inchon-Seoul campaign, size of armada,
     738
   as "infantry slugging match," 779
   Iron Triangle, 804
   Joint Chiefs nix bombing near Chinese
     border, 765
   Korean People's Army (KPA), 706, 708,
     723, 727, 728, 736–37, 743, 792
   lack of peace treaty, U.S. troops remain,
     837, 846

"Line Kansas," 835
low point for the U.S./UN forces (Nov.-
   Dec. 1950), 781–84
murder of civilians and POWs, 715, 745
North Korean air force wiped out, 719
People's Liberation Army (PLA), 752
Pusan, 4, 5, 721–22, 727, 733, 734, 736–37,
   738
Pyongyang, 636, 695, 696, 706, 708, 709,
   723, 743
Pyongyang campaign, 749, 750, 755–57,
   763
Pyongyang retreat, 780–81, 783, 788
Republic of Korea Army (ROKA), 706,
   708, 709, 714, 763, 764, 792, 795, 796,
   797, 835
retaking Kimpo and Inchon, 794, 795
Rhee restored to Seoul, 744
Ridgway's Operation Dauntless, 803–4
Ridgway's Operation Killer, 796
Ridgway's Operation Punch, 794
Ridgway's Operation Ripper, 797
Ridgway's Operation Thunderbolt, 794
Ridgway's Operation Wolfhound, 793–94
Seoul falls, 715
Seoul falls, second time, 789–90
Seoul liberated, 4, 735, 741–44
Seoul retaken by U.S./UN, 796
Seventh Infantry Division in, 722, 730,
   738, 743–44, 792
Smith Force, 717–18
Soviet military personnel in Pyongyang,
   709
Soviet war planes in, 751, 770, 772, 779
stalemate after DM's dismissal, 835
Stratemeyer drops propaganda leaflets,
   796
tanks, M4 Shermans, 3–4
38th parallel, 636, 693, 694, 696, 705, 706,
   710, 713, 714, 719, 743, 749, 750–51,
   753, 756, 765, 781, 788, 790, 796,
   797–98, 799, 802, 804, 805–6, 809, 829,
   833, 837
two strategies after Inchon, 749
UN forces, 719, 723, 728, 738, 739, 744,
   745, 756, 767, 771–73, 777, 783, 786,
   788, 792, 794–96, 835
UN policy on, 713, 719, 751, 769, 788
U.S. bombing, 717–18, 719
U.S. casualties, 718, 719, 763–64, 780, 781,
   787, 801, 801n, 835
U.S. Cavalry defeated at Nammyon river,
   767
U.S. fights delaying actions, 718–19,
   720–21
U.S. Marines in, 728, 730, 731, 736–44,
   756, 767, 777–79, 780, 783, 796
U.S. troops in, 730
Wonsan, 750–51, 756, 764, 768, 779
X Corps and, 755, 756, 764, 767, 768, 772,
   777–79, 780–82, 785, 792, 795–97, 835
Yalu River, 752, 764, 766, 767
Yalu River advance, xiv, 753, 772, 773,
   777–79
Yalu River retreat, 779–82
Krueger, Walter, 73, 285, 481–82, 493, 502,
   508–9
   Battle of Luzon, 562, 564, 569, 600, 601
   Battle of Manila, 570, 571, 572–73, 574, 576
   captures Carigara, 552–53
   casualties on Leyte and, 570
   as DM's strong left arm, 523
   Eleventh Airborne and, 557–58
   Japanese surrender ceremony and, 628
   leadership and, 523
   occupation forces, 637
   Ormoc Valley and, 553, 554
   Philippines Campaign (1944–45),
      invasion force, 523, 526, 541, 542,
      552–53
   promotion to four stars, 572
   retaking Corregidor (1945), 589
   Sixth Army, 542, 554, 557, 571, 572, 637
Kunzig, Colonel, 219
Kurita, Admiral, 542, 543, 544, 546, 548, 549
   flagship Yamata, 547
Kyushu invasion (code-named OLYMPIC),
   601, 606, 610, 611, 612

Lae, New Guinea, 439, 442, 465, 466, 467,
   479, 483, 484, 486, 607
   Japanese escape from, 488–89
La Follette, Philip, 513
La Follette, Robert "Fighting Bob," 513
La Guardia, Fiorello, 190
"Lament for General MacArthur" (Asahi
   Shimbun), 813
Langer, Walter, 129
Lanphier, Thomas, 478
Laos, 837
Laurel, Jose, 334
League of Nations, 206, 236
Leahy, William D., 241, 488, 529
   FDR summit, Pearl Harbor, 1944 and, 516
   invasion of Japan, casualty estimate, 612
   OLYMPIC invasion and, 606

Leary, Herbert, 435
Lee, Clark, 377
Lee, Robert E., 49, 52, 459
Leeds, Charles T., 52
Lehrbas, Lloyd, 495, 536, 552
LeMay, Curtis, 622
Lenihan, Charles, 115
Lenin, Vladimir, 160
Levin, Emmanuel, 224
Leyte, 516
    airfields problem at, 546
    Allied landing on, 534–38
    Allied troops, 534, 535, 537, 541, 546,
        553–54
    amphibious landing on, 535
    Battle of, 519–59
    Battle of Leyte Gulf, 542–49
    casualties, 541, 570
    ceremony at Tacloban, 541
    distance from Hollandia, 524
    DM landing scheduled, 518, 519, 520
    DM meets with two Eleventh Airborne
        privates, 557–58
    DM surveys Tacloban coast, 533, 536
    DM tours battlefield, 536–41
    Dulag airfield, 553
    famous photo, DM wading ashore,
        537–38, 845
    HQ (Price House), 551–52, 557–58,
        560–62
    invasion of the Philippines and, 523,
        526–27, 533
    Japanese forces in, 530, 532, 552, 553, 557
    Japanese naval assault and, 542
    Ormoc operation, 553, 557
    planes crash-landing at Tacloban, 549
    Red Beach, 534, 537
    Tacloban airfield, 551, 553
    U.S. ships in battle of, 534, 535
Liddell-Hart, Basil Henry, 601
Life magazine, 308, 377
    DM's memoirs in, 840
Liggett, Hunter, 124, 127, 145
Li Hung-chang, 18
Lincoln, Abraham, 45, 514, 668
    quote in DM's Tokyo office, 648
Little, Royal, 139, 140, 141–42
Livy, 647–58
Lloyd, John E., 449, 451
Lodge, Henry Cabot, 19, 34
Long, Gavin, xii, 387, 608, 845, 847
Lovett, Robert, 769, 804–5, 808
Luce, Clare Boothe, 306–8

Luce, Henry, 307, 308, 840
Ludendorff, Erich, 119
Lumsden, Herbert, 565
Lusitania, 90
Luzon, 275, 281, 295, 319, 379, 393, 516
    Allied battle to retake, 558, 562–76, 599,
        600, 601
    Allied casualties, 568
    Cagayan Valley, 570
    defense plan (1941), 302
    DM goes ashore at, 568
    DM's HQ in Dalugan, 569
    Filipinos greeting Allies and DM, 567–69,
        572
    I Corps, 570–71, 572, 573
    improvements (1922), 179
    invasion plan (1945), 528, 529, 556, 562,
        564
    invasion of the Philippines and, 533
    Japanese defense zones, 570–71
    Japanese forces in, 530, 559
    Japanese land on (1941), 324
    kamikaze attacks, 565, 566, 567, 568, 571
    kamikaze bases on, 553
    Lingayen Gulf landing, 562, 564, 565,
        566–68, 571
    operation L-3, 556
    Sixth Army, 571, 572
    strategic importance of, 517
    Wainwright assumes command (1942),
        401
    War Plan Orange Three (1941), 338, 340,
        401
    Yamashita's plan for (1944–1945), 559

MacArthur, Arthur (father), 7–27
    adjutant general, Department of the
        Dakotas, 30
    America's role in Asia and, 51, 633
    appearance, 62, 75–76
    applies for China post, 18–19, 21
    Asian tour with DM (1905–1906), 63–68
    "Chinese Memorandum," 19–22, 23, 54,
        56, 654
    Civil War and, xiv, 5, 7, 8–10, 26, 27,
        75–76, 185–86
    Commander, Division of the Pacific, 54
    concerns about Asia and the rise of Japan,
        68, 69, 150
    Congressional testimony on Philippines
        atrocities, 51
    death of, 75–78, 254
    death of son, Malcolm, 23

dispute with Taft over Philippines
   independence, 62–63
DM absorbs view of Filipinos, 54, 55
DM graduates from West Point and, 52
end of career disappointments, 76
guerrilla warfare and, 43–46
harbor for Los Angeles proposed, 56
hero of the Philippines, 47
intellectual attainment and, 29
lessons for his son from Philippines war,
   50–51
as lieutenant general, 68
love of war, 9–10
Medal of Honor, 26–27, 143
meets and marries "Pinky" Hardy, 12–14
military attaché in Japan, 60–62
military career and political patronage,
   10–11
officers of, DM later serves under, 46
Philippines, military governor
   appointment, 44–46
Philippines, Spanish American War, 34,
   35, 39–41, 43–44
post-Civil War posts, western frontier,
   11–12
posting, Camp Thomas, Georgia, 35
posting, Fort Selden, New Mexico, 24–25
posting, Fort Wingate, New Mexico, 15,
   24
posting, Jackson Barracks, New Orleans,
   12, 14
posting, Little Rock, Arkansas, 14
posting, San Antonio, Texas, 27–28
posting, Washington, D.C., 25–27
promotions and ranks of, 10, 11, 25, 30,
   45, 68
reading of, 12
as role model for DM, 53, 848–49
San Francisco earthquake and, 68
soldiers' respect for, 46
son Arthur III born, 14
son Douglas born, 14–15
son Malcom born, 14
Transcontinental Railway, Promontory
   Summit and, 12
Ulysses S. Grant and, 15, 18
West Point never attained by, 31
"On Wisconsin!" and other sayings, 8
MacArthur, Judge Arthur (grandfather), 7–8,
   10, 12, 14, 25–26, 29, 30
MacArthur, Arthur, III (brother), 14, 15, 28,
   30, 67, 79, 177, 303
   cadet on the USS *Philadelphia,* 30

death of, 254
in World War I, aboard the *Chattanooga,*
   103
MacArthur, Arthur, IV (nephew), 67
MacArthur, Arthur, IV (son), 282, 322,
   336
   Ah Cheu (ayah), 336, 364, 395, 403, 404,
      418, 474, 816
   Australia and, 418, 420, 473–74, 525
   on Corregidor, 362, 363–64
   daily life, Japan, 687
   DM meets Hirohito, 652
   DM sends spent bullets, 552
   escape from Corregidor, 395, 403, 404,
      407
   Japan farewell, 815
   musical talent, 525
   routine with DM in the Philippines, 305–6
   Tokyo residence, 647
   Waldorf Astoria Hotel as home, 831
MacArthur, Aurelia Belcher (grandmother),
   7, 9
MacArthur, Douglas
   as American hero, 377–80, 386, 425, 660,
      819, 820–21, 846
   appearance, the MacArthur look, 108,
      110, 111, 112, 128, 152, 496, 515
   archive sources, xii, xiii
   belief in destiny, 11, 134–35, 141, 149, 286,
      289, 348, 362–63, 377, 427, 532, 539,
      644, 731
   biographies about, xii, 844–46
   brushes with death, 57–58, 130, 134–35,
      141, 347, 551–52
   character and personality, 93, 102, 294,
      428–29, 447–48, 454, 662, 687–88,
      786, 793, 811, 817, 849
   core values and love of the army, 48–49,
      848–49
   corncob pipe, 515, 536, 561, 575, 714
   courage of, 151, 152, 621, 622, 846, 847
   (*see also specific wars*)
   decision-making and, 164
   "Dugout Doug" myth, 380–81, 382, 396,
      420, 495, 583, 639, 845
   fashioning a persona, 152, 161–62, 515,
      844
   father of modern American Olympic
      sports, 193–95
   favorite Bible passages, 534
   Greek tragic hero analogy, xiv–xv
   health of, 76, 265, 301
   historical impact of, 848–50

MacArthur, Douglas (*cont'd*):
  iconic images of, xi, 265, 537–38
  ingredients for a successful military career
    and, 10–11
  intelligence, prodigious memory, 36, 50,
    52, 100, 144, 160, 163
  invulnerability portrayed by, 110
  leadership and, 73, 80, 100, 105–6,
    111–12, 143, 154, 159, 161, 162, 194,
    363, 496, 524, 526, 610, 662, 747, 846
  as legend, 843, 844
  lesson of preparedness, 36
  loneliness at the top and, 266
  luck and, 134, 136, 301, 406, 464, 737, 740
  management style, 100–101, 106, 524, 526
  men's devotion to, 106, 128, 154, 163,
    237n, 453
  military philosophy, 190
  negative image, 217–18, 222–25, 843,
    844–47
  nervous reaction, 36, 629, 737
  "no substitute for victory," 827, 828, 830,
    835, 849
  obsession with Medal of Honor, 27
  "Old soldiers never die, they just fade
    away," 827, 830
  personal habits of, 265–66, 303–4, 306,
    474, 494, 561–62, 686–87
  personal vanity, 249, 265
  philosophy about soldiering, 208
  poetry by, 32, 71–73, 171, 176
  policy based in tolerance and, 202
  popularity of, 757
  power of, 637
  presidential hopes, 513–15, 656, 821, 830,
    832, 834–35, 836
  quip: "Sometimes it is the order one
    disobeys that makes one famous," 110,
    129
  reexamination of, 843–50
  refusal to carry a sidearm, 110
  relationship with his father, 53, 60, 63–69,
    78
  relationship with his mother, 13, 25, 36,
    38, 46–47, 53, 59, 71, 78, 102, 158, 159,
    172–73, 175, 177, 182, 203, 239–40,
    241, 248, 255, 259–60, 849
  relationship with the press, 93, 108, 152,
    154, 185, 199, 290, 378, 536, 559–60,
    781, 819, 844
  religion and, 32
  run-ins with superiors as lifelong habit,
    96–97

Scottish proverb about MacArthur, 7
self-confidence of, 6, 36, 97, 101, 137,
    282
self-control of, 234, 596
sense of pride, 88
as the single most powerful American
    general in history, 520
"the soldier faith," 672
strategic concepts of, 849
understanding of modern warfare, 164
views on the future of war, 633–34,
    826–27, 838–39, 841–42
vision for Asia and America's future in the
    Pacific, xiii, 51–52, 69, 560, 732, 822,
    824–25, 839, 850
wit of, 58
—1880–1917 (early life and military
    career), 7–102
  aide-de-camp for his father, Asian tour
    (1905–1906), 60, 63–68, 69
  aide-de-camp to Theodore Roosevelt, 70
  appearance, 37, 48, 79
  arrives in Japan (1905), 63
  birth, xiv, 14–15
  death of brother, Malcolm, 23, 25
  education, 28–32
  father's death and, 78
  father's Philippine briefing for, 54, 56
  father's posting to New Mexico and, 24–25
  father's posting to San Antonio and, 27–28
  father's posting to Washington, D.C.,
    25–27
  first memory, xiv
  intellectual attainment and, 29
  lesson about Asia and Communism, 65
  lessons learned from his father's Medal of
    Honor, 27
  lessons learned from his father's years in
    the Philippines, 50–51
  malaria and recuperation (1904–1905),
    59–60
  meets and becomes friends with FDR, 91
  military ambitions, 32
  military posting, General Wood's office,
    Washington, DC, 78–79
  military posting, Milwaukee, 70–73
  military posting, superintendent of the
    State, War, and Navy Building,
    Washington, DC, 79
  military posting, Third Engineer
    Battalion, Philippines, 54–60
  military posting, training men in Fort
    Leavenworth, Kansas, 73–74, 78

military posting, Washington Barracks, 70

officers of, Philippine veterans, 46

promotions, 58, 73–74, 88

recommended for Medal of Honor, 86, 87–88, 89

relationship with his grandfather, 25–26

romance with Fanniebelle Stuart, 71–72

romance with "Ramona," 173–74

secret mission, Mexico (1914), 80–86

view of Newton Baker, 91

on U.S. Army General Staff, 79–80, 90–91, 95–97

U.S. War Department's Bureau of Information chief, 91–92, 93

West Point admission prep, 30–33, 36

as West Point cadet, xiv, 37–38, 41–43, 46–50, 52–53

—1917–1918 (World War I), 103–49

Argonne, Kriemhild Redbout and the Côte de Châtillon, 132, 135–44

Baccarat line, 115–16

Baker tours the front and, 113–14

bravery of the Fighting Irish and, 127

bravery under fire, xv, 115, 116, 121, 130, 141, 142, 144

as "Bullet Proof," 149

Champagne front, 116, 118–19

Château-Thierry, 123–24

Chaumont, Pershing's headquarters, 104, 105, 117, 119, 128, 129

chooses to serve in the Infantry, 98

Croix Rouge Farm, 124

Eighty-fourth command, 126

"the Fighting Dude" nickname, 112, 114

France, conditions in war-torn, 105–6

France, first battle (Feb. 26, 1918), 108–10

France, gas attacks, 113, 136

France, leadership style, 100, 105–6, 111–12

lessons learned about command, 143

lesson learned from Pershing's refusal to advance, 132

as Mann's chief of staff, 98

meeting with Menoher, Reilly, at Neuve Forge Farm, 144–45

memory of German dead and belief in abolishing war forever, 122

as Menoher's chief of staff, 106, 108

Metz advance, 131–32

military decorations, 110, 112, 122, 127, 128, 135, 143, 144

National Defense Act and, 90–91

National Guard mobilization and, 95–98

Ourcq, 124–27

Patton with, 130

Pershing confrontation with, 116–17, 118

Pershing denies Medal of Honor, 143, 144, 151

Pershing refuses to advance, 131

press's assessment of (1917), 93

promotion to brigadier general, xv, 117–18, 119

promotion to colonel, 98

promotion to major general, 143–44

Rainbow Division (42nd) battle plans, 104–5

Rainbow Division (42nd) casualties, 116, 121, 126, 128, 142, 144, 149

Rainbow Division (42nd) command, 148

Rainbow Division (42nd) formed, 98–100

Rainbow Division (42nd) ships out, 101–2, 103

Rainbow Division (42nd) training, 99–101

recommends Pershing for AEF leader, 94

St. Benoit headquarters, 134

St. Mihiel, 128–31, 134

St. Mihiel illness, 129

St. Nazaire's harbor, arrival in France (Nov. 1, 1917), 103

Sedan and Marshall's mistake, 145–48

Selective Service creation and, 92–93

Souain (Second Battle of the Marne), 119–22, 151

as unmarried, 102

at Vaucouleurs, 104–5

—1919–1941 (Between the Wars), 151–287

air mail scandal and, 236–37, 237n

appearance, 161, 254, 265, 266

Atlanta posting (1925), 185–87

Bonus Army and, 214–25, 244, 249, 845

CCC and, 228–31

Chastleton-Isabella scandal, 237–42, 249

commitment to his army career, 191–92

description of, by Chase, 153–54

description of, by White, 154

FDR brands him "the most dangerous man in the country," 195, 212, 223, 225, 226, 228

FDR inauguration and, 226

FDR's military budget cuts and, 231–36

FDR's relationship with, 226–29, 231, 233–35, 237, 241, 244–45, 247, 251, 252, 258–59, 269, 272, 277–78, 285

—**1919–1941 (Between the Wars)** (*cont'd*):
  fight against disarming America, xv,
    196–252
  Fort McHenry posting (1925), 187
  French occupation and, 152, 154
  home at Quarters No. 1, Fort Myer, 203,
    239, 247
  honors and praise following World War I,
    151
  interview with Theodore White, 286–87,
    314
  marriage to Jean Faircloth, 253–56,
    264–66, 270–71, 273–74, 277, 282 (*see
    also* MacArthur, Jean Faircloth)
  marriage to Louise Brooks, 171–75, 177,
    178, 191, 193, 196
  military decorations, 151, 161, 249
  Mitchell court martial and, 187–90
  Pershing animosity, 152, 173, 175, 176–77,
    178
  Philippines (1922), 176, 177–85
  Philippines (1928), 196–99
  Philippines (1935–1941), Field Marshal of
    the Philippine Army, 256, 259, 266–87
  Philippines (1935), US military advisor in
    Manila, 246–52
  Philippines (1937), quits the U.S. Army to
    remain as Field Marshal, 276–77
  Philippines remuneration and salary,
    248
  promotion to major general, 152, 185
  Rainbow Division (42nd) and, 151–55
  Rainbow Division (42nd) veterans address
    (1935), 196, 250
  recognizes "growing arc of crisis" in Asia
    (1930), 201, 205, 206
  son Arthur IV born, 282
  Spanish flu and other health problems,
    152–53
  speech against disarmament (1927), 182
  on state of postwar Germany, 154
  on Treaty of Versailles, 155
  U.S. commander of the AEF in the Far
    East predicted by, 286–87
  U.S. in the Pacific, DM's strategic vision
    for, 262
  U.S. Olympics Committee president,
    193–95
  Waldorf Astoria altercation, 156
  War Department and, 187, 197, 204,
    208–10, 212, 222, 229–31, 235, 236,
    242, 245, 260, 261, 267, 268, 269, 272,
    277, 279
  West Point superintendent, xv, 157–71,
    175–77
—**1941–1945 (World War II)**, 288–615. *See
  also specific battles; specific countries;
  specific people*
  Admiralty Islands campaign, 491–97
  Admiralty Islands reconnaissance and,
    493–96
  airpower and, 298, 469, 485, 550–52 (*see
    also* Arnold, Hap; Kenney, George;
    specific battles)
  Allied assault on Kyushu (OLYMPIC),
    606
  Allied landings on Honshu (CORONET),
    606
  amphibious warfare and, 462–65, 485, 528
    (*see also* Barbey, Daniel)
  appearance, 307, 392, 420, 447, 496
  atomic bombing of Hiroshima and
    Nagasaki and, 613–14, 617
  awarded third Distinguished Service
    Cross, 574
  Bataan surrender and, 429–32
  Battle of Biak Island, 505–10
  Battle of the Bismarck Sea, 466–70
  Battle of Hollandia, 501–3, 506
  Battle of Noemfoor Island, 509–10
  Battles of Kiriwina and Woodlark, 471,
    472, 479, 480, 481, 482–83
  Borneo offensive and, 606–7, 609–10
  bravery under fire, 347, 362–63, 381, 493,
    495, 502, 575, 609–10
  "bypassing the enemy" strategy, 501,
    528
  CARTWHEEL operation (Elkton III),
    479–87
  Christmas (1944) and, 560–61
  crosses the line with FDR, 438
  demeanor of, 328
  description of, by Clare Booth Luce, 307
  description of, by Rogers, 301
  escape to Australia, 395–413
  Executive Order #1 controversy, 382–83
  FDR gives command of all ground forces
    in the Pacific, 605
  FDR meeting in Pearl Harbor, 512,
    515–18
  FDR showdown over return to the
    Philippines, 516–18
  FDR's relationship with, 289, 290–91,
    515–16, 605
  fog of war and, 316–17
  Halsey and, 479

"I shall return," 404, 419, 521, 538–39, 540
Japan invasion (DOWNFALL), 600, 601, 606, 611
Japan surrenders, xi, xv, 614–15
leadership style, 300, 348–49, 362–63, 609–10
liberation of Manila, 529, 570, 571–77, 579–88, 593–600
Medal of Honor awarded, 422–23
New Guinea Campaign, xv, 444, 471–72
news of declaration of war delayed, 322
Papuan Campaign, 438–60
Pearl Harbor attacked and, 314–15, 317
Philippines Campaign (1941–42), 314–94, 475. *See also* Bataan Peninsula; Corregidor Island; Philippines, World War II
    Washington misleads DM about relief forces, 354–55, 357–58, 364–65, 370–71
Philippines Campaign (1944–45), 499, 511, 517, 518, 519, 522–77, 579–601
plane, *Bataan,* 525–26
promotion, fourth star, 331
promotion to general of the army (five stars), 558–59
promotion to lieutenant general, 293
qualities for war command, 294–95
Rabaul offensive, 432, 437
retaking Bataan (1945), 588–89, 590–92
retaking Corregidor (1945), 589–93, 598–99
as "rock of strength," 363, 381
"Special Executive Order from President Quezon," 382–84, 608
Sutherland as chief of staff (*see* Sutherland, Richard K.)
SWPA, supreme commander of Allied Forces, 388, 390, 415, 416–653
USAFFE appointment (July, 1941), 289–92, 298
USAFFE command, 289–416
USAFFE staff, 299–300
War Department orders not to initiate hostilities against Japan, 308, 316–17
—**1945–1950 (Occupation of Japan),** xv, 615–704. *See also* Japan, Occupied
as AFPAC head, 637
airplane, *Bataan II,* 615, 618, 619, 693
American Embassy, Tokyo, and, 644
American Embassy compound, DM and

family's residence in, 647, 648, 686, 705
American Embassy luncheons, 687–88
arrival in Japan, 615–21
battle for final version of NSC 13/2, 691–92
confrontation with Soviets over occupation of Japan, 638–39
demobilization of Japanese army, 664–65
Democrats worry about DM's political appeal, 640, 642
description of, by Kase, 645
dogs and, 686
experience in military occupations, 654
feelings of cultural superiority, 655–56
first days in Japan, initial decisions, 621–23
goal of occupation of Japan, 647
Hirohito and, 645–47, 649–53, 654, 661–62, 703
home life and daily routine in Japan, 686–88
Japan's constitution, inclusion of renouncing war, now and forever (Article 9), 667–70, 692
Joint Chiefs directive to, 646
Kennan and, 689–92
Korea visit (1948), 692–97
lessons from his father in the Philippines, 655, 656
love of the Japanese people for, 676–77
"Magna Carta" for postwar Japan, 665
management style, 687–88
personal conduct and image, 677
Philippines trip (Aug. 1946), reburial of Quezon, 683–84
political reforms for Japan, 665–66, 675–76
power of, 637, 641, 646, 654, 662, 688, 691, 692, 703
press criticism and, 680–81, 688, 689
as SCAP (supreme commander of the Allied powers in Japan), 614, 646, 703
SCAP GHQ staff, 657–59, 661–62
SCAP headquarters, 647–48
as "Sir Boss," 660–61
size of occupation forces and, 642–44
strategy for occupation, 615, 618–19, 626, 627, 633–34, 643, 644–45
surrender ceremony and speeches, 625–26, 627–34, 682
Truman and, 639–40
war criminal trials, 649, 670–75, 697–703

MacArthur, Douglas (*cont'd*):
—**1950-1951 (Korean War)**, 705–813. *See also* Korean War
airplane, *Bataan II*, 714, 715, 742, 746, 761, 816
airpower, faith in, 714, 719, 770, 779, 786, 795
allies for the fight, 719, 723
appearance at seventy, 730–31
Bataan retreat remembered, 722
bombing north of the 38th parallel and, 719
bravery under fire, 715–16, 746, 774–75
call to Communist Chinese to face defeat, 804
Chiang Kai-shek-Formosa visit (July 31, 1950), 724–25
China entering the war miscalculated, 752–53, 754, 760–61
China in the Korean War, xii, xiv, 751–53, 766–806
Chinese aggression as expansionism, 776
Chinese Offensives (1950–1951), 767–72, 789–90, 791, 795–96
Collins meeting (Dec., 1950), 783
Commander-in-Chief, Far East (CINCFE), 3, 4, 764, 770, 783, 802–3, 807–13
Commander-in-Chief, UN Command and SCAP, 719–20
Commander of ROK forces, 720
Congressman Martin reads DM's criticism of Truman to Congress, 806–7, 811, 848
Distinguished Flying Cross, 764, 775
Dulles as political ally, 710, 712
evacuation of U.S. and UN forces from Korea contemplated, 784
Far Eastern Air Force (FEAF) and, 707, 719
first airdrop, 187th Airborne, 763
geopolitical forces in Korean conflict, 801–2
GHQ staff, 5, 715, 769, 791
Inchon landing opposition, 730, 731
Inchon-Seoul campaign (code-named CHROMITE), xv, 3–6, 727–42
Japan's farewell to, 813–16
Joint Chiefs review of strategy, 728–30, 732–36, 738, 740, 741, 750–51, 765–66, 777, 807–9
joint planning staff (JSPOG), 728, 730
Kim Il Sung's surrender called for, 753

Korean reunification goal, 749–50
Korean trip (Apr. 3, 1951), final visit, 805–6
Korean trips (Jan.–Mar., 1951), 793, 794
Korean victory, significance of, 746–48
Korean War outbreak, U.S. combat resources available, 707
low point for the U.S./UN forces (Nov.–Dec. 1950), 781–84
Nationalist China, stronger ties with, 725–27
New York Times interview on America's strategic position, 707
North Korea attack expected by, 708–9
nuclear weapons and, xiv, 799–800
orders air strikes north of 38th parallel, 714
orders American and UN personnel out of Korea, 712
predicts Sino-Soviet split, 776
press release (Nov. 1950), 775
Pyongyang campaign, 749, 750, 755–57
Ridgway's role and, 785–86, 793–97
sanity questioned, 799
Seoul liberation and speech, 744–47
Seoul trip (June 29, 1950), 714, 715–16
strategy, 719, 720–21, 727–28, 750–51, 755–56, 765, 767, 773, 783, 784, 786, 790, 791, 806
strategy, The Plan, four point plan using atomic bombs, 798–802, 826, 832–33
Suwon airfield press conference, 803
Syngman Rhee and, 712, 744, 746
Truman and animosity, 761–62
Truman and Joint Chief's cease-fire directive, Jan. 13, 1951, 798
Truman awards Distinguished Service Medal, 761
Truman criticized by DM, 802–4, 807, 834, 847, 847n
Truman dismissal of, xiv, 802, 804–5, 833–34, 847
Truman dismissal of, news of, 809–13
Truman meeting on Wake Island, 756–61, 847–48
Truman personal message (Jan. 13, 1951), 790–91
Truman response (Mar. 14, 1951), to DM's "insubordination," 805, 847
Truman rift, 724, 726
Truman thanked for supreme UN post, 720

urges defense of South Korea, 710, 712

U.S. News & World Report interview, 782–83

VFW statement on Formosa, 726, 727

war conference (Nov. 28, 1950), 779

Washington report (June 30, 1950), requesting U.S. boots on the ground, 716

Washington rift, 791, 797–98

Washington's rules of engagement, 770, 808

Willoughby fails to alert FECOM about major crisis in Korea, 710

Yalu River, faulty intelligence and losses, 779–80

Yalu River advance, xiv, 772, 773, 777–79

Yalu River reconnoiter, 774–75

Yalu River retreat and, 779–82

—1951–1964 (final years), 818–42

address to Congress (April 19, 1951), 821–30

advises against Vietnam War, 839

advises using nuclear threat against Communists, 838

Congressional testimony on Korea (May 3–5, 1951), 832

death of, xiv, 842

Eisenhower and, 834–35, 836

Eisenhower meets with, solution to Korea and, 837–38

as forgotten figure, 831

health decline, 840

international disarmament and end to war forever advocated, 838–39

Kennedy meets with (1961), xiii, 839

keynote address, Republican Convention, Chicago (1952), 836

Korean armistice, reaction to, 837

last trip to the Philippines (1961), 840

message of, tour to major U.S. cities, 831–32

mourning for, 843

public reaction to return to America (1951), 818–22, 823

retirement from the military, 827

return to America (1951), 818

state funeral of, 843

Sylvanus Thayer Award, 840

Waldorf Astoria Hotel as home, 831

West Point farewell speech (May 12, 1962), xiv, 53, 840, 841–42, 843

writes memoirs, 840–41, 843

MacArthur, Jean Faircloth (wife), 849

American Embassy luncheons, Japan, 687, 690

in Australia, 419, 420, 473–75

Australia (1942), two bizarre incidents, 416–18

background, 253–54

birthday wishes from DM (1944), 559

birthday wishes to DM (1945), 602

bombing of Clark Field and, 322

Bulkeley's PT boats and, 397–98

Christmas apart (1944), 561

Christmas in Manila (1941), 333

Corregidor, admiration for, 363

Corregidor, air attacks on and, 347, 348, 362

Corregidor, escape from, 395, 403–5, 407–13

Corregidor, house, 348

Corregidor, refusal to leave, 376–77

Corregidor, situation as hopeless, 365

Corregidor, tending the wounded on, 364

daily life, Japan, 687

death of, 843

devotion to DM, 274, 809–10

DM engagement and wedding, 273–74

DM as infallibly faithful, 306, 527

DM as "Sir Boss," 306, 333, 416, 534, 602, 604

DM meets Hirohito and, 652

DM quits the Army to stay in the Philippines and (1937), 277

DM's address to Congress (1951) and, 823

DM's devotion to, 604

DM's dismissal from Korea and, 810

DM's orders to leave Corregidor and, 391–92

DM's reaction to Battle of the Bismarck Sea, 469

DM's romance with, 254–56, 264–66, 270–71

Japan's farewell to, 814, 815–16

Korean War, effect of on, 809–10

liberation of Seoul and, 744

in Manila (1937), 276, 336–37

in Manila (1945), Casa Blanca, 602–5

in Manila (1945), hospital visits, 604

oral interview (1998), xiii

Philippines Campaign and, 525, 533–34

public reaction to DM's return to America (1951), 822, 823, 831

Quezon's inauguration and, 264

relationship with DM, 306–7, 602–5, 687

son Arthur IV born, 282

MacArthur, Jean Faircloth (wife) (cont'd):
   Tokyo residence, 647
   visits the Philippines (1926), 254
   Waldorf Astoria Hotel residence, 831
MacArthur, Louise Cromwell Brooks (wife),
      849
   DM's Baltimore posting and, 187
   DM's libel suit against Pearson's column,
      240
   DM's Philippine posting and, 177–85
   estate at Rainbow Hill, 187
   leaves and divorces DM, 193, 196
   life after DM, 240, 241
   lifestyle of, 191
   Manila society and, 181–82
   meets and marries DM, 171–75
   trial of Billy Mitchell and, 189
MacArthur, Malcolm (brother), 14, 15, 23
MacArthur, Mary Pinckney Hardy "Pinky"
      (mother), 19, 849
   advice before West Point admissions
      exam, 36
   background, 12–13
   death of, 259–60
   death of husband and, 78
   death of son, Malcolm, 23–24
   DM as superintendent, West Point, 158,
      159
   DM as the center of her life, 25, 29, 78,
      182, 239, 241, 255, 259
   DM faces anti-hazing court, poem for,
      46–47
   DM graduates from West Point, 52
   DM's admission to West Point and, 31–33,
      36
   DM's education and, 38
   DM's emotional well-being and, 53, 102
   DM's marriage to Louise Brooks and,
      172–73, 175, 177
   DM's return to the Philippines (1935) and,
      248, 254
   health of, 78, 177, 182, 241, 248, 255, 256,
      259
   interfering in DM's life, 71, 182
   in Japan (1905), 61
   letters to Pershing, 113, 117–18
   living with DM, Quarters Number One,
      Fort Myer, VA, 203, 239
   living with DM, Washington, D.C., 78
   marriage to Arthur MacArthur, 13–14
   mother's death and inheritance, 16
   move into Wardman Park Hotel, 177
   Pershing family friendship, 61

   photo of DM and (1922), 177
   posting, Fort Wingate, New Mexico, 15
   posting, San Antonio, Texas, 27–28
   in Santa Barbara, with son Arthur, 113
   scrapbook of DM in France, 108
   in Siam (1906), 66–67
   son Arthur III born, 14
   son DM born, 14–15
   son Malcolm born, 14
   at West Point when DM attends, 36
MacArthur, Mary (sister-in-law), 67, 249,
      254, 255
MacArthur: 1941–1951 (Willoughby and
      Chamberlain), xii
MacArthur as Military Commander (Long),
      xii
MacArthur: His Rendezvous with History
      (Whitney), xii
MacArthur Record, The (MacArthur and
      Whitney), 840
MacKenna, Major, 125
Madang-Salamaua-Finschhafen triangle, 472,
      481
   Japanese retreat, 488
Magnuson, Warren, 809
Mahan, Alfred Thayer, 19
Maher, Marty, 166
Mainichi Shimbun newspaper, 813
Malaya, 425, 607, 801, 802, 837
Manchester, William, xii, xiv–xv, 490, 845
   on Wake Island Truman-DM meeting,
      760–61
Manchuria, 201, 560, 583, 624
   Battle of Mukden, 61, 62
   Chinese arms buildup, for Korean War,
      752
   Japanese in, 532, 655, 665
   Japanese POWs in detention camps, 665
   Japanese takeover (1931), 205–6
   Korean War and, 750, 751, 752, 753, 764,
      769, 770, 772, 779, 783, 798, 799, 807
   Russian takeover (1945), 579, 611, 636,
      638
   Russo-Japanese War and, 60, 62, 149
   Soviet fighter planes in, 764
Maneuver in War (Willoughby), 299
Manila, Philippines. See also Philippines;
      Philippines Campaigns
   Allied hospital in, 613
   DM in (1903), 56–59
   DM residence, penthouse of the Manila
      Hotel, 256, 265, 276, 314, 324, 330,
      354, 595–96, 602–3

evacuation of, 328, 330, 333–37, 350
Intramuros (old city), 40, 56, 59, 181, 270, 273, 295, 300, 308, 309
Intramuros, battle for, 586, 588, 589, 593–95, 672
liberation of, 529, 570, 571–77, 579–89, 593–600, 735
Malacañan Palace, 264, 266, 285, 349, 597, 603
occupied by the Japanese, 354
as open city, 330–31, 333–34, 338, 343, 344
as smoldering ruin, 350
strategic importance of, 562, 564
war criminal trials, 670–75
worst-hit Allied capital in World War II, with the exception of Warsaw, 597
Mann, General, 97, 98
    DM as chief of staff, 98
Manzano, Narciso, 353
Mao Zedong, 201, 683, 695, 703, 706
    Kim Il Sung and, 751, 767
    Korea, Fifth Offensive, 805, 835
    Korea, First Offensive, 767–71
    Korea, Fourth Offensive, 795–96
    Korea, Second Offensive, 771
    Korea, Third Offensive, 789–90
    Korean armistice and, 837
    Korean War and, 751–53, 754, 766, 800
    Peng and ambush of the Eighth Army, 766, 773
    sends men to the North Korean army, 709
    split with the Soviets, 828
    Stalin and, 761
    support for invasion of South Korea, 709
March, Peyton, 31, 46, 60–61
    appoints DM to head West Point and, 157–58, 159, 161, 165, 177
    as Army Chief of Staff, 118, 152, 156–57
    recommends DM as Chief of Staff, 200
Mariana Islands, 150, 488, 500, 506, 518
Marianas Turkey Shoot, 542
Marquat, William "Billy," 299–300, 395, 551
    GHQ antiaircraft chief, 435
    SCAP Economic and Scientific Section head, 658–59
Marrett, Samuel, 325
Marshall, George Catlett, 291–92
    Allied resources for the Pacific, 461
    animosity between DM and, 73, 144
    as brigadier general, 294
    in charge of CCC camps, 230n

deadly mistake at Sedan, 144, 146
demobilization post-World War II and, 642
with DM, Fort Leavenworth, Kansas, 73
DM and Korean War, 769
DM as supreme commander, SWPA and, 426, 428
DM awarded Medal of Honor and, 422–23
DM in Philippines and, 302–3
DM intentionally misled by, 354–55, 370–71
DM ordered to leave Corregidor, 388–89
DM personal memo to (Nov. 8, 1950), 776
DM promised help in Corregidor, 345
DM pulled off Corregidor and, 385, 390, 393
DM reports on Bataan collapse, 368
DM's castigation of Allied strategy, 375
DM's confidence about China not entering Korean War and, 762
DM's crossing the 38th parallel and, 765–66
DM's dismissal and, 807–9, 833–34
DM sends last will and testament to, 377
DM's Executive Order #1 and, 383
DM's policy in Japan and, 660
DM's Rabaul campaign and, 437
DM's return to America, 822
DM's reversion to WPO-3, 340
invasion of Japan, casualty estimate, 611–12
invasion of the Philippines and, 326–27, 340, 529
Jean MacArthur and, 814
Kenney and, 449
message to DM after liberation of Seoul, 747
operation CARTWHEEL and, 480–81
Pacific Military Conference, 470–72
Papuan Campaign and, 459
Philippines abandoned by the U.S., 355
Rabaul plan and, 440–41
receives highest military rank, general of the army, 558
as Secretary of Defense, 4
size of occupation forces and, 643–44
tours SWPA, 488
Truman's Korean cease-fire plan and, 798
U.S. Navy and, 438
in World War I, on taking Metz, 131–32
Marshall, Richard "Dick," 299, 329, 367, 403
    in Australia, 418, 419
    Australian mistress, 527

Marshall, Richard "Dick," (cont'd):
    defense of Bataan and, 360
    as DM's chief of staff, Japan, 658
    escape from Corregidor, 395, 408
    as GHQ deputy chief of staff, 435
    Quezon and, 382
Marshall Islands, 150, 480, 500
Marshall Plan, 703
Martin, Joseph, 806, 811, 821, 823, 827, 848
Matsui, General, 698
Matsumoto, Joji, 666–67, 668
Matthews, Bill, 712
Mayo, Henry, 80
Maze, Paul, 416
McCain, John, 628
McCarthy, Joseph, 818, 819, 837
McCloy, John, 730
McCoy, Frank, 115, 125, 189, 200
    bravery of the Fighting Irish and, 127
McCreary, Betsy, 580–81, 584
McCutcheon, Frank, 32
McDuffie, John, 245
McKinley, William, 31, 34, 41, 43
McMahon, Brian, 679
Melbourne, Australia, 418, 475
    greets DM (1942), 419–20
    ULTRA decrypt office, 439, 442, 465, 466,
        478
Menoher, Charles, 106, 108, 109, 110, 112,
        116, 123, 127, 128, 144–45
    DM at Argonne and, 137, 138, 139, 142
Merisiecki, R. J., 557–58
Merritt, Wesley, 35, 40
Mexico
    Battle of Veracruz, 81
    DM mission to Veracruz (1914), 80–86
    Pershing's pursuit of Pancho Villa, 92
    Zimmerman affair, 94
Midway, Battle of, 434–35, 437
Midway Island, 434
Milbourne, General "Shrimp," 774
Miles, Perry, 216–22, 224
Miller, Albert L., 514, 515
Miller, Colonel, 368
Miller, Ernest B., 380
Miller, Merle, 848
Millett, Allan, 718
Milwaukee, Wisconsin
    death of Arthur MacArthur, 75–78
    DM and MacArthur family in, 31–32,
        70–71, 76
    DM's qualifying exam in, 36, 46
    pro-Spanish American war march in, 33

Mindanao, 197, 261–62, 308, 332, 385, 490,
        492
    battle for, 601
    destination of DM and party from
        Corregidor, 396, 411–12
    DM landing scheduled, 518
    DM push for, 512
    Japan invades, 331
    reconnaissance of, 507
    Reno IV plan, 500
Mindoro
    airfields, 557
    Allied attack on, 556–57
    operation L-3, 554–56
    schedule for attack on, 556
Mitchell, John L., 31, 32
Mitchell, William "Billy," 32–33, 140, 208,
        237, 485
    court martial of, 187–90
    death of, 244
    friendship with DM, 188–89, 190
    imitates DM's cap for classic headgear of
        bomber pilots, 108
    predicts Japanese attack on Pearl Harbor,
        188
Mitchell, William D., 217
Mitsubishi, 679, 681
Mitsui, 679, 681
Mollison, P. V., 482–83
Molotov, Vyacheslav, 636
Mongkut, King, 66n
Monroe Doctrine, 33
Moore, George, 341, 404
Mori, Takeshi, 616
Morotai Island, 519–20
Morse, William, 411
Morton, Louis, 316, 381
Moseley, George Van Horn, 216, 220–21, 224,
        487
Mountbatten, Louis Lord, 607
Muccio, John, 696, 811
Murfreesboro, Tennessee, 27, 253–54, 269,
        270, 273
Murphy, Frank, 262, 264, 671, 674
Murphy, Robert, 267
Mussolini, Benito, 160, 206, 236, 243
Mutsuhito, Emperor of Japan, 75

Nagano, Kameichiro, 431
Napoleon, 344, 379, 656
National Defense Act, 90, 210
NATO, 703
Nazdab, New Guinea, 485–86, 493

Nelson, Horatio, Duke of Wellington, 849
New Britain Island, 150, 472, 484
New Georgia, 479, 483, 484, 486
  Bougainville, 471, 472, 479, 481, 484, 487
  Munda airfield, 483, 484, 486
New Guinea, xv, 73, 150, 414, 437, 444,
  471–72, 488–89, 497, 499, 522. *See also*
  Hollandia; Papua; Papuan Campaign;
  Rabaul, New Britain; *specific battles*
  Admiralty Islands campaign and, 491–97
  Allied bombing of, 466, 488
  Allies victory in, 511
  Australian forces and, 526
  Battle of the Bismarck Sea and, 466–70
  Battle of the Coral Sea and, 434
  DM accompanies parachute drop, 485
  DM's desire for amphibious landing craft
    and, 463
  DM visits (Oct. 1, 1942), 449
  Fifth Air Force and, 448
  Japanese bombing (April 12, 1943), 477
  Japanese code books reveal strategy, 490
  Japanese in, 460
  Japanese land on, 413
  Japanese Operation I and, 475–76
  operation CARTWHEEL, 479–87, 499
  parachute drop into Nadzab, 485–86
  as South West Pacific Area (SWPA), 426
  strategic importance of, 439
Newman, Red, 535
Newsweek, article critical of DM's reforms in
  Japan, 680–81, 689
New York Herald Tribune, 782, 819
New York Journal, 33
New York Times
  as ally of DM, 185, 199
  DM's plans for Mindoro and, 555
  endorses DM as Commander-in-Chief,
    UN Command, 720
  supports Truman in dismissing DM, 819
  war threat seen (1935), 243
  Yalu River retreat and, 782
New York World, 33
New Zealand, 441
  Japanese threat to, 413
  as South West Pacific Area (SWPA), 426
Nimitz, Chester
  autonomy of, vs. MacArthur, 437, 550
  Battle of the Coral Sea, 433–34, 437
  Battle of Hollandia, 501
  Battle of Leyte, 519
  Battle of Midway, 434
  command of all naval forces, 605
  command of the Pacific Fleet, 350
  DM's Rabaul plan and, 462
  FDR meeting in Pearl Harbor and, 515–18
  invasion of Japan and, 601
  invasion of Japan and meeting with DM,
    605–6
  Japanese surrender ceremony and,
    628–29, 632
  Japan's formal surrender and, 618
  Manus and, 500
  Mariana Islands and, 500, 506, 518
  Marshall Islands and, 480
  Mindoro operation and, 555
  orders do not include help for the
    Philippines, 350
  Philippines Campaign (1944–45),
    invasion force, 524–25
  post-World War II and DM, 637–38
  as prioritized over DM, 438
  push to the Marshall and Palau Islands,
    500
  relationship with DM, 618
  Saipan and, 505
  sharing information with DM, 439
  strategy for Marianas and Palaus,
    Formosa, and China, 516–18
  strategy questioned by, 490
  as supreme commander in central Pacific,
    426, 429
  Tarawa and, 490
Nininger, Alex "Sandy" (first posthumous
  Medal of Honor), 358–59
Nishimura, Shoji, 542, 543, 545
Nixon, Richard, 819
Noble, Albert, 493
Noemfoor Island, 509–10
  fighting for Lone Tree Hill, 523
Norris, Revee, 139
Norstad, Lauris, 727

O'Ballance, Edgar, 799, 800
O'Daniel, Lee, 379
Ogden, Hugh, 110
Okazaki, Katsuo, 630
Okinawa, 517, 529, 601, 605
  casualties, 601, 610, 611, 787
  DM departs for Japan, 615
O'Laughlin, Charlie, 259
O'Laughlin, John, 211, 297–98
Oldendorf, Jesse, 544, 565
*Old Soldiers Never Die: The Life of Douglas
  MacArthur* (Perret), xii
Olson, John, 359

Olympic Games, Netherlands (1928), 193–95
On War (Clausewitz), 446
Ord, James "Jimmy," 249, 255, 257, 261, 264, 276, 278, 279, 281, 293
Organized Reserves, 192, 230, 232
Osmeña, Sergio, 59, 535, 536, 537, 539, 597, 608
Otis, Elwell E., 41, 44
Otjen, Theabald, 31, 33
Ozawa, Jisaburo, 542, 544

Pace, Frank, 759, 762, 811
Pace, John T., 213, 217, 224
Paddock, Charley, 193
Pal, Radhabinod, 700–701, 703
Palau Islands, 500, 528
Palmer, Fred, 129–30
Panikkar, K. M., 753, 754
Papua (Buna-Sanananda Operation), 438–60, 477, 484
  Allied casualties, 444, 451, 456, 460, 464
  Australian forces in, 449, 450, 451, 456, 457
  Buna, 440, 441–42, 444, 447, 450–51, 452, 454, 455–57, 458, 460, 476, 481
  conditions on, 444
  Dobodura, 440, 452, 484
  Fifth Air Force and, 448, 450, 451, 453, 454
  first defeat of a Japanese amphibious force by Allies, 444
  Gona, 450–51, 456
  Japanese casualties, 450, 460
  Japanese falling back, 450–51
  Japanese offensive against Port Moresby planned, 439–40, 442
  Kenney and, 448–60
  Kokoda Trail, 439, 444, 449, 450
  Milne Bay, 440, 442, 444, 458
  Operation PROVIDENCE, 441
  Port Moresby, 433, 439, 440, 442, 444, 448
  Sanananda, 450–51, 456, 458–59
  shortage of firepower, 456
  success of, 459
  SWPA HQ on, 451–52, 453, 454, 455, 456–57, 458, 459, 467, 477
  topography, 438–39
  Urbana Force, 456, 457, 458
  U.S. forces in, 440, 441, 449, 450, 451
  Warren Force, 457–58
Parker, David, 452
Parker, General, 146

Parker, George
  final battle on Bataan and, 430, 590
  II Corps of, 356, 357, 358, 360, 366, 367
  South Luzon Force, 340, 348
Parsons, Ed, 8, 9, 76, 77
Patman, Wright, 213, 215
Patton, George S.
  Bonus Army and, 216, 219
  with DM at St. Mihiel, 130
  leadership model, 846
  Medal of Honor, 151
  with Pershing in Mexico, 95
Payne, Frederick H., 212, 220–21
Pearl Harbor, 150, 286
  attack on, 314–15, 317
  damage from attack, 350
  ships that survived attack, 545
Pearson, Drew, 244
  Bonus Army story and DM's libel suit, 240
  DM payoff and, 241–42
  DM's Chastleton Apartments scandal and, 240–41
  "Washington Merry-Go-Round" column, 240
Peleliu, 528
Peng Dehuai, 766, 773
Percival, General Arthur, 625, 628, 632
Perret, Geoffrey, xii, 135, 178, 220, 248, 383, 384, 538
Perry, Commodore Matthew, 629–30, 633, 634
Pershing, John J. "Blackjack," 46
  animosity between DM and, 152, 173, 175, 200
  Argonne and, 132–44
  with Arthur MacArthur in Japan, 60–61
  background, 94–95
  battle at St. Mihiel and, 129, 131
  command of the Buffalo Soldiers, 95
  denies DM the Medal of Honor, 143, 144
  disagrees with DM about advance to Metz, 131
  DM outranks, 559
  DM saves his pension, 251
  entering Sedan and mistake, 145–48
  forced retirement of, 185
  heads U.S. Expeditionary Force in France, 94, 96, 114–15, 145–48, 156
  leadership model, 846
  Louise Brooks as hostess for, 172, 173
  as national hero, 95
  opinion of DM, 115, 150, 154–55
  Pinky MacArthur and, 113, 117–18, 182

plans for the Rainbow Division and DM, 104–5
reams out DM, then promotes him, 116–17
on reduction in armed forces, 203
removes DM as superintendent of West Point, 175, 176–77
report on DM, 178
sent to Mexico after Pancho Villa, 92, 95
temperament, 116–17
at West Point, 48, 94
Petillo, Carol, xii, 23, 171, 284
DM's Executive Order #1 and, 383–84
Petraeus, David, 44
Pfister, Dr. Franz, 31
Philippines, 35, 44, 150
Arthur MacArthur and, 35, 39–41, 43, 44–45
Arthur MacArthur's hopes for, 68–69
Arthur MacArthur's views on American presence in, 51–52
Camp Jossman, Panay, 57
coastal defense of, 281–82
defense plan, 256–58, 262, 268–69
Dewey sinks the Spanish fleet, 35, 39
disease and, 41
DM as Field Marshal of the Philippine Army, 256, 259, 266–87, 290
DM as national hero, 197, 840
DM as U.S. Military Advisor, 245–86
DM attends reburial of Quezon, 683–84
DM briefed by his father on, 54, 56
DM brings Eisenhower as chief of staff, 249
DM brings his mother and doctor, 248, 256
DM docks in Manila (Oct. 26, 1935), 255–56
DM gets malaria, 58, 59
DM gets war supplies from the U.S., 284
DM identified with, 54
DM in command of the Philippine Division, 182–83
DM leaves (1930), departing speech on need for tolerance, 202
DM quits the U.S. Army to stay, 276–77
DM's and Eisenhower's salaries in, 285
DM's attempt at building an air force in, 281
DM's brush with death in, 57–58
DM's defense plan, 245, 283
DM's falling out with Eisenhower, 278–80
DM's hopes for, 69

DM's last trip (1961), 840
DM's lessons learned from his father's experience in, 50–51
DM's posting to (1903), Third Engineer Battalion, 54–60
DM's posting to (1922), 177–85
DM's posting to (1928), 196–99
DM's training program and, 260–61, 268–69, 276, 280–81
DM support independence, 179, 181, 198
DM's vision for, 269, 307
DM's war materiel requests, 267, 268
DM tries to build a navy, 282
DM trip with Quezon to Washington, 270–73
Eisenhower leaves (1939), 284–85
exports, 179
fleets of four nations in Manila Harbor, 39
Fort William McKinley, 182
guerrilla war, 43–46
independence of, 245, 273, 683
Iowans of the 168th under Arthur MacArthur, 112
Japanese in Mandanao, 197, 261–62
Japanese threat to, 150, 196–97, 245, 257, 261, 268, 275, 283
Jean Faircloth visits (1926), 254
lack of U.S. plan for, 197
Manila Bay, 56, 198, 288
Moros people of, 179
Murphy as Governor-General, 262, 264
Philippine Army, 266–87, 290
Philippine Scouts, 182–84, 197, 256, 268, 295, 366
Philippine Scouts mutiny, 183–84
post-World War I economic depression, 179
Quezon as president, 245, 248, 256, 260–62
Quezon calls for neutrality in World War II and independence, 283
rebel insurgency, 40, 41, 43–45, 57, 179
rebel leader Aguinaldo and, 39–41, 44, 45, 683
Sayre as American Commissioner, 284, 290
Spanish surrender, 40
speculation on Japanese invasion, 197–98
Stimson as governor-general, 198–99
Thirty-first Infantry Regiment and, 268, 295, 331, 356, 357, 366, 368, 432, 511
two lawyers important to DM's career, 59
Tydings-McDuffie Act, 245

Philippines (cont'd):
   as U.S. ally, 68
   U.S. annexes, 41
   U.S. racism and, 269
   U.S. refuses resources for defense of, 263,
      267, 279–80, 283
   U.S. troops in, Spanish-American War,
      44
   War Plan Orange, 180, 263, 283, 302
   Washington Naval Treaty of 1921–22
      (Five-Power Treaty), 198
   Wood as governor-general, 179–80
Philippines Campaign (1941–1942), xiv,
     324–94, 414. *See also* Baatan;
     Corregidor Island; Luzon
   air defense, planes needed, 308
   airfields, 305, 308
   air power, 297, 302, 303, 305, 308, 318–21,
     325
   American casualties, 40
   American tanks in, 352–53
   animosity toward the U.S., 374
   B-17 bombers and, 298–99, 303, 305, 308,
     318, 320–21, 325, 329
   Brereton as air force commander, 303,
     315–20
   challenges of Philippine command,
     296–97
   Clark Field, 295, 299, 305, 308, 310
   Clark Field bombed (Dec 8., 1941),
     318–21, 322, 329
   DM abandons Rainbow Five and reverts
     to War Plan Orange, 333, 338–41
   DM and battle for, 324–77
   DM appointed Commanding General,
     United States Army Forces in the Far
     East (July 26, 1941), 289–92
   DM coins "Filamerican," 380
   DM coordinates U.S. and Philippine
     armies, 294
   DM loses his bomber force, 329
   DM meets with British admiral Phillips,
     310
   DM prepares for Japanese invasion, 294,
     296–305
   DM's code-breaking center (Station 6) and
     message ending in "STOP," 311–13
   DM's defense strategy, xiv, 296–305, 307–8
   DM's father's library and, 334
   DM's haunting memories of, 475
   evacuation of Manila, 328, 330, 333–37,
     350 (*see also* Bataan Peninsula;
     Corregidor)

   "fighting retreat" of troops, 338, 349,
     351–52
   Filipino troops, 296, 302, 303, 305, 331,
     332, 353
   Filipino troops, courage of, 298
   final reinforcements (1941), 308
   Fort McKinley, 311
   Fort Stotsenburg, 295, 341
   full alert (1941), 308–13
   Hart as navy commander, 303–5
   Homma's surrender ultimaturm, 360
   Japanese bombing of, 350
   Japanese bombing of Clark Field (Dec. 8,
     1941), 318–23
   Japanese capture of Legaspi, 329
   Krueger commands Sixth Army, 73
   Lingayen Gulf as site of Japanese landing,
     325, 330, 332, 353
   Manila as an open city, 330–31, 333–34,
     338, 343, 344
   Manila as smoldering ruin, 350
   Manila occupied by the Japanese, 354
   military forces, training problems, 308
   military importance of, 307, 338, 345, 354
   National Guardsmen with Company C,
     352–53
   navy of, 305
   Nichols Field, 319
   100th Coast Artillery Regiment, 297
   P-35s, 325
   P-40s and, 299, 308, 318, 319, 320
   Philippine Scouts, 295, 296, 332
   posthumous Distinguished Service
     Crosses awarded, 325
   PT boats, 305, 342, 371
   radar at Iba, 310, 318–19
   Rainbow Five plan, 301–2, 316, 324
   as South West Pacific Area (SWPA), 426
   United States Army Forces Far East
     (USAFFE), 296
   USAFFE headquarters (1 Calle Victoria),
     289, 299, 306, 307, 314, 315, 316, 328
   U.S.-Japan negotiations cease, war
     imminent, 308
   U.S. Navy orders to withdraw, 304–5, 324
   U.S. supplies for, 297, 298, 302
   U.S. troops in, 295, 296, 297, 298, 305,
     308, 318–19, 325, 340, 352
   Washington abandons DM and his men,
     354–55, 369–71
Philippines Campaign (1944–1945), xiv, 499,
     522–77, 579–601. *See also* Leyte;
     Luzon

banzai attacks, 591
Battle of Biak Island and, 507
Battle of Intramuros, 586, 588, 589, 593–95
Battle of Leyte and, 519, 534–59
Battle of Luzon, 562–76
Battle of Manila, 576–77, 579–89
biggest armada in the history of Pacific, 566–67
biggest invasion force the Pacific had ever seen, 536
Bilibid Prison, 581–82, 583–84
civilian casualties, 587, 593–95
Clark Field, 570, 572, 574–75
date for launching of, 500
DM angered by headline, 596
DM confronts FDR over, 516–18
DM fighting on same ground as his father, 575
DM landing scheduled, 518
DM on cruiser *Nashville*, 532–36
DM reinstalls legitimate government, 597
DM's first sight of Manila, Corregidor, Marivales, and Bataan, 566
DM shattered by the holocaust, 596, 598
DM's HQ at Hacienda Luisita, 573, 586
DM's impatience to get to Manila, 572–75
DM's landing at Leyte recorded, 536, 845
DM's memories and, 597
DM's message to FDR and FDR's reply, 539–40
DM's plane, *Bataan,* 525–26
DM's speech at Malacañan, 597–98
DM's speeches, 522, 536, 538–39, 540
DM visits liberated prisoners, 583–84
famous photo of DM wading ashore, 537–38
FDR's message to DM, 599
Fifth Air Force and, 550–52
Filipinos greeting Allies and DM, 579, 584
Hollandia as main staging base for, 499
intelligence about Japanese on, 519, 552
invasion of Japan staged from, 600
island of Morotai as last stepping stone to, 511
Iwabuchi's last stand, 576–77, 582–89
Japanese burn Manila Hotel penthouse, 595–96, 602–3
Japanese casualties, 593
Japanese forces in, 530, 532, 552, 593
Japanese savagery, 587, 593–95
Lingayen Gulf, 557
Malacañan Palace, 597, 603

Malacañan Palace and DM's limousine, 584–85
Manila, liberation of, 529, 562, 564, 570, 571–77, 579–89, 593–600, 735
Mindoro operation (code-named L-3), 554–56
Ormoc operation stalls, 553
Osmeña as new president, 597
preparations for, 523–25
prisoners and civilians in Japanese hands, 575–76, 579–82, 583
retaking Bataan, 588–89, 590–92
retaking Corregidor, 589–93
second-biggest amphibious landing in history, 528
strategic importance of, 517, 518
strategy for, 523–24
survivors of Bataan and Corregidor, 583–84
University of Santo Tomas, internment camp, 576, 579–80, 581, 582, 584
XIV Corps, 572, 573, 587–88, 593
Phillips, Tom, 310, 324
Plain Speaking (Miller), 848
Plato, 841–42
Poweleit, Alvin C., 406
Powell, Colin, 828
Powell Doctrine, 828, 846
Powers, Vincent, 561–62
Price, C. Ward, 707
Pulitzer, Joseph, 33
Puller, Lewis "Chesty," 741

Quezon, Manuel, 59, 104, 179, 181, 196, 197, 202, 245–46
on Corregidor, 341, 348, 349, 360
death of, 529
DM evacuates from Corregidor, 382, 389
DM instructs to evacuate Manila, 330, 334, 336, 340
DM letter to, 415
DM's promise to, 597
Eisenhower and, 285
FDR sends check for war relief, 328
fury of, at FDR's abandonment of the Philippines, 369–70, 376
greets DM, Manila (1935), 255
inauguration, 256, 258–59, 264, 349
Japanese in Davao and, 261–62
military training plan of, 260–61
neutrality proposed by, 373–75
neutrality stance, talks with the Japanese, 280–81, 283, 295

Quezon, Manuel (*cont'd*):
as Philippines president, 245, 248, 256, 260–62, 349
reburial in the Philippines, 683–84
relationship with DM, 164, 256, 258, 273, 278, 281, 284, 295, 306, 348, 349, 363, 389–90, 529–30, 683–84
second inauguration, 349
"Special Executive Order," 382–84, 608
successor to, 535
trip to U.S. with DM to meet with FDR, 270–73
U.S. support and, 263
Willoughby and, 299

Rabaul, New Britain, 364, 432–33, 437, 439, 440, 442, 460, 461, 470, 480, 492
Allied bombing of, 466, 486, 499
anonymous Navy poem and, 473
DM loses interest in, 499
DM's plan for (Elkton I), 461–62, 470–72
Japanese force at, 465, 466–67
New Guinea Campaign and, 471–72
raids on, 484
WATCHTOWER plan for, 440–41
Radford, Arthur, 732, 735
Randall, Alexander, 10, 11
Rants, Han, 535, 540–41
Ray, Harold, 398
Ray, James, 395, 408, 432
Read, George, 180, 183
Reed, Walter, 79
Reel, A. Frank, 673
Reeves, Hugh, 485
Reilly, Henry, 116, 129, 144, 145, 146
Reminiscences (MacArthur), xii, 357, 791, 793, 840–41, 843
Republican Party, 660, 679
communist conspiracy theory of DM's dismissal, 833–34
DM delivers keynote, RNC in Chicago, 836
DM's dismissal from all commands and, 808, 818–19
DM's presidential hopes and, 513–15, 656, 821, 823, 832
presidential election (1952), 834–35, 836
rising stars (1950s), 837
Reston, James, 720
Reyna, Siguion, 256–57
Rhee, Syngman, 692, 693, 694, 697, 706, 745, 749, 814
calls DM to save Korea, 712

division of Korea and, 749
DM and, 693
gives DM command of ROK forces, 720
gratitude for DM, 746
Korean War and, 714
moves government to Pusan, 722
restored to Seoul, 744
Rhoades, Weldon "Dusty," 525, 527, 539, 617, 618, 629
Sutherland and, 657–68
Rhodes, Charles, 143, 144, 148
Ridgway, Matthew, 300, 727, 784, 785, 835
character and personality, 793
as commander of SCAP and CINCFE, 814, 829
DM's dismissal from all commands, 811
DM visits in Korea (Apr. 3, 1951), 806
Eighth Army and, 786, 787, 789, 792, 796
farewell to DM, 815
initiative in Korea and, 792–93
Korean War after DM's dismissal, 835
legend of, as Korean War hero, 787
"the meat grinder" of, 796
nickname, "Iron Tits," 793
offensive strategy of, 789
Operation Dauntless, 803–4
Operation Killer, 796
Operation Punch, 794
Operation Ripper, 797
Operation Thunderbolt, 794
Operation Wolfhound, 793–94
replaces Walker in Korea, 785–86
Seoul withdrawal, 789–90
strategy for Korea, 809
strategy vs. DM's, 829
at West Point, 785
in World War II, 785
Roberts, William, 696, 709, 712
Robertson, Sir Horace, 815
Roche, James Jeffrey, 30
Rockwell, Francis, 334, 398
escape from Corregidor, 395, 408, 409
Roddock, Theodore, 554
Rodriguez, Paul, 510
Rodriguez, Rod, 485–86, 590, 592–93
Rogers, Paul, 288–89, 300–301, 338, 457
air attacks on Corregidor and, 347
Battle of Manila, 596
on Corregidor, 343, 362
DM evacuates Manila and, 335–36
escape from Corregidor, 403, 413–14
at Leyte, 551

"Special Executive Order from President Quezon," 382, 383, 384
Special Order 66, 402–3
taking of Intramuros and, 594
Romulo, Carlos, 362, 373, 394, 399
Roosevelt, Franklin Delano (FDR), 37, 349
accepts DM's resignation (1937), 277
addresses the Philippine people via shortwave radio, 346
air war in the Pacific, 472
American policy toward MacArthur and the Philippines, 327–28, 354–55, 370–71, 373, 375–76
animosity for Drew Pearson, 241
appearance and poor health (1944), 516
as Assistant Secretary of the Navy, 91
assumes DM will never return to the U.S., 277–78
Bonus Army and, 215–16
Brain Trust of, 228
Cairo conference, 693
calls DM "the most dangerous man in America," 195, 212, 223, 225, 226, 228
CCC and, 228–31, 232
death of, 235, 605
demonstration of power and, 235
DM appointed Commanding General, United States Army Forces in the Far East (July 26, 1941), 289–92, 298
DM as friend, 91, 226–27, 605
DM as sounding board for, 251–52
DM given command of all ground forces in the Pacific, 605
DM meeting at Pearl Harbor with (July 23, 1944), 512, 515–18
DM ordered to leave Corregidor, 388–89
DM promised help in Corregidor, 345, 346, 349–50
DM saves the army and, 251
DM's Executive Order #1 and, 383
DM's instructions about coming war, 252
DM's memorandum (Feb. 8, 1942), 374–75
DM's message from the beach at Leyte and FDR's reply, 539–40
DM's position and, 244–45
DM's requests for Philippine aid and, 269–70
election of 1932 and presidency, 224
election of 1944 and, 514, 517
Europe-first strategy, 354, 368–69, 390, 422, 438, 447
hypocrisy in Philippines policy, 264

inauguration (1933), 226
invasion of the Philippines and, 332
Japan's aggression in Indochina and, 292
King's strategy in the Pacific backed, 488
meeting with Quezon and DM, 272–73
message to DM after liberation of Manila, 599
military budget cuts and, 231–36
Neutrality Act, 236
opinion of DM, 223, 225, 228, 235
Philippines abandoned by, 369, 370–71
Philippines and DM, 245–46, 247
"quarantine" speech, 275
Quezon gun-salute controversy and, 258–59
Quezon's letter (Feb. 8, 1942), 374
recall of DM from the Philippines and, 386–87, 390, 393
showdown with Dern, DM, over budget, 233–35
Spanish flu and, 152
Truman and, 640
U.S. Navy, King, and, 437–38
war aid to China and, 275
Yalta Conference, 578–79
Roosevelt, Theodore, 18, 19, 679
Arthur MacArthur and, 76
brokers peace treaty, Russo-Japanese War, 62, 150, 693
DM as aide-de-camp to, 70
Philippines and, 62
Spanish American War and, 34, 35, 40
World War I and, 90
Ross, Colonel, 139, 141, 142–43
ROTC (Reserve Officers' Training Corps), 90, 185, 205, 209, 232, 250, 281
Rovere, Richard, xii, 844–45
Rowell, S. F., 444, 451
Roxas, Manuel, 202, 374, 609n
DM and release of, 608–9
Royal Australian Air Force (RAAF), 428, 483
Royal Navy, 414. See also specific battles; specific ships
Rusk, Dean, 637, 693, 749, 804
Wake Island meeting with DM, 759, 760
Russo-Japanese War, 18, 60–62, 150, 578, 693
Rutledge, Wiley, 671, 674
Ryukyus, 529

Saipan, 500, 505, 528
Sakai, Saburo, 318, 320
Salamaua, New Guinea, 439, 479, 483, 484
Sams, Crawford F., 659

San Antonio, Texas, 27–28
San Francisco
    DM in (1905), 59–60
    Earthquake (1906), 67–68
Sato, Naotake, 815
Saturday Evening Post, description of Manila
    under attack, 350
Sayre, Francis, 284, 290, 330, 336, 340,
    363–64, 374, 377
    escape from Corregidor, 385, 393
Schaller, Michael, xii, 383, 816, 845
Schlesinger, Arthur, Jr., xii, 844–45
Schumacher, Vincent, 407, 408, 409
Schuyler, Cortlandt, 688, 689–90
Scott, Admiral, 91
Scott, Hugh, 88, 96–97
Sebald, William, 687, 688
    farewell to DM, 814, 815
    Korea and, 696, 709, 753
    State Department man in Japan, 662
    war criminal sentences review and, 702
Selective Service Act, 92–93, 95
    peacetime draft and, 642–43
Selleck, Clyde, 289
Seoul, Korea
    destruction in, 744–75
    DM's speech at liberation ceremony,
        745–46
    DM trip (June 29, 1950), 714, 715–16
    fall of, 715
    Kim's secret police, murder of civilians,
        745
    liberation of, 4, 735, 741–44
    population flees from, freezes, 790
    retaking, 793, 796
    Rhee's government returns to, 744
    Ridgway retreats from, 789–90
    Russians defecate in room, 745
Shackleton, Robert, 697
Shanghai, 67
    American defense of, 206
    Japan attacks (1932), 206
    Japan conquers (1937), 275
    U.S. soldiers on leave in, 304
Sharp, William, 411–12
Shaw, Patrick, 702
Shedden, Fred, 428–29
Shepherd, Lemuel, 4, 728, 732, 733, 735
    Inchon and, 737, 740, 741
    Silver Star for, 742
Sheridan, Phillip, 49, 559
Sherman, Forrest, 4, 6, 732, 733, 735
Sherman, William Tecumseh, 9, 45, 559

Sherr, Joe, 311, 312
Shidehara, Baron
    DM's political reforms and, 665–66
    new constitution for Japan and, 666,
        669
Shigemitsu, Mamoru, 630, 631, 632
    DM meeting with, 645–46, 647
Shikoku, 601
Short, Dewey, 828
Siam (today's Thailand), 364
    Ayutthaya, 66
    Bangkok, 66, 67
    DM in (1906), 66–67
    king of, 66–67, 66n
Sibert, Franklin, 538, 552
Singapore, 364, 414
    DM in (1905), 64, 65
    surrender of, 385
Sio, Papua, New Guinea, 488–89
Skerry, Harry, 351, 355
Sladen, Fred Winchester, 177, 189, 197
Smith, Charles B. "Brad," 717, 767
Smith, O. P.
    battle of Chosin Reservoir and, 780
    Inchon-Seoul campaign, 730–31, 733, 735,
        737, 740, 743
    Silver Star for, 742
Snell, Bertrand, 210–11
Solomon Islands, 150, 426, 460, 472, 476
Sony, 685
Southern Philippines, 601
South West Pacific Area (SWPA), 426, 473,
    707
    AAF and, 447
    Admiralty Islands offensive, 491–97
    airpower and, 484–85
    Alamo Force, 482, 483, 493
    Allied assault on Kyushu plan
        (OLYMPIC), 606
    Allied casualties, 487
    Allied invasion of Japan plan
        (DOWNFALL), 606
    Allied landings on Honshu plan
        (CORONET), 606
    Australian Military Forces and, 607–8
    Battle of Biak Island, 505–10
    Battle of Hollandia, 501–3
    Battle of Leyte decision and, 519
    Battle of Morotai Island, 519–20
    Blamey's Allied forces, 427–28, 435, 449,
        476, 482
    CARTWHEEL (Elkton III), 479–87, 499
    Central Bureau (intelligence and code-

breaking), 436, 465, 466, 489–90, 491, 506, 510, 530 (*see also* Akin, Spencer)
decrypted radio messages reveal Japanese plans, 504
DM as supreme commander, 416–653
DM gets decryption of Japanese strategy, 491, 501
DM's American forces, 435, 444
DM's Australian forces, 435
DM's GHQ staff and the Bataan Gang, 299, 428–29, 435–36, 447, 474, 524, 525, 533, 564
DM's military requirements and, 427
DM's rebirth after Bataan debacle, 423
Elkton I plan, 461–62, 471, 499
Fifth Air Force, 449, 466, 476–77, 486, 501, 520, 523, 550
first major parachute drop of the Pacific war, 485
First Marines, "The Old Breed," 486–87, 501
headquarters (*see* Brisbane, Australia)
invasion of Japan plan (DOWNFALL), 606
Japanese code books recovered, 489–90
Japan's Operation I and, 475–76
Joint Chiefs plans for, 440
Kenney appointed head of SWPA Army Air Forces, 523
last amphibious landing of WWII at Balipapan, 613
as MacArthur's area, 437
Marshall tours, 488
naval forces for, 439, 465, 476
Philippines Campaign (1944–45), 522–77, 579–601
Reno IV plan, 499
resource allotment and, 438
Seventh Amphibious Force for, 462, 464–65, 476
Sixth Army, 482
size of combined forces, 520
size of DM's forces, 488
Third Amphibious Force, 484
turning point in the war, 500
USAFFE HQ, 482
U.S. Navy at odds with DM, 426, 438, 439, 463, 488, 498
Washington (FDR, Joint Chiefs) has to okay all plans and strategy, 427, 429, 437, 480, 491, 499, 501, 518, 529
Soviet Russia
air planes for China, 770
atomic bomb and, 704
China and, 560, 825, 828, 833
Communist Party's Third International, 160
containment policy and, 688, 703, 704, 833
DM's prescient vision of, 560
DM's reaction to being in occupied Japan and, 638–39
European countries occupied by, 683
fight against Japan and, 330
four-power occupation of Germany and, 638
Hitler invades (June 22, 1941), 292
invasion of Manchuria, 611
Japanese POWs in detention camps, 665
Korea and, 3, 693, 694, 695
post-World War II territory taken from Japan, 636, 638, 665
Russo-Japanese War and, 60–62, 693
threat to the Mediterranean, 703
as threat to the U.S., 642
U.S. foreign policy regarding Korea and, 708
U.S. tank designs sold to, 209n
Spaatz, Carl, 620
Spanish American War
Cuba and, 33, 35, 40
motives for U.S. going to war, 34
Philippines and, 39–41
sinking of the USS *Maine*, 33–34
Spanish surrender, 40
Sprague, Clifton, 520, 524, 546–47
baby flattops, 546, 547
flagship *Fanshaw Bay*, 547
miracles of Leyte battle, 547–48
Springfield, Massachusetts, 7
Stalin, Josef, 201, 560, 636, 665, 828
DM proposes Ike-Stalin summit, 838
Kim Il Sung and, 709, 751
Korea and, 697, 751, 772
non-support for wider Chinese war, 800–801
Potsdam Declaration, 641
Yalta Conference, 578–79
Stanford, Leland, 11
Stark, Harold, 286, 304, 324, 327
Starling, Edward, 220
Stassen, Harold, 515
Stern, Warren, 809
Stimson, Henry L., 78–79, 198–99, 206, 263, 291, 349
DM's Executive Order #1 and, 383

Stimson, Henry L. (*cont'd*):
   invasion of the Philippines and, 327, 332, 350–51
   at odds with U.S. Navy, 437
   Philippines abandoned by the U.S., 354–55, 370–71, 373
   pulling DM off Corregidor and, 390
Stivers, Charles, 435
Stivers, Paul, 395–96
Story, Anthony, 714, 715, 774, 775, 816
Stotesbury, Edward T., 171
Stratemeyer, George, 775, 786
   bombers in Korea, 717–18, 719
   DM's Formosa trip and, 724
   dropping propaganda leaflets, 796
   farewell to DM, 815
   as FEAF chief, 707, 714
   Fifth Air Force and, 719
   first airdrop, 187th Airborne, 763
   Korean bombing offensive and, 768–69, 770, 771
   landings at Inchon and, 733
   liberation of Seoul and, 744
   size of air force, 719
   war conference (Nov. 28, 1950), 779
Strubel, Arthur, 554–55, 556, 733
   DM's strategy in Korea and, 755
   Inchon and, 735, 740, 741
   Wonsan harbor, 756
Stuart, Fanniebelle, 71–72
Stuart, Jeb, 49
Sulzberger, C. L., 555
Sumatra, 426
Summerall, Charles, 46, 137, 139–40, 142, 189, 193, 195
   as Chief of Staff, 199, 204
   proposes DM to replace him as Chief of Staff, 199–200, 201
Sun Yat-sen, 59
Sutherland, Richard K., 289, 293–94, 299, 300, 303, 359, 442
   arrival in Australia, 417
   arrival in Japan (1945), 615
   attack on Pearl Harbor and, 314, 317
   Battle of Leyte decision and, 519, 520
   Brereton's preemptive raid on Formosa and, 315–16, 317
   on Corregidor, 342, 343, 361, 389
   Corregidor air attacks and, 347
   defense of Bataan and, 360, 367
   DM names successor in case of his death, 377
   with DM on Bataan, 357

   DM's break with, 627–28
   DM's orders to leave Corregidor and, 391, 392
   DM's Rabaul plan and, 462
   escape from Corregidor, 395, 398, 400, 401, 409, 413
   evacuation of Manila, 336
   evacuation of Quezon and, 382
   as GHQ chief of staff, 435, 436
   Japanese bombing of Clark Field and, 319–20, 321
   Japanese delegation to DM and surrender document, 614–15
   Japanese invasion of the Philippines and, 329
   Japanese surrender ceremony and, 618, 627–28, 632, 657
   Joint Chiefs and, 491
   Kenney and, 447, 450, 451
   on Krueger, 573
   Leyte and, 537, 551
   meeting with Joint Chiefs over DM's return to the Philippines, 518
   Mindoro operation and, 556
   mistress Elaine Clark and, 527–28, 627–28
   as obstructionist, 524
   Pacific Military Conference, 470–72
   Papua and, 451, 452, 454, 457, 460
   Reno IV plan, 499
   resignation of, 657
   rift with DM over Clark, 527–28, 627–28, 658
   trip to Papua, 444
   Wainwright and, 401
Suzuki, Sosaku, 578
Sverdrup, Lief "Jack," 569, 640
Swift, Innis, 492, 570, 571, 572, 573, 574
Swing, Joseph, 558, 588, 622–23

Taft, Robert, 836, 837
Taft, William Howard, 44, 45, 50, 62–63, 66
Taisho, Emperor of Japan, 75
Tametomo, Kuroki, 61
Taylor, Montgomery, 206
Thailand. *See* Siam
Thayer, Sylvanus, 170
Thomas, Scott, 379
Tibet, 776, 802
Timor, 414
Tinian, 500
Tinley, Matthew, 139
Togo, Heihachiro, 62, 63, 530
Tojo, Hideki, 292, 649, 651

war criminal trial and execution, 698,
699–703
Tokyo, Japan
American Embassy compound, DM and
family's residence in, 647, 686
American Embassy in, 623, 644
Dai-ichi Insurance building, 5
Dai-ichi Insurance building, as SCAP HQ,
623, 647–48, 655, 660, 670, 674, 676,
677, 686, 730, 732–33, 810
destruction in, 623, 630, 637
DM arrives in (1905), 63
Imperial Hotel, 623
MacArthur in (1950), 5
Toshiba, 685
Townsend, Glen, 296, 298
Toyota Motor Company, 685, 816
Trobriand Islands
Alamo Force and, 482, 483
combat teams land on, 482–83
Kiriwina and Woodlark, 471, 472, 479,
480, 481, 482–83
operation CARTWHEEL (Elkton III) and,
479
Truk Island, 437, 476, 499
Truman, Harry
advisor on Korea, 696
approval ratings, 757, 820
atomic bombing of Hiroshima and
Nagasaki, 612–13
atomic bomb strategy of, 783, 799–800,
829
China "lost" to Communists, 704
China policy, 708, 752
containment policy, 703, 830, 833
cuts aid to Chiang Kai-shek, 708
DM appointed Commander-in-Chief, UN
Command, 720
DM awarded third Distinguished Service
Medal, 761
DM reprimanded (Mar. 24, 1951), 805
DM rift and, 724, 726
DM's criticism of, 802–4, 807
DM's dismissal from all commands, xiv,
802, 804–5, 807–13, 834, 844, 847
DM's dismissal from all commands, public
and political reactions, 818, 820
DM sent message (Jan. 13, 1952), 790–91
DM sent message after liberation of Seoul,
747
DM's image attacked, 844
DM's Korean bombing campaign and, 769
on DM's presidential chances, 832

DM's request for Korea reinforcements
refused, 716–17
DM's return to U.S. and, 822
DM viewed with antagonism, 639–40,
643, 761–62, 847, 847n
draft reinstated, 722
on FDR and DM, 640
foreign policy team, 688
Formosa policy, 724, 725, 726
Harriman backs DM's Korea plans, 730,
748
Japanese surrender ceremony and, 628
Japan invasion plans (DOWNFALL), 611
Japan vs. Europe and, 660
Joint Chiefs and, 3–6 (*see* Joint Chiefs of
Staff)
Korean cease-fire plan, 798, 826, 829,
835
Korean War, final view of, 802, 829
Korean War and atomic bomb, 783
landing at Inchon opposed, 3, 4, 6
as least popular president, 844
military budget cuts and, 713, 716–17
NSC order 13/2 signed, 692
orders troops to Korea, 712–13
Potsdam Declaration, 641
press statements and, 783
size of occupation forces and, 642–44
South Korea supported by U.S., 784
Wake Island meeting with DM, 756–61,
847–48
war with the Soviets and, 708
Yalu River retreat and, 782
Tschepe, Moritz, 186
Tsukada, Rikichi, 570
Tugwell, Rex, 228
Tulagi, 440, 441
Tulsa, 440, 441
Turner, Frederick Jackson, 19
Twain, Mark, 306, 660–61
Twelve O'Clock High (film), 108
Tydings, Millard, 245

Ullom, Madeline, 371
ULTRA, 439
intel about Biak Island, 505
intel about Japanese forces in the
Philippines, 530
intel about Japanese on Halmahera,
519–20
intel about Morotaia, 520
intel on Japan's defending forces, 610–11,
612
Japanese attack on Buna and, 442

ULTRA (*cont'd*):
Japanese code books recovered at Sio, 489–90
Japanese convoy plans intercepted, 466, 467
Japanese convoy route and intercept, 506
Japanese expecting Lingayen Gulf landing, 564
Japanese fleets heading for Leyte missed, 542
Japanese reinforcements at Leyte missed, 532, 552
secret codes recovered at Aitape, 503–4
Yamamoto's itinerary incepted, 478
Umzedu, Yoshijiro, 630, 632
United Nations, 643
DM as Commander-in-Chief, UN Command, 719
Korean armistice and, 837
Korean Trusteeship Commission and, 695
Korean War and, 708, 712, 719, 720, 723, 745–46, 747, 749, 751, 766, 769, 786, 788, 804
Security Council resolution on Korean War, 713
United States
Alaska purchase, 17
anti-Communism in, 820
Arcadia Conference, 425
armed forces decline, post–World War I, 203–4
Asia and, 16–17, 54, 56, 62, 68, 560, 626
Asian policy and domino theory, 837
Asian populations in, 17
Black Tuesday and the Wall Street Crash, 201, 204
"Chinese Memorandum" of Arthur MacArthur and, 19–22
declaration of war (1917), 93
declaration of war (1941), 322
demobilization post–World War II, 641–42
DM's address to Congress and the nation (April 19, 1951), 821–30
expansionist foreign policy, 34
isolationism, 204
leadership in Pacific War and, 425
MacArthur for president movement, 513–15
Manifest Destiny, 34
Midway Island purchase, 17
mobilizing for war (1940), 284
Open Door Policy, 206

Pacific, strategic importance of, 64, 201, 202
pacifist movement, 192, 204, 207
peacetime draft and, 642–43
Philippines and, 68–69, 196–99
post-war changes in, 820
public opinion, post–World War I, 155–56
role in Asia to be symbol of freedom, 51
Soviet Russia becomes threat, 642
vanishing western frontier, 19, 25
war in Europe and, 286
war with Japan foreseen, 283
wealth of (1930s), 211
Untold Story of Douglas MacArthur, The (Hunt), xii
USAFFE (United States Army Forces Far East)
DM reinstatement and appointment Commanding General (July, 1941), 286–87, 289–92, 298
headquarters (1 Calle Victoria), 289, 299, 306, 307, 314, 315, 316, 328
staff, 299–300
U.S. Army. *See also* Almond, Edward "Ned"; Eichelberger, Robert "Bob"; Krueger, Walter; Ridgway, Matthew; Walker, Walton; *specific battles; specific generals; specific wars*
air mail scandal and, 236–37, 237n
American First Army, 132, 145, 146, 148
Arthur MacArthur and the Eighteenth Infantry, 12, 13, 14, 15
Arthur MacArthur and the Seventeenth Infantry, 10, 11
Arthur MacArthur and the Thirty-sixth Infantry, 11
budget cuts (1920s), 192
budget cuts (1930s), 204, 210–12, 231, 235–36
Buffalo Soldiers, 95
camels as pack animals, 24
CCC and, 228–31, 230n
Chaffee's experimental armored unit, 204, 209
at Civil War's end, 10
Command and General Staff College at Leavenworth, 249, 250, 299, 454, 661
Craig as Chief of Staff, 244, 276
creating a force for World War I, 95–96
demobilization post–World War I, 156
divisions in Korea, 3
DM advocates military aviation, 244

DM and increase in peacetime army (1936), 242–43
DM as Chief of Staff (1930-1935), 203–52
DM as Chief of Staff (1930-1935), evaluation of, 250–52
DM as supreme commander, SWPA, 426–653
DM heads Bureau of Information, 91–92, 93
DM on General Staff, 79–80
DM quits to stay in the Philippines (1937), 277
DM recalled from Philippines (1937), 276–77
DM reinstatement and appointment Commanding General ISAFFE (July, 1941), 286–87, 289–92, 298
DM's first principle as Chief, 204
DM's letter to Snell, 210–11
DM's response to budget cuts, 209–11
DM's second principle as Chief, 205
DM sworn in as Chief of Staff, 203
experimental mechanized force at Fort Meade, 204
First Army (Big Red One), 136, 137, 146, 462–63
General Staff and World War I plans, 89, 95–96
highest military rank, general of the army, 558–59
hostility to Mitchell's idea about the importance of airpower, 189
M-1 Garand rifle, 250
March as Chief of Staff, 118, 152, 156–57
medals and ribbons, 251
National Defense Act and, 90, 210
Old Army, 11
105 mm howitzer, 250
Pacific command split, 426, 490
Philippine Department, 267–68, 283, 284, 287, 289, 294, 296, 354
Reserve Officers' Training Corps (ROTC) created, 90
restructuring of, 250
size (1898), 34
size (1930s), 210, 211, 232, 244
size, post-World War II, 707
Summerall as Chief of Staff, 199
tanks, 250–51
War College, 250
U.S. Army Air Corps/U. S. Air Force. See also Arnold, Hap; Far Eastern Air Force (FEAF); Kenney, George; Mitchell,
William "Billy"; SWPA Army Air Forces; Whitehead, Ennis; specific battles
air mail scandal, 236–37
B-17 bomber, 250, 298, 303, 305 (see also specific battles)
B-29 bombers, 500, 605, 610, 622, 633
budget for, 204, 208–9
F-38 Sabre and, 789
Far Eastern Air Force (FEAF), 707
formation of, 188
Japanese surrender ceremony and greatest overflight in history, 633
in Korea, 714, 768–69, 770, 772, 779, 786, 792, 795–96
P-40s, 299
U.S. Army Corps of Engineers, Mississippi project, 211–12
U.S. Army Reserves, 250
U.S. Congress
Armed Services Committee, 204
Arthur MacArthur testimony on Philippines atrocities, 51
Congressman Martin reads DM's criticism of Truman to Congress, 806–7, 811, 848
cutting army's budget (1930), 204, 210–12
DM's address (April 19, 1951), 821–30
DM's letter to House Minority leader Snell, 210–11
DM's testimony on Korea (May 3–5, 1951), 832
House Subcommittee on Military Appropriations, 208, 242–43
Neutrality Act, 236
Patman Bill, 213, 215
World War I veterans and, 213
U.S. Department of Defense
budget cuts, 1950, 713, 716–17
NSC order 13/2 and DM, 691–92
U.S. Department of State. See also Sebald, William
civil war in China and, 695
DM and, 665
Eurocentricity and, 689
Kennan criticism of SCAP, 690–91
Korean Trusteeship Commission and, 695
memo on points of Japan's new constitution, 667–68
Sebald and DM, 662, 814, 815
Wake Island DM-Truman meeting and, 759
Yalu River retreat and, 782

U.S. mail, DM and scandal, 236–37
U.S. Marines, 482. *See also* Shepherd, Lemuel
    amphibious landings at Inchon, 4, 5, 6
    at Bougainville, 461
    at Cape Gloucester, 481, 486, 487, 501
    fighting style, 572
    First Marines under DM, 481, 482, 486, 501
    at Guadalcanal, 441, 486, 487
    at Iwo Jima, 600–601
    in Korea, 5, 728, 730, 731, 736–44, 756, 767, 777–79, 780, 783, 796
    M-1 rifle and, 250
    at Munda, 483
    on New Georgia, 461
    on Okinawa, 601
    in the Philippines, 309, 344, 349
    Seventh Marines under Walt, 497
    in Shanghai, 206
    Veracruz and, 81
    in World War I, 115, 149
U.S. National Guard, 123–24
    Alabamans of the 167th, 99, 138–39, 140, 141–42
    budget for, 205, 232, 233, 235
    Eighty-fourth Battalion (DM's men), 99, 128, 129, 130, 135, 138, 139, 143, 145, 152
    Eighty-third Battalion, 99, 115, 124, 137–38, 144, 146
    equipment shortage, 99–100
    Fourth Ohio, 99
    Iowans of the 168th, 110–12, 139, 140–41
    New York's 165th (old Sixty-ninth, "the Fighting Irish"), 99, 106, 115, 124, 125, 126, 127, 138, 156
    167th and 168th Infantry Regiment, 99, 124, 138–39
    Rainbow Division (Forty-second), 98–101
    Rainbow Division at Vaucouleurs, France, 104–5
    Rainbow Division comes home, 155
    Rainbow Division fighting in France, 110–49
    Rainbow Division occupation of France, 152, 154
    Rainbow Division ships out to France, 101, 103
    Rainbow Division training at Camp Mills, Long Island, 99–101
    Rainbow Division winter in France and, 105–6
    in World War I, 95–98, 103–49

World War I casualties, 116, 121, 126, 128, 142, 144, 149
U.S. Navy, 437. *See also* Halsey, William; Kinkaid, Thomas; Nimitz, Chester; *specific battles; specific ships*
    American Pacific Fleet in Tokyo Bay, single greatest armada in modern history, 618
    amphibious landing craft, 462–63
    animosity between DM and, 426, 438, 439, 463, 488, 498
    Asiatic Fleet, 206, 286, 304, 324
    Asiatic Naval Detachment, 198
    attack on Manila, Spanish American War, 35
    Battle of the Coral Sea, 433–34, 437
    Battle of Midway, 434, 437
    budget, 1930s, 211
    decryption by ULTRA, 439, 442, 466, 467, 478
    DM's Rabaul campaign vetoed, 437
    Halsey's Pacific command, 476
    Japanese surrender ceremony and greatest overflight in history, 633
    King commands the U.S. Fleet, 350
    loss of ships, Pearl Harbor, 419
    Nimitz as supreme commander in central Pacific, 426, 427
    Nimitz commands the Pacific Fleet, 350
    Operation ULTRA, 436, 442
    Pacific Fleet ordered to remain in Hawaii (1940), 283
    Pearl Harbor as closest base to the Philippines, 286
    Philippines Campaign (1944–45), invasion force, 524
    Philippines strategic importance, 263
    plan to bypass the Philippines, 516–18
    post–World War II and DM, 637–38
    PT boats for the Philippines, 282, 305
    ships in western Pacific, post–World War II, 707
    submarines operating in Lingayen Gulf, 332–33
    supplies DM a flotilla for his Philippine defense plan, 273
    U.S. Asiatic Fleet, 35
    USS *Akron* and dirigible air fleet, 226
    Washington Naval Treaty of 1921–1922 (Five-Power Treaty), 198, 236
    weakness of (1940), 286
U.S. News & World Report, 782–83
    DM interview with Hugh Baillie, 803

U.S. Olympic Committee, 193–95, 231
USS *Blue Ridge,* 566
USS *Boise,* 565–66
    DM aboard, Battle of Luzon, 566, 568
    DM and Borneo offensive, 609
    DM and Krueger conference on board,
       571
    DM's first sight of Manila, Corregidor,
       Marivales, and Bataan, 566
USS *Buchanan,* 628
USS *California,* 545
USS *Chattanooga,* 103
USS *Covington,* 103
USS *Dolphin,* 80
USS *Enterprise,* 434
USS *Fanshaw Bay,* 547
USS *Gambier Bay,* 548, 549
USS *Gurnard,* 506
USS *Heerman,* 547
USS *Hoel,* 547, 548
USS *Honolulu,* 539
USS *Hornet,* 434
USS *Houston,* 286
USS *John Land,* 537
USS *Johnston,* 547, 548
USS *Kalinin Bay,* 548
USS *Lexington,* 433, 437
USS *Louisville,* 545
USS *Maine,* 33–34
USS *Maryland,* 545
USS *Minneapolis,* 545
USS *Missouri,* xi
    DM's speech to the American public on,
       633–34, 826
    at Inchon, 742
    Japanese surrender ceremony and, 628–33
USS *Mount McKinley,* 737
    DM aboard, 737–38, 739
USS *Nashville,* 501, 532, 539, 543–44, 556,
    566
USS *Nebraska,* 81
USS *New Jersey,* 543
USS *New Mexico,* 565
USS *Olympia,* 39
USS *Ommaney Bay,* 565
USS *Pennsylvania,* 545
USS *Pensacola,* 324, 326
USS *Philadelphia,* 30
USS *Phoenix,* 493, 494–96
    LCVPs take DM ashore Los Negros, 495
USS *Portland,* 545
USS *President Harrison,* 308
USS *Richmond,* 17

USS *St. Lo,* 547, 548–49
USS *Santee,* 549
USS *Suwanee,* 549
USS *Tasker Bliss,* 289
USS *Tennessee,* 545
USS *Wasatch,* 544, 545, 549, 555, 556
USS *West Virginia,* 545
USS *White Plains,* 547, 548
USS *Yorktown,* 433, 434, 437
U.S. War Department. *See also* Marshall,
    George Catlett
    army post closings and other cuts
       (1931–1932), 210
    bad decision on developing tank forces,
       209, 209n
    budget for 1934, 231–32
    budget for 1936, 242
    CCC and, 229–30
    deny reinforcements for DM in the
       Philippines, 354
    DM at odds with, 204, 208, 211
    DM's war materiel requests for the
       Philippines, 267, 268, 269
    fate of Japan's four cyclotrons, 685–86
    FDR's budget cuts, 231–36
    Germany First strategy, 422
    MAGIC office, cracking Japanese code,
       PURPLE decryption effort, 311–12
    military aviation advanced, 244
    mislead DM about support for the
       Philippines, 345
    non-military expenditures, 212
    number of American forces in occupied
       Japan and, 643–44
    peacetime draft and, 642
    post-war forces, size of and, 641–42
    White Plan (on civil disorder), 216

Van Aduard, Baron Lewe, 701
Vandenberg, Hoyt, 732
    DM's dismissal from Korea and, 833
Van Volkenburgh, Robert, 441, 442
Vargas, Jorge, 334, 374
Vaughan, Harry, 822
Vietnam War, 802
    Communist insurgency in, 837
    DM's warning to JFK, xiii, 839
Villa, Pancho, 92

Wachi, Takeji, 397
Wainwright, Jonathan "Jim" or "Skinny," 296,
    300, 302, 308, 435, 583, 624
    appearance, 351

Wainwright, Jonathan "Jim" or "Skinny" (*cont'd*):
  Bataan and, 333, 367
  Calumpit Bridge and, 340, 351–53
  DM evacuating Corregidor and, 400–402
  DM promotes, 357
  DM's return to America, 822
  "fighting retreat" of troops, 338, 349,
    351–52, 357
  Homma's ultimatum to, 674
  Japanese invasion of the Philippines and,
    325–26
  Japanese surrender ceremony and, 628, 632
  last stand on Bataan and, 400, 590
  message to MacArthur on collapse of
    Bataan troops, 430
  North Luzon Force of, 329, 340, 348
  No Surrender order and, 431, 432
  as POW in Manchuria, 624
  retirement, 625
  reunion with DM in Tokyo, 624–25
  starvation on Bataan and, 372
  Truman and, 639–40
Wakde Island, 506–7
Wake Island, 364
  DM-Truman meeting on, 756–61, 847–48
Waldorf Astoria Hotel, New York, 156
  DM's home in retirement, 831
  fan mail waiting for DM at, 831
Waldron, Albert, 456
Walker, Walton, 3, 4, 5, 6, 702, 707, 767
  casualties at Pusan, 737
  Chinese in Korean War and, 766
  death of, 784–85
  DM arrives at Chongchon River HQ, 773
  DM's strategy in Korea and, 755
  as Eighth Army commander, 722, 723,
    727, 730, 736, 755, 756, 768, 770, 773,
    785
  First Marine Brigade at Pusan and, 733,
    737, 738
  Inchon-Seoul campaign, 728, 733, 741,
    742–44
  at Pusan, 722, 728, 729, 733, 736–37, 738
  in Pyongyang, 764
  Pyongyang campaign, 755, 756, 760
  retreat from Pyongyang, 781, 788
  Ridgway replaces, 785
  war conference (Nov. 28, 1950), 779
  Yalu River advance and retreat, 773,
    777–79
Walt, Lewis, 487
Washington Post, 782
Waters, Walter W., 213–15, 216, 217

Watson, Edwin, 290, 386
Wau, Papua New Guinea, 465, 467, 483
Wavell, Archibald, 388
Webb, Judge, 701
Weller, Reginald, 143
Wells, H. G., 213
Westmoreland, William, 841
West Point (U.S. Military Academy)
  Academy Board, 165, 169, 172
  Beast Barracks, 38, 49, 170
  Cadet Summer Camp, 164–65, 169, 170
  DM and Army-Navy baseball game (May
    18, 1901), 50
  DM and Ganoe, 160–65
  DM and hazing, 38, 41–43, 46–48, 170
  DM and sports at, 171, 193, 195
  DM as exceptional cadet, 48, 49, 50, 52
  DM as leader, 53
  DM as superintendent, xv, 157–71, 175
  DM as undergraduate, xiv, 36–38, 46–50,
    52–53, 160
  DM's admission to, 30–33, 36
  DM's classmates, 37, 38, 48, 49
  DM's core values and, 48–49
  DM's father's Philippine exploits and, 38
  DM's graduation address (1934), 232–33
  DM's last speech (May 12, 1962), xiv, 53,
    840, 841–42, 843
  DM's leadership style, 162–63
  DM's love for, 49, 53
  DM's mother and superintendent
    position, 159
  DM's mother rooming nearby, 36–37, 38
  DM's reforms for, 166, 168, 169–70, 176,
    177–78
  famous graduates of, 49
  Ganoe and, 160–68
  hazing, purpose of, 48
  hazing at, 94, 170
  hazing death and investigation, 43, 46–48
  Honor Committee and honor code,
    170–71
  jargon of, 37, 43
  motto, 165
  Pershing at, 48, 94
  Pershing removes DM as West Point
    superintendent, 175, 176–77
  physical conditions at, 37–38, 49
  Ridgway at, 785
  rules for cadets, 37
  Sladen as DM's successor, 177
  state of, post–World War I, 157, 158–59
  War Department and, 158–59, 168

West Texas Military Academy, 28–30
Wewak, Papua, New Guinea, 484, 491, 501
Wheaton, Lord, 51
White, Theodore H., 286
White, Thomas, 628
White, William Allen, 154, 666
Whitehead, Ennis, 449, 467, 468, 469, 492
   in charge of the Pacific Air Command, 637
   command of Fifth Air Force, 523
   Far Eastern Air Force (FEAF) and, 707
   Japanese surrender ceremony and, 628
   Mindoro airfields, 557
Whitlock, Lester, 435
Whitman, Walt, 16
Whitney, Courtney, 533
   biography by, xii, 840
   creation of Japan's constitution and, 667–68
   with DM, history of the war in the Pacific, 840
   as DM's confidant, 658
   DM's dismissal from Korea and, 810, 811
   fears about Japanese reception of Allies, 617–18, 622
   first airdrop, 187th Airborne, 763
   intelligence about Japanese strength on Luzon, 564
   Kades and, 659
   landing at Leyte, 536
   landing in Japan, 617–18
   landings at Inchon and, 737
   liberation of Seoul and, 744
   occupation of Japan and, 641
   passage of new constitution and, 668–69
   public reaction to DM's return to America (1951), 822
   return to America with DM, 816
   SCAP's Government Section head, 658, 659
   unpopularity of, 658
   on Wake Island Truman-DM meeting, 760–61
   war conference (Nov. 28, 1950), 779
Wilkie, Wendell, 384–85, 514, 515
Willcox, Cornelius, 166
Willoughby, Charles A., xii, 299, 312, 330, 435–36
   Banzai attack on Aitape and, 510–11
   biography by, 383
   Chinese PLA divisions in Manchuria and, 752, 753
   Clare Boothe Luce and, 306–7
   on Corregidor, 343, 361
   evacuation of Corregidor, 395, 408, 413
   faulty intelligence and losses at Yalu, 779–80
   GHQ intelligence chief (G-2), 435, 436, 442, 491, 505, 569
   Hollandia offensive and, 492
   intel about the Japanese buildup on Luzon and Leyte, 530
   intel about North Korea's military buildup and, 709–10
   intel estimates on South Korea attack, 708–9
   intel on Chinese in North Korea, 770
   intel on invading North Korea, 749
   intel on Japanese on Corregidor, 589, 590
   intel on Japan's defending forces, 610–11
   intel that China in Korea was "provisional," 766
   as Japan's J. Edgar Hoover, 658–59
   Jean MacArthur and, 814
   New Guinea Campaign, 467
   SCAP GHQ staff, Japan, 658, 690
   second-guessing himself, 442
   Seoul trip (June 29, 1950), 715
   war conference (Nov. 28, 1950), 779
Wilmott, H. P., 437
Wilson, Francis, 343
Wilson, John K., 347, 348, 413
Wilson, Warren, 584
Wilson, Woodrow, 80, 179, 227
   appoints Baker as Secretary of War, 90, 91
   creation of the Selective Service, 92
   declaration of war (1917), 94
   DM brings news of Funston's death, 94
   DM's plan to mobilize the National Guard and, 96
   invasion of Mexico and, 81, 82, 86
   Mexico's Huerta and, 80
   National Defense Act, 89, 90, 91
   pursuit of Pancho Villa, 92
   World War I and, 90
   Zimmerman affair and, 94
Winged Defense (Mitchell), 188
Winn, Cooper, 139, 140
Wolf, Walter, 105–6, 117, 131, 146
Women's Army Corps (WAC), 527
Wonju, Korea, 791–92
Wood, Leonard, 78, 79, 81, 82, 83, 85, 86, 87, 93, 200
   death of, 199
   as DM supporter, 179–80, 186

Wood, Leonard (*cont'd*):
  as Philippines governor-general, 179–80,
    198, 246
  World War I and, 89, 90, 91
Wood, Robert, 642–43
World Tomorrow, The, 207–8
World War I, 103–49. *See also* MacArthur,
    Douglas, 1917–1918
  AEF's favorite tune, 122
  American First Army, 132, 145, 146, 148
  American Second Army, 149
  Argonne, 132, 135–44
  Armistice, 148, 152
  Army Chief of Staff March as key in
    winning, 156
  Belleau Wood, 115
  carnage of, 89
  Champagne front, 116
  Château-Thierry and Ourq, 123–27
  DM and U.S.'s Rainbow Division, 98–149
  DM as youngest brigadier general, xv,
    117–18, 119
  DM's first battle, 109–10
  Flanders, 119
  Gallipoli, 427
  German casualties, 119
  Germans in retreat, 132, 145
  Germans on defense, 123–44
  German submarine attacks, 89, 90, 94
  Lost Battalion, 135
  low point for the Allies, October 1917,
    101–2
  mustard gas used in, 113
  outbreak of, 86
  Pershing as head of AEF, 96, 114–15,
    145–48, 156
  phosgene gas used in, 113
  Rainbow Division's first fighting, 110–12
  sinking of the *Lusitania,* 90
  Souain (Second Battle of the Marne),
    119–22
  St. Mihiel, 128–31, 134
  "take Sedan," 145–48
  Treaty of Versailles, 155, 159–60
  trench raids, 109, 115
  U.S. creates Selective Service and, 92
  U.S. declares war on Germany, 93
  U.S. desire to stay out of, 89
  U.S. First Division (Big Red One), 136,
    137, 146
  veterans of, Bonus Army and, 212–24
World War II, 288–615. *See also* MacArthur,
    Douglas, 1941–1945; Japan, World

War II; South West Pacific Area;
  specific battles; specific campaigns;
  specific countries
  Allied air power in the Pacific, 466–70,
    484–85
  Arcadia Conference, 425
  blitzkrieg warfare, 204–5, 209n, 291, 446
  Casablanca Conference, 461
  D-Day in Normandy, 528
  demobilization post–World War II, 641–42
  Dunkirk, 286
  Europe-first strategy, 354, 368–69, 390,
    422, 425, 438, 447, 526
  first posthumous Medal of Honor, 359
  four-power occupation of Germany, 638
  German panzer divisions, 209n
  Germany overruns Belgium, Holland, and
    France, 286, 290
  Hitler invades Russia (June 22, 1941), 292
  Japan aggression in China and the rape of
    Nanking, 275
  Japan attacks Swatow, 281
  Japan at war with the U.S. and Great
    Britain, 322
  Japanese conquests in the Pacific, 364,
    385, 413, 414, 425
  Japanese atrocities, 648–49
  Japanese attack on Pearl Harbor, 314–15,
    317
  Japanese surrender, xi, xv, 614–15
  Japan sinks *Prince of Wales* and the
    Repulse, 310, 324
  Poland and, 281, 283
  Potsdam Declaration, 617, 633–34, 638,
    641, 677
  South West Pacific Area (SWPA), 426–27
  Soviet T-34 tanks, 209n
  U.S.-Japan negotiations cease, war
    imminent, 308
  Yalta Conference, 578–79
Wright, Edward, 97
Wright, R. K. "Pinky," 727, 730
  DM expects removal as CINCFE, 802
  DM's strategy in Korea and, 755
  on DM's The Plan, 802
  DM's Yalu River reconnoiter and, 774
  first airdrop, 187th Airborne, 763
  G-3 in charge of planning, 715
  Joint Strategic Plans and Operations
    Group, 727–28
  landings at Inchon and, 733, 737
  war conference (Nov. 28, 1950), 779
Wright, William, 180

Yalta Conference, 578–79
Yamamoto, Isoroku, 434, 476, 477
  shot down, 478, 525
Yamashita, General, 385
Yamashita, Tomoyuki, 530, 532, 538n, 559,
    564
  HQ at Baguio, 574
  Manila and, 564–65, 570, 576–77, 582
  Philippine defense zones, 570, 572,
    585
  trial and execution of, 670–73, 698

Years of MacArthur, The (James), xii
Yokohama, Japan, 621
  destruction in, 622
  Grand Hotel, 622, 623–24
Yokoyama, General, 570
Yoshida, Shigeru, 668, 747, 813–14
  farewell to DM, 815, 816

Zhang Yu, 498
Zhou Enlai, 752, 753, 754
Zimmerman, Arthur, 94

ABOUT THE AUTHOR

Arthur Herman is the author of eight books, including the *New York Times* bestseller *How the Scots Invented the Modern World* (2001) and *Gandhi and Churchill: The Epic Rivalry That Destroyed an Empire and Forged Our Age* (2008), which was a finalist for the Pulitzer Prize. He is also senior fellow at the Hudson Institute, where he has become one of Washington, D.C.'s most dynamic writers and thinkers, with essays regularly appearing in *The Wall Street Journal, The Wall Street Journal Asia,* and *The Wall Street Journal Online.* He also publishes frequently in *Commentary, Foreign Policy, The American Interest, Mosaic* magazine, and *Nikkei Asian Review.*

Dr. Herman received a Ph.D. in history from the Johns Hopkins University and is a former visiting scholar at the American Enterprise Institute. He is a popular teacher and lecturer, both at the university level (George Mason, Georgetown, American University, and The University of the South) and in the famed Western Heritage Program, which he created for the Smithsonian's Campus on the Mall. His books have been nominated for numerous prestigious prizes on both sides of the Atlantic, and translated into seven languages, including Chinese and Japanese. His book *Freedom's Forge: How American Business Produced Victory in World War II* was named by *The Economist* as one of its Notable Books for 2012.

Arthur Herman is married to Beth Herman, poet, essayist, and writer/illustrator of children's books.

ABOUT THE TYPE

This book was set in Minion, a 1990 Adobe Originals typeface by Robert Slimbach (b. 1956). Minion is inspired by classical, old-style typefaces of the late Renaissance, a period of elegant, beautiful, and highly readable type designs. Created primarily for text setting, Minion combines the aesthetic and functional qualities that make text type highly readable with the versatility of digital technology.